D1751308

Building on Progress
Expanding the Research Infrastructure for the
Social, Economic, and Behavioral Sciences

Building on Progress

Expanding the Research Infrastructure
for the Social, Economic, and Behavioral
Sciences

edited by the
German Data Forum (RatSWD)

Vol. 1

Budrich UniPress Ltd.
Opladen & Farmington Hills, MI 2010

You must not circulate this book in any other binding or cover and you must impose this same condition on any acquirer.

A CIP catalogue record for this book is available from
Die Deutsche Bibliothek (The German Library)

© 2010 by Budrich UniPress Ltd. Opladen & Farmington Hills
www.budrich-unipress.eu

ISBN 978-3-940755-58-2
2 Vols. in slipcase

© These volumes are published by Budrich UniPress and are published under the Creative Commons licence:
http://creativecommons.org/licenses/by-nc-nd/3.0/de/deed.en_GB
You are free to copy, distribute, display, and perform the work as long as you tribute it to the original author/editors. No commercial use, or changes unless approved by Budrich UniPress.

Both volumes may be downloaded free of charge at the Budrich UniPress website www.budrich-unipress.com
The two volumes in slipcase may be ordered from your local bookseller or directly from the Budrich UniPress.

Budrich UniPress Ltd.
Stauffenbergstr. 7. D-51379 Leverkusen Opladen, Germany
28347 Ridgebrook. Farmington Hills, MI 48334. USA
www.budrich-unipress.eu

Jacket illustration by Walburga Fichtner, Cologne, Germany
Printed in Europe on acid-free paper by
paper & tinta, Warszaw, Poland

PREFACE BY THE FEDERAL MINISTRY OF EDUCATION AND RESEARCH (BMBF)

Nobel Prize-winning economists Amartya Sen and Joe Stiglitz, in collaboration with a number of co-authors of the internationally acclaimed report "On the Measurement of Economic Performance and Social Progress," noted that:

> "Those attempting to guide the economy and our societies are like pilots trying to steering a course without a reliable compass. The decisions they (and we as individual citizens) make depend on what we measure, how good our measurements are and how well our measures are understood. We are almost blind when the metrics on which action is based are ill-designed or when they are not well understood. For many purposes, we need better metrics. Fortunately, research in recent years has enabled us to improve our metrics, and it is time to incorporate in our measurement systems some of these advances. There is also consensus among the Commission members that better measures may enable us to steer our economies better through and out of crises."

The German Data Forum (RatSWD) was founded to address these needs for more reliable statistics and better empirical research in Germany and beyond. The German Data Forum advises the German federal government and *Länder* governments on issues that impact the expansion and improvement of the research data infrastructure in the empirical social, behavioral, and economic sciences. Since it was established in 2004 by the German Federal Ministry of Education and Research (BMBF, *Bundesministerium für Bildung und Forschung*), the German Data Forum has significantly advanced the agenda set forth by the Commission to Improve the Information Infrastructure (KVI, *Kommission zu Verbesserung der informationellen Infrastruktur zwischen Wissenschaft und Statistik*) and has supported the work of research funding agencies by making recommendations on how the KVI agenda can be most effectively implemented. The German Data Forum has hereby helped make a wide range of high-quality, reliable microdata available to empirical researchers in the social, behavioral, and economic sciences at Research Data Centers and Data Service Centers throughout Germany.

These data are enabling researchers to expand the frontiers of scientific knowledge. Viewed in isolation, findings from discrete research disciplines appear unspectacular; only on rare occasions do they yield a fundamentally new picture of the world or of society. It is for precisely this reason that patience and a long-term perspective are so crucial for research funding and support. Of the many new conclusions that have been developed on the basis of empirical data from the Research Data Centers, two groundbreaking findings can be cited as evidence of this: First, data from German pension insurance carriers have been used by several researchers to identify significant differences between male and female life expectancy depending on the level of education and corresponding differences in workplace health risks. Second, data from the Federal Labor Office, in which firm statistics were merged painstakingly with data on employment structures, have been used to show that exporting firms pay higher wages than non-exporting firms. This would be impossible to see from the raw statistical data, since exporting firms have a different product portfolio and personnel structure than non-exporters.

The development and distribution of "Campus Files", a noteworthy contribution to university education, is also among the achievements of the Research Data Centers and Data Service Centers established by German Data Forum and the German Ministry of Education and Research. By working with original statistical data, students obtain more advanced methodological training with greater practical relevance. This will undoubtedly pay off substantially in the years (and decades) to come – particularly when the graduates begin putting their statistical expertise to work professionally in such fields as policy analysis and market research.

Despite the gains it has already made in expanding the research infrastructure, the German Data Forum is not content to rest on past achievements. To the contrary, in 2008 it launched the project, "Developing the Research Data Infrastructure for the Social and Behavioral Sciences in Germany and Beyond: Progress since 2001, Current Situation, and Future Demands." Building on its work from the last several years, the German Data Forum now aims to develop the research infrastructure even further, to ensure that it can meet future demands, and to identify emerging data needs in the German, European, and international contexts. The Federal Ministry of Education and Research will continue to lend its support in this important undertaking.

The support of the Federal Ministry of Education and Research has made it possible to bring together over 100 renowned experts from a wide range of disciplines in an ongoing dialog. The current publication delivers the results of this concentrated effort in two volumes. The nearly 70 advisory reports in the second volume offer a detailed look at the situation from the perspective of various branches of the social, behavioral, and economic sciences in order to identify specific data needs. It is a comprehensive and systematic compendium designed for use by research organizations, funding agencies, and statistical offices.

Government policy alone cannot create optimal conditions for improving the research infrastructure. Dialog with the research community and the federal statistical agencies is critical. Acting as a platform for this dialog is one of the key tasks of the German Data Forum. The Federal Ministry of Education and Research looks forward to being a participant in this discussion.

Berlin, November 2010

Cornelia Quennet-Thielen
State Secretary
Federal Ministry of Education and Research (BMBF)

Table of Contents:

Volume 1:

PREFACE BY THE FEDERAL MINISTRY OF EDUCATION
AND RESEARCH (BMBF) .... i-iii

EDITORS 9

PREFACE BY THE GERMAN DATA FORUM (RATSWD) 11

RECOMMENDATIONS 17

EXECUTIVE SUMMARIES 41

ADVISORY REPORTS 95

TOWARDS AN IMPROVED RESEARCH INFRASTRUCTURE
FOR THE SOCIAL SCIENCES: FUTURE DEMANDS AND
NEEDS FOR ACTION 97

1. Providing a Permanent Institutional Guarantee for the German Information Infrastructure...*Johann Hahlen* 97
2. The European Dimension...*Klaus Reeh* 115
3. The Role of the German Research Foundation...*Eckard Kämper and Manfred Nießen* 127
4. Providing Data on the European Level...*Peter Elias* 139
5. Infrastructure for High-Quality and Large-Scale Surveys. Cooperation between Academic Research and Private-Sector Agencies...*Peter Ph. Mohler and Bernhard von Rosenbladt* 155
6. The Availability of Market Research Data and its Potential for Use in Empirical Social and Economic Research...*Erich Wiegand* 175

PROGRESS SINCE 2001 AND CURRENT STATE 189

1. The Recommendations of the 2001 KVI Report and Their Realizations up to 2008...*Gabriele Rolf-Engel* 189
2. Access to Microdata from Official Statistics...*Stefan Bender, Ralf Himmelreicher, Sylvia Zühlke and Markus Zwick* 215
3. Publicly Financed Survey Data: Access and Documentation *Wolfgang Jagodzinski and Christof Wolf* 231

4. Teaching and Statistical Training...*Ulrich Rendtel* 251
5. e- Infrastructure for the Social Sciences...*Ekkehard Mochmann* 265

CURRENT STATE OF AND FUTURE DEMANDS IN
DIFFERENT FIELDS 287

I. (NEW) DATA TYPES AND THEIR POTENTIALS 287

1. Macroeconomic Data...*Ulrich Heilemann* 289
2. Interdisciplinary Longitudinal Surveys...*Jürgen Schupp and Joachim Frick* 303
3. Geodata...*Tobia Lakes* 325
4. Regional Data...*Gerd Grözinger and Wenzel Matiaske* 341
5. Genetically Sensitive Sample Designs...*Frank M. Spinath* 353
6. Biological Variables in Social Surveys...*Rainer Schnell* 367
7. Administrative Transaction Data...*Julia Lane* 383
8. Transaction Data: Commercial Transaction Surveys and Test Market Data....*Bernhard Engel*..401
9. Time Use and Time Budgets....*Joachim Merz*...........................413

II. METHODS 451

1. Survey Methodology: International Developments...*Frauke Kreuter* 453
2. Improving Research Governance through Use of the Total Survey Error Framework...*Marek Fuchs* 471
3. Metadata....*Arofan Gregory, Pascal Heus and Jostein Ryssevik*.......487
4. Paradata...*Frauke Kreuter and Carolina Casas-Cordero* 509
5. Record Linkage from a Technical Point of View...*Rainer Schnell*...531
6. Experiments, Surveys, and the Use of Representative Samples as Reference Data...*Thomas Siedler and Bettina Sonnenberg* 547
7. Experimental Economics...*Simon Gächter* 563
8. Experience Sampling...*Michaela Riediger* 581
9. Virtual Worlds as Petri Dishes for the Social and Behavioral Sciences...*Edward Castronova and Matthew Falk* 595

10. Qualitative Interviewing of Respondents in Large Representative Surveys...*Olaf Groh-Samberg and Ingrid Tucci* 607

Volume 2:

III. DATA PROTECTION AND RESEARCH ETHICS 627

1. Data Protection and Statistics – A Dynamic and Tension-Filled Relationship...*Peter Schaar* 629
2. Record Linkage from the Perspective of Data Protection...*Rainer Metschke* 643
3. New Methods in Human Subjects Research: Do We Need a New Ethics?...*Karsten Weber*...657
4. Does Germany Need a (New) Research Ethics for the Social Sciences?...*Claudia Oellers and Eva Wegner* 673

IV. FIELDS 687

1. Migration and Demography...687
   1.1 Migration and Globalization...*Martin Kahanec and Klaus F. Zimmermann* 689
   1.2 Migration and Statistics...*Sonja Haug* 703
   1.3 Internal Migration...*Andreas Farwick* 723
   1.4 Fertility and Mortality Data for Germany...*Michaela Kreyenfeld and Rembrandt Scholz* 739
2. Measuring Competencies..753
   2.1 Measuring Cognitive Ability...*Roland H. Grabner and Elsbeth Stern*...753
   2.2 Measuring Cognitive Competencies...*Ulrich Trautwein* 769
   2.3 Measuring Vocational Competencies...*Martin Baethge and Lena Arends* 783
   2.4 Measuring Social Competencies...*Ingrid Schoon* 797
   2.5 Subjective Indicators...*Beatrice Rammstedt* 813
3. Education and Research...825
   3.1 Education Across the Life Course...*Hans-Peter Blossfeld*........825

3.2 Preschool Education...*C. Katharina Spieß*..................................841
3.3 Data in the Domain of Secondary School Education....
    Petra Stanat and Hans Döbert......................................859
3.4 Knowing More about Vocational Training...*Steffen Hillmert*..877
3.5 Higher Education...*Andrä Wolter*...............................891
3.6 Adult Education and Lifelong Learning...*Corinna Kleinert and Britta Matthes*..911
3.7 Research, Science, Development...*Stefan Hornbostel*..............929

4. Economy and Labor Markets.....................................943
    4.1 Data from the Federal Employment Agency...*Stefan Bender and Joachim Möller*..943
    4.2 More and Better Data for Labor Market Research. Proposals for Efficient Access to the Currently Unused Potential of Official Statistical Data...*Hilmar Schneider*..............959
    4.3 Interdisciplinary Longitudinal Surveys. Linking Individual Data to Organizational Data in Life-Course Analysis...*Stefan Liebig*...971
    4.4 Organizational Data...*Stefan Liebig*...........................985
    4.5 Firm-Level Data...*Joachim Wagner*..........................1001

5. State, Family, and Health..1015
    5.1 Public Finance...*Thiess Büttner*................................1015
    5.2 Household Income, Poverty, and Wealth...*Richard Hauser*...1027
    5.3 Family Research...*Johannes Huinink*..........................1041
    5.4 Intergenerational Relationships...*Bernhard Nauck and Anja Steinbach*..1057
    5.5 Administrative Data from Germany's Statutory Health Insurance Providers for Social, Economic, and Medical Research...*Günther Heller*..1081
    5.6 Provision for Old Age: National and International Survey Data to Support Research and Policy on Aging... *Hendrik Jürges*..1093
    5.7 Income Provisions and Retirement in Old Age...*Tatjana Mika, Uwe Rehfeld and Michael Stegmann*.................1107

6. Political and Cultural Participation and the Role of the Media 1123
   6.1 Political Participation – National Election Study... *Rüdiger Schmitt-Beck* 1123
   6.2 Civil Society...*Mareike Alscher and Eckart Priller* 1139
   6.3 Culture...*Jörg Rössel and Gunnar Otte* 1153
   6.4 Mass Media Research...*Heiner Meulemann and Jörg Hagenah* 1173
   6.5 Judicature...*Wolfgang Heinz* 1197
   6.6 Environment...*Cornelia Ohl and Bernd Hansjürgens* 1217

TERMINOLOGY 1231

EDITORS

Representatives of the empirical social and economic research community in the German Data Forum (RatSWD) between 2008 and 2011:

- Prof. Dr. Frank Kalter, University of Mannheim (Dec. 2008 – Jan. 2011)
- Prof. Dr. Eckhard Klieme, University of Frankfurt am Main (Nov. 2006 – Nov. 2008)
- Prof. Dr. Heiner Meulemann, University of Cologne (Nov. 2006 – Nov. 2008)
- Prof. Dr. Notburga Ott, Ruhr University Bochum – *Deputy Chairperson 2008 – 2011* (Dec. 2008 – Jan. 2011)
- Prof. Dr. Susanne Rässler, University of Bamberg (Dec. 2008 – Jan. 2011)
- Prof. Dr. Ulrich Rendtel, Free University of Berlin (Nov. 2006 – Nov. 2008; Dez. 2008 – Jan. 2011)
- Prof. Dr. Heike Solga, University of Göttingen – *Chairperson 2007 – 2008* (Nov. 2006 – Nov. 2008)
- Prof. Petra Stanat, Ph.D., Director of the Institute for Educational Progress (IQB, *Institut für Qualitätsentwicklung im Bildungswesen*) at Humboldt University of Berlin; and Free University of Berlin (Nov. 2006 – Nov. 2008; Dec. 2008 – Jan. 2011)
- Prof. Dr. Joachim Wagner, Leuphana University of Lueneburg (Dec. 2008 – Jan. 2011)
- Prof. Dr. Bettina Westle, University of Marburg (Nov. 2006 – Nov. 2008)

Representatives of the data production community in the German Data Forum (RatSWD) between 2008 and 2011:

- Roderich Egeler, President of the Federal Statistical Office (Dec. 2008 – Jan. 2011)
- Eckart Hohmann, President of the State Statistical Office of Hesse – *Deputy Chairperson 2007 – 2008* (Nov. 2006 – Nov. 2008; Dec. 2008 – Jan. 2011)

- Prof. Dr. Joachim Möller, Director of the Institute for Employment Research (IAB, *Institut für Arbeitsmarkt- und Berufsforschung*) of the Federal Employment Agency (BA, *Bundesagentur für Arbeit*) (Oct. 2007 – Nov. 2008; Dec. 2008 – Jan. 2011)
- Sibylle von Oppeln-Bronikowski, Federal Statistical Office (Aug. 2008 – Nov. 2008)
- Walter Radermacher, President of the Federal Statistical Office (Nov. 2006 – July 2008)
- Prof. Dr. Hans Rattinger, President of GESIS – Leibniz Institute for the Social Sciences (*Leibniz-Institut für Sozialwissenschaften*) (Dec. 2008 – Nov. 2009)
- Uwe G. Rehfeld, German Federal Pension Insurance (RV, *Deutsche Rentenversicherung*) (Nov. 2006 – Nov. 2008; Dec. 2008 – Jan. 2011)
- PD Dr. Hilmar Schneider, Director of Labor Market Policy at the Institute for the Study of Labor (IZA, *Institut zur Zukunft der Arbeit*) (Nov. 2006 – Nov 2008)
- Prof. Dr. York Sure, President of GESIS – Leibniz Institute for the Social Sciences (*Leibniz-Institut für Sozialwissenschaften*) (Dec. 2009 – Jan. 2011)
- Prof. Dr. Gert G. Wagner, Director of the German Socio-Economic Panel (SOEP, *Sozio-oekonomisches Panel*) at the German Institute for Economic Research (DIW Berlin, *Deutsches Institut für Wirtschaftsforschung*) – Chairperson 2008 – 2011 (Nov. 2006 – Nov. 2008; Dec. 2008 – Jan. 2011)

Business office of the German Data Forum (RatSWD) – scientific staff between 2008 and 2011:

- Denis Huschka (*Managing Director*)
- Claudia Oellers
- Dr. Gabriele Rolf-Engel

PREFACE BY THE GERMAN DATA FORUM (RATSWD)

"Valid and reliable data are the indispensable foundation for research in the social sciences and economics: they ensure that research is in line with contemporary realities and provide convincing arguments for actions by citizens, policy-makers, and business leaders."

This is the opening sentence of the 2001 evaluation report by the German Commission on Improving the Information Infrastructure between Science and Statistics (KVI, *Kommission zur Verbesserung der informationellen Infrastruktur zwischen Wissenschaft und Statistik*), prepared on behalf of the Federal Ministry of Education and Research (BMBF, *Bundesministerium für Bildung und Forschung*).[1] Ten years later, this statement still holds: the provision of valid and reliable data through a sophisticated and sustainable research infrastructure is an important task for both academic research and official statistical institutions, and will remain so in the years to come.

The German Data Forum (RatSWD) was founded by the BMBF in 2004. Its origins, however, date back to 1999, when the BMBF appointed the KVI to submit a comprehensive report with recommendations to improve the German research infrastructure for the social and economic sciences. This report, published in 2001, still constitutes the basis for a large part of the work performed by the German Data Forum. Although the Forum's tasks have gradually expanded, collaboration with the Research Data Centers and Data Service Centers, both of which have come into existence since the founding of the Forum, continues to form the backbone of its activities. However, since KVI report's publication, much has changed – and improved – in terms of data collection, preservation, access, and analysis. Thus, the time is ripe to systematically assess the progress made so far in Germany's information infrastructure and to discuss current challenges and future needs in the German, European, and international contexts.

One of the key tasks of the German Data Forum is to offer informed advice to the policy-makers, official data providers (especially state and federal statistical offices), and research funding bodies involved in building and

---

[1] Kommission zur Verbesserung der informationellen Infrastruktur zwischen Wissenschaft und Statistik (KVI) (Ed.) (2001): Wege zu einer besseren informationellen Infrastruktur. Baden-Baden, 37 [own translation]. See also the documentation of the recommendations: "Towards an Improved Statistical Infrastructure. Summary Report of the Commission set up by the Federal Ministry of Education and Research (Germany) to improve the statistical infrastructure in cooperation with the scientific community and official statistics", in: Schmollers Jahrbuch 121 (3), 443-468.

running national and international statistical and research infrastructures for the social, economic, and behavioral sciences. To this end, the German Data Forum promotes dialog between, as well as within, academic research infrastructures and official statistical services, facilitating the extensive communication and coordination processes required to identify and prioritize needs and to develop sustainable concepts for nationwide and international data provision.

The German Data Forum has made a major step towards achieving these objectives by commissioning advisory reports from internationally recognized scholars in the social, economic, and behavioral sciences. The 68 advisory reports contained in this final volume, "Building on Progress – Expanding the Research Infrastructure for the Social, Economic, and Behavioral Sciences," cover a broad range of topics. Their preparation began in the summer and autumn of 2008 with two international workshops at which authors exchanged ideas with members of the German Data Forum. The intensive discussions that took place there regarding current challenges and future demands facing Germany's research infrastructure revealed the need to include many more fields than initially planned. By 2010, the original number of about 60 advisory reports had increased to almost 70. Together, these advisory reports form a compendium of recent developments and data infrastructure needs in numerous fields – not only in the economic and social sciences, but to some extent also in the behavioral sciences. They touch on an array of methodological, ethical, and privacy issues related to data collection, preservation, and access, and take recent European and international developments into consideration. Although the German Data Forum (RatSWD) has attempted to make this a comprehensive overview, one cannot claim to have covered every issue of relevance to the German research infrastructure in the behavioral, economic, and social sciences; the infrastructure for public health research, for example, is not discussed here. Furthermore, since the majority of advisory reports in this publication were written in 2009, it should be noted that the information presented reflects the state of affairs at that point in time. In order to guarantee the timely publication and broad international scope of this work, all advisory reports were released as *RatSWD Working Papers* and placed online prior to their final publication here.

This compendium is published in two volumes divided into three main parts. The first part presents the German Data Forum's recommendations on the further development of the research infrastructure for the social, economic, and behavioral sciences. One of the overarching goals of these recommendations – and of the German Data Forum itself – is to create optimal infrastructural conditions in Germany for innovative research both at universities and independent research institutes and within the system of official statistics and government research institutes. This requires that researchers in all these institutions be equipped with the capabilities and tools they need to create and access databases in Germany and abroad. A second and equally important goal is to create and cultivate a research environment that allows young scholars, official researchers, and official statisticians with innovative ideas to achieve their full potential.

A vibrant, structurally sound, and highly productive research environment cannot be created using a top-down approach: the impetus must come from the research community itself. Scholars as well as official statisticians and researchers need formal procedures that promote competition and allow research entrepreneurship to flourish. The recommendations contained in Part I of this publication seek to facilitate these processes by communicating the needs of scientific researchers and statisticians to policy-makers and by promoting dialog among the various institutions involved

The second part of this publication, also contained in the first volume, provides "executive summaries" of all of the advisory reports, including detailed recommendations on how to meet current and future data needs. The summaries serve to provide the reader with a compact overview of current issues and needs in each research field.

The third part is comprised of the 68 advisory reports commissioned by the German Data Forum and makes up by far the largest section of this final volume. The advisory reports cover a wide range of fields in the social, economic, and behavioral sciences: economics, sociology, psychology, educational science, political science, geoscience, and communications and media research. Some reports focus mainly on substantive issues, some on survey methodology and issues of data linkage, some on ethical and legal issues, and others on the assurance of quality standards.

The third part begins with the assessment reports that address future demands likely to be placed on Germany's research infrastructure as well as the progress made since the first KVI report of 2001. One of the main topics dealt with here is the harmonization of European research infrastructures and possibilities for the permanent institutionalization of certain elements thereof. These are followed by reports on specific research fields, and on new data types and their potential applications in scientific research – for example, geodata, biodata, and transaction data. Many of these reports highlight recent advances in research methodology, such as the use of paradata ("data about data") and, for example, "qualitative methods" that can enrich quantitative data. Others are concerned with questions of data security and research ethics.

Further reports deal with specific fields: migration and demography; vocational competencies, education, and research; labor markets and the economy; the state, the family, and health; political and cultural participation; and the role of the media. Since these have been identified as crucial research fields for research infrastructure, key aspects of each are discussed in several advisory reports.

Most of the authors of advisory reports work in academic or governmental organizations in Germany, but important reports also came from private-sector experts and from European and US scholars. Because of the wide scope of expertise spanning many different fields and issues, this compendium is of value not only for policy-makers, research funding bodies, and institutional data providers, but indeed for anyone interested in gaining an overview of Germany's research infrastructure within its international contexts in the social, economic, and behavioral sciences.

The entire process of preparing this compendium for publication was driven by a sense of enthusiasm, which became particularly evident at the workshops and in numerous discussions among contributors and German Data Forum (RatSWD) members. We are grateful to everyone involved in bringing this publication to fruition.

First of all, we would like to thank the Federal Ministry of Education and Research (BMBF, *Bundesministerium für Bildung und Forschung*) for their generous support through project funding (grant number 01 UW 0805). This provided the basis for intensive and systematic critical engagement with the topic of research infrastructure for the social, economic, and behavioral sciences, the results of which are presented in this publication.

Our profound gratitude goes to the authors of the advisory reports, who, through their comments and suggestions at the two workshops, greatly assisted in developing a differentiated overview of the current data landscape. Without this crucial input and their advisory reports, this publication would not have been possible.

Further thanks go to all the members of the German Data Forum (RatSWD) for their help in summarizing the findings of the advisory reports and in formulating recommendations based on these results. Special thanks go to Bruce Headey of Melbourne University, who provided numerous valuable suggestions and was responsible for writing the executive summaries.

This publication would never have been possible without the support of the German Data Forum (RatSWD) business office, specifically Patricia Axt, Lena Gond, Toby Carrodus, and Simon Wolff, who provided organizational, proofreading, and indexing assistance. Christoph Beck monitored the advisory reports and did the final proofreading and layout, all with exceptional commitment and careful attention to detail.

Further special thanks go to Deborah Anne Bowen and Jennifer Dillon for the editing of numerous English-language manuscripts and for translating several contributions into English. It was a large and sometimes difficult project, and they completed it with perseverance, commitment, and analytical expertise.

We are especially grateful to Claudia Oellers for her tireless dedication, immense effort, and the overall coordination of "Building on Progress – Expanding the Research Infrastructure for the Social, Economic, and Behavioral Sciences."

The German Data Forum (RatSWD) adopted these recommendations at its 25th meeting on June 25, 2010, in Berlin.

Berlin, October 2010

Heike Solga	Gert G. Wagner
Chairperson of the German Data Forum (RatSWD) 2007 – 2008	Chairperson of the German Data Forum (RatSWD) 2009 – 2011

Denis Huschka
Managing Director of the
German Data Forum (RatSWD)

RECOMMENDATIONS

For Expanding the Research Infrastructure for the Social, Economic, and Behavioral Sciences

The big picture: Measuring the progress of societies

The importance of better data for the social, economic, and behavioral sciences is underscored by recent international developments. For decades, social progress was judged mainly by measures of economic performance; above all, by increases in gross domestic product (GDP). In 2009, the Commission on the Measurement of Economic Performance and Social Progress ("Stiglitz Commission")[1] published its report, which opens with the statement that "what we measure affects what we do." It sought to bring about a change in social and political priorities by advocating that greater emphasis be placed on measures of well-being and of environmental and economic sustainability.

The Stiglitz Commission's recommendations form a backdrop to this report.[2] Recommendation 6 in particular can serve as a unifying theme for our recommendations; we quote it below in full.

Both objective and subjective dimensions of well-being are important

> "*Quality of life depends on people's objective conditions and capabilities. Steps should be taken to improve measures of people's health, education, personal activities and environmental conditions. In particular, substantial effort should be devoted to developing and implementing robust, reliable measures of social connections, political voice, and insecurity that can be shown to predict life satisfaction.*"

In Germany, the Statistical Advisory Committee (*Statistischer Beirat)*, which advises the Federal Statistical Office, made the Stiglitz Commission's report the backbone of its recommendations for the next few years. The Committee writes:

---

1 Report by the Commission on the Measurement of Economic Performance and Social Progress, chaired by Joseph E. Stiglitz, Amartya Sen and Jean-Paul Fitoussi, http://www.stiglitz-sen-fitoussi.fr, and Stiglitz, J./Sen, A. and Fitoussi, J.-P. (2010): Mismeasuring Our Lives: Why GDP Doesn't Add Up. New York.
2 International organizations like the Organisation for Economic Co-operation and Development (OECD) are dealing with similar issues. For example OECD established the "Global Initiative on Data and Research Infrastructure for the Social Sciences (Global Data Initiative)" as part of its "Global Science Forum."

"Initiatives for the further development of national statistical programs – above all demands for new data – often come from supra- and international institutions: the EU Commission, the European Central Bank, the UN, OECD and the IMF. The Statistical Advisory Committee (*Statistischer Beirat*) believes that valuable key initiatives will come from the Stiglitz Commission and the theme *Beyond GDP* advanced by the European Commission. Official statistics, in cooperation with the scientific community, must react to these initiatives and their system of reporting must develop accordingly."[3]

We want to stress this point in particular: *Beyond GDP* will be a fruitful concept only if it is discussed and shaped collaboratively by government statistical agencies and academic scholars. As the Statistical Advisory Committee wrote:

"The Federal Statistical Office should take stock of the non-official data which may be available with a view to measuring the multi-dimensional phenomenon of *quality of life*. The development of statistical indicators should be undertaken in cooperation with the scientific community."[4]

Further, at the 12th German-French Council of Ministers in February 2010, President Sarkozy and Chancellor Merkel agreed on the *Agenda 2020*, which included joint work on new measures of social progress. This was yet another message that policy-makers are interested now more than ever in sound empirical evidence about a wide range of social and economic trends indicative of human progress or regress.

The following principles and themes are not intended to contribute directly to discussion of the Stiglitz Commission report or the initiative of the German-French Council of Ministers. But they do lay the groundwork for improved measurement of economic performance and social progress.

We strongly believe that recent improvements in survey methods and methods of data analysis hold promise of contributing substantially to improved measurement of social progress.

---

3 Statistischer Beirat (2010): Eckpunkte zur Weiterentwicklung der amtlichen Statistik in der 17. Legislaturperiode, p. 8 [own translation].
4 Ibid.

Background

This report is based on contributions by approximately one hundred social scientists[5] who were invited by the German Data Forum (RatSWD) to write advisory reports on key research issues and future infrastructure needs within their areas of expertise; their reports are published as part of this publication.[6] The number of experts who have contributed is even larger than it was when the predecessor of this report was published in 2001.[7]

The advisory reports cover a wide range of fields of the behavioral, economic, and social sciences: sub-fields of economics, sociology, psychology, educational science, political science, geoscience, communications, and media research. Some reports focus mainly on substantive issues, some on survey methodology and issues of data linkage, some on ethical and legal issues, some on quality standards. Most contributors work for German academic or governmental organizations, but important reports were also received from individuals in the private sector and from European and American academics. All had a focus on German infrastructural needs, but German as well as international contributors emphasized the importance of international collaborative and comparative research. All reports have been repeatedly peer reviewed; they have been discussed and amended at successive meetings and in working groups organized by the German Data Forum (RatSWD).

We first set out some *guiding principles* underlying the recommendations. The core of the recommendations is structured around a set of *principles* and *specific recommendations* regarding infrastructure for the social sciences.

Research in the fields of public health and social medicine is not reviewed. These are clearly such important and distinct fields that they require their own major reviews.

---

5 To avoid long-winded expressions, the term social sciences will be used in the remainder of this report to refer to all the behavioral, economic, educational, and social sciences, as well as related disciplines.

6 Some working papers that were not commissioned by the German Data Forum but that are of interest too are available on the homepage of the German Data Forum. See http://www.ratswd.de/eng/publ/workingpapers.html, especially Working Papers 50, 52, 79, 113, 131, 135, 137, 139, 141, 151, and 153.

7 Kommission zur Verbesserung der informationellen Infrastruktur zwischen Wissenschaft und Statistik (KVI) (Ed.) (2001): Wege zu einer besseren informationellen Infrastruktur. Baden-Baden. For an English translation of the recommendations, see: "Towards an Improved Statistical Infrastructure – Summary Report of the Commission set up by the Federal Ministry of Education and Research (Germany) to Improve the Statistical Infrastructure in Cooperation with the Scientific Community and Official Statistics." Schmollers Jahrbuch, 121 (3), 443-468.

Principles guiding the recommendations

Evidence-based research to address the major issues confronting humankind

The social sciences can and should provide *evidence-based research* to address many of the major issues confronting humankind: for example, turbulent financial markets, climate change, population growth, water shortages, AIDS, and poverty. In addressing some of these issues, social scientists in Germany need to cooperate with physical and biological scientists, with scholars in the humanities, and also with the *international community* of scientists and social scientists.

Competition and research entrepreneurs

In making recommendations about the future of research funding and research infrastructure, we recognize the importance of competition and research entrepreneurs. This may seem an unusual perspective. In many countries, including Germany, there is a tradition of centralizing research funding and infrastructure decisions. In our view, this is suboptimal. Science and the social sciences thrive on competition – competition of theory and ideas, and competition of methods, and competition of infrastructures.

Public funding of research infrastructure is certainly needed because research findings and research infrastructure are public goods and would be undersupplied in a free market.[8] But decisions should not be made in a centralized, top-down fashion – an approach that has the effect of stifling rather than promoting innovation. The experience of the last few years has demonstrated – notably in the field of empirical educational research – that many fruitful new ideas and initiatives can emerge from a decentralized structure that would almost certainly never have resulted from a "master plan." First of all, in Germany the National Educational Panel Study (NEPS) and the Panel Analysis of Intimate Relationships and Family Dynamics (pairfam) are worthy of mention. Both are new panel studies with a long time horizon.

The history of Germany's Research Data Centers and Data Service Centers illustrates the same point. All the Research Data Centers and Data Service Centers established in the last six years were the result of independent initiatives intended to meet distinctive research needs. The KVI laid the groundwork by initiating the establishment of the first four Research Data Centers and two Data Service Centers through central funding. All the later centers were bottom-up developments. The Federal Ministry of Education

---

[8] See also UK Data Forum (2009): UK Strategy for Data Resources for Social and Economic Research. RatSWD Working Paper No. 131.

and Research (BMBF, *Bundesministerium für Bildung und Forschung*) and other initiatives provided some project funding for a few centers. What was crucial was the basic concept for the Research Data Centers, and that was developed by the KVI in its 2001 report.

It is true that the German Data Forum (RatSWD) later institutionalized this framework by establishing a Standing Committee of the Research Data Centers and Data Service Centers (*Ständiger Ausschuss Forschungsdaten-Infrastruktur des RatSWD*). This committee helps the centers to work together and put forward common interests, but it does not initiate new centers. Indeed, the German Data Forum (RatSWD) is of the firm opinion that it should not do so. What is necessary is a common framework for new initiatives that aim to raise Germany's social science infrastructure to a higher level.

In this report we take some further steps towards developing a common framework for research infrastructure in the social sciences. In doing so, we bear in mind the increasing opportunities open to German researchers to contribute to European and international databases and projects, as well as to projects in Germany itself. We formulate some principles and highlight a range of concepts and ideas drawn from the advisory reports.

We do not make detailed recommendations about specific research fields or particular infrastructural facilities. This would run counter to our view that innovative research directions and new ideas develop mainly at the grass-roots of scientific and statistical communities. The advisory reports did include a large number of recommendations for promoting research in specific fields and on specific issues. A few of these recommendations are included in this report as examples, but in general our approach is to make recommendations about institutions and processes in which competition and research entrepreneurship can flourish. Nevertheless, by providing the advisory reports in this publication, we hope to give research funding bodies some idea about the budgets that may be needed if particular ideas are put forward by "scientific entrepreneurs."

The important role of younger researchers

Closely connected to the need for competition and innovation in science is the need to develop and foster excellent young researchers and ensure that they have sufficient influence in the research community for their ideas and research skills to flourish. It is, in general, true that a centralized research environment favors older, well-established researchers. Almost unavoidably, it is they who are appointed to the main decision-making positions. However eminent they are, their decisions may tend to favor well-established research topics and well-established methods. Innovation, on the other hand, is more likely to come from younger and mid-career researchers.

An important aim and principle underlying this report is to enhance the roles, influence, and opportunities of younger and mid-career researchers. They should be encouraged and given incentives to act as research entrepreneurs, competing amongst themselves as well as with older, established researchers to develop infrastructure. They may, however, have occasion to form research networks among themselves, and this should be supported.[9]

The need to encourage younger researchers is particularly clear in the official statistical offices. They need more freedom to improve official statistics by doing research. Further, with more research opportunities available, employment in official statistical offices will become more attractive to innovative post-doctoral researchers. Recommendations along these lines are developed under Theme 2 below, where we also suggest that it would be valuable to form new kinds of partnerships with private-sector data collection agencies for the performance of specific infrastructure tasks.

Social science requires improved theory and methods, not just more data

The main focus of this report is necessarily on research infrastructure and databases, but we want to highlight explicitly the importance of further improvements in social science theory and also in statistical and survey methods.

Social scientists in almost all fields complain about data deficiencies. The usually unstated assumption is that if only they had the right data, they could do the rest. This is self-serving, misleading and often used to defend a lack of pertinent results. Theory and method are also crucial, and new developments in these domains often go hand in hand with availability of new data sources. The advisory reports published in Part III of this compendium describe exciting new data sources available to social scientists, including data arising from "digitization," geo-referencing, and bio-medical tests. We make some recommendations about linkages between new and increasingly available data sources and potential improvements to social science theory and method.

Research ethics and data protection are of growing importance

Most data in the social sciences are of course data on human subjects. This means that principles of research ethics and privacy need to be observed. In Germany the right to privacy and data protection is enshrined in the Federal Data Protection Act (BDSG, *Bundesdatenschutzgesetz*), which protects individuals against the release of any information about their personal or material

---

9   See the editorial in *Science*, April 2, 2010, Vol. 328, 17, and letters in *Science*, August 6, 2010, Vol. 329, 626-627.

circumstances that could be used to identify them. Principles of research ethics, on the other hand, are not embodied in law but are dealt with by the scientific community through codes of ethics promulgated by their professional associations.

Due to new technological developments, data protection and research ethics are of growing importance. Two of the themes outlined below reflect this importance.

Specific recommendations

In this section, we summarize insights arising from the advisory reports and subsequent discussions within the German Data Forum (RatSWD). We do this by presenting ten themes. Most of them represent general ideas and fairly abstract recommendations. We aim to encourage debate in the scientific and policy-making communities.

Theme 1: Building on success: Cooperation between official statistics and academic researchers

The German Data Forum's (RatSWD) current activities, as well as the present compendium, build on substantial achievements flowing from the 2001 KVI report. A major theme of that report was the need for improved cooperation between academics and the official statistical agencies, particularly in regard to making official datasets available for academic research. Initially, four Research Data Centers and two Data Service Centers were set up to provide academics and other users with access to official data files and with training and advice on how to use them. The original Research Data Centers are associated with the Federal Statistical Office, the Statistical Offices of the German *Länder*, the Institute for Employment Research (IAB, *Institut für Arbeitsmarkt- und Berufsforschung*) of the Federal Employment Agency (BA, *Bundesagentur für Arbeit*), and the German Pension Insurance (RV, *Deutsche Rentenversicherung*). Since then, nine more Research Data Centers have been founded (June 2010) and, after being reviewed by the German Data Forum (RatSWD), they joined the group of certified Research Data Centers. It is also worth noting that, after their first three years, all the original Research Data Centers and Data Service Centers were formally reviewed and received positive evaluations.

One of the advisory reports provided for this review offered the observation that, as a result of the Research Data Centers, Germany went from the bottom to the top of the European league as an innovator in enabling scientific use of official data. It has also been suggested that the Research Data Centers have had benefits that were not entirely foreseen, in that civil servants and policy advisors are increasingly using research-based data from Research Data Centers to evaluate existing policy programs and plan future programs. Civil servants have more confidence in academic research findings knowing that they are based on high-quality official data sources and that the researchers have received advice on how to use and interpret the data.

Official data files have also become more readily available for teaching in the higher education sector as a result of the recommendations of the 2001 KVI report. CAMPUS-Files, based on the Research Data Center files, have been created for teaching purposes and are widely used around the country.

It is important to note that the Research Data Centers have made good progress in dealing with a range of privacy and data linkage concerns that loomed large ten years ago. Particular progress has been made in linking employer and employee data. Research Data Centers have also, in some cases, been able to develop procedures for enabling researchers to have remote access to data once they have worked with officials in the relevant agencies and gained experience in using the data.

Partly due to the progress already made, but mainly due to technological and inter-disciplinary advances, new and more complicated issues relating to data protection, privacy, and research ethics keep arising. Some of these issues emerge because of the increasing availability of types of data that most social scientists are not accustomed to handling, including biodata and geodata. Other issues emerge due to the rapidly increasing sophistication of methods of record-linkage and statistical matching. These issues are discussed in more detail under Theme 8 ("Privacy") and Theme 9 ("Ethical Issues").

Based on these considerations, it is recommended that work continues towards providing a permanent institutional guarantee for the existing Research Data Centers. In the best-case scenario, Research Data Centers that belong to the statistical offices and similar institutions should be regulated by law. At present, the costs of Research Data Centers are borne by the agencies that host them, and users are usually not required to pay more than a nominal fee. In fact, we believe that this is the best way to run the centers because it ensures maximum use of official data. In the event that funding issues pertaining to the Research Data Centers arise in public and policy discussions, it is recommended that cost-sharing and user-pays models be investigated.

It is recommended that methods of obtaining access to a number of important databases that are still de facto inaccessible to researchers be investigated. Examples include criminal statistics and data on young men collected through the military draft system.

In particular, it is recommended that methods of permitting remote data access to Research Data Center files continue to be investigated.

It is recommended that the microdata of the 2011 Census – the first Census in almost 30 years – should be accessible and analyzed in-depth by means of concerted efforts on the part of the scientific community and funding agencies for academic research.

It is recommended that peer review processes be established and sufficient resources allocated to provide "total quality management" also of the data produced by government research institutes (*Ressortforschungseinrichtungen*).

We are in favor of a coordinated and streamlined process. We take a critical view, however, of the current trend towards increasing numbers of evaluations: this is neither efficient nor beneficial to the scientific content.

It is recommended that data providers in Germany collaborate more closely with the European Union's statistical agency, Eurostat.

Theme 2: Inter-sector cooperation: cooperation between academic research, the government sector, and the private sector

A major theme of the 2001 KVI report was the need for greater cooperation and collaboration among academic social scientists, official statistical agencies, and government research institutes (*Ressortforschungseinrichtungen*). Since then, it has become clear that in many areas of data collection and analysis, official institutes and academic organizations can form effective partnerships. Such partnerships would be strengthened if younger researchers in all areas were permitted more independent roles.

Much remains to be done. Academic research teams and official statistical agencies and research institutes probably still do not always realize how much they have to gain from collaboration. But each side must pay a price.

Academics need to understand and respect the social, political, and accountability environments in which official agencies operate. The official agencies (including the ministries and parliaments behind them), for their part, need to be willing to give up monopoly roles in deciding what specific data to collect and disseminate.

A strong case can be made that the improved level of cooperation that has been seen in recent years between academic social scientists and official statistical agencies and authorities should now be extended to include the private sector as well. Many large social and economic datasets, especially surveys, are collected by private-sector agencies. Since these agencies operate in a competitive market, they need a reasonably steady and secure flow of work in order to be able to make the investments required to maintain high-quality standards in data collection and documentation. Public-private partnerships may be desirable for initiating, attracting funding for, and continuing long-term survey-based projects. The UK's Survey Resources Network has experience in these ventures and may be able to offer useful guidance. Last but not least, a permanent flow of sufficient amounts of work is necessary to ensure competition between private fieldwork firms.

There are many opportunities for methodological investigations carried out in cooperation among academics and government and private-sector survey agencies. One clear example is investigation of the advantages, disadvantages, and possible biases of mixed-mode surveys. Mixed-mode surveys, which are more and more widely used, involve collecting data using a variety of methods, for example, personal interviews, telephone, mail, and Internet. In practice, respondents are commonly offered a choice of method, and the choice they make may affect the evidence they report.

Leaving aside cooperative ventures with public sector and academic clients, it is clear that private sector fieldwork agencies already collect a vast amount of market research data of great potential value to academic researchers.

The potential of market research data for secondary analysis lies mostly in the fields of consumption patterns and media usage. The German market research industry is huge – it has an annual turnover of more than two billion euros – and over 90 percent of its research is quantitative. However, samples are often highly specialized; telephone interviewing is the most common mode of data collection; and data documentation standards are not as high as academic social scientists would wish. However, secondary data analyses seem to be worthwhile – last but not least as a kind of quality control for these data. Clearly, too, the commercial clients for whom data are collected would have to give permission for secondary analysis. The data would have to be anonymized not only to protect individuals, but also to protect commercially sensitive information about products.

In addition, transaction data (e.g., about purchasing behavior) that is generated by commercial firms can be of interest for scientific research. In this case, anonymization is extremely important. The German Data Forum (RatSWD) makes no specific recommendation about this issue beyond the view that recognition of market research data and transaction data merits consideration in the scientific and statistical communities.

Theme 3: The international dimension

The main focus of the detailed advisory reports contained in this publication is of course on German social science infrastructure and research needs, but the international dimension is critical too. Plainly, many of the problems with which social scientists as well as policy-makers deal transcend national borders; for example, turbulence in financial markets, climate change, and movements of immigrants and refugees. Furthermore, international comparative research is an important *method of learning*. Similar countries face similar issues, but have developed diverse and more or less satisfactory policy responses. To do valuable international comparative research, researchers usually need to work with skilled foreign colleagues.

International data collected by the EU and other supra-national organizations have important strengths but also important limitations. The data are at least partly "harmonized" and cross-nationally comparable. Generally, however, data coverage is restricted to policy fields for which international organizations have substantial responsibility. Data are much sparser in areas that are still mainly a national-level responsibility. Furthermore, the needs of policy-makers, for whom the data are collected, do not exactly match the needs of scientists.

For example, policy-makers require up-to-date information, whereas scientists give higher priority to accuracy. Policy-makers are often satisfied with use of administrative and aggregate data and accept "output harmonization," whereas scientists favor the collection of micro-level survey data and prefer "input harmonization," that is, data collection instruments that are the same in each country.

With regard to international cooperation, which still raises some difficult problems for German research – in part because of legal restrictions on data sharing – we recommend that a working group be set up by the German Data Forum (RatSWD) to find ways of making German official statistics available *in a simple manner* as anonymized microdata to reliable foreign research institutes.

There are several cooperative European ventures that will be discussed in an open and constructive manner. These include a new European household panel survey under academic direction, Europe-wide studies of birth and other age cohorts, and a Europe-wide longitudinal study of firms. It would also be of great benefit to comparative European research if access to micro-level datasets held by Eurostat could be improved. Ideally, these data would be made available by virtual remote access, with appropriate safeguards to ensure data security.

It is noted that, following a British initiative, an International Data Forum (IDF) has been proposed. Along the lines of the UK Data Forum and the German Data Forum (RatSWD), this body would aim to bring together academic researchers and official statistical institutes, including international organizations like the OECD. The plan is currently being developed via an Expert Group set up under the auspices of the OECD. It is recommended that Germany participate in this and related initiatives through the German Data Forum (RatSWD) and possibly other bodies.

Finally, it is clear that the academic data providers are not very well organized at the international and supra-national level. Most surveys are conducted only within the bounds of a country at each wave. Notable exceptions are international survey programs like the European Social Survey (ESS) and the Survey of Health, Ageing and Retirement in Europe (SHARE), and networks of archives like the Council of European Social Science Data Archives (CESSDA), "Data Without Boundaries," and the "Committee on Data for Science and Technology (CODATA)." We recommend that the academic sector consider setting up an independent organization to represent its interests at the European and worldwide levels. This academic organization would be one of the partners in the international bodies that are likely to be established following the OECD initiative.

Theme 4: Data on organizations and "contexts"

It is clear that, since the 2001 KVI report, a great deal of progress has been made in Germany to improve academic researchers' access to firm-level data – that is, to data on employers and employees. These are high-quality data mainly collected in official surveys; firms are required to respond and to provide accurate information about the firm and its employee structure. Most statistical data of this kind are now available from Research Data Centers. Progress has been made on issues of data linkage, while protecting confidentiality, with the result that it is now often possible for researchers to link data from successive official surveys of the same firm. It is not, however, at present legally possible to link surveys of German firms to international datasets. This would be a desirable development, given that many firms now have global reach.

Progress made in improving access to data on business organizations points the way towards what needs to be achieved in relation to the many other organizations and contexts in which people live and work. Individual citizens are typically linked to multiple organizations: firms, schools, universities, hospitals, and of course their households. Linking data on these organizations and contexts with survey data on individuals would be desirable. Yet technical problems concerning algorithms for linking data are certainly easier to solve than the important questions regarding research ethics and data confidentiality that are in need of discussion.

At present, then, there are no German datasets that have adequate statistical information on all the organizations in which individuals operate. Data thus need to be collected in surveys on persons and activities in multiple organizations, and where possible, linked to data about the organizations themselves. This could potentially be achieved by (1) adding additional questions about organizational roles to existing large-scale surveys, perhaps even including the large sample of the German Microcensus, as well as by (2) linking existing survey datasets on these organizations with Microcensus data and other surveys on individuals and households.

A very special kind of new data type is information about historical contexts, which can be linked to time series data or microdata with a longitudinal dimension. The European Social Survey (ESS), for instance, provides such a databank. It contains information on minor and major historical events, and is updated on a daily basis. It is worthwhile to think about offering such a centralized historical database to the research community at large.

Government and research-based statistical data on political and civil society organizations are in short supply in Germany. In many Western countries, evidence about political parties – the most important type of political organization – is regularly obtained from national election surveys. Election surveys are also the main source of evidence on mass political participation. We want to note that in Germany, there is no guaranteed funding for election surveys, although a major election project (GLES, *German Longitudinal Election Study*) is currently being undertaken. This project could develop into a national election study.

Several of the advisory reports prepared for the German Data Forum (RatSWD) discussed detailed practical ways of realizing these possibilities. The German Data Forum (RatSWD) recommends that funding agencies consult these advisory reports when assessing specific applications to conduct organizational research.

Theme 5: Making fuller use of existing large-scale datasets by adding special innovation modules and "related studies"

Many of the advisory reports recommended that fuller use could be made of existing large-scale German datasets (such as ALLBUS) by adding special innovation modules, thereby creating greater value for money. Suggestions were made both for *special samples* and for *special types of data* to be collected. In all cases, it was suggested that the particular benefit of adding modules was that the underlying survey could serve as a national benchmark or *reference dataset* against which the new, more specialized data could be assessed.

The availability of a reference dataset enables researchers to obtain a more contextualized understanding of the attitudes and behaviors of specific groups. Conversely, the availability of detailed and in-depth evidence about subsets of the population can strengthen the causal inferences that analysts of the main reference dataset are able to make.

The advisory reports covering international and internal migration document substantial data deficits, which, it is suggested, could be largely overcome by adding special modules to existing longitudinal surveys (such as the SOEP). It has been pointed out that existing datasets do not allow researchers to track the life-cycles of migrants over long periods. This is particularly a problem in relation to highly skilled migrants, a group of special interest to policy-makers. Migrant booster samples, added to existing large-scale surveys, would largely overcome the problem.

Reports written by experts in other fields made similar recommendations. For example, it was suggested that data deficits relating to pre-school education and vocational education and competencies could be partly overcome by adding short questionnaire modules to ongoing surveys.

It is more or less conventional in the social sciences to collect exploratory qualitative data – for example, open-ended interviews – to develop hypotheses and lay the basis for quantitative measures prior to embarking on a large-scale quantitative project. It is suggested that this sequence can also sensibly be reversed. Once a quantitative study has been analyzed, individuals or groups that are "typical" of certain subsets can be approached with a view to conducting qualitative case studies. The researcher then knows precisely what he/she has a "case of." Extended or in-depth interviews can then be undertaken to understand the decisions and actions that subjects have taken at particular junctures in their lives, and the values and attitudes underlying their decisions.[10]

In an advisory report it is proposed that innovation modules using "experience sampling methods" be added to existing large-scale surveys. Again, the procedure would be to approach purposively selected respondents, representing sub-sets of the main sample, and ask them to record their answers to a brief set of questions (e.g., about their current activities and moods) when a beep alerts them to do so.

Theme 6: Openness to new data sources and methods

Advisory reports prepared for the German Data Forum (RatSWD) highlighted the potential of several exciting new sources and methods of collecting data. We want to mention some of these new technical possibilities, but without making specific funding recommendations. We do, however, want to stress that Germany needs to develop funding schemes involving use of these new data sources and data collection methods.

Digitization

Survey data and publications in the social sciences have generally been available in digital form for some time. Thanks to the grid technology promoted by the Federal Ministry of Education and Research (BMBF) as part

---

10 It is important to address the privacy and ethical implications of approaching survey respondents for additional interview data. Clearly, the respondents must be asked for explicit consent to link the data sets.

of the D-Grid Initiative, it is now possible to work with these digital data on a much larger scale and – more crucially – in new research contexts, thus enabling completely new approaches in empirical research. Yet the possibilities offered by grid technology have not been exploited in the social sciences to any notable extent.

Large quantities of data that would be of interest in social sciences research are generated by the Internet (particularly online social networks) and by the use of mobile phone, GPS, and RFID technologies. To date, researchers have drawn little benefit from such data, as numerous questions concerning access and data confidentiality remain unclarified. A few initiatives have been undertaken. For example, the networking site Facebook reports that social scientists in all English-speaking countries are analyzing messages posted on the site each day to assess changes in moods and perhaps happiness levels.

However, it will not be possible to make substantial progress until access and privacy issues are resolved. The German Data Forum (RatSWD) notes that the UK's Economic and Social Research Council (ESRC) has set up an Administrative Data Liaison Service to deal with similar issues by linking academics to producers of administrative data.

Geodata – A multifaceted challenge

Most of the data used in the social sciences have a precise location in both space and time. While geodata are used widely in geography and spatial planning, this is generally not the case in the social sciences. Spatial data from various sources (e.g., concerning urban development or the weather) can readily be combined via the georeferences of the units under investigation. This makes georeferenced data a valuable resource both for research and for policy advice and evaluation. While administrative spatial base data have been widely available for Germany for a long time, there has been an enormous increase in recent years in the supply of spatial data collected by user communities (e.g., OpenStreetMap) and private data providers (e.g., Google Street View). Furthermore, remote sensing data (aerial photos or satellite data) have become more important. These data are provided by different sources, which makes it important to launch geodata infrastructure projects that bring together different geodata sets. It must be emphasized that data security is of high importance for this type of data; issues of personal rights are particularly sensitive.

Closely related to geodata are data for regions, which can be defined as areas as large as a German *Land* or as small as a municipality. Regional data have been available for many years and have been used for cross-regional investigations and as context variables in studies investigating the behavior of persons or firms. Access to many datasets at various levels of regional aggregation is straightforward in Germany through the use of cheap CDs/DVDs and the Web.[11] The main challenge is to offer access to geodata in ways that allow easy combination with other data. Both current and older data need to be made available to allow for longitudinal studies. Furthermore, data on households, and buildings should be entered with a direct spatial reference; this is especially important for the forthcoming 2011 Census.

An important recommendation for the future is to intensify collaboration between social science researchers and researchers in institutions in the currently rather segregated areas of geoinformation and information infrastructure. Thus, the German Data Forum (RatSWD) will set up a *working group* on geodata and regional data with a view to bringing the different data providers and users together.

Biodata – Research incorporating the effects of biological and genetic factors on social outcomes

In recent times, greater attention has been paid in the social sciences to biomedical variables, including genetic variables that influence social and economic behaviors. Many opportunities, and some serious risks, exist in this growing research field. Historically, social scientists have received no training in biomedical research and are unlikely to be aware of the possibilities. Certainly, they have little knowledge of appropriate methods of data collection and analysis. It is under discussion whether the German Data Forum (RatSWD) will set up a *working group* with a view to positioning German social scientists to be at the forefront of developments. The group would need to include biologists and medical scientists, as well as social scientists and – equally important – not only data protection specialists but also ethics specialists. In addition, one issue that such a working group would have to address is the difficulty that researchers who are working at the interface of the social and biomedical sciences currently have in attracting funding.

A role model for this kind of multidisciplinary data collection may be found in the SHARE study, which has already conducted several pilot studies, collecting biomedical data from sub-sets of its European-wide sample. It has been shown that, with adequate briefing, medically untrained interviewers can do a good job of getting high-quality data in biomedical surveys, without a significant increase in non-participation or drop-out rates.

Virtual worlds for macro-social experiments

Advocates of the use of computer-generated "virtual worlds" (such as "Second Life") for social science research believe that they offer the best

---

[11] http://www.geoportal.bund.de, http://www.raumbeobachtung.de, http://www.regionalstatistik.de. [Accessed on: August 7, 2010].

vehicle for developing and testing theories at a "macro-societal" level. Many of the problems facing humanity are international or threaten whole societies: climate change, nuclear weapons, water shortages, and unstable financial markets, to name just a few. By setting up virtual worlds with humans represented by avatars, it is possible to conduct controlled experiments dealing with problems on this scale. The experiments can be run for long periods, like panel studies, and they can allow for the involvement of unlimited numbers of players. They pose no serious risk to players and avoid the ethical issues that limit many experiments.

Advocates of macro-social experiments recognize that initial costs are high, but claim that the worlds they create hold the prospect of eventually being self-funding, paid for by the players themselves.

Theme 7: Data quality and quality management

An increasingly important role is being played by questions related to the quality of (1) available measurement instruments, and (2) documentation required to facilitate secondary analysis of existing datasets.

Experts in several areas in their advisory reports made the point that a fairly wide range of measurement instruments were available to them, but that researchers would benefit from guidance in assessing their comparative reliability, validity, and practicality in fieldwork situations. In the advisory reports, it was suggested that something like a *central clearing house* was needed with a mandate to assess and improve standards of measurement. It was noted that the recent founding of the Institute for Educational Progress (IQB, *Institut zur Qualitätsentwicklung im Bildungswesen*) could serve as a model for additional subfields.

The IQB was launched at a time when the poor performance of German students in standardized international tests led to increased concern with measuring learning outcomes. The institute is measuring the performance of representative samples of students in the 16 German *Länder*, and will also be available to serve as a source of advice on measurement issues

A related but somewhat separate concern mentioned in several advisory reports is the poor quality of documentation provided for many surveys and other datasets that, in principle, are available for secondary analysis. It appears that academic data collection has much to learn in this respect from official statistical agencies, which generally adhere to high standards in data collection and documentation.

In thinking about data storage and documentation, a distinction should probably be drawn between two types of academic projects: those that are of interest only to a small group of researchers and those that are of wider interest. A mode of self-archiving (self-documentation) should suffice for the former type, although even here minimum satisfactory uniform standards need to be established. The latter type should be required to meet high professional standards of documentation and archiving (see Theme 10).

To a large extent, improvement of survey data documentation is a matter of adopting high *metadata standards*. These are standards relating to the accurate description of surveys and other large-scale datasets that need to be met when data are archived. Historically, researchers paid little attention to the quality of metadata surrounding their work; archiving was left to archivists. This mind-set is changing. There have been rapid advances in the development and implementation of high-quality metadata standards, standards which apply to datasets throughout their life cycle from initial collection through to secondary use.

An important source of survey metadata is the information collected in the recruitment of survey participants and in the actual survey itself concerning survey methods, the administration of the survey, and, when applicable, geographic location. These data, sometimes termed *paradata*, are typically recorded by interviewers and stored at the surveying institute. The data are valuable for analyzing problems of survey non-response and for assessing the advantages and disadvantages of different data collection modes. Paradata can be used for "continuous quality improvement" in survey research. It is recommended that efforts be made to standardize and improve the quality of paradata collected by public and private-sector survey agencies. The European Statistical System has published a handbook on enhancing data quality through effective use of paradata.

In Germany, the Research Data Centers have taken the lead in trying to improve current standards of documentation. Based on their experience, it appears that there are two internationally acceptable sets of metadata standards – the Data Documentation Initiative (DDI) and the Statistical Data and Metadata Exchange (SDMX) Standard – which could be more widely used in Germany. Adoption of these standards requires the establishment of a IT infrastructure compatible with the industry standard for Web services. This infrastructure can then facilitate the management, exchange, harmonization, and re-use of data and metadata.

We would like to highlight in particular one potential means of improving documentation: the use of a unique identifier for datasets (e.g., a digital object identifier or DOI). Unique identifiers for particular measurement scales (e.g., the different versions of the "Big Five" inventory) could possibly also be helpful (see also Theme 10 below).

The need for high-quality metadata appears even more pressing when recalling that many Internet users who are not themselves scholars are making increased use of these data for their own analyses. Results generated by lay users are especially likely to be skewed or misleading if the strengths and limitations of the data are described inadequately or in jargon a layperson could not be expected to understand.

Theme 8: Privacy issues

This section deals with privacy issues, particularly those that arise due to increasingly sophisticated methods of data linkage. *Record linkage* refers to the possibility of linking up different datasets containing information about the same units (e.g., individuals or firms). Linkages may be made, for example, between different surveys or between survey data and administrative data. Normally, datasets can only be linked if a common identifier is available. However, linkage can be achieved by means of "statistical matching" when datasets either do not contain the same identifiers for particular individuals or datasets of similar yet not identical units.

When an individual or firm consents to take part in a specific research project, the commitment and its limits are usually reasonably clear. But what is the situation if researchers acquire the permission of respondents to link a file obtained for this specific project to other files about the respondent, which, for example, contain information about her employer, tax files, health, or precise geographical location? Clearly, such linked data are of immense value to researchers, both in conducting basic scientific research and in providing policy advice. While it is clear that such linking may only take place with the explicit consent of the concerned individuals, how "explicit" must this consent be? Do the individuals whose data are being linked need to provide specific consent prior to each new linkage?

The advisory reports written for the German Data Forum (RatSWD) express a wide variety of views on this matter. While some legal experts have described such data linking as a breach of law, we believe that these problems could be best resolved by passing legislation that would require researchers to observe a principle of "research confidentiality" (*Forschungsdatengeheimnis*). This legislation, which was recommended by the KVI in 2001, would require that if authorized researchers obtained knowledge of the identity of their research subjects – even by accident – they would be obliged not to reveal the identities under any circumstances. Most important, the act would prevent both police and any other authorities from seizing the data. When pushing forward the issue of "research confidentiality," it will be important to refer to the European legislation.

A further proposal discussed in one of the advisory reports, is for data stewards (*Treuhänder*) to be appointed for the purpose of protecting the privacy of research subjects. Data stewards would be responsible for keeping records of the identity of subjects and would only pass data on to researchers for analysis with the identifying information removed.

A more general recommendation given in the reports is that a "National Record Linkage Center" be set up with high security precautions to cover all fields in which record linkage is an issue. This has been proposed to avoid the duplication that would occur if each branch of social science made its own separate efforts. The German Data Forum (RatSWD) expressly abstains from making any specific recommendations, but believes that the mentioned problems and possibilities are worth detailed consideration.

Theme 9: Research Ethics

This theme deals with two separate sets of ethical issues: the ethics of research using human subjects, and the ethics of scientists in publicizing their results.

Research using human subjects

The need to define and enforce ethical standards in research using human subjects has always been urgent and has become more so in view of the increasing availability of new types of data highlighted in this report: administrative and commercial data, data from the Internet, geodata, and biodata.

In practical terms, Germany does not yet have a detailed set of ethical requirements specifically designed to protect individuals who take part in research projects in the social sciences – a field typically concerned, of course, with the administration of surveys, and not human experiments. However, all researchers have to abide by the requirements of the Federal Data Protection Act. Additionally, the main professional associations in sociology and psychology have issued ethical guidelines, but these mainly affect behavior towards peers, rather than towards research subjects.

A review of ethics procedures in the UK and the US was undertaken by an advisory report to see if they offered useful examples for Germany. British procedures appear worth consideration; US procedures are perhaps too heavily geared towards the natural sciences.

In the UK, beginning in 2006, the *Economic and Social Research Council* (ESRC), which is the main funding body for academic research, forced universities whose researchers were seeking funding from ESRC to set up ethics committees. In practice, committees have been put in place in all universities, usually operating at the departmental or faculty level and not always on a university-wide basis. The committees are required to implement six key principles, four of which protect human subjects. Subjects have to be fully informed about the purposes and use of the research in which they are participating; they have the right to be anonymous; the data they provide must remain confidential; participation must be voluntary, and the research must avoid harm to the subjects.

The principle of "avoiding harm" is particularly important in view of the increasing availability of Web data, geodata, and biodata. "Avoiding harm" appears to be a principle of more practical relevance than the principle of "beneficence," which German social scientists, borrowing from the biological sciences, have sometimes incorporated into ethical guidelines.

Above all, given that research is conducted increasingly on the basis of international exchange, and research data are exchanged between different countries and national research institutions, it is of growing importance that respondents be able to rely on researchers to handle their data responsibly. Due to differences in national data security regulations as well as in research ethics standards, this is a difficult task, which, at worst, can hinder research. However, universal data protection rules are desirable, but extremely unlikely. Thus, it is important that, at a minimum, the scientific and statistical expert communities seek to foster the development of ethical standards which are then voluntarily adopted by those engaged in research and statistical work.

Scientific responsibility in publicizing results

A key set of ethical issues surrounds the responsibility of scientists in publishing and publicizing their results. In a recent editorial in *Science*,[12] it is noted that "bridging science and society" is possible only if scientists behave properly – that is, in accordance with scientific standards. The editorial mentions not just the need to avoid obvious scientific misconduct relating to data fraud or undisclosed conflicts of interest, but also the importance of avoiding "over-interpretation" of scientific results.

It is worth noting that many economists appear to believe that over-interpretation (by simplifying results) is necessary if a scientist wants to reach the general public. The former Federal President of Germany, Mr. Köhler, an economist by training, appeared to endorse this approach by calling for social scientists to announce "significant" findings without burying important results under too many details.[13]

We believe that it would *not* be wise for social scientists to take this advice, precisely because scientific results often become the subject of contentious public policy debates. Empirical results *can* have the effect of making policy debates more rational, but only if the assumptions underlying research and shortcomings that mar obtained results are communicated honestly. It is a duty of the scientific community to promote this type of honesty.

---

12 *Science*, February 19, 2010, Vol. 327, 921.
13 Köhler, H. (2009): Ein Kompass für die Gesellschaft. Grußwort von Bundespräsident Horst Köhler beim Festakt zum 40jährigen Bestehen des Wissenschaftszentrums Berlin für Sozialforschung am 17. Februar 2009 in Berlin. In: http://www.bundespraesident.de/Anlage/original_652450/Grusswort-beim-Festakt-zum-40jaehrigen-Bestehen-des-Wissenschaftszentrums-Berlin-fuer-Sozialforschung.pdf. [Accessed on November 17, 2010].

Theme 10: Giving credit where credit is due

A key principle of these recommendations is *"to give credit where credit is due."* This principle[14] should apply to efforts at developing the research infrastructure just as much as to academic authorship in publications. In general, valuable new infrastructural initiatives will only be launched if the staff of infrastructures under academic direction, of official statistical agencies – and perhaps of private-sector organizations that collect and provide data as well – feel recognized and rewarded for undertaking this important work. Junior and senior staff of all types of organizations need to be clearly recognized for their important contributions.

Existing academic conventions about "authorship" are not entirely satisfactory, nor are "science metrics" that evaluate the output of researchers, universities, and research institutes. In a recent article in *Nature*[15] it is suggested:

> "Let's make science metrics more scientific. To capture the essence of good science, stakeholders must combine forces to create an open, sound and consistent system for measuring all the activities that make up academic productivity. ... The issue of a unique researcher identification system is one that needs urgent attention."

Effective partnerships and joint investments by academic research institutes, official statistical agencies, and private fieldwork organizations occur despite seriously inadequate incentives and recognition for the creation and maintenance of research infrastructure. However, in order to make such collaborations more than rare events, the "rules of the game" must be changed. The establishment and running of infrastructure resources like biobanks, large social surveys, and the Scientific Use Files of official data must be rewarded more adequately than at present. This applies to official statistics, public administrations, private organizations, and the entire scientific system.

The German Data Forum (RatSWD) sees itself as one of the key players in promoting discussion and proposing effective steps on this issue. Here we want to mention two instruments that might help to ensure that credit is given where it is due.

First, the establishment of a system for the persistent identification of datasets (e.g., the DOI system) would not only allow easier access to data, but also make datasets more visible and easily citable, thereby enabling the authors/compilers of the data to be clearly recognized. Even particular measurement "devices" (e.g., specific scales for the "Big Five" inventory) might be identified and citable by unique identifiers. And a digital object identifier makes it easier to see the links between a scholarly article, the relevant datasets, and the authors/compilers of the datasets. There are already

---

14   *Nature*, December 17, 2009, Vol 462, 825.
15   *Nature*, March 25, 2010, Vol. 464, 488-89.

some organizations that have assigned DOIs to datasets (e.g., CrossRef and DataCite).

Second, the issue of a unique researcher identification system is equally important and needs urgent attention. The recent launch of Open Researcher Contributor ID (ORCID) looks particularly promising. The use of a unique researcher ID makes the scientific contributions of each individual researcher who works on a dataset clearly visible.

Concluding remarks

In Germany, there are several organizations for funding scientific research. Due to this "fragmented" funding environment, some policy-makers, government officials, and senior researchers believe that a more centralized organization would perform better. However, we at the German Data Forum (RatSWD) disagree. We are convinced that competition opens up more space for new ideas than would be available under a centralized system.

Even though we do not support centralized organization of research, we nevertheless recognize an increasing need to provide long-term funding to establish and run large-scale social science infrastructure. Fortunately, the academic community, official statistical agencies, and government research institutes are thinking more than ever before about how to reorganize and finance infrastructure in research and statistics. So, for example, the German Council of Sciences and Humanities (WR, *Wissenschaftsrat*), and Germany's Joint Science Conference (GWK, *Gemeinsame WissenschaftsKommission*) have working groups underway that are considering matters of research infrastructure.[16]

The discussions in these working groups have already made obvious that not only Research Data Centers and data archives but also more and more libraries – university and research institute libraries as well as centralized specialist libraries (*Fachbibliotheken*) – are an important part of the research infrastructure, providing crucial data documentation and access services. The Federal Archive (*Bundesarchiv*) could also play a specific role. Nothing is

---

16 These are (in 2010) the "Research Infrastructure Coordination Group (*Koordinierungsgruppe Forschungsinfrastruktur*)" and the "Working Group on a Research Infrastructure for the Social Sciences and Humanities (*Arbeitsgruppe Infrastruktur für sozial- und geisteswissenschaftliche Forschung*)" of the German Council of Science and Humanities (WR, *Wissenschaftsrat*) as well as the "Commission on the Future of Information Infrastructure (KII, *Kommission Zukunft der Informationsinfrastruktur*)" of the Joint Science Conference by the Federal and Länder Governments (GWK, *Gemeinsame Wissenschaftskonferenz des Bundes und der Länder*).

settled yet. However, it is time to find a new and appropriate division of labor among these institutions.

Many approaches will no doubt be considered, but in our view it is preferable to develop *principles* for funding and managing research infrastructure, rather than to attempt the almost impossible task of formulating a detailed *master plan*.

The German Data Forum (RatSWD) is itself neither a research organization nor a funding organization. It exists to offer advice on research and data issues. This places it in an ideal position to moderate discussions and help find the most appropriate funding arrangements.[17]

---

[17] See also the "Science-Policy Statement on the Status and Future Development of the German Data Forum (RatSWD)" by the German Council of Science and Humanities (WR, *Wissenschaftsrat*). Schmollers Jahrbuch, 130 (2), 269-277.

Executive Summaries[*]

---

[*] The executive summaries have been compiled and edited by Bruce Headey. These summaries are not necessarily identical with those in the expert reports.

TOWARDS AN IMPROVED RESEARCH INFRASTRUCTURE FOR THE SOCIAL SCIENCES: FUTURE DEMANDS AND NEEDS FOR ACTION

1. Providing a Permanent Institutional Guarantee for the German Information Infrastructure *(Johann Hahlen)*

Background and current issues

Proposals relating to an institutional guarantee for social science infrastructure should be soundly based on an understanding of existing constitutional, legal, and other requirements in Germany. In particular, the Federal Constitution enshrines strict rights to "informational self-determination."

Following the last 2001 KVI report, and taking account of legal constraints, four Research Data Centers and two Data Service Centers were set up. These centers take responsibility for "anonymizing" data and are themselves organized on a subject-matter basis. Formal evaluations of these centers have been positive.

Start-up funds for the centers came mainly from the Federal Ministry of Education and Research (BMBF, *Bundesministerium für Bildung und Forschung*) with the intention that other relevant institutions would provide subsequent funding. A permanent funding solution is now required, and while users can cover some of the costs it is important that the prices they are charged do not deter research.

Recommendations

(1) Each of the four institutions that houses a Research Data Center should provide financial support for its "own" Research Data Center.

(2) Special research projects, including methodological research, should continue to receive project funding on a temporary basis.

(3) Users should pay some costs, but subsidies should be available for financially "weak" users, like PhD candidates. Better-off users (e.g., economic research institutes) should pay full costs, especially if they have the capacity to pass costs on to clients.

(4) It is suggested that new Research Data Centers are needed to cover additional subject areas (e.g., health, education, crime, migration).

(5) An additional Research Data Center may be desirable to hold data that covers more than one subject area. This Research Data Center could function as a "data trust," archiving data for future scientific use.

2. The European Dimension *(Klaus Reeh)*

Background and current issues:

A great deal of social and economic data is now collected at the European level. The data are at least partly "harmonized" and thus cross-nationally comparable. Generally, however, data are restricted to those policy areas for which European institutions have substantial responsibility. Much less data is available in areas that are still mainly a national-level responsibility. Furthermore, the needs of policy-makers for whom the data are collected do not entirely square with the needs of scientists. For example, policy-makers want up-to-date information, whereas scientists are more interested in accuracy. Policy-makers are often satisfied with use of administrative and aggregate data and accept "output harmonization," whereas scientists favor the collection of micro-level survey data and prefer "input harmonization," that is, data collection instruments that are the same in each country.

Recommendations

(1) The German Data Forum (RatSWD) needs to recognize that the provision of high-quality data for science is a higher priority in Germany than at the European level. It is therefore recommended that the German Data Forum take the lead in pressing for improved European level data and statistics and working with Eurostat and sympathetic national statistical agencies.

(2) The German Data Forum could also take the lead in developing agreements among scientists about how best to compromise between their own needs and the differing needs of policy-makers for statistical data.

3. The Role of the German Research Foundation (DFG) *(Eckard Kämper, Manfred Nießen)*

Background and current issues

The future strategy of the German Research Foundation (DFG, *Deutsche Forschungsgemeinschaft*) should be based on past achievements and lessons learned from those achievements. First, the focus of efforts should be mainly on generating valuable new data, not sharing existing data. Second, the leaders of projects whose primary purpose is to provide a collective good for the research community (e.g., large-scale surveys) should be required to build an effective infrastructure to assist the community of users. At present, compliance with requirements to deposit data in archives for use by other researchers is far below 100 percent. The reasons for non-compliance need to be investigated. They certainly include the considerable costs of compliance in both time and money, costs that active researchers are unwilling to bear.

The DFG has ample means to support its aims and is willing to play an active role under its elected leadership bodies.

Recommendation

It is up to the research community to adapt itself in cooperative ways to make effective use of available funding instruments. Cooperation is required (a) to identify research themes that merit priority, (b) to identify funding options to support these priorities, and (c) to help define a division of labor in research funding between different national (including ministries) and international funding bodies.

4. Providing Data on the European Level *(Peter Elias)*

Background and current issues

This advisory report reviews the potential demand for and provision of European data for social science research. The concept of data provision is defined broadly, covering the ease with which specific types of data can be found, interpreted, understood, and accessed by researchers. The advisory report first addresses the issue of why researchers need European (as opposed to national) data sources. This leads to a discussion of the potential demand for data at the European level. The main section focuses on the characteristics of data currently available or under development. The concluding section provides an assessment of the need for new and/or improved data infrastructures and suggests where efforts could be focused to meet such needs.

Recommendations

The major needs are:

(1) A new European Household Panel.
(2) Facilities to encourage analysis of birth and other age cohort studies.
(3) A European-based longitudinal study of business organizations.
(4) Improved access to micro datasets held by Eurostat. This should be feasible, ensuring appropriate data security via virtual remote access.

5. Infrastructure for High-Quality and Large-Scale Surveys. Cooperation between Academic Research and Private-Sector Agencies *(Peter Ph. Mohler, Bernhard von Rosenbladt)*

Background and current issues

Germany already has a fairly well established set of large-scale measurement instruments (LMIs) – mainly surveys – in the social sciences. The LMIs provide high-quality measurement of social and economic trends and should be viewed as a core element of the country's research infrastructure. The private sector is the main sector involved in designing surveys and collecting data, although the government and academic sectors are also important. The system works well at present but the degree of cooperation between the private sector and other sectors may not be adequate for the future.

Recommendation

Closer cooperation among government, the private sector, and academia would be beneficial for the development of LMIs. The private sector as a whole needs the assurance of a planned flow of work in order to undertake the large-scale investments in survey infrastructure that are required. The German Data Forum could take the lead in initiating closer cooperation and could look to the UK's Survey Resources Network as a useful example. Public-private partnerships are desirable for initiating, attracting funding, and continuing long-term survey-based projects. Such partnerships could promote methodological innovations, as well as collecting large datasets.

6. The Availability of Market Research Data and its Potential for Use in Empirical Social and Economic Research *(Erich Wiegand)*

Background and current issues

The potential of market research for secondary analysis lies mostly in the fields of consumer behavior, consumption patterns, and media usage. The German market research industry is huge – it has an annual turnover of more than two billion euros – and over 90 percent of its research is quantitative. However, samples are often highly specialized (rather than being representative and heterogeneous), telephone interviewing is the most common mode of data collection, and data documentation standards are not as high as academic social scientists would wish.

The chances of getting market research data released for secondary analysis would be improved if a win-win situation could be created by which, as a quid pro quo, the industry gained access to microdata from official statistical agencies. At present this is forbidden by law; individual data from official statistics are only available for scientific and not for commercial purposes.

Recommendation

It is recommended that the academic social and economic research community should consider supporting market research companies in their efforts to gain access to official statistics at the individual level. This would increase the readiness of companies and their clients to make data available for secondary analysis by social scientists. The appropriate body for the academic community (e.g., the German Data Forum) to negotiate with is the Working Group of German Market and Social Research Institutes (ADM, *Arbeitskreis Deutscher Markt- und Sozialforschungsinstitute*).

PROGRESS SINCE 2001 AND CURRENT STATE

1. The Recommendations of the 2001 KVI Report and Their Realizations up to 2008 *(Gabriele Rolf-Engel)*

Background and current issues

This advisory report describes the structure of the 2001 KVI report and lists the eight themes into which its 36 recommendations were categorized. It then reviews the extent to which each recommendation has or has not been implemented between 2001 and 2008. Each recommendation is assigned a green light (full implementation), a yellow light, or a red light. The advisory report makes no recommendations, but leaves it open to the German Data Forum to press for the implementation (or improved implementation) of 2001 recommendations that were either not implemented or only partly implemented. Key successes include:

(1) The foundation of four Research Data Centers, making confidentialized data files accessible for scientific purposes as well as CAMPUS-Files for teaching purposes.

(2) Establishment of two Data Service Centers.

(3) Access to business data via projects supported by the Federal Ministry of Education and Research (BMBF, *Bundesministerium für Bildung und Forschung*).

(4) Long-term funding for the German Socio-Economic Panel (SOEP, *Sozio-oekonomisches Panel*) and the National Educational Panel Study (NEPS).

2. Access to Microdata from Official Statistics *(Stefan Bender, Ralf Himmelreicher, Sylvia Zühlke, Markus Zwick)*

Background and current issues

A major outcome of the 2001 KVI report was the founding of four publicly funded Research Data Centers. These centers have greatly improved the access of researchers to official microdata. The centers have developed in constructive ways that were not entirely foreseen. Their services are widely used and many policy decisions are now planned and/or evaluated on the basis of data originating from them. Germany has gone from the bottom of the European league with regard to use of official statistical data for research purposes to the position of being an innovator. Innovations have been made, in particular, in providing access to data for teaching purposes via CAMPUS-Files, and in producing linked employer-employee datasets.

The Research Data Centers have developed strict criteria that provide for equal treatment of all data users, regardless of the subject/content of their research. Strict privacy and data protection conditions are in force. Researchers are required to spend substantial time working on the premises of a Research Data Center in order to learn about content and methodological issues relating to the data they are using. Access via controlled remote data sites may then be available.

Recommendations

(1) The four Research Data Centers should continue to increase their cooperation.

(2) One area of cooperation is the development of improved procedures for remote data access.

(3) Cooperative work is also underway to match survey data to administrative data.

It is noted that discussions are underway relating to the possible permanent establishment of the Research Data Centers of the Federal Statistical Office and the Statistical Offices of the German *Länder*.

3. Publicly Financed Survey Data: Access and Documentation
(Wolfgang Jagodzinski, Christof Wolf)

Background and current issues

Four types of publicly financed surveys are considered: (1) academic surveys, (2) surveys using data from projects funded by the German Research Foundation (DFG, *Deutsche Forschungsgemeinschaft*), (3) surveys utilizing data collected for research funded by the Federal State and the *Länder* (*Ressortforschung*), and (4) surveys employing data collected by national and international statistical agencies.

Recommendations

(1) Minimum standards of data accessibility should be required for all publicly funded scientific projects. All data should be stored in a digital repository provided by the social science infrastructure.

(2) A distinction should be drawn between two types of projects: those that are only of interest to a small group of researchers and those that are of wider interest. A mode of self-archiving (self-documentation) should be established for the former type, prior to data being lodged in a central depository. The latter type should be required to meet high professional standards of documentation and archiving. A pilot project should be established to define these standards.

(3) Access to data from the government research institutes (*Ressortforschung*) is at present quite limited and should be the standard expectation. Confidentiality requirements are often cited as the reason for restrictions but should rarely prevent access to an entire dataset.

(4) Access to data funded by national and international agencies is at present quite satisfactory, but it would be desirable for all documentation to reach the standard set by the European Social Survey (ESS).

4. Teaching and Statistical Training *(Ulrich Rendtel)*

Background and current issues

Well-educated researchers are needed for fruitful analysis of large social and economic datasets. Further, the creation of research data centers has generated increased demand for such analysts at the Diplom/Master's and PhD levels. But within the field of economics there is intense competition between sub-disciplines to attract students, and survey statistics has not fared well. The situation is better in sociology faculties.

Recommendations

(1) Some CAMPUS-Files (i.e., files freely available to teachers and students) are already available, including some from the Federal Statistical Office. However, the creation of new CAMPUS-Files, covering a wider range of subjects, is recommended as a way of attracting more high-quality students.

(2) It is recommended that new Master's programs be created in survey statistics, in part to compensate for the fact that, following the Bologna reforms, Bachelor-level students are not likely to have sufficient statistical training to undertake analysis of large datasets.

(3) Finally, it is recommended that it should become possible for students to receive academic credit for completing training courses in data analysis, which are currently offered by private sector data producers, the

Leibniz-Institute for the Social Sciences (GESIS, *Leibniz-Institut für Sozialwissenschaften*), and the Research Data Centers. This would be a sensible extension of the increasing collaboration between these organizations and universities.

5. e-Infrastructure for the Social Sciences *(Ekkehard Mochmann)*

Background and current issues

Social scientists have been slow to take advantage of collaborative research opportunities made possible by e-Science infrastructure. In principle, grids of fiber optic cable can link widely dispersed networks of researchers who can share data and undertake analyses using virtually unlimited computing capacity. For example, The EU research network Géant links 10,000 scientists at 300 sites in 50 countries and provides access to 80,000 CPU cores 24 hours a day.

The German Grid Initiative was launched in 2005, but so far social scientists have not contributed. Most social scientists appear to believe that Web 2.0 technology is adequate for their needs. A good example of technology at this level is the Council of European Social Science Data Archives (CESSDA) Portal, which holds important international datasets, including the European Social Survey (ESS) and the European Values Study. Documentation of studies is based on Data Documentation Initiative specifications (DDI), with Web software tools enabling users to browse and analyze data.

Recommendations

(1) The German social science community needs to decide whether it wants to take a concerted initiative to make use of data grid technology. If it does, then an institutional basis may be needed similar to the National Center for eSocial Science (NCeSS) in the UK. The Open Access Initiatives (e.g., the Berlin Declaration 2003) and the OECD (2004) declaration on open access to publicly financed data provide a basis for taking steps in this direction.

(2) If the social science community decides that it may wish to proceed, one way forward would be to set up a working group to make a needs assessment in relation to grid technology and to deal with a range of methodological, technical, and legal issues.

CURRENT STATE OF AND FUTURE DEMANDS IN DIFFERENT FIELDS

I. *(New) Data Types and their Potentials*

1. Macroeconomic Data *(Ulrich Heilemann)*

Background and current issues

No really lamentable or material gaps exist, and the cost of obtaining data is low. No major changes are likely before scheduled reforms to the National Accounts in 2011 and then 2014.

The provision of macro-data improved enormously 50 years ago when the National Accounts were introduced. In the last decade, we have seen huge improvements in research infrastructure for microeconomics, which perhaps has now "caught up" with macroeconomics. In many areas of social science, it is now no longer reasonable to regard data as a limiting factor.

2. Interdisciplinary Longitudinal Surveys *(Jürgen Schupp, Joachim Frick)*

Background and current issues

Household panel studies under academic direction are conducted in several countries. The Panel Study of Income Dynamics (PSID) in the US was the first to be launched and has been followed by similar major panel studies in Germany, Britain, and Australia. Experience shows that academic direction of these panel studies is beneficial for both the capacity to innovate and the capacity to extend their scope to include topics of interest to new disciplines. In practice, most of the current national panel studies were initially directed by economists and/or sociologists. But they now include questions and measures relating to psychological concepts, cognitive capabilities, and physical and mental health. They have also been extended to include age-specific modules of interest to developmental psychologists and biologists (e.g., mother and child and retirement modules). The German Socio-Economic Panel (SOEP, Sozio-oekonomisches Panel) will specifically add an innovation sample to try out new questionnaire modules and data collection methods, and will also conduct behavioral experiments with sample members as subjects. None of these changes were envisaged when the household panels started, but under academic direction innovation has been embraced.

The fact that data from these household panels are in continuously high demand from both the academic and policy communities is testimony to their capacity for innovation.

Recommendations

(1) It is recommended that increased attention be given in household panels to the earliest and last phases of human life – early childhood and late adulthood. Event-triggered modules (e.g., a module triggered by the birth of a child) should be designed to cover specific phases of the life course in more detail.

(2) Sample sizes need increasing to improve statistical power in analyzing data for population sub-sets (e.g., immigrants) and regions. It is recommended that sub-sample sizes of 500 per birth and age cohort should be considered an acceptable standard.

(3) It is recommended that national household panels be used as "reference" datasets for more specialized surveys. That is, they can effectively be used to provide comparisons (or baselines) for results from the more specialized studies.

3. Geodata *(Tobia Lakes)*

Background and current issues

In principle, all socio-economic data relate to a specific location in time and space. In practice, it is estimated that some geoinformation is provided for about 80 percent of all such data. The quantity, quality, and multidimensionality of geodata are improving rapidly in Germany and elsewhere, but are seriously under-exploited by social scientists. Large databases have been built up in both the public and private sectors. In Germany, the Federal Agency for Cartography and Geodesy (BKG, *Bundesamt für Kartographie und Geodäsie*) is a major source for users, but private-sector sources are also important. In both sectors it is common to charge fees for user access, especially when complex database searches are required, involving use of advanced mapping and spatio-temporal algorithms. However, some sources (e.g., GoogleEarth) provide free data and access to free software.

Recommendations

(1) There is a need for more cooperation between what, at present, are rather segregated public and private sector sources of geodata.

(2) The upcoming 2011 Census could be used as a focus for such cooperation, partly by efforts to link Census data to other sources.

(3) The German Data Forum could assist the process for social scientists whose work could benefit greatly from more sophisticated use of geoinformation.

(4) The German Data Forum could also facilitate international cooperation in the use of geodata.

4. Regional Data *(Gerd Grözinger, Wenzel Matiaske)*

Background and current issues

Space/location is an increasingly important dimension of social science analysis. It is clear that intra-national (or regional) comparisons can prove just as valuable as the more fashionable international comparisons. A great deal of high-quality regional data is available, provided by official and semi-official statistical agencies and generally in the form of user-friendly DVDs. Academic researchers and, especially, commercial firms also collect spatial data, often at a very detailed local level. Regional analysis has also been facilitated by methodological advances; in particular, the development of multilevel statistical analysis.

Recommendations

(1) It would be valuable for researchers if some existing datasets that are not yet available for spatial analysis could be released (e.g., the PISA E dataset).

(2) On many topics (e.g., criminal behavior) insufficient data are available at the regional and local level.

(3) An agreed classification of localities should be used in research. The European Nomenclature of Territorial Units for Statistics (NUTS, *Nomenclature des unites territoriales statistiques*) classification is the clear choice.

5. Genetically Sensitive Sample Designs *(Frank M. Spinath)*

Background and current issues

Many social and economic outcomes, including earnings, life satisfaction, and physical and mental health, result from the interplay of genetic and environmental factors. There is an opportunity to modify existing household panel studies in order to allow for state-of-the-art multi-group analyses of genetic and environmental effects. The panels already include respondents who are genetically related to each other in a wide variety of ways. What is needed is an additional over-sampling of twins. In Germany there is no central twin register, but previous studies have nevertheless had considerable success in recruiting twins. There is, however, usually some bias towards oversampling women and monozygotic twins.

Recommendation

It is recommended that twin cohorts be added to and integrated into panel studies, including the German Socio-Economic Panel (SOEP, *Socio-oekonomisches Panel*).

6. Biological Variables in Social Surveys *(Rainer Schnell)*

Background and current issues

Social scientists have almost completely ignored biological variables in their research. Yet it is clear that these variables are important in accounting for many aspects of social and economic behavior. There are, in fact, many biological measures that can be taken by medically untrained observers (e.g., survey interviewers) in standard surveys. These include body-mass index, grip strength, and simple pulmonary function tests. However, as a matter of law, blood samples can only be taken by a medical doctor in Germany. Small sized sensors and "intelligent clothing" may become increasingly important for use in surveys. Generally, respondents react favorably to the use of new instruments, but cooperation may later decline as the techniques become more common.

Recommendations

(1) Biological variables (biomarkers) should be collected in a wide range of surveys. With this in mind, biologists and behavioral scientists, for example, should become members on the advisory board of the Leibniz Institute for the Social Sciences (GESIS, *Leibniz-Institut für Sozialwissenschaften*). Graduate programs in the social sciences should alert students

to the value of biomarkers, and students should be trained in appropriate methods of analysis.

(2) Research is needed on the willingness of respondents to cooperate in providing biological measures and on possible biases resulting from differential cooperation. Ideally, controlled experiments should be conducted.

(3) Funding opportunities for cross-disciplinary work are limited in Germany. An interdisciplinary special research program of the German Research Foundation (DFG, *Deutsche Forschungsgemeinschaft*) would be a valuable first step. An EU project may also be a promising way forward.

7. Administrative Transaction Data *(Julia Lane)*

Background and current issues

This advisory report describes the potential for the social sciences of data from a wide range of sources, including Internet clickstreams (e.g., in the use of social networking sites), e-mails, cell phones, GPS systems and radio frequency identification devices, credit card purchases, telephone calls, retail store scanning records, health records including biomarkers, and employment records.

In sheer quantity, administrative data dwarf all other datasets, but at present social scientists make little use of them. Note, however, that the UK's Economic and Social Research Council (ESRC) has set up an Administrative Data Liaison Service to link academics to producers of administrative data, and the US National Science Foundation (NSF) has recently awarded large grants for the study of social and information networking. Peter Elias, on behalf of several international agencies, is working to establish the International Data Forum.

Recommendations

(1) Invest in new methods of data collection to harvest administrative data. It is necessary to solve issues of privacy and confidentiality, but considerable progress has already been made in this regard. Funding agencies are at present keen to fund such efforts. This opportunity should be taken advantage of.

(2) Devise new ways of analyzing transaction data. The data are often characterized by a high noise-to-signal ratio and by non-linearity. Standard tables and regression analyses tend to be of limited value. Visual representations are often preferable. Social scientists could learn much about such techniques from computer and behavioral scientists.

(3) The study of administrative data should be conducted by "virtual communities" of scientists using an open and transparent infrastructure for data sharing and dissemination. In this respect, social science communities should become more like "hard science" communities.

(4) Improved methods of communicating administrative data to policy-makers and broader communities need to be devised.

8. Transaction Data: Commercial Transaction Surveys and Test Market Data *(Bernhard Engel)*

Background and current issues

Commercial transaction surveys and test market data are virtually unused by the scientific community. Yet they are important sources for understanding consumer behavior. Their advantage is that they provide "hard" data on sales and marketing, not just "soft" data on consumer perceptions. There are three main problems facing scientists who may wish to use the data. First, the commercial owners need to give permission. Second, the data would need to be made anonymous with respect to both individuals and products, without losing information vital to research. Third, the quality of the data would need to be checked to determine their value for scientific research.

Recommendations

(1) In cooperation with the official statistical community and market researchers, the German Data Forum could facilitate *scientific use of commercial transaction and test market data* by initiating a project to investigate issues of data "anonymization," with respect to both the identity of products and the identity of consumers.

(2) The German Data Forum could also take the lead in proposing standards of data quality.

9. Time Use and Time Budgets *(Joachim Merz)*

Background and current issues

Time use studies are uniquely valuable for studying, *inter alia*, the division of labor within households, household production, and leisure activities. The Federal Statistical Office conducts a time use survey approximately every ten years, and this is now integrated with the EU's Harmonized European Time Use Surveys (HETUS).

Recommendations

(1) The next German national time use survey, due in 2011-12, should be conducted by the Federal Statistical Office and needs secure funding. It should again be embedded in the EU's HETUS. It is recommended that the German Data Forum support this view.

(2) Supplementary questions about infrequent activities should be appended to the main diary collection instrument.

(3) Mobile devices should be used to provide additional experience sampling data. This requires a pilot study before incorporation in the main survey.

(4) Expenditure data and subjective satisfaction data should be collected alongside time use data.

(5) A new longitudinal study on time use is recommended to answer questions about changes in individual time use profiles in response to major life events and changing environmental conditions.

II. Methods

1. Survey Methodology: International Developments *(Frauke Kreuter)*

Background and current issues

Survey methodology has been heavily influenced by two factors in recent years: falling response rates and technological advances in data collection. Falling response rates have led researchers to emphasize that these rates were never a valid guide to *response bias*. Two alternative measures of response bias are now receiving more attention: single indicators for an entire survey (e.g., the variance of non-response weights) and item-specific estimates (e.g., comparisons between survey results for a particular variable and interviewer observations or administrative data).

In order to counteract falling response rates, efforts are being made to reduce *response burden*. One approach is multiple matrix sampling, which involves putting different sub-sets of questions to sub-sets of respondents drawn from an initial sample.

Changing technology has allowed development of mixed-mode surveys (e.g., different sub-sets of respondents record their data using CAPI, or CATI, or by mail). Substantial research efforts are now being directed at methods of estimating response bias for each mode and, overall, for multi-mode surveys.

Recommendations

(1) Many recent developments, including deployment of mixed-mode surveys and requirements for interviewer observations, place increased demands on survey interviewers. This suggests a need for further research on interviewer performance and its consequences for response bias.

(2) German researchers are particularly well placed to investigate response bias in mixed-mode surveys, due to major efforts already undertaken in data linkage (e.g., between surveys and official sources).

(3) Randomized experiments that test alternative survey modes and methods could usefully be conducted within survey organizations that are already responsible for carrying out many surveys at the same time.

(4) All of the above recommendations require increased cooperation between researchers and survey organizations.

2. Improving Research Governance through Use of the Total Survey Error Framework *(Marek Fuchs)*

Background and current issues

The infrastructure for survey research has greatly improved in the last 20 years. It would now be valuable to conceive of survey methodology as a framework or "science for conducting and evaluating surveys." The specific framework proposed here revolves around the concept and measurement of *total survey error*. Total survey error includes both sampling or "representation" error and also measurement/response error (Groves et al, 2004). In practice, it is usually too expensive to calculate mean square errors for particular sample estimates because multiple repetitions of one's survey design are required. However, researchers can benefit greatly from using the total survey error framework because it alerts them to all possible components of error and serves as a guide in designing cost-effective surveys.

Recommendations

(1) It is recommended that the research community adopt the total survey error framework as a guide to survey design and evaluation.

(2) Survey methodology should be regarded as a valuable "cross-disciplinary discipline." The emergence of Master's degrees in this field should be encouraged.

3. Metadata *(Arofan Gregory, Pascal Heus, Jostein Ryssevik)*

Background and current issues

In the social sciences, *metadata* can be defined as available documentation of primary datasets. Historically, researchers paid little attention to the quality of metadata surrounding their work; archiving was left to archivists. This mindset is changing. There have been rapid advances in the development and actual implementation of high-quality metadata standards; standards which apply to datasets throughout their life cycle from initial collection through to secondary use, perhaps in conjunction with quite different datasets. The German Research Data Centers, which were set up following the 2001 KVI report, together with the Leibniz Institute for the Social Sciences (GESIS, *Leibniz-Institut für Sozialwissenschaften*), have taken a leading role in these developments.

This advisory report describes two sets of metadata standards in some detail: the Data Documentation Initiative (DDI) and the Statistical Data and Metadata Exchange (SDMX) Standard. These are seen as central to a potential global metadata management framework for social science data and official statistics.

Recommendations

(1) It is suggested that the German Data Forum endorse the importance of high-quality data documentation and the implementation of the metadata quality standards described above.

(2) Adoption of these standards requires the establishment of an industry standard, Web-service-oriented, and registry-based IT infrastructure. This infrastructure can then facilitate the management, exchange, harmonization, and re-use of data and metadata.

4. Paradata *(Frauke Kreuter, Carolina Casas-Cordero)*

Background and current issues

The use of computers in survey data collection generates a great deal of "paradata," a term coined by Mick Couper (1998). Paradata are data "surrounding" a survey and consist mostly of records of efforts to contact respondents, together with interviewer observations. Audio recordings made in the course of computer-assisted data collection also constitute paradata. The data are valuable for analyzing problems of survey non-response and for assessing the pros and cons of different data collection modes. Paradata can be used to achieve "continuous quality improvement" in survey research. In this context, the European Statistical System has developed a handbook on improving data quality through effective use of paradata.

In Germany, data collection agencies generate and disseminate fewer paradata than in some other Western countries.

Recommendations

(1) It is desirable that the research community as a whole demand high-quality paradata. This would encourage data collection agencies to make the necessary investments.

(2) Experimental survey designs – for example, to assess alternative data collection modes, or alternative respondent contact procedures – particularly benefit from the collection of paradata.

(3) Panel surveys provide special opportunities for the collection of valuable paradata because the same respondents are repeatedly interviewed under (potentially) varying conditions.

5. Record Linkage from a Technical Point of View *(Rainer Schnell)*

Background and current issues

Record linkage involves linking the same objects (e.g., survey respondents) in two or more databases using a set of common identifiers. These identifiers may include unique individual ID numbers, but other unique characteristics or combinations of characteristics may be used as well.

This advisory report reviews problems in record linkage and comments on available software.

Recommendations

(1) Research needs to be undertaken on the practical performance of record linkage programs and algorithms. Large real social science datasets – not simulated data – need to be used for this purpose.

(2) A European research program is needed on pre-processing keys for privacy-preserving record linkage.

(3) A National Record Linkage Center is needed in Germany. At present, different disciplines duplicate efforts in this area.

6. Experiments, Surveys, and the Use of Representative Samples as Reference Data *(Thomas Siedler, Bettina Sonnenberg)*

Background and current issues

In the last two decades social scientists have made increasing use of laboratory experiments to research social preferences and behavioral outcomes. A problem with most experiments is that the subjects are students and self-selected (volunteers). There is some evidence that this biases results, and that students who self-select into experiments are not even representative of the student body from which they are drawn. It is therefore valuable to compare the results of experiments with results of representative sample surveys that have investigated the same topic. Ideally, a sub-set of survey respondents should be found to take part in laboratory experiments. At the bare minimum, using the survey data as *reference data* allows the experimenter to estimate biases in his/her results. At best, the comparison may help to validate both sets of results. In this regard, the advisory report cites research on risk attitudes in which data from the German Socio-Economic Panel (SOEP, *Sozio-oekonomisches Panel*) and experimental results were compared. It transpired that survey respondents who rated high on willingness to take risks then actually took high-risk decisions in an experimental setting.

Recommendation

It is recommended that surveys be used as *reference data* for social and economic experiments.

7. Experimental Economics *(Simon Gächter)*

Background and current issues

Experimental economics should be regarded as a *method* applicable within many sub-fields economics, rather than as a sub-field itself. The aim is to use controlled laboratory-type conditions to answer *if-then* questions about the choices that economic agents face. Hypotheses can be more rigorously tested in the lab than by using observational data, but issues then arise about the generalizability of results to the "real world." One such issue arises because most studies use students as their laboratory subjects, with the German Socio-Economic Panel (SOEP, *Sozio-oekonomisches Panel*) and the British Household Panel Study (BHPS) being exceptions. This special form of sample selectivity/bias needs addressing.

Recommendations

(1) It would be valuable if experimental economists could develop an agreed questionnaire for administration to all subjects, which would document their specific socio-economic characteristics. Sample selectivity could then be assessed and taken into consideration in assessing empirical results.

(2) For recommendation (1) to be beneficial, it would be necessary to set up data depositories for experimental economics. At present, there appear to be only two journals that require authors to make data available, and there is only one major depository (in the US) at which data is available to other researchers. It would be desirable to set up depositories in Germany and elsewhere in Europe. The depositories would then be the right place to lodge the results of questionnaires completed by experimental subjects (Recommendation 1).

(3) The German Data Forum might wish to advocate these developments and facilitate their implementation. However, the difficulties are considerable. Many researchers feel they have strong property rights over their data. Further, the task of making subject samples and data more comparable across studies would be time-consuming for researchers.

8. Experience Sampling *(Michaela Riediger)*

Background and current issues

Experience sampling refers to the repeated capturing of experiences – such as feelings, thoughts, behaviors, and events – at or close to the moment at which they actually occur in an individual's life and in his or her normal/natural environment. Data are typically recorded by the subject in response to a cue (e.g., a beeper going off) using a hand-held computer. Compared with standard survey reports, which are based on recall, data produced by experience sampling have a high level of validity and are particularly valuable for assessing within-person changes across time. On the other hand, experience sampling studies are resource-intensive and place a heavy burden on subjects, who usually have to be paid. This means that small samples are the norm, with sample attrition still a problem. Further, subjects' responses may be affected by participation in a study (reactivity effects).

Experience sampling is going through a boom period, but few datasets are available for secondary analysis. Most studies are small-scale, conducted by psychologists. The use of experience sampling in large household panels is in its infancy. However, the German Socio-Economic Panel (SOEP, *Sozio-oekonomisches Panel*) has successfully piloted an experience sampling procedure with a small but representative sample.

Recommendations

(1) Experience sampling should be used in large-scale surveys as part of a multi-method approach. Similarly, it can be used to conduct "studies within a study."

(2) Mobile technology should be used to reduce the burden on respondents.

(3) Careful sample selection criteria should be used to minimize self-selection and other forms of sample bias. Control group designs are needed to assess reactivity effects.

(4) It should be a requirement of funded research that datasets be deposited for secondary use.

(5) Experience sampling could be included as a research topic in the Priority Program on Survey Methodology of the German Research Foundation (DFG, *Deutsche Forschungsgemeinschaft*).

9. Virtual Worlds as Petri Dishes for the Social and Behavioral Sciences *(Edward Castronova, Matthew Falk)*

Background and current issues

Social scientists need to develop theories and test hypotheses at the macro-societal level. Computer generated *virtual worlds*, with humans represented as avatars, should have priority as a tool for generating and testing these theories. Virtual worlds have many advantages. They can be used to conduct realistic controlled experiments, varying one or more parameters as the experimenter sees fit. They can be constructed to have a good fit with empirical reality and they allow for the interaction of numerous (even millions of) players. They can be run for long periods, like panel studies. Generally, they pose no serious risks to players, avoiding the ethical issues that limit many other types of studies. They are, however, initially expensive and time-consuming to set up, although, like the virtual worlds run by the gaming industry, they may eventually be self-funding.

Recommendations

(1) Virtual worlds should be recognized as a research tool for future research at the macro-societal level.
(2) Initial research funding is needed.
(3) Virtual worlds have good prospects of becoming self-funding or profitable by means of charging users both initial and ongoing fees, as happens with Internet worlds marketed by the gaming industry.

10. Qualitative Interviewing of Respondents in Large Representative Surveys *(Olaf Groh-Samberg, Ingrid Tucci)*

Background and current issues

Large representative surveys are using mixed methods to an ever-increasing degree. For example, biomarkers, register data, and experiments provide different types of evidence linked with survey data. However, the practice of conducting qualitative interviews with sub-sets of respondents from large scale surveys, including longitudinal surveys, is still quite rare. The key advantage of this approach, in contrast to many reported case studies, is that the researchers know precisely what they have "cases of."

Qualitative methods have proven just as valuable as quantitative methods in providing insights into social reality that reflect the multidimensionality of individual life courses and lived realities. Furthermore, in-depth interviews can provide an improved understanding of individual decision-making processes and behavior resulting from more or less unconscious strategies. They also provide insights into decisive turning points in people's lives. Finally, use of multiple methods to investigate the same issues enables researchers to "triangulate" their results and so assess their validity.

Recommendation

It is recommended that consideration be given to conducting qualitative interviews with purposively selected respondents from large-scale surveys, including longitudinal surveys.

III. Data Protection and Research Ethics

1. Data Protection and Statistics – A Dynamic and Tension-Filled Relationship *(Peter Schaar)*

Background and current issues

A balance has to be struck between the requirements of individual privacy and the research needs of the scientific community. Despite the development of ingenious methods of protecting privacy, including use of aliases, it is clear that recent decisions of the Federal Constitutional Court, interpreting the Basic Law, are likely to make it more difficult for researchers to collect comprehensive datasets, retain them, and make them available to others. The Court takes the view that individuals have a right to privacy, which can only be abrogated by informed consent for specific purposes. Further, the Court holds that informed consent given for one study does not allow datasets to be combined and regularly updated. "Profiling" of individuals via combining datasets is also clearly illegal. Posting data on the Internet runs such serious privacy risks that it can only be allowed if absolute anonymity is guaranteed.

Recommendation

The Research Data Centers of the Federal Statistical Office and other public agencies provide Scientific Use Files for research, teaching, and other specific uses. The files are created in such a way as to ensure virtual or full anonymity of subjects. This is one way forward.

2. Record Linkage from the Perspective of Data Protection
(Rainer Metschke)

Background and current issues

A cherished dream of social science researchers is to be able to link diverse survey datasets relating to the same individuals or households. The realization of this dream is beset with many obstacles, not least constitutional and legal provisions relating to data protection and privacy. This advisory report discusses current and potential future methods of making data available to the research community within the law. These methods include pseudonymization of respondents and data encoding, as well as the related use of "data stewards" (see below).

Recommendations

(1) Researchers and official statistics need to determine which datasets it is appropriate to link for research purposes, and then list the legal, technical, and methodological problems likely to be encountered.

(2) One method that is used for linking datasets, while still protecting privacy, is use of a legal entity known as a data steward (*Treuhänder*). The precise legal status of data stewards needs to be clarified.

(3) Additionally, the appropriate relationship between data stewards and Research Data Centers needs to be defined.

(4) Recommendations for the modernization of the law relating to statistics and data integration should eventually be drawn up. It would be sensible to conduct a pilot study first.

3. New Methods in Human Subjects Research: Do We Need a New Ethics? *(Karsten Weber)*

Background and current issues

New methods of data collection in the social sciences, including online research (e.g., data mining of websites) and use of biomarkers, pose *ethical issues* related to autonomy, beneficence, justice, privacy, and informed consent. These general ethical principles need to be more tightly defined or redefined by ethics committees dealing with modern data collection methods. For example, the principle of beneficence – promoting the good of others – appears to have few clear applications in social science research and needs to be redefined as preventing harm. Special consideration needs to be given to the development of ethical principles and practices relating to research on children and other vulnerable groups.

Recommendations

(1) Ethics committees should be established to approve and monitor human subjects research.

(2) The committees should employ risk assessment procedures to assess risks to research subjects.

(3) Particular attention should be paid to risk assessment and the application of ethical principles to research on children and other vulnerable groups.

4. Does Germany Need a (New) Research Ethics for the Social Sciences? *(Claudia Oellers, Eva Wegner)*

Background and current issues

In practical terms, Germany does not have a detailed set of ethical requirements that protects research subjects and is designed for the social sciences. However, all researchers have to abide by the requirements of the Federal Data Protection Act, and professional bodies in sociology and psychology have issued ethics guidelines affecting behavior towards peers rather than towards research subjects.

A review of ethics procedures in Britain and the US was undertaken to see if they offered useful examples for Germany. British procedures appear worth consideration; US procedures are perhaps too heavily geared towards the natural sciences.

In Britain, beginning in 2006, the Economic and Social Research Council (ESRC), which is the main funding body, forced universities seeking funding to set up ethics committees required to implement six key principles, four of which protect human subjects. Subjects have to be fully informed about the purposes and use of the research and have a right to remain anonymous, the data provided must remain confidential, participation must be voluntary, and the research must avoid harm to subjects. In practice, most universities have ethics committees in place at a faculty and/or departmental level and not just at the broader university-wide level.

Recommendation

Germany should consider the introduction of ethics principles and procedures similar to those in Britain.

IV. Fields

1. Migration and Demography

1.1 Migration and Globalization *(Martin Kahanec, Klaus F. Zimmermann)*

Background and current issues

Existing international migration datasets do not effectively capture the complexity of migration trajectories. Little is known about the prior experiences of immigrants in their home countries, about migrants who make more than one move, about the moves of additional family members, or about out-migration. The experiences of skilled migrants – the migrants that host countries are most keen to attract – are especially poorly documented because many make multiple (including circular) moves.

Lack of quality data about immigrants reduces the effectiveness of public policy, especially in education and job training.

International organizations, including the EU and the World Bank, have begun to make some datasets available to researchers, as have non-governmental organizations, for example, the Institute for the Study of Labor (IZA, *Forschungsinstitut zur Zukunft der Arbeit*). These organizations use advanced data management technologies to store data and provide access to users, but this does not remedy underlying data deficits.

Recommendations

(1) International coordination of data collection methods and standardization of immigrant identifiers.

(2) Guidelines for collecting adequate information about immigrants, including retrospective data on experiences in their home countries.

(3) Longitudinal data collection.

(4) Boosting immigrant samples in large social surveys.

(5) Appropriate anonymity standards relating to immigrant respondents.

(6) Data Service Centers using modern technologies to facilitate user access.

(7) Making arrangements for future data access a priority in planning data collection.

1.2 Migration and Statistics *(Sonja Haug)*

Background and current issues

Empirical research on migration is faced with problems relating to the fact that (1) most surveys under-sample some migrant groups, and (2) different sets of official statistics contain differing estimates of migrant numbers. However, several significant improvements have been made in migration statistics or are currently projected. The concept of "migration background," replacing the concept of foreign-born, has been adopted in the German Microcensus and is recommended for the main 2011 Census. If a projected central population register is set up, future migration researchers will have an ideal sampling frame from which to draw adequate and/or special migrant samples. At present, the most accessible large dataset is the German Socio-Economic Panel (SOEP, *Sozio-oekonomisches Panel*), which does over-sample migrants.

Recommendations

(1) Improvements are needed in sampling methods applied to migrant populations, especially small groups.

(2) New longitudinal studies focused on migrants should be a priority in Germany and internationally.

1.3 Internal Migration *(Andreas Farwick)*

Background and current issues

Research on internal (within-country) migration covers a wide range of issues relating to the reasons, distance, and direction of moves, as well as processes of decision-making. Both official aggregated data and cross-sectional data are useful for descriptive purposes but have limited value for explaining why households change residences. This advisory report describes longitudinal datasets that are valuable for understanding causal relations, but also notes their limitations. Retrospective longitudinal studies have the advantage of providing long histories of recalled events, including migration events. Their limitation is that they do not provide valid data on reasons for and attitudes to changes of residence. Prospective longitudinal studies are generally preferable in this respect, but could be improved by providing standardized data on aspects of migration (see below).

Recommendations

(1) Longitudinal (and other) studies should collect standardized data on place of residence and changes of residence at the smallest available spatial level, using the Nomenclature of Territorial Units for Statistics (NUTS, *Nomenclature des unites territoriales statistiques*) coding scheme.

(2) Data should be coded according to standard typologies of the characteristics of places/locations of residence, changes of residence, reasons for moving, intentions to move in future, the dwelling itself, the neighborhood, and commuting.

1.4 Fertility and Mortality Data for Germany *(Michaela Kreyenfeld, Rembrandt Scholz)*

Background and current issues

The data infrastructure for research on fertility and mortality in Germany has improved in recent years. In particular, several large datasets have been made available through Research Data Centers. Fertility data, in particular, have been improved through the Microcensus, which now collects information about the total number of children born to each woman during her life. There are still some "weak spots." Accurate counts and information about the exact composition of reconstituted families are lacking. Also, it is known that immigrants are healthier than average, but their mortality risks are inadequately understood.

Recommendation

Collecting information in the Microcensus via a household relationship matrix would considerably improve the quality of data on households/families and should, perhaps, be considered. Clearly, however, adoption of a matrix approach would represent a major change in the design of the Census instrument.

2. Measuring Competencies

2.1 Measuring Cognitive Ability *(Roland H. Grabner, Elsbeth Stern)*

Background and current issues

Many survey researchers want, in principle, to include cognitive tests in questionnaires. One quite common motive is to obtain unbiased estimates of the effects of socio-economic variables on some outcome (e.g., wages). The practical problem is that most cognitive tests that are regarded as valid by psychologists take too long to administer to be included in socio-economic surveys. This advisory report reviews a promising new type of cognitive test – the WM or working memory test. WM tests measure a person's ability to store and process information in working memory. There is considerable evidence showing that this ability is highly related to domain-specific abilities and to general cognitive abilities (the g factor). The advisory report reviews several promising WM tests; the shorter ones would take five to ten minutes to administer in a computer-assisted survey setting.

Recommendation

Working memory tests require further development and testing. There are several promising candidate tests, but few evaluations with large and diverse samples have been undertaken.

2.2 Measuring Cognitive Competencies *(Ulrich Trautwein)*

Background and current issues

In order to make well informed decisions in the educational arena, politicians and other decision-makers need high-quality data on the development of student competencies. This advisory report argues that there is often no substitute for well constructed standardized tests, and that it is important to measure a range of competencies and not just rely on measures of general cognitive ability.

Recommendations

(1) Policy-makers need better quality longitudinal data about the development of student competencies to inform their decisions.

(2) Data from multiple sources (e.g., school achievement studies and data from national agencies) need to be linked.

2.3 Measuring Vocational Competencies *(Martin Baethge, Lena Arends)*

Background and current issues

The EU has responded to the internationalization of labor markets in part by seeking to improve the quality and transparency of Vocational and Educational Training (VET). A European Qualifications Framework has been proposed, together with a European Credit System for VET. A logical extension of these policy initiatives is development of agreed measures of vocational competencies. It is clear that current international measures of adult literacy, numeracy, etc. are too broad to be termed measures of "vocational competencies." Beyond that, there is no consensus even about what types of measures are required. One school of thought favors measurement of *internal conditions* (dispositions and skill sets), which are taken to indicate capacity to perform vocational tasks. A second school of thought favors measurement of *external performance* of specific vocational tasks. The authors favor the first approach, which views individuals as carriers of skills that could be adapted to a variety of vocational tasks and may form a basis for lifelong learning.

At present, EU Member States are attempting to achieve convergence on these issues through the Copenhagen process. A Feasibility Study is currently underway, with participation by experts from interested countries. This study will provide a clear picture of national VET programs that might be included in international comparisons, but there is no immediate prospect of agreement on measurement issues.

2.4 Measuring Social Competencies *(Ingrid Schoon)*

Background and current issues

There are differences in the way social competencies are conceptualized and measured in psychology, education, sociology, and economics. In general, social competency requires adapting individual characteristics to social demands and specific situations. Limited data are available on the development of social competencies during individual lifetimes, or about their possible biological basis. Several archives hold national and/or international datasets that include some data on social competencies. These include the UK's Economic and Social Data Service (ESDS), the Council of European Social Science Data Archives (CESSDA), and the Inter-University Consortium for Political and Social Research (ICPSR).

Recommendations

(1) Existing data on social competencies need to be cataloged and documented in a consistent way in order to promote secondary analysis.

(2) Longitudinal data are needed to assess the acquisition of social competencies and their expression in specific contexts. Longitudinal data are also required to understand intergenerational transmission of competencies.

2.5 Subjective Indicators *(Beatrice Rammstedt)*

Background and current issues

Subjective indicators – the best-known relating to life satisfaction – are widely used in survey research and have been shown to be associated with a large array of social and economic outcomes. The psychometric properties of subjective indicators have not been adequately investigated. The main difficulty is that the validity of self-reports (e.g., reports of satisfaction, or worries, or trust in others) is hard to assess, even by peer and/or expert reports.

Recommendations

(1) Most large surveys, like the German Socio-Economic Panel (SOEP, *Sozio-oekonomisches Panel*) and the European Values Study (EVS), use single indicators. The reliability and validity of single indicators need to be assessed, and if they prove deficient, short multi-item measures should be developed and assessed.

(2) The cognitive processes used by respondents in making their subjective judgments require investigation.

3. Education and Research

3.1 Education Across the Life Course *(Hans-Peter Blossfeld)*

Background and current issues

There is enormous demand in Germany for high-quality longitudinal data on education through the life course and on returns to education. Until the National Educational Panel Study (NEPS) was set up in 2008, there was no long-term German panel study providing nationwide data on educational experiences, competences, and outcomes. Previous studies dealt primarily either with particular transitions (e.g., from secondary school to university) or were focused on particular areas of the country.

In planning the NEPS, it was considered that birth cohort studies take too long to bear fruit; it takes nearly 20 years before the first "subjects" enter the labor force. So, following the lead of the National Center for Education Statistics in the US, NEPS will have a "multi-cohort sequence design." This involves collecting data on "subjects" during key transitions: kindergarten to elementary school, elementary school to secondary school, and so on. At each transition, decisions are made about participation in different educational institutions and processes, and this participation leads to development or non-development of various competences. Varying outcomes and returns to education are recorded. Particular attention will be given in NEPS to immigrant educational experiences and outcomes.

NEPS will give high priority to preparation of a Scientific Use File for researchers and will offer training courses on how to make effective use of the data.

3.2 Preschool Education *(C. Katharina Spieß)*

Background and current issues

There is widespread international recognition of the importance of preschool education as a key determinant of later educational outcomes. However, there is a dearth of datasets in Germany that enable researchers to assess linkages between preschool educational experience and later outcomes. Existing datasets focus mainly on preschool attendance and are particularly deficient for children below the age of three and from migrant families. Two recent developments – the "Educational Processes, Competence Development, and Selection Decisions in Pre- and Primary School Age" (BiKS, *Bildungsprozesse, Kompetenzentwicklungen und Selektionsentscheidungen im Vor-*

und Grundschulalter) study at the University of Bamberg and the National Educational Panel Study (NEPS) – will improve matters somewhat, but the former study stops at the second grade of elementary school and the latter only includes children from age four onwards.

Recommendations

(1) Improved data are needed to measure the *quality* of preschool education, including the education of children under three.
(2) These data should be linked to cost data, so that cost-benefit studies can be undertaken.
(3) It is important to have adequate sub-sample sizes for disadvantaged children and children from migrant families.
(4) It may be beneficial to improve the preschool data infrastructure jointly with research infrastructure on families as well as on abilities and competencies in these other areas. Possibilities of data linkage need to be investigated.

3.3 Data in the Domain of Secondary School Education *(Petra Stanat, Hans Döbert)*

Background and current issues

Compared to most Western countries, Germany knows little about its school system. Data are lacking on how student competencies develop over time and on the factors which affect development. Official school statistics are at an aggregate level only. The Microcensus is valuable for some purposes but provides only cross-sectional data and has no information on preschool attendance or learning outcomes. The German Socio-Economic Panel (SOEP, *Sozio-oekonomisches Panel*) measures some aspects of cognitive abilities but not subject-specific competencies.

Partly as a result of the poor performance of German students in standardized international tests, there has been increased interest in measuring learning outcomes. Major recent innovations are the founding of the Institute for Educational Progress (IQB, *Institut zur Qualitätsentwicklung im Bildungswesen*) and the National Educational Panel Study (NEPS). The IQB will administer competency tests to representative samples of students in the 16 *Länder*. The NEPS is a multi-cohort study, starting in 2009, that will cover eight key educational and career transitions. Data from the IQB and the Panel Study will be available for secondary analysis through research data centers.

Recommendations

(1) School statistics should be reported at the individual-level in all *Länder*.

(2) To allow for longitudinal analysis, school statistics should ideally include unchanging student identifiers. The legal and practical feasibility of using such identifiers needs to be assessed.

3.4 Knowing More about Vocational Training *(Steffen Hillmert)*

Background and current issues

Vocational training is a key aspect of the lifelong learning required in modern economies.
 To understanding the costs and benefits of this training, it is essential to have *longitudinal data*, which can capture multiple periods of training undertaken by the same individual. However, at present, longitudinal evidence is limited. The German Socio-Economic Panel (SOEP, *Sozio-oekonomisches Panel*) and the German Life History Study (GLHS) are valuable sources, but evidence is still needed from administrative sources. The data records generated within the "dual system" of vocational training are quite comprehensive, but do not allow individuals to be traced from one period of training to another. In other sectors of vocational training, even more serious data deficiencies exist.

Recommendation

Each individual should have a common ID number within the vocational education system so that his/her education and training career can be traced over a lifetime.

3.5 Higher Education *(Andrä Wolter)*

Background and current issues

In the last five years, there has been a major increase in research on higher education in Germany. This has been partly due to the boom in education research generally, and partly due to the Bologna Reforms, which have led to increased demand for internationally comparable data.

Data come from two sources: official statistics and surveys. In principle, all data are available for secondary analysis, although some practical problems arise (see below).

Recommendations

(1) Access for secondary analysis of education surveys could be made more convenient by setting up a Research Data Center associated with the Higher Education Information System (HIS, *Hochschul-Informations-System*).

(2) Some specific sets of questions need to be integrated into all education studies. These include questions about migration status, learning competencies, and evidence of lifelong learning.

(3) Panel studies are a particularly important deficit, although this will be partly remedied by the establishment of the National Educational Panel Study (NEPS).

3.6 Adult Education and Lifelong Learning *(Corinna Kleinert, Britta Matthes)*

Background and current issues

Adult education and lifelong learning are regarded as increasingly important due to the emergence of a "knowledge society" and the increased economic competition resulting from globalization. Germany has many different sources of cross-sectional data on adult education, plus several longitudinal studies, including the new National Educational Panel Study (NEPS), the German Socio-Economic Panel (SOEP, *Sozio-oekonomisches Panel*), and the German Life History Study (GHLS). A major problem is that the sources provide contradictory evidence; for example, the Microcensus reported that only 13 percent were involved in adult education in 2003, while the Adult Education Survey (BWS, *Berichtssystem Weiterbildung*) reported 41 percent. Such large divergences highlight the need to develop standardized questions.

Recommendations

(1) It is *not* recommended that new sources of data be provided.

(2) The main requirement is to develop standardized questions that capture all aspects of lifelong learning: formal learning, on-the-job learning, informal learning, and development of measured competences. Also, the *household context,* in which decisions about continued learning are made, needs to be recorded.

3.7 Research, Science, Development *(Stefan Hornbostel)*

Background and current issues

Research institutions are under increasing pressure to measure and even predict ("foresight studies") their research performance. They need to do so in order to avoid being disadvantaged in national and international competition for funding.

Outcome measures are generally preferred (e.g., citations in high-impact journals). However, input measures, including attraction of third-party funding, are also often used. Germany's federal research report reflects the demand for evidence to assess research performance, but data are often delayed and are not appropriate for outcomes analysis. By contrast, the German Council of Science and Humanities (WR, *Wissenschaftsrat*) provides up-to-date and transparent ratings that are available for scientific use. Internationally, Google Scholar and other open access repositories are increasingly valuable.

Germany may be falling behind in its capacity to conduct "bibliometry analyses" of research performance. The Federal Ministry of Education and Research (BMBF, *Bundesministerium für Bildung und Forschung*) is currently promoting a consortium to try and close this gap.

Recommendation

Germany has a decentralized education and research system. Recognizing this, it is desirable to develop a decentralized data collection system (CRIS, *Current Research Information System*), which could then develop national standard definitions of research performance.

The Norwegian research information system (Frida) and Open Research Archives (NORA) provide a good example of what can be done. Institutions have to provide data to Frida and NORA in order to receive government funding.

4. Economy and Labor Markets

4.1 Data from the Federal Employment Agency *(Stefan Bender, Joachim Möller)*

Background and current issues

Access to labor market data was greatly improved as a result of the 2001 KVI report. The establishment of Research Data Centers and Data Service Centers has been particularly valuable. Anonymization techniques have developed rapidly and have facilitated access to data. Policy developments have provided researchers with new opportunities. Important examples are (1) the availability of data on active labor market programs required for evaluations of the Hartz reforms and (2) job search data generated as a result of the Social Code 11 reforms (2005). The research network of the German Research Foundation (DFG, *Deutsche Forschungsgemeinschaft*) "Flexibility of Heterogeneous Labor Markets" has used and generated a great deal of valuable data.

Recommendations

(1) Increased use of datasets that link different types of data: economic and environmental data (AFiD) and company data from official statistics, the Bundesbank, and the Federal Employment Agency (BA, *Bundesagentur für Arbeit*) / Institute for Employment Research (IAB, *Institut für Arbeitsmarkt- und Berufsforschung*) (KombiFID).

(2) Improvements in international datasets are also necessary, in part because of transnational movements of labor.

4.2 More and Better Data for Labor Market Research. Proposals for Efficient Access to the Currently Unused Potential of Official Statistical Data *(Hilmar Schneider)*

Background and current issues

The official labor market statistics are inadequate, primarily because they are based on the outdated idea of compiling aggregate statistics for specific purposes. The key need is for panel data at the individual and household levels. It is also important to have the possibility of making linkages between surveys. Existing deficits can be most clearly illustrated in regard to *hourly wage rates*. Accurate measurement of hourly wage rates is crucial for labor market research, but even the Income and Consumption Survey (EVS, *Einkommens- und Verbrauchsstichprobe*) does not permit accurate measurement because it only asks about wages earned during contractually stipulated, not actual work hours.

The situation has improved somewhat since Falk and Steiner made their recommendations for the 2001 KVI report, but even so, neither the Microcensus nor the Income and Consumption Survey have been developed into adequate surveys for labor market research.

Recommendations

(1) The Microcensus and the official Income and Consumption Survey (EVS, *Einkommens- und Verbrauchsstichprobe*) should contain the variables needed to calculate actual hourly wage rates. The laws governing these two surveys will be reviewed in 2012 and 2013 and should be amended to allow for this improvement.

(2) The design of official surveys should be coordinated to create possibilities for data linkage.

(3) Data linkage between surveys – including linkage between firm data and employee data – should be permitted for purely statistical purposes without the express agreement of individual respondents.

(4) Remote data access and processing should be made feasible for users of the Research Data Centers of the Federal Statistical Office and the Statistical Offices of the German *Länder*.

4.3 Interdisciplinary Longitudinal Surveys. Linking Individual Data to Organizational Data in Life-Course Analysis *(Stefan Liebig)*

Background and current issues

This advisory report is based on three fundamental insights from social science and economics: (1) The causes and consequences of individual behavior can only be satisfactorily studied with longitudinal data; (2) individual behavior is embedded in and strongly affected by social contexts and aggregates; and (3) formal organizations (e.g., firms and universities) are becoming more and more important for individual life courses. It follows from these premises that social and economic research needs a data infrastructure that provides information about individuals over time in the context of the organizations in which they live and work.

In the last eight years in Germany, there have been major efforts to provide the scientific community with linked individual and firm-level data. However, the main datasets which are currently available provide only limited information about individuals and firms and tell us nothing about the households in which individuals live. For many research purposes, including the study of social inequality, it is important to add household data to existing files.

A project currently underway at the University of Bielefeld is testing the feasibility of the proposed approach. It will assess both methods of maximizing firm/organizational participation and issues relating to confidentiality and data protection.

Recommendation

It is recommended that the German Socio-Economic Panel (SOEP, *Soziooekonomisches Panel*) shallcollect information about the firms and other organizations in which sample members live and work. An attempt would then need to be made to contact the organizations to collect data from them. If this project succeeded, it would yield a dataset unique in international terms.

4.4 Organizational Data *(Stefan Liebig)*

Background and current issues

Organizational data describe the central characteristics of organizations, their internal structures and processes, and their behavior as corporate actors. Data on business organizations – firms – are already widely used by researchers, and there is now increasing interest in studying other organizations, including schools, universities, and hospitals. In recent years, the official statistical organizations have made substantial improvements in providing data on firms for social science research. However, data from non-official sources are rarely available for secondary analysis. In fact, there are no adequate records of the datasets that exist, and documentation of methodological standards and quality is inadequate. These are serious deficits in view of increased demand for high-quality international comparative and longitudinal studies.

A current project at the University of Bielefeld is testing the feasibility of the approach. It will assess both methods of maximizing firm/organizational participation and issues relating to confidentiality and data protection.

Recommendations

(1) Documentation on existing non-official organizational datasets needs to be compiled and made readily accessible to researchers.
(2) Universities and publicly funded research institutes should be required to make their data available for secondary analysis.
(3) Methods and data quality indicators should be properly documented.
(4) Methods of conducting organizational surveys need to be taught in universities.
(5) A network of organizational research projects should be established, in part to deal with the implications of data protection laws and related issues of data linkage.
(6) It is proposed that a new Research Data Center be established for firm and organizational data. This center would take the lead in documenting existing surveys and archiving them. It would provide expertise in secondary analysis of organizational surveys and seek to improve methodological standards. A Research Data Center is essential for German research to come up to best international practice.

4.5 Firm-Level Data *(Joachim Wagner)*

Background and current issues

Researchers use firm-level data to document the stylized facts and assumptions used in formal models, and then to test hypotheses derived from the models. The most comprehensive data come from official sources: the Federal Statistical Office, the Federal Employment Agency (BA, *Bundesagentur für Arbeit*), and the Deutsche Bundesbank. Data from official surveys have the advantage that they cover all target firms. The firms are required to respond and respond accurately. Academic surveys have been valuable for specific purposes, but rely on small samples and limited response. Following the 2001 KVI report, the availability of data for research purposes improved markedly. Most of the important collectors of firm-level data established Research Data Centers and some offer Scientific Use Files. Furthermore, researchers can combine data from repeated surveys to produce longitudinal data on firms.

Recommendations

(1) From a research standpoint, it would be desirable to match data about firms collected by different agencies. This would require a change of law.

(2) It would also be desirable to create international datasets, in part because many firms now have global reach.

5. State, Family, and Health

5.1 Public Finance *(Thiess Büttner)*

Background and current issues

Public finance is concerned with the decisions of firms and households, not just governments. Budgetary statistics provide high-quality data relating to some government decisions and public services, but data on the *quality* of public services are generally lacking. Furthermore, tax arrangements are so complex that it is usually necessary to resort to simulation, rather than obtaining exact empirical data. The greatest future need is for datasets that combine governmental, firm, and household level data. The recent Combined Firm Data for Germany (KombiFiD, *Kombinierte Firmendaten für Deutschland*) initiative by the Federal Statistical Office, the Institute for Employment Research (IAB, *Institut für Arbeitsmarkt- und Berufsforschung*), and the Deutsche Bundesbank, is a major development along these lines.

Recommendation

Major research advances could be made by combining governmental, household, and firm-level data. The resulting datasets would be particularly valuable for studying the impact of taxes and assessing possible tax reforms.

5.2 Household Income, Poverty, and Wealth *(Richard Hauser)*

Background and current issues

This advisory report focuses on *official statistics* relating to household income, poverty, and wealth. It characterizes the main research questions in this field, and presents an overview of available statistics and Scientific Use Files produced by the four Research Data Centers.

The author underscores the importance of a European peer review group, applying standards based on the European Statistics Code of Practice, which has already detected some problems with the statistics produced by the Federal Statistical Office and the Statistical Offices of the German *Länder*.

Recommendations

(1) Peer review groups should be set up to assess the work of all data-producing agencies, including ministries.

(2) The recommendation of the 2001 KVI report is repeated to find ways in which Scientific Use Files could be made available to reliable foreign research institutes.

(3) Specific improvements are recommended in survey methods and questionnaire design in the Income and Consumption Survey (EVS, *Einkommens- und Verbauchsstichprobe*) and the German contribution to the European Union Statistics on Income and Living Conditions (EU-SILC).

(4) It is recommended that the statistics of the various minimum benefit programs be harmonized.

(5) A single Scientific Use File is recommended relating to all minimum benefit recipients.

5.3 Family Research *(Johannes Huinink)*

Background and current issues

A great deal of progress has been made in the availability of data for family research since the 2001 KVI report. The German Socio-Economic Panel (SOEP, *Sozio-oekonomisches Panel*) has received long-term funding, the German Life History Study (GLHS) continues to provide valuable data, and the new Panel Analysis of Intimate Relationships and Family Dynamics (pairfam) is underway. Access to the Microcensus has been much improved, which is of great benefit to family researchers.

The greatest remaining need is for improved longitudinal data. Improvements are needed at the regional, national, and international level. Data collection by official statistics could also be improved.

Recommendation

It would be valuable for the German Data Forum to provide the auspices for family researchers to work on developing an improved framework for family data collection.

This framework could be used to improve official statistics as well as surveys under academic direction.

5.4 Intergenerational Relationships *(Bernhard Nauck, Anja Steinbach)*

Background and current issues

Intergenerational relationships within families and kinship groups are a major topic of research in the social sciences. The impetus for research has come partly from changes in the family, including reduced fertility and longer life expectancy, and the implications of these changes for public policy and the welfare state. Six dimensions of social exchange are widely used in intergenerational analysis: structural, associative, affective, consensual, normative, and functional. However, despite general agreement on appropriate dimensions, there is no accepted overall theory of intergenerational relations.

Numerous large-scale German and international datasets are available for analysis. These include the German Socio-Economic Panel (SOEP, *Sozio-oekonomisches Panel*), the German Ageing Survey (DEAS, *Deutscher Alterssurvey*), the Survey of Health, Ageing and Retirement in Europe (SHARE), and the Panel Analysis of Intimate Relationships and Family Dynamics (pairfam).

Recommendation

The aim should be to develop an overarching theory of intergenerational relationships. This requires panel data with questions which enable researchers to take a lifespan perspective.

5.5 Administrative Data from Germany's Statutory Health Insurance Providers for Social, Economic, and Medical Research *(Günther Heller)*

Background and current issues

For the last 125 years, medical care in Germany has been financed under a statutory insurance system. Eighty-six percent of the population have statutory insurance, while 14 percent have private insurance. The data reviewed were mostly collected by statutory health insurers with the aim of making correct reimbursements to health providers. Hence, they are secondary data from the point of view of a social science user.

At present, the data are only available for research within the health insurance system, or to researchers working closely with a statutory insurer. Some insurers have established databases that are anonymized at the individual level and that link different health-related contacts and treatments. But it is not clear that all insurers have such a database.

There has been no comprehensive validity study conducted on the data, but its validity is checked for its primary purpose – information that bears directly on the accuracy of invoices for reimbursement. But other information that might interest social scientists (e.g., time of medical procedures or admission diagnoses) is not necessarily carefully checked because it does not substantially affect reimbursements.

Recommendation

A detailed handlingof legal privacy provisions is important in considering potential use of these datasets by social scientists.

5.6 Provision for Old Age: National and International Survey Data to Support Research and Policy on Aging *(Hendrik Jürges)*

Background and current issues

Population aging is a key trend in all developed countries. It poses major policy problems relating to the maintenance of economic growth and to provision of adequate living standards in old age. International comparative data are particularly valuable, because diverse "policy solutions" have already been (or are being) attempted, and their results can be assessed. A large number of German and international datasets are available, including the German Socio-Economic Panel (SOEP, *Sozio-oekonomisches Panel*) and the Cross-National Equivalent File (CNEF), which includes SOEP, the

German Ageing Survey (DEAS, *Deutscher Alterssurvey*), the Survey of Health, Ageing and Retirement in Europe (SHARE), and the Savings Behavior in Germany (SAVE) survey.

Recommendations

(1) There is a need to combine conventional survey data with two other types of data: administrative data and biomarkers.

(2) It is important to extend surveys to include institutionalized people, especially those in nursing homes.

5.7 Income Provisions and Retirement in Old Age *(Tatjana Mika, Uwe Rehfeld, Michael Stegmann)*

Background and current issues

The aim is to assess the incomes of current and future retirees. Historically, most retirees have mainly relied on federal social security pensions. This implies that estimation of retiree incomes depended on administrative data from the German Pension Insurance, which included information about employment and earnings histories, and also life events affecting pension entitlements.

Recent reforms have increased the importance of occupational pensions and private savings. Accordingly, additional sources of administrative data are now required, and these data need to be linked to the German Pension Insurance (RV, *Deutsche Rentenversicherung*) data. So far this has been done in a number of official datasets and surveys, including the Completed Insured Life Courses (VVL, *Vollendete Versichertenleben*), the Old-age Pension Schemes in Germany survey (ASID, *Alterssicherung in Deutschland*), and survey data from Retirement Pension Provision Schemes in Germany (AVID, *Altersvorsorge in Deutschland*). All but the last of these datasets are available for scientific research from the Research Data Centers or the Leibniz Institute for the Social Sciences (GESIS, *Leibniz-Institut für Sozialwissenschaften*).

Recommendations

(1) It is desirable to link official records – preferably from several sources – to survey data. Survey data could be particularly valuable in providing information on self-assessed health and retirement intentions.

(2) There is at present no regular procedure in place for making administrative record-to-record linkages, let alone linking to survey data. Privacy

requirements are onerous and the separate governing boards of pension funds all have to give separate approval. Nevertheless, if particular research projects using improved data could demonstrate the value of record-to-record linking, then a regular procedure might become possible.

6. Political and Cultural Participation and the Role of the Media

6.1 Political Participation – National Election Study *(Rüdiger Schmitt-Beck)*

Background and current issues

This advisory report provides an overview of recent developments in research on elections and mass political participation. Similar to other Western countries, Germany does not provide guaranteed funding for national election studies. This is a key deficit.

Recommendations

(1) A National Election Study should be established by providing the current German Longitudinal Election Study (GLES) project with continuing logistic and methodological support under the auspices of the Leibniz-Institute for the Social Sciences (GESIS, *Leibniz-Institut für Sozialwissenschaften*). Permanent long-term public funding, with the study institutionalized at GESIS, is the desirable long-term outcome.

(2) A small number of political variables should be tagged for inclusion in all surveys conducted in German General Social Survey (ALLBUS, *Allgemeine Bevölkerungsumfrage der Sozialwissenschaften*) and the German Socio-Economic Panel (SOEP, *Sozio-oekonomisches Panel*).

(3) The data services of the statistical offices should be modified to meet basic requirements of research on elections and political participation.

(4) Public agencies should be under a formal obligation to deposit survey data collected under their auspices into appropriate archives.

6.2 Civil Society   *(Mareike Alscher, Eckart Priller)*

Background and current issues

Available data on civil society organizations (CSOs) remain seriously inadequate. To a large extent, researchers have to compile data from other sources which were not primarily designed to provide valid data on CSOs. However, considerable progress has been made through Germany's participation in the Johns Hopkins Comparative Nonprofit Sector Project. This project sets out the data requirements that would need to be met in order to provide a valid description of CSOs and their activities. More recently, the Civil Society Data Collection Project has set out to provide a reporting system for Germany, using the concepts of the Johns Hopkins project and data (mainly) from the Federal Statistical Office. The mid-term goal is to establish a National Accounts satellite system for CSOs.

Recommendations

(1) The long-term goal should be to set up a comprehensive, self-contained data provision system for CSOs.

(2) This goal can be reached by using existing surveys and data sources, including improved data from the CSOs themselves, and by adding questions about civic engagement to ongoing surveys, especially the annual Microcensus.

6.3 Culture   *(Jörg Rössel, Gunnar Otte)*

Background and current issues

The expert report focuses on culture defined as the arts. Research on the arts falls into three categories: artistic production and its organization, the distribution and economic valuation of culture, and the consumption of culture. Sociology and economics are the two main social sciences in which the arts are studied.

Recommendations

(1) Two large baseline surveys are needed: (a) a survey providing life-course information on artists, as well as information about their current work, status, earnings, etc., and (b) a representative sample survey of cultural consumption.

(2) Development of a single national cultural statistic as set out in the study *Kultur in Deutschland* and compatible with efforts at the EU level.

(3) *Publicly* financed surveys on culture, including those conducted by statutory bodies, as well as citizen surveys and audience surveys, should be deposited at the Data Archive of the Leibniz Institute for the Social Sciences (GESIS, *Leibniz-Institut für Sozialwissenschaften*) and be available for secondary research.

6.4 Mass Media Research *(Heiner Meulemann, Jörg Hagenah)*

Background and current issues

Mass media research focuses on both the production of media "programs" and their consumption. Content analysis is the main method used to analyze programs. Surveys, including time budget surveys, are used to analyze consumption. Several archives store media programs. The German National Library (*Deutsche Bibliothek*) in Frankfurt holds a copy of every newspaper published. Various public and private agencies archive and analyze the content of television and radio media. The largest of the private agencies is *Media Tenor*, which has conducted content analysis of programs from about 700 sources since 1993. Both public and private agencies also analyze media consumption; the private agencies being motivated partly by demand for advice on communications and advertising outlets.

The Federal Statistical Office includes time spent consuming media in its Time Budget Studies (1991 and 2001). International data on media consumption have been collected by the Eurobarometer and the European Social Survey (ESS).

Recommendations

(1) It is recommended that a central media content archive be set up for Germany. This should include data collected by public and private agencies, and by individual researchers.

(2) Common content analysis categories should be developed, in part to facilitate international comparisons.

(3) The professional societies of the social and communication sciences should attempt to secure access to important surveys funded by media stations, as well as privately funded surveys.

6.5 Judicature   *(Wolfgang Heinz)*

Background and current issues

An adequate system of crime statistics would enable us to answer questions about: (1) trends in the incidence of different types of crime, (2) the decisions of the authorities relating to prosecution, (3) the numbers and types of criminal sentences/penalties imposed, (4) the extent to which penalties are enforced, and (5) rates of reconviction/recidivism.

Assessed by these standards, current official German crime statistics are seriously deficient. As a result, it is currently necessary to supplement official statistics with periodical crime and victimization surveys. Similarly, prison statistics need supplementing with statistics about suspects who face preliminary proceedings. Additional ways also have to be found to collect data on the enforcement of criminal sentences and on reconvictions.

Recommendations

(1) A comprehensive crime statistics database would need to contain all police data on crime and all relevant judicial decisions. Data on individuals would need to be "pseudonymized" and then linked.

(2) This database would need to be regularly updated, in particular with respect to enforcement of sentences and reconviction/recidivism. It would then be possible to assemble case flow statistics and to conduct cohort studies.

6.6 Environment   *(Cornelia Ohl, Bernd Hansjürgens)*

Background and current issues

Environmental problems are large in scale. They are typically long-lasting and also have wide geographical impacts. Furthermore, their impact is often subject to "true uncertainty"; that is, there is insufficient knowledge of damages and costs, and the probability of damages and costs is unknown. The complexity of the problems means that innovative research methods and modeling approaches are needed to supplement traditional monitoring methods used for assessing environmental impacts.

Recommendations

(1) Geographical Information System technology should be used to enhance mapping of environmental impacts. These impacts need to be shown in

relation to a range of socio-economic indicators mapped at the appropriate scale. The biggest challenge lies in mapping global climate change.

(2) It is also necessary to evaluate policy responses to environmental challenges and assess the vulnerability of affected social units.

(3) A nested data structure is needed in order for researchers to be able to assess developments from a polluter's point of view, a victim's point of view, and also a regulator's point of view.

ADVISORY REPORTS

TOWARDS AN IMPROVED RESEARCH INFRASTRUCTURE
FOR THE SOCIAL SCIENCES:
FUTURE DEMANDS AND NEEDS FOR ACTION

1. Providing a Permanent Institutional Guarantee for the German Information Infrastructure

Johann Hahlen

Contact:

Johann Hahlen, Staatssekretär a.D.
Am hohen Rain 52
50389 Wesseling-Urfeld
Germany
e-mail: johann.hahlen[at]web.de

1. A permanent information infrastructure must be tailored to the specific German data situation. This means it must – to the extent possible – take account of the variety of data, the multitude of data producers and, especially, the potential domestic and foreign users and ways they intend to use the data. Furthermore, it must be open to topics of future interest and new questions.

When setting up a permanent information infrastructure, it must be kept in mind that there is a network of interactions among the various datasets and data users, which in Germany is determined by a number of legal and structural conditions. It is realistic to say that these conditions cannot be changed and, consequently, it is reasonable to treat them as given. Any ideas for scientific policy regarding a permanent information infrastructure should take account of the following conditions:

- For natural persons, the German Constitution (GG, *Grundgesetz*) grants the right to informational self-determination protecting individuals from unlimited collection, storage, use and transmission of their personal data and safeguarding the individual's right to decide on the disclosure and use of personal data. Although the GG does not require data collected for statistical purposes to be strictly and concretely linked to a specific purpose, it does set limits on the information system. Transmitting statistical data for scientific use is permitted by the Constitution if limited to what is necessary for the particular scientific purpose, if no direct reference is made to individuals (no names or addresses), and if the recipient of the data does not have any additional information that could allow re-identification of the individual and thus result in a violation of the individual's right to informational self-determination. This was laid down by the Federal Constitutional Court in its fundamental population census judgment of 15 December 1983 (BVerfGE[1] 65, 1 et seqq.). This requirement is met by the clause relating to the scientific community in § 16 Abs. 6 of the Federal Statistics Law (BStatG, *Bundesstatistikgesetz*).[2] Local units, enterprises, and legal entities engaged in economic activity cannot claim the right to informational self-determination. However, they are protected by the right to perform business activities, which is also granted by the Constitution.

- The scientific use of personal data and of data on economic entities must comply with these constitutional principles, the numerous legal provisions on the collection and use of statistical data, and regulations protecting local units and enterprises with regard to their

---

[1] Decision of the Federal Constitutional Court (BVerfG, *Bundesverfassungsgericht*).
[2] The citations to German legal sources have been left in German to guarantee accuracy.

economic activity (e.g., the protection of business secrets or fair and open competition on the market).

- Data producers and data holders – to the extent that they are part of the public administration, for example, government authorities or institutions – are bound by the principle of the rule of law according to Art. 20 Abs. 3 GG. No information infrastructure of any kind and no scientific demand can exempt such data producers and data holders from complying with the above regulations.

- This remains unaffected by the freedom of science, research, and teaching guaranteed by Art. 5 Abs. 3 GG. It is true that the Federal Constitutional Court has interpreted the basic right of the freedom of science (Art. 5 Abs. 3 GG) to entail a government obligation to provide efficient institutions to ensure the freedom of science and the relevant teaching. However, this does not mean that an individual scholar can claim the right to access specific data stocks. Furthermore, it does not mean that a scholar's research might take priority over the legal protections afforded to individuals or enterprises.

- Germany is a federation (Art. 20 Abs. 1 GG) in which the exercise of state powers is generally a matter of the *Länder* (federal states) (Art. 30 GG). The *Länder* are generally responsible for executing federal laws (Art. 83 GG). The Federation, which – according to Art. 73 Abs. 1 Satz 11 GG – has the sole legislative power for "statistics for federal purposes," was allowed by Art. 87 Abs. 3 GG to establish the Federal Statistical Office as an independent superior federal authority. However, the federal legal provisions on official statistics are implemented by the *Länder* through their own administration (Art. 84 Abs. 1 GG). At the same time, Germany has committed to the project of European integration, and has transferred sovereign powers to the European Union (Art. 23 Abs. 1 GG), so that EU Regulations and Directives are directly applicable in Germany or have to be transformed into German law. Therefore, EU Regulation No. 223/2009 on European Statistics (former EU Regulation No. 322/97 on Community Statistics) and EU Regulation No. 831/2002 concerning access to confidential data (of the EU) for scientific purposes are directly applicable in Germany.

- Finally, the principle of democracy, which is explicitly referred to by the German Constitution (Art. 20 Abs. 1 and 2, Art. 21 Abs. 1, Art. 28 Abs. 1 and Art 38 Abs. 1 GG), requires a free, open, transparent and discursive process of forming opinions, which needs both the knowledge of the facts relevant for the decision-making concerned, especially the data available, and the scientific examination and processing of those facts.

2. There are many indications of the need for a permanent information infrastructure in Germany. What is needed is not just a free, non-government press and radio landscape and a free, self-determined research system but also access to data from official statistical institutions and – if possible – any other data stocks collected for government purposes. At the same time, it is crucial to safeguard the legal rights of the entities to which the data refer (individuals, local entities, enterprises). However, these needs – which are easy to reach consensus on in abstract terms – are confronted with a number of very real weaknesses:

- On the one hand, as Chancellor Angela Merkel once stated, any policy starts with the facts. On the other, we could just as easily quote the former Prime Minister of Saxony Biedenkopf, who talked about the widespread "resistance to facts" among politicians. On that point, Keynes said the following: "There is nothing a government hates more than to be well informed; for it makes the process of arriving at decisions much more complicated and difficult." Probably, however, the impression of a "resistance to facts" is merely due to the fact that those in power think they are sufficiently informed already, while frustrated statisticians and social scientists overestimate the importance of their findings.

- In any case, it is obvious that empirical social and economic research in Germany has been severely underfinanced for a relatively long time compared with other branches of empirical science, such as medicine and other natural sciences.

- What is more, in some areas, there has been obvious reluctance on the part of German economists to engage in empirical work.

- And finally, by no means only in Germany, there is a certain reluctance among scholars to scrutinize their own work for reproducibility and falsification. This, combined with the tendency – though perhaps simply a human one – towards competition and isolation, may prevent these scholars and institutions from obtaining the high infrastructural investments they need from government agencies.

3. Based on these conditions and structural constraints, the permanent information infrastructure that is needed can be defined in both negative and positive terms.

3.1 This is what a permanent information infrastructure in Germany should *not* be:

- The public data producers and data holders belong to different levels of state administration that are, in many cases, structured by *Länder* or other regional units. For example, in addition to the Federal Statistical Office there are 14 *Länder* offices producing and storing statistical data. The Federal Employment Agency (BA, *Bundesagentur für Arbeit*) and the German Pension Insurance (RV, *Deutsche Rentenversicherung*) are part of the indirect federal administration; education data are stored by the competent *Länder* ministries; the Central Register of Foreigners belongs to the Federal Office for Migration and Refugees (BAMF, *Bundesamt für Migration und Flüchtlinge*), which is a superior federal authority; the population registers are available at the towns and municipalities or at central *Länder* population registers. Health data come from some 100 widely varied sources.

    This patchwork is anything but convenient for anyone interested in data for scientific use; it is confusing and labor-intensive at best. The idea of an institution that is comprehensive both regionally and in terms of subject matter therefore seems obvious, but it turns out to be an unachievable vision.

    As experience shows, the various data producers and data archives in Germany are not willing to transmit their data to third parties or even to grant third parties the right of use. At most, they are willing to be represented by a regional partner (one *Land* for several or all other *Länder*). A highly structured information infrastructure is certainly not convenient, but modern information technology offers the potential for cross-referencing that can make things clearer and provide orientation in the maze of data providers.

- A register comprising all data, such as a large central archive where all the data producers and data archives store duplicates of their data, would theoretically be a solution to the dilemma described above – but it is impossible due to the legal situation. This is because, in Germany, data are strictly linked to a specific purpose in order to protect the individuals, local entitites, or enterprises referred to by the data. This means that, already during data collection, respondents must be informed what specific purposes their data are being collected for and who will receive access. Transmission of originals or duplicates to a "central scientific register" has not been dealt with legally and will only be possible to regulate in future legislation. Consequently, no stock data can be stored in such a register unless all respondents give their consent, which makes the whole matter unrealistic. Exceptions are not permitted by the clause relating to the scientific community as stated, for example, in § 4a Abs. 2 of the Federal Data Protection Act.

However, statistical data which are processed and used only in an anonymized form do not need to be linked to a specific purpose, so that they can be used for scientific purposes if anonymity (even de facto anonymity) is safeguarded. This does not yet make it possible to set up a comprehensive central scientific register because what could be stored there would only be aggregated data and microdata in a de facto anonymized form. Although the latter is possible – with sometimes considerable efforts – for specific data stocks such as the Microcensus, this is not possible for all official statistical data. Therefore, a central register limited to statistical data would be highly incomplete. The health monitoring system operated by the Robert Koch Institute and the Federal Statistical Office is not an example to the contrary because it uses only aggregated data from the various sources.

- What should not be envisaged to guarantee the information infrastructure is the creation of a new federal authority or – either in addition or alternatively – of new *Länder* offices. First, for the reasons shown above, they could not represent a central register. Second, this would involve considerable bureaucratic efforts; they would have to be integrated into existing divisions of responsibility and hierarchies, they would have to acquire the required wide range of special knowledge on the various data stocks and would be limited to coordinating activities, while scientific data users would still have to deal with the relevant data producers and data holders.

- The same reasons apply to attempts to establish an information infrastructure on a permanent basis through a university institute of some kind or through one or several professors. The existence of the Leibniz Institute for the Social Sciences (GESIS, *Leibniz-Institut für Sozialwissenschaften*) and its practical success at the same time show the limits of such institutions. A university institute or a team of scientists would not be able to cope with these requirements.

- Also, it is not promising to use externally funded private institutions to establish a permanent and secure foundation for the information infrastructure. As experience in Germany shows, the financial resources of potential users (from the scientific community) would not be sufficient to pay the considerable staff required for such institutions to offer services that meet the wide range of requirements. The empirical social and economic research community cannot be expected to obtain enough funding from the relevant organizations in the near future to permit such institutions to be established or maintained

3.2 What should a permanent information infrastructure in Germany look like if the models rejected here are not an option and if the goal is to achieve maximum use for data users, especially from the scientific community?

- Considering the possibilities of modern information technology, the infrastructure must be available online seven hours a day, 365 days a year. Where online use is not possible because of data protection and statistical confidentiality, local workstations should be kept available for use at common universities hours.

- The infrastructure should ensure that it is equally open to anyone interested and that it is neutral, i.e., that it does not assess or censor user requests. It should be independent in its methodological work and be based on accepted scientific standards. The openness, neutrality and methodological independence should each be ensured through supervision by a committee comprising representatives of data producers and scientific data users as well as the responsible data protection commissioner.

- The infrastructure should be sufficiently equipped with staff and material to fulfill its tasks. At the same time, it should be lean and economical, so that it can be used without insurmountable financial obstacles. Its work should be rationalized through permanent evaluation of its processes and through wide-ranging use of the appropriate information technologies.

- Considering the complex subject matter and regional structures of data production and storage in Germany, and the fact that centralization is unachievable, the infrastructure should be structured in terms of subject matter, it should cover all of Germany and it should be broken down into regions only to the extent absolutely required (e.g., by *Länder*).

- Although the infrastructure should be set up permanently, it should also be able – for example, through revision clauses – to react flexibly to changes in data availability and in the demand from the scientific community.

- In all these areas, in practical work it is necessary for the infrastructure institutions to achieve an optimal reconciliation between, on the one hand, the legitimate interests of data producers and data archives as well as the rights – protected by provisions on data protection and statistical confidentiality – of the individuals, local entities, and enterprises referred to by the data and, on the other hand, the interests of the scientific users. Constantly keeping this in mind will be one of the main tasks of the committee set up by the relevant infrastructure institution, in addition to the tasks mentioned above.

4. The institutions set up in Germany on the basis of the recommendations of the KVI report of March 13, 2001, and with considerable support from the Federal Ministry of Education and Research (BMBF, *Bundesministerium für Bildung und Forschung*) have basically proved successful:

4.1 The German Data Forum (RatSWD), where data producers and data users work together, has developed into an institution creatively enhancing the information infrastructure in Germany. In this council, representatives of the Federation and the *Länder* co-operate with individuals elected in a "grassroots" manner from the scientific community. Therefore, its proposals are practical and are welcomed by the community. Apart from its internal work, such as exchanging ideas with the major institution funding research (BMBF) and carrying out evaluations for official statistical institutions, the German Data Forum (RatSWD) is engaged in many external activities that have become important elements in the information infrastructure in Germany and should be continued.

What should be mentioned first of all here is the Conference for Social and Economic Data (KSWD, *Konferenz für Sozial- und Wirtschaftsdaten*). At this important event, which is held at regular intervals, council members are elected from the scientific community and research results are presented that have been obtained using the available data stocks. This provides a basis for discussing gaps identified in the information infrastructure.

Important suggestions towards improving the information infrastructure are given by the expertise contests organized by the German Data Forum (RatSWD) and the working papers and newsletters it publishes.

4.2 The most important progress that has been made since the 2001 KVI report, has been the establishment of the four Research Data Centers and the two Data Service Centers.

- The Research Data Center of the Federal Statistical Office was founded in 2001 – as the first Research Data Center in Germany –

and was positively assessed in 2004. It allows empirical social and economic researchers to access official statistical microdata, while safeguarding statistical confidentiality. For that purpose, the Research Data Center makes Public Use Files, Scientific Use Files, and CAMPUS-Files available for off-site use by the research and teaching community. Guest researchers can use less strongly anonymized data on the premises of the Federal Statistical Office in Wiesbaden, Bonn, and Berlin. Also, scholars can use data stocks of the Federal Statistical Office by means of controlled teleprocessing (on-site use).

- The decentralized Research Data Center of the Statistical Offices of the German *Länder* was set up in April 2002 and positively assessed in late 2006. It offers scientists the same access to official statistical data as shown above for the Research Data Center of the Federal Statistical Office. Subsequent to an amendment of the BStatG, the Statistical Offices of the German *Länder* established a system of centralized data storage for the whole of Germany for this purpose, with a breakdown by subject matter.

- The Research Data Center of the Federal Employment Agency (BA, *Bundesagentur für Arbeit*) was established in April 2004 at the Agency's Institute for Employment Research (IAB, *Institut für Arbeitsmarkt- und Berufsforschung*) in Nuremberg and has also been assessed positively. It makes the large data stocks of the Federal Employment Agency available for scientific analyses within the scope of Art. 75 of Volume X of the Social Code.

- The Research Data Center of the German Pension Insurance (RV, *Deutsche Rentenversicherung*) was also established in 2004 at two locations in Berlin and Würzburg. The Scientific Use Files produced there with regard to the statistics of new and existing pensions and the statistics of persons insured allow, for the first time, scientific evaluation of the vast data treasures of the German Pension Insurance.

- The two Data Service Centers – also based on the 2001 KVI report – were established in 2003 at GESIS in Mannheim and at the Institute for the Study of Labor (IZA, *Forschungsinstitut zur Zukunft der Arbeit*) in Bonn. The Data Service Center at GESIS works under the name of German Microdata Lab (GML) and offers a service and research infrastructure for official microdata. The International Data Service Center for Labor Market Relevant Data (IdZA, *Internationales Datenservicezentrum für arbeitsmarktrelevante Daten*) at the IZA provides labor market researchers with a metadata portal for existing data; it has developed a special web-based tool (JoSuA) for data access via controlled teleprocessing.

All Research Data Centers and Data Service Centers have been welcomed enthusiastically by the scientific community and are used extensively for research and teaching, with the two Research Data Centers of official statistics having observed a marked recent shift in the demand for means of access to their data stocks. While the – initially very high – demand for Scientific Use Files has been declining, demand is increasing for individual datasets, which guest researchers can access from protected scientific workstations at the Research Data Centers, and for controlled teleprocessing.

The encouraging practical efficiency of the Research Data Centers has been achieved in two ways:

- Thanks to start-up financing from the BMBF, the Research Data Centers have made a wealth of official statistical data stocks available to the research and teaching community by producing Public Use Files, Scientific Use Files, and CAMPUS-Files, by offering safe scientific workstations for guest scientists, and by offering controlled teleprocessing.

- The financial obstacles to use of data of official statistics that existed in the 1990s – which were insurmountable in some cases for empirical social scientists – have been removed, thanks in part to start-up financing provided to the Research Data Centers by the BMBF. For example, in the mid-1990s the Statistical Offices had to charge as much as DM 30,000 (about EUR 15,000) per Scientific Use File of the Microcensus to cover the considerable production costs. Since the emergence of Research Data Centers, a social scientist can obtain such a Scientific Use File for a "charge" of just EUR 90 including the CD and shipping.

4.3 The information infrastructure developed since the 2001 KVI report also includes many larger and smaller projects and initiatives of widely varied institutions. These include:

- Every year since 1999, the Federal Statistical Office has been granting the Gerhard Fürst Award for dissertations and diploma/master theses dealing with empirical questions and using official statistical data.

- The Statistical Offices of the German *Länder* have set up branches of its Research Data Center at the German Institute of Economic Research (DIW Berlin, *Deutsches Institut für Wirtschaftsforschung*) and at Dresden Technical University.

- At its conferences, the German Statistical Society (DStatG, *Deutsche Statistische Gesellschaft*) offers workshops for junior scholars to introduce them to empirical work with the various data stocks.

5. Despite all the progress made so far, there still is much to improve and numerous problems that remain to be solved. We have not yet succeeded in developing a firm institutional foundation for the information infrastructure in Germany. Financial and content-related problems need to be solved.

5.1 Financial problems appear to be the most urgent issue at present and, although they are not so excessive in volume (the Research Data Centers of the Statistical Offices of the German *Länder*, for instance, reckons with total costs of only about EUR 3.7 million for the 2 1/2 years from 1 July 2007 to 31 December 2009), they are difficult but can be solved.

- The structures created on the basis of the 2001 KVI report (especially the RatSWD with its business office in Berlin and the four Research Data Centers) owe their establishment to the support provided by the BMBF. This was temporary project support in the form of start-up financing that requires the relevant institution to contribute funds of its own, considering the benefit it draws from the project.

- The German Socio-Economic Panel (SOEP, *Sozio-oekonomisches Panel*), which meanwhile is 25 years "old," has been financed institutionally since 2004. Thus an important recommendation of the KVI has been implemented and its work can be regarded as permanently guaranteed. In contrast, such institutional support seems out of reach for the Research Data Centers but it is not strictly necessary.

- The financial situation of the Research Data Centers varies considerably at the present time.

- In the beginning, the Research Data Center of the Federal Statistical Office was financed mainly by the BMBF. Meanwhile its core business, answering and handling user requests from the scientific community, is funded completely out of its own budget. The Research Data Center receives BMBF funds only for research projects to extend the data supply it offers, for instance by anonymizing panel data from economic statistics.

- Most of the funds required for the Research Data Center of the Statistical Offices of the German *Länder* will be provided by the BMBF up to the end of 2009.
- The Research Data Center of the BA at the IAB was partly financed by the BMBF and since the beginning of 2007 has been funded entirely by the BA.
- The Research Data Center of the German Pension Insurance will be supported by the BMBF until the end of 2008.

Consolidation and a uniform financing line for the Research Data Centers are therefore urgently needed. On the one hand, they would have to guarantee the ongoing existence of the Research Data Centers and the further development of their data supply. On the other, the Research Data Centers should not charge prices that users cannot afford. It is thanks to the 2001 KVI report and the project support by the BMBF that this – harmful – situation no longer exists in Germany. After all, the scientific community should be able to use the respective data stocks for research and teaching purposes. At the same time, one will have to accept that the BMBF generally confines itself to temporary start-up financing and regards the respective data archives and scholars as responsible thereafter.

Therefore the organizations supporting the Research Data Centers, the empirical social and economic research institutions and the BMBF should agree on the following model, which should entail sustainable financing of the Research Data Centers at affordable prices for their users:

- The respective organizations supporting the Research Data Centers, for example of the Federal Statistical Office and the Statistical Offices of the German *Länder*, will take over the basic financing of their Research Data Centers.
- The further development of methodology and special research projects of the Research Data Centers will continue to receive project funding on a temporary basis, provided that these are important for an expansion of the information infrastructure.
- The Research Data Centers will charge users to cover the expenses incurred in each case, but there will be far-reaching possibilities to reduce prices for financially "weak" users such as PhD candidates or university institutes, while "well equipped" users, for instance economic research institutes, which can pass on their expenses to their clients, will have to pay prices fully covering the expenses.

For the Federal Statistical Office and the Statistical Offices of the German *Länder* to support this solution, it would be advisable to amend the Federal Statistics Law, making it clear that the mandate of official statistics also includes the provision of data (both aggregated data and microdata) to the scientific community. The inclusion of such a provision into one of the next bills on statistical issues should be supported at the Federal Ministry of the Interior (BMI, *Bundesministerium des Inneren*). Once the cooperation of the statistical offices in an Research Data Center with jointly held data is made possible by the Federal Statistics Law in 2005 (through its § 3a Abs. 2 and § 16 Abs. 2), the Research Data Centers of the official statistical agencies would thus be enshrined in law and their funding would be indirectly guaranteed.

5.2 As regards its contents, the information infrastructure that has emerged in Germany since 2001 provides numerous starting points for expansion and consolidation. Depending on the perspective, different institutions prioritize one point or another. Priorities and posteriorities should be discussed in the German Data Forum (RatSWD) and a medium-term consolidation and extension program should be set up, focusing not only on what would be desirable but also on what chances there are to implement it. The initiatives listed in the following are therefore not listed in order of preference.

- The existing four Research Data Centers are far from opening up all data stocks that are of interest to empirical social and economic research. This is why there should also be Research Data Centers, for instance, for health, education, and media data. Other major fields awaiting investigation are crime control and the administration of justice and penal administration, for example, using the criminal statistics of the police and judicial statistics. The situation is similar with the Central Register of Foreigners kept at the Federal Office for Migration and Refugees, the business register of the Federal Statistical Office, and the population registers of the municipalities and the *Länder*. Finally, provisions have to be made in time for the scientific use of the data that will be collected in the EU-wide population census scheduled for the year 2011. In each of these areas, it would have to be determined whether Research Data Centers should be set up and, if so, how this can be fostered.

- As there are different Research Data Centers, each of them restricted to specific data stocks, it is crucial that a "special" Research Data Center be set up that combines the data stocks of various data producers or makes it possible to work with the data from different producers. A similar goal is pursued by the proposal to create a kind of "data trust" keeping data stocks from various subject fields and making them accessible to the scientific community through the channels known from the Research Data Centers. Advantageous as both ideas may be from the viewpoint of empirical social and economic research, the obstacles of data protection legislation appear insurmountable so that one should not "fight a losing battle" here.

- Such a solution might be considered, if at all, for statistical data whose collection does not have to be strictly linked to a specific purpose. But then the data kept there would have to be at least de facto anonymized. This, however, would probably not be worthwhile. Also, it should be kept in mind that combining de facto anonymized personal data from different statistics increases the chances of reidentification, which is precisely what must be prevented.

- Non-statistical data, however, have to be strictly linked to a specific purpose. This means the following. First the data – and also the microdata – of the various producers would have to be transferred to the "special" Research Data Center or the "data trust." So far this would generally not be covered by the respective data collection purpose and would therefore be illegal. The clauses relating to the scientific community as contained in the German Federal Data Protection Act (e.g., § 14 Abs. 5 Satz 2) do not permit such data transmission and storage because the research purposes can actually be achieved with reasonable efforts even without a "special" Research Data Center or without a "data trust." The proposal to appoint the data protection commissioner in charge as trustee does not solve the problem. Apart from the fact that the Federal Commissioner for Data Protection has already dismissed such ideas for his institution, the unsolvable problem of having to alter the purpose would persist. If – despite all practical obstacles – the consent of all concerned to such a purpose-altering transfer could be obtained, reservations would remain because contrary to the order of the Federal Constitutional Court, the data would not be de facto anonymized at the earliest possible time.

- In view of this legal situation, it would be advisable to invite an expert, for example, from the Federal Employment Agency or its Institute for Employment Research (IAB) to the Research Data Center of the Federal Statistical Office and to entrust him or her with "data processing by order" – that is, with the evaluation of statistical data in combination with data of the Federal Employment Agency in relation to a specific issue. The Research Data Center of the Federal Statistical Office plans to do this with regard to the data of the Federal Employment Agency.

- Given the legal consensus that the clause on the scientific community in § 16 Abs. 6 of the Federal Statistics Law does not cover foreign universities or foreign scientists, the information infrastructures created in Germany to date have not furthered scientific cooperation with foreign countries, and this also holds true for the EU. It is true that there is now a "Safe Centre" at Eurostat in Luxembourg, whose establishment was made possible by Regulation (EC) No 831 / 2002 (concerning access to confidential data for scientific purposes). However, German statistical microdata would be available there only if they had been submitted to Eurostat, as well, which is an exception. The establishment of such an "EU Safe Centre" in Wiesbaden, which is planned by Eurostat together with the Federal Statistical Office, will therefore not bring any improvements for foreign scientists. To enable cross-border scientific work, empirical social and economic researchers should call for an extension of § 16 Abs. 6 of the Federal Statistics Law to cover foreign scientists. Article 23 of the new EU Regulation No. 223/2009 on European Statistics grants researchers access to confidential data which only allow for indirect identification of the statistical unit for scientific purposes.

- There has been no progress in the last few years regarding the 2001 KVI recommendation to introduce a research or scientific code of confidentiality. The restraint shown in responding to this suggestion may be due to the fact that such a research data secret would have to entail the scientist's right to decline to answer questions, and the prohibition of seizure. However, this recommendation still deserves to be studied in detail. Because of the complexity of the matter, the German Data Forum (RatSWD) should set up a working party for the purpose. After the recent cases of data abuse at a large telecommunication provider and in call centers, serious proposals have been put forward calling for a codification of the right to informational self-determination and of a right to privacy of information technology records. If these attempts should materialize, the scientific community would have to promote its interests in an elaborate proposal to introduce a research or scientific secret. Progress in this difficult matter might be easier if a code of conduct existed for scientists interested in using the data stocks, paired with the possibility to impose sanctions, which was also recommended by the 2001 KVI report. The RatSWD should also take steps in that direction, together with the other scientific institutions.

- Finally, the 2001 KVI report deserves further attention, since it aims at an expansion of empirical social and economic research (including university education on this type of research). Beyond the establishment of "empirical economic research" as a university subject, there is a sufficient number of current problems justifying, for instance, the creation of special research areas (e.g., on questions of health and education policies) or of professorships for empirical work (co-) financed by trusts.

- When the information infrastructure has been established on a permanent basis, it will be important to carry out continuous checks for "proliferation," overlaps, duplication of labor, and the like. This should take place in the course of, and apart from, the now common and rather strict periodical evaluation of the facilities created. Experience shows that these problems are likely to arise, especially with new developments, and that the readiness to make necessary changes may still be lacking. In particular, the informational structures resulting from the federal system should be analyzed in this respect.

2. The European Dimension

Klaus Reeh

Contact:

Klaus Reeh
Adviser to the Director-General, Eurostat
Bâtiment BECH
5, rue Alphonse Weicker
2721 Luxembourg
e-mail: klaus.reeh[at]ec.europa.eu

Abstract

The purpose of this report is to identify how to better meet the needs of scientists and take into account their concerns around the use of economic and social data at the European level without compromising or neglecting the legitimate needs and justified concerns of European policy-makers.

1. Background

The volume and type of data that can be made available to scientists depend increasingly on targeted initiatives and general developments at the European level. These initiatives and developments are primarily motivated by the need for official statistics to serve the purposes of (European) policy making. A number of scientific needs are met because they overlap with the needs of European policy-makers:

- Comparability across national borders is of central importance for both policy-makers and scientists.
- Policy-makers and scientists both benefit from coordinated program planning between the Member States since this is the only way to have corresponding statistics on hand for all Member States.

Other scientific needs and concerns, however, are either at least partially at odds with the (legitimate) needs and concerns of European policy-makers or have a significantly different priority level:

- In science, for example, accuracy is usually more important than how recent the information is; the opposite is true for policy making. While policy-makers are often under pressure to make snap decisions, the world of science faces such time pressure only in exceptional circumstances.
- Methodological stability over time is often more important in science than the ability to adequately address up-to-the-minute political and institutional situations; the opposite is true for policy making. While policy-makers normally have to base their arguments on what is at play in the current situation, scientific perspectives draw from longer periods of time.
- Complex statistical procedures do not pose a problem for science; scientists often even demand them. For policy making, however, there are limits to complexity because it complicates communication.

- Scientists are always looking for new concepts that must then also be described statistically, whereas policy-makers cannot but prefer to work with well-established concepts. Conceptual innovation is a necessity for science, but is subject to limitations in the field of policy making.

Scientists have needs that can be satisfied without obstructing the needs of European policy-makers. Nonetheless, these needs are often neglected. An important reason for this is that they have not been, and are still not sufficiently emphasized by scientists themselves.

- Access to (anonymized) microdata has become increasingly important for science. The behavior of individual actors or groups of actors has become increasingly interesting for economic and social science research, particularly with a view toward improving what are still too frequently the rather simplistic assumptions within economic science itself, and to overcome the divide between micro and macro analysis. In contrast, the use of microdata is of limited importance for European policy making (or for European administration), and is sometimes excluded entirely.

Although policy-makers and scientists often have overlapping interests in and needs for (European) statistics, it must nevertheless always be borne in mind that – to borrow from the language of sociology – the "science system" and the "political system" follow differing logics and principles. Science (empirical science) endeavors to adopt at least a denationalized or even global approach in order to avoid politicization. Policy making, on the other hand, must remain to a large extent national and, by definition, also political, even where there is an attempt at depoliticization, which is made not least by pointing to the inherent necessities that can be substantiated by statistical evidence. Furthermore, (empirical) science constantly strives for neutrality in its value system; in contrast, policy making cannot escape value judgments – indeed, value judgments are its business.

Official statistics, which are after all part of both systems, can easily risk being torn between the two different fields and end up satisfying neither of them. To make matters more difficult at the European level, official statisticians usually have a much more general mission at the national level and are much freer to decide how to accomplish their mission than would be legally possible at the European level. It is therefore desirable for scientific research policy in particular to look into this issue and to support a broader spectrum of responsibilities for European statistics, which would make it possible to provide European statistics also for domains without a specific *political* competence at EU level.

2. A few specific problem areas

A number of specific barriers stand in the way of both the extensive, appropriate supply and the sensible use of European economic and social data by scientists. Below is a non-exhaustive, brief outline of some of these barriers. They are not listed in order of importance. Reference is made first to more technical barriers and then to barriers which are more organizational in nature.

- The purpose of European statistical policy is to organize official statistics in such a way that the information needed to implement European policies (for the appropriate exercise of European competences) is available. It follows that European statistics can cover only those areas for which a European political competence exists. It is therefore not a comprehensive system, and has never been presented as such. This incompleteness is frequently regretted by scientists, but is difficult to remedy at the European level, since the European Union does not have full competence in the field of statistics and the European Commission does not have the corresponding right of initiative to create an all-encompassing European statistical system.

- The harmonization of official statistics is the main focus of the European statistical policy. However, each harmonization brings with it inevitable discontinuity, at least in some Member States. Temporal continuity is sacrificed in favor of improved geographical comparability. Yet continuity over time is particularly important for science (time series econometrics). Scientists (generally more than policy-makers) therefore press for retroactive calculations of harmonized statistics.[1] These are very costly and therefore cannot be carried out without a specific request.

- On the other hand, the harmonization of individual statistics repeatedly encounters various limitations which result not least from these statistics being anchored within the different national systems and their basic respective orientations. Even when policy-makers consider individual harmonization results to be acceptable, scientists often find fault with them: the process of "output harmonization" often suffices to achieve data convergence for analyzing problems of "practical policy making," whereas it is all too commonly believed that "rigorous science" requires "input harmonization" in order to obtain secure findings. However, the content

---

[1] The treatment of changes to territorial boundaries is a similar issue. Here again, scientists push for retroactive calculations or for the old territorial boundary to continue to be used.

superiority of "input harmonization" has not been clearly established and requires expensive comparisons, while the lower costs of "output harmonization" are a definite advantage.

- One technical (but also policy) problem is posed by the incoherence of data related to cross-border issues, such as flows between countries or entitlements with cross-border validity (e.g., rights). Particularly in the case of sample surveys due to the sampling error, but also in exhaustive surveys, exactly identical results in the country of arrival and the country of departure cannot be expected for a number of reasons when statistically measuring exactly the same flow. The same applies to the allocation of entitlements. This problem is indeed inconvenient for policy making, but is not considered too serious for the decision-making process, whereas in science it is seen to undermine research possibilities and the accuracy of conclusions.

- The growing complexity of official statistics has been brought about by the methodological and definition-related cross-linking of specialized statistics. On the one hand this is necessary, for instance, in order to develop a system of national accounts, which is important for policy making, and particularly for European policy. On the other hand, it impedes the targeted pursuit of specific scientific questions because it leads to conceptual definitions that are determined by considerations unrelated to the field of reference. Furthermore, the establishment of an omnipresent statistical *"perspective unique"* (single perspective) encourages the adoption of a *"pensée unique"* (single line of thought). This may even be helpful in European policy since it often makes decision making easier. However, it appears to endanger the safeguarding of a variety of perspectives, which is important in the world of science.

- Another problem for science is the general lack of flexibility of official statistics caused by their increasing codification, which is not least of all a consequence of their Europeanization. In many cases, European legislation is required where national legislation would never have been necessary. Think, for example, of the detailed regulations on the calculation of the HCPI (Harmonized Consumer Price Index). Without its functional significance for European policy even the calculation of national accounts would never have been codified. This to a large extent determines the demands on European statistics and considerably limits the possibilities for rapid, pragmatic action in the field of official statistics, with the result that new phenomena of particular interest for science are insufficiently recorded in European statistics and with a certain delay.

- Recently, policy-makers have insisted more on reducing the response burden (which is, on the whole, relatively undemanding) and in this context are pressing for the increased use of administrative sources in order to lighten the "burden" on respondents. This can lead to significant changes (and often also restrictions) in the availability of comparable data, as administrative structures and thus sources often differ enormously within the EU. This in turn can restrict scientific research possibilities. The partial substitution of observation by estimation is particularly problematic for (empirical) science in this regard. However, it must be borne in mind that these estimation procedures are also developed by the (methodological) sciences. The problem is thus not just a conflict between policy making and science, but also a conflict of interests between empiricists and theorists, possibly worsened by policy-makers.

- Policy-makers of course generally support a reduction in the cost of official statistics, especially at the European level. Here too, (methodological) science, in conjunction with technology, offers valuable cost-cutting assistance. But here again there is a conflict of interest between empiricists and theorists. The solid, suitably controlled, accurately targeted, and regular sample survey is still the most popular source for (empirical) science, but these surveys are very costly and are therefore becoming increasingly controversial, a trend reinforced by concerns about data protection. Science must come to terms with the fact that, in official statistics, the importance of the classic sample survey will diminish while that of administrative sources will increase.

- The functional use of official statistics for policy-making purposes has expanded at the European level in recent years. This has raised increasing doubts among scientists and others regarding the credibility of European statistics. It seems to be a widely-held belief (and probably also a basic assumption of the New Political Economy) that official statisticians angle their results, when necessary in the national interest, according to desired political outcomes. In this context, however, science all too often overlooks the harmony of interests between European policy making and science, and the fact that the Europeanization of statistics on the basis of trusting cooperation between the national statistical offices and Eurostat has led to the depoliticization of the statistical processes, from conceptualization to data collection, statistical preparation, and dissemination.

- In general, science seems to have difficulty dealing with the role of policy making in official statistics. As regards statistical methods, the influence of science is of course substantial; scientists are even asked for advice. But as far as the statistical program is concerned, it would be difficult for science to accept the primacy of policy making over statistics. Knowledge in many fields is desirable, but not everything can be researched on account of limited resources (aside from the fact that some things should simply not be officially recorded). Expense and yield, cost and benefit must first be weighed by official statistics within the framework of their legal remit, but ultimately this must always also be the duty of policy-makers as legislators and as the budgetary authority. It is therefore not enough for scientists to voice their concerns and needs to official statisticians; they must also seek support from policy-makers. In the European context, such efforts are two-tiered and therefore doubly expensive, and the world of science does not appear to be particularly well-equipped for this, since it must work at convincing official statisticians and policy-makers at both the national and European level.

- Finally, reference must be made to one more barrier which is particularly problematic in the European context: centralized (European) access to microdata. European legislation generally requires Member States only to provide tables, but not individual data. Microdata at the European level are therefore available for only a very limited number of statistics. These data are of course available to scientists, in accordance with Commission Regulation (EC) No. 831/2002. Access arrangements have admittedly become more user-friendly in recent years, but further improvements in the near future will be difficult to achieve owing to the pending change in the legal basis for European statistics. Instead, we can even expect the process of gaining access to data to become even longer, as a parliamentary inspection has been built into the approval procedure.

3. Possible solutions

For some of the difficulties listed here, there are no simple solutions (e.g., limitations and consequences of harmonization, changes to territorial boundaries) – science will simply have to live with them. It will doubtlessly be possible to find solutions to other problems, but this will take time and above all budgetary resources, and possibly also an amendment to the legal framework. However, these solutions can be found only through dialogue between scientists and official statisticians as well as between scientists and policy-makers.

3.1 Recommendations relating solely to science policy

Scientists without question believe there is room for improvement in the general policy on scientific research at the European level with respect to official statistics. The provision of economic and social statistics is not a particularly important issue for European research policy, unlike German policy, an importance demonstrated at least in recent years by the very existence of the German Data Forum (RatSWD). At the European level, whatever support is allocated is largely directed toward methodological research in the field of statistics. There are certainly good reasons for this, but the result is that Eurostat – the central authority for the provision of European data and the focal point of European statistics, or more precisely for official statistics at European level – is not and cannot be very active in the provision of statistics for (European) policy and the public. There is no body (as yet) comparable to Germany's national and regional Research Data Centers, which specifically address the needs of science. Likewise, there is no infrastructure (as yet) to connect all the relevant data holders and thereby facilitate the use of European data through different channels and different sites. The following recommendations are therefore proposed:

- First recommendation: German research policy (BMBF, *Federal Ministry of Education and Research*) should more actively represent the needs and concerns of scientific users of economic and social data at the European level. If it is appropriate in a national context to give science better access to available data, which has been difficult or impossible to access or use until now, then the same applies to the European context. The German Data Forum (RatSWD) should be called upon to draft recommendations for the further development of a truly European data infrastructure (not only access to data but also data type and volume).

- Second recommendation: in light of the forthcoming amendment to the Commission Regulation (EC) No 831/2002, German research policy (BMBF) and German official statistics should push for simplified access and a greater variety of forms of access. The German Data Forum (RatSWD) could be asked to give an opinion on this in the context of the European amendment procedure.

- Third recommendation: in the summer of 2009, the European Statistical Advisory Committee (ESAC) will take over from the European Advisory Committee on Statistical Information in the Economic and Social Spheres (CEIES). German scientists must lobby the 24 members of this body, some of whom will be representatives from the sciences, for improvement to data access and data volume at the European level (for instance via the

RatSWD). Furthermore, German scientists could urge this body to provide incentives for improved cooperation between official statisticians and scientists (both empirical and methodological scientists).

- Fourth recommendation: scientists should in general make targeted use of the opportunities to voice their views offered under the new "governance structure" of European statistics that has taken shape in recent months. Their efforts will be even more effective if other Member States share these views. It would therefore be a good idea for the RatSWD to establish closer contacts with user bodies in other Member States.

- Fifth recommendation: lastly, it could be helpful for researchers to look into the social and political processes that generate the need for statistical information and tried to analyze these processes. This would certainly also make it easier for scientists to take part in these processes and influence them in such a way as to ensure that greater account is taken of their own concerns. Such processes have, after all, become considerably more complex in recent years and, with the new media, also more participatory, not least at the European level.

3.2 Practical steps

While policy initiatives to improve the legal framework conditions are important, significant improvements are nevertheless also possible under the current conditions.

- Sixth recommendation: German official statistics should engage in technical cooperation with those national statistical offices which also want to improve access for scientists to European data and, as sponsors (where appropriate through the European structures that have been created for that purpose), should take the initiative. Particular consideration should be given here to whether the data made available in the context of this cooperation would go beyond the already Europeanized microdata (on the basis of EU legislation). Data which has not been harmonized owing to a lack of Community competence and which Eurostat cannot take care of are also of interest to empirical science.

- Seventh recommendation: at the same time, German official statisticians should increase their efforts to lobby for improved access to, and an extended scope of, economic and social data at the European level. The European Commission (Eurostat) is of course restricted in the exercise of its right of initiative to those statistical fields that relate to policy areas where the Community is competent. However, when it is a matter of infrastructure that, once created, will be used both for Europeanized and non-Europeanized statistics, it should be possible for the European Commission (Eurostat) to at least assume the role of a catalyst.

Perhaps it will also be necessary to break new ground and separate content, access, and control possibilities from infrastructure. The infrastructure could then be used to provide access to European microdata through Eurostat and at the same time also provide Europe-wide access to national microdata under the joint control of the national statistical offices – in whatever form such a joint structure might take. German national and regional Research Data Centers are probably best placed and suited to submit proposals.

- Eighth recommendation: the use of European statistics presents a number of particular difficulties, some of which have already been mentioned (structural breaks caused by harmonization, contradictions in the double recording of intra-Community flows and entitlements, etc.). Science can make important contributions in how to deal with these difficulties by making them a research subject in their own right. Here again, the German Data Forum (RatSWD) could provide valuable stimulus.

- Ninth recommendation: the German Data Forum (RatSWD) could also be a driving force when it comes to the provision of data on statistical units without a clear national affiliation (e.g., multinational companies). The EuroGroups Register is currently being developed and one objective could be to improve the data on multinationals so that they can be subjected to systematic empirical analysis.

- Tenth recommendation: lastly, it must be pointed out that, not least for its own benefit, science should actively support the statistical policy of the European Commission (Eurostat). Successful harmonization, coordinated and forward-looking program planning, efficient collection and processing procedures, and widespread dissemination of the results generally also improve possibilities scientific research. However, this should apply not only to the core area of European responsibilities and those fields in which the open method of coordination is used, but also for purely national fields. The research avenues open to empirical science depend on the availability not only of temporal but also of spatial data. The European Commission (Eurostat) is of central importance for making the latter type of data available and should therefore be actively and enthusiastically supported by the scientific community.

To sum up, we wish to restate and thereby emphasize the following: in order to improve data for the economic and social sciences, the German Data Forum (RatSWD) should first begin to become a more Europeanized organization. Establishing contacts with partners in the European Union is necessary to allow for their common interests to be asserted jointly, based on the broadest possible coalitions. Secondly, German Research Data Centers at national and regional levels should cooperate with partners in other EU Member States, not least of all to maintain the drive generated by their creation. And, thirdly, representatives of German policy on scientific research (BMBF) should push for European policies to improve the supply and use of economic and social data across Europe.

3. The Role of the German Research Foundation

Eckard Kämper and Manfred Nießen

Contact:

Eckard Kämper
Kennedyallee 40
53175 Bonn
Germany
e-mail: Eckard.Kaemper[at]dfg.de

Abstract

The strategy adopted by the German Research Foundation (DFG) for future data research infrastructures should be based on what has been achieved thus far and the lessons that can be learned from that. First, the focus of effort should be on providing data rather than on sharing data. Second, projects whose primary purpose is to provide a common good should seek to build research infrastructure. The DFG has powerful means at its disposal to fund outstanding infrastructure projects. It is up to the scientific community to adapt and utilize these funding instruments. Different types of strategic cooperation are required among interested parties in the field. These include: cooperation on identifying thematic priorities within the research community; cooperation between the research community and funding institutions in determining funding options; cooperation around defining the division of labor between different funding institutions (including ministries) on the national and international level. The DFG is prepared to play an active role in this cooperative effort under the leadership of its elected bodies (the *Fachkollegien* and *Senat*).

Keywords: large scale studies; strategic cooperation

The research infrastructure of the social sciences, like that of other disciplines, has long had a place on the agenda of the German Research Foundation (DFG, *Deutsche Forschungsgemeinschaft*), both in terms of its funding policies and its funding activities. The DFG provided the funding for both ZUMA[1] and SOEP[2], for example, and nurtured them through their formative years. The DFG has also funded activities at the ZA[3], IZ[4] and ZPID[5]. All these activities have been about data – about methods and methodologies for collecting and analyzing data, and about organizations and structures for preserving data and making them accessible.

Data-related research infrastructure has become a more prominent topic in research policy over recent months and years, nationally as well as internationally. In the general science policy debate, much emphasis has been placed on "sharing data," often also referring to open access initiatives.

---

1   ZUMA: Center for Survey Design and Methodology & Social Monitoring and Social Change. See: http://www.gesis.org/en/institute/gesis-scientific-sections/center-for-survey-design-and-methodology/ and http://www.gesis.org/en/institute/gesis-scientific-sections/social-monitoring-social-change/.
2   SOEP: German Socio-Economic Panel. See: www.diw.de/gsoep.
3   ZA: Data Archive and Data Analysis. See: http://www.gesis.org/en/institute/gesis-scientific-sections/data-archive-data-analysis/.
4   IZ: Specialized Information for the Social Sciences & Information Processes in the Social Sciences. See: http://www.gesis.org/en/institute/gesis-scientific-sections/specialized-information-for-the-social-sciences/ and http://www.gesis.org/en/institute/gesis-scientific-sections/information-processes-in-the-social-sciences/.
5   ZPID is the psychology information center for the German-speaking countries. See: http://www.zpid.de/index.php?lang=EN.

1. Sharing data: a realistic approach

The idea of sharing data focuses on data produced in research projects that pursue specific hypotheses and generate the data accordingly. That is, the data are generated or collected to answer the specific questions of the project at hand; thus, the data are project-specific.

It is taken for granted that sharing data will increase efficiency and reduce research costs by necessitating replication studies and reducing duplication in data production. However, data sharing is by no means a new idea. It has a long history that is well worth examining more closely.

The DFG has long required that all funded projects transfer their data to public data archives, for example, to the ZA or ZPID. But relatively few datasets have actually been transferred. As a result, some of the DFG's national programs (SPP, *Schwerpunktprogramme*) have imposed strict time limits on the transfer of data to public archives for every project funded. While the success rate – the number of projects complying with this provision – has increased, it still is far below 100 percent.

We may lament the discrepancy between official policy and the actual behavior of the research community, exert more pressure, and impose tighter controls. But we should also ask: what are the reasons for this discrepancy? Why do relatively few projects "share" their data by transferring them to a data archive?

Project-specific data, generated to answer specific research questions, do not necessarily lend themselves to use by others. Both contextualization and specification are a necessary provision for sharing these kinds of data. After completion of the research project, scarce resources – researchers' time in particular – must be further invested to produce a dataset that is potentially valuable to others and that can be transferred to an archive for their use. The question is: can the reluctance of the research community to invest in this type of data sharing be understood as an indicator of the low value ascribed to shared data?

And what about the datasets that *have* been transferred to archives – data from projects whose primary aim was not to produce data "for others" but to pursue specific research questions? To what degree are these data being used by the research community? In other words: is there sufficient demand?

Both of these questions – why the research community is reluctant to invest in sharing data and how high is the actual demand for shared data – need to be analyzed in more detail. Data generated with public money should, of course, be made available to the public (that is, in the case of sensitive individual or company data subject to data protection restrictions, made available to the research community). However, keeping in mind the overall goal of a data infrastructure, for some projects it may not be a top priority to invest in data sharing, given the high transaction costs and limited value of the data to the scientific community. More pragmatic approaches to secure access to individual project data are being discussed more in the context of "research integrity" than in the context of infrastructure.

The goal of providing data is a markedly different approach from data sharing, and it has become increasingly prominent in the DFG's funding activities over the past few years. With the term "data provision," we refer to a type of project or program whose primary aim is not to answer a specific, narrowly delimited research question and to collect data for this purpose, but to collect and/or generate data for wider use and thus act as a "research infrastructure." The focus and theoretical foundation of this form of data production is not a set of specific hypotheses, but a wider research topic or area. Data production for wider use is the main purpose of the DFG's projects and programs, which are designed as a service to the scientific community. Increasingly, data production is taking the form of large-scale longitudinal studies.

The DFG has long been regarded as lacking adequate funding instruments for longitudinal studies. In 1995, however, the DFG began considering how to remedy this problem, and held a workshop convening experts from the field of large-scale longitudinal studies and members of the DFG's committees. The workshop resulted in a paper that specified the criteria that would need to be fulfilled in order for longitudinal studies to seek DFG funding, and that encouraged researchers to develop their ideas for such studies.[6] While this did not produce any significant immediate effect, the situation has changed dramatically in recent years. Large-scale longitudinal studies providing research infrastructure for the social sciences have become a major activity. Various factors have contributed to this change:

(1) Emerging activities in the national research community, closely linked to similar activities in Europe and elsewhere;

(2) Increased attention to these developments in European programs and European institutions;

(3) Adjustments of DFG instruments to foster and promote these activities.

---

[6] The paper was widely published: Kölner Zeitschrift für Soziologie, Psychologische Rundschau, Zeitschrift für Entwicklungspsychologie und Pädagogische Psychologie, Zeitschrift für Wirtschafts- und Sozialpsychologie, and ZUMA-Nachrichten.

2. Providing data: shaping the instruments

What did the DFG do to bring about this reorientation and why? It all goes back to the workshop of 1995, where the first strategic debate took place on how the DFG could improve opportunities for funding longitudinal studies. The workshop brought together representatives from all disciplines of the social and behavioral sciences. Its recommendations addressed the scientific community as well as the DFG as a funding organization.

This initial input did not produce systematic changes, however, either within the scientific community or at the DFG. This changed, however, with a major strategic initiative launched by the DFG in 2002, called the Funding Initiative for the Humanities (*Förderinitiative Geisteswissenschaften*). This initiative addressed the specific needs of the humanities, but also created new funding opportunities open to both the humanities and the social sciences. One of the four pillars of the strategic initiative was to reshape and modernize the DFG's strategic initiative long-term program or *Langfristprogramm*, whose effects became visible as early as 2003.

The *Langfristprogramm* had been in existence since the DFG was founded, but was initially designed only for the humanities. In 2003, the DFG's *Senat* and Joint Committee resolved to implement a reform of this program with the following elements:

(1) Limits were placed on the formerly open-ended time frame: the program is now only for research activities requiring seven to twelve years of funding.

(2) Only projects of potentially high scientific impact and importance will be funded. A longer-term perspective is necessary, but is by no means the sole requirement.

(3) The *Langfristprogramm* is no longer confined to the humanities, but is now open to both the humanities and the social sciences. The strategic decision to open up the *Langfristprogramm* to the social and behavioral sciences was based, among other things, on the recommendations from 1995. Longitudinal studies are invited to seek funding within the *Langfristprogramm*.

(4) As a consequence of provisions (2) and (3) (aiming at high-impact activities and opening up to the social sciences in general and longitudinal studies in particular), the scale of funding per individual project has been expanded: substantial funding is available depending on the individual project needs. As a consequence, fewer projects will be funded, but they will come from a broader range of disciplines – humanities and social sciences – and with a broader range of budgets.

The first project in which this new funding option was put to use was the European Social Survey (ESS), an internationally comparative study of repeated cross-sections, with more than twenty countries participating. The European Commission provides the core funding for this project, and more than twenty national funding agencies finance the national data collection. The *Langfristprogramm* was essential in making the German part of the European Social Survey possible, and allowed the DFG to fully participate in the European program. When the DFG makes a decision to approve a project as part of the *Langfristprogramm*, this includes a commitment to provide funding for the entire duration of the activity. Because the ESS was part of the *Langfristprogramm*, the DFG was able to stand in for the ESS in the network of national support institutions, the European Commission, and the European Science Foundation, and to formally sign commitments. This provided the groundwork for the ESS to become a truly European infrastructure that eventually became part of the road map of the European Strategy Forum on Research Infrastructure (ESFRI). As a consequence, the ESS may become a "European Research Infrastructure," which will require a new legal form. The aim is to become a kind of international organization. This will certainly have implications for the role of national funding organizations that are still unknown to us.

Just recently, in December 2008, the German Longitudinal Election Study (GLES) was adopted as part of the *Langfristprogramm*, with the potential to be funded for nine years. After that time, and after having gathered data on three successive national elections, it is intended that the GLES will be taken on board at GESIS. Whereas the future perspective for the ESS beyond its funding as part of the *Langfristprogramm* remains open, the future of the GLES is relatively secure: provided that the DFG-funded project proves to be a success in scientific terms, it will be continued under the institutional umbrella of GESIS.

The situation of pairfam, the panel study of intimate relations and family members, is unique in another respect as well: a national research program (SPP) was set up by DFG to develop and implement the study. Normally, national programs aim at rather loose cooperation between projects around a common topic. With pairfam, however, the very idea of the program was to develop a common product. This required a clearly defined division of labor between the individual projects within the program, a high level of coordination, clear leadership, and intense collaboration across the fields of sociological, economic, and psychological research on family and relationships. Although the funding instrument that was used, the SPP, normally aims at supporting a different kind of scientific cooperation, the adaptive use of this instrument was successful, and indeed innovative: the first four years of the SPP were used for the development of the panel study, and the final two years are currently being devoted to carrying out the first two waves of the panel.

Before giving a green light to these final two years and releasing the actual funding for the first two waves, the *Senat* and Joint Committee of DFG carefully considered the future prospects for pairfam. After all, it would not have made sense to finance the first two waves without a perspective on future steps. The deliberation was based on a review panel's assessment of pairfam's plans. Reviewers, the *Senat*, and the Joint Committee came to the conclusion that pairfam should be invited to seek future funding as part of the *Langfristprogramm*. This opened up a perspective of twelve years for pairfam and confirmed the strategic decision to design the *Langfristprogramm* in a way that would allow for substantial funding of individual projects. pairfam, which started as part of a SPP, demonstrates that the new *Langfristprogramm* is not the only instrument in the DFG's portfolio that can be used to support large-scale longitudinal studies.

In principle, all funding instruments should be considered. The German Socio-Economic Panel (SOEP, *Sozio-oekonomisches Panel*) is a prominent example. SOEP, which has become a cornerstone of the German research infrastructure in the social and behavioral sciences, was initiated and developed many years ago as part of a collaborative research center (SFB). When this SFB ended (in 1991) after an initial twelve-year funding period, funding for the SOEP was continued under the individual-project funding mode (refinanced by special funds from the German federal and state governments). However, given the importance of the SOEP as a research infrastructure, an institutional solution was needed that could provide long-term stability. A solution was negotiated by the Federal Ministry of Education and Research (BMBF, *Bundesministerium für Bildung und Forschung*), the respective ministries of the states, and the DFG: after more than twelve years in the individual-project funding mode, the SOEP was established as a special "service unit" at DIW Berlin, a member of the Leibniz Association (WGL, *Leibniz Gemeinschaft*). SOEP's success story – with regard to funding and institutional solutions – is rooted in the adaptive use of several funding instruments and cooperation among the funding institutions (BMBF, DFG, WGL). pairfam, on the other hand, is currently in the process of adapting several funding instruments to its needs.

A final example of both adaptation of funding instruments and co-operation among funding institutions is the National Educational Panel Study (NEPS). The idea for NEPS was first presented and discussed at the symposium in 2004 that was organized by the DFG as part of its "Program on Empirical Research on Education." The symposium brought together researchers from Germany and other European countries as well as representatives of government ministries. At its conclusion, the program's Scientific Board gave advice that formed the basis for the DFG's position on

NEPS. Following the Scientific Board's recommendation, the DFG's Governing Board agreed that the DFG would play an active role in the future process, in close collaboration with BMBF, whereby the funding for NEPS would come solely from the BMBF.

The DFG organized preparatory expert meetings, an international expert workshop to assess the pilot study, and a full-scale international peer review for the full proposal. Based on this peer-review, the BMBF made the formal decision to finance NEPS as a data-providing research infrastructure. The DFG's *Senat* simultaneously decided to allocate a substantial budget for a national research program (SPP) in which projects would be funded that make scientific use of the NEPS data. In other words, the DFG, by implementing its mechanisms for independent assessment of scientific quality, provided the mechanism to firmly root NEPS in the scientific community. For the implementation of peer-review results, the BMBF and DFG agreed on a division of labor: the BMBF finances the research infrastructure, the DFG funds the scientific use of the data through its national research program.

3. The role of the German Research Foundation (DFG)

The major large-scale longitudinal studies that currently serve as the foundation for the data research infrastructure in the social sciences have developed into a major field of activity at the DFG. This development, however, was not the result of a strategic master plan. Of course, there was the policy statement of 1995 and the strategy decision of 2003 to redesign the *Langfristprogramm* specifically geared towards longitudinal studies in the social sciences. Nonetheless, the individual activities and projects that emerged within the scientific community were pursued in a relatively uncoordinated way. This is not surprising, given that the DFG is owned by the scientific community and firmly founded on the principle that strategic initiatives as well as individual funding decisions must be driven by research questions and by researchers themselves. The case of NEPS does not follow this principle to the letter, but nevertheless provides a good illustration of the DFG's role: NEPS was initiated and, at least in its early stage, conceptualized by the BMBF. Furthermore, it is the BMBF, not the DFG, that funds this research infrastructure. Close cooperation and partnership with the DFG was sought to provide scientific quality control through independent peer review and thereby scientific legitimation. The DFG's role in the partnership with BMBF has been to ensure that this externally initiated panel study is and will continue to be essentially science-driven.

Closely related to the principle of being "science-driven" is the fact that the DFG cannot provide institutional funding, but is confined to project funding. The major strategy decision to redesign the *Langfristprogramm*, therefore, meant redefining it as a tool for project funding and introducing the twelve-year limit for each cycle of funding. This means that longitudinal studies can be funded by the DFG under one of the following provisions: (1) the study will come to an end within twelve years; (2) the topic of the study demands a longer perspective than twelve years, but if no continuation can be secured, the scientific outcome of twelve years alone will justify the investment – in other words, the second-best solution can stand alone; or, (3) if the study is planned from the outset as a truly longitudinal one, going beyond twelve years, initial funding by the DFG can be granted if follow-up funding (i.e., institutional funding) can be expected. SOEP (which was not planned as such a long-term project, but rather became one) and GLES (which was planned as such from the very beginning) are examples of the DFG strategy of enabling a potentially long-lasting project to be launched. This brings us to our first conclusion regarding the role of the DFG: projects that seek funding from the DFG have to be driven by the scientific community; that is, they must be well-planned scientifically and they must be organized in a form suited to project funding – at least for the duration of DFG funding period. If these two provisions are fulfilled, the DFG is well-equipped to find adaptive solutions.

Projects like ESS, GLES, and pairfam are data research infrastructures of central importance to the research community; yet, they are expensive and put considerable strain on the budgets available for funding the social sciences. Up to now, these projects have been proposed individually and dealt with on a case-by-case basis. However, if data research infrastructures are going to establish themselves as a major line of activity and funding, some degree of coordination and even strategy might be necessary. The DFG's elected bodies – the *Fachkollegien* and *Senat* – will be able to provide leadership for this process of addressing key questions within the scientific community: mapping the field, defining thematic priorities, co-ordinating projects and programs in order to maximize effects and economize resources, etc.

Coordination and strategy also pose challenges to the DFG as a funding organization, to the ministries, and to research organizations like the Leibniz Association (WGL) universities. Coordination and collaboration between the institutions have up to now also taken place on a case-by-case basis: SOEP (DFG/BMBF/WGL), GLES (DFG/WGL) and NEPS (DFG/BMBF/University) have each resulted in individual constellations and solutions that we regard as success stories.

Yet, it must also be reiterated, we have witnessed increased activities in this field and the momentum has been building. Not only because of the financial implications, but also in view of the long-term perspective of each individual activity, coordination and collaboration between the major players in the field may become necessary. A division of labor and development of institutional perspectives are the keywords here. The DFG is prepared to play an active role in this coordination process.

Coordination and collaboration between institutions is not only appropriate in view of the division of labor and sharing of responsibilities on the national level, but also in view of the international activities. ESFRI is but one field, however important it may be. If "European Research Infrastructures" come into existence as new legal entities, we as national institutions will have to redefine our position vis-à-vis these new entities as well as in relation to each other. The national institutions will have to cooperate in order to maximize the effects on the European and international level – and of course, in the best interests of the research community.

The International Data Forum (IDF), as a final example, goes beyond the European level. The DFG has supported the initial phase of this idea, together with our partner organizations from the UK, the US, Canada, the Netherlands, and China. The goal of the IDF is to facilitate and coordinate international production and sharing of data for research in the social sciences. It strives to align its aims with the strategic directions and priorities of prominent organizations representing the producers, managers, and research users of data relevant to the social sciences. One of its tasks is to facilitate collaboration and mutual understanding between key data stakeholders in the social sciences. Following the founding conference for the International Data Forum, the next steps are set to establish interagency agreement on the need for IDF and the scale of its operations. Decisions will be sought in 2009.

DFG has nominated the chair of the RatSWD as a member and the German representative of the Founding Committee of the IDF. This is already a concrete example of coordination between national institutions.

4. Summary

The DFG strategy for data research infrastructures will be based on what has already been achieved and on the lessons that can be learned:

(1) The guiding perspective should be on providing data, rather than sharing data. Projects whose primary purpose is to provide a common good should focus on building research infrastructure.

(2) The DFG has powerful programs at its disposal to fund outstanding infrastructure projects. It is up to the scientific community to adapt and utilize the diverse funding instruments of the DFG to its needs.

(3) Strategic cooperation is needed among all interested parties: cooperation within the research community on identifying thematic priorities; cooperation between the research community and funding institutions on the options for funding; and cooperation between the funding institutions on the division of labor, on the national as well as on the international level.

(4) The DFG is prepared to play an active role in this cooperative effort under the leadership of its elected bodies (*Fachkollegien* and *Senat*).

4. Providing Data on the European Level

Peter Elias

Contact:

Peter Elias
University of Warwick
Institute for Employment Research
Coventry CV4 7AL
UK
e-mail: Peter.Elias[at]warwick.ac.uk

Abstract

This paper reviews the potential demand for and the provision of European data for social scientific research. The concept of data provision is defined broadly, covering the ease with which specific types of data can be discovered, interpreted, readily understood and accessed by researchers.

The paper is structured as follows. First, it addresses the issue of why researchers need European (as opposed to national) data resources. This leads in to a short section discussing the potential demand for data at the European level. The main section focuses on the nature of various data resources currently available or under development. Finally, it concludes with an assessment of the need for new and/or improved data infrastructures and suggests where efforts could be focused in order to respond to such needs.

Four areas are identified where there is a clear need for new European research data resources to be developed. These are:

- a European Household Panel
- facilities to encourage comparative analysis of birth and other age cohort studies
- a European organization-based longitudinal survey
- improved access to microdata records held by Eurostat

Keywords: European data infrastructures, social science data needs

1. Introduction

This paper reviews the potential demand for and the provision of European data for social scientific research. The concept of *data provision* is defined broadly, covering the ease with which specific types of data can be discovered, interpreted, readily understood and accessed by researchers.

The paper is structured in the following way. The next section addresses the issue of why researchers need European (as opposed to national data resources). This leads in to a short section discussing the potential demand for data at the European level. The main section focuses on the nature of various data resources. Finally, the paper concludes with an assessment of the need for new and/or improved data infrastructures and suggests where efforts could be focused to realize such needs.

2. Why do we need data at the European level?

There are two main reasons for supporting the development of Europe-wide data infrastructures. The first relates to the need to inform social and economic policies which are pan-European in design or operation. As the European Union continues to integrate its economic and social structures, there is a need to understand how such integration operates across the EU, and to identify both strengths and weaknesses in policy implementation. It is primarily for this reason that the European Union, through its statistical agency (Eurostat), coordinates the production and collection of census, survey, and administrative data across the EU. The second need for European data relates more to the nature of research in the social sciences which, for the most part, cannot make use of the kind of randomized and controlled experiments that typify research in the physical sciences and must rely more on variations across groups and through time to investigate causality. Europe provides wide cultural diversity not simply in the obvious dimensions (language, politics, legal systems, etc.) but also across more difficult to measure traits such as cultural values, traditions, beliefs. To the researcher this provides variations that help inform the research process. "Europe" thus affords the research environment that the physical scientists would otherwise harness in the laboratory.

3. What kinds of data do we need for research in the social sciences at the European level?

European-level research has the same basic needs for data as research at the national level. However, the very nature of the European Union dictates that there will be specific research interests that may not have any national counterpart. For example, research on cross-national migration within the EU or across its external borders. Equally, understanding economic growth and decline within a European context (e.g., transnational investment, impact studies for the location of large-scale infrastructures, economic stability within the eurozone) requires a specific Europe-wide focus whilst drawing upon what are essentially national data resources.

4. Pan-European data resources

This section illustrates the available data resources designed to facilitate European research. No distinction is made here between data resources which are purpose-built for comparative research at the European level (input harmonized) and those which have arisen as research groups have attempted to meld a number of separate resources into a pan-European resource (output harmonized).

To document the variety of data resources that are available, the following typology has been adopted:

- *cross-sectional micro resources* – information which is descriptive of a unit of observation at a single point in time. Cross-sectional microdata observations may be repeated in order to monitor change at the macro-level;

- *longitudinal microdata resources* – information which describes the evolution of a unit of observation (e.g., a person, a family, an organization) through time. Such data resources are powerful instruments in the study of cause and effect;

- *macro databanks* – derived from cross-sectional survey or administrative data sources, "databanks" are repositories of tabulated data, usually providing a wide range of social and economic indicators.

Macro databanks are not covered in detail in this paper. While they constitute important resources for a variety of research interests, access to these resources and their use is relatively easy and uncontroversial.[1] However, for most research purposes, researchers want access to the underlying microdata resources from which the statistical indicators in macro databanks are constructed.

Other typologies are also useful, for example the distinction between administrative and transaction data – the former referring to data generated as a by-product of an administrator process (registration for social security benefits) or the latter from a transaction (e.g., purchase or sale of goods or services). Reference to such data types is made in the concluding section.

---

1 As an example of a research resource dedicated to providing access to and information about a wide variety of macro databanks, see ESDS International: http://www.esds.ac.uk/international/access/dataset_overview.asp. [Last visited: 03/02/2010].

4.1 Cross-sectional microdata resources

4.1.1 Resources available via Eurostat

Figure 1: Cross-sectional microdata resources available through Eurostat

EU Labour Force Survey

The EU-LFS is the longest running EU-wide statistical survey. Conducted by National Statistical Offices in Member States, the LFS has, since 1992, had a common output requirement in terms of the employment-related information it provides on individuals and households. Data currently available covers the period 1983–2006. In Spring 2002 the total sample size was approximately 1.5m persons. Data are available as anonymized micro records.[2]

EU Structure of Earnings Survey

The EU-SES is a large enterprise-based sample survey designed to provide accurate and harmonized data on earnings across the EU. The survey was held in 1995, 1999, 2002, and 2006. Results for 1995 are not comparable with later years.

Data collected includes earnings, age, gender, occupation, sector, hours worked, education, and training for employees of enterprise with 10+ employees. The latest data available for research purposes is the 2002 survey.

Access to SES data is through the SAFE Centre in Luxembourg.[3]

EU Community Innovation Survey

Community Innovation Statistics are produced in all 27 EU countries, 3 EFTA countries, and candidate countries. Data are collected on a four-year cycle. The first (pilot) survey was held in 1993, the second survey held in 1997/98 and the third survey in 2000/01. The fourth survey, conducted in 2006 with a reference year of 2004 will be available shortly. Anonymized microdata are available via CD-ROM. Access to non-anonymized data is possible through the SAFE Centre facility in Luxembourg.[4]

The CIS provides information on the characteristics of innovation at the enterprise level.

EU Statistics on Income and Living Conditions

The EU-SILC was designed as a successor to the European Community Household Panel which ran from 1994 to 2001. The first release of EU-SILC was in 2004, with a 2003 reference year.

Anonymized microdata from 2004 and 2005 are available via CD-ROM.

The EU-SILC contains a longitudinal element covering a four year period. The first longitudinal database was made available late in 2007.[5]

---

2 For further information on access conditions, see EU-LFS: http://epp.eurostat.ec.europa.eu/portal/page/portal/eurostat/home. [Last visited: 03/02/2010].
3 See EU-SES: http://epp.eurostat.ec.europa.eu/portal/page/portal/eurostat/home.
4 See EU-CIS: http://epp.eurostat.ec.europa.eu/portal/page/portal/eurostat/home.
5 For details see EU-SILC: http://epp.eurostat.ec.europa.eu/portal/page/portal/eurostat/home.

Since the late 1960s, the European Union (formerly the European Community) has sought to develop comparable microdata resources in order to measure and progress social, political, and economic integration. These efforts have given rise to a number of major data resources. However, access to these resources has, until recently, been severely restricted.

Cross-sectional microdata collected by Eurostat from National Statistical Offices across the EU include:

- EU Labour Force Survey (EU-LFS)
- Community Innovation Survey (EU-CIS)
- Structure of Earnings Survey (EU-SES)
- Statistics on Income and Living Conditions (EU-SILC)

Brief details of each of these sources are shown in the boxes below. Further information can be gained by following the hyperlinks.

4.1.2 Resources available via other data providers

4.1.2.1 Luxembourg Income Study (LIS)

The LIS began in 1983 under the joint sponsorship of the government of Luxembourg and the Centre for Population, Poverty and Policy Studies (CEPS), which became an independent body in 2001. The LIS archive contains two databases, the Luxembourg Income Study database and the Luxembourg Wealth Study (LWS), covering cross-national micro datasets on incomes, wealth, employment, and demography. The LIS database contains nearly 200 datasets organized in six time periods (waves) spanning the years from 1968 to 2005.[6]

With the exceptions of Portugal and Romania for Wave VI (around 2004) and Slovenia for Wave V (around 2000), income microdata are available for all EU countries, North America, Australia, Israel and Taiwan. The newer LWS database (released in December 2007) contains 13 wealth datasets from 10 countries.[7]

No direct access to the micro datasets is permitted. Registered users submit syntax (SAS, SPSS, and STATA) which LIS staff run on their behalf. Planned developments for the period 2008–2013 include a web-based user

---

[6] Microdata held by Eurostat are confidential data about individual statistical units. The release of these data to bona fide researchers is governed by Commission Regulations EU Nos. 83/2002, 1104/2006 and 1000/2007, which implement Council Regulation (EU) No. 322/97. Article 17 allows the EU to grant access to data it has collected from national statistical authorities if the national statistical authority gives explicit permission for such use.

[7] Austria, Canada, Cyprus, Finland, Germany, Italy, Norway, Sweden, UK, and the US.

interface for syntax submission, storage of and access to prior programs, and an online tabulator.[8]

4.1.2.2 Council of European Social Science Data Archives (CESSDA)

CESSDA is a network which promotes the acquisition, archiving, and distribution of electronic data. The network now extends to 20+ countries across Europe, providing access to and delivering over 50,000 data collections per annum and acquiring over 1,000 data collections each year. The CESSDA portal provides easy access to the catalogues of member organizations.

Via its multilingual search interface, CESSDA guides enquirers to appropriate datasets at specific data archives.[9] Enquirers can browse datasets by topic and by keywords before linking to specific archive websites to determine access conditions.

In 2007, CESSDA acquired FP7 Preparatory Phase funding to facilitate a significant upgrade in its functionality. This three-year phase will result in a plan to facilitate and coordinate national funding to provide a European research infrastructure. CESSDA also provides access gateways to other important EU-wide data resources, including the European Social Survey,[10] the Eurobarometers,[11] the International Social Survey Programme and the European Values Study (see below for further details about these sources).[12]

4.1.2.3 Integrated Public Use Microdata Series-International (IPUMSI)

IPUMSI is a project funded by the US National Science Foundation, based at the University of Minnesota, dedicated to the collection and distribution of census data from around the world.

To date, 35 countries have donated microdata from 111 censuses, totaling 263 million person records. The eight European countries which have so far contributed to the IPUMSI database are Austria, France, Greece, Hungary, Netherlands, Romania, Spain, and the United Kingdom. Census data for Slovenia will be available in 2009. Plans are also underway for the addition of censuses from Czech Republic, Germany, Ireland, Italy, Switzerland, and Turkey. The IPUMSI website maintains good metadata documentation stan-

---

8   For further information about LIS see: http://www.lisproject.org/.
9   CESSDA facilitates keyword searches across the following data publishers:
    UK Data Archive, SSD (Sweden), SIDOS (Switzerland), NSD (Norway), GSDB (Greece), GESIS-ZA (Germany), FSD (Finland), DDA (Denmark), DANS (Netherlands), ADPSS-Sociodata (Italy), ADP (Slovenia).
10 http://www.europeansocialsurvey.org/.
11 http://www.esds.ac.uk/international/access/I33089.asp.
12 For further information about CESSDA, see: http://www.cessda.org/index.html. [Last visited: 03/02/2010].

dards that allow users to appreciate differences in the ways in which censuses have been carried out, differences in the definition of key variables, etc.[13]

4.1.2.4 European Social Survey (ESS)

The ESS is an academically directed social survey designed to provide information on the attitudes, beliefs, and behaviors of Europe's changing population. Now in its fourth round, the ESS maps long-term attitudinal and behavioral changes in European society. Over 30 European countries now participate in the survey, with sample sizes ranging from 1,000 to 2,000 persons in each country.[14]

A major strength of the ESS is its attention to methodological weaknesses in the generation and its use of cross-national comparative data. Particular emphasis is placed on the interpretation of key concepts in the survey research instruments and their translation into different linguistic and cultural contexts.

4.1.2.5 Eurobarometer

The Eurobarometer surveys were established in 1973, designed to provide the European Commission with data on social trends, values, and public opinion generally, helping in the preparation of EU-wide policy and to inform the evaluation of its work. Surveys are conducted annually, with each survey covering approximately 1,000 face-to-face interviews[15] in each EU country.

Eurobarometer microdata are available from a variety of sources, including the Inter University Consortium for Political and Social Research (ICPSR) at the University of Michigan and the GESIS[16] Data Archive.[17]

4.1.2.6 International Social Survey Programme (ISSP)

Since 1983, the ISSP has promoted cross-national collaboration in the creation of research instruments and methods to generate a wide variety of data about social, economic, and political change, as well as values, beliefs, and motivations. While individual country samples are fairly small, the ISSP

---

13 Census data are freely available to registered users at: https://international.ipums.org/international/ [Last visited: 03/02/2010].
14 The minimum number of achieved interviews is set at 2,000 persons, except in countries with a population of less than 2 million, where the minimum number is 1,000.
15 Variations are Germany (2,000), Luxembourg (600), UK (1,300 of which 300 in Northern Ireland).
16 Leibniz Institute for the Social Sciences (GESIS, *Leibniz-Institut für Sozialwissenschaften*).
17 Links to these sources can be made through CESSDA (see above).

devotes considerable resources to ensuring good comparability between countries.[18]

4.1.2.7 European Values Study

The European Values Studies (and its companion, the World Values Surveys) are designed to enable a cross-national, cross-cultural comparison of values and norms on a wide variety of topics and to monitor changes in values and attitudes across the globe. Topics covered include perception of life, family, work, traditional values, personal finances, religion and morale, the economy, politics and society, the environment, allocation of resources, contemporary social issues, national identity, and technology and its impact on society. To date, four waves have been conducted in 1981–1984, 1990–1993, 1995–1997, and 1999–2004. Not all of the earlier surveys employed probability sampling procedures. These survey responses have been integrated into one dataset, to facilitate time series analysis.[19]

4.1.2.8 European Working Conditions Survey (EWCS)

The EWCS series began in 1990–91 and is usually conducted every five years. The survey utilizes a face-to-face questionnaire administered to a random sample of employed people (employees and self-employed), who serve as representatives of the working population in each EU country. The latest survey, held in 2005, covered the EU27 plus Croatia, Turkey, Switzerland, and Norway.

The questionnaire covers many aspects of working conditions, including violence, harassment and intimidation at the workplace, management and communication, work-life balance, and payment systems.

The EWCS datasets for 1991, 1995, 2000, and 2005 are available from the UK Data Archive (ESDS, Economic and Social Data Service). For further information, see EWCS or EWCS at ESDS.

---

18 Further information about the ISSP is available at: http://www.issp.org/ [Last visited: 03/02/2010].

19 Further information about the EVS can be found at: http://www.europeanvaluesstudy.eu/ [Last visited: 03/02/2010].

4.2 Longitudinal microdata resources

4.2.1 European Community Household Panel (ECHP)

The European Community Household Panel (ECHP) is a panel survey in which samples of households and persons have been interviewed year after year. These interviews cover a wide range of topics concerning living conditions. They include detailed income information, financial situation in a wider sense, working life, housing situation, social relations, health, and biographical information of the interviewed. The total duration of the ECHP was 8 years, running from 1994–2001 (8 waves).[20]

4.2.2 Survey of Health, Ageing and Retirement in Europe (SHARE)

The Survey of Health, Ageing and Retirement in Europe (SHARE) is a multidisciplinary and cross-national panel database of microdata on health, socio-economic status, and social and family networks of more than 30,000 individuals aged 50 or over. Eleven countries have contributed data to the 2004 SHARE baseline study, ranging from Scandinavia (Denmark and Sweden) through Central Europe (Austria, France, Germany, Switzerland, Belgium, and the Netherlands) to the Mediterranean (Spain, Italy and Greece). Further data have been collected in 2005–06 in Israel. Two "new" EU Member States – the Czech Republic and Poland – as well as Ireland, joined SHARE in 2006 and participated in the second wave of data collection in 2006–07. The survey's third wave of data collection will collect detailed retrospective life-histories in sixteen countries in 2008–09, with Slovenia joining in as a new member.[21]

5. Summary: future needs for a European data infrastructure

Table 1 attempts to briefly summarize this review of available *European* data resources which are likely to be of interest to social scientists. The list covers microdata resources only. Macro databanks, providing indicators of trends and yielding information on country and regional differences across Europe, are useful research resources, but do not provide the flexibility needed for exploring social, economic, and demographic processes in depth, nor are they adequate for most scientific modeling purposes. The table also excludes CESSDA, which (amongst other functions currently under development) acts

---

20 For further information: http://epp.eurostat.ec.europa.eu/portal/page/portal/eurostat/home
21 For further information: http://www.share-project.org/ [Last visited: 03/02/2010].

primarily as a networked intermediary organization. The facility it offers – to search data catalogs in different ways across a range of archives in various countries for specific sources of data – makes CESSDA a powerful tool for data discovery and for comparative research where data permits. CESSDA also provides links to many of the resources shown in table 1, but it is not, in itself, a producer of pan-European data for research purposes.

The issues that are raised about sample sizes, data accessibility, and/or data quality paint a none-too-inspiring picture of the range and availability of European data resources for research across the social sciences and in related disciplines. Despite the efforts made by individuals, research teams, and by some national bodies, the availability, accessibility, and quality of these data resources are fairly limited. There are a number of notable exceptions here, particularly ESS and SHARE, both of which, like CESSDA, have been recognized by the European Strategy Forum for Research Infrastructures (ESFRI) and the European Commission as major research infrastructures in need of further support and development. However, in a number of EU countries and North America, major advances are being made to facilitate a broader social science research agenda which encompasses research in the fields of environmental sciences (climate change, air soil and water pollution, and crop modification), medical sciences (genetic expression and human behavior, spread of contagious diseases, impact of ageing), and engineering (transport systems and congestion, housing design, personal and collective security). This broader agenda has required new types of data structures that are significantly larger than any of the resources currently available, are longitudinal in nature, and which can be readily enhanced via linkage to administrative and/or transactional data. Simultaneously, new access procedures have been developed which take advantage of technical developments to provide better and more secure access to complex and sensitive data sources, as well as facilitating a more "hands-on" approach to research[22] than has been the case with, say, the Luxembourg Income Study or the Eurostat SAFE access procedures.

Possibly the most disappointing aspect of this review relates to the continued barriers to widespread access by the research community to the purpose-built European statistical databases held by Eurostat. Notwithstanding renewed legislative efforts to improve matters from within Eurostat, access remains slow, costly, and restrictive. No remote access is provided by Eurostat, despite the proven technology, the security this approach offers compared with the proliferation of data via physical media, the reduced

---

22 http://www.norc.org/projects/data+enclave+project.htm [Last visited: 03/02/2010], and http://www.ons.gov.uk/about/who-we-are/our-services/vml/index.html. [Last visited: 03/02/2010].

Table 1: European microdata requirements: sources and issues relating to access, coverage and quality

Type of microdata required	Source	Data access, coverage, quality issues
Census data (demography and housing)	IPUMSI	Incomplete coverage across the EU.
Labor force, income data, living conditions	Eurostat (EU-LFS; EU-SILC; EU-SES)	High costs of access, complex bureaucracy, some data to be accessed on site, no record linkage possible.
Values, beliefs, attitudes	Eurobarometer; ISSP; European Values Study	Relatively small sample sizes.
Social and political behavior	European Social Survey; ISSP	High quality, but relatively small samples.
Longitudinal individual and household data	Eurostat (ECHP); SHARE	ECHP discontinued after 2001. SHARE has high-quality longitudinal data but is still fairly new.
Organization-based data (structure, pay, working conditions)	Eurostat (EU-CIS); European Working Conditions Survey (EWCS)	Only available at 5-year intervals, no longitudinal measures.

costs, and the convenience it provides to the research community. The costs currently incurred by researchers working on publicly funded research are hardly defensible.[23]

This suggests where efforts should be focused to improve these essential research resources. Four major new initiatives are proposed:

5.1 A new European household panel

This should build upon the latest developments in a number of countries, to establish larger and better household panels than has hitherto been the case. The obvious first step here is to determine how certain countries can take the household panels they currently have under academic direction, and align their activities to facilitate cross-panel analysis. There is nothing new in this approach. Indeed, the demand for cross-national equivalent files based upon the US Panel Study of Income Dynamics, the German Socio-Economic Panel (SOEP, *Sozio-oekonomisches Panel*), and the British Household Panel Survey (BHPS) testifies to the values of such resources. However, the new UK Household Longitudinal Study Understanding Society, the SOEP, and the Swiss Household Panel (SHP) are candidates for renewed efforts to build bigger, better, and more comprehensive household panel studies for a number of European countries than has hitherto been possible.

5.2 Comparative birth cohort studies

A number of countries[24] have commenced work to develop new and bigger birth cohort studies than have been available previously. The opportunity to exploit the rich variety of data these studies will provide and the disciplines that must combine to make this happen (genetics, psychology, economics, sociology, education) provide a world-class opportunity that Europe should grasp.

---

23 An example of this is the €8,000 cost for a DVD and CD-Rom(s) containing a set of quarterly/yearly files covering available data in 26 countries and all years from 1983 to 2006.

24 These include the UK (a 2012 birth cohort of up to 60,000 persons), Germany (a proposed national birth cohort beginning in 2011), France (a cohort commencing in 2009), the US (a cohort commencing from 2008 to 2012) and other cohorts in Ireland, Sweden, etc.

5.3 Longitudinal studies of organizations

Comparative longitudinal studies of organizations are required to provide valuable insights into the ways in which enterprises grow, succeed, prosper, and decline in an increasingly risky global business environment. The framework for such a development exists in a number of countries (e.g., the Workplace Employee Relations Studies in the UK, the REPONSE surveys in France, the database of organization data held by the German Institute for Employment Research (IAB, *Institut für Arbeitsmarkt- und Berufsforschung*)) and could form the core of a proposal to develop such a comparative research resource built upon existing surveys and research expertise.

5.4 Improved access to Eurostat data

Last, but not the least of these proposals, is the need to improve access to data held by Eurostat. In part, the problems of access currently faced by researchers are the responsibilities of the National Statistical Institutes which supply the data to Eurostat and which stipulate conditions for their release. This results in what is termed the "lowest common denominator" problem. For example 26 out of 27 countries stipulated that identifying information on individual records (e.g., names of individuals, names of organizations) should never be made available to researchers. But good research proceeds by allowing researchers to link between data sources, maximizing their utility and facilitating new and important research to be conducted. Concerns about data security can now be addressed via the new forms of control and access that virtual remote access provides. There is a now-pressing need to address these issues and to find innovative solutions to unlock the research potential of these truly European resources that cost the EU taxpayer many millions of Euros to create.

In addition to these specific proposals to develop new or to build on existing research infrastructures at the European level, there is a need to determine the feasibility of promoting access to some less well-established types of data within a European context. The two most obvious sources of information here are *administrative data* sources and *transaction data*. The former are derived from the administration of systems or programs (e.g., social security benefit, school records) and can often be mapped onto other resources to enhance their research potential. As a by-product of systems which are not primarily designed to provide research data, and because they are national in character, potential here may be limited, but further investigation of their research potential is warranted. Transaction data are often held by private-sector organizations and relate to the delivery of services or customer-initiated transactions (e.g., mobile phone records, shopping data). Where such companies are providing services across the European Union, the potential to use such information for Europe-wide research purposes becomes feasible. However, companies are likely to restrict access and to limit the nature of research that can be conducted from such sources. Again, some preliminary work needs to be undertaken to investigate the feasibility of using such data as Europe-wide research resources.

5. Infrastructure for High-Quality and Large-Scale Surveys

Cooperation between Academic Research and Private-Sector Agencies

Peter Ph. Mohler and Bernhard von Rosenbladt

Contact:

Peter Ph. Mohler
University of Mannheim
e-mail: peter.mohler[at]uni-mannheim.de

Bernhard von Rosenbladt
TNS Infratest Sozialforschung, Munich
e-mail: bernhard.rosenbladt[at]tns-infratest.com

Abstract

High-quality data from large-scale surveys provide a solid basis for outstanding research in the social sciences. Because of the unique demands of survey measurement in terms of the resources and skills required, it should be viewed as a specific sector of the research data infrastructure. In Germany, large-scale surveys have been established both within and outside academia, and major new projects are underway. Clearly, the sector is expanding. There is a need to discuss future challenges, not only with a focus on individual large projects, but with a view to the sector of large-scale surveys and high-quality survey measurement in general.

One aspect is the segmentation of large-scale measurement instruments in Germany along institutional lines (statistical offices, government agency research, public research institutions, and the academic community). Here, we recommend that an overall framework be developed covering all sub-sectors. A second aspect is the infrastructure required for large-scale, high-quality data collection. In Germany (outside the sector of statistical offices), this infrastructure is provided by private survey organizations. We argue that these should be recognised as relevant actors within the research data infrastructure. They have to invest in technological and human resources in order to provide the professional services required, and they need conditions and forms of cooperation that encourage this investment.

Keywords: survey research, research infrastructure, Germany

1. The notion of large-scale surveys' measurement

The survey-based analysis of social and economic structures, behaviour, and attitudes is among the great innovations of the social sciences. Today infrastructures exist for surveys of individuals, households, firms and other institutions in all developed countries, although such surveys may differ in size and quality. The present paper focuses on the subset of large-scale, high-quality surveys. This segment of survey research is one of the foundations of excellence in the social sciences. Only with a comprehensive system of large-scale measurement instruments (LMI) will the social sciences be in the position to continue and even expand their work as providers of evidence-based information and advice to citizens, political leaders, and other decision-makers (Mohler 2008). And indeed, the demand for this type of survey measurement is growing. The notion of LMI implies three elements of a social survey:

(1) "Large-scale" refers to sample size. Large samples of respondents are necessary to heighten the survey's statistical power and precision. "Large-scale" also indicates the resulting need for an effective field-force for data collection. The lower limit of "large" is not fixed but may

be illustrated by the German General Social Survey (ALLBUS, *Allgemeine Bevölkerungsumfrage der Sozialwissenschaften*) with a sample of 3,500 respondents. Examples of medium-sized samples are the German Socio-Economic Panel (SOEP, *Sozio-oekonomisches Panel*), with about 10-12,000 households and the new pairfam Panel (*Panel Analysis of Intimate Relationships and Family Dynamics*) with a starting sample of 12,000 respondents. At the upper end, there is the German Microcensus with a sample of more than 300,000 households surveyed annually.

(2) "High-quality" refers to quality standards for survey methodology. Normally this implies some form of probability sampling and, beyond this, a commitment to quality criteria at all stages of the survey process, in accordance with the Total Survey Error (TSE) quality framework. It also implies "quality costs" in terms of higher financial budgets compared to the normal survey business.

(3) The third element is some form of continuous measurement. This may be implemented by repeated cross-sections or by longitudinal panel surveys. In organizational terms, the survey will normally be part of a medium or long-term research programme with a perspective of observing social trends or individual biographies or other issues of stability and change.

Within the range of these criteria, large-scale measurement instruments may cover different populations, such as households, individuals, enterprises, etc., and may be based on different modes of data collection, such as face-to-face interviewing, telephone interviewing, mail and web surveys, or – increasingly – mixed-mode approaches. We would like to underline that the segment of large-scale surveys discussed here covers a specific though essential part of quantitative research in the social sciences. There are many small surveys, studies of special groups or topics, ad-hoc surveys at a lower budget level – all of them are necessary and may satisfy their respective research purposes. When discussing issues of the research data infrastructure, however, the challenges of large-scale measurement instruments require specific attention.

This paper reconsiders how research needs for large-scale, high-quality survey data can be met in the future within the German social science infrastructure. We argue for treating this issue as one of strategic importance. The agenda of the German Data Forum (RatSWD) in its starting phase mainly aimed at gaining better access for the research community to the microdata collected by Statistical Offices and other public agencies. This initiative was highly successful. The work program may now move to a broader agenda, envisaging the overall architecture of data supply for the social sciences. Large-scale measurement instruments are a core segment of that data supply.

2. Review of large-scale survey measurement in Germany

Large-scale measurement instruments need an effective infrastructure for data collection. Whether this infrastructure exists, how it is organized in institutional terms, and how powerful it is may vary across countries. In order to evaluate the German situation we start with a brief review of large-scale surveys in Germany. Subsequently we look at organizational arrangements and quality standards in a comparative perspective, taking the US and the UK as points of reference.

In general terms, survey-based data can be collected by different kinds of data providers. In most countries there are governmental or semi-governmental agencies (statistical offices) conducting "official" or governmental surveys. Aside from this, in most developed countries there are independent survey organizations. These may be organized within public institutions, e.g., universities, or as professional survey research companies within the private sector. Individual survey organizations may or may not have the capacity for large-scale, high-quality measurement instruments as defined above.

Another aspect of data supply is how large-scale surveys are initiated, funded, and governed. One should be aware of the fact that academic research institutions are only one of several actors here. Government and research institutions within the public administration play an important role as well. The specific needs and institutional arrangements of academia should be discussed in this broader context.

We will now briefly review the main actors initiating LMI in Germany, just mentioning the large surveys under their respective responsibility:[1]

Type 1: Government surveys under specific legal regulation (amtliche Statistik)

In Germany, such surveys are conducted by the Statistical Offices. In organizational terms this means that the Federal Statistical Office acts as a kind of coordinator and clearing agency for 16 autonomous Statistical Offices of the German *Länder*, which normally are the actual data collection agencies. The main surveys are the annual Microcensus, a number of smaller population surveys, and a number of establishment surveys. Continuous population surveys include the Household Expenditure Survey (EVS, *Einkommens- und Verbrauchsstichprobe*, every five years) and EU-SILC (annually) dealing with income and living conditions. Special surveys conducted only once or at longer time intervals include the Time-Budget Survey and the Survey on ICT Usage. For most of these surveys, scientific

---

[1] More information about a range of projects is provided in Rosenbladt (2008).

user files are currently available. Enabling researchers to access these datasets was the main objective of the KVI initiative and the original agenda of the German Data Forum (RatSWD).

Type 2: Government agencies research in particular policy areas (Ressortforschung)

During the last few decades, federal ministries have initiated a number of social surveys that are of general interest for social monitoring in various areas and that meet the criteria of large-scale, high-quality measurement instruments. They are designed as repeated cross-sectional surveys with sample sizes between 5,000 and 20,000 respondents. Examples are the surveys on income of the elderly (ASID, *Alterssicherung in Deutschland*, and AVID, *Altersvorsorge in Deutschland*), on vocational training and adult learning (AES, *Adult Education Survey*), on long-term care (MuG, *Möglichkeiten und Grenzen selbstständiger Lebensführung*), or on volunteering (*Freiwilligensurvey*). All these projects include extensive reporting to the public as well as Scientific Use Files for secondary analysis.

Type 3: Surveys governed by federal and state research institutes

Federal and state research institutes have initiated and funded a number of large-scale, high-quality surveys that are of general interest to the scientific community. Examples are

- the Institute for Employment Research (IAB, *Institut für Arbeitsmarkt- und Berufsforschung*) with a broad range of projects, such as the annual Establishment Panel Survey (*IAB Betriebspanel*) or, more recently, the household panel on employment and social security (PASS) or the survey on employment biographies, qualification and competences (ALWA)
- the Federal Institute for Vocational Education and Training (BIBB, *Bundesinstitut für Berufsbildung*) with large cross-section surveys such as the survey on employment and qualification
- the Higher Education Information System (HIS, *Hochschulinformationssystem*) with its surveys of a variety of student populations
- the German Youth Institute (DJI, *Deutsches Jugendinstitut*) with its Family Surveys and Youth Surveys, now being redefined to form part of an Integrated Survey starting in 2009

- the Federal Institute for Population Research (BIB, *Bundesinstitut für Bevölkerungsforschung*) with its Gender and Generations Surveys (GGS)
- the Federal Office for Migration and Refugees (BAMF, *Bundesamt für Migration und Flüchtlinge*) with its recent survey of migrants in Germany
- the Robert Koch Institute (RKI, *Robert Koch-Institut*) with its health surveys.

Type 4: Surveys governed by the scientific community (academic research)

In Germany, there are very few surveys created and run by academic research organizations that meet the criteria of large-scale, high-quality measurement instruments. The few that can be mentioned here are ALLBUS, including the incorporated German part of the International Social Survey Programme (ISSP) conducted every two years; the German part of the European Social Survey (ESS) conducted every two years; the SOEP, a household panel with annual interviewing; the German part of the European Survey on Health, Ageing and Retirement in Europe (SHARE), a panel survey with bi-annual interviewing.

The need for such large-scale measurement instruments is recognised increasingly in the scientific community and its funding institutions. This will result in a much broader data supply in the future. In 2008, a new panel survey on family and pair relationships was started (pairfam). In 2009 a series of cohort panel surveys under the common label of the National Educational Panel Study (NEPS) will start. The German National Election Study (GNES), a system of elections surveys, will also start in 2009.

Structures of funding and governing large-scale surveys as reviewed above are related to typical patterns of data collection:

- Surveys of type 1 are designed and conducted by Statistical Offices.[2]
- Surveys of type 2 are tendered by ministries and contracted to survey organizations, which in this case often take over full research responsibility from design to reporting.
- Surveys of type 3 and type 4 are designed and governed by the respective research institutions. These institutions typically do not have their own

---

[2] There are exceptions to this rule. For instance, in case of telephone surveys, data collection is contracted out to survey organizations because the statistical offices do not have their own infrastructure for large-scale CATI operations. The most prominent example was the ILO survey of 2002-2006.

infrastructure for large-scale data collection; therefore, by way of subcontracting, data collection is handed over to a survey organization.[3]

- These survey organizations are private-sector companies. This is to say that, aside from surveys of the Statistical Offices (type 1), data collection for large-scale surveys in Germany relies on the professional services provided by private firms. The scientific community and the public are often not aware of this fact because the publicly known owner of the survey data is the respective public research institution.

There are two conclusions from the review:

(1) In Germany, large-scale measurement instruments are not a vision for the future but an existing, well-developed segment of data supply for public bodies and the social sciences. Based on this, German research groups have been able to play a leading role in social research at the international level as well. It is true, though, that the academic community has lagged behind in establishing large-scale, high-quality measurement instruments of their own. With the major new projects launched recently, the situation is changing: academia is taking a more active role. The objective for the future is to widen the scope of large-sale survey measurement, establishing new surveys and approaching new research questions.

(2) The institutional basis of large-scale measurement instruments in Germany is a combination of public and private organizations. On the public side one finds, besides governmental agencies, research institutions working in different organizational contexts (public administration as well as academia) but all operating as part of the scientific community. On the private side, one finds survey research institutes organized as professional service companies.

The question is how to evaluate this overall structure. One may argue that it has apparently operated quite well so far, as demonstrated by the fact that LMI is well established. In recent years, much progress has been made in survey technology and measurement methods. The question remains, however, whether the existing infrastructure is sufficient for the future. The demand for large-scale surveys that provide high-quality survey measurement is rising. The number of such projects is increasing, accompanied by a tendency towards larger sample sizes, more complex survey designs, and

---

3   There are two main exceptions to this pattern: 1) RKI organizes data collection for its Health Surveys, which include some medical treatment, on its own. 2) HIS conducts surveys of student populations, normally implemented through mail or web surveys, on its own. Similarly surveys and assessments implemented in schools normally are conducted by specialized agencies or institutes affiliated to the respective ministry of education.

more demanding methodological techniques and standards. All of these developments will require significantly expanded survey measurement capacities.

3. Organization and standards: Germany compared to the US and the UK

Large-scale social science surveys belong to the class of high-precision scientific instruments, similar to those used in the natural sciences. In order to measure social structures, individual behavior, and social change properly, surveys must not only be large-scale but also high-quality Conducting a large-scale survey at a poor quality level means misallocating money. Quality standards and how to implement them in practice must therefore be part of the discussion on large-scale measurement instruments.

Sample surveys may be viewed as a communication process. They are complex instruments generated in a structured and dynamic interplay of several thousand people. They must be organized in production processes requiring intensive, continuous process quality control.

To understand the enormous task of making a large-scale survey, let us consider the (relatively simple) case of an ALLBUS-type survey, a one-nation cross-sectional survey. After having designed and properly tested a questionnaire, a fielding team of about 200 interviewers (plus back-office staff) will be handed the addresses of about 7,000 selected target persons. Most of them have to be contacted several times to achieve the final net of about 3,200 respondents. Let us assume the average contact rate is 2.5. This means that some 17,500 contacts or contact attempts have to be made. The net sample of 3,200 respondents will, on average, communicate with an interviewer in a face-to-face situation for about 70 minutes (i.e., all in all about 460 working days). The instrument measures about 400 variables per respondent resulting in about 800,000 single data points or measurements, which make up the data file.

To design, implement, and successfully conduct such a survey, a number of quite distinct methods and techniques have to be combined into a single streamlined survey process. Among these are communication and cognition methods which allow the transfer of substantive research questions into appropriate survey items; sample statistics, which govern the design, implementation and assessment of actual samples; logistics and process quality methods, which guarantee transparent fielding processes; content analysis as a special field for all open-ended items and coding; documentation methods which relate numerical information with "what it means," and statistical analysis combined with other quality measures to assess the validity and reliability of the data obtained, to mention just the major research areas.

In contrast to the sheer endless number of possible errors or distortions that can happen in this process, one can observe a remarkable robustness in many high-quality surveys over longer periods of time. This indicates that the process can be successfully managed – with ample opportunities for improvement. There is, for instance, the issue of declining response rates in combination with higher aspirations to include all strata of a society (i.e., less integrated groups), which must be tackled by future large-scale surveys.

Only the best survey organizations are able to manage this process observing rigorous scientific standards. For obvious reasons, the number of such organizations is small in all countries. Institutional settings may vary between countries; thus, for a compact overview, we will discuss the situation in the United States and the United Kingdom compared to Germany.

United States

The number of private and university affiliated agencies which are able to run large-scale measurement instruments is actually very limited in the US. Apart from the two university-affiliated agencies NORC (*National Opinion Research Center*) and ISR (*Institute for Social Research*), there are two other private sector institutes, namely Westat and RTI (*Research Triangle Institute*).

Centers like NORC or ISR in the United States, though affiliated with universities, organize their data collection in profit centers, whose aim is obviously to earn a profit. As soon as they require subsidies from the university or their head organization, they are either quickly downsized or, as was the case with some smaller survey research centers in the past, simply shut down. As profit centers, they compete for tendered and non-tendered surveys. They carry out surveys in the social sciences as well as government surveys. One can also observe a division of labor within such centers. Often principal investigators and analysts are faculty members, while data collection is dealt with by separate units, which themselves are defined as profit centers. Sometimes, the university data collection organization will compete for contracts from their own university with other agencies, say Westat or RTI.

Concerning standards and methodological rigor, the US has been in the lead for a long time. Discussions about the precision of large-scale measurement instruments (non-response, measurement error, total survey error, etc.) were initiated at US research institutions, which turn down low-quality proposals and are prepared to invest substantial sums in high-quality instruments. In general, considerably larger amounts of money are spent on high-quality surveys in the United States than in Germany.[4]

United Kingdom

The United Kingdom has a highly developed culture of survey research and considerable public spending for all kinds of surveys, whether evaluation studies of government programs or more basic monitoring of social trends. In contrast to the US, but similar to Germany, there are no academic data collection institutions. Instead, large-scale measurement instruments co-operate with private sector institutes in the data collection phase. The number of agencies powerful enough to run large-scale surveys is also very limited. The dominant data collection agency is NATCEN (*National Centre for Social Research*), a private, not-for-profit organization. Others include large survey companies such as BMRB Ltd. (*British Market Research Bureau Limited*), TNS (*Taylor Nelson Sofres*) or Ipsos.

Regarding standards, it is noteworthy that many UK agencies have introduced quality concepts and have been certified according to ISO or other standards. The Economic and Social Research Council (ESRC) has made great efforts to improve instrument quality for quantitative research in the last decade. This has produced several programs, conferences, projects, etc. targeting higher standards and better quality in social surveys. Increasingly, competitive structures are being introduced for long-term projects as well, i.e., calls for bids for long-term surveys at regular intervals. The bidders for these are academic groups, which in turn collaborate on data collection with private-sector data collection agencies. As in the US, the price level for high-quality surveys is considerably higher in the UK than in Germany.

Germany

Like the United Kingdom, Germany has no academically affiliated data collection agency with the capacity to run large-scale surveys such as ALLBUS, SOEP, ESS, EVS, ISSP, etc. Data collection thus has to be delegated to private-sector agencies. One should note here that "data collection" as a catchword covers a wide range of services that can include instrument design, sampling frame, fieldwork, data editing and processing, documentation, websites, and so on.

---

[4] There is little public information on actual survey costs. Krosnik cited the price of $1,000 per interview in a 2006 press statement. Other sources include non-disclosed bids in international surveys and private information. The same holds for the UK.

Similar to the US and the UK, the number of survey agencies that can manage large-scale, high-quality surveys is very limited. This is particularly true for surveys based on face-to-face interviewing. Although there exist a number of well-known survey companies in Germany, a closer look at the list of large-scale surveys reviewed above reveals that in recent years there were mainly two agencies involved in this segment of research: TNS Infratest and infas. Others have reduced or even cut their face-to-face field force entirely, or are not trained for probability sampling or methodological documentation as required for high-quality surveys.

Despite the small number of actors, the market for large-scale, high-quality surveys is fairly competitive. The two survey companies mentioned have demonstrated their ability to conduct demanding social surveys successfully. Both companies provide "full service"; that is, they are able to offer data collection by all interview modes (face-to-face, telephone, mail, Internet) and to provide far more than just fieldwork: their professional services include the complete range of data collection steps as well as methodological consulting or writing research reports for clients requesting such services.

As mentioned above, the price level for conducting surveys is lower in Germany than in countries like the US or UK. Survey companies in Germany have invested a great deal in conducting "lean production" surveys in order to cope with clients' expectations of good quality at low budget levels. This is achieved partly by productivity gains through technology or very tight resource management. And partly it is achieved by cost-saving adaptations of methodological procedures (e.g., variations of random route procedures in face-to-face surveys). Relatively few surveys are budgeted sufficiently to meet the highest quality standards according to state-of-the-art social science methodology. At the same time, academic clients and survey methodologists have not really tried to understand the differences in survey production at different cost levels or to assess the quality achieved in the different types of surveys using the Total Survey Error framework.

Given the trend towards lower response rates in surveys – which is a problem in other countries as well – this has led to some concern in academia about the quality of surveys provided by "commercial" agencies. For many years there have been discussions about potential alternative structures, with a marked preference for academically affiliated survey organizations. We will come back to this issue later. At this juncture, we would like to underscore that the problems addressed in these discussions mainly affect the operation of "normal" surveys, whereas the sub-sector of large-scale surveys is by necessity more quality-driven. The growing demand for large-scale, high-quality measurement instruments makes it all the more important to establish quality standards that can be applied to all the various survey types discussed here.

4. Issues of infrastructure: Assessment and recommendations

When discussing the future of large-scale measurement instruments in Germany (and beyond), various infrastructural issues must be taken into consideration. We suggest discussing such issues on three levels: (1) infrastructure in terms of an overall framework for LMI, (2) infrastructure in terms of resources and know-how for data collection, (3) infrastructure in terms of individual LMI.

(1) Infrastructure in terms of an overall framework for large-scale survey measurement

Large-scale, high-quality measurement instruments must be defined as a core element in the research data infrastructure for the social sciences. Large-scale surveys offer a particular class of data, distinct from others such as administrative statistics on the one hand and survey or observational data for special (often ad-hoc or smaller-scope) studies on the other hand.

A crucial point is to develop an overview of the field as a whole, covering all of the types and sub-sectors of large-scale measurement instruments reviewed above. So far, such a broad view is not common. Instead, large-scale measurement instruments are segmented along institutional lines, that is, statistical offices (*Amtliche Statistik*) (type 1), government agencies research (type 2), state and federal research institutes (type 3) and the academic community (type 4). All these institutions have their specific responsibilities, budgets, and procedures, and will therefore all carry out their own large-scale surveys in the future. Yet one can imagine that there could be some kind of overarching framework or coordination.

Objectives would be to articulate the common interest in strengthening the basis for large-scale, high-quality measurement instruments in Germany; to avoid overlaps or conflicts of interest; to identify problems or needs for action; to develop institutional arrangements for the governance of large-scale measurement instruments; to serve as a platform to discuss issues of technological developments and resources with (public and private) data collection agencies; to support linkages of LMI in Germany with European and international structures, etc.

We will refrain from making organizational proposals here. It is evident that the German Data Forum (RatSWD) forms a kind of institutional nucleus for the representation of all those involved in LMI and high-quality survey measurement. It would be worth discussing how to integrate the private survey companies because of their crucial contribution to an effective research data infrastructure. It would also be useful to have a closer look at comparable institutional arrangements in other countries. A number of countries have established structures for a more coordinated or focused development of large-scale surveys. Among recent initiatives one may mention, in particular, the Survey Resources Network[5] in the UK. The institutional framework here is combined with efforts to promote survey methodology (on an comparative level see the International Workshop on Comparative Survey Design and Implementation (CSDI)).

One may discuss whether the (academic) social science community should focus on its "own" large-scale surveys, which are governed by scientific objectives and academic institutions, or whether this should be part of a broader approach. One argument for a broader approach is social science community's interest in obtaining access to all large-scale survey data, irrespective of their origin in other institutional sectors. A second point is that all institutional sectors use the same "production basis" for large-scale surveys, i.e., the resources and know-how of survey organizations. It should be a matter of common interest to assess future demands for large-scale data collection and to help existing suppliers reach their potential.

(2) Infrastructure in terms of resources and know-how for data collection

Large-scale, high-quality measurement instruments require technical resources and know-how beyond the scope of what universities or research institutions or even most of the existing survey or market research organizations have at their disposal.

As we have described above, conducting large-scale surveys means organizing complex communication processes according to methodological standards, but also as quickly and as affordably as possible. The revolution in communications media and the resulting changes in communication behavior heavily affect how surveys can be conducted today. The logistics of a survey, and partly the interviewing process as such, make use of advanced technology and need streamlined production processes.

Consequently, large-scale measurement instruments are also a matter of economic resources and economic efficiency. To build up and maintain data collection operations of the required scope requires substantial financial resources and continuous operating capacities, as well as ongoing investments and innovations to maintain competitiveness. This includes investment in the highly qualified staff who are necessary to offer comprehensive professional services and research experience.

It does not go without saying that such resources exist. To give an example, one can design a new survey of 10,000 randomly selected respon-

---

5   http://surveynet.essex.ac.uk/

dents who will take part in a 60-minute personal interview. It is by no means a given that such a survey can simply be "ordered" at some agency.

In Germany, the infrastructure for data collection of this scope does exist. Apart from government surveys conducted by statistical offices, the infrastructure is provided by private survey organizations. Whether the given supply satisfies all needs and whether it is advanced and stable enough to meet future requirements, however, is subject to debate.

In academia, "for-profit" survey companies are sometimes regarded as service providers that belong to the commercial sphere and are not really part of the research process. Potential alternative structures have been discussed. Theoretically, there are two alternatives:

- The first are the statistical offices (the Federal Statistical Office and 16 Statistical Offices of the German *Länder*), which could act as fieldwork organizations. Indeed one may ask whether the present division of labor between the statistical offices and survey organizations will remain the same in the future. Is it conceivable that the statistical offices might take over data collection functions for large-scale surveys in the social sciences? There are no signs indicating this. Statistical offices work under tight legal, budgetary, and organizational restrictions, which make arrangements of this sort unlikely. Moreover, the German statistical offices do not use the survey design preferred for social science projects.[6] One should also mention here the difference between the "enumerators" who work at statistical offices and are trained to list facts, and the "interviewers" in survey research who are trained to facilitate measurement of respondents' characteristics. Given the outcomes of this distinction for survey quality, researchers have criticised how key projects such as EU-SILC are being implemented in Germany.[7]

- A second alternative would be to establish an academically affiliated data collection organization. The vision is to bundle all current and future academically governed surveys to create the critical mass necessary to establish and run a large-scale data collection enterprise profitably. Is this a realistic option for the future? There are numerous obstacles to an academic survey organization. One is the enormous investment required to set

---

[6] Social science surveys normally combine probability sampling with the condition of voluntary participation of respondents. By contrast, population surveys of the statistical offices in Germany either rely on the legal obligation of respondents to take part (Microcensus) or, if participation is voluntary, they use quota sampling.

[7] Richard Hauser (2009: 11) recommends that EU-SILC "should be improved by using truly random samples, … face-to-face-interviews with multilingual questionnaires, sole responsibility of the German Federal Statistical Office, and outsourcing fieldwork to a private market research company with a well-trained and permanent staff of interviewers."

up and maintain large-scale survey operations. A second is the segmented institutional structure of the German political, administrative, and research system, which is not favorable to centralized solutions. A third problem is how to organize competition of suppliers in such a structure: would the academic fieldwork organization be protected from competition? Would it be publicly subsidized? Or would it have to act under market conditions like a private company?

Other aspects of this debate deal with the academic world itself. Motivation and career paths within the academic social sciences would have to support an academic fieldwork organization. In the United States, there have been pioneers in survey research who wanted to collect data on their terms, who thus wanted to define standards themselves and who, consequently, spent time and effort in the thicket of fieldwork. To implement the vision of an academic field organization in Germany, one must, first and foremost, create such a culture, which would be a lengthy and thus most unlikely process.

Following from this, our recommendation is to acknowledge the co-operation between public and academic research institutions and private-sector survey agencies as an integral part of the research data infrastructure.[8] Challenges of the future must be met within this framework. This strategy is in line with developments in other European countries.

It may be useful to think about institutional mechanisms to strengthen the public-private cooperation. Basically, however, the economic mechanisms of supply and demand will rule the game. The private economy will supply the required resources insofar as there is sufficient demand and the services are profitable. Investment will be encouraged if there is sufficient planning security and a price level that promises return on investment. Competition among suppliers will be a driving force to improve the effectiveness and quality of the service.

At the same time, the cooperation can take advantage of the professional competence, research experience, and scientific ambitions of many survey managers in those survey agencies that are involved in the large-scale survey business. In fact, there are examples of excellent cooperation between survey managers in data collection agencies and survey directors and their teams in public or academic research institutions. Such cooperation is an important element in the research data infrastructure. Both sides should be aware of their common interest in maintaining and developing a strong infrastructure for data collection. They are both in the same boat, sailing to new horizons.

---

8 One could envisage such a structure along the lines of the partnership between astronomers and the optical industry: the two work together to design telescopes; the industry produces and maintains the instruments and the astronomers use them for their observations.

5. Infrastructures in terms of individual large-scale survey instruments

There are many aspects to "infrastructure," and the term is used in a number of different ways. The EU, for instance, has set up a European Strategy Forum on Research Infrastructures (ESFRI). Here infrastructure means a large individual project of general importance. In the ESFRI case, the focus is on research infrastructures of pan-European interest. The program is not restricted to the sciences, but also includes the social sciences. The framework is not restricted to survey research projects, but out of a list of six acknowledged infrastructures of European importance there are two large-scale surveys: the European Social Survey and SHARE.

We suggest that, all large-scale measurement instruments are defined as "infrastructures" in this sense. This would emphasize a number of characteristics that are crucial for such projects: their strategic role in enhancing research in the respective fields; the perspective of continuity, including the need for secure funding; governance structures and institutional arrangements for conceptual decisions, data production, and data access; their function of creating communities of researchers in the respective field, at both the national and the international level.

Large-scale measurement instruments must be embedded in an appropriate scientific infrastructure. They should be located in a more comprehensive network of high-quality social surveys, allowing existing elements and missing crucial areas to be easily identified. Moreover, the core instrument – the survey itself – must not work as a closed shop; it should be wide open to its scientific environment. Crucial functions to enable this are R&D for continuous improvement of the core instrument, and outreach to inform the scientific community and the society at large about the potential of the core instrument.

Data collection agencies, which are usually private survey organizations, should be viewed as part of the respective "infrastructure." Selecting the most suitable survey organization will require a competitive procedure. However, after the decision is made, continuity will normally be the most favorable framework for cooperation. Stable working relationships enable learning effects on both sides. Involving survey managers in decisions about methodological design and instrument development can help to optimize the survey. Contract periods of, say, three or six years facilitate investments and returns on investment (both financial resources and know-how).[9]

One might also imagine more innovative forms of cooperation. For instance, imagine that scientists applying for funds for a future large-scale

---

9   Our arguments put forward here on sustainable knowledge accumulation are similar to those which led to the foundation of ZUMA in 1974.

infrastructure were to form a research alliance with a private-sector agency of their choice. It would then be up to the funders to decide whether the quality and originality of the survey justifies the funds asked for. There may even be competing proposals. Price bargaining would be part of proposal development and not part of ex post subsequent funding decisions. Or, imagine that funders were to accept the need for better quality and in turn be prepared to spend more on methodological improvement and innovation than they have so far. The effects on how surveys are organised and how quality is achieved would be tremendous. Third, imagine that the quality promised were controlled independently by the funding agencies. We leave it to the reader's imagination what a major change in actual survey measurement quality that could be.

6. Conclusions and recommendations

- Large-scale, high-quality survey measurement is a crucial foundation for excellence in the social sciences. Because of its unique demands in terms of resources and skills, it should be viewed as a specific sector of the research data infrastructure.

- In Germany, a range of surveys of this type have been established, inside and outside academia, and new large projects are being created. Clearly, the sector is expanding. While this is no doubt a positive development, there is a need to discuss future challenges not only with a focus on individual large projects, but with a view to the sector of large-scale survey measurement in general. Understanding the various meanings of "infrastructure" may help to conceptualize the issue.

- Large-scale surveys are initiated, funded, and governed in different ways. In Germany, the field is segmented along institutional lines. The key actors include the statistical offices (*Amtliche Statistik*), governmental agencies and research institutes (*Ressortforschung*) and the academic community. It would be reasonable – in terms of resources, quality standards, and access to the data – to develop an overall framework covering all these subsectors. The German Data Forum (RatSWD) is a kind of nucleus for the infrastructure needed for networking and coordination. Institutional arrangements or programs in other countries may provide additional experience and models.

- Large-scale, high-quality measurement instruments require a well-developed infrastructure for data collection. In Germany, this infrastructure exists. For surveys other than those of the statistical offices, it is supplied by private-sector survey organizations. It may be discussed whether this structure is stable and effective enough for future demands. However, alternative structures are not realistically in sight. Private survey organizations should, therefore, be recognised as relevant actors within the research data infrastructure. They have to invest in technological and human resources in order to provide the professional services required, and they need conditions and forms of cooperation which encourage this investment.

- Single large-scale survey measurement instruments may be defined as "infrastructures" in line with the use of the term at the European level (ESFRI). Compared to normal research projects, such programs need a more highly developed institutional infrastructure and must be embedded in the scientific environment. A well-defined map of such infrastructures is a prerequisite for the long-term coherent planning of a national social science infrastructure in Germany and beyond.[10]

---

10 "Beyond" mainly refers to the European level, which is of particular importance for large-scale survey measurement. A vision for a European System of Social Science Instruments was set out by Mohler and Wagner (2004).

References:

Hauser, R. (2009): Household income, poverty and wealth. RatSWD Working Paper No. 53.
Mohler, P.P. (2008): Große sozialwissenschaftliche Infrastruktureinrichtungen für das 21. Jahrhundert. Manuskript.
Mohler, P.P. and Wagner, G.G. (2004): ESSI – The European System of Social Science Instruments. Foundations of Continuous Measurement on a European Level using Survey Technology. Working Paper.
Rosenbladt, B. v. (2008): Die Rolle der Umfrageinstitute in der sozialwissenschaftlichen Dateninfrastruktur. RatSWD Working Paper No. 36.

6. The Availability of Market Research Data and its Potential for Use in Empirical Social and Economic Research

Erich Wiegand

Contact:

Erich Wiegand
ADM Arbeitskreis Deutscher Markt- und Sozialforschungsinstitute e.V.
Langer Weg 18
60489 Frankfurt am Main
Germany
e-mail: wiegand[at]adm-ev.de

Abstract

The great usefulness of market research data for secondary analyses lays mainly in the fields of consumer behavior, consumption patterns, and media usage. Making this data available for secondary analysis in empirical social and economic research depends on the professional codes and regulations of the market research industry, and on the readiness of private agencies and their clients to make the data available.

Many market research projects focus on specific target groups. Their potential use for secondary analyses resides in deriving representative insights from these specific groups as well as in basic and methodological research. In most cases, public access to market research data must be contractually agreed upon with the client of the research project.

For methodological reasons, access to official statistics is also important for a number of market research projects. Therefore, private research agencies should have the same privileges and access to official data as academic research institutions. As long as this access has not been established, it is unlikely that these private agencies will be eager to make their market research data publicly available.

1. Introduction

Although market research projects are commissioned and conducted in response to the problems and questions of individual clients, they can be of great interest for empirical social and economic research. In fact, many market research data contain significant potential for secondary analyses. The availability of market research data for empirical social and economic research depends not only on the relevant legal provisions and professional regulations, but also on the readiness of the market research agencies themselves and their clients to make these data available for secondary analyses. Therefore, it is critical to create a win-win situation for market research providers and clients on one side, and for researchers in the relevant fields on the other.

2. The market of market research in Germany

In developed countries, research-based information is gaining importance for decision making; the German market research industry is growing continuously – both economically and in its social reach. An empirical expression of the current state of market research can be gleaned from the following:[1]

- In 2007, the total revenue of market and social research agencies in Germany was approximately 2.1 billion Euros.
- Less than half of this revenue was associated with German-based activity, which demonstrates that market research has become a global business.
- More than 90 percent of the revenue came from quantitative research projects which have a higher potential for secondary analyses than qualitative projects.
- About two-thirds of the revenue was achieved by so-called "ad hoc studies" specially designed and conducted to solve a single problem.
- The most important clients of the market research agencies come from the consumer goods industry, the pharmaceutical industry, and the media. Clients from the public sector play a relatively minor role.
- More than 40 percent of all quantitative interviews have been conducted by telephone.

These figures indicate that the potential of market research data for secondary analyses in empirical social and economic research lays specifically in the broad field of consumer behavior, patterns of consumption (including goods and services as well as time use), and media usage.

3. Potential uses of market research data in empirical social and economic research

The potential of market research data for secondary analyses in empirical social and economic research depends on several key factors:

3.1 Information and knowledge about market research

Despite the close cooperation of associations representing market and social research interests respectively (see clause 5, below), many social and economic researchers have relatively limited information and knowledge about the market of market research and its current and future developments. This

---

1   http://www.adm-ev.de. [Last visited: 03/02/2010].

lack of information limits the potential uses of market research data for secondary analyses. Therefore, the situation looks like a treasure hunt: "Study the map carefully, dig deeply and you will find the treasure!" The situation is also true in reverse – the knowledge gap also applies to many market researchers with regard to the potential of empirical social and economic data from academic and non-profit research institutions.

3.2 Representativeness of market research data

As a consequence of the individualization of lifestyles and of consumption patterns, an increasing number of market research projects are focused on specifically defined and sometimes relatively small target groups. Accordingly, the sample designs of these research projects are not intended to be representative for the whole population in Germany. This does not significantly reduce the potential for using such market research data for secondary analyses in social and economic research. The research data of market research projects on specific target groups still allows for structural insights into a large number of social and economic issues regarding these target groups, as well as for basic and methodological research.

3.3 Space of time between data collection and public availability

In many cases, market research clients need research results at short notice for fast and ever-accelerating decision making. As a consequence, the "half-life" of market research data for the private-sector clients is an ever-shorter time period (i.e., market research results become outdated in an ever-shorter period of time). In principle, this development increases the potential of market research data for the purpose of social and economic research. Faster outdating of market research means a shorter time from the collection of research data to their availability for secondary analyses – provided that market research agencies and clients are prepared to make them available publicly.

3.4 Infrastructure and documentation

Academic survey research in Germany has a well-established infrastructure for secondary analyses of survey data. But for the "outside" world – including parts of the market research industry – this is all but unknown. Since the public availability of market research data for secondary analyses is not only the responsibility of the market research agencies and their clients, the

GESIS[2] Data Archive, the primary institution in charge of the data, should work to increase awareness of its activities and raise its visibility outside of the research community. For example, the introduction of a GESIS exhibition stand at the annual market research trade fair in 2008 was an important step in gaining recognition and raising the profile of this public institution within the market research industry.

In order to assess the possibilities and limitations of the research results from a single project, and to determine their comparability with the research results of other projects, detailed methodological information about the project should be made available. According to DIN ISO 20252:2006, "Market, Opinion and Social Research – Vocabulary and Service requirements," the technical description of a quantitative research project shall comprise the following details (where applicable):

- client name
- research service provider
- research objectives
- target group
- actual sample size versus projected sample size and reasons, if relevant, for not obtaining the projected sample
- date of fieldwork
- sampling method, including the procedure for selecting respondents
- data collection method
- response rate (in the case of probability samples) and the definition and method of calculating it
- type of incentives
- number of interviewers
- interviewer validation methods
- questionnaires, visual exhibits, or show cards, in addition to other relevant data collection documents
- documents, materials, or products used as part of the research project
- weighting procedures
- estimating and imputation procedures
- the reliability of the results, including (when probability samples are used) estimates of sampling variance and estimates of non-sampling errors or indicators thereof
- results based on subgroups and the number of cases used in subgroup analysis

It is the responsibility of market, opinion, and social research service providers and their clients to establish and promote these standards for documentation of research projects and research results.

---

2   Leibniz Institute for the Social Sciences (GESIS, *Leibniz-Institut für Sozialwissenschaften*).

4. Availability of market research data for empirical social and economic research

Besides the factors described above, the potential for the use of market research data in empirical social and economic research is affected by the availability of these data for secondary analyses. The actual availability of market research data depends on the professional rules of market research and the applicable legal provisions, as well as on the readiness of market research agencies and their private and public clients to make the data available. This readiness, in turn, depends on the benefits that are connected to public availability of privately commissioned market research data.

In order to exhaust the potential of market research data it is necessary to create a mutually beneficial situation for the market research agencies and their clients as data providers on the one hand, and for the empirical social and economic researchers as data users on the other.

4.1 Professional rules and legal provisions

The already mentioned international quality standard for market, opinion, and social research (DIN ISO 20252:2006) does not contain specific requirements regarding public availability of research data. With regard to the publication of research results, the following is stipulated:

> "Research service providers may publish research results for scientific or other purposes if they have conducted the research project at their own expense, or if such publication has been contractually agreed with the client commissioning the research project, or if the latter has consented to such publication" (see DIN ISO 20252:2006, clause 4.8.4).

If this international quality standard had also addressed the public availability of research data, the corresponding requirements would probably have been defined as fully as those pertaining to the publication of research results.

The "ICC/ESOMAR International Code of Market and Social Research" (last revised in December 2007) does not contain specific professional rules regarding public availability of market research data. With regard to the publication of research results, however, it points out the mutual responsibilities of researchers and clients. Both shall "ensure that published results are not misleading" (see Article 11b).

However, it belongs to the professional responsibilities of market research agencies to safeguard the confidentiality of their clients and all documents and materials that have been provided to or produced by them in the context of research projects. This requirement applies to the research data, too. In the international quality standard for market, opinion, and social research (DIN ISO 20252:2006), the following is stipulated:

"Every effort shall be made to store records in a manner adequate to ensure...that their confidential nature is not compromised. Unless otherwise agreed, all research records shall only be available to the client..." (see DIN ISO 20252:2006, clauses 4.9.3 and 4.9.4).

Since nearly all market research industry research is commissioned by private or public clients, it is crucial that the availability of market research data is contractually agreed with the clients. Without such an agreement, the market research agencies in most cases are not allowed to make their data available for secondary analyses as part of their professional responsibility to their clients.

According to professional principles and industry rules of market research, data must be processed and transmitted to clients and any other third parties in an anonymized form in order to safeguard respondent privacy. Such research data are no longer personal data. That is, analyzing them does not allow for re-identification of single respondents and the data protection laws do not apply. However, when making research data available for secondary analyses, market research agencies shall undertake specific efforts to check and to avoid any potential problems with regard to re-identification of single respondents, especially since secondary analyses might be conducted by foreign researchers abroad.

Whether the intention to make research data publicly available for secondary analyses is something that must be integrated into the required consent of the data subjects (i.e., the respondents from whom the research data are collected), must be considered from a legal point of view. According to the Federal Data Protection Act (BDSG, *Bundesdatenschutzgesetz*), the data subjects shall be informed of the purpose of collection, processing, and use of their data. The important question is: does this legal provision mean that respondents also shall be informed of and must agree to subsequent secondary analyses when asking them to participate in a certain market research project?

4.2 Readiness of the market research agencies

Without doubt, making market research data available for social and economic research by way of secondary analyses contributes to an increased awareness and perhaps reputation of market research agencies – provided they are quoted in publications in accordance with the professional rules of the scientific community. But is this possible increase in awareness and reputation alone perceived as a (relevant) benefit from their point of view?

For a number of market research projects, the data collected by official statistics are not relevant. For other projects, however, access to the individual – of course anonymized – data collected by the statistical offices are important for methodological reasons (e.g., to calculate benchmarks or weighting factors). In these cases, the private market research agencies should have the same privileges and access to the official statistical data as academic research institutions. As long as this access is not established, it is unlikely that there will by any great willingness on behalf of the market research agencies to make their data publicly available for secondary analyses. In principle, however, this willingness already exists – in both market research agencies as well as their clients – a fact that is evident from numerous examples and illustrated by the following:

In 2005, a conference on data fusion and data integration was organized jointly by the Federal Statistical Office, the Working Group of German Market and Social Research Institutes (ADM, *Arbeitskreis Deutscher Markt- und Sozialforschungsinstitute*), and the Working Group of Social Science Institutes (ASI, *Arbeitsgemeinschaft Sozialwissenschaftlicher Institute*). A presentation was given by Heiner Meulemann and others on the potential of media consumption data for secondary analyses. These data have been collected since 1954 in order to provide a reliable empirical basis for the commercial purposes of media planning. These data have been archived at the Central Archive for Empirical Social Research at the University of Cologne (ZA, *Zentralarchiv für Empirische Sozialforschung*) from the very beginning. Therefore, they comprise a valuable source for secondary analyses, especially in the fields of media usage, social structure, and social change in addition to research methodology.

4.3 Readiness of the market research clients

The readiness of private-sector market research clients to share research data from projects they have commissioned and to make it available for the secondary analyses of social and economic research depends largely on the value of the data. As long as market research results are contributing to the success of a client's business, this readiness does not exist at all. Only when the research data no longer provide a competitive business advantage are clients potentially willing to make research data available to the broader scientific community. At this point, the readiness of market research clients to make privately purchased research data available largely depends on hearing a persuasive argument that it is of mutual benefit for both sides.

4.4 Establishing the win-win situation

For the market research industry, regular access to data from official statistics is a key factor influencing the readiness of research agencies as well as their clients to make their data available for secondary analyses. In order to create a truly win-win situation, access to market research data might be attached to certain conditions; for example, a commitment to making the research data from single projects publicly available for subsequent analyses might be granted where individual statistical data from official sources have been used in order to conduct the research project.

It is clear that in order for private market agencies to have regular access to official statistical data, the Federal Statistics Law (BStatG, *Bundesstatistikgesetz*) would have to be revised, since § 16 Abs. 6[3] stipulates that access to individual data is restricted to institutions that carry out independent scientific research. Since the Basic Law for the Federal Republic of Germany (*Grundgesetz für die Bundesrepublik Deutschland*) does not differentiate between basic and applied research but protects the freedom to conduct both types of research in the same manner, however, the restriction of access to individual statistical data for "independent scientific research" seems inappropriate.

Of course, in the long term, it is the responsibility of ADM to negotiate with the relevant political bodies in order to revise the BStatG accordingly. However, the political representation of interests in this field probably will not be successful without a strategic alliance with the associations and institutions representing empirical social and economic research.

5. The role of the associations

In Germany, the close cooperation of professional and trade associations representing market, opinion, and social research has a long tradition and is more intensive than in many other countries. This cooperation is focused mainly on self-regulation in a broad sense by defining professional rules and developing quality standards, including the formation of a joint disciplinary body as well as organizing common conferences on a regular basis. In the case of the latter, the Federal Statistical Office is involved, too. In the future, the comparatively few contacts between associations representing the private-sector and the academic research community and their respective bodies need to be intensified.

In terms of the potential use and availability of market research data for social and economic research, these points of contact between the associations representing private-sector and academic empirical survey research respectively provides the following advantages:

---

[3] The citations to German legal sources have been left in German to guarantee accuracy.

- They help increase mutual understanding between market research agencies and the social and economic research community, a precondition for exhausting the potential of market research data for secondary analyses.
- They help maintain the research data infrastructure of empirical survey research and thus improve its mutual benefit for research data suppliers and users as well.
- They are a precondition for organizing joint conferences, meetings, and workshops – offering important means for ensuring the above two bullet points.
- They intensify relations between suppliers and users of research data, an important step toward ensuring the public availability of data for secondary analyses.
- They help establish the strategic alliance in political representation of interests in order to create the win-win situation described above.

6. Summary

The potential for market research data to contribute to the field of empirical social and economic research lies mainly in research areas dealing with consumer behavior, consumption patterns, and media use. The practical availability of market research data for secondary analyses is affected by professional rules within market research, legal provisions, and the readiness of market research agencies and their clients. A key factor determining the readiness of the market research industry to make its data publicly available is whether it has regular access to official statistical data for private market research agencies, similar to the privileges academic research institutions enjoy. The cooperation of professional and trade associations which represent market, opinion, and social research interests in Germany will play a major role defining the future possibilities for secondary analyses of market research data.

7. Recommendations

(1) There should be continued effort on both sides and by various means (e.g., joint conferences, workshops, newsletters, etc.) to improve understanding and knowledge between market research agencies and the research community.

(2) The data infrastructure of empirical survey research should be promoted more actively outside the academic scientific community to increase its visibility for market research agencies and their clients.

(3) Existing standards for documentation of the methodological and technical details of research projects both by the market research industry as well as by empirical social and economic research need to be more strongly reinforced.

(4) The availability of market research data for secondary analyses for purposes of empirical social and economic research should be agreed upon contractually when a research project is commissioned.

(5) In order to improve the readiness of private market research agencies and their clients to make market research data publicly available for secondary analyses, the bodies representing academic social and economic research should actively support the efforts by private market research agencies to acquire regular access to statistical data.

(6) The bodies representing the empirical economic research community should be included in the forms of cooperation that already exist between the associations representing market, opinion, and social research in Germany and public-sector agencies.

References:

ADM Arbeitskreis Deutscher Markt- und Sozialforschungsinstitute e.V. (www.adm-ev.de, 2008).

DIN ISO 20252:2006 Market, opinion and social research – Vocabulary and service requirements.

ICC/ESOMAR International code on market and social research (last revised December 2007).

Meulemann, H./Hagenah, J. and Akinci, H. (2005): Die Media-Analysen. Synopse des Datenbestands und Nutzungschancen für Sekundäranalysen des sozialen Wandels in Deutschland seit 1954. In: König, Ch./Stahl, M. and Wiegand, E. (Eds.): Datenfusion und Datenintegration. 6. Wissenschaftliche Tagung.

PROGRESS SINCE 2001 AND CURRENT STATE

1. The Recommendations of the 2001 KVI Report and Their Realizations up to 2008

Gabriele Rolf-Engel

Contact:

Gabriele Rolf-Engel
Business Office of the German Data Forum (RatSWD)
c/o DIW Berlin
10108 Berlin
Germany
e-mail: grolf-engel[at]ratswd.de

In 1999 the German Federal Ministry of Education and Research (BMBF, *Bundesministerium für Bildung und Forschung*) appointed a commission to examine the information infrastructure in Germany and to make proposals for its improvement. The central objective was to improve the cooperation between the scientific community and official statistical agencies. The German Commission on Improving the Information Infrastructure between Science and Statistics (KVI) presented its final report in 2001 (KVI 2001).

The Commission's report consisted of:

- a stocktaking of deficits and data needs in different fields (e.g., population, employment, income and wealth data, etc.),
- an overview of the major data producers, data providers, and statistical databases (e.g., official statistics, social security statistics, government ministry data, administrative data, scientific data, private market data, and data from social research institutes and commercial providers) and the practice of providing access to anonymized microdata,
- an international comparison of the best statistics and best practices of statistical analysis, and
- recommendations on improving the performance of the information infrastructure for empirical economic and social research in Germany.

The Commission developed 36 recommendations on:

- improving cooperation between the scientific community and official statistical agencies,
- expanding participation of the scientific community in developing survey and data processing programs (by official statistical agencies as well as by ministries and non-statistical institutions conducting surveys),
- priorities for continuing and developing important statistics,
- supporting research on data collection, processing, and archiving,
- higher education and training,
- data access, especially access to microdata,
- confidentiality of research data, and
- implementation and funding.

The following synopsis gives an overview of the Commission's recommendations. The second column lists the objectives of the recommendations, some of which are formulated explicitly in the Commission's report, and some of which I have deduced from the proposed solutions listed in the third column. The traffic signals in the fourth column illustrate the extent to which results of the recommended action are already evident: green indicates that the objectives have been fully achieved; yellow indicates that work is still in progress; and red indicates that there remains significant further work to be done. Since these conclusions may be in dispute, the fifth column provides additional explanatory comments.

As the traffic signals in the following synopsis show, many of the Commission's recommendations have already been put into effect, some of the most important being:

- the establishment of the German Data Forum (RatSWD) and its predecessor the Founding Committee of the Council for Social and Economic Data,
- the establishment and evaluation of several Research Data Centers and Data Service Centers that are working to improve access to microdata and facilitate data analysis,
- new means of data access. In addition to the distribution of Scientific Use Files and Public Use Files, controlled remote data access is provided. Furthermore, workplaces are being provided for guest researchers in the Research Data Centers,
- improved cooperation and information exchange between the scientific community and official statistics through:
  - the German Data Forum (RatSWD), as a platform for communication,
  - the biennial Conference for Social and Economic Data (KSWD, *Konferenz für Sozial- und Wirtschaftsdaten*),
  - dialog workshops in the fields of media data, crime statistics, household statistics, and globalization,
  - joint research projects on data access, statistical development, and methodological development,
  - the appointment of three working groups by the German Data Forum (RatSWD) dealing with crime statistics, new means of access to microdata for Germany, and preparation of a German National Death Index, and
  - the establishment of the Census Commission,
- access to anonymous firm-level data and opening up longitudinal microdata, and

- capacity-building (young scholar workshops, expert report competitions for young researchers, CAMPUS-Files using realistic datasets).

Nevertheless, there is still a substantial need for action, especially when implementing the Commission's recommendations, in terms of:

- legislative action,
- international activities,
- coordination within and between organizations on a voluntary basis and/or without sufficient budget (e.g., facilitating dialog within the scientific community).

Last but not least, continuous funding of the existing infrastructure remains a problem. This applies both to the permanent institutionalization of the German Data Forum (RatSWD), which has been financed up to now as a pilot project of the BMBF, and to permanent funding for the Research Data Center of the Statistical Offices of the German *Länder*.

Synopsis: Recommendations of the Commission

🔴 Task completed or on schedule — green	🟡 Room for improvement — yellow	🔴 Project structure not yet visible — red

Recommendation			
No.	**Objective**	**Solution**	**Traffic signal**
\multicolumn{4}{l}{*Improved cooperation between science and statistics is necessary for data users and data producers*}			
1	To improve cooperation between the scientific community and official statistical agencies based on the traditional model of a division of labor	Adopt and enforce institutional regulations	🔴 red
2	To assess and to improve the information infrastructure based on input from data producers and data users To develop a platform for structured dialog between data producers and data users	Establish a Council for Social and Economic Data, whose main functions are: • assessing and improving the data infrastructure and advising the federal and state governments on programs of science-based statistics and their funding • promoting social and economic reporting • recommending the establishment of Research Data Centers and Data Service Centers and evaluating their activities • suggesting how project funds should be allocated These tasks need coordinators in the group of data producers, in the group of data users, and between the two groups.	🔴 red

Status
Comment
Several important activities have been carried out, especially the establishment of the German Data Forum (RatSWD), which offers a platform for dialog between data providers and data users (see recommendation 2) and the KSWD, which takes place every two years.
Measures In 2004 the German Federal Ministry of Education and Research (BMBF) set up the RatSWD. This Council includes empirical researchers from universities, colleges, and other independent research institutions as well as data producers and representatives of service centers. The predecessor of the RatSWD, the Founding Committee of the Council for Social and Economic Data (GA, *Gründungsausschuss*), was founded in 2001. The GA and the RatSWD have undertaken a great number of activities to improve the research data infrastructure in Germany (Rolf et al. 2008; Solga and Wagner 2007), particularly by offering a platform for dialog between data providers and data users and by advising Germany's federal and state governments on the establishment of Research Data Centers and Data Service Centers and by evaluating their work. Additionally, the GA and the RatSWD have contributed to improving the research data infrastructure by assessing projects in terms of data access and methodological developments in the social and economic sciences. In its first few years of work, the RatSWD's activities have focused on improving data access for empirical research. Now, the need to improve survey development and processing programs has moved to the forefront of the RatSWD's agenda. *To be done:* Ensure permanent funding for the RatSWD, which has funding from the BMBF for an initial period. The German Council of Science and Humanities (*Wissenschaftsrat*) has evaluated the RatSWD positively and recommends its permanent funding (Wissenschaftsrat 2009a).

Recommendation			Traffic signal
No.	Objective	Solution	
Participation by the scientific community in developing survey and processing programs			
3	To involve the scientific community both in improving the survey and processing programs of the official statistical agencies and in special hearings by German parliament on this subject	Adopt institutional regulations Improve coordination in the scientific community (in discussions of the Council for Social and Economic Data in cooperation with the relevant scientific associations)	🟡 (amber)
4	To make survey and processing programs of the official statistical agencies more flexible	Reduce strict legal regulations and expand the scope for statistical offices and their advisory bodies to shape survey programs	🔴 (red)
5	To expand the influence of the scientific community in proposing modifications of official statistical programs	• Broaden the definition of the Statistical Advisory Committee's tasks (including medium-term program planning)	🔴 (red)
		• Achieve fuller representation of the scientific community in the Statistical Advisory Committee (increase the number of representatives of empirical social and economic research)	🟢 (green)
		• Hold mandatory hearings as part of the legislative process on official statistics	🔴 (red)

Status
Comment
Official statistical agencies are open to advice, but the scientific community has still not made sufficient use of this opportunity. *Measures* Appointment of the Census Commission (*Zensuskommission*), a scientific commission that advises the federal government and official statistical agencies on preparing, processing, and analyzing the 2011 Census. Nomination of the Census Commission's members on recommendation from the RatSWD No institutional regulations are in place, but a number of joint activities are underway, such as a series of workshops *"Dialog von Wissenschaft und amtlicher Statistik"* dealing with the 2011 register-based census, household surveys, and globalization. *To be done:* Fostering dialog in the social, economic, and behavioral sciences and mobilizing the respective scientific associations to improve their information infrastructure. Holding regular hearings with the scientific community as part of the legislative process.
Not yet visible The Statistical Advisory Committee (*Statistischer Beirat*), an organization of the users, respondents, and producers of federal statistics, has called for more flexibility in designing the statistical system (Statistisches Bundesamt 2003).
Not yet visible The Statistical Advisory Committee has recommended medium-term program planning (Statistisches Bundesamt 2003).   The scientific community has attained greater influence on the Statistical Advisory Committee through an additional representative of empirical social and economic research appointed by the RatSWD.   Not yet visible

Recommendation			Traffic signal
No.	Objective	Solution	
6	To increase the influence of the scientific community on surveys conducted by ministries and non-statistical authorities (e.g., Deutsche Bundesbank, Federal Employment Agency, and the social security institutions)	Provide structured opportunities for scientific advice	○ ○ ○
Priorities in continuing and developing important statistics			
7	To continue collecting important official statistics	Conduct a population census	○ ○ ●
8	To enhance and to develop important official statistics	Further develop the German Microcensus by <ul><li>introducing a rotating panel</li><li>developing an access panel</li><li>presenting exact data on gross earned income</li><li>providing Scientific Use Files</li></ul>	○ ○ ●
9	To enhance and develop important official statistics	Improve the sample survey of income and consumption (EVS, *Einkommens- und Verbrauchsstichprobe*) by <ul><li>reducing the time intervals between the sample surveys</li><li>introducing a rotating panel</li><li>presenting detailed wealth data</li></ul>	○ ○ ○
10	To bridge serious gaps in business sector statistics	<ul><li>Further develop statistics on the service economy</li><li>Achieve better statistical coverage of business modifications</li></ul>	○ ○ ○

Status
Comment
As of yet there exist no structured opportunities for science to exert greater influence over official surveys, but informal steps have been taken, for example, by including scientific advisory councils in survey planning.
The 2011 Census is on schedule: http://www.destatis.de/jetspeed/portal/cms/Sites/destatis/Internet/DE/Navigation/Zensus/Zensus,templateId=renderPrint.psml__nnn=true
The Microcensuses are available as Scientific Use Files. The joint project "Preparation and Provision of the Microcensus as a Panel Sample" has been carried out with participation of the German Federal Statistical Office, the Research Data Centers of the German Federal Statistical Office and the Statistical Offices of the German *Länder*, the Freie Universität Berlin, and the Centre for Survey Research and Methodology (ZUMA) funded by the BMBF and the German Research Foundation (DFG, *Deutsche Forschungsgemeinschaft*). Today, the 1996-1999 Microcensus panel and the 2001-2004 Microcensus panel are available for research as Scientific Use Files. As of yet, exact data on gross earned income are not available.
The proposed measures have not been implemented so far. This must be seen within the overall context of household surveys: a discussion is underway between the scientific community and official statistical agencies concerning new concepts of household surveys (both in Germany and abroad). A workshop, entitled *"Dialog von Wissenschaft und amtlicher Statistik zum Erhebungsprogramm der amtlichen Haushaltsstichproben in Deutschland,"* has been organized by the RatSWD and ZUMA: http://www.ratswd.de/ver/mannheimWS.php
The research potential of firm-level data has been improved through data matching (see recommendation 27).

Recommendation			
No.	Objective	Solution	Traffic signal
11	To maintain and develop important science-based statistics	• Ensure permanent institutionalization and funding of the German Socio-Economic Panel (SOEP, *Sozio-oekonomisches Panel*) • Extend the sample	🔴
12	To continue important science-based statistics	Continuing the • German General Social Survey (ALLBUS, *Allgemeine Bevölkerungsumfrage der Sozialwissenschaften*) • International Social Survey Programme (ISSP) and • Welfare Surveys (*Wohlfahrtssurveys*)	🔴
13	To provide stronger support for cohort studies such as longitudinal studies of human development	Continue existing cohort studies and generate new cohort studies that cover early childhood, adolescence, and early adulthood	🔴
Supporting research on data collection, processing, and archiving			
14	To improve university-level teaching on the methodologies of empirical social and economic research	• Set up a special commission for the German Council of Science and Humanities on the current state of affairs in higher education and research regarding the methods of empirical social and economic research (or defining this area as a task of the High Commission on Empirical Economic Research) • Establish professorships or research centers at universities to focus on methodological problems of survey and official statistics	🔴

Status
Comment
Since 2003 the SOEP has been receiving ongoing funding through the Bund-Länder Commission for Educational Planning and Research Promotion (BLK, *Bund-Länder-Kommission für Bildungsplanung und Forschungsförderung*) by Germany's federal and state governments. Several additional subsamples have expanded the possibilities for studying small societal groups. The SOEP has proposed to considerably enlarge the sample. The German Council of Science and Humanities approves of this proposal (Wissenschaftsrat 2009b).
The ALLBUS and the ISSP are conducted regularly: the ALLBUS is a continuous biennial survey, the ISSP a continuous annual program. Welfare Surveys were conducted from 1978 to 1998. Since 2002, the European Social Survey (ESS) has taken place every two years.
Existing cohort studies are continuing, such as: - the SOEP, an annual survey conducted since 1984 (see recommendation 11), and - the IAB Establishment Panel, an annual survey conducted since 1993. Examples of new panel studies are: - the project "Educational Processes, Competence Development and Selection Decisions in Pre- and Primary School Age" (BiKS, *Bildungsprozesse, Kompetenzentwicklung und Selektionsentscheidungen im Vor- und Grundschulalter*), which is funded by the DFG, - the National Educational Panel Study (NEPS), measuring competencies of children, adolescents, and adults over an extended period, which is funded by the BMBF, - the Panel Analysis of Intimate Relationships and Family Dynamics (pairfam) funded by the DFG, and - the Survey of Health, Ageing, and Retirement in Europe (SHARE).
In 2002, the German Council of Science and Humanities published the report "*Empfehlungen zur Stärkung wirtschaftswissenschaftlicher Forschung an den Hochschulen*" (Wissenschaftsrat 2002). The Priority Program of the DFG "Survey Methodology" has been launched: http://www.survey-methodology.de/de/projekte.html Examples of further activities enhancing higher education and research in methods of empirical social and economic research are: - workshops for young researchers dealing with technical and methodological problems with complex datasets provided by the RatSWD in conjunction with official statistics and non-university research institutes, and - the "European Data Watch" section of *Schmollers Jahrbuch*, which offers descriptions and discussions of micro databases that are of interest to empirical researchers: http://www.ratswd.de/publ/datawatch.php.

Recommendation			Traffic signal
No.	Objective	Solution	
15	To support methodological research in official statistics	• Strengthen the involvement of the scientific community in the further development of methodological instruments	🔴
		• Include sustained methodological research in the tasks and budgets of official statistics	⚪
		• Expand joint research projects by scientific and official statistical agencies	🔴
16	To ensure the long-term preservation of statistical data	Commission the Council for Economic and Social Data to deal with the problem of archiving statistical data	⚪
17	To promote the subject of Empirical Economic Research and to make it more visible	Recommend that the DFG establish the subject of Empirical Economic Research as a sub-discipline (or as an extension of the sub-discipline statistics)	🟡
Higher education and training			
18	To improve education in areas such as statistics, econometrics, applied computer science, empirical methods, data collection, data	Recommend that universities and faculties improve education for • undergraduates (statistics, econometrics, and applied computer science by using realistic datasets) • graduate studies (statistics, econometrics, data collection, data	🟡

Status
Comment

See recommendation 14

Efforts have been made to assign the task of "research" to official statistics in the Law on Statistics for Federal Purposes (BStatG, *Bundesstatistikgesetz*) (Hohmann 2007).

Several joint research projects have been funded by the BMBF or the DFG (see recommendation 27 for an example).

The problem of archiving primary research data is currently being debated. The issues being discussed include
- *Rundgespräch "Forschungsprimärdaten"* of the DFG, Bonn, January 2008
  http://www.dfg.de/download/pdf/foerderung/programme/lis/forschungsprimaerdaten_0108.pdf
- The Priority Initiative "Digital Information" of the Alliance of German Science Organizations, Berlin, June 2008
  http://www.dfg.de/download/pdf/foerderung/programme/lis/allianz_initiative_digital_information_en.pdf

There is consensus on not attempting to establish central rules for data archiving. Each discipline should develop its own individual solution to the problem.

The recommendation listed in column 3 has not been taken up by the DFG or the respective scientific associations. But this does not mean that the DFG does not promote empirical economic research, as the Priority Program of the DFG "Flexibility in Heterogeneous Labor Markets" shows
http://kooperationen.zew.de/en/dfgflex/home.html

Curriculum development is difficult to assess because of changes in the German educational system (bachelor, master, doctorate).

Positive development can be observed in the fields of post-graduate programs and teaching appointments to the staff of Research Data Centers.

Measures improving the education for students and young researchers mostly taken by non-university stakeholders include:

\multicolumn{3}{c	}{Recommendation}	Traffic signal
No.	Objective	Solution	
	editing, data protection, and data analysis To improve statistical knowledge transfer to students	editing, data protection, and data analysis) • post-graduate-programs (new empirical methods and more in-depth study of statistics and econometrics) Increasing teaching posts on the staff of official statistical agencies	
19	To make working in empirical social and economic research, statistics, and econometrics more attractive	Recommend that universities and ministries of science • increase the number of professorships in empirical social and economic research, statistics, and econometrics • upgrade existing associate professorships to full professorships	🟢⚪⚪
20	To bring together universities, non-university research institutes, and official statistical agencies	Organize seminars, advanced training courses, and interdisciplinary summer schools in cooperation between universities, non-university research institutes, and official statistical agencies	🟢⚪⚪
\multicolumn{4}{l	}{*Economic aspects of data access*}
21	To provide low-cost access to aggregated data of official statistics	Enable low-cost access to aggregated data of official statistics via Internet	⚪⚪🔴
22	To provide low-cost access to Scientific Use Files and Public Use Files	Enable low-cost access to Scientific Use Files and Public Use Files Follow the example of the BMBF-funded pilot projects (providing flat-rate financing for the fixed costs of anonymization and covering the marginal costs of data delivery to the researcher)	⚪🟡⚪
\multicolumn{4}{l	}{*Access to aggregated data*}
23	To promote convenient access to regionalized data via Internet	Set up a joint database system of official statistics that contains data from all federal statistical sources, broken down by region	⚪🟡⚪

Status
Comment
<ul><li>Supply of CAMPUS-Files (free Public Use Files for teaching purposes)</li><li>"European Data Watch" section of *Schmollers Jahrbuch*, presenting micro databases (see recommendation 14)</li><li>Expert report competitions for young researchers announced by the RatSWD</li><li>Supplying a teaching module which focuses on data protection in the social sciences http://www.ratswd.de/publ/ratswd_dokumente.php</li><li>Organizing young scholars' workshops (see recommendation 20)</li></ul>
In the social, educational, and behavioral sciences, an empirical focus seems to play a major role in professorship appointments.
Workshops on technical and methodological problems in dealing with complex data are being offered to young researchers by the RatSWD in conjunction with official statistical agencies, universities, and non-university research institutes.
Free or low-cost access to aggregated data is being provided by official statistical agencies via Internet.
Low-cost access to a large number of Scientific Use Files for scientific purposes is available; CAMPUS-Files can be downloaded for free. Costs of combining several complex datasets or of analyzing panel data are rather high.
Microdata: recommendation implemented as far as possible Macrodata: GENESIS-Online, room for improvement

Recommendation			Traffic signal
No.	Objective	Solution	
Microdata access and data protection			
24	To ensure respondents' trust in data protection and to enable unlimited re-analyses	Use of different ways of access to micro datasets depending on the kind of data	🔴
25	To guarantee confidentiality of data To ensure data protection and privacy	Periodically revise the list of technical measures developed as part of the German Anonymization Project (University of Mannheim)	🔴
		Develop of a code of conduct describing the obligations of scientists and research institutions under data protection regulations. The code of conduct should be developed jointly by the disciplines concerned.	🟢
		Provide certification of institutions that would benefit from the *"Wissenschaftsprivileg"* (§ 16 Abs. 6 BStatG)[1]	🟢
26	To improve access to confidential microdata	- Enhance the development of Scientific Use Files - Provide Scientific Use Files of older data to allow analysis of social change - Provide similar files such as regional Microcensus files and Microcensus panel files	🔴
27	To permit access to business microdata	Develop anonymization strategies for data on businesses and local bodies (joint research project of the scientific and official statistical communities)	🔴

---

[1] The citations to German legal sources have been left in German to guarantee accuracy.

Status
Comment

Various options of data access exist depending on the degree of anonymity of the data:
- dissemination of Public Use Files (absolutely anonymous microdata files)
- dissemination of Scientific Use Files (factually anonymous microdata files)
- workplaces for guest researchers in the Research Data Centers
- controlled remote data access

Work is underway in the field of anonymization and data protection, e.g., Wirth (2006) and several anonymization projects (see recommendation 27).

Several discipline specific codes of conduct, but no common code of conduct (e.g., *Ethik-Kodex der Deutschen Gesellschaft für Soziologie (DGS) und des Berufsverbandes Deutscher Soziologen (BDS)*; *Erklärung für das Gebiet der Bundesrepublik Deutschland zum ICC/ESOMAR Internationalen Kodex für die Markt- und Sozialforschung*
http://www.soziologie.de/index.php?id=19
http://www.adm-ev.de/fileadmin/user_upload/PDFS/Erklaerung_2008.pdf

It has proven difficult to find a common solution for the Research Data Centers (see recommendation 29) because of different legal foundations (BStatG, SGB).

To be done:
Develop a list of criteria for identifying institutions with the task of independent scientific research under § 16 Abs. 6 BStatG

Since their foundation, the first four Research Data Centers (see recommendation 29) have provided a large number of Scientific Use Files. For an overview, see:
http://www.forschungsdatenzentrum.de/datenangebot.asp
http://fdz.iab.de/de/FDZ_Overview_of_Data.aspx
http://forschung.deutsche-rentenversicherung.de/ForschPortalWeb/contentAction.do?key=main_fdz_forschung

The BMBF has financed the creation of Scientific Use Files by other data producers, too, through pilot projects such as the SUF HIS-Absolventenpanel:
http://www.his.de/abt2/ab22/archiv/abs12

A number of projects (finished, in progress, or planned) have been supported by the BMBF:
- "Factual Anonymization of business microdata" (FAWE)
- "Anonymization of business panel data" (FAWE-Panel: *Anonymisierung wirtschaftsstatistischer Paneldaten*)

Combining data from different surveys (and from different data producers)
- "Official Firm Data for Germany" (AFiD, *Amtliche Firmendaten für Deutschland*)
- "Combined Firm Data for Germany" (KombiFiD, *Kombinierte Firmendaten für Deutschland*)

Recommendation			Traffic signal
No.	Objective	Solution	
28	To improve access to microdata and to learn how to analyze microdata	Develop Public Use Files • to train students, • to meet commercial users' needs, • to enable foreign scholars to access German microdata	🔴 (red)
29	To improve and facilitate access to microdata	Establish Research Data Centers with controlled remote data access to enable use of microdata that is difficult to anonymize (i.e., when factual anonymization would impair the information in the data) and in the case of matching various datasets	🔴 (red)
30	To improve and facilitate access to microdata	• Establish workplaces for guest researchers in the Research Data Centers • Develop transparent procedures for the selection of guest researchers	🔴 (red)
Using international microdata			
31	To improve the situation for research in economic and social sciences at the international level	Here a great number of measures are necessary, including • developing and passing on Eurostat databases to the scientific community in the form of anonymized Scientific Use Files	⚪ (none filled)

Status
Comment
Absolutely anonymous Public Use Files are provided for teaching purposes (CAMPUS-Files). See: http://www.forschungsdatenzentrum.de/campus-file.asp An internationally integrated microdata-orientated infrastructure for census research has been established: "Integrated Public Use Microdata Series – International" (IPUMS-International). See: https://international.ipums.org/international/
Measures Four Research Data Centers have been established and evaluated by the RatSWD and its predecessor, the GA: - Research Data Center of the German Federal Statistical Office - Research Data Center of the Statistical Offices of the German *Länder* - Research Data Center of the Federal Employment Agency at the Institute for Employment Research - Research Data Center of the German Federal Pension Insurance The Research Data Centers offer different means of data access, including controlled remote access. For the datasets provided, see the relevant homepages (see recommendation 26). To ensure the quality of the Research Data Centers, the RatSWD has developed a list of criteria to be met by Research Data Centers. For example, Research Data Centers should not evaluate the content of research projects applying for data access, and data producers should not maintain exclusive access to their data: http://www.ratswd.de/download/publikationen_rat/RatSWD_FDZKriterien.PDF Meanwhile, nine further Research Data Centers have adopted these standards and further data centers are scheduled to do so: http://www.ratswd.de/eng/dat/fdz.html *To be done:* Funding of the Research Data Center of the Statistical Offices of the German *Länder* on a permanent basis
Tasks completed.
A network of centers is to be established in Europe that allows access to microdata. At the end of the process, Eurostat will aim to provide remote data access to the statistics community. Examples of international projects harmonizing data from different countries: - "Integrated Public Use Microdata Series – International" (IPUMS-International)"; construction of an internationally integrated microdata-orientated infrastructure for census research https://international.ipums.org/international/

Recommendation			Traffic signal
No.	Objective	Solution	
		• harmonizing data from different countries	
32	To support data exchange with research institutions in non-EU Member States	Recommend that the federal government implement a "Safe Harbor" mechanism	● ○ ○
Demand for services and service agency for microdata			
33	To enhance the efficiency of using microdata for research purposes	Maintain research service institutions in Germany in the future as part of the information infrastructure	○ ○ ●
Data linkage			
34	To reduce the costs of data acquisition and the burden on respondents	Develop legal provisions on the possibility of precisely linking microdata for statistical purposes without the explicit consent of each respondent (matching only in completely shielded research and statistics areas)	○ ○ ○

Status
Comment
- "Survey of Health, Ageing and Retirement in Europe (SHARE)"; cross-national panel database of microdata on health, socio-economic status, and social and family networks http://www.share-project.org/   CESSDA: One of the objectives of the Council of European Social Science Data Archives (CESSDA) is to promote the integration of the European database.   http://www.cessda.org/doc/cessdaconstitution20040402.pdf   ESFRI: The objective of the European Strategy Forum on Research Infrastructures (ESFRI) is to support a coherent approach to policy-making on research infrastructure in Europe. http://cordis.europa.eu/esfri/   IDF: There is an initiative to establish an International Data Forum (IDF) to facilitate the production and dissemination of social and economic data at the international level. http://www.esrcsocietytoday.ac.uk/ESRCInfoCentre/Images/IDF%20Conference%20report%202007_tcm6-21126.pdf   Establishing a European Data Forum is in discussion.
Not yet visible, but progress has been made below the level of a law.

Two Data Service Centers have been established and evaluated by the RatSWD and its predecessor, the GA, to make data analysis more convenient. These are the: - German Microdata Lab, which is part of the Leibniz Institute for the Social Sciences (GESIS, *Leibniz-Institut für Sozialwissenschaften*), and the   - International Data Service Center at the Institute for the Study of Labor (IZA, *Forschungsinstitut zur Zukunft der Arbeit*)   http://www.gesis.org/das-institut/wissenschaftliche-arbeitsbereiche/dauerbeobachtung-der-gesellschaft/german-microdata-lab/   http://www.iza.org/   New developments to be mentioned here are: - MISSY "Microdata Information System"   http://www.gesis.org/en/services/data/official-microdata/microcensus/missy/   - JoSuA "Job Submission Application"   http://idsc.iza.org/metadata/
Not yet visible   The project "Biographical data of selected social insurance agencies in Germany" (BASiD: *Biografiedaten ausgewählter Sozialversicherungsträger in Deutschland*) is in its early stages. The project's aim is to construct a combined dataset for research purposes based on data from the German Pension Insurance, the Federal Employment Agency, and the Institute for Employment Research.   Other approaches (statistical matching) are under discussion or in use.

Recommendation			
No.	Objective	Solution	Traffic signal
Confidentiality of research data			
35	To avoid trade-offs between the freedom of science and the need for data protection	Recommend that legislators introduce the principle of "research data confidentiality": the scientist's privilege to refuse testimony as a witness on research data and prohibition of seizure (*Zeugnisverweigerungsrecht und Beschlagnahmeverbot*)	🔴
Implementation and funding			
36	To provide sufficient funds to implement the Commission's recommendations	Recommend that the institutions responsible for research and science funding sponsor the activities mentioned above	⚪

Status
Comment
Not yet visible
The BMBF has offered financial support for many of the recommended activities for a starting phase (pilot project financing). *To be done:* Permanent funding of the RatSWD and of the Research Data Center of the Statistical Offices of the German *Länder*

References:

Hohmann, E. (2007): Zur Weiterentwicklung der Forschungsdatenzentren der amtlichen Statistik. Verankerung der Aufgabe „Forschung" im Statistikrecht von Bund und Ländern, 22. Februar 2007. http://www.ratswd.de/download/veranstaltungen/Nachtrag_Hohmann.pdf.

Kommission zur Verbesserung der informationellen Infrastruktur zwischen Wissenschaft und Statistik (KVI) (Ed.) (2001): Wege zu einer besseren informationellen Infrastruktur. Baden-Baden.

Rolf, G./Zwick, M. and Wagner, G.G. (2008): Fortschritte der informationellen Infrastruktur in Deutschland: Ein Überblick über die Jahre 1998 bis 2008. In: Rolf, G./Zwick, M. and Wagner, G.G. (Eds.): Fortschritte der informationellen Infrastruktur in Deutschland. Festschrift für Johann Hahlen zum 65. Geburtstag und Hans-Jürgen Krupp zum 75. Geburtstag. Baden-Baden.

Solga, H. and Wagner, G.G. (2007): A Modern Statistical Infrastructure for Excellent Research and Policy Advice. Report on the German Council for Social and Economic Data during Its First Period in Office (2004 – 2006). Schmollers Jahrbuch 127 (2), 315-320.

Statistisches Bundesamt (2003): Statistischer Beirat empfiehlt Novellierung des Bundesstatistikgesetzes. Pressemitteilung vom 18. Juni 2003.

Wirth, H. (2006): Anonymisierung des Mikrozensuspanels im Kontext der Bereitstellung als Scientific-Use-File. Arbeitspapier 11 des Methodenverbundes "Aufbereitung und Bereitstellung des Mikrozensus als Panelstichprobe". http://www.destatis.de/jetspeed/portal/cms/Sites/destatis/Internet/DE/Content/Wissenschaftsforum/MethodenVerfahren/Mikrozensus/Arbeitspapiere/Arbeitspapier 11,property=file.pdf.

Wissenschaftsrat (2002): Empfehlungen zur Stärkung wirtschaftswissenschaftlicher Forschung an den Hochschulen. Drs. 5455-02. Saarbrücken, 15. November 2002. http://www.wissenschaftsrat.de/texte/5455-02-1.pdf.

Wissenschaftsrat (2009a): Stellungnahme zum Status und der zukünftigen Entwicklung des Rates für Sozial- und Wirtschaftsdaten (RatSWD), Berlin. Drs. 9504-09. Aachen, 13.11.2009. http://www.wissenschaftsrat.de/texte/9504-09.pdf.

Wissenschaftsrat (2009b): Stellungnahme zum Status und der zukünftigen Entwicklung des Sozio-oekonomischen Panels (SOEP), Berlin. Drs. 9503-09. Aachen, 13.11.2009 http://www.wissenschaftsrat.de/texte/9503-09.pdf.

2. Access to Microdata from official statistics

Stefan Bender, Ralf Himmelreicher, Sylvia Zühlke and Markus Zwick

Contact:

Stefan Bender
Research Data Center of the Federal Employment Agency at the Institute for Employment Research
Regensburger Str. 104
90478 Nuremberg
Germany
e-mail: stefan.bender[at]iab.de

Ralf Himmelreicher
Research Data Center of the German Pension Insurance
Ruhrstr. 2
10709 Berlin
Germany
e-mail: ralf.himmelreicher[at]drv-bund.de

Sylvia Zühlke
Research Data Center of the Statistical Offices of the *Länder*
c/o IT North Rhine-Westphalia
Mauerstraße 51
40476 Düsseldorf
Germany
e-mail: sylvia.zuehlke[at]it.nrw.de

Markus Zwick
Research Data Center of the Federal Statistical Office
65180 Wiesbaden
Germany
e-mail: markus.zwick[at]destatis.de

Abstract

The four publicly funded Research Data Centers in Germany – the Research Data Center of the Federal Employment Agency, the Research Data Center of the German Pension Insurance, the Research Data Center of the Statistical Offices of the German *Länder* and the Research Data Center of the Federal Statistical Office – have made a significant improvement to the data and services available to researchers over the past few years. Their services are widely used, empirical findings lead to refereed publications and the state of research in rendering microdata anonymous has made great leaps. Many policy decisions are now planned and evaluated on the basis of data originating from the Research Data Centers. Germany has gone from the bottom of Europe's league with regard to the use of individual data to an innovative provider of new ideas, such as on access to individual data for teaching purposes and linked employer-employee datasets.

In 2007, the Research Data Centers developed criteria for their specific design in conjunction with the German Data Forum (RatSWD).

The aim of this paper is to describe the key criteria for a common working basis for the Research Data Centers, detailed descriptions of the four Research Data Centers and an outlook over future German developments.

Keywords: Research Data Center, data access, data protection, microdata

1. Introduction

The four publicly funded Research Data Centers in Germany – the Research Data Center of the Federal Employment Agency at the Institute for Employment Research (IAB, *Institut für Arbeitsmarkt- und Berufsforschung* within the BA, *Bundesagentur für Arbeit*), the Research Data Center of the German Pension Insurance (RV, *Deutsche Rentenversicherung*), the Research Data Center of the Statistical Offices of the German *Länder*, and the Research Data Center of the Federal Statistical Office – have made significant improvements to the data and services available to researchers over the past few years.[1] Founded on the recommendation of the 2001 KVI report, and funded in the project phases by the Federal Ministry of Education and Research (BMBF, *Bundesministerium für Bildung und Forschung*), the centers have developed in a way that was not initially anticipated. Their services are widely used, empirical findings lead to refereed publications, and the state of research in rendering microdata anonymous has made great leaps. Many poli-

---

1 Two Data Service Centers – the German Microdata Lab (GML) at ZUMA and the International Data Service Center (IDSC) at the Institut for the Study of Labor (IZA, *Forschungsinstitut zur Zukunft der Arbeit*) – were also set up as part of this initiative, and have also worked very successfully, see Schneider and Wolf 2008.

cy decisions are now planned and evaluated on the basis of data originating from the Research Data Centers. Germany has gone from a position at the bottom of Europe's league with regard to the use of individual data produced by empirical research with public funding, to a role as an innovative provider of new ideas, such as providing access to individual data for teaching purposes and linked employer-employee datasets.

In 2007, the Research Data Centers, in conjunction with the German Data Forum (RatSWD), developed criteria specifically focused on the design of Research Data Centers in Germany.[2] These criteria are based on the experiences of the four Research Data Centers mentioned above, which have now all been positively evaluated according to the regulations of the Leibniz Association (WGL, *Leibniz Gemeinschaft*). The criteria catalogue is designed as a guideline for other data producers planning to set up a Research Data Center.

Section 2 of this report presents the key criteria for a common working basis for Research Data Centers. Section 3 consists of more detailed descriptions of the four existing Research Data Centers as they are today. These include the respective data provided alongside further services and usage intensity. The article closes with an outlook over future developments.

2. The RatSWD criteria for Research Data Centers

Research Data Centers are institutions with the main purpose of providing simple, transparent, and high-quality access to microdata suitable for statistical analysis, while maintaining data protection and data security. Moreover, the Research Data Centers are intended to contribute to improving cooperation between the data users from the scientific community and the respective data producers. The Research Data Centers are thus an interface between the data producers' supply of data and the demand for these data from the research side. Strictly observing data protection regulations, they enable the following individual data access:

- anonymous microdata files
- controlled remote data access
- workplaces for guest researchers in the Research Data Centers

In order to provide these central services, the four publicly funded Research Data Centers have developed the following basic characteristics as criteria, in conjunction with the German Data Forum (RatSWD):

---

2 http://www.ratswd.de/download/publikationen_rat/RatSWD_FDZKriterien.PDF

(1) The data made available to the scientific community arise for statistical purposes as part of public administration processes, research, and evaluation, and are produced using public funding.

(2) Access to the data is subject to the legal provisions of data protection and data security in the specific area. The task of the Research Data Centers is to provide easier access through specific regulations.

(3) Access to microdata is subject to legal regulations guaranteeing equal treatment of data users. Correspondingly, the Research Data Centers ensure transparent and standardized access regulations. This also includes the regulation that no application for use shall be privileged or disadvantaged on grounds of its content. The Research Data Centers do not undertake any evaluation of the content of the research projects applying for access, but merely check for data protection or contractual permissibility. Should there be contractual or legal restrictions on the analysis of the data, these shall be published simultaneously with the provision of the data. Evaluations that give no cause for concern on grounds of data protection (i.e., are contractually permissible) may be published independently and autonomously by the users.

(4) As well as providing access possibilities, the Research Data Centers also produce data products for easy analysis and comprehensive data documentation. Moreover, information is provided via the available data and via the Research Data Centers in standardized form through websites, data, and method reports, as well as through individual consulting. The Research Data Centers' tasks also include organizing and participating in academic events in order to present the available data material, and presenting the available data and access to potentially interested parties (particularly non-university research institutes, specialized colleges of higher education, and universities). The Research Data Centers actively participate in academic discussion on the potential for analysis of existing data and in dialogues on use and development possibilities of the data infrastructure for scientific purposes.

(5) A specific amount of research must take place within the Research Data Centers. Practical research is essential to become familiar with the data and the latest methodological and content-related discussions, and thus to be able to provide users with adequate advice and instructions. The work within the Research Data Centers must not be restricted to service activities, as this would ultimately be equivalent to an exit from the scientific stage. Scientific research within the Research Data Centers enables access to further skills and qualifications and participation in scientific events, and also the publication of own work in the relevant journals.

(6) Research within the Research Data Centers is not coupled with exclusive access for the data producers. The anonymous microdata is made available simultaneously to all researchers, at least via controlled remote data access or at workplaces for guest researchers.

3. The four publicly funded Research Data Centers

From 1999 to 2001, the KVI report developed proposals for improving the data infrastructure between the scientific and statistics communities, on behalf of the BMBF. One of the commission's central recommendations was to set up Research Data Centers. There are currently four Research Data Centers in Germany that were recommended by the German Data Forum (RatSWD), which are described in detail below.

3.1 Research Data Center of the Federal Statistical Office

The Research Data Center of the Federal Statistical Office was the first center to be set up on the recommendation of the 2001 KVI report, and it was given a positive evaluation in summer 2004. The core activity of the Research Data Center of the Federal Statistical Office, processing user requests, is now funded completely from original in-house sources. The Research Data Center also receives funding from the BMBF within scientific projects, for example for rendering panel data on economic statistics anonymous.[3]

The most important official statistics are now available in the Research Data Centers of the Federal Statistical Office and the Statistical Offices of the German *Länder*, as a joint service. Access to the data, which is growing in volume, is possible in four forms, differing with regard to the type of anonymity and form of data provided. Absolutely anonymous Public Use Files (PUFs) and factually anonymous Scientific Use Files (SUFs) can be used outside of the statistical offices (off-site use). Data rendered less anonymous and containing less reduced information are made available at workplaces for guest researchers on the premises. Moreover, researchers may also work with formally anonymous individual data using their own syntax via controlled remote data access (on-site use).[4]

The most intensively used form of data are the SUFs. Approximately 710 standardized SUFs have been provided for 328 different projects since mid-2004, when the Research Data Center of the Federal Statistical Office was

---

3 For the problem of permanent establishment see Zwick (2006).
4 www.forschungsdatenzentrum.de

first evaluated. The most frequently used dataset is the Microcensus. Overall, however, demand for standardized SUFs is stagnating, whereas demand for individual datasets at the workplaces for guest researchers and via controlled remote data access is increasing. Controlled remote data access is now widely popular as a form of access available to researchers abroad and to commercial users. Thirty researchers have visited the Research Data Center since 2004, with controlled remote data access used in 55 projects. Eighteen further projects are currently taking place using the two forms of access.

The *Research Data Center Working Papers* series was initiated to present the wide use of the official microdata. To date, nearly thirty such working papers have been published in this series, available at the website. The Federal Statistical Office's book series, *Statistik und Wissenschaft*, also includes various volumes of articles reflecting the dialogue between the Research Data Center and the scientific community.

The Research Data Center of the Federal Statistical Office developed the series *CAMPUS-Files* especially for teaching at the university level. These files consist of absolutely anonymous microdata, allowing students to learn methodological skills and analyze sociological and economic issues. These data are available free of charge via the website of the Research Data Centers of the German Federal Statistical Office and the Statistical Offices of the German *Länder*.[5]

The Research Data Center's work focuses on further development of the access routes, anonymity methodology, and conceptional development. In order to strengthen its anchoring in the scientific community, the Research Data Center of the Federal Statistical Office is strongly present at relevant conferences (e.g., *Statistische Woche, Jahrestagung des Vereins für Socialpolitik, Kongress der DGS*). It also offers its staff the possibility to gain PhDs using the Research Data Center's resources, via two-thirds contracts.

3.2 Research Data Center of the Statistical Offices of the German Länder

The Research Data Center of the Statistical Offices of the German *Länder* took up work on 1 April 2002. Up to 2003, it focused on solving basic issues concerning funding, data access, and conditions for use. The Research Data Center has been funded by the BMBF since the beginning of 2004. Its core task is to provide easier access to the individual data of the Statistical Offices of the German *Länder*, for scientific research. In order to realize this task, a regional infrastructure was set up, enabling nationwide access to official microdata for the scientific community in sixteen regional locations. Moreover, a centralized data administration was established, which simplifies in-

---

5 For further information, see Zwick (2007).

terregional use of the microdata of the Statistical Offices of the German *Länder*.[6]

The Research Data Center of the Statistical Offices of the German *Länder* was evaluated in October 2006. The assessors gave a positive evaluation of the services and recommended extending the project funding and establishing the facility on a permanent basis. The project's term was thus extended up to the end of 2009 on the basis of a new funding application. The second project phase focuses on integrating economic and environmental statistical data, implementing knowledge transfer at university level, and improving ease of access to the regional locations by setting up branch offices at universities and other scientific institutions. The Research Data Center is also working towards establishing its services on a permanent basis.

The activities of the Research Data Center of the Statistical Offices of the German *Länder* have led to a broad range of microdata on various subjects for the scientific community. A total of over sixty statistics are currently available for use in academic research projects from the fields of social issues, the economy, agriculture, the environment, justice administration, and taxation. The range of data is continually extended to meet research needs. Demand in the field of economic and environmental statistical data has shown a particularly dynamic development. The demand for integrated datasets based on different statistics and survey years presents particular challenges. There are various access routes available for users.[7]

Use of the Research Data Center has increased steadily since 2004, with the number of applications for use multiplying fourfold by 2007 – from 31 to 133. On average, each application requires access to six different datasets, so that more than 2721 datasets have been provided for research purposes to date. Due to the decentralized infrastructure, most data use takes place at the workplaces for guest researchers or via controlled remote data access, and is thus particularly labor-intensive for the Research Data Center.

The previous work of the Research Data Center of the Statistical Offices of the German *Länder* has shown that the official statistical microdata are an important basis for innovative scientific analyses[8] and the users are very satisfied with the new range of services. The Research Data Center is therefore working very hard to establish its services on a permanent basis.

---

6   For further information, see Zühlke et al. (2004), and Zühlke et al. (2007).
7   www.forschungsdatenzentrum.de
8   Selective datasets are discussed in detail by Kaiser and Wagner (2008), Wirth and Müller (2006), Zühlke and Christians (2006).

3.3 The Research Data Center of the Federal Employment Agency at the Institute for Employment Research

The Research Data Center of the Federal Employment Agency at the Institute for Employment Research[9] was founded in December 2003, as there had been no systematic access to social data up until this point. Following a positive evaluation by the German Data Forum (RatSWD) in April 2006, the Research Data Center was permanently established as an independent Research Data Center of the BA at the IAB.[10] An evaluation by the German Council of Science and Humanities in 2007 confirmed that the Research Data Center was an internationally unique institution:

"The Research Data Center (focusing on methods and data access) is an internationally visible, indispensable service institution, unique in Europe and a prime example to other institutions, possessing large datasets of scientific importance" (Report of the German Council of Science and Humanities for the IAB 2007: 55).

The Research Data Center prepares individual datasets developed in the sphere of social security and in employment research and makes them available for research purposes – primarily for external researchers. Through documentation and working tools such as the "FDZ Datenreport" and "FDZ Methodenreport" that are available online[11] and its workshops and user conferences, the Research Data Center makes it easier for external researchers to work with datasets.

The Research Data Center micro datasets include the IAB Establishment Panel, die IAB Employment Sample (IABS), the BA Employment Panel (BAP), the Integrated Employment Biographies Sample (IEBS), the Establishment History Panel (BHP), the Linked-Employer-Employee Data for the IAB (LIAB), the cross-sectional survey "Life Situation and Social Security 2005" (LSS 2005) and the first wave of the panel study "Labor Market and Social Security'" (IAB-PASS, *Panel "Arbeitsmarkt und soziale Sicherung"*).[12]

Before the Research Data Center data can be used for the first time, researchers must submit a request to use the data. Following approval by the Federal Ministry for Labor and Social Affairs (BMAS, *Bundesministerium für Arbeit und Soziales*), a use agreement is concluded between the scientist and the IAB. The number of approvals for dataset and data access has increased continuously from 81 (in 2005) to 116 (in 2007). It should also be

---

9   More information on the Research Data Center is available in Kohlmann (2005), Bender et al. (2008).
10 The Research Data Center has basic financing for a Head (exempt from collectively agreed terms), five positions for (senior) researchers, and three for non-academic staff and student assistants (40 hours per week).
11 http://fdz.iab.de
12 There is an English documentation on the website for nearly every dataset and a publication in the data watch section of *Schmollers Jahrbuch*.

noted that the projects normally last for over a year and thus projects from 2005 and 2006 were also continued in 2007. Two other very important parameters are the number of cases of remote data access and the number of guest stays (normally lasting several days) at the Research Data Center for on-site use. Both figures have approximately quadrupled or almost quintupled as compared to 2005 (on-site use rising from 22 in 2005 to 133 in 2007; remote data access from 359 in 2005 to 1328 in 2007). Up to 2007, researchers had published, for example, 246 articles or papers on the basis of the IAB Employment Sample, 82 using the LIAB and 1,999 using the IAB Establishment Panel, within and outside the IAB.[13]

The Research Data Center serves not only the national but also the international market. One important step towards internationalization in 2007 was the online publication of web pages in English and the translation of nearly every data documentation. The use of the Research Data Center by researchers abroad has thus increased.[14] In 2006, the Research Data Center had 16 contractual partners based abroad, including two who visited as guest researchers. In 2007, the Research Data Center counted 34 contractual partners based abroad and welcomed nine guest researchers from abroad. Guest researchers from abroad can access Research Data Center data relatively easily. It is no more difficult for them than for researchers from Germany. Since the cost of a stay in Nuremberg for visitors from abroad is higher than it is for locals, the Research Data Center established a grant to aid guest researchers in 2007. In 2007, four visitors made use of this service. The establishment of this grant was evaluated positively by the German Council of Science and Humanities in its report.

The Research Data Center is now networking more strongly with Research Data Centers in other countries. This ensures that new and innovative developments can be applied more quickly in the Research Data Center. These include, for example, anonymization of datasets through multiple imputation (Drechsler et al. 2008) or metadata databases.

For the quality of the data supply and the advisory service it is crucial, however, for Research Data Center employees to carry out empirical research themselves. The Research Data Center's research activities are well documented by its publication record. In both 2006 and 2007, Research Data Center employees published a total of ten research articles. These also include two publications in top scientific journals listed in the Social Sciences Citation Index (SSCI). This picture has been completed by numerous lectures about their research activities given in Germany and abroad.

---

13 The figures refer to all publications with the relevant dataset since the dataset first became available in the IAB. Some of the datasets were already available within and outside the IAB long before the existence of the Research Data Center.
14 The categorization of researchers abroad refers to their place of work, not to their nationality.

In addition, the Research Data Center of the BA participates in a number of externally funded projects, co-financed by the German Research Foundation (DFG, *Deutsche Forschungsgemeinschaft*), the BMBF or the Leibniz Association and carried out in cooperation with universities, research institutes and, of course, with the other Research Data Centers. Each of these externally funded projects also included funding for personnel.

3.4 Research Data Center of the German Pension Insurance

The Research Data Center of the German Pension Insurance was founded in January 2004 and is now based in Berlin and Würzburg. During its initial setup phase – from 2004 to 2008 – the Research Data Center was funded by the BMBF.

The core task of the Research Data Center is to recover the data treasures of the German Pension Insurance (Rehfeld and Mika 2006). Alongside the microdata itself, the Research Data Center provides methodological information and commentaries intended to help simplify analyses using data from the German Federal Pension Insurance.[15]

The Research Data Center of the German Pension Insurance has realized the projects it agreed on with the funding institution (BMBF). Firstly, it has established an infrastructure within the Research Data Center, and secondly, it has taken the Research Data Center from a pilot project to a permanent institution. Thirdly, the range of data and the use possibilities have been extended considerably. In both Berlin and Würzburg, the micro datasets of the German Pension Insurance are processed in cooperation with the respective departments and the data users, to make them available to researchers particularly in the form of user-friendly Scientific Use Files.

Figure 1 gives an overview of cross-sectional and longitudinal microdata from the German Pension Insurance in the fields of retirement, insured persons and rehabilitation, with the corresponding names of the microdata. This data, highlighted in grey, is generated from the Research Data Center as anonymous SUFs, which scientists working in research units may access free of charge, the only requirement being a signed contract with the Research Data Center.

The statistics of the German Pension Insurance can be divided into datasets that focus on biographical information in combination with retirement and insurance and in a special dataset for rehabilitation. The datasets listed with a reference period of one day mean that this day represents the monitoring date in a specific year. Some statistics have both daily and annual reference periods.

---

15 Current information on the range of data, access routes, workshops and publications is available at www.RDC-rv.de.

The data range offered by the Research Data Center now also includes the SUFs of the two longitudinal datasets Completed Insured Life Courses 2005 (VVL, *Vollendete Versichertenleben*) and the insurance account sample 2005 (VSKT, *Versicherungskontenstichprobe*) (Himmelreicher and Stegmann 2008). Please note that it is particularly complicated to prepare the longitudinal data as SUFs, since many modifications have to be undertaken in order to render the longitudinal information anonymous (Stegmann and Himmelreicher 2008).

Figure 1: Micro datasets of the German Pension Insurance

Topic of the micro dataset				
Retirement			Insurance	Rehabilitation
Retirement inflow	Retirement stock	Retirement cash-stock		
Cross-sectional data				
Pension awarded within a certain period/ cessation of pension payment (reference period 31.12.)	**Pension payments** (reference period 31.12.)	**Pensioners with one or more pension payments** (reference period 30.06.)	**Insured persons** (reference period 31.12. and within reference year)	**Medical and occupational rehabilitation** (reference period 31.12. and within reference year)
Longitudinal data				
Completed Insured Life Courses (reference period 31.12.)			**Insurance account sample** (reference period 31.12.)	**Longitudinal dataset for rehabilitation**

☐ Dataset available as SUF via Research Data Center of the German Pension Insurance (February 2010)

Source: Following Himmereicher and Radl (2006).

The extended data range provided free of charge by the Research Data Center, which now also includes longitudinal data, represents a considerable improvement in usage possibilities for research. As the Research Data Center data have now been used in numerous scientific disciplines by more than two hundred and fifty researchers and an increasing number of presentations and publications are being written on the basis of the data, the Research Data Center is becoming increasingly well known in the scientific community. However, once the BMBF funding expires at the end of 2008, it will become difficult to provide the familiar standard of services to an increasing number of researchers with fewer staff.

The services of the Research Data Center and its plans for the future clearly show that the Research Data Center has recovered the large data treasures of the German Pension Insurance for research use. The newly created institution is thus on the right path. It has considerably extended possibilities for scientific analysis, while deepening the empirical knowledge in the fields of pensions, demography, and above all employment biographies.

4. Outlook

At the end of the phases funded by the BMBF, the Research Data Centers are facing new challenges. The Research Data Center of the Federal Employment Agency at the Institute for Employment Research has meanwhile been integrated into the Federal Employment Agency with all capacities from the funding phase, and now carries out its work as an organizational unit of the Federal Employment Agency at the Institute for Employment Research. The Research Data Center of the German Pension Insurance has been established as a permanent institution in the German Pension Insurance, equipped with basic funding to meet the key infrastructural needs. Additional third-party funding has to be obtained for research projects. For the Research Data Centers of the Federal Statistical Office and the Statistical Offices of the German *Länder*, possibilities for establishment on a permanent basis are still under discussion.

The Research Data Centers coordinate basic issues of data access for research purposes among each other, and work in close conjunction on various projects to extend the range of data available and the access routes. Further development of the data range will focus on integrating statistics in the near future. The projects Official Firm Data for Germany (AFiD, *Amtliche Firmendaten für Deutschland*) and Combined Firm Data for Germany (KombiFiD, *Kombinierte Firmendaten für Deutschland*) will extend the range of data in two directions: AFiD will bring together economic and environmental data from the Statistical Offices by means of the German Company Register (URS, *Unternehmensregister*) on the microdata level. KombiFiD goes one step further, uniting company data across the boundaries of the individual data producers as part of a feasibility study on a joint dataset. In addition, processes for statistical matching of survey and process-produced data are being tested, for example, between longitudinal data of the Research Data Center of the German Pension Insurance and the DIW's Socio-Economic Panel (SOEP, *Sozio-oekonomisches Panel*) (Rasner et al. 2007) or the IAB's longitudinal data or in several of the IAB's own projects (Bender et al. 2009, to quote one example).

In the field of data access, the Research Data Centers are looking into the procedure of remote data access. This access route has already been put to successful use in other European countries. The researchers are provided with direct access to the microdata at a specially set-up workplace in their own institutions via a secure internet connection. The Research Data Centers are currently checking the requirements for introducing this access route in Germany.

References:

Bender, S./Hartmann, B. and Herrlinger, D. (2008): FDZ Annual Report 2007. RDC Methodenreport 02/2008. Nuremberg.
Bender, S./Fertig, M./Görlitz, K./Huber, M. and Schmucker, A. (2009): WeLL - unique linked employer-employee data on further training in Germany. In: Schmollers Jahrbuch 129 (4), 637-643.
Drechsler, J./Dundler, A./Bender, S./Rässler, S. and Zwick, T. (2008): A new approach for disclosure control in the IAB Establishment Panel. Multiple imputation for a better data access. Advances in Statistical Analysis 92, 439-458
Kohlmann, A. (2005): The Research Data Center of the Federal Employment Service in the Institute for Employment Research. Schmollers Jahrbuch 125 (3), 437-447.
Kommission zur Verbesserung der informationellen Infrastruktur zwischen Wissenschaft und Statistik (KVI) (Ed.) (2001): Wege zu einer besseren informationellen Infrastruktur. Baden-Baden.
Himmelreicher, R. and Radl, J. (2006): Zusammenfassung und Ausblick auf die weitere Entwicklung des FDZ-RV. DRV-Schriften 55/2005, 281-286.
Himmelreicher, R. and Stegmann, M. (2008): New possibilities for socio-economic research through longitudinal data from the Research Data Center of the German Federal Pension Insurance (RDC-RV). Schmollers Jahrbuch 128 (4).
Kaiser, U. and Wagner, J. (2008): Neue Möglichkeiten zur Nutzung vertraulicher amtlicher Personen- und Firmendaten. Perspektiven der Wirtschaftspolitik 9, 329-349.
Rasner, A./Himmelreicher, R./Grabka, M. and Frick, J. (2007): Best of Both Worlds: Preparatory Steps in Matching Survey Data with Administrative Pension Records – The Case of the German Socio-Economic Panel and the Scientific Use File Completed Insurance Biographies 2004. SOEP Data Documentation.
Rehfeld, U. and Mika, T. (2006): The Research Data Center of the German Statutory Pension Insurance (RDC-RV). Schmollers Jahrbuch 126 (1), 122-127.
Schneider, H. and Wolf, C. (2008): Die Datenservicezentren als Teil der informationellen Infrastruktur. In: Rolf, G./Zwick, M. and Wagner, G. (Eds.): Fortschritte der informationellen Infrastruktur in Deutschland. Baden-Baden.
Stegmann, M. and Himmelreicher, R. (2008): Aufbereitung der prozessproduzierten Daten der gesetzlichen Rentenversicherung im FDZ-RV. DRV-Schriften 79, 7-13.
Wirth, H. and Müller, W. (2006): Mikrodaten der amtlichen Statistik – Ihr Potenzial in der empirischen Sozialforschung. In: Dieckmann, A. (Ed.): Methoden der empirischen Sozialforschung. Wiesbaden.
Zühlke, S./Zwick, M./Scharnhorst, S. and Wende, T. (2004): The research data Centers of the Federal Statistical Office and the statistical offices of the *Länder*. Schmollers Jahrbuch 124 (4), 567ff.
Zühlke, S. and Christians, H. (2006): Datenangebot und Datenzugang im Forschungsdatenzentrum der Statistischen Landesämter. In: Landesamt für Datenverarbeitung und Statistik (Ed.): Statistische Analysen und Studien Nordrhein-Westfalen. Düsseldorf.

Zühlke, S./Christians, H. and Cramer, K. (2007): Das Forschungsdatenzentrum der Statistischen Landesämter – eine Serviceeinrichtung für die Wissenschaft. Wirtschafts- und sozialstatistisches Archiv 1 (3-4), 169-178.

Zwick, M. (2006): Forschungsdatenzentren – Nutzen und Kosten einer informationellen Infrastruktur für Wissenschaft, Politik und Datenproduzenten. Wirtschaft und Statistik 12, 1233-1240.

Zwick, M. (2007): CAMPUS-Files, Free Public Use Files for Teaching Purposes. Schmollers Jahrbuch 127 (4), 655-668.

3. Publicly Financed Survey Data: Access and Documentation

Wolfgang Jagodzinski and Christof Wolf

Contact:

Christof Wolf
GESIS – Leibniz Institute for the Social Sciences
B2, 1
68159 Mannheim
Germany
e-mail: Christof.Wolf[at]gesis.org

Abstract

This paper will address the issue of access to and documentation of survey data financed through public funds. We distinguish between four types of publicly financed survey data: (1) academic survey data from the national or international research infrastructures, (2) data from projects funded by the German Research Foundation (DFG, *Deutsche Forschungsgemeinschaft*) or similarly funded projects, (3) survey data collected in research projects funded by the federal government and the German states, or *Länder* (*Ressortforschung*), and (4) population and household surveys from national and international statistical agencies. For each of these types of data we describe the current situation and present recommendations for future development.

Keywords: survey data, data access, data documentation, data archive

1. Introduction: Four data types

Our recommendations refer to four data types: (1) academic survey data from the national (such as ALLBUS[1] or SOEP[2]) or international (such as ESS,[3] SHARE,[4] ISSP,[5] European Values Study, or CSES[6]) research infrastructure; (2) data from the German Research Foundation (DFG, *Deutsche Forschungsgemeinschaft*) projects or similarly funded projects; (3) data collected in research projects funded by the federal government and the German states (*Ressortforschung*); (4) population and household surveys from national and international statistical agencies. We will briefly describe the current situation and make suggestions for the future development of each of these data types. We do not attempt to give a comprehensive overview of all existing survey programs, however. We also do not address problems concerning register data.

---

1 German General Social Survey (ALLBUS, *Allgemeine Bevölkerungsumfrage der Sozialwissenschaften*).
2 German Socio-Economic Panel (SOEP, Sozio-oekonomisches Panel).
3 European Social Survey.
4 Suvey on Health, Ageing and Retirement in Europe.
5 International Social Survey Programme.
6 Comparative Study of Electoral Systems.

2. National and international research infrastructure

2.1 Present situation

Surveys conducted in connection with academic research are part of the research infrastructure (national and international survey programs) and provide the main source of comparative studies either in a longitudinal or in a comparative perspective. In Germany, national programs such as ALLBUS and SOEP are seen as part of the research infrastructure for the social sciences and thus they are fully funded. With regard to international surveys the situation is more heterogeneous. As far as ISSP is concerned, the costs for the German survey as well as a large share of the costs for processing the international dataset are seen as investments in the international research infrastructure and publicly funded. The European Values Study has recently reached a similar status. The last wave has been publicly funded and the costs of data processing are divided between Tilburg and the GESIS[7] Data Archive.[8]

Panel studies like SOEP are optimally suited for analyzing individual change over time. They are not only expensive, however, but also require a highly developed infrastructure for data collection and data processing. It is therefore difficult to organize multi-wave panel studies on an international level. Apart from very few exceptions, like SHARE, the large international survey programs are therefore still cross-sectional. In the meantime, most of them have built up sequences of cross-sections that permit cohort studies for the analysis of change. Standards for international surveys have recently been published by the Institute for Social Research in Michigan.[9]

There is a high demand for these studies. This is evident from the large number of data downloads and distributed copies as well as from the numerous citations of the datasets in publications. Almost all survey programs publish their own bibliography.

This demand justifies a larger investment in data documentation and data improvement. There has been some progress made in the standardization and harmonization of data. The ESS has set new standards for the documentation of international studies. Several programs have started to add contextual data to the microdata files.

Both the continuous growth and improvement of the database as well as the high demand for data in the scientific community guarantee the application of the most recent technologies in data processing and therefore an almost optimal access to the data. Although some of these programs are based on a mixed funding they largely follow the recommendations of the

---

7   Leibniz Institute for the Social Sciences (GESIS, Leibniz-Institut für Sozialwissenschaften).
8   http://www.europeanvaluesstudy.eu
9   http://ccsg.isr.umich.edu

OECD for fully publicly funded research data.[10] In a few survey programs the time point of general data access is still a point of discussion. As long as primary investigators are also responsible for the national funding they sometimes postpone the open data access in time. However, the situation has improved considerably over the last years. This problem would immediately be solved on a contractual basis if an international infrastructure for academic survey programs could be established. To our knowledge ESS and SHARE are so far the only science driven survey programs which receive the funding of the overhead costs from an international organization.

The other restrictions come from data protection laws. Datasets which are offered for free download on the internet therefore usually do not include fine-graded regional or occupational variables. A reduced version of the ALLBUS (ALLBUScompact) is freely accessible. Larger versions of the ALLBUS and of international social surveys like ESS, the European Values Study, or ISSP can be downloaded for free for scientific use. If data protection requires a special contract between the researcher and the user, data are distributed individually. The scientist has only to pay handling charges for data delivery.

2.2 Recommendations

It would be highly desirable if the data quality of other international survey programs could reach the quality of the ESS in the future. This would require, however, larger budgets for the international research infrastructure. The ESS has also set new standards for the documentation of sampling and data collection which should be gradually adopted by other programs. Furthermore, the translation process as well as its documentation can be improved. Until recently the translation of international surveys was under the responsibility of the national teams and largely terra incognita for secondary analysts. They could only get the final questionnaire which often did not even include interviewer instructions. Recent developments attempt to reach a higher degree of standardization and transparency.[11]

Other activities would require the institutionalization of a larger international infrastructure that would not only advise researchers in data collection and data processing but also coordinate different survey programs. In particular, the input standardization of socio-demographic variables should be achieved. It would also be desirable to improve comparability by includ-

---

10   http://www.oecd.org/dataoecd/9/61/38500813.pdf
11   Thus, the European Values Study 2008 has recently used the web-based translation module WEBTRANS developed by Gallup Europe for reaching a centralized control of the translation process, better comparability of the translations in different languages, more uniformity of the final questionnaires, and better documentation for comparative analyses.

ing sub-modules of items from time to time into different research programs or by integrating different surveys into a common database.

3. DFG projects and other scientific projects

3.1 Present situation

While the data access to publicly funded national and international survey programs that belong to the research infrastructure is fairly satisfying, the access to data of singular scientific projects funded by the DFG and other comparable foundations still leaves quite a lot to be desired.[12] GESIS has recently attempted to identify DFG projects from the years 2003 to 2005 that are likely to meet the acquisition criteria of the GESIS Data Archive.[13] Due to the limitations of the project documentation, however, it cannot be decided in all instances whether the project meets the criteria or not. What can be safely said, however, is that more than half of the studies which almost certainly meet the criteria are not sent to the Data Archive.[14]

Basic rules for scientific conduct require that data have to be made accessible for replication. However, they do not require delivering the data to an archive. On the one hand, in light of the cost of archival work, it is debatable whether all project data should be deposited in an archive. On the other hand, there are serious doubts whether empirical data – even if they have been stored on floppy disks or tapes years ago – still are accessible. The serious limitations of meta-analyses clearly show that access to the original data is always preferable over confining oneself to published results of statistical analysis.

3.2 Recommendations

In our view, modern information technologies allow for a substantial improvement of the present situation in two directions.

First of all, we propose the definition of a minimum standard of data accessibility that must be guaranteed by all publicly funded scientific projects: all data must be stored in a digital repository provided by the social science infrastructure. The researcher does not store the data on a disk in the

---

12 For a detailed description of the perspective of the German Research Foundation on the development of social science infrastructure, see Nießen and Kämper in this volume.
13 In principle, the GESIS Data Archive only accepts representative studies of populations or larger subpopulations which are relevant to social science research. It does not acquire experimental studies, for instance.
14 The results can be obtained from the authors.

university but in a domain that is maintained by a publicly funded institution. The obvious advantage of this solution for the researchers is that they do not have to concern themselves with backups and data transfer onto new computers. All these tasks are in the responsibility of the institution hosting the data repository. Special agreements between data producers and the hosting institution will address all questions concerning data ownership, data access, and data distribution. The data producer is free to choose between different options; that is, the rights to the data do not automatically go to the data host. The advantages offered by such a system would be an incentive for storing the data in a central place.

Second, we should distinguish at least between two different types of project data: those which are only relevant to a small group of scientists and data of broader interest. For the former type of data, a mode of *self-archiving* should be established. This is based on a clear division of labor: the data are stored in a central location such as the GESIS Data Archive in Cologne, but data processing and documentation are done by the primary investigator. The social science infrastructure should provide the researchers with attractive self-storage tools which help them to document and preserve the data. These tools could allow for lower and higher standards of data processing. They could also enable the researcher to build up both simple and more sophisticated databases as well as to combine data and publications. However, the project has the main responsibility for data deposition and the Data Archive should not be involved to a larger extent in this process.

Clearly, a number of questions have to be clarified before a mode of self-archiving can be established. What exactly is the division of labor between the social science infrastructure and the primary investigators? Who is responsible for the migration of data to new computer systems? Who protects the primary investigator against the violation of laws, in particular laws of data confidentiality? What kind of facilitating tools for data processing should be developed?

Self-archiving and self-documentation are not sufficient for datasets that will be of probable interest for a larger group of researchers. These data should not only be stored in the data archive but should be processed in accordance with the most advanced standards of data processing and documentation. It is advisable to consult the archive in the early stages of the project, a standard practice in all important international survey programs. The involvement of an archive requires additional resources. These resources should be included in the budget calculations of the research project from the very beginning.

One immediate objection that will be made to our proposal is that the distinction between data of restricted and broader interest is artificial and vague. For example, hasn't it sometimes turned out that a study like the election study of 1953[15] – almost forgotten in the 1950s – became extremely important for the analysis of long-term change in later decades? Yes, this happens from time to time. We would counter, however, that reviewers of project applications have good judgment and can determine whether a dataset has the potential for secondary analyses or not. Collaborative research units, for instance, will usually produce datasets that are highly salient for the scientific community at large. Moreover, if half a million or more Euros are granted for a representative national sample, it is often at least implicitly assumed that these data will not be used exclusively by the primary investigators. Details of this procedure have of course to be further elaborated.

We recommend a pilot project that will further clarify the terms and modalities of assisted self-archiving within a central data repository and professional data archiving. Such a project should also come up with proposals for self-archiving tools.

4. Research projects funded by federal or state governments (*Ressortforschung*)

4.1 Present situation

Research in this category is largely carried out by Governmental Research Agencies (GRA) and in smaller part by external researchers. GRAs have recently been evaluated by a research committee of the German Council of Science and Humanities (*Wissenschaftsrat*).[16] Besides containing evaluation reports on twenty-eight institutes, this committee has published a comprehensive report, "Recommendations on the Role and Future Development of Governmental Research Agencies with R&D Activities," in May 2006, January 2007, May 2008, and November 2008.[17] Further reports and additional recommendations were published in 2009. As far as the service of research and development infrastructure (R&D infrastructure) and data access is concerned, the recommendations from 1 April 2007 on page 11 state:

"All Federal Ministries and their agencies should avoid installing redundant and expensive R&D infrastructure. The R&D infrastructure should instead be subject to use by scientists from all kinds of R&D establishments. Such joint use requires that information on the infrastructure be readily available. Therefore, within the next two years, the BMBF in cooperation with all other federal ministries should compile a compendium listing all R&D infrastructure in GRAs (especially instruments and data). This compendium should be made available to all universities and research establishments in Germany. The Govern-

---

15 ZA-Study number S0145, so called Reigrotzki-Study.
16 http://www.wissenschaftsrat.de/engl_rechts.htm#EVAL
17 http://www.wissenschaftsrat.de/texte/7854-07.pdf

ment is also advised to release scientific use files to research data centers, thus granting external scientists access to specific data collections. If such data centers cannot be created, other instruments such as work places for visiting scientists should be used to facilitate access."[18]

The establishment of Research Data Centers at a subset of the GRAs will improve the accessibility of data to smaller or larger extents. Some institutes – such as the German Youth Institute (DJI, *Deutsches Jugendnstitut*) – already routinely deliver their data to the GESIS data archive. In these cases, the scientific community will benefit from new Research Data Centers mainly by having access to single and cumulative data files that so far have not been made accessible. In other instances, however, the establishment of Research Data Centers will lead to more dramatic improvements.

The research committee of the *Wissenschaftsrat* so far has focused primarily on the research of GRAs; however, quite a number of its recommendations either directly address or also apply to research projects carried out by external researchers. Therefore, we do not need to go into additional detail here but can confine ourselves to two minor issues which to our knowledge have not been systematically addressed.

The first is the Scientific Use File (SUF). It is expensive to produce and requires technical and methodological skills that often are not available at a GRA. It is more difficult to provide SUFs to the scientific community continuously than it is to establish one or two work places for visiting scientists. As a result, SUFs might actually be set at a low priority in the emerging Research Data Centers. At the same time, work places for scientists are not substitutes for SUFs, because the latter allow for more flexible and less time-consuming data analysis. SUFs therefore act as a much lower barrier against secondary analysis than workplaces in remote institutions. The report of the *Wissenschaftsrat* neither lists potential SUFs nor defines selection criteria; it does not discuss the cost-effective production of SUFs. It is particularly ambiguous in the latter respect: while the second-to-last sentence in the upper quotation can be interpreted as an indication that externally produced SUFs should be released to the new Research Data Centers, the German version by contrast defines the production of SUFs as a task of the Research Data Centers themselves.[19]

---

18 http://www.wissenschaftsrat.de/texte/7854-07.pdf
19 "Im Rahmen von Forschungsdatenzentren sollen 'scientific use files' erstellt werden, die externen Wissenschaftlern die Auswertung ausgewählter Datensammlungen erleichtern sollen. Wo 'scientific use files' nicht möglich sind, sollen die Forschungsdatenzentren mit Hilfe anderer Instrumente (z.B. Fernrechnen und Gastwissenschaftlerarbeitsplätze) Daten auf geeignete Weise zugänglich machen." (Within the framework of these Research Data Centers, "scientific use files" are to be created, so as to make it easier for external researchers to evaluate selected data collections. Where these files are unable to be provided, Research Data Centers are to make data appropriately accessible with the assistance of

The second problem concerns the release of data from projects which are funded by the federal or state governments. While some government departments, in particular the Federal Ministry of Family Affairs, Senior Citizens, Women and Youth (BMFSFJ, *Bundesministerium für Familie, Senioren, Frauen und Jugend*),[20] follow a fairly open policy, others are more restrictive. There is no general regulation so far.[21] If research projects of this type become visible in the media, the GESIS Data Archive directly approaches the primary investigators. Sometimes these attempts are successful and the data are acquired by the archive. Quite a few datasets, however, never become accessible for the scientific community.

4.2 Recommendations

Our recommendations focus on the two topics mentioned above. As far as SUFs are concerned, we share the preference of the *Wissenschaftsrat*. In order to secure an optimal number of SUFs, experts should first ascertain the demand for SUFs and define priorities. If the SUF is a sufficiently high priority, the most cost-efficient mode of file production has to be determined. SUFs can be produced by the Research Data Center alone, in close cooperation with an experienced external organization, or by an external organization alone. It can be distributed by the Research Data Center, by the external organization, or by both. The "Recommendations" of the *Wissenschaftsrat* and its English translation suggest two different modes of SUF production: while the German text aims at the creation of SUFs by a Research Data Center of the GRA, the English translation alludes to SUF production by the external agency. Both interpretations are correct insofar as cost-efficient solutions will differ from GRA to GRA. Presumably there is no general solution to the problem, but in any case it is highly desirable that the cost-efficient production of SUFs in this area is tackled as quickly as possible.

The question of data release should be investigated more systematically by the committee of the *Wissenschaftsrat*. In our view, the previous considerations should hold: if data from *Ressortforschung* are in the interest of the scientific community, they should in general be accessible. Data confidentiality regulations, often seen as an obstacle to data access, actually are rarely a reason for withholding a complete dataset. More often, they only require

---

other means, such as, for example, the allocation of visiting research positions or remote computing).

20 Negotiations between the Zentralarchiv (now: GESIS Data Archive) and the BMFSFJ have resulted in the decision that data of research projects which are funded by this government department are regularly delivered to the GESIS Data Archive at the end of the project. The datasets which the archive obtains are usually of high quality and well documented.

21 The Eurobarometers are another example of publicly funded surveys which are regularly delivered to the GESIS Data Archive.

the cutoff of some information and variables. In addition, access to sensible data may be offered in safe data centers. Free access to data for scientific purposes, in any case, should be the general rule and exceptions should be allowed only in a few, well-founded instances.

5. Household surveys from official statistics

Large-scale data collections produced under the auspices of national statistical agencies have specific strengths that make them especially interesting for social and economic research. With respect to population or household surveys, the large sample sizes and the usually very low non-response rates make these data a valuable source for economic and social-structural investigation.[22] They are regularly used for purposes of social monitoring – such as the *Datenreport* (Statistisches Bundesamt et al. 2008) – or for the construction of social indicators – as in the "Education at a Glance" (OECD 2007) or the Social Indicators Monitor SIMon.[23] However, these data are also used for a wide range of different analytical purposes, evident in the extensive bibliographies of articles based on the Scientific Use Files of the German Labor Force Survey, for example, or the German Income and Consumption Survey.

5.1 Present situation

The most important household surveys for socio-economic research from official statistics in Germany are the Microcensus, the German Income and Consumption Survey (EVS, *Einkommens- und Verbrauchsstichprobe*), and the German Time Budget Survey (*Zeitbudgeterhebung*).

The Microcensus – Germany's Labor Force Survey – is an annual random sample survey of one percent of the German population. It has been carried out in West Germany since 1957 and in reunified Germany since 1991. Integrated into the Microcensus is the German part of the European Labor Force Survey. Because participation in the Microcensus is obligatory, response rates are close to 100 percent. With over 800,000 individuals it is the largest population survey in Europe.

The EVS has been conducted every fifth year since 1963. The survey is based on a quota sample and participation is voluntary.

The Time Budget Survey is Germany's time use survey. It was conducted for the first time in 1991/92 and repeated 10 years later in 2001/2002.

---

22 Other data from official statistics include business surveys and process-produced data; these are dealt with in other chapters in this volume.
23 http://gesis-simon.de

The Time Budget Survey is a quota sample of over 12,000 individuals living in 5,400 households. The questionnaire of the survey complies with Eurostat's recommendations for time-use surveys and participation in the survey is voluntary.

In addition to these databases, microdata from the Censuses of 1970 and 1987 (West Germany) and from 1981 (East Germany) are currently available or will shortly be available for academic research.

In general, there are four different ways to access German microdata from official statistics:

- In the case of most of the surveys mentioned above, Scientific Use Files (SUFs) can be ordered from the Federal Statistical Office by academic or research institutions for the purpose of predefined scientific research purposes. Usage within these institutions is not restricted to German nationals, although each individual working with a SUF has to be registered as data user with the Statistical Office. SUFs are microdata files that have been reasonably anonymized. According to the Law on Statistics for Federal Purposes, this means that the files have been anonymized in such a way that any identification of individuals is only possible by excessive expenditures of time, costs, and personnel (Wirth 2008). This is typically achieved by providing only a subsample of the original dataset. In the case of the Microcensus, for instance, only a 70 percent sample is provided, deleting most of the regional information and collapsing categories with small frequencies (see also Müller et al. 1995).[24] For the Microcensus, a total of 21 SUFs are currently available, the earliest coming from 1973, the latest from 2006.[25] For the Income and Consumption Survey there are currently data from seven years, the first from 1962/1963, the latest from 2003. The data from the two waves of the Time Budget Survey are also available as SUFs.

- A second option for accessing data from official statistics is offered by the Research Data Centers of the Federal Statistical Office and the Satistical Ofices of the German *Länder*. Both offer facilities for on-site use.

- Thirdly, official microdata can be accessed remotely. In this case, the analyst provides syntax to the Research Data Centers of the Federal Statistical Office and the Satistical Ofices of the German *Länder*, the Research Data Centers execute the syntax and check if the output complies

---

24 Alternatively, when detailed regional information is kept, other attributes such as occupation, industry or nationality are recoded into larger categories (see Wirth et al. 2005).
25 The SUFs are created by the statistical agencies in close cooperation with the German Microdata Lab at GESIS in Mannheim (see Lüttinger et al. 2004; Schneider and Wolf 2008).

with data confidentiality requirements. This form of access is especially valuable if direct access to microdata cannot be granted due to problems of data confidentiality. This kind of problem, however, is mainly only relevant to establishment data and does not usually pose a problem for the use of household or population data. If, however, a researcher does not have the option of obtaining a SUF, for example because he or she is not working at a national research organization, then remote access might be a helpful service.

- Finally, the statistical agencies provide so called CAMPUS-Files which are Public Use Files (PUFs). These files are absolutely anonymized and can therefore be used without restriction. They are especially useful for training purposes. With respect to household surveys there are currently four CAMPUS-Files for different waves of the Microcensus and the Microcensus panel file available from the website of the Research Data Centers of the Federal Statistical Office and the Statistical Ofices of the German *Länder*.[26]

According to a recent survey among users of German microdata from official statistics, scientists clearly prefer the SUF as mode of data access. *All* respondents have used SUFs. In addition, one-fifth of users has made use of remotely processing the data and 10 percent have accessed the data in at least one of the Research Data Centers of the Federal Statistical Office and the Satistical Ofices of the German *Länder* (Lüttinger et al. 2007).

More and more researchers are interested in international comparative research. Regarding this growing demand, official microdata provided by Eurostat – the Statistical Office of the European Union – comes into focus. Eurostat currently provides access to microdata of four household surveys. These are the European Community Household Panel (ECHP), the European Union Labour Force Survey (EU-LFS), and the European Union Statistics on Income and Living Conditions (EU-SILC) (for a broader overview of European data, see Elias in this publication).

The ECHP is a panel survey that started in the twelve Member States of the European Union in 1994 and continued on an annual basis until 2001 (8 waves; some additional countries joined the survey after its initial launch). The survey covers a wide range of topics concerning living conditions including detailed income information, financial situation in a wider sense, working life, housing situation, social relations, health, and biographical information of the interviewed. The ECHP was Eurostat's attempt to create a comparative database following the principal of input harmonization (for the

---

26 http://www.forschungsdatenzentrum.de/campus-file.asp

different harmonization strategies see below and Ehling 2003; Granda, Wolf and Hadorn 2010).

The European Union Labour Force Survey is a rotating random sample survey covering the population in private households in currently thirty European countries. The sampling units are dwellings, households or individuals depending on the country-specific sampling frames. The collection of microdata, or individual data, started in 1983. Since 1998, the EU-LFS has developed into a continuous quarterly survey. The EU-LFS is conducted by the national statistical institutes across Europe and is centrally processed by Eurostat. The main aim of the EU-LFS is to provide comparable information on employed, unemployed, and inactive persons of working age (15 years and above) in European countries. The definitions of employment and unemployment used in the EU-LFS closely follow the guidelines put out by the International Labour Organisation. However, it follows an ex-ante output harmonization approach.

EU-SILC is an annual statistic and was launched in 2004 in thirteen Member States. From 2005 onwards the data are available for all EU25 Member States plus Iceland and Norway. Romania, Bulgaria, Turkey and Switzerland launched the EU-SILC in 2006. The EU-SILC provides cross-sectional and longitudinal microdata on income, poverty, social exclusion, living conditions and health. It can be viewed as a successor of the ECHP, though it employs an ex-ante output harmonization approach. The reference population of EU-SILC is defined as all private households and includes all persons aged 16 and over within a private household residing in the territory of the Member States at the time of data collection.

Other datasets initiated by the European Union or coordinated by Eurostat are either not available as an integrated microdata file or they are not distributed by Eurostat even though these data may be of great interest for social research (for details see the next section).

5.2 Recommendations

Among the manifold challenges we face with respect to further development in the area of population and household surveys from official statistics, there are three that seem especially pertinent from the perspective of socio-economic research: (1) continued improvement of data access, (2) adjustment of procedures to anonymize new data sources, and (3) enhancement of inter-temporal and cross-national comparability of data.

The improvement of data access can be divided into two main areas: improvement in documentation in order to ease access to data already available to the research community and the generation of access to new data sources. As is true for all secondary research, analyses of official microdata also depend on extensive documentation of the data and the data generation process. In addition, to be useful, this information has to be formatted in a standardized form and organized in such a way that it can be accessed seamlessly (e.g., a document that is stored under a pile of other documents and that can be only read with a pair of "magic glasses" obviously is of no use). An example for a very thoroughly documented statistic is the German Microcensus. The microdata information system MISSY[27], developed by GESIS, combines all available metadata for this survey and offers them in a coherently organized form through a web-based system (see Janßen and Bohr 2006).

Data access should also be improved with respect to information on field procedures. Compared to what we know about the process of data collection in social surveys such as the European Social Survey, the field work procedures utilized by the different Statistical Offices of the German *Länder* or in the different national offices of the EU are mostly terra incognita, paradata is mostly missing. The situation has improved somewhat over the last ten years, at least for the Labour Force Survey. Today we at least know the mode of interviewing (self-administered, CAPI, or CATI), the date of the interview, and if the interview is a proxy interview.

A significant problem that remains is the difficulty of access to data sources collected under the regulation of or at least coordinated by the European Union. Currently, only microdata from the above mentioned EU-LFS, ECHP, and EU-SILC are available for research outside of Eurostat. Other data such as the Adult Education Survey, the Time Use Survey, Household Budget Survey, Statistics on Information and Communications Technologies (Household Survey) or Europe's Health Survey are currently not available for comparative research. If the Lisbon goal of the European Council is to be met, namely Europe becoming the "most competitive and dynamic knowledge-based economy in the world, capable of sustainable economic growth with more and better jobs and greater social cohesion," then research monitoring this progress is mandatory and this research requires access to the relevant data.

A new challenge for data access is posed by register data that will become increasingly important over the next years. In this context, problems of integrating data from different registers and from registers and surveys has to be solved (Alda et al. 2005). Furthermore, the currently applied methods of data anonymization have to be adapted to these new data sources. However, this is not totally new terrain.

A final issue we would like to address concerning the most critical improvements to micro databases from official statistics is that of inter-temporal and especially cross-national comparability. At present, EU data is collected on the basis of regulations detailing the variables that Member States have to provide to Eurostat. This approach, called ex-ante output harmonization (Eh-

---

[27] http://www.gesis.org/MISSY

ling 2003), leaves the concrete process of data collection to the data producer (i.e., each country has its own questionnaire and applies their own field procedures). This flexibility of data collection makes it easier for the national statistical offices to integrate the data collection process into their national programs. The comparability of data for demographic and socio-economic variables yielded by this approach is generally satisfactory. This is especially the case where international standard classifications such as the International Standard Classification of Occupations (ISCO) or the Nomenclature générale des activités economiques dans les Communautés Européennes (NACE) are available and the countries agree on their interpretation and application. However, even with such "factual" information as highest educational degree (Schneider 2008) or supervisory status (Pollak et al. 2009), output harmonization may lead to incomparable data. Naturally this is much more true for subjective data such as health status, life satisfaction or happiness, all of which are included in the EU-SILC program.

The analytical potential of microdata collected under EU regulations and integrated by Eurostat could be improved without greater cost if the following three recommendations were applied: first, although it might not be feasible and for some variables even impossible to strictly apply input harmonization, we believe that these pan-European programs have to move in this direction. Even if, as can be assumed, not all Member States agree on a blueprint for a questionnaire or on a set of data collection procedures, Eurostat could propose such a blueprint and develop a set of best practice rules for data collection.[28] Although these documents would not be legally binding, their existence would lead to them being adopted by many countries because doing so will save time and money. Second, to be able to assess data quality in more detail, all survey documents should be made available. In addition to questionnaires, these would ideally include interviewer instructions and data on the data collection process as is common practice in social surveys. Third, the harmonized and integrated datasets distributed by Eurostat should also contain the original country-specific measures at least for variables for which the harmonization process necessarily leads to a high information loss. The availability of these data would enable researchers to assess the quality of the harmonized measures and it would allow the construction of alternatively harmonized variables.

---

28 This strategy has been already applied with respect to the ICT Business Survey (Eurostat 2007).

6. Conclusions

In this section we have dealt with selected problems of data documentation and data access. We have not addressed the data exchange on the international level that has by and large positively developed in Germany. Foreign scientists currently have a variety of opportunities to analyze German data. International research and data centers would be a further step for improving cooperation in research and teaching.

We have only briefly touched on the progress that has been made in broadening the bases of empirical research. A number of activities aim at the generation of complex databases which combine different data types. The typical micro-macro dataset is only one example of a large variety of new sources for analysis. Empirical data can be combined with literature and publications, survey data can be combined with regional information, media data, etc. In order to create these new databases, metadata standards, in particular the DDI standard, have to be further developed (see Heus et al. in this publication). New tools enabling the linkage of different meta-databases are necessary. Some of these tools are currently developed in the context of the Preparatory Phase Project of the Council of European Social Science Data Archives (CESSDA). Interoperable meta databases finally will help to combine datasets from different years and/or different countries, thereby enlarging our resources for inter-temporal and comparative research.

References:

Alda, H./Bender, S. and Gartner. H. (2005): The linked employer-employee dataset created from the IAB establishment panel and the process-produced data of the IAB (LIAB). Schmollers Jahrbuch 125 (2), 327-336.
Ehling, M. (2003): Harmonising Data in Official Statistics: Development, Procedures, and Data Quality. In: Hoffmeyer-Zlotnik, J.H.-P. and Wolf, Ch. (Eds.): Advances in Cross-National Comparison. A European Working Book for Demographic and Socio-Economic Variables. New York.
Eurostat (2007): Methodological Manual for Statistics on the Information Society. Survey year 2007, v2.0. Luxembourg.
http://europa.eu.int/estatref/info/sdds/en/isoc/isoc_metmanual_2007.pdf. [Last visited 09/30/2008].
Granda, P./Wolf, Ch./Hadorn, R. (2010): Harmonizing Survey Data. In: Harkness, J. et al. (Eds.): Survey Methods in Multicultural, Multinational, and Multiregional Contexts. New York. [In print].
Janßen, A. and Bohr, J. (2006): Microdata Information System MISSY. Iassist Quaterly 30 (2), 5-11.
Lüttinger, P./Köhne-Finster, S. and Urban, J. (2007): Ergebnisse der dritten Befragung von Nutzern der Mikrozensus Scientific Use Files. GESIS Methodenbericht Nr. 1/2007. Mannheim.
Lüttinger, P./Schimpl-Neimanns, B./Wirth, H. and Papastefanou, G. (2004): The German Microdata Lab at ZUMA: Services provided to the scientific community. Schmollers Jahrbuch 124 (3), 455-467.
Müller, W./Blien, U. and Wirth, H. (1995): Identification Risks of Microdata. Evidence from experimental studies. Sociological Methods & Research 24 (2), 131-157.
OECD (2007): Education at a Glance 2007. OECD Indicators. Paris.
Pollak, R./Wirth, H./Weiss, F./Bauer, G. and Müller, W. (2009): Issues in the Comparative Measurement of the Supervisory Function using the examples of the ESS and the EU-LFS. In: Pfau-Effinger, B./Magdalenić, S.S. and Wolf, Ch. (Eds.): International vergleichende Sozialforschung: Ansätze und Messkonzepte unter den Bedingungen der Globalisierung. Wiesbaden.
Schneider, H. and Wolf, Ch. (2008): Die Datenservicezentren als Teil der informationellen Infrastruktur. In: Rolf, G./Zwick, M. and Wagner, G.G. (Eds.): Fortschritte der informationellen Infrastruktur in Deutschland. Festschrift für Johann Hahlen zum 65. Geburtstag und Hans Jürgen Krupp zum 75. Geburtstag. Baden-Baden.
Schneider, S.L. (2008): Suggestions for the cross-national measurement of educational attainment: refining the ISCED-97 and improving data collection and coding procedures. In: Schneider, S.L. (Ed.): The International Standard Classification of Education (ISCED-97). An Evaluation of Content and Criterion Validity for 15 European Countries. Mannheim.
Statistisches Bundesamt, GESIS, and WZB (Eds.) (2008): Datenreport 2008. Ein Sozialbericht für die Bundesrepublik Deutschland. Bonn.

Wirth, H. (2008): Microdata access and confidentiality issues in Germany. Presentation at the meeting "Census Microdata: findings and futures", University of Manchester, 1 - 3 September 2008.

Wirth, H./Zühlke, S. and Christians, H. (2005): Der Mikrozensus als Datenbasis für die Regionalforschung. In: Grözinger, G. and Matiaske, W. (Eds.): Deutschland regional. Sozialwissenschaftlichen Daten im Forschungsverbund. München.

Wissenschaftsrat (2007): Recommendations on the Role and Future Development of Governmental Research Agencies with R&D Activities. http://www.wissenschaftsrat.de/texte/7854-07.pdf. [Last visited 02/03/2010].

4. Teaching and Statistical Training

Ulrich Rendtel

Contact:

Ulrich Rendtel
Freie Universität Berlin
Institut für Statistik und Ökonometrie / Fachbereich Wirtschaftswissenschaft
Gary Str. 21
14195 Berlin
Germany
e-mail: Ulrich.Rendtel[at]fu-berlin.de

Abstract

The availability of well-educated researchers is necessary for the fruitful analysis of social and economic data. The increased data offer made possible by the creation of the Research Data Centers has resulted in an increased demand for PhD students at the master's or *Diplom* levels. Especially in economics, where we find intense competition among the various individual subjects within the course of study, survey statistics has not been very successful in laying claim to a substantial proportion of the coursework and training. The situation is more favorable in sociology faculties.

This article argues that the creation of new CAMPUS-Files would help foster statistical education by providing Public Use Files covering a wider range of subjects. It also presents some suggestions for new CAMPUS-Files along these lines. Additionally, it argues for the establishment of master's programs in survey statistics to increase the availability of well-trained statisticians. An outline of such a master's program is presented and current PhD programs are evaluated with respect to training in survey statistics.

Training courses are also offered outside the university that promote the use of new datasets as well as expanding the knowledge of new statistical methods or methods that lie outside standard education. These training courses are organized by the Research Data Centers, (i.e. the data producers), the Data Service Centers, or by GESIS (*Leibniz Institute for the Social Sciences*). The current tendency to strengthen ties and collaborate with universities should be supported by making it possible to earn academic credit for such courses.

Keywords: master's programs, survey statistics, CAMPUS-Files, statistical training.

1. Introduction

A major issue identified by the German Commission on Improving the Information Infrastructure between Science and Statistics (KVI, *Kommission zur Verbesserung der informationellen Infrastruktur zwischen Wissenschaft und Statistik*), is the relationship between data access and the ability to analyze these data competently. For this reason, the original KVI proposal voted for the creation of CAMPUS-Files, free Public Use Files (PUFs) to support academic teaching, as well as new training courses on Scientific Use Files (SUFs) (KVI 2001: 32). In this paper I review the current state of statistical teaching and training in Germany with respect to the use of new information sources that became available during the first phase of the German Data Forum (RatSWD).

Several aspects of university training in statistics will be addressed. First, both economics and the social sciences are affected by the transition from the educational model of the German *Diplom* to the bachelor's and master's program model. This transition, which is ongoing, has strong implications for university curricula. The impact of this change was not foreseen by the 2001 KVI report and is analyzed in section 4. One new feature of German university education today is the obligatory emphasis on structured doctoral programs and graduate schools. The relationship between these new branches to the present availability of statistical training is discussed in the section 5. In this context, I will also introduce the role of training courses held outside the university, namely courses run by GESIS and the Research Data Centers. Finally, some concluding remarks will be made with respect to international comparisons.

2. Consequences of improved data access

During the first phase of the RatSWD there was a strong emphasis placed on data access; namely, the development and production of SUFs and their deployment by the Research Data Centers. Corresponding to the federal structure of Germany, there is a total of sixteen state agencies and one federal state agency that offer SUFs as well as on-site access to datasets where no SUFs exist, such as firm-level data or household data with detailed regional information. This expanding data supply has resulted in a sharp increase of users. From the beginning of 2004 to 2007, the number of new data contracts rose by a factor of seven. Given that this process of improved data access has not yet come to an end, one may reasonably predict an additional dramatic increase in the number of data user contracts.

A further consequence of the increased number of research contracts at the Research Data Centers has been an increased number of job openings in the area of applied data analysis. As a register of this increased demand, I have looked to the SOEP mailing list, a forum for advertising job openings in the field of applied data analysis.[1] In this venue, the number of job offers (including academic research) has risen from eleven (in the second half of 2004) to thirty (in the first half of 2008). The positions offered are mainly part-time jobs (half or two-third positions) that include the opportunity of writing a doctoral thesis.[2]

The principal qualifications required for these positions include: competence in handling data generated by complex surveys, background in statisti-

---

1 The mailing list has existed in its present form since March 2004. The results reported here should be interpreted with some caution. Other effects, such as a potential increase of list subscribers, may also have induced a larger number of job offers. Help from the SOEP group, especially Uta Rahmann, in providing this information is gratefully acknowledged.
2 Compared to job offers from the private sector, the income earned in these positions is quite unattractive.

cal methodology, the ability to run statistical analysis packages (i.e., STATA, SPSS, R, or SAS), and some familiarity with a special substantial topic, such as labor economics or gender diversity. In these areas, however, representatives of the Federal Statistical Office in Germany have complained of a lack of skills and education, especially among economists who have recently left the university (see Rendtel 2008). Specifically, it is said that young economists aren't familiar with the important surveys in official statistics, that they don't know the framework of survey methodology, and have limited experience handling empirical data – for example in dealing with item nonresponse or coding errors. Sociologists, on the other hand, are regarded as better trained. They seem to profit from mandatory courses on empirical methods in surveying in their field, which are not included in the standard program of economic study.

To summarize, there is a gap created by the increased demand for young researchers with a sound knowledge of important surveys and data handling and an insufficient amount of statistical training. This observation, however, is more characteristic of university programs in economics than it is of sociology departments.

3. CAMPUS-Files

One measure taken to narrow this gap is the use of CAMPUS-Files in academic teaching. These files are created for use in statistical training. Because of the lack of controls in their use by students, the level of anonymization should be higher than in the case of SUFs. In general, they are regarded as absolutely anonymous PUFs, which restricts their power for analysis (see Zwick 2008).

At the moment (August, 2008), there are eight CAMPUS-Files offered by the Research Data Center of the Federal Statistical Office: two from the German Microcensus (1998, 2002), two taxation data files (*Lohn- und Einkommenssteuerstatistik* 1998, 2001), a file of employee and firm-level data on wages (*Gehalts- und Lohnstrukturerhebung* 2001), a file of the German subsample of the European firm-level panel data on the impact of job training, a file of social aid recipients (*Sozialhilfestatistik* 1998), and finally, a file of small and medium-sized firms on cost structure (*Kostenstrukturerhebung kleine und mittlere Unternehmen* 1999).[3] Since they allow no identification of units in the files, there is no control over what is done with the file data.

---

3   These files can be downloaded from the website of the Research Data Center (http://www.forschungsdaten zentrum.de/campus-file.asp).

A more restrictive use of data is offered by the Research Data Center of the German Pension Insurance (RV, *Deutsche Rentenversicherung*). In this case, the instructor must apply for a CAMPUS-File and notify each student who receives a copy of the file.[4] There are four of these files offered for teachers: two on the stock of the retired persons (2003, 2005) and two on recently retired persons (2003, 2004). For the social sciences, the German General Social Survey (ALLBUS, *Allgemeine Bevölkerungsumfrage der Sozialwissenschaften*) is also offered as a CAMPUS-File, although this title is not explicitly used.[5] Other surveys are offered for a modest fee by the GESIS Data Archive and Data Analysis for use in teaching.

It is relatively surprising that one of the most frequently analyzed data files, the German Socio-Economic Panel (SOEP, *Sozio-oekonomisches Panel*), is not represented as a CAMPUS-File. Teachers are allowed to use a 50 percent subset of the SOEP that they must construct themselves. However, this file cannot be given away to the students, which makes it unsatisfactory as a teaching option. Moreover, the SOEP is a collection of more than one hundred flat files across six subsamples. The complexity of this data structure is overwhelming for untrained students. Thus it seems desirable to have a SOEP file that can be distributed to students and that has a simpler structure than the full SOEP.[6] Nevertheless researchers who run analyses with the SOEP need to be trained on a SOEP version that has the full complexity of a long-running household panel. A CAMPUS-File version of the SOEP would arguably present an educational tool at a level somewhere between the full complexity of the original file and that of a collection of mere analysis files to demonstrate the syntax and outcome of statistical program packages.[7]

In response to the broader range of data sources that can be analyzed now, the topics covered by CAMPUS-Files should be correspondingly enlarged. For example, the German Income and Consumption Survey (EVS, *Einkommens und Verbrauchsstichprobe)* is a basic source of poverty research. Also the German Microcensus, which has followed a continuous sampling scheme since 2005, is not represented by a CAMPUS-File, nor is it used as a rotating panel over three years.[8]

---

4 See www.RDC-rv.de
5 The ALLBUScompact Cumulation 1980-2006 covers 13 biannual cross-sectional surveys, see http://www.gesis.org/en/services/data/survey-data/allbus/
6 The complexity of the data structure is to some extent buffered by the retrieval system, the SOEPinfo meta analysis program (see http://www.diw.de/de/soep). One easy way to reduce the complexity of the full SOEP might be to put aside all subsamples with the exception of the Subsample F, which was started in 2000.
7 See for example the collection of SOEP files in STATA format used to support Kohler and Kreuter's textbook, Datenanalyse mit Stata (www.stata.com/datenanalyse/).
8 For more information, use the search tool on the website of the Federal Statistical Office, (http://www.destatis.de) for the Microcensus Panel Project (MZ-Panel).

Generally speaking, a good infrastructure should offer a CAMPUS-File for each subject area. For example, the data of the Federal Employment Agency have become a must for a labor economist, yet there is no CAMPUS-File offered by the Research Data Center of the Federal Employment Agency at the Institute for Employment Research (IAB, *Institut für Arbeitsmark- und Berufsforschung* within the BA, *Bundesagentur für Arbeit*). Alternatively, European datasets such as the EU Statistics on Income and Living Conditions (EU-SILC), a rotating panel started in 2005, would offer another good candidate for a European CAMPUS-File.

For sociologists, the European Social Survey (ESS) is an important international data source. Compared with EU-SILC, the situation is again much more advantageous. The ESS EduNet is an internet-based analysis training program developed by Norwegian Social Science Data Services. It not only provides data access but also a teaching environment.[9] Further areas that deserve more attention include health surveys and educational data.[10]

The downloadable format is very convenient for teachers and students. However, other formats may be equally attractive for the dissemination of data for seminars and projects. For example, the British Economic and Social Data Service (ESDS) offers a data sharing option that allows the teacher to distribute data to his or her students under the condition that the students are registered and have signed an agreement concerning the terms of data usage.[11] More information on this can be found on the ESDS website.

4. After Bologna: The situation of statistical education in Germany

The most important outcome of the Bologna Process is the transition from a single phase *Diplom* curriculum to a two-phase scheme with a three-year bachelor's and a two-year master's phase. Compared with the German *Diplom* and its four-year schedule, the bachelor's phase is significantly shorter.[12] However, this has given rise to competition between the individual subjects within a faculty over their representation in the shorter bachelor's framework.

---

9   See http://essedunet.usd.uib.no/cms/edunet/about.html
10 The large-scale Educational Panel Study (*Bildungspanel*), for example, might be a good candidate for demonstrating the difficulty of analyzing school data.
11 http://www.esds.ac.uk/ordering Data/sharing Data.asp
12 This effect is reinforced by mandatory general occupational skills training, comprised of languages, internships, or word-processing. At the Freie Universität Berlin this block of required study amounts to 30 credits, equal to the workload of a semester.

There are two models for coping with such a situation: (a) all courses are required to cut their curriculum by approximately 30 percent; and (b) a narrower selection of courses lead to a more specific BA (*Bachelor of Arts*) exam. The decision in favour of either model depends on the individual preferences and composition of local faculties. An empirical analysis of the economic curricula in various faculties was presented by Rendtel (2008). This study compared 117 BA degree programs at economic faculties in universities and universities of applied sciences (*Fachhochschulen*). In one quarter of the cases the percentage of mandatory credits to be earned from quantitative courses was found to be less than 5.5 percent! At the other extreme, a small number of some BA programs required 25 percent or even up to 30 percent of course credits from mandatory quantitative courses.

In addition to changes in course requirements, the format of the written diploma thesis, a final year project, has changed from one that would have been finished within four to six months, to one that must be completed in nine weeks.[13] Such a short time frame excludes examination topics requiring substantial empirical data analysis.

The large disparity in required quantitative credits illustrates the extreme diversity of different subjects within economic faculties. In these faculties, business administration recruits the majority of students and often has interest in subjects that do not use statistical inference or survey data. For example, in the bachelor's program in Business Administration at the Freie Universität Berlin, statistical inference is no longer a mandatory course. As a result, one may expect a large variation in the statistical skills of new BAs graduating from different economic faculties. In the case of sociology, university departments seem more homogeneous. In this discipline the role of survey data and empirical statistical analysis in the educational program seems to be well recognized.

Nonetheless, it does seem that at the moment students with a bachelor's degree are not qualified for research projects in empirical data analysis. The usual qualifications that are listed in the job descriptions correspond rather to the *Diplom* or the master's level of study. Thus, unless there is a substantial progression of students from the bachelor's into the master's level, one may predict a decrease in candidates qualified for high-level data analysis.

The heterogeneity of qualifications increases at the master's level. There is a trend toward highly specialized master's degrees. Again the diversity of master's degrees seems to be much greater in economics than in other faculties. This trend towards tailored master's degrees has given rise to highly specialized courses in the curricula, such as "Quantitative Methods in Finance." These replace statistical courses of general relevance, such as "Multivariate Analysis." Unless the master's program is geared specifically

---

13   12 credit points equal a total of 12 x 30 = 360 working hours. With a weekly workload of 40 hours one obtains 360/40 = 9 weeks.

toward statistics and data analysis there will be no possibility of obtaining a sound education, for example, in survey statistics.

This article therefore proposes the establishment of master's programs tailored to the needs of empirical data analysis with a special emphasis on survey data. Such a program should cover the framework of design-based statistics, i.e., sampling from a finite population with known inclusion probabilities, since most of the Research Data Center files come from surveys with informative sampling. The calibration of survey data – often simplified as "weighting," which is the standard routine in official statistics – should also be given more attention. Furthermore, the issue of nonresponse and some strategies to cope with it is an important topic for everyone who utilizes survey data. In fact, missing data not only occur as nonresponse but they also occur in evaluation studies as one missing observation in treatment-control pairs.[14] Measurement error is another important issue for everyone who analyses survey data.[15] Measurement errors overlap with survey techniques and questionnaire design. This is an area in which social scientists are well-trained but it is much less familiar to economists. Last but not least, there should be extensive training in basic skills (i.e., data management, model selection, data presentation, and interpretation). This can be supplemented, for example, with internships at the Research Data Centers or other research institutes, such as the Institute for Employment Research or the German Institute for Economic Research (DIW, *Deutsches Institut für Wirtschaftsforschung*).

One of the big statistical events in the near future, i.e. the German Census in 2011, will be a mixture of data from different sources. Such a design, which is complicated by overcoverage (*Karteileichen*) and undercoverage (*Fehlbestände*), is a methodological challenge for the Federal Statistical Office and it will be a challenge for those who analyze a SUF based on this census. Moreover, as regional counts are one of the most important issues of the census, the use of small area estimates is on the agenda. Whether it is accessed on-site or via the installation of platform for remote access, small area estimation will become a topic for data users.

However, none of these topics are the focus of a master's program in Germany. Neither has survey statistics been prioritized at the two German statistical faculties in Dortmund and Munich. Almost no graduates from the Dortmund program, of the some 1000 *Diplom* statisticians the department has produced, are working in official statistics (see Thöne and Weihs 2008). Here biometrics, computational statistics and, not least, the facilities own demand for doctoral candidates were the largest fields where the graduates were employed.

---

14 See Rässler (2006) for an overview of this in the context of data from the Federal Employment Agency (Bundesagentur für Arbeit).
15 For illustrative examples see Raghunathan (2006) and Durrant (2006)

There are obvious problems in terms of teaching capacity with trying to establish this type of intensive focus on surveys statistics at one site. To run a master's program like this would require the teaching power of at least three chairs in statistics who had a close affiliation to survey statistics. At the moment no German university offers such a concentration of energies in survey specialization. However, one might assemble the teaching resources residing at different universities in a joint master's program as a second-best solution. There are still problems with teleteaching from different sites, but given the technical possibilities that exist, teleteaching survey statistics at the master's level seems a feasible solution.

5. After the Master's: Vocational training and PhD programs

It is clear that the new datasets that have been generated by the Research Data Centers require some introduction for interested users to acquaint them with the potentials and risks of the dataset. In general, this type of training units last about three days and includes practical exercises with the data. The standard clients are young researchers who are at the beginning of some empirical project and/or their thesis project. Most participants have just finished their *Diplom*. The level of statistical proficiency is quite mixed. Very often researchers lack even an elementary knowledge of the design-based approach, and models beyond the linear regression model (e.g., Logit model or Loglinear models) are unknown. To my knowledge there is no systematic test of the statistical knowledge given to participants of such training courses.

The need for data training courses was recognized early on by the SOEP project, which has offered an annual training course at the German Institute for Economic Research (DIW) in Berlin since 1989. This opportunity has now been expanded by its integration into the university framework and for the two years they have organized a workshop series, SOEP@campus, in collaboration with other universities.[16] The participation is partly sponsored by the Federal Ministry of Education and Research (BMBF) as a part of the KVI process. The Research Data Center of the IAB within the BA has offered a workshop on spell data on the basis of some of its test data. Again with sponsorship from the BMBF, the Research Data Center of the Federal Statistical Office and the Data Service Center of the German Microdata Lab at GESIS have been offering workshops on newly released data files. Here the Microcensus and the Microcensus Panel have played an important part.

---

16 See, for example, http://www.uni-due.de/soziologie/-soepatcampus/index.php

Often data producers have established user groups that convene for regular meetings (annual or biannual), where results can be presented and discussed. The user group can be regarded as an academic network for the exchange of knowledge and experience. Therefore it can support statistical training in multiple ways.

Within the framework of statistical training, GESIS plays an important part. GESIS is a member of the Leibniz-Gemeinschaft and provides statistical education on subjects that are not routinely offered at university. Thus it supplements university education, for example, by presenting courses on latent class analysis, multilevel models or mixture models. Their "Spring Seminar" is devoted to an intensive training on special methods, usually presented in a sequence of three blocks of one week each.

The ZUMA (*Zentrum für Umfragen, Methoden und Analysen*) branch of GESIS offers workshops in different fields (new datasets, interview techniques and questionnaire design, sampling, editing, and statistical methods). The workshops are presented in a three-day format at Mannheim. The participants have to pay a moderate fee. The number of participants is limited (14–18), so waiting lists have been created. The demand is such that the average waiting list is as long as the number of participants, numbering about 400 per year. There is nothing similar to GESIS in economics. One reason is probably the greater heterogeneity of the research areas.

At the international level, there are similar bodies that offer training and statistical instruction in survey statistics and the analysis of survey data; however, their organization differs. The National Survey Research Center in the US is affiliated with the University of Michigan and involves the development, refinement, and propagation of the scientific method of survey research through teaching and training.[17] The National Center for Research Methods (NCRM) in the UK is a network of research groups, each conducting research and training in an area of social science research methods.[18] It acts under the auspices of the Economic and Social Research Council (ESRC), the British funding organization that integrates research activities in this field.[19] The network is organized according to a "hub-model," where the Southampton School of Social Science serves as the hub that connects six nodes. These nodes are located at separate universities and each specializes in certain topics or methods. The whole project runs under a four-year funding scheme.

Under the auspices of the German Research Foundation (DFG, *Deutsche Forschungsgemeinschaft*) several PhD programs are offered for statistical teaching and training. However, these programs are only open to those few students who were accepted in the program. Moreover, most of these

---

17 See isr.umich.edu/src/
18 See www.ncrm.ac.uk
19 In Germany this council would cover the activities of DFG, the BMBF and the RatSWD.

graduate schools, such as the Mannheim Graduate School of Economic and Social Sciences or the Bremen International Graduate School of Social Sciences are integrated into the German Universities Excellence Initiative.[20] Thus they are not oriented toward broader participation like the GESIS training courses.[21]

A different approach was proposed in the DFG-funded Priority Program on Survey Methodology which was started in 2007. Here the intention was to establish survey methodology as an independent subject. For this purpose the program plans to establish a "German School of Survey Methodology."[22] The proposal incorporates international experts in survey methodology as teachers and includes a nationwide recruitment of students. This proposal is similar to the proposal for the establishment of a master's program in survey statistics.

A few comments need to be made concerning the relationship of university teaching within the bachelor's and master's scheme and those training programs that lie outside this scheme:

(1) The two levels should be adapted to each other. It is my impression that sometimes the participants of training courses lack both an elementary knowledge of statistics and experience with empirical data analysis.

(2) Quite often the motivation of students to participate in a training course is low because they cannot earn credits toward their master's degree. The credit system is very flexible, however, which makes it easy to grant credit for participation in training courses. A necessary prerequisite to this, of course, would be some kind of examination of the attendees by the trainers.

6. Conclusions and recommendations

The availability of well-educated researchers is necessary for the fruitful analysis of social and economic data. The increased data offer made possible by the establishment of the Research Data Centers has resulted in an increased demand for PhD students at the master's or *Diplom* level. Even today it is not an easy task to recruit young researchers with a sound education in the methods of data analysis who also have some practical experience in this business. Especially in economics, where we find intense competition among

---

20 Gess.uni-mannheim.de; www.bigsss-bremen.de
21 One may regard low admission numbers as intrinsic to excellence. However, with respect to the need of a higher number of well trained researchers this might be also regarded as a kind of luxury.
22 See www.survey-methodology.de/

the various subjects within the course of study, survey statistics has not been very successful in laying claim to a substantial proportion of the course work and training. The situation is more favorable in the sociological faculties.

This article proposes the creation of new CAMPUS-Files, free PUFs that would help foster statistical education by covering a wider range of subjects. It also advances some specific suggestions for new CAMPUS-Files along these lines. Additionally, it argues for the establishment of master's programs in survey statistics that can help increase the availability of well-trained statisticians, and provides an outline of such a master's program.

There is also a widespread network of training courses that address the needs of young researchers. These programs provide training in the introduction of new datasets as well as in non-standard analysis techniques. These training courses are organized by the Research Data Centers (i.e., the data producers), the Data Service Centers or by GESIS. Recently, there has been a greater tendency toward collaboration with universities. In order to attract students before their exam – and thus enlarging the number of applicants for research projects – one should investigate the possibility of granting academic credit for bachelor's and master's students.

The close cooperation between the SOEP group and universities is regarded as a fruitful model of this approach. Likewise, the Research Data Centers offer not only data but also support for the analysis of these data. They should be encouraged to reinforce and expand their training activities. This will not only improve statistical education in the university but will help widen the scope of official statistics from a mere data producer to an information provider.

References:

Durrant, G. (2006): Missing data Methods in Official Statistics in the United Kingdom: Some Recent Developments. ASTA Advances in Statistical Analysis 90 (4), 577-593.

Kommission zur Verbesserung der informationellen Infrastruktur zwischen Wissenschaft und Statistik (KVI) (Ed.) (2001): Wege zu einer besseren informationellen Infrastruktur. Baden-Baden.

Rässler, S. (2006): Der Einsatz von Missing Data Techniken in der Arbeitsmarktforchung des IAB. ASTA Advances in Statistical Analysis 90 (4), 527-552.

Raghunathan, T. (2006): Combining Information from Multiple Surveys for Assessing Health Disparities. ASTA Advances in Statistical Analysis 90 (4), 515-526.

Rendtel, U. (2008): Statistikausbildung und Amtliche Statistik. Kritik und Perspektiven. ASTA Wirtschafts- und Sozialstatistisches Archiv 2 (1/2), 5-20.

Thöne, M. and Weihs, C. (2008): Vielseitig und gefragt. Absolventen und Absolventinnen der Dortmunder Studiengangs Statistik. ASTA Wirtschafts- und Sozialstatistisches Archiv 2 (1/2), 75-92.

Zwick, M. (2008): Campus-Files – Kostenfreie Public-Use-Files für die Lehre. ASTA Wirtschafts- und Sozialstatistisches Archiv 2 (1/2), 175-188.

5. e- Infrastructure for the Social Sciences

Ekkehard Mochmann

Contact:

Ekkehard Mochmann
e-mail: E.Mochmann[at]web.de

Abstract

When the term "e-Science" became popular, it frequently was referred to as "enhanced science" or "electronic science." More revealing, however, is the definition, "e-Science is about global collaboration in key areas of science and the next generation of infrastructure that will enable it" (Taylor 2001). The question arises to what extent can the social sciences profit from recent developments in e-Science infrastructure?

While available computing, storage, and network capacities have so far been able to accommodate and access social science databases, new capacities and technologies will support new types of research, such as linking and analyzing transactional or audio-visual data. Increasingly, collaborative work among researchers in distributed networks is efficiently supported by information technology and new resources have been made available for e-learning. Whether these new developments will be transformative or merely helpful will very much depend on whether their full potential is recognized and creatively integrated into new research designs by theoretically innovative scientists.

Progress in e-Science was closely linked to the vision of the Grid as "a software infrastructure that enables flexible, secure, coordinated resource sharing among dynamic collections of individuals, institutions and resources" with virtually unlimited computing capacities (Foster et al. 2000). In the social sciences there has been considerable progress made in the use of modern information technologies (IT) for multilingual access to virtual distributed research databases across Europe and beyond (e.g., NESSTAR, CESSDA-Portal), data portals for access to statistical offices, and for linking access to data, literature, project, expert, and other databases (e.g., Digital Libraries, VASCODA/SOWIPORT). Whether future developments will require Grid enabling of social science databases or can be further developed using WEB 2.0 support is currently an open question. The challenges that must be met are the need for seamless integration and interoperability of databases, a requirement further mandated by internationalization and transdisciplinary research. This goes along with the need for standards and harmonization of data and metadata.

Progress powered by e-Infrastructure is, among other things, dependent on both regulatory frameworks and human capital well trained in both data science and research methods. It is also dependent on a sufficient critical mass of the institutional infrastructure to efficiently support a dynamic research community that wants to "take the lead without catching up."

1. Introduction

Are advances in socio-economic research driven by data or technology? Claims in one direction and inspired deliberations pondering these alternatives are not new. While Norman Nie asserted without reservation "that all science is fundamentally data driven" (Nie 1989: 2) others have argued "that progress in science rather depends on formal modelling" (Rockwell 1999: 157). More recently "methodological and substantive rigour"[1] have been emphasized as necessary preconditions for the creation of reliable sources of knowledge about social change. Both information technology and the social science database have developed remarkably over the past few decades – from poverty of data to the rapidly expanding production of all kinds of empirical evidence beyond the survey and statistical microdata. These now include, for example, electronic texts, event databases, videos, geo-information, and new kinds of data, as in the case of transaction data (Lane 2010; Engel 2010) or biomarkers (Schnell 2010). Access to comprehensive databases and advanced data analysis increasingly allow modeling of complex social processes.

To efficiently support future empirical research

"[t]he present major task is [...] to create pan-European infrastructural systems that are needed by the social sciences [...] to utilise the vast amount of data and information that already exist or should be generated in Europe. Today the social sciences [...] are hampered by the fragmentation of the scientific information space. Data, information and knowledge are scattered in space and divided by language, cultural, economic, legal and institutional barriers" (ESFRI 2006).

2. e-Science, e-Social Science, the Grid and Web 2.0

Though there has already been evident progress fuelled by new kinds of measurement, expanding databases, and technological support for the past few decades, new and revolutionary systematic approaches can now be used to analyze research challenges. Based on the results of the resulting analyses, comprehensive technological infrastructures can be implemented to facilitate innovative research. These "e-Science" approaches were initially referred to as "enhanced science" or "electronic science." More revealing, however, is the definition "e-Science is about global collaboration in key areas of science and the next generation of infrastructure that will enable it" (Taylor 1999). Basically, e-Social Science follows these ideas, with emphasis on providing advanced IT services to "enable" social research. The National Centre for e-Social Science at Manchester (NCeSS) states:

"e-Social Science is a term which encompasses technological developments and approaches within Social Science. We are working with Social Scientists and Computer Scientists on tools and research which Social Scientists can take and use to help their research. These tools might either allow a Social Science Researcher to conduct new research or else conduct research more quickly These tools can be used across a variety of

---

1   http://www.europeansocialsurvey.org/

Social Science domains. [...] Within NCeSS, we refer to the 'e' in e-Social Science as 'enabling'."[2]

Progress in e-Science was closely linked to the vision of the Grid as "a software infrastructure that enables flexible, secure, coordinated resource sharing among dynamic collections of individuals, institutions and resources and virtually unlimited computing capacities" (Foster et al. 2000). As such, it was based on multi gigabit broad band width fiber cables connecting distributed and loosely coupled computing resources, using open standards in the Grid. In coordination with the National Research and Educational Networks (NRENs), they would provide a globe-spanning net with virtually unlimited computing capacity, intelligent middleware to support interoperability of network services, and control of access and authentication. To support information handling and support for knowledge processing within the e-scientific process, future developments point toward the Semantic Grid (De Roure et al. 2003: 9).

The Enabling Grids for E-SciencE (EGEE) project is a prominent and globally expansive example of the impetus to build a secure, reliable, and robust Grid infrastructure with a light-weight middleware solution intended to be used by many different scientific disciplines. It is built on the EU Research Network (GÉANT), and exploits Grid expertise generated by many EU, national, and international Grid projects, including the EU Data Grid.[3] Just to show the new dimensions: at present, it consists of approximately 300 sites in 50 countries and gives its 10,000 users access to 80,000 CPU[4] cores, 24 hours a day, 7 days a week. This project came to the conclusion that the state of computer and networking technology today facilitates extensive computing grids that integrate geographically distributed computer clusters, instruments, scientific communities, and large data storage facilities. The resulting benefits include a large increase in the peak capacity, the total computing available, and data management power for various scientific projects, in a secure environment.[5] Critics, however, point to the fact that these new developments cannot be used outside high energy physics so far.

The Grid idea followed the computer scientists' blueprint for a perfectly designed distributed infrastructure. Lessons learned from early developments emphasize that it is very important to have application scientists collaborate closely with computer scientists.

"Successful projects were mostly application and user driven, with a focus on the development of standard and commodity components, open source, and results easy to understand and to use" (Gentzsch 2007: 17).

---

2   http://www.ncess.ac.uk/about_eSS/
3   http://eu-datagrid.web.cern.ch/eu-datagrid/
4   Central Processing Unit.
5   http://www.eu-egee.org

It is significant that the German Grid initiative (D-Grid)[6], which started in 2005 with six science projects, now also includes Text Grid[7] from the humanities but none from the social sciences. Over the past few years more than ten new projects from the sciences have been added. In this area, at least, the social sciences certainly do not belong among those who adopted technology early. This pattern can be observed in most other countries, with the exception of the UK and the US, where the social science communities have made particular efforts to boost their e-Infrastructure. In this context it may also be worth noting that the first attempt to support retrieval of data by machine was actually conceived in the context of a social science project already described in 1964 (Scheuch and Stone 1964). Ideas for researcher dialogue with interactive data analysis and retrieval systems date back to 1972 (Scheuch and Mochmann 1972: 154f). With respect to transnational data infrastructure, the Council of European Social Science Data Archives (CESSDA) is studying the feasibility of Grid enabling. This investigation examines current developments and applications in Grid technologies in order to find efficient and sustainable ways for the implementation of a cyberinfrastructure for the social sciences and humanities and to identify the issues for implementing Grid technology.

Instead of an enthusiastic uptake of Grid technologies, a number of initiatives have followed a bottom-up approach in collaborative systems development, for example, creating access to virtually distributed databases using the World Wide Web in a more sophisticated way. These new trends in the use of WWW technology to enhance collaboration as well as information and data sharing are referred to as Web 2.0 technologies. They are still based on the so far known World Wide Web specifications. Results of these developments are possibly less perfect than those designed for Grid applications, but they are facilitated by cooperative approaches within the science community and they take usually much less time to implement.

3. Social research infrastructure, e-infrastructure, cyberinfrastructure

The social sciences have a long record of infrastructure development in terms of service institutions, databases, data laboratories, and researcher networks in the field of international comparative research (Scheuch 2003). Thus, it was no surprise that the social scientists pointed to the need to distinguish the preexisting infrastructure from the emerging IT-based infrastructure (Sere-

---

6   http://www.d-grid.de/
7   http://www.textgrid.de/

nate 2003b). The e-infrastructure concept was thus proposed in 2003 to coin a term for the development of the next generation of transnational Information and Communication Technology (ICT) research infrastructure in Europe:

> "e-Infrastructure refers to this new research environment in which all researchers – whether working in the context of their home institutions or in national or multinational scientific initiatives – have shared access to unique or distributed scientific facilities (including data, instruments, computing and communications), regardless of their type and location in the world" (European Commission IST 2005).

At the same time, the National Science Foundation Blue-Ribbon Advisory Panel identified similar objectives for what they called "Cyberinfrastructure":

> "We envision an environment in which raw data and recent results are easily shared, not just within a research group or institution but also between scientific disciplines and locations. There is an exciting opportunity to share insights, software, and knowledge, to reduce wasteful re-creation and repetition. Key applications and software that are used to analyze and simulate phenomena in one field can be utilized broadly. This will only take place if all share standards and underlying technical infrastructures" (Atkins et al. 2003: 12).

Cyberinfrastructure is defined in relation to already known infrastructures:

> "Although good infrastructure is often taken for granted and noticed only when it stops functioning, it is among the most complex and expensive things that society creates. The newer term cyber-infrastructure refers to infrastructure based upon distributed computer, information and communication technology. If infrastructure is required for an industrial economy, then we could say that cyberinfrastructure is required for a knowledge economy" (Atkins et al. 2003: 5).

In Europe, the provision of network services to research and education is organized at three levels: the Local Area Network to which the end-user is connected, the national infrastructure provided by the National Research and Education Network (NREN), and the pan-European level provided by GÉANT.

GÉANT currently interconnects the national research and education networks (NRENs) from all over Europe, including Russia. In terms of geographical coverage, technology used, and services made available, GÉANT considers itself the number one research network in the world, which attracts requests for interconnection from all over the world. Under the GÉANT2 project it has grown to include more than 100 partners already. This is much more than the social sciences need so far, but it gains in importance when we think about the potential for International Data Federations to support continuous global comparative and transdisciplinary research. While the technical backbone of the network is in place, many application tools, standards, and content with rich metadata have to be developed in order to make full use of these technologies.

World Class Research Networking
GÉANT: The Multi-Gigabit pan-European Research Network
GÉANT is operated by DANTE, The European Research Networking Organisation
GÉANT
www.geant.net
1993
2003
DANTE
www.dante.net
Information Society Technologies
Global Connectivity October 2003
10 Gbit/s
2.5 Gbit/s
Interconnections
existing
planned
GÉANT & NORDUnet networks

4. Data infrastructure needs of the social sciences
(Major results of the SERENATE project and the AVROSS study)

Exciting visions of the future potential of new technologies like to travel with appealing descriptions of how it is actually implemented in working environments. Closer examination, however, frequently shows that, in practice, services that are needed by end-users on a continuous basis are often far from satisfactory. The economic potential to implement new technologies, the level of expertise in different societies that is available to support these technologies and to adjust them to the specific needs of their user communities, as well as data management and methodological skills vary from country to country.

Needs, challenges, and obstacles in relation to these new technologies have been analyzed by the Study into European Research and Education Networking as Targeted by *e*Europe (SERENATE). Security features were highlighted by a large number of the respondents who deal with sensitive data or even medical images. Another critical element is mobile access to network services – including both home access for researchers, particularly for non-laboratory based research such as humanities and social sciences, and access when abroad. As a consequence of these usage patterns, the deployment of "Authentication, Authorization and Accounting" (AAA) services across the various networks was stipulated to provide the necessary controls on access. The report from the final workshop also noted that access to a rich variety of data from many sources is possible and identified the potential for software to support collaborative working, the sharing of databases, and data integration at many levels. Finally, the networks offer the means to include the "future generation of scientists in schools" (Serenate 2003b: 14).

In the spirit of e-Science approaches to systematically examining options and challenges for enhancing scientific research, SERENATE includes some tough observations on contextual requirements into its findings:

"We have learned that many people – national and European politicians, ministries and agencies in the national governments, the European Commission, telecoms vendors, equipment vendors, various service suppliers, local and regional authorities, universities and user communities all have to be mobilized, and to move in the same direction, if we are to make progress. If we do not make plans to maintain and even improve the situation over the next 5–10 years, then the sustained pace of technical, organisational and political change will inevitably lead to rapid decay" (Serenate 2003a).

Analyses based on the Accelerating Transition to Virtual Research Organisation in Social Science (AVROSS) study concluded that efforts by the US and the UK appear to be an exception, since no other European country has adopted an initiative that promotes e-infrastructure uptake by the social sciences or the humanities. At the same time, the European Strategy Forum on Research Infrastructures (ESFRI) has recognized the importance of including these domains of science in the ESFRI Roadmap report. This foundational report identified three long-term strategic goals for Social Science and Humanities (SSH) research infrastructures: comparative data and modeling, data integration and language tools, and coordination (European Strategy Forum on Research Infrastructures 2006). These aims create a potential for researchers in SSH who want to develop or use e-infrastructure.

5. Status quo and best practice examples from the social sciences

For the most part, social scientists do not see a particular need to use the Grid technology for e-Social Science developments, since most of their data and computation needs could be handled by the existing Internet capacities. There are numerous Internet solutions for access to specific collections, even with local AAA procedures. While many of them grant sufficient user support for their constituency, it is rarely possible for them to provide interoperability of databases and metadata (see the report on Metadata in this publication) or world wide networked access. There are, however, a few remarkable examples for transnational data access in virtually distributed databases.

Building on extensive experience in international data transfer, the Council of European Social Science Data Archives (CESSDA) worked towards networked solutions that ideally would allow interested researchers to access the holdings of member archives from any point in the world. This is operational now as the CESSDA Portal, providing seamless access to datasets from currently twelve social science data archives across Europe.[8] Among other things, it includes prominent reference studies from international comparative research, such as the European Social Survey, Eurobarometers, the International Social Survey Programme, and the European Values Studies.[9] The Data Portal builds on the work of the EU-funded MADIERA project.[10] All content is based on the Data Documentation Initiative (DDI) specifications for documenting datasets including relevant metadata.[11] Multilingual functionality is supported by the European Language Social Science Thesaurus (ELSST) and the NESSTAR technology provides functionality to the user for browsing and analyzing data.[12] The software consists of tools

---

8   http://www.cessda.org/
9   http://www.cessda.org/accessing/catalogue/
10 http://www.madiera.net/
11 http://www.ddialliance.org/org/
12 http://www.nesstar.com/

which enable data providers to disseminate their data on the Web. NESSTAR handles survey data and multi-dimensional tables as well as text resources.

A recent user survey conducted by the Institute for Social Research (ISR, Ann Arbor, Michigan) in cooperation with the Leibniz Institute for the Social Sciences (GESIS, *Leibniz-Institut für Sozialwissenschaften*) under the auspices of the European Science Foundation, with more than 2000 users, shows that there is a high level of satisfaction with these new technologies. These are efficiently supporting simultaneous data access to thousands of studies in a virtual distributed network, frequently including the option to check the measurement instrument, get methodological and technical background information, and then proceed to data analysis in the same session. As a precondition for taking advantage of this functionality on the output side, there are nontrivial investments on the input side. To close the knowledge gap between principle investigators – who designed the study and followed the steps through fieldwork and data management – up to the provision of analysis-ready files, a lot of methodological and technical details covering the research process up to that point have to be communicated to enable further informed analysis.[13]

A frequently discussed area of development is the integration of data, literature, project documentation, and expert databases. One development in this direction is SOWIPORT, which includes among other things references to social science literature and data resources offered by different providers.[14] The Dutch Data Archiving and Networked Services (DANS) have started to store data for long-term preservation and access in the Grid.[15]

There are several other technological developments that have been successfully applied to social science data service for larger international user communities. These include, for example, the Data Service for the European Social Survey (ESS);[16] the ZACAT Data Portal of GESIS,[17] which provides access to most of the continuous international survey programs; the JD-Systems Survey Explorer;[18] or Survey Data and Analysis (SDA), a set of programs for the documentation and web-based analysis of survey data[19] that includes, for example, the German General Social Survey (ALLBUS, *Allgemeine Bevölkerungsumfrage der Sozialwissenschaften*) and the American National Election Study (ANES).

---

13   MetaDater project: http://www.metadater.org/
14   http://www.sowiport.de
15   http://www.dans.knaw.nl/en
16   http://www.europeansocialsurvey.de/)
17   http://zacat.gesis.org
18   http://www.jdcomunicacion.com/ ISSPSpain.asp
19   http://sda.berkeley.edu/

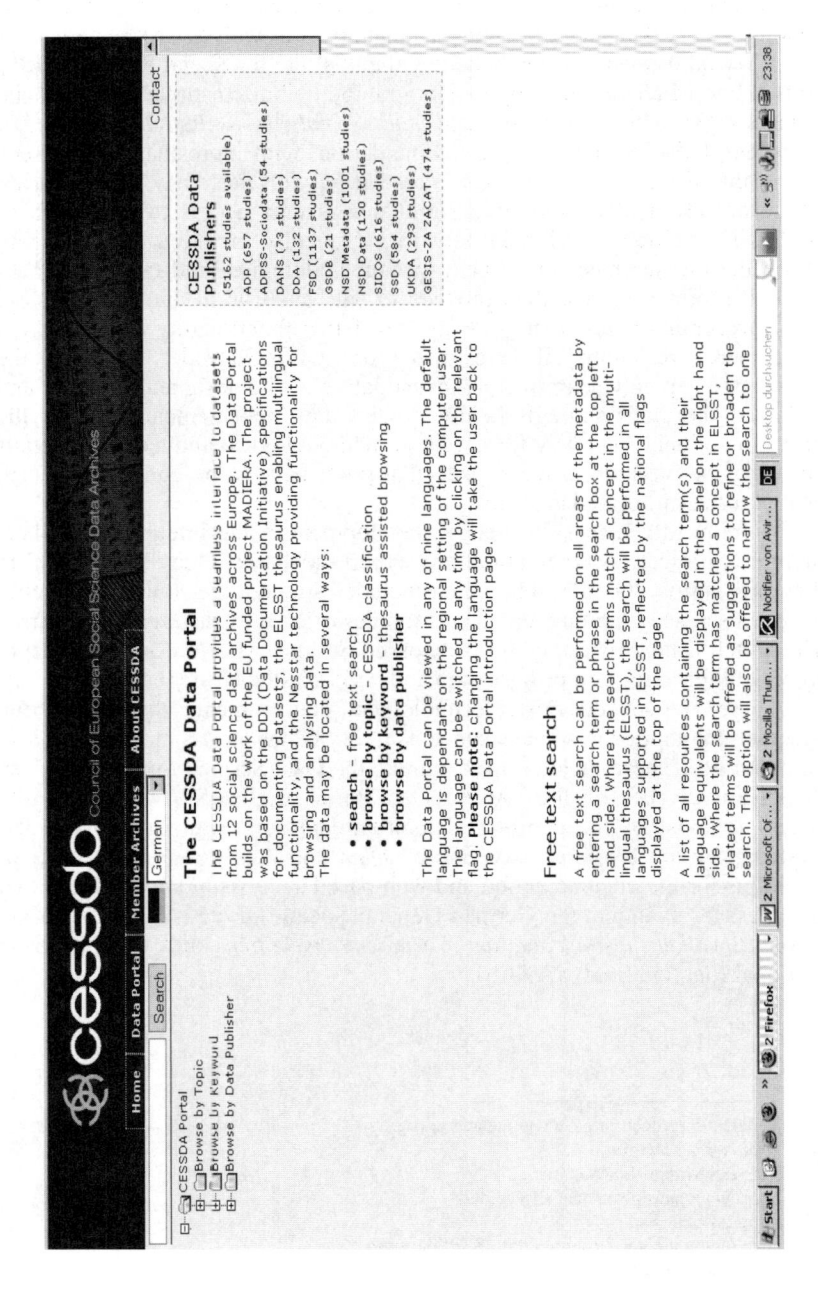

cessda
Council of European Social Science Data Archives

| Home | Data Portal | Member Archives | About CESSDA |

Search German

- CESSDA Portal
  - Browse by Topic
  - Browse by Keyword
  - Browse by Data Publisher

Contact

The CESSDA Data Portal

The CESSDA Data Portal provides a seamless interface to datasets from 12 social science data archives across Europe. The Data Portal builds on the work of the EU funded project MADIERA. The project was based on the DDI (Data Documentation Initiative) specifications for documenting datasets, the ELSST thesaurus enabling multilingual functionality, and the Nesstar technology providing functionality for browsing and analysing data.

The data may be located in several ways:

- **search** – free text search
- **browse by topic** – CESSDA classification
- **browse by keyword** – thesaurus assisted browsing
- **browse by data publisher**

The Data Portal can be viewed in any of nine languages. The default language is dependant on the regional setting of the computer user. The language can be switched at any time by clicking on the relevant flag. **Please note**: changing the language will take the user back to the CESSDA Data Portal introduction page.

Free text search

A free text search can be performed on all areas of the metadata by entering a search term or phrase in the search box at the top left hand side. Where the search terms match a concept in the multi-lingual thesaurus (ELSST), the search will be performed in all languages supported in ELSST, reflected by the national flags displayed at the top of the page.

A list of all resources containing the search term(s) and their language equivalents will be displayed in the panel on the right hand side. Where the search term has matched a concept in ELSST, related terms will be offered as suggestions to refine or broaden the search. The option will also be offered to narrow the search to one

CESSDA Data Publishers
(5162 studies available)
ADP (657 studies)
ADPSS-Sociodata (54 studies)
DANS (73 studies)
DDA (132 studies)
FSD (1137 studies)
GSDB (21 studies)
NSD Metadata (1001 studies)
NSD Data (120 studies)
SIDOS (616 studies)
SSD (584 studies)
UKDA (293 studies)
GESIS-ZACAT (474 studies)

A more recent development is the Dataverse Network supported by the Institute for Quantitative Social Science (IQSS) of Harvard University.[20]

"The Dataverse project aimed to solve some of the political and sociological problems of data sharing via technological means, with the result intended to benefit both the scientific community and the sometimes apparently contradictory goals of individual researchers" (King 2007: 1).

Dataverse provides open source software to host Dataverse networks at larger institutes or to create individual "dataverses" as archives of individual owners that may be just for long-term archiving and analysis, or for access by other users over the Internet. In this way, individually created databases and trusted archives can be networked as the Networks homepage depicts.[21]

As software is only part of the solution, IQSS also provides citation standards for the content to be stored. The digital library services of each dataverse include data archiving, preservation formatting, cataloguing, data citation, searching, conversion, subsetting, online statistical analysis, and dissemination.

6. Conclusions

As we can observe already today, a comprehensive infrastructure based on advanced data communications, computing, and information systems are extremely supportive for conducting high-quality research. They are indispensable for progress, which so far has been unlikely to be achieved in many fields of research. Outstanding examples are the mapping of the human genome and the discovery of new elementary particles, which were facilitated by advanced computational, data storage, and network technologies. Being in touch with widely dispersed research communities, collaborative working and data access in globe-spanning comparative social survey programs that include over 40 countries are already strongly supported by these new technologies. The rapidly growing social science database, including methodologically controlled databases and new kinds of data with related metadata, increasingly leans toward making data linkages across topical domains. This modeling of complex social processes – which may require collaboration in dispersed researcher networks and large-scale data access and computation resources – can be supported more effectively than ever before. One example for creating that kind of research environment is a design study, "Provi-

---

20 http://dvn.iq.harvard.edu/dvn/
21 http://dvn.iq.harvard.edu/dvn/

IQSS Dataverse Network

Search | User Guides | Report Issue | Log in

POWERED BY THE **Dataverse Network** PROJECT

Welcome to the IQSS Dataverse Network!

Access the world's largest collection of social science research data here by searching across or browsing through one of the virtual data archives (called "dataverses") listed below. You may also create a dataverse of your own which may easily be customized to appear as if it is on your web page, but in fact is served by the IQSS Dataverse Network. This means that all the scholarly credit, web visibility, and access control for the data devolve to you, but all the work, preservation guarantees, and software and hardware upgrades and maintenance are taken care of by IQSS. Learn more about the Dataverse Network Project...

Search Studies

Cataloging Information [▼] [   ] Go

Advanced Search | Tips

Show All Dataverses >
Filter by Organization >
Filter by Type >

All Dataverses

Create your own Dataverse ▶

| ALL | A | B | C | D | E | F | G | H | I | J | K | L | M | N | O | P | Q | R | S | T | U | V | W | X | Y | Z |

Dataverses: 243 | Studies: 36,525 | Files: 644,355

|◀ ◀◀ ◀ 1 2 3 4 ▶ ▶▶ ▶|

Name		Affiliation	Released ▼	Activity
Center for Geographic Analysis		Harvard University	May 11, 2010	
Malesky, Edmund	View Info [+]	UCSD	May 3, 2010	
Grimmer, Justin	View Info [+]	Harvard University	Apr 30, 2010	
Enns, Peter	View Info [+]	Cornell University	Apr 26, 2010	
Tol, Richard	View Info [+]	Economic and Social Research Institute and Vrije U Amsterdam	Apr 21, 2010	
Gov2001	View Info [+]	Harvard University	Apr 21, 2010	
Fernandez, Paz	View Info [+]	Instituto Juan March	Apr 21, 2010	
O'Donovan, Michael	View Info [+]	Hlakanphila Analytics	Apr 12, 2010	
Ur, Jason	View Info [+]	Harvard University	Apr 7, 2010	
Schwartz, Alan	View Info [+]	University of Illinois at Chicago	Mar 26, 2010	

ding an Infrastructure for Research on Electoral Democracy in the European Union" (PIREDEU),[22] which brings together all kinds of empirical evidence ranging from survey data to aggregate statistics to party manifestoes on a European level, while the Comparative Study of Electoral Systems is taking a global approach.[23]

The technical backbone and the e-Infrastructure for advanced Grid applications are in place and are currently in use by many international and national science communities. In principle, as well as in practice, there are technological solutions to provide researchers with computational resources on demand; the capability to share complex, heterogeneous and widely distributed data repositories; and the means to enable researchers to collaborate easily and effectively with colleagues around the world. These functionalities, which are available now, have been part of the e-Research Vision that took shape at the beginning of this millennium. This gives an indication of the incredible speed at which these new technologies develop and are adopted in some disciplines.

By and large, the social sciences have so far opted for Web 2.0 solutions. The appeal of Web 2.0 solutions lies in the ease of "ready to use applications." So far, they seem powerful enough to support most data access and analysis needs in domains. This is currently not the case with sensitive microdata from statistical offices and with panel data. Research is underway to integrate disclosure procedures into data access and analysis systems, which pose particular data protection problems. With increasing data availability and research crossing traditional disciplinary boundaries on a global scale, new technologies for large-scale data access and high speed computing may be required.

It is up to each scientific community to assess its specific needs and to decide at what speed it wants to move. Sometimes there are advantages to being a latecomer in adopting new technologies, as many detours may be avoided (Schroeder et al. 2007). Nevertheless, it is obvious that ground laying work needs to be done. A combination of methodological and technical expertise is required to adopt or design and implement the new infrastructures. As has been emphasized in almost all prominent studies quoted, the combination of experts from the social research community working closely with IT specialists is required. Practical experiences from many international projects prove, however, that it is difficult to find the required expertise for limited project lifetimes and that it is even more difficult to keep the additional expertise acquired during the project accessible for further research and development. So, needs assessments, user community studies, and capacity building at the interface of social research methodology and computer science are a prerequisite for viable and sustainable developments.

---

22 http://www.piredeu.eu/
23 http://www.umich.edu/~cses/

It may be a healthy step to combine future research methodology curricula with modules of what might be called "data science," which is about data structures, data management, access and interoperability of databases.

The Open Access Initiatives (e.g., the Berlin Declaration 2003) and the OECD declaration on open access to publicly financed data (OECD 2004) certainly support the creation of a culture of data sharing and ease of access to information and data, including metadata. The challenges and development needs in e-Infrastructure are beyond what a normal research institute can afford to invest in order to keep up on its own with the developments and to cover its long-term needs. Forming alliances or multilateral institutional cooperation have been solutions of academic self organization so far. The National Center for e-Social Science in the UK is an example of how to create a competence center designed to serve the social science community in this respect.

Whether future developments will need Grid enabling of social science databases or can be adequately developed using WEB 2.0 support is currently an open question. The challenge here is the seamless integration and interoperability of databases, a requirement that is also stipulated by internationalization and transdisciplinary research.

Progress in e-Infrastructure is also dependent on regulatory frameworks (Hahlen 2010) and data policies (e.g., NERC Data Policy 2002). The best technical solutions may provide some routines and intelligent algorisms to control access to sensitive data. International access, which is technically possible, can be out of question if statistical confidentially or statistics law prohibit outside use. Last but not least, the organizational infrastructure requires sufficient critical mass in terms of expertise, networking capacities, and sustainable resources to efficiently support a research community that wants to "take the lead without catching up."

7. Recommendations

The present assessment of socio-economic databases does show, once again, that impressive amounts of data are available in many fields of research. It is not surprising, however, that the database as it exists is rather scattered, not well-integrated, and does not lean easily to intranational or international comparative research or even the combination of different sources for analyses with transdisciplinary perspective. Apart from harmonizing data on the measurement level, nontrivial investment is required to get databases organized and to get the metadata in place.

For the most part, social scientists do not see a particular need to use the Grid technology in the development of e-Social Science, since most of their data and computation needs can be handled by the existing Internet capacities. Numerous Internet solutions exist for access to specific collections, even with local AAA procedures in place. While many of them provide sufficient user support for their constituency, the interoperability of databases and metadata (see the report on Metadata in this publication), as well as world wide networked access are rarely possible. There are, however, a few noteworthy examples of transnational data access in virtually distributed databases.

7.1 Data policy and strategic plans for research data management

Some scientific communities have formulated comprehensive *strategic plans* or even published explicit *data policies*. It might provide a good starting point in the social sciences to assess needs in an international context and to identify challenges, drivers, and impediments for the development of a future German e-Infrastructure for the social sciences, which would also provide interfaces to and interoperability with leading international networks.

7.2 Needs assessment and framework conditions

Like other countries, Germany has the technical infrastructure for modern data services in place. Whether there is the *need* and whether the *regulatory framework* conditions will permit the installation of an integrated *German Data Net* has yet to be determined. This could best be done by a *working group* that includes experts on methodological, legal, and technical issues.

7.3 Measurement and metadata standards

Good documentation is a decisive factor that will impact the potential of future data analyses. The Association of German Market Researchers (ADM, *Arbeitskreis Deutscher Markt- und Sozialforschungsinstitute*), the Association of Social Science Institutes (ASI, *Arbeitsgemeinschaft Sozialwissenschaftlicher Institute*), and the Federal Statistical Office agreed on *minimal standards for demographic variables* (*Standarddemographie*) long ago to allow for better comparability of measurements across the three sectors. Likewise, there are standards for metadata that would allow easier identification of and access to data that is related to the concepts central to the respective research questions. It might be advantageous to follow a single metadata standard, but this is not absolutely required. Nevertheless, to follow at least some metadata standard is a precondition for the development of interoperability at a later stage. DDI is being used by several institutes in

Germany already. Working towards wider consensus on adopting metadata standards and agreeing on interfaces is one milestone along the infrastructure highway.

7.4 Best practice in data management and documentation

Efficient database management will require the close cooperation of researcher networks and data services. Best practices have to be communicated to implement metadata capture already at the point of data collection and to cover the whole life cycle from research design via data collection to publication and reuse.

7.5 Capacity building

Training of researchers in best practices of supplying all relevant information from the research process (e.g., the *OAIS model*) and training of data professionals should be oriented toward what could be named "data science" in future curricula. Substantial investment in sound databases needs to be based on the highest level of methodological, data management, and IT expertise. This is hard to find on the labor market in this combination and equally difficult to combine in research teams, simply because there is a serious lack of professionally trained people in this field. Data management, documentation, and access could become one module of "*data science*" in studies of social science research methods. There is a huge market and demand for these skills – such as social and market research, insurance companies, media centers and media archives, data providers, etc.

7.6 Research funding should also cover data management

It is not always easy to assess the relevance of data for future needs. Nevertheless, a vast uninspired *omnium gatherum* should be avoided. At least reference studies and data collections that allow comparability over time or space should be properly documented for further use. This is a nontrivial and labor intensive phase in the research process.

Frequently, the data management required to create high-quality databases demands a lot of methodological and technical expertise. This should be acknowledged by funding authorities and evaluation committees, which tend to honor the analyses but not the investment in preparing the data for it. So future funding of data collection should include *a line on data management and documentation*. Likewise *evaluation criteria* should also include whether databases have been created following *methodological and technical best practice*.

7.7 Technical developments

The question of whether current institution-specific data portals, remote access to individual databases, product catalogues in integrated literature, and data portals like SOWIPORT or networked solutions with central data repositories, such as the DRIVER development on global level, or even Data Grid solutions are the needs of the future has to be assessed with a mid-term and a long-term perspective.

7.8 e- Infrastructure competence center for the social sciences

The Open Access Initiatives (e.g., the Berlin Declaration 2003) and the OECD declaration on open access to publicly financed data (OECD 2004) certainly support the creation of a culture of data sharing and ease of access to information and data, including metadata. The challenges and development needs in e-Infrastructure are beyond what a normal research institute can afford to invest in order to keep up on its own with the developments and to cover its long-term needs. The formation of alliances or multilateral institutional cooperation agreements have been solutions of academic self-organization to date. The National Center for e-Social Science in the UK is an example of creating a competence center designed to serve the social science community in this respect.

References:

Atkins, D.E. et al. (2003): Revolutionizing Science and Engineering through Cyberinfrastructure. Report of the National Science Foundation. Blue-Ribbon Advisory Panel on Cyberinfrastructure. January 2003, 5 and 12.
Berlin Declaration on Open Access to Knowledge in the Sciences and Humanities, Max-Planck-Gesellschaft. Berlin 2003.
Berman, F. and Brady, H. (2005): Final Report: NSF SBE-CISE Workshop on Cyberinfrastructure and the Social Sciences.
De Roure, D./Jennings, N.R. and Shadbolt, N.R. (2003): The Semantic Grid: A Future e-Science Infrastructure. In: Berman, F./Fox, G. and Hey, T. (Eds.): Grid Computing – Making the Global Infrastructure a Reality. Chichester.
Engel, B. (2010): Transaction Data: Commercial Transaction Surveys and Test Market Data. [In this publication].
European Strategy Forum on Research Infrastructures (ESFRI) (2006): European Roadmap for Research Infrastructures. Report 2006.
European Commission IST (2005): Building the e-infrastructure. Computer and network infrastructures for research and education in Europe. A pocket guide to the activities of the Unit. ftp://ftp.cordis.europa.eu/pub/ist/docs/rn/leaflet-2005 en.pdf. [Last visited: 02/23/2010].
Foster, I. and Kesselmann, C. (1999): The Grid: Blueprint for a New Computing Infrastructure San Francisco.
Foster, I./Kesselmann, C. and Tuecke, S. (2000): The Anatomy of the Grid. http://www.globus.org/alliance/publications/papers/anatomy.pdf. [Last visited: 02/23/2010].
Gentzsch, Wolfgang (2007): Grid Initiatives: Lessons Learned and Recommendations version 2.0. http://www.ogf.org/UnderstandingGrids/documents/Grid_Initiatives_July_12_2007.pdf
Hahlen, J. (2010): Providing a Permanent Institutional Guarantee for the German Information Infrastructure [In this publication].
Hey, T. [The Corporate Vice President for Technical Computing, Microsoft] (2008): "eScience, Semantic Computing and the Cloud: Towards a Smart Cyberinfrastructure for eScience" auf der 38. Jahrestagung der Gesellschaft für Informatik: Informatik 2008 – Beherrschbare Systeme – dank Informatik, 08.-13.09. Munich.
King, G. (2007): An Introduction to the Dataverse Network as an Infrastructure for Data Sharing. Sociological Methods and Research 32 (2), 173-199.
Lane, J. (2010): Administrative transaction data. [In this publication].
Meulemann, H. (Ed.) (2004): Erwin K. Scheuch. Infrastrukturen für die sozialwissenschaftliche Forschung. Gesammelte Aufsätze. Bonn.
Mochmann, E. (2001): Infrastruktur für die Komparative Sozialforschung in Europa. In: Hasebrink, U. and Matzen, Ch. (Eds.): Forschungsgegenstand Öffentliche Kommunikation. Funktionen, Aufgaben und Strukturen der Medienforschung. Symposien des Hans-Bredow-Instituts, Band 20. Baden-Baden/Hamburg.
Natural Environmental Research Council (NERC) (2002): Data Policy Handbook Version 2.2, 2002.

Neuroth, H./Kerzel, M. and Gentzsch, W. (Eds.) (2007): Die D-Grid Initiative. Göttingen.
Nie, N. (1989): Model vs. data driven science and the role of the ICPSR in the progress of the social sciences. Adress delivered to the 27th Annual Conference of Official Representatives of the ICPSR. Ann Arbor.
OECD (Ed.) (2004): Science, Technology and Innovation for the 21st Century. Meeting of the OECD Committee for Scientific and Technological Policy at Ministerial Level, 29.-30. January, Paris – Final Communique.
Rockwell, R.C. (1999): Data and statistics: empirical bases for the social sciences. In: Kazangicil, A. and Makinson, D. (Eds.): World Social Science Report. Paris.
Scheuch, E.K. (2003): History and visions in the development of data services for the social sciences. International Social Science Journal 177, 385-399.
Scheuch, E.K. and Mochmann, E. (1972): Sozialforschung. In: Merten, P. (Ed.): Angewandte Informatik. Berlin/New York.
Scheuch, E.K. and Stone, P.J. (1964): The General Inquirer Approach to an International Retrieval System for Survey Archives. American Behavioural Scientist 8 (10), 23-28.
Schnell, R. (2009): Biological Variables in Social Surveys. [In this publication].
Schroeder, R. den Besten, M. and Fry, J. (2007): Catching Up or Latecomer Advantage? Lessons from e-Research Strategies in Germany, in the UK and Beyond. Paper presented at the German e-Science Conference 2007. Baden-Baden.
Serenate (2003a): Flyer. http://www.serenate.org/publications/flyer.pdf
Serenate (2003b): Report on Final Workshop results IST-2001-34925. Study into European Research and Education Networking As Targeted by eEurope. SERENATE Deliverable no. D19. [Authors: Vietsch, K. and Martin, J. (Eds.), Cavalli, V./Dyer, J./Robertson, D./Saugstrup, D./Scott, M. and Wood, Sh.].
Taylor, J. (2001): Presentation given at UK e-Science Meeting, London, July.
Tanenbaum, E. and Mochmann, E. (Eds.) (1994): Integrating the European database: Infrastructure services and the need for integration. International Social Science Journal 46/1994, 4 (142), 499-511.

CURRENT STATE OF AND FUTURE DEMANDS IN DIFFERENT FIELDS

I. (NEW) DATA TYPES AND THEIR POTENTIALS

1. Macroeconomic Data

Ullrich Heilemann[*]

---

[*] For information on current developments of German official statistics, the author is indebted to *Thomas Luh*, Federal Statistical Office, and Dr. *Wolf-Dietmar Speich*, Statistical Office of the Free State of Saxony. For critical comments the author thanks Prof. Dr. *Roland Döhrn*, RWI, Prof. Dr. *Peter von der Lippe*, Universität Essen-Duisburg and *Klaus Löbbe*, Duisburg.

Contact:

Ullrich Heilemann
Institut für Empirische Wirtschaftsforschung (IEW)
Universität Leipzig
Grimmaische Str. 12
04109 Leipzig
e-mail: heilemann[at]wifa.uni-leipzig.de

Abstract

Germany's macroeconomic statistical infrastructure is well-developed: availability and access (including cost) are reasonable and do not leave much to be desired. Beside old demands of more and better information on stocks and flows, sectoral foreign direct investment, on new technologies, and the service sector, the present crisis will cause new requests with respect to the interaction between the monetary and the real sector. The recent trend of improving actuality of data will continue, although requests from a research perspective reliability, validity, and completeness should not get out of sight. A further strand of improvement might be the production of monthly national account (NA) data by German official statistics to improve short-term analysis and forecasting. Besides, the informational gain could be considerably enhanced by following US practice and publishing the indicator data on which the flash estimates are based. The present crisis may speed up the fulfillment of some of these demands, but given that the financial restrictions of the past decade will continue to apply, this may mean only a shift in priorities. This is even more likely with the new NA system scheduled for implementation in 2014 and it would be surprising if more were to happen than has been planned so far (e.g., the great NA-revision 2011).

1. Introduction

The following look at the current state and the future of macroeconomic data is likely to fail. For one thing, researchers will be disappointed to find that their claims for more and "better" data are not adequately supported; official statistics, while to some degree perhaps sharing this disappointment, may miss suggestions and specific comments on old and new data needs. In a material sense, the situation does not appear lamentable and no case can be made requiring immediate action. In addition, few of the following remarks are new or unique. Indeed, as an empirical macroeconomist, and as a member of various statistical advisory bodies, the present author is impressed by the progress made in numerous areas of research infrastructure that were inconceivable only a decade ago. Within the triad of data, methods, and theory, for an increasing number of areas of the social and behavioral sciences, "data" no longer appear to be the limiting factor (here appetite comes with eating, too) – especially not when also looking at cost, returns, and setting negative priorities. It is true that improvements to the macroeconomic information infrastructure over the last two decades were much smaller than the progress made in microeconomics and many of its sub-categories (for labor economics, e.g., Bender and Möller 2010; Schneider 2010). However, these other areas were only catching up with the state of macroeconomic data, which had experienced a similar jump with the launch of the system of national accounts (NA) in Germany some 50 years ago. Given the breadth of the topic, at least in the context of this publication, the following remarks will be cursory and the references rather general.

2. General remarks

At present, German macroeconomic research appears to be largely content with the existing data supply. Government interventions (e.g., in price statistics) or manipulation of statistics, not exactly uncommon in other Western countries, are more than rare here. More importantly, the general supply differs only slightly in substance or style – consistency, comparability, timeliness, etc. – from that of most other industrial countries. For nearly forty years (1920–1960), the driving forces behind the launch and completion of the present macroeconomic infrastructure (notably the national account system, or NA) had been research institutes, especially the German Institute for Economic Research, (DIW Berlin, *Deutsches Institut für Wirtschaftsforschung*) and some of its offspring. Nevertheless, large parts of the research community within and outside these institutes were all too happy when, in the 1960s, official statistics started to take over most of the business of data production and dissemination. This put an end to some institutes' quasi monopolies on some data but, obviously more important for the institutes, they felt relieved at being released from a never-ending and, in terms of academic reputation, poorly rewarded occupation.

Looking back, there has been a great deal accomplished since the 1970s to broaden and deepen the scope of the NA, for example, by using much more elaborate satellite systems for household production and the environment, and still more are to come (health economy, civil society, etc.). Of course, macroeconomists who rely heavily on the NA do have a number of requests on their agenda (see below). However, neither researchers and research institutes nor the German Social Policy Association (*Verein für Socialpolitik*) have expressed much concern about deficits (or about the state of the information infrastructure in general). For statisticians and the German Statistical Society (*Deutsche Statistische Gesellschaft*), of course, things are different (for a somewhat agnostic view, see Richter 2002). Above all, in recent years there has been enormous energy expended on all sides by the development of new concepts of the System of National Accounts (SNA), price statistics, etc., as well as by the microdata revolution.

Despite all this, the economists' gospel is still: *more and better data*, with "better" meaning "more up-to-date" (i.e., more speedily publicized data). Requests for more reliable, more valid or more compatible data are rarely heard. When one takes methods and theory into consideration, however, the priorities seem less clear. Few economists would agree that the marginal return of a Euro spent for investment in research would yield the most if it were spent on data.

Many recent improvements, notably the speeding-up of publication of NA data can be traced back to international financial markets and policy (in particular on the level of EU). It should have been clear right from the beginning that this might have consequences for data reliability and might increase the amount of revisions necessary. However, at the time, this did not really matter. Of course, it would have helped users of this data to know the actual trade-off between timeliness and "accuracy" – its size, whether it changed over time, what might be done to improve accuracy, which aggregates are the most relevant,[1] whether there are differences from other national statistical systems, and if so, can these differences be linked to particular procedures and models, and what can be done to reduce them. So far, only a few users seem to have asked these questions, and no answers have been given.[2] The same questions might be asked with respect to the new SNA (ESA[3] 95): did the list of trade-offs change, in which direction, etc.? Again, no such questions are being asked.

Requests for more and better data are usually answered by the statistical authorities by pointing at the cost involved, their limited resources, and fixed priorities, all of which are hard to contradict by third parties.[4] In general, the cost-benefit ratios of German official statistics and the approximately 10 Euro spent per capita for statistics appear favorable. However, specific information on the cost, including the burden on respondents, on specific fields (macro- and microeconomic, business cycle-growth analyses and forecasts, etc.) is not available for outsiders (Heilemann 1999). Even more difficult to clarify is the utility of (additional) investment in the various segments of the information infrastructure, most of all from a research perspective. The economic and fiscal savings from precise and timely macro data may be enormous; however, the privilege of setting official statistics' priorities will remain with policy.

Generally, the need to improve consistency, comparability, and timeliness, etc. – factors associated with data "style" – of the available macroeconomic data is more urgent than the need for new data, which is limited to a few areas. This is different from the last ten to fifteen years, which were

---

1   For the unfulfilled quest for metadata, see Gregory et al. (2010).
2   As an example for such a study (for the UK), see Maitland-Smith (2003), recently for Germany also Kholodilin and Siliverstovs (2009). Leigh and Stehn (2009) rank Germany surprisingly low in a comparison of temporal stability (1965Q1-2004Q4/ 1995Q1-2004Q4) of revisions in the G7 countries. Similary, so does the European Central Bank (2009) in a Euro area comparison of revisions of NA demand aggregates.
3   European System of Accounts.
4   For some elements of the recent discussions regarding the costs of statistics in Germany, see v. d. Lippe (2006) and Schupp et al. (2003).

characterized by rapidly changing needs that made their way onto the agenda of official statistics, of which many items have been settled. What remains open, however, is the degree to which the hugely increased supply of microdata can improve the *empirical* foundation of macrodata (see, for example, Becker et al. 2006), and in turn, thus testing the "macro compatibility" of microdata.

3. Specific demands

A detailed appraisal of current research interests and the resulting demands on the present and future data situations faces a number of challenges.[5] First, with respect to macroeconomic data, there is still a large backlog of "unfilled orders." To mention just a few: data requirements that came with the advent of globalization, such as the need for detailed information on stocks and flows of foreign direct investment coming from a number of sectors; data on new technologies, and the service economy.[6] Second and more fundamentally, researcher data requests are necessarily stimulated by impending problems, as a closer look at the "backlog" of orders demonstrates. Of course, sometimes things also go the other way and, for a number of reasons, new data may stimulate new questions. Present data needs could hardly have been foreseen five years ago. Even harder to anticipate are data needs that may arise in reaction to the present mixture of crises – financial, regulatory, macroeconomic, sector, currency, etc. Economic "theory" will hardly serve as a guide, as some may be hoping: it may march to the beat of the same drummer as empirical research, but its empirical zeal has usually been modest. Despite the availability of more and "better" data, experience tells us that this limited interest in empirical analysis will hardly change in the near future. It is true that growth theories – both old and new – articulate their needs for a better coverage of human capital,[7] but by now these are old requests and part of the "backlog." Third, it should be remembered that the main thrust for improving official statistics are policy needs on the national and, increasingly, on the international level – certainly if monetary or other

---

5 See also from an US perspective, the Jubilee Volume of The Conference on Research in Income and Wealth (Berndt and Triplett 1990).
6 For details, see, for example, CEIES 2002 and the website of the former 'European Advisory Committee on Statistical Information in the Economic and Social Spheres (CEIES)', now ESAC (European Statistical Advisory Committee) http://forum.europa.eu.int/Public/irc/dsisi/ceies/home, see also Heilemann (2003). For a more (US) research-oriented listing, see http://www.nber.org/CRIW/general. For migration, see also Kahanec and Zimmermann (2010) and Haug (2010), both in this volume.
7 See the various education related papers in this volume.

costs are involved. In the end, all users will benefit from this. The progress of information technology has reduced all these costs (another way is to make better use of administrative data) and will continue to do so, not least because of the government's goal of a "slim state," which will continue to require fiscal prudence. An exception may be the financial sector (including statistics) – crisis is the father of progress.

The ever-increasing interest in data on the service sector was a natural extension of its mounting size. Additional impulses came in the 1990s, when supply factors such as the Information Technology and the demand of the finance industry and of the information/knowledge society shaped the "New Economy." Its direct and indirect links with the rest of the economy intensified, notably with industry, as illustrated by the 1990s productivity miracle in the US. By now, many disputes about the role and scale of technical progress have since been settled, although some of the questions raised – measuring output, hours worked-productivity, prices – still lack convincing answers, particularly in Europe and Germany. National and international statistical bodies have made considerable efforts to overcome some of these difficulties.[8] Germany, for example, employed annual structural surveys in the service sector (activities in transport and communication, real estate, etc.).[9] However, in other parts of the service sector, notably in banking and insurance, such surveys, as well as reliable short-term indicators for the service sector, are still missing.

Other avenues for research (and policy) that were opened by globalization are the causes, forms, and consequences on intra-firm and intra-group trade, FDI proprietorship, trade restrictions, and – strange as this may sound – information on the size, development, forms, and structure of illegal activities (including the shadow economy). While the material and substantial dimensions of these problems are already difficult enough to cover, arguments about "style" pose even greater difficulties given their transnational, all-embracing nature. While by now the problem is recognized, attempts to tackle it have only just started.[10]

Looking more closely at researcher demands, most of them seem to be related to the need for a broader and more fully integrated macroeconomic perspective. Starting with a traditional model of business cycle analysis of the *Keynes/Klein* type as a core model and a general framework of (multi-purpose) macroeconomic analysis, since the 1980s a number of subsystems

---

8   For example, the EU Commission funded the EU Klems project that aims to create a database on measures of economic growth, productivity, employment creation, capital formation and technological change at the industry level for all European Union Member States from 1970 onwards (http://www.euklems.net).
9   It should be noticed that the "great" NA revision in 2011 will picture, among others, the service sector in a more detailed way.
10 For a detailed outline of the problems, user needs, and approaches followed by national and international statistical bodies, see, for example, CEIES (2000).

or satellite systems have been added that interdependently explain demographic developments, human resources and human capital, energy, mobility of capital and people, etc.[11] Clearly, this requires a high compatibility of data, and long time series within or at least compatible with the NA framework.

The needs of business cycle research proper deserve more attention, quite independent from the present crisis (Löbbe 2002). More precisely, while the indicator approach already enjoys a great deal of attention – at least at the level of the Economic and Monetary Union (EMU) of the European Union (Eurostat 2005) – the analytical branch of business cycle analysis seems to be lagging behind. From the point of view of both theoretical and applied analysis, it would be a great step forward if, first, primary data on stocks were freed from the stigma of being residuals; and, second, if inventories were disaggregated – both of which have been demanded for over forty years (Fürst 1967).[12] An even more important leap forward would be an integrated accounting of the distribution of financial and real income and wealth within the NA or compatible with it.[13] This would allow for a detailed examination of the consequences of the functional, as well as personal, distribution of income and wealth as suggested by macroeconomic theory, in particular in mature economies like that of Germany. Whether it will result in an improved explanation (or even more accurate forecasts) of private consumption or private investment remains to be seen. In any case, the information itself would be valuable.

Again, similar ideas have been put forward with respect to a better understanding and modeling of financial motives and financial markets, their actors and institutions (e.g., Eckstein 1983: 77ff). While some flow of funds models have been developed for the German monetary sector, their explanatory power, for a number of reasons, has not been very convincing. However, from a macroeconomic perspective, what is more troublesome is that they have not been linked to the real sector, because the data for the closure of the various channels of transmission – the many forms in which wealth is held – are missing.[14] Of course, things will become even more difficult if we look for a proper inclusion of the international dimension (i.e., globalization and its consequences, not to mention the European Monetary Union). Currently, the first vintage of actual data on international trade in goods is reported about two years after the fact, though preliminary data are not generally

---

11 While the 1983 version of the DRI model of the US economy (Eckstein 1983) can serve as an early example for such a concept and its implementation, the Dutch CORE model (e.g., CPB 1999) may be seen as an illustration of present demands and possibilities.

12 US official statistics have long since published disaggregated inventory data. German OS acknowledges this need as established in ESA 1995, but because of the high cost has thus far declined to do.

13 For a current synopsis of the aggregated and sectoral non-financial wealth accounting, see, for example, Schmalwasser and Müller (2009).

14 Ibid.

criticized as being particularly deficient. However, neither monetary flows, nor data of (other) assets (including human capital or property rights) are reported with the necessary detail or quality.

A more complete system, linking the flow of funds and asset data from the international economy, would greatly improve our understanding of how the financial sector functions and would make, for example, the current demand for a contagion-related stress test of the financial system more realistic and reliable. Only then will we be able to examine the number and roles of the channels of transmission of various crises and their effects. Again, to analyze such influences on investment, consumption, government, distribution, and the foreign sector[15] requires more information on wealth and income, its composition, and distribution (Hauser 2010), at least as much as possible within the framework of the NA. All of these requests had already been made in the first report of the Council of Economic Experts (1964), and have been repeated many times since (e.g., Hax 1998; Glöckler 2003). In this context, the many discrepancies between financial accounting and NA should also be mentioned. Often, the differences are only the consequence of an incongruent dating of transactions, but this is sufficient to hamper economic analysis and assessment.

While the now easy and nearly cost-free access to official data (journals may soon follow) has been much welcomed by the academic community, equally impressive progress with regard to databases is often overlooked. The timeliness of publication of NA data has been greatly improved and harmonized between EU Member States, developments that may especially benefit forecasters. There is now a continuous quality monitoring process, in particular with respect to revision.[16] However, it would be interesting to know, for example, whether revision needs have been increased by the now shorter publication periods or by the new System of National Accounts (SNA) (ESA 1995). Besides, the informational gain could be considerably enhanced by following US practice and publishing the indicator data on which the flash estimates are based. Forecasters are not the only ones who should benefit from knowing the past and present trade-offs between timeliness and revision practices and needs. It remains to be seen whether the current greater timeliness of the NA data is – from a broader quality perspective – a net gain, not just for policy and the financial markets, but for the academic community as well. Finally, official statistics might also reflect on the handling of chain index-based SNA data by the US and others: the loss of precision when using absolute terms instead of indices is small while computation is greatly eased.

---

15 For example, how large would Germany's or Japan's net exports be in terms of proprietorship?
16 See Körner and Schmidt (2006). This is a welcome first step but, of course, it could be extended to metadata, once they are reported. See also FN 2.

Even if the previous list is incomplete with respect to both data substance and style, there is still an old and long list of demands made of official statistics.[17] Again, we should realize that considerable returns on investment might come from improving foreign information supply and infrastructures. This holds from both a research perspective – particularly comparative perspectives – as well as from a policy perspective. The support given in the wake of the EU's southern and eastern enlargements were of considerable help, even if, as with any harmonization, we may have to at least temporarily pay for this with a reduction of national standards.[18]

4. How to move forward

Goals and means are dependent on each other, and the quality of data is largely determined by who is collecting and who is processing them. The current crises will shift present priorities in the direction suggested above, even if, so far, there have been no hints that the German government is willing to commit more resources to this purpose, financial or administrative, its own or that of respondents. At present and for the near future, financial resources appear, at best, fixed. Negative priorities will be hard to set, and the potential to increase productivity appears for outsiders to be rather limited, as privatization and outsourcing experiments in other countries during the past decade have shown. To reduce costs, the use of administrative data might be increased, while the use of primary data is reduced – hardly a reason to expect improvements in data quality. Another ambivalent example is the increase in the cut-off limits for enterprises, which has consequences for intermediate consumption, and our picture of the size and the dynamics of the economy, especially in Eastern Germany. At first, this will affect only the structural perspective, but ultimately it will also affect the aggregate level and its dynamics. On the other side, a wider reliance on administrative data may augment the coherence and compatibility of OS data.

Leaving aside the overall comfortable situation for macroeconomics, a way toward further improvement would be to renew researcher interest in data production and their passion for statistics, a source that thus far seems to have been addressed in the discussion of the "information infrastructure"

---

17 See on this, for example, Richter (2002) and his often very demanding requests.
18 While there is no doubt that in recent years the European Commission (policy!) became increasingly important for national statistics, for a number of reasons not all researchers may be happy with that. For a European policy view on the statistical infrastructure, see Reeh (2010).

only in an indirect way.[19] This is not to overlook the fact that some of the major research institutes are trying to come back to their roots in the creation and improvement of specific research infrastructures.[20] Ignoring policy institutions like central banks and international institutions like the OECD, it is only outside of official statistics that these institutes have enough expertise and motivation to engage in questions of macroeconomic data. More engagement and more reputational reward by the (German) academic community would benefit both their work and the information infrastructure. This is a view supported not only by a look at the US, but also by looking back at German experiences before and after WWII (see above).

5. Conclusions and recommendations

Germany's macroeconomic statistical infrastructure is comparatively well-developed: availability and access (including cost) are reasonable and do not leave much to be desired. The list of proposals for extension and improvements is long and comprehensive, although, once again, this is not that different from the lists drawn up in most other highly developed countries. The present crisis may speed up the fulfillment of some of these demands, but given that the same financial restrictions of the past decade will continue to apply, and the opportunities for additional productivity gains are small, we need a shift in priorities which we did not see so far – despite all of the rhetoric on the statistical needs of the "information society." This is more likely with the new NA system scheduled for implementation in 2014[21] but it would be surprising if more were to happen than has been planned so far (e.g., the great NA-revision 2011).

A new way to diminish this dilemma would be to stimulate, if not a passion at least a stronger interest in questions of macroeconomic data within the academic community. All sides involved would gain much by bringing the academic community closer to this, the forefront of empirical statistical research, making it a closer ally of official statistics, as witnessed in microeconomics over the past twenty years.

---

19 See KVI (2001): 137ff, 146ff. Improving university education may be one strand, improving research standards another. See also, for example, Richter (2002): 293ff.
20 To mention just one example, the efforts of the DIW Berlin (Cors and Kouzine 2003) to bridge the gap between quarterly data may be cited. For a more complete overview, see KVI (2001): 102ff.
21 In 2003 the Statistical Commission of the United Nations (UNSC) initialized a revision of the SNA 1993 http://unstats.un.org/unsd/sna1993/issues. In the course of this process, ESA 95 will be revised. Different from SNA, this will not be mandatory for EU Member States.

The suggestions made here, if implemented, would broaden and improve the data infrastructure. They would help to find better solutions for our problems, primarily for old problems. Scope, frequency, and timeliness of macroeconomic forecasts will further increase and, with some luck, the amount of revisions will be reduced. In the end, monthly data may trigger a jump of insight in macroeconomic dynamics similar to the one that came with the transition from annual to quarterly data.[22] However, whether the accuracy of rate of growth forecasts of real GDP will increase more than by one or two digits is doubtful. The experience of the last 40 years – not just in Germany – does not support such hopes. However, not to worry: neither do theory nor new methods.

---

22 The DIW Berlin started reporting quarterly NA data in 1953. OS began publishing complete sets of NA data in 1978. For an exposition of the possible gains of monthly NA-data, as well as the experiments conducted by a number of forecasters to produce this data, see Klein (2009). This exposition also includes principle component analysis.

References:

Becker, R.A./Haltiwanger, J./Jarmin, R.S./Klimek, S.D. and Wilson, D.J. (2006): Micro and macro data integration: the case of capital. In: Jorgenson, D.W./Landefeld, J.S. and Nordhaus, W.D. (Eds.): A new architecture for the U.S. national accounts. Chicago.

Bender, S. and Möller, J. (2010): Data from the Federal Employment Agency. [In this publication].

Berndt, E.R. and Triplett, J.E. (Eds.) (1990): Fifty years of economic measurement – the Jubilee of the Conference on Research in Income and Wealth. (NBER Studies in Income and Wealth, (54). Chicago.

CEIES (Ed.) (2000): Proceedings of the eighth seminar – Foreign direct investment, Venice, Italy, 11 and 12 November 1999. Luxembourg: European Communities. http://forum.europa.eu.int/Public/irc/dsisi/ceies/home.

CEIES (Ed.) (2002): Proceedings of the seventeenth seminar – The new economy – key measurement issues, Rome, Italy, 4 and 5 March 2002. Luxembourg: European Communities. http://forum.europa.eu.int/Public/irc/dsisi/ceies/home.

Cors, A. and Kouzine, V. (2003): An approach for timely estimations of the German GDP. Allgemeines Statistisches Archiv, (87), 201-220.

CPB Netherlands Bureau for Economic Policy Analysis (Ed.) (1999): WorldScan – the core version. The Hague.

Eckstein, O. (1983): The DRI-model of the U.S. economy, New York.

European Central Bank (2009): Revisions to GDP estimates in the Euro Area. ECB Monthly Bulletin, April, 85-90.

Eurostat (Ed.) (2005): Short-term indicators – Priority assessment, quality, revisions and timeliness – 90th DGINS Conference – Paris, 13-14 September 2004. Luxembourg.

Fürst, G. (1967): Reichen die Informationen über den Konjunkturverlauf aus? Der Volkswirt [seit 1973: Die Wirtschaftswoche], Jg. 21, 2853-2856.

Glöckler, W. (2003): Sachverständigenrat und Statistisches Bundesamt. In: Statistisches Bundesamt (Ed.): 40 Jahre Sachverständigenrat zur Begutachtung der gesamtwirtschaftlichen Entwicklung 1963 – 2003. Wiesbaden.

Gregory, A./Heuss, P. and Ryssevik, J. (2010): Metadata. [In this publication].

Haug, S. (2010): Migration and Statistics. [In this publication].

Hauser, R. (2010): Household Income, Poverty, and Wealth. [In this publication].

Hax, H. (1998): Anforderungen an die Statistik zur Konjunkturbeobachtung und Konjunkturprognose durch den Sachverständigenrat. Allgemeines Statistisches Archiv, (82), 15-24.

Heilemann, U. (1999): Die amtliche Statistik – Dienstleiter in der Informationsgesellschaft. In: Statistisches Bundesamt (Ed.): 50 Jahre Bundesrepublik Deutschland: Amtliche Statistik – Ein konstitutives Element des demokratischen Staates. Wiesbaden.

Heilemann, U. (2003): Globalisation and statistics – a movable target. Statistical Journal of the United Nations Economic Commission for Europe 20 (2), 83-88.

Kahanec, M. and Zimmermann, K.F. (2010): Migration and Globalization. [In this publication].

Kholodilin, K.A. and Siliverstovs, B. (2009): Do forecasters inform or reassure? Evaluation of German real time data. DIW-Discussion Papers No. 888.

Klein, L.R. (Ed.) (2009): The making of national forcasts. Cheltenham.

Kommission zur Verbesserung der informationellen Infrastruktur zwischen Wissenschaft und Statistik (KVI) (Ed.) (2001): Wege zu einer besseren informationellen Infrastruktur. Baden-Baden.

Körner, T. and Schmidt, J. (2006): Qualitätsberichte – ein neues Informationsangebot über Methoden, Definitionen und Datenqualitäten der Bundesstatistiken. Wirtschaft und Statistik, 109-117.

Leigh, D. and Stehn, S.J. (2009): Fiscal and monetary policy during downturns: evidence from G7. IMF Working Paper WP/09/50.

Löbbe, K. (2002): Möglichkeiten und Grenzen der Konjunkturanalyse anhand der amtlichen Statistik. Kurzgutachten im Auftrag der Hans-Böckler-Stiftung. Düsseldorf.

Maitland-Smith, F. (2003): Revisions analysis – Quarterly GDP. Presentation at the OECD/IMF Workshop „Assessing + Improving Statistical Quality", 5-7 Nov. 2003, http://www.oecd.org/dataoecd/26/14/18989859.ppt. [Last visited: 02/19/2010].

Reeh, K. (2010): The European Dimension. [In this publication].

Richter, J. (2002): Kategorien und Grenzen der empirischen Wirtschaftsforschung. Stuttgart.

Schupp, J./Stäglin, R. and Wagner, G.G. (2003): Entbürokratisierung der Statistik durch Flexibilisierung. DIW-Wochenbericht, (24), 396-399.

Schmalwasser, O. and Müller, A. (2009): Gesamtwirtschaftliche und sektorale nichtfinanzielle Vermögensbilanzen. Wirtschaft und Statistik, 137-147.

Schneider, H. (2010): More and Better Data for Labor Market Research. Proposals for Efficient Access to the Currently Unused Potential of Official Statistical Data. [In this publication].

von der Lippe, P. (2006): Ist der Föderalismus in der Statistik noch zeitgemäß? Allgemeines Statistisches Archiv, (90), 341-355.

2. Interdisciplinary Longitudinal Surveys

Jürgen Schupp and Joachim R. Frick

Contact:

Jürgen Schupp
Joachim R. Frick
German Socio-Economic Panel (SOEP)
DIW Berlin
Mohrenstr. 58
10117 Berlin
Germany
e-mail: jschupp[at]diw.de
         jfrick[at]diw.de

Abstract

This paper concentrates on the trends in peer-reviewed longitudinal panel studies under scientific direction. Household panel studies have succeeded in broadening their disciplinary scope. Numerous innovations such as questions dealing with psychological concepts, and age-specific topical modules, physical health measures, measures of cognitive capabilities, and behavioral experiments have been incorporated into various panel studies or are soon to be introduced. In the UK, the household panel study Understanding Society comprising 40,000 households was launched in 2009 and recently added an "innovation sample"; in the Netherlands, the new Longitudinal Internet Studies for the Social sciences (LISS) launched in 2006 with over 5,000 households will be used for the testing of innovative measurement methods.

The microdata from household panel studies like the US Panel Study of Income Dynamics (PSID), the British Household Panel Study (BHPS, the predecessor of UK HLS), the Household, Income and Labour Dynamics in Australia (HILDA) Survey, and the German Socio-Economic Panel (SOEP, *Sozio-oekonomisches Panel*) are in continuously high demand by the research and policy advisory community. More important than "discovering" entirely new survey areas is "tailoring" the details of existing survey content to new, more specific (theoretical) questions, and thus maintaining proven and widely used elements of survey content. In the years to come, "tailoring" survey content will be the real challenge facing surveys that are integrated into the existing research infrastructure like HILDA, LISS, PSID, the Swiss Household Panel (SHP, *Schweizer Haushaltspanel*), SOEP, and the British study Understanding Society.

We argue that, in the future, household panel studies should be designed to take the "margins" of the life course more fully into account. Indeed, household surveys are ideally suited to gather comprehensive data on these life phases. They can be improved, on the one hand, by including specific topics about the fetal phase of life and early childhood of children born into the panel, and on the other hand, by including better information about late life and death. In the middle of the life course, improved questions on income, savings, consumption, and wealth, as well as psychological constructs will play a central role, as will specific "event-triggered" questionnaires on central life occurrences such as marriage, divorce, and entry into and exit from unemployment.

In order to substantially improve the statistical power of long-term longitudinal data, we propose an absolute minimum number of observations of about 500 persons per birth and age cohort. As of now, only the British study Understanding Society will meet this target. A positive side-effect of such an enlargement is a significantly improved potential for analyses of relatively small groups within the population: for example, lone parents or specific immigrant groups. Another positive side-effect would be an improved potential for regional analyses. For example, in Germany, a cohort size of about 500 persons implies a survey sample size of about 20,000 households, which is large enough for analyses in the majority of federal states.

Multidisciplinary panel studies will become even more important if they are accepted as reference datasets for specialized surveys that are independent of the original panel study (e.g., observational studies such as twin studies and laboratory or intervention studies). To enhance this important function, new types of service are needed, including advice on special surveys and possibly also data preparation for special surveys.

Keywords: household panels, multidisciplinary surveys, reference datasets
JEL Classification: A12, C81, C83, C93, C99, H2, H3, H5, I12, I21, I3, J1, J2, J3, J6, J71

1. Introduction

"Longitudinal surveys, which collect information about the same persons over many years, have given the social sciences their Hubble telescope. Both allow the observing researcher to look back in time and record the antecedents of current events and transitions" (Butz and Boyle Torrey 2006: 1899).

If we look back in survey history, social scientists began as early as the 1930s to design a new kind of longitudinal study: the panel survey (Lazarsfeld and Fiske 1938). Panel surveys measure the same variables in the same individuals at two or more points in time. One of the first panel studies was conducted in the US in 1940 in the field of political science (Lazarsfeld et al. 1944). The focus was on the effect of election campaigns, the mass media, and personal communication about politics and causal relationships. Known as the "Erie County Study," Lazarsfeld's study was conducted on a sample of about 600 persons who were surveyed repeatedly over a period of more than six months in seven panel waves. This study remains a model for election studies in political science up to the present day.

In the methodological literature, panel surveys are often described as having a "prospective longitudinal design" (Featherman 1980). In such a design, a group of individuals are interviewed, tracked, and reinterviewed at least once at some future point in time. A "retrospective" panel design, on the other hand, entails collecting data on only one occasion. The longitudinal dimension of such a study is obtained by asking people to recall what things were like at some earlier point in time, as well as at present (de Vaus 2001). This means that it is not strictly necessary to use a longitudinal research design to collect longitudinal data, although there are conceptual distinctions among different types of longitudinal data (Featherman 1980). Here, a crucial question is how reliable retrospective data are as substitutes for direct observations of the past (e.g., concurrent respondent reports in longitudinal panels, independent records, etc.). Such retrospective designs have been used in sociology to collect event history data covering the entire life course. An example of such a study is the German Life History Study (GLHS) (Brückner and Mayer 1998).

In developmental psychology, longitudinal surveys have a clear prospective focus:

"Longitudinal methodology involves repeated time-ordered observation of an individual or individuals with the goal of identifying processes and causes of intraindividual change and of interindividual patterns of intraindividual change in behavioral development" (Baltes and Nesselroade 1979: 7).

Together with total population designs, which are representative from both a cross-sectional and a longitudinal perspective, longitudinal panel surveys are described as advantageous in several respects:

"Total population designs and longitudinal panel designs can be used for practically any type of longitudinal analysis, given a sufficient number of cohorts and measurement periods. Other designs are more limited, and their appropriateness must be judged in the context of a particular research problem" (Menard 2002: 33).

High-quality household panel surveys begin, like cross-sectional surveys, with a random sample of a set of households and of the individuals within those households. For decades, the only mode of data collection was through face-to-face, paper-and-pencil interviews. But an increasing variety of other modes of data collection have become common, some reflecting technological advances. For example, mail surveys and web-based surveys are now also being used (e.g., in the Dutch LISS panel). In addition, different modes of assessment are used. In panel surveys, trained interviewers conduct health tests and tests of cognitive ability (e.g., in SHARE[1]). Panel surveys differ from cross-sectional surveys in that they continue to follow sampled individuals at regular intervals, usually once per year (wave). Adhering to the basic "follow-up rules" determining who to contact and interview again, household panel surveys produce data on changes in the demographic, economic, and social conditions of their members and thus attempt to remain representative of the cross-sectional population as well. This is in contrast to individual panel studies covering entire birth cohorts of individuals in the population.[2] These panels represent their cohorts as they age and may gradually decline in representativity for the original age group. The household panel surveys discussed in the following section can be defined as: multiple repeated observations (usually once per calendar year) for age-heterogeneous individuals within their household context and based on a random sample of all (private) households of a country. Their theoretical concept and variables cover a wide range of social and economic issues.

---

1   Survey of Health, Ageing and Retirement in Europe.
2   Like the longitudinal design of the 1958 National Child Development Study and the 1970 British Cohort Study (BCH) (Schoon 2006) and the Millenium Cohort Study (MCS) or the British birth cohort in 2012 ('Olympic Cohort').

One may ask whether the Hubble telescope (by Butz and Boyle Torrey 2006: 1899) really is the right metaphor for panel studies. After all, since microdata is involved, the comparison with a microscope might seem more appropriate.[3] The answer is twofold. First, panel data have a temporal dimension (as noted by Butz and Boyle Torrey): they do not deliver just a "snapshot," but allow us to actually look back in time (just as telescopes do). Second, panel studies are expensive compared to other studies in economics and the social sciences. Thus, in terms of money, the comparison with a highly sophisticated but expensive device such as the Hubble telescope is much more appropriate than the comparison with more economical microscopes.

This paper gives a summary of current developments in longitudinal household surveys under academic direction. For an overview covering all the various types of panel and cohort studies, see Wissenschaftsrat (2010).

2. Status quo of multidisciplinary household panel studies under academic direction

The success story of large-scale household panels started about 40 years ago, with the US Panel Study of Income Dynamics (PSID) (Brown et al. 1996). Only household panel designs like the PSID, or the designs of the German Socio-Economic Panel (SOEP, *Sozio-oekonomisches Panel*) and British Household Panel Study (BHPS), represent all individuals and households in the population and contain an endogenous mechanism for representing demographic changes in existing households caused, for example, by new entrants (birth, immigration, regional mobility) as well as drop-outs (death, emigration) reflecting the dynamics of the underlying population.

Household panels start with a representative sample of households and a representative set of individuals residing in those households. If the tracking and following rules used in household panels call for attempted interviews with all household members in the original sample, all individuals born to the original sample members, and any individuals who have moved into those households in the meantime (see Kroh et al. 2008), then this prospective panel design continues to provide a representative cross-sectional picture of the underlying population over the life of the panel. Except for immigration into newly founded households from outside the sampling frame, all demographic events (births, deaths, emigration, and events like divorce and the departure of children from their parents' homes) are covered by a high-

---

3   Senator Jürgen Zöllner, who is responsible in Berlin's government for education and research, once asked this question.

quality household panel design. Immigration has to be handled through supplemental samples (see Schupp and Wagner 1995).

Due to initial non-response and attrition of panel respondents over the course of time, high-quality response and attrition analyses and carefully designed re-weighting strategies are crucial to achieve representative population estimates in panel studies (Ernst 1989; Rendtel and Harms 2009). Population estimates (indicating representativity) are an important issue, because all longitudinal and cross-sectional results of the household panel survey are in continuously high demand in both the research and policy advisory community (e.g., Wissenschaftsrat 2009: 56).

Today, some of the most widely used long-running household panel studies that seek to provide a representative view of the entire population of a given society include the BHPS, the Household Income and Labour Dynamics in Australia (HILDA) Survey, the Swiss Household Panel (SHP, *Schweizer Haushaltspanel*), and SOEP. These panels differ from the individual longitudinal studies developed by sociologists in both design and scope, using an extended household concept to measure subjective as well as objective variables. They also differ from the longitudinal cohort studies developed by epidemiologists and psychologists.

Over the course of time, household panel studies have expanded in scope – driven by new research questions of their Principal Investigators (PI) and by the demands of their scientific user communities – and now cover a number of new research questions, some dealing empirically with the "utility" of respondents and the parameters of their utility function. These include happiness and satisfaction with life, health, "other preferences" (trust, fairness, and reciprocity), risk, and inequality aversion.

"Biomarkers" are another exciting new area of research providing non-standard measurement of a respondent's "biological and medical status." One such biomarker is "grip strength," which can be used as an indicator of health (Hank et al. 2009).

"Indeed, biomarkers on social surveys may well reveal more about subjects' predispositions and their ancestry than do their verbal responses on which social scientists have historically depended. Over the past two decades, the theory of evolution has influenced parts of economics and psychology, and to a lesser extent sociology, anthropology, and political science" (Butz and Boyle Torrey 2006: 1899).

In other words, socio-economic panel studies are incorporating an increasing number of concepts from the fields of medicine and psychology. This development has been propelled by the emergence of new research questions, and its pioneers include the Health and Retirement Survey (HRS), the English Longitudinal Study of Ageing (ELSA), and the Survey of Health,

Ageing and Retirement in Europe (SHARE)[4]. The latter study provides a new, comprehensive, international view on aging, but does not cover the population under 50 years of age.

The research community unanimously supports the call for more complete data on the individual life course within the household context, and for improved opportunities to analyze intergenerational transmissions of behavior and social structures and thus to disentangle the impacts of "nature" and "nurture." Outside of the social sciences, this kind of analysis is called "behavioral genetics" (e.g., Plomin et al. 2008). And, in fact, household panel data expand the possibilities for doing research along this line because of the variety of different intergenerational relationships captured in the households surveyed.

Another methodological advantage of panel data is the possibility to make causal inferences: natural experiments created through inherent differences between institutions and countries. The international comparability of data is therefore a central objective in the governance of social statistics and longitudinal studies, and this can only be guaranteed through the optimal design of organizational and financial structures.

The Cross-National Equivalent File (CNEF, based at Cornell University in Ithaca, NY, US) provides a common database derived from existing national panels, namely PSID (US), SOEP (Germany), BHPS (UK), the Survey of Labour and Income Dynamics (SLID; Canada), SHP (Switzerland), and HILDA (Australia) (see Frick et al. 2007). And all successful household panel studies under academic direction demonstrate that the real added value of panel studies can be reaped only after ten waves or more.

To put it succinctly, the major household panel studies under academic direction (as mentioned above) stand for *theory-based data collection*, not just for more data and better statistics. And because such household panels are expensive, all of them are part of the national and/or international research infrastructure (Elias 2010).

---

4   Thus, while SHARE is also a prospective panel study, it is not a fully-fledged household panel, but rather an extended cohort study. The strength of SHARE is its worldwide multi-country coverage (http://www.share-project.org/).

3. Recommendations

3.1 Governance

Two prime examples of good governance in large-scale surveys are the European Social Survey (ESS, a set of repeated cross-sectional surveys run by political scientists) and SHARE (a truly interdisciplinary longitudinal study of economics, sociology, and health). Both surveys provide datasets that form an infrastructure for addressing theory-driven research questions. Unfortunately, initiatives for cross-nationally harmonized household panels, which are more expensive than studies like ESS, are often not research-driven – for example, the European Community Household Panel (ECHP), which provides annual panel data for the period 1994 to 2001. The European Statistics on Income and Living Conditions (EU-SILC), the follow-up survey of ECHP, has a reduced panel component of just four waves focusing on short-term measurement of income and poverty dynamics. EU-SILC will not, however, allow for the kind of in-depth life-course analysis necessary for testing theoretical concepts and hypotheses in the social and behavioral sciences.

We believe that the following list of recommendations can help to ensure good governance of household panel studies under academic direction:

- *Ensure medium-term funding!*
  Household panels – like other prospective longitudinal studies – crucially require stable research questions, survey content, and fieldwork. Annual funding – for example, one-year contracts with fieldwork organizations – cannot guarantee the necessary degree of stability and reliability. Although auditors and accountants may not like medium-term and especially not long-term funding or contracts, medium-term funding (covering at least five years) is the absolute minimum in the case of household panels. And to ensure the quality of the fieldwork and the longitudinal data, ten-year periods of funding and contracting are even better. Other means of quality control than short funding periods must be found to ensure the quality of the panel. In case of panels under academic direction, this is not difficult to achieve because all academic panel studies are under the permanent supervision of advisory boards (and under the "supervision" of users).

- *Get the user community involved!*
  Ongoing panel studies need ideas from their users. However, it is an open question how best to gather user input. Funding agencies are attempting more and more to promote competition. In our opinion – based not least of all on the experience of the British Household Panel Study (BHPS) – the theoretical and methodological standards of major

household panels cannot be raised simply by holding an annual competition among users to suggest an additional "One Minute Question."[5] This was used occasionally by BHPS, but is no longer being used in the new British panel study Understanding Society. While such an approach may produce mainstream add-ons, we feel it is less promising than the approach adopted by the SOEP (which has already undergone pilot testing in recent years): that of focusing on close cooperation with users who are prepared to invest their time, energy, and even resources in pre-testing, with the explicit aim of increasing the SOEP's *long-term longitudinal potential*.

- *Oversample subgroups!*
  While gigantic sample sizes of 100,000 households would ensure sufficient sample sizes in the near and more distant future, with high statistical accuracy for all relevant subgroups of the population, they are not realistic in terms of funding. Thus, the oversampling of subgroups is a permanent issue for the governance of household panel studies. The new British panel study Understanding Society, with a sample size of 40,000 households covering all of the British regions, is a good example, because even this large sample cannot cover immigrants in a sufficient manner. As a result, immigrants are over-sampled. In terms of governance and funding, it is a difficult question whether oversampling of special groups should be done with household panels themselves or through related studies (with external funding) that use a fully-fledged household panel as a "reference sample." There is no clear-cut answer to this question. Whether oversampling should take place within a major household survey or by means of related studies must be discussed on a case-by-case basis.

- *Be innovative!*
  The same is true for the use of "innovation samples" to address highly specified, theory-driven research questions that require specific variables and possibly also specific survey methods. Incorporating such aspects into an ongoing longitudinal survey has the advantage that one need not wait for many years before doing longitudinal analysis. A longitudinal innovation sample that is open to new kinds of measurement is of much higher research value than a new cross-sectional innovation sample. The Dutch LISS panel could possibly become a model for future innovation samples.[6]

---

5   This refers to a competition to create special questions, for which a specific amount of time will be allocated in the survey.
6   The governance of this innovative household panel is documented at http://www.lissdata.nl/lissdata/.

- *Push for related studies!*
  A representative, large-scale household panel sample can serve as a control sample for intervention studies that may be carried out using parts of the innovation sample or as related studies (Anger et al. 2009; Siedler et al. 2009).

3.2 Important areas for substantive enlargements and methodological improvements in the survey programs of household panels[7]

In order to understand human life and human society better, we need to understand human beings as fundamentally social beings. It is thus important to study the range of networks (and areas) in which humans live. But at the same time, there is increasing evidence that sociality is not only a cultural phenomenon (highlighting the importance of intergenerational networks as mentioned above), but that it is also – to a degree that varies between individuals – "hard-wired" into our genome through epigenetic inheritance (Fehr 2009). International developments suggest the value of more systematically surveying a number of variables on the biological foundations of human life (biological and personality characteristics) in a number of areas, and of studying the networks in which individuals, their families, and their households are embedded.

This systematic approach to measurement is not only the result of theoretical improvements but is also driven largely by new technological opportunities for measurement and analysis (e.g., experiments in the lab and in the field, surveys using the Internet and mobile phones, methods of collecting biomarkers and analyzing the genome). In fact, this new analytical approach currently appears to be driven even more by new technologies than by new theoretical insights. This might seem to contradict textbook reasoning about the primacy of scientific theory over pure measurement possibilities, based on the idea that empirical methods should only be used to test the empirical implications of specific theories. "Measurement without theory" is an old and serious criticism lodged against empirical research and data collection. However, in the history of science, we find numerous examples demonstrating that new measurement methods often precede and indeed pave the way for theoretical reasoning. One prominent example is Galileo's telescope, first used 400 years ago, in the year 1609 in Padua. Although it was invented for

---

7   Without challenging the importance of the following issues, we do not address here questions of improved data management (e.g., by means of the "long format" and the Data Documentation Initiative (DDI)), data distribution (Rendtel 2009), and improved IT technologies (see, e.g., www.opendatafoundation.org). We also do not discuss the possiblities of "paradata," which deliver information about the fieldwork process (Kreuter and Casas-Cordero 2010). We do believe that paradata are of utmost importance for the analysis and control of fieldwork processes, attrition analyses, and weighting (Schräpler et al. 2010).

practical purposes, it revolutionized not only the measurement of the visible universe, but a lot of theories too. In the future, "new eyes" will show us further "new skies" (Kanipe 2009).

It is self-evident that the ambitious goal of comprehensively measuring human life trajectories could easily overtax respondents and lead to declining and, in particular, selective response rates. For this reason, we propose that for household panels requiring a high cooperation rate among long-term respondents, new survey methodologies should be tested, such as a standardized "multi-method approach" and "matrix sampling." In matrix sampling, missing values are deliberately created (and later replaced with imputed values) by randomly assigning certain questions that are *not* to be asked to particular subsamples. This reduces the burden of the number of questions to be answered. Though appealing in theory, this method will be challenging to implement successfully in a long-running survey. It may also be worthwhile to use more special proxy questionnaires for the youngest panel "members" who are not able to respond on their own in early childhood, or for those who cannot participate due to temporary absence or bad health.

The comprehensive survey program developed for, and partly realized in, the classic social scientific survey of the "Unemployed of Marienthal" (see Jahoda et al. 1933) appears more promising than ever. Yet since the 1970s, with the growing popularity of standardized survey research, the methodology used in the Marienthal Study has been gradually abandoned. Today, new technologies make more accurate and comprehensive empirical research possible.

Among geneticists, who focus on heritable influences on human behavior, it is broadly accepted that social context is essential for understanding human outcomes. Typically, several different genes and environments play a role in certain outcomes, and it is therefore crucial to study the interactions between the two mechanisms to understand the complexities and dynamics of human behavior. On the other hand, recent work by sociologists and economists provides further evidence that individuals do not respond to societal contextual influences in a unique or socially contingent way. This means that only multidisciplinary collaboration integrating genetic approaches can be expected to produce new insights into this complex relationship (Freese 2009; Guo et al. 2008). The SOEP study has already taken initial steps in this direction, aimed at an interdisciplinary enlargement of the research design (Schupp and Wagner 2010).

- *Better data on the start and end of life*
  Thanks to their longitudinal design, household panel studies are ideally suited to trace the biographies of birth cohorts from the very beginning to the terminal phases of life.

  In an ongoing household panel study, membership does not begin at birth (as is the case in conventional cohort studies) but indeed prior to birth, through the participation of one or both parents in the study. The potential of this unique feature of household panels can be exploited by asking mothers-to-be questions about pregnancy and (very) early childhood. These data allow the economic and social conditions at conception and during pregnancy to be taken into account as aspects defining the individual life course.

Household panels not only provide the opportunity to observe the life course from the very beginning, but also shed light on the terminal phase of life.[8] However, when health declines in later years, respondents often become unwilling or incapable of responding on their own. In these cases, proxy interviews are a useful alternative, yet they remain relatively uncommon. Furthermore, it is often necessary to follow respondents from private households into retirement or nursing homes (Jürges 2010).

- *Consumption and savings*

  Up to now, consumption has generally not been covered well by household surveys. However, in theoretical terms, consumption is an important measure of economic well-being at the individual and the household level. Due to the complexity and respondent burden involved in surveying high-quality data on consumption (levels and patterns), it is widely believed that well-being can be proxied by income. Obviously, this is less than adequate, since income may indeed be much more volatile than consumption, necessitating information on income (a flow measure) as well as on the process of (dis)saving to smooth consumption.

  In order to better understand human behavior in this context, the collection of information on wealth (stock measure), as well as on changes in wealth holdings over time, appears to be especially fruitful for long-running household panel surveys like SOEP (see Frick et al. 2007). Recent advancements in the collection of expenditure data, rather than consumption data, have been made in the Australian HILDA survey, providing clear evidence that income poverty is different from consumption poverty as well as from low wealth (see, e.g., Headey 2008). The 2010 wave of SOEP will, for the first time, include a short assessment of expenditures in the most important domains (housing, nutrition, education, family transfers, and savings).

- *Better measures of competencies*

  In all household panel surveys, human capital has traditionally been operationalized solely by measuring educational attainment as the highest level of schooling or vocational training completed. It seems "natural" to

---

8   See also Romeu Gordo et al. (2009) about household panels as a resource for research on aging, and Kröger (2008) for a pretest of the SOEP exit questionnaire.

improve household panel survey instruments by collecting better data on the cognitive competencies of respondents using standardized measurement procedures (Schupp et al. 2008). In addition, there should be increased efforts to record what are known as non-cognitive capabilities, that is, competencies that are not necessarily acquired in educational institutions but (to a greater extent) at home during early childhood. The SOEP survey program will be extended in a number of ways in the coming years to cover the area of skills (Grabner and Stern 2010; Uhlig et al. 2009).[9]

- *Health and the biological foundations of social and economic behavior*
  Despite the growing interest in integrating biomarkers into surveys, we are convinced that the collection of biomarkers in household panel studies in an unrestricted manner, and solely to address medical research questions, would not be useful or even practicable. Attempting to move in the direction of medical research would impose too high a burden on respondents (as regards the scope and duration of the survey) and would impede the useful division of labor between different methodological approaches and surveys. Rather, a survey of this kind would be a perfect example of a "related study."

  However, biomarkers that can be used to enhance social and behavioral science analyses, and in some cases consolidate their results considerably, promise to be highly useful (National Research Council 2008). One of the reasons is that longitudinal surveys deliver, through repeated measurement, very reliable pictures of phenotypes (the term used by life scientists to describe organisms as the result of the interaction between genotype and environment). Thus, with longitudinal data produced by social scientists, we are much more likely to identify the biological foundations of human behavior than with converse approaches: for example, if life scientists tried to enrich biobanks with social variables.

- *Other measurement improvements*
  A new technology, and an alternative to item sets, is what are known as factorial designs with vignettes. These questions ask respondents very detailed questions about fictitious situations and decisions. This approach is a kind of quasi-experiment (Sauer et al. 2009).

  New technologies have opened up completely new possibilities for measuring human behavior and biographies in the context of personal networks and local environment. We believe that these new measurement possibilities are especially valuable within prospective panel

---

9 See the research network "Nicht-kognitive Fähigkeiten: Erwerb und ökonomische Konsequenzen" (Non-Cognitive Skills: Acquisition and Economic Consequences). For more information, see http://www.zew.de.

studies: such new technologies can help to measure behavior between regular panel waves (which are usually conducted once per calendar year) and to measure networks and environments. We briefly mention some of these new opportunities without having the space to discuss them in depth. Mobile phones can be used as devices for sampling between regular panel waves. In fact, this is being done already (Riediger 2010; Riediger et al. 2009). It will be relativeley straightforward to use the same technology to locate respondents who have moved and collecting photos and sound bytes from their everyday life (Mehl et al. 2007). Even monitoring the physical status of respondents over the course of a day (or several days) with systems currently used by physicians to monitor their patients would be possible (Wrzus et al. 2010).

Networks and local environments of respondents can be measured by links to their Facebook accounts (if respondents give permission). And on the basis of respondents' statements, links can be created to organizational data (e.g., on employers or childcare facilities) (Liebig 2010).

In addition, panel studies can gradually be enhanced by carrying out internal surveys of contextual data. At SOEP, we intend to start with specific surveys that gather data on organizational contexts from 2011 onwards. These will include targeted surveys in childcare centers, schools, and at respondents' workplaces. In 2007, we administered such a pre-test and obtained positive results. It showed that respondents are by and large willing to pass on the addresses of their childcare centers, schools, and employers (Schupp et al. 2008). In 2008, the German General Social Survey (ALLBUS, *Allgemeine Bevölkerungsumfrage*) carried out its first survey of this kind[10] at the workplaces of all employed survey respondents; the results will be used to lay the groundwork for similar questions.

Based on the private addresses of respondents, records can be linked to an increasing number of geo-coded databases, providing information on the local weather or availability of local infrastructure, for example (Lakes 2010, Goebel et al. 2010).

Survey data and behavioral experiments also can be combined (Gächter 2010; Naef and Schupp 2009). Online games, for example, can be used to run behavioral experiments (Bell et al. 2009; Castronova and Falk 2010). And for special subsamples, in-depth studies are possible based on approaches of "qualitative social research" (Tedclie and Tashakorri 2003; Laurie and Sullivan 1991).

---

10 The ALLBUS Organisational survey is being led by Stefan Liebig, who also provided advice to the SOEP when first pilots were being carried out during pretesting (for first results on such an Linked Employer-Employee (LEE) dataset, see Meyermann et al. 2009).

3.3 Developments in sample design and fieldwork

Sufficiently large cohort subsamples allow researchers to analyze the impact of new retirement regulations or measures like the "child-raising allowance" in Germany. To meet our objective of providing statistically reliable information on groups of individuals born in the same year (age cohorts), we consider 500 cases per cohort to be a minimum. With about 500 observations per birth cohort, a researcher can analyze how the new policy instrument works for two very similar birth cohorts: one that is affected by the new law and one that is not. Another example is migration research, which profits similarly from larger samples (Haug 2010; Farwick 2010).

Possible developments in household panel samples are not limited to just enlarging sample size and overall statistical power. The inclusion of special populations (in the case of SOEP, groups like immigrants and high-income households) is another possibility. And not only socio-economic subgroups of the population can be of interest: twins are also candidates for oversampling as a genetically interesting subgroup (Spinath 2010).

In the context of aging societies in Germany and many other Western countries, the coverage of persons in institutions needs to be improved – particularly individuals in (residential) nursing homes. Here the main focus should not be on achieving representative coverage of the institutional population as such, but on covering the life transition from private household to institutional care. This kind of longitudinal data is of high scientific and practical importance for better understanding health changes in old age, intergenerational relations, the relevance of institutional care arrangements for the individual life course, and, last but not least, the process of dying in modern societies. At present, household panels tend to be confronted with non-response when elderly respondents move into (nursing) homes. Here, the difficulties of interviewing persons affected by dementia constitutes a major hurdle; in this special case, the option of having care providers conduct proxy interviews requires further investigation.

International migration and migration dynamics play an increasingly significant role in society. In 2006, more Germans left their native country than ever before, except for the emigration wave of the 1950s. In household panel surveys, respondents moving abroad are no longer included in the sample. At SOEP, groundwork has already been undertaken for surveying abroad. Respondents who have left Germany since 2004 have been contacted, and surveys have been conducted in writing.[11] The hope is that this will make it easier to re-integrate these individuals into the standard sample when and if they return to Germany, since they will never have left the sample completely. Obviously, following internationally mobile indi-

---

11 "Living outside Germany." See, for first results, Schupp et al. (2008).

viduals will require very sophisticated fieldwork. However, in light of the harmonization of household panel surveys within the European Union, we expect increasing research interest in following mobile EU citizens across national borders to gain a better understanding of the motives and the consequences of mobility.

4. Concluding remarks

Datasets generated from multidisciplinary panel surveys are usually extremely rich in analytical potential. At the same time

"(t)he richness of panel data is of value only to the extent that the dataset is analyzed, and analyzed in a timely manner. Running a panel survey is like being on a treadmill: the operations of questionnaire design, data collection, processing and analysis have to be undertaken repeatedly for each successive wave. There is a real danger that the survey team will become overwhelmed by this process with the result that the data are not fully analyzed. To avoid this danger, adequate staffing is needed and a well-integrated organization needs to be established" (Kalton and Citro 1993: 212).

Multidisciplinary household panel surveys need an institutionalized organizational setting, and they are outstanding examples of the research infrastructure that is vital for the social and behavioral sciences. Aside from the group of principal investigators running these kinds of panel studies, they also crucially require a multidisciplinary user group active in analyzing the data and publishing results. An exchange of experiences between data producers and data users is also important. Data producers can work to lower the burdens on users – for example, the challenges of learning to work with complex data structures – by providing new technologies of data distribution, documentation, and training courses. On the other side, feedback from data users on their experiences with the data can act as the scientific foundation for improving multidisciplinary household surveys. A future prospect will be the establishment of a European network of household panels under *academic direction*, with the HLS in the UK and SOEP providing key longitudinal data on the European level (Elias 2010).

References:

Anger, S. et al. (2009): Developing SOEPsurvey and SOEPservice: The (Near) Future of the German Socio-Economic Panel Study (SOEP). SOEPpaper No. 155.
Baltes, P.B. and Nesselroade, J.R. (1979): History and Rationale of Longitudinal Research. In: Nesselroade, J.R. and Baltes, P.B. (Eds.): Longitudinal Research in the Study of Behavior and Development. New York
Bearman, P. (2008): Introduction (Exploring Genetics and Social Structure). American Journal of Sociology 114 (S1), v-x.
Bell, M.W./Castronova, E. and Wagner, G.G. (2009): Surveying the Virtual World: A Large Scale Survey in Second Life Using the Virtual Data Collection Interface (VDCI). DIW Data Documentation No. 44.
Borghans, L./Duckworth, A./Heckman, J.J. and ter Weel, B. (2008): The Economics and Psychology of Personality Traits. The Journal of Human Resources 43 (4), 972-1059.
Brown, Ch./Duncan, G.J. and Stafford, F.P. (1996): Data Watch: The Panel Study of Income Dynamics. Journal of Economic Perspectives 10 (2): 155-168.
Brückner, E. and Mayer, K.U. (1998): Collecting Life History Data – Experiences From the German Life History Study. In: Giele, J.Z. and Elder, G.H. Jr. (Eds.): Methods of Life Course Research. Thousand Oaks.
Butz, W.P. and Boyle Torrey, B. (2006): Some Frontiers in Social Science. Science 312, 1898-1900.
Castronova, E. and Falk, M. (2010): Virtual Worlds as Petri Dishes for the Social and Behavioral Sciences. [In this publication].
de Vaus, D.A. (2001): Research Design in Social Research. London.
Diewald, M. and Mayer, K.U. (2008): The Sociology of the Life Course and Life Span Psychology: Integrated Paradigm or Complementing Pathways? DIW Discussion Papers No. 772.
Elias, P. (2010): Providing Data on the European Level. [In this publication].
Ermisch, J./Gambetta, D./Laurie, H./Siedler, Th. and Uhrig, S.C.N. (2007): Measuring People's Trust. ISER Working Papers No. 2007-32.
Ernst, L. (1989): Weighting Issues for Longitudinal Household and Family Estimates. In: Kasprzyk, D./Duncan, G./Kalton, G. et al. (Eds.): Panel Surveys. New York.
Farwick, A. (2010): Internal Migration. [In this publication].
Featherman, D.L. (1980): Retrospective Longitudinal Research: Methodological Considerations. Journal of Economics and Business 32 (2), 152-169.
Fehr, E. (2009): On the Economics and Biology of Trust. Journal of the European Economic Association 7 (2-3), 235-266.
Freese, J. and Shostak, S. (2009): Genetics and Social Inquiry. Annual Review of Sociology 35, 107-128.
Frick, J.R. and Grabka, M.M. (2005): Item-non-response on income questions in panel surveys: incidence, imputation and the impact on inequality and mobility. Allgemeines Statistisches Archiv 89 (1), 49-60
Frick, J.R. and Grabka, M.M. (2007): Item Non-Response and Imputation of Annual Labor Income in Panel Surveys from a Cross-National Perspective. SOEPpaper No. 49.

Frick, J.R./Goebel, J./Schechtman, E./Wagner, G.G. and Yitzhaki, Sh. (2006): Using Analysis of Gini (ANoGi) for detecting whether two sub-samples represent the same universe: The German Socio-Economic Panel Study (SOEP) Experience. Sociological Methods & Research 34 (4), 427-468

Frick, J.R./Jenkins, S.P./Lillard, D.R./Lipps, O. and Wooden, M. (2007): The Cross-National Equivalent File (CNEF) and its Member Country Household Panel Studies. Schmollers Jahrbuch 127 (4), 627-654.

Frick, J.R./Grabka, M.M. and Sierminska, E. (2007): Representative wealth data for Germany: The impact of methodological decisions around imputation and the choice of the aggregation unit. SOEPpaper No. 3.

Frick, J.R./Grabka, M.M. and Groh-Samberg, O. (2007): Estimates of Imputed Rent and Analysis of their Distributional Impact in Germany. (Research project "Accurate Income Measurement for the Assessment of Public Policies" (AIM-AP), funded by European Commission, 6th Framework Programme, 2006-2009, Contract Nr. CIT5-CT-2005-028412).

Gächter, S. (2010): Experimental Economics. [In this publication].

Geyer, S./Norozi, K./Buchhorn, R. and Wessel, A. (2008): Chances of employment in a population of women and men after surgery of congenital heart disease: Gender-specific comparisons between patients and the general population. SOEPpaper No. 91.

Goebel, J./Wagner, G.G. und Wurm, M. (2010): Exploring the Linkage of Spatial Indicators from Remote Sensing Data with Data from the Socio-Economic Panel (SOEP). SOEPpaper [forthcoming].

Guo, G. (2008): Introduction to the special issue on society and genetics. Sociological Methods & Research 37 (2), 159-163.

Guo, G./Tong, Y. and Cai, T. (2008): Gene by Social Context Interactions for Number of Sexual Partners among White Male Youths: Genetics-Informed Sociology. American Journal of Sociology 114 (Supplement), S36-S66.

Grabner, R.H. and Stern, E. (2010): Measuring Cognitive Ability. [In this publication].

Hank, K./Jürges, H./Schupp, J. and Wagner, G.G. (2009): Isometrische Greifkraft und sozialgerontologische Forschung: Ergebnisse und Analysepotentiale des SHARE und SOEP. Zeitschrift für Gerontologie und Geriatrie 42, 117-126.

Haug, S. (2010): Migration and Statistics. [In this publication].

Headey, B. (2008): Poverty Is Low Consumption and Low Wealth, Not Just Low Income. Social Indicators Research 89, 23-39.

Jahoda, M./Lazarsfeld, P.F. and Zeisel, H. (1933): Marienthal: The Sociography of an Unemployed Community – Translated by the authors with John Reginait and Thomas Elsaesser. Chicago 1971.

Jürges, H. (2010): Provision for Old Age: National and International Survey Data to Support Research and Policy on Aging. [In this publication].

Kämper, Eckhard and Manfred Nießen. (2010): The Role of the German Research Foundation. [In this publication].

Kalton, G. and Citro, C.F. (1993): Panel Survey: Adding the Forth Dimension. Survey Methodology 19 (2), 205-215.

Kanipe, J. (2009): New Eyes, New Skies. Nature 457 (7225), 18.

Kreuter, F. and Casas-Cordero, C. (2010): Paradata. [In this publication].

Kroeger, K. (2008): "Exit-Interviews" in SOEP und SHARE. DIW Data Documentation No. 40.

Kroh, M./Pischner, R./Spieß, M. and Wagner, G.G. (2008): On the Treatment of Non-Original Sample Members in the German Household Panel Study (SOEP). Methoden – Daten – Analysen 2 (2), 179-198.

Krupp, H.-J. (2008): The German Socio-Economic Panel: How It All Began. SOEPpaper No. 75.

Kruppe, Th./Müller, E./Wichert, L. and Wilke, R.A. (2008): On the Definition of Unemployment and its Implementation in Register Data – The Case of Germany. Schmollers Jahrbuch 128 (3), 461-488.

Laurie, H. and Sullivan, O. (1991): Combining Qualitative and Quantitative Data in the Longitudinal Study of Household Allocations. ISER Working Paper 1991-07.

Lakes, T. (2010): Geodata. [In this publication].

Lazarsfeld, P. and Fiske, M. (1938): The "Panel" as a New Tool for Measuring Opinion. Public Opinion Quarterly 2 (4), 596-612.

Lazarsfeld, P.F./Berelson, B. and Gaudet, H. (1944): The People's Choice – How the Voters makes up his Mind in a Presidential Campaign. New York/London.

Liebig, S. (2010): Interdisciplinary Longitudinal Surveys. Linking Individual Data to Organizational Data in Life Course Analysis. [In this publication].

Mayer, K.U. (2009): New Directions in Life Course Research. Annual Review of Sociology 35, 413-433.

Mehl, M.R. et al. (2007): Are Women Really More Talkative Than Men? Science 317, 82.

Menard, S. (2002): Longitudinal Research. Second Edition Thousand Oaks.

Merz, J. (2010): Time Use and Time Budgets. [In this publication].

Meyermann, A./Elsner, J./Schupp, J. and Liebig, S. (2009): Pilotstudie einer surveybasierten Verknüpfung von Personen- und Betriebsdaten – Durchführung sowie Generierung einer Betriebsstudie als nachgelagerte Organisationserhebung zum SOEP-Pretest 2006. DIW Research Notes No. 31.

Naef, M. and Schupp, J. (2009): Measuring Trust: Experiments and Surveys in Contrast and Combination. SOEP Papers on Multidisciplinary Panel Data Research at DIW Berlin No. 167.

National Research Council (2008): Biosocial Surveys. Committee on Advances in Collecting and Utilizing Biological Indicators and Genetic Information in Social Science Surveys. In: Weinstein, M./Vaupel, J.W. and Wachter, K.W. (Eds.): Committee on Population, Division of Behavioral and Social Sciences and Education. Washington.

Plomin, R./DeFries, J.C./McClearn, G.E. and McGuffin, P. (2008): Behavioral Genetics, Fifth Edition. New York.

Rasner, A./Himmelreicher, R.K./Grabka, M.M. and Frick, J.R. (2007): Best of Both Worlds: Preparatory Steps in Matching Survey Data with Administrative Pension Records; The Case of the German Socio-Economic Panel and the Scientific Use File Completed Insurance Biographies 2004. SOEPpaper No. 70.

Rendtel, U. (2010): Teaching and Statistical Training. [In this publication].

Rendtel, U. and Harms, Th. (2009): Weighting and Calibration for Household Surveys. In: Lynn. P. (Ed.): Methodology of Longitudinal Surveys. Chichester.

Riediger, M. (2010): Experience Sampling. [In this publication].

Riediger, M./Schmiedek, F./Wagner, G.G. and Lindenberger, U. (2009): Seeking Pleasure and Seeking Pain: Differences in Prohedonic and Contra-Hedonic Motivation From Adolescence to Old Age. Psychological Science 20 (12), 1529-1535.

Rodgers, J.L./Bard, D.E./Johnson, A./D'Onofrio, B. and Miller, W.B. (2008): The Cross-Generational Mother–Daughter–Aunt–Niece Design: Establishing Validity of the MDAN Design with NLSY Fertility Variables. Behavioral Genetics 38, 567-578.

Romeu Gordo, L./Motel-Klingebiel, A./Wurm, S. (2009): SOEP as a Source for Research on Ageing – Issues, Measures and Possibilities for Improvement. RatSWD Working Paper No. 83.

Sauer, C./Auspurg, K./Hinz, Th./Liebig, S. and Schupp, J. (2009): Die Bewertung von Erwerbseinkommen: methodische und inhaltliche Analysen zu einer Vignettenstudie im Rahmen des SOEP-Pretest 2008. DIW Data Documentation No. 44.

Schäfer, Ch./Schräpler, J.-P./Müller, K.-R. and Wagner, G.G. (2005): Automatic Identification of Faked and Fraudulent Interviews in Surveys by Two Different Methods. Schmollers Jahrbuch 125 (1), 183-193.

Schoon, I. (2006): Risk and Resilience. Cambridge.

Schräpler, J.-P./Schupp, J. and Wagner, G.G. (2010): Individual and Neighborhood Determinants os Survey Nonresponse – An Analysis Based on a New Subsample of the German Socio-Economic Panel (SOEP), Microgeographic Characteristics and Survey-Based Interviewer Characteristic. SOEPpaper [forthcoming].

Schupp, J. and Wagner, G.G. (1995): Die Zuwanderer-Stichprobe des Sozio-oekonomischen Panels (SOEP). Vierteljahrshefte zur Wirtschaftsforschung 64 (1), 16-25.

Schupp, J. and Wagner, G.G. (2010): Zum „Warum" und „Wie" der Erhebung von (genetischen) ‚Biomarkern' in sozialwissenschaftlichen Surveys. SOEPpapers on Multidisciplinary Panel Data Research No. 260.

Schupp, J./Siegel, N.A./Erlinghagen, M./Stegmann, T. and Wagner, G.G. (2008): Leben außerhalb Deutschlands – Eine Machbarkeitsstudie zur Realisierung von Auslandsbefragungen auf Basis des Sozio-oekonomischen Panels (SOEP). SOEPpapers on Multidisciplinary Panel Data Research No. 120.

Schupp, J./Spieß, C.K. and Wagner, G.G. (2008): Die verhaltenswissenschaftliche Weiterentwicklung des Erhebungsprogramms des SOEP. Vierteljahrshefte zur Wirtschaftsforschung 77 (3), 63-76. [English Version is forthcoming as a SOEPpaper in 2010].

Schupp, J. (2009): 25 Jahre Sozio-oekonomisches Panel – Ein Infrastrukturprojekt der empirischen Sozial- und Wirtschaftsforschung in Deutschland. Zeitschrift für Soziologie 38 (5), 350-357.

Siedler, Th./Schupp, J./Spieß, C.K. and Wagner, G.G. (2009): SOEP as „Reference Data". Schmollers Jahrbuch 129 (2), 367-374.

Siegrist, J. (2001): Zukünftige Aufgaben der Sozial-Epidemiologie. In: Mielck, A. and Bloomfield, K. (Eds.): Sozial-Epidemiologie. Weinheim/Munich.

Spinath, F.M. (2010): Genetically Sensitive Sample Designs. [In this publication].

Teddlie, Ch. and Tashakorri, A. (2003): Major Isues and Controversies in the Use of Mixed Mothods in the Social and Behavioral Sciences. In: Tashakorri, A. and

Teddlie, Ch. (Eds.): Handbook of Mixed Methods in the Social and Behavioral Research. Thousand Oakes/London/New Delhi.

Uhlig, J./Solga, H. and Schupp, J. (2009): Bildungsungleichheiten und blockierte Lernpotenziale: Welche Bedeutung hat die Persönlichkeitsstruktur für diesen Zusammenhang? Zeitschrift für Soziologie 38 (5), 418-440.

Wagner, G.G./Frick, J.R. and Schupp, J. (2006): Enhancing the Power of Household Panel Studies: The Case of the German Socio-Economic Panel Study (SOEP). Schmollers Jahrbuch 127 (1), 139-169

Wissenschaftsrat (2003): Strategische Forschungsförderung – Empfehlungen zu Kommunikation, Kooperation und Wettbewerb im Wissenschaftssystem. http://www.wissenschaftsrat.de/texte/5654-03.pdf.

Wissenschaftsrat (2009): Science-Policy Statement on the Status and Future Development of the Socio-Economic Panel (SOEP).
http://www.wissenschaftsrat.de/texte/9503-09.pdf.

Wissenschaftsrat (2010): Overview of International Household Panel Studies. RatSWD Working Paper 135.

Wrzus, C. et al. (2010): Do Associations Between "Sleeping Well" and "Feeling Well" Become Weaker with Age? Results from the SOEP and an Ambulatory Monitoring Study. Berlin. [Manuscript in preparation].

3. Geodata

Tobia Lakes

Contact:

Tobia Lakes
Humboldt Universität zu Berlin
Geographisches Institut
Unter den Linden 6
10099 Berlin
Germany
e-mail: Tobia.Lakes[at]geo.hu-berlin.de

Abstract

Empirical data can be characterized by its precise location in space and time. An estimated 80 percent of all data contain such spatio-temporal references and are termed geodata. This paper starts with the question: how does it benefit the socio-economic sciences to use geodata and the spatial dimension respectively? In the following report, a multidimensional approach is taken to outline the current situation of geodata and the use of spatial techniques in Germany. The ever-growing volume and variety of available geodata is given particular emphasis. Data security is another issue of great importance when using geodata. Furthermore, the present developments in price and user concepts, accessibility, technical standards, and institutionalization are addressed. A number of challenges facing the field of geodata are identified including open access to geodata, data security issues, and standardization. The main challenge, however, seems to be cooperation and exchange between the rather segregated fields of geoinformation and the information infrastructure. Furthermore, the German Census in 2011 is identified as a major challenge for the acquisition and management of geodata. Geodata and the use of spatial techniques are a field that is rapidly developing due to technological developments as well as due to a recent surge in public interest. The benefits they hold for socio-economic research should be exploited in the future.

Keywords: geodata, geoinformation, Web GIS, geodata infrastructure, spatial techniques

1. Introduction

Many of the foremost research issues to emerge in recent years – climate change and its impact on human life, megacity development, disparities between the rich and the poor, environmental justice, and security – have one element in common: they benefit from empirical study and therefore rely critically on empirical data (IPCC 2007; UN Habitat 2008; EC 2008). Empirical data about households, the sources and targets of migration, meteorological data, the accessibility of education, and the range of environmental pollution are examples of where empirical data are needed, data that can be characterized by a precise location in space and time. An estimated 80 percent of all data contain such spatio-temporal references and are termed geodata. The use of geodata and spatially explicit techniques is well-established in geography or spatial planning as well as in specific subdisciplines such as social geography or economical geography (Longley et al. 2005). However, until recently, the benefit of using geodata and geoinformatics techniques to develop spatially explicit approaches has rarely been exploited in the socio-economic sciences and policy-related research (Goodchild and

Janelle 2004). In addition to regional data approaches (i.e., the report by Grözinger and Matiaske in this publication), the explicit linkage of data to a location has become an area of growing interest, for example, in the context of the next German Census in 2011.

What are the added benefits for the socio-economic sciences in using geodata and the spatial dimension respectively? First of all, geodata is data like every other dataset, hence *spatial data can provide additional information* and therefore should be valued and included in empirical research. In Germany, a large pool of geodata already exists that is continuously being enlarged – something that is described in detail below – and is waiting to be exploited by new users. Second, geodata can add fundamental advantages by *allowing for visualizations in the form of maps and database search algorithms based on location*. Third, the spatial information *makes it possible to integrate various datasets via the spatial location* and examine possible interrelationships between datasets. In a recent study, for example, the life satisfaction approach is used to evaluate air quality: individual-level panel and high-resolution SO_2 data are combined to identify the effect of SO_2 concentration on life satisfaction, housing rents, and the total willingness-to-pay for improvements in air quality (Lüchinger 2009). Directly georeferenced data are also of particular interest as a means of creating comparability to repeatedly collected data based on modified statistical units. The final and perhaps most important benefit is that *spatial analyses* enable the inclusion of the context via concepts of proximity, range, containment, overlap, adjacency, or connectedness. The visualization and statistical analyses of these properties is one way of detecting patterns, anomalies, outliers, and sometimes even causation, and thus to generate new insights. Of course, underlying processes cannot be detected, but they can sometimes be approximated. In a recent study, for example, the factors influencing choices about tertiary education among recently graduated students was modeled: the distance between the students' households and the universities turns out to be very significant (Spiess and Wrohlich 2008). These spatially explicit analyses can be extended to *spatio-temporal modeling approaches* that aim at modeling spatial processes in time, including probable future developments such as land-use change at the interface between the human and environmental systems (Lakes and Müller 2008).

The access to and analysis of geodata on national, European, and global scales are necessary in order to undertake the type of cross-disciplinary research required for developing policy-relevant strategies. Such data therefore can be regarded as not only beneficial, but essential. In Germany, "geoinformation" is now regarded as one of the most important crosssectional technologies of this century and a policy field with an outstanding future (Bundesregierung 2008).

2. Status quo: Geodata and spatial techniques

An outline of the research that would potentially benefit from geodata shows not only that the available geodatasets are of interest, but also that there are techniques available for handling and exploiting the spatial dimension of geodata. This paper describes the data and techniques that exist in Germany in a national and international context. The discussion takes a multi-dimensional approach, addressing data availability, factors influencing data availability (accessibility, technical standards, price and user concepts, data security, and institutionalization), and spatial techniques.

2.1 Present situation of geodata

The amount and the variety of available geodata in Germany is continuously expanding. In terms of content, geodata can be divided into spatial base data and spatial thematic data that are acquired and provided by official or private sources. The *spatial base data* contain general topographical and property information and hence offer the basis for most research studies.

Excursus:
Geodata can either contain a **direct spatial reference** or an **indirect spatial reference**. In the case of a **direct spatial reference** – such as the geodata used most frequently in Germany, the Gauss-Krüger and ETRS 89 systems – the information about the location is defined by two- or three-dimensional coordinates within a coordinate reference system. Data that contain an **indirect spatial reference** include systems closer to everyday human experience, such as administrative areas, postal addresses, or place names. In order to digitally process the complexity of real world objects, they must be generalized and simplified. Discrete objects and continuous fields are two approaches to modelling space that each correspond to a data model – the vector or raster model respectively. Points (e.g., trees, cities), lines (e.g., roads, rivers) and areas or polygons (e.g., city-parcels, administrative boundaries) are examples of the **vector model**. **Raster data** consists of cells within a rectangular grid, such as the remote sensing data of airborne or satellite systems.

The acquisition and management of spatial base datasets is predominately the task of public organizations, and are accessible at the Federal Agency for Cartography and Geodesy (BKG, *Bundesamt für Kartographie und Geodäsie*) and at the survey administrations of the Länder and municipalities, in keeping with the federal system in Germany. The two most important Germany-wide standardized spatial base datasets are:

- **The Authoritative Topographic-Cartographic Information System,** (ATKIS, *Amtliches Topographisch-Kartographisches Informationssystem*) that includes digital landscape models, digital terrain models, digital topographical maps, digital orthophotos, digital street names, geographic names, and administrative boundaries.

- **The Authoritative Real Estate Cadastre Information System** (ALKIS, *Amtliches Liegenschaftskataster Informationssystem*) that contains the Real Estate Map, the Real Estate Book, and the Official House Coordinates.

Within these standardized systems, objects are classified according to a specific hierarchical object catalogue and numbering system, such as 2000 – Residential and Infrastructural Areas (*Siedlungsflächen*), with subclasses including 2100 – More Developed Areas (*baulich geprägte Flächen*), 2111 – Areas with Residential Structures (*Wohnbauflächen*), and 2121 – Sport Facilities (*Sportanlage*). In recent years, *spatial base data from official sources have been increasingly replaced* by new methods of data provision. On the one hand, the *geodata acquired and provided by a worldwide user community via the Internet* is of growing importance. The OpenStreetMap Project is an example of this Wikipedia-style open information source that can be used and updated by anyone in a collaborative way. On the other hand, the influence of *private data providers* within the geodata market is also beyond question. Up-to-date road networks data (e.g., Navteq, Tele-Atlas), household address data, aerial photos, and satellite data are increasingly provided by private companies. While aerial photos are still predominately produced by German companies (e.g., Hansa Luftbild), the market for satellite data is a global one, as seen, for example, in the way that data from satellites being distributed worldwide are useful for local studies. Over the past few years, too, *remote sensing data has captured user interest*. In part initiated by the arrival of new internet-based technologies such as GoogleEarth, it has become obvious that aerial photos as well as satellite data constitute a good data source even at first sight, not to mention with the possibilities opened up by sophisticated remote sensing data for analyses in social science research (Rindfuss and Stern 1998; Goodchild and Janelle 2004). The variety of remote sensing datasets available is growing, each offering specific advantages depending on the objective and context of the study. One can choose, for example, between very high spatial resolution (Quickbird) or very high temporal resolution (Rapid Eye) versus satellite data covering very large areas (Landsat TM). A few companies in Germany have specialized in providing remote sensing data, such as GAF or EuroMap. Remote sensing datasets are also available at the German Remote Sensing Data Center (DFD, *Deutsches Fernerkundungsdatenzentrum*) of the German Aerospace Center (DLR, *Deutsches Zentrum für Luft- und Raumfahrt*).

In addition to the topographical and property information of geospatial base data, the focus in research and application has predominately been on *spatial thematic data*. This can cover a wide variety of fields, including environmental data, employment data, or business data depending on the specific research objective. On the side of government data, these are collected and used *at the federal level, by the Länder, and by municipalities.* While some federal agencies are experienced in working with a spatially explicit approach – such as the German Federal Ministry for the Environment, Nature Conservation, and Nuclear Safety or the Federal Office for Building and Regional Planning – others traditionally provide data either without or with only very aggregated spatial references (e.g., the Federal Employment Agency or the Federal Statistical Office). Particularly important official sources of spatial thematic data for researchers resides at the communal level, in areas such as planning, forestry, environment, statistics, and the police. Of particular interest in this regard is the German Census in 2011, which will provide macro-census information that can be precisely linked to location for further analysis. In addition to government data, a large amount of geospatial thematic data is collected by the research sector itself. Furthermore, both non-profit organizations and commercial data providers hold and provide a significant amount of spatial thematic data. It is particularly in the area of commerce that data needs are not sufficiently covered by public data provision, including branch specific information, as well as data on building, communication, and lifestyle and socio-demographic, market, and consumer data (Fornefeld et al. 2003). Another important source of data comes from the field of *geomarketing*, with companies such as Pitney Bowes Inc. that offer worldwide services in direct marketing and postal services based on a geographic information system (GIS), MapInfo.

2.2 The present situation and factors influencing data availability

The most decisive challenge confronting the current use of spatial base data and spatial thematic data in Germany and elsewhere is the accessibility of a large amount of available geodata, which is distributed in several places and acquired and provided by different sources. The problems inherent in this situation are well recognized by the scientific, business, administration, and political communities in the field of geoinformation. A number of measures have been taken to enhance accessibility. First, *geodata infrastructures and geodatabases have been established on different levels within government agencies and other institutions.* The aim of these geodata infrastructures (GDI) is to improve the accessibility and use of available geodata. Geodata infrastructure projects are very often connected to the management of geodatabases and internet-based geoportals for user-friendly data provision. A Germany-wide national geodatabase has been set up to hold all the geodata needed for legal purposes, government activities, economic development, and research. Its purpose is to provide access to data from different sectors of the federal government, the *Länder,* and municipalities via standardized web services (as a first step, federal geodata is now accessible through the website: www.geoportal.bund.de). A second significant instrument for enabling access to spatial thematic data is the German Environmental Information Portal, PortalU, which allows users to search for environmental information from 120 public agencies and organizations via thematic, spatial, and temporal criteria.

One important issue to emerge recently is the need to create *price and user concepts of geodata that will promote transparent and market-oriented development* without putting the ownership or responsibility for the data into question. The basic approach that the federal government has taken is to charge fees for the use of public geodata based on the cost of data provision (Bundesregierung 2008). The primary building blocks of this policy of data access include the introduction of eGovernment procedures, (e.g., ePayment), legal guidelines such as the Geodata Access Act (*Geodatenzugangsgesetz*) and the Environmental Information Act (*Umweltinformationsgesetz*), and the fees structure established by the Working Committee of the Surveying Authorities of the States of the Federal Republic of Germany (AdV, *Arbeitsgemeinschaft der Vermessungsverwaltungen der Länder der Bundesrepublik Deutschland*).

The technical difficulties arising from varying specifications and formats have been an ongoing challenge. This has been dealt with by developing standards for geoinformation technology that also need to fit eGovernment strategies. The system of independent access to geodata of different levels requires the definition and adoption of standards based on European (CEN) and international standards (ISO, Open Geospatial Consortium). In 2007, the GDI-DE (Spatial Data Infrastructure Germany) introduced an architectural concept for geodata infrastructure, which contains information on functionality, services, and technology for developing the future infrastructure in Germany.

Data security is of ongoing importance for all types of data. Aside from being generally regulated by the foundational Freedom of Information and Reuse of Public Sector Information Act (*Informationsfreiheits- und Informationsweiterverwendungsgesetz*), geodata presents a specific case for which the issue of personal rights is particularly sensitive. Up to now there has been no consistent approach developed for finding a balance between the release and non-disclosure of geodata. In general it depends on the extent to which the personal right of the persons concerned are invaded (Karg and Weichert 2007). Google's recent activity photographing street panoramas for use in 3-D city models available online has provoked new discussions about data security. Specifically relevant to geodata is the Environmental Information Act (*Umweltinformationsgesetz*), which is the national manifestation of European guidelines on public access to information about the environment. Remote sensing data represent a particular type of data with many advantages due to the area-wide, comparable, and up-to-date information they provide on multiple aspects of the earth's surface. However, this data may also pose critical data security risks, as addressed in the recent Satellite Data Security Act (*Satellitendatensicherheitsgesetz*). The issue of data security is of great importance, but it is very complex as it pertains to the provision of social and economic data and, therefore, cannot be fully explored in this paper (see the report by Schaar on data protection and by Metschke on record linkage in this publication).

The measures that have been taken to assure the accessibility and efficient use of geodata have been strengthened by *major achievements in institutionalizing cooperation* between different levels and types of public administration in Germany, as well as within the economic and research sectors that use geodata. To name only the most important: the Interdepartmental Committee for Geoinformation (IMAG, *Interministerieller Ausschuss für Geoinformationswesen*), the Steering Committee of Spatial Data Infrastructure Germany (*Lenkungsgremium GDI-DE*), the Commission for Geoinformation Business (*GIW-Kommission*), the AdV,[1] and the "Deutschland Online" initiative, in coordination with the Working Group of State Secretaries Responsible for eGovernment in the Federation and the *Länder* (*Arbeitskreis der Staatssekretäre für eGovernment des Bundes und der Länder*).

Not only in Germany but also internationally, the cross-border exchange of geodata is of growing importance. The *international interoperability of geodata and geoinformation* has been particularly strengthened by the European INSPIRE initiative, which has developed a set of basic guidelines for interoperability in terms of geodata management and provision as well as for the development of a European geodata infrastructure.

Furthermore, three major *innovations for newly available data* are of importance in the international context: Galileo, the European satellite navigation system, will provide the basis for the future referencing of geodata, the localization and positioning of objects. In 2013, Galileo is expected to offer positioning data which will be of interest for multiple user groups. A central platform for the future usage of Galileo has been set up with the "Forum for Satellite Navigation" by the Federal Ministry of Transport, Building, and Urban Affairs. A second initiative is the Global Monitoring for Environment and Security, which is supposed to integrate terrestrial, satellite, airborne, maritime, and other data sources for environmental policy, climate measures, and sustainable development, as well as for humanitarian, development, and security relevant issues. It is a joint initiative of the European Commission and the European Space Agency. Third, the Group on Earth Observation (GEO) should be mentioned, which was initiated in 2005 to build a "Global Earth Observation System of Systems" (GEOSS) that offers

---

1 http://www.adv-online.de.

better access to earth observation information. A central access point (GEO Portal) as well as a catalogue service (GEO Clearinghouse) is envisaged.

2.3 Present situation in spatial techniques

Geodata can be used like any other dataset in a statistical software application to extract the thematic information it holds. However, in addition to the techniques mentioned above for geodata access and distribution, specific spatial extensions are needed to exploit the spatio-temporal dimension of geodata. The specific type of professional software that offers the required spatial techniques is called GIS (geographical information system). It is a computer system used for capturing, management, analyzing, and displaying Geodata. GIS includes hardware, software, networks, standards, and protocols for data handling and analysis (Longley et al. 2005).

Apart from proprietary software, *Open Source GIS and databases* increasingly provide an interesting alternative (e.g., PostGIS, PostgreSQL, GRASS). In addition, *spatial extensions for frequently used database systems* are being employed, such as Oracle Spatial and new releases of SQL Servers. Whether a professional GIS is needed or whether basic tools suffice depends to a large extent on user interests and requirements. Of particular interest are *Web Services*, which offer basic spatial services without the need for an installed GIS software on the user's PC. While basic functions such as map visualization of decentralized servers via Web Services are well-established, more sophisticated techniques are still in development and need further research. Finally, *freely available Internet tools* are a growing sector, including sponsored user-community portals, such as Picasa – which offers a service to place photos in Google Earth – or portals financed by advertisements, such as Map24.de, which offers navigation data and services. These go along with *navigation and mobile services* that have reached operational application level. Accompanied by the development of GPS sensors in mobile phones and widely spread mobile phone cameras, these open up new opportunities for location-based services as well as for research.

3. Future developments

Looking ahead from the current situation there are manifold developments on the horizon concerning geodata and spatial techniques. Only a few examples will be addressed here (see also Bundesregierung 2008).

The *amount of available datasets will continue to grow*, and the variety of thematic, spatial, and temporal characteristics will increase. The development of *new data acquisition* technologies in particular will contribute to the growing amount of data. These include the more frequent use of positioning systems and new remote sensing technologies, to name only the German development of Terra-SAR-X, RapidEye, and EnMAP. Geodata will increasingly be acquired by both public and private data providers. Hence, new forms of *public-private partnerships and cooperation* for data acquisition, including collaborative web-based initiatives, need special attention. A project of major significance in terms of georeferenced data acquisition and provision within Germany is the next *German Census in 2011.*

The already initiated *development of internet-based access points for geodata, or geoportals will continue*, whether they are government or business portals. The overall objective of building up a national geo-database with the goal of establishing a demand-oriented geodata supply will be a major task for the future. The Geodata Center of the Federal Agency for Cartography and Geodesy (*Geodatenzentrum of the Bundesamt für Kartographie und Geodäsie*) envisages a further extension of the www.geoportal.bund.de, with the current access to data from the Federal State expanding to include data from the *Länder* and municipalities as a geoportal for Germany. In addition to the development of geoportals for official data, business geoportals will also grow in number (MICUS 2008).

Another recent trend that will continue is the creation of portals that are not limited to data or metadata, but that include *Web Services*, enabling direct access to data and thematic map visualizations via the Internet without requiring specialized software. In keeping with this, the principle of decentralized data within specific organizations and centralized data provision for the user will continue. With the growing importance of the Internet, coordinated efforts with *eGovernment*, such as ePayment, will be of interest for geodata. Technical standards need further attention not only within the field of geoinformation but also beyond specialized science and as part of the eGovernment concept developed by the Working Group of the GDI-DE.

In addition to new spatial Internet-based technologies, spatial extensions of widely used database systems support the trend, *"GIS Goes Mainstream."* Hence, the user community is expected to grow constantly, spurred on by free and open source products. Furthermore, *new spatial techniques* in professional GIS software offer the potential to integrate different datasets or to support spatio-temporal modeling.

Cost and usage concepts will continue to be an important issue for public sources of data – a centralized tool for assessing geodata fees at all levels of government as well as for private data providers will be a long-term objective. According to the federal government (Bundesregierung 2008), the cost for data acquired by tax money will be limited to the actual cost of provision, which will enlarge the geodata user group.

Discussions about *data security and the need to legally and consistently define data access rights* will continue to increase, for example in the context of the 2011 Census. A consultancy rating of the most frequently used data and a categorization based on data security relevance will be undertaken (Bundesregierung 2008). A draft of geodata access legislation (*Geodatenzugangsgesetz*) is under development, aiming at the free provision of geodata and geodata services by the federal government and the European Union providing there is no further business usage of the data.

In the near future, *Germany will also have to address the requirements of international developments* (INSPIRE,[2] GMES,[3] GEOSS[4]) and take concrete actions to fulfill them. The INSPIRE guideline has to be transferred into German law by May 15, 2009. The spatial datasets proposed in the annex of the INSPIRE program must be implemented by 2019 in all levels of public administration.

4. European and international challenges

In comparison with Germany, there are similar and yet diverging tendencies that prevail in international contexts (Fornefeld et al. 2003). The strategy of developing geodata infrastructures as a way of optimizing access to geodata from public sources through interministerial organization is an ongoing task in European countries and beyond, for example in the United States. While in the US this goal has reached a well-established level, in most other countries it remains in a development phase. Since internationalization occurs both in the field of private data acquisition as well as in the provision of spatial techniques, the global market is converging. In addition, an increasing number of international guidelines in Europe and across European borders require the comparable use of thematic geodata, such as the European Union Water Framework Directive. International initiatives, such as the INSPIRE guideline, GMES, and GEOSS will thoroughly change the handling of geodata in Germany and Europe. The resulting potential for geodata usage in research and business must be exploited as much as possible. These cross-border developments are leading to the increasing importance of international exchange of geodata beyond the infrastructure of specific government ministries.

---

2   Infrastructure for Spacial Information in Europe.
3   Global Monitoring for Environment and Security.
4   Global Earth Observation System of Systems.

5. Conclusions and recommendations

The collection of geodata and the use of spatial techniques comprise a rapidly developing field due to developments in data technology and methodology, as well as the new level of political attention it has attracted. This makes it difficult to keep track of current developments, although it is more important than ever to regularly analyze the situation and develop recommendations. After all, it needs to be stressed that geodata is data like any other dataset and the artificial separation between geodata and meteorological, juridical, and demographic data for example is no longer adequate, considering that 80 percent of all information has a spatial reference. It is only the combination of information that offers multiple benefits. Hence, most of the issues addressed by the other reports in this publication are also relevant to geodata. The following section will present selected recommendations concerning geodata, the factors influencing geodata accessibility, and spatial techniques.

5.1 Geodata and factors influencing geodata

The amount and variety of geodata is constantly growing. Hence, the main challenge is to *provide access to geodata* in such a way that they can be combined with other forms of data to provide information for research and public policy (Bundesregierung 2008). A *geodata infrastructure based on geoportals* is very significant, but new sources of internet-based and private data provision must also be considered (MICUS 2003; Bundesregierung 2008).

In terms of the data, a *reliable update of official sources of spatial base data* is lacking. Although a five-year rhythm may be what is envisioned, in reality it is often less frequent. Furthermore, the provision of historical data is also of relevance to longitudinal studies, in the best case, comparable data. This may be a task for public agencies since it is not covered by private data providers. Data gaps in *area-wide coverage of spatial base data* in Germany (not to mention Europe or even beyond) need to be closed, for example, in the very different quality of urban and rural topographical data. In addition, research requires comparable data; hence, *object catalogues for spatial base data and spatial thematic data should be developed in greater detail.* Since linking geodata has been identified as a major task, conversion codes between different datasets should be available. Spatial reference is one key to possible data integration; therefore, *data should be equipped with a spatial reference as far as possible.* While indirect reference via postal codes or election districts might be more feasible, the spatial outline and position can change. Therefore, direct spatial reference seems to present a better solution since it leaves data security issues either untouched or at least manageable (see Schaar in this publication) and only then can the spatial benefits of thematic data such as official statistics, Microcensus, and particularly the 2011 Census be fully exploited. *More thinking must be done about the 2011 Census* in order to enable the linkage and integration of census data with further datasets based on explicit georeferencing via the personal address, and at the same time preventing the extraction of individual-level information via techniques such as data aggregation on the grid level or the thematic-object based level.

User rights, particularly for reuse and further use of data, as well as *regulations for fees and price models* in Germany, Europe, and internationally need to be pursued.

Consistent and up-to-date technical standards continue to be an important subject.

With the growing amount of data available, and the enhanced combination of data from different sources, *quality measures for geodatasets* must be developed. Users miss reliable measures of available datasets for data from both official sources and privately offered data. Imperfect data is better than no data; however, it is essential to be able to estimate the possible limits of explanatory power.

5.2 Spatial techniques

On one side, sophisticated spatial analysis and integration of geodata with additional data within interdisciplinary projects open up new research opportunities and need to be exploited. On the other side, mapping techniques for non-professionals offering user-oriented techniques for their specific tasks are a challenge and require an overview of existing software and tools for non-professional spatial analysis supported by best-case studies.

New techniques such as the freely available GoogleMaps, Picasa, or GoogleEarth open up a wide field for *internet-based data access and tools* that need to be exploited. However, issues around the *quality and reliability of publicly available and free tools* need to be investigated.

5.3 Politics

The main challenge in this area seems to be the *need for exchange between the rather segregated fields of geoinformation and the information infrastructure*, such as the German Data Forum (RatSWD). Parallel developments in terms of geodata infrastructures, geodata portals, and geoinformation management should be integrated into a national approach for the overall information infrastructure. A *round table on geodata and regional data together with the German Data Forum (RatSWD)* should be established to bring together the different methods and initiatives taken by data providers and researchers.

The primary issues to be addressed include user and price concepts, data security, and technical standards development to further enhance data exchange. Also, exchange is needed between the public, private, and research sectors in the field of geoinformation in order to get new impulses for and from research.

An awareness of the great potential of geodata and the use of spatial techniques is the prerequisite for their successful use in transdisciplinary, if not interdisciplinary, socio-economic and policy-related research. *Joint research projects* along with a presence in journals and media should be initiated to exploit the potential of integrating geodata in integrated analyses. Integrative modules across departmental (and thematic data) boundaries within universities may be one possibility. *International exchange* should include successful initiatives of geodata usage in the context of scientific infrastructures such as the Center for Spatially Integrated Social Science (US)[5]; SEDAC, the Socioeconomic Data and Applications Center (US)[6]; or the Center for Geoinformation (Ireland)[7].

---

5   http://www.csiss.org/
6   http://sedac.ciesin.columbia.edu/
7   http://ncg.nuim.ie/

References:

Bundesregierung (2008): Zweiter Bericht der Bundesregierung über die Fortschritte zur Entwicklung der verschiedenen Felder des Geoinformationswesens im nationalen, europäischen und internationalen Kontext. Drucksache 16/10080.
EU Commission (EC) (2008): Global Monitoring for Environment and Security (GMES): we care for a safer planet. Communication from the Commission to the European Parliament, Council, EESC and CoR. OM(2008)748.
Fornefeld, M. et al. (2003): Der Markt für Geoinformationen: Potenziale für Beschäftigung, Innovation und Wertschöpfung. Studie im Auftrag des Bundesministerium für Wirtschaft und Arbeit. Düsseldorf.
Goodchild, M.F. and Janelle, D.G. (2004): Thinking spatially in the Social Science. In: Goodchild, M.F. and Janelle, D.G. (Eds.): Spatially Integrated Social Science. New York.
INSPIRE (2007): Richtlinie des Europäischen Parlamentes und des Rates zur Schaffung einer Geodateninfrastruktur in der Europäischen Gemeinschaft vom 14. März 2007 (2007/2/EG) (ABl. L 108/1 v. 25. April 2007).
IPCC (2007): Impacts, Adaptation & Vulnerability. Contribution of Working Group II to the Fourth Assessment Report of the Intergovernmental Panel on Climate Change (IPCC). Cambridge.
Karg, M. and Weichert, T. (2007): Datenschutz und Geoinformation. Studie im Auftrag des Bundesministeriums für Wirtschaft und Technologie. Unabhängiges Landeszentrum für Datenschutz Schleswig-Holstein. Hannover.
Lakes, T./Müller, D. and Krüger, C (2009): Cropland change in southern Romania – a comparison of logistic regressions and artificial neural networks. Landscape Ecology 24 (9), 1195-1206.
Longley, P. et al. (2005): Geographic Information Systems and Science. New York.
Lüchinger, S. (2009): Valuing Air Quality Using the Life Satisfaction Approach. Economic Journal 119 (536), 482-515.
MICUS (2003): Der Markt für Geoinformationen: Potenziale für Beschäftigung, Innovation und Wertschöpfung. Studie im Auftrag des Bundesministerium für Wirtschaft und Technologie.
Rindfuss, R.R. and Stern, P.C. (1998): Linking Remote Sensing and Social Science: The Need and the Challenges. In: Liverman, D. et al. (Eds.): People and Pixels: Linking Remote Sensing and Social Science. Washington.
Spiess, K. and Wrohlich, K. (2008): Does distance determine who attends a University in Germany? SOEPpapers on Multidisciplinary Panel Data Research 118.
UN-HABITAT (2008): The State of the World's Cities 2008/9. United Nations. [Published 2009].

4. Regional Data

Gerd Grözinger and Wenzel Matiaske

Contact:

Wenzel Matiaske
Helmut-Schmidt-University /
University of the Federal Armed Forces Hamburg
Faculty for Economics and Social Sciences
Holstenhofweg 85
22043 Hamburg
Germany
e-mail: matiaske[at]hsu-hh.de

Abstract

The spatial dimension is an increasingly important aspect of research in the social sciences, as a new wave of recent publications shows. In this work, intra-national comparisons have proven to be as fruitful as the more common international analyses, and regional characteristics are shown to have considerable influence on individual behavior. This movement has been fostered by methodological advances, e.g., in multilevel techniques. Germany has a good basic infrastructure for spatial analysis providing easy access to official and semi-official data. In addition, both scientific researchers and commercial marketing firms are active in collecting valuable information, in some cases on a very detailed local level – even down to just a handful of households. However, there is ample room for improvement: huge existing datasets (e.g., PISA-E) are not open for spatial analysis purposes; in many cases sufficient regional information is not available (e.g., on criminal behavior); and systematic oversampling in sparsely inhabited areas to allow additional regional analysis is relatively uncommon.

1. Research questions

Regional analyses of social behavior have a long tradition in the social sciences. In sociology, Durkheim's famous book on suicide was one of the earliest works addressing the impact of regional characteristics – religiosity, urbanization, and social control – on individual anomic behavior (Durkheim 1952). The basic idea of modeling regional characteristics as independent variables influencing social behavior has been taken up repeatedly since then. But early sociology is also known for studies that concentrate on the regional context, embedding social relationships in a group or community (*Gemeinschaft*). Whyte's well-known case study of "Street Corner Society" in Boston's Little Italy brings the spatial dimension into the tradition of the Chicago School (Whyte 1943). Economic theory contains both approaches to regional analysis as well – the use of regional features as independent variables affecting individual behavior, and their use as dependent variables defining social contexts. In one of the first such economic studies, Marshall emphasized the importance of regional characteristics in shaping industrial districts and their role as a core determinant of economic development (Marshall 1898). Regional aspects have also long been discussed from a business management point of view as a problem of site selection: von Thünen's concentric model of land use may be read as an early precursor of industrial location theory (Thünen 1826).

Both strands of theory still profoundly influence the debate. Their impact has been magnified by theoretical and methodological developments. On the theoretical side, recent work has attempted to more clearly distinguish between macro- and micro-levels of social behavior (Alexander et al. 1987). In the words of contemporary rational choice theory, the context of action on the macro-level of social systems – regions in our context – constrain the "logic of the situation." Regional conditions on the macro-level influence how individual or corporate actors choose goal-oriented actions on the micro- (or meso-) level. The logic of aggregation also leads back from the micro- to the macro-level of the social system. There, it shows emergent effects that are not always collective goods created by the "invisible hand," but may also include situations of collective damage (Coleman 1990).

These theoretical developments correspond with methodological progress. Hierarchical regression models – fixed and random effect models (the terminology differs between sociology and economic methodology) – have had a particularly important impact. These models take the hierarchical structure of the analysis explicitly into account: behavior or attitudes are not only explained by individual properties (micro-level) but also by regional circumstances (macro-level) (Snidjders and Bosker 1993). Examining the different degrees of freedom on the various hierarchical levels increases the reliability of the test statistic. These models often include cross-level interactions. Depending on the subject of analysis, different estimators are available (Blien 2005). However, there is a danger of overextending such analyses and thereby falling victim to the "ecological fallacy" problem. To model the macro-constraints of the logic of the situation, individual data and structural (regional) data must either directly mirror each other or be linked in another way.

Whereas this group of multilevel models is predestined to analyze the macro-micro link, there is no standard model available to describe the micro-macro link. In many cases one can use a microeconomic model of market exchange to analyze the logic of aggregation, typically to study price or power effects (Braun 2008). But the assumption of more or less perfect markets does not always hold true. Therefore, a multiplicity of methods like game theory models, Markov models, and simulation studies are employed. Currently social network analysis is being used more and more in the multilevel context (Wasserman and Faust 1994). Furthermore, multivariate techniques developed or modified for ecological analysis, e.g., restricted or detrended correspondence analysis and other eigenvalue techniques or multi-dimensional scaling, seem to be extremely useful in the case of regional data (Leyer and Wesche 2005).

In addition to its pure scientific interest, the analysis of regional data has always been of interest to policy-makers. After World War II, the collection of German regional data experienced its first renaissance in the late 1960s and early 1970s (at least in West Germany). This was connected with the new public interest in planning policy (Schäfers 1973). Scientific organizations responded to the rising demand with increased professionalization, and as a result many current research activities date back to this decade. The section of the German society of sociology (DGS, *Deutsche Gesellschaft für Soziologie*) on urban and regional sociology was officially established in 1975, the same year that another user group with regional interests was founded – the planners' association (*Informationskreis für Raumplanung*) – with now over 1,500 members. In 1976, the German Economic Association (*Verein für Socialpolitik*) followed with the establishment of a commission on regional theory and regional policy.

With the deepening and enlargement of the European Union, new themes and issues have arisen. Instruments like the Cohesion Fund, the Social Fund, and the Regional Development Fund all need regular data for implementation and evaluation of measures. International comparisons have been facilitated by common definitions of regional units: in 2003, a framework on the definitions of NUTS (Nomenclature des unités territoriales statistiques) was legally enacted in the EU based on past cooperation and experiences among the national statistical offices (Brunner 2008).

Interest in the regional dimension increased further with German unification. Given the strong and persistent differences between East and West, the social sciences began to seek explanations of different development paths (e.g., Bertram et al. 2000). Public interest has increased as well, leading to numerous activities. A huge German national atlas project has been launched in which in twelve volumes with CDs offer a comprehensive view of life in the German regions (*Leibniz-Institut für Länderkunde*). This has been conducted mostly on the level of spatial planning regions (ROR, *Raumordnungsregionen*). Also on the ROR level an online survey was conducted and has served as a basis for many comparisons in the media (Faßbender and Kluge 2006).

The labor market is of key importance for policy making. In Germany, the labor market is characterized by extensive regional disparities, especially in terms of the extent of employment and unemployment, but also in terms of income levels. The Institute for Employment Research (IAB, *Institut für Arbeitsmarkt- und Berufsforschung*) collects and analyses labor market data – employment statistics, unemployment statistics, the IAB Establishment Panel – on different levels (Blien et al. 2001). IAB contains its own research department on regional labor markets and also coordinates a regional research network among the former state employment offices (Eckey et al. 2007).

In specialized spatial and regional research, economic research, and current business administration research – that is, in the development of regional clusters – the region is understood as an independent object of research. However, in behaviorally oriented research fields, the macro-level – i.e., aggregate data on the social environment – is linked with micro-level data on behavior, attitudes, and preferences (see Grözinger and Matiaske

2005; Grözinger et al. 2008 for a summary of current studies). These fields usually use micro and macro data derived from different sources. Below we will highlight research facilities providing such data and discuss characteristic aspects of spatial data and problems of bringing it together with individual data. The potential capacity of datasets containing small-scale coordinates is huge, especially by fusion of data. Matchable datasets are not only from public or scientific sources, but also – especially in commercial research – primarily from other sources.

It is primarily private enterprises that have an interest in regional economic or marketing policies. For such decisions, they frequently make use of databases provided by private research facilities and business consultancies. The Society for Consumer Research (GfK, *Gesellschaft für Konsumforschung*) in Nuremberg is one of the biggest European providers of geomarketing data and support analysis, planning, and evaluation of locations in Germany and abroad. Their regional data based on point-of-sale surveys and socio-demographic and sector-specific data are of interest not only for practical purposes but also for general research. GfK's indicators for purchasing power can be analyzed at all regional levels down to individual street sections (Lochschmidt 2005). Similar data are provided by other companies; Microm, for example, calculates "social milieus" from such data, which are used by the German Socio-Economic Panel (SOEP, *Sozio-oekonomisches Panel)* to complement the survey data (Kueppers 2005).

2. Status quo: Databases and access

For research in the tradition described above, where data are needed for planning purposes, a good basic regional data infrastructure is provided by official sources. This is partly done by the Federal Statistical Office, often in cooperation with the Statistical Offices of the German *Länder*, and a special federal research unit, the Federal Office for Building and Regional Planning (BBR, *Bundesamt für Bauwesen und Raumordnung*). The BBR publishes widely-used regular reports on the structure of regional differences in Germany (2005) and forecasts for future development (2004).

Data from the Federal Statistical Office and the BBR can be usually found on the following hierarchically ordered levels (numbers show the respective amount of entities):

- States (*Bundesländer*): 16
- Regional Planning Units (ROR, *Raumordnungsregionen*): 97
- Cities and Counties (SG, *Städte* und *Gemeinden*): 439.

Three data compilations should be highlighted. All are convenient for scientific use since they are available on CD/DVD; both come without user restrictions, are more or less reasonably priced (approx. €75) and regularly updated. In addition, there are linked websites where the variables are defined and maps provided,[1] or where data updates can even be downloaded.[2]

- INKAR[3] (Bundesamt für Bauwesen und Raumordnung 2007) with approximately 800 indicators
- Statistik Regional (Statistische Ämter des Bundes und der Länder 2008b) with approximately 1,100 indicators
- Statistik Lokal (Statistische Ämter des Bundes und der Länder 2008a) with more than 300 indicators.

In many cases, these datasets fulfill the interest of social researchers in regional background information. Where appropriate, differentiation along the lines of gender and migration is often included. In the case of unemployment, INKAR provides the female unemployment rate, the absolute number, the percentage, and the trend. For foreigners, rate, percentage, and trends are given.

Regional information can often be broken down further into an even more detailed grid. Some of the German states are rather large in population und therefore consist of different administrative areas (*Regierungsbezirke*). Many, especially bigger cities have information broken down on boroughs (*Stadtteile/Bezirke*). And on the most detailed level, every municipality provides a land registry (*Kataster*). Whereas such data can only be obtained from the regional or local administrations, detailed general information about the approx. 12,000 municipalities (*Gemeinden*) is conveniently available on a special DVD:

- Statistik Lokal (Statistische Ämter des Bundes und der Länder 2007a).

However, it must be mentioned that the statistical units used are defined either following political traditions or for planning purposes, which are also based on political boundaries. For scientific questions, one therefore has to deal with huge variations in both the population and area, which can make analysis rather difficult. In many contests, the number of inhabitants – an important piece of information – ranges from:

- On the state level, the minimum is 0.7 million (Bremen); the maximum 18 million (North Rhine-Westphalia).

---

1 http://www.raumbeobachtung.de
2 http://www.regionalstatistik.de
3 Indikatoren und Karten zur Raum- und Stadtentwicklung.

- On the ROR level, the minimum is less than 300,000; the maximum is Berlin with over 3 million.
- On the SG level, the minimum is barely over 50,000; the maximum again Berlin with over 3 million.

Besides these official statistical entities, there are other principles of classification, mostly used by scientific or marketing institutions for sampling, such as:

- ZIP codes (*Postleitzahlen*)
- Electoral districts (*Wahlbezirke*)
- Telephone area codes (*Telefonvorwahlen*)
- Labor market regions (*Arbeitsmarktregionen*)
- License plates (*Autokennzeichen*)
- Households (*Haushalte*).

Some of them can also be (dis)aggregated according to the needs of the user. For example, the ZIP code has five digits and is hierarchically ordered. It can therefore be used in its entirety or just the first or first two, three, or four digits.

Households are the smallest unit of information sampled by marketing institutions. Although not set out in law, it is generally understood that to meet German privacy protection mandates all local statistical information has to be based on at least five households (Mietzner 2005). It is permitted to combine information on such clusters, however. On this basis, information collected using consumer marketing techniques provides a wealth of data that can be assembled to describe a certain area according to sociological criteria.

Whereas both of the lists above rely on the principle of physical proximity, it is also possible to classify regional entities by common properties. Frequently used principles in the social sciences are:

- Number of inhabitants
- Income levels
- Types of urbanization.

The latter category can be differentiated according to the needs and the levels of regional aggregation. The BBR, for example, offers a classification of three general regional types of settlements, seven types on the ROR level, and nine on the SG level.

The SOEP deserves special mention. It is by far the most widely-used dataset for social science questions in Germany. Registered users with appropriate data safety measures can obtain access to a version on the ROR level. On the SOEP premises in Berlin, one can even work with a version on the state level.[4]

---

4 http://www.diw.de/english/soep/29012.html

Basically, every special dataset that contains information on the sampling point is a potential source for aggregation to some regional level. For example, one can estimate the regional religious distribution (not available from official statistical sources) on the basis of a survey (Dülmer 2005). But the regionalized sample size must exceed a critical number to provide reliable estimators (Bliese 2000).

Finally, not all data is available on the appropriate regional level, as one may reasonably expect. Three examples are found in areas that are the subject of widespread public debate: (1) the Criminal Statistic is not published regularly or in comprehensive form (Bundeskriminalamt 2008), (2) the PISA-E study, which in Germany refers to the national supplement to the international PISA study, is not provided for secondary analysis below the state level, (3) the outcome of the IQ tests of young men in connection with the military draft system is also seen as private property although it can be successfully linked to regional variables (Ebenrett et al. 2003).

3. Future developments and challenges

The historical dimension of regional characteristics is frequently underestimated, often exceeding the periods of official data. A recent study on the impact of social capital analyzed regional crime rates using historical data on household, population, occupation, etc. as instrumental variables, from 1795 to 1970 (Akcomak and Weel 2008). The Netherlands Volkstellingen Archive (Dutch census) provides this data and more.[5] It would be an improvement if Germany's historical regional data from different sources – church and land registers, historical reports, etc. – were also properly edited and made available for quantitative analysis.

Looking over the border leads to another area for future research improvement. The European NUTS classification has been available for several years, which facilitates comparative research. However, this classification system is more appropriate for planning purposes than for social research. On the European level, a future challenge will therefore be the development of a more detailed classification system, based on the needs of social scientists.

Generally, there is a trade-off between a highly detailed classification system and data privacy. In particular, providing household data for geo-marketing may have the negative side-effect of discriminating against the inhabitants of certain areas ("scoring"). In the long run, the effect may not only lead to intra-regional migration and a self-perpetuating vicious cycle of

---

5 http://www.volkstellingen.nl/en/

discrimination; it may also increase public distrust in data collection and endanger the legitimacy of social science research. Furthermore, problems may arise in the reliability of measured datasets when the data from different reference levels are brought together or methods of data fusion are applied (Zimmermann 2005).

4. Conclusions and recommendations

The following list contains the most important measures to improve the infrastructure on regional data in Germany. From an organizational point of view, the most relevant are:

- In addition to its publications, the BBR has a huge amount of unpublished data on different regional levels on file. They should provide at least a regularly updated list of these data with proper descriptions and a well-defined policy on data access for scientific purposes.
- The GESIS Data Archive, where many of the German survey data are stored, should be granted extra funding to classify all surveys according to their appropriateness for regional analysis.
- Future surveys aimed at being nationally representative should be sampled in such a way that detailed regional analysis is also possible at least on the ROR level. Due to the different population levels, this would need some systematic oversampling in sparsely inhabited areas.
- The five-household entity – currently not formalized – could be used as a basis for any detailed data structuring. Notwithstanding the aforementioned danger of illegitimate use of such information, it would be useful if marketing firms would cooperate to work out a single list of blocks that then could be used universally. Alternatively, the eight-household grid of the Microcensus – which is due to be renewed for the 2011 Census – could be used for this purpose.
- A concordance should then be provided in which the different levels and principles could be easily transferred upward (e.g., a particular ROR, ZIP code, etc. consists of certain numbers of blocks).
- Finally, the wide range of research interests in regional and geographical information from scientific, administrative, and commercial users and data producers leads to the recommendation of a roundtable where common interests could be defined. The German Data Forum (RatSWD) should initiate such a group.

References:

Akcomak, I.S. and Weel, B.T. (2008): The Impact of Social Capital on Crime: Evidence from the Netherlands. Maastricht.
Alexander, J.C./Giesen, G./Münch, R. and Smelser, N.S. (Eds.) (1987): The Micromacro Link. Berkely.
Bertram, H./Nauck, B./Klein, T. (Eds.) (2000): Solidarität, Lebensformen und regionale Entwicklung. Opladen.
Blien, U. (2005): Die Mehrebenenanalyse regionaler Fragestellungen. In: Grözinger, G. and Matiaske, W. (Eds.): Deutschland regional. Sozialwissenschaftliche Daten im Forschungsverbund. Munich.
Blien, U./Haas, A./Hirschenauer, F./Meierhofer, E./Tassinopoulos, A./Vollkommer, D. and Wolf, K. (2001): Regionale Arbeitsmarktforschung im IAB. Mitteilungen aus der Arbeitsmarkt- und Berufsforschung 1, 45-73.
Bliese, P.D. (2000): Within-group agreement, non-independence, and reliability: Implications for data aggregation and analysis. In: Klein, K.J. and Kozlowski, S.W. (Eds.): Multilevel Theory, Research, and Methods in Organizations. San Francisco.
Braun, N. (2008): Sozialkapital aus Sicht der Rational Choice Soziologie. In: Matiaske, W. and Grözinger, G. (Eds.): Sozialkapital: eine (un)bequeme Kategorie [Jahrbuch Ökonomie und Gesellschaft, Band 20]. Marburg.
Brunner, C. (2008): European Datasets: Regional and Urban Statistics. In: Grözinger, G./Matiaske, W. and Spieß, C.K. (Eds.): Europe and its Regions. The Usage of European Regionalized Social Science Data. Cambridge.
Bundesinstitut für Bau-, Stadt- und Raumforschung (2004): Raumordnungsprognose 2020. Informationen zur Raumentwicklung 3/4.
Bundesinstitut für Bau-, Stadt- und Raumforschung (2005): Raumordnungsbericht 2005. Berichte 21.
Bundesinstitut für Bau-, Stadt- und Raumforschung (2007): INKAR – Indikatoren und Karten zur Raum- und Stadtentwicklung. Bonn.
Bundeskriminalamt (2008): Polizeiliche Kriminalstatistik 2007. Wiesbaden.
Coleman, J.S. (1990): Foundations of Social Theory. Cambridge.
Dülmer, H. (2005): Die Schätzung von kleinräumigen Kontextinformationen aus Umfragedaten. In: Grözinger, G. and Matiaske, W. (Eds.): Deutschland regional. Sozialwissenschaftliche Daten im Forschungsverbund. Munich.
Durkheim, E. (1952): Suicide. A Study in Sociology. London.
Ebenrett, H.J./Hansen, D. and Puzicha, K.J. (2003): Verlust von Humankapital in Regionen mit hoher Arbeitslosigkeit. Aus Politik und Zeitgeschichte B 6-7, 25-31.
Eckey, H.-F./Schwengler, B. and Türck, M. (2007): Vergleich von deutschen Arbeitsmarktregionen. Nuremberg.
Faßbender, H. and Kluge, J. (2006): Perspektive Deutschland. Was die Deutschen wirklich wollen. Berlin.
Grözinger, G. and Matiaske, W. (Eds.) (2005): Deutschland regional. Sozialwissenschaftliche Daten im Forschungsverbund. Munich.
Grözinger, G./Matiaske, W. and Spiess, K.C. (Eds.) (2008): Europe and its Regions: The Usage of European Regionalized Social Science Data. Cambridge.

Kueppers, R. (2005): MOSAIC von microm. In: Grözinger, G. and Matiaske, W. (Eds.): Deutschland regional: Sozialwissenschaftliche Daten im Forschungsverbund. Munich/Mering.

Leibniz-Institut für Länderkunde (Eds.). (Div.): Der Nationalatlas Bundesrepublik Deutschland. Heidelberg.

Leyer, I. and Wesche, K. (2005): Ordinationsmethoden zur Analyse ökologischer Daten. In: Grözinger, G. and Matiaske, W. (Eds.): Deutschland regional: Sozialwissenschaftliche Daten im Forschungsverbund. Munich/Mering.

Lochschmidt, B. (2005): Wissen gesucht? Wissen gefunden: GfK Regionalforschung. In: Grözinger, G. and Matiaske, W. (Eds.): Deutschland regional: Sozialwissenschaftliche Daten im Forschungsverbund. Munich/Mering.

Marshall, A. (1898): The Principles of Economics. London.

Mietzner, L. (2005): Anwendungsfelder für mikrogeographische Daten im Marketing In: Sokol, B. (Ed.): Living by Numbers. Leben zwischen Statistik und Wirklichkeit. Düsseldorf.

Schäfers, B. (Ed.) (1973): Gesellschaftliche Planung. Stuttgart.

Snidjders, T. and Bosker, R. (1993): Multilevel analysis. An introduction to basic and advanced multilevel modelling. London.

Statistische Ämter des Bundes und der Länder (2008a): Statistik lokal. Gemeindedaten für ganz Deutschland. Düsseldorf.

Statistische Ämter des Bundes und der Länder (2008b): Statistik regional. Daten für die Kreise und kreisfreien Städte Deutschlands. Düsseldorf.

Thünen, J.H. v. (1825): Der isolierte Staat in Beziehung auf Landwirtschaft und Nationalökonomie. Hamburg.

Wasserman, S. and Faust, K. (1994): Social network analysis: Methods and Applications. Cambridge.

Whyte, W.F. (1943): Street corner society: the social structure of an Italian slum. Chicago.

Zimmermann, E.J. (2005): Möglichkeiten und Grenzen der Datenfusion. In: Grözinger, G. and Matiaske, W. (Eds.): Deutschland regional. Sozialwissenschaftliche Daten im Forschungsverbund. Munich.

5. Genetically Sensitive Sample Designs

Frank M. Spinath

Contact:

Frank M. Spinath
Differentielle Psychologie und psychologische Diagnostik
Universität des Saarlandes
66123 Saarbrücken
Germany
e-mail:　f.spinath[at]mx.uni-saarland.de

Abstract

Understanding the sources of individual differences beyond social and economic effects has become a research area of growing interest in psychology, sociology, and economics. A quantitative genetic research design provides the necessary tools for this type of analysis. For a state-of-the-art approach, multigroup data is required. Household panel studies, such as Understanding Society in the UK or the SOEP in Germany, combined with an oversampling of twins, provide a powerful starting point since data from a reasonably large number of non-twin relatives is readily available. In addition to advances in our understanding of genetic and environmental influences on key variables in the social sciences, quantitative genetic analyses of target variables can guide molecular genetic research in the field of employment, earnings, health, and satisfaction, as combined twin and sibling or parent data can help overcome serious caveats in molecular genetic research.

Keywords: genetics, twins, psychology, sociology, economics, heritability, environment, multigroup design, BHPS, SOEP
JEL Classification: B40, B49, C51, C83

1. Motivation (research questions)

The present report argues that household panel studies that were initiated for the analysis of household income offer a unique opportunity to study the importance of genetic and environmental influences on variation across individuals in key areas of social, economic, and psychological research. It should be noted that, from a genetic point of view, the "environment" includes all influences other than inheritance – a much broader use of the term than is usual in the behavioral sciences. By this definition, environment includes, for example, prenatal events and biological events such as nutrition and illness, not just family socialization factors. Similarly, in this paper, the term environment encompasses a wide variety of biological, natural, social, and economic environments.

Research questions like the origin of earnings variation, life satisfaction, health, and their interrelation with psychological variables such as personality can be addressed. By disentangling the interplay of genes and environmental factors (social scientists may call those effects "socio-economic"), the analyses of genetically informative samples make it possible to derive more accurate estimates of social and economic effects on behavior than social and economic studies, which ignore the influence of genes. A recent Special Issue on "Society and Genetics" in the journal *Sociological Methods & Research* illustrates the growing interdisciplinary readiness to stop treating the differences across individuals at birth as a black box (Guo 2008). In a similar vein, Diewald (2008) argues that genetically sensitive research designs can be of immense value to sociological research in providing evidence to test sociological hypotheses against competing explanations. As a result, more sophisticated methodological approaches in the social sciences should become best-practice, acknowledging and involving genetically informative samples.

Since the inherent design of household panels includes participants of varying genetic and environmental similarity (biological full siblings, biological half-siblings, parent-child dyads, and to a smaller extent adoptive children, twins, and triplets), such panel studies are an ideal – and up to now underutilized – starting point for state-of-the-art quantitative genetic analyses. This report illustrates how household panel studies enriched with an oversampling of twin participants can even address dynamic gene-environment interplay.

This report focuses on the quantitative genetic approach. Molecular genetic research strategies (e.g., genetic association and candidate gene studies) constitute a different methodological approach that is not addressed here (for an outlook on possible combinations of both methods, see section 5 below). Due to the fact that genetically sensitive sample designs are a relatively new topic in the discussion of the research infrastructure and future needs in social and economic research, this report also provides a basic theoretical and methodological background to the understanding of quantitative genetic analyses.

The benefit of utilizing genetically informative data is not limited to research of a predominantly psychological nature, and the number of studies on the etiology of key variables in economic and social research is growing. For example, twin data indicates that basic political attitudes like liberalism and conservatism are likely to be heritable (Hatemi et al. 2007). In two further independent twin studies, Fowler, Baker, and Dawes (2008) showed that voter turnout and political participation have very high heritabilities.

In a recent multigroup analysis, Björklund, Jäntti, and Solon (2005) studied the influences of nature (genes) and nurture (socio-economic characteristics) on earnings variation using observed sibling correlations in earnings for nine types of sibling pairs: monozygotic (MZ) twins reared together, monozygotic twins reared apart, dizygotic (DZ) twins reared together, dizygotic twins reared apart, non-twin full siblings reared together, non-twin full siblings reared apart, half-siblings reared together, half-siblings reared apart, and adoptive siblings. On the basis of this variety of sibling types in the analyses, the authors were able to estimate models that involved less restrictive assumptions and provided opportunities to examine the sensitivity of their results to variation in modeling assumptions; namely, the introduction of nonzero GE correlation, of estimates for the genetic relatedness of DZ twins, non-twin full siblings, half-siblings, and adoptive siblings, and varying sibling correlation in environmental influences. The results turned out to be sensitive to flexibility in modeling the variation across types of sibling pairs in the similarity of their environments. Even the smallest estimate of the genetic component of earnings variation, however, suggested that it accounts for about 20 percent of earnings inequality among men and more than 10 percent among women. The largest environmental influence was of the nonshared variety, which is in line with the results of many quantitative studies on personality. In the present study, even among MZ twin brothers, an estimated 64 percent of their earnings variation was explained by neither genetic nor shared environmental resemblance.

The latter study is also a good example of how quantitative genetic methods can be used to target key research topics in labor economics, that is, understanding the sources of earnings inequality and accounting for the rise in earnings inequality that has occurred in most developed countries over the last quarter-century (Katz and Autor 1999). Inequality research focusing on the role of family and community origins ties in particularly well with the quantitative genetic understanding of shared and nonshared environmental factors. The basic idea is that if family and community origins account for a large portion of earnings inequality, siblings will show a strong similarity in earnings; if family and community background hardly matters at all, siblings will show little more resemblance than would randomly selected unrelated individuals.

2. Theoretical and methodological background

Results from classical twin studies have made a remarkable contribution to one of the most dramatic developments in psychology during the past few decades: the increased recognition of the important contribution of genetic factors to virtually every psychological trait (Plomin et al. 2008). However, enriching classical twin studies by data from additional dyads (non-twin siblings, parents-children, etc) can improve behavioral genetic analyses for the following reasons.

The classical twin design compares the phenotypic resemblances of identical or MZ and fraternal or DZ twins. MZ twins derive from the splitting of one fertilized zygote and therefore inherit identical genetic material. DZ twins are first-degree relatives because they develop from separately fertilized eggs and are 50 percent genetically identical on average. It follows that a greater within-pair similarity in MZ compared to DZ twins suggests that genetic variance influences the trait under study.

To disentangle and to quantify the contributions that genes and the environment make to human complex traits, data are required either from relatives who are genetically related but who grow up in unrelated environments ("twin adoption design"), or from relatives who grow up in similar environments but are of differing genetic relatedness ("twin design"). Most twin studies that have been conducted over the past 80 years are of the latter type. Only two major studies of the former type have been conducted, one in Minnesota (Bouchard et al. 1990) and one in Sweden (Pedersen et al. 1992). These studies have found, for example, that monozygotic twins reared apart from early in life are almost as similar in terms of general cognitive ability as are monozygotic twins reared together, a result suggesting strong genetic influence and little environmental influence caused by growing up together in the same family. These influences are typically called *shared environment influences* because they refer to environmental factors contributing to the resemblance between individuals who grow up together. *Nonshared environmental influences*, on the other hand, refer to environmental factors that make individuals who grow up together different from one another.

One reason why a predominant number of twin studies have utilized the twin design instead of the twin adoption design is that twins typically grow up together, thus it is much easier to find a large number of participants for the classic twin study. In humans, about 1 in 85 live births are twins. The numbers of identical and same-sex fraternal twins are approximately equal. That is, of all twin pairs, about one-third are identical twins, one-third are same-sex fraternal twins, and one-third are opposite-sex fraternal twins. The rate of twinning differs across countries, increases with maternal age, and may even be inherited in some families. Greater numbers of fraternal twins are the result of the increased use of fertility drugs and in vitro fertilization, whereas the rate of identical twinning is not affected by these factors.

Comparing the phenotypic resemblance of MZ and DZ twins for a trait or measure under study offers a rough estimate of the extent to which genetic variance is associated with phenotypic variation of that trait. If MZ twins resemble each other to a greater extent than do DZ twins, the heritability (h^2) of the trait can be estimated by doubling the difference between MZ and DZ correlations, that is, $h^2 = 2(r_{MZ} - r_{DZ})$ (Falconer 1960). *Heritability* is defined as the proportion of phenotypic differences among individuals that can be attributed to genetic differences in a particular population. It should be noted that for a meaningful interpretation of twin correlations in the described manner, a number of assumptions have to be met: the absence of assortative mating for the trait in question, the absence of G(enotype) × E(nvironment) correlation and interaction, and the viability of the Equal Environments Assumption. A more detailed discussion of these assumptions as well as the effects of variation attributable to chorionicity differences is available elsewhere (Spinath 2005), so a short introduction should suffice here:

Assortative mating describes nonrandom mating that results in similarity between spouses and increases correlations and the genetic similarity for first-degree relatives if the trait under study shows genetic influence. Assortative mating can be inferred from spouse correlations which are comparably low for some psychological traits (e.g., personality), yet are substantial for others (e.g., intelligence), with average spouse correlations of about 40 (Jensen 1998). In twin studies, assortative mating results in underestimates of heritability because it raises the DZ correlation but does not affect the MZ correlation. If assortative mating is not taken into account, its effects are attributed to the shared environment.

Gene-Environment (GE) correlation describes the phenomenon that genetic propensities can be correlated with individual differences in experiences. Three types of GE correlations are distinguished: passive, evocative, and active. Previous research indicates that genetic factors often contribute substantially to measures of the environment, especially the family environment (Plomin 1994). In the classic twin study, however, GE correlation is assumed to be zero because it is essentially an analysis of main effects.

Gene-Environment (G × E) interaction is often conceptualized as the genetic control of sensitivity to the environment. Heritability that is conditional on environmental exposure can indicate the presence of a G × E interaction. The classic twin study does not address G × E interaction and the classic twin model assumes the equality of pre- and postnatal environmental influences within the two types of twins.

Finally, the classic twin model assumes the equality of pre- and postnatal environmental influences within the two types of twins. In other words, the *Equal Environments Assumption (EEA)* assumes that environmentally caused similarity is roughly the same for both types of twins reared in the same family. Violations of the EEA in the sense that MZ twins experience more similar environments than DZ twins would inflate estimates of genetic influences.

3. Methodological advances and new research questions

The comparison of correlations between MZ versus DZ twins can be regarded as a reasonable first step in our understanding of the etiology of particular traits. To model genetic and environmental effects as the contribution of unmeasured (latent) variables to phenotypic differences, Structural Equation Modeling (SEM) is required. Analyzing univariate data from MZ and DZ twins by means of SEM offers numerous advances over the mere use of correlations, including an overall statistical fit of the model, tests of parsimonious submodels, and maximum likelihood confidence intervals for each latent influence included in the model.

The true strength of SEM, however, lies in its application to multivariate and multigroup data. During the last decade powerful models and programs to efficiently run these models have been developed (Neale et al. 2003). Extended twin designs and the simultaneous analysis of correlated traits are among the most important developments that go beyond the classic twin study (Plomin et al. 2008).

Multigroup designs using a wider variety of sibling types bring more power to bear on quantitative genetic analyses (e.g., Coventry and Keller 2005). For example, it is useful to include non-twin siblings in twin studies to test whether twins differ statistically from singletons, and whether fraternal twins are more similar than non-twin siblings.

Multigroup designs also enable the application of more general (i.e., less restrictive) models, such as relaxation of the EEA or the introduction of GE correlation, as well as to examine the sensitivity of results to variations in modeling assumptions. Furthermore, results from multigroup analyses are less prone to systematic method bias and sampling error.

4. Status quo: Databases and access

More than 5,000 papers on twins were published during the five years from 2001 to 2006, and more than 500 of these involve behavior (Plomin et al. 2008). The value of the twin method explains why most developed countries have twin registers (Bartels 2007).

About a decade ago, Boomsma (1998) published the first paper in a series aimed at giving an overview of existing twin registers worldwide. A short description of 16 registries in nine European countries was presented. At the time, these registries had access to over 350,000 pairs providing a resource for genetic-epidemiological research. In the years 2002 and 2006, special issues of the scientific journal *Twin Research and Human Genetics* documented further progress in this field. Currently, worldwide registers of extensive twin data are being established and combined with data from additional family members, offering completely new perspectives in a refined behavioral genetic research (Boomsma et al. 2002).

However, datasets required for multigroup analyses are typically not readily available, especially in countries without official twin or extensive population registers such as Germany. Even in Sweden, home of one of the most extensive twin registers in the world, samples for multigroup data have to be matched from different sources (Björklund et al. 2005). In the study described in the introduction, data on non-twin siblings came from random samples of the Swedish population drawn by Statistics Sweden whereas the twin sample came from the Swedish Twin Registry (Medlund et al. 1977).

The situation in Germany is even more complicated because a central twin register is not available. The Bielefeld Longitudinal Study of Adult Twins (BiLSAT; Spinath et al. 2002), the first large-scale twin study in Germany, was initiated in 1993. Twins were recruited through newspaper and media announcements as well as twin organizations. A telephone hotline was installed and twins who expressed interest in the BiLSAT were informed about the aims of the study and the approximate time required to complete the questionnaire sets. Names, addresses, date of birth, and self-reported zygosity of twin pairs who decided to participate were entered into the database. Within six months, approximately 1,500 twin pairs were enrolled in the BiLSAT and questionnaire data was collected for approximately 75 percent of the initial sample. The twins' age varied between 14 and 80 years ($M = 32$, $SD = 13$ years) and the sample was heterogeneous with regard to education and employment status. As is typically observed with voluntary twin samples, females participated more frequently than males and MZ twins participated more frequently than DZ twins.

In two more recent twin studies (Spinath and Wolf 2006), a different recruitment procedure aimed at reducing self-selective sampling was applied: through individual inquiries at registrations offices in two German federal states (North Rhine-Westphalia and Thuringia), contact information on persons with the same birth name, the same birthday, and also the same birthplace was gathered. These requests resulted in 36,574 addresses of potential twin pairs – adult twins as well as parents of twins. From this list, people in the relevant age-groups for the planned projects (birth cohorts 1995–1998 and 1955–1970) were selected. After matching the provided addresses with data found in public telephone directories, 1,014 adult twins and 715 families with children twins were contacted by phone in 2005. An additional 3,832 households were contacted by mail. First contact by phone turned out to be more efficient, because almost two-thirds of all personally contacted twins agreed to participate as compared to only 26 percent (children sample) and 10 percent (adult sample) participations when first contact was made by mail. The total number of false positive contacts (people born on the same day and with the same surname who claimed not to be twins) was relatively small, yielding 2.4 percent for the children sample and 4.3 percent for the adult sample and rendering the chosen way of recruitment feasible.

5. Future developments

Interdisciplinary efforts to collect data of relevance to psychologists, sociologists, and economists alike, using genetically sensitive designs are highly desirable since the challenges of recruiting a multigroup sample can be met with greater ease in a collaborative effort combining household panel study data and data from traditional twin samples.

Studies such as the British Household Panel Study (BHPS) and the German Socio-Economic Panel (SOEP, *Sozio-oekonomisches Panel*), representative longitudinal studies of private households providing information on all household members and covering a range of topics including employment, earnings, health, and satisfaction indicators, are ideal for many reasons:

First of all, household panels naturally include biological full-siblings, biological half-siblings, parent-child dyads, and to a smaller extent adoptive children, twins, and triplets.

Second, an explorative analysis showed that with nearly 11,000 households and more than 20,000 persons sampled in the SOEP, data from a reasonably large number of non-twin relatives is readily available. In the SOEP data collected in 2007, for example, it was possible to identify 2,209 individuals from 983 families who have at least one sibling as well as 179 adopted children. With 47 individuals in twin or triplet pairs from 20 families, the number of twins who are already enrolled in SOEP is not large enough for a multigroup analysis. However, the recruitment of twins who participate in the assessment of SOEP variables and who could ultimately be enrolled in the regular longitudinal assessment offers a unique opportunity to enrich an already powerful dataset to allow for quantitative genetic analyses.

Studying the families of identical twins, for example, has come to be known as the families-of-twins method (D'Onofrio et al. 2003). When identical twins become adults and have their own children, interesting family relationships emerge. For example, in families of male identical twins, nephews are as related genetically to their twin uncle as they are to their own father. Furthermore, the cousins are as closely related to one another as half siblings are. Studying twins and their family members is a powerful method in differentiating and quantifying environmental and genetic processes underlying associations between family-level risk factors and child adjustment to environmental stimuli. In addition to refined modeling opportunities for estimating genetic and environmental influences on target variables in such samples, repeated measurements provide the opportunity to address genetic and environmental influences to stability and change over time as well as covariance among variables of interest. To summarize: in principle, household panel studies which trace individuals with their families and households for decades are ideal databases for such studies. However, up to now the number of twins assessed in such studies is too small.

Finally, twin and multigroup samples are valuable for determining behavioral areas in which molecular genetic research efforts and candidate gene studies are more likely to be fruitful. As an example, Fowler and Dawes (2008) recently reported that a polymorphism of the MAOA gene significantly increases the likelihood of voting. Additional household information as well as twin and parent data combined (also known as the Nuclear Twin Family Design, NTFD), allow for a separation of environmental factors shared only between siblings (S) and familial environmental factors passed from parents to offspring (F).

Two possible ways to establish an oversampling of twins (i.e., to arrive at a sufficiently large number of twin participants) in Germany have already been outlined above. These possibilities can be combined with a third recruitment strategy: the screening of people by survey research. In cooperation with TNS Infratest, a feasibility check was carried out in which a random sample was contacted via telephone.[1] As part of a larger interview, respondents were asked whether they happened to be a member of a twin pair. If this was the case, a second question addressed the willingness to be contacted and informed about a twin research project. A total of 17,529 interviews yielded 312 members of twin pairs (1.8 percent). From this sample, 149 individuals (48 percent) agreed to be contacted by phone or mail. The twins' age varied between 14 and 75 years (M = 43, SD = 16 years). In contrast to the voluntary twin sample in BiLSAT mentioned above, male and female twins agreed to be contacted with equal frequency.

The fact that twin and non-twin sibling pairs need to be matched in a pairwise fashion requires the introduction of suitable pointer variables into the dataset. Quantitative genetic analyses also require zygosity information for same-sex twin pairs. The best way to determine twin zygosity is by means of DNA markers (polymorphisms in DNA itself). If a pair of twins differs for any DNA marker, they must be fraternal because identical twins are identical genetically. If a reasonable number of markers are examined and no differences are found, it can be concluded that the twin pair is identical. Physical similarity on highly heritable traits such as eye color, hair color, or hair texture, as well as reports about twin confusion are also often used for zygosity determination. If twins are highly similar for a number of physical traits, they are likely to be identical. Using physical similarity to determine twin zygosity typically yields accuracy of more than 90 percent when compared to genotyping data from DNA markers (e.g., Chen et al. 1999).

---

[1]   This study is supported by a BMBF grant (Grant Number 01UW0706).

6. Conclusions and recommendations

Understanding the sources of individual differences – compared to social and economic effects – has become a research area of growing interest in psychology, sociology, and economics. A quantitative genetic research design provides the necessary tools for this type of analysis. For a state-of-the-art approach, multigroup data is required. Household panel studies, such as the SOEP in Germany or BHPS in UK,[2] combined with an oversampling of twins, provide a powerful starting point since data from a reasonably large number of non-twin relatives is readily available.

Quantitative genetic analyses of target variables can guide molecular genetic research in the field of employment, earnings, health, and satisfaction, and combined twin and sibling or parent data can help overcome serious caveats in molecular genetic research.

The implementation of a pilot assessment of key socio-economic variables in a special sample of MZ and DZ twins that is comparable to BHPS or SOEP is highly recommended. Initial data collection in the twin sample including zygosity diagnosis can be realized online to minimize attrition. A total of approximately 400 twin pairs of each group of twins (that is, MZ, same-sex DZ, and opposite-sex DZ twins) enrolled in such a pilot assessment can provide a meaningful basis for the development of a more refined strategic plan, such as the integration of a twin cohort into the regular interview-based assessment in the British panel study Understanding Society and SOEP.

---

2   Where the new panel "Understanding Society" with a larger number of households will provide even better research opportunities.

References:

Bartels, M. (2007): An update on longitudinal twin and family studies. Twin Research and Human Genetics 10, 3-12.

Björklund, A./Jäntti, M. and Solon, G. (2005): Influences of nature and nurture on earnings variation: a report on a study of various sibling types in Sweden. In: Bowles, S./Gintis, H. and Osborne, M. (Eds.), Unequal chances: family background and economic success. New York.

Boomsma, D.A. (1998): Twin registers in Europe: an overview. Twin Research 1, 34-51.

Boomsma, D./Busjahn, A. and Peltonen, L. (2002): Classical twin studies and beyond. Nature Reviews Genetics 3, 872-882.

Bouchard Jr, T.J./Lykken, D.T./McGue, M./Segal, N.L. and Tellegen, A. (1990): Sources of human psychological differences: the Minnesota study of twins reared apart. Science 250, 223-228.

Chen, W.J./Chang, H.W./Lin, C.C.H./Chang, C./Chiu, Y.N. and Soong, W.T. (1999): Diagnosis of zygosity by questionnaire and polymarker polymerase chain reaction in young twins. Behavior Genetics 29, 115-123.

Coventry, W.L. and Keller, M. C. (2005): Estimating the extent of parameter bias in the classical twin design: A comparison of parameter estimates from Extended Twin-Family and classical twin designs. Twin Research and Human Genetics 8, 214-223.

D'Onofrio, B.M./Turkheimer, E.N./Eaves, L.J./Corey, L.A./Berg, K./Solaas, M.H. and Emery, R.E. (2003): The role of the children of twins design in elucidating causal relations between parent characteristics and child outcomes. Journal of Child Psychology and Psychiatry and Allied Disciplines 44, 1130-1144.

Diewald, M. (2008): Zwillings- und Adoptivkinder-Stichproben für soziologische Analysen? Zum Ertrag verhaltensgenetischer Ansätze für sozialwissenschaftliche Fragestellungen und Erklärungen [Using twin and adoptive child samples for sociological analysis? On the value of behavioral genetics approaches for social scientific issues and interpretations]. DIW Research Notes No. 27.

Falconer, D.S. (1960): Introduction to quantitative genetics. New York.

Fowler, J.H./Baker, L.A. and Dawes, C.T. (2008): The genetic basis of political participation. American Political Science Review 102, 233-248.

Fowler, J.H. and Dawes, C.T. (2008): Two genes predict voter turnout. Journal of Politics 70, 579-594.

Guo, G. (2008): Introduction to the special issue on society and genetics. Sociological Methods and Research 37, 159-163.

Hatemi, P.K./Medland, S.E./Morley, K.I./Heath, A.C. and Martin. N.G. (2007): The genetics of voting: an Australian twin study. Behavior Genetics 37, 435-448.

Jensen, A.R. (1998): The g factor: the science of mental ability. London.

Katz, L.F. and Autor, D.H. (1999). Changes in the wage structure and earnings inequality. In: Ashenfelter, O.A. and Card, D. (Eds.): Handbook of Labor Economics (Vol. 3). Amsterdam.

Medlund, P./Cederlof, R./Floderus-Myrhed, B./Friberg, L. and Sorensen, S. (1977): A new Swedish twin registry. Acta Medica Scandinavica Supplementum 60, 1-11.

Neale, M.C./Boker, S.M./Xie, G. and Maes, H. (2003): Mx: Statistical Modeling (6th Edition). VCU Box 900126, Department of Psychiatry, Richmond, 23298.

Pedersen, N.L./McClearn, G.E./Plomin, R. and Nesselroade, J.R. (1992): Effects of early rearing environment on twin similarity in the last half of the life span. British Journal of Developmental Psychology 10, 255-267.

Plomin, R. (1994): Genetics and experience: the Interplay between nature and nurture. Thousand Oaks.

Plomin, R./DeFries, J.C./McClearn, G.E. and McGuffin, P. (2008): Behavioural genetics (5th Edition). New York.

Spinath, F.M. (2005): Twin Designs. In: Everitt, B.S. and Howell, D.C. (Eds.): Encyclopedia of Statistics in Behavioral Science (Vol. 4). Chichester.

Spinath, F.M./Angleitner, A./Borkenau, P./Riemann, R. and Wolf, H. (2002): German Observational Study of Adult Twins: a multimodal investigation of personality, temperament and cognitive ability. Twin Research 5, 372-375.

Spinath, F.M. and Wolf, H. (2006): CoSMoS and TwinPaW: initial report on two new German twin studies. Twin Research and Human Genetics 9, 787-790.

6. Biological Variables in Social Surveys

*Rainer Schnell**

---

* For helpful comments on an earlier draft I am indebted to Günther Heller and Johannes Kopp.

Contact:

Rainer Schnell
University of Duisburg-Essen
Institute for Sociology
Lotharstr. 65
47057 Duisburg
Germany
e-mail: rainer.schnell[at]uni-due.de

Abstract

Social scientists have long virtually ignored the biological constraints of human behavior. Yet if the prediction of behavior is considered essential to a social science, neglecting any variable that might influence human behavior is unacceptable. This paper provides examples of important biological variables and describes their measurement in social surveys.

1. Introduction

Social surveys today are collecting increasing amounts of data on biological variables that might influence social behavior. I will refer to such variables in the following as "biologically relevant variables" or "biological variables" for short. These include biometric features (e.g., fingerprints), biomarkers (e.g., cortisone levels), biomaterial (e.g., hair), and measures of anthropometric variables (e.g., body-mass index, or BMI).

Historical background. Social scientists have long virtually ignored the biological constraints of human behavior.[1] This historical development culminated in the qualitative conception of sociology as a "text science" dealing solely with how social actors understand and interpret one another. For this kind of sociology, the goal of social science is not to develop predictive models of social behavior but to reconstruct meaning. As such, quantitative and qualitative sociology do not differ methodologically but in their scientific objectives. If the prediction of behavior is considered essential for a social science, it cannot afford to neglect any variable that might influence human behavior. This paper will cite examples of important biological variables and describe their measurement in social surveys.

Biosocial surveys. The combination of questionnaire data and biological variables measured in a random sample of a population is increasingly denoted as a "biosocial survey." Such surveys have the advantage of every large sample: population parameters can be estimated even for small subgroups of a population. In general, this is impossible with the small sample sizes common in biopsychology, biology, and medicine. Furthermore, in many cases, samples in these disciplines are not random samples of a population but convenience samples of self-selected populations. Finally, most medical surveys are restricted to health variables, thereby lacking biographical data and those dependent variables of most interest for social scientists: employment history, mating behavior, value systems, and fertility. On the other hand, biological variables are usually not measured in social science

---

[1] Steven Pinker (2002) has discussed this at length in "The blank slate".

surveys. Even studies on divorce seldom measure the obviously relevant and time-varying variables like body and face symmetries, BMI, fertility indicators, testosterone levels, etc.

Using biological variables affecting social behavior as independent variables together with sociologically relevant dependent variables in large-scale surveys will allow more detailed examination of longstanding sociological problems. More technically: the goal of including biological variables in social science population surveys is to reduce unexplained variance and the amount of misspecification in social science models.[2]

2. Increase of studies with biosocial variables in core social-science journals

Sociobiological hypotheses and biosocial surveys are still considered exotic by many social scientists, and prominent sociobiologists are often regarded with some suspicion. This will change very slowly. Two books published by the National Academy Press are of particular importance for this process. The first was the book *Cells and Surveys*, edited by Finch et al. (2001), with the rhetorical subtitle "Should Biological Measurements be included in Social Science Research?". The follow-up volume, *Biosocial Surveys*, was edited by Weinstein et al. (2008).

A review by Freese et al. (2003), appearing in the *Annual Review of Sociology*, was the beginning of a series of publications on biosocial variables in core journals of the social sciences. The *American Political Science Review* published an article on the genetic transmission of political orientations in 2005 (Alford et al. 2005), followed in 2008 by an article on genetic variations in political participation (Fowler et al. 2008). *Social Forces* published an issue in September 2006 with the editorial "The Linking of Sociology and Biology" (Guo 2006), containing four articles on biosocial variables. *Sociological Methods Research* had a "Special Issue on Society and Genetics" in 2008. Even the *American Journal of Sociology* released a special issue in 2008 on "Exploring Genetics and Social Structure" (Volume 114, Supplement 2008). Parallel to these publications, the steering groups of the large-scale panel studies in the social sciences published recommen-

---

[2] The self-restriction of model builders on likelihood-ratios and Wald-statistics as inferior substitutes for model testing and residual diagnostics keep them forgetting about the small explanatory power of social sciences models. Even for simple problems like voting, fertility decisions or divorce, the proportional reduction of error of the model compared with the marginal distribution is rarely larger than 10 percent. After 40 years of multivariate research this is quite shameful.

dations for the inclusion of biosocial indicators in surveys (Lillard and Wagner 2006; Kumari et al. 2006).

To sum up, biosocial problems, hypotheses, and studies can now be found even in the core social science journals – at least the American ones. The technical and statistical level of these publications is still not up to the standards of the medical literature, but given sociology's longstanding neglect of biology, this was to be expected.

3. Biosocial data for social sciences applications

There are many examples of sociological problems in which biological variables set constraints for human behavior. Among them are genetic factors, variables on mating behavior, and perinatal variables. Only a few examples will be given; a complete and systematic review is still missing in scientific literature.

Genetic factors. For many traditional social science problems, empirical evidence of genetic effects has been found. Examples are suicide (Voracek and Loibl 2007), aggressive behavior (Craig and Halton 2009), and "antisocial behavior" in general (Moffitt 2005).

The list of dependent variables of social science interest for which genetic effects or gene-environment interactions have been reported is growing daily: from the frequency of life events (Bemmels et al. 2008) to economic decision making (Zhong et al. 2009) and the preference for coffee (Vink et al. 2009). Particularly interesting are genetic variations that correlate with numerous dependent behavioral variables. Another politically relevant topic in this context is attention-deficit hyperactivity disorder (ADHD): there are a considerable number of candidate genes for ADHD.[3] At the Bremen Institute for Prevention Research and Social Medicine (BIPS, *Bremer Institut für Präventionsforschung und Sozialmedizin*), the new study "German Population Based Long Term Follow Up of ADHD" was launched in July 2009. This study will track treated and non-treated children displaying ADHD over 12 years. Variables of interest are medical aspects, like symptoms of ADHD and other psychiatric diseases, as well as accidents, drug abuse, school achievement, juvenile crime, professional careers, and indicators of life quality.

Mating and marital stability. A surprising amount of research in German sociology over the last 15 years had been done on divorce. Even more surprising is the almost complete lack of biological variables associated with mating behavior in this literature. Even obvious factors, which might be

---

3 see Gizer et al. (2009).

varying with time, like differential attractiveness of the partners, have seldom been considered.[4] Despite the fact that many of the possibly relevant measurements (for example: BMI, facial and body symmetry, waist-to-hip ratio, fertility indicators) could have been measured easily and inexpensively,[5] these variables have been included in almost no study to date. Other variables associated with mating behavior, such as odor (Ebberfeld 2005), are much more difficult to measure within a survey context, but still not impossible. Due to technical problems and circadian effects, interpersonal and intrapersonal hormonal differences are even harder to measure within surveys. Nevertheless examples do exist in the sociological literature (for testosterone levels, see Booth et al. 2006).

Perinatal variables. Different perinatal variables have been associated with human behavior in later life. An important example is the level of intrauterine testosterone (see Manning 2002). The clinical quality of births is often accessed with the so called Apgar Score; furthermore, birth weight and size of the newborn are considered as predictors of many mortality events. There are studies on long-term effects, for example, of birth weight on cognitive development (Goosby and Cheadle 2009). Even effects of birth order have been studied, for example, with regard to school achievements (Booth and Kee 2009) and homosexuality (Blanchard 2008).

4. Biorelevant data in medical surveys

Medical surveys measure numerous variables on health status. To clarify the discussion, we should distinguish between medical surveys and examination surveys. Examination surveys usually ask medical survey respondents to visit an examination center. Due to the required technical equipment for techniques like sonography, CT, radiology, MRI, EEG and ECG, mobile examination centers have sometimes been used. These high-tech exams are hardly the most practicable measures for use in social surveys. Measurements that can be conducted by medically untrained interviewers in respondent households are of prime interest. These include respondent weight and height, waist-to-hip ratio, and blood pressure. Even more interesting for social scientists are measurements of a more general state of health, for example, grip strength with a dynamometer or a simple pulmonary function test ("peak flow meter").[6] A simple but useful test of limited mobility that is occasionally

---

4   see Hill and Kopp (2006).
5   see Zebrowitz (1997), Rhodes and Zebrowitz (2002), and Swami and Furnham (2008).
6   see ibid.

used in surveys of the elderly is how long it takes the respondent to pick up a pencil from the floor.

5. Bio-materials in the true meaning of the word

Blood. Perhaps the most versatile bio-material usable in surveys is blood. Many analyses can be done with venous blood. Unfortunately, to draw blood, German law requires the presence of an MD. The collection of blood samples thus faces practical restrictions. Even preparing blood samples for transport to a laboratory is an unusual task for non-medical fieldworkers and requires special training. Finally, the long-term storage of blood samples requires significant technical effort and costs. Taking blood using the "finger prick" method, where a drop of blood from a fingertip is dried on a small piece of paper (dried blood spot, DBS) is much easier. The analytical options are restricted compared to those of venous blood, but sampling, transport, and storage of the samples is considerably simpler. So far – with the exception of pure medical surveys – little is known about the general willingness to participate in blood samples and the long-term storage of the samples.

Saliva. Collecting saliva is the easiest way to obtain material for DNA analysis. Saliva may be used for other tests such as the level of cortisol (as a stress indicator or in the context of aggressive behavior; see Yu and Shi 2009) and cotinin (as an indicator of nicotine exposure; see Shahab et al. 2008). Saliva is usually collected from the mouth using a cotton swab. Today, a number of analyses are even possible on material collected with chewing gum. This method is non-invasive and has the potential to become widely accepted to collect such data in random samples of the population.

Hair. Hair and fingernails can be collected without any problems even under survey conditions. These materials can be used for the analysis of absorbed contaminants ("biomonitoring") and consumed drugs.[7]

Urine. McCadden et al. (2005) report on a random sample of 5105 men and women (aged 16-44), who were asked for a urine sample after a CAPI interview. Of these, 3628 (71 percent) agreed, and 3608 samples were collected successfully. The samples are used to screen for "chlamydia trachomatis," a sexually transmittable bacteria that causes almost no immediate but serious long-term problems in women. Another noteworthy study collected urine in a mail survey of a random sample of 21,000 Dutch men and women (age 15-29), for whom van Bergen et al. (2006) reports a response rate of

---

7   The book edited by Tobin (2005) gives an overview on the chemical analysis of human hair. For potential usages of other noninvasive bio-materials, see Esteban and Castano (2009).

almost 41 percent. A number of other similar studies are now available; Low et al. (2007) give an overview.

6. Long-term measurements

For studies on specific population such as overweight children or diabetics, long-term measurement instruments are used. These include instruments for recording blood pressure, heart rate, and intensity of movement (more specifically acceleration, using a device called an accelerometer).[8] Small-sized sensors like SmartPatch and SmartBand allow wireless measurements of heart rate (via WLAN), breathing rate, oxygen saturation of the blood, and temperature for 24 hours, even on infants.[9] Although such instruments are becoming much smaller, more portable, and less onerous, they still affect daily routine. Technical developments open up new perspectives every day, for example, the use of mobile phones with GPS as a substitute for accelerometers, since subjects carry mobile phones anyway. Another example is "intelligent clothing," where sensors in the clothes provide information on temperature, pulse rate, skin resistance, and transpiration (see Solaz et al. 2006).[10] For many cognitive tasks (and of course for diabetics), glucose levels throughout the day are important. A newly developed probe that can be mounted by trained persons in abdominal fat allows continuous recording of glucose levels. The corresponding electronic device is currently carried in a waist bag and barely affects daily activities (Dye et al. 2010).

7. Environmental data

Many health surveys collect samples of environmental materials to determine environmental pollution. These include samples of soil, tap water, and air. In Switzerland there is a nationwide noise map in which the objective magnitude of noise exposure is measured or interpolated (Ingold and Koepfli 2009). Such maps exist in other countries as well, but covering only particular regions.[11] With the consent of the respondents, some studies collect items

---

8   For accelerometers, see Puyau et al. (2004) and Murphy (2009).
9   www.intelligentclothing.com/wireless.html
10 Another example might be „intelligent shoes," where sensors measure speed or pressure distribution. An early example is the „Adidas Micropacer".
11 EU- directive 2002/49/EG (June 25th 2002) states that communities with a population over 250.000 people are committed to publish regional noise maps, see also www.lärmkarte.de.

of daily practical use, like toothbrushes, washcloths, combs, and vacuum cleaner bags.[12] In at least one older American study, household garbage was collected for response validation without the consent of the respondents (see Rathje 1984).

8. Research needs

Extensive research is needed on the use of biosocial variables in social surveys. This is especially true for problems of respondent cooperation in biosocial surveys.

Cooperation problems. Few studies exist on the willingness of respondents to cooperate in the collection of biological indicators within social surveys. If respondents correctly identify the purpose of a survey as nonmedical, this will have strong effects on the perceived cost/benefit ratio of participation. Nearly nothing is known up to now on the resulting biases. Most biological variables in social surveys are measured in panel studies. Repeated participation in a panel may result in a biased remaining sample, but the repeated participation may also increase respondents' trust that their participation will not entail negative consequences. Results based on panels should therefore be treated with care when generalized to standard surveys. Furthermore it has to be taken into consideration that, as a rule, respondents (as well as scholars) react positively to most new methods: cooperation rates are initially high for most data collection modes (in person, by phone, and by the Internet), but deteriorate quickly with the widespread use of these techniques. This also seems plausible for the measurement of biosocial variables in social surveys. For this reason, experimental studies are urgently needed on response rates in the general population depending on organi-

---

12 The German environmental survey of 1990/1992 collected (for subsamples) respondents hair in order to measure aluminium, barium, plumb, boron, cadmium, calcium, chrome, copper, magnesium, phosphorus, platinum, strontium, thallium, zinc, caesium, palladium, uranium, vanadium as well as nicotine and cotinin. In the environmental survey of 1998 blood and urine samples were taken for "human biomonitoring". In subsamples, tap water was analysed for arsenic, plumbum, boron, cadmium, copper, nickel and zinc. Dustbags content was analysed for PCB, biocides, phtalates and triphosphates. The surprisingly short list of publications based on the survey can be found on the homepage of "Umweltbundesamt" at www.Umweltbundesamt.de/gesundheit/publikationen. More interesting for social scientists may be a volume on environmental justice by another federal agency (Bundesamt für Strahlenschutz et al. 2008).

zation conducting the survey, type of biological indicator, incentives used, and explanations of the survey given to respondents.[13]

Collecting and processing biosocial variables. In medical surveys, medically trained staff members are available for collecting and processing biological materials. Very little is known about whether medically untrained persons who do the fieldwork in social science surveys can be used for collecting biosocial information, ranging from the simple measurement of the BMI to collecting dried blood spots. Recent experiences with the low quality of paradata recorded by interviewers may raise some doubt as to the feasibility of traditionally trained interviewers collecting non-standard data. This doubt is even greater since the results of such fieldwork can hardly be controlled at this stage of research: after all, nothing is known about the data quality that can be expected under such field conditions.[14]

The standard procedure for special survey measurements with high technical demands is the use of few, but highly trained qualified interviewers. Adoption of this procedure for biological variables will result in considerable interviewer effects, since measurement errors are clustered within interviewers. Therefore, intraclass correlations are high. Usually, the effective decrease in sample size due to interviewer effects is computed by multiplication of interviewer workload with the intraclass correlation (Schnell and Kreuter 2005). High intraclass correlations multiplied with high workloads will yield a considerable underestimation of population variance. Therefore, more highly trained interviewers than usual will be needed for biosocial surveys, further increasing the cost of such surveys. Finally, neglect of these kinds of interviewer effects will increase the amount of errors of the first kind (alpha error rate) in biosocial surveys. Therefore, detailed studies of interviewer effects on biosocial variables are needed.

Long-term storage. For research with biological material, long-term storage of the samples is highly desirable. This allows the material to be tested at a later stage using analytical techniques that currently do not exist or on research problems that are still unknown. Long-term storage of biological samples creates considerable technical and logistical problems, however, and these remain unresolved, even for medical research in Germany.[15]

By comparison with other countries in Europe, the situation in Germany is disheartening: due to the large number of federal statistical agencies and the oligarchic structure of German academic medicine, the country still does not even have a mortality register, which would provide fascinating research

---

13 The comparison of stated cooperation in factorial surveys and actual cooperation in factorial experiments might be interesting in itself: I expect only a small amount of agreement.
14 Exceptions are Kroh (2005) and Jaszczak et al. (2009).
15 On technical requirements for the storage of human tissue see Troyer (2008). Helpful advice on storing other biomaterials can be found in *Cancer Epidemiology, Biomarkers and Prevention*, 15 (9) of September 2006.

opportunities if it were linked to samples on long-term storage in a biobank. The UK Biobank[16] is based on precisely this concept. More than 10 assessment centers will collect biosamples of 500,000 persons (at present between 40 and 69 years) across the entire United Kingdom. The resulting biodata will be combined with environmental and lifestyle data. The corresponding German project (the "Helmholtz cohort") has just completed the stage of identifying institutions willing and able to recruit participants for the study.

Data protection problems. The German Ethics Council (*Deutscher Ethikrat*)[17] published a detailed statement on the ethical problems and legal restrictions of biobanks in 2004. A special problem of biobanks results from the fact that persons could raise objections to the use of their samples for scientific projects that were not foreseen at the time of their consent to sample storage. Scientific progress may require disclosure of biological information to third parties. The German Ethics Council reminded researchers that biological samples may reveal information not only about the person from whom the sample was taken but also about his genetic relatives, perhaps even subgroups of the population or the total population of a country (2004, 109). Finally, the protection of persons unable to consent must be taken into account. The German Ethics Council noted, in conclusion, that collecting, storing, handling, and analysis of biological samples must be carried out in accordance with the protection of the individual. A corresponding legal framework has to be developed at an international level.[18]

The absence of a clear legal framework imposes considerable problems on social scientists seeking approval of biosocial projects from university ethics review boards, and resistance has to be expected, especially from other social scientists. In order to promote this kind of research, we need some successful examples of biosocial surveys – preferably not conducted by social scientists – to overcome institutional resistance. Under the current conditions in Germany, I personally consider cooperation with foreign research groups more promising.

Lack of biosocial theories for biological variables in surveys. A theoretical foundation for the use of biological variables in social surveys is lacking. Sociobiologists have proposed plausible hypotheses on generative behavior, some on hormonal differences, morbidity differences, and deviant behavior, and a few isolated results on trust, justice, risk behavior, and even voting behavior.[19] But by and large, we simply have very few theories on biological constraints of human behavior at present. Filling this research gap

---

16 www.ukbiobank.ac.uk.
17 Bevore 2008: *Nationaler Ethikrat*.
18 For an European discussion, see the book edited by Hayry et al. (2007).
19 The frequent publications of a small number of cases with surprisingly strong effects underscores the importance of publishing only significant effects after thorough testing. Without independent replications the statistical problems of multiple testing must be kept in mind.

will require far closer cooperation among biologists, psychologists, and social scientists than ever before. Without a corresponding new infrastructure for research, this seems impossible to me.

9. Recommendations

Inclusion of biosocial hypotheses and techniques in graduate studies. Due to the very slow adoption of new techniques in the social sciences in general and the tentative reception of sociobiological considerations in particular, the fastest way to promote biosocial research in the social sciences may be to include sociobiological theories and techniques in graduate studies and summer schools.

- In order to promote this kind of research, expertise is needed in the committees deciding on the topics in large-scale social science projects.
- The Leibniz Institute for the Social Sciences (GESIS, *Leibniz-Institut für Sozialwissenschaften*) should therefore, for the first time, include biologists and behavioral scientists on their committees.
- Since the technical details of collecting, processing, analyzing, and storing biomarkers are unknown outside the scientific fields from which they originate, appropriate training seminars should be included in the list of the standard GESIS summer schools.

Research on the willingness to cooperate. Research is necessary on respondents' willingness to cooperate in the collection of biosocial information and indicators in non-health surveys.

- We urgently need experiments on respondents' willingness to cooperate in the collection of different biomarkers, depending on the explanation given of the purpose of the survey, the organization conducting the survey and different incentives.

Funding opportunities. German research traditions make interdisciplinary research fields like sociobiology quite difficult. None of the traditional academic fields (medicine, biology, psychology, anthropology, the social sciences, etc.) consider human sociobiology a central research topic. Therefore, this seemingly exotic field is competing for research grants under relatively unfavorable conditions.

- To promote biosocial research we will need new tools for granting research proposals.

- An interdisciplinary priority program of the German Research Foundation (*Schwerpunktprogramm* of the DFG, *Deutsche Forschungsgemeinschaft*) in human sociobiology or even better on biosocial surveys would be a first step.
- Due to the resistance from German sociologists and the organizational structure of German university medicine, an EU project on human sociobiology seems more promising to me than an attempt to change German decision-making structures.

References:

Alford, J.R./Funk, C.L. and Hibbing, J.R. (2005): Are political orientations genetically transmitted? American Political Science Review 99 (2), 153-167.
Bemmels, H.R./Burt, S.A./Legrand, L.N./Iacono, W.G. and McGue, M. (2008): The heritability of life events: an adolescent twin and adoption study. Twin Research and Human Genetics 11 (3), 257-265.
Blanchard, R. (2008): Review and theory of handedness, birth order, and homosexuality in men. Laterality 13 (1), 51-70.
Booth, A./Granger, D.A./Mazur, A. and Kivlighan, K.T. (2006): Testosterone and social behavior. Social Forces 85 (1), 167-191.
Booth, A.L. and Kee, H.J. (2009): Birth order matters: the effect of family size and birth order on educational attainment. Journal of Population Economics 22 (2), 367-397.
Bundesamt für Strahlenschutz (BfS) et al. (Ed.) (2008): Umweltgerechtigkeit – Umwelt, Gesundheit und soziale Lage. Nummer 2, Umweltmedizinischer Informationsdienst (UMID). Umweltbundesamt.
Craig, I. and Halton, K. (2009): Genetics of human aggressive behaviour. Human Genetics. [Electronic prepublication on 9. June].
Dye, L./Mansfield, M./Lasikiewicz, N./Mahawish, L./Schnell, R./Talbot, D./Chauhan, H./Croden, F. and Lawton, C. (2010): Correspondence of continuous interstitial glucose measurement against arterialised and capillary glucose following an oral glucose tolerance test in healthy volunteers. British Journal of Nutrition 103, 134-140.
Ebberfeld, I. (2005): Botenstoffe der Liebe: Über das innige Verhältnis von Geruch und Sexualität. Münster.
Esteban, M. and Castano, A. (2009): Non-invasive matrices in human biomonitoring: a review. Environ Int. 35 (2), 438-449.
Finch, C. et al. (Eds.) (2001): Cells and surveys: should biological measures be included in social science research? Washington.
Fowler, J.H./Baker, L.A. and Dawes, C.T. (2008): Genetic variation in political participation. American Political Science Review 102 (2), 233-248.
Freese, J./Li, J.-C.A. and Wade, L.D. (2003): The potential relevances of biology to social inquiry. Annual Review of Sociology 29, 233-256.
Gizer, I./Ficks, C. and Waldman, I. (2009): Candidate gene studies of ADHD: a metaanalytic review. Human Genetics. [Electronic prepublication on 9. June].
Goosby, B.J. and Cheadle, J.E. (2009): Birth weight, math and reading achievement growth: a multilevel between-sibling, between-families approach. Social Forces 87 (3), 1291-1320.
Guo, G. (2006): The linking of sociology and biology. Social Forces 85, 145-149.
Hank, K./Jürges, H. and Schaan, B. (2009): Die Erhebung biometrischer Daten im Survey of Health, Ageing and Retirement in Europe. Methoden – Daten – Analysen 3 (1), 97-108.
Hayry, M./Chadwick, R./Arnason, V. and Arnason, G. (Ed.) (2007): The ethics and governance of human genetic databases. European perspectives. Cambridge.
Hill, P. and Kopp, J. (2006): Familiensoziologie. Wiesbaden, 4th edition.

Ingold, K. and Köpfli, M. (2009): Lärmbelastung in der Schweiz. Ergebnisse des nationalen Lärmmonitorings SonBase. Bern.

Jaszczak, A./Lundeen, K. and Smith, S. (2009): Using nonmedically trained interviewers to collect biomeasures in a national in-home survey. Field Methods 21 (1), 26-48.

Kroh, M. (2005): Intervieweffekte bei der Erhebung des Körpergewichts in Bevölkerungsumfragen. Das Gesundheitswesen 67, 646-655.

Kumari, M./Wadsworth, M./Blake, M./Bynner, J. and Wagner, G.G. (2006): Biomarkers in the proposed UK longitudinal household study. Technischer Bericht, Economic & Social Research Council.

Lillard, D. and Wagner, G.G. (2006): The value added of biomarkers in household panelstudies. DIW Data Documentation 14, 1-12.

Low, N. et al. (2007): Epidemiological, social, diagnostic and economic evaluation of population screening for genital chlamydial infection. Health Technol Assess 11 (8), iii-iv, ix-xii, 1-165.

Manning, J.T. (2002): Digit ratio: a pointer to fertility, behavior, and health. New Brunswick.

McCadden, A./Fenton, K.A./McManus, S./Mercer, C.H./Erens, B./Carder, C./ Ridgway, G./Macdowall, W./Nanchahal, K./Byron, C.L./Copas, A./Wellings, K. and Johnson, A.M. (2005): Chlamydia trachomatis testing in the second British national survey of sexual attitudes and lifestyles: respondent uptake and treatment outcomes. Sexually Transmitted Diseases 32 (6), 387-394.

Moffitt, T.E. (2005): Genetic and environmental influences on antisocial behaviors: evidence from behavioral-genetic research. Adv Genet 55, 41-104.

Murphy, S.L. (2009): Review of physical activity measurement using accelerometers in older adults: considerations for research design and conduct. Preventive Medicine 48 (2), 108-114.

Nationaler Ethikrat (Ed.) (2004): Biobanken für die Forschung. Berlin.

Pinker, S. (2002): The blank slate: the modern denial of human nature. London.

Puyau, M.R./Adolph, A.L./Vohra, F.A./Zakeri, I. and Butte, N.F. (2004): Prediction of activity energy expenditure using accelerometers in children. Medicine and science in sports and exercise 36 (9), 1625-1631.

Rathje, W.L. (1984): "Where's the beef?": red meat and reactivity. American Behavioral Scientist 28, 71-91.

Rhodes, G. and Zebrowitz, L. (Ed.) (2002): Facial attractiveness. Evolutionary, cognitive, and social perspectives. Westport.

Rylander-Rudqvist, T./Håkansson, N./Tybring, G. and Wolk, A. (2006): Quality and quantity of saliva DNA obtained from the self-administered oragene method – a pilot study on the cohort of Swedish men. Cancer Epidemiology, Biomarkers and Prevention 15 (9), 1742-1745.

Schnell, R. and Kreuter, F. (2005): Separating Interviewer and Sampling-Point Effects. Journal of Official Statistics 21 (3), 389-410.

Shahab, L./Hammond, D./O'Connor, R.J./Cummings, K.M./Borland, R./King, B. and McNeill, A. (2008): The reliability and validity of self-reported puffing behavior: evidence from a cross-national study. Nicotine & Tobacco Research 10 (5), 867-874.

Solaz, J./Belda-Lois, J./Garcia, A./Barbera, R./Dura, J.V./Gomez, J.A./Soler, C. and Prat, J. (2006): Intelligent textiles for medical and monitoring applications. In: Mattila, H.R. (Ed.): Intelligent textiles and clothing. Cambridge.

Swami, V. and Furnham, A. (2008): The psychology of physical attraction. London.

Tobin, D.J. (Ed.) (2005): Hair in toxicology. An important bio-monitor. Cambridge.

Troyer, D. (2008): Biorepository standards and protocols for collecting, processing, and storing human tissues. In: Liu, B.C.-S. and Ehrlich, J.R. (Eds.): Tissue proteomics. New York. [Methods in molecular biology, vol. 441].

van Bergen, J./Götz, H./Richardus, J.H./Hoebe, C./Broer, J./Coenen, T. et al. (2006): Prevalence of urogenital Chlamydia trachomatis infections in the Netherlands suggests selective screening approaches. Results from the PILOT CT population study. Drugs Today (Barc), 42 Suppl A, 25-33.

Vink, J.M./Staphorsius, A.S. and Boomsma, D.I. (2009): A genetic analysis of coffee consumption in a sample of Dutch twins. Twin Research in Human Genetics 12 (2), 127-131.

Voracek, M. and Loibl, L.M. (2007): Genetics of suicide: a systematic review of twin studies. Wiener Klinische Wochenschrift 119, 15-16, 463-475.

Weinstein, M. et al. (Eds.) (2008): Biosocial surveys. Washington.

Wong, D.T. (Ed.) (2008): Salivary diagnostics. Ames.

Yu, Y.-Z. and Shi, J.-X. (2009): Relationship between levels of testosterone and cortisol in saliva and aggressive behaviors of adolescents. Biomedical and Environmental Sciences 22 (1), 44-49.

Zebrowitz, L.A. (1997): Reading faces: window to the soul? Boulder.

Zhong, S./Chew, S.H./Set, E./Zhang, J./Xue, H./Sham, P.C./Ebstein, R.P. and Israel, S. (2009): The heritability of attitude toward economic risk. Twin Research in Human Genetics 12 (1), 103-107.

7. Administrative Transaction Data

Julia Lane

Contact:

Julia Lane
e-mail: jlane[at]nsf.gov

The New Astronomy

"All astronomers observe the same sky, but with different techniques, from the ground and from space, each showing different facets of the Universe. The result is a plurality of disciplines (e.g., radio, optical or X-ray astronomy and computational theory), all producing large volumes of digital data. The opportunities for new discoveries are greatest in the comparison and combination of data from different parts of the spectrum, from different telescopes and archives."[1]

1. Introduction

The value of administrative transaction data, such as financial transactions, credit card purchases, telephone calls, and retail store scanning data, to study social behavior, has long been recognized (Engle and Russell 1998). Now new types of transaction data made possible by advances in cyber-technology have the potential to further expand social scientists' research frontier. For example, a person's interests and social networks can be uncovered through their online behavior documented by the major search engines, such as Yahoo! and Google, as "data collection events."[2] Geographic movements can be tracked by cell phones which include GPS location information.[3] Health, work, and learning information can be tracked by the use of administrative data from hospital records, employment records, and education records (Jones and Elias 2006). In sum, the new cyber-enabled ability to collect information from a wide variety of sources, which has transformed many disciplines ranging from astronomy to medical science, can potentially transform research on social behavior.

To be sure, the use of some transaction data for research and statistical purposes is becoming routine.[4] The *Handbook of Survey Research* will include a chapter on linking administrative records to survey data. The United Kingdom's Economic and Social Research Council (ESRC) has established

---

1 NVO: http://www.us-vo.org/; IVOA: http://www.ivoa.net/.
2 http://bits.blogs.nytimes.com/2008/03/09/how-do-they-track-you-let-us-count-the-ways/?scp=17&sq=privacy%20yahoo!&st=cse accessed Sept 19, 2008.
3 http://www.nytimes.com/2008/06/22/technology/22proto.html?scp=3&sq=gps%20privacy&st=cse accessed Sept 19, 2008.
4 The term "transaction data" is broadly used in this chapter to include administrative records which are "information that is routinely collected by organizations, institutions, companies and other agencies in order that the organization can carry out, monitor, archive or evaluate the function or service it provides" (Calderwood and Lessof 2006: 2). The term as used here also includes the enormous amount of transaction datasets that are becoming available from, for example, credit card records, and stock trading, as well as the location information stored from cellular telephone and the clickstreams derived from online activity.

an Administrative Data Liaison Service to link the producers of administrative data to the academic community. Furthermore, both the OECD and the Conference of European Statisticians are examining ways to use administrative data for the production of official statistics.

The opportunities are immense. The social sciences could be transformed by access to new and complex datasets on human interactions. The impact of social science on policy could also be transformed as a result of new abilities to collect and analyze real-time data. In addition, the funding exists: the United States has invested heavily in cyberinfrastructure[5] and the United Kingdom has established a National Centre for eSocial Science.[6] A good review of European Union activity is provided in a recent report by Barjak et al. (2007).[7]

A number of important issues remain.

- What is the potential for new data (e.g., citation tracking, web-scraping, biomarkers, geospatial information, through radio frequency identification devices (RFIDs) and sensors, web-based social interactions) to be included in the scientific data infrastructure? How can such data be validated, analyzed, matched and disseminated?

- How have new approaches to data dissemination (e.g., protected remote access, combined with organizational, educational, and legal protocols) advanced the potential for using transaction data in scientific research?

- What is the optimal infrastructure to promote the scientific analysis of administrative data – so that research can be generalized and replicated? What can we learn from the study of virtual organizations?

2. Background

The value of administrative data has long been recognized by the research community (Hotz et al. 2000). The study of medical outcomes, for example, has been transformed by the use of administrative records (Skinner and Wennberg 2000). Administrative data vastly expands the potential to examine the employment and earnings outcomes of low-wage workers (Autor 2009). Of course, there are a number of challenges: a detailed discussion of

---

5   The Office of Cyberinfrastructure was established at the National Science Foundation in 2006.
6   http://www.ncess.ac.uk.
7   http://ww3.unipark.de/uc/avross/.

the issues associated with using administrative data is provided in Lane (2009).

Increasingly, statistical agencies are also using administrative records because of the considerable pressures to keep costs down at the same time as creating new information. Indeed, the Public Policy Program of the Washington Statistical Society, in partnership with the Federal Committee on Statistical Methodology's Subcommittee on the Statistical Uses of Administrative Records, is pleased to have launched a seminar series on "Administrative Data in Support of Policy Relevant Statistics." More concrete examples are provided by the LEHD program in the United States,[8] and the LEED program in New Zealand.[9] Because an infrastructure based on administrative records created a new sample frame for economic dynamics, it has been used in its own right to create new measures of workforce dynamics at detailed geography and industry levels ranging from earnings for incumbent workers, new hires, and separated workers, to the number of quarters of non-employment of separated workers and measures of job retention and stability.

Another reason that the approach has been attractive is that administrative data have a breadth of information that is simply unattainable from other sources. For example, outside of manufacturing industries, the United States Census Bureau's measurement of inputs does not even distinguish between production and supervisory employees. After the implementation of the LEHD program, however, economic entities in all sectors (establishments or enterprises, as appropriate) were used to create detailed summaries of the distribution of observable (demographic) and unobservable characteristics of the workforce in terms of earnings, external earnings potential, and mobility.

Finally, administrative records shed new light on new economic structures. For example, using the LEHD program as an illustrative example, such data can be used to create new ways of classifying firms into particular industries based on worker activities (Benedetto et al. 2007); new ways of identifying the changing structures of firm mergers, acquisitions, and births and deaths, based on worker flows (Benedetto et al. 2007); new approaches to providing place of work and industry coding on demographic surveys such as the American Community Survey (Freedman et al. 2008), more accurate and complete coding of individual outcomes (Abowd and Vilhuber 2005) and new measures of demand side factors on household and individual surveys. Statistics on individual and household income and income mobility now include factors like whether the employer was growing or shrinking, whether the employer was profitable, and what other kinds of employees were also at the employer (Andersson et al. 2005).

---

8   http://lehd.did.census.gov/led/ [Last visited:10/20/2008].
9   http://www.stats.govt.nz/leed/default.htm.

3. What is the potential for transaction data to inform research?

In 2006, the amount of digital information created, captured, and replicated (worldwide) was 1,288 x 1018 bits. In computer parlance, that's 161 exabytes or 161 billion gigabytes. This is about 3 million times the information in all the books ever written.[10] The sheer magnitude of this information means that this paper can only provide an illustrative, rather than exhaustive review of the types of data that can be collected and used to describe human behavior: here we describe what can be captured using RFID's, web archiving, web-scraping and data mining of electronic communications.

The potential to describe minute-by-minute human interactions with the physical environment became reality with the development of RFID and video technologies. RFID's can be produced for pennies a unit and emit a wireless signal that enables the bearer to be tracked. Businesses now use the technology routinely to track employees (e.g., to ensure that night guards do their assorted tours at the assorted times) and to track their customer behavior (see figure 1). The potential for social science research is clear – ranging from tracking time-use information in a far more granular fashion than from survey data, to the environmental impacts on social behavior, to measuring

Figure 1:

PARIS: Thousands of garments in the sprawling men's department at the Galeria Kaufhof are equipped with tiny wireless chips that can forestall fashion disaster by relaying information from the garment to a dressing-room screen. The garments in the department store, in Essen, Germany, contain radio frequency identification chips, small circuits that communicate by radio waves through portable readers and more than 200 antennas that can not only recommend a brown belt for those tweed slacks but also track garments from the racks, shelves and dressing rooms on the store's third floor. ... But the rapid development of RFID technology is also being regarded cautiously by the authorities in the European Union, who are moving quickly to establish privacy guidelines because the chips – and the information being collected – are not always visible. Their goal is to raise awareness among consumers that the data-gathering chips are becoming embedded in their lives – in items like credit cards, public transportation passes, work access badges, borrowed library books and supermarket loyalty cards.

Source: International Herald Tribune 2 March 2008.

---

10 The Expanding Digital Universe, March 2007, IDC White Paper sponsored by EMC Corporation.

the number and quality of human interactions. In fact, similar technologies are already being used for research purposes to great advantage. For example, Schunn uses video data collected from a recent highly successful case of science and engineering, the Mars Exploration Rover, to study the way in which human interactions contributed to the success of the project. While the project both wildly exceeded engineering requirements for the mission and produced many important scientific discoveries, not all days of the mission were equally successful. Schunn uses the video records to trace the path from the structure of different subgroups (such as having formal roles and diversity of knowledge in the subgroups) to the occurrence of different social processes (such as task conflict, breadth of participation, communication norms, and shared mental models) to the occurrence of different cognitive processes (such as analogy, information search, and evaluation) and finally to outcomes (such as new methods for rover control and new hypotheses regarding the nature of Mars) (2008).

Of course, human behavior is increasingly captured through transactions on the internet. For example, most businesses, as well as registering with the tax authority, also create a website. It is now entirely possible to use web-scraping technologies to capture up-to-date information on what businesses are doing, rather than relying on administrative records and survey information. Historical records on businesses can also be created by delving into the repository of webpages on the Wayback Machine (see figure 2 for an example of the webpages for Citibank). This archive takes snapshots of the web every two months and stores them in the manner shown, providing a rich archive of hundreds of billions of web pages. Individual as well as business behavior can be studied using this archive. Indeed, major NSF (National Science Foundation) grants, such as the Cornell Cybertools ward,[11] have funded the study of social and information networks using these very large semi structured datasets.

Figure 2:

The Wayback Machine:
http://www.archive.org/index.php

Other ways of collecting information on human behavior from the Web include capturing clickstreams from usage statistics. The MESUR project,[12]

---

11 Very Large Semi-Structured Datasets for Social Science Research, NSF award 0537606 http://www.infosci.cornell.edu/SIN/cybertools.
12 MESUR: Metrics from Scholarly Usage of Resources http://www.mesur.org/MESUR.html.

for example, has created a semantic model of the ways in which scholars communicate based on creating a set of relational and semantic web databases from over one billion usage events and over ten billion semantic statements. The combination of usage, citation, and bibliographic data (see figure 3) can be used to develop metrics of scholarly impact that go well beyond the standard bibliometric approaches used by academics (Bollen et al. 2007).

Figure 3:

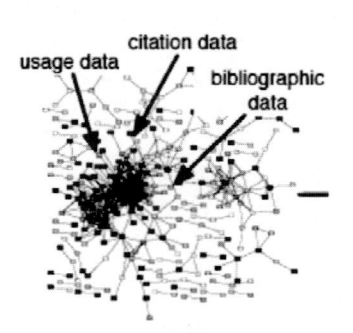

PHASES 1 & 2:
Modeling and data aggregation

A final illustration of the value of capturing transaction data is evident from the work of Noshir Contractor. He studies a variety of ways in which humans interact with each other, including cell phone and email interactions. In a recent study he examined the emergency response of key agencies and individuals to Hurricane Katrina. The first slide in figure 4 shows the result of analytical work based on the "Data to Knowledge" application at the National Center for Supercomputing Applications (NCSA) at the University of Illinois. This is a rapid, flexible data mining and machine learning system which allows automated processing by creating itineraries that combine processing modules into a workflow. This procedure was first applied to the body of communication between 8/23/2003 and 8/25/2005 (as Katrina was approaching Florida). An examination of the top panel of figure 4 shows the American Red Cross (ARC) on the top. FEMA interactions only exist at FEMA Administration (Middle Left). Florida and Palm Beach have many mentions. At the bottom of the figure, it is clear that Oil and Power groupings are quite important, as is the pocket of National Parks in the middle. The location flags are heavily based in Florida, except for the Petroleum Network. New Orleans is very much on the fringe at the bottom.

The second slice of time that was examined was 3 September 2005 to 4 September 2005 – as the hurricane was hitting New Orleans. As is evident from the pictorial description of the analysis, Mississippi and Louisiana are the most frequently mentioned states. Urban Search and Rescue has joined the network as a key concept. The topic of power has changed to Outages, Alabama Power is still at the margin, and Shelter has moved back to the middle. FEMA and ARC have essentially swapped positions and the National Guard is moving towards the center (Contractor 2008).

This vividly illustrates how new approaches to capturing information could transform social scientists ability to provide information to policy-makers. Imagine a similar exercise being done in the study of financial markets, for example. Real-time data collected from the web analysis of online blogs and newspaper articles could have picked up clusters of concern about Lehman Brothers, Goldman Sachs, and Bear Stearns, and could potentially have described the information cascades that transformed the financial infrastructure in September and October of 2008. Or, in another example, new data could be collected on the innovation processes that generate competitive advantage within firms.[13]

Figure 4:

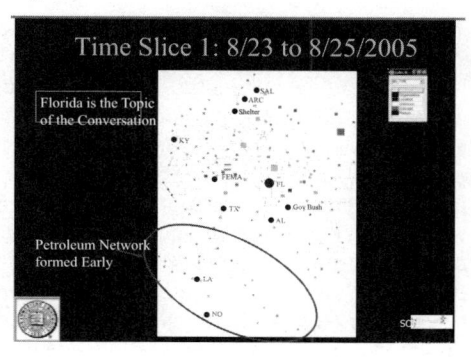

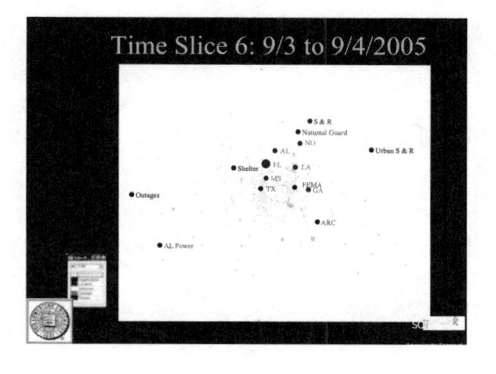

Of course, together with new data, new analytical techniques need to be developed. Standard regression analysis and tabular presentations are often inadequate representations of the complexity of the underlying data generation function. There are a variety of reasons for this inadequacy. First, the units of analysis are often amorphous – social networks rather than indivi-

---

13 http://www.conference-board.org/nsf. Carol Corrado "Workshop on developing a new national research data infrastructure for the study of organizations and innovation".

duals, firm ecosystems rather than establishments. Second, the structural relationships are typically highly nonlinear, with multiple feedback loops. Third, theory has not developed sufficiently to describe the underlying structural relationships. Therefore, making sense of the vast amounts of data is a substantive challenge. There has been considerable effort invested in developing new models and tools to address the challenge, however. For example, since a major national priority is understanding the formation and evolution of terrorist networks through the internet and other communication channels, substantial resources have been devoted to the field of visual analytics. Their research agenda aligns very closely with a potential research agenda for social scientists, focusing as it does on the science of analytical reasoning, visual representations and interaction techniques, data representations and transformations, as well as the production, presentation, and dissemination of complex relationships (Thomas and Cook 2005). It is also worth noting that new partnerships are being formed to address the nontrivial computing challenges.[14]

4. The effect of new data dissemination protocols

Both transaction and administrative data are often highly sensitive. The dissemination of such data is, however, critical for a number of reasons. The first is that data only have utility if they are used. Data utility is a function of both the data quality and the number and quality of the data analysts. The second is replicability. It is imperative that scientific analysis be able to be replicated and validated by other researchers. The third is communication. Social behavior is complex and subject to multiple interpretations: the concrete application of scientific concepts must be transparently communicated through shared code and metadata documentation. The fourth is building a collective knowledge base, particularly with new data whose statistical properties are unknown. The fifth is capacity building. Junior researchers, policy-makers, and practitioners need to have the capacity to go beyond examining tables and graphs and develop their understanding of the complex response of humans to rapidly changing social and legal environments. Access to complex microdata provides an essential platform for evidence based decision-making. Finally, access to microdata permits researchers to examine outliers in human and economic behavior – which is often the basis for the most provocative analysis.

A major barrier to the use of administrative data is the difficulty of getting permission to use administrative data for purposes other than which it

---

14 http://www.nsf.gov/news/news_summ.jsp?cntn_id=111470.

was collected. This is an extremely time-consuming process: since the data are collected to administer programs and not for research purposes. Legal, ethical, and financial issues similarly act to restrict access.

However, new data dissemination protocols are being developed. Remote access approaches use modern computer science technology, together with researcher certification and screening, to replace the burdensome, costly, and slow human intervention associated with buffered remote access (Lane et al. 2008). The Office for National Statistics (ONS) (Ritchie 2005) for example, instituted a full "remote laboratory" service in January 2004. Their approach is to use a thin client service, which means there is no data transfer at the user end. They have also centralized data management operations, which makes it much more efficient to work across different sites. Statistics Denmark (Borchsenius 2005) has found that remote access arrangements are now the dominant mode of access to microdata. Statistics Sweden's system for remote access to microdata (MONA; Söderberg 2005) provides users with secure access to databases at Statistics Sweden from almost any place with internet access. In this manner, Statistics Sweden has increased the accessibility of microdata for external users at the same time that it has increased security precisely because the client's computer functions like an input-output terminal. All application processing is done in the server. Statistics Netherlands (Hundepohl and de Wolf 2005) has gone even further in terms of its remote access. It has begun a pilot project, called the OnSite@Home facility,[15] which makes use of biometric identification – the researcher's fingerprint – to ensure that the researcher who is trying to connect to the facility is indeed the person he or she claims to be.

The NORC (National Opinion Research Center) data enclave has taken the remote access approach one step further. Recognizing that a remote access environment also permits the development of an environment that allows the sharing of information about data in the same fashion as that adopted by the physical and biological sciences, it has created virtual organizations (Foster et al. 2001; Pang 2001). Tools such as the Grid, MySpace, and Second Life have changed how people congregate, collaborate, and communicate: the NORC enclave offers social scientists the same opportunities. Promoting virtual collaboration not only serves the function of ensuring the generalizability and replicability of work that is fundamental to high-quality research, but also promotes a healthy interaction between data collectors, data producers, and data users. In particular, the NORC enclave allows multiple people on a team access to the data, and team members are set up with individual workspaces that are complemented by team workspaces. Each workspace allows the user to save their result sets and related

---

15 Hundepohl, Anco, and Paul-Peter de Wolf "OnSite@Home: Remote Access at Statistics Netherlands," paper presented at the Joint UNECE/Eurostat work session on statistical data confidentiality (Geneva, Switzerland, 9-11 November 2005).

notes. NORC supports the ongoing collaborative annotation of data analysis and results through wikis and blogs and discussion spaces. There is also a group portal environment that enables the collaborative development of research deliverables such as journal articles. Figure 5 gives a visual idea of the enclave approach.

The social science community could potentially transform its empirical foundations if it adopted such a collaborative framework. It could use remote access to a common dataset to move away from the current practice of individual, or artisan, science, towards the more generally accepted community-based approach adopted by the physical and biological sciences. Such an approach would provide the community with a chance to combine knowledge about data (through metadata documentation), augment the data infrastructure (through adding data), deepen knowledge (through wikis, blogs, and discussion groups) and build a community of practice (through information sharing). Adopting the type of organizational infrastructure made possible by remote access could potentially be as far-reaching as the changes that have taken place in the astronomical sciences, and cited in the opening section. It could lead to the "democratization of science" opening up the potential for junior and senior researchers from large and small institutions to participate in a research field.

However, it is worth noting that the establishment of a virtual community to advance the development of a data infrastructure is itself a social science challenge. Indeed, the study of virtual organizations is attracting attention in its own right as a way of advancing scientific knowledge and developing scientific communities. As Cummings et al. note:

"A virtual organization (VO) is a group of individuals whose members and resources may be dispersed geographically and institutionally, yet who function as a coherent unit through the use of cyberinfrastructure. A VO is typically enabled by, and provides shared and often real-time access to, centralized or distributed resources, such as community-specific tools, applications, data, and sensors, and experimental operations. A VO may be known as or composed of systems known as collaboratories, e-Science or e-Research, distributed workgroups or virtual teams, virtual environments, and online communities. VOs enable system-level science, facilitate access to resources, enhance problem-solving processes, and are a key to national economic and scientific competitiveness" (2008:1).

It is clearly an open research question for the social science data community to determine how such an organization should be established, how data should be accessed, how privacy should be protected, and whether the data should be shared on a central server or distributed servers. Some approaches can be centralized, like the approach taken by the ESRC in the UK in creating a specific call for a secure data archive,[16] or decentralized, such as

---

16 http://www.esrc.ac.uk/ESRCInfoCentre/opportunities/current_funding_opportunities/ads_sds.aspx?ComponentId=25870&SourcePageId=5964.

Figure 5:

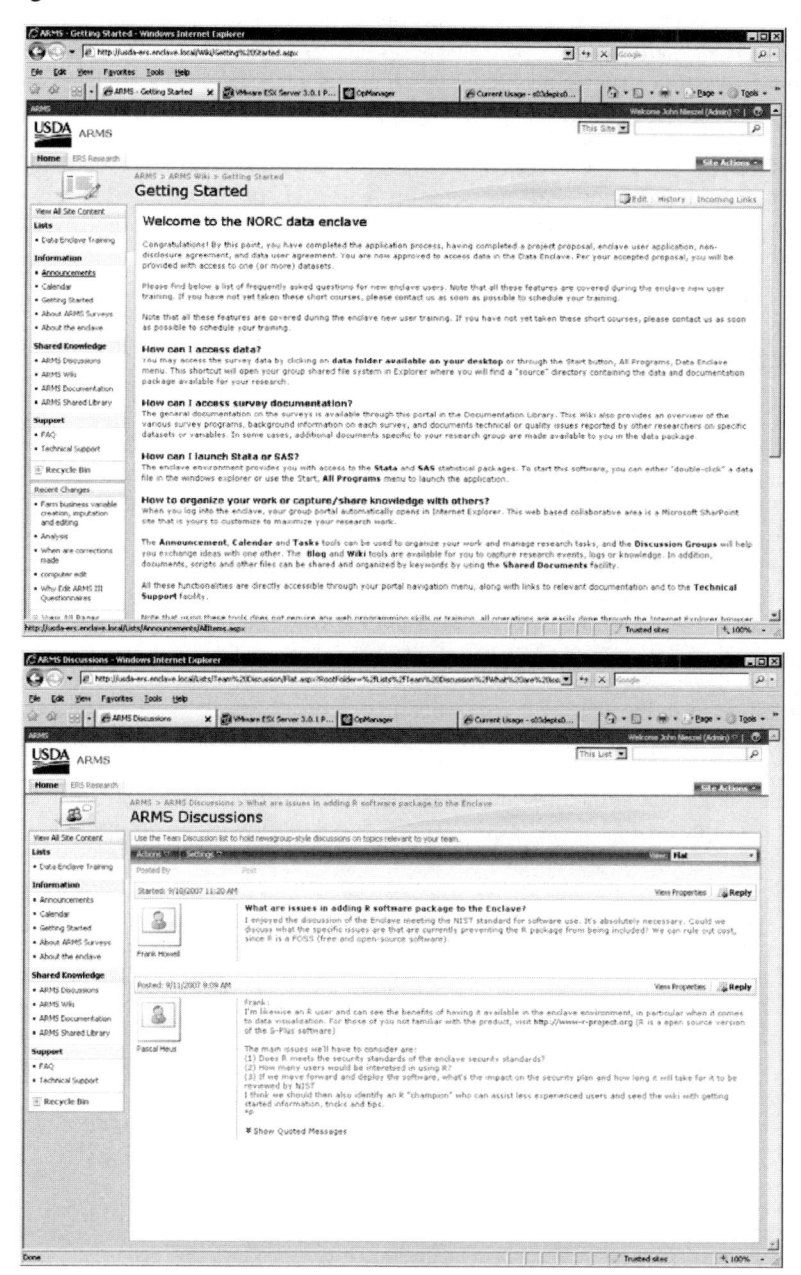

the US National Science Foundation approach that lets the community decide.[17] Certainly both the users and the owners of the data, whether the data be survey, administrative, transaction based, qualitative or derived from the application of cybertools, would need be engaged in the process.

Similarly, it is an open research question as to the appropriate metrics of success, and the best incentives to put in place to achieve success (Cummings and Kiesler 2007). However, a recent solicitation[18], as well as the highlighting of the importance of the topic in NSF's vision statement,[19] suggests that there is substantial opportunity for social science researchers to investigate the research issues.

5. Ethics and privacy issues

A related social science research challenge that the new cyber-technologies pose, as well as potentially help to solve, is the ethical issues raised by the new capacities to collect data on human beings, particularly a focus on the privacy and confidentiality issues raised by collecting data on the interaction of human subjects.

The philosophical issues are well summarized by Madsen (2003). He identifies a "privacy paradox" in confidentiality research – occurring when data managers, in interpreting the right to privacy very narrowly, results in less social benefit, rather than in more. Two factors contribute to this paradox. One is the fear of a panopticon society, in which an all-seeing few monitor the behavior of many, which has been exacerbated since September 11, 2001. The second is a fundamental uncertainty about data ownership – whether data constitute private or public property. It is possible that the tension in the core paradox results from a framework which simply includes rights and responsibilities into the decision-making mix, rather than including social utility. But much more research must be done in this area.

The second set of issues is economic in nature (Lane 2003). Given the clear public good aspects of data collection and dissemination, how can the costs and benefits of the social investment in data be tallied to identify the optimal level of data collection? A partial list of the social benefits would include: improved decision making, avoidance of the moral hazard associated with monopoly government control of information, and improved data quality. A similar list of the social costs would include legal sanctions, the cost of breaches of confidentiality (which might substantially reduce data

---

17 http://www.nsf.gov/funding/pgm_summ.jsp?pims_id=503141.
18 www.nsf.gov/pubs/2008/nsf08550/nsf08550.htm.
19 NSF Cyberinfrastructure Vision for 21st Century Discovery, March 2007.

quality), and support costs. Simply refusing to collect and analyze data which could inform public decision making – with tremendous public benefit – may not be a socially optimal decision.

Also of interest is how to convey the quality of such confidentiality measures to the humans who are the subject of study. Social scientists could expand their current interest in confidentiality to develop approaches that ensure the collaboration and engagement of individuals and organizations in providing data to the research community, as well as permit the data to be shared so that empirical analyses can be generalized and replicated.

It is worth noting that there is increasing interest by computer scientists in ways of protecting confidentiality so that sensitive data can be collected and analyzed without revealing individual identities – and so that researchers can generalize and replicate scientific results.[20] This interest includes policies for the anonymization and sanitization of the data, retention and storage protocols, transformation prior to dissemination, and retaining usability.

6. Recommendations

The social science community should act to address these challenges. Some work is already being done, such as the work by Peter Elias on behalf of a number of international agencies to establish the International Data Forum. However, specific, targeted activities could be undertaken to develop a new social science data infrastructure capable of answering new scientific and policy issues.

Recommendation 1: Invest in new methods of collecting transaction data

The community should take advantage of the interest that funding agencies have in funding cyberinfrastructure for the social sciences to collect new data sources. These would include clickstream information, data from web-archives, email transactions, firm administrative records, social interactions in cyberspace (such as Facebook and MySpace), and video data. The social science community should partner with data collectors, such as Google, Yahoo!, Facebook and the business community to create joint value.

Recommendation 2: Invest in new ways of analyzing transaction data

The social science community should recognize that while new units of interest to social scientists can now be studied, such as social networks, there

---

[20] http://www.nsf.gov/funding/pgm_summ.jsp?pims_id=5033268&org=CNS.

are a number of analytical challenges. The units of analysis are amorphous and change rapidly over time. The information that is collected is no longer precisely measured: there is a high noise to signal ratio. There are large amounts of heterogeneous data. The social science community should partner with other disciplines to develop new analytical techniques. Computer and behavioral scientists have substantial expertise in creating analytical datasets in this environment; the visual analytics community has experience in making sense of such data.

Recommendation 3: Invest in new ways of disseminating transaction data

In order to develop the scientific basis for studying transaction data, the social science community needs to develop an open and transparent data infrastructure. A scientific dialogue needs to be developed about the establishment of a scientific frame, the integrity of the data, and the validation of results. In other words, social scientists must join the "hard" sciences in ensuring that their work is generalizable and replicable (i.e. scientific). A number of remote access sites are being established by leading data disseminators, such as the NORC data enclave, the UK ESDS (Economic and Social Data Service) and CESSDA (Council of European Social Science Data Archives) that promote the development of virtual organizations around data. These new access modalities offer the social sciences a way of creating virtual organizations that have new ways of collecting, accessing, and analyzing transaction microdata.

Recommendation 4: Invest in new ways of conveying complex information

The social science community should invest in new ways of conveying complex information to the broader policy making and lay communities. Tabular techniques may no longer adequately provide sufficient clarity: further investment in such visualization techniques as maps and graphs is warranted.

References:

Abowd, J. and Vilhuber, L. (2005): The Sensitivity of Economic Statistics to Coding Errors in Personal Identifiers. Journal of Business and Economic Statistics 23 (2), 133-152.

Andersson, F./Lane, J. and McEntarfer, E. (2005): Successful Transitions out of Low-Wage Work for Temporary Assistance for Needy Families (TANF) Recipients: The Role of Employers, Coworkers, and Location. http://aspe.hhs.gov/hsp/low-wage-workers-transitions04/index.htm [Vol.: http://aspe.hhs.gov/hsp/low-wage-workers-transitions04/index.htm]. Washington.

Autor, D. (2009): Labor Market Intermediaries. Chicago.

Barjak, F./Lane, J./Procter, R. and Robinson, S. (2007): Accelerating Transition to Virtual Research Organisation in Social Science (AVROSS). Brussels.

Benedetto, G./Haltiwanger, J./Lane, J. and McKinney, K. (2007): Using Worker Flows in the Analysis of the Firm. Journal of Business and Economic Statistics 25 (3), 299-313.

Bollen, J./Rodriguez, M. and Sompel, H.V.D. (2007): MESUR: usage-based metrics of scholarly impact. Paper presented at the Joint Conference on Digital LIbraries, Vancouver.

Borchsenius, L. (2005): New Developments In The Danish System For Access To Microdata, Joint UNECE/Eurostat work session on statistical data confidentiality. Geneva.

Calderwood, L. and Lessof, C. (2006): Enhancing longitudinal surveys by linking to administrative data. Centre for Longitudinal Studies Working Paper.

Contractor, N. (2008): CI-KNOW: A Tool for Understanding and Enabling the Transformative Power of Cyberinfrastructure in Virtual Communities, Presentation at the National Science Foundation, September 15, 2008.

Cummings, J./Finholt, T./Foster, I./Kesselman, C. and Lawrence, K. (2008): Beyond Being There: A Blueprint for Advancing the Design, Development and Evaluation of Virtual Organizations.

Cummings, J. and Kiesler, S. (2007): Coordination costs and project outcomes in multi-university collaborations. Research Policy 36 (10), 1620-1634.

Engle, R. and Russell, J. (1998): Autoregressive Conditional Duration: A New Model for Irregularly Spaced Transaction Data. Econometrica 66 (5), 1127-1162.

Foster, I./Kesselman, C. and Tuecke, S. (2001): The Anatomy of the Grid: Enabling Scalable Virtual Organizations. International Journal of Supercomputer Applications 15 (3), 200-222.

Freedman, M./Lane, J. and Roemer, M. (2008): New Approaches to Creating Data for Economic Geographers. Journal of Official Statistics 24 (1), 133-156.

Hotz, J./Goerge, R./Balzekas, J. and Margolin, F. (2000): Administrative Data for Policy-Relevant Research: Assessment of Current Utility and Recommendations for Development. Evanston.

Hundepohl, A. and de Wolf, P.-P. (2005): OnSite@Home: Remote Access at Statistics Netherlands, Joint UNECE/Eurostat work session on statistical data confidentiality. Geneva.

Jones, P. and Elias, P. (2006): Administrative data as research resources: a selected audit. Swindon.

Lane, J. (2003): The Uses of Microdata: Keynote Speech, Conference of European Statisticians. Geneva.

Lane, J. (2009): Administrative and Survey Data. In: Marsden, P. and Wright, J. (Eds.): Handbook of Survey Research. Oxford.

Lane, J./Heus, P. and Mulcahy, T. (2008): Data Confidentiality in a Cyber World: Making Use of Cyberinfrastructure. Transactions on Data Privacy 1 (1), 2-16.

Madsen, P. (2003): The Ethics of Confidentiality: The Tension Between Confidentiality and the Integrity of Data Analysis in Social Science Research, NSF Workshop on Confidentiality Research. Arlington.

Pang, L. (2001): Understanding Virtual Organizations. Information Systems Control Journal 6/2001.

Ritchie, F. (2005): Access to Business Microdata in the United Kingdom, Joint UNECE/Eurostat work session on statistical data confidentiality. Geneva.

Schunn, C. (2008): Integrating Social and Cognitive Elements of Discovery and Innovation. In: N.S. Foundation (Ed.) [Vol. Award number 0830210].

Skinner, J. and Wennberg, J. (2000): Regional Inequality in Medicare Spending: The Key to Medicare Reform? In: Garber, A. (Ed.): Frontiers in Health Economics. Cambridge.

Söderberg, L.-J. (2005): MONA – Microdata On-Line Access At Statistics Sweden, Joint UNECE/Eurostat work session on statistical data confidentiality Geneva.

Thomas, J.J. and Cook, K.A. (2005): Illuminating the Path: The Research and Development Agenda for Visual Analytics. http://nvac.pnl.gov/docs/RD_ Agenda_VisualAnalytics.pdf. [Last visited: 03/02/2010].

8. Transaction Data: Commercial Transaction Surveys and Test Market Data

Bernhard Engel

Contact:

Bernhard Engel
German Television ZDF
Media Research Department
ZDF Strasse 1
55100 Mainz
Germany
e-mail: Engel[at]zdf.de

Abstract

Commercial transaction surveys and test market data are important sources for the analysis of consumer behavior in various markets. The advantage of these surveys is that they do not simply rely on the "weak" data of consumers but also on "measured" data (e.g., sales information, marketing information). The key questions for the analysis of commercial transaction surveys and test market data concern the prospective evaluation of market success for launched or relaunched products and services, the influence of marketing and media on product purchases under "real market conditions," and the comparison between the test market and the total market. These data are not yet used by the scientific community. There are three major challenges to getting access to the data. First, the owners of the data (market research institutes and their clients) need to allow data access. Second, the data must be anonymized in various ways (individuals and households, brands and products) without losing relevant information. Furthermore, quality guidelines for commercial transaction surveys and test market data must be developed. The German Data Forum (RatSWD) could get this process underway by initiating a project that included the participation of official statistics, the scientific community, and commercial market research.

Keywords: consumer behavior, test market

1. Introduction

Until recently, commercial transaction surveys have not been a focal point of interest for either the RatSWD or research funding agencies like the German Research Foundation (DFG, *Deutsche Forschungsgemeinschaft*) or the Federal Ministry of Education and Research (BMBF, *Bundesministerium für Bildung und Forschung*). The term "commercial transaction survey" is not common even in market research. In order to define commercial transaction surveys for this advisory report, we will introduce some of the main characteristics and uses of this type of data infrastructure and also provide examples of what is *not* a commercial transaction survey.

Topics related to this report can be found in other contributions to this publication, including:

- Administrative Transaction Data (Lane)
- Interdisciplinary Longitudinal Surveys. Linking Individual Data to Organizational Data in Life-Course Analysis (Liebig)
- The Availability of Market Research Data and its Potential for Use in Empirical Social and Economic Research (Wiegand)

Also the keywords "access panels" and "(micro-)geographical data" may be useful links to this advisory report.

Commercial transaction surveys are surveys where transactions from business to consumers (B2C) are observed under controlled conditions. The extent of control, the unit of measurement, and the unit of analysis may vary. The typical commercial transaction survey is known as a "test market."[1]

In test markets, there is statistical control of variables not only on the demand side, but also on the supply side of the market. On the supply side, there is information collected about product properties, pricing, marketing activities, etc. On the demand side, consumers give information about their shopping behavior (e.g., shopping baskets, frequency of shopping, preferred package sizes), demographics, preferences, etc. Hence, it is possible to set up a test environment with single or multiple stimulus response models under controlled conditions. Test markets may be representative samples or not. It is necessary, however, for some degree of "functional representativeness" to be established. This term is used in qualitative research and means that all relevant influence factors are covered by the sample. Test markets are normally defined as surveys in a clearly defined area.

There are, however, various other survey and research methods that use the name "test market" that we will not discuss in this paper. For this report, we will *not* discuss test markets such as:

(1) *Surveys in a single store.* These surveys are often very small and are not relevant data sources for a scientific data structure.

(2) *Surveys and test markets for a single client.* The access to customer-specific surveys is difficult and the market research focus of these surveys is not always well documented.

(3) *Virtual Test Markets.* These test markets are statistical models and the database is completely derived from a calculation model, so there are no data at the respondent level.

(4) *Test markets that are fully developed markets* (e.g., Austria as a quasi test market for Germany,[2] or the use of Ireland as a quasi test market for the US through the introduction of special digital TV services).

The following sections of this expert report will concentrate on the specific characteristics of test markets as defined in this introduction. The basic research questions around such test markets concern

- the prospective evaluation of market success for launched or relaunched products and services;

---

1   The NHS (Nielsen Home Scan single source), a major transaction survey completed at the end of 2005, measured TV viewing behavior (electronic measurement) and consumer behavior (scanning of purchases).
2   See "T-mobile bestätigt UMTS-iPhone: Österreich wird TestMarkt." In: Der Standard. 09.06.2008.

- the influence of marketing and media on product purchases;
- the influence of these under "real market conditions"; and,
- a comparison between the test market and the total market.

Test markets are one instrument among others in the product development process. The industry will never use the results from a test market as the only criterion for decisions. This should be kept in mind when one has access to data from test markets.

There are different stages in the product development cycle where market research helps to optimize the launch to market (e.g., focus groups for concept and packaging tests, standardized procedures to evaluate an adequate market price). The last step before launch to market is very often the launch in a test market.

2. Test markets in Germany: Relevant cases

There are few sources of information about test markets in Germany that are available for general use. For the purposes of this report, there are three examples that provide *descriptions* of test markets, but not data; namely, the GfK Behavior Scan, the TNS Bonsai Deutschland, and IP Test Market Friedrichshafen. The data providers are market research institutes and the results are confidential to their clients.

GfK Behavior Scan (Hassloch)[3]

The GfK Group's test market is the largest in Germany. Focusing on the town of Hassloch (approx. 20,000 inhabitants), mainly fast moving consumer goods (hereafter FMCG) are tested. The sample size is 3,500 households. In approximately 2,500 households, it is possible to change television advertising to include targeted test spots. Between 90 percent and 95 percent of the total expenditures for FMCG is spent in stores within the Hassloch area.

The following overview illustrates the basic structure of the Hassloch test market based on the types of data collected in this project. The project produces extensive data. All purchased products are labeled with the EAN (European Article Number) Code. There are identifiers for the household, the store, the basket of all purchases, and a time stamp. The EAN Code can also be linked to additional product information. On the household level, it is

---

3   The GfK (*Gesellschaft für Konsumforschung*) Group is one of the largest market research companies in the world. The Group has a staff complement of 10,000+ employees working in 115 operating companies covering more than 100 countries of the world. (Högl and Hertle 2009).

possible to identify exposure to advertisements and sales promotion. Clients do not have access to raw data. The delivery of data is on an aggregated level.

The Hassloch test market is connected with other test possibilities in a larger area called *Vorderpfalz*, or the Anterior Palatinate region. In this area, the sample size is very large. There are, however, no data on a respondent level, but only on an aggregate level (testing television advertisements and store turnover) available for clients.

Normally, the structure of the Hassloch test market is compared with that of Rhineland-Palatinate. Relevant variables include age, sex, housing conditions, household type (single, family with or without children, foreigners) and spending power. According to these variables Hassloch has a similar structure to Rhineland-Palatinate, although the spending power is slightly higher (Index = 104).

TNS Bonsai Deutschland[4]

The TNS Bonsai Deutschland is another test panel in Germany. The basic objective of this project is to optimize product lifecycles. TNS Bonsai Deutschland has no continuous consumer panel but offers client-specific surveys with data integration from other sources. The test market is located in Bremen.

The specific "unique selling proposition" (hereafter USP) or, said simply, value, of TNS Bonsai Deutschland is the OTC optimizer. TNS Bonsai Deutschland has a cooperation with about 150 pharmacies in Bremen. Bonsai Deutschland continuously generates sales data of pharmacies in the OTC and free choice area (Wawi, *Warenwirtschaft*). In combination with a nationwide pharmacy panel, there are various testing opportunities for the launch and relaunch of products but also for marketing activities at the point of sale. Although these data are very important for the success of products in the OTC sector and for category management in pharmacies, they are probably not as useful more generally as a source of data for the German data infrastructure.

---

[4] TNS Bonsai Deutschland is part of TNS Group. TNS is one of the top five market research companies worldwide. The shareholder of TNS Bonsai Deutschland is TNS Infratest. Generally, only very little information from TNS Bonsai-Deutschland is accessible.

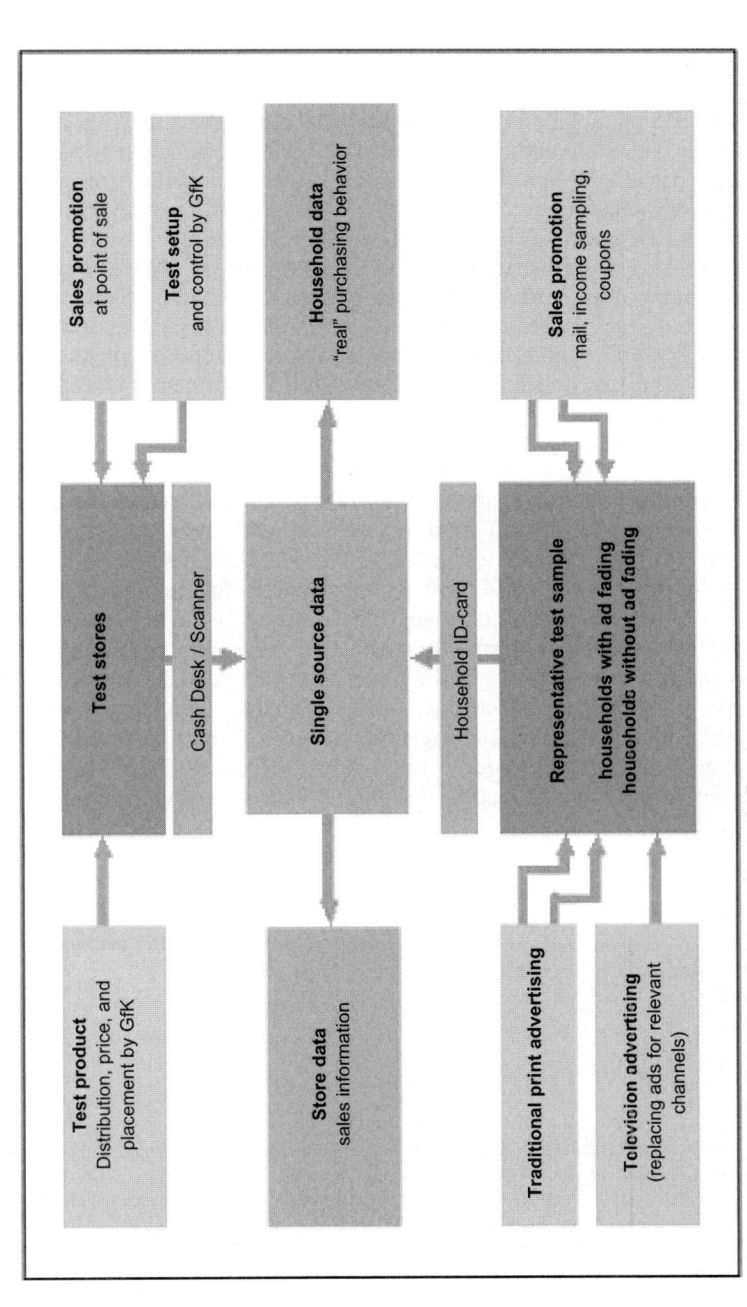

Figure 1: Overview of the GfK Test System in Hassloch/Pfalz

Source: Högl and Hertle 2009, English translation by B. Engel
Arrows indicate possibility of experimental influence

IP Test Market Friedrichshafen[5]

The IP test market in Friedrichshafen was established in August 2007 by Deutsche Telekom and the city of Friedrichshafen. Friedrichshafen was selected because it won the T-City contest for the best ideas on how to use modern broadband networks to improve the quality of everyday life. Consequently, Deutsche Telekom will invest €35 million into the IP infrastructure in Friedrichshafen and will spend another €80 million for the development of new products and services on the broadband network. There are various ongoing projects in this test market in areas such as education and searching, mobility and traffic control, tourism and culture, citizen and state, economy and job, and health and healthcare. The project has a cooperative agreement with Zeppelin University in Friedrichshafen (Deutsche Telekom Institute for Connected Cities – TICC)

The IP test market in Friedrichshafen can also be seen as Deutsche Telekom's contribution to the German IT Summit.[6] Activities are in place to establish continuous evaluation of projects and their acceptance in the market. Testing in the IP test market of Friedrichshafen not only evaluates consumer behavior, but also presents opportunities for testing technology.

The IP test market in Friedrichshafen is probably the most interesting test market for broader research questions. IP technology will change our everyday life in the future with its diverse array of services. In the context of this program, the IP platform allows a continuous tracking of user actions without added burden for the users. However, it should be noted that the IP test market in Friedrichshafen is not a public service. Rather, Deutsche Telekom has set up this test market to improve its competitive position in the IP market.

---

5   The IP Test market is a project led by Deutsche Telekom for testing and implementing new services based on internet protocol (IP based services).
6   The German IT Summit (*Nationaler IT-Gipfel*) was initiated by German Chancellor Angela Merkel in December 2006 to improve the position of Germany's IT industry. The second summit was held on December 10, 2007. There are several working groups that report to chancellor Merkel. One group, headed by René Obermann, CEO of Deutsche Telekom, works on the "Convergence of Media: The Future of Networks and Services."

3. Conclusions and recommendations

Changes in social and economic life are complex processes. In test markets, this complexity is reduced to the influence of certain measures (e.g., effects of marketing, changes in the quality or the prices of products, influence of the media on consumer behavior). The analysis of test market data can help to develop hypotheses about social and economic change.

Test markets are also used in other European countries and are extensively used in the US. The GfK Group, for example, follows test markets for FMCG that are comparable to Hassloch in Angers and le Mans (France). Insofar as sources allowing more general access to the data do exist, the US is the leader in the methodology and usage of test markets. In the system that has developed there, extensive rankings designate whether a specific MSA (Metropolitan and Micropolitan Statistical Area, according to the definition of the US Census Bureau) is a good consumer test market. There are about 150 named MSAs in the US that can be used as test markets. The determining criteria include not only demographics, but also consumer and media behavior, leisure activities, etc.[7]

3.1 Access to existing test market data

Gaining access to existing test market data in Germany presents three major obstacles. First, market research institutes and clients are the owners of the data. In many cases, more then one client is involved in the project. Data protection and anonymization are necessary not only at a respondent level, but also for other entities associated with the database, such as stores, products, producers of the products, etc. The German Data Forum (RatSWD) could provide assistance with adapting existing rules for data protection and anonymization to the specific case of test market data. In the case of the IP test market Friedrichshafen, the RatSWD could contact the TICC Institute at Zeppelin University in Friedrichshafen to promote further collaboration.

3.2 Initiatives to establish test market quality guidelines and transparency for Germany

Test markets have specific sampling requirements. It is difficult for the users of data to decide whether a test market is a "best practice" sample or not. On the one hand, it is necessary to establish a test environment under controlled

---

7 See Acxiom (2004). Acxiom Deutschland also offers similar data, especially to direct marketing.

conditions; on the other hand, the results from a test market should be transferable to the real world. Because a test market has multiple "entities," a representative population sample cannot meet the standards for a test market. Additional information – like infrastructure information about the town or region where the test market is located – could help to improve the value of a test market sample. Perhaps it would be useful to discuss the problem in the context of "representative sampling beyond demographics." The German Data Forum (RatSWD) could play a role by suggesting a project bringing together official statistics, the scientific community, and commercial market research with the objective to develop quality guidelines and transparency for German test markets.

References:

BMWI (2007): Konvergenz gestalten – Chancen nutzen. Broschüre zum Arbeitsauftrag der AG 2 „Konvergenz der Medien – Zukunft der Netze und Dienste" im Rahmen des 2. IT Gipfels.

Högl, S. and Hertle, Th. (2009): MarketingLab – Evaluatives Pretesting mit der GfK Testmarktwelt. In: Bruhn, M./Esch, F.-R./Langner, T. (Eds.): Handbuch Kommunikation. Grundlagen – Innovative Ansätze – Praktische Umsetzungen. Wiesbaden.

Deutsche Telekom (2007): Testmarkt Friedrichshafen. Pressemeldung dpa vom 24.08.2007 14:33 „Friedrichshafen wird Musterstadt – Vertrag mit Telekom". Mediaversuch am lebenden Objekt. Media & Marketing 6/2004, 44-49.

Acxiom (2004): Which American City Provides The Best Consumer Test Market? "Mirror on America" Provides Ranking of Top 150 Cities.

www.t-city.de IP-Testmarkt Friedrichshafen. [Last visited: 12/03/2010].

www.bonsai-deutschland.de TNS Bonsai-Deutschland, Bremen. [Last visited: 12/03/2010].

http://www.gfk.com/group/services/instruments_and_services/contact_dates/00141/index.en.html GfK Behavior Scan, Hassloch. [Last visited: 12/03/2010].

9. Time Use and Time Budgets

*Joachim Merz**

---

* Acknowledgement: I would like to thank Dr. Markus Zwick and Heike Habla from the Research Data Center of the Federal Statistical Office as well as Erlend Holz, Prof. Dr. Manfred Ehling, and Dr. Daniel Vorgrimler (all from the Federal Statistical Office), and Dr. Kimberly Fisher (University of Oxford, UK), for their very helpful support.

Contact:

Joachim Merz
Leuphana University Lueneburg
Research Institute on Professions
(FFB, *Forschungsinstitut Freie Berufe*)
Department of Economics, Behavioural and Law Sciences
Scharnhorststr. 1
21335 Lueneburg
Germany
e-mail: merz[at]uni-lueneburg.de

Abstract

"Time use statistics offer a unique tool for exploring a wide range of policy concerns including social change; division of labor; allocation of time for household work; the estimation of the value of household production; transportation; leisure and recreation; pension plans; and health-care programmes, among others" (United Nations). This advisory report will discuss recent developments, improvements and future challenges of time use and time budgets for policy and research with a focus on international but especially national developments in Germany that have emerged in the wake of the 2001 KVI report.

The topics to be addressed are: recently established international time use institutions, data archives, and surveys; German time use databases and their accessibility, current time use research fields and studies; time use for economic and social policy; new methods in time use survey sampling; future developments; and European and international challenges. The conclusions and recommendations first urge the implementation of the new German Time Use Survey (GTUS 2011/12) and urgently call for its financing and support for its active organization. Specific GTUS improvements, SOEP time use issues, a brand new time use panel, and the permanent establishment of the German Research Data Centers are also recommended.

Keywords: time use, time budgets and time use surveys, time use data
JEL classification: C81, J2D1, I3, O15, O17

1. Time use and time budgets: General concerns

Time is the encompassing and compound dimension and resource of individual activities and living arrangements. Very generally speaking, any characteristic or information is only complete where time is a factor that is considered in addition to the factual socio-economic and geographic attributes. Quantitative-statistical based knowledge about the use of time for all conceivable activities – from the labor market to the leisure world – is thus of central importance not only for the individual but also for the economy, for governmental economic and social policy, and for society at large:

"Time use statistics offer a unique tool for exploring a wide range of policy concerns including social change; division of labour; allocation of time for household work; the estimation of the value of household production; transportation; leisure and recreation; pension plans; and health-care programmes, among others" (United Nations Statistics Division).[1]

Time use surveys collect information about activity sequences in time spells over a period lasting from one day to a week. At the core of a time use survey is the time use diary, which registers an individual's activity sequence.

---

[1] http://unstats.un.org/unsd/demographic/sconcerns/tuse/

For each main activity in such a time period additional information is entered – such as secondary activity – and information about "where" and "with whom" this activity was done. In addition to the diary information, a time use survey typically includes a questionnaire about background socio-economic individual and household variables. Sometimes specific information is included in the questionnaire about less frequent activities for a period longer than a day and/or item-specific questions like a seven-day work schedule proposed by the Harmonised European Time Use Study (HETUS, see Eurostat 2009).

Time budgets in a strong sense refer to activity specific to aggregated time used over the course of the entire day. Time budgets as a set of time taking up activities thus are comparable to income budgets spending for a set of consumption expenditures (Harms and Gershuny 2009: 1). However, the terminus time budget or time budget survey is often synonymous with the diary information itself or with the diary-based complete time use survey (diaries plus socio-economic background); this is the interpretation we will adopt here. The overall advantage of a time budget is its more accurate time use measurement than can be recorded by stylized data, and the temporal location of an activity within a given day. This offers the possibility of analyzing the timing of activities (like working hours); moreover, information about the sequence of activity patterns is an extraordinary surplus when compared to all other surveys asking for daily or weekly individual activities in the labor market or in any field of daily life.

Time use research analyses the individual's use of time. As Andrew Harvey, a longstanding mentor of time use research states,

"Time use research is the study of how people use their time. Minimally, time use studies show what activities people do week to week or day to day. Maximally, they show what people are doing, where they are, who they are with, and how they feel from minute to minute."[2]

Time use: Background and literature

Some examples of early time use studies are the American study "How Working Men Spend Their Time" (Bevans 1913) and the British studies "Round About a Pound a Week" (Pembers-Reeves 1913). A classic German time use study is the 1933 Marienthal Study "Die Arbeitslosen von Marienthal – Ein soziographischer Versuch über die Wirkungen langandauernder Arbeitslosigkeit" (Jahoda, Felix and Lazarsfeld 1933).

Since the beginning of the 20th century, time use research has developed with respect to methodological as well as to substantive issues. Meanwhile

---

2   http://www.stmarys.ca/partners/turp/pages/whatistimeuse.htm

there are a number of comprehensive studies about the interest in and the international development of time use research. Kramer (2005) has recently provided an historic overview, Harms and Gershuny (2009) focus on time budgets and time use issues, Gershuny (2001) covers time use methods, Harvey (2004, 1999), Harvey, Merz and Mukhopadhyay (2006), Harvey, Szalai, Elliott, Stone and Clark (1984), Gershuny (1995), (Andorka 1987) or the volume on "Time Use – Research, Data and Policy" (Merz and Ehling 1999) give a general overview about the current state of the field.

Although within a time use diary the respondent is characterizing his or her activity in a time spell in his or her own words, only coded activities are available for the data user. Thus, the creation of appropriate coding for all conceivable research interests is a challenging task. However, there are international harmonizing approaches, such as the HETUS project (Eurostat 2009), the United Nations (Bediako and Vanek 1999), or alternative approaches (Hoffmann and Mata 1999). Actual scientific articles with in-depth time use analyses, books and projects can be found in particular in the new electronic *International Journal of Time Use Research*.[3] Andrew Harvey with his TURP project at St. Mary's University in Halifax, Canada, provides a substantial bibliography of time use studies. Since 2007, the Centre for Time Use Research (CTUR) has offered information about current time use publications.[4]

This advisory report will discuss improvements in and future challenges for time use and time budgets with a focus on recent international and, in particular, national developments since 2000 in the wake of the 2001 KVI report.[5] The discussion is organized as follows: section 2 sketches internationally important time use institutions, data archives, and surveys, followed by time use databases and their accessibility in Germany (section 3). Time use research fields with international and national improvements, developments, and studies are presented in section 4. Time use in and for economic and social policy is the topic in section 5. New methods in time use survey sampling are presented in section 6. Section 7 examines future developments within European and international challenges. Section 8 draws conclusions and offers some recommendations.

---

3 http://www.eIJTUR.org
4 http://www.timeuse.orgh c/information
5 Kommission zur Verbesserung der informationellen Infrastruktur zwischen Wissenschaft und Statistik 2001, Merz 2001.

417

2. Time use international: Institutions, data archives and surveys

The following represent the most significant of the recently established time use institutions, data archives, and international surveys forming the improved international background in which German time use activities are embedded.

International time use institutions. Important international time use institutions are compiled in table 1.

Table 1: International Time Use Institutions

IATUR: The International Association for Time Use Research	www.iatur.org
TURP: Time Use Research Program at St. Mary's University, Halifax, Canada	www.stmarys.ca/partners/turp
UNSTATS: United Nations Statistics: Allocation of Time and Time Use	http://unstats.un.org/unsd/demographic/sconcerns/tuse/
RNTU: Research Network on Time Use at Lüneburg University, Germany	http://ffb.uni-lueneburg.de/rntu
eIJTUR: electronic International Journal of Time Use Research	www.eIJTUR.org
CTUR: Centre for Time Use Research at Oxford University, UK	www.timeuse.org

Major developments. The time use community is growing since 1970[6] and has grown increasingly within the last decade. Its annual conference in 2009 – following earlier conferences in the US and Sydney, Australia – will be at the Leuphana University of Lüneburg, Germany,[7] hosted by our Research Institute on Professions (FBB, *Forschungsinstitut Freie Berufe*) and the German Federal Statistical Office. Since 1985 TURP at St. Mary's University in Halifax (Canada) has provided a worldwide time use bibliography and is a new pioneer in spatial time use research with its 2007–2009 *Halifax Regional Space-Time Activity Research (STAR)* Project, a GPS-assisted household time use survey. Besides the recent UNSTATS activities and the time use research network RNTU activities at Lüneburg, a new peer-reviewed scientific time use journal, the electronic *International Journal of Time Use Research*[8] hosted by FFB (University of Lüneburg) was founded in 2003. Worldwide time use datasets are archived and harmonized by CTUR/MTUS at Oxford University, representing enormous progress in the ability to make international comparisons.

---

6   http://www.iatur.org
7   http://www.leuphana.de/ffb/iatur 2009
8   http://www.eIJTUR.org

International time use data archives. The first international time budget study was the Multinational Time Budget Study coordinated in the 1960s by Alexander Szalai (1972). This project developed standardized diaries and survey methods and was implemented by twelve countries[9] in 1965. Since then new time use and time budget surveys have increasingly been created. Recent main studies and archives since 2000 are compiled in table 2.

Table 2: International Time Use Data Archives

MTUS: Multinational Time Use Study	www.timeuse.org/mtus
MHES: Multinational Household Expenditures Study	www.economics.unimelb.edu.au/SITE/household/MTUS1.shtml
HETUS: Harmonised European Time Use Study HETUS table generating tool	http://ec.europa.eu/eurostat/ https://www.testh2.scb.se/tus
CHAD: Consolidated Human Activity Database	www.epa.gov/chadnet1/index.html

Major developments. The most comprehensive and enduring data archives of international time use studies since is the Multinational Time Use Study (MTUS) at CTUR now at Oxford University (Prof. Jonathan Gershuny, see Gershuny et al. 2000). MTUS is harmonizing time use studies based on diaries from many countries with now about 60 studies from about twenty-six countries worldwide. MHES, the Multinational Household Expenditures Study (MHES) (Prof. Duncan Ironmonger, University of Melbourne, Australia), provides individual and household information about time use *and* expenditures.

The European Union begun to support the harmonization of time use surveys and statistics in Europe in the early 1990s (HETUS, Eurostat 2009; Rydenstam 1999). Now major European time use surveys are harmonized by HETUS, an enormous advantage for the development of international comparisons. Updated HETUS guidelines are available from 2009. Based on the HETUS, Statistics Finland and Statistics Sweden have developed the *HETUS table generating tool,* an interactive, internet-based, user-friendly tool for producing user-defined statistical tables.[10] The Consolidated Human Activity Database (CHAD) will serve as an example for a specific individual time use

---

9   USSR, US, BRD, DDR, Bulgaria, Czechoslovakia, Hungary, Poland, Yugoslavia, Belgium, France, Peru.
10 Credentials are necessary to access the tool. Klas Rydenstam, from Statistics Sweden (https://www.testh2.scb.se/tus/tus/ and klas.rydenstam@scb.se) has to be contacted (Rydenstam 2007, 118).

database dedicated to a certain substantive aim, in this case environmental protection.[11]

International time use surveys since 2000. At the turn of the millennium around twenty European countries conducted time use surveys according to the harmonized HETUS guidelines. More than 40 international time use surveys worldwide have been conducted since 2000 (see table 3).[12]

Table 3: International Time Use Surveys since 2000

Country	Time Use Survey	Year
Argentina	Encuesta de Uso del Tiempo de Buenos Aires	2005
Australia	Time Use Survey of New Mothers	2005-2006
Austria	Austrian Time Use Survey 2008-2009	2008-2009
Belgium	Belgian Time Use Survey	2000, 2005
Brazil	Belo Horizonte Time Use Survey	2001
Bulgaria	Time Use Survey	2001-2002
Canada	General Social Survey, 19 Time Use	2000, 2005
Denmark	The Time Use of Households	2001
Estonia	Time Use Survey	1999-2000
European Union	Harmonised European Union Time Use Surveys	1999-2002
Finland	Time Use Survey: Everyday Life in Finland	2000
Germany	German Time Use Study	2001-2002
Guatemala	National Survey of Living Conditions	2002
Hungary	Time Use Survey	2000
Ireland	Adolescent Time Use and Well-Being	2007-2008
Ireland	Time Use in Ireland	2005
Italy	National Time Use Survey	2002-2003
Japan	Japanese Time Use Survey	2000, 01, 05
Mongoloia	Pilot Time Use Survey	2000
Netherlands	Time Budget Survey of the SCP Office	2000

---

11 CHAD is developed by the US Environmental Protection Agency (EPA) CHAD harmonizes about 10 databases with frequency and duration information of an activity (e.g., under pollution) with further daily and spatial information.
12 Detailed information about earlier harmonized international time use studies are made available by MTUS of the Centre of Time Use Research at Oxford University (http://www.timeuse.org/ information/studies/data). A list of the MTUS harmonized time use activities is available at http://www.timeuse.org/mtus/documentation/appendix.

Country	Time Use Survey	Year
New Zealand	Time Use Study	2008-2009
Norway	Tidsnyttingsundersokelsen	2000-2001
Poland	Time Use Survey	2001
Portugal	Teachers Time	2001-2003
Republic of Kiribati	Time Use Survey Gilbert Island	2001-2002
Republic of Korea	Time Use Survey	2000, 2005
Romania	National Time Use Study	2001
Slovak Republic	Time Use Survey	2006
Slovenia	Time Use Survey	2000-2001
South Africa	Time Use in South Africa	2000
Spain	Encuesta de Empleo del Tiempo	2002-2003
Sweden	Time Use Survey	2000-2001
Switzerland	Emploi du temps en Suisse	2001
Taiwan	National Time Use Survey	2004
Thailand	National Time Use Survey	2000-2001
Turkey	Time Use Survey 2006	2006
United Kingdom	Omnibus, One Day Diary Module	2001, 2005
United Kingdom	The National Survey of Time Use	2000-2001
USA	ATUS: American Time Use Survey	2003-2007

Source: CTUR/MTUS harmonized data (http://www.timeuse.org/information/studies/data) and author research.

Major developments. In addition to these recent, national cross-sectional time use surveys since 2000, other important developments can be noted. First, the Harmonised European Time Use Surveys (HETUS) were a milestone in concerted multinational sampling and activity coding of time use diary data. Second, the new US time use engagement through the annual American Time Use Study (ATUS)[13] includes work on the ATUS ancestor, The American Heritage Time Use Study (AHTUS, 1965, 1975, 1989, 1992–94 and 1998/99) which is harmonized by the Centre for Time Use Research (CTUR) at Oxford University.[14] The American Heritage Time Use Data (AHTUD) is the database for the five respective time use studies and was assessed by a

---

13 http://www.bls.gov/tus/
14 http://www.timeuse.org/ahtus

multinational group of experts[15] that provided calibration (Merz and Stolze 2008), evaluation, and recommendations for further time use surveys (Harvey 2006)[16]. Third, some countries are following a quinquennial period of collecting new time use surveys (Canada, Japan, Korea). Altogether, the almost exponential increase of new time use studies since 2000 worldwide emphasizes the internationally recognized importance of time use data for research and policy.

3. Time use data in Germany: Databases and data access

The most important development in providing time use diary data nationally is the official German Time Use Survey GTUS 2001/02 (predecessor GTUS 1991/92). In addition, summarized working hour information is provided by the German Microcensus. Average time use data stylized by a "normal day"[17] are part of the German Socio-Economic Panel (SOEP, *Sozio-oekonomisches Panel*). Finally, some other topic-specific, smaller-sized surveys and firm time use data have been collected in Germany since 2000.

Time use databases in Germany

German Time Use Survey 2001/02. The 2001/02 German Time Use Survey consists of approximately 5,400 households, 37,700 diary days, and 270 activity codes classified by household work and do-it-yourself activities, paid job or job seeking, voluntary and community work, qualification and education, physiological recreation, social life and contacts, use of media and leisure time activities, child care, taking care of and attending to people, and preparation time and travel time including the means of transport. The GTUS design follows Eurostat's Guidelines on Harmonised European Time Use Surveys (HETUS). All household members aged ten years and older were asked to fill out diaries based on 10-minute intervals on three days – two days during the week from Monday to Friday, and one day on the weekend. Data were collected on primary and secondary activities, persons involved or present, the location, and mode of transport. A wide range of household and

---

15 Multinational project "Assessing American Heritage Time Use Studies" by Prof. Dr. Andrew Harvey, St. Mary's University, Halifax, NS, Canada, Prof. Dr. Dr. Ignace Glorieux, Vrije Universiteit Brussel, Brussels, Belgium, Prof. Dr. Joachim Merz, University of Lüneburg, Germany, Klas Rydenstam, Statistics Sweden.
16 http://pna.yale.edu
17 The benefits and challenges of diary vs. stylized time use information are discussed for example in Robinson 1985, Niemi 1993, and Schulz and Grunow 2007.

individual data (socio-demographic, economic, and other background variables) were collected in additional questionnaires.

The GTUS microdata themselves and information about the survey are available from the Research Data Centers of the Federal Statistical Office and the Statistical Offices of the German *Länder*.[18] In addition, the Institute for the Study of Labor (IZA, *Forschungsinstitut zur Zukunft der Arbeit*) in Bonn offers metadata about this and other surveys.[19] A comprehensive *GTUS-Compass* describing the broad range of GTUS 2001/02 information and its usage is provided by the Federal Statistical Office (2006a).[20]

German Socio-Economic Panel (1984–ongoing). Since 1984, the SOEP of living in Germany has annually collected a broad set of individual subjective and objective information from each household member sixteen years and older.[21] The SOEP, hosted by the German Institute for Economic Research, (DIW Berlin, *Deutsches Institut für Wirtschaftforschung*),[22] registers only "typical" or "normal" work and non-work daytime time use information for each of the following activities: paid work (including commuting and secondary occupational activities), housework and shopping, childcare, do-it-yourself, education/learning, watching television or videos, and hobbies and other leisure activities. In addition, the SOEP asks for information about less frequent activities and how often they were done within different longer time periods.

One advantage of the SOEP (among others) is its truly longitudinal character and its broad range of socio-economic variables for testing behavioral hypotheses. The disadvantage (besides having exclusively stylized information) is that it only permits information on full hours of activity (no minutes or smaller units of time) when collecting data. A simple extension by minutes is strongly recommended for further SOEP waves and for international comparisons.

German Microcensus: The large-scale German Microcensus[23] (1 percent sample of the population) is focused around the labor market and has asked for in-depth information about a variety of "typical" or "normal" working hours since 2005, as well as for current as well as desired working hour arrangement.

---

18 http://www.forschungsdatenzentrum.de
19 http://idsc.iza.org/metadata/
20 Compass topics: Publications of government, ministries, and research facilities, conferences, journals and other media; Master thesis, final diploma, doctoral dissertations; Eurostat: Harmonised European Time Use Study (HETUS); Federal Statistical Office publications; United Nations (UN); Journals about time use and related topics; Associations, conferences, data archives and research facilities about time use and related topics; General research facilities and data archives; Contact about the Time Use Surveys at the Federal Statistical Office of Germany.
21 http://www.diw.de/soep
22 http://www.diw.de/english
23 http://www.destatis.de

Further studies with time use information. Time use information gathered by private firms, such as Nielsen Marketing or the Society for Consumer Research (GfK, *Gesellschaft für Konsumforschung*) will be discussed in the "Time Use Research Fields" section below. Television and broadcast services (like ARD or ZDF) and other media firms have developed their own large-scale survey system about media use with a significant amount of process-based time use information. The situation and the suitability of diary-based time use research for media use have recently been analyzed by Merz (2009). Smaller-sized or topic-specific studies include the "Berliner Längsschnitt Medien," a project to analyze media use and school performance by the Criminological Research Institute of Lower Saxony (KFN, *Kriminologisches Forschungsinstitut Niedersachsen*)[24] or, in another example, the time use study focused on intra-family relations conducted by the State Institute for Family Research at the University of Bamberg.[25] Although there are important private firms and other institutions that collect time use data in Germany, in general, the data are not available to other institutions or researchers, in general.

Time use microdata access in Germany

While the SOEP and its time use data have been made available for scientists since its inception in 1984 via the DIW Berlin, official microdata have also been provided for some years by new Research Data Centers for the public and the scientific community.[26] The official German Time Use Surveys GTUS 2001/02 and GTUS 1991/92 are provided and serviced by the Research Data Centers of the Federal Statistical Office and the Statistical Offices of the German *Länder*. These Research Data Centers provide four different forms of access to selected microdata of official statistics: Public Use Files (PUFs), Scientific Use Files (SUFs), safe scientific workstations and data laboratories, and controlled remote data processing. These four options differ with regard to both the anonymity of the microdata that can be used and the form of data provision.[27] Access to German official microdata is possible for foreign institutions and scientists not subject to German law.

New microdata access developments after 2000 and in the future. The entire system of microdata access via the Research Data Centers is a new one and has created very successful options for working with official microdata, such as the creation of SUFs. However, SUFs are still anonymized; a "final run" with the original data held within the Federal Statistical Office is

---

24 http://www.kfn.de
25 http://www.ifb.bayern.de/ forschung /inapf-deu.html
26 http://www.ratswd.de/engl/dat/RDC.html
27 http://www.forschungsdatenzentrum de/en/anonymisierung.asp

necessary for many final results and publications. The new *onsite secured possibilities* (similar to those at the DIW Berlin for geo-coded SOEP data) is a promising avenue for providing advanced access. The possibility for *remote access to micro- and metadata*, which, for instance, is provided by the Luxembourg Income Study (LIS), will also be important in the future. The most important future issue, however, is that the Research Data Center of the Federal Statistical Office must be permanently established in order to continue to provide this necessary, well-accredited service!

4. Time use research fields: International and national improvements, developments, and studies since 2000

In principle, time use research fields encompass the whole range of human activity. However, particularly in the specific time use diary type of data, they focus on and allow for activity analyses incorporating attributes of the timing, duration, and sequence of activities with all its effects and causalities of daily life activities. Stylized time use data also give insight into a normal or average day and/or less frequent activities within a desired period of time.

From this perspective, the international and national time use research fields that have emerged since 2000 can be said to include substantive contributions from economic, sociology, and other sciences and also to have addressed methodological issues on a national and multinational level. Though there are a multitude of studies behind each time use research field over the past decade, and certainly behind those dating before this,[28] in assembling table 4 only one international and one national reference will characterize each issue. My taxonomy of time use research fields tries to capture recent international and national research activities and a variety of sources could be cited.[29]

---

28 See for example Merz and Ehling 1999.
29 National: For GTUS 2001/02 based studies the excellent GTUS-Compass by the German Federal Statistical Office (Statistisches Bundesamt 2006) and further actual information provided by its author Erlend Holz; Research Project Summary and literature from the Reserach Data Center of the Federal Statistical Office (http://www.Forschungsdaten zentrum.de). International: CTUR publication list (http://www.timeuse.org/informa tion/publications/; Information by the Research Network on Time Use Research (RNTU: http://www.rntu.org; electronic International Journal of Time Use Research (http://www. eIJTUR.org) and other Journals.

Table 4: Time Use Research Fields since 2000 – International and National

Time Use Research Field	International Reference	International Time Use Data	National Reference	National Time Use Data
Labor Market/ Paid Work Timing, Fragmentation of Work/ Work-life balance/ Sequencing	Hamermesh 2002/Fisher and Layte 2004/ Lesnard 2004	MTUS Version 5.0.1 (D), British TUS 2000-01 (D), HETUS 2003 (D)/ French TUS 1985-86, 1998-99 (D)/.	Merz and Böhm 2005; Merz and Burgert 2004; Merz, Böhm, Burgert 2004	GTUS 2001/02 (D)
Unpaid work/ Nonmarket Activities/ Household Production	Deding and Lausten 2006, Harvey 2006, Ironmonger 2001	Danish TUS 2001 (D), American (Heritage) TUS (D), Australian TUS (D)	Schäfer 2004	GTUS 2001/02 (D)
Gender Perspectives	World's Women Report UNIFEM 2009	Multiple time use data worldwide (D/Q)	Cornelißen 2005, Sellach et al. 2004	GTUS 2001/02 (D)
Division of Housework	Anxo and Carlin 2004, Bonke and McIntosh 2005	French TUD 1999 (D)	Gille and Marbach 2004	GTUS 2001/02 (D)
Child Care/ Day Care/ Care giving	Joesch and Spiess 2006, Chalasani 2006	ECHP 1996 (Q)	Kahle 2004, Fendrich and Schillig 2005	GTUS 2001/02 (D)
Family Interactions/ Parental Time and Leisure	Anxo and Carlin 2004/ Guryan, J., Hurst, E. and M.S. Kearney 2008	French TUS 1999/ American TUS 2006	Bundesministerium für Familie, Senioren, Frauen und Jugend 2006	GTUS 2001/02 (D)
Nutrition/ Household Economics	US Department of Agriculture	American TUS 2005, 2006	Gwodz et al. 2006	GTUS 2001/02 (D)
Consumption/ Shopping	Jacobson and Kooreman 2004	Netherland SCP Survey 2000 (D/Q)	Merz, Hanglberger and Rucha 2009	GTUS 2001/02 (D)
Education	Guryan et al. 2007	ATUS 2005	Wilhelm and Wingerter 2004	GTUS 2001/02 (D)
Leisure/ Culture/ Quality of Life	Torres et al. 2007	European Quality of Life Survey (25 countries)	Statistisches Bundesamt 2008, Weick 2004	GTUS 2001/02 (D)

Time Use Research Field	International		National	
	Reference	Time Use Data	Reference	Time Use Data
Media use/ Play/ IT	Deal 2008	Digital Games Survey 2006 (D/Q)	Merz 2009, Jäckel and Wollscheid 2004, 2007, Fritz and Klingler 2006, Kleinmann and Mößle 2008	GTUS 2000/01 (D), ARD/ZDF-Studie 2005 (Q), BL 2005-2010 (D/Q)
Space/ Geography/ Environment	Harvey 2009	STAR: GPS Time Use Survey 2008	Kramer 2005	GTUS 2001/02 (D)
Mobility/ Transport/ Travel	Keall and Baker 2008	Travel Survey New Zealand 2001 (D)	Kramer 2004	GTUS 2001/02 (D)
Social Contacts/ Networks / Volunteering	Bittman et al. 2005	Australian TUS 1997 (D), Australian SDAC 1998 (Q)	Merz and Osberg 2009, Gabriel et al. 2004	GTUS 2001/02 (D)
Time Crunch/ Time Stress/ Harriedness	Sullivan 2007, Bonke and Gerstoft 2007	Danish TUS 2001 (Q), Home OnLine 1998 (Q/D)	Gille and Marbach 2004	GTUS 2001/02 (D)
Poverty/ Extended well-being/ Inequality	Akarro 2008, Folbre 2009	Time Use Study and Advanced Census Analysis in Tanzania 2002 (D)	Holz 2004, Kettschau et al. 2004, Merz and Rathjen 2009 ISG 2004	GTUS 2001/02 (D)
Special Populations Children/ Adolescent, Youth/ Elderly, Retirement	Pääkkönen 2008/ Mulligan, Schneider and Wolfe 2005/ Piekkola and Leijola 2006	Finnish TUS 1999/00 (Q)/ CPS 1992 (Q), NELS 1992, SDAC 1992/93 (ESM)/ MTUS: 1987, 1991, 1995, 1999 2000 (D)	Cornelißen and Blanke 2004, Engstler et al. 2004	GTUS 2001/02 (D)
Economic Accounting/ Valuing/ Sustainable Society	Landefeld and Culla 2000, Eurostat 2003	Country time use study aggregated to Natinal Accounts	Schäfer 2004, Stahmer 2003, Stäglin 2003	GTUS 2001/02 (D). Time-Input-Output Tables

	International		National	
Time Use Research Field	Reference	Time Use Data	Reference	Time Use Data
New Methods Visualization/ Sequence Analysis Timing/ Profiling/ Heterogeneity/ Entropy	Michelson and Crouse 2004, Ellegard and Cooper 2004/ Wilson 2001/ Stewart 2006/ Gonzales-Chapela 2006/	ALLBUS 12 1998 (D), FAMITEL 2001 (D/Q), Swedish TUDPS 1996 (D)/ ALLBUS 1998 (D)/ EPA TDS 1992-1994 (D), ATUS 2006 (Q)	Hufnagel 2008	GTUS 2001/02 (D)
Methodology Diary versus Questionnaire/ Representa-tivity	Kitterod and Lyngstadt 2005, Niemi 1993/	Norwegian TUS 2000/01 (D/Q)/	Schulz and Grunow 2007/ Merz and Stolze 2008	ifb TUS 2006/ AHTUD 1965-99

AHTUD: American Heritage Time Use Data, ALLBUS: German General Social Survey, ATUS: American Time Use Survey, ARD/ZDF 2005: ARD/ZDF-Studie Massenkommunikation 2005 (Q), BL: Berliner Längsschnitt Medien, CPS: Current population survey, ECHP: European Community Household Panel, HETUS: Harmonised European Time Use Studies, MTUS: Multinational Time Use Study, NELS: National Education Longitudinal Study, TUS: Time Use Survey, SDAC: Survey of Disability, Ageing and Carers, Sloan Study: Study of Youth and Social Development Wave 1, GTUS: German Time Use Survey
Source: Author taxonomy based on various national and international data (see Footnote 10).

Major improvements and developments. Altogether, the table 4 overview shows a wide range of research fields relating to important economic and social issues. For instance, specific time use information provided by diaries allows particular *labor market analyses* that are not available in other labor market surveys: the sequencing, timing, and fragmentation of daily working hour arrangements, multiple jobs per day. These are important for new forms of labor contracts in the development of labor market flexibility. *Unpaid work and nonmarket activities* are significant for understanding the importance of the informal economy and underscore women's economic importance and gender approaches to labor in particular. The *total leisure activities*, including social networking and volunteer work, family interaction, media use, culture, sports, and genuine leisure (to mention only a few) are important in many respects for understanding economic, social, individual, and societal living conditions. For example, recent psychology time use studies (via experience sampling) have been used to study affect regulation (Riediger et al. 2009).

For the German context this overview also demonstrates that the recent German Time Use Study GTUS 2001/02 enabled a broad spectrum of in-depth activity research in a wide range of research fields. However, the primary German database GTUS 2001/02 is no longer up to date; there is an urgent need for a new German time use diary survey. Further information about the over fifty substantive research projects that have been reported to date that are served by the Research Data Centers and based on GTUS 2001/02 (with a great number more using data from GTUS 1991/92) emphasizes the critical importance of the German Time Use Survey for scientific as well as for administrative purposes (see the list of the Research Data Center research projects in the Appendix table A1).

In addition to the spectrum of time-use based scientific research activities that have been discussed, there are many other fields in private enterprises and administrative or governmental activities that ask for or would gain from time use information.

Private firms and time use information. Besides all the working hour time use data within any given private firm, private organizations in the field of consumer surveying also collect item- and time-specific information. To mention only the two important of these private firms: The Nielsen Consumer Panel survey, for example, which now includes 300,000 households in twenty-eight countries, collects information on consumption activities[30] scanned by the respondents via bar-codes. The GfK runs its ConsumerScope with even more explicit time use information, including specific studies on gardening, media use, etc., thus deepening the activity-specific time use information.[31]

Time use and downsizing bureaucracy by reducing administrative burdens: The Standard Cost Model (SCM) of the Federal Statistical Office, a tool for downsizing bureaucracy, measures the administrative costs imposed on businesses and individuals by central government regulation. Specific SCM time use surveys and interviews provide the data to this end and data from GTUS 2001/02 is used for further investigation. The German efforts are integrated in an international SCM network.[32]

Time Use, National Accounts, and Nonmarket Production: Though the main focus of time use research is on individual behavior, there are substantial longstanding international and national efforts to record the contribution of nonmarket production to the national product and national accounts. Emphasis in this area is placed on valuing individual time use using various methods, such as market replacement costs with global or specialized substitutes, opportunity costs, and self-evaluation (Chadeau 1985; Goldschmidt-Clermont 1993). Recent international nonmarket national accounts efforts are described by Landefeld and Culla (2000) and Eurostat (2003). An interesting new way to describe the macro situation of a society is the "Great Day," an aggregated time use picture proposed by Gershuny (1999).

---

30 http://www.acnielsen._de/products/cps_homescan.shtml
31 http://www. gfkps.com/scope/infopool/chartofthe week/index.de.html
32 http://www.administrative-burdens.com/

Recent German national accounts by nonmarket satellite systems focus on time pattern in a Social Accounting Framework (see Stahmer 2003, Stahmer and Schaffer 2004, Stäglin and Schindtke 2003 for time input-output tables). Schäfer 2004 provides an estimate of a nonmarket production contribution for the German national accounts based on the GTUS 2001/02.

5. Economic and social policy and time use

Targeted economic and social policy needs accurate individual information about the population. The comprehensive range of time use data on individual activities can provide genuine information to support almost any sound economic and social policy and to accompany the daily temporal coordination of life. Against the substantive background of our time use research field overview (Table 4), one can identify a few main policy areas and new activities – of international importance but cited here with German references – that gain in particular from individual time use information:

- *Family and time use policy.* For almost all activities considered in the recent Seventh Family Report of the Federal Ministry of Family Affairs, Senior Citizens, Women and Youth (BMFSFJ, *Bundesministerium für Familie, Senioren, Frauen und Jugend*) (2006) with time policy for child care, child-rearing allowances, balancing family and work, education and other aspects of individual living conditions.[33]

- *Public transport, traffic, mobility, and time use policy.* There is increasing interest in individual transport and traffic time aspects of working and leisure activities (see Kramer 2005).

- *Bureaucracy downsizing and time use.* Reducing administrative costs and time burden imposed on businesses and individuals (see the discussed SCM project).[34]

- *Poverty and time use policy.* See the reports in this publication for a discussion of the three German Federal Richness and Poverty Reports (Armuts- und Reichtumsberichte der Bundesregierung, Bundesministerium für Arbeit und Soziales 2008; in particular: ISG 2004; Kettschau et al. 2004).

- *Working hours, labor market flexibility and time use policy.* Setting administrative general regulations on working hours and working conditions with particular daily working time regulations.

---

33 http://www.bmfsfj.de
34 http://www.administrative-burdens.com

- *Time policy in urban and rural areas.* To support the temporal coordination of public services and the private and firm sector.

The Time Use Compass by the Federal Statistical Office (2006a) mentioned above provides an additional range of time use information used by the German administration for economic and social policy.

New and future time use policy developments. The temporal aspect regarding family affairs and working-hour arrangements is a longstanding policy focus. Time use policy interests are new with regard to urban and rural temporal coordination of daily life, such as the time policy project for the metropolitan area Hamburg (Mückenberger 2008) and the new time policy of Europe-wide activities (Garhammer 2008). For further examples, see the activities of the German Society for Temporal Governance (DGfZP, *Deutsche Gesellschaft für Zeitpolitik e.V.*).[35]

6. New methods in time use survey sampling

All the substantive time use approaches and research fields are based on the following instruments and methods:

- *Direct time use questions (stylized approach)* record the number of times that an individual participated in a given activity or the amount of time denoted for that activity in a typical day – either time constrained (must cover a defined time period) or time unconstrained.

- *Activity lists* are typically selective rather than exhaustive; mostly time-unconstrained.

- *Beepers* (experienced sampling) collect information via signaling devices that call for immediate information randomly over a given period (day) to register immediate subjective and context-sensitive information.

- *Time use diary* is an exhaustive record of all activities and patterns of associations between people and locations; this allows for sequence analyses; a highly recommended approach.

Time use research uses all kinds of time use data, but the diary is the preferred method of sampling, followed by stylized data. Both have benefits and challenges: diaries allow the investigation of activity timing during a day, stylized data capture less frequent information and disregard the randomness of situations occurring on a single day, to mention only the main issues (see Harvey

---

35 http://www.zeitpolitik.de

1999 for more). There are some beeper data-based results, like those of the ISR Michigan group, but beeper data is not the dominant sampling instrument that is used. However, experience sampling, by a beeper or another instrument, which collects context-sensitive data by a self-reported momentary experience, by a random or other scheme over a day, for instance, is increasingly used at least in psychological investigations (Riediger 2009).

Within this methodological framework, many new sampling tools connected with the growth of handheld devices and mobile phones have been developed (see the conference volume about new sampling technologies with focus on time use surveying by Ehling and Merz 2002).

Table 5: New time use sampling technologies by surveying principles

Come and Go
PZE-Master [Working hour per terminal] www.zeit-reporter.de/article_info.php?articles_id=154
NovaCHRON [Workers time per web client] http://www.novachron-zeiterfassung.de/personalzeiterfassung.php
diTime [Working hours per web-client] http://www.disoft-solutions.de/
timeCard [Working hours per chipcard/token] www.easy-technology.de/software/timecard/
Micades [Mobile per barcodescanner and GPRS/GSM] www.mobile-zeiterfassung.info/Fahrzeug.html
MOBILDAT [Mobile per software] www.mobile-zeiterfassung.info/Fahrzeug.html
Webalizer [Media/IT use per software] www.tobias-schwarz.net/webalizer_gui.html
Web-Zählpixel [Internet use per plugin/software] www.ivw.de
User tracking [Internet use per cookies/software] www.agof.de/

Project Precise
MobilZeit SERVICE [Working hours per terminal] http://www.mobile-zeiterfassung.info/Fahrzeug.html
TimeLog Project [Working hours per software] http://www.timelog.de/produkte/zeiterfassung.html
TIM / TIM Mobile [Mobile per cell phone (GPRS/GSM) and software] www.pressebox.de/pressemeldungen/echtzeit-zeitmanagement/boxid-108393.html

Task Precise
Zeittagebücher [per diary]
Time-Soft [Working Hours per web-client] www.lewald.com
Micro-Kiosk-System [Working Hours per terminal / PDA] www.softguide.de/prog_g/pg_2252.htm
diTime [per Barcodescanner] http://www.disoft.de/index.htm
SMS-Methode [per cell phone and software]
Mobile Zeiterfassung [per cell phone and software]http://www.virtic.com/?u=mobile_zeiterfassung
Halifax Regional Space-Time Activity Research (Star) Project [activity per cell phone (GPS) and diary] http://www.stmarys.ca/partners/turp/pages/projects/STAR/STAR_Main.htm
TimeCorder [activity per hardware] http://www.paceproductivity.com/timecorder.html
Timeboy [per Hardware] www.datafox.de
mQuest [per PC, PDA or smartphone] www.mquest.info

Source: Merz 2009.

Many new sampling instruments, mainly developed to collect individual working-hour information, can be classified – according to the taxonomy of Merz 2009 – by three principles: Come and Go, Project Precise, and Task

Precise. Come and Go measures the total daily working time (when and how long). Project Precise measures the time information for a certain project (when and how long). Task Precise might measure a certain (sub-)task of a project. Table 5 provides examples of new time use sampling devices for each of these principles.

For a discussion of the benefits and challenges of these new time use data sampling instruments see Merz (2009). They certainly have to be considered and tested before they might be used for a future German Time Use Survey.

7. Future developments: European and international challenges

The worldwide financial and economic crisis accentuates the importance of the effective use of scarce resources. Since time use surveys encompass many (or all) individual activities incorporating temporal information, they are a very efficient "all-in-one" tool that provides a broad scope of detailed individual data in a household context for a multitude of substantive interests with minimal investment. Therefore, one could expect that the current crisis favors the implementation of new time use surveys; however, policy-makers still need to be convinced of its enormous practical value.

In Europe, great efforts have been invested and still have to be invested in order to get a full HETUS every ten years (as Norway, among other countries, has been doing for decades). Following approximately twenty new time use surveys from the beginning of the millennium (2000–2002), the next European Harmonised Time Use Study (HETUS) in 2010–12 will be a cornerstone not only in national surveying and research but also for the development of the European community as a whole.

In the UK, "light" diaries have been discussed for the multiple intervening years between the full-scale surveys every ten years (in Japan and Korea there are only five intervening years). According to the IATUR secretary Dr. Kimberly Fisher, there are a growing number of diary surveys on specific topics linked to longitudinal data – several studies focus on children, for example, notably the Child Development Supplement of the PSID (*US Panel Study of Income Dynamics*)[36] and the "Growing Up Longitudinal Study of Australian Children."[37] These narrowly focused studies represent another way to collect individual time use data.

---

36 http://psidonline.isr.umich.edu/CDS/
37 http://www.aifs.gov.au/growingup/

Internationally, new countries and new time use surveys are on the agenda worldwide. A new UN-sponsored series of studies in developing countries is being discussed. Based on the experiences and the efforts of the annual American Time Use Studies, the international time use community will succeed in more frequent cross-sectional time use surveys. A comprehensive survey by the German Federal Statistical Office about *Time Use Survey – National Plans for the next wave of surveys 2008-2010 for 32 countries* is included in Appendix 2.

Periodic cross-sectional time use surveys with intervals of five or ten years will be very important in the upcoming years. The invention of an annual time use panel of regularly surveyed individuals and/or households with all its longitudinal information is on the international agenda. The panel option will be an enormous step forward in time use research that will provide – among others things – specific event-driven micro information for up-to-date and targeted policy and research. New electronic devices allow more precise and at the same time less expensive time use data sampling. Future developments and challenges for the time use survey situation in Germany will be outlined in our conclusions and recommendations.

8. Conclusions and recommendations

This advisory report on the current situation in international and national recent time use, recent improvements and future developments has underscored the following: time use surveys – with time as the comprehensive dimension of any individual activity – allow new insight into daily living activities, incorporating the timing and sequence of lived events. The central time diary methodology cues respondents to walk through the sequence of events in a given day, which has significant advantages in ensuring the completeness and consistency of responses. Time use diaries thus support an understanding of causality, and the interdependence that exists between all market and nonmarket activities and their individual synchronization. The disadvantage, however, is the high cost of administration, which mandates relatively few days observed per respondent with the resulting possibility that a survey will miss low frequency events. Therefore, additional summary questions about the "work week" (HETUS) have already been added to the GTUS 2001/02 as well as in some other time use surveys.

Against the background of growing international experience in the field of successful time use survey methodology, the following recommendations are indicated, with a particular focus on Germany. They will support research and targeted policy with more advanced, substantive as well as methodological investigations on modeling individual and household behavior at the micro-level and on developing new and sound national accounts data at the macro-level:

- *Recommendation 1a (GTUS 2011/12):* it is essential that the next official German Time Use Survey (GTUS) is conducted in the years 2011–2012 nationwide by the Federal Statistical Office. The financing for GTUS 2011/12 is not yet assured and it must be organized as soon as possible. The next GTUS has again to be embedded in the European Harmonised Time Use Surveys (HETUS, Eurostat 2009). The next GTUS 2011/12 would assure information in a ten years interval context together with GTUS 1991/92, GTUS 2001/02 with precious time use information including socio-economic background available for targeted policy and research.

- *Recommendation 1b:* new methods in sampling time diaries based on mobile devices – including beeper and/or experience sampling methods for even more context-sensitive questions – should be incorporated in the next GTUS after a proper pilot study. This will fulfill three objectives: first, to gain more context-sensitive data; second, to reduce the burden of filling out a traditional diary booklet; and third, it will reduce the overall expense. The sampling procedure should use mixed-mode data collection (internet, cell- or telephone, mail, pre-coded diaries, etc.) and the advantages of the Access Panel (Körner et al. 2008) with voluntary information from the German Federal Statistical Office.

- *Recommendation 1c:* the single activity spell with its "where" and "with whom" attributes should be extended by expenditure information. This would provide new data about expenditures associated with each activity and the intensity for all related activity fields (transport, shopping, etc.).[38] A suitable way must be found to characterize a second or third job within a daily activity spell.

- *Recommendation 1d:* the time use diary information should be extended by questions concerning less frequent activities. First, with information about the work week consistent with the recent HETUS recommendation (Eurostat 2009, Guidelines Annex VI). Second, by information about a longer period than a day (different week diaries, frequencies, etc.). Third, by information about a "typical" or "normal" period (day, week, month).

- *Recommendation 1e:* the time use diary supplementary information should be extended by more objective background individual and household questions and questions about the living environment. The supplementary data should contain information about the income situation from

---

38 For example, with brackets for a sequence of equal activity spells.

labor market activities (occupational status, wages, and detailed income including unemployment benefits, etc.) or from other income sources (capital income, further third-party payments, etc.). The environmental information should encompass external child care possibilities and external living conditions (residence environment, exposure to environmental risks, and social life participation including social networks, social "inclusion" etc.).

- *Recommendation 1f:* the time use diary supplementary information should also be extended by subjective information about satisfaction (of life in general and other items beyond time type and stress information) and health (subjective and objective). In addition, the "Big Five" personal characteristics items[39] should be added to create an approximate measurement of unobserved heterogeneity, for instance. All this subjective data will allow researchers to value and qualify the time use information.

- *Recommendation 1g:* the time use diary supplementary information should be closely adjusted and harmonized with the respective socio-economic questions of the SOEP to allow for high quality merged new datasets.

- *Recommendation 2:* a brand new annual Time Use Survey Panel should be started to answer important longitudinal questions. A TUS Panel – for example in the wake of GTUS 2011/12 – will allow the investigation of changing individual time uses and time use profiles in changing environments with extended causality and sequential event analyses. The TUS Panel thus has a different focus than the SOEP.

- *Recommendation 3:* the SOEP should continue to ask for both "typical day" as well as less frequent time use information. First, this will allow continuing longitudinal analyses. Second, it will enable the use of the enormous socio-economic background information on the labor market and additional information present in the SOEP to explain time use behaviour. The SOEP should not only ask for full hours but should allow minutes' information as well.

- *Recommendation 4:* the Research Data Center of the Federal Statistical Office should in any case be advanced to a permanent standing. However, particularly for its time use data service and its role developing new time use data it should be established permanently. The new onsite secure data access possibilities should be further developed. Particularly,

---

39 See for a short Big Five Inventory, the SOEP version of the Big Five (Schupp and Gerlitz 2008).

remote access to micro- and metadata should be expanded for fast and secure access.

- *Recommendation 5:* in general, the German Data Forum (RatSWD) should actively support and strengthen all activities related to ensuring that the GTUS 2011/12 will be financed and organized. Because a time use survey provides such a multitude of substantive answers for policy and research in a single, "all-in-one" tool, because it is harmonized now within Europe and offers an efficient use of scarce resources, the next GTUS 2011/12 should be rigorously and tenaciously promoted.

Appendix A1: Current registered research projects registered with the Research Data Center of the Federal Statistical Office and based on GTUS 2001/02

No.	Research Projects: Registered with the Research Data Center of the Federal Statistical Office and based on GTUS 2001/02 (March 2009)
1	Arbeitstitel: Haushalt: Kleine Fabrik oder gender factory
2	Zeitverwendung von Arbeitslosen und Vollzeiterwerbstätigen. Eine vergleichende Analyse mit den Zeitbudgetdaten des Statistischen Bundesamtes von 2002.
3	Inklusionsprofile
4	Zeitverwendung in Haushalten
5	FrauenDatenReport 2005
6	Feiertage, Freizeit und Soziales Kapital
7	Soziale Netzwerke und Hilfebeziehungen im unteren Einkommensbereich
8	Consumption and Time Allocation
9	Female labor market supply and home work in Germany
10	Bayerischer Familienreport 2006 – Schwerpunkt "Väter in Deutschland"
11	Kooperative Demokratie – Kritik der Arbeit und der Arbeitslosigkeit
12	1. Erwerbsverhalten und Home Production / 2. Zeitverwendung im Alter
13	Der soziale Dienstleistungsbereich als Chance für eine höhere Arbeitsmarktintegration und Professionalisierung weiblicher Erwerbskarrieren
14	Zeitverwendung und Work-Life-Balance in Großbritannien und Deutschland
15	Das Arbeitsangebotsverhalten von Frauen in Deutschland
16	A. Mobilitäts- und Freizeitverhalten von Kindern und Jugendlichen B. Verbesserung der Methoden zur Prognose der KFZ-Bemessungsverkehrsstärken
17	Zeitverwendung und soziale Schichten
18	Klartext reden oder Farbe bekennen: Der Einfluss von Sprachkenntnissen und Aussehen auf gesellschaftliche Integration von Migranten in Deutschland
19	Der Einfluss von Kindern auf Zeitallokation von Haushalten
20	Effekt von Zeitverwendung auf die Ausbildung von nicht-kognitiven Fähigkeiten
21	Arbeitszeit & Zeitbudgetanalysen – Analyse täglicher Arbeitszeiten und Nachfragearrangements
22	Soziale Ungleichheit und Prävention
23	Das Konzept der Europäischen Sozioökonomischen Klassifikation und seine Anwendung auf die in der Zeitbudgeterhebung 2001/02 befragten Haushalte
24	Renewbility
25	Substitutability of Partner's Productive Activities
26	Einkommensabhängiges Freizeitverhalten unter älteren Menschen
27	Zeit und soziale Ungleichheit. Die schichtspezifische Strukturierung sozialer Zeit – unter besonderer Beobachtung von Geschlecht und Generation
28	Schulz-Borck/Hofmann: Schadenersatz bei Ausfall von Hausfrauen und Müttern im Haushalt – mit Berechnungstabellen, 6. Aufl.-Karlsruhe: VVW 2000, ISBN 3-58487-89487-894-8
29	"Integration of Rebound Effects into Life-Cycle Assessment" (finanziert durch BFE und Nationalfonds)
30	Ruhestandsmigration in Deutschland
31	Assisted Living – Technisch unterstüztes Wohnen im Alter, Teilprojekt: Sozialwissenschaftliche Begleitforschung
32	Sozioökonomische Berichterstattung (soeb.de)
33	"Einkommen und Freizeit – Eine empirische Analyse des Freizeitverhaltens älterer Menschen mit Daten der Zeitbudgeterhebung des Statistischen Bundesamtes"

34	Ökonomische Analyse der Zeitverwendung für Ernährung
35	Integrierter Survey
36	International Evidence on housework and market work by husbands and wives
37	Entwicklungstendenzen im Online-Printmedienbereich in Deutschland – Arbeitsmarktstatistische und Arbeitsorganisatorische Analyse der Srukturveränderungen durch das Internet für Journalisten, 1990 - Gegenwart
38	Erstellung von Tabellen für das Seminar zur Wirtschaftslehre des Haushalts, in dem Studierende den Zeitaufwand für Kinder in den unterschiedlichen Haushaltstypen vergleichen sollen
39	Stochaistische Modellierung von Nutzerverhalten in Wohngebäuden
40	A cross-cultural analysis of overreporting of socially desirable behavior
41	Bezogenes Verkehrsverhalten von Beschäftigten im sekundären und tertiären Sektor
42	Potentiale der Zeitbudgeterhebung 2001/02 Eine Bestandsaufnahne anhand der Zeitverwendung "Junger Alter"
43	Berichtete und tatsächliche Kirchgangshäufigkeit in Ost- und Westdeutschland
44	Comparative Study on the Double Burden of Working Parents; Gender Differences in Time Poverty
45	Zeitverwendung von Arbeitslosen für Arbeitssuche
46	Soziale Netzwerke und Hilfebeziehungen im unteren Einkommensbereich
47	Zeitbudgeterhebungen – Methodik und Anwendungen
48	Analyse der Verschiebungen zwischen Wegezeiten und Zeiten für andere Aktivitäten in Abhängigkeit von der Raumstruktur
49	PACT (Pathways for carbon transitions)
50	Der zweite demographische Übergang

Source: The Research Data Center of the Federal Statistical Office, Wiesbaden 3/2009.

Appendix A2: Time Use Survey – National plans for the next wave of surveys 2008–2010

Country	Foreseen schedule	Comment
Belgium (BE)	2010	Statistics Belgium collects TUS data and Vrije Universiteit Brussel analyzes them. Next data collection will take place in 2010, analysis in 2011.
Bulgaria (BG)	2009/2010	Survey will be included into the National Program for Statistical Surveys 2009/2010.
Czech Republic (CZ)	Not before 2010	The implementation of TUS has not yet begun (no plan exists). There is a lack of financial resources and human capacity, the respondents' burden is still increasing, and neither TUS nor related activities are the priority of Czech Statistical Office in the area of social statistics.
Denmark (DK)	2008/2009	DTUC-Danish Time Use and Consumption Survey by Rockwool Foundation (Pilot ongoing).
Germany (DE)	No schedule	The next wave of the TUS survey is not yet organized and financed.
Estonia (EE)	2009/2010	EE is planning a TUS by 2009/2010.
Ireland (IE)	Not before 2010	The National Development Plan Gender Equality Unit, which was based in the Department of Justice, Equality and Law Reform, engaged the ESRI to carry out a pilot light diary survey in 2005. The report is available to download at: http://www.justice.ie/en/JELR/Pages/Time_use_survey_report Anonymized microdata is available through the Irish Social Science Data Archive (ISSDA), see: http://www.ucd.ie/issda/ dataset-info/timeuse.htm However, with the exception of this 2005 light diary pilot and a small CSO HETUS pilot carried out in one region of Ireland (Munster) in 1998, to date no national time use study has been carried out in Ireland. There are no definite plans to carry out a HETUS based or light diary survey at present.
Greece (EL)	No schedule	There is a lack of "economic and human resources."
Spain (ES)	2009/2010	ES plans a TUS in 2009/2010. Fieldwork between 10/2009 and 9/2010.
France (FR)	September 2009- August 2010	
Italy (IT)	2008/2009	Fieldwork between February 2008 and January 2009.
Cyprus (CY)	Not before 2013	It is unlikely that TUS will be launched before 2013.
Latvia (LV)	Not before 2011	It is difficult to have a precise plan at this moment. This depends on financial resources.

Country	Foreseen schedule	Comment
Lithuania (LT)	Not before 2010	It is difficult to have precise plan at this moment. This depends on financial resources.
Luxembourg (LU)	Not before 2010/2011	First, they have to integrate the Time Use Survey in their national plan. Thus, it is difficult to have a precise plan for the moment (financing and human resources must be confirmed). It is unlikely that the survey will be launched before 2010–2011.
Hungary (HU)	2009 or 2010	They plan to organize a TUS during 2009 or 2010. Only a pilot (with a n=100 sample) will be made. If it is successful, the results of this pilot can be used to emphasize the importance of such a survey. It is not easy to find financial sources for a survey in Hungary, as it is not compulsory there.
Malta (MT)	No updated information	The previous TUS survey was carried out in 2002.
Netherlands (NL)	2010	Previous TUS surveys: 1. 2005 applying national methodology 2. 2006 according to HETUS guidelines In 2010, they will either apply their national methodology or the Hetus methodology. They have to weight the pros and cons of both methodologies before they reach a decision.
Austria (AT)	2008/2009	Fieldwork from March 2008 until February 2009. The sample for TUS will be a subsample of the Austrian Microcensus. In addition to the Microcensus questionnaire, persons in the selected households will be asked to fill in a diary for one day (aim: net sample of 8,000 persons being 10 years and older). There will be no special TUS questionnaire.
Poland (PL)	(2012) 2014	It is impossible for Poland to carry out TUS in 2010 because of the Agricultural Census in 2010 and the National Census in 2011. The most likely and convenient time for the Polish CSO is 2013/2014, but it will be considered in 2012. This depends on financial resources.
Portugal (PT)	No schedule	It is not planned and depends on financial resources.
Romania (RO)	2009/2010?	The Romanian National Institute of Statistics could not carry out TUS in 2008/2009 due to a lack of financial and human resources. They provisionally planned the survey to be launched in 2009/2010, which depends on financial and human resources.
Slovenia (SI)	No schedule	Slovenia did not plan to incorporate financial resources and employees for the TUS in the medium term plan. A TUS will not be conducted in the near future.
Slovakia (SK)	Not before 2010	Previous TUS surveys: In 2006, the Pilot project on TUS, in accord with the 2004 HETUS guidelines, was carried out. A plan for regular TUS (not earlier than 2010) depends on obtaining of financial resources.

Country	Foreseen schedule	Comment
Finland (FI)	2009/2010	Fieldwork between April 2009 and March 2010.
Sweden (SE)	2010 if resources available	Regarding the next round of TUS, there is an ongoing discussion with the Ministry for Integration and Gender concerning financing. There is a great interest in taking part in the next round.
United Kingdom (UK)	Full survey: not before 2013. Exploring lower cost options (e.g., collecting basic data via an existing survey)	The UK carried out a light diary survey over 4 months in 2005. With regard to a HETUS survey, there appears to be no prospect of funding a full survey in the current planning period (2008-2012) given other priorities and budgetary pressures. ONS is still exploring lower cost options (e.g., collecting basic data via an existing survey), but this will also depend on the provision of financial resources from government and the ESRC.
Croatia (HR)	No schedule	National plan to be confirmed.
FYROM (MK)	2009	According to the working plan 2008-2012, TUS will be carried out in 2009. Fieldwork will start on 1 January 2009.
Turkey (TR)	2011	The previous TUS survey was carried out in 2006 and the results published in July 2007. The Turkish Statistical Institution, TURKSTAT, has planned to carry out TUS for a 5-year-period in line with HETUS guidelines.
Norway (NO)	2010	
Switzerland (CH)	Not before 2011	No TUS is planned at the Swiss Federal Statistical Office (FSO). In the context of the new Statistical System on Households and Persons, the possibility of a mini-TUS added to the omnibus survey is being examined (light diary, CATI-interviews with precoded activities). It would be realized in 2011 at the earliest. The decision is still open.

Source: German Federal Statistical Office 2009 (situation as of November 4, 2008)

References:

Akarro, R. (2008): The Impact of Time Use Differentials on Poverty levels in the Eastern and Northern Zones of Tanzania. European Journal of Economics, Finance and Administrative Sciences 13, 108-120.

Andorka, R. (1987): Time budgets and their uses. Annual Review of Sociology 13, 149-164.

Anxo, D. and Carlin, P. (2004): Intra-family time allocation to housework: French evidence. electronic International Journal of Time Use Research 1, 14-36. www.eIJTUR.org.

Ås, D. (1978): Studies of time use: Problems and prospects. Acta Sociologica 21 (2), 125-141.

Bediako, G. and Vanek, J. (1999): Trial International Classification of Activities for Time Use Statistics. In: Merz, J. and Ehling, M. (Eds.): Time Use – Research, Data and Policy. FFB-Book Series 10, 151-164.

Bevans, G.E. (1913): How Working Men Spend Their Spare Time. New York.

Bundesministerium für Arbeit und Soziales (2008): Der 3. Armuts- und Reichtumsbericht der Bundesregierung. Berlin. http://www.bmas.de/coremedia/ generator/26896/lebenslagen-in-deutschland-der-3-armuts-und-reichtums-bericht-der-bundesregierung.html.

Bundesministerium für Familie, Senioren, Frauen und Jugend (2006): Familie zwischen Flexibilität und Verlässlichkeit – Perspektiven für eine lebenslaufbezogene Familienpolitik. Siebter Familienbericht, Deutscher Bundestag, Drucksache 16/1360.

Chadeau, A. (1985): Measuring Household Activities – Some International Comparisons. Review on Income and Wealth 31, 237-254.

Cornelißen, W. (Ed.) (2005): Gender-Datenreport, 1. Datenreport zur Gleichstellung von Frauen und Männern in der Bundesrepublik Deutschland. Im Auftrag des Bundesministeriums für Familie, Senioren, Frauen und Jugend. 2. Fassung. Munich.

Cornelißen, W. and Blanke, K. (2004): Zeitverwendung von Mädchen und Jungen. In: Statistisches Bundesamt (Ed.): Alltag in Deutschland – Analysen zur Zeitverwendung. Wiesbaden.

Dressel, Chr./Cornelißen, W. and Wol, K. (2005): Vereinbarkeit von Familie und Beruf. In: Cornelißen, W. (Ed.) (2005): Gender-Datenreport, 1. Datenreport zur Gleichstellung von Frauen und Männern in der Bundesrepublik Deutschland. Im Auftrag des Bundesministeriums für Familie, Senioren, Frauen und Jugend. 2. Fassung. Munich. http://www.bmfsfj.de/Publikationen/genderreport/root.html.

Ehling, M. and Merz, J. (Eds.) (2002): Neue Technologien in der Umfrageforschung – Anwendungen bei der Erhebung von Zeitverwendung [New Technologies in Survey Research – Applications for Time Use Studies]. FFB-Schriftenreihe Band 14. Baden-Baden.

Ehling, M. et al. (2001): Zeitbudget in Deutschland – Erfahrungsberichte der Wissenschaft. Spektrum der Bundesstatistik, Bd. 17. Wiesbaden

Engstler, H./Mennin, S./Hoffmann, E. and Tesch-Römer, C. (2004): Die Zeitverwendung älterer Menschen. In: Statistisches Bundesamt (Ed.): Alltag in Deutschland – Analysen zur Zeitverwendung. Wiesbaden.

Eurostat (2009): Harmonised European Time Use Surveys – 2008 Guidelines, EUROSTAT Methodologies and Working papers. http://epp.eurostat. ec.europa.eu/cache/ITY_OFFPUB/KS-RA-08-014/EN/KS-RA-08-014-EN.PDF.

Eurostat, Task Force Household Satellite Accounts (2003): Household Production and Consumption, Proposal for a Methodology of the Household Satellite Accounts. Task Force Report for EUROSTAT, Division E1.

Fahr, R. (2005): Loafing or Learning? The Demand for Informal Education. European Economic Review 49 (1), 75-98.

Fendrich, S. and Schilling, M. (2004): Informelle Betreuungssettings in der ausserfamilialen Kinderbetreuung. In: Statistisches Bundesamt (Ed.): Alltag in Deutschland – Analysen zur Zeitverwendung. Wiesbaden.

Folbre, N. (2009): Inequality, Consumption, and Time Use. In: Nolan, B. and Smeeding, T.M. (Eds.): The Oxford Handbook of Economic Inequality. Wiemer Salverda, Chapter 14.

Fritz, I. und Klingler, W. (2006): Medienzeitbudgets und Tagesablaufverhalten. Media Perspektiven 4/2006. http://www.media-perspektiven.de/uploads/tx_mppublications/04-2006_Fritz.pdf.

Gabriel, O./Trüdinger, E.-M. and Völkl, K. (2004): Bürgerengagement in Form von ehrenamtlicher Tätigkeit und sozialen Hilfsleistungen. In: Statistisches Bundesamt (Ed.): Alltag in Deutschland – Analysen zur Zeitverwendung. Wiesbaden.

Garhammer, M. (2008): Arbeitszeit, Zeitnutzung von Familien und Zeitpolitiken in Europa. http://www.opus-bayern.de/ohm-hochschule/frontdoor.php?source_opus=12.

Gershuny, J. (1995): Time budget research in Europe. Statistics in Transition 2 (4), 529-531.

Gershuny, J. (1999): Informal Economic Activity and Time Use Evidence. In: Merz, J. and Ehling, M. (Eds.): Time Use – Research, Data and Policy.

Gershuny, J. (2001): Time Use Research Methods. In: Baltes, P. and Smelser, N. (Eds.): International Encyclopedia of the Social & Behavioral Sciences. Amsterdam.

Gershuny, J. and Sullivan, O. (1998): The Sociological Uses of Time use Diary Analysis. European Sociological Review 14 (1), 69-85.

Gershuny, J./Fisher, K./Jones, S. and Gauthier, A. (2000): A Multinational Longitudinal Time use Data Archive. In: Gershuny, J. (Ed.): Changing Times: Work and Leisure in Postindustrial Society. Oxford.

Gille, M. and Marbach, J. (2004): Arbeitsteilung von Paaren und ihre Belastung mit Zeitstress. In: Statistisches Bundesamt (Ed.): Alltag in Deutschland – Analysen zur Zeitverwendung. Wiesbaden.

Goldschmidt-Clermont, L. (1993): Monetary Valuation of Non-Market Productive Time – Methodological Considerations. Review of Income and Wealth 4, 419-433.

Guryan, J./Hurst, E. and Kearney, M.S. (2008): Parental Education and Parental Time With Children. NBER Working Paper No. 13993. New York. http://www.nber.org/papers/w13993.

Gwozdz, W./Hufnagel, R./Seel, B. and Wahrig, L. (2006): Messung der Entwicklung der geschlechtsspezifischen Arbeitsteilung mit den Daten der Zeitbudgeterhebungen 1991/92 und 2001/02. Hauswirtschaft and Wissenschaft 1, 22-28.

Hamermesh, D. (2002): Timing, togetherness and time windfalls. Journal of Population Economics 15, 321-325.

Hamermesh, D.S. and Pfann, G.A. (2005). The Economics of Time Use. North-Holland.

Harms, T. and Gershuny, J. (2009): Time Budgets and Time Use. RatSWD Working Paper No. 45.

Harvey, A. (1999): Time Use Research: The Roots to the Future. In: Merz, J. and Ehling, M. (Eds.): Time Use – Research, Data and Policy. FFB-Schriftenreihe 10. Baden-Baden.

Harvey, A. (2004): Welcome Address of the IATUR President: eIJTUR and Time use: Past, Present and Future. electronic International Journal of Time Use Research 1 (1), I-IV. www.eIJTUR.org.

Harvey, A. (2009): Halifax Regional Space-Time Activity Research (STAR) Project – A GPS-Assisted Household Time use Survey, St. Mary's University. Halifax. www.stmarys.ca/partners/turp/main.html.

Harvey, A./Szalai, A./Elliott, D.H../Stone, P.J. and Clark, S. (1984): Time Budget Research: An ISSC Workbook in Comparative Analysis. New York.

Harvey, A. (2006): Nonmarket Production and Historical Time use Data: Potential and Issues, Yale Program on Nonmarket Accounts: A Project on Assessing Time Use Survey Datasets. Halifax.

Hoffmann, E. and Mata, A. (1999): Measuring Working Time: An Alterbnative Approach to Classifying Time Use. In: Merz, J. and Ehling, M. (Eds.): Time Use – Research, Data and Policy. FFB-Book Series 10.

Holz, E. (2004): Poverty and family life: Time use of families with and without poverty risk, Proceedings of the Annual IATUR Conference 2004, International Association for Time Use Research – IATUR and Italian National Statistical Institute – ISTAT. Rome.

Institut für Sozialforschung und Gesellschaftspolitik (ISG), Köln (Ed.) (2004): Aspekte der Armuts- und Reichtumsberichterstattung: Reichtum und Eliten – Haushaltsproduktion und Armutsprävention. 2. Wissenschaftliches Kolloquium am 8. und 9. Oktober 2003 in Rüdesheim am Rhein. Veranstaltung des Bundesministeriums für Gesundheit und Soziale Sicherung. Durchführung und Dokumentation: Institut für Sozialforschung und Gesellschaftspolitik. http://www.isg-institut.de/index.php?b=single&id_B=6&id_UB=8&id_Nummer=83.

Ironmonger, D. (2001): Household Production and the Household Economy. Department of Economics Research Paper No. 759. University of Melbourne.

Jäckel, M. and Wollscheid, S. (2004): Mediennutzung im Tagesverlauf: Ausweitung des Angebots und Strukturen der Zeitverwendung. In: Statistisches Bundesamt (Ed.): Alltag in Deutschland – Analysen zur Zeitverwendung. Wiesbaden.

Jäckel, M. and Wollscheid, S. (2007): Time Is Money and Money Needs Time? A Secondary Analysis of Time-Budget Data in Germany. Journal of Leisure Research 39 (1), 86-108.

Jacobsen, J. and Kooreman, P. (2004): Timing Constraints and the Allocation of Time: The Effect of the Changing Shopping Hours Regulations in the Netherlands. IZA Discussion Paper No. 130.

Jahoda, M./Lazarsfeld, P.F. and Zeisel, H. (1933): Marienthal: The Sociography of an Unemployed Community – Translated by the authors with John Reginait and Thomas Elsaesser. Chicago 1971.

Juster, F.Th. (1999): The Future of Research on Time Use. In: Merz, J. and Ehling, M. (Eds.): Time Use – Research, Data and Policy. FFB-Schriftenreihe Band 10. Baden-Baden.

Juster, F.Th. and Stafford, F.P. (1991): The allocation of time: empirical findings, behavioural models and problems of measurement. In: Journal of Economic Literature 29, 471-522.

Kahle, I. (2004): Alleinerziehende im Spannungsfeld zwischen Beruf und Familie. In: Statistisches Bundesamt (Ed.): Alltag in Deutschland – Analysen zur Zeitverwendung. Wiesbaden.

Keall, M.D. and Baker, M.G. (2008): Travel Survey Data to Estimate Time Spent at Important Settings. electronic International Journal of Time Use Research 5, 127-129.

Kettschau, I./Hufnagel, R. and Holz, E. (2004): Lebensgestaltung auf Haushaltsebene – Verknüpfung zwischen Armutsforschung und Zeitbudgetdaten. Expertise für das Bundesministerium für Familie, Senioren, Frauen und Jugend, Beitrag zum Berichtskapitel für den 2. Armuts- und Reichtumsbericht der Bundesregierung. Fachhochschule Münster, Fachbereich Oecotrophologie. Münster.

Kleimann, M. and Mößle, T. (2008): The Logs of Eliza and Other Media Stories. Behavioral and Developmental Effects of a School Based Media Education Program – Berlin Longitudinal Study Media. International Journal of Behavioral Development 32 (6), Supplement 2 (54), 55-59.

Klevmarken, A. (1999): Microeconomic Analysis of Time Use Data: Did We Reach the Promised Land? In: Merz, J. and Ehling, M. (Eds.): Time Use – Research, Data and Policy. FFB-Schriftenreihe Band 10. Baden-Baden.

Kommission zur Verbesserung der informationellen Infrastruktur zwischen Wissenschaft und Statistik (KVI) (Ed.) (2001): Wege zu einer besseren informationellen Infrastruktur. Baden-Baden

Körner, T./Nimmergut, A./Nökel, J. and Rohloff, S. (2008): Die Dauerstichprobe befragungsbereiter Haushalte – Die neue Auswahlgrundlage für freiwillige Haushaltsbefragungen. Wirtschaft und Statistik 5/2008, 451-487.

Kramer, C. (2004): Zeitverwendung. In: Statistisches Bundesamt (Ed.): Datenreport 2004.

Kramer, C. (2005): Verkehrsverhalten, Wegezeiten und Mobilität. Expertise für den Siebten Familienbericht der Bundesregierung. Berlin.

Kramer, C. (2005): Zeit für Mobilität – Räumliche Disparitäten der individuellen Zeitverwendung für Mobilität in Deutschland. Reihe Erdkundliches Wissen, Band 138. Stuttgart.

Landefeld, J.S. and Culla, S. (2000): Accounting for Nonmarket Household Production within a National Accounts Framework. Review of Income and Wealth 46 (3).

Lindqvist, M. (2001): The Finnish System of Official Social Surveys, Statistics Finland, Official Social Surveys in Europe. Edited by F. Kraus and G. Schmaus. EuReporting Working Paper No. 25.

Meier, U./Küster, Chr. and Zander, U. (2004): Alles wie gehabt? – Geschlechtsspezifische Arbeitsteilung und Mahlzeitenmuster im Zeitvergleich. In: Statistisches Bundesamt (Ed.): Alltag in Deutschland – Analysen zur Zeitverwendung. Wiesbaden.

Merz, J. (1990): Zur Notwendigkeit und Nutzung von Zeitbudgetdaten in der Sozialökonomie. In: v. Schweitzer, R./Ehling, M. and Schäfer, D. (Eds.): Zeitbudgeterhebungen. Ziele, Methoden und neue Konzepte. Stuttgart.

Merz, J. (1992): Zur Dynamik markt- und nichtmarktmäßigen Arbeitsangebots: Zeitverwendung verheirateter Frauen in Beruf und Haushalt – Eine Panelanalyse. In: Hujer, R./Schneider, H. and Zapf, W. (Eds.): Herausforderungen an den Wohlfahrtsstaat im strukturellen Wandel. Frankfurt/New York.

Merz, J. (1997): Zeitverwendung in Erwerbstätigkeit und Haushaltsproduktion – Dynamische Mikroanalysen mit Paneldaten, DFG-Endbericht, FFB-Dokumentation Nr. 7, Fachbereich Wirtschafts- und Sozialwissenschaften, Universität Lüneburg.

Merz, J. (2001): Informationsfeld Zeitverwendung. In: Kommission zur Verbesserung der informationellen Infrastruktur zwischen Wissenschaft und Statistik (KVI) (Ed.): Wege zu einer besseren informationellen Infrastruktur. Baden-Baden.

Merz, J. (2002): Time Use Research and Time Use Data – Actual Topics and New Frontiers. In: Ehling, M. and Merz, J. (Eds.): Neue Technologien in der Umfrageforschung – Anwendungen bei der Erhebung von Zeitverwendung (New Technologies in Survey Research – Applications for Time Use Studies). FFB-Schriftenreihe Band 14. Baden-Baden.

Merz, J. (2009): Zeitverwendungsforschung und Mediennutzung, Gutachten für das Zweite Deutsche Fernsehen (ZDF). FFB-Diskussionspapier Nr. 75, Leuphana Universität Lüneburg.

Merz, J. and Böhm, P. (2005): Arbeitszeitarrangements und Entlohnung – Ein Treatment-Effects-Ansatz für Freiberufler, Unternehmer und abhängig Beschäftigte. In: Schulte, R. (Ed.): Ergebnisse der Mittelstandsforschung. Münster.

Merz, J. and Burgert, D. (2004): Arbeitszeitarrangements – Neue Ergebnisse aus der Zeitbudgeterhebung 2001/02 im Zeitvergleich zu 1991/92. In: Statistisches Bundesamt (Ed.): Alltag in Deutschland – Analysen zur Zeitverwendung. FORUM Band 43. Wiesbaden.

Merz, J. and Ehling, M (Eds.) (1999): Time Use – Research, Data and Policy. FFB-Schriftenreihe Band 10. Baden-Baden.

Merz, J. and Rathjen, T. (2009): Time and Economic Poverty – Interdependent Multidimensional Poverty with the German Time Use Survey 2001/02. Manuscript, Research Institute on Professions (FFB), University of Lüneburg.

Merz, J. Hanglberger, D. and Rucha, R. (2009): The Timing of Daily Demand for Goods and Services – Multivariate Probit Estimates and Microsimulation Results for an Aged Population with German Time Use Diary Data. FFB Discussion Paper No. 75, Department of Economics, Behavioural and Law Sciences, Leuphana University.

Merz, J./Böhm, P. and Burgert, D. (2004): Timing, Fragmentation of Work and Income Inequality – An Earnings Treatment Effects Approach. FFB Discussion Paper No. 47, Department of Economics and Social Sciences, University of Lueneburg.

Mückenberger, U. (2008): Zeitpolitik in der Metropolregion Hamburg, Projektantrag „Wissenschaftliche Begleitung des Projektverbunds ‚Zeitpolitik in der Metropolregion Hamburg'". Hamburg.

Niemi, I. (1993): Systematic error in behavioral measurement: Comparing results from interview and time budget studies. Social Indicators Research 30 (2-3), 229-244.

Pember Reeves, M. (1913): Round About a Pound a Week, Bell. London. New Edition: 1990.

Pinl, Cl. (2004): Wo bleibt die Zeit? Die Zeitbudgeterhebung 2001/02 des Statistischen Bundesamts. Aus Politik und Zeitgeschichte Nr. 31-32. http://www.bpb.de/publikationen/CRWJ8M,0,Wo_bleibt_die_Zeit.html.

Riediger, M. (2009): Experience Sampling, Federal Ministry of Education and Research. RatSWD Working Paper No. 62.

Riediger, M. et al. (2009): Seeking Pleaseure and Seeking Pain. Psychological Science 20 (12), 1529-1535.

Robinson, J.P. (1985): The validity and reliability of diaries versus alternative time use measures. In: Juster, F.T. and Stafford, F.P. (Eds.): Time, Goods and Well-Being. Ann Arbour.

Robinson, J.P. and Godbey, G. (1997): Time for Life – The Surprising Ways Americans Use Their Time.

Rydenstam, K. (1999): The EUROSTAT Project on Harmonising Time Use Statistics. In: Merz, J. and Ehling, M. (Eds.): Time Use – Research, Data and Policy. FFB-Book Series, Vol. 10.

Rydenstam, K. (2007): The Harmonised European Time Use Database and the Table Generating Tool. electronic International Journal of Time Use Research (4-1), 118-119. www.eIJTUR.org.

Schäfer, D. (2004): Unbezahlte Arbeit und Haushaltsproduktion im Zeitvergleich. In: Statistisches Bundesamt (Ed.): Alltag in Deutschland – Analysen zur Zeitverwendung. Wiesbaden.

Schäffer, S.M. (2003): Die Zeitverwendung von Konsumenten – Implikationen für das Dienstleistungsmarketing. Wiesbaden.

Schriftreihe Media Perspektiven (2006): Massenkommunikation VII, Eine Langzeitstudie zur Mediennutzung und Medienbewertung 1964 – 2005. Baden-Baden.

Schulz, F. and Grunow, D. (2007): Time-diary versus time-estimation data. A comparison of two different methods of measuring the time spent on housework. Zeitschrift für Familienforschung 1/2007, 106-128.

Schupp, J. and Gerlitz, J.-Y. (2008): Big Five Inventory-SOEP. In: Glöckner-Rist, A. (Ed.): Zusammenstellung sozialwissenschaftlicher Items und Skalen. ZIS Version 12.00. Bonn.

Sellach, B./Enders-Dragässer, U. and Libuda-Köster, A. (2004): Geschlechtsspezifische Besonderheiten der Zeitverwendung – Zeitstrukturierung im theoretischen Konzept des Lebenslagen-Ansatzes. In: Statistisches Bundesamt (Ed.): Alltag in Deutschland – Analysen zur Zeitverwendung. Wiesbaden.

Stäglin, R. and Schintke, J. (2003): Monetäre, physische und Zeit-Input-Output-Tabellen, Teil 2: Analytische Auswertung, Sozio-ökonomisches Berichtssystem für eine nachhaltige Gesellschaft, Bd. 2. http://www-ec.destatis.de/csp/shop/sfg/vollanzeige.csp?ID=1011818.

Stahmer, C. (2003): Aufbau eines sozio-ökonomischen Berichtssystems für eine nachhaltige Gesellschaft. In: Statistisches Bundesamt (Ed.): Sozialer Wandel – Daten, Analysen, Gesamtrechnungen, Band 41 der Schriftenreihe „Forum der Bundesstatistik". Wiesbaden.

Stahmer, C. and Schaffer, A. (2004): Time Pattern in a Social Accounting Framework, Paper prepared for International Association for Research in Income and Wealth – IARIW, 28th General Conference, August 22-28, 2004, Cork, Ireland, http://www.iariw.org/papers/2004/axel.pdf.

Stahmer, C./Mecke, I. and Herrchen, I. (2003): Zeit für Kinder. Betreuung und Ausbildung von Kindern und Jugendlichen, Sozio-ökonomisches Berichtssystem für eine nachhaltige Gesellschaft, Bd. 3.

Statistisches Bundesamt (2004): Alltag in Deutschland – Analysen zur Zeitverwendung, Forum der Bundesstatistik. Wiesbaden.

Statistisches Bundesamt (Ed.) (2006a): Compass 2001/02 Time Use Survey: Publications, Links and Prints incl. Data Files and Research Facilities

Statistisches Bundesamt (Ed.) (2006b): Zeitbudgets – Tabellenband I, Zeitbudgeterhebung: Aktivitäten in Stunden und Minuten nach Geschlecht, Alter und Haushaltstyp 2001/02. Wiesbaden. https://www-ec.destatis.de/csp/shop/sfg/bpm.html.cms.cBroker.cls?cmspath=struktur,vollanzeige.csp&ID=1019589.

Statistisches Bundesamt (Ed.) (2008): Statistisches Jahrbuch 2008, Tabelle 7 Kultur, Freizeit, Sport, 7.15 Zeitaufwand pro Woche für Unterhaltung und Kultur 2001/2002 nach Geschlecht und Alter, 185. https://www-ec.destatis.de/shop sfg/bpm.html.cms.cBroker.cls?cmspath=struktur,vollanzeige.csp&ID=1022845.

Szalai, A. et al. (Eds.) (1972): The use of time: Daily activities of urban and suburban populations in twelve countries. The Hague.

Torres, A./Brites, R./Haas, B. and Steiber, N. (2007): First European Quality of Life Survey: Time use and work–life options over the life course, European Foundation for the Improvement of Living and Working Conditions. Dublin. www.eurofound.europa.eu.

UNIFEM United Nations Development Funds for Women (2008): Who Answers to Women? Progress of the World's Women 2008/2009 – Gender & Accountability. http://www.unifem.org/progress/2008/.

US Department of Agriculture (2009): American Time Use Survey: Food & Eating Module. http://www.ers.usda.gov/emphases/ healthy/atus/questions.htm.

Weick, S. (2004): Lebensbedingungen, Lebensqualität und Zeitverwendung. In: Statistisches Bundesamt (Ed.): Alltag in Deutschland – Analysen zur Zeitverwendung. Wiesbaden.

Wilhelm, R. and Wingerter, Ch. (2004): Lebenslanges Lernen – Statistischer Ansatz und empirische Ergebnisse der Zeitbudgeterhebung 2001/2002. In: Statistisches Bundesamt (Ed.): Alltag in Deutschland – Analysen zur Zeitverwendung. Wiesbaden.

Wilson, C. (1999): Sequence Alignment Analysis of Daily Activities. In: Merz, J. and Ehling, M. (Eds.): Time Use – Research, Data and Policy. FFB-Schriftenreihe Band 10. Baden-Baden.

Wilson, C. (2001): Activity patterns of Canadian women: An application of ClustalG sequence alignment software, Canada Mortgage and Housing Corporation, Paper 01-2292. Ottawa.

II. METHODS

1. Survey Methodology: International Developments

Frauke Kreuter

Contact:

Frauke Kreuter
Joint Program in Survey Methodology
1218 LeFrak Hall
College Park, MD 20742
US
e-mail: fkreuter[at]survey.umd.edu

Abstract

Falling response rates and the advancement of technology have shaped discussions in survey methodology for the last few years. Both have led to a notable change in data collection efforts. Survey organizations are currently exploring adaptive recruitment and survey designs and have increased their collection of non-survey data for sampled cases. While the first strategy represents an attempt to increase response rates and save on cost, the latter shift can be seen as part of the effort to reduce the potential bias and response burden of those interviewed. To successfully implement adaptive designs and alternative data collection efforts, researchers need to understand the error properties of mixed-mode and multiple-frame surveys. Randomized experiments might be needed to gain that knowledge. In addition, there is a need for close collaboration between survey organizations and researchers, including the ability and willingness to share data. The expanding options for graduate and post-graduate education in survey methodology could also help to increase the potential for implementing high-quality surveys.

Keywords: survey methodology, responsive design, paradata

1. Introduction

Falling response rates (Schnell 1997; Groves and Couper 1998; de Leeuw and de Heer 2002) and the advancement of technology (Couper 2005) have shaped discussions in survey methodology for the last few years. This report will highlight some of the developments that have resulted from these two trends and discuss the increasing difficulty of conducting surveys in the same way that had been common throughout the 1970s, 1980s, and 1990s. It is impossible to capture all of the changes in survey practice that took place during that time. However, this report will address several of the most prominent developments that have been discussed within the survey methodology research community, and those that are not addressed in the other contributions to this publication.

All of the developments that will be discussed here share an increased flexibility in data collection efforts. At the same time, they illustrate design changes implemented in a controlled or even randomized way in order to assess their effects on individual error sources. The result is less of a streamlined, recipe-style approach to data collection. Unlike in Germany, the data infrastructure in the US and UK allows for this type of flexibility in contexts where survey organizations are closely tied to scientists at universities (e.g., University of Michigan) or in survey research organizations that act as primary investigators (for example, with NORC, the National Opinion Research Center, and the General Social Survey). In both countries, most of the data collection agencies used for social science research are organizations that specialize in surveys for research projects. The companies therefore tend to have an incentive to invest in developing the expertise necessary for conducting high-quality surveys.

The present report begins with a discussion of how response rates have functioned as a quality indicator for surveys, and then summarizes the current discussion of alternatives to response rates as indicators. I will then highlight recent developments within survey operations. Many of these developments are reactions to falling response rates and increased concerns about nonresponse bias; others are motivated more broadly by the larger issue of total survey error (Groves et al. 2004) or as a reaction to technological changes. The main question behind all these developments, however, is: "How can we ensure high-quality data collection in a changing survey environment and increase quality in existing studies?"

2. Response rates and other survey quality indicators

For years, both survey methodologists as well as the general public have focused on response rates as indicators of survey quality (Groves et al. 2008). This focus has changed in recent years. For one thing, even in surveys with traditionally high response rates, participation has fallen below expectations. In addition, empirical evidence over the last decade has increasingly demonstrated that nonresponse rates are poor indicators of nonresponse bias for single survey estimates (Keeter et al. 2000; Curtin et al. 2000; Groves 2006). The shift in focus away from nonresponse rates toward bias is evident in a number of areas. It can be seen, for example, in the guidelines established by the US Office of Management and Budget, which require a detailed plan for the evaluation of nonresponse bias before they approve data collection sponsored by federal statistical agencies.[1] It is also evidenced by

---

1   All data collections conducted or sponsored by the US federal statistical agencies have to be approved by the Office of Management and Budget (OMB), which ensures that performance standards developed by the Interagency Council on Statistical Policy (ICSP) are met (Graham 2006). Conducting or sponsoring is defined here as any information that the agency collects using (1) its own staff and resources, or (2) another agency or entity through a contract or cooperative agreement. The approval by OMB is not just an attempt to reduce burden on the respondents (see Paperwork Reduction Act) but to ensure "that the concepts that are being measured are well known and understood, and shown to be reliable and valid" (Graham 2006). OMB applications require information from the data collection agency on questionnaire design procedures, field tests of alternative versions of their measures, reinterviews with subsamples of respondents, and the like. Pretests and pilot studies are encouraged, and the OMB guidelines spell out how those can be conducted. No criteria are specified to quantify potential measurement error. The development of a plan to

research initiatives to develop alternative indicators for survey quality (Groves et al. 2008).

Alternative indicators of survey quality can be grouped into two sets (Groves et al. 2008): single indicators at the survey level (which is similar to the current use of the response rate), and individual indicators at the estimate level. Single indicators include *variance functions of nonresponse weights* (e.g., coefficients of variation of nonresponse weights), *variance functions of post-stratification weights* (e.g., coefficients of variation of poststratification weights), *variance functions of response rates* on subgroups defined for all sample cases (both respondents and nonrespondents), *goodness of fit statistics on propensity models,* and *R-indexes* (Shouten and Cobben 2007), which are model-based equivalents of the above. Researchers from the Netherlands, the UK, Belgium, Norway, and Slovenia formed a joint project (RISQ) to develop and study such R-indexes.

The second set of indicators is produced on the survey estimate level. It is evident that nonresponse bias is item-specific (Groves and Peytcheva 2008) and thus estimate-level indicators would have the soundest theoretical basis. Examples of estimate-specific indicators are: *comparisons of respondents and nonrespondents on auxiliary variables; correlation between post-survey nonresponse adjustment weights and the analysis variable of interest (y) measured on the respondent cases; variation of means of a survey variable y within deciles of the survey weights;* and *fraction of missing information on y.* The latter is based on the ratio of the between-imputation variance of an estimate and the total variance of an estimate based on imputing values for all the nonrespondent cases in a sample (Little and Rubin 2002; Wagner 2008; Andrige and Little 2008).

All of these attempts rely heavily on the availability of auxiliary variables, such as enriched sampling frames, interviewer observations, or other paradata correlated with the survey variables of interest. Thus, we cannot revise our survey quality indicators without also changing survey operations.

Survey operations – the procedures of data collection – are themselves subject to quality assessment and quality indicators. O'Muircheartaigh and Heeringa (2008) presented a set of criteria at the 3MC conference in Berlin. Another example for quality assessment of survey operations are the OMB guidelines.[2] Independent of those guidelines, there are a couple of recent developments in survey operations that are informative for the German data collection context.

---

evaluate nonresponse bias is required only in cases where projected unit response rate falls below 80 percent.

2   http://www.whitehouse.gov/omb/inforeg/statpolicy.html#pr. [Last visited: 03/02/2010].

3. Survey operations

While survey methodologists and statisticians are aware of the fact that response rates are a poor indicator of nonresponse error (Keeter et al. 2000; Groves 2006) and are even less suitable as an indicator of the overall survey quality (Groves et al. 2004), a drop in response rates has nevertheless been the catalyst that has engaged survey researchers in rethinking current practices. In the light of the increasing difficulty that has been encountered, growing cooperation has heightened the awareness of potential biases in surveys and created the need to evaluate survey procedures, which are faced with the threat of losing precision through decreasing sample sizes. Changes in fieldwork procedures require cost-quality trade-off decisions.

Surveys conducted with a *responsive design* use *paradata* to carry out these cost-quality trade-off decisions during the fieldwork stage. Such paradata are not only used as criteria for decision-making during field operations, but are increasingly seen as tools for evaluating measurement error or conducting post-survey bias adjustments. *Multiple-mode* surveys are often a response to cost-quality trade-off analyses prior to the start of the survey, but they are also a reaction to coverage problems that arise when mode-specific frames do not cover the entire population. An extreme form of multiple-mode surveys are those where the respondent recruitment is separated from the actual data capture. The most prominent examples are access panels or opt-in polls (discussed in other chapters of this publication and therefore omitted here).

3.1 Responsive design

Survey organizations have been using subsampling and two-phase designs for a long time. However, the design decisions were often only based on estimates of current response rates and qualitative information from field supervisors. These approaches were further hampered by the inability to reach every sample unit in the subsample, and thus the statistical properties of the two-phase design were not necessarily unbiased. Over the last decade, survey organizations in the US and some European countries have begun to systematically base design decisions on quantitative information gathered during early phases of the fieldwork. The most prominent and detailed published example of this comes from the Social Research Center at Institute for Social Research of the University of Michigan, in an article outlining the use of "responsive design" (Groves and Heeringa 2006). Responsive design is characterized by four stages in the survey process. First, design characteristics are identified that may affect survey cost and error. Second, this set of indicators is monitored during the initial stages of data collection. Third, in subsequent phases of data collection, the features of the survey are altered based on cost-error trade-off decision rules. Finally, data from the separate phases are combined into a single estimator. One example of the kinds of data collected are the hours spent by an interviewer calling on sample households, driving to sample areas, conversing with household members, and interviewing individuals in the sample.

One critical element of this type of responsive design is the ability to track key estimates as a function of estimated response propensities (conditioned on a design protocol). If survey variables can be identified that are highly correlated with the response propensity, and if it can be seen that point estimates of such key variables are no longer affected by extending the field period, then one can conclude that the first phase of a survey (with a given protocol) has reached its phase capacity and a switch in recruitment protocol is advisable. Using non-contact error as an example, one can expect that a given recruitment protocol has reached its capacity if the percentage of households with access impediments stabilizes with repeated application of the recruitment protocol (e.g., repeated callbacks). Applying this method, Groves and Heeringa (2006) concluded that, for the National Survey of Family Growth (NSFG) cycle-6 field period, 10–14 calls produced stable cumulative estimates on the vast majority of the key estimates. A necessary condition for tracking key survey estimates concurrently is the ability and willingness of interviewers not only to record respondent data and paradata electronically, but also to submit the data to the survey managers in a timely manner. In the case of NSFG, the submissions occurred every evening (Wagner 2008).

3.2 Paradata

Paradata (data about the process of data collection) were already mentioned as an important tool for guiding fieldwork decisions (see Kreuter 2010). Increasingly, paradata are also used as tools for survey nonresponse adjustment and for the detection and modeling of measurement error. The latter is already more common in online surveys, where keystroke files are readily available due to the nature of the task. Even face-to-face surveys now have the capacity to electronically capture survey process data. Some examples of this include keystroke files obtained from computer-assisted personal interviews (CAPI), the audio computer-assisted self interview (Audio-CASI) surveys (Couper et al. 2008), and digital recordings of the (partial) interviews.

Paradata of potential use for nonresponse adjustments are collected in conjunction with household listings and when contact attempts to sample units are made. Recently, the US Census Bureau began to employ an automated system for collecting contact histories for CAPI surveys (Bates et al. 2008). Other governments have started using similar procedures. For example, the Research Center of the Flemish Government (Belgium) began to use contact forms in their surveys based on the work of Campanelli et al. (1997). The time of contact (day and time), the data collection method (in person or by telephone), and other information is recorded for each contact attempt with each sample unit (Heerwegh et al. 2007). A standard contact form has also been implemented since 2002 (round one) of the European Social Survey, and contact data were recently released publicly by the US National Center for Health Statistics (NCHS) for the 2006 National Health Interview Survey (NHIS). Thus, contact protocol data are increasingly available for each sample unit, which makes those data an attractive source for nonresponse-adjustment variables. Other large survey projects that collect observations of neighborhoods and housing unit characteristics include the 2006 Health and Retirement Study (HRS), Phase IV of the Study of Early Child Care (SECC), the Survey of Consumer Finances (SCF), the National Survey on Drug Use and Health, the British Election Study (BES), the British Crime Survey, the British Social Attitudes Survey (BSA), and the Survey of Health, Ageing and Retirement in Europe (SHARE).

Inspired by Groves and Couper (1998), some researchers have been able to use interviewer observations to assess the likelihood of response. Copas and Farewall (1998) successfully used the interviewer-assessed interest of sample members about participating in the British National Survey of Sexual Attitudes and Lifestyle as a predictor of response. Lynn (2003) demonstrated that the presence of multi-unit structures and door intercoms predicted the amount of effort required to contact sample households in the British Crime Survey. Bates et al. (2006) used contact information from the 2005 NHIS to predict survey participation. They examined the effect of various respondent questions, concerns, and reasons given for reluctance as they were recorded by interviewers on the survey response. For the US National Survey of Family Growth, Groves and Heeringa (2006) used a series of process and auxiliary variables to predict the screening and interview propensity for each active case. The expected screening and interview propensities were summed over all cases within a sample segment and grouped into propensity strata. The propensity strata were used by supervisors to direct the work of interviewers. Propensity models using call record paradata were also estimated for the Wisconsin Divorce Study (Olson 2007) and the US Current Population Survey (Fricker 2007). Both Olson (2007) and Fricker (2007) then examined measurement error as a function of response propensity. Lately, more studies have tried to establish a relationship between paradata collected during the contact process (or as interviewer observations) and key survey variables (Schnell and Kreuter 2000; Asef and Riede 2006; Peytchev and

Olson 2007; Groves et al. 2007; Yan and Raghunathan 2007; Kreuter et al. 2007).
A systematic evaluation of the quality of such paradata, however, is very limited. For example, measurement error properties of these data, collected either through interviewer observation or through digital recordings of timing or speech, are currently being studied by Casas-Cordero (2008) and Jans (2008).

3.3 Auxiliary variables and alternative frames

Next to paradata there is a second set of data sources that is now of increasing interest to survey designers – commercial mass mailing vendors. These lists are of interest for their use in the creation of sampling frames, to enhance survey information and to evaluate nonresponse bias.

In face-to-face surveys in the US, two methods of infield housing unit listing are most common. Traditional listing provides listers with maps showing the selected area and an estimate of the number of housing units they will find. Dependent listing gives listers sheets preprinted with addresses believed to lie inside the selected area. Those addresses come either from a previous listing or from a commercial vendor. Listers travel around the segment and make corrections to the list to match what they see in the field. The latter appears to be less expensive (O'Muircheartaigh et al. 2003). There is a third method of creating a housing unit frame, which involves procuring lists of residential addresses from a commercial vendor and identifying those that fall within the selected areas. Here, geocoding is used instead of actual listings. The coverage properties of such frames are still under study (Iannacchione et al. 2003; O'Muircheartaigh et al. 2006; Dohrmann et al. 2007; O'Muircheartaigh et al. 2007; Eckmann 2008). Survey research organizations are currently exploring the US Postal Service delivery sequence files to replace traditionally used PSUs (Census blocks) with zip codes. While this last development is specific to the US, it is nevertheless of interest as it holds out the potential to stratify with rich datasets, or to inform interviewers in advance about potential residents and their characteristics. This information can be used for tailored designs. In Germany, dependent listing and enhanced stratification was already used for the IAB-PASS study (Schnell 2007).

3.4 Multiple modes

Several US federal statistical agencies have explored the use of mixed mode surveys. The two main reasons that mixed mode studies are usually considered relate to survey cost and response rates. There are three prominent types of multiple-mode studies: modes are administered in sequence, modes are implemented simultaneously, or a primary mode is supplemented with a secondary mode (de Leeuw 2005).

The American Community Survey (ACS), which replaced the Census long form, is an example of a sequential application of modes. Respondents are first contacted by mail, nonrespondents to the mail survey are contacted on the phone (if telephone numbers can be obtained), and finally in-person follow-ups are made to a sample of addresses that have not yet been interviewed. Parallel to the primary data collection, a method sample is available to examine various error sources (Griffin 2008). The Bureau of Labor Statistics (BLS) is currently using multiple modes for the Current Employment Statistics (CES) program. Firms are initiated into the survey via a computer-assisted telephone interview (CATI), kept on CATI for several months, and are then rolled over to touchtone data entry, the internet, fax, etc.[3] Experiments are undertaken to evaluate measurement error separately from nonresponse error for each of these modes (Mockovak 2008). The National Survey of Family Growth has CAPI as its primary mode, although sensitive information (e.g., number of abortions) is collected through Audio-CASI.

With their responsive design and the acknowledgement of imperfect sampling frames, mixed-mode surveys present some attractive advantages. Research is underway to explore the interaction between nonresponse and measurement error for these designs (Voogt and Saris 2005; Krosnick 2005). The European Social Survey program just launched a special mixed-mode design in four countries to examine appropriate ways of tailoring data collection strategies and to disentangle mode effects into elements arising from measurement, coverage, and sample selection. Another large scale study within Europe that experiments with mixed-modes is the UK Household Longitudinal Study (UKHLS), under the supervision of the Institute for Social and Economic Research. On the administrative side, the Social Research Center at the University of Michigan is currently constructing a new sample management system that will allow more efficient ways of carrying out mixed-mode surveys (Axinn et al. 2008). The new system will manage samples across data collection modes (F2F, telephone, Internet, and supplementary data modes such as biomarkers, soil samples, etc.) and will allow easy transfer of samples between modes and interviewers (e.g., between CAPI and centralized CATI).

---

3   http://www.bls.gov/web/cestn1.htm. [Last visited: 03/02/2010].

3.5 Reduction of response burden

Another development related to measurement error can be seen most recently in the context of large-scale surveys. Researchers at the Bureau of Labor Statistics (BLS) are investigating survey re-design approaches to reduce respondent burden in the Consumer Expenditure Survey (Gonzalez and Eltinge 2008). One proposed method is multiple matrix sampling, a technique for dividing a questionnaire into subsets of questions and then administering them to random subsamples of the initial sample. Matrix sampling has been used for a long time in large-scale educational testing. This method is growing in popularity for other types of surveys (Couper et al. 2008) where respondent burden is an increasing concern. Another method from educational testing that is currently under exploration is adaptive testing. Most applications of this method are currently tested in health surveys but survey issues regarding context effects arise (Kenny-McCoullough 2008).

3.6 Interviewer

All of the above mentioned developments have one feature in common – they alter and extend the task interviewers have to perform. In the past, there was already a tension between the dual role of interviewers. On the one hand, they have to be adaptive and flexible when recruiting respondents into the sample (Groves and McGonagle 2001; Maynard et al. 2002), and on the other hand, interviewers are asked to deliver questions as standardized as possible to reduce interviewer effects (Schnell and Kreuter 2005). Now, however, the number of tasks that one interviewer is required to perform is even higher, including recording observations, bookkeeping, handling technology, explaining technology, switching between different questionnaire flows, etc. Considering this increased burden and the resulting higher expectations placed on the interviewer, a more careful look at interviewer performance seems necessary. Survey organizations (NORC in the US, NatCen and ONS in the UK) have already started to analyze interviewer performance across various surveys (Yan et al. 2008) combined with census data (Durrant et al. 2008) or questionnaires given to the interviewer (Jäckle et al. 2008); others investigate alternatives to conventional interviewers (Conrad and Schober 2007).

Compared to Germany, it seems more common for US data collection firms to employ interviewers that work for one particular survey organization (and thus become acclimated to a particular survey house culture), or, if they do work with other organizations, these would also be social survey research organizations. More importantly, it is common in the US for interviewers to be centrally trained from the survey agency at the beginning of their employment and also at the beginning of new large-scale assignments. Unlike in Germany, face-to-face survey interviewers tend to be paid by the hour rather than by completed cases. This results in a different incentive structure and also opens the possibility for interviewers to spend time on the additional tasks mentioned above. It goes without saying that the cost of face-to-face surveys in the US is often tenfold that of what is typical in Germany.

4. Summary

In conclusion, survey methodologists are conducting new and exciting research into the trade-offs between cost and response rates. As part of these efforts, research is being done on how best to use non-survey data to provide information about nonresponse bias or measurement error, but also to supplement data collection and reduce respondent burden. Research is underway to gain a better understanding of the error properties of mixed-mode and multiple-frame surveys, but conclusive results are still lacking. The German data infrastructure initiative has the potential to contribute to this research. An overarching theme in all of the above mentioned developments has been the increased interest in the relationship between various error sources (Biemer et al. 2008). In Germany, there are several good opportunities to engage in research related to the intersection of error sources, especially given the exceptional data linkage efforts that have been undertaken. In this area, Germany is clearly taking the lead compared to the US. However, what could be improved in Germany is the collaboration between survey organizations and researchers, the amount of data shared between those organizations, and the willingness to systematically allow for randomized experiments in data collection protocols. In short, I would recommend the following:

- Work toward higher quality surveys, particularly in the face-to-face field. One step in this direction would be the development of survey methodology standards and the commitment to adhere to these standards. Those standards should include a minimum set of process indicators (metadata), and variables created in the data collection (paradata).

- Expanding options for graduate and post-graduate education in survey methodology could increase the potential for implementing high-quality surveys.

- Carefully examine interviewer hiring, payment, and training structures in German survey organizations. Recommendations or minimum requirements regarding these issues might also be needed for German government surveys.

- Use the potential inherent in having multiple surveys run within (or across) the same survey organizations for coordinated survey methodology experiments. As we increase the burden on interviewers and try to reduce the burden on respondents, many questions will be left open in the research area of survey methodology, such as the effect of question context through matrix sampling, or the effect of interviewer shortcuts when creating sampling frames, or collecting paradata for nonresponse adjustment.

References:

Andridge, R. and Little, R. (2008): Proxy pattern-mixture analysis for survey nonresponse. Paper presented at the 2008 Joint Statistical Meeting. Denver.

Asef, D. and Riede, T. (2006): Contact times: what is their impact on the measurement of employment by use of a telephone survey? Paper presented at Q2006 European Conference on Quality in Survey Statistics. Cardiff.

Atrostic, B.K./Bates, N./Burt, G. and Silberstein, A. (2001): Nonresponse in US Government Household Surveys: Consistent Measures, Recent Trends, and New Insights. Journal of Official Statistics 17 (2), 209-226.

Axinn, W. et al. (2008): SRC Building New Software to Facilitate Mixed Mode Data Collection Projects. Center Survey 18 (6), 8.

Bates, N./Dahlhamer, J. and Singer, E. (2008): Privacy concerns, too busy, or just not interested: Using doorstep concerns to predict survey nonresponse. Journal of Official Statistics 24 (4), 591-612.

Biemer, P./Beerten, R./Japec, L./Karr, A./Mulry, M./Reiter, J. and Tucker, C. (2008): Recent Research in Total Survey Error: A Synopsis of 2008 International Total Survey Error Workshop (ITSEW2008).

Campanelli, P./Sturgis, P. and Purdon, S. (1997): Can you hear me knocking: An investigation into the impact of interviewers on response rates. London.

Casas-Cordero, C. (2008): Errors in Observational Data Collected by Survey Interviewers. Comprehensive Examination Paper, Joint Program in Survey Methodology.

Conrad, F. and Schober, M. (2007): Envisioning the Survey Interview of the Future. New York.

Copas, A.J. and Farewell, V.T. (1998): Dealing with non-ignorable non-response by using an 'enthusiasm-to-respond' variable. Journal of the Royal Statistical Society Series A-Statistics In Society 161 (3), 385-396.

Couper, M. (2005): Technology Trends in Survey Data Collection. Social Science Computer Review 23 (4), 486-501.

Couper, M. and Lyberg, L. (2005): The use of paradata in survey research. Paper presented at the 54th Session of the International Statistical Institute. Sydney.

Couper, M./Raghunathan, T./Van Hoewyk, J. and Ziniel, S. (2008): An Application of Matrix Sampling and Multiple Imputation: The Decisions Survey. Paper presented at the 2008 Joint Statistical Meeting. Denver.

Curtin, R./Presser, S. and Singer, E. (2000): The effects of response rate changes on the index of consumer sentiment. Public Opinion Quarterly 64 (4), 413-428.

de Leeuw, E.D. and de Heer, W. (2002): Trends in household survey nonresponse: A longitudinal and international comparison. In: Groves, R.M./Dillman, D.A./Eltinge, J.L. and Little, R.J.A. (Eds.): Survey nonresponse. New York.

de Leeuw, E.D. (2005): To Mix or Not to Mix Data Collection Modes in Surveys. Journal of Official Statistics 21 (2), 233-255.

Dohrmann, S./Han, D. and Mohadjer, L. (2007): Improving coverage of residential address lists in multistage area samples. Proceedings of the Section on Survey Research Methods. American Statistical Association.

Durrant, G.B./Arrigo J. D. and Steele, F. (2008): Using Paradata to Develop Hierarchical Response Propensity Models 19th International Workshop on Household Survey Nonresponse. Ljubljana, Slovenia, 15-17 September 2008.

Eckman, S. (2008): Errors in Housing Unit Listing and their Effects on Survey Estimates, Comprehensive Examination Paper, Joint Program in Survey Methodology.

Fricker, S. (2007): The relationship between response propensity and data quality in the Current Population Survey and the American Time Use Survey. Doctoral dissertation. University of Maryland.

Gonzalez, J. and Eltinge, J. (2008): Adaptive Matrix Sampling for the Consumer Expenditure Interview Survey. Paper presented at the Joint Statistical Meeting, American Statistical Association.

Graham, J.D. (2006): Memorandum for the President's Management Council. January 20, 2006. Executive Office of the President, Office of Management and Budget. Washington, D.C. 20503.

Griffin, D. (2008): Measuring Mode Bias in the American Community Survey. Paper presented at the JSPM Design Seminar Spring.

Groves, R.M. (2006): Nonresponse rates and nonresponse bias in household surveys. Public Opinion Quarterly 70 (5), 646-675.

Groves, R.M. and Couper, M. (1998): Nonresponse in Household Interview Surveys. New York.

Groves, R.M. and Heeringa, S. (2006): Responsive design for household surveys: tools for actively controlling survey errors and costs. Journal of the Royal Statistical Society Series A: Statistics in Society 169 (3), 439-457.

Groves, R.M. and McGonagle, K. (2001): A theory-guided interviewer training protocol regarding survey participation. Journal of Official Statistics 17 (2), 249-266.

Groves, R.M. and Peytcheva, E. (2008). The impact of nonresponse rates on nonresponse bias: A meta-analysis. Public Opinion Quarterly 72 (2), 167-189.

Groves, R.M./Wagner, J. and Peytcheva, E. (2007): Use of Interviewer Judgments About Attributes of Selected Respondents in Post-Survey Adjustment for Unit Nonresponse: An Illustration with the National Survey of Family Growth. American Statistical Association.

Groves, R.M./Fowler, J.F./Couper, M.P./Lepkowski, J.M./Tourangeau, R. and Singer, E. (2004): Survey Methodology. New York.

Groves, R.M./Brick, J.M./Couper, M./Kalsbeek, W./Harris-Kojetin, B./Kreuter, F./Pennell, B./Raghunathan, T./Schouten, B./Smith, T./Tourangeau, R./Bowers, A./Jans, M./Kennedy, C./Levenstein, R./Olson, K./Peytcheva, E./Ziniel, S. and Wagner, J. (2008): Issues Facing the Field: Alternative Practical Measures of Representativeness of Survey Respondent Pools. Survey Practice, October 2008 http://surveypractice.org/2008/10/30/issues-facing-the-field/ [Last visited: 03/02/2010].

Heerwegh, D./Abts, K. and Loosveldt, G. (2007): Minimizing survey refusal and noncontact rates: do our efforts pay off? Center for Survey Methodology, Katholieke Universiteit Leuven. Survey Research Methods 1 (1), 3-10.

Iannacchione, V.G./Staab, J.M. and Redden, D.T. (2003): Evaluating the use of residential mailing addresses in a metropolitan household survey. Public Opinion Quarterly 67 (2), 202-210.

Jäckle, A./Lynn, P./Nicolaas, G./Sinibaldi, J. and Taylor, R. (2008): Interviewer characteristics, their behaviours, and survey outcomes. Paper presented at the 2008 International Workshop on Household Nonresponse.

Jans, M. (2008): Can Speech Cues and Voice Qualities Predict Item Nonresponse and Inaccuracy in Answers to Income Questions? Prospectus for Dissertation Research, Michigan Program in Survey Methodology.

Keeter, S./Miller, C./Kohut, A./Groves, R. and Presser, S. (2000): Consequences of Reducing Nonresponse in a National Telephone Survey. Public Opinion Quarterly 64 (2), 125-148.

Kenny-McCulloch, S. (2008): Pretesting Surveys with Traditional and Emerging Statistical Methods: Understanding their Differential Contributions and Affects on Question Performance in Standardized and Adaptive Measurement. Prospectus for Dissertation Research, Joint Program in Survey Methodology.

Kreuter, F. (2010): Paradata. [In this publication].

Kreuter, F./Lemay, M. and Casas-Cordero, C. (2007): Using proxy measures of survey outcomes in post-survey adjustments: Examples from the European Social Survey (ESS). Proceedings of the Survey Research Methods Section. American Statistical Association.

Krosnick, J. (2005): Effects of survey data collection mode on response quality: Implications for mixing modes in cross-national studies. Conference on Mixed Mode Methods in Comparative Social Surveys. City University London, 15. Sept. 2005.

Little, R.J.A. and Rubin, D.B. (2002): Statistical Analysis with Missing Data, 2nd edition. New York.

Lynn, P. (2003): PEDAKSI: Methodology for collecting data about survey non-respondents. Quality and Quantity 37 (3), 239-261.

Maynard, D.W./Houtkoop-Steenstra, H./Schaeffer, N.C. and van der Zouwen, J. (2002): Standardization and Tacit Knowledge: Interaction and Practice in the Survey Interview. New York.

Mockovak, B. (2008): Mixed-Mode Survey Design. What are the effects on data quality? Challenging Research Issues in Statistics and Survey Methodology at the BLS. U.S. Bureau of Labor Statistics. www.bls.gov/osmr/challenging_issues/mixedmode.htm.

Olson, K. (2007): An investigation of the nonresponse – measurement error nexus. Doctoral dissertation. University of Michigan.

Office of Management and Budget (2006): Questions and answers when designing surveys for information collections. www.whitehouse.gov/omb/inforeg/pmc_survey_guidance_2006.pdf. [Last visited: 03/02/2010].

O'Muircheartaigh, C./Eckman, S. and Weiss, C. (2003): Traditional and enhanced listing for probability sampling. Proceedings of the Section on Survey Research Methods. American Statistical Association.

O'Muircheartaigh, C./English, E./Eckman, S./Upchurch, H./Garcia, E. and Lepkowski, J. (2006): Validating a sampling revolution: Benchmarking address lists against traditional listing. Proceedings of the Section on Survey Research Methods American Statistical Association.

O'Muircheartaigh, C./English, E. and Eckman, S. (2007): Predicting the relative quality of alternative sampling frames. Proceedings of the Section on Survey Research Methods. American Statistical Association.

O'Muircheartaigh, C. and Heeringa, S. (2008): Sampling Designs for Cross-cultural and Cross National Studies. Paper presented at Multinational, Multiregional, and Multicultural Contexts. Berlin from June 25–28, 2008.

Peytchev, A., and Olson, K. (2007): Using interviewer observations to improve non-response adjustments: NES 2004. Proceedings of the Survey Research Methods Section. American Statistical Association.

Schnell, R. (1997): Nonresponse in Bevölkerungsumfragen. Opladen.

Schnell, R. (2007): Alternative Verfahren zur Stichprobengewinnung für ein IAB-Haushaltspanel mit Schwerpunkt im Niedrigeinkommens- und Transferleistungsbezug. In: Promberger, M. (Ed.): Neue Daten für die Sozialstaatsforschung: Zur Konzeption der IAB-Panelerhebung „Arbeitsmarkt und Soziale Sicherung". Nuremberg. IAB Forschungsbericht No. 5/2007.

Schnell, R. and Kreuter, F. (2000): Untersuchungen zur Ursache unterschiedlicher Ergebnisse sehr ähnlicher Viktimisierungs-surveys. Kölner Zeitschrift für Soziologie und Sozialpsychologie 52 (1), 96-117.

Schnell, R. and Kreuter, F. (2005): Separating Interviewer and Sampling-Point Effects. Journal of Official Statistics 21 (3), 389-410.

Schouten, B. and Cobben, F. (2007): R-Indexes for the Comparison of Different Fieldwork Strategies and Data Collection Modes. Paper presented at the International Workshop for Household Survey Nonresponse.

Spar, E. (2008): Federal Statistics in the FY 2009 Budget. In: American Association for the Advancement of Science, Report on Research and Development in the Fiscal Year 2009. http://www.aaas.org/spp/rd/rd09main.htm. [Last visited: 03/02/2010].

Staab, J.M. and Iannacchione, V.G. (2003): Evaluating the Use of Residential Mailing Addresses in a National Household Survey, Joint Statistical Meetings – Section on Survey Research Methods.

Voogt, R.J.J. and Saris, W.E. (2005): Mixed Mode Designs: Finding the Balance Between. Nonresponse Bias and Mode Effects. Journal of Official Statistics, 21 (3), 367-387.

Wagner, J. (2008): Adaptive Survey Design to Reduce Nonresponse Bias. Doctoral dissertation. University of Michigan.

Yan, T. and Raghunathan, T. (2007): Using Proxy Measures of the Survey Variables in Post-Survey Adjustments in a Transportation Survey, Joint Statistical Meetings – Section on Survey Research Methods.

Yan, T./Rasinski, K./O'Muircheartaigh, C./Kelly, J./Cagney, P./Jessoe, R. and Euler, G. (2008): The Dual Tasks of Interviewers, International Total Survey Error Workshop (ITSEW), North Carolina.

2. Improving Research Governance through Use of the Total Survey Error Framework

Marek Fuchs

Contact:

Marek Fuchs
Darmstadt University of Technology
Institute of Sociology
Residenzschloss
Marktplatz 15
64283 Darmstadt
Germany
e-mail: fuchs[at]ifs.tu-darmstadt.de

Abstract

Survey research is an integral element of modern social science. The German survey research infrastructure – in terms of research institutes, surveys, conferences, and journals – has greatly improved over the past 20 years, and recently several important European initiatives in this area have gained momentum. This has brought about the need for an integrated theoretical concept to assess and evaluate the quality of surveys and survey estimates. In our view, survey methodology is an interdisciplinary body of knowledge and expertise that describes the "science of conducting and evaluating surveys." It is a theory-driven empirical approach used to assess the quality of survey research. Thus, it applies the principles of survey research and experimental research to the development and assessment of survey methodologies themselves. Even though surveys have been conducted in a highly professional manner for decades, survey methodology offers the opportunity to use a universal theoretical approach when planning and assessing surveys as well as shared terminology. The integrated theoretical concept and joint terminology both foster the professionalization of survey methods and stimulate methodological research on the improvement of survey methods.

One key element of survey methodology is the total survey error framework. This will be described in greater detail below (section 1). Then we will discuss some limitations of this concept (section 2) and mechanisms and organizational issues that arise in promoting the use of this concept (section 3).

1. The total survey error framework

Multiple criteria are used to assess the quality of survey statistics; these include reporting timeliness, the relevance of the findings, the credibility of researchers and results, and finally, the accuracy and precision of the estimates. While timeliness of reporting and the credibility of researchers and results are rather soft indicators that require qualitative assessments, the accuracy of a survey statistic is an objective quantitative quality indicator. It is determined by the survey estimate's distance or deviation from the true population parameter. If, for example, a survey aimed to determine the average household income of a certain population, any deviation of the sample estimate from the true value – the one that would have been obtained if all members of the target population had provided error-free income data – would decrease the survey's accuracy. By contrast, the precision of a survey estimate is determined by the size of the margin of error (or confidence interval) and thus by the standard error. The standard error is a function of the sample size, of the alpha error, and of the variance of the measure in question. Accuracy and precision offer an integrated view of the quality of a survey estimate. While the precision is discussed in almost every introductory statistics textbook, the accuracy is not always considered to the same extent when evaluating the quality of a survey estimate. Rather, most survey researchers generally determine the margin of error or the standard error in order to assess the quality of an estimate. The accuracy of the estimate is considered less rigorous and is also less often determined explicitly. In survey methodology, accuracy and precision are treated as concepts of equal importance. However, given the lack of attention devoted to the accuracy of estimates so far, we focus on this facet in the present paper. In the following, we use the total survey error framework (e.g., Biemer and Lyberg 2003) to provide a comprehensive discussion of a survey estimate's accuracy.

There are two types of survey error that harm the accuracy of a survey estimate: variable or random error, and systematic error. While random errors are assumed to cancel each other out – that is, a negative deviation of the measurement from the true value would be compensated by a positive deviation – systematic errors shift the sample estimate systematically away from the true value. The latter would be the case, for example, if with a certain question wording, all respondents to a survey reported a higher number of doctor visits than actually occurred during a given reference period. For linear estimates (such as means, percentages, and population totals), it is safe to state that an increase in the random error leads to an increased variance, while a rise in any systematic error results in a larger bias of the estimate. Using this terminology, one can state that the accuracy of a survey estimate is affected by an increase in the bias.

From a traditional point of view, the driving factors or sources of survey error fall into two groups: sampling error and non-sampling error. Non-sampling error would then be further differentiated into coverage error, non-response error, and measurement error. A theory-driven modern approach distinguishes between observational errors and non-observational errors. While observational errors are related to the measurement of a particular variable for a particular sample unit, non-observational errors occur when an incomplete net sample is created that is supposed to represent the target population. Building upon this, Groves and colleagues (2009) classify sources of error into two groups: the first sources of error result from the representation of the target population in the weighted net sample ("representation"), and the second from effects on the survey responses obtained from a respondent ("measurement"). This extension of the traditional total survey error concept allows for detailed analysis of the mechanisms, and considers several sources of error as well as possible interaction effects.

1.1 Total survey error components affecting representation

(1) Before a sample can be drawn, a sampling frame is necessary that allows access to the members of the target population. The completeness of this frame and possible biases in its composition cause misrepresentations of the population by the sample. If a group is underrepresented in the frame – for example, if individuals who own mobile phones as their only communication device are missing from traditional random digit dialing (RDD) sampling frames because they do not have a landline telephone – the socio-demographic or substantive characteristics of this group are not considered when computing the survey statistic. This underrepresentation of some groups (coverage bias) causes a lack of accuracy of survey estimates (e.g., Blumberg and Luke 2007).

(2) Once a frame is available, one needs to draw a random sample, using a simple random sample, a stratified sample, a cluster sample, or more complex sample designs (Kish 1965; Lohr 1999). Based on this sample, the standard error is computed by taking the square root of the quotient of the variance in the sample and the number of cases in the sample. The standard error is then used to compute the confidence limits and the margin of error – both are indicators for the precision of the estimate. The sampling error depends heavily on the design of the sample: for a fixed number of sample cases, the standard error usually decreases if stratification is applied. By contrast, a clustered sample is generally characterized by larger design effects, which in turn raises the sampling error for a particular estimate. However, on a fixed budget, clustering usually increases the precision since the effective sample size can be increased even though the variance estimate suffers from the design effect caused by clustering.

(3) Unit non-response is probably the form of error that has been studied best of all the bias components in the total survey error framework (Groves and Couper 1998; Groves et al. 2002). Since the early days of survey methodology, researchers have been aware of the fact that some portions of the gross sample cannot be reached in the field phase of a survey or are not willing to comply with the survey request for cooperation. Since the responses of these groups may differ considerably from the responses of those members of the gross sample who can be reached and who are willing to cooperate, unit non-response is considered a serious source of systematic error that yields a non-response bias. The literature provides comprehensive theoretical approaches to explain the various stages of respondent cooperation and also findings that can be generalized beyond particular surveys. In part, this is due to the fact that a potential non-response bias can be assessed for variables for which parameters are

available from official statistics. Compared to other sources of error, this leaves survey researchers in a comfortable situation, since a possible bias can be observed more easily.

(4) Finally, the net sample needs to be adjusted for design effects introduced by the sample design. If the sample design, for example, asked for a disproportional stratified sample, an appropriate weighting procedure would have to compensate for the unequal selection probabilities when estimating the population parameter. In addition, the net sample may be adjusted for a possible non-response bias (redressment), although this procedure is questionable (Schnell 1997). Both procedures require complex computations considering information from the gross sample and from official statistics. While the first approach may potentially increase the random error of the estimate, correcting for bias may introduce systematic errors into the sample and thus bias the estimate.

1.2 Total survey error components affecting measurement

The four sources of error discussed so far are related to the representation of the target population by the weighted net sample. Coverage error, sampling error, non-response error, and adjustment error all potentially contribute to the random error or systematic error of the survey estimate. The next three sources of error are concerned with the measurement process. First, we will discuss the specification error, then the measurement error, and finally the processing error.

(5) Most concepts of interest in survey research cannot be observed directly. Measurement requires researchers to operationalize and translate the concept into questionnaire items that can be asked by interviewers and answered by respondents. For example, the general public's attitudes on illegal immigration need to be decomposed into several items describing various aspect and dimensions of illegal immigration. Respondents are then asked to report their degree of agreement with these items. The combined score of all items on this subject would then be treated as a measurement of the attitudes on illegal immigration. If an important aspect of this concept were missing on the scale, the validity of the operationalization would be compromised because the scale would not measure the defined concept completely and a specification error would occur. Usually, this results in a serious bias because the estimates based on an incomplete scale would not mirror the complete true attitudes of the members of the target population on illegal immigration. Unfortunately, the specification error is hard to determine: it requires a qualitative assessment, and standard procedures are rarely available to date.

(6) Measurement error is a rather complex component of total survey error (Lyberg et al. 1997). It consists of various elements that may cause systematic survey error as well as random survey error, both individually and jointly. Accordingly, measurement error may contribute to an increase in the estimate's variance as well as to its bias. Measurement error arises from the mode of survey administration, from the questionnaire or survey instrument, from the setting in which the instrument is administered, from the interviewers (if present), and also from the respondents (Lyberg et al. 1997).

Survey mode: the traditional trichotomy differentiates among face-to-face surveys, telephone surveys, and self-administered surveys. These modes differ with respect to the presence or absence of an interviewer – this allows for various degrees of standardization of the measurement process and also for different types of motivational support, as well as explanation and help to the respondent – and the dominant communicative channel (audio-visual, audio-only, visual-only). In recent years, many new survey modes have evolved with the introduction of modern information and communication technologies. Some of these modes transfer an established methodology into a computer-assisted mode (Couper et al. 1998); whereas other new modes have evolved as a consequence of merging survey modes (Conrad and Schober 2008). Each of these survey modes has its particular strengths and weaknesses for specific survey topics and survey designs. While a web-based survey might increase the variance of an estimate because respondents tend to answer a frequency question more superficially than in a face-to-face interview, the response to a face-to-face version of the very same questions might be prone to a higher degree of social desirability distortion, which in turn contributes to measurement bias.

Questionnaires: over the past 25 years, questionnaire design has evolved from an "art of asking questions" into a "science of asking questions" (Schaeffer and Presser 2003). This line of research has demonstrated on innumerable occasions that slight modifications in the wording of a question or response categories, in the order of the questions and response categories, and also in the visual design of the whole questionnaire as well as of single questions, affect the answers obtained from the respondents. Since the early days of the CASM movement (CASM=Cognitive Aspect of Survey Measurement), a multiplicity of research papers and textbooks (Sudman et al. 1996; Tourangeau et al. 2000) have contributed to a coherent theoretical approach that helps explain and predict random measurement error and systematic measurement error related to the questionnaire.

Respondent: also within the framework of the CASM movement, a detailed theoretical approach on how respondents consider and answer survey questions has been developed. As a result, the question-answer process has been described in great detail. Using this framework, several systematic and random respondent errors when answering survey questions have been identified. For example, satisficing behavior – as opposed to optimizing response behavior (Krosnick and Alwin 1987) – as well as mood effects and a "need for cognition" have been demonstrated by methodological research.

Interviewer: finally, it has been demonstrated that personal and social characteristics of interviewers – if present in the interview situation – as well as their task-related and non-task-related behaviors may have a considerable influence on the answers obtained from respondents. Accordingly, not only study-specific instructions are needed, but also improved professional interviewer training that focuses on general aspects of the interviewers' duties and responsibilities. However, one has to be aware that it is impossible to avoid individual respondent reactions to an interviewer's personal and/or social characteristics, since interviewer-administered surveys require a personal meeting of respondents and interviewers.

(7) Processing and editing the responses: in addition to the error components mentioned so far, the errors that occur when editing the survey responses obtained from respondents have been included in the total survey error framework. A few examples of possible error in the editing stage of a survey include poor handwriting with open questions, the treatment of inconsistent responses and of answers that were initially not codable, as well as incorrect classification of occupations. Also, scanning paper questionnaires with optical character recognition (OCR) technology and keying the answers from questionnaires into a database are prone to errors. In addition, some crucial responses may be imputed in the presence of item non-response, which is also susceptible to random or systematic error. Accordingly, these survey steps and the errors associated with them may either increase the variance of a variable – which in turn inflates the standard error and the margin of error – or compromise the accuracy of a response because a bias is introduced.

1.3 A simplified formula for the mean squared error

Technically speaking, the total survey error is the difference between a sample estimate and the respective parameter in the target population. This difference is measured by the mean squared error (MSE), which in turn consists of two components: the squared sum of the bias components plus the sum of the variance components (Biemer and Lyberg 2003, for an intuitive discussion of this concept). For the mean squared error, we need to combine the bias and variance from all sources in order to obtain an estimate of the total survey error. Although most sources of error can contribute to bias and variance simultaneously, some sources are primarily responsible for the increase of either variance or bias. Thus, a simplified formula for the mean squared error is as follows:

$$MSE = (B_{spec} + B_{meas} + B_{proc} + B_{cov} + B_{nr})^2 + VAR_{meas} + VAR_{samp} + VAR_{adj}$$

where the abbreviations have the following meaning:

B_{spec}	Specification bias/reduced validity
B_{meas}	Measurement bias
B_{proc}	Processing bias
B_{cov}	Coverage bias
B_{nr}	Non-response bias
VAR_{meas}	Measurement variance
VAR_{samp}	Sampling variance
VAR_{adj}	Adjustment variance

Although it is easy to estimate sampling variance – every introductory statistics textbook outlines the basic approaches – estimating the other types of variance and especially the biases is much more ambitious. The mean squared error as a measure for the total survey error is often only of heuristic value because the exact value of a particular variance or bias component cannot be computed.

The mean squared error offers the opportunity to evaluate survey designs and the estimates computed based on these survey designs. Thus, the "users" of a particular survey can assess the quality of reported results not only based on sampling error and the margin of error, but also based on other error components. This is especially important since the bias component of the mean squared error is assumed to exceed the sampling error. Thus, the sample estimate of the population parameter departs potentially more pronouncedly from the true value than has been assumed based on the sampling error alone.

1.4 Some pros and cons of the total survey error framework

Although total survey error offers a convincing framework to evaluate the accuracy of a survey estimate, it also suffers from a serious drawback. The effort necessary to compute a reasonable estimate of the magnitude of a particular error component usually exceeds the available resources. The estimation of the mean square error requires multiple repetitions of the survey design, which is usually too costly and also not feasible since the target population does not remain unchanged between repetitions. Also, for many survey designs, some error components are not accessible because of the field procedures applied or legal constraints (e.g., privacy laws prohibit extensive non-response follow-up studies in many countries). Also, it should be noted that for the exact computation of the mean squared error the parameter needs to be accessible. Because this is usually not the case, the mean squared error is seldom explicitly determined in practice. More often, only a few key components are estimated or a survey design is rated along the various components of bias and variance on a scale from "low" to "high." The decision for a particular survey design is then made based on a detailed computation of some error components and a rough assessment of the magnitude of the other error components. This leaves the researcher as well as the user of a survey statistic in a situation where a qualitative assessment of the magnitude of the total survey error is the best available assessment.

Regardless of this serious limitation of the total survey error framework, survey research and survey methodology have greatly benefited from the emerging total survey error approach.

(1) The total survey error framework makes researchers aware of possible errors in their survey statistics. If the response rate and the size of the net sample are the only available indicators for a given survey, many likely biases remain undetermined. Here, the total survey error framework allows for systematic reflection on possible limitations to survey quality and thereby fosters professional evaluation of ongoing surveys in terms of data quality and provides a common language and terminology for critical discussion.

(2) In addition, the total survey error framework provides a theoretical explanation for the various types of possible errors (variance and bias) and also for the underlying mechanisms (random error vs. systematic error). It also names a wide range of possible sources for problems in data quality. Hence the total survey error framework puts forward a more comprehensive theoretical approach to further developments of survey methods, beyond the traditional "keep at it" approach. In addition, it provides measurable indicators for evaluating the improvements introduced by these new survey methods.

(3) The total survey error framework also provides a basis for interdisciplinary discourse across the boundaries of traditional disciplines. Among others, surveys have been used for a long time in the fields of sociology, psychology, economy, and educational research. Although it is too early to say that the specific methodologies of these various fields have been completely integrated, one can say that these various methodologies have merged to some extent or are in the process of integration based on the total survey error framework and the survey methodology.

(4) From an international perspective, the integrated concept of total survey error has contributed to the dissemination of high criteria and a set of methods to meet those criteria. International surveys like the Programme for International Student Assessment (PISA), the International Social Survey Programme (ISSP), and the European Social Survey (ESS) would

not be feasible if researchers from diverse cultural and disciplinary backgrounds were not able to interact and cooperate in a common framework. Although there are still many national differences in the design and administration of surveys, the total survey error framework does promote a minimum degree of conformity in the assessment of data quality.

2. Survey error and survey cost

The survey designer's goal is to reduce the total survey error through proper design decisions in the preparatory stages for the survey as well as during the fieldwork. Most of the time, however, design decisions – regarding the mode of administration, question format, interviewer training procedures, and so on – do not only affect one specific source of error, but rather multiple sources. Thus, every improvement in eliminating one error source may be accompanied by an increase in another. Hence, survey designers need to compromise and balance different sources of error.

The total survey error framework offers the opportunity to determine the relative importance and weight of various error components in a given survey. Although not every component can be determined for each survey, an evidence-based assessment of multiple error sources is possible. As the body of literature on the various error components expands, researchers will be able to choose cost-efficient strategies that help reduce the total survey error (Groves 1989). However, in practice, survey designs are not only evaluated in the presence of fixed constraints on time and money. For example, survey design A may be chosen over survey design B despite the fact that it produces data of lower quality in terms of the mean squared error. But because the estimated cost of survey design B is considerably higher, the person responsible nevertheless decides to use survey design A.

Thus, the total survey error framework also relates to cost and requires survey designers to consider the accuracy of their surveys in relation to cost and timeliness of reporting. This raises the danger that researchers will sacrifice the quality of their survey to cost. However, since the total survey error approach requires researchers to document and publish key characteristics of each survey, the scientific community can easily assess to what extent survey quality is compromised to cost constraints. It is hoped that this will prevent researchers from making design decisions solely or predominantly based on the costs involved. The acceptance of the total survey error framework would be greatly increased if funding agencies required applicants to make use of this approach in their proposals.

3. Organizational issues

Although the total survey error approach offers a set of standardized terms, concepts, and measures, it needs to be adapted to the respective surveys, topics, and country-specific conditions. In addition, the total survey error framework involves evidence-based discussions of methodological issues conducive to producing advice and rules based on empirical tests and evaluations. Thus, a thorough country-specific assessment of the various components of the total survey error is needed, either in the form of an evaluation of ongoing surveys in the field or of lab- or field-based independent experimental studies. While experimental studies on methodological issues provide basic knowledge and allow for the testing of methodological concepts, they lack applied results that could directly benefit ongoing surveys. By contrast, in an evaluation embedded in an ongoing survey, researchers are limited in the degree to which the experimental methodological design is able to test innovative approaches since highly risky designs might harm the quality of the production data. Based on this reasoning, improvements in the total survey error approach should be promoted through a strategy combining methodological evaluations of ongoing large-scale surveys and of stand-alone experimental studies or laboratory experiments.

Until recently, the resources allocated to methodological research have not been adequate. Methodological studies have been conducted only as addendums to substantive surveys – which limits the scope and design of the study – or with student populations, or with other factors limiting their generalizability. Of course, the former ZUMA[1] (now continued as a department of GESIS[2]) has a long tradition in methodological research. Nevertheless, given the lack of resources, studies conducted elsewhere have usually been either focused on specific surveys or – if conducted independently – limited in their size and thus in the broader impact of the results in the scientific community. In the past few years, however, two important developments have been taken place. On the one hand, several large-scale surveys have taken over their own survey operation in order to evaluate new modes, innovative instruments, and means of reducing non-response. On the other hand, the projects funded by the German Research Foundation (DFG, *Deutsche Forschungsgemeinschaft*) since 2008 in the Priority Program 1292 "Survey Methodology" have shown potential to function as a nucleus for a broader movement towards basic methodological research. Based on these experiences it seems advisable to promote a twofold strategy: methodological research should be implemented as part of every large-scale survey funded by public resources. A research plan for methodological studies should

---

1   Zentrum für Umfragen, Methoden und Analysen.
2   Leibniz Institute for the Social Sciences (*Leibniz-Institut für Sozialwissenschaften*).

already be developed in the design stage of the respective surveys and should be covered by a certain percentage of the overall funding (e.g., 5 percent of the total funds allocated to a particular survey). The research plan for the methodological study should already be specified in the proposal for the survey and evaluated by survey methodology experts according the same high standards as the proposal for the substantive study.

Unlike in the US and some other countries, German academic researchers do not have a wide range of field organizations at their disposal. Although several universities have built small to medium-sized computer-assisted telephone interview (CATI) facilities and some medium-sized online access panels are available as well, the majority of the fieldwork is conducted by private market research institutes. In order to promote the total survey error framework, a universal application of this concept is needed across all sectors including academia, official statistics, and the private sector. At present, the General Online Research conferences (with respect to web surveys), the meetings of the Section on Quantitative Research Methods in the German Sociological Association (DGS, *Deutsche Gesellschaft für Soziologie*) and a few other small-scale events are the only settings in which researchers from academia, the private sector, and official statistics come together and engage in joint methodological discussion. This is completely unsatisfactory. The annual conference of the American Association for Public Opinion Research might serve as a model for a similar conference scheme in Germany.

So far, high ranking permanent academic positions in the field of survey research are usually filled with experts in substantive research areas who are also qualified as survey experts and, in particular, as survey statisticians. Thus, for junior researchers, it is hard to build a career predominantly on survey methodology or even on a specialization in this field (e.g., sampling, measurement, or non-response). However, professionalizing the field of survey methodology will require an infrastructure of experts who focus on the various components of total survey error. Thus, in addition to survey experts in substantive fields and survey statisticians, experts in data collection and survey methodology should be considered more often for permanent academic positions. In the past few years, a few positions have been deliberately offered to this group. Further action should be taken to provide survey methodology with a sufficient human resource basis.

In order to disseminate survey methodology and the total survey error framework, a few specialized master study programs are beginning to emerge in Germany. Given the longstanding tradition of such programs in the US (e.g., Ann Arbor and the Joint Program in Survey Methodology, or JPSM) and the UK (e.g., Essex), one could expect positive effects in Germany as well. Also, doctoral education in the field of methods research has been offered so far on an individual basis only. Accordingly, a structured doctoral program that offers a set of integrated courses in survey methodology needs to be established.

A key challenge for the development of high-quality survey research lies in adopting joint quality indicators and common standards for each of the qualitative measures. The rather disparate use of response rates and measures of non-response in Germany is a good example of how survey research could benefit from an integrated quality concept. Whether we should adopt the English terminology or develop German terminology for the same concepts also needs further discussion. In our view, the use of the English terms has the advantage that the words are clearly identifiable as technical terms. In addition, the use of a shared English language terminology facilitates collaboration in international surveys such as the ESS or EU-SILC. Finally, when using the international terminology it is easier to participate in international discussion at conferences and in journals.

4. Summary of recommendations

In sum, this paper does not suggest a completely new approach to the methodological research on survey methods. Instead, it proposes that the existing work be integrated into the total survey error framework and that this concept and other knowledge from the field of survey methodology be applied rigorously to the planning and assessment of surveys. Also, it recommends the increased use of evidence-based rules and strategies to improve surveys. This will require evaluation and validation studies embedded in ongoing surveys as well as independent experimental studies in the field or in the lab that are not bound by the same limits as ongoing surveys. The following recommendations are the key elements of a strategy for achieving these objectives:

- The total survey error framework should be adopted as standard to describe and assess the quality of surveys. Since this concept requires the documentation of different variance and bias components associated with a particular survey, this will promote the methodological considerations in the planning phase of a survey, in its field phase, as well as during the analysis.
- The error components of a particular survey should be assessed based on evidence from evaluation studies or experimental work.
- Strategies und rules on how to improve the quality of surveys in general should be evidence-based. Experiments in the field and in the lab are key elements in support of evidence-based rules and strategies.
- Funding for methodological research in the total survey error framework should be provided in the context of ongoing large-scale surveys (a minimum of 5 percent of the overall budget for a particular survey) as

well as by national funding agencies for independent experimental studies in the field and in the lab.

- Accordingly, the total survey error framework should be mandated by funding agencies. Applicants should be required to make use of this approach in their proposals.
- For academic positions in the field of survey research (associate and full professorships), universities and similar research institutions should not only recruit candidates from substantive areas or from the field of survey statistics, but should also consider survey methodologists with a record of publications and projects in the various components of total survey error. This will help establish expertise in survey methodology and contribute to the professionalization of survey methodology.
- In order to maintain a consistent flow of graduates and postgraduates in the field of survey methodology, the emerging specialized master programs should be strengthened. Also, at least one structured doctoral program with an international teaching staff should be established in Germany.
- The further development of survey methodology in Germany should be fostered by launching a new international journal that offers survey methodologists a forum by publishing peer-reviewed papers on data collection in English.
- An annual conference of survey methodology experts from the academic sector, the private sector, and official statistical agencies should be established to promote and foster the use of the total survey error framework in survey research across these three sectors in Germany.

As these recommendations are gradually put into practice, survey methodology will evolve as a professional cross-disciplinary discipline contributing to survey research in economics, sociology, political science, health research, educational research, consumer and market research, and many other fields in the academic sector, the private sector, and also in the official statistical agencies.

References:

Biemer, P.P. and Lyberg, L.E. (2003): Introduction to Survey Quality. New York.
Blumberg, S.J. and Luke, J.V. (2007): Coverage bias in traditional telephone surveys of low-income and young adults. Public Opinion Quarterly 71 (5), 734-749.
Conrad, F.G. and Schober, M. (2008): Envisioning the survey interview of the future. Hoboken.
Couper, M.P./Baker, R.P./Bethlehem, J./Clark, C.Z.F./Martin, J./Nicholls, W.L., et al. (Eds.) (1998): Computer Assissted Survey Information Collection. New York.
Groves, R.M. (1989): Survey errors and survey costs. New York.
Groves, R.M. and Couper, M.P. (1998): Nonresponse in household interview surveys. New York.
Groves, R.M./Fowler, F.J./Couper, M.P./Lepkowski, J.M./Singer, E. and Tourangeau, R. (2009): Survey Methodology (2nd edition). New York.
Groves, R.M./Dillman, D.A./Eltinge, J.L. and Little, R.J.A. (Eds.) (2002): Survey Nonresponse. New York.
Kish, L. (1965): Survey Sampling. New York.
Krosnick, J.A. and Alwin, D.F. (1987): An evaluation of a cognitive theory on response-order effects in survey measurement. Public Opinion Quarterly 51 (2), 201.
Lessler, J.T. and Kalsbeek, W.D. (1992): Nonsampling Errors in Surveys. New York.
Lohr, S.L. (1999): Sampling: Design and Analysis. Pacific Grove.
Lyberg, L./Biemer, P./Collins, M./De Leeuw, E./Dippo, C./Schwarz, N. et al. (Eds.) (1997): Survey measurement and process quality. New York.
Schaeffer, N.C. and Presser, S. (2003): The science of asking questions. Annual Review of Sociology 29 (1), 89-113.
Schnell, R. (1997): Nonresponse in Bevölkerungsumfragen. Ausmaß, Entwicklung und Ursachen. Opladen.
Sudman, S./Bradburn, N. and Schwarz, N. (1996): Thinking about answers. The application of cognitive Processes to survey methodology. San Francisco.
Tourangeau, R./Rips, L. and Rasinski, K. (2000): The psychology of survey response. Cambridge.

3. Metadata

Arofan Gregory, Pascal Heus and Jostein Ryssevik

Contact:

Pascal Heus
Open Data Foundation
5335 North Nina Drive
Tucson, AZ 85704
US
e-mail: info[at]opendatafoundation.org

Abstract

Metadata, or data about data, play a crucial role in the social sciences, ensuring that the data collected are accompanied by thorough documentation and grounded in community knowledge across their entire life cycle – from the early stages of data production to secondary analysis by researchers or use by policy-makers and other key stakeholders. This chapter provides an overview of the social sciences metadata landscape, including best practices and related information technologies. It focuses in particular on two measures – the Data Documentation Initiative (DDI) and the Statistical Data and Metadata Exchange (SDMX) Standard – that appear central to a global metadata management framework for social data and official statistics. It also highlights current trends and challenges to integration and provides a set of high-level recommendations for producers, archives, researchers, and sponsors with the aim of fostering the adoption of metadata standards and best practices in the years to come.

Keywords: social sciences, metadata, data, statistics, documentation, data quality, XML, DDI, SDMX, archive, preservation, production, access, dissemination, analysis

1. What is metadata?

Metadata is a difficult term to define; it means many things to many different audiences. If we turn to Wikipedia, we find: "Metadata (meta data, or sometimes metainformation) is 'data about data,' of any sort in any media."[1] While broadly true, the Wikipedia definition does not capture the real importance of metadata to those involved in social science research.

Within any domain, the term *metadata* can be more usefully defined by describing its agreed use. In the case of social science research, there exists a well-developed metadata culture, which allows us to be very specific. Researchers understand what data are: the full range of information that is collected, processed, analyzed, and used in the conduct of research. *Metadata* covers all forms of documentation about this data.

Even so, we are left with a definition of the term that is still incredibly broad. It is sometimes helpful to think about the different types of metadata, using common terms:

- *Structural metadata* describes the structure of datasets, whether these are tabular in nature or simply files of raw data or microdata. Which variable's value appears in which column? Which row represents which case? Are there hierarchical relationships? Etcetera.

---

[1] http://en.wikipedia.org/wiki/Metadata

- *Reference metadata (also known as "descriptive" metadata)* consists of what is often thought of as "footnote" metadata, whether relating to methodology, sampling, quality measurements, production notes, or other aspects. This is a very broad term that can cover a range of information dealing with everything from individual values to entire collections of data.

- *Administrative metadata* is the data created through the process of administering data, covering its collection, production, publication, and archiving.

- *Behavioral metadata (also known as "paradata")* is information about the reaction and behavior of users when working with data, and that of respondents when the data is being collected (in this case, it is paradata about a collection instrument). This can be of interest to those who act as data librarians, enabling them to better manage their data collections, but can also be of direct interest to researchers seeking to address the questions: what did other researchers do with the data? How did respondents react when asked a question?

It is worth noting that metadata are for human as well as machine consumption. Whereas most of the structural metadata exist to allow software processes to read, manipulate, and exchange data files, the purpose of reference and behavioral metadata is to enable human researchers to find, understand, and assess the quality of the data.

One of the criticisms of metadata as a broad discipline is that it is context-dependent, especially in terms of its use to help navigate the contents of the Internet as a whole. Indeed, there is a long and ongoing debate about the value of metadata. This debate – while both entertaining and instructive – is not particularly useful to those in social sciences research, because very specific definitions of the relevant metadata exist in the form of standard metadata models: the Data Documentation Initiative[2] (DDI), ISO-TS 17369 Statistical Data and Metadata Exchange[3] (SDMX), Dublin Core Metadata Initiative[4] (DCMI), ISO/IEC 11179,[5] the Neuchatel models for variables and classifications, and others.

The benefit of having such standards is that they allow for *direct implementation* of metadata-driven systems and management systems for metadata – and thus realization of the benefits – without having to answer questions about the precise value and meaning of metadata in its broadest sense.

---

2   http://ddialliance.org/
3   http://sdmx.org/
4   http://dublincore.org/
5   http://metadata-standards.org/

2. Metadata and technology

2.1 Historical technological approaches

Metadata is a natural part of most current data implementations, given the strong focus modern technology places on information. If technology depends on the *exchange and use of information* – or data – then the metadata describing that information can be critical in the creation of systems that perform tasks in an automated way.

Many of the early discussions about metadata dealt with describing the structure of data, whether it be the simple textual format of a data file or the structural information about a relational database schema. Other discussions were concerned more with the content of the data – that is, the type of file and what it contains. This focus arose naturally out of computers' ability to compute at ever increasing speed: the first challenge was to handle the data itself and to perform some operation with it. Once this was achieved, the question was how to retain enough information about the data so that it could be *exchanged with others or used in the future*. This was where the interest in metadata arose.

It is interesting to note how little the metadata capabilities of many statistical tools have grown since the era before the Internet. While many other types of applications have developed the ability to process and understand files from other users based on standard formats and models, statistical processing applications do not share this rich, "networked" view of the world. Many statistical tools today are reminiscent of applications dating from the 1980s – they understand enough metadata to handle specific data files and to interpret their contents and format or perform analytical operations, but have little ability to exchange this information with other systems or describe the context in which the data was produced.

2.2 Metadata and the Internet

The single most important development driving the current interest in metadata is the advent of the Internet. A vast network of interconnected computers requires a large set of standard protocols to allow computers to use files throughout the network. Most of these protocols are metadata.

To give a simple example: when a browser on your computer encounters a webpage, it gets a set of information from the server – metadata – which it uses to properly display that page. The webpage will probably be in HTML[6], but it might also be a Word document or a PDF file, or even a video clip. Each of these files requires a different application behavior. Thus, part of the

---

6   http://en.wikipedia.org/wiki/HTML

metadata given to the browser is the MIME-type[7] of the file, which tells the computer which application to launch.

Early Internet protocols provided enough metadata to allow for human users to exchange files, but there was typically insufficient metadata for computer applications to directly perform tasks without human intervention. Because the emphasis was on people viewing files from around the network, there emerged metadata standards that supported this type of application – the best-known of these were a set of citation fields for describing any kind of resource, the Dublin Core.

As the Internet has evolved, there has been an increasing emphasis on interactions between applications – a phenomenon termed "distributed computing." This development revealed that the available metadata – even with the help of standards such as the Dublin Core – were insufficient. In all of its applications, however, the Internet has placed strong emphasis on the use of remote resources without the need for explicit, human-guided integration, thus demanding a large amount of metadata and increasingly requiring metadata standards.

2.3 Metadata and XML-based technologies

One of the biggest developments in the growth of the Internet – and for distributed computing generally – was the advent of the eXtensible Markup Language[8] (XML) and the suite of related technologies and standards. Derived from a technology standard for marking up print documents – the Standard Generalized Markup Language[9] (SGML) – the original focus of XML was to better describe documents of all sorts so they could be used more effectively by applications discovering them on the Internet.

XML is a meta-language used to describe tag sets, effectively injecting additional information into a document. Unlike HTML (which was also based on SGML), however, there was no fixed list of tags – the whole point is that documents could be designed to carry specific additional information about their contents. Thus, XML document types could be designed to carry any sort of metadata in line with the contents of the document.

XML is not only a language but also a collection of technologies available to perform various operations on the underlying data or metadata: the XML schema for describing document structure; XPath[10] and XQuery[11] for

---

7   http://en.wikipedia.org/wiki/MIME.
8   http://en.wikipedia.org/wiki/XML and http://www.w3.org/XML/
9   http://en.wikipedia.org/wiki/SGML.
10   http://en.wikipedia.org/wiki/XPath.
11   http://en.wikipedia.org/wiki/XQuery.

querying and searching XML; SOAP[12] and REST[13] for facilitating the exchange of information; and many others.

Most importantly, the above technologies are often readily available on most computers and are free to use. The XML standards themselves are maintained by the World Wide Web Consortium[14] and publicly available. This implies that XML not only provides a common language and facilitates metadata management but is also easy to adopt as a technology. While XML does not preclude the existence of legacy metadata management systems, it has shifted the way we model the information structure and expose the metadata to the outside world. Harmonized models have emerged in various fields of expertise, including the social sciences.

The Dublin Core was quickly realized in an XML format, and other standards also used the new format, notably the DDI (see below). At first, these standards were designed very much with human users in mind, but those involved in solving problems related to distributed computing realized that XML was a very powerful tool as well.

These developments led to a set of Web services[15] standards (SOAP, WSDL, etc.) as well as a new type of service-oriented architecture[16] (SOA). The development of Web services technology and service-oriented architectures continued the demand within applications for precisely defined metadata exchanged using standard protocols. Some of the later standards such as SDMX – and later versions of existing standards (such as DDI version 3.0) are designed to leverage these developments.

Today, we have a powerful set of technology tools and metadata models that are directly relevant to the applications used by the social sciences researcher. While not all of the statistical software packages have utilized these developments, we are increasingly seeing these new metadata-rich technologies used to provide researchers and those who support them with functionalities that were not possible in earlier generations of technology.

---

12   http://en.wikipedia.org/wiki/SOAP.
13   http://en.wikipedia.org/wiki/Representational_State_Transfer.
14   http://www.w3.org/
15   http://en.wikipedia.org/wiki/Web_service.
16   http://en.wikipedia.org/wiki/Service-oriented_architecture.

3. Metadata and the social sciences

3.1 Why metadata?

In the social sciences, data quality has a direct impact on the soundness of policies and the validity of research outputs. Data quality is typically measured using criteria such as accessibility, coherence, relevance, timeliness, integrity, consistency, and coherence. These indicators are generally accepted as a good measure of the overall usefulness of the data. Meeting these criteria not only means making data available but also requires comprehensive documentation of the data structures, production processes, statistical methodologies, data sources, contexts, and many other aspects. This is necessary not only to ensure usability but also for purposes of discovery, accessibility, preservation, and information exchange.

In the social sciences, metadata is essential for several reasons:

- It is needed to ensure that users have sufficient information to properly *understand* and *use* the data. Without relevant documentation, researchers are unable to accurately interpret the meaning of the data. A lack of information also places an extra burden on data providers, who need to be able to respond to users' questions.

- It is required to facilitate *data discovery* and *access* by the intended consumers. The best data in the world is useless if no one is aware of its existence.

- It supports the long-term *preservation* of data by ensuring that the relevant information remains with the data for future use or for conversion into new archival formats.

- Common metadata languages and structures are also essential to support the *exchange* of information between agencies and/or individuals.

In general, better documentation makes for more useful data, and ultimately better research. The usability of data is intricately tied up with issues about how thoroughly it is documented: rich metadata about a dataset allows for easier access and use of the data. Researchers want better data, and one way to help improve data quality is to provide better documentation.

3.2 Metadata and the data lifecycle

The data lifecycle in the social sciences is quite complex as the data flowing from the survey respondents or administrative systems to the researchers and policy-makers goes through several stages and transformation processes involving many different actors. Furthermore, secondary or derivative data and research findings often themselves become data sources for others.

Any description of the purpose of metadata within the data lifecycle should start with an analysis of the users' requirements:

- The majority of data users are not involved in the creation of the data they use.
- Data are frequently used for other research purposes than intended by the creators (secondary analysis).
- Data are frequently used many years after they were created.
- Data users often compare and combine data from a broad range of sources (across time and space).

The common denominator of the four characteristics is their emphasis on the relative distance between the end users of statistical material and the production process. Whereas the creators and primary users of statistics might possess "undocumented" and informal knowledge that will guide them in the analysis process, secondary users must rely on the formal metadata accompanying the data to exploit their full potential. For this reason it might be said that social science data only become accessible through the metadata accompanying the dataset. Without written descriptions of the various elements comprising a dataset, it will appear to the end user as a more or less meaningless collection of numbers. The metadata provides the bridges between the producers of data and their users and convey information that is essential for secondary analysis.

Ideally, data providers should abide by Gary King's replication standard,[17] which holds that "sufficient information exists with which to understand, evaluate, and build upon a prior work if a third party can replicate the results without any additional information from the author." Note that from this perspective, researchers as much as producers are defined as "data providers," and should therefore abide by the same documentation principles.

Traditionally, however, metadata has not been the focus of data producing agencies and the responsibility for documenting data was often left to the data archive, data librarians, or Research Data Centers. Such "after-the-fact" efforts require substantial resources and typically lead to a considerable amount of information loss and sparsely documented data.

This mindset has changed in recent years, and considerable efforts are now being made by data producers and archives to improve the overall quality of metadata. The idea is also being extended to the researchers or end

---

17 "Replication, Replication," Gary King, PS: Political Science and Politics, Vol. XXVIII, No. 3 (September 1995), 443–499 and "A Revised Proposal, Proposal," Vol. XXVIII, No. 3 (September 1995), 443–499. See also http://gking.harvard.edu/projects/repl.shtml.

users, whose contribution to metadata is often nonexistent. Collecting inputs from the users themselves should lead to a better understanding of data usage, reduce the duplication of efforts, and promote the sharing of knowledge. This shift from a centralized maintenance of metadata by the archive to a distributed approach, where many entities contribute to the knowledge, seems only natural: it is better and easier to capture information about an event at the time of its occurrence than after the fact.

There is another view of the data lifecycle that is not so much concerned with the collection and production of data for research as it is with the aggregation and harmonization of data. This view can be termed the *information chain* because it describes the flow of data from its original micro-level source(s) through the various aggregation and harmonization processes, as the data flows upward from its source through the hierarchy of primary and secondary users. Data collected through surveys or from administrative sources at a regional level might be aggregated at a national level, combined with other sources, and then further aggregated at the international level.

This view of the data lifecycle also places importance on the distance between those collecting the original data, and its eventual use at a higher level of aggregation. Without sufficient documentation about the aggregation and harmonization processes, it is difficult for end users to fully understand the aggregates they are using.

The main goal of capturing metadata at each stage in the lifecycle is to maintain it throughout a single cycle from collection to publication (and hence to archiving), but also to capture each secondary use of the data, so that any dataset will be accompanied by as complete a set of documentation as possible. Information captured as it comes into existence is higher in quality and more complete, which directly benefits the user of the data.

There are also less obvious benefits to having a consistent set of metadata accompanying a dataset through the lifecycle: good metadata can be used to help drive the processing of the data as it goes through its lifecycle, and well-documented data collections make it possible to compare similar datasets. Complete information about the content and processing of a collection of data can provide valuable information to those who want to re-purpose or manage the data within that collection. Thus, the beneficiaries of good metadata, captured as the data is collected, processed, and published, include not only researchers but also secondary users, archivists, and data producers.

Very often, good metadata can form the basis for code generation, whether that code runs inside a statistical package or is used for some other purpose (such as automatic generation of forms for data collection). It can also be used for the automated production of documentation or publications that can be customized to the end user's needs. Although not immediately apparent, the benefit of having good metadata is that the systems which support the researcher, data producer, and archivist can all be made much more efficient and produce higher-quality data.

3.3 Standard metadata models

The recent emphasis on the data lifecycle, and on capturing metadata from the beginning, has driven the development of two standard models, each designed around one of the data lifecycle views described above. The DDI is, in its most recent version, based on a lifecycle model that describes the collection and sourcing of data through the stages of publication, archiving, and secondary use. ISO TS-17369, the SDMX standard is based on a view of the information chain, with a stronger focus on aggregate data products. These standards – along with a number of others in various important areas – create a common view of how metadata within the social sciences domain can be described and exchanged to facilitate the flow of metadata accompanying the relevant datasets.

4. The Data Documentation Initiative

4.1 DDI – early history

The DDI[18] is an international program to produce a metadata specification for the description of social science data resources. The program was initiated in 1994 by the Inter-University Consortium for Political and Social Research (ICPSR). Contributors to the project come mostly from social science data archives and libraries in the US, Canada, and Europe.

The original aim of the DDI was to replace the widely used OSIRIS codebook specification with a more modern and Web-aware specification that could be used to structure the description of the content of social science data archives. The first preliminary version came in the form of an SGML Document Type Definition[19] (DTD), which in 1997 was converted to an XML DTD. The migration to XML took place just a few months after the W3C released the first working draft of the XML specification. The DDI was consequently one of the very first major metadata initiatives using the new framework. Several data archives started to use the DDI to describe their data collections, and software was developed to support its use. However, it soon became apparent that the first versions of the DDI had several severe limitations:

---

18 http://www.ddialliance.org.
19 http://en.wikipedia.org/wiki/Document_Type_Definition.

4.1.1 A pure "bottom-up" approach

The DDI specification was developed to describe concrete files or products coming out of the statistical production process. Given its roots in social science data archiving, this is quite natural. The information objects in the data archives were final products whose lifeline to the various production processes had been severed and which were given individually to users, outside their original production context.

As a consequence there was a one-to-one relationship between a DDI instance and the physical data it was meant to describe. The DDI was tied to the dataset, and there were no methods to describe abstract statistical concepts that might be represented in more than one concrete study. It was therefore impossible to reference identical variables across datasets, and even series of survey instances where the majority of variables are identical from wave to wave had to be described instance by instance.

4.1.2 Modularity

The first versions of DDI had their roots in a "book" metaphor. It was seen as the digital equivalent of a paper document – the well-established codebook or data dictionary. The specification was not built according to a modular architecture that would have allowed information and application providers to select bits and pieces and "snap" them together on a freer basis.

4.1.3 Extensibility

Another critical limitation was the lack of a proper extensibility mechanism. Within the confines of an XML DTD there is no way to add local extensions without compromising the interoperability of the core specification. You either accept the specification as it is without any additions or you break it. For a big and complex specification like the DDI, this is a major problem that can easily damage the adoption process. Without a mechanism that allows extensions to be made without breaking the standard, the chances are high that application providers will sacrifice interoperability for local efficiency and relevance.

Despite these limitations, the DDI met the fundamental needs of data archives for documenting survey datasets and has been widely adopted by agencies around the world.

4.2 DDI version 3.0

Version 3.0 of the DDI was released in April of 2008, representing a major revision to the standard that solved the problems of earlier versions as described above. Based on a survey lifecycle model, it is designed to describe groups and series of studies, to define degrees of comparison within and across studies, and to allow for reuse of metadata where appropriate. It uses a modular approach, with modules which are related to each step of the data lifecycle. Different types of metadata are organized into packages relating to their contents. All the metadata about a survey instrument, for example, are found in the "data collection" module, represented by an XML namespace.

DDI 3.0 represents an approach to the metadata that is more in line with the capabilities of modern information technology: it is relational in nature rather than document-centric so that metadata can be easily referenced and reused. This is important because modern Web services technology utilizes the idea of distributed computing. DDI 3.0 is designed explicitly to support the concept of having a collection of metadata be distributed and reused by reference.

The combination of the lifecycle approach, a modular design, and metadata reusability has transformed the specification from a product intended for archiving datasets by a single agency into a highly flexible standard that can be used by all actors in the survey lifecycle for different purposes. Expected uses of DDI 3.0 include study design and survey instrumentation, questionnaire generation, support for data collection and processing operations, capturing data aggregation or recoding, managing question or concept banks, data discovery, research projects, data comparability, metadata mining, and probably a number of other purposes that cannot yet be foreseen. For each case, a subset of the specification is used either for the specific purpose or to provide a customized view of the information. A strength of DDI 3 is that it maintains a common language and metadata consistency across the lifecycle stages and among contributors.

The new version has also been designed to work with standards such as SDMX, ISO 11179, Dublin Core, and others, which ensure that the metadata can be connected to other domains or stages of the lifecycle. It takes into account backward compatibility with previous versions of DDI to ensure that current users can continue to use their existing framework or metadata.

Overall, DDI 3.0 has broadened the scope of the specification and made the standard attractive to a broader range of users across the entire survey lifecycle, from data producers to researchers.

4.3 Adoption of the DDI

In its early stage of existence, the DDI specification was primarily used by the data archive community in North America and Europe. With only a handful of tools available, the first DDI users relied on proprietary solutions to manage their metadata or even compiled the metadata by hand! The advent of the Nesstar[20] software played a key role in the adoption and success of the DDI as the only production-grade solution. In 2006, the International Household Survey Network (IHSN) integrated the Nesstar Publisher as one of the components of its Microdata Management Toolkit,[21] a set of tools targeted towards national statistical agencies in developing countries for the preservation and dissemination of survey microdata. Supported by the PARIS21 / World Bank Accelerated Data Program,[22] the toolkit has met with great success and is now in use in dozens of countries across Africa, the Middle East, Latin America, and Asia. DDI is now a truly global specification.

With the publication of DDI version 3.0, the DDI Alliance has broadened the potential user base of the specification to all agencies and individuals involved in the survey lifecycle. While no official implementation of 3.0 is currently in use, several organizations (primarily producers and Research Data Centers) have expressed interest in adopting it or are already in the initial stages of implementation. The availability of generic tools will play a major role in the success of 3.0, but once this initial hurdle is passed, a large uptake of the new version is expected.

5. The Statistical Data and Metadata Exchange

In 2001, seven international and supranational organizations organized the SDMX[23] Initiative: the Bank for International Settlements (BIS), the Organization for Economic Cooperation and Development (OECD), the European Central Bank (ECB), Eurostat, the World Bank, the International Monetary Fund (IMF), and the United Nations Statistical Division (UNSD). The initiative was formed to examine how new technologies could be used to better support the reporting and dissemination of aggregate statistics, which all of these organizations use to support policy and development activities.

In 2005, the first version of the SDMX technical standards (that is, technology standards) became an ISO Technical Specification, ISO TS-

---

20 http://www.nesstar.com.
21 http://www.surveynetwork.org/toolkit.
22 http://www.surveynetwork.org/adp.
23 http://www.sdmx.org.

17369. They provided an information model and XML formats for all types of aggregate data and related structural metadata, along with guidelines about how Web services should be supported. There is also a legacy format in UN/EDIFACT syntax, formerly known as GESMES/TS (but now SDMX-EDI), which is still supported under the SDMX model.

Having standard XML formats for data and structural metadata made the process of exchanging data more efficient because the data were now predictable and accompanied by rich metadata. SDMX has been implemented by many additional international organizations, and national-level institutions such as central banks and statistical offices. Adoption is global.

In 2008, the SDMX Initiative released two other important sets of products: a second and significantly expanded version of the technical specifications SDMX 2.0 (now being submitted to ISO for acceptance as an International Standard) and a set of content-oriented guidelines, which recommend how various statistical concepts in broad use can be defined, named, represented, and used.

In addition to support for aggregate datasets and related structural metadata, version 2.0 of the technical specifications provide support for all types of reference metadata, including the ability to mimic the contents of other related standards for the purposes of cross-walking. There is also a standard for providing registry services, a feature of Web services architecture that allows for the easy location of data and metadata resources around a distributed network.

It is important to note that both SDMX and DDI were designed to be aligned and to work well with other related standards – SDMX was designed with a knowledge of DDI (version 3.0 and earlier versions), and vice-versa. An effort was made to ensure that these standards are complementary rather than competitive.

6. Other specifications

There are several other standards that are of interest to the social sciences researcher. These will be given a brief mention here, and the list provided is not exhaustive.

- *ISO/IEC 11179:* This standard provides a model for understanding what it terms "data elements," which are as applicable to metadata as they are to data. The model provided gives a standard way of defining terms, the concepts they represent, the value domains they encompass, and how those value domains are represented. Additionally, a model for lifecycle management is provided. Ultimately, this is a powerful model for defining the semantics of different terms and concepts used with social sciences data.

- *ISO 19115:* This standard provides a model for defining geographies and is used by many other systems that care about geography, maps, etc. This model is embedded in DDI, for example, but is widely used.
- *Dublin Core:* Dublin core provides a set of fields for providing the citations of resources and has a core set and an extension mechanism, expressed in XML.
- *METS:* This is a standard from the world of digital archives, which provides for the packaging of a set of related objects (e.g., a webpage and the image files it references). It allows for other standard metadata formats to be embedded in it (DDI is one example of this).
- *PREMIS:* This is an XML format for expressing metadata about the archival lifecycle, and is meant to be used in combination with the OAI archival reference model.

Given the many stages data that and metadata go through in the social sciences and the different perspectives taken by the various actors, it is clear that a single metadata specification cannot be used to cover the entire life cycle. Using the DDI and SDMX as core standards and extending their functionalities through combination with the other standards mentioned above offers data producers, librarians, researchers, and other consumers a robust set of tools for the management of data and metadata across the entire lifecycle. The often non-trivial job of mapping these standards correctly to one another is being undertaken in forums such as the UN/ECE's METIS[24] conference and elsewhere.

One example of this is the use of DDI to document micro-level data sources, with resulting aggregates described using SDMX. Each standard is best suited to a different set of processes – having them well-aligned, and mapped, allows for the combined use of the standards in an efficient and consistent manner.

---

24 http://www.unece.org/stats/archive/04.01d.e.htm.

7. Metadata in Germany

There has been much involvement from some German organizations in the development and use of metadata standards, and today, Germany is one of the leading countries in terms of adoption of the standards described in this paper. Our impression is that the increased recent interest in DDI and other standards such as SDMX is being driven at least partly by legislative changes regarding the exchange of data between state-sponsored institutes, but we are not familiar enough with German law to make any definite pronouncement. Certainly, German involvement in metadata standards has a long history.

The involvement of Germany in the creation of metadata standards focuses mostly on DDI – some German institutes such as GESIS (*Leibniz Institute for the Social Sciences*) were very involved in both the development of past versions of the standards and also in their implementation. The German Microcensus is a good example of how DDI was – and continues to be – used for data documentation, but there are many others.

More recently, some of the other German institutes involved in social sciences and economics have started using DDI and participating actively in the DDI community. Most notably at the Research Data Centers, where an application must be submitted to gain access to confidential data, there has been an increasing uptake of and interest in the use of DDI 3.0. This reflects an international trend, but thanks to the Research Data Centers and other research institutes, Germany is one of the most active countries in the use of DDI. At the IASSIST 2008[25] conference at Stanford University, the Institute for Employment Research (IAB, *Institut für Arbeitsmarkt und Berufsforschung*)[26] presented a prototype for using the DDI 3.0 metadata model as the basis for a documentation system that will serve both the Research Data Centers and the internal research departments. At the International Data Service Center of the Institute for the Study of Labor (IZA, *Forschungsinstitut zur Zukunft der Arbeit*)[27] in Bonn, DDI 2.1 is used as the standard metadata model, and in the future DDI 3.0 will be used.

One reason for Germany's leadership role within the social sciences metadata community is the hosting of DDI-related events for the past two years at Schloss Daghstul, the Leibniz Center for Informatics. Organized by GESIS, with some co-sponsors, seminars have been held to provide an in-depth understanding of DDI 3.0, and other DDI-related meetings have taken place on related themes (in 2008, the topic was DDI 3.0 best practices). These events took place in the fall of 2007 and 2008, and it appears that they

---

25 http://iassist08.stanford.edu.
26 http://www.iab.de/
27 http://idsc.iza.org/

will become an annual feature of the DDI community calendar. They have attracted attendees from all over the world.

In 2009, the first European DDI User's Group meeting will be hosted by IZA, which has also played a significant role in organizing the group. Thus, it can be seen that German institutes have had a significant role in the development and use of DDI, and this role appears to be growing with the advent of DDI 3.0.

SDMX has also been supported within Germany. The Federal Statistical Office in Wiesbaden was an early participant in the SDMX Open Data Interchange (SODI) project run by Eurostat, along with a small number of other European national statistical organizations. The European Central Bank in Frankfurt – although not a German organization as such, but a European one – is one of the sponsors of SDMX (along with the BIS,[28] the IMF,[29] the OECD,[30] Eurostat, the World Bank, and the UN Statistical Division), and was also a major user of the standard on which SDMX was based, GESMES/TS.

Increasingly, there is a growing interest in the exchange of research data and statistical data both within countries and across national borders. Metadata standards such as DDI and SDMX are a critical ingredient in facilitating these exchanges. Germany has emerged as one of the more forward-looking countries in this respect.

8. Directions, challenges, and recommendations

The availability of high-quality metadata promises to drive many positive changes within the social sciences in the near future. Better metadata allows for better use of technology, which can fundamentally impact what is possible for researchers: (1) data that is better documented, easier to find and use, and of greater consistency and higher quality; (2) heightened visibility for researchers' findings and the ability to replicate and validate those findings using the actual data and processes; (3) new techniques for identifying comparable datasets and an increased level of granularity in working with data from multiple sources; (4) improved tools for data management to assist data producers, librarians, and archives; (5) and the establishment of virtual research communities.

It is worth noting that important components of the technology suite needed to achieve these benefits are *Web services[31] based architectures* and

---

28 Bank for International Settlements.
29 International Monetary Fund.
30 Organisation for Economic Co-Operation and Development.
31 http://en.wikipedia.org/wiki/Web_service.

registries.[32] The first is the industry standard technology essential for allowing applications to effectively communicate with each other and exchange information. The second implements public catalogs for applications within a domain to facilitate searching and locating data and metadata resources wherever they are located on the Internet or network. This combination is essential to support the establishment of dynamic portals and federated spaces that provide users with a virtual view of the statistical information and effective mechanisms for timely publication of data, documents, and research outputs. It also unlocks powerful features such as notification services (whereby the information automatically flows towards its intended users, not the other way around), comparability and harmonization, researcher feedback, and community-driven knowledge spaces.

Another significant emerging idea is the concept of *enhanced publications*, which combine research findings, data, and metadata as a single package, providing support for the replication standard within the social sciences. Given a collection of such publications, it becomes possible to maintain linkages between primary and secondary datasets and publications, providing for richer comparisons and broader knowledge. Well-packaged information also allows for the use of data at the level of the variable, rather than just the monolithic dataset, supporting more granular comparison and exploration by topic.

These benefits will not be achieved without meeting some significant challenges, however. These can be broken down into three categories: (1) tools, (2) metadata quality, and (3) practice. Most agencies or individuals will likely confront issues in each of these areas, but it is important to know that they do not need to do so in isolation. Organizations such as the Open Data Foundation, the DDI Alliance, the IHSN and others are working towards bringing users together for the purpose of sharing resources and expertise to jointly address metadata challenges.

(1) *Tools:* An XML specification by itself is not something that can be used out of the box. It requires software to allow for the capture, storage, publication, and exchange of the metadata. Building such products can be an expensive effort, and this problem was recognized by the DDI and SDMX sponsors. To address the issue, several initiatives are ongoing for the development of open source solutions to facilitate the use and adoption of DDI and SDMX. The DDI Foundation Tools Program[33] aims at the implementation of a DDI 3.0 core framework and utilities for implementers as well as the production of a generic DDI 3.0 editor. The Open Data Foundation is working with its partners to release a free SDMX browser tool and provides a source code repository to anyone

---

32 http://en.wikipedia.org/wiki/Metadata_registry.
33 http://tools.ddialliance.org.

interested in developing open source software for social science metadata management. The IHSN has also developed a DDI 2 based Microdata Management Toolkit targeted at statistical agencies in developing countries.

We therefore recommend that anyone interested in adopting a metadata standard check with the relevant organizations regarding the availability of tools and even contribute to the joint development efforts.

(2) *Metadata quality:* Having tools available does not mean that the metadata will be sound and reliable. In the end, it is the content that counts, and compiling high-quality comprehensive metadata also requires good techniques, guidelines, and a significant amount of discipline. While some of the work can be automated or semi-automated using software utilities, it is often necessary to compile information by hand and chase down metadata to find the missing piece of knowledge or document. This is particularly true when the metadata is captured after the fact or after back-logging. This implies that human error and missing information are a factor. Quality assurance is therefore a very important aspect of metadata management, and any organizations adopting standards should thoroughly document these processes. As a general rule, metadata should be treated as an official publication and should therefore follow the same institutional rules.

Harmonization of practices across organizations also plays a major role when the metadata leaves the institution and is shared with users or other partners. If the same metadata elements are documented using different principles, they will no longer be coherent, which can confuse users, impact comparability, and reduce system interoperability.

Agencies such as the DDI Alliance, the IHSN, or SDMX sponsors produce generic guidelines and best practices for the preparation of metadata. They also work closely with metadata producers toward the harmonization of metadata elements. When looking into metadata quality assurance issues, we therefore suggest that users consult the existing websites and literature for references or join existing initiatives. We also recommend that agencies working in smaller communities actively collaborate on metadata harmonization.

(3) *Practice:* Adopting new standards and technologies implies a change in the way the organizations and individuals have been operating. While the benefits of a sound metadata management framework are extensive, this inevitably meets some resistance and requires a certain amount of resources to foster acceptance. Just because the tools and guidelines exist to help realize the benefits does not mean that people will use them. Researchers in particular are often reluctant to recognize that new techniques and discipline are necessary. Awareness, training, and integration

are all adoption issues facing researchers, archives, and data providers. Highlighting the benefits and providing incentives will be necessary to achieve successful integration.

Given the strong interest of data providers in metadata standards, we anticipate the adoption of DDI and SDMX to continue accelerating strongly in the coming years. A key to this success will be the availability of generic software tools. Sponsors and community-driven open source initiatives are expected to contribute a wide range of generic products for the management, publication, and sharing of metadata that will foster adoption of standards. These initial efforts will likely start to produce significant results in 2009–2010. In the meantime, statistical agencies and Research Data Centers with strong internal IT capacities will likely design their own tools in parallel to manage metadata. As the potential market grows in size, it is also possible that statistical packages or other commercial vendors will begin to provide solutions as well.

While the metadata will initially continue to emerge primarily from data archives, the uptake among producers should increase, improving overall quality as the information is captured closer to its source. Researchers will also likely begin to contribute to the metadata knowledge. Such end user adoption may be slow at first, but incentives and benefits should quickly overcome the resistance to change, and we should see an increase in user based metadata. This overall will foster the existence of shared knowledge spaces through metadata and bridge the communication gap that often exists between user and producer.

Given that many actors will now be contributing to the metadata, best practices and harmonization will play a crucial role in the overall quality and consistency of the information. Led by sponsors and major statistical agencies, national and international initiatives will likely emerge to draft metadata management guidelines and work towards the harmonization of common metadata elements. This will not only lead to improved metadata but will also foster better and more comparable data.

As more and more standard metadata is being produced, the need for exchange, sharing, and publication will quickly increase. As end users prefer to have single point of entry, national, regional, and international catalogs or registries will grow in importance. This aggregation of information will support the development of large collections of information that could potentially support complex searches and metadata mining operations. Note that such registries do not store the actual data. They act as "lookup points" that are used to retrieve the location where the information actually is (just like a phone or address book).

In order to foster broad adoption of metadata and related best practices in social sciences, we recommend the following:

(1) Promote the importance of high-quality data documentation and its capture using metadata standards.

(2) Familiarize producers, archives, and researchers with metadata standards, related best practices, and technologies.

(3) Support the development of standards-based tools, preferably under an open source license and aligned on community recommendations.

(4) Do not undertake metadata adoption activities in isolation. Instead, join and sponsor community or government-backed initiatives.

(5) For data and metadata managers and providers, support the establishment of an industry standard, Web service-oriented, and registry-based IT infrastructure to facilitate the management, exchange, reuse, and harmonization of metadata and data.

(6) Integrate metadata capture at all stages of the life cycle. Document events as they happen, not after the fact.

(7) Leverage on the availability of metadata to automate the production of documentation or generation of statistical scripts to reduce the overall production costs, increase quality, and deliver user-customized products.

(8) Support the establishment of virtual research and collaborative spaces to allow for user-driven metadata and foster community knowledge capture.

Overall, the future of social science metadata looks very bright. The availability of robust standards combined with modern technologies has laid the foundation of a global harmonized framework for the management of social science data and documentation. Just as the Internet has revolutionized and connected our world, social science metadata has the potential to open new possibilities for producers, archives, and users.

4. Paradata

Frauke Kreuter and Carolina Casas-Cordero

Contact:

Frauke Kreuter
University of Maryland
Joint Program in Survey Methodology
1218 Lefrak Hall
College Park, MD 20742
US
e-mail: fkreuter[at]survey.umd.edu

Abstract

Paradata – data about the process of survey production – have drawn increasing attention as the statistical world moves towards the implementation of quality metrics and measures to improve quality and save costs. This paper gives examples of various uses of paradata and discusses access to paradata, as well as future developments.

Keywords: paradata, process data, responsive design, measurement error, non-response, adjustment

1. Introduction

During the last two decades, survey researchers have begun to use computer-assisted methods to collect social science data. This trend is most obvious in web surveys, but is equally present in telephone surveys that use automated call scheduling systems or mail surveys that take advantage of logs provided by postal services. All of these systems produce data about the survey process as a by-product, which Mick Couper coined paradata in a presentation at the Joint Statistical Meeting in Dallas (Couper, 1998). Inspired by Couper's suggestions to use data automatically generated by computer-aided systems to evaluate survey quality, survey methodologists have since then broadened the concept of paradata to other aspects of the survey process and other modes of collection.

Data about survey process have drawn increasing attention as the statistical world moves towards the implementation of quality metrics, measures to improve quality and save costs, and a framework in which to measure total survey error (Biemer and Caspar 1994; Lyberg et al. 1997; Aitken et al. 2004; Couper and Lyberg 2005). Both data users and data producers are now aware of the potential benefits of paradata. This has been reflected by growing interest at invited paper sessions at international conferences such as the International Workshop on Household Survey Nonresponse, bi-annual conferences of the European Survey Research Association (ESRA), annual conferences of the American Association of Public Opinion Research (AAPOR), Joint Statistical Meetings (JSM), and the Sessions of the International Statistical Institute (ISI), as well as the quality conferences co-organized by Eurostat.

2. Examples for paradata and their use

There is no standard definition in the literature of what constitutes paradata. Several papers attempt to systematize data that are not part of the actual interview (Scheuren 2000; Couper and Lyberg 2005; Scheuren 2005; O'Reilly 2009), but each of these papers varies slightly in terminology and in what is considered paradata. Paradata was originally conceptualized as the data automatically generated as the by-product of the computer-assisted survey process (e.g., call record data and keystrokes), but the term has more recently been expanded to include information that may be recorded by interviewers (e.g., observations), or captured through additional systems (e.g., digital audio recording) (Couper 1998).

For this review we do not seek to provide a fixed definition of paradata. What is important in our opinion is the concept of data collected during and about the survey process. These data can be used to understand and improve the process (and subsequently the end result). Thus, instead of a definition, we give some examples of how paradata is currently being used around the world.

One set of data typically referred to as paradata are call records collected during the process of contacting a sample case. The time of contact (day and time), as well as the outcome of a call (non-contact, refusal, ineligible, interview, appointment, etc.) are almost always available on these call records (Heerwegh et al. 2007; Blom et al. forthcoming). These variables are either recorded by the interviewer (with PAPI or CAPI systems) or automatically, as is commonly the case for call schedulers in computer-aided telephone interviews (CATI). The recording of the date and time of a prior contact allows call schedulers to vary contact attempts with the hope of increasing the probability of a successful contact (Weeks et al. 1987; Kulka and Weeks 1998; Greenberg and Stokes 1990; Stokes and Greenberg 1990; Brick et al. 1996; Sangster and Meekins 2004; Wagner and Raghunathan 2007), and ideally to reduce the cost (Groves 1989; Triplett 2002; Murphy et al. 2003). Prominent examples of call record data collected in face-to-face surveys are the Contact History Instrument (CHI) implemented in surveys by the US Census Bureau (Bates 2003), or the standard contact forms that have been requisite since round one of the European Social Survey (Stoop et al. 2003). In some instances, call record data are used to guide decisions on responsive or two-phase sampling designs (Groves et al. 2003; Kennickell 2003; Groves and Heeringa 2006; Eckman and O'Muircheartaigh 2008), or to gain knowledge about optimal calling patterns in face-to-face surveys in general (Matsuo et al. 2006; Durrant et al. 2009). To our knowledge, there is so far only one survey, the US National Survey of Family Growth (Lepkowski et al. 2009), in which call record data from face-to-face surveys are used to drive centralized day-to-day field decisions similar to those in supervised call centers. For most surveys, face-to-face call record data are analyzed after the fact to assess interviewer efforts and compliance with pre-specified design requests (Billiet and Pleysier 2007; Lipps 2007; Koch et al. 2009).

Regardless of the mode of data collection, survey methodologists use call record data to study various aspects of survey participation. Call record data are available for both respondents and non-respondents to nay given survey and are thus prime candidates for the study of nonresponse bias, for example, through level-of-effort analyses, in which early respondents are compared to late responders assuming that later responders are more similar to non-responders than early responders (Stinchcombe et al. 1981; Smith 1984; Schnell, 1998; Kennickell 1999; Chiu et al. 2001; Duhart et al. 2001; Lynn et al. 2002; Lynn 2003; Wang et al. 2005; Stoop 2005; Voogt and Saris 2005; Billiet et al. 2007; for a meta-analysis of the results, see Olson 2010). With the goal of assessing net quality gains, researchers have used call record data to shed light on the relationship between nonresponse and measurement error (Green 1991; Yan et al. 2004; Olson 2006; Peytchev and Peytcheva 2007; Yu and Yan 2007).

A second set of data subsumed under the concept of paradata is also collected during the initial phase of establishing contact and convincing sample units to participate in the survey. These paradata are observations made by the interviewer. Like call record data, these interviewer observations are available on all sampled cases and thus suitable to inform survey design decisions (Copas and Farewell 1998; Lynn 2003; Groves et al. 2007) and assess nonresponse bias (Maitland et al. 2009). In recent face-to-face surveys, interviewers are charged with collecting observations of neighborhoods and housing unit characteristics in a number of surveys usually along the lines suggested by Campanelli et al. (1997), Groves and Couper (1998), or Lynn (2003). Examples are the US Health and Retirement Study, the US Study of Early Child Care, the US Survey of Consumer Finances, the US National Survey on Drug Use and Health, the British Election Study, the British Crime Survey, the British Social Attitudes Survey, the European Social Survey, and the Survey of Health, Ageing and Retirement in Europe. Some rather novel interviewer observations are those that are tailored to the survey topic and thus have higher potential to be useful for adaptive survey design decisions or nonresponse adjustment. Again, a prime example is the National Survey of Family Growth, in which interviewers are asked to guess whether or not the sample person is currently in an active sexual relationship (with an opposite-sex partner), and whether or not children are present in the household Groves et al. (2007). Other sets of interviewer observations made at the doorstep are those capturing the interaction between interviewer and respondent and respondents' reasons for refusal (Campanelli et al. 1997; Bates and Piani 2005; Bates et al. 2008).

Both call record data and interviewer observations have the potential to enhance current nonresponse adjustments. Not only are they available for both respondents and nonrespondents, but ideally are they predictive of the sampled person's probability of responding to a survey and of the survey variables of interest. Over the years, survey methodologists have extensively researched and developed covariates of survey participation (Schnell, 2005; Groves and Couper 1998), many of which are now part of call record and contact data forms. The possibility of using call record data for nonresponse adjustment has been discussed for quite some time (Drew and Fuller 1980; Potthoff et al. 1993), and current papers demonstrate the relationship between information in call records and the probability of responding to a survey request (Beaumont 2005; Biemer and Wang 2007; Blom 2009; Kreuter and Kohler 2009). Interviewer observations of variables close to the survey (such as the presence of children in a fertility survey) can complement call record data in response propensity models due to their likely stronger relationship to survey variables of interest (Kreuter et al. 2010). Difficult issues in modeling may, however, arise when strong predictors of response are combined with strong predictors of survey outcome variables (Kreuter and Olson 2010).

In computer-aided surveys, a third set of paradata can be captured: audio-recordings of the interaction between interviewer and respondent. Researchers have suggested that vocal characteristics of the respondent and interviewer are in part responsible for successful recruitment attempts. Especially during telephone interviews, potential respondents have very little information about the interviewer, aside from how he/she sounds, speaks, and interacts when they decide whether or not to participate in a telephone interview (Groves et al. 2007; Best et al. 2009). Yet interviewers vary widely in how often their invitations lead to participation, suggesting that potential respondents may give considerable weight to interviewers' verbal attributes. Recordings and paradata derived from them are of interest, not only because they can shed light on survey participation, but also because they can be used to assess measurement errors on a question level (Jans 2010). Recordings become more common as digital storage becomes less expensive (Couper 2005; Thissen et al. 2007). However, the post-processing of such recordings into usable paradata is a large task and has been undertaken in only a few methodological studies. Those studies make use of recent developments in the field of acoustical engineering and new software, which makes it possible for researchers to automatically process audio files and obtain objective data on voice characteristics such as disfluencies, pauses, interruptions, speech rate, and pitch (Jans 2010; Conrad et al. 2010).

In addition to audio-recordings, computer-assisted survey instruments facilitate the automated collection of paradata that can be used to assess measurement error at the question level. Most data collection software records the time used to complete a question, a set of questions, or the whole interview (response times), and capture key strokes, with which researchers can, for example, measure how often a respondent backed up and changed an answer and whether supplementary definitions are used (Couper 1998). All of these measures are available for computer-aided personal interviews (CAPI), computer-aided telephone interviews (CATI) and Web surveys. Web surveys also differentiate between paradata that include characteristics of a respondent browser captured from server logs (server-side paradata) and respondent behavior captured by embedding JavaScript code into the instrument (client-side paradata). Response times and key stroke measures have been used to study aspects of the response process (Bassili and Fletcher 1991; Kreuter, 2002; Heerwegh 2003; Kaminska and Billiet 2007; Yan and Tourangeau 2008; Couper et al., 2009; Lenzner et al. 2009; Peytchev 2009), to guide interventions in Web surveys (Conrad et al. 2009), evaluate interviewers (Couper et al. 1997; Mockovak and Powers 2008), and review the performance of questions in pretests (Couper 2000; Stern 2008; Hicks et al. 2009).

Our list of examples is by no means complete, but it does give a flavor of the many uses of data auxiliary to the main data collection that contain information about the process with which the data are collected. There is, in addition, an entirely different usage of paradata beyond monitoring, managing, modeling, and improving the data collection process. Summary statistics of paradata are also used to describe the dataset as a whole: response rates (created out of recordings of the final status in call records) are examples of such survey-level statistics. While paradata contribute to such summary statistics, the summary statistics themselves are usually not referred to as paradata but called metadata instead (Couper and Lyberg 2005; Scheuren 2005).

Auxiliary data available on the case level that come from an entirely different source are also usually not considered paradata (i.e., administrative data, data from commercial lists, or data available on sampling frames). A more borderline case are separate surveys of the interviewers themselves (Siegel and Stimmel 2007). To the extent that information from interviewers can help to understand the survey process, they can be viewed as paradata (like interviewer observations, for example). Metadata and auxiliary data also play increasing roles in monitoring and enhancing data quality. For some recent initiatives in using such auxiliary data, see Smith (2007; 2009).

2.1 Databases and data access

Unlike survey data themselves and metadata about those surveys, paradata are usually not made publicly available for several reasons. For one, it is not common to release gross-sample data, i.e., data records that include all sampled units, both those that respond to the survey request and those that do not. Second, paradata are often not collected on the same unit of analysis as the survey data are, making the release of such datasets more complicated. Call record data are usually collected at each call attempt, which could easily generate up to fifty records for cases fielded in a telephone survey. Response times are collected at an item level and sometimes twice within one item (if the time to administer the item is measured separately from the time the respondent took to answer the question). Vocal properties of an interviewer are recorded on a finer level and could generate several records even within the administration of a single item. Third, the format of these paradata varies a great deal by data collection agency and system: for example, outcome codes on call record data vary across agencies and modes of contact available to the interviewer (Blom et al. 2008). While the lack of standards for the collection and release of paradata is not a problem per se (except for making data preparation work more burdensome for analysts), it does require proper documentation, which is usually not covered by data collection grants. Fourth, for some of the paradata, there are open legal and ethical questions. Detailed observations of the neighborhood or housing unit might facilitate the de-identification of survey respondents. For Web surveys, Couper and Singer (2009) raise the question of whether respondents should be informed about the capturing of client-side paradata in particular if they are used to understand or even control respondent behavior, and not just used for improvement of the design or performance of the instrument.

Some important surveys do release their paradata to the public. Examples are contact protocol data from the European Social Survey, paradata from the US National Health Interview Survey, and paradata from the American National Election Survey (the latter being available for secondary analysis upon request).

3. Future developments

3.1 Data provision

As the previous section showed, the potential uses of paradata are wide-ranging. Survey methodologists have started to exploit paradata to guide intervention decisions during data collection and to provide opportunities for cost savings. To the extent that errors cannot be prevented, paradata also help us to detect errors after the fact (thus providing guidance for the next survey) and to model and adjust for them. So far, a series of paradata have been used to assess or model measurement error, nonresponse error, and even the interaction of the two. Until now, very few paradata have been collected for other parts of the process. If we match the most commonly collected paradata to the various error sources in a total survey error framework (see figure 1), we see that for several process steps in the generation of survey statistics, no paradata are currently available. The systematic documentation of questionnaire development by Schnell et al. (2008) could lead to new paradata for the creation of measurement indicators.

From a quality monitoring and improvement perspective, a more structured approach towards the selection, measurement, and analysis of key process variables would be desirable (Morganstein and Marker 1997). Ideally, survey researchers would specify a set of product characteristics and underlying processes associated with these characteristics, and then these processes would be checked by means of key process variables.

The virtue of paradata as a by-product of the survey process is that they come cheap to the data collector. If paradata are used systematically for process improvement and postprocess analyses, then their structure will probably change: variables will be added (e.g., new interviewer observations) and requests for standardization might turn out to conflict with existing collection systems. Paradata might then no longer be just a by-product, but a product with costs attached to it. It is up to survey methodologists to prove that paradata provide the cost control (or even cost savings) and performance increases that they have promised. Without the demonstration of repeated and successful use, survey methodologists will face difficulties in convincing data collection agencies to routinely collect such data.

One obstacle to demonstrating the usefulness of paradata is the quality of the data itself. While paradata might help to address some of the errors present in survey data, the data may suffer from measurement error, missing data, etc. Interviewers can erroneously record certain housing unit characteristics, can misjudge features about the respondents, or can fail to record a contact attempt altogether (Casas-Cordero 2010; Sinibaldi 2010; West 2010). For example, it is possible that paradata are subject to high variation in the way the information is recorded by different interviewers (e.g., evaluation of the condition of the house relative to other houses in the area) or some interviewers may simply not place high priority on filling in the interviewer observation questionnaires because they are not paid for doing so. Some studies have shown high levels of missing data in interviewer observations, indicating a lack of data quality (Kreuter et al. 2007; Durrant et al. 2009). Such missings may occur, for example, if the interviewer does not have enough time or does not feel the need to fully record every contact attempt to the household. Likewise, scripts embedded in Web surveys can fail to install properly and client-side data are not captured as intended, and recordings of interviewer administered surveys can be inaudible due to background noise or loose microphones (McGee and Gray 2007; Sala et al. 2008).

Figure 1: Total Survey Error components and paradata for their assessment (modified graph from Groves et al. 2004)

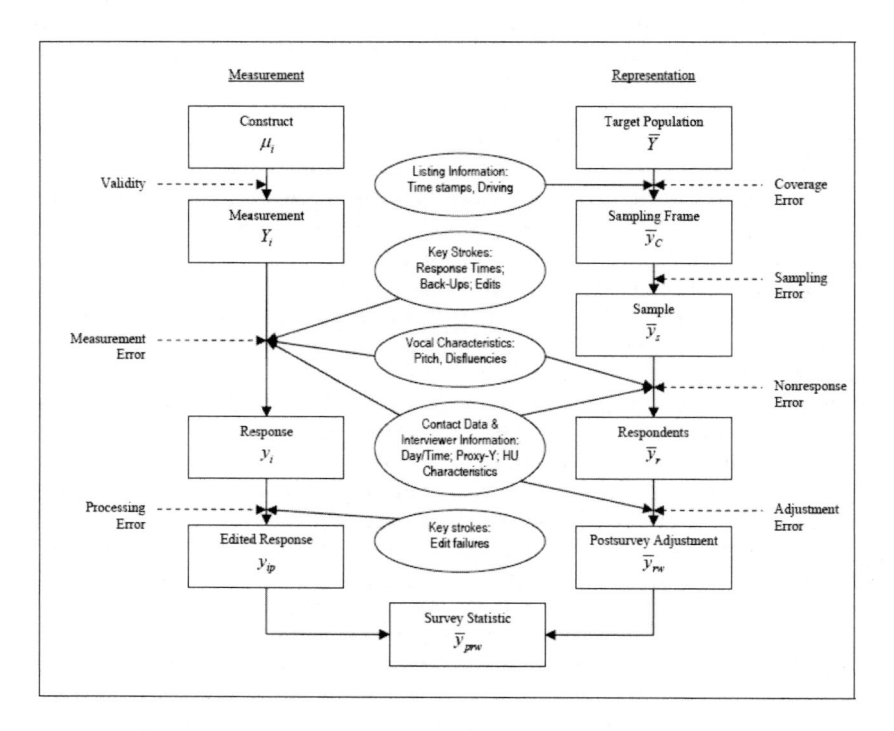

[Figure: Diagram showing Measurement side (Construct μ_i → Measurement Y_i → Response y_i → Edited Response y_{ip}) with errors Validity, Measurement Error, Processing Error; and Representation side (Target Population $\bar{Y}$ → Sampling Frame $\bar{y}_c$ → Sample $\bar{y}_s$ → Respondents $\bar{y}_r$ → Postsurvey Adjustment $\bar{y}_{rw}$) with Coverage Error, Sampling Error, Nonresponse Error, Adjustment Error; both converging to Survey Statistic $\bar{y}_{prw}$. Central paradata ovals: Listing Information: Time stamps, Driving; Key Strokes: Response Times; Back-Ups; Edits; Vocal Characteristics: Pitch, Disfluencies; Contact Data & Interviewer Information: Day/Time; Proxy-Y; HU Characteristics; Key strokes: Edit failures.]

As long as these recording errors and missing data patterns are not systematic, they will reduce the effectiveness of paradata for process improvement and error modeling, but should not threaten them altogether. If errors appear systematically (e.g., savvy users in Web surveys prevent scripts from capturing key strokes), resulting conclusions are threatened to be biased. Currently, not enough is known about the measurement error properties of paradata.

3.2 Data usage

As mentioned before, a key challenge to the use of paradata is their unusual data structure, with time-dependent observations on multiple levels collected through various modes with varying instruments. If we again take call record data as an example, the literature is still dominated by analyses using case-level aggregate statistics of call-level data (e.g., total number of contact attempts, total number of refusals), while some more recent examples take advantage of the multilevel structure by using survival models or multilevel discrete time event history models in predicting propensities to respond (Durrant and Steele 2009; Olson and Groves 2009; Wagner 2009).

Many methodological questions concerning how to make best use of paradata are still unsolved. In the estimation of response propensity models, we do not know yet if time should be modeled discretely as active day in the field or relative to the time since beginning of the field period. Nor is it clear how to best combine paradata into nonresponse propensity models with the aim of adjusting for survey nonresponse (Kreuter and Olson 2010). When dealing with response latencies, we do not yet know how best to handle unusually long response times, how best to model time dependency within the process of answering multiple subsequent survey questions, etc. Closer collaboration among survey methodologists, statisticians, and econometric modelers could benefit the research in this area.

Methodologists who use paradata for management and monitoring are still experimenting with tools for displaying the constant flow of process information. A "dashboard" was developed at the Institute for Social Research in Michigan (Groves et al. 2008; Lepkowski et al. 2009) to provide survey managers and principal investigators with timely access to data, and tools to facilitate decision-making – but there is still room for improvement (Couper 2009). The use of process control charts has been proposed before (Deming 1986; Morganstein and Marker 1997; Couper and Lyberg 2005), but so far, no standard charts have been developed to monitor survey data collection. Increased access to paradata and in particular timely update of such data streams will increase the need for good tools to display and analyze paradata.

3.3 Data access

To address the risk of de-identification of respondents, the paradata that pose this danger could be made available in Research Data Centers where access and usage of data is monitored. Given the potential of certain paradata to improve nonresponse adjustment, an entirely new data retrieval system might be worth considering. Given appropriate paradata, nonresponse adjustment can be tailored to individual analyses. Usually, only one set of nonresponse adjustment weights is created and distributed with survey data. Growing nonresponse has made the assumption that a single adjustment strategy is sufficient for all statistics produced by a survey less tenable. A data retrieval system could be conceptualized that allows the on-demand creation of adjustment weights based on the planned analysis.

Public access to paradata also allows a post-hoc examination of the procedures followed by the data collection institutes. If survey organizations are aware that process information will become public, this might lead overall to a higher data collection standard. Obviously higher-quality work will come with a price. However, some survey organizations might not want to release paradata, as it discloses information about their fieldwork procedures. If these procedures are considered to be proprietary, the disclosure could be seen as an impingement on their comparative advantage.

4. Discussion

Survey data collection is essentially a production process with a product. Surveys do not differ in this respect from other organizations that produce products or services and are concerned about their quality. Management strategies for such organizations have moved to what are called continuous quality improvement methods (Imai 1986; Deming 1986), in which measures of the process are monitored along the way so that error sources can be located and interventions planned (examples of such strategies are Total Quality Method, TQM, or Six Sigma). Several researchers have suggested the application of such strategies to the process of survey operations (Biemer and Caspar 1994; Morganstein and Marker 1997). Paradata, as discussed here, can play an important role in the application of such strategies. The European Statistical System has developed a handbook on improving quality through the analysis of paradata (Aitken et al. 2004), but the work is still not done, and individual surveys might do well to identify key process variables for their specific circumstances (Couper and Lyberg 2005).

Survey data collection faces major uncertainties in the planning stages. It is difficult to estimate the effectiveness of measures taken to establish contact with households, identify eligible persons, select a respondent, gain that person's cooperation, and complete the interview. Likewise, estimates of the cost implications of any of these steps are often difficult to make. Responsive designs (Groves and Heeringa 2006) seek to address this uncertainty by measuring the results of various survey design features, often experimentally, and then use these measurements to intervene in the field data collection process. This monitoring includes both the paradata as well as key survey estimates. To the extent that the paradata provide information about the risk of nonresponse bias, the responsive design is capable of reducing the risk of this bias. Much more effort is needed to manage the costs of alternative design features.

To increase the conditions for high-quality collection of paradata, a survey climate is necessary that allows for experimental manipulation within the field process. Pooling data across studies can also help to disentangle confounding elements; for this, some standardization of paradata would be necessary (Blom et al. 2008). Panel data enjoy the luxury of repeated measures of observations. Researchers only recently started to explore the potential of paradata to examine attrition (Lepkowski and Couper 2002; Kreuter and Jäckle 2008) and measurement error in relation to interviewer characteristics (Jaeckle et al. 2009; Weinhardt and Kreuter 2009; Yan and Datta 2009).

Compared to other countries, data collection in Germany is not as "paradata-rich" as it could be. Since 1995, Schnell and his colleagues suggested the inclusion of contact protocol data for the gross sample to be a standard deliverable (Schnell et al. 1995). Very few surveys followed this suggestion. Furthermore, systems should be developed and put in place that allow data collection agencies to engage in data-driven interventions into the fieldwork process. For a single survey, the start-up costs might be too high and survey organizations might not see the need for such investments. If, however, the German social science data community as a whole demands paradata for process controls, investments in the respective systems might be economical. Investment into the development of new statistical tools and methods is also needed to help make sense of the vast amount of unstructured paradata generated by modern survey process. The standard analytic tools we use for survey data are not appropriate for much of the paradata we need to analyze. Here, too, collaboration throughout the social science data community would be a good first step.

References:

Aitken, A./Hörngren, J./Jones, N./Lewis, D. and Zilhão, M.J. (2004): Handbook on improving quality by analysis of process variables. Technical report, Eurostat.

Bassili, J.N. and Fletcher, J.F. (1991): Response-time measurement in survey research a method for CATI and a new look at nonattitudes. Public Opinion Quarterly 55 (3), 331-346.

Bates, N. (2003): Contact histories in personal visit surveys: The Survey of Income and Program Participation (SIPP) methods panel. In: Proceedings of the Section on Survey Research Methods of the American Statistical Association.

Bates, N./Dahlhamer, J. and Singer, E. (2008): Privacy concerns, too busy, or just not interested: Using doorstep concerns to predict survey nonresponse. Journal of Official Statistics 24 (4), 591-612.

Bates, N. and Piani, A. (2005): Participation in the National Health Interview Survey: Exploring reasons for reluctance using contact history process data. In: Proceedings of the Federal Committee on Statistical Methodology (FCSM) Research Conference.

Beaumont, J. (2005): On the use of data collection process information for the treatment of unit nonresponse through weight adjustment. Survey Methodology 31 (2), 227-231.

Best, H./Bauer, G. and Steinkopf, L. (2009): Interviewer voice characteristics and productivity in telephone surveys. Paper presented at the European Survey Research Association (ESRA) Conference, Warsaw, Poland.

Biemer, P. and Caspar, R. (1994): Continuous quality improvement for survey operations: Some general principles and applications. Journal of Official Statistics 10 (3), 307-326.

Biemer, P. and Wang, K. (2007): Using callback models to adjust for nonignorable nonresponse in face-to-face surveys. In: Proceedings of the Section on Survey Research Methods of the American Statistical Association.

Billiet, J./Philippens, M./Fitzgerald, R. and Stoop, I. (2007): Estimation of nonresponse bias in the European Social Survey: Using information from reluctant respondents. Journal of Official Statistics 23 (2), 135-162.

Billiet, J. and Pleysier, S. (2007): Response based quality assessment in the ESS – Round 2. An update for 26 countries. Technical report, Center for Sociological Research (CeSO), K.U. Leuven.

Blom, A. (2009): Nonresponse bias adjustments: What can process data contribute? Iser working paper 2009-21, Institute of Social research (ISER), Essex University.

Blom, A./Lynn, P. and Jäckle, A. (2008): Understanding cross-national differences in unit nonresponse: The role of contact data. Technical report, Institute for Social and Economic Research ISER.

Blom, A./Lynn, P. and Jäckle, A. (forthcoming): Understanding cross-national differences in unit nonresponse: The role of contact data. In: Harkness, J.A./Edwards, B./Braun, M./Johnson, T.P./Lyberg, L.E./Mohler, P.P./Pennell, B.-E. and Smith, T. (Eds.): Survey Methods in Multinational, Multiregional, and Multicultural Contexts. New York.

Brick, J.M./Allen, B./Cunningham, P. and Maklan, D. (1996): Outcomes of a calling protocol in a telephone survey. In: Proceedings of the Section on Survey Research Methods of the American Statistical Association.

Campanelli, P./Sturgis, P. and Purdon, S. (1997): Can you hear me knocking: An investigation into the impact of interviewers on survey response rates. Technical report, The Survey Methods Centre at SCPR, London.

Casas-Cordero, C. (2010): Testing competing neighborhood mechanisms influencing participation in household surveys. Paper to be presented at the Annual Conference of the American Association of Public Opinion and Research (AAPOR), Chicago, IL.

Chiu, P./Riddick, H. and Hardy, A. (2001): A comparison of characteristics between late/difficult and non-late/difficult interviews in the National Health Interview Survey. In: Proceedings of the Section on Survey Research Methods of the American Statistical Association.

Conrad, F./Broome, J./Benki, J./Groves, R.M./Kreuter, F. and Vannette, D. (2010): To agree or not to agree: Effects of spoken language on survey participation decisions. Paper to be presented at the Annual Conference of the American Association of Public Opinion and Research (AAPOR), Chicago, IL.

Conrad, F./Couper, M./Tourangeau, R./Galesic, M. and Yan, T. (2009): Interactive feedback can improve accuracy of responses in web surveys. Paper presented at the European Survey Research Association (ESRA) Conference, Warsaw, Poland.

Copas, A. and Farewell, V. (1998): Dealing with non-ignorable nonresponse by using an 'enthusiasm-to-respond' variable. Journal of the Royal Statistical Society, Series A 161 (3), 385-396.

Couper, M. (1998): Measuring survey quality in a CASIC environment. In: Proceedings of the Section on Survey Research Methods of the American Statistical Association.

Couper, M. (2000): Usability evaluation of computer-assisted survey instruments. Social Science Computer Review 18 (4), 384-396.

Couper, M. (2005): Technology trends in survey data collection. Social Science Computer Review 23, 486-501.

Couper, M. (2009): Measurement error in objective and subjective interviewer observations. Modernisation of Statistics Production, Standardisation, Efficiency, Quality assurance and Customer Focus, 2-4 November 2009, Stockholm, Sweden.

Couper, M./Hansen, S. and Sadosky, S. (1997): Evaluating interviewer performance in a CAPI survey. In: Lyberg, L./Biemer, P./Collins, M./de Leeuw, E./Dippo, C./Schwarz, N. and Trewin, D. (Eds.): Survey Measurement and Process Quality. New York.

Couper, M. and Lyberg, L. (2005): The use of paradata in survey research. In: Proceedings of the 55th Session of the International Statistical Institute, Sydney, Australia.

Couper, M. and Singer, E. (2009): Ethical considerations in the use of paradata in web surveys. Paper presented at the European Survey Research Association (ESRA) Conference, Warsaw, Poland.

Couper, M./Tourangeau, R. and Marvin, T. (2009): Taking the audio out of Audio-CASI. Public Opinion Quarterly 73 (2), 281-303.

Deming, W. (1986): Out of the Crisis. Cambridge.
Drew, J. and Fuller, W. (1980): Modeling nonresponse in surveys with callbacks. In: Proceedings of the Section on Survey Research Methods of the American Statistical Association.
Duhart, D./Bates, N./Williams, B./Diffendal, G. and Chiu, P. (2001): Are late/difficult cases in demographic survey interviews worth the effort? A review of several federal surveys. In: Proceedings of the Federal Committee on Statistical Methodology (FCSM) Research Conference.
Durrant, G./D'Arrigo, J.and Steele, F. (2009): Using field process data to predict best times of contact conditioning on household and interviewer influences. Technical report, Southampton Statistical Science Research Institute.
Durrant, G. and Steele, F. (2009): Multilevel modelling of refusal and noncontact in household surveys: Evidence from six UK government surveys. Journal of the Royal Statistical Society, Series A 172 (2), 361-381.
Eckman, S. and O'Muircheartaigh, C. (2008): Optimal subsampling strategies in the General Social Survey. In: Proceedings of the Section on Survey Research Methods of the American Statistical Association.
Eifler, S./Thume, S. and Schnell, R. (2009): Unterschiede zwischen subjektiven und objektiven Messungen von Zeichen öffentlicher Unordnung. In: Weichbold, M./Bacher, J. and Wolf, Ch. (Eds.): Umfrageforschung. Herausforderungen und Grenzen. Wiesbaden. (Sonderheft 9 der Österreichischen Zeitschrift für Soziologie).
Green, K.E. (1991): Reluctant respondents: Differences between early, late and nonrespondents to a mail survey. Journal of Experimental Education 56, 268-276.
Greenberg, B. and Stokes, S. (1990): Developing an optimal call scheduling strategy for a telephone survey. Journal of Official Statistics 6 (4), 421-435.
Groves, R.M. (1989): Survey Errors and Survey Costs. New York.
Groves, R.M. and Couper, M. (1998): Nonresponse in Household Interview Surveys. New York.
Groves, R.M./Fowler, F./Couper, M. and Lepkowski, J. (2004): Survey Methodology. New York.
Groves, R.M. and Heeringa, S. (2006): Responsive design for household surveys: Tools for actively controlling survey errors and costs. Journal of the Royal Statistical Society, Series A 169 (3), 439-457.
Groves, R.M./Wagner, J. and Peytcheva, E. (2007): Use of interviewer judgments about attributes of selected respondents in post-survey adjustment for unit nonresponse: An illustration with the National Survey of Family Growth. In: Proceedings of the Section on Survey Research Methods of the American Statistical Association.
Groves, R.M./Kirgis, N./Peytcheva, E./Wagner, J./Axinn, B. and Mosher, W. (2008): Responsive design for household surveys: Illustration of management interventions based on survey paradata. NCRM Research Methods Festival, St Catherine's College, Oxford, UK.
Groves, R.M./Van Hoewyk, J./Benson, F./Schultz, P./Maher, P./Hoelter, L./Mosher, W./Abma, J. and Chandra, A. (2003): Using process data from computer-assisted face to face surveys to help make survey management decisions. Paper to be

presented at the Annual Conference of the American Association of Public Opinion and Research (AAPOR), Nashville, TN.

Heerwegh, D. (2003): Explaining response latencies and changing answers using client-side paradata from a web survey. Social Science Computer Review 21 (3), 360-373.

Heerwegh, D./Abts, K. and Loosveldt, G. (2007): Minimizing survey refusal and noncontact rates: Do our efforts pay off? Survey Research Methods 1 (1), 3-10.

Herget, D./Biemer, P./Morton, J. and Sand, K. (2005): Computer audio recorded interviewing (CARI): Additional feasibility efforts of monitoring field interview performance. Paper presented at the U.S. Federal Conference on Statistical Method.

Hicks, W./Edwards, B./Tourangeau, K./Branden, L./Kistler, D./McBride, B./Harris-Kojetin, L. and Moss, A. (2009): A system approach for using CARI in pretesting, evaluation and training. Paper presented at the FedCasic Conference, Delray Beach, FL.

Imai, M. (1986): Kaizen: The Key to Japan's Competitive Success. New York.

Jaeckle, A./Sinibaldi, J./Tipping, S./Lynn, P. and Nicolaas, G. (2009): Interviewer characteristics, their behaviours, and survey outcomes.

Jans, M. (2010): Verbal Paradata and Survey Error: Respondent Speech, Voice, and Question-Answering Behavior Can Predict Income Item Nonresponse. Ph.D. thesis, University of Michigan, United States.

Kaminska, O. and Billiet, J. (2007): Satisficing for reluctant respondents in a cross-national context. Paper presented at the European Survey Research Association (ESRA) Conference, Prague, Czech Republic.

Kennickell, A. (1999): What do the 'late' cases tell us? Evidence from the 1998 Survey of Consumer Finances. Paper presented at the International Conference on Survey Nonresponse, Portland, OR.

Kennickell, A. (2003): Reordering the darkness: Application of effort and unit nonrepsonse in the Survey of Consumer Finances. In: Proceedings of the Section on Survey Research Methods of the American Statistical Association.

Koch, A./Blom, A./Stoop, I. and Kappelhof, J. (2009): Data collection quality assurance in cross-national surveys: The example of the ESS. Methoden, Daten, Analysen 3 (2), 219-247.

Kreuter, F. (2002): Kriminalitätsfurcht: Messung und methodische Probleme. Opladen.

Kreuter, F. and Jäckle, A. (2008): Are contact protocol data informative for non-response bias in panel studies? A case study form the Northern Ireland subset of the British Household Panel Survey. Panel Survey Methods Workshop, University of Essex, Colchester, UK.

Kreuter, F. and Kohler, U. (2009): Analyzing contact sequences in call record data. Potential and limitation of sequence indicators for nonresponse adjustment in the European Social Survey. Journal of Official Statistics 25 (2), 203-226.

Kreuter, F./Lemay, M. and Casas-Cordero, C. (2007): Using proxy measures of survey outcomes in post-survey adjustments: Examples from the European Social Survey (ESS). In: Proceedings of the Section on Survey Research Methods of the American Statistical Association.

Kreuter, F. and Olson, K. (2010): Multiple auxiliary variables in nonresponse adjustment. [Manuscript under review].

Kreuter, F./Olson, K./Wagner, J./Yan, T./Ezzati-Rice, T./Casas-Cordero, C./Lemay, M./Peytchev, A./Groves, R.M. and Raghunathan, T. (2010): Using proxy measures and other correlates of survey outcomes to adjust for nonresponse: Examples from multiple surveys. Journal of the Royal Statistical Society, Series A.

Kulka, R. and Weeks, M. (1998): Toward the development of optimal calling protocols for telephone surveys: A conditional probabilities approach. Journal of Official Statistics 4 (4), 319-332.

Lenzner, T./Kaczmirek, L. and Lenzner, A. (2009): Cognitive burden of survey questions and response times: A psycholinguistic experiment. Applied Cognitive Psychology.

Lepkowski, J. and Couper, M. (2002): Nonresponse in longitudinal household surveys. In: Groves, R.M./Dillman, D./Eltinge, J. and Little, R. (Eds.): Survey Nonresponse. New York.

Lepkowski, J./Groves, R.M./Axinn, W./Kirgis, N. and Mosher, W. (2009): Use of paradata to manage a field data collection. In: Proceedings of the Section on Survey Research Methods of the American Statistical Association.

Lipps, O. (2007): Cooperation in centralised CATI panels – A contact based multilevel analysis to examine interviewer, respondent, and contact effects. Paper presented at the European Survey Research Association (ESRA) Conference, Prague, Czech Republic.

Lyberg, L./Biemer, P./Collins, M./de Leeuw, E./Dippo, C./Schwarz, N. and Trewin, D. (1997): Survey Measurement and Process Quality. New York.

Lynn, P. (2003): PEDAKSI: Methodology for collecting data about survey non-respondents. Quality and Quantity 37 (3), 239-261.

Lynn, P./Clarke, P./Martin, J. and Sturgis, P. (2002): The effects of extended interviewer efforts on nonresponse bias. In: Dillman, D./Eltinge, J./Groves, R.M. and Little, R. (Eds.): Survey nonresponse. New York.

Maitland, A./Casas-Cordero, C. and Kreuter, F. (2009): An evaluation of nonresponse bias using paradata from a health survey. In: Proceedings of the Section on Survey Research Methods of the American Statistical Association.

Matsuo, H./Loosveldt, G. and Billiet, J. (2006): The history of the contact procedure and survey cooperation – Applying demographic methods to European Social Survey contact forms round 2 in Belgium. Louvain-la-Neuve, Belgium. Paper presented at the Quetelet Conference.

McGee, A. and Gray, M. (2007): Designing and using a behaviour code frame to assess multiple styles of survey items. Technical report, National Centre for Social Research (NatCen), London, UK.

Mockovak, W. and Powers, R. (2008): The use of paradata for evaluating interviewer training and performance. In: Proceedings of the Section on Survey Research Methods of the American Statistical Association.

Morganstein, D. and Marker, D. (1997): Continuous quality improvement in statistical agencies. In: Lyberg, L./Biemer, P./Collins, M./de Leeuw, E./Dippo, C./Schwarz, N. and Trewin, D. (Eds.): Survey Measurement and Process Quality. New York.

Murphy, W./O'Muircheartaigh, C./Emmons, C./Pedlow, S. and Harter, R. (2003): Optimizing call strategies in RDD: Differential nonresponse bias and costs in

REACH 2010. In: Proceedings of the Section on Survey Research Methods of the American Statistical Association.

Olson, K. (2006): Survey participation, nonresponse bias, measurement error bias, and total bias. Public Opinion Quarterly 70 (5), 737-758.

Olson, K. (2010): When do nonresponse follow-ups improve or reduce data quality? A synthesis of the existing literature. [Manuscript].

Olson, K. and Groves, R.M. (2009): The lifecycle of response propensities in fertility and family demography surveys. Paper presented at the annual meeting of the Population Association of America, Detroit, MI.

O'Reilly, J. (2009): Paradata and Blaise: A review of recent applications and research. Paper presented at the International Blaise Users Conference (IBUC), Latvia.

Peytchev, A. (2009): Survey breakoff. Public Opinion Quarterly 73 (1), 74-97.

Peytchev, A. and Peytcheva, E. (2007): Relationship between measurement error and unit nonresponse in household surveys: An approach in the absence of validation data. In: Proceedings of the Section on Survey Research Methods of the American Statistical Association.

Potthoff, R.,/Manton, K. and Woodbury, M. (1993): Correcting for nonavailability bias in surveys by weighting based on number of callbacks. Journal of the American Statistical Association 88 (424), 1197-1207.

Sala, E./Uhrig, S. and Lynn, P. (2008): The development and implementation of a coding scheme to analyse interview dynamics in the British Household Panel Survey. Technical report, Institute for Social and Economic Research ISER, University of Essex.

Sangster, R. and Meekins, B. (2004): Modeling the likelihood of interviews and refusals: Using call history data to improve efficiency of effort in a national RDD survey. In: Proceedings of the Section on Survey Research Methods of the American Statistical Association.

Scheuren, F. (2000): Macro and micro paradata for survey assessment. [Manuscript].

Scheuren, F. (2005): Paradata from concept to completion. In: Proceedings of the Statistics Canada Symposium. Methodological Challenges for Future Information Needs.

Schnell, R. (1998): Besuchs- und Berichtsverhalten der Interviewer. In: Statistisches Bundesamt (Ed.): Interviewereinsatz und –qualifikation. Stuttgart.

Schnell, R. (2005): Nonresponse in Bevölkerungsumfragen. Opladen. www.ub.uni-konstanz.de/kops/volltexte/2008/5614. [Last visited: 03/10/2010].

Schnell, R./Hill, P. and Esser, E. (1995): Methoden der empirischen Sozialforschung. 5th Edition [latest edition 2008]. Munic.

Schnell, R./Krause, J./Stempfhuber, M./Zwingenberger, A. and Hopt, O. (2008): Softwarewerkzeuge zur Dokumentation der Fragebogenentwicklung – QDDS – 2. Technical report, Endbericht des Projekts an die DFG.

Siegel, N. and Stimmel, S. (2007): SOEP-Interviewerbefragung 2006. Methodenbericht. Technical report, Munich.

Sinibaldi, J. (2010): Measurement error in objective and subjective interviewer observations. Paper to be presented at the Annual Conference of the American Association of Public Opinion and Research (AAPOR), Chicago, MI.

Smith, T. (1984): Estimating nonresponse bias with temporary refusals. Sociological Perspectives 27 (4), 473-489.

Smith, T. (2007): The Multi-level Integrated Database Approach (MIDA) for improving response rates: Adjusting for nonresponse error, and contextualizing analysis. Paper presented at the European Survey Research Association (ESRA) Conference, Prague, Czeck Republic.

Smith, T. (2009): The Multi-level Integrated Database Approach for detecting and adjusting for nonresponse bias. Paper presented at the European Survey Research Association (ESRA) Conference, Warsaw, Poland.

Stern, M. (2008): The use of client-side paradata in analyzing the effects of visual layout on changing responses in web surveys. Field Methods 20 (4), 377-398.

Stinchcombe, A./Jones, C. and Sheatsley, P. (1981): Nonresponse bias for attitude questions. Public Opinion Quarterly 45, 359-375.

Stokes, S. and Greenberg, B. (1990): A priority system to improve callback success in telephone surveys. In: Proceedings of the Section on Survey Research Methods of the American Statistical Association.

Stoop, I. (2005): The Hunt for the Last Respondent. The Hague.

Stoop, I./Devacht, S./Billiet, J./Loosveldt, G. and Philippens, M. (2003): The development of a uniform contact description form in the ESS. Paper presented at the International Workshop for Household Survey Nonresponse, Leuven, Belgium.

Thissen, R./Sattaluri, S./McFarlane, E. and Biemer, P.P. (2007): Evolution of audio recording in field surveys. Paper presented at The American Association for Public Opinion Research (AAPOR) 62th Annual Conference.

Triplett, T. (2002): What is gained from additional call attempts and refusal conversion and what are the cost implications? Technical report, The Urban Institute, Washington DC.

Voogt, R. and Saris, W. (2005): Mixed mode designs: Finding the balance between nonresponse bias and mode effects. Journal of Official Statistics 21, 367-387.

Wagner, J. (2009): Adaptive contact strategies in a telephone survey. In: Proceedings of the Federal Committee on Statistical Methodology (FCSM) Research Conference.

Wagner, J. and Raghunathan, T. (2007): Bayesian approaches to sequential selection of survey design protocols. In: Proceedings of the Section on Survey Research Methods of the American Statistical Association.

Wang, K./Murphy, J./Baxter, R. and Aldworth, J. (2005): Are two feet in the door better than one? Using process data to examine interviewer effort and nonresponse bias. In: Proceedings of the Federal Committee on Statistical Methodology (FCSM) Research Conference.

Weeks, M./Kulka, R. and Pierson, S. (1987): Optimal call scheduling for a telephone survey. Public Opinion Quarterly 51, 540-549.

Weinhardt, M. and Kreuter, F. (2009): The different roles of interviewers: How does interviewer personality affect respondents' survey participation and response behavior?

West, B. (2010): An examination of the quality and utility of interviewer estimates of household characteristics in the National Survey of Family Growth. Paper to be presented at the Annual Conference of the American Association of Public Opinion and Research (AAPOR), Chicago, MI.

Yan, T. and Datta, R. (2009): Estimating the value of project-specific and respondent specific interviewer experience: Evidence from longitudinal and repeated cross-section surveys.

Yan, T. and Tourangeau, R. (2008): Fast times and easy questions: The effects of age, experience and question complexity on web survey response times. Applied Cognitive Psychology 22 (1), 51-68.

Yan, T./Tourangeau, R. and Arens, Z. (2004): When less is more: Are reluctant respondents poor reporters? In: Proceedings of the Section on Survey Research Methods of the American Statistical Association.

Yu, M. and Yan, T. (2007): Are nonrespondents necessarily bad reporters? Using imputation techniques to investigate measurement error of nonrespondents in an alumni survey. In: Proceedings of the Section on Survey Research Methods of the American Statistical Association.

5. Record Linkage from a Technical Point of View

Rainer Schnell

Contact:

Rainer Schnell
University of Duisburg-Essen
Institute for Sociology
Lotharstr. 65
47057 Duisburg
Germany
e-Mail: rainer.schnell[at]uni-due.de

Abstract

Record linkage is used in preparing sampling frames, deduplicating lists, and combining information from two different databases on the same object. If the identifiers of the same objects in two different databases have error-free unique common identifiers like personal identification numbers (PID), record linkage is a simple file merge operation. If the identifiers contain errors, record linkage is a challenging task. In many applications, the numbers of observations in the files differ widely: a sample survey may contain a few thousand records while an administrative database of social security numbers may contain a few million. Available software, privacy issues, and future research topics are discussed.

Keywords: record linkage, data mining, privacy-preserving protocols

1. Introduction

Record linkage seeks to identify the same objects in two different databases using a set of common identifiers.[1] If the files have error-free unique common identifiers like personal identification numbers (PID), record linkage is a simple file merge operation. If the identifiers contain errors, record linkage is a challenging task. In many applications, the numbers of observations in the files differ widely: a sample survey may contain a few thousand records while an administrative database of social security numbers may contain a few million. Most research applications of record linkage use the linking process to prepare sampling frames, deduplicate lists, and combine information from two different databases on the same object.[2]

2. Current applications

Searching for the keyword "record linkage" will currently yield a few thousand papers on applications in medicine (mainly epidemiology), but only a few dozen papers in the social sciences. Nevertheless, record linkage is often used by social science research organizations as part of their fieldwork

---

1   The term "record linkage" is the one most commonly used by statisticians. In computer science, there are a variety of different terms for this process: "deduplication," "reconciliation," and "merge/purge processing."

2   Record linkage tries to identify the same objects in two databases. Do not confuse record linkage with statistical matching: statistical matching (or data fusion) tries to find records of very similar values for different objects; thereby deliberately joining data files with no common objects. For applications of statistical matching, see D'Orazio et al. (2006).

activities; in many such cases the client does not even know that a record linkage process has been used. In practice, constructing sampling frames often implies linking records from different databases referring to the same entities, such as names, addresses, birthdates, phone numbers, and geodata.[3] Record linkage is often used to combine information based on a survey with information from a database. This is often the case with business surveys, where information on the performance, size, and type of business are combined with business survey data through record linkage.[4]

Record linkage may be used to build panels after data collection, for example by using historical data as in the Victorian Panel Study (VPS). The VPS is intended as a longitudinal dataset based on the British censuses from 1851 to 1901 (Crockett et al.: 2006). Such linkages are possible in many cases, even without the use of unique personal identifiers. One such application is the Statistical Longitudinal Census Dataset (SLCD). The Australian Bureau of Statistics (ABS) will build the SLCD by linking a 5 percent sample of people from the 2006 population census to subsequent censuses. To minimize privacy problems, the ABS will link records without using names or addresses (Bishop and Khoo 2006). Record linkage is also an essential tool for conducting general censuses, and indeed is the most important tool used in registry-based censuses – like the German Census in 2011 – where record linkage is required to estimate coverage rates.[5] As a final example, in nonresponse research, linking the data of nonrespondents to administrative data files is one of the few methods of assessing nonresponse bias with empirical data.

3. Record linkage process

Record linkage is the process of linking two files that contain data on the same entity using common identifiers. This process follows a standard sequence (see figure 1). Usually, the identifiers must be standardized, which is called "pre-processing." Since the number of comparisons is generally too high to be computed directly, the computations are split up between disjunct subsets of observations (called "blocks") and repeated for different blocking criteria.[6] The similarity of records within a block is computed using similarity functions, most often today either with an edit-distance or Jaro-Winkler

---

3 Some examples for German surveys may be found in Schnell (2008).
4 Details on such application can be found in a paper by Winkler (1995).
5 There is a rich literature on using record linkage for census undercount estimates, starting with Winkler/Thibaudeau (1991) and Ding/Feinberg (1996).
6 For example, in a cancer registry, persons living within an area with a common postal code are treated as a block.

string similarity function.[7] Then a decision has to be made on thresholds of similarity: records above a threshold are considered as a link; records below the threshold are considered as a non-link. Records between the thresholds are usually submitted for clerical review. The statistically most interesting part of the process is the decision on which pairs of elements in the two files to consider as true links. This decision may be made based on different computational models, for example, classification trees (CART), support vector classifiers (SVM), or statistical decision rules.[8] Most record linkage programs today use a probabilistic decision rule based on the model proposed by Fellegi/Sunter (1969). The parameters of the model are usually estimated by some variant of an EM algorithm (Herzog et al.: 2007). Special situations (for example, a known one-to-one correspondence between the two files) require modifications of the decision rules.

Figure 1: The linking process

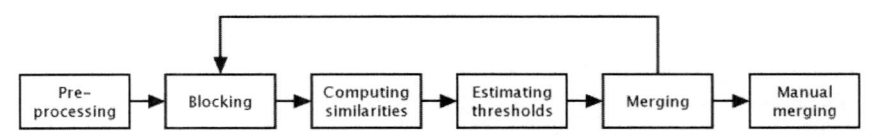

Pre-processing → Blocking → Computing similarities → Estimating thresholds → Merging → Manual merging

4. Available software

There are many record linkage systems available. Most of these are special purpose programs for use in official statistics or cancer registries.[9] Furthermore, there are a few commercial programs for office applications. Of course, there also exist academic proof-of-concept implementations of special algorithms. In the following, the historically most important program and three contemporary programs in the public domain will be described in some detail.

---

[7] Details on the computation and performance of string similarity functions can be found in Herzog et al. (2007) and Schnell et al. (2003).
[8] Detail on SVMs and CART can be found in any textbook on statistical learning, for example, Bishop (2006).
[9] A highly selective review from an official statistics point of view can be found in Herzog et al. (2007), which also includes a list of criteria that should be used in evaluations of record-linkage software.

4.1 Automatch

The most widely known probabilistic record linkage program is "Automatch." The last version (4.2) was released in 1992. Automatch is now a part of a large collection of programs (IBM's "WebSphere QualityStage") and cannot be licensed or purchased as a stand-alone program. The cost of the IBM Web-Sphere is far beyond the scope of research groups; therefore Automatch is no longer used in research contexts. Only a few cancer registries use the old DOS version of Automatch with special permission from IBM. Automatch is often used to validate the other programs. It should be noted that the limitations of old DOS programs have been evaded by some clever programming shortcuts; therefore Automatch is not a perfect baseline for comparisons.

4.2 Link Plus

Link Plus is primarily a probabilistic record linkage program for cancer registries. The program has been developed for the "National Program of Cancer Registries" (NPCR) of the Center for Disease Control and Prevention. It is a Windows-based program for detecting duplicates and linking cancer registry files with external files.[10] The program offers different similarity functions and phonetic encodings. Furthermore, it handles missing data and special cases like middle initials.[11]

4.3 Link King

"Link King" is an SAS-based probabilistic record linkage program developed by Kevin M. Campbell. The program requires a base SAS license. The program can work with SAS files, SPSS portable files, and CSV files. The most interesting features are nickname matching, gender imputation for 20,000 (American) names, and the calculation of distances between (American) zip codes.[12]

---

[10] Since the development team wants to include the Microsoft.NET framework and Access databases, the binding of Link Plus to windows will be even closer in the future.
[11] The program is available for no charge at
http://www.cdc.gov/cancer/npcr/tools/registryplus/lp.htm
[12] The program is available for no charge at http://www.the-link-king.com

4.4 The Merge Toolbox: MTB

A project group of the author (funded by a research grant from the German Research Foundation) has developed a "merge toolbox" (MTB) for probabilistic record linkage (Schnell et al.: 2005). MTB is written in JAVA and is therefore highly portable to any modern computer system. The program consists of a preprocessing module, a linkage module, and a manual editing module. The program can read and write STATA and CSV files, computes nearly all known string similarity functions, and can perform deterministic and probabilistic record linkage. MTB is being used by cancer registries and research groups in epidemiology, sociology, and economics in Germany.[13]

4.5 Empirical comparisons of programs

Since most record-linkage programs for probabilistic linkage use the same algorithms for making link decisions, the programs should yield very similar results, given the same input. Since the programs differ in preprocessing, some studies compare different parts of the linkage process. Only identically preprocessed data files should be used for linking; but this is often of no practical relevance. For practical applications, the complete linkage process between optimally tuned programs should be compared: this is no small task, and as a result, such studies are rare (Campbell et al.: 2008). From a theoretical point of view, it would be interesting to compare different programs using different decision rules (for example, CART, SVM, and Fellegi-Sunter) on non-preprocessed data and identically preprocessed data. However, systematic studies of this kind are still lacking. For the future, it seems more promising to work on an optimized combination or sequence of decision rules after extensive standardization and preprocessing than to make naive empirical comparisons.

---

13 A restricted version of the program is available for no charge at http://www.uni-konstanz.de/FuF/Verwiss/Schnell/mtb. For scientific purposes, the full program is available for no charge by writing to the author.

5. Privacy issues

Record linkage may be misused for de-anonymization of scientific research files. This possibility of misuse is simply due to the fact that the programs try to minimize distances between objects in a high-dimensional space. Therefore, de-anonymization by minimizing distances can be done by every program for cluster analysis.[14] This misuse is therefore not specific to record-linkage programs.

The result of a successful record linkage is a dataset C with more known characteristics of the objects than in the original data files A and B. Using this enhanced data file C to compare these characteristics with another data file D makes identification of objects in D much more likely than identification using A or B alone, since the number of observations with a given combination of characteristics is declining with every added variable.[15] The risk of disclosure is therefore higher after record linkage. It might be necessary to use additional standard disclosurerisk measures for the enhanced data file C.[16]

6. Research perspectives

From a statistical perspective, the theoretical problems of record linkage are well defined and some interesting solutions have been found. Many applied researchers consider record linkage a simple task. In practice, it is not. In fact, the lay user is often disappointed with the performance of record linkage programs.[17] The main reason for this poor performance is usually the quality of the input data: if many identifiers are missing or poorly standardized, any automatic method will fail. Therefore, we need more work on preprocessing of identifiers. Since preprocessing depends on language- and country-specific details, programs and algorithms must be fine-tuned with local datasets and expert systems. Experts from the fields of statistics and computer science need to use real data from actual data-generating processes.

---

14 For an application, see Torra et al. (2006).
15 This can be seen as a direct consequence of the definition of k-anonymity: in a k-anonymized dataset, each record is indistinguishable from at least (k-1) other records.
16 Examples of such techniques can be found in Willenborg/de Waal (1996) and Domingo-Ferrer (2002); for record linkage and privacy issues in general, see United States General Accounting Office (2001).
17 For example, Gomatam et al. (2002) note higher sensitivity and a higher match rate but a lower positive predicted value of Automatch in comparison to a stepwise deterministic strategy. These results could be changed easily by changing the matching parameters and the preprocessing.

6.1 Real-world test datasets

Interestingly, a standard dataset for comparing record linkage procedures has not been published. Instead, some research groups build data generators with specified error-generating mechanisms. Since such error structures may be different from those of real-world applications, a collection of test datasets based on real world data would be highly desirable. Since the details of name conventions, addresses, postal codes, etc. differ between countries and databases, a German reference database is needed.

6.2 Expert systems and key standardization

Database fields contain many different ways of storing information of key values used for record linkage. These fields must be standardized based on expertise with the distinctive features of German addresses, phone numbers (land lines and mobile), name conventions (for example, historical rules for name changes after marriage), academic titles, historical hereditary titles, legal business forms, etc. Compiling such lists and generating transformation rules is a tedious and labor-intensive task. Currently, the huge amount of work required to generate such exhaustive lists and standardization rules is only done by private companies.[18] Of course, the cumulated commercial knowledge bases are not available for academic use. Therefore, German official statistics will have to buy such standardization services for large-scale operations like the 2011 Census on the commercial market with obvious consequences. In the long run, statistical offices, cancer registries, and other publicly funded research organizations will need common knowledge bases for key standardization.

6.3 Reference databases

For practical record linkage, several reference databases are needed that are currently not publicly available for research purposes. At present, simple lists of all German municipalities with old and new German zip codes, correspondence lists of zip codes and phone numbers, regional identifiers like city codes (*Gemeindekennziffer*), Gauss-Krüger coordinates, and street addresses are not available for public use. Every record linkage group has to compile

---

18 The unit on "Postal Automation" of Siemens I&S (Constance) employs more mathematicians and computer scientists for producing such expert systems than all German cancer registries together. Given the published lists of customers of other companies in the same sector in Germany (for example, "Fuzzy Informatik," a spin-off of Daimler), it is safe to assume that currently more than 50 experts in Germany are working on such standardization tasks.

its own rough version of these reference lists. Since some of these lists are quite expensive, there should be a common scientific license for this data.[19] Furthermore, frequency tables of names and surnames conditioned on gender, nationality, and year of birth would be very useful for imputing gender, nationality, and age based on a given name. Other databases can be used for the same purpose, for example, gender can be imputed with certain ICD or ISCO codes. This imputed information can be used for record linkage with incomplete keys.

6.4 Candidate generation

One interesting idea that has not been studied in detail so far is the generation of candidates for matching based on a search string. The candidates can be generated by introducing random errors or according to pre-specified rules (Arusu et al.: 2008). The resulting candidates will be compared to the existing identifiers. This step should follow unsuccessful standard linkage attempts.

6.5 Blocking

Data files for record linkage are usually quite large. In many applications, we have a small file (for example, a survey) with about 1000 observations and an administrative database with, for example, 10 million records. This would result in 10^{10} comparisons, taking 278 hours at 10,000 comparisons per second. Using standard hardware and standard programs, this is unacceptable. The computation time is usually reduced by using a simple idea: compute the similarity matrix only within subgroups. These subgroups are called "blocks" and the strategy is called "blocking." For example, instead of comparing all company names in Germany with one another, we compare all pairs of company names within each city. Using a suitable blocking variable reduces the computing time for one typical record linkage run (10,000 observations linked to a five million record database) to less than a hour. Of course, this speed comes at a price. The variable used for blocking must be considered a perfect classification variable: exhaustive and disjunct- and error-free. Since blocking variables are in many cases proxy variables of geographical identifiers like dial prefixes, postal codes, or administrative units, there is no guarantee for error-free perfect classification of units. Currently, there is a great deal of research activity in computer science on modifications of blocking algorithms to im-

---

19 For example, a list of all the geo-coordinates of all German buildings, which would be useful for many research purposes in record linkage and epidemiology, is a considerable expense, amounting to about the cost of one research assistant per year.

prove on simple blocking schemes (for example, "adaptive blocking," Bilenko et al.: 2006). These new blocking techniques still have yet to be implemented in production software for record linkage.

6.6 Algorithms for large similarity matrices

As an alternative to blocking, algorithms for computing approximate similarity matrices could be used. Such algorithms have been proposed in the technical literature, for example, "Sparsemap" (Hristescu and Farach-Colton: 1999), "Boostmap" (Athitsos et al.: 2004) and "WEBSOM" (Lagus et al.: 2004). Another interesting approximation was recently suggested by Brandes/Pich (2007). None of these techniques has been systematically used for record linkage up to now. Special data structures or algorithms used for high-dimensional indexing (Yu 2002) have rarely been applied to large-scale record linkage projects.

6.7 Special hardware

Since the blocking of datasets reduces the task of computing an $n*n$ similarity matrix to the independent computation of k matrices of size $m*m$, the computation can be done by several independent machines or processors. This is a very simple version of a parallel computing process, which requires only a minor modification of existing programs. Of course, parallel searching of similarity index structures by special algorithms (Zezula et al: 2006: Chapter 5) or the separate standardization of each record may also be done with such hardware. However, the resulting program can be run on the shelf hardware like standard PC boards. Since such a system should be portable, a compact server rack can be used. Currently available server boards house four processors with four cores each, so a special machine with 64 cores can be built by using only four server boards. In order to reduce power consumption, smaller mobile processor boards may be used instead, requiring eight boards with two quad-core mobile processors. Such a system will drain less than 1000 watts in total, so it does not require special cooling or power supply. The machine should be equipped with at least 1 Gbyte RAM for each processor. In order to minimize the risk of data leaking, the machine can be built as a diskless server: it needs no hard disk at all, since the operating system can be booted from a memory stick and the data to be processed may be kept on removable memory sticks.[20] The sticks should be destroyed after reading; the linked data file should be saved to an empty new stick. In slightly less de-

---

20 Even a data file with 30 million records and 100 bytes of ID-information per record fits on a 10 EUR 4 Gbyte USB stick.

manding computer security environments, the input files may be copied to the machine by using VPN. Such a portable secure special purpose record-linkage machine can be built for the price of three small enterprise servers. It would be highly desirable to have at least one such machine within a trusted computing center with restricted access, for example, within one of the Research Data Centers.

6.8 Privacy-preserving record linkage

In most practical applications, record linkage has to be done with the standard keys: name, surname, gender, date of birth, and place of birth. Since people hesitate to use such identifiers, in many applications encrypted keys have to be used. Since the input data for encryption is prone to errors, a slight deviation between the keys of a true link pair is probable. Such slight deviations result in keys that cannot be matched, since similarity distances between encrypted keys are pointless. Therefore, privacy-preserving record linkage requires special algorithms. Starting with the publication by Churches/Christen (2004), some protocols for record linkage with encrypted alphanumeric keys with errors have been suggested (Pang and Hansen: 2006; Scannapieco et al.: 2007). Independent comparisons of these protocols have not been published and are badly needed. All protocols seem to be awkward to implement with mistrustful database owners. To overcome these problems, we have developed a new protocol that has proven to be fast and reliable (Schnell et al.: 2009). We are currently testing the protocol on different simulated datasets. A complete record linkage solution for encrypted keys must include a protocol for computing distances between encrypted metric data. One very interesting protocol has been proposed by Inan et al. (2006). A highly secure record linkage program for error prone numeric and alphanumeric keys will require a few years of testing and programming. This seems to be the most important research task still to be carried out before record linkage can be used widely given the increasing privacy concerns in western populations.

7. Three recommendations

7.1 Training datasets and reference datasets

In order to improve the performance of record-linkage programs and algorithms, large training and reference datasets should be produced. These should be real-life datasets containing only linkage variables. The links have to be established with a common error-free key or through careful clerical work. Simulated datasets are no substitute for such datasets. Therefore, privacy concerns must be addressed by standard procedures of statistical disclosure control.

7.2 Research program on preprocessing and privacy-preserving record linkage

We need a European research program on preprocessing keys for privacy preserving record linkage. Such a research program should be multinational, since European countries differ in ethnic composition and therefore in the distribution of ethnic surnames. Furthermore, the legal situation of record linkage differs widely within Europe. A multinational and multi-disciplinary research group of computer scientists, lawyers, linguists, historians, and social scientists is therefore needed to solve the problems of privacy-preserving record linkage using standard identifiers like names and surnames.

7.3 National Record Linkage Center

We currently have no research centers for record linkage in Germany, only the cancer registries, which perform a very limited kind of record linkage for a single purpose. Every research team in criminology, sociology, medicine and economics must build its own record linkage infrastructure. In many cases, the cost of doing so exceeds the available research funds. Therefore, at least one National Record Linkage Center is needed. This center should have special machines (massive parallel processors), a team trained in record linkage, and the data protection facilities necessary to act as a data trustee for large-scale projects.

References:

Arasu, A./Chaudhuri, S. and Kaushik, R. (2008): Transformation-based Framework for Record Matching, International Conference on Data Engineering.
Athitsos, V./Alon, J./Sclaroff, S. and Kollios, G. (2004): BoostMap: a method for efficient approximate similarity rankings. CVPR, 268-275.
Bilenko, M./Kamath, B. and Mooney, R.J. (2006): Adaptive Blocking: Learning to Scale Up Record Linkage, ICDM06: Sixth International Conference on Data Mining, 87-96.
Bishop, C.M. (2006): Pattern Recognition and Machine Learning. Berlin.
Bishop, G. and Khoo, J. (2006): Methodology of Evaluating the Quality of Probabilistic Linking, Proceedings of Statistics Canada Symposium 2006. www.statcan.ca/english/freepub/11-522-XIE/2006001/article/10401-en.pdf. [Last visited: 02/10/2010].
Brandes, U. and Pich, C. (2007): Eigensolver Methods for Progressive Multidimensional Scaling of Large Data. Proc. 14th Intl. Symp. Graph Drawing (GD '06). LNCS 4372, 42-53.
Campbell, K.M./Deck, D. and Krupski, A. (2008): Record linkage software in the public domain: a comparison of Link Plus, The Link King, and a 'basic' deterministic algorithm. Health Informatics Journal 14, 1-15.
Churches, T. and Christen, P. (2004): Some methods for blindfolded record linkage. BMC Medical Informatics and Decision Making 4, 1-17.
Crockett, A./Jones, C.E. and Schürer, K. (2006): The Victorian Panel Study. University of Essex. [Unpublished manuscript].
Ding, Y. and Feinberg, S.E. (1996): Multiple sample estimation of population and census undercount in the presence of matching errors. Survey Methodology 22, 55-64.
Domingo-Ferrer, J. (Ed.) (2002): Inference control in statistical databases: from theory to practice. Lecture notes in computer science Vol. 2316. Berlin.
D'Orazio, M./DiZio, M. and Scanu, M. (2006): Statistical Matching: Theory and Practice. New York.
Elmagarmid, I.A./Ipeirotis, P.G. and Verykios, V. (2006): Duplicate Record Detection: A Survey. IEEE Transactions on Knowledge and Data Engineering, 19/2006, 1-16.
Fellegi, I.P. and Sunter, A.B. (1969): A Theory for Record Linkage. Journal of the American Statistical Association 64.
Gomatam, S./Carter, R./Ariet, M. and Mitchell, G. (2002): An empirical comparison of record linkage procedures. Statistics in Medicine 21 (10), 1485-1496.
CMIS Technical Report No. 03/83, CSIRO Mathematical and Information Sciences.
Herzog, T.N./Scheuren, J.J. and Winkler, W.E. (2007): Data Quality and Record Linkage Techniques. New York/Berlin.
Hristescu, G. and Farach-Colton, M. (1999): Cluster-preserving embedding of proteins. Technical report. Rutgers University.
Inan, A./Saygin, Y./Savas, E./Hintoglu, A.A. and Levi, A. (2006): Privacy Preserving Clustering on Horizontally Partitioned Data. Proceedings of the 22nd International Conference on Data Engineering Workshops (ICDEW'06).

Lagus, K./Kaski, S. and Kohonen, T. (2004): Mining massive document collections by the WEBSOM method. Information Sciences 163 (1-3), 135-156.

Pang, C. and Hansen, D. (2006): Improved record linkage for encrypted identifying data. HIC 2006 and HINZ 2006 Proceedings. Brunswick, 164-168.

Scannapieco, M./Figotin, I./Bertino, E. and Elmagarmid, A.K. (2007): Privacy preserving schema and data matching, Proceedings of the 2007 ACM SIGMOD international conference on Management of data, 653-664.

Schnell, R./Bachteler, T. and Bender, S. (2003): Record linkage using error prone strings. American Statistical Association, Proceedings of the Joint Statistical Meetings, 3713-3717.

Schnell, R./Bachteler, T. and Reiher, J. (2005): MTB: Ein Record-Linkage-Programm für die empirische Sozialforschung. ZA-Information 56, 93-103.

Schnell, R. (2008): Avoiding Problems of Traditional Sampling Strategies for Household Surveys in Germany: Some New Suggestions. Discussion paper for the GSOEP. www.diw.de/documents/publikationen/73/86107/diw_datadoc_2008-033.pdf. [Last visited: 02/10/2010].

Schnell, R./Bachteler, T. and Reiher, J. (2009): Privacy-preserving record linkage using Bloom filters. BMC Medical Informatics and Decision Making 2009, 9-41.

Torra, V./Abowd, J.M. and Domingo-Ferrer, J. (2006): Using Mahalanobis Distance-Based Record Linkage for Disclosure Risk Assessment. Privacy in Statistical Databases, 233-242.

United States General Accounting Office (GAO) (2001): Record Linkage and Privacy. Issues in Creating New Federal Research and Statistical Information, April 2001, GAO-01-126SP. Washington.

Willenborg, L. and de Waal, T. (1996): Statistical Disclosure Control in Practice. New York.

Winkler, W.E. (1995): Matching and Record Linkage. In: Cox, B. et al. (Eds.): Business Survey Methods. New York, 355-384

Winkler, W.E. and Thibaudeau, Y. (1991): An application of the Fellegi-Sunter model of record linkage to the 1990 U.S. decennial census technical report, US Bureau of the Census. www.census.gov/srd/papers/pdf/rr91-9.pdf. [Last visited: 02/10/2010].

Yu, C. (2002): High-Dimensional Indexing. Transformational Approaches to High-Dimensional Range and Similarity Searches. Berlin.

Zezula, P./Amato, G./Dohnal, V. and Batko, M. (2006): Similarity Search. The Metric Space Approach. New York.

6. Experiments, Surveys and the Use of Representative Samples as Reference Data

Thomas Siedler and Bettina Sonnenberg

Contact:

Thomas Siedler
Bettina Sonnenberg
DIW Berlin
Mohrenstr. 58
10117 Berlin
Germany
e-mail: tsiedler[at]diw.de
          bsonnenberg[at]diw.de

Abstract

During the last two decades, laboratory experiments have come into increasing prominence and constitute a popular method of research to examine behavioral outcomes and social preferences. However, it has been debated whether results from these experiments can be extrapolated to the real world and whether, for example, sample selection into the experiment might constitute a major shortcoming of this methodology. This note discusses potential benefits of combining experimental methods and representative datasets as a means to overcome some of the limitations of lab experiments. We also outline how large representative surveys can serve as reference data for researchers collecting their own datasets in order to explore potential sample selection biases.

Keywords: experiments, survey, representativity
JEL-Classification: C01, C52, C8, C9, D0, D6, D81, D84

1. Introduction

During the last two decades, laboratory experiments have come into increasing prominence and now constitute a popular method of research to examine behavioral outcomes and social preferences. There are obvious advantages of laboratory experiments. First, researchers can control the environment under which individuals make their decisions and allow causal inferences by exogenously varying one parameter while holding all others constant. Second, the simplicity of many such experiments makes it easy to explain the findings to non-academics and policy-makers. However, major limitations of most experiments are that they are administered to students, who usually self-select themselves into the study and are therefore not representative of the entire adult population. In fact, due to self-selection, experimental studies with student subjects might not even be representative of the entire student population. For example, Eckel and Grossman (2000) investigate the impact of recruitment methods on behavior in a series of dictator experiments with a charitable organization as a recipient in laboratory sessions. The authors compare altruistic behavior among student subjects recruited voluntarily through announcements in graduate and undergraduate courses ("voluntary sample") with students in which the experiment was conducted during class time ("pseudo-voluntary sample"). They find that pseudo-volunteers are significantly more generous on average than their volunteer counterparts, and that socio-economic characteristics such as religion or survey measures of altruistic preferences have a larger effect on giving behavior among students recruited pseudo-voluntarily. Similarly, Harrison et al. (2007) examine potential self-selection bias in both a field experiment and a laboratory experiment with student subjects. The authors start with the observation that samples observed in the experiment might suffer from randomization bias (Heckman and Smith 1995). Being interested in individuals' risk attitudes, the authors note that the likelihood to participate in the experiment might be higher for individuals with on average higher risk attitudes than among the general population. On the other hand, the researchers offer participants a fixed show-up fee that might encourage individuals that are more risk-averse to participate in the experiment, potentially outweighing sample selection into the experiment in their study due to randomization bias. The authors report significant self-selection into both the field experiment and the laboratory experiment with adult subjects drawn from the general Dutch population, arguing that their sample is on average more risk-averse than the general population (see also Roe et al. 2009). In addition, most laboratory experiments are conducted on very homogenous samples (typically students studying the same subject at the same university) and often information on potentially important socio-economic background characteristics is missing or lacks sufficient variation. Another shortcoming of laboratory experiments is the lack of anonymity. In most laboratory studies, students play against each other and know that the other player is a student. Hence, the degree of anonymity is rather low. Both the degree of homogeneity and anonymity in the subject pool might influence revealed social preferences (Sapienza et al. 2007). The question has also been raised whether laboratory experiments are externally valid and to what extent laboratory findings can be extrapolated to the general population (Levitt and List 2007). A branch of the recent literature examines the external validity of laboratory experiments by comparing behavior in laboratory sessions with experimental outcomes in more heterogeneous and representative samples (Bosch-Domenech et al. 2002; Haigh and List 2005; Benz and Meier 2006). The majority of these studies report that the behavior in the lab differs from that observed in other contexts. For a detailed discussion of potential limitations of laboratory experiments measuring social preferences, see Levitt and List (2007). For a recent discussion regarding potential improvements and future challenges in the field of experimental economics, see Gächter (2009).

Another strand of research in economics and the social sciences makes use of survey questions from large representative cross-sectional or household panel datasets. One criticism of using attitudinal questions from these surveys concerns the lack of behavioral underpinnings and the absence of meaningful survey questions in certain contexts. For example, Glaeser et al. (2000) and Ermisch et al. (2009) discuss the difficulties of measuring respondents' trustworthiness by means of survey questions. Combining attitudinal survey questions with behavioral experiments that include monetary rewards can potentially provide a fuller understanding of economic behavior and help to overcome some of these shortcomings. This note briefly discusses potential benefits of combining experimental methods and representative datasets when studying economic outcomes and social behavior. We also provide a short overview about the recent literature combining the experimental approach with survey methods. Finally, we discuss potential benefits of using large representative surveys as reference data for researchers collecting their own datasets. An overview of recent selected studies combining behavioral experiments with survey questions or using representative surveys as reference datasets is provided in table 1.

2. Combining behavioral experiments and survey methods

2.1 Trust and trustworthiness

A new research strand combines behavioral experiments and survey methods. Fehr et al. (2002) incorporate the standard trust-game experiment (Berg et al. 1995) into a representative survey of the German population and asked respondents several survey measures of trust. Fehr et al. (2002) find a positive association between attitudinal survey measures of trust and sender's behavior, but no significant correlation between survey-based measures of trust and trustworthiness in the experiment. In addition, the authors report that individuals aged 65 and above, highly skilled workers, and those living in larger households exhibit less trusting behavior in the experiment.

Using nationally representative data for Germany, Naef and Schupp (2009) compare survey and behavioral measures of trust. The authors create a new survey measure of trust and find that it is significantly correlated with the experimental trust measure. Moreover, they report that their experimental measure of trust is not subject to a social desirability bias and is robust to variations in stakes and the use of strategy method. This study demonstrates how survey measures can be tested by combining the experimental approach with survey methods.

In a representative sample of the Dutch population, Bellemare and Kröger (2007) measure levels of trust and trustworthiness elicited through an experiment similar to those presented by Berg et al. (1995) in a representative sample of the Dutch population. The authors also compare their representative trust experiment with a sample of college students in an equivalent laboratory experiment. They find that college students have considerably lower levels of trust and trustworthiness than individuals in the representative sample and that these differences can be explained mainly by differences in socio-economic and background characteristics, in particular age, gender, and education. For example, the authors find that women have higher levels of trust than men, but display lower levels of trustworthiness. In line with

Fehr et al. (2002), Bellemare and Kröger (2007) find a positive, inverted U-shaped association between age and trust. The authors do not find evidence of a participation bias in their trust experiment with student subjects, and therefore argue that trust and trustworthiness as measured in the laboratory are informative about the behavior in the general population.

Ermisch et al. (2009) integrate a new experimental trust design into a sample of the British population. The authors' rationale for using an alternative trust design is based on observations that the sender's behavior in the standard trust-game experiment (Berg et al. 1995) is not only influenced by trust but also depends on other motivations such as sender's reciprocity, risk aversion, altruism, or inequality aversion (Cox 2004; Karlan 2005; Ermisch and Gambetta 2006 and Sapienza et al. 2007). In their "one-shot" trust experiment, the sender faces the decision as to whether or not to pass on a fixed amount of money (e.g., whether or not to send £10. If £10 are sent, the experimenter increases it by £30 so that the second person receives £40) and the receiver must decide whether or not to pay back a fixed amount of money (e.g., the sender has the choice of either paying back £22 or keeping all £40). Thus, the players cannot choose whether or not to transfer a certain amount of money between, say, £1-£10; rather they face the decision whether to transfer the entire amount or nothing. The authors argue that this binary trust game is more likely to measure revealed trust and trustworthiness than the standard trust game experiment, in which the possibility of sending "any amount favours the intrusion of other motives such as 'gift giving', 'let's risk part of it' and 'I like to gamble'." Ermisch et al. (2009) find that the experiment is more likely to reveal trust if people are older, if they are homeowners, if their financial situation is "comfortable," or if they are divorced or separated. Trustworthiness is lower if a person's financial situation is perceived by them as difficult or as "just getting by."

2.2 Risk attitudes

Another recent example demonstrating the benefits of combining incentive-compatible experimental measures with survey methods is the study by Dohmen et al. (2009). In a previous related study, Dohmen et al. (2007) examine the relationship between individual's risk aversion, impatience, and cognitive abilities. They find that lower cognitive abilities are significantly associated with greater risk aversion and more pronounced impatience. These relationships are found to be robust to controlling for a broad set of socio-economic characteristics, such as age, gender, education, and income, which are measured through standard survey questions. In their study, both risk aversion and impatience are measured by choice experiments that involve real monetary choices and relatively large stakes. Respondents were told in advance that the experiment was about financial decisions, that they would have the chance to win money, and that the earned amount would depend on their choices in the experiment. Subjects were also informed that every seventh participant would win. For instance, in the lottery experiment, a financial decision is represented by the choice between a certain payoff (*Option A*) and a risky lottery (*Option B*). Participants were also informed that, for each paired lottery, *Option B* always implies a 50 percent chance of winning €300 and a 50 percent chance of winning nothing. The experiment starts with the following lottery choice: respondents can choose between a certain payoff of €0 (*Option A)* and *Option B*. If participants choose *Option B*, the amount of *Option A* is increased by €10 in the next decision round. Thus, the second lottery choice is between the "safe" payoff of €10 and Option *B*. Similarly, conditional on prior decisions, a third lottery choice is between a certain payoff of €20 and *Option B*. The experiment ends when subjects choose *Option A* for the first time, or when the maximum amount of €190 for *Option A* is reached. This study is another example demonstrating the potential benefits of combining experimental and survey measures in a representative sample of the population.

3. Using representative surveys as reference data

In this section, we briefly discuss potential benefits of using large representative surveys as reference datasets for researchers collecting their own data. Household panels might offer a useful reference point for experimental studies, thanks to their longitudinal character and the sampling of all household members – for example, the British Household Panel Study (BHPS), the new household panel study *Understanding Society* in the United Kingdom, and the German Socio-Economic Panel (SOEP, *Sozio-oekonomisches Panel*). Register data can constitute another fruitful source of reference data (Harrison et al. 2007). The basic idea here is that large representative surveys can serve as reference data for researchers collecting datasets that do not represent the full universe of the population of interest (e.g., through clinical trials, intervention studies, laboratory and behavioral experiments, and cohort studies). An important issue when investigators collect their own data is whether the sample represents the general population, or conversely, whether it is selective (for example, by design or through choice-based sampling). This approach might offer several benefits. First, by asking participants similar questions to those in representative surveys, researchers can compare their sample with either a sub-sample or the whole representative survey. Second, in contrast to many of the scales and questionnaire instruments developed by psychologists, for instance, questions in household panel surveys like the SOEP or BHPS are not copyrighted and can be used by other researchers free of charge. Thus, these datasets can be a valuable point of reference for designing new questionnaires. Combining experimental sessions with a questionnaire collecting basic individuals' socio-demographic characteristics used in representative surveys gives researchers valid information as to the representativeness of their sample with respect to the individual characteristics surveyed.

Two recent studies exemplify the potential for using questions from a panel survey when researchers collect their own data. In Germany, Geyer et al. (2009) examine whether individuals aged 17-45 with operated congenital heart disease have adverse employment chances compared to people without heart problems. The authors compare their sample of patients (N=314; treatment group) with a sample drawn from the SOEP, which serves as a comparison group. The treatment group consisted of women and men who had a congenital heart disease and were operated on at the University Hospital of Göttingen. The authors conducted a face-to-face interview with patients using several SOEP questions. Comparing their hospital sample with the SOEP as reference data they found considerable differences between the two samples with respect to gender, age, and employment status.

Two recent projects that also follow the idea of using a representative household panel study (SOEP) as reference data are the Berlin Aging Study II and the Brain Gene Behavior Project. The Berlin Aging Study II, collecting data on objective socio-economic and biological characteristics like objective health, functional capacity, subjective health, and well-being, draws on SOEP questions with regard to health and life satisfaction to enable comparisons with the SOEP data (Max Planck Institute for Human Development 2009). Likewise, the Brain Gene Behavior Project, a large-scale study on the molecular genetic basis for personality, cognitive, and individual behavioral differences, makes use of the SOEP questionnaire to exploit comparable reference data (Neuroeconomics Lab Bonn and Socio-Economic Panel 2009).

In the United Kingdom, the study by Ermisch et al. (2009) demonstrates how a panel survey can help in determining the extent to which a particular sample is representative of the general population. The authors integrate a new experimental trust design into a former sample of the British population and compare their trust sample with a sample from the BHPS. By using a questionnaire similar to the BHPS, the authors are able to determine that their trust sample over-represents women, people who are retired, older, divorced, or separated. Together, these two studies show that household panel studies can serve as useful reference data for researchers collecting their own samples and can help to reveal the representativeness of their own collected data.

4. Conclusion

The studies reviewed demonstrate that enormous academic benefits can be derived from combining experimental studies with representative surveys.[1] First, experiments based on representative samples help to assess potential biases of studies based on student subjects who self-select themselves into the sample. This advances our knowledge on whether and to what extent experimental studies on student samples can be generalized. Second, research measuring both revealed preferences and stated preferences allows researchers to validate their measures. For example, Fehr et al. (2002), Ermisch et al. (2009), and Naef and Schupp (2009) report that answers to attitudinal questions on trust toward strangers do predict real trusting behavior in the experiment.

The recent studies by Eckel and Grossman (2000) and Roe et al. (2009) demonstrate the importance of self-selection into experimental studies, and their studies suggest that results from laboratory experiments might not be generalized to the entire population. In this note, we briefly discussed potential benefits of using large representative survey as reference data for researchers who are collecting their own datasets and point readers to two recent examples in the literature.

---

1   See also Falk et al. (2009).

Table 1: Studies Combining an Experimental Design with Survey Methods

Author(s)	Topic	Method
Bellemare and Kröger 2007	Measure levels of trust and trustworthiness elicited through an experiment similar to those presented by Berg et al. (1995) in a representative sample of the Dutch population.	Trust and trustworthiness measured by an invest- and-reward experiment.
Benz and Meier 2006	Explore the correlation between individual behavior in laboratory experiments and in a similar situation in the field.	Donation lab experiments with college students.
Dohmen et al. 2009	Investigate the relevance of survey questions on risk-taking behavior in field experiments and actual behavior in the real world.	Risk-taking measured by a lottery game in a field experiment and SOEP survey questions with a representative sample of 450 participants.
Eckel and Grossman 2000	Compare the effect of recruitment method in dictator experiments with student subjects.	Altruism measured by means of dictator games.
Ermisch et al. 2009	Measure trust and trustworthiness in Great Britain using an experimental and survey design.	One-shot trust experiment with former respondents of the BHPS in combination with survey questionnaires.
Fehr et al. 2002	Investigate trust and trustworthiness by comparing behavioral experimental outcomes and representative survey data.	Implementation of a trust experiment in a representative survey of the German population in 2002.
Gächter et al. 2004	The authors present survey and experimental evidence on trust and voluntary cooperation in Russia using both a student and a non-student sample.	One-shot public goods experiment.
Geyer et al. 2009	Examine the effect of congenital heart disease on employment status.	Sample of 628 patients surveyed in clinic combined with medical check-up (treatment group).

Data	Finding
Representative sample of the Dutch population and a laboratory sample with college students.	The smaller amount of students' investments predominantly demonstrates differences in socio-economic and background characteristics. While these characteristics can explain different revealed behavior, they have almost no impact on stated trust. Return ratios are significantly lower in the lab sample as well.
Secret use of the real donation spending behavior of the students.	The authors find a rather moderate or weak relationship between lab and field behavior.
Comparison with representative data of the whole SOEP sample on seven different survey questions with regard to risk attitudes.	The general risk attitude survey questions are significantly correlated with behavior in the lottery game as well as with actual behavior in the real world, e.g., with regard to financial, sports, and health-related behavior. Simultaneously, specific behavior is best predicted by context-specific risk survey measures in the respective domain.
Laboratory experiment with self-recruited students (voluntary sample) and in classroom recruited college students during the class period (pseudo-voluntary sample).	Volunteers are less generous in distributing endowments and are more motivated by incentives than classroom-recruited students. Respondents' characteristics such as sex, religion, and altruism influence the behavior of pseudo-volunteers more than that of volunteers. The authors conclude that self-selection into the sample matters.
Comparison with representative BHPS sample allows the authors to examine whether their experimental sample is representative of the general population.	For example, the authors report that their experimental sample over-represents women, people who are retired, divorced, or separated. Individual behavior in experiments is found to be a reliable and superior measure compared to standard common trust survey questions.
—	Trust in strangers and past trusting behavior correlate with trust behavior in the experiment, but no survey measure predicts trustworthiness.
Not fully representative survey data of Russian non-students and a student subject pool.	Non-students display higher levels of trust than students, and also contribute more to the public good as long as socio-economic background is not controlled for. Individuals who believe that most other people are fair contribute significantly more to the public good game than those without such beliefs. Likewise, optimists make higher contributions than pessimists.
Their comparison group is a 10 percent sample drawn from the German SOEP.	The authors find significant differences between male patients and male control subjects. Those with congenital heart disease are less likely to be employed full-time, more likely to be employed part-time, and in marginal employment. The differences between treatment and control group depend on the severity of the disease.

Author(s)	Topic	Method
Glaeser et al. 2000	Examine the validity of trust survey questions with a behavioral trust experiment.	Laboratory experiment with Harvard undergraduates.
Harrison et al. 2007	Investigate whether experiment samples are biased because of the risk of randomization. The authors undertake both a laboratory experiment and a field experiment to examine whether selection into the experiment influences measures of risk attitudes.	Eliciting individual risk attitudes through an experimental lottery game in both a field experiment and a laboratory experiment.
Levitt and List 2007	Discuss whether estimates on pro-social behavior from laboratory experiments can be extrapolated to the real world.	Literature review.
Naef and Schupp 2009	Test the correlation and validity of trust survey questions with experimental measures of trust.	Trust experiment with survey respondents, representative for Germany.

Data	Finding
Survey measures on trust (self-reported attitudes and behavior) of 258 Harvard undergraduates.	Ten out of 12 GSS trust questions do not predict trust, but are related to trustworthiness as measured in the experiment. Trust in the experiment is associated with past trusting behavior. Trust and trustworthiness rise with closer social distance.
First, the authors collect information on subjects' socio-economic characteristics by means of questionnaires and use this information to correct for potential self-selection into the field experiment. Second, in their laboratory experiment, they investigate the impact of variation in recruitment information on individual risk attitudes.	The authors find that the use of show-up fees generates a more risk-averse sample. Participants in both the field and laboratory experiment are found to be more risk-averse than the general population once they control for selection into the experiment.
	The authors argue that pro-social behavior in experiments depends on a number of experimental situation and design factors, e.g., stakes, sample recruitment, anonymity, as well as unobserved respondents' characteristics. They caution against generalizing results from laboratory to real-world situations.
Self-reported trust and trustworthiness by different measurements with a representative survey sample.	GSS Survey question do not measure trust in the experiment. However, the authors find a significant correlation between self-reported SOEP trust measures and experimental measures of trust. Students are found to be slightly more trustful than non-students.

References:

Bosch-Domenech, A./Montalvo, J.G./Nagel, R. and Satorra, A. (2002): One, two, (three), infinity,...: Newspaper and lab beauty-contest experiments. American Economic Review 92 (5), 1687–1701.

Bellemare, C. and Kroeger, S. (2007): On representative social capital. European Economic Review 51, 183-202.

Benz, M. and Meier, S. (2006): Do people behave in experiments as in the field? Evidence from donations. Working Paper No. 248, Institute for Empirical Research in Economics, University of Zurich.

Berg, J./Dickhaut, J. and McCabe, K. (1995): Trust, reciprocity, and social history. Games and Economic Behavior 10, 122-142.

Cox, J.C. (2004): How to identify trust and reciprocity. Games and Economic Behavior 46, 260-281.

Dhami, M.K./Hertwig, R. and Hoffrage, U. (2004): The Role of Representative Design in an Ecological Approach to Cognition. Psychological Bulletin 130 (6), 959-988.

Dohmen, T./Falk, A./Huffman, D. and Sunde, U. (2007): Are risk aversion and impatience related to cognitive ability? IZA discussion paper No. 2735. [Forthcoming in the American Economic Review].

Dohmen, T./Falk, A./Huffman, D./Sunde, U./Schupp, J. and Wagner, G.G. (2009): Individual Risk Attitudes: New Evidence from a Large, Representative, Experimentally-Validated Survey. [Forthcoming in Journal of the European Economic Association].

Eckel, C.E. and Grossman, P.J. (2000): Volunteers and pseudo-volunteers: The effect of recruitment method in dictator experiments. Experimental Economics 3, 107-120.

Ermisch, J. and Gambetta, D. (2006): People's trust: the design of a survey-based experiment. ISER Working Paper 34/2006.

Ermisch, J./Gambetta, D./Laurie, H./Siedler, T. and Uhrig, N. (2009): Measuring people's trust. Journal of the Royal Statistical Society: Series A (Statistics in Society) 172 (4), 749-769.

Falk, A./Dohmen, T. and Sunde, U. (2009): Kontrolliert und repräsentativ: Beispiele zur Komplementarität von Labor- und Felddaten. Perspektiven der Wirtschaftspolitik 10 (1), 54-74.

Fehr, E./Fischerbach, U./von Rosenbladt, B./Schupp, J. and Wagner, G.G. (2002): A Nation-Wide Laboratory. Schmollers Jahrbuch 122 (4), 519-542.

Gächter, S./Herrmann, B. and Thöni, C. (2004): Trust, voluntary cooperation, and socio-economic background: survey and experimental evidence. Journal of Behavior & Organisation 55, 505-531.

Gächter, S. (2009): Experimental Economics. [In this publication].

Geyer, S./Norozi, K./Buchhorn, R. and Wessel, A. (2009): Chances of employment in a population of women and men after surgery of congenital heart disease: Gender-specific comparisons between patients and the general population. Congenital Heart Disease 4 (1), 25-33.

Glaeser E.L./Laibson, D.I./Scheinkman, J.A. and Soutter, C.L. (2000): Measuring trust. Quarterly Journal of Economics 115, 811-846.

Haigh, M. and List, J. (2005): Do professional traders exhibit myopic loss aversion? Journal of Finance 60 (1), 523-534.

Harrison, G.W./Lau, M.I. and Rutström, E.E. (2007): Risk attitudes, randomization to treatment, and self-selection into experiments. Working Paper 05-01, Department of Economics, University of Central Florida.

Heckman, J.J. and Smith, J.A. (1995): Assessing the case for social experiments. Journal of Economic Perspectives 9 (2), 85-110.

Hogarth, R.M. (2005): The challenge of representative design in psychology and economics. Journal of Economic Methodology 12 (2), 253-263.

Karlan, D.S. (2005): Using experimental economics to measure social capital and predict financial decisions. American Economic Review 95 (5), 1688-1699.

Levitt, S.D. and List, J.A. (2007): What do laboratory experiments measuring social preferences reveal about the real world? Journal of Economic Perspectives 21, 153-174.

Max-Planck-Institute for Human Development (2009): Berlin Aging Study II (BASE II): Health and Cognitive Functioning across the Lifespan. http://www.base-berlin.mpg.de/BASE_II.html. [Last visited: 02/10/2010].

Naef, M. and Schupp, J. (2009): Measuring trust: Experiments and surveys in contrast and combination. IZA discussion paper No. 4087.

Neuroeconomics Lab Bonn, Socio-Economic Panel (2009): Bonn Gene Brain Behavior Project. http://www.neuroeconomics-bonn.org/cms/front_content.php?idcat=4. [Last visited: 02/10/2010].

Roe, B.E./Haab, T.C./Beversdorf, D.Q./Gu, H.H. and Tilley, M.R. (2009): Risk-Attitude Selection Bias in Subject Pools for Experiments involving Neuroimaging and Blood Samples. Journal of Economic Psychology 30 (2), 181-189.

Sapienza, P./Toldra, A. and Zingales, L. (2007): Understanding Trust. NBER Working Paper No. 13387.

Siedler, T./Schupp, J./Spieß, C.K. and Wagner, G.G. (2009): The German Socio-Economic Panel as Reference Data Set. Schmollers Jahrbuch 129 (2), 367-374.

7. Experimental Economics

Simon Gächter

Contact:

Simon Gächter
Centre for Decision Research and Experimental Economics
School of Economics
Sir Clive Granger Building, University Park
NG7 2RD
Nottingham
UK
e-mail: simon.gaechter[at]nottingham.ac.uk

Abstract

Experimental economics has become an established method for generating controlled and replicable empirical information that is complementary to other empirical methods in the social sciences. There is a strong research infrastructure for laboratory experimentation in Europe and also in Germany. A valuable instrument in the development of this methodology would be the creation of a short socio-economic survey integrating questions already used in existing surveys, which experimental economists could then administer to their participants. This would make it relatively easy to analyze the selectivity of subject pools. However, among experimental economists there is as yet no existing standard questionnaire for collecting this information, which limits the ability to compare respective datasets. The effort shall be made, therefore, to create such a common questionnaire. Furthermore, there is at present no across-the-board standard for data reporting in this area. There is one data repository in the United States that currently does collect experimental data and makes them freely available. Building up a data archive that integrates (merges) existing data, however, is a very laborious undertaking and requires substantial scientific input from interested researchers.

Keywords: experimental economics, data archives, selectivity of subject pools
JEL Classification: C81, C9

Key points and recommendations

(1) Experimental economics is an established method for the generation of controlled and replicable empirical knowledge that is complementary to other empirical methods in the social sciences. There is a strong research infrastructure for laboratory experimentation in Europe and also in Germany.

(2) Most of the experiments that have been conducted by experimental economists have used students as subjects. A recent research interest to emerge thus raises the question of whether the results from the laboratory (i.e., using students) can be generalized to other social groups. Of particular interest in answering this question are experiments conducted as part of representative surveys, such as the German Socio-Economic Panel (SOEP, *Sozio-oekonomisches Panel*) or the British Household Panel Study (BHPS, part of the longitudinal study Understanding Society). The advantage of these studies is that representative socio-demographic information can be connected to experimentally observed behavior. This method has enormous future potential and research has only just begun. In Europe, the German SOEP has played a pioneering role.

(3) There is currently no general standard for data reporting. The release of data after publication is voluntary, with the exception of two top professional journals that require accepted papers to publish their data. Only one data repository exists (in the United States) where experimental data are collected and made freely available.

(4) Building up a data archive that integrates (merges) existing data is very laborious and requires substantial scientific input from interested researchers. The construction of such a database is complex due to the multidimensionality of the data, the different interests of researchers, and their various property rights to the use of data.

(5) One valuable instrument in the development of this methodology would be the creation of a short socio-economic questionnaire drawing from questions used in existing surveys – such as the BHPS or SOEP – which experimental economists could administer to their participants. It would then be relatively simple to analyze the selectivity of subject pools. However, since no standard yet exists among experimental economists, there is limited comparability among respective datasets. An effort shall be undertaken to create such a common questionnaire.

In order to provide the necessary background for an understanding of the issues being addressed in subsequent sections, this article will first introduce the nature of experimental data. In section 2, I will then describe what I see as the current situation in experimental economics and discuss the state of data reporting and recording today. Section 3 explores some interesting future developments. Section 4 describes what I see as the main challenges facing experimental economics, and section 5 offers some concluding recommendations.

1. Research questions and data in experimental economics

Economic experiments are a method of observing economic decision making under controlled conditions. Thus, experimental economics is not a subfield of economics but rather an empirical method used to answer specific research questions. These questions come from all parts of the discipline of economics (Kagel and Roth 1995; Plott and Smith 2008; Camerer 2003; Duffy 2008; Falk and Gächter 2008; Shogren 2008). Experiments have been used to test theories, to uncover empirical regularities, to test the behavioral implications of institutions and incentives, to uncover the structure of peoples' attitudes towards risk and uncertainty, their time preferences and their social preferences. Many of these experiments can be considered basic research, but research on how experimental data might be used for consulting, policy advice, and economic engineering is growing (Roth 2002).

The methods of experimental economics are used not only within economics, but also increasingly in management science, anthropology, political science, biology, social neuroscience, and psychology. As such, experimental economics is a platform for interdisciplinary research. There are also close links to psychology, not least because experimental economics is frequently used as a toolbox by behavioral economists interested in improving the psychological realism of economics (Camerer et al. 2004). Although experimental economics and experimental approaches in psychology have a great deal in common, there are some significant differences in their respective methodologies (Hertwig and Ortmann 2001).

A large part of empirical research in economics is the use of field data, that is, naturally occurring data which accrue in daily economic life. These data are typically collected for recording purposes (e.g., by statistical offices) and are often not directly useful for answering scientific questions, in particular those that are motivated by economic theory. The reason is that economic theories (and most research questions derived from them) are typically "if-then" statements, and naturally occurring data do not exist in this fashion. In experiments these "if-then" conditions can be implemented by way of experimental design.

In addition to laboratory experiments, field experiments are also conducted where the experiment takes place in the natural decision making environment of the participants (Harrison and List 2004). Of particular interest are experiments conducted as part of representative surveys, where the advantages of experiments and survey data are combined (Fehr et al. 2002). Some recent studies also take advantage of the new range of possibilities offered by the Internet.

In the following section, I describe the procedures typically followed in a laboratory experiment. In a large majority of cases the participants are undergraduate students at the respective university. Specialized web-based software is now available for managing recruitment (Greiner 2004).[1] When participants decide to take part they normally do not know what the experiment will be about; they are invited "to take part in an experiment on economic decision making." Thus, self-selection depending on the type of experiment is not an issue. Upon arrival at the lab, the participants receive written instructions which contain the complete rules for the particular experiments.

The large majority of experiments are those conducted in networked computer laboratories and the interactions take place using specially-designed professional software, such as, for example, the popular toolbox "z-Tree" (Fischbacher 2004). In addition to being fully scripted (written

---

[1] Exlab. University of Central Florida. http://exlab.bus.ucf.edu/.

instructions and rules ensure that experiments are always conducted in a comparable way), two further standards exist for conducting experiments: first, participants get paid on the basis of their decisions; and second, the use of deception in the design of experiments is forbidden (Hertwig and Ortmann 2001; Friedman and Sunder).[2] Thus, experiments are real decisions, not hypothetical ones, as they are in questionnaire-based research, or in simulations.

The ability to control and replicate the data generating process is one of the decisive advantages of experimentation over other methods of data collection. Naturally occurring decision situations are complex; many conditions under which natural decisions occur are unknown to the researcher and cannot be influenced or occur simultaneously with other conditions, such that it becomes impossible to say anything about causality. By contrast, in an experiment the experimenter designs ("controls") the decision situation and therefore causal inferences can be made when conditions ("treatments") change.

Replicability refers to the degree to which it is possible to run the exact same experiment – whether in the same research lab or in any other lab. This is a very important feature that is normally not feasible with other methods of data generation. There are various forms of replication. Researchers typically replicate the same experiments several times, simply to collect enough data. Sometimes researchers replicate their experiments in different participant pools (within and even across cultures) to see the robustness of findings across different social groups (Güth et al. 2003; Gächter et al. 2004; Carpenter et al. 2005; Hermann et al. 2008). Another type of replication occurs if other scientists want to run the same experiment in their own lab. This is usually quite easy, because it is an established standard of good practice to include documentation of the instructions used in the appendix of the research paper. Similarly, the software code is also frequently available. Exact replication is quite rare because it is hard to publish, but it is common to replicate previous results alongside new treatments, for instance, to create comparisons (Smith 1994). The ability to replicate results is a particular advantage of laboratory data and may not be feasible with field experiments because they take place in naturally occurring decision-making situations that may change over time in a way that cannot be controlled.

A common critique of laboratory experiments (i.e., those using undergraduates as subjects) is that undergraduates are a very specific portion of the population. Furthermore, laboratory experiments are associated with the potential drawback of being artificial situations that do not greatly resemble natural decision-making contexts (this can also be a decisive advantage of the lab experiment, however). For these reasons, it has become increasingly

---

2   Experiments in which participants are not paid on the basis of their decisions or that employ deception are normally not publishable in economics journals.

popular for researchers to conduct experiments using non-student participant pools and outside university labs.

Doing experiments with non-students, cross-culturally, and in a much noisier "field" has consequences for both the design of experiments and how they are statistically analyzed. Simple comparisons of means often do not suffice because the use of varied participant pools requires controlling for their characteristics. To the extent that subject pool characteristics are important, or even the focus of research there are two suggested implications: first, the requirements concerning the amount of data collected increases and, second, simple non-parametric statistics are not powerful enough for the data analysis. Multivariate regression techniques are needed. The rapid development of microeconometrics is certainly very valuable here but these techniques have to be adapted to the nature of experimental data (Andersen et al. 2007).

2. Status quo

In this section I will address the following issues: (1) the status of experimental economics, (2) the standards used in conducting experiments, and (3) the current situation in reporting data. Finally, I will describe one repository of experimental data, called "ExLab."

Status of experimental economics. Experimental economics is now an established method of empirical economic research.[3] The number of publications in this area has increased tremendously since the mid-1980s. Experimental papers are now published in all of the major journals as well as in field journals in the discipline. Since 1998 there has also been a specialized field journal (*Experimental Economics*) devoted to the development of experimental economics, broadly conceived.[4] Meanwhile, there are also textbooks (Friedman and Sunder 1994; Davis and Holt 1993), monographs (Camerer 2003; Guala 2005), and handbooks (Kagel and Roth; Plott and Smith 2008). There is a professional association of experimental economists, the "Economic Science Association,"[5] to which most experimental economists belong. Many universities, too, now run experimental economics laboratories, and the European infrastructure, including Germany, is excellent, generally speaking, and competitive with the existing infrastructure in the US.

---

3   The contribution of experimental economics to the economic sciences was further recognized when the 2002 Nobel Prize was awarded to Vernon Smith and Daniel Kahneman.
4   Experimental Economics. Springer. http://www.springer.com/economics/economic+theory/journal/10683.
5   Economic Science Association. https://www.economicscience.org/.

Standards for conducting experiments. I have described the current situation with regard to the rules of conduct for the types of experimentation mentioned above. The standard is quite uniform and is normally enforced through editorial policies. There is no standard for eliciting socio-demographic background information. In the past, these variables were often of little interest to researchers, because the related experiments were focused on testing behavioral theories and used convenience samples of sociologically homogeneous undergraduates for that purpose. The only notable exception to this was where there was a particular interest in gender differences. The situation today is somewhat different. Many researchers now routinely collect socio-demographic data, in particular if they are using non-student participant pools. Thanks to software that is both specialized and easy-to-use (like "z-Tree"),[6] administering these questionnaires has become relatively easy. However, no standard questionnaire for gathering background data has yet emerged.

Status quo for data reporting. It is common practice to attach the written instructions of an experiment to the manuscript when submitting it to a journal. The instructions are important in the evaluation of the validity of a given experimental design. Often these instructions are published alongside with the article or on the website of either the journal in which it is published or the author. It is uncommon, however, to submit the data itself at the review stage.

There is currently no uniform standard for reporting the data of *published* papers. At present, the three top journals in the field – the *American Economic Review*, *Econometrica*, and the *Review of Economic Studies* – publish the data (from any empirical paper, not only experimental ones) and require authors to submit the data (raw data, software, and code for analyzing the data) for publication on their websites.[7] Apart from these journals I am not aware of any other economics journal that publishes the data of empirical studies on its website. However, since the *American Economic Review* and the *Review of Economic Studies* are highly respected journals, other journals may adopt the same standard.

Some researchers publish the instructions, software, and data on their websites voluntarily alongside the paper itself, yet no homogeneous standard has emerged. There is an informal expectation that the instructions, software, and raw data from *published* papers will be supplied if requested by another researcher. It appears that people normally comply with this expectation as a social norm. When they do not agree to release data, it is usually because they intend to utilize the collected data further in new research projects.

---

6 Z-Tree. http://www.iew.unizh.ch/ztree/index.php.
7 American Economic Review. http://www.aeaweb.org/articles/issues_datasets.php; Review of Economic Studies. http://www.restud.com/supplementary.asp; Econometric Society. http://www.econometricsociety.org/

The ExLab data repository. To my knowledge, "ExLab" is the only repository for experimental data currently in existence. ExLab is run by the College of Business Administration of the University of Central Florida. It may be used by all researchers in the experimental social sciences.[8]

ExLab consists of three modules. The "Experiment Manager" provides a platform for organizing experiments (scheduling sessions, recruitment, registration of participants, etc.). The "Questionnaire Builder" can be used to develop online questionnaires. The most interesting function in the context of this report is the "Digital Library" module. Here, registered researchers can upload their data, instructions, software, and paper, whether the experiment is published or not. It is also possible simply to download selected materials.

There are roughly 150 projects currently registered (the projects are usually published papers). Many of them contain raw data; however, there is no common format. Some data are just a pdf-file, some are xls-files, some are Stata data files, and some refer the viewer to an external website. The quality of data documentation is variable, partly depending on how old the data are. Because the "Digital Library" is not centrally managed, the quality of data documentation depends on the researchers who upload data. In some cases socio-demographic information of participants is available.

3. Future developments

Experimental economics is clearly here to stay. It has become a valuable tool for economic research that complements existing tools. An important task of previous research was testing theories, and undergraduates were often sufficient for this purpose. Many experiments returned highly regular results, raising the important issue of whether they are generalizable to other social groups. Some developments on the horizon are a response to this question. Here I will discuss future developments (1) in field experiments, (2) in the integration of experiments into representative surveys, and (3) in the cross-fertilization with other behavioral sciences. A recent development (4) is the use of the Internet for conducting experiments.

(1) *Field experiments* are certainly the fastest growing area of experimental economics. Researchers conduct field experiments in almost all areas in the field of economics, with the possible exception of experiments that are purely theoretical that are best conducted in the lab. Field experiments are an important addition to the methodological toolbox because they enhance our understanding of economic decision making outside

---

8 Exlab. University of Central Florida. http://exlab.bus.ucf.edu/.

the artificial (though indispensible!) worlds of lab experiments. Field experiments can also give us a richer picture of the importance of socio-demographic variables in economic decision making. Therefore, I expect field experiments to continue to grow in importance.

(2) *Integration of experiments into representative surveys.* While running experiments in the field with non-student participants can give us important insight into the generalizability of laboratory findings, only representative samples allow us to draw more general conclusions. The integration of experiments into representative surveys is an exciting development. The SOEP[9] has played a pioneering role in this area. In the Netherlands, CentERdata has also facilitated studies with representative participant pools.[10] In the US, TESS (*Time-Sharing Experiments for the Social Sciences*) allows researchers to run experiments on representative participant pools.[11]

Recent experimental research has focused on issues of trust, fairness, and attitudes toward risk (Fehr et al. 2002; Bellemare and Kröger 2007; Mellemare et al. 2008; Dohmen et al. 2005; Naef et al. 2007). Research in this area is a promising new development and I expect it to expand rapidly, especially considering the ever-expanding body of experience with the process of conducting experiments in the surveys.

(3) *Cross-fertilization of experiments from other behavioral sciences.* Economic experiments (in particular, in simple games) are now used in all of the behavioral sciences. The datasets produced depend on the specific research environment and questions of the respective science. For example, anthropologists have run experiments in small-scale societies where people naturally have significantly different socio-economic backgrounds from those people living in modern, highly developed societies (Heinrich et al. 2006; 2005). But apart from these exceptional instances, the data are not that different than those we already know.

The situation is somewhat different in the emerging field of neuro-economics and the closely related field of social neuroscience, both of which represent exciting new directions in the field (Sanfey et al. 2006; Fehr and Camerer 2007). Up to this point, the datasets have typically been relatively small, in particular where scanning methods (e.g., fMRI) are used. Representativeness (with regard to socio-demographics) has not yet become an issue because most research has simply tried to establish some basic facts. In this respect neuroeconomics is in the same pioneering situation that standard experimental economics was in fifteen

---

9   German Socio-Economic Panel. http://www.diw.de/english/soep/29012.html.
10 Centerdata. http://www.centerdata.nl/en.
11 Time-Sharing Experiments for the Social Sciences. http://www.experimentcentral.org/.

to twenty years ago. For example, research at this time sought to establish basic facts about trust and reciprocity (in rather small-scale lab studies using student-subjects). Today, experiments are run with potentially thousands of participants in representative surveys like the SOEP. It is conceivable that a similar development will occur in neuroeconomics, provided some of its basic findings are replicated in other studies and appropriate techniques (e.g., biomarkers) are developed.

(4) *Experiments using the Internet.* In principle, the Internet offers the possibility of reaching large (worldwide) participant pools, in some cases of several thousand participants (Drehmann et al. 2005) who come from diverse socio-economic backgrounds (Egas and Riedl 2008). Thus, Internet experiments present a potentially attractive research tool. The drawback is that an Internet experiment allows for less control than a lab experiment. Participants might also perceive the decision making situation as more anonymous, compared to a lab environment where there are usually other people are in the room. Whether increased anonymity is a problem or perhaps an advantage depends on the research question. Some research has started to compare decision making in the lab and on the Internet (Güth et al. 2003; Anderhub et al. 2001; Charness et al. 2007). As the Internet gains in importance, combining lab and online experiments will be a fruitful area of research. The lab can provide the (small-scale) benchmark and be used to generate hypotheses about what should happen in the (large-scale) Internet experiment (or in a representative experiment).

A novel area that seems very promising consists of experiments conducted using virtual interactive platforms such as "Second Life."[12] Some researchers see great potential in using such virtual worlds for economic (Castranova 2008) or social science research (Bainbridge 2007) because experiments that are not feasible in the real world can be conducted on the Internet, and because these virtual worlds have millions of users. From the perspective of experimental economics, the question is whether experiments that are set within virtual platforms have scientific value, due to the potential for selection biases of virtual world participants and the inability to control who actually participates. Research on the comparability of results from well-known laboratory findings has just begun, but seems encouraging (Chesney et al. 2007). Thus, I expect research on virtual platforms to continue and to produce some important findings in the near future.

---

12 Second Life. http://secondlife.com/.

4. European and international challenges

The challenges of conducting cross-national research exist on two levels – funding and comparability of methods. The funding issue is beyond the scope of this particular report, but the question of methodology deserves some comment.

Some of the most serious challenges to methodology in experimental economics arise from conducting cross-cultural research. Ensuring the comparability of procedures and participant pools are the key problems that need to be solved in order to move forward. Of the two, comparability of participant pools is the more challenging problem. If representative experiments are not feasible, one approach is to maximize participant pool comparability by running all experiments with the same social groups (Herrmann et al. 2008).

Since participant pools will never be perfectly homogenous across locations it is important to control statistically for the socio-demographic background characteristics. For a proposal on such questions, see Siedler et al. (2008). If representative experiments are feasible the challenge is reduced to ensuring the comparability of procedures and obtaining sufficiently large numbers of participants. Previous research has shown that this can be done (see Naef et al. 2007 comparing Germany and the US). The challenges of course increase with the number of societies compared. Here, some type of collaboration, for example among different household panels, in running these experiments would be essential.

5. Conclusions and recommendations

The gold standard of any experimental science is having control over the environment and replicability of results. This holds true for experimental economics. The laboratory offers a high degree of control and many useful and replicable insights have been gained in that context. Experimental economics is an established tool that has become part of mainstream economics.

Most previous experiments have been conducted using undergraduates as subjects. The question of how these results generalize to other social groups is an interesting one. Running experiments in the field, via the Internet or as part of representative surveys, therefore, are all exciting and fruitful new tools for research that can help to answer this question.

With regard to availability of data, the situation is mixed and probably will remain so for some time. Some journals publish the data on their websites and some researchers do the same voluntarily on their individual websites. There is no "universally accepted" database or repository I am aware of where people post their data after results have been published, with the exception of the ExLab data repository described above. The question is, how desirable is such a data archive? A repository offers the advantage of creating one place where data can be found, so costs of searching are low. However, given the search machines and specialized mailing lists available today, it is also relatively cheap and easy to track down existing datasets, and most researchers are willing to send data upon request.[13] Those who are not willing to share information in this way would also likely be unwilling to submit their data to a repository as well. Maintaining a data archive and getting people to contribute to it is a very costly undertaking that probably would, due to its mainly administrative character, not be of great scientific advantage for those who maintain it.

Another issue concerns the quantitative comparison of research findings across studies (meta-analysis). This is not yet common in experimental economics, although some examples exist (Oosterbeek et al. 2004; Zelmer 2003). A meta-analysis looks at the means or medians of published findings and compares them. Even more scientifically interesting is where they merge all the data from a particular type of experiment into one database, and then perform the analysis on the combined observations (that is, all data points) of all the studies involved. Two types of analyses can be done: comparing the impact of different experimental rules on outcomes, and investigating the role of socio-demographics and other survey variables on decision making (that is, performing on a small scale what the representative experiments can do on the large scale). Being able to do this kind of research requires much more than a mere data repository can deliver. It requires building up a data archive (using database tools) that keeps track of all the dimensions and variables of the original studies (data and paradata).[14] The main problem is the nature of experimental data, which are multidimensional and very specific to a particular research question. Thus, in practice even experiments of one type (for example, trust games or public goods games) differ across multiple dimensions. Merging data from different experiments into one database and also thereby ensuring comparability is a very laborious and scientifically challenging task.

I am particularly aware of these challenges because, working together with my PhD student Eva Poen, I am currently constructing a database of all the public goods experiments I have been involved over the last fifteen years. Simply developing this database took more than one year and it is now only tailor-made for the public goods experiments I have been involved in. This database contains experimental data as well as socio-demographic information and questionnaire responses from more than 6000 participants from

---

13 ESA Experimental Methods Discussion. http://groups.google.com/group/esa-discuss/about.
14 Paradata are "data about data," that is, the details of (experimental) data generation.

(only) eighteen different studies. This database will not be publicly available until we have answered our main research questions ourselves.

In summary, from my own experience I think that merging data (drawn from one type of experiment) into one database would be scientifically desirable. However, I do not think it is feasible without substantial scientific input from interested parties who then also will have property rights to the use of the database. These problems become even more profound when there is a larger number of involved scientists. A one-size-fits-all, or top-down solution to these problems will probably not work.

As I have already mentioned several times, the integration of experiments into representative surveys is an exciting new development in the field of experimental economics. This procedure allows researchers to investigate the impact of socio-demographics on experimentally observed behavior. Some researchers, including myself, have always elicited socio-demographics and responses to psychological questionnaires (similar to personality questionnaires) from the participants in their experiments. However, these efforts have not been coordinated between researchers. Moreover, (experimental) economists were only marginally interested in socio-demographics and therefore eliciting these variables was more of a subsidiary interest, which sometimes led to inconsistencies in the questionnaire design and thereby compromised comparability. Providing the scientific community with a standard set of well-conceived questions that can be administered after any experiment (and that does not last longer than 10 minutes) would be very helpful. A useful step in that direction would be if survey experts and experimental economists would collaboratively propose such a questionnaire and argue for its usefulness in the relevant and appropriate scientific forum.

References:

Anderhub, V./Müller, R. and Schmidt, C. (2001): Design and Evaluation of an Economic Experiment Via the Internet. Journal of Economic Behavior and Organization (46), 227-47.
Andersen, S./Harrison, G./Lau, M.I. and Rutström, E.E. (2007): Behavioral Econometrics for Psychologists. Working Paper 07-04, Department of Economics, College of Business Administration, University of Central Florida.
Bainbridge, W.S. (2007): The Scientific Research Potential of Virtual Worlds. Science 317 (5837), 472-76.
Bellemare, Ch. and Kröger, S. (2007): On Representative Social Capital. European Economic Review 51 (1), 183-202.
Bellemare, Ch./Kröger, S. and Van Soest, A. (2008): Measuring Inequity Aversion in a Heterogeneous Population Using Experimental Decisions and Subjective Probabilities. Econometrica 76 (4), 815-39.
Camerer, C./Loewenstein, G. and Rabin, M. (Eds.) (2004): Advances in Behavioral Economics. Princeton.
Camerer, C.F. (2003): Behavioral Game Theory. Princeton.
Carpenter, J.P./Burks, S. and Verhoogen, E. (2005): Comparing Students to Workers: The Effect of Stakes, Social Framing, and Demographics on Bargaining Outcomes. In: Carpenter, J.P./Harrison, G. and List, J. (Eds.): Field Experiments in Economics. Research in Experimental Economics. Amsterdam.
Castranova, E. (2008): A Test of the Law of Demand in a Virtual World: Exploring the Petri Dish Approach to Social Science. CESifo Working Paper No. 2355.
Charness, G./Haruvy, E. and Sonsino, D. (2007): Social Distance and Reciprocity: An Internet Experiment. Journal of Economic Behavior & Organization 63 (1), 88-103.
Chesney, Th./Chuah, S.-H. and Hoffmann, R. (2007): Virtual World Experimentation: An Exploratory Study. CeDEx Discussion Paper No. 2007 (14).
Davis, D.D. and Holt, Ch.A. (1993): Experimental Economics. Princeton.
Dohmen, Th./Falk, A./Huffman, D./Sunde, U./Schupp, J. and Wagner, G.G. (2005): Individual Risk Attitudes: New Evidence from a Large, Representative, Experimentally-Validated Survey. IZA Discussion Paper Series No. 1730.
Drehmann, M./Oechssler, J. and Roider, A. (2005): Herding and Contrarian Behaviour in Financial Markets – an Internet Experiment. American Economic Review 95 (5), 1403-1426.
Duffy, J. (2008): Experimental Macroeconomics. In: Durlauf, S. and Blume, L.E. (Eds.): The New Palgrave Dictionary of Economics Online. Basingstoke.
Egas, M. and Riedl, A. (2008): The Economics of Altruistic Punishment and the Maintenance of Cooperation. Proceedings of the Royal Society B – Biological Sciences 275 (1637), 871-878.
Falk, A. and Gächter, S. (2008): Experimental Labour Economics. In: Durlauf, S. and Blume, L.E. (Eds.): The New Palgrave Dictionary of Economics Online. Basingstoke.
Fehr, E. and Camerer, C. (2007): Social Neuroeconomics: The Neural Circuitry of Social Preferences. Trends in Cognitive Sciences 11 (10), 419-427.

Fehr, E./Fischbacher, U./Rosenbladt, B. von/Schupp, J. and Wagner, G.G. (2002): A Nationwide Laboratory. Examining Trust and Trustworthiness by Integrating Behavioral Experiments into Representative Surveys. Schmollers Jahrbuch 122 (4), 519-542.

Fischbacher, U. (2007): Z-Tree: Zurich Toolbox for Readymade Economic Experiments. Experimental Economics 10 (2), 171-178.

Friedman, D. and Sunder, Sh. (1994): Experimental Methods. A Primer for Economists. Cambridge.

Gächter, S./Herrmann, B. and Thöni, Ch. (2004): Trust, Voluntary Cooperation, and Socio-Economic Background: Survey and Experimental Evidence. Journal of Economic Behavior and Organization 55 (4), 505-531.

Greiner, B. (2004): An Online Recruitment System for Economic Experiments. In: Kremer, K. Macho, V. (Eds.): Forschung Und Wissenschaftliches Rechnen. Gwdg Bericht 63. Göttingen.

Guala, F. (2005): The Methodology of Experimental Economics. Cambridge.

Güth, W./Schmidt, C. and Sutter, M. (2003): Fairness in the Mail and Opportunism in the Internet – a Newspaper Experiment on Ultimatum Bargaining. German Economic Review 4 (2), 243-265.

Harrison, G.W. and List, J.A. (2004): Field Experiments. Journal of Economic Literature 42 (4), 1009-1055.

Henrich, J./Boyd, R./Bowles, S./Camerer, C.F./Fehr, E./Gintis, H./McElreath, R./Alvard, M./Barr, A./Ensminger, J./Henrich, N./Hill, K./Gil-White, F./Gurven, M./Marlowe, F.W./Patton, J.Q. and Tracer, D. (2005): Economic Man in Cross-Cultural Perspective: Behavioral Experiments in 15 Small-Scale Societies. Behavioral and Brain Sciences 28 (6), 795-855.

Henrich, J./McElreath, R./Barr, A./Ensminger, J./Barrett, C./Bolyanatz, A./Cardenas, J.-C./Gurven, M./Gwako, E./Henrich, N./Lesorogol, C./Marlowe, F./David, T. and Ziker, J. (2006): Costly Punishment across Human Societies. Science 312 (5781), 1767-1770.

Herrmann, B./Thöni, Ch. and Gächter, S. (2008): Antisocial Punishment across Societies. Science 319 (5868), 1362-1367.

Hertwig, R. and Ortmann, A. (2001): Experimental Practices in Economics: A Methodological Challenge for Psychologists? Behavioral and Brain Sciences 24 (3), 383ff.

Kagel, J. and Roth, A.E. (1995): The Handbook of Experimental Economics. Princeton.

Naef, M./Fehr, E./Fischbacher, U./Schupp, J. and Wagner, G.G. (2007): Decomposing Trust: Explaining National and Ethnical Trust Differences. [Unpublished manuscript].

Oosterbeek, H./Sloof, R. and van de Kuilen, G. (2004): Cultural Differences in Ultimatum Game Experiments: Evidence from a Meta-Analysis. Experimental Economics 7 (2), 171-188.

Plott, Ch.R. and Smith, V.L. (Eds.) (2008): Handbook of Experimental Economic Results, Vol. 1. Amsterdam.

Roth, A.E. (2002): The Economist as Engineer: Game Theory, Experimentation, and Computation as Tools for Design Economics. Econometrica 70 (4), 1341-1378.

Sanfey, A.G./Loewenstein, G./McClure, S.M. and Cohen, J.D. (2006): Neuroeconomics: Cross-Currents in Research on Decision-Making. Trends in Cognitive Sciences 10 (3), 108-116.

Shogren, J.F. (2008): Experimental Methods in Environmental Economics. In: Durlauf, S. and Blume, L.E. (Eds.): The New Palgrave Dictionary of Economics Online. Basingstoke.

Siedler, T./Schupp, J./Spiess, C.K. and Wagner, G.G. (2008): The German Socio-Economic Panel as Reference Data Set. RatSWD Working Paper No. 48.

Smith, V.L. (1994): Economics in the Laboratory. Journal of Economic Perspectives 8 (1), 113-131.

Zelmer, J. (2003): Linear Public Goods Experiments: A Meta-Analysis. Experimental Economics 6 (3), 299-310.

8. Experience Sampling

Michaela Riediger

Contact:

Michaela Riediger
Max Planck Institute for Human Development
Max Planck Research Group "Affect Across the Lifespan"
Lentzeallee 94
14195 Berlin
Germany
e-mail: riediger[at]mpib-berlin.mpg.de

Abstract

Experience sampling refers to the repeated sampling of momentary experiences in the individual's natural environment. The methodological advantages of this approach include the minimization of retrospective response biases and the maximization of the validity of the assessment. The conceptual benefits it offers include insights into short-term processes and into the daily-life contexts of the phenomena under study. Making use of the benefits of experience sampling while taking its methodological challenges into consideration allows researchers to address important research questions in the social and behavioral sciences with great precision and clarity. Despite this, experience sampling information is rarely found in the data infrastructure publicly available to researchers. This situation is in stark contrast to the way this methodology is thriving today in research-producing datasets that are not publicly available, for instance, in many psychological investigations. After a discussion of the benefits and challenges of experience sampling, this report outlines its potential uses in social science and economic research and characterizes the status quo in experience-sampling applications in the currently available datasets, focusing primarily on household surveys conducted after 2001. Recommendations are offered for an intensified use of experience sampling in large-scale data collections and how this might be facilitated in the future.

Keywords: experience sampling in the social and behavioural sciences

1. What is experience sampling?

Experience sampling refers to the capturing of experiences – such as events, behaviors, feelings, or thoughts – at the moment of, or close to, their occurrence, and within the context of a person's everyday life. The distinctive characteristic that sets this methodology apart from other assessment approaches is the *repeated* sampling of *momentary* experiences in the individual's *natural* environment (as opposed to, for example, single-time retrospective reconstructions of past experiences in questionnaires or interviews). Many labels, such as event sampling, real-time data capture, time-situated method, ambulatory assessment, diary method, or ecological-momentary assessment, have been used to refer to this methodology. In this report, I use the term *experience sampling* coined by Mihaly Csikszentmihalyi and colleagues in the 1970s, which has since been widely adopted.

The core method in experience sampling, and hence the primary emphasis of this report, is the acquisition of repeated self-reports of momentary experiences or of experiences that occurred during short preceding time intervals (typically covering no more than 24 hours). Assessment schedules in experience sampling research include (a) *interval-contingent sampling* (assessments at fixed points in time, such as before going to bed at night), (b) *signal-contingent sampling* (assessments triggered by signals that typically occur at varying time intervals throughout the day and that are given by electronic assessment devices, such as handheld computers), (c) *event-contingent sampling* (assessments triggered by the occurrence of pre-specified events, such as expenditures), and (d) any combinations of the above. Which assessment schedule is most appropriate in a given study context depends on the specific research question at hand, the prevalence of the particular experience under study, and on feasibility considerations.

Although self-report is the core assessment method in experience sampling and the primary focus of this report, it should be noted that other assessment techniques originating from diverse scientific disciplines can be used as complementary assessment strategies to capture the multiple facets of naturally unfolding experiences and their contexts. These techniques include the ambulatory monitoring of physiological processes or physical activities (see the advisory report on bio-markers in this publication), the recording of behavioral information (e.g., performance in cognitive tasks), the recording of ambient environmental parameters (e.g., sound recordings, photographs of the environment), or the recording of the individual's geographical locations (e.g., geo-tracking, see report on geographical data).

This report opens with a discussion of the benefits and challenges of experience sampling, followed by an outline of its potential uses in social science and economic research. I will then characterize the current situation by looking at experience sampling applications in available datasets, focusing primarily on household surveys conducted after 2001. Based on this assessment, I will draw some conclusions about the future development of experience sampling and its contribution to the data infrastructure and offer some suggestions for how this methodology can address present and future research needs in the social and behavioral sciences.

2. The benefits and challenges of experience sampling methodology

When compared to retrospective self-report – the most widely used assessment approach in social and economic data surveys – experience sampling offers compelling benefits, both from a methodological and a conceptual perspective. At the same time, it is accompanied by some significant challenges, including being a more resource-intensive methodology. Hence, careful consideration of both its benefits and challenges is necessary in order to take full advantage of this powerful methodology.

There are important *methodological* advantages in experience sampling that are brought about by the immediacy of the measurement and the fact that it takes place in the participants' natural environments. It is well known that human memory imposes limits on the validity of what people can report retrospectively. In most questionnaires or interviews, respondents have to rely on partial recall and inference strategies when asked to report on their past behavior or experiences. There is ample empirical evidence that this results in retrospective memory biases and aggregation effects that impair the validity of the information assessed, sometimes profoundly. Experience sampling provides a promising alternative by obtaining reports of experiences at the moment of, or close to, their occurrence. Furthermore, the fact that this information is collected within the natural context of the participants' day-to-day lives further enhances the validity of the assessment, offering unique opportunities to understand experiences and behaviors in their ecological context (Schwarz 2007). Today, experience sampling assessment is typically implemented with the help of electronic assessment devices such as handheld computers, which provide the added methodological benefit of allowing close monitoring of participant response adherence to the measurement scheme.

The prevailing emphasis in most available data collections in the social and economic sciences to date is on differences *between* individuals at given points in time. A fundamental dimension of many aspects in human life – their inherently fluctuating nature as reflected in short-term *within*-person variations – has not yet received much attention, even though the importance of within-person processes for understanding many social and behavioral phenomena has been acknowledged in theory. Hence, a compelling *conceptual* benefit of experience sampling results from the fact that assessments are repeated with short time intervals between them. This makes short-term processes and fluctuations – which cannot be studied with the traditional fixed annual assessment schedules – accessible to scientific investigation. Another conceptual benefit of experience sampling is that it provides insight into the role of everyday contexts for the target phenomena under study, such as the respective roles played by the individual's educational, work, or social environments.

Despite these methodological and conceptual benefits, there are significant challenges that need to be considered when implementing the experience sampling method. Of these challenges, three stand out as particularly critical. First, experience sampling is resource-intensive. Because motivation plays such a significant role in determining whether a participant will successfully complete an experience sampling study or not, close contact with the participants throughout the entire study and adequate remuneration are indispensable. Second, the burden for the participants (e.g., the necessary time commitment) is comparatively large. This creates difficulties in terms of both representativeness and attrition of the sample. The demanding nature of experience sampling studies could lead certain types of individuals to be over- or underrepresented in the sample from the beginning, or to drop out during the study interval. Finally, repeated measuring of a given phenomenon can cause reactivity effects. That is, it is possible that the phenomenon under study may change as a result of measurement or reporting. Although reactivity is a challenge for all social and behavioral research, it can be even more relevant in experience sampling research because the repeated assessments may lead people to pay unusual attention to their experiences and behaviors.

In short, experience sampling carries immense methodological and conceptual advantages. Nonetheless, it also presents a number of challenges that need to be considered, which I will discuss in detail in the concluding section of this report. When adequately applied, however, experience sampling indisputably represents a powerful tool with which to tackle new questions and investigate research questions in greater depth. In the following section I will describe the ways that experience sampling can be applied to social science and economic research.

3. Potential uses of experience sampling in social science and economic research

Generally speaking, experience sampling can provide fine-grained and ecologically valid information on

- the *Who*, *What*, *Where*, *When*, or *How* of experiences and behaviors as they occur in daily life and in natural environments,
- the naturally occurring *variation* and *co-variation* of experiences, behaviors, events, and contextual characteristics over time (both *within* and *between* individuals), and
- the within-person *variability* of experiences and behaviors (i.e., short-term fluctuations or changes) that, depending on the research domain under study, can be indicative either of people's flexibility or adaptability, or of their instability and vulnerability.

Obviously, these are questions that are of immense relevance and importance for a large variety of domains in social, behavioral, and economic research. There are a vast number of potential applications that could provide new insight into diverse phenomena. These include the investigation of life transitions (e.g., divorce, unemployment, childbirth, entering the workforce, or retirement), social interactions, investment or buying behaviors, health behaviors and health-care use and effectiveness, well-being and life satisfaction, family life, work life, availability, use and effectiveness of the educational system, major life events and stressors, as well as investigations of many other research domains. Despite the wide spectrum of potential applications, experience sampling information is still rare in the data infrastructure that is publicly available to researchers in the social and behavioral sciences. This stands in stark contrast to the growing application of this methodology in research activities which produce datasets that are not publicly available, as is the case in many psychological investigations. The following section provides an analysis of the current state of experience sampling applications in the social and behavioral sciences.

4. Status quo of experience sampling in the data infrastructure

The purpose of the following analysis is to characterize the status of experience sampling information in the available data infrastructure. The first part of this analysis addresses the present use of experience sampling in household surveys. It illustrates the scarcity of experience sampling information in the datasets that are accessible to the public and interested researchers. The second part of this analysis addresses the status of experience sampling in psychological research. The purpose of this section is to illustrate how the methodology is actively involved in the production of datasets, but these are available only to a small number of scientists connected to the original research. The concluding section of this report will build on this analysis of the status quo to formulate some recommendations for future research needs and challenges.

4.1 Experience sampling in household surveys with ongoing data collection since 2001

To identify contemporary household surveys employing experience sampling methodology, I conducted a search using the keywords "experience sampling," "diary/diaries," and "ambulatory assessment" in the following databases:

- Data Catalogue of the GESIS Data Archive[1]

---

[1] http://www.gesis.org/Datenservice/Suche/Daten/index.htm

- Survey Databank of the German Youth Institute (*Surveydatenbank des Deutschen Jugendinstituts*)[2]
- National Statistics' Database of Longitudinal Studies[3]
- Data Catalogue of the Economic and Social Data Service[4]

Table 1 lists household surveys that apply experience sampling based on the results of this search strategy and that also demonstrate ongoing data collection since 2001 (up until June 20, 2008). The table shows that only a few household panels currently integrate experience sampling. All of the identified applications of this methodology in household surveys used experience sampling in the form of diaries; that is, in the form of interval-contingent, short-term retrospective assessments. Table 1 also shows that the methodology is applicable in large-scale data collections and well-suited for the investigation of a wide array of phenomena. This is further demonstrated by the fact that the German Federal Statistical Office in collaboration with the Statistical Offices of the *Länder* successfully obtains household expenditure diaries in the German Income and Consumption Survey (EVS, *Einkommens- und Verbrauchsstichprobe*).

None of the most prominent international prospective household panels – the US Panel Study of Income Dynamics (PSID), the German Socio-Economic Panel (SOEP, *Sozio-oekonomisches Panel*), the British Household Panel Study (BHPS, to be succeeded by the UK HLS), and the Multidisciplinary Facility for Measurement and Experimentation in the Social Sciences (MESS, Netherlands) – have yet employed experience sampling methodology. Nonetheless there are clear signs of a growing awareness of, and interest in the powerful potential of this methodology. The study proposal of the Dutch household panel MESS, for example, highlights experience sampling as a potential method for future assessment waves. Furthermore, the German Socio-Economic Panel has recently developed a mobile-phone based experience sampling technology in cooperation with Max Planck Institute for Human Development (Berlin) that makes the application of signal-contingent experience sampling possible in heterogeneous and widely distributed samples. The feasibility of this technology has already been demonstrated in a first model study involving a sample of $N = 378$ participants ranging in age from 14 to 83 years. Participants were provided with mobile phones that they carried with them while pursuing their daily routines. Testing software was installed on the mobile phones that caused the phones to ring at certain points throughout the day and signaled the participant to complete an assessment instrument that referred to his or her mo-

---

2   http://db.dji.de/surveys/index.php?m=msa,0
3   http://www.iser.essex.ac.uk/ulsc/keeptrack/index.php
4   http://www.esds.ac.uk/search/searchStart.asp

mentary experiences. Participant responses were then immediately uploaded via the Internet to a central server. The server interface was also used to set up the study design, to manage the data collection, and to monitor participant response compliance.

Table 1. Experience Sampling in Household Panels with Ongoing Data Collection since 2001

Country	Panel	Experience sampling	Data accessibility
UK	Expenditure and Food Survey Start: 2001–2002 Most recent data: 2005–2006 Sample size: 6,164 households in Great Britain, and 527 in Northern Ireland Design: repeated cross-sectional	Diaries of personal expenditures, homegrown and wild food brought into the home. Kept by each adult for two weeks; simplified diaries kept by children aged 7 to 15 years for two weeks.	Derived variables from the diary are included in the dataset, as the raw diary data are not released to the public for confidentiality reasons (access contingent upon registration).
UK	Home On-Line Survey (HoL) 1998–2001 (finished) Sample size: 999 households, all household members older than 9	Seven end-of day diaries (comprehensive activity diaries).	Access contingent upon registration.
UK	Scottish Household Survey Start: 1999 Most recent data: 2007 Sample size: 27,000 in 2003–2004 (diaries) Design: repeated cross-sectional	One travel diary provided on day prior to interview by one randomly selected adult of the household.	Access contingent upon registration.
Denmark	Time Use of Households: A Scheduling of Danes Daily Use of Time Started: 1987 Most recent data: 2001 Sample size: 4,000 Design: longitudinal (2 occasions)	Diaries kept by respondents and their partners for two days, one randomly selected weekday, and one randomly selected weekend day (activities, social partners).	Application to Danish National Institute of Social Research.
Ireland	Household Budget Survey Started: 1951 Most recent data: 2004–2005 Sample size: 6,884 households in 2004–2005 Design: repeated cross-sectional	Detailed diary of household expenditure over a two-week period.	From 1987 on request to Irish Social Science Data Archive.

4.2 Experience sampling in psychological research

The relatively rare use of experience sampling in large-scale data collections such as household surveys – surveys that are designed to contribute to a broadly accessible data infrastructure – stands in stark contrast to the way the methodology has been taken up in research activities designed to produce smaller datasets and available to a limited number of researchers. One example, which is discussed in this section, can be found in the field of psychological research. Other examples of fields where experience sampling is frequently used – in time use studies and transportation research – are the focus of other advisory reports in this publication so they are not addressed here.

The methodological and conceptual strengths of experience sampling are well-recognized in psychological research. This has led to a recent upsurge in the use of experience sampling methodology for psychological investigations. Hundreds of papers on experience sampling investigations have been published since 2001. As of 20 June 2008, for example, and taking into account only publications that have appeared between 2001 and 2008, the database PsycINFO yielded 355 hits for the keyword "experience sampling," 175 hits for the keyword "diary method," and 188 hits for the keyword "ambulatory assessment." Other indications of the dynamic growth of experience sampling methodology in this area is the recent publication of several monographs on experience sampling methodology and special issues dedicated to this theme in international psychology journals (e.g., Ebner-Priemer et al. in press; Hektner et al. 2007; Stone et al. 2007; Westmeyer 2007); and the recent foundation of the "Society of Ambulatory Assessment" in 2008[5]).

Although experience sampling in psychological research is most often applied in small samples (i.e., $N < 200$) that are queried only once, experience sampling has also been successfully included as an assessment method in comparatively larger and longitudinal research projects, particularly those conducted in the US. Examples of these include:

- the "National Survey of Midlife Development in the USA" (MIDUS, $N = 7,189$) in which experience sampling in the form of eight subsequent telephone interviews on daily life was administered in a subproject entitled, "National Study of Daily Experiences" (NSDE, $N = 1,483$);

- the "Normative Aging Study" (NAS, $N = 2,280$) in which experience sampling in the form of eight consecutive daily diaries on stressful events, memory failures, etc. was administered in a subsample of $N = 333$ participants; and,

---

5 http://www.ambulatory-assessment.org/

- the "Alfred P. Sloan Study of Youth and Social Development" in which signal-contingent sampling of momentary experiences was repeatedly administered in a sample of $N = 877$ adolescents.

Taken together, the recent increase in the use of experience sampling methodology in psychological research underscores the methodological and conceptual strengths of this approach and demonstrates its applicability to a variety of populations. However, these uses in psychological research have not yet contributed to an enrichment of a wider data infrastructure available to a community of interested researchers at large. Rather, access to experience sampling datasets in psychology typically remains limited to a narrow group of researchers within the network of those involved in the conceptualization of the study and the collection of the data. Release of those data to the research community is not yet common practice in psychological research.

5. Recommendations for future developments and challenges

To summarize, experience sampling is a promising research tool that has profound methodological and conceptual benefits compared to standard survey methodologies of retrospective or general self-reports. It has the potential to provide important and ecologically valid insights into a large array of research domains in the social and behavioral sciences. Although experience sampling currently occupies a lively position in psychological research, only a few applications of experience sampling are available in data collections that feed into the publicly available data infrastructure. There are, however, indications of a growing awareness of the potential of experience sampling in the international research landscape.

A broad conclusion that can be drawn from these analyses is that making use of the benefits of experience sampling, while taking its methodological challenges into consideration, will contribute to the creation of a data infrastructure that makes it possible to address current and future research questions with greater precision and clarity. In the following section I offer six concluding recommendations focused on facilitating the intensified use of experience sampling in large-scale data collections now and into the future.

(1) *Strengthen multi-method approach in large-scale surveys.* Experience sampling is a potent methodology that can supplement standard survey methodology such as global or long-term retrospective self-reports. Its methodological advantages (e.g., minimization of response biases and

maximization of ecological validity) allow for the investigation of existing research questions in great depth. Its conceptual advantages (e.g., accessibility of short-term fluctuations and change within and between individuals, the respective role of contextual characteristics) generate opportunities for tackling new research questions.

(2) *Consider a 'study within a study' solution in large-scale data collections.* Experience sampling is resource-intensive. Theory-driven applications in selected subsamples of participants will therefore increase the feasibility of experience sampling in large-scale data collections.

(3) *Make use of technological advances in experience sampling applications.* Technological advances can be used to increase the feasibility of experience sampling in large-scale and heterogeneous samples and also to decrease the burden of experience sampling for the participants. Particularly promising for large-scale data collections is the use of mobile technology. Among its advantages are (a) the potential to use the participants' own mobile phones as assessment devices, (b) the central control of study content and assessment schedules via web-interfaces in server-client systems, (c) the immediate upload of data to central servers allows the monitoring of participant response compliance, (d) the relative unobtrusiveness and feasibility of measurement completion in daily life contexts (provided assessment instruments are of adequate length), and (e) the easy combination with follow-up interviews or other assessment strategies stemming from diverse scientific areas (e.g., for ambulatory bio-monitoring see the advisory report on bio-markers in this publication; for location-tracking, see the report on geographical data).

(4) *Address the methodological challenges of experience sampling.* Study designs should adopt appropriate measures to address the methodological challenges of experience sampling. Control group designs are necessary to assess potential reactivity effects, to note possible changes in the phenomenon under study caused by its measurement. Careful sample recruitment strategies are needed to minimize potential self-selection biases that would result in limited sample representativeness. Sample attrition, or participant drop-out, can be minimized by maintaining close contact to the participants during the study interval and by implementing reasonable study characteristics, such as those pertaining to the number of measurement occasions and the length of the assessment instruments.

(5) *Increase the accessibility of experience sampling datasets.* To increase the availability of experience sampling datasets in the data infrastructure of the social and behavioral sciences, it is essential to foster the release of datasets to the larger research community. One possible form this

could take is to make research funding grants contingent upon the researcher consenting to release the obtained dataset to the research community after a reasonable amount of time (e.g., after 7–10 years).

(6) *Advance research on experience sampling methodology.* Methodological research will support the greater implementation of experience sampling methodology in survey designs. One way to promote research on experience sampling methodology is to include it as a research topic in the Priority Programme on Survey Methodology of the German Research Foundation (DFG, *Deutsche Forschungsgemeinschaft*).

References:

Ebner-Priemer, U./Pawlik, K. and Kubiak, Th.E. (Eds.) (in press): Ambulatory Assessment [Special issue]. European Psychologist.
Hektner, J.M./Schmidt, J.A. and Csikszentmihalyi, M. (2007): Experience sampling Method: Measuring the quality of everyday life. Thousand Oaks.
Schwarz, N. (2007): Retrospective and concurrent self-reports: The rationale for real-time data capture. In: Stone, A.A./Shiffman, S./Atienza, A.A. and Nebeling, L. (Eds.): The science of real-time data capture. New York.
Stone, A.A./Shiffman, S./Atienza, A.A. and Nebeling, L. (Eds.) (2007): The science of real-time data capture. New York.
Westmeyer, H.E. (Ed.) (2007): Advances in the methodology of ambulatory assessment [Special issue]. European Journal of Psychological Assessment 23 (4).

9. Virtual Worlds as Petri Dishes for the Social and Behavioral Sciences

Edward Castronova and Matthew Falk

Contact:

Edward Castronova
1229 East 7th Street
Bloomington, IN 47405
US
e-mail: castro[at]indiana.edu

Abstract

The next tool developed for social science experimentation should allow for macro level, generalizable scientific research. In the past, devices such as rat mazes, petri dishes and supercolliders were developed when scientists needed new tools to do research. We believe that virtual worlds are the modern equivalent to supercolliders for social scientists, and that they should be the next area to receive significant attention and funding. The advantages provided by virtual worlds research outweigh the costs. Virtual worlds allow for societal level research with no harm to humans, large numbers of experiments and participants, and make long term and panel studies possible. Virtual worlds do have some drawbacks in that they are expensive and time-consuming to build. These obstacles can be overcome, however, by adopting the models of revenue and maintenance practiced by the current game industry. The returns from using virtual worlds as scientific tools could reach levels that would self fund future research for decades to come. At the outset, however, an initial investment from funding agencies appears to be necessary.

Keywords: virtual worlds, macro-level experiments, research infrastructure
JEL Classification: C15, C59, C82, C99

1. Introduction

In the past, science developed new tools for research as the need arose. From petri dishes to rat mazes, and continuing on even to the construction of supercolliders, scientists require specific tools to answer the questions they ask. These devices all influence specific micro-level observations. But when it comes to social science and research questions on the societal level, tools for empirical research had not developed much beyond where they were two centuries ago until recently. Developments in the collection of survey data began to take place after "World War II." In the 1990s, "experimental economics" started to become a new and popular tool for empirical research (although, surprisingly, seldom applied by sociologists). Now, however, social scientists should be looking toward a new area: virtual worlds (VW).

To be considered a virtual world, a game or social networking site must: be computer generated, persistent (i.e., always there even if no one is currently logged into it), and have humans represented in the form of avatars (the embodiment of the user in the virtual space) capable of taking actions on behalf of their human counterpart. Only in virtual worlds do we find the proper tool set for large scale social science research, something previously unavailable to scientists. These defining features combine to allow scientists access to long-running persistent societies of users, all engaged in actions that resemble what we see in the real world (Castronova and Falk 2009).[1] Please note that what we are discussing in this paper are experiments on the macro- level of a society. We are not addressing the issue of using virtual worlds for conducting experiments on the micro-level of individual players (see, for example, Chesney et al. 2007). For an even simpler approach using virtual worlds like "Second Life" for social surveys, see Bell et al. (2008).

Because of the large-scale commercial success and now widespread use of VWs, it is possible to collect large amounts of data from large numbers of users. Instead of a few hundred people in one place for a short time, as in current experimental economics, for example, and other lab-based research, we can draw from populations that range from thousands to millions and take measurements over time. Because of the size of the populations involved, VWs let us look at causation at the macro or societal level.

Virtual worlds range in scope from small-scale, internet browser based games with perhaps a few hundred players to the massively successful game "World of Warcraft," which has had ten million subscriptions purchased in its four years of existence and has an estimated consistent player base of eight million. The populations of these worlds span the globe, and it is just as possible to meet someone from thousands of miles away as it is to join your friends from down the street when exploring the virtual world (Castronova 2005; 2007).

2. Petri dishes, rat mazes, supercolliders

While the virtual world is not a sealed vacuum, it does resemble a petri dish in its functionality (Castronova and Falk 2009). Many users, millions at a time in fact, can exist in a game like "World of Warcraft." These users are not, however, all interacting with each other in one space. Like petri dishes in the laboratory, individual servers – digital copies of the same world with unique users interacting – make it possible for technology to handle the demand. The servers, or individual petri dishes, contain the same ingredients in them. It is the bacteria – in this case the players – that differ based on the server they choose.

Because the servers all inherently begin as exactly the same world, it is possible to make one small change to the composition of the goo in the petri dish – a single variable on one server – to create experimental conditions. Server after server, side by side, can resemble rows of petri dishes in a lab. One group contains a set of control conditions, another group one experimental condition, and so on. The underlying code, or the thing that makes it

---

1 See also Giles (2007) and Miller (2007).

all work, does not change. The color of the sky, the names of the places, and the sizes of the oceans do not differ, unless of course that is what the scientist chooses to change. The only restriction to the number of servers and amount of players is monetary, something we will return to below.

Just because all this is possible does not make virtual worlds perfect for answering all questions. In fact, there are some types of questions that virtual worlds are poor at answering. Like all experimental tools, the tool must be designed to answer the types of questions that the researcher wants to ask.

For instance, mammalian cognition is a frequently studied topic. Some scientists use rat mazes to test the cognitive habits of rats and others recreate the mediated environments humans encounter every day to examine what effects they have on the brain. Both of these cases provide good examples of how scientific tools are shaped to correspond to the questions at hand.

Figure 1 demonstrates the relationship between type of question asked and the tools used to study them. The horizontal axis in figure 1 arrays experimental environments according to their fidelity to reality. An environment that is very concrete replicates reality quite well. It is a simulation. A media effects environment that places a TV with current programming in an American living room – replicated right down to the six-pack of beer and the cat odor – is concrete. A media effects environment that attaches wires to individuals' heads and has them watch triangles on a small screen while holding a buzzer is abstract.

The dashed line running diagonally across figure 1 registers the set of ideal experiments – where the conceptual level of the question is well-matched by the concreteness of the experimental environment. If the research question is specific, the experimental environment must be concrete. If the question is general, the experimental environment must be abstract. The area labeled "Bad Experiments" in the figure refers to the attempt to study a specific question within an abstract research environment. You cannot conclude much about the reaction of typical American families to last night's newscast by wiring their heads and asking them to watch triangles on a screen. Bad experiments can go the other way too: you cannot learn much about the general rate of response times to visual stimulus just by watching people in their living rooms.

The point of the diagram is this: it is senseless to make claims about the validity of a research environment unless you know what sort of question is being studied. A rat maze is a terribly abstract environment, yet would anyone say, "You can't learn anything about anything in a rat maze. A rat maze is too unlike the real world." It is possible to learn a great deal about mammalian cognition from rat mazes. When research questions involve societies, or have macro-level implications, we must build a more concrete and specific environment.

Figure 1. Experimental Tools and Scientific Questions

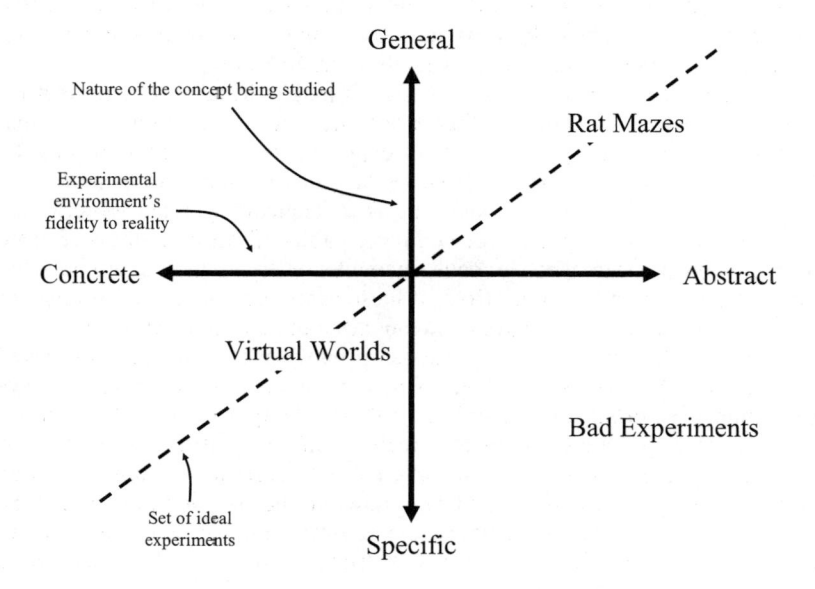

```
                            General
                              ▲                    ╱
   Nature of the concept being studied          ╱
                              │           Rat Mazes
                              │        ╱
   Experimental               │     ╱
   environment's              │  ╱
   fidelity to reality        │╱
   Concrete ◄─────────────────┼─────────────────► Abstract
                            ╱ │
              Virtual Worlds  │
                         ╱    │
                      ╱       │       Bad Experiments
                   ╱          │
                ╱             │
             ╱  ↑             │
       Set of ideal           │
       experiments          Specific
```

Source: Castronova and Falk (2009).

3. Current state of the research field

While many researchers examine communications and media in the form of virtual worlds, only a very small number are using empirical methods to do so. Much of the research is concerned with theory creation, observational and ethnographic methods, including observational analyses by means of regression analysis. All of these methods are valid and collect pieces of information, but none of them are experimental and as such do not lead to the concrete, generalizable, macro-level information about human behavior that social science is seeking.

Social and behavioral scientists seek to understand how humans interact. Social scientists, specifically, want to explore the large questions of human interactions: war, disease, starvation, ecological disaster, economic stability, etc. The only way to solve macro-level problems is with macro-level science. *Controlled experimentation at the societal level* is not being conducted, and in fact would be impossible to conduct under normal circumstances. It is inadvisable and indeed impossible to remove real humans from society, place them in a vacuum for months or years at a time and then experiment on them. There are some attempts being made at this type of science, known to economists as "field experiments" (Harrison and List 2004; Hausman and Wise 1985; List 2008) but they are often derided for their inability to produce controlled and generalized results.

Field experiments take one of three forms: artificial field experiments, framed field experiments, and natural field experiments. Artificial field experiments tend to resemble laboratory experiments as closely as possible, but with a sample drawn from a specific population of interest. This eliminates generalizability unless that group is itself representative of the general population. Framed field experiments entail placing experimental differences in their natural habitat, such as providing different social programs for groups and determining which choice worked better overall. These again target a specific population (i.e., those participating in that particular choice at that location at that time). While less abstract than artificial field experiments, they do not hold up to the rigor of laboratory testing standards. The closest of the three to laboratory science are natural field experiments, which combine the anonymity on the part of the subject with the experimental manipulation of framed field experimentation. They fall short again, however. Due to the interaction of natural environment and the lack of available opportunities to produce works, researchers are limited by their reliance on the presence of naturally occurring phenomena that they can get approval to study.

Governmental interest in research generally falls into a category all of its own: simulation research. On the surface, simulation research looks like the virtual worlds research we propose here, but there is a fundamental difference between the two. Simulations are essentially computer-run models, in which the players (known as "agents") are also computerized. Each behaves in a manner that is simple and is predictive of how an individual would act, assuming that each individual will always make the most "rational" choice. This is problematic, however, since many believe that humans do not react rationally to many situations, if any at all, and therefore consider the interactions of simple, rational models to be incomplete. A fundamental improvement to this model would be to use real humans in place of the agents – which is exactly what virtual worlds offer.

Building what amounts to the social science equivalent to a supercollider, however, appears both necessary and expensive. Preliminary forays into this research field are already being conducted. Our group, the Synthetic Worlds Initiative of Indiana University, has already completed the construction of a small-scale virtual world and the subsequent experimentation process within.

Funded by a USD $250,000 grant from the MacArthur Foundation, "Arden" – a world based loosely on the works of William Shakespeare – took a student team almost two years to build. It then required another several months to run an experiment within the world and to compile those results for publication (Castronova et al. 2008). The experimental test run of Arden was an investigation of the economic theory of supply and demand. Having found that the law of supply and demand holds true in a virtual world, Arden was deemed a successful first step towards the creation of a virtual petri dish, or supercollider. But it was, in fact, only a first step.

The next logical step is to create another virtual world, capable of housing more users and answering bigger questions. Along these lines, we are currently developing a game called Greenland that will be used to test the emergence of currency in the form of a web browser based resource collection game. But even this project, which can expect somewhere between several hundred to several thousand subjects, is merely another small development. The ideal supercollider-level virtual world would be more like "World of Warcraft," and consequently cost much more.

4. Development costs, future research and recommendations

Developing a persistent A-list, or top quality, virtual world game requires not only a significant investment of time and personnel, but also involves large overhead costs for startup. This can be an insurmountable obstacle in terms of current social science research funding awards. Other areas of research and public service, however, provide models for the research and development of extremely expensive projects that get results and, in the end, generate profits to replenish those research and development costs.

The cost of developing virtual worlds are typically held in secrecy, since game design companies do not want to publicize exactly how much they've spent developing their projects. However, on the basis of the knowledge shared by former and current leaders in that industry, it is quite possible to infer how much one should cost. Game development costs come primarily from three areas: the game design team (development), game launch, and customer service during the years in which a world operates.

Game design teams are typically small at the beginning, possibly five or so people, but rapidly expand to include teams of 25–40 people, depending on the size of the project. This expansion occurs over a couple of years, and projects regularly take more than thirty months from the initial design meeting to the end of testing, or launch. For example, in 2005, the rule of thumb was that it cost approximately USD $10,000 per month per person on the team. This does not match up with the current size of research funding in the field – remember that Arden was created on a USD $250,000 grant over the course of two years by a team of approximately fifteen people. Professional game developers also work longer than forty-hour weeks, and are dedicated staff, whereas Arden and Greenland are being developed by graduate students working part time. Hiring professional staff would greatly speed up projects like this and allow for faster game development and more experimentation.

In addition to the cost of personnel, each of the servers (i.e., the petri dishes) discussed earlier is quite an expensive investment and requires a large amount of expensive bandwidth to run. Setting all this up and making sure it works before releasing it to the public is the next step in game development. In 2003, for example, the average cost for game "launch" (as it is known in the industry) was USD $7 million, with amounts in the USD $10–12 million range being more the rule than the exception. Current research is being performed on two small servers hosted on university campuses. These servers simply cannot handle the mass numbers of players as the servers game companies use. Therefore, this limits both the number of study participants and variations of the virtual world it is possible to have.

After the game goes public and research and play commence, there is still a significant amount of time and money required on the part of the game support staff. They must maintain player relations, collect subscription fees (if using one of the fee-based models we discuss below), and take care to maintain the software and hardware that allow users to access the world.

There are, however, two examples of ways through which it would be possible to fund large public projects, pay back the funding agencies, and create profits for further research and projects. These examples can be gleaned from parallels between nuclear power plants, the pharmaceutical research industry, and our vision of a virtual world as a supercollider.

Nuclear power plants, like new experimental drugs, are initially funded on public money. These infrastructures, once built, begin to sell their services to customers (in the form of power and pills, respectively). Through this revenue stream, the companies that undertook the burden of building and maintaining the facilities (in the case of nuclear power), or developing, researching, and testing (in the case of drugs) pay back the startup money they required to make those advances.

This is also the model used by the game industry around the world today. Games are launched to the public with both a "box fee" (the price the consumer pays in the store for the software) and then a monthly subscription fee. For example, upon release, "World of Warcraft" cost approximately USD $50 US dollars, and also costs users around USD $15 a month to play. These fees mean that Blizzard Entertainment, the parent company that financed the creation of the project, has seen its money back and more. Blizzard continues to use profits from "World of Warcraft" not only to pay the aforementioned support staff, but to fund new projects as well. It is important to remember though that it does take time to see this return on investment – typically twelve months at a minimum if a game is a large commercial success. If it is not, this process can take much longer. This does present a valid and established format for funding agencies to consider when making choices about funding large projects of this nature.

5. Conclusion

The next tool for social science experimentation should allow for macro level, generalizable scientific research. In the past, devices such as rat mazes, petri dishes, and supercolliders have been developed when scientists needed new tools to do research. We believe that virtual worlds are the modern equivalent to supercolliders for social scientists, and feel they should be the next area to receive significant attention and funding. The advantages provided by virtual worlds research outweigh the costs. Virtual worlds allow for societal level research with no harm to humans, incorporate large numbers of experiments and participants, and make long term and panel studies possible.

Virtual worlds do have some drawbacks; they are expensive and time consuming to build. These obstacles can be overcome, however, by adopting the models of revenue and maintenance practiced by the current game industry. The returns from virtual worlds being used as scientific tools could reach levels that would self fund future research for decades to come. At the outset, however, an initial investment from funding agencies appears to be necessary.

References:

Bell, M./Castronova, E. and Wagner, G.G. (2008): Virtual Assisted Self Interviewing (VASI): An Expansion of Survey Data Collection Methods to the Virtual Worlds by Means of VDCI. RatSWD Working Paper No. 42.
Castronova, E. et al. (2008): A Test of the Law of Demand in a Virtual World: Exploring the Petri Dish Approach to Social Science. International Journal of Gaming and Computer-Mediated Simulations (2), 1-14.
Castronova, E. (2007): Exodus to the Virtual World How Online Fun is Changing Reality. New York.
Castronova, E. (2005): Synthetic Worlds. Chicago.
Castronova, E and Falk, M. (2009): Virtual Worlds: Petri Dishes, Rat Mazes, Supercolliders. Games and Culture 4 (4), 396-407.
Chesney, Th./Chuah, S.-H. and Hoffmann, R. (2007): Virtual world experimentation: An exploratory study. Nottingham University Business School – Industrial Economics Division Occasional Paper Series No. 2007-21. Nottingham.
Giles, J. (2007): Life's a Game. Nature 445 (7123), 18-20.
Harrison, G.W. and List, J.A. (2004): Field experiments. Journal of Economic Literature 42 (4).
Hausman, J.A. and Wise, D.A. (1985): Social Experimentation. Chicago.
List, J.A. (2008): Homo experimentalis evolves. Science 321 (5886), 207-208.
Miller, G. (2007): The Promise of Parallel Universes. Science 317 (5843), 1341-1343.

10. Qualitative Interviewing of Respondents in Large Representative Surveys

Olaf Groh-Samberg and Ingrid Tucci

Contact:

Olaf Groh-Samberg
BIGSSS, University of Bremen
FVG-West, Wiener Straße
28359 Bremen
Germany
e-mail: ogrohsamberg[at]bigsss.uni-bremen.de

Ingrid Tucci
Sozio-Economic Panel Study (SOEP)
DIW Berlin
Mohrenstrasse 58
10117 Berlin
Germany
e-mail: itucci[at]diw.de

Abstract

Large representative surveys are using mixed methods to an ever-increasing degree. Biomarkers, register data, and experiments, for example, provide different types of data that can be linked with survey data. The use of qualitative interviewing of participants in longitudinal surveys is, however, still rare in the social sciences. Yet qualitative methods have proven just as valuable as quantitative methods in providing insights into social reality by reflecting the multidimensionality of individual life courses and lived realities. Furthermore, in-depth interviews can provide a better understanding of individual decision-making processes and behavior resulting from more or less unconscious strategies. They also provide insights into decisive turning points in people's lives. Finally, by linking quantitative and qualitative data, the reliability of longitudinal information can be analyzed thoroughly in terms of accuracy as well as meaningfulness.

Keywords: mixed methods, qualitative data, longitudinal data, life course
JEL Code: C81, C83, Z13

1. Introduction

In the social and behavioral sciences, the use of mixed methods to address a particular research question typically involves a combination of quantitative and qualitative methodologies (Brannen 2005; Bryman 2006; Tashakkori and Teddlie 2003). As an increasing range of data becomes available for scientific research – as documented throughout this publication and in the Working Paper Series of the German Data Forum (RatSWD) – the possibilities for mixed method approaches are growing. However, the use of mixed methods to link data from large representative surveys to qualitative data is still rare. A recent trend in longitudinal surveys worldwide consists of the linkage of survey data with data from different sources using diverse methodologies. For example, birth cohort studies or household panels like BHPS,[1] HILDA,[2] PSID,[3] and SOEP,[4] are collecting biomarkers, objective health measures, data from experiments, daily experience sampling or register and institutional context data to survey respondents (see the respective chapters in this publication and, e.g., the new UK Household Longitudinal Study Understanding Society, or UKHLS). In this context of methodological innovations of longitudinal surveys, conducting in-depth qualitative inter-

---

[1] British Household Panel Study.
[2] Household, Income and Labour Dynamics in Australia.
[3] US Panel Study of Income Dynamics.
[4] German Sozio-Economic Panel (SOEP, *Sozio-oekonomisches Panel*).

views with sub-samples of respondents is one important and promising, yet only recently developing issue.

Up to now, qualitative methods have been used primarily with quantitative data to "embellish" analyses (Mason 2006a). However, mixed methods approaches in the sense of a triangulation of quantitative and qualitative data collected from the same respondents might help to understand the mechanisms underlying human behavior and individual life courses (e.g., Giele and Elder 1998). This is particularly true with respect to individual decision-making processes, coping strategies, and biographical "turning points," i.e., events or experiences that play a decisive role an individual's life course by correcting trajectories (Abbot 1997). The importance of decision-making is not only central to the so-called *rational actor model* that has become a common reference model in the economic and social sciences and is typically associated with the large-scale quantitative data analysis (Goldthorpe 2000); it is even considered a broader "unifying framework" for the behavioral sciences (Gintis 2007).

However, as quantitative research along these lines only observes the contexts, determinants, and outcomes of individual decisions – which are measured at least indirectly by means of proxy information – the decision-making process itself can only be modeled in a "reduced form" due to the lack of information on what is really going on in the individual's mind. This is exactly where qualitative in-depth interviews with sub-samples of survey respondents offer possibilities for new research prospects. Qualitative interviews may provide insights into how people select relevant information, what relevance they assign to them, and how their values, attitudes, perceptions, states of knowledge, and conscious as well as unconscious strategies are shaped by and shape their behavior.

Thus, qualitative methods can provide insights into something that still remains a "black box" for quantitative methods that aim to connect measured "inputs" with measured "outcomes" of human decisions and behavior and strive to establish a "causal link" by testing the theoretically derived hypotheses. From a qualitative perspective, this causal link appears to present itself as a dynamic and recursive system of "meanings." This does not mean, however, that the two methods are incompatible (Brannen 2005; Kelle 2001). Rather, by developing explanations of human behavior – for example, regarding educational decisions – the assumptions of quantitative research typically derived from the rational actor model, or any other theory, can be more directly tested, specified, and enriched or even rejected by means of qualitative methods that allow a deeper understanding of how choices come about.

2. The state of the art

Although still rather rare, the linkage of survey data with qualitative interviews seems to have reached scientific maturity, and is being discussed increasingly within the scientific community (Tashakkori and Teddlie 2003). Although there are still forces at work promoting the separation of quantitative and qualitative methods – separate training courses, academic journals, funding schemes, and university chairs – efforts are also underway seeking to actively press forward with mixed method research (e.g., Bryman 2006; Mason 2006b).

It has become apparent that mixed methods are not a third way, or even a third methodology in their own right, and that there exists a broad variety of means by which mixed method approaches can be rationalized and employed in empirical research. A meta-analysis by Bryman (2006) of more than 200 research projects employing mixed methods reveals that mixed methods are mainly employed in sociology, and that they combine self-administered questionnaire surveys with semi-structured interviews to address specific research questions. Mixed methods are typically used to produce "complementary" data or to "enhance" data, facilitating the examination of different perspectives or different aspects of a particular research question. However, there is no strict methodology that determines how different methods should be linked. Rather, there are good arguments for designing and linking mixed methods based on theoretical principles in order to produce non-redundant and non-trivial results (Kelle 2001).

Mixed methods approaches were formerly used primarily in larger-scale research projects aiming to explore new, uncharted research fields. The seminal work of Marie Jahoda, Paul Lazarsfeld et al. (1933) "Marienthal: The Sociography of an Unemployed Community" dealt with the challenges posed by the external economic shock of mass unemployment during the 1930s. The sociology and psychology of the time was entirely incapable of predicting how modern society might respond to such a shock, so the research team attempted to collect as wide a variety of data as possible, ranging from the observation of walking speed, conventional household interviews to content analysis of school essays. Once testable concepts had been produced – such as the concept of individual stages of unemployment experiences – they could then easily be tested using standard quantitative methods or more focused qualitative interviews from predefined samples. This gave rise to Lazarsfeld's idea that qualitative methods could be used to *develop hypotheses* and that quantitative methods could be used to *test hypotheses*. Following this idea, mixed methods research designs often use qualitative interviews and ethnographic research to develop a hypothesis, and survey questionnaires to test the hypothesis. However, the strict two-stage model of sequentially combining qualitative and quantitative methods has not become widespread (Leech and Onwuegbuzie 2009; Creswell et al. 2003). Rather, many larger mixed methods research projects use qualitative methods to supplement quantitative surveys in order to gain a fuller understanding of the "real lives" of the individuals and households surveyed (e.g., Portes and Fernández-Kelly 2008; Mayer and Schulze 2009a; 2009b).

3. The unique potential of qualitative projects based on longitudinal survey respondents

In some sense, longitudinal surveys such as household panel or birth cohort studies can be said to follow in the tradition of Jahoda et al. (1933) in establishing a large survey to analyze how households adapt to social and economic changes and in turn contribute to social change. Longitudinal surveys provide a constantly expanding body of diverse data and are therefore becoming multiple or mixed method enterprises to an increasing degree. Conducting qualitative interviews with long-term survey respondents provides a unique opportunity for a real triangulation of different types of data on people's life courses. In long-running longitudinal studies, it is possible to conduct biographical interviews with long-term respondents for whom more than a decade of prospectively collected panel data are available. In principle, the longitudinal data can also be linked with register data from employment or social insurance agencies.

Triangulations like these would make it possible to thoroughly analyze the validity, reliability, and meaningfulness of panel data. Biographical crises or "turning points" in the life course as reported in qualitative interviews can be checked against the standardized yearly measures collected in longitudinal surveys (e.g., life satisfaction). Is it possible to detect biographical crisis through quantitative longitudinal data? Are respondents able to remember negative events like unemployment or the timing of a divorce? Does the use of combined methodologies affect non-response behavior (item non-response as well as partial unit non-response or panel attrition)?

Mixed method research designs are often used for validation purposes: this is the case with qualitative interviews or experiments being used to validate and/or improve measures in survey questionnaires (e.g., Dohmen et al. 2010 for measuring risk aversion). Cognitive interviewing has been developed as a qualitative tool for this purpose (Willis 2005). Moreover, by drawing on a large ongoing survey, one can systematically select respondents who appeared to be particularly interesting in the quantitative analysis for qualitative interviews. A common feature of such designs is the construction of typologies by clustering survey data and then selecting "representative" respondents for each cluster, or by selecting extreme cases or even outliers for more in-depth analysis (see Portes and Fernández-Kelly 2008 for an outlier analysis).

Apart from investigating the methodological effects arising from the type of data, qualitative interviewing of respondents to longitudinal surveys allows insights in a wide range of particular research questions, such as school choice, educational and occupational aspirations, and family formation. Qualitative interviews can be carried out with entire households and address issues such as family relations within and across households, social networks, perceptions of neighborhoods, schools, employers, and how these shape life goals and individual behavior. However, these rich opportunities have only recently entered the research agenda of longitudinal surveys.

4. Review of qualitative projects based on longitudinal survey respondents

To date, very few projects have been carried out involving qualitative interviews with respondents to longitudinal surveys, but a growing number of such projects have started recently or are currently under planning:

- For the German context, about three dozen interviews were conducted with respondents from the 1971 birth cohort of the German Life History Study (GLHS). Using narrative interviews, Mayer and Schulze (2009a) used a "modest mixed-methods strategy" to analyze the life courses of this generation in West and East Germany and, in another study, to study parenthood processes in order to provide evidence of mechanisms resulting in delayed family formation (Mayer and Schulze 2009b: 12).

- In a project at the University of Manchester on interactions between and within generations, data from the English Longitudinal Study of Ageing (ELSA) were linked to qualitative interviews of between 25 and 30 respondents and approximately 20 of their descendants.[5] The goal of the study was to understand intergenerational transfers and communication and the role played by older people.

- In a project conducted at the Center for Longitudinal Studies at the University of Manchester, qualitative interviews are planned with about 180 respondents (aged 50) from the 1958 British Birth Cohort Study in order

---

5   More details on this project are available at http://www.socialsciences.manchester.ac.uk/realities/research/generations/

to understand the driving forces and the dynamics underlying voluntary social engagement.

- In the UK, qualitative interviews are planned for the new UKHLS.[6]
- In the US, Portes and Fernández-Kelly (2008) also used mixed methodologies to analyze data from the Children of Immigrants Longitudinal Study (CILS). They conducted narrative interviews with 50 second-generation youths and their families to understand how young respondents have coped with disadvantages during their childhood and teen years and to examine their educational success.
- Also in the US, researchers linked data from the Women's Employment Study (WES) with qualitative data gathered from a sub-sample of the survey's respondents (approximately 70) in order to analyze processes of union formation among low-income women and to formulate hypotheses that can be tested by the use of panel data (see Seefeldt 2008).[7]
- Researchers have used mixed methodologies on data from the South African KwaZulu-Natal Income Dynamics Study (KIDS) in order to understand the factors explaining transitions into or out of poverty (Adato et al. 2006). Qualitative data was collected on members of eight households selected from this first large-scale longitudinal study of household poverty in South Africa.

5. Challenges

Linking qualitative in-depth interviews to quantitative surveys poses new challenges. First of all, ethical and data protection issues have to be considered and resolved (Leahey 2007). For legal reasons, survey respondents have to declare their willingness to participate in the survey, and this declaration should explicitly include their agreement to participate in personal in-depth interviews. Moreover, respondents need to understand exactly how qualitative interviews – or the transcript, audio, or video file – will be linked with the quantitative microdata.

---

6 For more details, see http://www.understandingsociety.org.uk/design/features/qualitative.aspx as well as http://www.understandingsociety.org.uk/news/latest/ and http://www.esrc.ac.uk/ESRCInfoCentre/research/resources/UKHLS.aspx

7 More details on this project are available at http://cairo.pop.psu.edu/allen/Project.cfm?ProjectID=189.

For longitudinal survey respondents, time-consuming in-depth interviews may negatively affect survey participation, and requests to divulge intimate biographical details could impair the respondent's relationship to the interviewer. From what we know so far about the effects of introducing new and more demanding kinds of surveying in ongoing longitudinal studies, they seem to strengthen rather than weaken respondents' personal commitment to the survey.

An important challenge in developing the social science research infrastructure in the future relates to the rules of access to qualitative data on survey respondents. Those responsible for managing longitudinal surveys need to establish working models that can provide external researchers the opportunity to interview respondents.

6. Recommendations

The inclusion of qualitative in-depth interviewing in the repertoire of data collection methods used in sample surveys is a highly promising innovation in terms of both methodological and substantial research. However, there is still a long way to go in laying the foundations and exploring the possibilities and limits of such an approach.

- Theory & methodology: more extensive use of qualitative methods in surveys should be based on theoretical and methodological proposals that guide the triangulation of qualitative and quantitative methods.

- Ethics, data protection, and access: ethical and data protection issues need to be addressed. Rules for access to samples of respondents should be established.

- Exploration: the possibilities and problems of conducting semi-structured and biographical interviews should be explored with rather small test samples of long-term survey respondents, focusing on methodological issues of "triangulating" life courses.

References:

Abbott, A. (1997): On the Concept of Turning Point. Comparative Social Research 16/1997, 89-109.
Adato, M./Lund, F. and Mhlongo, P. (2007): Methodological Innovations in Research on the Dynamics of Poverty: A Longitudinal Study in KwaZulu-Natal, South Africa. World Development 35 (2), 247-263.
Brannen, J. (2005): Mixing methods: the entry of qualitative and quantitative approaches into the research process. International Journal of Social Research Methodology 8 (3), 173-84.
Bryman, A. (2006): Integrating quantitative and qualitative research: how is it done? Qualitative Research 6 (1), 97-113.
Creswell, J.W./Plano-Clark, V.L./Gutmann, M.L. and Hanson, W.E. (2003): Advanced mixed methods research designs. In: Tashakkori, A. and Teddlie, Ch.B. (Eds.): Handbook of mixed methods in social and behavioral research. Thousand Oaks.
Dohmen, Th./Falk, A./Huffman, D./Sunde, U./Schupp, J. and Wagner, G.G. (2010): Individual Risk Attitudes: New Evidence from a Large, Representative Experimentally-Validated Survey. Journal of the European Economic Association 7. [Forthcoming].
Giele, J.Z. and Elder, G.H. (Eds.) (1998): Methods of Life Course Research: Quantitative and Qualitative Approaches. Thousand Oakes/London/New Delhi.
Gintis, H. (2007): A framework for the unification of the behavioral sciences. Behavioral and Brain Sciences 30 (1), 1-61.
Goldthorpe, J.H. (2000): The Quantitative Analysis of Large-scale Data Sets and Rational Action Theory: For a Sociological Alliance. In: Goldthorpe, J.H.: On Sociology: Numbers, Narratives, and the Integration of Research and Theory. Oxford University Press.
Jahoda, M./Lazarsfeld, P.L. and Zeisel, H. (1933): Marienthal: The Sociography of an Unemployed Community – Translated by the authors with John Reginait and Thomas Elsaesser. Chicago 1971.
Kelle, U. (2001): Sociological Explanations Between Micro and Macro and the Integration of Qualitative and Quantitative Methods. Forum: Qualitative Social Research 2 (1). http://www.qualitative-research.net/index.php/fqs/article/viewArticle/966/2108. [Last visited: 5/19/2010].
Laurie, H. and Sullivan, O. (1991): Combining qualitative and quantitative methods in the longitudinal study of household allocations. Sociological Review 39 (1), 113-139.
Leahey, E. (2007): Convergence and confidentiality? Limits to the implementation of mixed methodology. Social Science Research 36 (1), 149-158.
Mason, J. (2006a): Six strategies for mixing methods and linking data in social science research. Real Life Methods Working Paper.
Mason, J. (2006b): Mixing methods in a qualitatively driven way. Qualitative Research 6 (1), 9-25.
Mayer, K.U. and Schulze, E. (2009a): Die Wendegeneration. Lebensverläufe des Jahrgangs 1971. Frankfurt am Main/New York.

Mayer, K.U. and Schulze, E. (2009b): Delaying Parenthood in East and West Germany. A Mixed-Methods Study of the Onset of Childbirth and the Vocabulary of Motives of Women of the Birth Cohort of 1971. In: Andersson, G./Bernardi, L./Kulu, H. and Neyer, G. (Eds.): The Demography of Europe: Trends and Perspectives. Berlin.

Leech, N.L. and Onwuegbuzie, A.J. (2009): A typology of mixed methods research designs. Quality and Quantity 43 (2), 265-75.

Portes, A. and Fernández-Kelly, P. (2008): No Margin for Error: Educational and Occupational Achievement among Disadvantaged Children of Immigrants. The Annals of the American Academy of Political and Social Science 620 (1), 12-36.

Seefeldt, K.S. (2008): Working after welfare: how women balance jobs and family in the wake of welfare reform. W.E. Upjohn Institute for Employment Research, Michigan.

Tashakkori A. and Teddlie Ch.B. (Eds.) (2003): Handbook of Mixed Methods in Social and Behavioural Research. Thousand Oaks.

Willis, G.B. (2005): Cognitive Interviewing: A Tool for Improving Questionnaire Design. Thousand Oaks.

Aktuell • profund • lesenswert

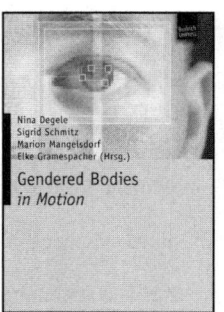

Budrich UniPress

NINA DEGELE
SIGRID SCHMITZ
MARION MANGELSDORF
ELKE GRAMESPACHER (HRSG.)
Gendered Bodies *in Motion*
2010. 206 S. Kt. 24,90 € (D), 25,60 € (A), 37,90 SFr
ISBN 978-940755-57-5

MARIAM IRENE TAZI-PREVE (HRSG.)
Familienpolitik
Nationale und internationale Perspektiven
Familienforschung – Schriftenreihe des Österreichischen Instituts für Familienforschung (ÖIF), Band 20
2010. 161 S. Kt. 19,90 € (D), 20,50 € (A), 30,50 SFr
ISBN 978-3-940755-45-2

CHRISTIANE RILLE-PFEIFFER
Kinder – jetzt, später oder nie?
Familienforschung –
Schriftenreihe des Österreichischen
Instituts für Familienforschung (ÖIF), Band 21
2010. 192 S. Kt. 19,90 € (D), 20,50 € (A), 30,50 SFr
ISBN 978-3-940755-54-4

Bestellen Sie jetzt:
Budrich UniPress Ltd. Stauffenbergstr. 7. D-51379 Leverkusen-Opladen.
ph +49.2171.344.694. fx +49.2171.344.693. buch@budrich-unipress.de

www.budrich-unipress.de

Building on Progress
Expanding the Research Infrastructure for the
Social, Economic, and Behavioral Sciences

Building on Progress

Expanding the Research Infrastructure for the Social, Economic, and Behavioral Sciences

edited by the
German Data Forum (RatSWD)

Vol. 2

Budrich UniPress Ltd.
Opladen & Farmington Hills, MI 2010

You must not circulate this book in any other binding or cover and you must impose this same condition on any acquirer.

A CIP catalogue record for this book is available from
Die Deutsche Bibliothek (The German Library)

© 2010 by Budrich UniPress Ltd. Opladen & Farmington Hills
www.budrich-unipress.eu

ISBN 978-3-940755-58-2
2 Vols. in slipcase

© These volumes are published by Budrich UniPress and are published under the Creative Commons licence:
http://creativecommons.org/licenses/by-nc-nd/3.0/de/deed.en_GB
You are free to copy, distribute, display, and perform the work as long as you tribute it to the original author/editors. No commercial use, or changes unless approved by Budrich UniPress.

Both volumes may be downloaded free of charge at the Budrich UniPress website www.budrich-unipress.com
The two volumes in slipcase may be ordered from your local bookseller or directly from the Budrich UniPress.

Budrich UniPress Ltd.
Stauffenbergstr. 7. D-51379 Leverkusen Opladen, Germany
28347 Ridgebrook. Farmington Hills, MI 48334. USA
www.budrich-unipress.eu

Jacket illustration by Walburga Fichtner, Cologne, Germany
Printed in Europe on acid-free paper by
paper & tinta, Warszaw, Poland

Table of Contents:

Volume 1:

PREFACE BY THE FEDERAL MINISTRY OF EDUCATION AND RESEARCH (BMBF) .... i-iii

EDITORS 9

PREFACE BY THE GERMAN DATA FORUM (RATSWD) 11

RECOMMENDATIONS 17

EXECUTIVE SUMMARIES 41

ADVISORY REPORTS 95

TOWARDS AN IMPROVED RESEARCH INFRASTRUCTURE FOR THE SOCIAL SCIENCES: FUTURE DEMANDS AND NEEDS FOR ACTION 97

    1. Providing a Permanent Institutional Guarantee for the German Information Infrastructure...*Johann Hahlen* 97

    2. The European Dimension...*Klaus Reeh* 115

    3. The Role of the German Research Foundation...*Eckard Kämper and Manfred Nießen* 127

    4. Providing Data on the European Level...*Peter Elias* 139

    5. Infrastructure for High-Quality and Large-Scale Surveys. Cooperation between Academic Research and Private-Sector Agencies...*Peter Ph. Mohler and Bernhard von Rosenbladt* 155

    6. The Availability of Market Research Data and its Potential for Use in Empirical Social and Economic Research...*Erich Wiegand* 175

PROGRESS SINCE 2001 AND CURRENT STATE 189

    1. The Recommendations of the 2001 KVI Report and Their Realizations up to 2008...*Gabriele Rolf-Engel* 189

    2. Access to Microdata from Official Statistics...*Stefan Bender, Ralf Himmelreicher, Sylvia Zühlke and Markus Zwick* 215

    3. Publicly Financed Survey Data: Access and Documentation *Wolfgang Jagodzinski and Christof Wolf* 231

4. Teaching and Statistical Training...*Ulrich Rendtel* 251
5. e- Infrastructure for the Social Sciences...*Ekkehard Mochmann* 265

CURRENT STATE OF AND FUTURE DEMANDS IN DIFFERENT FIELDS 287

I. (NEW) DATA TYPES AND THEIR POTENTIALS 287

1. Macroeconomic Data...*Ulrich Heilemann* 289
2. Interdisciplinary Longitudinal Surveys...*Jürgen Schupp and Joachim Frick* 303
3. Geodata...*Tobia Lakes* 325
4. Regional Data...*Gerd Grözinger and Wenzel Matiaske* 341
5. Genetically Sensitive Sample Designs...*Frank M. Spinath* 353
6. Biological Variables in Social Surveys...*Rainer Schnell* 367
7. Administrative Transaction Data...*Julia Lane* 383
8. Transaction Data: Commercial Transaction Surveys and Test Market Data....*Bernhard Engel* 401
9. Time Use and Time Budgets....*Joachim Merz* 413

II. METHODS 451

1. Survey Methodology: International Developments...*Frauke Kreuter* 453
2. Improving Research Governance through Use of the Total Survey Error Framework...*Marek Fuchs* 471
3. Metadata....*Arofan Gregory, Pascal Heus and Jostein Ryssevik* 487
4. Paradata...*Frauke Kreuter and Carolina Casas-Cordero* 509
5. Record Linkage from a Technical Point of View...*Rainer Schnell* 531
6. Experiments, Surveys, and the Use of Representative Samples as Reference Data...*Thomas Siedler and Bettina Sonnenberg* 547
7. Experimental Economics...*Simon Gächter* 563
8. Experience Sampling...*Michaela Riediger* 581
9. Virtual Worlds as Petri Dishes for the Social and Behavioral Sciences...*Edward Castronova and Matthew Falk* 595

10. Qualitative Interviewing of Respondents in Large Representative Surveys...*Olaf Groh-Samberg and Ingrid Tucci* 607

Volume 2:

III. *DATA PROTECTION AND RESEARCH ETHICS* 627

1. Data Protection and Statistics – A Dynamic and Tension-Filled Relationship...*Peter Schaar* 629
2. Record Linkage from the Perspective of Data Protection... *Rainer Metschke* 643
3. New Methods in Human Subjects Research: Do We Need a New Ethics?...*Karsten Weber*..657
4. Does Germany Need a (New) Research Ethics for the Social Sciences?...*Claudia Oellers and Eva Wegner* 673

IV. *FIELDS* 687

1. Migration and Demography...687
   - 1.1 Migration and Globalization...*Martin Kahanec and Klaus F. Zimmermann*..689
   - 1.2 Migration and Statistics...*Sonja Haug* 703
   - 1.3 Internal Migration...*Andreas Farwick* 723
   - 1.4 Fertility and Mortality Data for Germany...*Michaela Kreyenfeld and Rembrandt Scholz*....................................739

2. Measuring Competencies...753
   - 2.1 Measuring Cognitive Ability...*Roland H. Grabner and Elsbeth Stern*..753
   - 2.2 Measuring Cognitive Competencies...*Ulrich Trautwein* 769
   - 2.3 Measuring Vocational Competencies...*Martin Baethge and Lena Arends*..783
   - 2.4 Measuring Social Competencies...*Ingrid Schoon* 797
   - 2.5 Subjective Indicators...*Beatrice Rammstedt* 813

3. Education and Research..825
   - 3.1 Education Across the Life Course...*Hans-Peter Blossfeld*.........825

3.2 Preschool Education...*C. Katharina Spieß*..................................841
3.3 Data in the Domain of Secondary School Education....
Petra Stanat and Hans Döbert..859
3.4 Knowing More about Vocational Training...*Steffen Hillmert*..877
3.5 Higher Education...*Andrä Wolter*..............................891
3.6 Adult Education and Lifelong Learning...*Corinna Kleinert and Britta Matthes*...911
3.7 Research, Science, Development...*Stefan Hornbostel*...............929

4. Economy and Labor Markets.....................................943
4.1 Data from the Federal Employment Agency...*Stefan Bender and Joachim Möller*...943
4.2 More and Better Data for Labor Market Research. Proposals for Efficient Access to the Currently Unused Potential of Official Statistical Data...*Hilmar Schneider*...............959
4.3 Interdisciplinary Longitudinal Surveys. Linking Individual Data to Organizational Data in Life-Course Analysis...*Stefan Liebig*..971
4.4 Organizational Data...*Stefan Liebig*..........................985
4.5 Firm-Level Data...*Joachim Wagner*.........................1001

5. State, Family, and Health...1015
5.1 Public Finance...*Thiess Büttner*..............................1015
5.2 Household Income, Poverty, and Wealth...*Richard Hauser*...1027
5.3 Family Research...*Johannes Huinink*......................1041
5.4 Intergenerational Relationships...*Bernhard Nauck and Anja Steinbach*..1057
5.5 Administrative Data from Germany's Statutory Health Insurance Providers for Social, Economic, and Medical Research...*Günther Heller*..1081
5.6 Provision for Old Age: National and International Survey Data to Support Research and Policy on Aging...*Hendrik Jürges*..1093
5.7 Income Provisions and Retirement in Old Age...*Tatjana Mika, Uwe Rehfeld and Michael Stegmann*......................1107

6. Political and Cultural Participation and the Role of the Media 1123
   6.1 Political Participation – National Election Study... *Rüdiger Schmitt-Beck* 1123
   6.2 Civil Society...*Mareike Alscher and Eckart Priller* 1139
   6.3 Culture...*Jörg Rössel and Gunnar Otte* 1153
   6.4 Mass Media Research...*Heiner Meulemann and Jörg Hagenah* 1173
   6.5 Judicature...*Wolfgang Heinz* 1197
   6.6 Environment...*Cornelia Ohl and Bernd Hansjürgens* 1217

TERMINOLOGY 1231

III. DATA PROTECTION AND RESEARCH ETHICS

1. Data Protection and Statistics – A Dynamic and Tension-Filled Relationship

Peter Schaar

Contact:

Peter Schaar
The Federal Commissioner for Data Protection and Freedom of Information
Der Bundesbeauftragte für den Datenschutz und die Informationsfreiheit
Husarenstraße 30
53117 Bonn
Germany
e-mail: peter.schaar[at]bfdi.bund.de

Abstract

New statistical methods have been developed for long-term storage of microdata. These methods must comply, however, with the fundamental right to informational self-determination and the legal regulations imposed by the Federal Constitutional Court. Thus, it is crucial to develop effective and coherent methods for protecting personal data collected for statistical purposes.

Recent decisions by the Federal Constitutional Court are likely to result in the outlawing of comprehensive, permanent statistical compilations comprised of microdata from a wide range of sources that are updated regularly. However, aside from such comprehensive methods, there are certainly other ways of using microdata that cannot be dismissed from the outset as violating constitutional legal norms.

Internet access to statistical microdata is likely to take on increased importance for scientific research in the near future. Yet this would radically change the entire landscape of data protection: the vast amount of additional information now available on the Internet makes it almost impossible to judge whether individuals can be rendered identifiable. In view of this almost unlimited information, individual data can only be offered over the Internet if the absolute anonymity of the data can be guaranteed.

Keywords: right to informational self-determination, census ruling of December 15, 1983, longer-term storage of microdata, primary statistics, secondary statistics, statistical confidentiality, absolute anonymization, de facto anonymization, additional information, pseudonymization, personal data profiles

1. Introduction

Statistics traditionally deals with the collection and evaluation of data on the personal or material situations of a large number of individuals or organizations: "Statistics means ... activity aimed both at measuring mass phenomena, combining the data into groups and publishing them."[1] A more recent textbook contains the following definition, "Statistics is a combination of mathematical methods used to assess mass phenomena. The data collected serves to describe the environment numerically and/or in the event of uncertainty to use this data as a decision-making aid."[2]

The purpose of data protection is, according to the Federal Data Protection Act, "to protect the individual against impairment of his right to

---

1   Meyers Konversationslexikon (Meyer's Conversational Encyclopedia) (1907), volume 18, under the term "Statistik".
2   Bücker, R. (1997): Statistik für Wirtschaftswissenschaftler (Statistics for Economists), 3rd Edition, 11.

privacy through the handling of his personal data."³ "Personal data means any information concerning the personal or material circumstances of an identified or identifiable individual (the data subject)."⁴

If and when statistics are used merely to evaluate information relating to institutions (government agencies, companies) or natural phenomena (e.g., weather), data protection issues are irrelevant. However, the situation is much more complex with data on personal circumstances, as the heated debate on the 1983/87 census showed. This "individual data" is linked to the data subject at least during the data collection phase, and may also involve personal data. Only in the course of further data processing and evaluation is the personal reference eliminated partially or completely. In the final analysis, data may only be published if it can be ruled out in all likelihood that conclusions can be drawn about individuals. Personal data are therefore rendered (de facto) anonymous within the framework of traditional statistics.

Data protection requirements are changing as new statistical methods focused on long-term storage of individual data (microdata) become available (especially in the context of longitudinal studies). This means the described method of data collection – in which the data are rendered anonymous, preventing access to personal data and publishing only aggregated results – is no longer adequate under all circumstances, and thus no longer practicable.

2. The right to informational self-determination

With its census ruling of December 15, 1983, the Federal Constitutional Court (BVerfG, *Bundesverfassungsgericht*) formulated the "fundamental right to informational self-determination":

"Under the terms of modern data processing, the protection of the individual against the unlimited collection, storage, use and passing on of his/her personal data comes under the general right to free development of one's personality set forth in Art. 2 Abs. 1 of the Basic Law in conjunction with Art. 1 Abs. 1 of the Basic Law [inviolability of human dignity]. The basic right warrants [...] the capacity of the individual to determine in principle the disclosure and use of his/her personal data."⁵

The ruling defined the requirements that need to be met in order to ensure that personal data are processed in accordance with the German Constitution (*Grundgesetz*). It ruled that any risks of misuse must be taken into account

---

3 § 1 Abs. 1 BDSG (*Bundesdatenschutzgesetz*). The citations to German legal sources have been left in German to guarantee accuracy.
4 § 3 Abs. 1 BDSG.
5 BVerfGE [decision] 65, 1, 1.

when data are processed. Even data that may seem irrelevant in an isolated context has the capacity to become relevant in a different context (by data fusion and data matching). The Federal Constitutional Court hence ruled that "considering the fact that individual data can be stored without any technical restraint with the help of automatic data processing ... there is no longer any such thing as irrelevant data."[6] According to the German Constitution, the collection and processing of data must be justified by reasons of compelling public interest; the prerequisites and scope of data processing must be regulated comprehensibly for citizens, and the principle of proportionality must apply.

Last but by no means least, the further processing of data must, in principle, be limited to the purpose for which it was originally collected, which is particularly relevant for the collection of data for statistical purposes. Contrary to the collection of personal data for a specific administrative task, the need to collect data for statistical purposes can only be described in abstract terms, as the results can and indeed should be used for multiple purposes. It is hence all the more important to ensure that statistical data processing is separated strictly from the processing of data for administrative tasks. The envisaged use of data to correct information in the identity register in the 1983 census was the main reason for the negative ruling by the Federal Constitutional Court.[7]

One of the major risks in terms of data protection is that personal data profiles can emerge that are capable of presenting a complete picture of an individual. Any such personality profiles are incompatible with the Basic Law. The Federal Constitutional Court already established this in 1969, in its Microcensus ruling on personality profiles:

"It would be incompatible with human dignity if the state claimed the right to register and catalogue people in their whole personality coercively, even if the data collected in a statistical survey was rendered anonymous, as this would treat people like objects that are accessible for data collection in every respect."[8]

Pursuant to this case ruling, it is now compulsory to protect personal data collected for statistical purposes in an effective and coherent manner. As such, it is important that the measures taken be oriented to the concrete threat situation and take the risks associated with rapid technological advancement into account.

---

6 BVerfGE 65, 1, 45.
7 BVerfGE 65, 1, 63.
8 BVerfGE 27, 1, 6.

3. Technological change

The main regulatory approaches to data protection originate from the time of mainframe computers, when electronic data processing took place at remote computing centers in accordance with rigid principles. Storage units the size of refrigerators, punch cards, and continuous printing paper dominated the scene when the Federal Constitutional Court issued its census decision in 1983.

Three main changes have taken place that are important in this context: the dramatic increase in storage capacities, the flexible evaluation possibilities, even of huge databases ("data mining"), and the "liberation" of computers from computing centers, offering 24/7 access to databases via networks, particularly the Internet.

In view of these trends, certain protection concepts that date back to the 1980s and 1990s are no longer realistic in today's world. This applies, for instance, to the approach of physically sealing off the use of statistical data processing from processing for other purposes. Nowadays, statistical data can, of course, be processed on separate systems.

When data users are to be offered the benefits of computer technology, it is virtually impossible to do so without giving them electronic access to statistical data – e.g., through networks. It is difficult, if not impossible, to explain to users in the scientific and political communities why they are confined to rigid evaluations in the form of statistical aggregates and why they are denied access to microdata. After all, it is precisely microdata that offer a wide range of opportunities for obtaining new information. Nonetheless, the risks associated with these convenient types of use must be considered carefully. If data are processed outside the "walls" of statistical offices, it is virtually impossible to control how it is used – for instance, whether it is being used in combination with other databases.

What is needed are concepts that develop new, flexible possibilities for utilization that meet the expectations of data users and that simultaneously safeguard effective, modern data protection.

Statistical confidentiality as a special data protection requirement

When developing data protection measures, it is crucial that the various legal, organizational, and technical measures are well coordinated. As such, the starting point is the obligation to maintain the statistical confidentiality, which aims first and foremost at ensuring – like all other regulations governing secrecy[9] – that only authorised "insiders" have access to the data and that the data are safe from use by unauthorised persons. The regulations governing the obligation to maintain statistical confidentiality represent special data protection regulations that override the general data protection legislation. They are intended not only to take the special sensitivity of the respective data into account, but also to build trust between the data subject and those who collect the data, who are obligated to maintain the confidentiality of statistical data on individuals without the individual having to fear negative consequences. According to the Law on Statistics for Federal Purposes (BStatG, *Bundesstatistikgesetz*):

> "Individual data on personal circumstances or the material situation provided for federal statistics shall not be disclosed by the incumbents and the persons specially sworn in to public service who are entrusted with the operation of federal statistics, unless otherwise stipulated by a special legal provision."[10]

In principle, personal data may only be used for certain tasks defined by law. It is prohibited and a punishable offence to use data for any purposes other than those expressly permitted by law. The same applies to passing on data to third parties outside the respective area. However, the principle of purpose limitation does not apply to statistical results that do not contain any personal reference. Individual statistical data may also be used for scientific purposes under certain circumstances:

> "For the purpose of scientific projects, the Federal Statistical Office and the Statistical Offices of the German *Länder* may transfer microdata to institutions of higher education or other institutions entrusted with tasks of independent scientific research if an allocation of the individual data are possible only with an excessive amount of time, expenses and manpower, and if the recipients are elected officials, persons specially sworn in for public service, or persons obligated according to Abs. 7."[11]

Contrary to this exemption for scientific purposes, the BStatG does not contain any explicit obligation to render individual data anonymous when these data are stored at statistical offices; however, this obligation arises implicitly from the jurisprudence of the Federal Constitutional Court, particularly in its census ruling. The legislator took these terms of reference into account by issuing detailed regulations on the rendering anonymous of data in a large number of individual statistical regulations on the deletion of calculation input features. After all, § 10 of the BStatG defines certain minimum (albeit merely geographical) requirements specifying precisely what individual data can be stored for extended periods by saying exactly what is prohibited and by prohibiting the use of precise address details. Finally, § 21 of the BStatG

---

9   Examples: the duty to treat medical records confidentially, confessional secrets, secrecy of postsostal and telecommunications secrecy.
10 § 16 Abs. 1 Satz 1 BStatG.
11 § 16 Abs. 6 BStatG.

stipulates that it is prohibited to match individual data from federal statistics or to combine any such individual data with other information:

> "It is prohibited to match individual data from federal statistics or to combine such individual data with other information for establishing a reference to persons, enterprises, establishments or local units for other than the statistical purposes of this Law or of a legal provision ordering a federal statistics."

4. Statistical methods and data protection

Even though traditional statistics are based, by and large, on data that refer to individual survey units, they do not rely on having retroactive access to individual data – with the exception of checks carried out during the data collection and data processing phase (to ensure the data are complete, plausible and, to a limited extent, correct). Rather, statistics involve aggregates, namely numerical values that are analysed and matched, with comparison and evaluation of any changes in this data over time. In principle, any such aggregates do not contain personal data unless it is possible to trace the results back to persons indirectly. It may, for instance, be possible to draw indirect inferences about individuals from statistical results if the respective table cell relates to a small number of people. The same applies to special characteristic values – for instance, if all members of a group have the same characteristic values.

Statistics are not matched at the case level. Only when statistics are published must it be ensured that none of the above-mentioned scenarios occur and that relevant countermeasures are undertaken (for instance, combining survey units, less distinctive characteristic values). As a rule, the loss of information associated with this rendering anonymous of data does not have any serious consequences and can certainly be tolerated (as long as different tabulations are not restricted, so to allow flexible tabulations).

The further development of statistical methods has led to heightened data protection requirements. The evaluation of statistical aggregates is supplemented by a more detailed analysis of patterns of individual statistical units at the so-called "micro-level." Group patterns are traced back to patterns in the lives of individuals, who may have been observed over an extended period of time. To this end, data on the individual need to be collected and, if applicable, matched over time (into a longitudinal dataset). The annual Microcensus surveys that are carried out on the households under review at regular intervals over four consecutive years are based on this model.

Generally speaking, these new methods involve microdata that can be linked multifunctionally and can be evaluated over time (as, for example, in clinical studies). There are numerous ways of accessing so-called "microdata files" – for example, through personal references in case scenarios in which the data are linked by a general personal identifier that can be used in a wide range of surveys.[12] However, there is no doubt that any such personal identifier is incompatible with the above-mentioned requirements of the Federal Constitutional Court in Germany.[13] For this reason, the court is likely to declare comprehensive, permanent microdata statistics comprising regularly updated data from a wide range of sources to be unlawful. However, aside from these comprehensive methods, there are certainly ways of using microdata that cannot be dismissed from the outset as violating the constitutional requirements.

5. Measures aimed at safeguarding data protection

It goes without saying that the traditional method of rendering data anonymous and deleting individual statistics based on a type of "stage model" is not compatible with a method that links microdata. It may be possible to trace the individual data back to the data subject even at the micro-level in the long term, which means the data do actually represent personal data in the majority of cases.

As such, one very interesting option would be to randomly link data collected within the framework of completely different statistical surveys in order to gain new information. In addition to the additional informative value such a method would yield, another argument in favor of it is the flexibility of the results it would generate.

In terms of data protection, any such method would involve major risks, given the apparent difficulty – if not impossibility – of rendering data anonymous in order to prevent inferences being drawn about identifiable statistical units. This risk could be mitigated by effectively ensuring that the data are protected against unauthorised access. However, whether this could achieve adequate protection is questionable, at least where particularly comprehensive or diverse microdata files containing personal features are concerned.

The type and size of the database is important when it comes to gauging the risk of abuse. Generally speaking, it can be said that the more comprehensive the database and the more sensitive the data, the greater the risk. This explains why censuses (which cover full populations) must be rated differ-

---

12 Lenz, R. and Zwick, M. (2005): Integrierte Mikrodatenfiles – Methoden zur Verknüpfung von Einzeldaten (integrated microdata files – methods of linking individual data). In: Statistisches Bundesamt (Ed.): Statistik und Wissenschaft 10, 100.
13 See. n. 6, BVerfGE 27, 1, 6.

ently than surveys in which small random samples of an entire population are taken. Data abuse also occurs with random sampling, albeit only to the extent of the sampling units included. Thus, the "abuser" needs to know who is included in the survey.[14]

It is also important to distinguish between primary and secondary statistics. It is not possible to state simply which of the two methods is more data protection-friendly. Occasionally, it is claimed that primary statistics, which collect data on the data subject are much more intrusive than secondary statistics, which do not collect any "new" data. This is only partly true. With secondary statistics, data are used and linked that were generally collected for another purpose altogether. This explains why most secondary files go hand in hand with data being used for a different purpose. Besides, the data subjects are "unaware" of the fact that their data are being used. Thus, they never gave informed consent. They are hence unable to check whether the data collection is lawful, and are unable to influence the process. In data protection terms, reference is made to deviation from the "Principle of Primary Collection" (ethical principle of informed consent). After all, more comprehensive secondary statistics – for instance, the census envisaged for 2011 – presupposes that it is possible to link data from different sources in which a particular type of infrastructure is needed. The question must therefore be raised how it can be prevented that infrastructures set up to collect statistics can also be used to link databases outside of statistics, with potentially far-reaching consequences for the data subject.

5.1 Rendering persons anonymous: absolute or de facto?

During the census debate of the 1980s, the most important question raised was: when do data lose their personal reference and when are they deemed anonymous or at least "de facto anonymous"?[15] Only data that are completely anonymous contain no personal reference whatsoever, and therefore do not come under data protection regulations, whereas with de facto anonymous data it cannot be ruled out that the personal reference can be made/restored if relevant additional information is available. Additional information describes the information needed to identify a person even if neither the person's name nor any other direct personal data (e.g., telephone number) can be linked

---

14 It is easy to make this impossible by deleting some cases that were sampled from the file that is available for analysis.
15 Fischer-Hübner, S. (1986): Zur Anonymität und Reidentifizierbarkeit statistischer Daten (Anonymity and reidentifiability of statistical data). In: Mitteilungen des Fachbereichs Informatik der Universität Hamburg 143; Brunnstein, K. (1987): Über die Möglichkeit der Re-Identifikation von Personen aus Volkszählungsdaten (The possibility of reidentifying persons from census data). In: Appel, R. (Ed.): Vorsicht Volkszählung! 2nd Edition, Cologne.

with other information that uniquely identifies the person. With individual statistics, it is possible to restore the personal reference if certain characteristic values are disclosed and if these characteristic values can be associated with the data subject. As such it must be borne in mind that the boundaries between personal and anonymous data are fading in view of the rapid increase in data volumes, as ever more powerful computers are making it easier and easier to restore the personal reference retroactively.[16]

With fully anonymous data, there is no case scenario in which third parties can associate data with a person. Complete or genuine anonymization hence means that personal data is altered in such a way as to ensure that the data can no longer be assigned to the person (even if there is additional information available). Only data that have been rendered fully anonymous contain no personal references whatsoever.

According to the definition of the Federal Data Protection Act, "rendering anonymous" means the modification of personal data so that the information concerning personal or material circumstances can no longer be attributed to an identified or identifiable individual, or only with a disproportionate amount of time, expense or labour.[17] This statutory definition is confined to rendering data de facto anonymous. Pursuant to § 3a of the BDSG, the data controller must implement data reduction and data economy measures. Pursuant to § 3a (2) of the BDSG, use is to be made of the possibilities for aliasing and rendering persons anonymous, insofar as this is possible and the effort involved is reasonable in relation to the desired level of protection to be achieved. This also applies to statistics.

5.2 Pseudonyms as an expedient?

The use of pseudonyms is appropriate in cases where it is necessary to identify a person but where an assumed identity is sufficient, namely when the real personal details do not need to be known and when, on the other hand, (actual or absolute) rendering anonymous is not possible. This type of case scenario frequently arises in statistics if data are stored at the micro-level (for instance for longitudinal analyses).

Aliasing means replacing a person's name and other identifying characteristics (e.g., name, account number or personnel number) with a label in order to preclude identification of the data subject or to render such identification substantially difficult.[18] Data stored under an alias generally contains

---

16 Mattern, F. and Langheinrich, M. (2001): Allgegenwärtigkeit des Computers – Datenschutz in einer Welt intelligenter Alltagsdinge (Omnipresence of computers – data protection in a world of intelligent everyday objects), 13.
17 § 3 Abs. 6 BDSG.
18 § 3 Abs. 6a BDSG.

some kind of personal reference – albeit indirect. As such, it is important to distinguish between various types of aliases that are used in various contexts:

With reference aliasing, the allocation feature is assigned to the data subject using a reference list (or reference file). Reference aliases can always be deleted by the data controller using the reference list. With disposable aliases, the assignment features are derived from personal data using special computing functions (hash functions). The methods used must be selected to ensure that inferences cannot be drawn from the result about the individual persons or the identification features used. Disposable aliases are particularly suitable for longitudinal analyses in scientific research projects and statistics. With this type of aliasing, however, the data stored under the alias can only be assigned to the person using the alias if the original data used to create the alias is known and if the attacker knows how the alias was created ("Brute-Force Attack").

5.3 Research Data Centers

The Research Data Centers run by the Federal Statistical Office, the Statistical Offices of the German *Länder*, the Institute for Employment Research (IAB, *Institut für Arbeitsmarkt- und Berufsforschung*) within the Federal Employment Agency (BA, *Bundesagentur für Arbeit*), and the Statistics of the German Pension Insurance (RV, *Deutsche Rentenversicherung*), have for a number of years made an attempt to balance data protection requirements against the interests of the scientific community in using microdata. The statistical offices give scientists direct access to individual data, observing general data protection requirements.

The Research Data Centers focus on microdata that have been cleared for remote data access.

However, the scientists do not access the statistical raw data or individual data managed by the offices directly, they access micro datasets, so-called Scientific Use Files (SUFs) generated for various purposes in which only virtually or fully anonymous data are stored.

SUFs can be accessed on-site or off-site. With on-site access, the data are accessed in the protected facilities of the Research Data Centers, whereas with off-site use, the data are accessed outside the Research Data Center for a specifically defined research project.

As the statistical offices have no way of ensuring the data are used properly, extreme caution must be taken when rendering data files anonymous, taking all of the additional information available to science into account. Access to official individual data are hence subject to the provisions set forth in the Law on Statistics for Federal Purposes.

Intensive use is being made of the newly established Research Data Centers.[19] Yet this is certainly not where developments will end, as there continues to be a keen interest in making the utilization of data even more flexible and above all in facilitating access from any location. Access via the Internet will likely be of key importance in the future. However, this would change the whole environment in terms of data protection, as it would no longer be possible to estimate the additional knowledge that might have been used to render individuals anonymous. In view of the unlimited amount of additional information available, individual data can hence only be used for uncontrolled Internet access if their absolute anonymity can be guaranteed. Anonymity "of a lesser quality" is not sufficient in view of the unlimited possibilities that exist for linking the widest range of databases.

---

19   Federal Data Protection Commissioner, TB 21, no. 7.6.

2. Record Linkage from the Perspective of Data Protection

Rainer Metschke[*†]

---

[*] This advisory report was translated for consistency, however, only the German version has been authorized by the author.
[†] Rainer Metschke passed away in August 2010. He was Advisor for the Berlin Commission for Data Protection and Informational Freedom.

Abstract

This article will discuss record linkage from the perspective of data protection. To begin with, it will examine data fusion, a prominent form of which is "statistical matching." This procedure occurs anonymously and in this respect, hardly appears to be relevant for protection of information issues. This changes, however, when results released as scoring values can be linked back to the individuals from which they stem.

For data integration, the term "record linkage" refers to a condition in which data stemming from two or more collections but related to a single entity must be combined so as to yield a unitary dataset. This dataset then allows for, for example, inferences about individuals. Notably, however, the combining of individual entries from official statistics with other official or even general statistics so as to attempt to trace these to back to any particular person is a criminal offence. Nonetheless, there do exist exceptions where penalties do not apply; the most notable of these are the laws pertaining to the Microcensus. Even so, the specificity of such statutory statistics essentially ensures that these data cannot be effectively combined by other parties. However, the informational and transparency obligations that the state imposes upon statistical authorities is said to erode the legal protection afforded to these authorities when combining data. With that, this erosion hinders the creation of any basis for constructing quality data.

In addition to discussing the aforementioned, this article presents a thought experiment. This experiment highlights a situation in which data depositaries, defined as third-parties independent of both researchers and statistics authorities, can be used to link statistics back to individuals in a legally feasible manner. Further, this article will offer an example of how legal protection of relevant parties may be maintained whilst still allowing for the combining of data for research purposes.

Keywords: data fusion, statistical matching, data integration, record linkage, reanalysis, census judgment, 2011 Census, reidentification ban, data depositary, statistical confidentiality

Preliminary remarks

It is perhaps one of the most cherished dreams of an empirical social researcher to be able to link datasets from diverse surveys relating to individuals, families, and households. If, for example, three attributes are collected in a survey, the researcher can evaluate them by analyzing one attribute three times, two attributes three times, or all three attributes once. If it is possible to link this set of data with yet another set from an additional survey – one that also has three attributes – rather than yielding seven analytical combinations, there would be... etc., etc.

This is also the ideal of criminologists, intelligence agencies, credit agencies, personnel managers, and epidemiologists, among many others. In light of current circumstances, one should not forget those who deal in address and bank account information. At the same time, this potential is the nightmare of civil liberties advocates, employee and personnel representatives, labor unionists, and those professions involved in data protection.

A brief introduction to data fusion

At first glance, data fusion hardly seems relevant to the subject of data protection. "Statistical matching" functions through the anonymity of individual datasets, derived from diverse sources and whose data either do not, or only incidentally, describe one and the same person. Common attributes or variables are used as linking elements using probabilities. This results in synthetic and thus artificial people. However, in terms of data protection, the application of this technique can be dangerous. Should these data be used to develop scoring values with which one evaluates real people or households, there are potentially serious consequences. If the probability is high enough that belonging to a group of individuals leads to a particular pattern of behavior, the individual can hardly defend himself against it. Lawmakers have recently begun to recognize this as well. In this context, one might think of the planned prohibition of the use of genetic data in the signing of insurance and work contracts. In addition, the upcoming amendment to the German Federal Data Protection Act will purportedly include the obligation, when using scoring methods, to disclose the methods used and the economic value of the data to those who will be affected.

Because of the constitutional status that guarantees their freedom, science and research should not be affected by such regulations. However, such research institutions are in fact the source of these methods of data fusion and the resulting evaluations. The fruit of scientific research becomes common property through publication and, as such, becomes available for use.

Data integration

A precondition for record linkage is the existence of identifying data or keys to code individuals, but also codes to unique attribute values or attribute combinations, such as unchanging medical values or DNA sequences. The content data on identical persons, households, or businesses from various sources are integrated, and the body of information expands.

Current situation and recommendations for data linkage in the 2001 KVI report

In 2001, the KVI report estimated that the current situation regarding the linkage of statistical data was inadequate and that the only acceptable solution from the standpoint of data protection – that of explicit consent – was impracticable and inefficient. This conclusion was based on concerns about the potential non-agreement of respondents, even though the linked data can no longer be matched to individuals. This would infringe on the public right to independent testing of statistical microdata through reanalysis.

The 2001 KVI report proposed that the efficiency of statistical production be increased through the linking of microdata, for which a legal authorization would be required instead of the consent of the respondent. Exact data linking would then be considered legally harmless if it was undertaken in an isolated area with subsequent anonymization. In particular, primary data collections and process statistics could be integrated and, as a result, the respondents would be released from the statistical duty of disclosure.

An indirect modification of the reidentification ban in statistics for federal purposes

With the penal provision in § 22 of the Law on Statistics for Federal Purposes (BstatG, *Bundesstatistikgesetz*),[1] the ban on reidentification of personal information from federal statistics under § 21 is enforced by penalty. § 21 of the BStatG forbids the merging of personal data from federal statistics with other federal statistics or general information for the production of an individual reference. For purposes in accordance with the BstatG, or for a one-time statistical legal ruling, the ban does not apply. It first comes into effect when the identifying data is at least separated from the personal information, if not completely deleted. There must therefore have been a process of factual anonymization undertaken in the isolated inner domain of the statistical office. In 1987, this prohibition was evaluated by the Federal Constitutional Court, who declared it to be a supplementary, confidence-building provision in the service of data protection.

On the other hand, if the stipulated statistical legal provisions imply tasks that permit data integration or even dictate it, this cannot be fundamentally classified as constitutionally dangerous. At the time of the 2001 KVI report, these regulations did not exist.

---

1   The citations to German legal sources have been left in German to guarantee accuracy.

In 2005, § 13a of the BStatG was rewritten as follows:

"Data records from statistics pursuant to § 13 Abs. 1, data from the statistical register, data specified in the Law on the Use of Administrative Data, and data obtained by the Federal Statistical Office and the Statistical Offices of the German *Länder* from generally accessible sources may be matched, provided that matching is required in order to obtain statistical information without conducting additional statistical surveys."

The reference in § 13a BStatG limits the permitted data integration to economic and environmental statistics relating to corporations, businesses, and workplaces. The Federal Statistical Office and the Statistical Offices of the German *Länder* are making increasing use of these new possibilities.

Sensitive data security issues regarding the integration of personal data in official statistics

In the German Microcensus resolution of 1969, the Federal Constitutional Court made a deliberation weighing the fundamental law guaranteeing inviolable areas of private life against the collective need for information from the individual citizen. This inviolable private domain escaped public authority. It is incompatible with human dignity, which must be guaranteed to all without restriction, for the state to reduce the person to a mere object and to mandate the registration and categorization of the entire private individual.

In their evaluation, the judges in the constitutional court stressed that not every statistical survey with the duty of disclosure is injurious to human dignity and the right to self-determination in this protected domain. As citizens bound to the collective, each person must accept the necessity of statistical collection within certain parameters and, what is more, as a precondition for systematic state governance.

It should be noted that the theory underlying this concept of individual rights to privacy and the first laws on data protection were developed in different spheres of constitutional law. In the census decision of 1983, the Federal Constitutional Court drew from the right to privacy in Art. 2 Abs. 1, in connection with the duty to preserve the inviolability of human dignity pursuant to Art. 1 Abs. 1, to create the foundational law for the protection of the individual against unrestricted collection, storage, use, and disclosure of his or her personal data. Particularly, under the conditions of modern data processing, state incursions into the right to "informational self-determination" are subject to an overriding collective interest, and must conform to the relevant norms as well as have a constitutionally legal foundation. An intervention must be of reasonable scope and must include technical and organizational means of protection.

The principle of the primacy of consent is common to almost all legal provisions surrounding data protection, which may only be restricted in cases of overwhelming collective interest, the principle of adhering to the strict purposes of collection and the imperative of data economy.

In this context, the census decision (VZU, *Volkszählungsurteil*) stipulates the following:

"It would be incompatible with informational self-determination if a legal order should permit a social order in which the citizens would no longer know who, what, and under what circumstances something is known about him. [...] This would not only compromise the individual opportunities for personal development, but also the common good, because self-determination is a basic functional requirement of a liberal democratic society founded on trade and the capacity of its citizens to participate" (VZU, 43.).

So, if the official statistical agencies intentionally link data on citizens from different sources without their knowledge or agreement, in actual fact behind their backs, for the portrayal of relatively large temporal and factual spheres of people's lives, can this be constitutionally acceptable?

Once again, on the census decision:

"The data collection program may portray individual spheres of life, for example the citizen's place of residence, but not his private information. Anything other than this would only be permissible if it were possible to unrestrictedly link the data collected with those maintained by administrative agencies, which maintain in part very sensitive datasets, or even to access such a data-sharing facility through a uniform personal ID or other identifier would be possible; a comprehensive registration and cataloging of personal data through the merging of individual circumstantial and personal data for the construction of personal data profiles of the citizenry is, even with the anonymity of statistical records, unacceptable" (VZU 65, 53.).

The specific nature of official statistics speaks against the permissibility of the exact matching of data from different sources. Duty of disclosure, enforceable by state law, is the rule – agreement to provide information tends to be the exception. There is no concrete purpose for the collection of data. New analyses are constantly being generated by data research centers in particular. Inflexible table programs are no longer the only modes of evaluation, making them easily controlled. Statistics is always data collection for the future. Frugality in data collection results only from limited resources for official statistics and from the efforts to downsize bureaucracy at the expense of official statistics.

This does not make the collection of official statistics inherently unconstitutional, however. To the contrary, the tendency described above is balanced by an official statistical policy of confidentiality with regard to personal data, which includes the imperative of keeping a strict separation of statistics from administrative processes, the resulting freedom from self-incrimination owing to the fulfillment of the duty of disclosure, the internal and external partitioning of the statistical offices, the earliest possible division and deletion of auxiliary identifiers, and the wide-ranging obligation to inform the respondents of their legal rights.

To sum up these observations, weighing both sides according to the principle of "practical concordance," it appears that the integration of individual statistical sets of personal data in this legal framework can result in an imbalance to the disadvantage of the individual citizen.

2011 Census: The largest integration of data in federal statistics

As many are already aware, the pending law regulating the census through multi-stage matching of personal data is derived from an administrative process. This is supplemented by a very large sample as well as a census of buildings and housing as primary surveys, and is expected to fulfill the preconditions for the generation of census datasets that largely correspond to the demands of a classic population count. Geodata will be matched with address data, population information from the data stores of municipal registers, the Federal Employment Agency (BA, *Bundesagentur für Arbeit*), and from the public administration for civil servants and judges. By means of "statistical matching," the data from the population sample is then used as a supplement in order to fill gaps in the data from administrative processes, or to carry out in-depth regionalized evaluations. A consistent personal identifier is not available by reason of constitutional law as outlined above. Thus, the matching will proceed through clearly identifiable data, such as names, birthdays, etc. Aside from the logistical problems associated with this approach, those in data protection are interested in whether this operation is one whose depth of intervention is acceptable, and whether the legal and technological-organizational securities to which statistical offices are bound could not somehow be reduced.

The majority of those entrusted with data protection see to it that the duties of constitutional law described in the preceding section are being fulfilled and the requirements of the statistical offices are being adhered to. On individual points, however, there is still disagreement.

It has hardly been discussed that the methods developed for the 2011 Census have given rise to instruments that, should they come into use in administrative processes, would no longer guarantee citizens freedom from disadvantage. One need only to observe the generation of households. The obligation to collect data primarily from the relevant individual – whether they are collected for the receipt of social services, the obligation to provide information, or for the preparation of an official document – has been countered for several years by the development toward widespread matching of administrative data. However, proposed statutory regulations on the storage and preservation of data, as well as restrictions on intended use, are increasingly coming under the scrutiny of constitutional law. Already at the time of the census test legislation, our public agency had called for an expansion of statistical confidentiality to extend to and include methods of data integration developed by the statistical offices and commissioned by them. Fully developed and functioning methods of data collection and processing systems awaken new desires – one need only think of the "LKW-Maut" (German toll system for heavy commercial vehicles) that politicians are now seeking to use for personal vehicles.

Research with personal data without consent on the basis of legal privileges for non-statistical research

Should research be undertaken with a single one-time authorization or sweeping research privileges using data without explicit agreement of the respondents, the following mandatory checks and authorization steps must be followed:

- The urgent necessity of the data for the research project must be established.
- Can the research project only be successfully carried out using the personal data, or also with pseudonymized or even only with anonymized data?
- Can anonymization or pseudonymization be carried out step by step?
- What agency will carry out the anonymization or pseudonymization (researchers, a neutral trusted third party, address procurement, data steward)?
- In research using primarily personal data, authorization from upper federal or state agencies, and frequently also from an informational or qualified data protection agency, is mandatory.

After extensive consultation and through the oversight of our agency over the last two decades, a three-digit number of research projects were successfully carried out, accompanied by consultation and testing, all based on the integration of longitudinal or cross-sectional data.

The boundaries of the research privilege pursuant to § 16 Abs. 6 of the Law on Statistics for Federal Purposes

The dilemma with regard to the use of personal statistical data for scholarly research lies in the fact that gradual anonymization or pseudonymization in the research process is ruled out. The data are permitted to leave the sealed-off area of the statistical office only when they have been factually anonymized. Reidentification, as stated above, is forbidden under penalty of law (see above), and thus longitudinal and cross-sectional data integration is forbidden as well. Only within the statistical office is integration of personal data not completely unacceptable, as both the pending Census Regulation Law and the Microcensus Law show.

A data model with a data steward function

A hypothetical exercise – even today

Take the case of a scientific research project in which the statistical probability and margin of error of the two datasets collected on the basis of the obligation to provide information need to be statistically verified: on the one hand, income data from the Microcensus, and on the other, data from the respective tax office (*Finanzamt*) – which soon may become the Federal Financial Supervisory Authority (BAFin, *Bundesanstalt für Finanzdienstleistungsaufsicht*).

What follows is a brief observation on the use of currently established identification numbers for the tax authorities. Observing the principles of the population census judgment of the Federal Constitutional Court, the regulations contained in 139b of the tax code stipulate that this individual personal identifier may only be permitted for the fulfillment of the legal tasks of the tax authorities. This pertains also for the use by other public and non-public offices. The legislators, however, built a loophole into the tax code with the formulation, "or a statutory provision that explicitly allows or imposes the collection of data and use of the identification number." It is extremely doubtful, however, that this regulation conforms to constitutional law. Should such a proviso succeed in being brought off, it would have to be quickly brought to trial before the Federal Constitution Court. In everyone's interest, as much for social and economic research as for the acceptance of official statistics, I would like to urgently advise against the demand for the use of tax identification numbers for the purposes of data integration outside of the legal tasks of the tax authorities. According to the wording of the law – and this underscores doubts about this regulation – it is even possible to allow uses within a legitimate, government-sanctioned objective that are foreign to the intended purpose. And now back to the theme of this advisory report.

Statistical offices do of course receive personal data from the tax authorities – but anonymously. Strictly speaking, the quality of this data already excludes the possibility of data integration. How can the data on individuals from the Microcensus and tax authorities be clearly linked to individuals in reanalysis?

The statistical office pulls a sample from the address data of the current sample census with file numbers. The desired attribute data with file numbers are stored separately in a parallel file. The address data with birth year and file numbers are transmitted to a data steward, who determines the tax office responsible for the particular address and assigns a pseudonym to the file number. The data steward conveys the address data of the individuals, the birth year, and the pseudonym to the appropriate tax office so that no connection to the household may be identified. After the data steward has transmitted this information, the data containing addresses and birth years are deleted. Based on this transmitted information, the tax office determines the tax data and correlates these with a minimal margin of error to the pseudonym. The address data and birth year are then deleted by the tax office. The tax office then encrypts the tax data and hands it back to the data steward with pseudonyms. The data steward then tells the statistics office which file numbers have pseudonyms, without passing on the pseudonyms themselves. The statistical office then passes the personal data from the Microcensus on to the data steward coded in yet a different way, but with the file number clearly provided. The data steward is then not in a position to decipher the attribute data. He replaces the file numbers with pseudonyms and then merges the variously coded personal data from the sample census and tax offices. The corresponding pseudonym is then deleted. What remains is only an anonymous and arbitrary dataset number. Any existing data referring to the tax office and regional offices within the German states are also deleted at this stage. The data are then transferred to the researchers in this form. With the private keys exclusively given to them, the data content can only be read and evaluated in this factually anonymized context. Even greater anonymization arises as a result of deficiencies in matching at the various tax offices.

Problems:

The tax offices find out that data have been prepared on specific individuals for data integration. The fact that these are data from official statistics can be kept confidential by the data steward (these might also be data from the BA or other sources, as in the case of data integration around questions of marginal employment). The allocation of the public and private keys to the tax and statistical offices should be conducted by the researchers themselves or by a second data steward. The public key can only be given by the first data steward to the data provider.

The statistical office learns indirectly which of their data have no exact correlations at the tax offices (are these just retirees?).

Is a legally acceptable framework for integration of statistical data to support scientific research conceivable?

Among researchers, data can be classified as factually anonymized if the integration of the data content does not present any fundamental potential for further de-anonymization. In the domain of official statistics, the basic imperative of separation is not harmed. For data from preliminary data collections, this method may no longer be appropriate if it is not possible to reconnect separate auxiliary identifiers with survey characteristics using a file number, as per § 9 Abs. 2 BStatG.

Legal consideration is required to determine whether this method prohibits reidentification of the attribute data "for the creation of an individual reference" (§ 21 BStatG). This seems to me to be the case. The question remains open whether this is covered under the tasks delineated in the Law on Statistics for Federal Purposes (§ 21 BStatG). If a legal research contract is signed for the use of federal statistics and this includes the rights to "auxiliary functions" according to § 16 Abs. 6 BStatG, then this would be possible.

At this point in my reflections, it appears that the principles of the division of official statistics and administrative processes, as well as the mandatory freedom from self-incrimination for respondents, are not infringed upon in the construct discussed above. To legally reinforce these principles, it is essential to provide legal legitimacy for the legal entity of the data steward. It is widely recognized that conceptions of a privileged right to confidential information for research purposes are of little use.

If, however, there were some broad legal parameters established for the three functions of data stewards (anonymization or pseudonymization; the relevant linking function; and functions of data preservation, preparation, and archiving), the situation would look significantly different. Even today, if a data steward takes on these functions immediately as a lawyer or notary in the service of and with the knowledge of the respondents, the data would be subject not only to a pledge of confidentiality, but also to the right to refuse to give evidence and the prohibition of seizure.

The individual respondents in the hypothetical construct above know nothing of the task the data steward is carrying out to protect their informational self-determination. A data steward is not their "trusted confidant." I argue that these gaps can be bridged by lawmakers. A main point of criticism about the efforts and claims for research privileges on the side of the federal government is that, with this, the legally privileged and protected domain will become vastly expanded. To the critics of this new "secrecy," with their restrictions on the security and criminal departments, it may be replied that this does not produce any new domain that cannot be controlled by these agencies.

For the official statistics, an opening clause might be integrated into the Law on Statistics for Federal Purposes (§16 Abs. 6) dealing with data stewards or such institutions operating as public authorities under the direction of a notary (distinct from but comparable to a hospital under the direction of a physician).

To sum up, I propose using the hypothetical scenario outlined above as a model for a discussion that can be considered from numerous perspectives.

Prospects and perspectives on the model

Assuming the above described legal parameters, the model can be integrated, either directly or in modified form, into a range of possible solutions for the problem as it is laid out in the following statements. It should be theoretically possible to analyze the representativity of voluntary surveys among persons who had previously participated in the Microcensus on a mandatory basis. In term of data protection laws, however, this should presuppose a linkage of compliance of those being surveyed with an initially strong pseudonymization and a concluding process of anonymization secured by a data steward. The analysis then yields data about statistical errors in the totals and aggregate of the voluntary surveys. There are, however, erasure deadlines for the Microcensus for voluntarily modifying things later on. The model can be assessed in this context too, for which is it highly suitable, as far as it concerns survey data with data from official registers such as the local population registry, which are very precise but not linked to or used to identify individuals.

With the integration of personal data of different dimensions, levels, and content, the model can provide an instrument that can be used at specifically designated points of crossing and linkage in order to secure anonymity at every level. This would be particularly useful in connection with work and personnel data from various sources.

A personal afterword on the hypothetical construct

For political counsel based on complex analysis and not only for alleged failures, which can supposedly only be uncovered by reanalysis in the official statistical agencies, independent research projects such as that called for in the 1998 memorandum ("Prerequisites for success in empirical economic research and empirically based economic and social policy advice") appear both necessary and promising. In my opinion, such projects will become possible with the involvement of the relevant data protection agencies following strict interdisciplinary assessments of their necessity. Also desirable for such projects would be something akin to the Swiss model of an open and accessible public dialogue on the content of these projects. If details were brought into the public discourse, however, the freedom from self-incrimination could be indirectly affected. I propose that this be discussed as well.

If Professors R. Hauser, G. G. Wagner, and K. F. Zimmermann had written their memorandum in English, the language that now appears to be compulsory, the 2001 KVI report and the German Data Forum (RatSWD) would probably not developed so successfully thus far. For this reason, only the German version of this essay is authorized.

Recommendations

Official statistics should determine, on the basis of the specific information needs of social and economic research, for which data stores data integration is recommended. Additionally, official statistics should highlight general legal, technical and methodological problems.

On the basis of the examples provided in this report, it should be determined whether, and with what necessary requirements, including legal requirements, the present constitutional barriers might remain untouched through the use of independent and legally chartered data stewards. This structure would allow for the use of data through the diverse possibilities available for pseudonymization and encoding.

The relationship between the Research Data Centers and data stewards is yet to be defined. Both must occupy different positions of responsibility from a data protection perspective in order to preserve the integrity of the ban against reidentification.

Recommendations for the modernization of statistical law for the creation of clear and fixed parameters to enable data integration should be set as the goal for an initial conceptual phase and a pilot project.

3. New Methods in Human Subjects Research: Do We Need a New Ethics?

Karsten Weber

Contact:

Karsten Weber
Technische Universität Berlin
Informatik und Gesellschaft
Sekretariat FR 5-10
Franklinstraße 28/29
10587 Berlin
Germany
e-mail: kweber[at]cs.tu-berlin.de

Abstract

Online surveys and interviews, the observations of chat rooms or online games, data mining, knowledge discovery in databases (KDD), collecting biomarkers, employing biometrics, using Radio Frequency Identification Device (RFID) technology – even as implants in the human body – and other related processes, all seem to be more promising, cheaper, faster, and comprehensive than conventional methods of human subjects research. But at the same time these new means of gathering information may pose powerful threats to privacy, autonomy, and informed consent. Online research, particularly involving children and minors as well as individuals belonging to other vulnerable groups such as ethnic or religious minorities, is in urgent need of an adequate research ethics that can provide reasonable and morally justified constraints for human subjects research. The paper at hand seeks to provide some clarification of these new means of information gathering and the challenges they present to moral concepts like privacy, autonomy, informed consent, beneficence, and justice. Some existing codes of conduct and ethical guidelines are examined to determine whether they provide answers to those challenges and/or whether they can be helpful in the development of principles and regulations governing human subjects research. Finally, some conclusions and recommendations are presented that can help in the task of formulating an adequate research ethics for human subjects research.

Keywords: human subjects research, online research, biomarkers, biometrics, autonomy, privacy, informed consent, research ethics

1. Preface

Social researchers today regularly use questionnaires, interviews, or observation in the conventional paper-and-pen style to gather data (including methods like Computer Aided Telephone Interviews (CATI)). Yet it seems more promising, cheaper, faster, and comprehensive to deploy new means of collecting information: online surveys and interviews, observations in chat rooms or online games (see papers in Hine 2005; Kaye and Johnson 1999; Lyons et al. 2005), data mining in online social networks like Facebook or on individual websites, knowledge discovery in databases (KDD, see Tavani 1999a; 1999b; Vedder 1999), collecting biomarkers such as tissue samples or hairs, employing biometrics like face recognition to identify persons (e.g., Clarke and Furnell 2005; Crosbie 2005), using RFID[1] technology to monitor,

---

1   In their rather technical article, Goodrum et al. (2006) provide an overview of what RFID technology (Radio Frequency Identification) is, how it works, and how it can be used. Roughly speaking, RFIDs are very small computer chips which can store and process information as well as receive and transmit data wirelessly across distances. In the case of passive devices without a power source, this distance ranges from a few centimeters to as

for instance, consumer behavior in supermarkets (e.g., Lockton and Rosenberg 2005), or even implanting RFIDs into the human body. (see EGE 2005).

With the exception of online surveys and interviews, as well as the implantation of RFIDs, these methods can be employed without the awareness and knowledge of those who are being scrutinized. These new techniques are urgently in need of an adequate research ethics. The ethical dimension is critical, for it is almost impossible to administer research completely by legal precepts. Moreover, this option is even not desirable since it implies interference with academic freedom, reduces flexibility, and delays research projects. In addition, national law cannot typically be applied to international research programs. Thus, a research ethics that is widely acceptable across national and cultural borders could potentially serve as a kind of soft law. It is important to stress that, while ethics can be effective in controlling human behavior in general and academic research in particular, it cannot replace law, something made clear by the recent data crime violations in Germany. If people are willing to break the law, laws will not inhibit them and ethics will not either. Nevertheless, the following discussion will deal with ethics rather than law, under the assumption that all means and actions deployed in human subjects research have met all legal requirements.

2. Research ethics

2.1 Different understandings of research ethics

In the search for an adequate research ethics one does not have to start from scratch. Certain organizations, institutions, and professional associations have already done valuable work in this area that will be referenced in this expert report (e.g., AAAS 1999; AoIR 2002). And yet it is clear that what is understood by research ethics is sometimes quite different in different cases, if one compares, for instance, Germany and the United States.

Research ethics in Germany (*Forschungsethik*) is often used in reference to principles first proposed by Max Weber (1904) or Robert K. Merton (1942). Merton's CUDOS scheme in particular is often cited, according to which science must fulfill the demands of: *communism* or *communalism* (results must be shared with the scientific community), *universality* (everybody shall be able to participate in science regardless of nationality, religion, culture, etc.), *disinterestedness* (scientists shall present results as if they had

---

far as one or two meters. In the case of active devices with a power source, the broadcasting range can be increased to around ten meters. RFIDs can be used as identification labels for products, animals, and even human beings; they often are mentioned as serious threats to privacy (e.g., Lockton and Rosenberg 2005).

no personal interest in their rejection or acceptance), *originality* (researchers shall aim to develop novel claims), and *skepticism* (science and its claims shall always be subject to critical examination).

Of course, these demands are widely accepted in the United States too, but they are complemented by principles and rules that guide daily research routines and the application of research methods. These principles and rules will be identified below. It is important also to note that German codes of conduct and ethical guidelines regarding social science or marketing research (ADM 2001; DGS/BDS 1992) already include some similar rules. However, these documents seem more concerned with the relationship of principal and agent rather than with the relationship of researcher and research subject – for instance in the DIN ISO 20252.

2.2 Principles in research ethics

It does not make sense to try to find moral rules specifically for guiding either online surveys, data mining, collecting biomarkers, or the application of RFIDs. Instead, it is important to identify more general principles that can be applied to all new techniques of gathering information. Since these principles are, of course, principles, it should not make a big difference whether they are being applied to conventional social science methods or to newer ones.

At the same time, principles are abstract in that they do not tell us which action to take in a certain situation. For instance, Immanuel Kant's moral imperative demands generalizability of reasons for taking a certain action but is silent with regard to morally acceptable actions. Thus, it is necessary to supplement principles with advice on how to implement them in the research process.

In its *Scientific Freedom, Responsibility and Law Program* (AAAS 1999), the American Association for the Advancement of Science identifies three basic principles to guide research on human subjects: autonomy, beneficence, and justice. This document also introduces supporting principles such as privacy and informed consent. Thus, in the first section of this article, these principles are described in general and then applied to new techniques of gathering information. This is followed by a short discussion and concludes with the presentation of some conclusions and recommendations. Due to a lack of space, it is impossible to provide a comprehensive discussion on the problem of new techniques in human subjects research. Therefore, this text focuses on some of the most pressing issues.

3. Basic principles and their application

In approaching the following discussion, it is important to note that the way that concepts like autonomy, beneficence, and privacy are understood is culturally determined. This does not necessarily imply moral relativism; however, the understanding advanced here is not the only possible and existing one. Nonetheless, this paper takes the position that respect for the following ethical principles should form a kind of default option in human subjects research. It is always possible to reduce the requirements that have to be respected, but a research ethics based upon universal human rights and dignity should not allow research that does not respect these principles. They can be understood as absolutes that can only be abandoned if, and only if, research subjects deliberately consent. Such a position makes it possible to adapt these principles to other cultural contexts without diminishing the core values of our own ethics.

3.1 Autonomy, informed consent, and privacy

Whether a person is to be granted autonomy or is already, by virtue of being a person, autonomous, is a question that has been discussed at least since the beginnings of Greek philosophy. The debate over informed consent has a more recent twentieth-century history, particularly as it pertains to the ethics of medicine and bioethics (see Sade 2001). The significance of privacy has been formulated at least since the hallmark paper of Warren and Brandeis, "The Right to Privacy," published in 1890.

3.1.1 General remarks

The concept of autonomy is a versatile one that can be filled with diverse meanings. In general, one can use "autonomy" as a descriptive term as well as ascriptive term. As *descriptive* term, it "[...] refers to people's actual condition and signifies the extent to which they are meaningfully 'self-governed' in a universe shaped by causal forces" (Fallon 1994: 877). To be autonomous, a person must meet certain criteria like being able to make decisions on rational grounds. Simultaneously, the term presupposes a set of conditions, such as the absence of coercion. Used as an *ascriptive* term, "[...] autonomy represents [...] their right to make and act on their own decisions, even if those decisions are ill-considered or substantively unwise" (ibid.: 878). It is important to stress that this understanding of autonomy focuses on the individual. At least in some non-Western societies it is the case that either some adults, frequently women, are not granted autonomy, or the idea that individuals should or do have the opportunity to make independent decisions is essentially denied (see Olinger et al. 2005). Since autonomy in its descriptive sense is a matter of degree, it has often been argued even in Western societies that certain circumstances allow for interference with a person's individual decision; such a perspective is often called "paternalism" (see Scoccia 1990) and will be discussed with reference to beneficence below.

In order to make autonomous decisions, some conditions must be met; being informed is one of these basic requirements. But informed consent is not always required of human subjects research. Gathering information that is publicly accessible – for instance, the content of television and radio programs or conducting observation in public spaces – does not require consent (see ASSS 1999: 7). That means that the distinction between private and public sphere is extremely important to human subjects research. If a researcher interferes with a person's private sphere or privacy, informed consent must be obtained (see Jacobson 1999: 135).

The shortest definition of privacy probably was coined by Samuel D. Warren and Louis D. Brandeis in 1890, who defined privacy as "the right to be let alone." Although their definition was and remains influential, far more detailed theorizations of privacy have emerged in recent years. In the context of human subjects research, and particularly with regard to new techniques of information gathering, the "control theory" and the "restricted access theory" of privacy (Tavani 1999b) should be mentioned. In control theory "[...] one has privacy if and only if one has control over information about oneself." (ibid.: 267). According to restricted access theory, "[...] an individual has privacy in a 'situation' if in that particular situation the individual is 'protected from intrusion, interference, and information access by others'" (ibid.). It must be again stressed here that the notion of privacy, like that of autonomy, is culturally biased.[2]

3.1.2 Application

Although autonomy has been discussed for a much longer time than informed consent and privacy, the latter two seem to be more important for human subjects research ethics. Privacy and informed consent are necessary prerequisites of autonomy insofar as it concerns the application of the new methods of information gathering mentioned above.

To respect privacy, it is essential to develop at least a working definition of private and public spheres. For instance, there is currently an intense debate about whether web pages, chat rooms, Usenet forums, and the like are public or private spaces. Often web pages are compared to radio and tele-

---

[2] See, for example, the papers in the journal *Ethics and Information Technology* 7 (1) 2005. Yet, with reference to Newell (1998) one can arguably deny that such differences really exist.

vision broadcasting, which are publicly accessible and therefore allowed to be scrutinized without asking for any kind of consent from the broadcaster (AAAS 1999: 7).

However, without further indications one cannot presume that the creation and publication of Internet web pages automatically implies consent to their use for research purposes. One indication, for example, that authors of web pages do not consent to certain types of research use is when their pages contain so-called meta-tags which say that the respective web page must not be included in the index of a search engine like Google.[3] According to the control/restricted access theories of privacy, the use of such technical strategies is a way that authors of web pages try to take control over the flow of information.

Additionally, a main difference between radio and television broadcasting on the one hand and web pages on the other, is that web pages regularly contain information directly related to identifiable persons. Since human subjects research must meet the requirement of beneficence (see below), collecting information from such web pages potentially can cause harm to their authors. Clearly, these are cases that call out for informed consent. Finally, gathering data from web pages might interfere with copyright and intellectual property rights, which would also make informed consent mandatory (see Allen et al. 2008; Berry 2004; Carusi 2008; Grimes 2008; Hudson and Bruckman 2004; Jacobson 1999).

Some of the arguments mentioned above imply that the information to be collected is publicly accessible and that public accessibility already offers necessary as well as sufficient criteria for abandoning the requirement of informed consent. Conclusively, if information is not publicly disclosed, consent that this information may be used in human subjects research cannot be taken for granted. Thus, new methods of gathering data, like observations in chat rooms or online games, data mining in online social networks, or knowledge discovery in databases, all demand that informed consent is acquired explicitly. Because access to such data is regularly restricted by passwords and other technical and organizational means, it cannot be presumed that these sources of data are supposed to be publicly accessible (see Tavani 1999a; 1999b; Vedder 1999). Rather, they must be understood as belonging to the private sphere of a certain group of individuals or a subculture. Consequently, to support autonomous decision making with regard to participation in human subjects research, it is vital to ask for consent.

With regard to other methods, like collecting biomarkers such as tissue samples or hairs, employing biometrics, or using RFID technology to monitor persons' behavior, researchers must regularly assume that those who are being observed conceive of their behavior as something that belongs to their private sphere. Typically, biomarkers are not intentionally, but rather

---

3   Or in cases the website includes a file called "robots.txt," again with specific entries.

accidentally, put into circulation. Therefore, one cannot assume consent has been given to further investigation in human subjects research. The collection of biomarkers in the context of medical treatment proves this as a general rule, for it is mandatory to ask explicitly for consent and to inform the individual of potential risks and consequences. Therefore, if human subjects research conducted outside contexts like medical treatment is at stake, particularly if information about health status or the consuming habits of individuals are being gathered, informed consent, from an ethical point of view, seems mandatory (see Bayertz et al. 2001; see also below on "Beneficence").

Lastly, using RFID implants for research purposes seems entirely inappropriate. After implantation, subjects have virtually lost their ability to autonomously stop the research process. Simultaneously, the risks of scarring, infection, and other health risks are quite difficult to evaluate, particularly for non-specialists (EGE 2005: 18; see below). Thus, for the application of RFIDs, well informed consent is difficult or even impossible to obtain.

3.2 Beneficence

3.2.1 General remarks

Generally speaking, beneficence as a moral claim means that with our actions we aim to promote the good of others and increase their benefits, and also try to prevent harm from others. As a guiding principle for our behavior, beneficence requires us to take the consequences of our actions into account. Therefore, it is necessary to try to forecast the possible and likely outcomes of current and future decisions. Obviously, such forecasts are often difficult or even impossible.[4] However, that is not the main problem posed by beneficence; rather, it is that beneficence may collide with the principle of autonomy. In moral as well as in political philosophy there is rigorous debate over whether the benefit to a person can be objectively measured or whether it can only be evaluated from an individual point of view. The latter view purports that, for instance, what is harmful for one person could be a benefit for another.

3.2.2 Application

Human subjects research in general can expose individuals to certain risks of harm. Although it might be difficult or even impossible to define one single

---

[4] One important response to this problem is represented by the "precautionary principle" (see Morris 2000). Except for the EGE Opinion No. 20 (EGE 2005: 17), the precautionary principle has not been explicitly taken into account in those codes of conduct or ethical guidelines referred to in the text at hand.

standard of good and harm that is acceptable for every person, it is obvious that some consequences of human subjects research are unambiguously intolerable: mental or physical harm, discrimination, damage or loss of property, and the like. Particularly where methods are employed that make subjects (potentially) identifiable, and thus may expose them to such consequences, it is extremely important to take the principle of beneficence into account. With regard to, for instance, data mining, KDD, biomarkers, or biometrics, the risk assessment of possible identification is therefore mandatory. It could be that a single set of data does not allow for identification of subjects, but a combination of several different databases would present this possibility. In such cases, research subjects must be informed and asked for their consent – regardless of whether publicly accessible data is used or not. Particularly if risk assessment is impossible or does not provide viable evidence, the principle of beneficence may even require a cessation of research.

3.3 Justice

3.3.1 General remarks

The third basic principle that shall guide research is justice, which demands a fair distribution of risks and benefits resulting from our actions. As described in the report of the AAAS (1999: 3): "Since the fruits of knowledge can come at a cost to those participating in research […] justice […] seeks a fair distribution of the burdens and benefits associated with research, so that certain individuals or groups do not bear disproportionate risks while others reap the benefits." In fact, justice can be interpreted as impartial beneficence. It is important to stress that a fair distribution of burdens and benefits does not necessarily imply equality but equity in distribution.

3.3.2 Application

With regard to human subjects research "[…] justice is perhaps the most elusive [principle] in terms of application and understanding" (AAAS 1999: 14). As already mentioned, it is quite difficult to make exact determinations around the notions of good, harm, and beneficence. If the term "justice" is understood as impartial beneficence, it is still unclear how benefits and burdens of human subjects research might be shared. In fact, it might be argued that since it is difficult to determine positive as well as negative outcomes of research, it would not make sense to talk about the just distribution of these outcomes. Nonetheless, there is one notion of justice that has a direct impact on human subjects research: the principle of justice does not allow for the instrumentalization of individuals or groups of individuals who certainly will never be, not even potentially, beneficiaries of a specific research program.[5]

4. A special problem

A very important question concerning autonomy, privacy, and informed consent is the problem of research on children and minors, for example, in the behavioral sciences, social sciences, epidemiology, or pedagogy and educational sciences. This kind of research is continuously growing as the critical importance of the first years of the life course becomes more and more obvious, for example, in research pertaining to school and preschool education. Yet, if one takes a closer look at the existing codes of ethics and codes of conduct as well as at the literature concerning ethics in general, children and minors are occasionally mentioned, but it is very difficult to find concrete advice for research.

For instance, in the report, *Ethical and Legal Aspects of Human Subjects Research on the Internet*, only two sentences on minors can be found: "For example, minors could respond to a study involving inappropriate materials for their age without the researcher's knowledge" (AAAS 1999: 8) and "Researchers are obligated by federal policies and professional ethics to provide special consideration for vulnerable members of the community, such as children and persons of diminished mental capacity" (ibid.: 5).

In the *ICC/ESOMAR International Code on Market and Social Research* one comes across statements like, "Market researchers shall take special care when carrying out research among children and young people" (ICC/ESOMAR 2007: 2), or "Researchers shall take special care when interviewing children and young people. The consent of the parent or responsible adult shall first be obtained before interviewing children" (ibid.: 6).

The *EGE Opinion No. 20* says that "ICT devices should be implanted in minors and legally incapacitated only if this is done in accordance with the principles set out in the Council of Europe Convention on Biomedicine and Human Rights" (EGE 2005: 31).

Finally, both the code of ethics adopted by the German Sociological Association (DGS/BDS 1992) as well as the 2001 report, "Standards for Quality Assurance for Online Surveys" (*Standards zur Qualitätssicherung für Online-Befragungen*) by the Working Group of German Market and

---

5 To use an example from biomedical research: pharmaceutical tests in developing countries which test drugs that will not be sold in the respective countries or that are not affordable for the research subjects themselves.

Social Research Institutes (ADM, *Arbeitskreis Deutscher Markt- und Sozialforschungsinstitute*), are almost completely silent on the question of ethics in human subjects research. Furthermore, neither the ADM's "Guidelines on the Use of Mystery Research in Market and Social Research" (*Richtlinie für den Einsatz von Mystery Research[6] in der Markt- und Sozialforschung*) from 1995, nor its "Guidelines for Online Surveys" (*Richtlinie für Online-Befragungen*) from 2000 refer to children or minors at all.

To summarize, scholars will on the whole find few if any references to legal regulation, but even fewer instructions concerning the design of research on children and minors. However, one can find detailed recommendations in "Ethical Decision-Making and Internet Research", a document put out by the Association of Internet Researchers in 2002.[7] Unfortunately, one must derive these recommendations from three sample consent forms for parents and children involved in Internet research. Nevertheless, this might be a useful point of departure for considering this question in individual contexts.

5. Conclusions, requirements, and recommendations

The above-mentioned principles of autonomy, privacy, informed consent, beneficence, and justice are just as important as ethical principles themselves. As guiding principles for human subjects research, they have particular potency. However, they must be supplemented by rules for their application in research design and on research processes. So far, some deficits can be identified that point directly to some specific requirements and recommendations.

- Human subjects research programs should employ risk assessment procedures concerning the potential for identification of research subjects if multiple databases are combined;

---

[6] "Mystery Research" includes covert observations in chat rooms and other similar online sites. Significantly, the ADM assumes that mystery research does not require informed consent. Nevertheless, it should be noted that the ADM does provide "Guidelines for Interviewing Minors" (*Richtlinie für die Befragung von Minderjährigen*) (ADM 1996) that contain comparable recommendations to those of the AoIR (2002). However, a detailed interpretation of all the ADM's guidelines would probably reveal some incompatibilities and even contradictions, for example with regard to informed consent in the case of online ("mystery") research on children and minors.

[7] Association of Internet Researchers, for more information refer to <http://www.aoir.org>, last visited 01/05/2009.

- Thresholds must be defined concerning acceptable risks for research subjects that also differentiate between children, minors, and adults;[8]
- A more appropriate definition of beneficence must be developed that focuses on preventing individual harm. The goal of working for the good for each research subject is highly implausible, difficult, and perhaps even impossible to obtain;
- Specific and concrete rules concerning human subjects research on children and minors must be developed and then incorporated into codes of ethics and codes of conduct. Specific attention must be given to the issue of data collection that involves children and minors who are now adults, particularly with regard to panel surveys. In such situations it is recommended that research subjects be asked for the renewal of informed consent. In the case of a denial it would then be mandatory to delete all personal data, for example, names and addresses, out of respect for autonomy, privacy, and beneficence (sometimes it might even be necessary to consider to delete *all* existing data to comply with copyright and intellectual property rights);
- As far as possible, thresholds, definitions, and rules concerning human subjects research must not be based on particular, culturally determined customs and traditions. Reference to customs and traditions makes it more difficult to adopt a general research ethics to different cultural contexts;
- Because such definitions and thresholds are often difficult to generalize, particularly in case of long-term research projects – projects involving a very large number of participants, or projects involving subjects with greater vulnerability like children or members of ethnic or religious minorities (because, for instance, if such groups are small it might be easy to deanonymize data and identify individuals) – it might be necessary to establish ethics committees specifically for human subjects survey research, similar to those that exist in (bio-)medical research programs.

---

8 Such thresholds already exist in animal research but are probably not sufficient for human subjects research. Animal-related research does not deal with questions concerning autonomy, privacy, and informed consent. However, it might be helpful to study the history of how such thresholds developed.

References:

AAAS (1999): Ethical and Legal Aspects of Human Subjects Research on the Internet. American Association for the Advancement of Science. http://www.aaas.org/spp/sfrl/projects/intres/report.pdf. [Last visited 08/21/2008].
ADM (1995): Richtlinie für die Befragung von Minderjährigen. Arbeitskreis Deutscher Markt- und Sozialforschungsinstitute e.V. http://www.adm-ev.de/pdf/R05_D.pdf. [Last visited 01/05/2009].
ADM (1996): Richtlinie für den Einsatz von Mystery Research in der Markt- und Sozialforschung. Arbeitskreis Deutscher Markt- und Sozialforschungsinstitute e.V. http://www.adm-ev.de/pdf/R02_D.pdf. [Last visited 01/05/2009].
ADM (2000): Richtlinie für Online-Befragungen. Arbeitskreis Deutscher Markt- und Sozialforschungsinstitute e.V. http://www.adm-ev.de/pdf/R08_D_07_08.pdf. [Last visited 01/05/2008].
ADM (2001): Standards zur Qualitätssicherung für Online-Befragungen. Arbeitskreis Deutscher Markt- und Sozialforschungsinstitute e.V. http://www.adm-ev.de/pdf/Onlinestandards_D.PDF. [Last visited 08/21/2008].
Allen, G.N./Burk, D.L. and Ess, Ch. (2008): Ethical Approaches to Robotic Data Gathering in Academic Research. International Journal of Internet Research Ethics 1 (1), 9-36. http://www.uwm.edu/Dept/SOIS/cipr/ijire/ijire_1.1_allen.pdf. [Last visited 08/27/2008].
AoIR (2002): Charles Ess & AoIR ethics working committee. Ethical decision-making and Internet research: Recommendations from the AoIR ethics working committee. http://www.aoir.org/reports/ethics.pdf. [Last visited 08/27/2008].
Bayertz, K./Ach, J.S. and Paslack, R. (2001): Wissen mit Folgen. Zukunftsperspektiven und Regelungsbedarf der genetischen Diagnostik innerhalb und außerhalb der Humangenetik. Jahrbuch für Wissenschaft und Ethik, Band 6, 271-307.
Berry, D.M. (2004): Internet research: privacy, ethics and alienation: an open source approach. Internet Research 14 (4), 323-332.
Carusi, A. (2008): Data as Representation: Beyond Anonymity in E-Research Ethics. International Journal of Internet Research Ethics 1 (1), 37-65. http://www.uwm.edu/Dept/SOIS/cipr/ijire/ijire_1.1_carusi.pdf. [Last visited 08/27/2008].
Clarke, N. and Furnell, S. (2005): Biometrics – The promise versus the practice. Computer Fraud & Security 9, 12-16.
Crosbie, M. (2005): Biometrics for enterprise security. Network Security 11, 4-8.
DGS/BDS (1992): Ethik-Kodex der Deutschen Gesellschaft für Soziologie (DGS) und des Berufsverbandes Deutscher Soziologen (BDS). Berufsverband Deutscher Soziologinnen und Soziologen e.V. http://www.bds-soz.de/images/stories/formulare/ethik.pdf. [Last visited 08/21/2008].
EGE (2005): European Group on Ethics in Science and New Technologies to the European Commission: Opinion on the ethical aspects of ICT implants in the human body. Opinion No. 20. http://ec.europa.eu/european_group_ethics/docs/avis20compl_en.pdf. [Last visited 08/19/2008].
Fallon, R.H. Jr. (1994): Two Senses of Autonomy. Stanford Law Review 46 (4), 875-905.
Goodrum, P.M./McLaren, M.A. and Durfee, Adam (2006): The application of active radio frequency identification technology for tool tracking on construction job sites. Automation in Construction 15 (3), 292-302.

Grimes, S.M. (2008): Researching the Researchers: Market Researchers, Child Subjects and the Problem of "Informed" Consent. International Journal of Internet Research Ethics 1 (1), 66-91. http://www.uwm.edu/Dept/SOIS/cipr/ijire/ijire1.1_grimes.pdf. [Last visited 08/27/2008].

Hine, Ch. (Ed.) (2005.): Virtual Methods. Issues in Social Research on the Internet. Oxford/New York.

Hudson, J.M. and Bruckman, A. (2004): "Go Away": Participant Objections to Being Studied and the Ethics of Chatroom Research. The Information Society 20, 127-139.

ICC/ESOMAR (2007): ICC/ESOMAR International Code on Market and Social Research. International Chamber of Commerce. http://www.iccwbo.org/uploadedFiles/ICC/policy/marketing/Statements/ICCESOMAR_Code_English.pdf. [Last visited 08/29/2008].

Jacobson, D. (1999): Doing Research in Cyberspace. Field Methods 11 (2), 127-145.

Kaye, B.K. and Johnson, Th.J. (1999): Research Methodology: Taming the Cyber Frontier. Techniques for Improving Online Surveys. Social Science Computer Review 17 (3), 323-337.

Lockton, V. and Rosenberg, R.S. (2005): RFID: The next serious threat to privacy. Ethics and Information Technology 7, 221-231.

Lyons, A.C./Cude, B./Lawrence; F.C. and Gutter, M. (2005): Conducting Research Online: Challenges Facing Researchers in Family and Consumer Sciences. Family and Consumer Sciences Research Journal 33 (4), 341-356.

Merton, R.K. (1942): Science and Technology in a Democratic Order. Journal of Legal and Political Sociology 1, 115-126. [Reprinted as "The Normative Structure of Science" in Merton, R.K. (1974): The Sociology of Science. Chicago].

Morris, J. (Ed.) (2000): Rethinking Risk and the Precautionary Principle. Oxford.

Newell, P.B. (1998): A Cross-Cultural Comparison of Privacy Definitions and Functions: A Systems Approach. Journal of Environmental Psychology 18, 357-371.

Olinger, H.N./Britz, J.J. and Olivier, M.S. (2005): Western privacy and ubuntu: influence in the forthcoming data privacy bill. In: Brey, Ph./Grodzinsky, F./Introna, L. (Eds.): Ethics of New Information Technology. Enschede.

Sade, R.M. (2001): Autonomy and Beneficence in an Information Age. Health Care Analysis 9, 247-254.

Scoccia, D. (1990): Paternalism and the Respect for Autonomy. Ethics 100 (2), 318-334.

Tavani, H.T. (1999a): Informational privacy, data mining, and the Internet. Ethics and Information Technology 1, 137-145.

Tavani, H.T. (1999b): KDD, data mining, and the challenge for normative privacy. Ethics and Information Technology 1, 265-273.

Vedder, A. (1999): KDD: The challenge to individualism. Ethics and Information Technology 1, 275-281.

Warren, S.D. and Brandeis, L.D. (1890): The Right to Privacy. Harvard Law Review IV (5), 193ff.

Weber, M. (1904): Die "Objektivität" sozialwissenschaftlicher und sozialpolitischer Erkenntnis. Archiv für Sozialwissenschaft und Sozialpolitik 19, 22-87.

4. Does Germany Need a (New) Research Ethics for the Social Sciences?

Claudia Oellers and Eva Wegner

Contact:

Claudia Oellers
Business Office of the German Data Forum (RatSWD)
c/o DIW Berlin
10108 Berlin
Germany
e-mail: coellers[at]ratswd.de

Eva Wegner
University of Cape Town
Department of Political Studies
Rondebosch, 7700
South Africa
e-mail: wegner.eva[at]gmail.com

Abstract

This paper evaluates the German, UK, and US approaches to dealing with research ethics in the social sciences. It focuses (1) on the extent to which these research ethics frameworks protect the key rights of research subjects and (2) the extent to which they take into account the methodology and approaches used in the social sciences and do not simply emulate those of the natural sciences.

The US approach represents a highly regulated and partly bureaucratic approach where the ethics review is modeled on the methodologies of the natural sciences. In the UK, in contrast, a social science research ethics framework has been developed that remedies some of these shortcomings. It is implemented through pressure from funding institutions and is designed to respond to the needs of social science research. The German social science ethics framework consists of non-binding codes of conduct, guidelines about good scientific practice, and ethics codes of the German professional associations and funding institutions. We find that ethical behavior in Germany is typically understood as ethical behavior towards peers. We recommend the establishment of a new research ethics framework for the social sciences in Germany that is modeled on the approach developed in the UK.

Keywords: research ethics, good scientific practice, institutional review boards

1. Introduction

Several recent papers have addressed the need for rethinking research ethics in the social sciences (e.g., Lane 2009, Weber 2010). Two reasons are typically given special emphasis. The first is based on new forms of collaboration among social scientists and researchers from other fields that are judged ethically more sensitive, especially biomedical research. Research that looks, for instance, at the behavioral consequences of genetic configurations can easily confront social scientists with new ethical dilemmas. The second reason given is that technological developments now allow for a large amount of data to be exchanged through or are freely accessible on the Internet. Data that are either available from agencies or that citizens themselves make accessible – for instance, on their websites or in online forums – create new possibilities for data matching. This produces new challenges for an obviously fundamental principle in research ethics – the anonymity of research subjects. Indeed, these two developments are among the key motivations that gave rise to a new research ethics framework for the Economic and Social Research Council in the UK (see ESRC 2005).

These developments are certainly important and invite the reconsideration and revision of research ethics in the social sciences. At the same time, an exclusive focus on such new developments may bury the fact that the existing framework for social science research ethics may already be inadequate for "standard" empirical work in the social sciences.[1] Our paper thus evaluates different ways of dealing with research ethics, focusing on two questions that must be at the core of any discussion and revision of social science research ethics. First, to what extent does a research ethics framework protect the key rights of research subjects, such as information and anonymity? Second, to what extent is that framework appropriate for social science research? That is, is it simply modeled on the natural sciences, or does it respond to the different methodologies and approaches used in the social sciences?

This report looks first at the German social science ethics framework, which is essentially one of non-binding codes of conduct, guidelines about good scientific practice, and ethics codes of the German professional associations and funding institutions. We find that ethical behavior is typically understood as ethical behavior towards one's peers. Second, we discuss US and British approaches to research ethics in the social sciences.

The US approach can be seen as a highly regulated and relatively bureaucratic approach where the ethics review is modeled on the methodologies of natural sciences. The above-mentioned new framework used in the UK, in contrast, represents a reformist approach that is implemented through pressure from funding institutions and aims to respond to the needs of social science research. Finally, we address the question of whether either of these could serve as a role model for the social sciences in Germany.

2. The research ethics infrastructure in Germany

In Germany, ethical requirements for research vary widely across research fields. Requirements are rigorous and legally binding in medical or biomedical research and much less so in the social sciences, where the only compulsory legal standard is the Data Protection Act (see Schaar 2010).

As in other countries, ethical questions in Germany have always been more prominent in the natural sciences than the social sciences. In the early 1970s, some universities had already established research ethics committees (RECs). In 1979 the German Medical Association, following an initiative of the German Research Foundation (DFG, *Deutsche Forschungsgemeinschaft*), recommended the introduction of RECs. In 1994, approval by a research ethics committee became compulsory for clinical trials following the Medi-

---

[1] Whether these new trends do indeed constitute new challenges for social science is also contested. Greely (2008), for instance, argues that although many feel differently about it, the data commonly used in the social sciences is not less sensitive than information about health issues.

cinal Product Act (MPG) and the fifth amendment to the Drugs Act (AMG). In 2004 a further amendment was enacted that implemented the good clinical practice directive of the EU (2001/20/EC). As a result, a majority of German medical faculties and medical research institutes now possess RECs.[2]

For the social sciences there is no comparable legal regulation for approval of research through a research ethics committee. No important funding institution or state agency has made it its mission or a priority to further, or to systematically address such standards in the social sciences. The only legal requirement to take into account in the social sciences is the federal law on data protection. This law addresses issues of consent, data gathering, storage, and processing for all kinds of research. It is an articulation of some general standards for data-related issues in scientific research, such as the duty to anonymize information.[3]

It is rather in the framework of professional self-regulation by professional associations of sociologists or psychologists that ethics questions are addressed in the social sciences in Germany. These professional associations have created ethics committees and established codes of ethics. For example, there is the joint code of ethics of the two professional associations of sociologists, the German Sociological Association (DGS, *Deutsche Gesellschaft für Soziologie*) and the Professional Association of German Sociologists (BDS, *Berufsverband Deutscher Soziologen*), which dates back to 1992. It addresses ethical standards in research – issues of integrity and objectivity as well as the protection of the research subjects – and also deals with relationships among academics, such as the duty of referees to state conflicts of interest. These two professional associations have established a joint ethics committee to which complaints on misconduct in all the areas covered by the ethics code can be brought. This ethics committee is supposed to help find consensual solutions, but it also has the prerogative to suggest sanctions, such as the temporary exclusion of a member or her full expulsion.

While this ethics committee may advise the professional associations on ethical questions, it is in no way involved with approving research projects from an ethical point of view. This type of ethical evaluation is performed, however, by the professional association of German psychologists, the German Psychological Society (DGPs, *Deutsche Gesellschaft für Psychologie*). Its ethics committee evaluates applications for which a funding institution has required a review. In this case, and for a fee, the ethics committee evaluates whether the goals and procedures of the project comply with

---

2   The tendency to consider ethical issues more important in biomedical research than in social sciences is also evident in the work of the National Ethics Council, established by the Federal Government in 2001 (since 2007, the German Ethics Council). The council has published reports and recommendations on several topics, but most of them concern the field of biomedical research.

3   For more details on legal requirements regarding data protection, see Schaar 2009.

ethical standards. A few social science departments in Germany, for example at the universities of Mannheim and Jena, have also established local ethics committees on their own initiative that review the research projects of faculty members.

More general standards for good scientific practice were defined in a set of guidelines established by the DFG, following a series of research misconduct cases in 1997 (DFG 1997). These guidelines encompass all fields of scientific research and focus strongly on questions of ethical behavior among researchers. The DFG recommended that universities establish their own principles on the basis of the DFG guidelines, and in 1998 decided that research institutions receiving funding from the DFG had to establish rules ensuring good scientific practice. In 1999, the DFG also created an institution – an ombudsmen committee – to investigate cases of scientific misconduct and to monitor the implementation of ethics guidelines.

After more than ten years it seems fair to say that the DFG guidelines have remained relatively inconsequential for promoting good scientific practice in research and teaching. Indeed, the reports of the ombudsmen themselves lament that there is little awareness of good practice and scientific misconduct.

Although German universities quickly adopted either the DFG rules or developed their own, they have made little effort to promote them.[4] By and large, researchers are unaware of the existence of these rules. This lack of awareness among researchers and the sorry efforts of universities to promote the rules was already pointed out by the DFG in 2001 and, according to the latest report in 2008, little progress has been made since. This report suggests that the awareness of good scientific practice could be increased via the implementation of another principle in the original guidelines (rule no. 2), namely making issues pertaining to good scientific conduct a standard item in the teaching and training of junior researchers. However, given that this suggestion has been largely ignored for the last ten years, it seems questionable whether this suggestion will have much effect.

The implementation of ethics guidelines has so far almost exclusively focused on conflicts within the scientific community. The statistics published by the ombudsmen show that the vast majority of cases concern conflicts between scientists concerning authorship or university appointments. The largest number of these cases concerned authorship and plagiarism (48/162 accepted cases), followed by cases concerning ownership of research equipment and of data (35/162) and those concerning obstruction of research (27/162).[5] The committee's dedication to conflicts among the scientific

---

4 According to the second report of the ombudsmen committee from June 2001, 58% of German universities had adopted such rules.
5 These statistics are from the first six years of the committee's work. They, as well as yearly reports can be found at http://www1.uni-hamburg.de/dfg_ombud/. Given that researchers

community and the absence of cases concerning the rights of research subjects follows logically from the structure and procedures of the committee. Because the committee does not initiate investigations, it is naturally left with cases where colleagues accuse their peers and typically this concerns issues where one academic career is hindered by the other. Indeed, in Germany good practice appears to almost exclusively cover the rights of researchers and how they are treated by their community. Good scientific conduct thus becomes an ethos of scientific honesty towards one's colleagues rather than towards the research subjects. In short, it is unlikely that such voluntary rules that give priority to "self-monitoring" will be sufficient to promote research ethics for empirical research and teaching in the social sciences.

3. Social science research ethics in the United States and Britain

3.1 US: the legal approach

In the US, federal regulations have made ethical standards for research involving human subjects mandatory since the early 1970s, in cases where research is conducted at federal institutions or is funded by federal agencies (National Research Act 1974).

The National Research Act, on which the current rules are based, was a reaction to abuses in human subjects research.[6] It led to the establishment of the *National Commission for the Protection of Human Subjects of Biomedical and Behavioral Research*, which had two main tasks. First, it identified the basic ethical principles that should underlie the conduct of biomedical and behavioral research involving human subjects. Second, it developed guidelines assuring that such research was conducted in accordance with those principles. In 1978, the Commission established the "Ethical Principles and Guidelines for the Protection of Human Subjects of Research," better known as the "Belmont Report."

Important parts of the Belmont Report were included in the current legal framework for ethical research, the Code of Federal Regulations (CFR), in particular Title 45 CFR part 46 (The Code of Federal Regulations Governing

---

seem to appeal to the DFG ombudsmen rather to those of their own institutions (seen as too partial), the statistics published by the DFG are of some generality.

[6] One of the most infamous cases of ethical misconduct of research is the Tuskegee Syphilis Study, which was a longitudinal project conducted between 1932 and 1972 by the US Public Health Service on poor, illiterate black men in rural Alabama. During this study 28 participants died.

the Protection of Human Subjects in Research). This framework was enacted in 1991 by the US Department of Health and Human Services (HHS), specifically its Office for Human Research Protections (OHRP). It includes the requirements for assuring compliance by research institutions,[7] for researchers obtaining and documenting informed consent, and for ethics review committees (Institutional Review Boards or IRBs) membership, function, operations, review of research, and record keeping.

In 1991, seventeen other Federal Agencies and Departments also adopted a uniform set of rules for the protection of human subjects, almost identical to Title 45 CFR part 46 (Subpart A).[8] This joint agreement on regulations is named the Federal Policy for Protection of Human Subjects, better known as the "Common Rule."

The Common Rule is based on three fundamental principles for ethical research:

- Respect for a person's autonomy: the researcher has to give adequate and comprehensive information about the research project and possible risks

- Beneficence: research has to maximize benefits for society and minimize risks for research subjects

- Justice: research must not exploit or ignore one group in order to benefit another group

Based on these principles, there are three core criteria for evaluating human subjects research: informed consent, risk-benefit assessment, and equitability of subject selection. Institutional Review Boards (IRBs) are the instrument for approving whether research is following these criteria. Most large universities and hospitals conducting research have established their own IRBs.

There are three different types of IRB (Parvizi et al 2007): (a) local IRBs are affiliated with the institution or organization conducting research, (b) central IRBs deal with large scale multi-site research, and (c) commercial IRBs are paid to review research with human subjects.[9] In the last few decades, the impact of IRBs on the research infrastructure has increased enormously. Indications of this development can be found in the increasing number of IRBs and the increase in their power. Although universities in the

---

[7] Institutions normally make an agreement with the appropriate federal agency that funds their research. Most universities have an agreement with the HHS.

[8] Further subparts of the 45 CFR part 46 outline rules for research on fetuses, neonates, and pregnant women (Subpart B); rules for research with prisoners (Subpart C); and rules regarding research involving children (Subpart D).

[9] Commercial IRBs have become more common in recent years. The responsibilities of these IRBs as for-profit organizations are identical to those based at academic or medical institutions and they are governed by the same federal regulations.

US are generally confronted with numerous regulations and bureaucracies, the IRB system is the only one that has the direct power to stop, delay, or change the character of research (see Bledsoe et al. 2007).

At first glance it seems that the regulation of ethical research standards through the IRBs is an appropriate model, not only to ensure the protection of research subjects but also to bring binding ethical standards to the social sciences. However, the IRBs' practices for approving research projects in the social sciences is by no means undisputed. More to the point, IRBs have been directly criticized along three main lines.

First and most particularly, IRBs have been criticized as being inappropriate for the social science. Their composition and their requirements are seen to privilege research methods similar to the natural sciences. Indeed, the Common Rule regulations and the Belmont principles were developed with biomedical and laboratory science methods in mind. As Milne (2005) emphasizes, the type of research documentation to be brought to the IRB, such as informed consent protocols, asks for objectivity, prediction, and control rather than description, interpretation, and discovery. Using this approach, there would seem to be little room for qualitative forms of data collection and research. This general critique holds true despite some noteworthy exemptions from full IRB review in the case of research that is particularly relevant to social science investigation. Such exemptions apply, for instance, to research about educational practices or research involving the collection or study of existing data if publicly available or unidentifiable.[10]

Secondly, the research review boards have been criticized for their strong bent towards legal issues. As the process of research review focuses heavily on producing a legally valid written consent form, Bledsoe et al. (2007: 631) argue that the main goals of these reviews appears to be not so much to protect the research subjects but rather to deflect as much risk as possible from the institution. As a legal contract between the investigator and the university, the IRB protocol is an instrument to place as much legal responsibility on the investigator by defining as many risks as possible that have to be considered prior to research. In other words, universities turn to delegating legal risk to their faculty members.

Finally, ethics reviews have suffered from an externalization and professionalization of ethical problems from the point of view of the researchers. Faced with extensive IRB protocols, researchers tend to simply do their paperwork in the required manner, rather than thinking through the ethical issues related to their work.

---

10 For more detailed information, see NSF (National Science Foundation) "What exemptions of the Common Rule are most appropriate to social science research?" (http://www.nsf.gov/bfa/dias/policy/hsfaqs.jsp)

3.2 United Kingdom: The reformist approach

Since 2006, the explicit guidelines of the *Economic and Social Research Council* (ESRC), the main sponsor of social science research in the UK, have forced universities seeking its funding to consider ethical issues in research and teaching alike. These guidelines seek to establish rules suitable for the social sciences, stating that extant guidelines like those for medical research may not be appropriate for the social sciences with its diverse methodologies. They also seek to respond to new challenges in social sciences research ethics that arise from, among other things, interdisciplinary research, globalization, and technological change (see ESRC 2005).

This *Research Ethics Framework* (REF) is the result of consultations with the UK social science community, including other funding institutions and professional associations. The resulting six key principles of ethical research require (1) that research be designed, reviewed, and undertaken to ensure integrity and quality, (2) that research staff and subjects be fully informed about the purpose, methods, and intended possible uses of the research as well as its risks, (3) confidentiality of information and anonymity of respondents, (4) voluntary participation, (5) the avoidance of harm to research participants, and (6) independent research and explicit statements of conflict of interest or partiality. It is noteworthy that four of these key principles deal with the protection of research subjects (rather than with misconduct among peers).

The implementation of these ethical standards is delegated to universities or research institutes. Ensuring research ethics goes beyond a particular research project for which a research institution seeks funding. Indeed, only those institutions that have put mechanisms and procedures in place to ensure minimal ethical standards can apply for funding from the ESRC.

Although the ESRC does not impose a particular model to ensure ethical standards, it stipulates that the minimal mechanisms must include, most importantly, a REC that looks at ethical issues in research applications and monitors the implementation of the project.[11] Moreover, any application to the ESRC has to explain if and why it needs a review by the RECs. The reviewers from the ESRC have to comment on these ethical self-assessments in the proposal and may reject a proposal or give a conditional award only. Additional "incentives" to ensure ethical standards in social science research are provided by the possible loss of funding by the ESRC, even if other non-ESRC funded projects in a research institution breach ethical standards.

Among the minimal standards in the ESRC guidelines are, however, not only research ethics for the actual research process but also for training. At

---

11 Members of RECs need to be trained to deal with ethical issues and have to be compensated for their work. The REF leaves it open whether social science sub-RECs are to be created or if ethical issues in social science research are to be treated by the general RECs.

the very least, social science postgraduate training programs have to incorporate the range of issues addressed in the REF. This requires the development of minimum standards of training and competence in ethical issues over time. According to the REF, such minimum training requirements are likely to include: training for individual researchers, training for members of local and institution-wide RECs, and training for postgraduate students in local ethics review requirements – in addition to more general ethics training as well as training for undergraduate students whose projects may require an ethics review (see ESRC 2005, 16).

As a relatively recent framework compared to the US system, the REF is probably more suitable to serve as a model for research ethics in the social sciences for four main reasons. First, the ensuring of research ethics is delegated to research institutions (although it is monitored by the ESRC). This decentralized approach could be more suitable for Germany because it would respect the independence of universities. Second, because the REF seeks to decrease delays and unnecessary efforts, the evaluation and approval of the REC is not necessary for the actual application, but only for the beginning of the project. Third, the REF not only creates negative incentives but introduces ethical issues into training. The purpose thus appears to be not to simply create a lengthy procedure to be complied with on the way to obtaining funding, but also to contribute to a research culture where ethical issues are viewed as an important part of research and training. Fourth, the REF recognizes explicitly that qualitative methodology may require a different type of ethical review than quantitative methodology.[12]

4. Discussion

The three ethics frameworks for the social sciences discussed here vary widely in their treatment of both of our two key criteria – the protection of research subjects and their appropriateness for the social sciences. They also differ in how they address various important sub-issues such as the degree of bindingness, the locus of implementation, and the weight given to raising awareness of ethical issues in the training of researchers.

Obviously, the German approach is the most underdeveloped one. Ethical principles are strongly considered in (bio)medical research, but this has not been extended to the social sciences. Those guidelines that address the whole scientific community in Germany, such as the DFG guidelines on

---

[12] On the negative side, obviously, are the greater costs for research institutions, since they need to create new bodies – the RECs – and compensate its members for their work. The ESRC, however, argues that the cost of reviewing ESRC-funded projects is also eligible for funding.

good scientific practice, focus almost exclusively on ethical behavior among peers rather than on the protection of research subjects. Providing few constraints, they have moreover received little promotion within the university. The ethics codes of professional associations do include sections on the protection of research subjects. No ethics reviews of research projects protect, however, the rights of research subjects *ex ante* and their ethics committees as well as the DFG ombudsmen are, structurally, unlikely to be summoned by research subjects *ex post*.

The US approach, in contrast, with its requirement for projects to have approval by IRBs, is highly protective of research subjects in the natural and social sciences alike. At the same time, the framework does not consider methods specific to the social sciences that make the issue of informed consent particularly complicated in its implementation. As a result of the origin of the IRBs in and membership bent towards the natural sciences, US social science research tends to lean towards "standard methods" in order to receive IRB approval. In this way, research ethics has a strong and not always beneficial effect on the content of social science research. Moreover, the significant bureaucratic work involved in getting IRB approval makes data gathering cumbersome and is therefore only encouraged at the post-graduate level.

The UK approach seeks to strike a balance. Given that the largest social science funding institution makes ethics reviews and ethics committees a requirement, it gives considerably more protection to the research subjects than the German system. Being designed for social science research, it is also much more open towards qualitative methodology than the US approach. Requiring an ethics review only for approved research projects, it also entails a less lengthy procedure than the US model, even though it requires researchers to think about ethical issues (i.e., the type of necessary review) when designing their project. Of the three approaches, it is also the one that most energetically stresses the need to raise the awareness of ethical principles during training.

5. Recommendations

Research ethics is about social responsibility and thus goes beyond a simple set of legal regulations. An ethics framework should thus give priority to raising awareness of ethical principles in research. This means that research ethics, and, more importantly, learning to think about the ethical dimension of their work, should be an integral part of the training of young researchers. Germany would benefit from a new research ethics framework for the social sciences. This framework should focus on protecting the rights of the research subjects and encompass data access, gathering, and processing. But it should also make it a priority to accommodate social science methodologies. Like the UK approach, it could be enforced by making it a mandatory step in the funding process. The US example shows that legal requirements may create many bureaucratic hurdles for research as well as having an undesired streamlining effect on its content.

This ethics framework could be modeled on the UK, but should be developed in consultation with the relevant professional associations, key funding institutions, universities, and independent research institutions in Germany. It should be reviewed upon request, following methodological innovations.

A German research ethics framework should give the responsibility for implementation to the universities. Independent research institutes should cooperate with the universities. At present, social science departments have neglected questions relating to research ethics in training and research practice. "Local" ethics committees with alternating members would bring the discussion and consideration of ethical principles into the universities. Such a system would integrate researchers into the implementation process of ethical standards rather than suspecting them *a priori* of misconduct.

References:

Bledsoe, C.H./Sherin, B./Galinsky, A.G./Headley, N.M./Heimer, C.A./Kjeldgaard, E./Lindgren, J./Miller, J.D./Roloff, M.E. and Uttal, D.H (2007): Regulating Creativity: Research and Survival in the IRB Iron Cage. Northwestern University Law Review 101 (2), 593-641.
Carpenter, D. (2007): Institutional Review Boards, Regulatory Incentives, and Some Modest Proposals for Reform (2007). Northwestern University Law Review 101 (2). Minnesota Legal Studies Research Paper No. 06-64. http://ssrn.com/abstract =948739. [Last visited: 01/18/2010].
Department of Health and Human Services – Office for Protection from Research Risks, Code of Federal Regulations Title 45, Public Welfare, Part 46, Protection of Human Subjects, Revised: June 18, 1991, Effective: August 19, 1991. https://irb.llnl.gov/appendices/Appendix03.pdf. [Last visited: 01/18/2010].
DFG (1997): Vorschläge zur Sicherung guter wissenschaftlicher Praxis. Bonn.
ESRC (2005): Research Ethics Framework. http://www.esrcsocietytoday.ac.uk/ ESRCInfoCentre/Images/ESRC_Re_Ethics_Frame_tcm6-11291.pdf. [Last visited: 01/18/2010].
Greely, H.T. (2008): Collecting Biomeasures in the PSID: Ethical and Legal Concerns. Mimeo
Haggerty, K.D. (2004): Ethics Creep: Governing Social Science Research in the Name of Ethics. Qualitative Sociology 27 (4), 391-414.
Lindgren, J./Murashko, D. and Ford M.R. (2007): Symposium, Foreword: Symposium on Censorship and Institutional Review Boards. Northwestern University Law Review 101 (2), 399-403
Milne, C. (2005): Overseeing Research: Ethics and the Institutional Review Board, Forum Qualitative Sozialforschung/ Forum: Qualitative Social Research 6 (1), Art. 41. http://nbn-resolving.de/urn:nbn:de:0114-fqs0501412. [Last visited: 01/18/2010].
National Commission for the Protection of Human Subjects of Biomedical and Behavioral Research, The Belmont Report, Ethical Principles and Guidelines for the Protection of Human Subjects of Research, April 18, 1979. http://ohsr.od.nih.gov/guidelines/belmont.html. [Last visited: 01/18/2010].
National Science Foundation (NSF): Frequently Asked Questions and Vignettes, Interpreting the Common Rule for the Protection of Human Subjects for Behavioral and Social Science Research. http://www.nsf.gov/bfa/dias/policy/ hsfaqs.jsp. [Last visited 01/18/2010].
Parvizi, J./Tarity, T./Conner, K. and Smith, B. (2007): Institutional review board approval: Why it matters. The Journal of Bone and Joint Surgery, 89-A (2), 418-426.
United States Department of Health & Human Services/Office for Human Research Protection (OHRP): Frequently Asked Questions. http://www.hhs.gov/ohrp/ 45CFRpt46faq.html. [Last visited 01/18/2010].
Schaar, P. (2010): Data protection and statistics – a dynamic and tension-filled relationship. [In this publication].
Weber, K. (2010): New Methods in Human Subjects Research – Do We Need a New Ethics? [In this publication].

IV. Fields

1. Migration and Demography

1.1 Migration and Globalization

Martin Kahanec and Klaus F. Zimmermann[*]

---

[*] The views expressed are the authors' alone and do not necessarily correspond to those of the German Data Forum (RatSWD). We thank Uwe G. Rehfeld and the participants to the Second Workshop of the German Data Forum (RatSWD) for helpful comments.

Contact:

Klaus F. Zimmermann
IZA, P.O. Box 7240
53072 Bonn
Germany
e-mail: Zimmermann[at]iza.org

Abstract

The international migration of people is a momentous and complex phenomenon. Research on its causes and consequences requires sufficient data. While some datasets are available, the nature of migration makes it complicated to use them for scientific research. There is currently no existing dataset that effectively captures international migration trajectories. To alleviate these difficulties, we recommend: (1) the international coordination of data collection methodologies and standardization of immigrant identifiers; (2) a longitudinal approach to data collection; (3) the inclusion of adequate information about relevant characteristics of migrants in surveys, including retrospective information; (4) minimal anonymization; (5) immigrant boosters in existing surveys; (6) the use of modern technologies and facilitation of Data Service Centers; and (7) making data access a priority of data collection.

Keywords: migration, immigrants, data collection, data access, data infrastructure

1. Introduction

The international migration of people lies at the core of the ongoing process of globalization. People migrate to improve their economic prospects, ensure a more secure living environment, reunite with their family members, or avoid persecution in their country of origin. For these and other reasons 3 percent of the world's population found themselves on an international migration trajectory in 2005. Since a large proportion of these migrants head towards developed countries, the share of international migrants in these countries reached as much as 9.5 percent in 2005.[1] These individuals experience not only important economic and social consequences of their move, but also psychological ones. Migration may involve a new job with higher pay, the loss of old social ties and the establishment of new ones, as well as the psychological costs of missing the homeland.

Migration, however, does not only affect the fates of those who are directly involved. Various effects emerge at the interface of migrant and native populations. Immigrants may bring with them new cultures or preferences, they may compete for certain jobs and create others, or claim publicly financed social security benefits. More broadly, migrants contribute to a more efficient allocation of resources and often become a driving force behind knowledge transfer and technological advancement. All these effects have repercussions for the native population, who may react to migrant inflows not only in determining their current actions, but also in making

---

[1] See United Nations, Department of Economic and Social Affairs, World Migrant Stock: The 2005 Revision Population Database.

long-term investment plans, such as those concerning education. Finally, natives may view immigrants positively or negatively and shape their attitudes accordingly.

Migration is a dynamic phenomenon involving many twists and turns. Driven by a multitude of possible reasons, migrants may move temporarily or permanently, transnationally and nationally, individually or in groups, return to their countries of origin or migrate to another country, or move between two or more countries in a circular way. The complex underlying processes driving migration and its effects have attracted significant and growing attention from scientists. Chiswick (1978) and Borjas (1985) have pioneered the scientific work on immigrant adjustment in host societies, highlighting the significance of the host country experience and stressing the importance of cohort effects, country of origin, religion, education, as well as a number of demographic characteristics such as age and gender. From a different perspective, research on the migration decision has been inspired and advanced by Harris and Todaro (1970), Becker (1964), Mincer (1978), and Borjas (1985). Immigrant self-selection discussed by Borjas (1987) and Chiswick (1999) implies the need for specific techniques (Heckman 1979) to consistently evaluate causal mechanisms behind immigrant adjustment.

The impact of immigration on the host labor market has been modeled by Chiswick, Chiswick, and Karras (1992) and Chiswick (1998). A large body of empirical literature, summarized by Kahanec and Zimmermann (2009), provides mixed evidence on the sign and determinants of these effects on wages and employment.[2] More recently, the roles of intermarriage (Meng and Gregory 2005), citizenship (Bratsberg et al. 2002), social networks (Munshi 2003), and attitudes (Bauer et al. 2000; Kahanec and Tosun 2009) pertaining to immigrant adjustment have received significant attention. The concept of ethnic identity has been extended by Constant and Zimmermann (2008), who elaborate on how attachment to the country of origin and the host country affect immigrant adjustment.

Although measuring the effects of migration is by no means an easy or straight-forward job, migration is a phenomenon that undoubtedly affects the well-being of the whole society and as such, has become an important and sensitive policy issue. Questions about the labor market consequences of migration, immigrant adjustment in host societies, and welfare competition have received particularly significant policy attention.

Understanding the causes and effects of international migration flows requires a sound and in-depth analysis. The need for such analysis is most conspicuous in the study of causal relationships, as these are difficult to establish empirically and their misrepresentation compromises both scientific and policy analyses. In fact, it may lead to incorrect policy recommendations,

---

2 The evidence on migration effects in source countries is mainly related to remittances (e.g., Barham and Boucher 1998), and wage and employment effects (Brücker 2007).

which may in turn lead to unpredictable consequences or even effects contrary to those intended. Since such analysis is impossible without high-quality data, such data are indispensable for policy analysts as well as scientists.

2. Relevant and available data

Despite the general scarcity of migration data, scientists and analysts have been able to use some existing survey or administrative datasets as well as small-scale dedicated survey data to study migration issues. While these datasets have facilitated valuable research, missing variables, excessive anonymization, and flaws in data collection design often compromise scientists' efforts to broaden and deepen our knowledge of migration causes and effects. In this section we focus on some large-scale datasets collected at the European level, since they, in contrast to small-scale surveys, have an intrinsic potential to provide the necessary transnational, longitudinal, and systematic data collection framework.

There are four extensive datasets that in some dimension provide coverage of European migration trajectories: the European Community Household Panel (ECHP), the EU Statistics on Income and Living Conditions (EU-SILC), the EU Labour Force Survey (EU-LFS), and the OECD/ SOPEMI (*Système d'Observation Permanente des Migrations*) dataset. Each of these datasets contains information about demography, labor force participation, employment, unemployment, self-employment, and educational attainment of immigrants. In addition, the European Social Survey (ESS) covers people's attitudes toward immigrants as well as their voting preferences, thus addressing migration indirectly.

Table 1 depicts the character of these datasets, highlighting some of their strengths and weaknesses. We can identify at least three major gaps in the available data.[3] First, these datasets provide either none or only a very limited account of migration trajectories. Transnational migration trajectories may involve simple or repetitive moves between two or more countries with temporary periods of residence of varying length as well as permanent moves. It is almost impossible to track such trajectories – with all their spells, stops, and circularities – within Europe or between Europe and third countries. In particular, little or no information is available on migrant experience prior to their arrival in the country of current residence or their intentions for further moves. Secondly, the data typically permit determining immigrant status based on an individual's citizenship and country of origin,

---

3 See also the discussion in Bauer and Zimmermann (1998).

neglecting the large groups of people with an immigrant background who are native citizens or those with dual citizenships. Finally, anonymization often renders any valuable analysis impossible, for example when immigrants from very different origins (e.g., Zimbabwe and Japan) are grouped into one category (e.g., non-EU).

3. Data access issues and needs

Inadequate access to existing datasets is one of the most limiting factors for scientific and policy analysis. Due to restrictive data access policies, a lack of interest on the side of the officials responsible, misinterpreted data protection rules, or simply the lack of adequate data access infrastructure, the use of datasets for scientific and policy purposes is, in general, severely limited. Since migration is, by definition, a transnational and dynamic phenomenon (i.e., involving one-way as well as repeat, sequential, and circular movement between more countries), its proper analysis requires a combination of information from multiple countries and across multiple periods.[4] Therefore, restrictions on data access and a lack of coordination in establishing access rules are particularly detrimental to the analysis of migration issues. Below we list some of the most pressing issues that obstruct availability of data for migration analysis and determine the needs concerning collection of adequate data on migration.

One of the main problems is that identifying and defining migrants in the existing datasets is not a trivial matter. The migration background, a foreign origin (foreign birthplace), citizenship, or ethnicity can be used to determine whether or not someone is an immigrant. Unfortunately, only a subset of this information, if any, is available in existing datasets. Only rarely can one identify first, second, and further generations of immigrants, citizens and non-citizens, and distinguish immigrants of different origin and ethnicity.

It is even more seldom that it is possible to obtain information that can be used to characterize migration trajectories. Perhaps with the exception of length of stay in the host country, pre-migration experience, tracking of all migration moves, or migration trajectories of family members (spouses) are rarely available. While the lack of data describing migration trajectories of those who make more frequent, possibly circular, moves is a general problem, it is particularly problematic in the case of highly skilled migrants, since these are the most fluid and mobile segment of the migrant population.

---

[4] Bauer, Pereira, Vogler and Zimmermann (2002) have merged Portuguese data and German data on Portuguese migrants to be able to compare migrants in the sending and a receiving country. See Crul and Vermeulen (2006) for another project in this spirit.

Other relevant and often missing information include language, religion, and attachment to the host society and the country of origin.

A further and related problem is that the effects of out-migration are hard to capture, since we typically do not observe people who leave or record their characteristics (they do not de-register and are in a different country when data are collected). In fact, this deficiency creates problems for the analysis of the entire population as well, since it compromises the representativeness of datasets. For example, according to the Weekly Report of the German Institute for Economic Research ("Wochenbericht des DIW") (2008, 382), doubts have arisen in Germany as to whether the official census statistics still represented the actual reality of the German population. Since the German national census data has only been based on registers since 1987 – which depend on the proper *registration* and *deregistration* of people – those who leave the country and do not deregister are erroneously counted. An example of the magnitude of the measurement error which can result from failing to track out-migration of those who have not deregistered was revealed in a clean-up of the data from the German Central Register of Foreigners (*Ausländerzentralregister*) in 2004, which showed that the official census statistics had overstated the number of foreigners in Germany by about 600,000.

Another problem with the current situation is that most datasets are representative of the total population and contain a limited number of observations. While this is not necessarily a problem in other contexts, in the context of migration it often implies insufficient samples of the immigrant population. In addition, many datasets are cross-sectional and thus do not capture the dynamic nature of migration. In particular, the snapshot picture that such datasets provide can only capture the most recent move and cannot distinguish some important effects, such as those of host country experience and immigrant cohort on immigrant adjustment.

Finally, knowledge of migration intentions and reasons, and their relationship to actual migration decisions is indispensable for predicting future migration flows as well as for understanding the social and economic outcomes of migrants in the host societies. Precise estimates of the directions and characteristics of such flows are crucial for designing effective and efficient immigration policies, for instance in the context of EU enlargement. The intention to stay, namely, whether migrants perceive their situation as temporary or come to settle in the host country permanently, carries important consequences for their labor market behavior and thus the effects they have on the host economy. Similarly, migrants who come for economic reasons and those who come as refugees or asylum seekers have very different labor market opportunities as well as intentions in the host country.

These issues concerning the availability of and access to adequate migration data define the primary needs concerning the collection of relevant data. In particular, collected data should properly identify migrants and people with immigrant backgrounds, and contain sufficient samples of migrants. They should cover (transnational) migration trajectories and, in particular, capture pre-migration experience and out-migration, as well as measure intentions and reasons for migration.

4. Future developments and challenges

The enlargement of the European Union and the concurrent expansion of the European Economic Area as well as the persistent economic and social hardship and insecurity in large parts of the world will continue to fuel substantial international flows of people. High-quality data are and will remain a key ingredient to understanding the causes and effects of these migration flows. Given the traditional prominence of quantitative techniques in economics and the growing emphasis on such techniques in other social sciences, especially sociology, we can project increasing demand for such data among scientists in the future. This demand will be further intensified by the increasing need for well-founded policy analysis at the European and national levels. Another contributing factor may be the business sector, which may seek to exploit the potential benefits from precise information about their current and potential customers.

The provision of high-quality migration data is in general insufficient, although it has somewhat improved over the last decade or two. This improvement has been enabled by the emergence of advanced information and data management technologies that can facilitate a wide access to existing datasets. This development particularly relates to a group of international institutions that have started to provide online access to some of their datasets (European Union, World Bank, ILO,[5] UN) as well as private and non-governmental organizations (IZA)[6] that use innovative technologies to promote access to own and third-party datasets. While some improvements have been made at the national level, government institutions still lag behind in data access provision. More recently, some remarkable developments have taken place, however, involving a partnership between public and non-governmental or private institutions aiming at a wider dissemination of valuable data collected by public institutions. For instance, the International Data Service Center of the IZA offers onsite computing via ultra thin access, and remote computing by means of a remote computing solution (JoSuA)

---

5   International Labour Organization.
6   Institute for the Study of Labor (IZA, *Forschungsinstitut zur Zukunft der Arbeit*).

facilitating the use of scientific use data of the German Federal Statistical Office.[7]

These positive developments should not hide the difficult reality of migration research and analysis as concerns data availability. Besides the various difficulties that migration researchers face regarding identification of migrants in existing datasets as well as a lack of relevant information about them, virtually no existing dataset has the necessary transnational and longitudinal perspective to capture complete migration trajectories. Thus, the key challenge in this respect is to track migrants and their migration experience as they move internationally. The associated practical challenge is to coordinate data collection methodologies across Europe and, even more complicated, between Europe and third countries.

5. Conclusions and recommendations

This essay summarizes some of the key problems and challenges related to the availability of data for the study of migration issues. Having considered the long-standing as well as more recent developments in migration research, it is clear that access to data of good quality, harmonized across time and countries, is one of the main bottlenecks hindering advances in our understanding of the causes and effects of migration. To alleviate this problem, there are a number of policy tools that may help.

First, coordination of data collection methodologies and standardization of immigrant identifiers across the EU would facilitate international comparability. It is necessary to harmonize data collection methods so that migration trajectories in Europe-wide datasets can be observed. In particular, unique individual identifiers need to be traceable across European countries. An open method of coordination, transparent indicators, benchmarking, and an efficient exchange of best practices seem to be the way to go in this regard. This also involves merging datasets transnationally and across time, including proper harmonization and linking of data, records, and topics. In particular, given the advancement in data management and storage techno-

---

[7] The International Data Service Center of the IZA, one of the Data Service Centers facilitated by the "KVI Commission," offers an integrated service which consists of a metadata portal and a remote computing solution. The International Data Service Center of the IZA's metadata service comprises a detailed, in depth, searchable and standardized information and documentation service on a growing number of datasets currently in the areas of employment and wages, education and training, and demographics and migration. The International Data Service Center of the IZA remote computing solution, known as JoSuA, facilitates usage of restricted datasets bridging the otherwise wide gap between legal constraints and scientific freedom without violating the former or constraining the latter. For further details see Schneider and Wolf (2008).

logies, this objective entails not only prospective but also retrospective harmonization and merging of datasets as well, involving digitalization of old datasets whenever necessary.

Second, whenever possible, a longitudinal approach should be adopted, both to facilitate the separation of spurious effects driven by unobserved cross-sectional variation from true causal relationships as well as to capture the dynamic nature of migration. In this regard, one should also consider extending selected existing cross-sectional datasets by surveying the covered individuals in one or more additional waves.

Third, adequate information about the relevant characteristics of migrants – experience in the host society (years since migration), country of origin, citizenship, ethnicity, language, religion, attachment to the host society and the country of origin, and migration intentions and reasons – is requisite. For example, it is of key importance to distinguish temporary and permanent migrants as well as economic migrants from those that come as refugees or asylum seekers, or as tied movers. Retrospective questions in survey questionnaires are necessary to track migrants' pre-migration experience (i.e., experience prior to the last observed move).

Fourth, anonymization should be limited to the smallest possible degree. As an option, alternative anonymization procedures could be applied to the same dataset, allowing two or more versions to be accessible to the researcher, each facilitating research on different research questions.

Fifth, immigrant boosters in existing surveys with a well-defined control group would facilitate sufficient immigrant sample sizes.

Sixth, online Data Service Centers, data registers and metadatabases can provide an invaluable service to the research community. In fact, the Internet is itself becoming a rich source of data and a tool to collect new data that still needs to be properly exploited.

Seventh, the use of modern data information technologies should be promoted to facilitate the collection, management, and storage of good quality data, as well as, importantly, enabling access to it. As part of this objective, the creation of Data Service Centers facilitating prudent access to such data is desirable.

Finally, the facilitation of data access for researchers should be embraced as one of the main objectives of data collection. Adequate effort by all the actors involved is necessary not only to facilitate knowledge about migration as such, but also, to the extent that suitable policies are adopted, to improve the welfare of substantial numbers of people who are directly or indirectly affected by migration.

Table 1: Datasets

Dataset	Type	Years	Countries	Measures of immigrant status	Weakness (selected)
ECHP	Longitudinal	1994 - 2001	EU 15	Year of arrival (region/country), country of birth, first and second citizenship, mother tongue	No information on immigrant experience prior to his/her arrival to the country of present residence.
EU-SILC	Longitudinal	2004 - 2006	Until 2004 EU15 Since 2006 EU25	Country of birth, citizenship (first)	Anonymization leading to a mixing of immigrants from very different origins.
EU-LFS	Survey	1983 - 2006	BE, CZ, DK, DE, EE, GR, ES, FR, IE, IT, CY, LV, LT, LU, HU, MT, NL, AT, PL, PT, SI, SK, FI, SE, UK, BG, RO (+HR, TR, IS, NO, CH)	Nationality (citizenship), years of residence, country of birth (anonymized), country of residence one year before the survey	Anonymization leading to a mixing of immigrants from very different origins.
OECD/ SOPEMI	Macro-data	1983- 2008	OECD	Stocks of foreign nationality and foreign born populations, country of birth, flows of foreign-born workers	While the dataset provides aggregate data, no information about the individual characteristics of migrants is available.
ESS	Cross-sectional	2002, 2004, 2006	EU25	Voting preferences, attitudes toward immigrants and ethnic minorities	The cross-sectional nature of the dataset does not capture the dynamic nature of migration.

References:

Barham, B. and Boucher. S. (1998): Migration, Remittances and Inequality: Estimating the Net Effects of Migration on Income Distribution. In: Journal of Development Economics 55 (2), 307-331.
Bauer, T./Lofstrom, M. and Zimmermann, K.F. (2000): Immigration Policy, Assimilation of Immigrants, and Natives' Sentiments towards Immigrants: Evidence from 12 OECD Countries. Swedish Economic Policy Review 7 (2), 11-53.
Bauer, T. and Zimmermann, K.F. (1998): Causes of International Migration: A Survey. In: Gorter, C./Nijkamp, P. and Poot, J. (Eds.): Crossing Borders: Regional and Urban Perspectives on International Migration. Aldershot.
Bauer, T./Pereira, P.T./Vogler, M. and Zimmermann, K.F. (2002): Portuguese Migrants in the German Labor Market: Performance and Self-Selection. International Migration Review 36 (2), 467-491.
Becker, G.S. (1964): Human Capital. A theoretical and empirical Analysis. New York.
Borjas, G.J. (1985): Assimilation, Changes in Cohort Quality, and the Earnings of Immigrants. Journal of Labor Economics 3 (4), 463-489.
Borjas, G.J. (1987): Self-Selection and the Earnings of Immigrants. American Economic Review 77 (4), 531-553.
Bratsberg, B./Ragan, J.F. and Nasir, Z.M. (2002): The Effect of Naturalization on Wage Growth: A Panel Study of Young Male Immigrants. Journal of Labor Economics 20 (3), 568–597.
Brücker, H. (2007): Migration after the EU's Eastern Enlargement: Who Wins, Who Loses? [Paper presented at Second IZA Migration Workshop: EU Enlargement and the Labor Markets, Bonn 7.-8. September 2007].
Chiswick, B.R. (1978): The Effect of Americanization on the Earnings of Foreign-born Men. Journal of Political Economy 86 (5), 897-921.
Chiswick, B.R. (1998): The Economic Consequences of Immigration: Application to the United States and Japan. In: Weiner, M. and Hanami, T. (Eds.): Temporary Workers or Future Citizens? Japanese and U.S. Migration Policies. New York.
Chiswick, B.R. (1999): Are Immigrants Favorably Self-Selected? American Economic Review 89 (2), 181-185.
Chiswick, C.U./Chiswick, B.R. and Karras, G. (1992): The Impact of Immigrants on the Macroeconomy. Carnegie-Rochester Conference Series on Public Policy 37 (1), 279-316.
Constant, A. and Zimmermann, K.F. (2008): Measuring Ethnic Identity and Its Impact on Economic Behavior. Journal of the European Economic Association 6 (2-3), 424-433.
Crul, M. and Vermeulen, H. (2006): Immigration, education and the Turkish second generation in five European nations: a comparative study. In: Parsons, C.A. and Smeeding, T.M. (Eds.): Immigration and the Transformation of Europe. Cambridge.
Harris, J.R. and Todaro, M.P. (1970): Migration, Unemployment and Development: A Two-Sector Analysis. The American Economic Review 60 (1), 126-142.

Heckman, J.J. (1979): Sample Selection Bias as a Specification Error. Econometrica 47 (1), 153-161.
Kahanec, M. and Tosun, M. (2009): Political Economy of Immigration in Germany: Attitudes and Citizenship Aspirations. International Migration Review 43 (2), 263-291.
Kahanec, M. and Zimmermann, K.F. (2009): International Migration, Ethnicity and Economic Inequality. In: Salverda, W./Nolan, B. and Smeeding, T.M. (Eds.): Oxford Handbook on Economic Inequality. Oxford.
Meng, X. and Gregory, R.G. (2005): Intermarriage and economic assimilation of immigrants. Journal of Labor Economics 23 (1), 135-175.
Mincer, J. (1978): Family Migration Decisions. Journal of Political Economy 86 (5), 749-773.
Munshi, K. (2003): Networks in the Modern Economy: Mexican Migrants in the U.S. Labor Market. The Quarterly Journal of Economics 118 (2), 549-599.
Schneider, H. and Wolf, C. (2008): Die Datenservicezentren als Teil der informationellen Infrastruktur. In: Rolf, G./Zwick, M. and Wagner, G.G. (Eds.): Fortschritte der informationellen Infrastruktur in Deutschland. Festschrift für Johann Hahlen zum 65. Geburtstag und Hans Jürgen Krupp zum 75. Geburtstag. Baden-Baden.
Weekly Report of the German Institute for Economic Research (Wochenbericht des DIW) Nr. 27-28/2008, DIW Berlin.

1.2 Migration and Statistics

Sonja Haug

Contact:

Sonja Haug
Hochschule Regensburg
Fakultät Angewandte Sozialwissenschaften
Postfach 12 03 27
93025 Regensburg
Germany
e-mail: sonja.haug[at]hs-regensburg.de

Abstract

The field of empirical research on migration and integration encompasses a wide range of research questions, theoretical approaches, and datasets. Research based on official statistics has to deal with diverse datasets for information on migration and foreign populations, resulting in miscellaneous statements. Recent developments in official statistics have concentrated on the improvement of data quality. The 2011 Census and the projected creation of a central population register are both important issues, for example, for the sampling and weighting of migrants in surveys. The concept of migration background, too, as it has become integrated into the German Microcensus, represents a major development in population statistics and is now widely accepted. This report recommends implementing questions on migration background into the 2011 Census. The most important and accessible datasets in the field of empirical integration research are the German Microcensus and the German Socio-Economic Panel (SOEP, *Sozio-oekonomisches Panel*); there is still untapped potential for analysis. The addition of a migrant sample as a supplement to large surveys is another valuable innovation. The most important challenges for empirical research in migration and integration are the development of sampling methods for migrant population (including onomastics and topomastics), studies of new and small migrant groups, research projects focused on the country of origin, longitudinal migrant surveys, and the development of adequate tools for measurement.

Keywords: population, migration, integration, migration background

1. Research questions

The field of empirical migration and integration research is characterized by a wide range of research questions, theoretical approaches, and datasets.

1.1 Established research questions

Migration research tends to center around a group of well-established questions: how many migrants are on the move? What are their countries of origin and destination? What are the determinants of migration? Integration research in Germany has paid particular attention to the population of "guest workers." Empirical research has focused on a descriptive analysis of integration (Mehrländer et al. 1996), or on explaining the migration and integration process (Esser 1980).

1.2 Theoretical developments and new research questions

Migration research today is more differentiated and has multiple points of focus. New research fields in international migration include: migration from Central and Eastern European countries, questions relating to demography and the concept of "replacement migration," return migration, and irregular migration. New interdisciplinary approaches in sociology or economics employ theories of social capital and social networks to explain migration decisions (e.g., Boswell and Mueser 2008). Transnational migration, chain migration, circular migration, and migrant communities are other important areas of research (Pries 1997). Theoretical and empirical progress in this area allows, for example, for an analysis of international migration dynamics from a development perspective using a micro-level decision model and event history methodology (Massey et al. 2008). New developments in migration and integration theory have also arisen through discussions about a general model for intergenerational integration (Esser 2008; Kalter 2008). Current research concentrates on the different dimensions of integration and the mechanisms underlying the observable types of integration (e.g., Kalter 2008b).

Empirical research on migrant integration is an emerging field and frequently overlaps with issues like social inequality and exclusion (Kalter 2003). Theories relating to the sociology and economy of migration are increasingly being incorporated into this area of research. In addition, the integration of the second generation of migrant families is a core issue (Haug and Diehl 2005). The Programme for International Student Assessment (PISA) study and other research studies highlight the problems faced by migrant children in the educational system (Stanat and Christensen 2006; Kristen 2005); labor market integration is yet another topic of inquiry (Granato 2003). New research can be said to focus on the transition from primary to secondary school and/or the transition from vocational education to occupation. Analysis of the integration process is a key trend in this area, and panel surveys and longitudinal studies play an ever greater role in this, although adequate datasets are rare. Evidence shows that naturalized migrants integrate more successfully than non-naturalized migrants, but they still differ from people without a migration background (Haug 2002; Salentin and Wilkening 2003). As a result of these insights, the formerly widespread concept of "foreigners" is losing ground, and the concept of "migration background" becoming generally accepted (for an overview of measurement aspects, see Diefenbach and Weiß 2006).

Research on internal migration is another topic to emerge in recent years, for example, looking at migration decision making in terms of the labor market and the life cycle (Huinink and Kley 2008; Kalter 1997; Wagner 1989; Windzio 2004).

1.3 Policy-related research questions

The analysis of legal migration and the estimation of illegal migration is one of the central policy-related issues in migration research (BAMF 2010). In Germany, the national contact point of the European Migration Network (EMN) is the Federal Office for Migration and Refugees (BAMF, *Bundesamt für Migration und Flüchtlinge*). Their aim is to improve the availability of and access to information on migration and asylum at the EU level; to facilitate work on annual policy reports, small scale studies, and annual reports on migration, asylum, and return migration statistics; and to support the policy and decision-making process. The target population for policy-related surveys is made up of former labor migrants and their families (Venema and Grimm 2002; Babka von Gostomski 2008; Weidacher 2000) or ethnic German repatriates (Haug and Sauer 2007), while special research projects have a narrower focus, such as studies on female migrants (Boos-Nünning and Karakasoglu 2006), the "second generation" (Haug and Diehl 2005), or Muslims (Brettfeld and Wetzels 2007). Integration policy-makers often tend to think of migration in terms of deficits, such as deficits in German language knowledge, in educational success, or in the labor market integration of migrants. What is needed, however, is a totally new approach towards prioritizing resources for migrants in areas such as language and professional skills. One emerging field of policy-related data analysis is the development of integration indicator sets in municipalities, the federal states, and on the national level (Siegert 2006; Worbs and Friedrich 2008; KGSt 2006; Filsinger 2008). The BAMF Integration Report Working Papers series provides an overview of official statistics and empirical social research covering a wide range of fields of integration. The Federal Government Commissioner for Migration, Refugees, and Integration has published a set of integration indicators and will publish a more detailed report at a later date. Comprehensive data analysis on integration aspects is also conducted in different fields of policy-related research; examples include the official reports on education (*Bildung in Deutschland*), poverty (*Armuts- und Reichtumsbericht*) or families (*Familienbericht*).

2. Status quo: Databases and access

Different databases are available for different research purposes (Diehl and Haug 2003; Haug 2005; Schönwälder et al. 2008).

2.1 Databases for research into immigration and emigration (population flow)

Since registration with the local authorities is obligatory in Germany, legal migration can be measured directly. Flow data result from decentralized local resident registration offices, which supply aggregate data on immigration and emigration – categorized by citizenship, country of origin or destination, age, and gender – to the Statistical Offices of the *Länder* and to the Federal Statistical Office. The lack of reliable figures on the number of irregular migrants leads to an underestimation of immigration and the size of the foreign population. Moreover, register information generally produces case-based statistics, so official aggregate migration statistics tend to overestimate migration. The restructuring of migration statistics for foreigners is ongoing, with the result that persons crossing the border several times a year are no longer counted multiple times. The migration data does not include specifics on the duration of stay or the residence permit status, so it is not possible to differentiate between long-term and short-term migrants.

A second source of migration flow data is the Central Register of Foreigners (AZR, *Ausländerzentralregister*; BAMF 2010). The major drawback of this register is that it only records the immigration of foreigners, and it cannot therefore be considered a comprehensive migration register. The main advantage of the register is that it provides person-based statistics and the option of distinguishing between short-term and long-term migrants (persons who have stayed for at least one year). In 2004, the register was adjusted and this resulted in a reduction in the number of foreigners in Germany from 7.3 million to 6.7 million (Opfermann et al. 2006).

Alongside these comprehensive migration statistics, there are also statistical systems for the registration of different groups of immigrants using specific entrance options such as those for ethnic German repatriates, Jewish migrants, family reunification or asylum seekers, short-term labor migrants, highly qualified labor migrants, or students (BAMF 2010).

2.2 Databases for research on foreigners and migrants (population stock)

There are three kinds of official databases. Data on population stocks are collected by the local authorities, who adjust the census data of 1987 by adding or subtracting national and international migration flows and natural population events (births and deaths) to or from the population projections of the Federal Statistical Office (*Bevölkerungsfortschreibung*). The population projections contain basic data on the demographic development of the German and foreign population, including statistics on population differentiated according to German and foreign citizenship. We know that the figure of 7.3 million foreigners listed in the population projections is higher than the actual figure. Another shortcoming concerns the very important concept of "foreigners," according to which German citizens such as the large groups of naturalized migrants and ethnic German repatriates are not identified as migrants. Moreover, new legislation on citizenship includes elements of *Jus soli* for children of foreigners, which will result in a significant decline in the number of "foreigners" over the next few years. This means that the population projections are less and less suitable as a basis for depicting the migrant population.

The BAMF is responsible for the AZR. Data on the foreign population is collected by the local authorities responsible for alien registration and includes the personal details used for administrative purposes such as name, gender, date of birth, date of immigration, country and place of birth, and citizenship. The register has several advantages, the most important of which is the "legal status" parameter, which is useful for differentiating temporary or permanent residents. In addition, unlike the population register, this register permits the identification of first and second generations as well as the duration of stay. The quality of the data was enhanced in 2004 by the clearing up of the AZR, and this resulted in a decrease in the number of foreigners calculated – from 7.3 million to 6.7 million (Opfermann et al. 2006).

A third database for migrant information is the German Microcensus, a mandatory survey of a one percent sample of the German population conducted each year. The last census in Germany was conducted in 1987, and the next one will be in 2011. Until then, the sole official source of information on migrant population households is the Microcensus (Statistisches Bundesamt 2008). The Microcensus is also part of the European Labour Force Survey. Before 2005, migrants were identified by foreign citizenship. To ensure that the figures also covered German migrants, the new concept of "migratory background" was incorporated in the 2005 Microcensus. This concept covers all foreigners, naturalized foreigners, ethnic German repatriates, and immigrants, as well as their descendants (Statistisches Bundesamt 2008). Under the new definitions, around 15 million persons have a migration background.

Information on religious minorities is not contained in official datasets. The Muslim population in Germany is estimated at 4 million, based on a survey of persons with migration background (Haug et al. 2009).

2.3 Databases for integration research

There is an even broader range of options in the field of migrant integration. All the datasets including those providing information on nationality or migration background can be used for social and economic research on integration issues.

At the national, regional, state, and municipal levels, various models are in place for the classification of aggregate data collected for administrative purposes and used in the implementation of an integration monitoring system. Various datasets exist on structural integration, such as education statistics, employment statistics from the Federal Employment Agency (BA, *Bundesagentur für Arbeit*), the datasets of the Institute for Employment Research (IAB, *Institut für Arbeitsmarkt- und Berufsforschung*), and statistics on social security recipients and crime statistics, which also cover German repatriates in some of the states or *Länder*.

The Microcensus is the largest official microdata file and one of the most important resources for integration research. It primarily supports research on the structural integration of migrants and, since 2005, the analysis of persons with a migration background. Researchers interested in aspects other than structural integration are likely to conduct their own surveys or to turn to unofficial data sources.

A second important dataset for the analysis of different aspects of integration is the German Socio-Economic Panel (SOEP, *Sozio-oekonomisches Panel*), a representative longitudinal study of private households conducted annually since 1984 by the German Institute for Economic Research (DIW Berlin, *Deutsches Institut für Wirtschaftsforschung*) (Wagner et al. 2007). Migrants are generally included in the former labor migrant household sample, supplemented by samples of ethnic German repatriates and migrants from a variety of countries.

Many institutes and universities are active in the field of integration research. An overview of ongoing projects and publications can be found in the GESIS-IZ research database (2008). Some institutes have also conducted surveys on the largest migrant groups such as the integration survey of the Federal Institute for Population Research (BiB, *Bundesinstitut für Bevölkerungsforschung*) (Haug and Diehl 2005), the Foreigner Survey of the German Youth Institute (DJI, *Deutsches Jugendinstitut*) (Weidacher 2000) or the representative survey "Selected Groups of Migrants in Germany" (RAM)

(Babka von Gostomski 2008). One current trend is to include a sample of Turkish migrants parallel to an ongoing study, such as in the study on participation and volunteering (Halm and Sauer 2007). Another method of research into integration is to survey migrants in studies on pupils conducted in schools, like the PISA study (Stanat and Christensen 2006), the studies of the Institute for Interdisciplinary Research on Conflict and Violence (IKG, *Institut für interdisziplinäre Konflikt- und Gewaltforschung*) or the Criminological Research Institute of Lower Saxony (KfN, *Kriminologisches Forschungsinstitut Niedersachsen*).

3. Future developments in Germany

3.1 Data collection and data provision

The most important actors in the field of official statistics are the Federal Statistical Office, the Statistical Offices of the *Länder*, and the BAMF. As in other demographic fields, the most important future developments for migration research are, first, the 2011 Census and, second, the plans currently under discussion to compile a central population register. Both developments will result in a revision of the official number of foreigners.

Private research institutes play an important role in data collection and are involved in almost every large empirical research project (Mohler and Rosenbladt 2008). There is a trend toward including a migrant sample in new survey projects, as in the National Educational Panel Study (NEPS) at the University of Bamberg, or in the Panel Analysis of Intimate Relationships and Family Dynamics (pairfam) at the University of Bremen, or in the Generations and Gender Survey (GGS) of the BiB. The most appropriate methodology for research on the migration process draws from combined surveys in both the country of origin and destination, for example on Mexican-US migration and the Polish migration to Germany (Massey et al. 2008), or the SOEP study on emigrants (Schupp et al. 2008).

In view of the growing migrant population with German citizenship, another trend that can be seen is the use of a name-based sampling method (onomastics, see Humpert and Schneiderheinze 2000; Haug and Diehl 2005; Haug et al. 2009). Another sampling method is based on the birthplace of migrants (topomastics), see for example studies on ethnic German repatriates in the local population register (Haug and Sauer 2007; Salentin 2007).

3.2 Data usage and data access

For data protection reasons, there is no free access to local population registers and to the AZR. The registry data is used for administrative purposes, and options for statistical analysis are strictly regulated by law. Aggregate data is available at each office responsible for the register. The local statistical offices give access to population register data for research purposes, which is especially the case for registration-based sampling in survey research.

Aggregate migration and population data can be found in the annual publications of the Federal Statistical Office. Other migration data is published by the BAMF or the BA. Access to the data files can be requested at the local statistical offices or the Statistical Offices of the *Länder*. The Federal Statistical Office publishes data on migration at local level (*Statistik lokal*). Population datasets on the district level are available at the Federal Statistical Office (*Statistik regional*) and through the Federal Office for Building and Regional Planning (BBR, *Bundesamt für Bauwesen und Raumordnung*; INKAR PRO offers up-to-date regional monitoring including future projections). There are many options for researchers who want to access aggregate data on structural integration. Statistics are published by the relevant authorities and by the Federal Statistical Office. For scientific purposes, researchers can access the 2005 Microcensus file at the Research Data Centers of the Federal Statistical Office and the Statistical Offices of the German *Länder*. Access is also possible through the German Microdata Lab at the Leibniz-Intsitute for the Social Sciences (GESIS, *Leibniz-Institut für Sozialwissenschaften*) in Mannheim. Access to the Microcensus is exemplary, and this option is widely used by researchers.

The most important actors in the research field are the following: the European Forum on Migration Studies (efms), BiB, DIW, DJI, the Migration Research Group of the Hamburg Institute of International Economics (HWWI, *Hamburgisches WeltWirtschaftsInstitut*), IAB, IKG, the Institute for Migration Research and Intercultural Studies (IMIS, *Institut für Migrationsforschung und Interkulturelle Studien*), the Institute for the Study of Labor (IZA, *Forschungsinstitut zur Zukunft der Arbeit*), the Mannheim Center of European Social Research (MZES, *Mannheimer Zentrum für europäische Sozialforschung*), the Social Science Research Center in Berlin (WZB, *Wissenschaftszentrum Berlin für Sozialforschung*), and the BAMF Research Group. A new research institution is the Advisory Board of German Foundations on Integration and Migration (Sachverständigenrat deutscher Stiftungen für Integration und Migration). Moreover, several universities conduct empirical projects on migration or integration.

Research institutes collecting datasets have their own release strategy. Data surveyed for policy-related reasons is generally not available to researchers. The exceptions are the SOEP data, which can be directly ordered from the DIW, or numerous files of the Research Data Center of the BA at the IAB, which are prepared for scientific purposes. The GESIS Data Archive lists other migrant surveys which can be ordered. The most important of these is the repeated MARPLAN survey on foreigners in Germany (latest dataset: 2002). Since 1991, the German General Social Survey (ALLBUS, *Allgemeine Bevölkerungsumfrage der Sozialwissenschaften*) conducted every second year by GESIS has also included foreigners if they speak German. Even if the migrant subgroup is too small to use in integration research, the ALLBUS is an important dataset for the analysis of attitudes among migrant populations.

4. Future developments: European and international challenges

International migration researchers are faced with differences in key concepts, data collection methods, and databases. As critics have long pointed out (Lederer 2004; Sachverständigenrat 2004), the German system of statistics does not conform to UN recommendations for conceptualizing international migration statistics (determination of long-term and short-term migrants) or international statistics for population stocks (foreign-born persons) (UN 1998; 2007). The established common rules for the collection of statistics by the Member States of the European Community refers to the concept of long-term resident, which is not applied in Germany (EU 2007).
The aim of several follow-up international projects (COMPSTAT, THESIM, PROMINSTAT) has been to collect metadata for the comparison of migration and integration of migrants in the EU (Poulain et al. 2006; Fassmann et al. 2008). Clearly, attempts to harmonize migration statistics in the EU have not been very successful to date, making comparisons difficult. The variations reflect differences in the definition of what constitutes a migrant and differences in the data sources – surveys or administrative records (Thierry 2008). However, the duration of stay, the country of birth or the migration background are added to nationality of migrants in some German official statistics (BAMF 2010).

In the field of internationally comparative research on integration, the SOEP is one of the most suitable resources. The SEOP contributes the German section of the household panel of the EU (ECHP). Other datasets that contain information on migrants are the European Statistics on Income and Living Conditions (EU-SILC), the EU Labour Force Survey, the OECD/ SOPEMI dataset, the Eurobarometer, and the European Social Survey (see Kahanec and Zimmermann 2008). International projects focusing on migrants, such as EFFNATIS (efms) or PIONEUR (GESIS, formerly ZUMA), incorporate data on migrants in a comparative perspective. The research program of the IMISCOE network (International Migration, Integration and Social Cohesion), comprised of 23 European research institutes, includes a number of comparative projects, for example the TIES project on the Integration of the European Second Generation.

5. Conclusions and recommendations

Generally speaking, the research infrastructure for migration and integration in Germany is very comprehensive. Nevertheless, there are several problems that need to be addressed.

Relating to official migration and integration statistics:

(1) When using data on migration and migrant population, researchers must deal with the under representation of certain groups of international or internal migrants due to non-registered migration. Studies on irregular migrants can provide an important supplement to knowledge about migration (Cyrus 2008). A more serious problem is the substantial difference between the number of foreigners listed in the population update and the Microcensus on the one hand, and the number registered in the AZR on the other. The lawful adjustment of the local resident registration offices and the central register of foreigners will improve the data quality in the future. The problem may also be tackled by the *2011 Census* and the population update revision. The census will be a new basis for the extrapolation of the migrant population in the Microcensus and also for the weighting of migrants in surveys. Researchers and private research institutes should take heed of these results for present and future projects on migrants.

(2) The creation of a *central population register* additionally to the local population registers of the municipalities would be another way of improving migration statistics. Researchers should have ensured access to such a central register for the analysis and sampling of foreigners and foreign-born persons – which is currently the case with local population registers. A central population register is cost- and time-effective, and would be a great improvement for survey research. Due to the decentralized register, a nationwide population sampling procedure, for example the ALLBUS, takes five or six months (Babka von Gostomski and Pupeter 2008).

(3) The *concept of migration background* is now widely accepted. Partial replacement of the term "foreigner" by the concept of "migration background" in official statistics represents a much-needed improvement, that more accurately reflects the reality of the population. In keeping with the recommendations of the working group on Coordinated Household and Population Statistics (HHSTAT) of the Union of Communal Statistical Information Systems (KOSIS-Verbund), statisticians analyze local population registers for persons with migration backgrounds (Härle 2004; Bömermann et al. 2008). There are also approaches that have been developed to make use of the concept of migration background in education and labor-market statistics. Yet there is no agreement or common use of the concept in several key respects, such as the migration status of third-generation migrants, or children who have only one parent with a migration background. It is still not possible to definitively identify ethnic German repatriates in the Microcensus 2007 (Seifert 2008). Furthermore, it is clear in the literature that researchers use slightly different definitions of migration background. Variations in how this concept is operationalized complicate the interpretation of results, and researchers should carefully consider the implications of their specific definitions of migration background.

(4) In general, data for *international comparative research* on migration is unsatisfactory. Unlike other countries, the concept of ethnicity is not used in official German statistics (see Schönwälder et al. 2008 for an overview of ethnicity measurements in empirical research). The extension of the "foreigner" and "foreign-born" concepts and the inclusion of "descendants of foreign-born" is suggested for the 2011 Census in the EU (UN 2006). Germany will participate in the EU-wide population census scheduled for 2011. After a long-lasting debate on the use of the concept of migration background, recommendations of experts and advice of researchers have been taken. The questionnaire of the 2011 Census will entail questions on migration background. The Census data will be a solid foundation for extrapolation of persons with migration background in the Microcensus in the future and facilitate comparative research on international migration as well as studies on integration of migrants.

(5) German migration statistics do not include information on the duration of stay, so the concept of *short-term/long-term migration* is not practicable. The AZR supports an analysis of long-term foreign migrants but excludes German citizens. A new law on population statistics was passed in 2008, stipulating that immigrants must be asked about their date of emigration. In this way, long-term emigrants who stay out of the country for longer than one year can be identified when they return to Germany,

and circular migration can be identified. This is an improvement for German migration statistics, but a more comprehensive solution for the analysis of long-term migration is preferable. A central population register would enhance the data situation.

(6) The implementation of the *"foreign-born" concept*, as it stands now, is inadequate. This problem will be addressed by entering the country of birth of foreigners in the local registers. The new rule is applied for foreigners registering as from 2009 on. This solution represents a real improvement in population statistics, since the current practice is to record only the place of birth.

Relating to empirical migration and integration research:

(7) In order to improve the validity of social research and social structure analysis, migrants should, in general, be included in *representative population surveys*. One reason for the implicit or explicit exclusion of migrants is that first-generation migrants in particular frequently do not have sufficient German language knowledge to participate in a survey. Translations of questions should thus be available for interviewers, at a minimum in the most prevalent migrant languages, Turkish and Russian.

(8) The accessible datasets of the Microcensus, the SOEP, or the IAB Employment Sample are adequate for integration research that deals with large migrant groups, and there is still untapped potential for analysis in this area. But even where population surveys like the Microcensus cover the full range of immigrant groups living in Germany, subgroup analyses soon run into case number problems, since data protection regulations make research into smaller migrant groups or small regions difficult. In order to acquire an adequate case number of migrants for analysis, we recommend that *specific large-scale survey studies be supplemented by a migrant sample*. Some possible examples are the Network for integrated European population studies (NIEPS), pairfam, or GGS. The advantage of this is that it enables comparisons between non-migrants and migrants. The majority of projects based on this kind of research design focus on Turkish migrants; however, the number of immigrants from Russia and other CIS countries is even larger.

(9) Some of the important questions in migration and integration research cannot be adequately studied through the available general surveys. Complex questions on migration biography, for example, refer only to migrants and therefore are not included in the ALLBUS. Also there is a lack of data in the Microcensus on indicators of emotional integration, on attitudes or religion. Instruments for the analysis of particular constraints on and resources available to migrants are important for the

analysis of the causal mechanisms of integration processes. *Adequate instruments* must be developed for these topics in conducting empirical research on migration and integration, and to implement these instruments into large studies.

(10) Most research results in the German context provide information about the integration of the large and very important group of Turkish migrants. Over and above questions about integration, research has to face the challenges presented by *new groups of migrants,* such as the large and rapidly growing group of Polish migrants or the groups with a unique profile like Jewish or Vietnamese migrants or refugees. One possible way to cope with this problem is to conduct special surveys for these migrant groups. The sampling of small migrant groups in a nationwide context, however, is more complicated. Difficulties arise with the sampling of migrant groups comprised of German citizens – such as ethnic German repatriates and naturalized persons. The identification of the minority population using name-based sampling methods is the preferred option in all these cases. A challenge for future research, therefore, is the development and methodological assessment of new sampling methods based on surnames or place of birth (onomastics and topomastics).

(11) For the analysis of causal mechanisms in the integration process, more panel studies like the SOEP are needed. Therefore, the implementation of a *longitudinal migrant study* in Germany is in the discussion stage.

(12) *Access* to most of the important datasets is possible by subscription (SOEP, ALLBUS) or by the Research Data Centers (Microcensus, IAB datasets). Yet, even if access to official data or to datasets of other research institutes can be granted upon request on a case-by-case basis, general access can represent a serious impediment for researchers.

(13) Internationally comparable datasets on migration are rare and migration research is in most cases restricted to the country of destination. With the growing importance of *circular migration,* however, the collection of data in the migrant country of origin and/or on the biographies of transnational migrants are becoming wide fields for future research.

(14) Since data collection is typically delegated to *private-sector agencies,* a competent partner is needed for the complex field work and ensurement of high data quality (Rosenbladt 2008; Mohler and Rosenbladt 2009). Energy and resources need to be invested in the continuous improvement of migrant survey methodology in cooperation with researchers and private research institutes.

References:

Babka von Gostomski, C. (2008): Türkische, griechische, italienische und polnische Personen sowie Personen aus den Nachfolgestaaten des ehemaligen Jugoslawien in Deutschland. BAMF Working Paper Nr. 11.
Babka von Gostomski, C. and Pupeter, M. (2008): Zufallsbefragung von Ausländern auf Basis des Ausländerzentralregisters. Methoden – Daten – Analysen 2/2008, 149-177.
BAMF (Bundesamt für Migration und Flüchtlinge) (2010): Migrationsbericht 2008. Nuremberg.
Bömermann, H./Rehkämper, K. and Rockmann, U. (2008): Neue Daten zur Bevölkerung mit Migrationshintergrund in Berlin zum Stand 31.12.2007. Zeitschrift für amtliche Statistik Berlin Brandenburg 3, 20-28.
Boos-Nünning, U. and Karakasoglu, Y. (2006): Viele Welten leben. Münster.
Boswell, C. and Mueser, P. (Eds.) (2008): Journal of Ethnic and Migration Studies. Special Issue: Economics in Migration Research: Towards Disciplinary Integration? 34 (4).
Brettfeld, K. and Wetzels, P. (2007): Muslime in Deutschland. Berlin.
Cyrus, N. (2008): Country report Germany: Undocumented Migration Counting the Uncountable. Data and Trends across Europe. HWWI. Hamburg.
Diefenbach, H. and Weiß, A. (2006): Menschen mit Migrationshintergrund. Datenerfassung für die Integrationsberichterstattung. Gutachten für das Statistische Amt & die Stelle für interkulturelle Arbeit der Landeshauptstadt München. Munich.
Diehl, C. and Haug, S. (2003): Assessing migration and integration in an immigration hesitant country: the sources and problems of data in Germany. Studi Emigrazione/International Journal of Migration Studies 40 (152), 747-771.
Esser, H. (1980): Aspekte der Wanderungssoziologie. Darmstadt.
Esser, H. (2008): Assimilation, ethnische Schichtung oder selektive Akkulturation? Neuere Theorien der Eingliederung von Migranten und das Modell der intergenerationalen Integration. Kölner Zeitschrift für Soziologie und Sozialpsychologie, Sonderheft 48, 81-107.
EU (2007): EU regulation (EC) No 862/2007 of the European Parliament and the council, Community statistics on migration and international protection and repealing Council Regulation (EEC) No 311/76 on the compilation of statistics on foreign workers.
Fassmann, H./Reeger, U. and Sievers, W. (2008): Statistics and Reality: Concepts and Measurements of Migration in Europe (IMISCOE Reports). Amsterdam.
Filsinger, D. (2008): Bedingungen erfolgreicher Integration: Integrationsmonitoring und Evaluation; Expertise im Auftrag der Friedrich-Ebert-Stiftung. Bonn.
GESIS-IZ Sozialwissenschaften und BAMF (2008): Migration und ethnische Minderheiten, SoFid. Bonn.
Granato, N. (2003): Ethnische Ungleichheit auf dem deutschen Arbeitsmarkt. Opladen.
Halm, D. and Sauer, M. (2007): Bürgerschaftliches Engagement von Türkinnen und Türken in Deutschland. Wiesbaden.

Härle, J. (2004): Personen mit Migrationshintergrund. Stadtforschung und Statistik 1/2004, 16-18.
Haug, S. (2002): Familienstand, Schulbildung und Erwerbstätigkeit junger Erwachsener. Erste Ergebnisse des Integrationssurveys des BiB. Zeitschrift für Bevölkerungswissenschaft 27 (1), 115-144
Haug, S. (2005): Die Datenlage im Bereich der Migrations- und Integrationsforschung. BAMF Working Paper Nr. 1.
Haug, S. and Diehl, C. (2005): Aspekte der Integration. Wiesbaden.
Haug, S. and Sauer, L. (2007): Zuwanderung und Integration von (Spät-)Aussiedlern. BAMF Forschungsbericht Nr. 3.
Haug, S./Stichs, A. and Müssig, S. (2009): Muslim Life in Germany. A study conducted on behalf of the German Conference on Islam. Research Report No. 6. Nuremberg.
Huinink, J. and Kley, S. (2008): Regionaler Kontext und Migrationsentscheidungen im Lebensverlauf. Kölner Zeitschrift für Soziologie und Sozialpsychologie, Sonderheft 48, 162-184.
Humpert, A. and Schneiderheinze, K. (2000): Stichprobenziehung für telefonische Zuwandererumfragen. Einsatzmöglichkeiten der Namensforschung. ZUMA Nachrichten 24 (47), 36-64.
Kahanec, M. and Zimmermann, K. (2008): Migration and Globalization: Challenges and Perspectives for the Research Infrastructure, RatSWD Working Paper No. 51.
Kalter, F. (Ed.) (2008a): Migration und Integration. Kölner Zeitschrift für Soziologie und Sozialpsychologie, Sonderheft 48.
Kalter, F. (1997): Wohnortwechsel in Deutschland. Opladen.
Kalter, F. (2003): Stand und Perspektiven der Migrationssoziologie. In: Orth, B. et al. (Eds.): Soziologische Forschung. Stand und Perspektiven. Opladen.
Kalter, F. (2008b): Einleitung. Stand, Herausforderungen und Perspektiven der empirischen Migrationsforschung. Kölner Zeitschrift für Soziologie und Sozialpsychologie, Sonderheft 48, 11-36.
KGSt (Kommunale Gemeinschaftsstelle für Verwaltungsmanagement) (2006): Integrationsmonitoring. Materialien Nr. 2/2006. Cologne.
Kristen, C. (2005): School choice and ethnic school segregation. Primary school selection in Germany. Münster.
Lederer, H. (2004): Indikatoren der Migration. Bamberg.
Massey, D./Kalter, F. and Pren, K. (2008): Structural Economic Change and International Migration from Mexico and Poland. Kölner Zeitschrift für Soziologie und Sozialpsychologie, Sonderheft 48, 134-161.
Mehrländer, U./Ascheberg, C. and Ueltzhöffer, J. (1996): Situation der ausländischen Arbeitnehmer und ihrer Familienangehörigen in der BRD. Repräsentativuntersuchung '95. Berlin.
Mohler, P. and Rosenbladt, B. von (2009): Infrastructure for large-scale survey measurement: cooperation of academic research and private sector agencies. RatSWD Working Papers No. 69.
Nauck, B. (2008): Akkulturation: Theoretische Ansätze und Perspektiven in Psychologie und Soziologie. Kölner Zeitschrift für Soziologie und Sozialpsychologie, Sonderheft 48, 108-133.

Opfermann, H./Grobecker, C. and Krack-Roberg, E. (2006): Auswirkungen der Bereinigung des Ausländerzentralregisters auf die amtliche Ausländerstatistik. Wirtschaft und Statistik 5, 480-494.
Poulain, M./Perrin, M. and Singleton, A. (2006): THESIM: Towards Harmonised European Statistics on International Migration. Louvain.
Pries, L. (1997): Einleitung. Neue Migration im transnationalen Raum. Transnationale Migration. Soziale Welt, Sonderband 12, 15-46.
Rosenbladt, B. von (2008): Die Rolle der Umfrageinstitute in der sozialwissenschaftlichen Dateninfrastruktur. RatSWD Working Paper No. 36.
Sachverständigenrat für Zuwanderung und Integration (2004): Migration und Integration – Erfahrungen nutzen, Neues wagen. Jahresgutachten 2004. Nuremberg.
Salentin, K. (2007): Die Aussiedler- Stichprobenziehung. Methoden – Daten – Analysen 1 (1), 25-44.
Salentin, K. and Wilkening, F. (2003): Ausländer, Eingebürgerte und das Problem einer realistischen Zuwanderer-Integrationsbilanz. Kölner Zeitschrift für Soziologie und Sozialpsychologie 55 (2), 278-298.
Schönwälder, K./Baykara-Krumme, H. and Schmid, N. (2008): Ethnizität in der Zuwanderungsgesellschaft Deutschland: Zur Beobachtung ethnischer Identifizierungen, Loyalitäten und Gruppenbildungen. SOEB Arbeitspapier 1. Forschungsverbund Berichterstattung zur sozioökonomischen Entwicklung der Bundesrepublik Deutschland.
Schupp, J./Siegel, N./Erlinghagen, M./Stegmann, T. and Wagner, G.G. (2008): Leben außerhalb Deutschlands: eine Machbarkeitsstudie zur Realisierung von Auslandsbefragungen auf Basis des Sozio-oekonomischen Panels (SOEP). SOEP Papers No. 120.
Seifert, W. (2008): Aussiedlerinnen und Aussiedler – neue Erfassungsmöglichkeiten und sozioökonomisches Profil. Statistische Analysen und Studien, Band 53, 11-23.
Siegert, M. (2006): Integrationsmonitoring – State of the Art in internationaler Perspektive. Nuremberg.
Stanat, P. and Christensen, G. (2006): Schulerfolg von Jugendlichen mit Migrationshintergrund im internationalen Vergleich. Eine Analyse von Voraussetzungen und Erträgen schulischen Lernens im Rahmen von PISA 2003. Berlin.
Statistisches Bundesamt (with WZB and ZUMA) (2006): Datenreport 2006. Bonn.
Statistisches Bundesamt (2008): Bevölkerung mit Migrationshintergrund. Ergebnisse des Mikrozensus 2007. Fachserie 1. Reihe 2.2. Wiesbaden.
Thierry, X. (2008): Towards a harmonization of European Statistics on International Migration. Population & Societies No. 442.
UN (1998): Recommendations on Statistics of International Migration. Rev. 1. New York.
UN (2006): Conference of European Statisticians. Recommendations for the 2010 Censuses of Population and Housing. New York.
UN (2007): Principles and Recommendations for Population and Housing Censuses, Rev. 2. New York.
Venema, M. and Grimm, C. (2002): Situation der ausländischen Arbeitnehmer und ihrer Familienangehörigen in der BRD. Repräsentativuntersuchung 2001. Offenbach.

Wagner, G.G./Frick, J.R. and Schupp, J. (2007): The German Socio-Economic Panel Study (SOEP) – Scope, Evolution and Enhancements. Schmollers Jahrbuch 127 (1), 139-169.
Wagner, M. (1989): Räumliche Mobilität im Lebensverlauf. Eine empirische Untersuchung zu sozialen Bedingungen der Migration. Stuttgart.
Weidacher, A. (2000): In Deutschland zu Hause. Opladen.
Windzio, M. (2004): Kann der regionale Kontext zur „Arbeitslosenfalle" werden? Der Einfluss der Arbeitslosigkeit auf die Mobilität zwischen regionalen Arbeitsmärkten in Westdeutschland. Kölner Zeitschrift für Soziologie und Sozialpsychologie 56 (2), 257-278.
Worbs, S. and Friedrich, L. (2008): Integrationsberichterstattung in Deutschland. Eine Bestandsaufnahme. Sozialwissenschaften und Berufspraxis 2/2008, 250-269.

1.3 Internal Migration

Andreas Farwick

Contact:

Andreas Farwick
Ruhr University Bochum
Geography Department
Universitätsstraße 150
44780 Bochum
Germany
e-mail: andreas.farwick[at]ruhr-uni-bochum.de

Abstract

Research on internal migration covers a wide range of issues that pertain to the reasons for moving, the distance and direction of movement within a country, and the process of decision making involved in undertaking these moves. Given the rich field of relevant research objectives and the substantial developments in migration theory, it is clear that the availability of a broad set of data that includes detailed information on various aspects of life is one of the key factors in ensuring continued progress in the analysis of internal migration and its development. The available official aggregated data are useful for descriptive structural analyses; however, they are limited in their ability to explain causal relations. The same holds true for cross-sectional data. Some of the longitudinal datasets discussed consist of retrospectively collected event history data that are not suitable for acquiring essential information about the attitudes and psychological states of the respondents over time. Several prospective longitudinal survey data do not represent essential aspects of internal migration. Data should at least include information on the place of residence (on the smallest possible spatial level), typologies pertaining to the characteristics of the place of residence, any change in residence, reasons for a move, the plan to migrate, the type of dwelling and the neighborhood, as well as on commuting.

Keywords: internal migration, regional migration, migration theory, official data, cross-sectional data, longitudinal data

1. Research objectives

The main fields of research in the study of internal migration can be addressed by posing the following basic questions: (a) who moves, (b) why do they move, (c) from what origin, (d) to what destination, (e) how are the decision-making processes involved in the move determined, and finally (f) how does this process change over time? These essential issues structure the field of research.

Issues a and b refer to the reasons and motives to change residence. One can make some rough distinctions between education-related movers, workplace-related movers, housing-related movers, and retirement-related movers (Gatzweiler 1975). This classification scheme runs parallel to specific stages in the life course (Rossi 1955) and can be related to different age groups: education-related movers (age 16 to 20 years), workplace-related movers (age 21 to 34 years), housing-related movers (age 25 to 49 years) and retirement-related movers (age 49 and above). Whether this classification of movers as an explanatory characteristic will remain adequate over time is an open question.

With regard to the origin and destination of movers (questions c and d), distinctions can be made between short- and long-distance migration and moves between different types of regions (e.g., rural to urban and vice versa). These migration patterns are again to some extent related to the reasons for the move. Education-related movers mostly stem from peripheral rural regions with an unattractive and relatively undifferentiated range of educational facilities. Workplace-related movers stem from peripheral or declining old industrial regions with shrinking opportunities for qualified workers ("rust belts") to the metropolitan centers of growth industries ("sun belts"). In Germany this workplace-related interregional migration has taken on a major significance since the early 1970s in the form of a North to South shift (Friedrichs et al. 1986; Windzio 2004) and – following the reunification of Germany – in the form of a massive East to West movement, especially in the first two years (Büchel and Schwarze 1994; Burda 1993; Wagner 1992; Windzio 2007; 2009).

Housing-related migration patterns are predominantly intra-regional or intra-urban. One of the major intra-regional migration patterns is the process of suburbanization, which began in the early 1960s. Particularly during the 1970s, increasing family income, improved transportation systems, and public incentive programs that encouraged individual housing, led to a first wave of the population shift away from the central cities. A second wave of suburbanization took place at the end of the 1980s. Increasing population densities and the extension of suburban areas pushed the new suburbanites further and further into the urban peripheries, causing substantial urban sprawl (Bleck and Wagner 2006). Due to the recent rebirth of inner-city housing for broad sections of the population, there is now a notable trend towards reurbanization (Brühl et al. 2005).

Currently, retirement-related movement in Germany does not have the magnitude that it has in the United States or in France, but it is becoming more and more significant. Retirement seekers notably favor regions with attractive landscapes, such as the northern foothills of the Alps (*Alpenvorland*) (Friedrich 1995).

Over time these population shifts will cumulatively increase regional disparities and may have substantial negative consequences for demographic and economic development, since all of the types of migration described are highly selective with respect to age, gender, and economic status. The migration of younger individuals, for example, results in the massive aging of peripheral regions, with consequences for the natural reproduction of the population. Population losses in East Germany and in the traditionally industrial areas of West Germany, combined with an ongoing suburbanization cause a considerable shrinking of central cities (Eichstädt-Bohlig et al. 2006). Furthermore, extensive out-migration of highly skilled labor from decreasing to prosperous regions ("brain drain") leads to a decrease in the human capital necessary for further development (Friedrich and Schultz 2008). Competing for highly skilled employees, some city business development agencies profile themselves as an attractive destination for qualified workers by stimulating – according to the thesis of Florida (2004) – a tolerant and cultural diverse climate in their regions.

The selectivity of migration patterns also raises a problem with regard to intra-urban migration. While well-educated, high-income city dwellers ("yuppies" and "dinkies") tend to rent or buy apartments or houses in the renovated and upgraded nineteenth-century inner city residential areas (thus contributing to a process of gentrification), an increasing number of lower income groups must move to the more run-down sections of the traditional working-class areas, or to peripheral public housing estates at the outskirts of the central cities to find less expensive rentals. This pattern of selective intra-urban migration causes a high degree of residential segregation and leads to the rise of poverty areas in which the social problems of the residents – due to negative neighborhood effects – accumulate (Farwick 2001).

While the decision to move can be partially explained by a typology of reasons and differences in opportunity structures (supply with infrastructure, labor market, housing market, climate, landscape, etc.), it remains difficult to explain why some people move and others do not. This issue is linked to the questions introduced at the opening of this discussion, that pertain to decision-making processes. On the one side, objective individual characteristics (age, gender, educational attainment, occupational or family related conditions, as well as housing conditions) are important factors in explaining these processes. On the other side, subjective factors like motives, information, and the evaluation of the situation, play an important role too. According to Kalter (1997), the decision to move can be divided into three stages: the idea of moving, the plan to move, and the actual move. The challenge is thus to explain the factors that determine each stage in the overall decision-making process. The complexity of analyzing the decision-making process becomes apparent when one considers that it is embedded in the life course and therefore related to many other events that take place during the lifetime (Wagner 1989).

Moreover – like every social action – the decision to change residence is framed by the social, political, and economic conditions of society. Since these social conditions change continuously over time, research questions seek to explain how different migration processes refer to these ongoing changes in the social environment.

Theoretical concepts approach the investigation of the phenomenon of internal migration on both the macro- and on the micro-level. Based on Ravenstein's classic "Laws of Migration" (1885/1889, reprint 1995), which emphasize the significance of the distance between the origin and destination in migration as a means of estimating population flows – the gravity model is the most important concept explaining internal migration patterns at the macro-level (Birg et al. 1993). Introducing other regional characteristics in addition to population size and distance, however, would extend this model. For example, neoclassical economic theories stress the role of regional income and job vacancy differentials particularly for an explanation of interregional migration patterns (Todaro 1969). With regard to intra-urban migration, concepts focusing on structures of supply and demand on the regional housing market are of particular relevance (Farwick 2001).

A major shortcoming of migration theories on the macro-level is that they cannot explain exactly how the decision to change residence is affected by regional characteristics. In this context, Lee (1972) outlined the impact of intervening obstacles. He argued that diverse variables – such as distance, physical and political barriers, and having dependents – could impede or even prevent migration.

Sjaastads (1962) seminal work considers migration as a particularly important investment decision in human capital. In the simplest model of wealth maximization, the fixed costs of moving are balanced against the net present value of earnings streams available in the alternative location. Furthermore, the social psychological approach adopted by Wolpert (1965) characterizes migration as a form of individual or group adaptation to perceived changes in environment.

A synthesis of different approaches to explain migration behaviors has given rise to the "value-expectancy model" (De Jong and Fawcett 1981). According to this, the decision to move is based on a specification of the personally valued goals that might be achieved by moving (or staying) and the perceived linkage, in terms of expectancy, between migration behavior and the attainment of these goals in alternative locations. Kalter (1997) enhanced this model in three ways: by incorporating the cost-benefit calculus of households, by accounting for the tendency toward inertia, and by integrating the problems of constraints and facilitators of the environment. Consequently, the decision to move has to be operationalized as a significant part of the life course characterized by a high degree of interdependence with other areas of life (Huinink and Kley 2008; Wagner 1989).

The described research objectives and theoretical developments show that studies on internal migration remain on the scientific frontier. Particularly, attention must be given to the development of theoretical models and empirical methods able to connect the decision-making process involved in migration to the complexity of events in a life-course perspective. We need more insight into the process of considering a change in residence or, alternatively, into the choice to commute – even over long distances – increasingly in the form of multi-local living arrangements.

Investigating migration as a combined and complex decision-making process influenced by a variety of family members is another important research area. The influence of broader social networks on the decision to move and on the destination of a move must also be considered.

An ongoing methodological challenge for studying migration decisions is the problem of self-selection, which has been noted by Borjas (1987). Since characteristics that influence wages also influence migration, specific methods – such as those described in Heckman (1979) for example – are needed to deal with this bias (Massey and Espinosa 1997; Windzio 2007; see also the report by Kahanec and Zimmermann on migration and globalization in this publication).

2. Status quo: Databases and accessibility

Over the last few decades we have seen considerable theoretical and methodological progress in this area of research. Yet to render these developments fruitful and to adequately meet the relevant research objectives, a rich pool of data is needed that can be applied to all kinds of analysis on the macro- or micro-level, with cross-sectional or panel design respectively.

2.1 Official statistics

Data from official statistics are used to describe structures of internal migration and to analyze processes on the macro-level (e.g., Schlömer and Bucher 2001). Data on population flows that result from residential moves are based on registration and deregistration within specific municipalities and are available from the Federal Statistical Office in the form of migration matrixes on different administrative levels, ranging from the federal states (*Bundesländer*) to rural and city districts (*ländliche Kreise* and *kreisfreie Städte*). The Statistical Offices of the German *Länder* provide migration matrixes at the spatial level of cities and communities. In case of many cities, migration matrixes are also available for intra-urban moves.

On an aggregated level these official data differentiate between the individual characteristics of age, gender, nationality, and employment status. The data serve to calculate various descriptive measures of migration, to identify interdependencies between regions, and to adopt gravity models (Birg et al. 1993). Since in the gravity models, the distance between the sources and destinations of movements is used, it would be a substantial improvement if migration matrixes from the Federal Statistical Office could include data on distances between the corresponding regions.

Spatial context information at different spatial levels down to the rural or city districts are available from the Federal Statistical Office and the Statistical Offices of the German *Länder*. Together these offices provide a data collection called "Regio-Stat-Katalog" which contains a variety of different regional characteristics (Arbeitsgruppe Regionale Standards 2005). The same information is also available on CD-ROM under the label "CD-ROM Statistik Regional." Data on an even smaller level of the more than 12,000 German cities and communities are provided by a collection called "DVD Statistik Lokal" which is annually updated. Another excellent source of regional data with a broad range of spatial characteristics with respect to different areas of life is a collection published on CD-ROM by the Federal Office for Building and Regional Planning (BBR, *Bundesamt für Bauwesen und Raumordnung*) called "INKAR."

A source of official data at the individual level is the German Microcensus (Wirth et al. 2005). For research purposes the data can be obtained from the Federal Statistical Office in the form of a Scientific Use File (SUF) that describes the place of residence of the respondents at the level of federal states, or *Länder*, and in form of a typology of communities by population size (*Gemeindegrößenklasse*). The data also contain the ID of the sample district (*Auswahlbezirk*) from which each individual in the sample is drawn. Of importance for internal migration research is information on residential change (since the previous year) and housing conditions. Comprehensive data on commuting to work is available for the years 1996, 2000, and 2004. The data include no information on reasons for a move or the plan to migrate. The Federal Statistical Office is planning to release a Microcensus Regional File that will include regional information at the level of 349 Microcensus districts (MZKR, *Mikrozensus-Kreisregionen*). Unfortunately, this file will not include information about residential changes undertaken since the previous year.

The Microcensus is a rotating panel sample in which every household within the sample district is included for a four-year time period (Lüttinger and Riede 1997). However, because households that change their residence during that period drop out of the sample (Rendtel 2005; see also the report on Family included in this publication), the panel is more or less useless for internal migration research.

Labor migration can be studied using the IAB Regional Sample, a regional version of the IAB Employment Sample provided by the Institute of Employment Research (IAB, *Institut für Arbeitsmarkt- und Berufsforschung*) (e.g., Windzio 2004; 2007; 2009). The data consists of a two-percent subsample of all employees in Germany subject to social insurance contribution, supplemented by information on benefit recipients. The file includes information from 1975 (in West Germany) to 2004 (Drews 2008). The sample covers a continuous flow of data on employment subject to social security as well as on the receipt of unemployment benefits, unemployment assistance, and maintenance allowance. Data include the district number

(*Kreiskennziffer*) of the workplace. They do not provide information on the place of residence. Because of this fact it is not possible to distinguish whether a change in workplace is connected with a residential move or a change in commuting to work. Therefore, the inclusion of the place of residence into the dataset should be taken into consideration. The data could take the form of a Scientific Use File delivered via the Leibniz Institute for the Social Sciences (GESIS, *Leibniz-Institut für Sozialwissenschaften*).

2.2 Survey data

One of the most important data for research on internal migration is the German Socio-Economic Panel (SOEP, *Sozio-oekonomisches Panel*) (Wagner et al. 2007), a representative longitudinal study of private households conducted annually by the German Institute for Economic Research (DIW Berlin, *Deutsches Institut für Wirtschaftsforschung*) (Burda 1993; Büchel and Schwarze 1994; Hunt 2004; Jürges 1998; Kalter 1994; Wagner 1992). Regional information about the place of residence is available on different spatial levels down to the German zip code areas (Spieß 2005). Regional typologies (community type, community size) are also available. Since 2004, the information on the place of residence is matched with geographical microdata from MICROM Consumer Marketing. These data – in the form of various MOSAIC typologies – contain information for housing blocks concerning demographic characteristics, housing type, car use, mobility, consumer behavior, social milieus, and purchasing power (Goebel et al. 2007). The SOEP dataset itself includes key indicators like date of move, reasons for move, and the plan to migrate. In addition, the data give information about housing status, quality of dwelling, and neighborhood characteristics. Since the SOEP allows for combining information on all household members, it is possible to apply multi-actor analytical designs. The usefulness of the SOEP dataset is greatly enhanced by this wide variety of structural characteristics as well as the inclusion of attitude indicators.

Another longitudinal dataset is the German Life History Study (GLHS) originally conducted by the Max Planck Institute for Human Development in Berlin (MPIB) and now continued at Yale University. The GLHS comprises the life histories of some 8,500 men and women from twenty selected birth cohorts in West Germany and of more than 2,900 men and women from thirteen selected birth cohorts in East Germany. West Germans born in 1964 and 1971 were interviewed in 1998–99 with a sample size of 2,909 respondents. A follow-up with the 1971 cohort was completed in 2005. The GLHS has an explicit focus on residential and migration history (Wagner 1989; Rusconi 2006). Detailed retrospective life-course information is available for all moves, including reasons to move, housing conditions, type of residential place, and type of neighborhood. Information on intentions to move in the future is lacking. In the Public Use Files available at GESIS, direct references to places and all open-ended responses have been removed.

The German Youth Institute (DJI, *Deutsches Jugendinstitut*) has conducted the Family Survey that is to some extent useful for migration research. It is a recurring survey of approximately 10,000 respondents that was conducted in an interval of six years (1988, 1994, and 2000). For a subsample of about 2,000 respondents it includes a three-wave panel. Regional information on the place of residence is available on different spatial levels down to the rural or city districts (*Kreise*). Moreover regional typologies of the places of residence are available in the form of the BIK typology (Hoffmeyer-Zlotnik 2005) and – for the third wave in the year 2000 – in form of the MOSAIC typologies from MICROM Consumer Marketing (see SOEP). In addition, the data include information on housing status and characteristics, quality of dwelling, and neighborhood characteristics. The cross-sectional dataset of the year 2000 contains also questions about reasons for leaving, respectively returning to the parental home and reasons for the first three changes of residence since age of 16. The data are available directly via the German Youth Institute website.

A more recent longitudinal dataset is the German Generations and Gender Survey (GGS), an international comparative panel study coordinated by the United Nations Economic Commission for Europe (UNECE) in Geneva. The Federal Institute for Population Research conducts the German part of the survey (Ruckdeschel et al. 2006). The first wave of the GGS was collected in 2005. In 2006 another sample of Turkish migrants was undertaken. Data collection for the second wave began in 2008. The data contain housing characteristics and questions about the intention to change residence. The data can be requested at the Federal Institute for Population Research.

In analyzing mobility patterns of the elderly, the Survey of Health, Ageing and Retirement in Europe (SHARE) (Börsch-Supan et al. 2003) is useful. To date, two waves with respondents aged 50 and over have been conducted in 2004 and in 2006. A third wave is currently in progress. The data include regional information about the place of residence on different spatial levels down to the rural or city districts (*Kreise*). Unfortunately for the German sample, data on residential location are only provided on the level of the *Länder*. Information on the housing situation, a change of the place of residence, and the main reasons for a move are available but information on the plan to migrate does not exist.

The German General Social Survey (ALLBUS, *Allgemeine Bevölkerungsumfrage der Sozialwissenschaften*), a cross-sectional database also provided by GESIS, is not applicable to research in the field of internal migration. Questions about the duration of habitation – in both a specific apartment or house and the location of residence – as well as the distance from the former place of residence, have only been included since 2000. It would be worthwhile to consider adding additional questions about possible intentions to change residence and the assessment of living conditions at the current domicile.

3. Future developments

One very welcome development in gaining access to data for migration studies is the increasing availability of official data via the Internet provided by various public institutions. The Federal Statistical Office together with the Statistical Offices of the German *Länder* offer migration statistics on the level of the *Länder* and rural or city districts respectively through their Internet platform, the "German Regional Database" ("Regionaldatenbank Deutschland"). Moreover, the Lower Saxony Institute for Statistics and Communication Technology (LSKN, *Landesbetrieb für Statistik und Kommunikationstechnologie Niedersachsen)* has made particularly successful efforts to provide comprehensive regional migration data for the state of Lower Saxony that includes data all the way down to the level of the city and community, which are accessible via its system "LSKN Online." Intra-urban migration data are, for example, provided by the Statistical Office of the city of Bremen (*Statistisches Landesamt Bremen*) through its excellent information system "Bremen on a Small Scale" ("Bremen Kleinräumig"). These examples should encourage other federal states, cities, and communities to offer regional data in a comprehensive way through the Internet.

Another advance in the access of data relating to the study of internal migration has accompanied the establishment of the Research Data Center of the Federal Statistical Office, which provides on-site use of official survey data (e.g., the German Census or Microcensus) and off-site use of different Public or Scientific Use Files. The same holds for the Research Data Center of the Federal Employment Agency at the Institute of Employment Research (IAB, *Institut für Arbeitsmarkt- und Berufsforschung* within the BA, *Bundesagentur für Arbeit*). These efforts need not only to be continued but also expanded.

Since the possibilities for in-depth analysis on the causal relations of migration through the use of official data are currently very limited, survey data will continue to play a major role. One future challenge in the field of internal migration research is to further the understanding of interdependencies between migration decisions and regional opportunity structures in the context of the life course. With regard to this question, Huinink and Kley (2008) stress that the significance of contextual impacts is strongly related to the aims and demands of actors in specific stages of their life course, a fact that has only been given rudimental theoretical and empirical analysis. Studies that want to address these issues require comprehensive longitudinal datasets including information on the place of residence that can be combined with an adequate variety of regional characteristics. Positive developments in this direction can be seen by the efforts of the DIW Berlin to make small-scale regional information of the SOEP available for analyses and to link them with spatial information from other datasets (see above).

4. Conclusion and recommendations

Given the range of research objectives and developments in migration theory, it is apparent that the availability of a broad set of data, including detailed information on various aspects of life (in particular educational and occupational biographies as well as changes in household structure), combined with information on the regional structure of the place of residence, is one of the key factors for ongoing progress in research on internal migration. The datasets described here are more or less sufficient to meet these demands.

Official aggregated data are particularly useful for descriptive structural analyses. As far as possible they should be made accessible via the Internet. For explaining causal relations, however, the value of aggregated data is limited. Therefore, cross-sectional survey data and especially longitudinal datasets are needed.

Among the cross-sectional survey data described, the German Microcensus is of immense importance – not least because of its huge sample size. Its value could be improved by collecting information on the reasons behind a given move and intentions to move. It is therefore strongly recommended that the Microcensus Regional File include information on residential change (since the previous year), reasons for a move, and the plan to migrate. In terms of migration studies, the usefulness of the IAB Regional Sample, the regional version of the IAB Employment Sample, would be greatly enhanced by including information on the place of residence.

Some of the described longitudinal datasets (the GHLS or the DJI Family Survey) consist of retrospectively collected event history data. The problem with this data lies in the inability of the surveys to collect information about the attitudes and psychological states of the respondents over time. Therefore, they do not provide characteristics like the subjective evaluation of what opportunities exist in the residential environment, or the emotional closeness to the place of residence, which are both highly relevant factors in migration intentions and actual migration. In light of these problems, the continuation and optimization in particular of *prospective* longitudinal panel studies is recommended.

In this regard, one major shortcoming of many of the prospective panel studies described above relates to the fact that several key aspects of internal migration are not represented. It is recommended that datasets should at least include information on the place of residence (at the smallest possible spatial level), typologies of the characteristics of the place of residence, information on a change of residence, reasons for moving, the plan to migrate, information on the dwelling and the neighborhood, as well as on commuting and multi-local living arrangements. For the purpose of cross-national comparisons, information on the place of residence should be made available in form of the EU's Nomenclature of Territorial Units for Statistics, or NUTS (*Nomenclature des unités territoriales statistiques*) where the level three NUTS code corresponds to rural or city districts (*ländliche Kreise* and *kreisfreie Städte*).

If the structural characteristics of the residential environment are not included, information on the location of individual residences should at least be combinable with spatial context information from other aggregated regional datasets. Particularly for the analysis of intra-urban moves, regional context information must be provided on a very small scale. Matching survey data with geographical microdata from MICROM is a significant step forward. Consideration should also be given to matching survey data with small-scale spatial data from the Inner City Spatial Monitoring (IRB, *Innerstädtische Raumbeobachtung*) of the BBR. Moreover, the typology of inner-city location types (*innerstädtische Lagetypen*) used by Inner City Spatial Monitoring should be implemented in the datasets.

Since the decision to migrate is very complex, further opportunities to analyze this process by using a multi-actor design should be provided. This implies accounting for structural characteristics, attitudes, and the decisions of other individuals in the person's household or even in their larger social network.

The most comprehensive longitudinal dataset is the SOEP, which collects structural and non-structural information on the dynamics of housing conditions and residential moves. Still, the value of this dataset is restricted by the general fact that residential moves do not occur that often during the lifetime. It thus follows that for some research issues, notably analyses of specific migration types (e.g., intra-urban moves), the size of the (sub)-sample becomes too small and therefore is no longer representative. One solution of this limitation could be to increase the sample size of the SOEP.

In general, regional multi-stage cluster sampling techniques should be used to collect data for internal migration research to assure regional type-specific analyses. A possible typology especially for inner-city cluster sampling could be the inner-city location types used by the Inner City Spatial Monitoring of the BBR.

References:

Arbeitsgruppe Regionale Standards (2005): Regionale Standards – Eine gemeinsame Empfehlung des Arbeitskreises Deutscher Markt- und Sozialforschungsinstitute e.V. (ADM), der Arbeitsgemeinschaft Sozialwissenschaftlicher Institute e.V. (ASI) und des Statistischen Bundesamtes, ZUMA. Mannheim.
Birg, H./Flöthmann, E.J./Heins, F. and Reiter, I. (1993): Migrationsanalyse. Forschungen zur Raumentwicklung, vol. 22. Bonn.
Bleck, M. and Wagner, M. (2006): Stadt-Umland-Wanderung in Nordrhein-Westfalen – eine Meta-Analyse. Raumforschung und Raumordnung 2/2006, 104-115.
Borjas, G.J. (1987): Self-selection and the earnings of immigrants. American Economic Review 77 (4), 531-553.
Börsch-Supan, A./Jürges, H. and Lipps, O. (2003): SHARE – Measuring the ageing process in Europe. Zuma Nachrichten 53, 96-113.
Brühl, H./Echter, C.P./Frölich von Bodelschwingh, F. and Jekel, G. (2005): Wohnen in der Innenstadt – eine Renaissance? Difu-Beiträge zur Stadtforschung. Berlin.
Büchel, F. and Schwarze, J. (1994): Die Migration von Ost- nach Westdeutschland – Absicht und Realität. Mitteilungen aus der Arbeitsmarkt- und Berufsforschung 27 (1), 43-52.
Bundesamt für Bauwesen und Raumordnung (Ed.) (2007): Innerstädtische Raumbeobachtung: Methoden und Analysen. Bonn.
Burda, M.C. (1993): The determinants of East-West German migration: Some first results. European Economic Review 37 (2-3), 452-461.
De Jong, G.F. and Fawcett, J.T. (1981): Motivations for migration: an assessment and a value-expectancy research model. In: De Jong, G.F. and Gardner, R.W. (Eds.): migration decision making. New York.
Drews, N. (2008): Das Regionalfile der IAB-Beschäftigtenstichprobe 1975-2004. Handbuch-Version 1.0.0, FDZ Datenreport. Nuremberg.
Eichstädt-Bohlig, F./Hannemann, Ch. and Bohne, R. (2006): Die Gestaltung der schrumpfenden Stadt. In: Heinrich-Böll-Stiftung (Ed.): Das neue Gesicht der Stadt. Berlin.
Farwick, A. (2001): Segregierte Armut in der Stadt. Ursachen und soziale Folgen der räumlichen Konzentration von Sozialhilfeempfängern. Opladen.
Florida, R. (2004): The rise of the creative class. New York.
Friedrich, K. (1995): Altern in räumlicher Umwelt. Sozialräumliche Interaktionsmuster älterer Menschen in Deutschland und den USA. Darmstadt.
Friedrich, K. and Schultz, A. (Eds.) (2008): Brain drain oder brain circulation? Konsequenzen und Perspektiven der Ost West Migration, Leibnitz-Institut für Länderkunde. Leipzig.
Friedrichs, J./Häußermann, H. and Siebel, W. (Eds.) (1986): Süd-Nord Gefälle in der Bundesrepublik? Opladen/Wiesbaden.
Gatzweiler, H.P. (1975): Zur Selektivität interregionaler Wanderung. Ein theoretisch-empirischer Beitrag zur Analyse und Prognose altersspezifischer interregionaler Wanderung, vol. 1. Bonn.
Goebel J./Spieß C.K./Witte, N. and Gerstenberg, S. (2007): Die Verknüpfung des SOEP mit MICROM-Indikatoren: Der MICROM-SOEP Datensatz. DIW Data Documentation 26.

Heckman, J.J. (1979): Sample selection bias as a specification error. Econometrica 47, 153-161.
Hoffmeyer-Zlotnik, J.H.P. (2005): Regionalisierung sozialwissenschaftlicher Umfragedaten – Eine Einführung. In: Grötzinger, G. and Matiaske, W. (Eds.): Deutschland regional. Munich, 3-28.
Huinink, J. and Kley, S. (2008): Regionaler Kontext und Migrationsentscheidungen im Lebensverlauf. In: Kalter, F. (Ed.): Migration, Integration und ethnische Grenzen. Sonderband der Kölner Zeitschrift für Soziologie, 162-184.
Hunt, J. (2004): Are migrants more skilled than non-migrants? Repeat, return, and same-employer migrants. Canadian Journal of Economics 37 (4), 830-849.
Jürges, H. (1998): Beruflich bedingte Umzüge von Doppelverdienern. Eine empirische Analyse mit Daten des SOEP. Zeitschrift für Soziologie 27, 358-377.
Kalter, F. (1994): Pendeln statt Migration? Die Wahl und Stabilität von Wohnort-Arbeitsort-Kombinationen. Zeitschrift für Soziologie 23, 460-476.
Kalter, F. (1997): Wohnortwechsel in Deutschland. Ein Beitrag zur Migrationstheorie und zur empirischen Anwendung von rational-choice Modellen. Opladen.
Lee, E.S. (1972): A theory of migration. Demography, 45-57.
Lüttinger, P. and Riede, Th. (1997): Der Mikrozensus: amtliche Daten für die Sozialforschung. ZUMA-Nachrichten 41, 19-43.
Massey, D.S. and Espinosa, K.E. (1997): What's driving Mexico-U.S. migration? A theoretical, empirical, and policy analysis. The American Journal of Sociology 102 (4), 939-999.
Ravenstein, E.G. (1995): The Laws of Migration. [Reprint of the title originally publ. in 2 parts in vol. 48, pt. 2, June 1885 and vol. 52, pt. 2, June 1889 of the Journal of the Royal Statistical Society. North Stratford].
Rendtel, U. (2005): Wie geeignet ist der Mikrozensus als Datenbasis für Längsschnittanalysen? Methodenverbund „Aufbereitung und Bereitstellung des Mikrozensus als Panelstichprobe". Arbeitspapier Nr. 7. Wiesbaden.
Rossi, P.H. (1955): Why families move: A study in the social psychology of urban residential mobility. Illinois.
Ruckdeschel, K./Ette, A./Hullen, G. and Leven, I. (2006): Generations and Gender Survey. Dokumentation der ersten Welle der Hauptbefragung in Deutschland. Materialien zur Bevölkerungswissenschaft. Wiesbaden.
Rusconi, A. (2006): Leaving the parental home in Italy and West Germany: Opportunities and constraints. Aachen.
Schlömer, C. and Bucher, H. (2001): Arbeitslosigkeit und Binnenwanderungen. Auf der Suche nach einem theoriegestützten Zusammenhang. Informationen zur Raumentwicklung 1, 33-47.
Sjastaad, L.A. (1962): The Costs and Returns of Human Migration. The Journal of Political Economy 70, 80-93.
Spieß, C.K. (2005): Das Sozio-oekonomische Panel (SOEP) und die Möglichkeiten regionalbezogener Analysen. In: Grötzinger, G. and Matiaske, W. (Eds.): Deutschland regional. Munich.
Todaro, M.P. (1969): A model of labor migration and urban unemployment in less developed countries. American Economic Review 59, 138-48.
Wagner, G.G. (1992): Arbeitslosigkeit, Abwanderung und Pendeln von Arbeitskräften der neuen Bundesländer. Sozialer Fortschritt 4, 84-89.

Wagner, G.G./Frick, J.R. and Schupp, J. (2007): The German Socio-Economic Panel Study (SOEP) – Scope, Evolution and Enhancements. Schmollers Jahrbuch 127 (1), 139-169.

Wagner, M. (1989): Räumliche Mobilität im Lebensverlauf. Stuttgart.

Windzio, M. (2004): Zwischen Nord- und Süddeutschland: Die Überwindung räumlicher Distanzen bei der Arbeitsmarktmobilität. Zeitschrift für Arbeitmarktforschung 1, 29-44.

Windzio, M. (2007): Regionale Arbeitslosigkeit und Distanz zur Grenze: Individual- und Konexteffekte auf die Abwanderung von Arbeitskräften von Ost- nach Westdeutschland. Schmollers Jahrbuch 127 (4), 553-583.

Windzio, M. (2009): The "Exit Option" of Labour Migration from East to West-Germany: Individual and Contextual Determinants of Geographic Mobility of Unemployed Workers. In: Egbert, H. and Kolb, H. (Eds.): Migrants and Markets: Perspectives from Economics and the Other Social Sciences. Amsterdam.

Wirth, H./Zühlke, S. and Christians, H. (2005): Der Mikrozensus als Datenbasis für die Regionalforschung. In: Grötzinger, G. and Matiaske, W. (Eds.): Deutschland regional. Munich.

Wolpert, J. (1965): Behavioral Aspects of the Decision to Migrate. Papers and Proceedings of the Regional Science Association 15, 159-169.

1.4 Fertility and Mortality Data for Germany

*Michaela Kreyenfeld and Rembrandt Scholz**

---

* We would like to thank Klaus Duschek for his detailed and friendly responses to our various inquiries about the Microcensus. For language editing, we would like to thank Miriam Hils.

Contact:

Michaela Kreyenfeld
Rembrandt Scholz
Max Planck Institute for Demographic Research
Konrad-Zuse-Str. 1
18057 Rostock
Germany
e-mail: kreyenfeld[at]demogr.mpg.de
        scholz[at]demogr.mpg.de

Abstract

There has been considerable progress made in the improvement of the data infrastructure for fertility and morality researchers in Germany in recent years. Several large-scale datasets have been made available through the establishment of Research Data Centers. The Microcensuses of the 1970s and 1980s, the censuses of the German Democratic Republic and the Federal Republic of Germany, the Microcensus panel, data from the pension registers, individual-level data from vital statistics, and the central foreigner registers are now available for scientific use. Vital statistics have been reformed, and the Microcensus now collects information on the number of children a woman has given birth to during her life. Despite these improvements, there are still some "weak spots" in Germany's data infrastructure. Germany is lacking official counts of reconstituted families. We know little about the mortality risks of immigrants. In addition, the data infrastructure for studying socio-economic differences in mortality risks could be improved, enabling Germany to catch up with international developments in this area. This paper concludes by making some suggestions for improving the available data.

Keywords: fertility, mortality, demographic data

1. Introduction

Since the turn of the last century, demographic change has been a popular topic among journalists and policy-makers alike. Yet despite the considerable level of public interest in this topic, the available data was rather poor in Germany: important fertility indicators were lacking, official mortality rates for the "oldest old" were of poor quality, and population counts were inaccurate. Today, however, we can state that the data situation for researchers interested in the field of demographic change has improved tremendously. Germany is about to conduct a register-based census which is expected to give an accurate account of the population size in Germany. Furthermore, new micro-level datasets have become available for scientific use that will enhance our understanding of demographic processes.

This paper provides an overview of what we believe are the most important recent innovations in the field of fertility and mortality research. Obviously, such an overview is subjective and can not be considered comprehensive. Nevertheless, we believe that we have included the most significant and critical datasets in this brief overview. Part 2 presents data and discusses applications. In Part 3 we discuss what could be done to improve data availability in the future. Part 4 concludes the overview, and provides a list of recommendations for the future.

2. Recent progress in the data infrastructure

2.1 Fertility and family research

In the field of family and fertility research, an important step forward was made recently with the amendment of the German Population Statistics Law (*Bevölkerungsstatistik-Gesetz*), which prescribes which data are to be collected for population statistics. For centuries, German vital statistics did not collect births by biological order. Since 2008, German vital statistics includes this type of information (Deutscher Bundestag 2007). Another important amendment provides that the Microcensus will ask female respondents to give the number of their biological children.[1]

Age at first birth and childlessness

The groundbreaking changes in the law will enable researchers to generate important structural fertility indicators, such as the mean age at first birth. The postponement of first birth is one of the most important changes in fertility behavior of the recent years (Sobotka 2004; Billari et al. 2006). Germany has been a forerunner in this development, but official indicators documenting this process were lacking. Due to the amendment of the German Population Statistics Law, it is now possible to generate a (period) mean age at first birth. This indicator is of great public interest. Furthermore, it is a measure that will enter international demographic statistics.

In addition to changes in the age at first birth, the level of childlessness is an indicator that is in great demand and frequently discussed (Berth 2005; Mönch 2007; Schwentker 2007). However, the ultimate level of childlessness cannot yet be calculated based on German vital statistics.[2] This gap in vital statistics can be filled through other sources, however. The *Frauenbefragung Geburten* has been an important source of indicators of permanent childlessness (Pötzsch 2007). In the future, the Microcensus will provide this information, too.

---

[1] The plan is to collect this information every four years. The Microcensus 2008 is the first to include a question on whether the respondent has ever given birth to a child and another one on the total number of children ever born. The question will be asked of female respondents aged 15 to 75.

[2] Since 2008, German vital statistics provide birth order-specific fertility information, which is needed to calculate indicators of childlessness. However, birth order specific fertility information for the entire reproductive life of a cohort must be collected first before an ultimate level of childlessness can be generated. The cohort 1993 will be the first one for which birth order information will be available for their entire reproductive lives. This cohort reaches the end of their fertile years in 2038.

Fertility of migrants

From 2008 onwards, the Microcensus will enable researchers to generate fertility indicators according to the socio-economic characteristics of the respondents. This will also enable us to generate the total number of children by nationality and migration background. In addition to the Microcensus, the Turkish sample of the Generations and Gender Survey (GGS) will complement our understanding of the demographic behavior of non-citizens and migrants. The fertility of migrants is an aspect worth pointing out, not only because this topic is of great scientific interest (see Nauck 2007; Milewski 2007), but also because vital statistics are not very useful for understanding the fertility dynamics of non-citizens and migrants. This is partly because population counts of non-German citizens have been imprecise. But this also relates to the fact that it is difficult to generate fertility indicators for a highly mobile population with aggregate level data.

Panel studies in the field of family and fertility

In the past, the Socio-Economic Panel (SOEP, *Sozio-oekonomisches Panel*) has been the major panel study for family and fertility researchers. Although this data provides a rich battery of socio-economic variables, it does not provide much information on the quality of partnership or the intention to become parent. This has limited our opportunities to study, for example, how fertility intentions transfer into behavior. Germany now provides two important datasets – the GGS and the Panel Analysis of Intimate Relationships and Family Dynamics (pairfam) – that will help shed light on the decision-making processes that underlie fertility and nuptiality behaviors. The first wave of the GGS has been released (Ruckdeschel et al. 2006). Data from the second round of the GGS, as well as data of the pairfam, were collected in autumn 2008 (Feldhaus and Huinink 2008).

Fertility and large-scale datasets

For demographic studies, having access to large-scale data is indispensable. In this context, the great achievement of the Research Data Centers must be acknowledged. The Research Data Centers of the Federal Statistical Office and the Statistical Offices of the German *Länder* have made available individual-level data for births and marriages. Additionally, the Microcensuses of the 1970s and 1980s and the censuses of the German Democratic Republic and the Federal Republic of Germany have been made available for scientific purposes. The Scientific Use File of the Microcensus, which opens up new potential for fertility and family analysis, is also now accessible (Schmidtke et al. 2008). Finally, the Research Data Center of the German

Pension Insurance (RV, *Deutsche Rentenversicherung*) provides researchers access to Scientific Use Files of pension records, which can also be used for fertility and family research (in particular, the *Versicherungskontenstichprobe*) (Kreyenfeld and Mika 2008). Fertility analyses with register data, like those that have previously been undertaken mainly for Scandinavian countries, can now be replicated using German data.

2.2 Aging and mortality

It is as crucial in the field of mortality and aging to have access to large-scale datasets as it is for demographic studies. After all, death is quite a rare event. Therefore, large datasets are needed in the calculation of robust mortality estimates. Fortunately, there has been considerable progress made in recent years in terms of the availability of large-scale datasets. New computer techniques and opportunities offered by installed process data sources enable researchers to conduct mortality analyses on large-scale datasets.

Human Mortality Database, population size and census

The Human Mortality Database (HMD) is a collaborative project which has been conducted since 2002 by the University of California at Berkeley (US) and the Max Planck Institute for Demographic Research (Rostock, Germany). The purpose of the database is to provide researchers around the world with easy access to detailed and comparable national mortality data via the Internet.[3] The HMD methodology has been used to validate German population statistics. In Germany, the last census was conducted in the West in 1987, and in the former East Germany in 1990.[4] In order to generate the population size, German vital statistics largely relies on the results from the last census and a component-method by births, immigrations, out-migrations, and deaths (*Bevölkerungsfortschreibung*). There is reason to believe that the population estimates that are generated from the *Bevölkerungsfortschreibung* are particularly distorted with growing distance to the last census, especially among the highest ages.

---

3   The database will contain original life tables for thirty-five countries, as well as all raw data used in constructing those tables. The raw data generally consist of birth and death counts from vital statistics, population counts from periodic censuses, and official population estimates. The general documentation and the steps followed in computing mortality rates are described in the methods protocol. There are datasets for East Germany, West Germany, and Germany Total for the period of 1955-2007 (http://www.mortality.org/).
4   The last "conventional" census of the German Democratic Republic was conducted in 1981. However, there were population registers in East Germany which provide reliable population counts. These registers were discontinued in 1990.

As shown in figure 1, the difference between the official and the recalculated population for men age 90+ in West Germany grows with the amount of time that has passed since the last census. Just after the West German Census in 1987, a sudden jump can be seen in the official population. This suggests that the population of males age 90 and over is strongly overestimated in German vital statistics (for more detail, see Jdanov et al. 2005; Scholz and Jdanov 2006). It may be hoped that the new census will improve the quality of the data available for studying mortality at higher ages.

Figure 1: Comparison of relative differences in population estimates in Germany 1960-2005 between official statistics and HMD

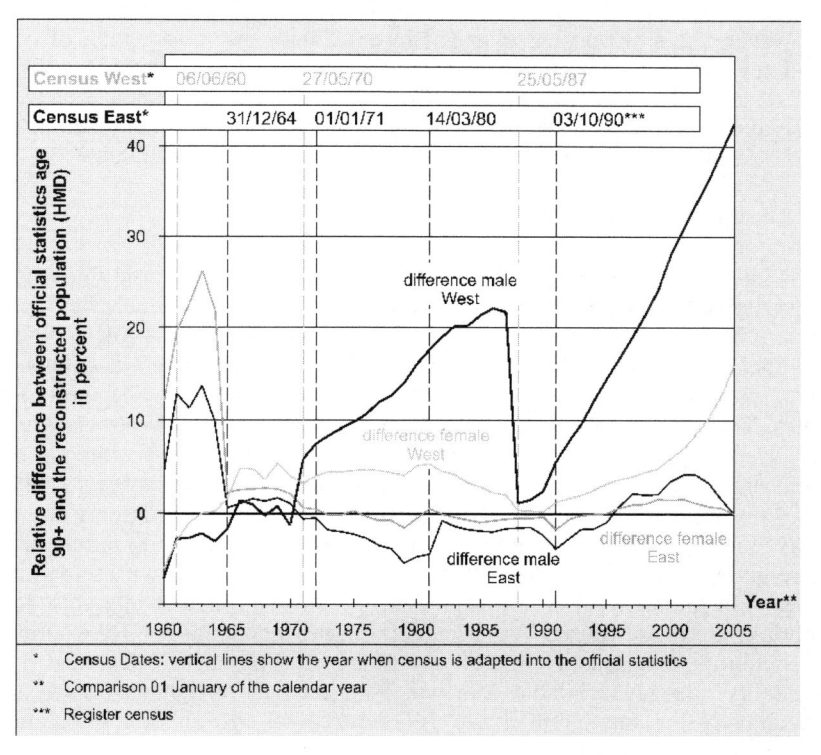

* Census Dates: vertical lines show the year when census is adapted into the official statistics
** Comparison 01 January of the calendar year
*** Register census

Source: own estimations

Socio-economic inequality in old age mortality

Relative socio-economic inequality in old age mortality is a major public health issue given the growing size of the elderly population and the sharp rise in absolute mortality with age. In the past, the international literature in this area was marked by the persistent absence of Germany. In many reviews of socio-economic mortality differences in Europe, Germany was not included. One reason for this is that, unlike in many other countries, German population statistics do not provide suitable data for mortality estimation by socio-economic status. Social science surveys can only partially fill this gap since the number of elderly subjects is too small for a robust estimation of mortality differentials in this kind of data. Furthermore, the survey data suffer from recruitment bias and the absence of people living in institutions. However, the situation has changed recently with the introduction of new policies enabling scientific analyses of administrative microdata. Data from the Research Data Center of the German Pension Insurance can now be used to evaluate mortality differentials among men aged 65 and older (Gaudecker and Scholz 2007; Shkolnikov et al. 2008; Himmelreicher et al. 2008).

The healthy migrant effect

It is known from several studies that migrants are healthier, and thus show lower mortality than the native population. This phenomenon has been described for various countries and ethnic groups, and holds true for both internal and international migrants. Generally, this development is explained by a special selection effect which may influence mortality and morbidity rates. This selective migration is thought to operate in two directions, which involve the movement of a "select group" of either the healthy or the unhealthy. The movement of healthier individuals is known as the so-called "healthy migrant effect." Conversely, it appears that sick migrants are involved in return migration, in order, for example, to be closer to family or to care-giving institutions. The latter phenomenon is also known as "salmon bias." For Germany, it is also important to consider whether migrants' low mortality rates are caused by inaccuracies in the vital statistics, for example, if doubtful data quality might contribute to migrants' "statistical immortality." Newly available data will help shed more light on this issue, specifically the Immigrant Survey of the Federal Institute for Population Research (BiB, *Bundesinstitut für Bevölkerungsforschung*) in Wiesbaden (Luy 2007), data from the German Pension Insurance (Kibele et al. 2008), and data from the German Central Register of Aliens (AZR, *Ausländerzentralregister*) (Kohls 2008).

3. Challenges and recommendations

Overall, the infrastructure for conducting fertility and mortality research has improved tremendously in recent years. Nevertheless, there are some "weak spots" in Germany's data infrastructure, which we will discuss in the following.

Family change and official statistics

Official statistics have always been slow in catching up to changes in the family. For a long time, the official UN definition of what is a family ignored new family forms, such as non-marital unions with children. This has changed in the recent years. In the UN recommendations for what is to be included in the census, co-residential partnerships are named among the core concerns (UN 2006: 113). Germany will be able to provide counts on co-residential unions based on data from the Microcensus. One drawback is that the question about partnership status, which is needed to identify a non-marital union, is voluntary, and about five percent of respondents refuse to answer the question (Heidenreich and Nöthen 2002). Since the share of non-marital unions has become such an integral demographic indicator, it seems odd that partnership status is one of the few questions in the Microcensus for which a response is not compulsory.

A related issue concerns stepfamilies. Families in which children live with biological and/or non-biological parents are on the rise, and they pose important new social policy questions. However, we do not have an accurate account of the share of reconstituted families in Germany. In the census, more complex living arrangements, such as stepfamilies, cannot be identified – despite the fact that the UN (2006) requested that this information be included in the census. Survey data, such as data from the Generations and Gender Survey, provide detailed information on family structure and living arrangements. However, sample sizes are too small to provide good "structural indicators" on the prevalence of reconstituted families. In the Microcensus, it is difficult to identify "stepfamily constellations," because the kinship status of the household members is only surveyed in reference to the head of the household.

It is difficult to make recommendations for resolving this problem. The household relationship matrix is usually seen as a superior method for surveying living arrangements (Statistical Commission and UN Economic Commission for Europe / Statistical Office of the European Communities; UN 2006: 107). If this method were introduced into the Microcensus, the share of stepfamilies in Germany could be established. However, this would obviously require a fundamental change in the Microcensus questionnaire.

Another solution could be to find out whether respondents may be asked if the stepparent, adoptive parent, or foster mother or father lives in the same household.[5]

Piecemeal changes in the field of family and fertility

While there has been significant progress made in improving Germany's data infrastructure, some changes remain incomplete. For example, it is certainly a great achievement that the number of biological children is now counted in the German Microcensus. However, it seems unfortunate that only women are asked about their fertility careers, since male fertility is also an important area for fertility and family researchers (Tölke and Hank 2005). In the social science dataset, it has become standard to ask both female and male respondents about their fertility careers. It seems socially regressive that, in the Microcensus, males have been filtered around the question concerning the number of biological children.

Finally, the Microcensus for fertility research would be tremendously enhanced if it included information on the ages at first, second, and additional births. Such a suggestion would certainly provoke another heated debate about whether the Microcensus questionnaire is already overloaded. However, a simpler solution could be found by repeating the *Frauenbefragung Geburten* on a regular basis to provide structural indicators of fertility change in Germany.

Socio-economic differences in mortality risks

In the field of mortality research, we must conclude that we still know too little about the mortality risks of immigrant populations. The data infrastructure for studying socio-economic differences in mortality risk could also be improved to keep pace with international developments in this area. We simply know too little about how mortality risks differ in Germany by educational level and socio-economic status. One way to improve this situation could be to establish a central mortality register similar to those that exist in other countries, such as Sweden or the US (Mueller 2008). However, this type of initiative will surely have to pass several administrative hurdles. An easier solution may be found by investigating ways that the Microcensus panel could be used for mortality research. Currently, it cannot be used for

---

5   The Microcensus already includes a question on whether the mother or father lives in the same household. However, it does not allow the respondent to distinguish whether he or she is a stepparent, adoptive parent, or foster parent. Legal regulations might make it impossible to ask respondents whether they have adoptive parents. However, a distinction between foster parents, stepparents, and biological or adoptive parents might present less of a legal problem.

this purpose because there is no systematic documentation of information on respondents who drop out – whether because they die or move to a different location. Finding a way to collect this information would not only increase the potential for using the Microcensus panel in mortality research, but would also expand the possibilities for employing the Microcensus panel in many other kinds of longitudinal research.

4. Conclusion

In this paper, we have described the significant progress that has been made in improving the data infrastructure for research on fertility and mortality in Germany. Nevertheless, additional changes and improvements could be made that would further increase our understanding of fertility and mortality processes. In terms of furthering research in these areas, we have argued that we need better structural indicators to capture family change in Germany. This would include making official counts of *reconstituted families* and also raises the possibility of making the question on *partnership status* compulsory in the Microcensus. In the field of mortality research, we stressed that we need better estimates of the *mortality risks of migrants,* and a better understanding of the *socio-economic determinants of death*. In this context, we pointed out the potential of the Microcensus to help fill the gap in data collection.

References:

Berth, F. (2005): Die demografischen Märchen: eine neue Gebärstreik-Debatte in Deutschland. Süddeutsche Zeitung: November 8, 2005.
Billari, F.C./Liefbroer, A.C. and Philipov, D. (2006): The postponement of childbearing in Europe: Driving forces and implications. Vienna Yearbook of Population Research 2006, 1-17.
Deutscher Bundestag (2007): Entwurf eines Gesetzes zur Änderung des Mikrozensusgesetzes 2005 und des Bevölkerungsstatistikgesetzes. Drucksache 16/5239.
Feldhaus, M. and Huinink, J. (2008): Neuere Entwicklungen in der Beziehungs- und Familienforschung. Schriften zum Beziehungs- und Familienentwicklungspanel. Band 1. Würzburg.
Fishbein, M. and Ajzen, I. (1980): Understanding attitudes and predicting social behavior. Upper Saddle River.
Gaudecker, H.-M. v. and Scholz, R.D. (2007): Differential mortality by lifetime earnings in Germany. Demographic Research 17 (4), 83-108.
Heidenreich, H.-J. and Nöthen, M. (2002): Der Wandel der Lebensformen im Spiegel des Mikrozensus. Wirtschaft und Statistik 1/2002, 26-38.
Himmelreicher, R./Sewöster, D./Scholz, R.D. and Schulz, A. (2008): Die fernere Lebenserwartung von Rentnern und Pensionären im Vergleich. WSI-Mitteilungen 5/2008, 274-280.
Jdanov, D.A./Scholz, R.D./Shkolnikov, V.M. (2005): Official population statistics and the Human Mortality Database estimates of populations aged 80+ in Germany and nine other European countries. Demographic Research 13, 335-362.
Kibele, E./Scholz, R.D. and Shkolnikov, V.M. (2008): Low migrant mortality in Germany for men aged 65 and older: fact or artifact? European Journal of Epidemiology 23 (6), 389-393.
Kohls, M. (2008): Leben Migranten wirklich länger? Bundesamt für Migration und Flüchtlinge. Working Paper der Forschungsgruppe des Bundesamtes / Bundesamt für Migration und Flüchtlinge No. 16.
Kreyenfeld, M. and Mika, T. (2008): Erwerbstätigkeit und Fertilität: Analysen mit der Versicherungskontenstichprobe der deutschen Rentenversicherung. Deutsche Rentenversicherung (Sonderausgabe) Band 79, 71-95.
Luy, M. (2007): Estimating the migrant survival advantage from orphanhood of second generation migrants. Rostocker Zentrum – Diskussionspapier No. 17 (November 2007).
Milewski, N. (2007): First child of immigrant workers and their descendants in West Germany: Interrelation of events, disruption, or adaptation? Demographic Research 17, 859-896.
Mönch, R. (2007): Frau Doktors unsichtbares Kind. Frankfurter Allgemeine Sonntagszeitung: June 10, 2007
Mueller, U. (2008): Argumente für die Einrichtung eines nationalen Mortalitätsregisters. RatSWD Working Paper No. 40.
Nauck, B. (2007): Immigrant families in Germany. Family change between situational adaptation, acculturation, segregation and remigration. Zeitschrift für Familienforschung 19 (1), 34-54.

Pötzsch, O. (2007): Neue Datenquelle zu Geburten und Kinderlosigkeit. Wirtschaft und Statistik 3/2007, 260-263.

Ruckdeschel, K./Ette, A./Hullen, G. and Leven, I. (2006): Generations and Gender Survey. Dokumetation der ersten Welle der Hauptbefragung Deutschland. Wiesbaden.

Schmidtke, K./Kreyenfeld, M. and Zühlke, S. (2008): Ökonomische Basis der Familiengründung – Analysen mit den Daten des Mikrozensus-Panels. [Paper presented at the „Statistische Woche", Cologne 2008].

Scholz, R.D. and Jdanov, D.A. (2006): The use of the data of the Forschungsdatenzentrum (FDZ) of the pension system in Germany – A correction method for population estimates in old age. In: DRV (Ed.): Bericht vom dritten Workshop des FDZ der Rentenversicherung (FDZ-RV). DRV-Schriften Band 55/2006, 200-211.

Schwentker, B. (2007): Ende einer Diskriminierung. ZEIT online: July 6, 2007.

Shkolnikov, V.M./Scholz, R.D./Jdanov, D.A./Stegmann, M. and Gaudecker, H.M. v. (2008): Length of life and the pensions of five million retired German men. The European Journal of Public Health 18 (3), 264-269.

Sobotka, T. (2004): Is Lowest-Low Fertility in Europe Explained by the Postponement of Childbearing? Population and Development Review 30 (2), 195-220.

Statistical Commission and UN Economic Commission for Europe/Statistical Office of the European Communities (2004): Towards possible changes to the census recommendations on families and household. Geneva.

Tölke, A. and Hank, K. (2005): Männer – Das "vernachlässigte" Geschlecht in der Familienforschung. Wiesbaden.

United Nations (UN) (2006): Conference of European Statisticians Recommendations for the 2010 Censuses of Population and Housing. Geneva

2. MEASURING COMPETENCIES

2.1 Measuring Cognitive Ability

Roland H. Grabner and Elsbeth Stern

Contact:

Roland H. Grabner
Elsbeth Stern
Swiss Federal Institute of Technology (ETH) Zurich
Institute for Behavioral Sciences
Universitätsstrasse 6
8092 Zurich
Switzerland
e-mail: grabner[at]ifv.gess.ethz.ch
 stern[at]ifv.gess.ethz.ch

Abstract

The assessment of cognitive abilities is critical in large-scale survey studies that aim at elucidating the longitudinal interplay between the individual's cognitive potential and socio-economic variables. The format of such studies calls for assessment methods that not only can be efficiently administered, but also show a high level of (psychometric) measurement quality. In consideration of recent theoretical and empirical advances in intelligence research, we recommend the implementation of tests drawing on working memory in large-scale survey studies. Working memory is a limited-capacity system for the temporary storage and processing of information that is currently considered to be the key cognitive system underlying intellectual abilities. Examples of four types of working memory tests are described and critically evaluated with regard to their psychometric quality and the need for further evaluation.

Keywords: cognitive abilities, intelligence, knowledge, information processing, mental speed, working memory

1. Research questions and theoretical developments

The analyses of gene-environment interaction and evolution are becoming more and more accepted as a research focus in the social sciences (see Spinath 2008). The basic argument is that without the "control" of genetic effects one cannot be sure that he or she is estimating unbiased socio-economic effects (Guo 2008; Diewald 2008). In this context, cognitive abilities play an important role. Cognitive abilities are the raw material for developing individual resources and are both promoted as well as constrained by socio-economic context. Research on cognitive abilities has revealed considerable associations between an individual's cognitive abilities ("general intelligence") and numerous indicators of life success – ranging from educational and vocational performance to delinquency, morbidity, and mortality (Jensen 1998; Deary et al. 2004). The causal nature of most of these correlations is still unknown, as is the mediating role of socio-economic variables. This underlines the importance of including cognitive ability measurements in large-scale survey studies to enhance our knowledge about the longitudinal interplay between individual cognitive resources and socio-economic variables.

1.1 A brief history of cognitive ability assessment

The first systematic approach to objectively measuring cognitive abilities can be traced back to Sir Francis Galton at the end of the nineteenth century (e.g., Jensen 1998). Galton developed a variety of tests to measure elementary mental functions such as sensory discrimination and perception speed, guided by the assumption that differences in intellectual ability result from a differential efficiency of the central nervous system. Galton's tests were presented to the public in his Anthropometric Laboratory at the International Health Exhibition in London. The interest into the new anthropometric measurements was enormous; between 1884 and 1890, the data of more than 9000 persons were collected. The validity of the tests for measuring cognitive abilities, however, was disappointing. The test results turned out to be only poorly correlated with commonsense criteria of intellectual abilities and educational success.

A more promising approach was pursued by Alfred Binet at the beginning of the twentieth century (1905). Commissioned by the French Ministry of Public Instruction, Binet was charged with developing a quick and reliable method of distinguishing mentally retarded children – who were not expected to profit from normal instruction in school – from those with mere behavior problems. In contrast to Galton, Binet and his colleague Simon devised a battery of tasks drawing on practical knowledge and skills rather than on elementary mental functions. Children were instructed to point at various parts of their body, name objects seen in a picture, give definitions, repeat series of digits or a complete sentence, tell the time of a clock, etc. Besides their focus on relatively practical skills, Binet and Simon's approach was innovative in that they used the children's age as an external criterion for cognitive abilities. By empirically assigning the tasks to different age groups, their intelligence scales allowed the objective assessment of whether a child was advanced or backward for his or her chronological age and, thus, to distinguish mentally retarded children from others. This comparison of mental with chronological age provided the basis for the advent of the intelligence quotient (IQ) (Stern 1912), until it was replaced by the concept of today's statistical deviation IQ (Wechsler 1944).

The Binet scales were soon translated and distributed in America and England and became the norm against which later intelligence tests were evaluated. The further development of intelligence tests was strongly related to the question of the structure of cognitive abilities. At a gross level, two different views can be distinguished. Some researchers (e.g., Jensen) emphasized the existence and importance of a general intelligence (g) factor, which was originally discovered by Spearman (1904). If a large and random sample of participants completes a number of diverse cognitive tests, the correlations among the different test scores will be almost entirely positive and, in most of the cases, of moderate size. This means that a person who does well in one test also has a high probability of achieving a good performance level in the other tests. Using statistical methods, this correlation pattern can be reduced to one single factor (the *g* factor), which usually accounts for about 50 percent of the entire test variance.

Other researchers (e.g., Thurstone or Gardner), in contrast, questioned the existence of the *g* factor. This diverging view predominantly resulted from the application of different statistical methods in analyzing cognitive test performance data or from the expansion of the intelligence concept to non-academic skills (such as interpersonal and bodily-kinaesthetic intelligence; Gardner 1983).

At present, there is a wide consensus on a hierarchical model of cognitive abilities, consisting of three levels of different generality (Carroll 1993; Gustafsson 1984). At the top and most general level is Spearman's *g* factor, reflecting the fact that diverse cognitive abilities show near-universal positive correlations.

Group factors for cognitive abilities such as fluid and crystallized intelligence are located at the second level. Fluid intelligence is conceptualized as the ability to solve novel problems and is typically assessed by tasks drawing on abstract reasoning (inductive or deductive) or complex problem solving. Crystallized intelligence reflects the breadth and depth of general knowledge and is usually measured by tests on vocabulary, spelling ability, or general information.

Finally, at the lowest level, there are specific cognitive abilities such as quantitative reasoning (for fluid intelligence) or lexical knowledge (for crystallized intelligence), accounting for variance that is neither attributable to factor *g* nor to the group factors. Although hierarchical models with *g* at the top and second- and third-order factors below might best describe the structure of individual differences in cognitive abilities, it is also widely accepted that most of the predictive value of intelligence tests derives from the *g* factor, which is strongly related to fluid intelligence (Brody 1999; Deary 1998; Jensen 1998).

1.2 Bases of cognitive abilities

Over the past decades, a great deal of research has been conducted to better understand the bases of individual differences in cognitive abilities. At present, two cognitive components are discussed that show consistent associations with intelligence and might, therefore, be considered as potential bases of human intelligence. The first component is *mental speed* (e.g., Neubauer 1995). There is a large body of evidence showing consistent negative associations between intelligence and reaction times in so-called elementary cognitive tasks (ECTs). ECTs are designed to place only minimal requirements on the participant and, thus, are less likely to be influenced by differential strategies or prior knowledge. As an example, in the letter-matching task by Posner and Mitchell (1967), the participants have to judge whether two letters are *semantically* identical or not (e.g., semantically identical: "Aa" or "AA" vs. semantically different: "Ab" or "AB"). In a meta-analysis, Neubauer (1995) reported an average correlation of -.33 between mean reaction times and psychometric intelligence test scores. This suggests that brighter individuals display a higher speed of information processing than less intelligent individuals, probably due to a more efficient functioning of their central nervous systems (Jensen 1998). A central restriction of ECTs represents the rather low effect sizes of the observed correlations. In most cases, correlations do not exceed absolute values of .30; a recent meta-analysis reports a mean correlation of -.24 (Sheppard and Vernon 2008). Thus, mental speed usually accounts for scarcely more than 10 percent of the variance in intelligence tests.

The second potential basis of individual differences in cognitive abilities is *working memory*. Working memory (WM) can be regarded as a limited-capacity system responsible for temporary storage (or maintenance) and processing of information (Baddeley 2002; 2003). The inclusion of a processing component distinguishes WM from short-term memory (STM) which only supports temporary storage of information. As an example, in a prototypical STM task (forward span), two to nine words are presented sequentially, and the participants are required to recall the words afterwards in the same order. WM tests usually require the execution of a second, additional task. In the original reading span task, for instance, participants read aloud sentences while trying to remember the last word of each sentence for later recall (Daneman and Carpenter 1980). Individuals differ in the capacity of WM, and these differences have proven to be related to several higher-order cognitive functions ranging from rather domain-specific skills (like reading comprehension; Daneman and Carpenter 1980; vocabulary learning; Daneman and Green 1986; or numeracy; De Rammelaere et al. 1999) to (domain-general) intelligence. The actual size of correlation between WM capacity and intelligence as well as the appropriate statistical approach to determine their true relationship are matters of intensive debate (Ackerman et al. 2005; Beier and Ackerman 2005; Kane et al. 2005; Oberauer et al. 2005). The current estimates range between about .40 and .80; single previous studies reported even higher correlations (up to .96) which led some authors to conclude that WM may be the psychological mechanism underlying (fluid) intelligence (Kyllonen and Christal 1990; Colom et al. 2004).

The distinction between storage and processing is also reflected in cognitive theories of WM. Probably the most prominent theory was put forward by Baddeley and colleagues already in the 1970s (Baddeley and

Hitch 1974). According to their tripartite model, WM consists of two "slave systems" which are coordinated and controlled by a third system, the "central executive." The slave systems enable the temporary storage of information and are domain-specific: phonologically coded material (verbal and numerical material) is maintained in the phonological loop, visuo-spatial information in the visuo-spatial sketchpad. The central executive component was considered to be an attention-control mechanism which is responsible for focusing attention to (task-) relevant information, dividing attention if two tasks are performed, and switching attention between different processes and information (Baddeley 2002).

There is considerable evidence that the central executive component of WM is domain-independent and drives the relationship between WM capacity and intelligence (e.g., Engle et al. 1999; Kane et al. 2004; but see also Colom et al. 2005). More specifically, Conway and colleagues (2003) regarded the "active maintenance of goal-relevant information in the face of interference" (p. 549) as the critical cognitive basis that is shared between intelligence and WM tasks. Support for their view comes from findings that individuals with high and low WM capacity also differ in the performance of low-level attention-control tasks that place practically no memory demands on the participants. In the anti-saccade task, for example, participants have to make an eye movement (saccade) in the opposite direction of a visual cue (e.g., a flashing light in the periphery). Since the reflexive response would be to orient towards the cue, the attention control demand consists of suppressing this habitual response. Individuals with higher WM capacity were found to display faster and more correct saccades than individuals with lower WM capacity.

2. Status quo

At present, numerous psychometric "intelligence tests" are available. Virtually all of the currently available market tests do a good job with measuring individual differences in cognitive abilities in that they meet the main criteria required for a psychometric test: objectivity, reliability, and validity.

A test displays *objectivity* if the result is independent of the person who administers, analyzes, and interprets the participant's performance. Objectivity is ensured by standardized instructions during administration as well as by clear-cut instructions for how test scores are determined and interpreted.

Reliability builds upon objectivity and reflects the measurement precision of a test. Reliability is never perfect (1.0) as the test performance is not only influenced by the true cognitive ability of the person but also by random factors such as momentary fluctuations of attention or mood, fatigue, etc. Usually, intelligence tests display reliabilities around .90, indicating that 10 percent of the total variance in test performance is due to random factors (i.e., measurement error) and 90 percent reflects true variance in intelligence.

Finally, the *validity* of a test reflects to what extent the test measures the trait or ability that it should measure. The validity of intelligence tests is typically evaluated by relating the performance in the test under investigation to an external criterion, either to the performance in a well-established intelligence test or to criteria such as school grades. The great success of the concept of intelligence primarily originates in the high validity of intelligence test performance for a lot of performance indicators in diverse areas of life (e.g., Jensen 1998).

In line with the originally intended purpose of intelligence tests, the strongest associations are found with educational variables. Intelligence correlates with school grades at about .50 and with years of education at about .55 (Neisser et al. 1996). Intelligence can also be regarded as a good predictor of vocational success; in a meta-analysis Schmidt and Hunter (1998) reported an average validity of .51 for overall job performance. Another quality criterion of psychometric tests is the availability of norms so that the individual test performance can be compared with the performance of an age-matched reference sample. The norms in intelligence tests allow the determination of the IQ, reflecting the standardized position of an individual relative to a reference population with a mean of 100 and a standard deviation of 15.

Given their high reliability and validity, intelligence tests can be definitively regarded as the best choice for assessing cognitive abilities. Many of the available market tests not only provide an estimate of the general intelligence of an individual (the IQ) but also inform about his or her cognitive ability structure. The Berlin Intelligence Structure Test (BIS-T) (Jäger et al. 1997), for instance, assesses three content facets (verbal, numerical, spatial-figural) and four operational facets (processing capacity, creativity, memory, and speed) of cognitive abilities with general intelligence as the integral of all ability facets.

The administration of such an intelligence structure test, however, is very costly, predominantly in terms of time. The full version of the BIS-T takes over 2 hours. But even one-dimensional intelligence tests focusing on general intelligence, such as the Raven's Advanced Progressive Matrices (Raven 1958) require a test time of at least 20-30 minutes in their short version. Thus, if we want to disentangle the impact of cognitive abilities and socio-economic effects on the outcomes of human lives, there is a strong need for the development of shorter cognitive ability assessment procedures that can be applied in large-scale surveys.

Lang and colleagues (2007) recently proposed two ultra-short tests for the measurement of intellectual abilities in the German Socio-Economic

Panel (SOEP, *Sozio-oekonomisches Panel*). One test (the symbol-digit test, or SDT) requires the fast assignment of numbers to symbols following a predefined number-symbol pairing. In the other test (the Animal Naming Task, or ANT), participants have to produce as many animal names as possible within a 90 second time interval. The reliabilities of these tests were reported to be around .90 for the SDT and around .65 for the ANT respectively. Their validities for general intelligence however, were not investigated, but can be expected to be rather low. The SDT draws on mental speed, and the performance in similar task versions was found to be only weakly related to intelligence (Conway et al. 2002). Likewise, the ANT only samples knowledge in a certain domain which turned out to be correlated only between .33 and .39 with broader vocabulary knowledge (Lang et al. 2007).

3. Future developments

In consideration of the recent theoretical insights into the cognitive bases of intelligence and the consistently strong relationship between WM capacity scores and higher-order intellectual abilities, it seems very promising to further develop short tests that draw on WM or its sub-components. In contrast to intelligence problems, WM tasks typically require only simple cognitive operations whose sequence is highly restricted by the instructions. The difficulty of working-memory tasks arises from the additional load on some facets of the cognitive architecture (Süß et al. 2002). The reading-span task described above, for example, requires continuous updating of the content of WM (with every sentence one new word needs to be memorized) and the maintenance of the words in spite of interference (i.e., reading sentences aloud).

Overall, WM tests offer the following advantages:

(1) They take a shorter time to administer than intelligence tests.

(2) Most of the tasks involved can be implemented in computer-aided testing environments.

(3) According to current research, they tap the central basis of cognitive abilities.

(4) WM tasks are typically less influenced by prior knowledge than intelligence tests.

(5) The limiting factor of WM capacity (central executive) seems to be domain-independent.

At this point, the development of WM tests lags far behind the development of intelligence tests. WM span tasks (such as the reading span task described above) are among the first WM measures to have been developed and are already well understood, a fact reflected in the existence of methodological reviews and user guides (Conway et al., 2005). The psychometric quality of other WM tasks (e.g., focusing on executive processes) is more difficult to evaluate due to the scarcity of studies with larger samples. In the following, an overview of WM tasks that could be employed in the large-scale survey studies is provided.

3.1 Traditional WM span tasks

Since the early reading-span task described above, several versions of WM span tasks have been developed. Three key tasks can be identified (Conway et al. 2005; Kane et al. 2004). In the (newer version of the) *reading span task*, the participant is presented with a meaningful or meaningless sentence and a to-be-remembered letter (e.g., "We were fifty lawns out at sea before we lost sight of land. ? X"). The participant's task is to read the sentence, judge whether it makes sense or not, read, and remember the letter. The *operation span task* requires judging the correctness of an arithmetic equation and to remember an additionally presented word (e.g., "Is (6 x 2) − 5 = 7? class"). In the *counting span task* participants have to count the number of dark blue circles in displays with other distracting objects (dark blue squares and green circles) and to remember the counted number. All these tasks are designed to force storage of information in the face of processing.

Conway et al. (2005) emphasized three critical task features: first, rehearsal must be avoided by presenting the next stimulus immediately after completion of the preceding one. Second, the timing of the task needs to be adaptive. Both properties are met in current computer versions in which the to-be-remembered stimulus is displayed immediately after completion of the interfering task (e.g., judging the correctness of an equation). Third, the number of stimuli within one item needs to be sufficient. A range from two to five stimuli per item turned out to be adequate for most college students.

The administration of a WM span task with 12 items (with two to five stimuli each) including instruction and practice items takes about 10 minutes. Besides the verbal WM span measures described above, a number of figural-spatial versions have been devised (Kane et al. 2004). As an example, in the symmetry span task, participants have to judge whether a figure in an 8 x 8 matrix is symmetrical or not and to remember the position of a red square in a subsequently presented 4 x 4 matrix.

The reliabilities of WM span tasks are usually in the range between .70 and .90, suggesting good measurement precision for a single test. Their validity for intelligence test performance lies around .50 (Kane et al. 2004).

3.2 Transformation span tasks

In this type of WM task, participants are not required to simultaneously store and process information but rather to perform some mental transformation on the stored information. A promising example is the alpha span task, originally developed by Craik (1986). Three to seven words are successively presented to the participant who is required to memorize them. After presenting the last word, the participant has to repeat the first letter of each word in alphabetical order, thus requiring an alphabetical reordering of the memorized words. Süß et al. (2002) presented one item with three words and two items with four, five, six, and seven words each, requiring an estimated test time of about 5 minutes including instruction.

The authors reported a reliability of .81 and a validity for general intelligence of .55. Other studies, however, report much lower validities for similar transformation tasks (e.g., the backward span task requiring the recall of the presented words in reverse order; Engle et al. 1999).

3.3 Dynamic WM tasks

A separate class of WM tasks that are frequently used in neuroscience research require the continuous monitoring and updating of the maintained information. In the prominent n-back task, a list of stimuli (words, numbers, or figures) is successively presented, and the individual has to continuously report whether each stimulus matches the one that had appeared n items ago (n-back). In a 2-back task, for instance, participants have to continuously maintain the last 2 stimuli of the list which means that they have to update the content of their WM with every new stimulus and to drop out the least recent one. Even though the n-back task is considered the gold standard in neuroscience research, there is mixed empirical evidence on the question whether this task draws on the same cognitive resources as the well-established WM span tasks (Conway et al. 2005; Kane et al. 2007).

Kane et al. (2007) investigated the construct validity of the n-back task in a sample of 129 young adults and found that the performance in the operation span task and the n-back task was only weakly associated (correlations did not exceed .25). In addition, both tasks accounted for independent variance in general intelligence. These findings suggest that the n-back task does not measure the same WM processes as the operation span task.

3.4 Executive control tasks

Executive processes related to attentional control are central in Baddeley's model of WM and are assumed to play a critical role in the relationship between WM capacity and intelligence. The development of tasks demanding these processes without strong reliance on storage, however, appears to be a great challenge. Süß et al. (2002) as well as Oberauer et al. (2003) have devised tasks requiring task set switching (i.e., the inhibition of an active action schema and the selection of another). In the numerical switching task by Süß et al. (2002), displays with varying number of digits are presented. The participant is required to alternate between reading the digits and counting them; the specific task to be performed is displayed on the top of the display. In the figural version, a round and an angular figure appears in each display, one left and one right. Participants have to indicate the side of either the angular or the round figure. Finally, in the verbal version, participants have to switch between two semantic categories in determining the presentation side of words. Similar to the transformation span tasks, these tasks can be administered within a few minutes.

Süß et al. (2002) report reliabilities between .78 (numerical) to .94 (verbal and figural) and validities between .33 (figural) and .58 (numerical) for general intelligence. Later research, however, has questioned the construct validity of these tasks as they are only weakly related to traditional WM span tasks (Oberauer et al. 2003; 2005) and reflect processing speed more strongly than reasoning abilities (Süß et al. 2002).

4. Conclusions and recommendations

In the past decades, considerable advances have taken place in understanding the individual differences in cognitive abilities and in the development of psychometric tests for ability assessment. Present research regards WM, reflecting a limited-capacity system supporting temporary storage and processing of information, as the cognitive key system underlying intellectual abilities.

Measures of WM capacity have been found to display substantial correlations with several domain-specific intellectual abilities as well as with intelligence, representing the epitome of domain-general cognitive abilities. Thus, tests assessing WM capacity or executive functions appear to be a more promising method for the cognitive ability assessment in large-scale survey studies than tests focusing on mental speed or surface knowledge in a certain domain.

Several candidate tasks have been described above which can be administered in considerably shorter time than psychometric intelligence tests. In addition, their task characteristics allow the presentation in computer-aided testing environments. The Internet seems to offer the ideal infrastructure for the implementation of the cognitive ability screening. The coverage is very high, and it is meanwhile not longer only accessible from the personal computer (at home or at the office) but increasingly also from mobile devices such as netbooks, mobile phones, or personal digital assistants (PDAs). So it becomes ever more unproblematic to administer those tests in large-scale surveys.[1]

However, it should be noted that most of these WM tasks are still in the development phase, and that studies with larger samples, which would allow a more accurate evaluation of their reliability and (construct) validity, are very scarce. Thus, some initial steps would be very helpful. Although the future challenge is to improve the psychometric quality of these tests, they also need to be administered in large-scale surveys. In fact, the data of the large-scale surveys can further contribute to their improvement. The actual reliability of these tests could be accurately quantified and norms for age-matched reference samples, which are presently almost completely missing for WM tests, could be easily established. In addition, the data from large-scale studies can also inform about their validity for indicators of life success. Parallel to these criteria, their validity for intelligence needs to be further investigated.

---

[1] The tests could be offered and advertized, for instance, in virtual social networks such as Facebook.

References:

Ackerman, P.L./Beier, M.E. and Boyle, M.O. (2005): Working memory and intelligence: The same or different constructs? Psychological Bulletin 131, 30-60.
Baddeley, A.D. (2002): Is working memory still working? European Psychologist 7 (2), 85-97.
Baddeley, A.D. (2003): Working memory: Looking back and looking forward. Nature Reviews Neuroscience 4 (10), 829-839.
Baddeley, A.D. and Hitch, G.J. (1974): Working memory. In: Bower, G.A. (Ed.): Recent advances in learning and motivation, Vol. 8. New York.
Beier, M.E. and Ackerman, P.L. (2005): Working memory and intelligence: Different constructs. Reply to Oberauer et al. (2005) and Kane et al. (2005). Psychological Bulletin 131 (1), 72-75.
Binet, A. (1905): New methods for the diagnosis of the intellectual level of subnormals. L'Année Psychologique 12, 191-244. [Translated in 1916 by Kite, E.S. in: Development of intelligence in children. Vineland, NJ: Publications of the Training School at Vineland].
Brody, N. (1999): What is intelligence? International Review of Psychiatry 11 (1), 19-25.
Carroll, J.B. (1993): Human cognitive abilities: A survey of factor analytic studies. Cambridge.
Colom, R./Flores-Mendoza, C./Quiroga, M.A. and Privado, J. (2005): Working memory and general intelligence: The role of short-term storage. Personality and Individual Differences 39 (5), 1005-1014.
Colom, R./Rebollo, I./Palacios, A./Juan-Espinosa, M. and Kyllonen, P.C. (2004): Working memory is (almost) perfectly predicted by g. Intelligence 32 (3), 277-296.
Conway, A.R.A./Cowan, N./Bunting, M.F./Therriault, D.J. and Minkoff, S.R.B. (2002): A latent variable analysis of working memory capacity, short-term memory capacity, processing speed, and general fluid intelligence. Intelligence 30 (2), 163-183.
Conway, A.R.A./Kane, M.J. and Engle, R.W. (2003): Working memory capacity and its relation to general intelligence. Trends in Cognitive Sciences 7 (12), 547-552.
Conway, A.R.A./Kane, M.J./Bunting, M.F./Hambrick, D.Z./Wilhelm, O. and Engle, R.W. (2005): Working memory span tasks: A methodological review and user's guide. Psychonomic Bulletin & Review 12 (5), 769-786.
Craik, F.I.M. (1986): A functional account of age differences in memory. In: Klix, F. and Hagendorf, H. (Eds.): Human memory and cognitive capabilities. Amsterdam.
Daneman, M. and Carpenter, P.A. (1980): Individual differences in working memory and reading. Journal of Verbal Learning and Verbal Behavior 19, 450-466.
Daneman, M. and Green, I. (1986): Individual-differences in comprehending and producing words in context. Journal of Memory and Language 25, 1-18.
De Rammelaere, S./Stuyven, E. and Vandierendonck, A. (1999): The contribution of working memory resources in the verification of simple mental arithmetic sums. Psychological Research-Psychologische Forschung 62 (1), 72-77.

Deary, I.J. (1998): Differences in mental abilities. British Medical Journal 317, 1701-1703.
Deary, I.J./Whiteman, M.C./Starr, J.M./Whalley, L.J. and Fox, H.C. (2004): The Impact of Childhood Intelligence on Later Life: Following up the Scottish Mental Surveys of 1932 and 1947. Journal of Personality and Social Psychology 86 (1), 130-147.
Diewald, M. (2008): Zwillings- und Adoptivkinder-Stichproben für soziologische Analysen? Zum Ertrag verhaltensgenetischer Ansätze für sozialwissenschaftliche Fragestellungen und Erklärungen [Using twin and adoptive child samples for sociological analysis? On the value of behavioral genetics approaches for social scientific issues and interpretations]. DIW Research Notes 27.
Engle, R.W./Tuholski, S.W./Laughlin, J.E. and Conway, A.R.A. (1999): Working memory, short-term memory, and general fluid intelligence: A latent-variable approach. Journal of Experimental Psychology 128 (3), 309-331.
Gardner, H. (1983): Frames of mind. New York.
Grigorenko, E.L. (2007): How Can Genomics Inform Education? Mind, Brain, and Education 1 (1), 20-27.
Guo, G. (2008): Introduction to the special issue on society and genetics. Sociological Methods & Research 37 (2), 159-163.
Gustafsson, J.-E. (1984): A unifying model for the structure of mental abilities. Intelligence 8, 179-203.
Jäger, O.A./Süß, H.M. and Beauducel, A. (1997). Berliner Intelligenzstruktur-Test [Berlin Intelligence Structure Test]. Göttingen.
Jensen, A.R. (1998): The g factor: The science of mental ability. Westport.
Kane, M.J./Conway, A.R.A./Miura, T.K. and Colflesh, G.J.H. (2007): Working memory, attention control, and the N-back task: A question of construct validity. Journal of Experimental Psychology-Learning Memory and Cognition 33 (3), 615-622.
Kane, M.J./Hambrick, D.Z. and Conway, A.R.A. (2005): Working memory capacity and fluid intelligence are strongly related constructs: Comment on Ackerman, Beier, and Boyle (2005). Psychological Bulletin 131, 66-71.
Kane, M.J./Hambrick, D.Z./Tuholski, S.W./Wilhelm, O./Payne, T.W. and Engle, R.W. (2004): The generality of working memory capacity: A latent-variable approach to verbal and visuospatial memory span and reasoning. Journal of Experimental Psychology: General 133, 189-217.
Kyllonen, P.C. and Christal, R.E. (1990): Reasoning ability is (little more than) working memory capacity?! Intelligence 14, 389-433.
Lang, F.R./Weiss, D./Stocker, A. and von Rosenbladt, B. (2007): Assessing Cognitive Capacities in Computer-Assisted Survey Research: Two Ultra-Short Tests of Intellectual Ability in the German Socio-Economic Panel (SOEP). Schmollers Jahrbuch 127 (1), 183-192.
Neisser, U./Boodoo, G./Bouchard, T.J./Boykin, A.W./Brody, N./Ceci, S.J./Halpern, D.F./Loehlin, J.C./Perloff, R./Sternberg, R.J. and Urbina, S. (1996): Intelligence: Knowns and unknowns. American Psychologist 51, 77-101.
Neubauer, A. (1995): Intelligenz und Geschwindigkeit der Informationsverarbeitung. Wien.

Oberauer, K./Schulze, R./Wilhelm, O. and Süss, H.M. (2005): Working memory and intelligence – their correlation and their relation: Comment on Ackerman, Beier, and Boyle (2005). Psychological Bulletin 131, 61-65.

Oberauer, K./Suss, H.M./Wilhelm, O. and Wittman, W.W. (2003): The multiple faces of working memory: Storage, processing, supervision, and coordination. Intelligence 31 (2), 167-193.

Posner, M.I. and Mitchell, R.F. (1967). Chronometric analysis of classification. Psychological Review 74 (5), 392-409.

Raven, J.C. (1958): Advanced Progressive Matrices. London.

Schmidt, F.L. and Hunter, J.E. (1998): The Validity and Utility of Selection Methods in Personnel Psychology: Practical and Theoretical Implications of 85 Years of Research Findings. Psychological Bulletin 124 (2), 262-274.

Sheppard, L.D. and Vernon, P.A. (2008): Intelligence and speed of information-processing: A review of 50 years of research. Personality and Individual Differences 44 (3), 535-551.

Spearman, C. (1904): "General intelligence", objectively determined and measured. American Journal of Psychology 15, 201-293.

Spinath, F.M. (2008): Improvements and Future Challenges in the Field of Genetically Sensitive Sample Designs. RatSWD Working Paper No. 45.

Stern, W. (1912): Die psychologischen Methoden der Intelligenzprüfung. Leipzig.

Süß, H.-M./Oberauer, K./Wittmann, W.W./Wilhelm, O. and Schulze, R. (2002): Working memory capacity explains reasoning ability – and a little bit more. Intelligence 30, 261-288.

Wechsler, D. (1944): Measurement of adult intelligence. Baltimore.

2.2 Measuring Cognitive Competencies

Ulrich Trautwein

Contact:

Ulrich Trautwein
University of Tuebingen
Institute of Education
Europastraße 6
72072 Tuebingen
Germany
e-mail: ulrich.trautwein[at]uni-tuebingen.de

Abstract

The systematic assessment of key cognitive competencies is of great scientific and societal interest, as is the availability of high-quality data on cognitive competencies. In order to make well informed decisions, politicians and educational authorities need reliable data about the effectiveness of formal and non-formal educational environments. Similarly, researchers need strong data to test complex theoretical models about how individual biographies are shaped by the interplay between individual and institutional affordances and constraints.

There are countless datasets that offer some form of information on competencies, such as the respondents' years at school and their school grades. Such data are relatively easy to collect. When it comes to making informed political and educational decisions, however, there are increasing calls for a more systematic use of standardized competency tests. Yet the production, storage, and use of standardized test data on competencies in specific domains is expensive, complex, and time-consuming.

This advisory report argues that there is a paucity of adequate data on cognitive competencies in important domains, and especially a lack of longitudinal data from standardized competency tests. Moreover, in the case of many important questions there are no good alternatives to high-quality standardized tests of cognitive competencies. Finally, it outlines some challenges in the construction and application of standardized competency tests and makes several recommendations.

Keywords: cognitive competencies, assessment, intelligence, school grades

1. The need for systematic assessments of cognitive competencies

Competencies are abilities that allow an individual to master the complex demands of particular contexts. There are many components of competent performance, including knowledge, cognitive and practical skills, attitudes, emotions, values, and motivations (for a detailed definition of competencies, see Rychen and Salganik 2001; Weinert 2001). The scope of this report is restricted to cognitive competencies that are taught and learned in formal and non-formal learning environments. These cognitive competencies include, for instance, subject-specific knowledge, reading and mathematical literacy, computer literacy, and job-related knowledge.

The systematic and rigorous assessment of key cognitive competencies is of high scientific and societal relevance, as is the availability of high-quality data on cognitive competencies. It is now widely accepted that in modern knowledge societies the economic prosperity of individuals, communities, and countries is associated with the cognitive competencies an individual has acquired. In order to make well informed decisions, politicians and educational authorities need high-quality data about the effectiveness of formal and non-formal educational environments. Similarly, researchers need strong data to test complex theoretical models about how individual biographies are shaped by the interplay between individual and institutional opportunities and constraints. Some questions that require high-quality data on cognitive competencies include: has mathematics and reading literacy generally increased or decreased among high school students in recent years and decades (see Becker et al. 2006)? Are *Abitur* (the school-leaving certificate in the academic track) standards and related competence levels comparable across the German federal states, or *Länder* (Trautwein et al. 2007)? Do female and male students and students from different family and ethnic backgrounds have the same access to high-quality education? Which domain-specific competencies are important for success in different domains at university and in the workplace (e.g., Nagy 2006)?

There is general agreement about the importance of assessing and documenting the competence levels achieved by learners in formal and non-formal learning environments; innumerable datasets offer some form of information on competencies. For instance, official statistics report the number of students who leave school with specific school-leaving certificates; school authorities document the distribution of school grades assigned within different grade levels and school types in each school year; and scientific studies ask students about their academic standing relative to their peers.

Such data on school-leaving certificates, grades attained in various learning environments, and self-reports of achievement are relatively easy to collect. They can be used to inform many questions and add to the body of knowledge about educational systems. When it comes to making informed political and educational decisions, however, there are a growing number of calls for a more systematic use of standardized competency tests. In the wake of international benchmarking studies such as PISA (OECD Programme for International Student Assessment) (Baumert et al. 2001), there has been increased scientific interest in Germany in the conceptualization, psychometric modeling, operationalization, and description of cognitive competencies. The production, storage, and use of standardized test data on competencies in specific domains is expensive, complex, and time-consuming, however. The question therefore arises of whether standardized competency tests might be replaced by cheaper and more readily available alternatives.

This report argues that there is a paucity of adequate data on cognitive competencies in important domains. There is, in particular, a lack of longitudinal data from standardized competency tests, and for many important questions there are no good alternatives to high-quality standardized tests of cognitive competencies. This chapter is structured as follows: the following section provides a short description of standardized cognitive competency tests. Section 3 highlights the differences between domain-specific cognitive competencies and intelligence tests. Three frequently used but qualitatively different approaches to measuring cognitive competencies (grades or certificates; self-reports of competence; self-concepts) are compared and contrasted in section 4, and their advantages and disadvantages discussed. Challenges in the construction and application of standardized competency tests are subsequently outlined. Finally, several recommendations are made. For the sake of brevity and drawing from available data, the chapter draws primarily on data collected in schools and universities.

2. Standardized tests of cognitive competencies

Standardized tests of cognitive competencies use student responses to certain stimuli (or "items") to infer competence levels. Carefully constructed standardized assessments such as those used in the PISA study are based on a conceptual model of what is being assessed, and their construction and evaluation is informed by psychometric models and state-of-the-art statistical analyses. Psychometrically constructed standardized tests have to fulfill a number of criteria. Most importantly, they must be objective (i.e., the resulting test scores must be independent of the person who administers and scores the test), reliable (i.e., the test must be internally consistent and give consistent results over time), and valid (i.e., the test must actually measure what it sets out to measure). When standardized tests with high validity are used, the competence levels of all test takers can be compared directly, independent of where they live or their learning environment. Some well-known standardized tests of cognitive competencies include the TOEFL test assessing the English-language skills of non-native speakers and the PISA tests assessing verbal, mathematical, and scientific literacy.

Tests can be distinguished along several dimensions. *Curriculum-oriented tests* are based on material defined in the learners' curriculum. For instance, a curriculum-oriented mathematics test would implement tasks covered in the mathematics curriculum. In contrast, tests such as those implemented in PISA, which are based on the *literacy concept*, probe for competencies considered essential for full participation in society. Ideally, tests of cognitive competencies allow comparison across test takers (*"norm-referenced tests"*) and inform on the individual test taker's absolute level of competence (*"criterion-referenced tests"* or tests with *"competence levels"*).

Standardized tests such as PISA have helped to close the knowledge gap surrounding the cognitive competencies of various student groups (e.g., boys vs. girls; students with different immigration status). For instance, findings have shown that immigrant groups are differentially successful in different school systems. When carefully constructed, standardized tests have a high degree of fairness because all students receive a similar "treatment". Moreover, it is possible to discern items that may place some subgroups at a disadvantage and to eliminate these items from the test.

A specific advantage of carefully constructed standardized competency tests is that they allow the development of competence to be tracked over time. Forms of "anchoring" allow test scores to be compared longitudinally, provided that the conceptual model is good and the quality of measurement is high.

To date, longitudinal data on the development of cognitive competencies over time are in short supply in Germany. Although some datasets contain such information, they tend to be relatively small, restricted to some areas of Germany, and/or the competency tests used are of limited quality (Blossfeld 2008). The National Educational Panel Study (NEPS; Blossfeld 2008) commencing in 2009 will help to overcome this deficit by examining students' mathematics, verbal, scientific, and ICT literacy as well as their literacy in English as a foreign language. Furthermore, some domain-specific tests will be administered to subgroups (e.g., business students).

3. Cognitive competencies vs. intelligence

The construction of psychometrically sound tests of domain-specific cognitive competencies is complex and expensive. Some critics have questioned whether these efforts are strictly necessary or whether cheaper alternatives are available. One proposed alternative is to use measures of general, decontextualized cognitive dispositions, such as intelligence (Rindermann 2006). Rindermann claimed that the competency tests used in large-scale assessment studies such as TIMSS (Trends in International Mathematics and Science Study) and PISA measure a single cognitive ability that is practically identical to general intelligence. Given the relatively high intercorrelations observed between mathematics literacy, reading literacy, and cognitive ability, it might therefore be argued that it would be easier and cheaper to use intelligence tests instead of tests of domain-specific competencies in large-scale assessments.

This line of argumentation has major limitations, however (Baumert et al. 2007). First, there are clear conceptual differences between domain-specific cognitive competencies and general, decontextualized cognitive dispositions such as intelligence (e.g., in processes of knowledge acquisition and information processing and in dependence on the quality of educational environments). Second, although there is a statistically significant correlation between intelligence and scores on domain-specific competency tests, the results of construct validation studies provide strong empirical support for the multidimensionality (i.e., empirical separability) of cognitive measures applied in large-scale educational assessments (see Baumert et al. 2007). Third, evaluations of the educational effectiveness of a specific school, state, or country differ across domains, as shown, for instance, by a recent study (Trautwein et al. 2007) comparing educational outcomes at the end of the academic track in two German states (Baden-Württemberg and Hamburg). Although the Baden-Württemberg students clearly outperformed the Hamburg students in mathematics, with an effect size of Cohen's $d = .98$, the respective differences in English achievement ($d = .16$) and reasoning ($d = .07$) were negligible. Fourth, intelligence and domain-specific competencies differentially predict academic outcomes such as success at university (Nagy 2006).

Taken together, domain-specific cognitive competencies are theoretically and empirically separable from general, decontextualized cognitive dispositions such as intelligence, which are less amenable to educational interventions (see the expertise by Stern, in this publication). Tests of intelligence cannot replace psychometric tests of cognitive competencies in assessments of educational effectiveness.

4. Other measures of cognitive competencies

4.1 Grades and (school-leaving) certificates

Many datasets contain information on teacher-assigned school grades and/or (school-leaving) certificates. For example, official statistics in Germany document in detail a broad range of certificates acquired in formal education (e.g., school-leaving certificates; university diplomas; completed apprenticeships). Similarly, many datasets contain information on teacher-assigned grades or teacher evaluations of student progress (e.g., school grades; university grades). Without question, grades and certificates affect individuals' academic biographies and long-term success on the job market, and thus represent important information that should be documented. However, to what extent can these easily available data replace information obtained using complex and expensive standardized achievement tests? Three aspects are critical here: reference group effects, the association between background variables and teacher-assigned grades, and the reliability of self-reports.

4.1.1 Reference group effects: restricted comparability

Prior research has clearly documented that achievement scores collected via standardized achievement tests correlate only moderately with teacher-assigned school grades (Baumert et al. 2003; Ingenkamp 1971). Although teacher-assigned grades typically give a rather accurate (but not perfect) estimate of the position of each student within a class, teachers' differential grading standards mean that grades do not typically provide a valid basis for gauging achievement across classes or schools. The majority of teachers in Germany and in many other education systems do not use an absolute criterion for achievement when assigning grades (as is the case in standardized achievement tests). Rather, they tend to grade on a norm-referenced basis (Ingenkamp 1971), with the best student in the class receiving a very good grade and the weakest student a bad grade or a "fail." As a consequence, "grading-on-a-curve" effects can be observed in most schools in Germany. The size of the correlation between school grades and standardized competency tests typically ranges from about $r = .30$ to $r = .60$ (e.g., Baumert et al. 2003; Trautwein et al. 2007). When individual achievement is controlled, higher class-average achievement is associated with lower grades (Trautwein et al. 2006). Clearly, it is important to distinguish theoretically and empirically between these two indicators of achievement. Furthermore, teacher-assigned grades cannot easily be used to measure learning gains over time.

Given that school grades are not on a common metric across teachers and schools, it is hardly surprising that students who acquire the same school-leaving certificate in different schools or states do not necessarily exhibit the same level of cognitive competencies. Moreover, although qualifications such as the *Hauptschulabschluss* (lower-school certificate) and *Abitur* (certificate giving access to higher education) are awarded at various school types in Germany, little is known about the comparability of these certificates across school types.

4.1.2 Effects of sex, family background, and immigration status

Teacher-assigned grades have been shown to be influenced not only by cognitive competencies, but also by various student characteristics. Importantly, it is well documented that teacher evaluations of students' cognitive competencies are associated with the students' family backgrounds (e.g., Baumert et al. 2001) and influenced by teachers' gender stereotypes. Teachers' evaluations of students from immigrant families are also likely to be affected by stereotypes, but these effects may be compensated by grading leniency. More empirical studies are needed in this context.

4.1.3 Validity of self-report data

Information on school grades and certificates can be collected via either self-reports or school records. Are student self-reports of their grades reliable indicators of their actual grades or should school records be consulted? Several recent studies have reported high associations between self-reported and teacher-reported grades. For instance, Dickhäuser and Plenter (2005) reported a correlation of $r = .88$ for the last mathematics grade. It must be noted, however, that participants in these studies did not have anything to gain from reporting higher school grades than they actually attained. In a different context, the association between self-reported and teacher-reported grades may well be lower.

4.2 Self-assessments of cognitive competencies: restricted validity and group differences

A quick, easy, and direct approach to assessing cognitive competencies is to ask individuals for an "objective" evaluation of their own competencies. For instance, students might be asked to report their competencies in logical reasoning or grammar (e.g., Kruger and Dunning 1999) and these self-ratings are then correlated with data from a standardized test or an expert rating. As shown in a meta-analysis by Mabe and West (1982), the resulting associations are typically moderate in magnitude and vary from study to study. Mabe and West were able to identify some characteristics of studies that moderate the association between self-ratings and other indicators of competencies. Higher associations are found, for instance, if respondents expect their self-reports to be compared with objective evaluations and if some guarantee of anonymity is given in the study instructions. Even under such favorable conditions, however, the associations between self-reported competencies and external information on these competencies were far from perfect. Looking at various domains, moreover, Kruger and Dunning (1999) showed that people with low abilities in these domains were particularly likely to overestimate their abilities. Kruger and Dunning attributed these misjudgments partly to the lower metacognitive competencies of these respondents. Taken together, the validity of self-evaluations of cognitive competencies is restricted.

4.3 Domain-specific self-concepts

Domain-specific self-concepts are another frequently used construct in many empirical studies. Domain-specific academic self-concepts reflect a person's self-evaluation regarding a specific academic domain or ability (see Trautwein et al. 2006). These self-concepts are usually collected via self-report measures. Typical self-concept items are "I am quite good at mathematics" (mathematics self-concept) and "I have a poor vocabulary" (verbal self-concept). Although self-concepts share some similarities with self-evaluations of competencies, there is one crucial difference. Self-concept instruments ask specifically for a person's subjective self-evaluation, not for an "objective" self-evaluation. It is therefore not surprising that these instruments elicit external frame of reference effects (e.g., respondents compare their accomplishments with those of their friends or schoolmates rather than using an "average" comparison group) as well as internal frame of reference effects (e.g., respondents compare their competencies in mathematics with their competencies in English), yielding a complex pattern of associations with other assessments of competencies. Domain-specific self-concepts have proven to be predictive with regard to the competency development. However, they are no substitute for standardized tests of cognitive competencies.

4.4 The need for multiple indicators: a research example

Which indicator of cognitive competence is the best predictor of a successful transition from school to university or the labor market? Modern educational systems work on the assumption that competence levels predict future success in higher education and the workforce. However, it has also been argued (e.g., Solga 2005) that employers rely heavily on the type of school-leaving certificate as a "signal" when hiring apprentices or employees. These certificates are more easily accessible than, for instance, test scores, and may thus have more influence in determining applicants' professional success than their actual level of competence. There is indeed some reason to believe that – given their easy availability to employers – school-leaving certificates and school grades have more pronounced effects on success in the application process, whereas competencies predict success during vocational training and occupational careers. As plausible as this reasoning may seem, however, there is a need for empirical studies that empirically tease apart the confounding effects of certificates and competence levels cross-sectionally and longitudinally. Moreover, there is a need to distinguish among facets of cognitive abilities. Some studies from the United States seem to indicate that general ability (intelligence) plays a more important role in training success than do specific competencies (e.g., Ree and Earles 1991). Convincing empirical support for such a pattern of results is still lacking in the German context, however, primarily because of the lack of datasets including information on competencies measured by standardized tests as well as teacher-assigned grades and certificates.

5. Standardized competency tests: Challenges

The empirical assessment of competencies is more difficult than it may appear at first glance. Theoretically and empirically sound competence models are required as a basis for the development of measurement procedures. The systematic integration of theoretical frameworks, psychometric models, and measurement approaches often requires interdisciplinary cooperation, which introduces another level of complexity. The challenges facing longitudinal competence measurement outlined below are among those currently being addressed.

As yet, there is disagreement over which *domains of cognitive competencies* can be meaningfully measured by standardized tests and how differentiated the measurement should be. These questions are, for instance, very relevant to job-related cognitive competencies. Similarly, with regard to *criterion-referenced tests and competence levels*, there is also some disagreement over which competence levels can be considered sufficient, which levels can the majority of learners realistically achieve, and who should be responsible for establishing these standards in different domains.

Another challenge pertains to *possible positive and negative effects of competence testing*. What are the effects of systematic competence assessment in learning environments? For instance, do teachers make changes to the learning content covered or to their methods of teaching in response to the introduction of competency tests, and are the overall effects positive or negative? Moreover, to date, in standardized educational assessments such as PISA, *unmotivated test taking* might have been the exception rather than the rule in Germany (Baumert and Demmrich 2001). However, it is not clear if this may change in the future if standardized competency tests are administered more frequently.

Finally, *longitudinal measurement* is one of the most difficult and crucial challenges in the context of competence testing. Challenges include choosing an appropriate linking procedure, possible retest effects, the danger of ceiling and floor effects, and the question of whether the construct being measured remains the "same" over time (e.g., are multiplication tables in elementary school and complex numbers at upper secondary level part of the "same" mathematics?).

6. Recommendations

(1) Broader use of standardized tests of cognitive competencies can help to evaluate the effectiveness of educational institutions. Wherever feasible, standardized competency tests – in addition to or instead of measures such as teacher-assigned grades and self-assessed competence – should be used.

(2) Some effort should be put into investigating domains of cognitive competencies for which competency tests can be easily constructed (based on either the curriculum or the literacy concept) and domains for which standardized competency tests are not feasible.

(3) There is a need for more high-quality tests that are available for researchers for use in their own projects (e.g., intervention studies). In this sense, there should be broader access not only to data but also to measurement instruments.

(4) When reporting "competence" data, researchers should always specify whether standardized tests or alternatives were used. It is especially important to critically address possible reference group effects and whether specific groups (e.g., gender or immigrant groups) might be at a disadvantage.

(5) Concerted efforts should be made to strengthen expertise in constructing and interpreting standardized competency tests in the scientific and non-scientific communities. There has been considerable progress in recent years (e.g., the German Research Foundation's (DFG, *Deutsche Forschungsgemeinschaft*) priority program on "Competence models for recording individual learning outcomes and for reviewing educational progress"), but more expertise is needed across a broader population of researchers.

(6) Ways must be found of linking competence data collected in empirical studies (e.g., school achievement studies) with other datasets (e.g., data available from national agencies).

References:

Baumert, J./Brunner, M./Lüdtke, O. and Trautwein, U. (2007): Was messen international Schulleistungsstudien? – Resultate kumulativer Wissenserwerbsprozesse. Eine Antwort auf Heiner Rindermann [What do international student achievements measure? – Results of cumulative learning. A reply to Heiner Rindermann.] Psychologische Rundschau 58, 118-129.

Baumert, J. and Demmrich, A. (2001): Test motivation in the assessment of student skills: The effects of incentives on motivation and performance. European Journal of Psychology of Education 16, 441-462.

Baumert, J./Klieme, E./Neubrand, M./Schiefele, U./Schneider, W./Stanat, P./Tillmann, K.-J. and Weiß, M. (Eds.) (2001): PISA 2000: Basiskompetenzen von Schülerinnen und Schülern im internationalen Vergleich [PISA 2000: Student literacy in international comparison]. Opladen.

Baumert, J./Trautwein, U. and Artelt, C. (2003): Schulumwelten: Institutionelle Bedingungen des Lehrens und Lernens [School environments: Institutional conditions of learning and instruction]. In: Baumert, J./Artelt, C./Klieme, E./Neubrand, M./Prenzel, M./Schiefele, U./Schneider, W./Tillmann, K.J. and Weiß, M. (Eds.): PISA 2000: Ein differenzierter Blick auf die Länder der Bundesrepublik Deutschland. Opladen.

Becker, M./Trautwein, U./Lüdtke, O./Cortina, K.S. and Baumert, J. (2006): Bildungsexpansion und kognitive Mobilisierung [Educational expansion and cognitive mobilization]. In: Hadjar, A. and Becker, R. (Eds.): Die Bildungsexpansion. Erwartete und unerwartete Folgen. Wiesbaden.

Blossfeld, H.-P. (2008): Education as a lifelong process. A proposal for a National Educational Panel Study (NEPS) in Germany. Bamberg.

Dickhäuser, O. and Plenter, I. (2005): "Letztes Halbjahr stand ich zwei": Zur Akkuratheit selbst berichteter Noten [On the accuracy of self-reported school marks]. Zeitschrift für Pädagogische Psychologie 19, 219-224.

Ingenkamp, K. (1971): Die Fragwürdigkeit der Zensurengebung [The dubiousness of school grades]. Weinheim.

Kruger, J. and Dunning, D. (1999): Unskilled and unaware of it: How difficulties in recognizing one's own incompetence lead to inflated self-assessments. Journal of Personality and Social Psychology 77, 1121-1134.

Mabe, P.A. and West, S.G. (1982): Validity of self-evaluation of ability: A review and meta-analysis. Journal of Applied Psychology 67, 280-296.

Nagy, G. (2006): Berufliche Interessen, kognitive und fachgebundene Kompetenzen: Ihre Bedeutung für die Studienfachwahl und die Bewährung im Studium [Vocational interests, cognitive and scholastic abilities: Their role in choice of major and success at university]. Unpublished doctoral dissertation, Freie Universität Berlin.

Ree, M.J. and Earles, J.A. (1991): Predicting training success: Not much more than g. Personnel Psychology 44, 321-332.

Rindermann, H. (2006): Was messen internationale Schulleistungsstudien? Schulleistungen, Schülerfähigkeiten, kognitive Fähigkeiten, Wissen oder allgemeine Intelligenz? [What do international student assessment studies measure? School

performance, student abilities, cognitive abilities, knowledge, or general intelligence?]. Psychologische Rundschau 57, 69-86.
Rychen, D.S. and Salganik, L.H. (2001): Defining and selecting key competencies. Göttingen.
Solga, H. (2005): Ohne Abschluss in die Bildungsgesellschaft: Die Erwerbschancen gering qualifizierter Personen aus soziologischer und ökonomischer Perspektive [Entering the education society without qualifications. The employment opportunities of lower qualified individuals from the sociological and economic perspectives]. Opladen.
Trautwein, U./Köller, O./Lehmann, R. and Lüdtke, O. (Eds.) (2007): Schulleistungen von Abiturienten: Regionale, schulformbezogene und soziale Disparitäten [School achievement of students at Gymnasium schools: Regional, track-specific, and social disparaties]. Münster.
Trautwein, U./Lüdtke, O./Marsh, H.W./Köller, O. and Baumert, J. (2006): Tracking, grading, and student motivation: Using group composition and status to predict self-concept and interest in ninth grade mathematics. Journal of Educational Psychology 98, 788-806.
Weinert, F.E. (2001): Vergleichende Leistungsmessung in Schulen – eine umstrittene Selbstverständlichkeit [Comparative measurement of achievement in schools]. In: F. E. Weinert (Ed.): Leistungsmessungen in Schulen. Weinheim.

2.3 Measuring Vocational Competencies

Martin Baethge and Lena Arends

Contact:

Martin Baethge
Sociological Research Institute (SOFI)
University of Goettingen
Friedlaenderweg 31
37085 Goettingen
Germany
e-mail: martin.baethge[at]sofi-uni-goettingen.de

Abstract

International large scale assessment programmes mostly concentrate on measuring and comparing general competences of students in compulsory education or adults in everyday life; concepts for measuring young adults' competences in specific vocational domains are lacking. The paper addresses the need for competence measurement in vocational education and training and illustrates future demands for the implementation of an international large-scale assessment of vocational education and training (VET-LSA). It discusses possible measurement approaches for vocational competences and outlines why methods for measuring internal conditions (dispositions) by tests instead of external measurement by observation are the favourite option. The measurement of cross-country differences in the level and distribution of vocational competences could break new grounds and provide standardised and internationally comparable indicators for benchmarking of VET and a basis for adequate classification of learning outcomes in classification systems, such as the EQF.

Keywords: international large scale assessment, vocational education and training, VET, competence measurement, VET-LSA, large-scale assessment in VET

1. The political dimension of measurement in Vocational Education and Training (VET)

The increasing internationalization of labor markets and vocational education and training (VET), as well as recent initiatives to improve transparency in VET such as the proposals for a European Qualification Framework (EQF) and a European Credit System for Vocational Education and Training (ECVET), have shifted the debate on transparency and quality standards in VET to the policy level.

The European Commission has put forward the ambitious economic and social goal of becoming "the most competitive and dynamic knowledge-based economy in the world" (European Commission 2004). In the field of VET this aim is being pursued through the Copenhagen Process. The European Commission's proposal for a EQF offers opportunities to increase mobility and enhance permeability between educational sectors. The recent progress report by the European Commission outlining advancement towards the Lisbon objectives emphasized that "internationally comparable large scale assessments programmes often concentrate on general competences (e.g., reading, information processing, numeracy and problem solving) whereas many employers argue that [...] there is an increasing need to conduct surveys which focus as well on the assessment of vocational skills and competences" (European Commission 2008: 61).

There are no indicators for international benchmarking of VET (see Higher Education below). The International Standards Classification of Education (ISCED, UNESCO 2006) does not provide a tool for comparing the performance of VET systems in different countries because the levels for classifying different VET programs are not transparent enough[1] (Mueller and Klein 2008).

An internationally comparable, objective, valid, and reliable assessment of cross-country differences in the level and distribution of vocational competences could provide a scientific basis for the debates on the EQF and the ECVET. The results would allow for a better classification of national educational programs within existing classification systems (e.g., NQF/EQF, ISCED) on an empirical basis.

2. Current state of competence measurement in VET

2.1 Large-scale assessments in education

There is a general consensus that indicators for measuring quality are key instruments for improving the quality of education and training necessary for the good governance of education systems and structures (European Commission – DG EAC 2004). Internationally comparative studies (e.g., PISA,[2] IALS[3]) provide standardized and internationally comparable indicators that give insight into the factors influencing the development of competences of students in compulsory education and adults in everyday life. These indicators provide policy-makers with a tool on which to base future policy choices.

The measurement of competences has become an instrument for benchmarking the performance of educational systems. During the past fifteen years, considerable experience has been gained in the development and implementation of large-scale assessments in education. International tests have been developed for measuring basic skills of students in compulsory education and generic skills of adults in everyday life; however, tests for measuring competences in specific vocational areas are still missing.

There are three major surveys for the measurement of basic skills of students in compulsory education: the TIMSS[4] survey, which focuses on the mathematics and science aptitudes of students in the fourth and the eighth

---

[1] In particular ISCED 3B/3C, 4 and 5B.
[2] The Programme for International Student Assessment (PISA) started in the mid 1990s.
[3] The International Adult Literacy Survey (IALS) was administered in 1994, 1996, and 1998.
[4] The Trends in International Mathematics and Science Study (TIMSS) was implemented first in 1995.

grade in a number of countries; the PIRLS[5] survey, in which reading literacy among fourth graders is measured; and the PISA study, which assesses the literacy, numeracy, science, and problem-solving performance of fifteen-year-olds. PISA has become a major policy tool for measuring student competencies in an internationally comparative perspective, for establishing benchmarks of educational improvement, and for representing the strengths and weaknesses of national educational systems.

For measuring the skills of adults, two surveys have been implemented: the IALS survey was the first attempt to implement a large-scale adult skills assessment based on tests on an international basis (OECD and Statistics Canada 2005). The Adult Literacy and Lifeskills (ALL) Survey builds on the IALS survey by extending the range of competency domains and improving the quality of assessment methods (Murray and Clermont 2005). The ALL Survey[6] is the most comprehensive program for measuring adult skills (16–65 years) in the following domains:

- prose literacy,
- document literacy,
- numeracy, and
- problem solving.

The ALL framework is based on an all-encompassing skill typology involving a comprehensive groups of skills relevant for everybody in a variety of life contexts (e.g., community, home, work). Skills for work are based on employability skill models derived from general skill categories that are applicable across a variety of working situations.

Building on the ALL survey, the OECD has launched an international study of financial literacy of adults in twelve OECD countries. The assessment is focused on financial literacy in the context of everyday life among adults as consumers, workers, and citizens (OECD 2005; 2008).

Following up on the IALS and ALL surveys, the OECD is also currently developing a strategy for assessing the literacy skills of adults, including familiarity with information and communication technologies, and the ability to manage information, construct new knowledge, and communicate with others (Schleicher 2008). In the first cycle, measurement in PIAAC[7] will be implemented in three areas:

---

5 The Progress in International Reading Literacy Study (PIRLS) was implemented in 2001.
6 The assessment was conducted in 2003 in people's homes in seven countries: Bermuda, Canada, Italy, Norway, Switzerland, United States, Nuevo León.
7 Programme for the International Assessment of Adult Competencies. PIAAC is currently being implemented with a view to undertake a first assessment in 2011. The main survey design is based on a minimum main study sample size per country of 5,000 adults, aged 16-64.

- *Direct assessment of cognitive skills.* Integrated measurement of broad literacy competence encompassing the range of performance from mastery of the basic building blocks of literacy to the capacity of effectively managing complex information processing tasks embedded in an Information Technology (IT) setting. Up to four areas of competences will be assessed, including "Problem-solving in a technology-rich environment," "Literacy," "Numeracy," and "Literacy component skills."
- *Indirect assessment of skills used in the workplace.* The JRA[8] module seeks to assess the level and use of a number of generic skills such as communication, presentation, and teamwork skills in the workplace. With the JRA module, individuals will be asked a set of questions relating to their job and the requirements of that job in terms of the intensity and frequency of the use of certain skills.[9]
- *Background questionnaire.* The aim here is to collect information relating to the antecedents and outcomes of adult literacy competences, including information on literacy practices and familiarity with and usage of information technology.
- None of the illustrated surveys for cross-country differences measuring the level and distribution of competences of students and adults is focused on the assessment of domain-specific competences in specific vocational areas.

Approaches for measurement in VET

The term "competence" is one of the most internally diverse concepts in the field of education and educational policy. Efforts to define the term have remained unsuccessful because a variety of topics are addressed under the heading of "competence" (e.g., Descy and Tessaring 2005; Arends 2006). In some contexts "competences" refer to the internal conditions of individuals that allow them to master tasks in different situations successfully. In others, "competences" refer to the tasks and situational requirements themselves. To compare the performance of different VET systems and programs, we differentiate between these two approaches for measuring competences: the measurement of the *internal conditions* that allow the individual to master (occupational) tasks successfully, and the measurement of the individual's

---

8   Jobs Requirement Approach (JRA).
9   Given that the approach is untested in an international survey, a pilot of the JRA module is currently taking place to test the validity and reliability of this approach in a cross-country and cross-cultural context.

external performance in different (occupational) situations. Following PISA, we are in favor of approaches that measure internal conditions in different occupational fields. This approach perceives individuals as carriers of competences who have developed the ability and willingness to successfully apply their knowledge, abilities, and experiences to authentic (occupational) situations. To measure internal conditions, however, internationally valid models of the structure and development of competences in specific domains (e.g., literacy, numeracy in PISA) at different levels of complexity are needed.[10]

The development and implementation of internationally valid tests for measuring internal conditions is considered a time-consuming, expensive, and methodologically challenging task (e.g., item development in PISA). To overcome this, many skills surveys have tried to identify less time-consuming and cheaper approaches to measuring competence on the basis of external performance. Typically, external measurement is implemented through the direct observation of individuals during work performance (e.g., work samples) or self-assessment of work activities (e.g., JRA approach). For example, the UK Skills Survey (Ashton et al. 1999; Felstead et al. 2002) and the O*NET database (US Occupational Information Network) are based on the Job Requirement Approach (JRA), a self-assessment instrument for individuals to rate their competences at the workplace.

Toolsema (2003) adopted the Generalized Work Activities (GWA) concept from O*NET[11] for identifying and comparing competences. In O*NET, GWA are "aggregations of similar job activities/behaviors that underlie the accomplishment of major work functions" (Jeanneret et al. 1999: 106). The central assumption is that work behavior is not necessarily linked to specific tasks and techniques and, therefore, can be located at a higher level of aggregation. Activities are considered competence indicators at a higher level of abstraction, indicating the purpose of competences. Toolsema derived six competence categories – social, participative, cognitive, physical-technical, learning, and employability – and linked them with GWAs. The instrument was applied for measuring cognitive, affective, and meta-cognitive aspects of performance at different levels of abstraction in the field of Higher Education, not in VET.

A different external approach was used in the VQTS model.[12] Here, the aim was to provide a structured description of work-related competences and their acquisition. By using a competence matrix, which displays the competences of a specific occupational field at different levels, the model aims to provide an instrument for VET providers to transfer and recognize competen-

---

10 In VET, models for measuring competences in different vocational areas are currently being developed (e.g., Winther and Achtenhagen 2008; Nickolaus et al. 2008).
11 Occupational Information Network from the US.
12 Leonardo da Vinci project "VQTS – Vocational Qualification Transfer System".

ces acquired within the official VET systems in foreign countries (Luomi-Messerer and Markowitsch 2006; Markowitsch et al. 2006). The model can be used for descriptions of qualification requirements in different occupational fields, but not for measuring individuals' abilities to successfully master occupational tasks in different occupational situations.

Approaches for external measurement of vocational competences are not recommendable for measuring competences in specific vocation areas:

(1) Self-assessment instruments, such as JRA or GWA, produce a picture of individual activities within a particular workplace, not of the competences used to successfully master occupational tasks in different situations.[13] Individual competences cannot be inferred from descriptions of performance in different working environments because work activities are linked to concepts of specific work organizations, which differ between firms and occupational sectors as well as between national settings.

(2) The greatest disadvantage of self-assessment as a method of obtaining data is the greater chance of measurement error, resulting from a more or less "intentional" manipulation of answers by respondents and unintentional discrepancies between the real and reported values, resulting in low reliability. To measure and compare young adults' performance across countries in a valid and reliable way, objective measures of internal conditions are highly recommendable.

(3) Performance-based measurement of specific, workplace-related tasks must be based on an agreement of the performance levels in different occupations in terms of occupational tasks, and must be relevant in specific vocational areas across countries.

(4) The overarching goals of VET are not sufficiently incorporated into external approaches: although aspects of work-related qualifications are included, those pertaining to individual development and societal participation are not.

(5) Some external approaches are very time-consuming, which is problematic in large-scale assessments in terms of reaching valid, reliable, and objective results at a low cost (e.g., skills tests in the World Skills competition amount to twenty hours total testing time).

(6) The most striking criticism that has been made of external measurement is the fact that data of students' performance cannot be linked to the organization and contents of VET and that it is not possible to assess the development of individual learning during VET.

---

13 GWAs could be used for triangulations in a large-scale assessment of VET.

3. Future demands for competence measurement in VET

To use competence measurement as an instrument for international benchmarking of VET systems and programs, we need an international large-scale assessment based on concepts for measuring internal dispositions using Item Response Theory models (Rost 2006). During its council presidency, the German government (Federal Ministry of Education and Research) adapted the discussion on quality in VET to launch an initiative for an "International Large-Scale Assessment of Vocational Education and Training" (VET-LSA).[14] The main benefit of a VET-LSA is to expand the knowledge for steering VET processes at different policy levels. The proposed VET-LSA will increase valid and reliable steering knowledge:

- to determine the relationship between individual (biographic) characteristics, training forms, and skill building;
- to improve transparency with regard to the performance of European VET programs;
- to link VET outcomes and institutional orders of VET systems;
- to determine the correlation between the competences certified in final examinations and competences actually measured;
- to assess the comparative strength and weaknesses of different training forms in different countries to learn from each other;
- to classify different vocational training qualifications in international classification schemes (ISCED, EQF) in order to support the comparability of certification processes at the European level;

and others.

The development and implementation of this type of international large-scale assessment of VET is much more complex than it is for compulsory education. Whereas international student assessment programs (e.g., PISA) are based on well-grounded research traditions and internationally validated concepts (e.g., world curriculum for mathematics, standards in education), VET cannot draw upon any similarly comparable concepts. In a VET-LSA, the focus is on the measurement of competences in specific occupational domains rather than on all occupations. Contrary to international assessment programs of students and adults (e.g., PISA, PIAAC), VET-LSA does not

---

14 On the policy level, the following representatives from European countries and institutions are members in the international Steering Group: Sweden, Denmark, Norway, Slovenia, Finland, Switzerland, Germany, Austria, Spain, CEDEFOP, ETF, EC.

claim to be an overall representative survey. The aim is to rather include some of the most important industrial–technical, commercial–administrative, and care occupations in the sample (Baethge et al. 2008; Baethge et al. 2007; Baethge et al. 2006).

VET systems in different countries or even in sectors within the same country are unlikely to be drawn into convergence through the Copenhagen Process (2002); there is a variety of outcomes rather than conformity. To measure the same construct, common elements in VET have to be identified at the outset. A VET-LSA feasibility study, which is currently being developed in cooperation with experts from all participating countries,[15] will provide a clear picture of those national programs that are comparable and might be included in an international comparison (Baethge et al. 2008). As a first step in making comparisons, international classification systems (ISCED, ISCO, O*NET) are used as a frame of reference for identifying a set of core occupational tasks and qualification requirements within all participating countries, not as a tool for competence measurement.

One of the central requirements for an international comparison of VET with a focus on competence measurement is a common understanding of the appropriate objectives for VET. This common understanding must be mutually developed, taking into consideration different scientific and policy perspectives. The definition of objectives for VET can be based on either a relatively limited or a broader approach. A broader approach encompasses individual competences in specific occupational domains and competences that individuals need to participate effectively as members of a flexible, adaptable, and competitive workforce and as lifelong learners. In a limited approach, competences are rather focused on the requirements of the workplace. In accordance with the ongoing scientific discussion, three objectives for educational systems at the systemic level were determined with an international group of VET researchers (Baethge et al. 2007). These objectives function as reference points for the definition of competences in vocational education and training and for the development of measurement tools in a VET-LSA:

- First, the development of individual vocational adjustment from an individual user perspective that takes into account the critical aspect of autonomy in working situations (individual perspective).

- Second, the ability to deal with today's labor market requirements and develop one's career (human resources perspective).

- Third, the ability to participate in organizational processes of work and work-related interactions (social perspective).

---

15   Sweden, Denmark, Norway, Finland, Slovenia, Switzerland, Austria, and Germany. France and Spain are interested in participating in the VET-LSA.

To determine to what extent VET systems are able to achieve these objectives, they have been operationalized within the concept of the VET-LSA in cooperation with experts from different countries. The concept of the VET-LSA comprises two major areas of measurement:

- *Vocational and occupational domain-specific competences* refer to young adults' abilities to successfully apply their knowledge and experience to authentic occupational situations in specific vocational fields (Car Mechatronics, Electricians, Business & Administration, Social & Health Care).
- *Cross-occupational competences* are related to successful performance in the labor market. They refer to the notion of key skills or "core competencies," which comprise knowledge, skills, and abilities, for example, about the structures of organizations and labor markets, or acting autonomously in work environments.[16]

To illuminate interdependencies between domain-specific vocational and basic competencies, a third area is included in the concept for VET-LSA:

- *Basic competences*, such as reading, writing, and mathematics, which are being tested in international programs for student or adult assessments.

In addition to the measurement of young adults' competences in VET, institutional and individual contextual factors impacting the development of competences during VET are included in the concept for the VET-LSA:

Institutional conditions on a macro and meso level refer to

- coordination and steering (actors in VET and their responsibilities, e.g., state or social partners),
- standards and norms (e.g., curricula and exams),
- resources (e.g., financing, professionalism of teaching staff), and
- institutional cooperation of educational service providers.

Whereas institutional conditions of VET should be measured in terms of average conditions in occupational fields (not at the institutional level) on the basis of expert interviews, organizational conditions of VET should be measured in terms of young adults' perceptions derived from questionnaires.

---

16 The measurement approach for cross-occupational competences in VET-LSA differs from the approach for generic workplace skills in PIAAC. Whereas in PIAAC assessment is based on self-assessment of work activities with the JRA approach, cross-occupational competences in VET-LSA will be assessed on the basis of approaches for internal conditions.

Individual conditions of educational development and background consist of:
- socio-economic status of the family (including migration),
- social and cultural capital of young adults and their families,
- educational and career development,
- information behavior and learning activities (including non-formal learning activities), and
- educational or career aspirations.

For the quality of educational processes, the following aspects are considered important:
- a focus on problem solving and task complexity within occupational contents,
- variability (multiple working tasks and tools),
- possibilities for independent task solving,
- support,
- learning climate,
- team integration, and
- quality control.

An international large-scale assessment of vocational education and training will provide a number of indicators to compare and evaluate VET systems and institutional arrangements in VET according to quality, including young adults' competence levels in different competence domains, and information about occupations and their relation to individual and institutional factors, among others.

References:

Arends, L. (2006): Vocational competencies from a life-span perspective: Theoretical considerations and practical implications for an international large-scale assessment of vocational education and training. Norderstedt.

Ashton, D./Davies, B./Felstead, A. and Green, F. (1999): Work Skills In Britain. Oxford.

Baethge M./ Arends, L. and Winther, E. (2008): First international workshop Feasibility Study VET-LSA, Discussion paper, workshop 3.-4. July, 2008 in Bonn. SOFI Göttingen.

Baethge, M./Achtenhagen, F. and Arends, L. (2008): How to Compare the Performance of VET Systems in Skill Formation. In: Mayer, K.-U. and Solga, H. (Eds.): Skill Formation – Interdisciplinary and Cross-National Perspectives. New York.

Baethge M./Achtenhagen, F./Arends, L./Winther, E./Nickolaus, R./Gschwendtner, T./Onna, M. van/Béguin, A./Sibberns, H. and Watermann, R. (2007): Concept for an International Large Scale Assessment of Vocational Education and Training (VET-LSA). Working paper for the international workshop, 29.-30. October, 2007 in Bonn. SOFI Göttingen.

Baethge, M./Achtenhagen, F./Arends, L./Babic, E./Baethge-Kinsky, V. and Weber, S. (2006): PISA-VET. A Feasibility-Study. Stuttgart.

Copenhagen Declaration (2002): Declaration of the European Ministers of Vocational Education and Training, and the European Commission, convened in Copenhagen on 29 and 30 November 2002, on enhanced European cooperation in vocational education and training. http://ec.europa.eu/education/pdf/ doc125en.pdf.

Descy, P. and Tessaring, M. (2005): The value of learning: evaluation and impact of education and training: third report on vocational training research in Europe: synthesis report. Luxembourg: Office for official publications of the European Communities (Cedefop reference series; 61).

European Commission (2004): Maastricht communiqué on the future priorities of enhanced European co-operation in vocational education and training: a review of the Copenhagen declaration of 30 November 2002. Brussels.

European Union (2008): The Bordeaux Communiqué on enhanced European cooperation in vocational education and training. http://www.eua.be/ fileadmin/user_upload/files/Newsletter_new/Bordeaux_Communique_EN.pdf. [Last visited: 03/10/2010].

Felstead, A./Gallie, D. and Green, F. (2002): Work Skills In Britain 1986-2001. Nottingham.

Helsinki Communiqué (2006): The Helsinki Communiqué on Enhanced European Cooperation in Vocational Education and Training. Communiqué of the European Ministers of Vocational Education and Training1, the European Social partners and the European Commission, convened in Helsinki on 5 December 2006 to review the priorities and strategies of the Copenhagen Process. http://ec.europa.eu/education/policies/2010/doc/helsinkicomen.pdf. [Last visited: 03/10/2010].

Jeanneret, P.R./Borman, W.C./Kubisiak, U.C. and Hanson, M.A. (1999): Generalized Work Activities. In: Peterson, N.G./Mumford, M.D./Borman, W.C./Jeanneret,

P.R. and Fleishman, E.A. (Eds.): An occupational information system for the 21st century: The development of O*NET. Washington.

Luomi-Messerer, K. and Markowitsch, J. (Eds.) (2006): VQTS model. A proposal for a structured description of work-related competences and their acquisition. Vienna: 3s research laboratory.

Markowitsch, J./Becker, M. and Spöttl, G. (2006): Zur Problematik eines European Credit Transfer System in Vocational Education and Training (ECVET). In: Grollmann, P./Rauner, F. and Spöttl, G.; (Eds.): Europäisierung Beruflicher Bildung – eine Gestaltungsaufgabe. Hamburg.

Mueller, W. and Klein, M. (2008): Von Schmollers-Vorlesung 2008: Schein oder Sein: Bildungsdisparitäten in der europäischen Statistik. Eine Illustration am Beispiel Deutschlands. Schmollers Jahrbuch 128 (4), 511-543.

Murray, T.S. and Clermont, Y. (2005): The origins and objectives of the ALL study. In Murray, T.S./Clermont, Y. and Brinkley, M.: Measuring adult literacy and life skills. New frameworks for assessment. Ottawa.

Nickolaus, R./Gschwendtner, T. and Geißel, B. (2008): Modellierung und Entwicklung beruflicher Fachkompetenz in der gewerblich-technischen Erstausbildung. Zeitschrift für Berufs- und Wirtschaftspädagogik 104 (1), 48-73.

OECD (2005): Improving financial literacy: Analysis of issues and policies. Paris.

OECD (2008): Improving financial education and awareness on insurance and private pensions. Paris.

OECD and Statistics Canada (2005): Learning a Living. First results of the adult literacy and life skills survey. Paris.

Rost, J. (2006): Using Item-Response-Theorie for measuring vocational competences in an international large-scale assessment in VET – Expert report. In: Baethge, M./Achtenhagen, F./Arends, L./Babic, E./Baethge-Kinsky, V. and Weber, S. (Eds.): PISA-VET. A Feasibility-Study. Stuttgart.

Schleicher, A. (2008): PIAAC: a new strategy for assessing adult competencies. International Review of Education.

Toolsema, B. (2003): Werken met competenties. Naar een instrument voor de identificatie van competenties. Enschede.

UNESCO (2006): ISCED 1997 International Strandard Classification of Education. Re-edition. http://www.uis.unesco.org/TEMPLATE/pdf/isced/ISCEDA.pdf.

Winther, E. and Achtenhagen, F. (2008): Kompetenzstrukturmodell für die kaufmännische Bildung. Adaptierbare Forschungslinien und theoretische Ausgestaltung [Competence model in the field of business and administration: state of the art and directions for further research]. Zeitschrift für Berufs- und Wirtschaftspädagogik 104 (4), 511-538.

2.4 Measuring Social Competencies

Ingrid Schoon

Contact:

Ingrid Schoon
Institute of Education
University of London
Department of Quantitative Social Science
20 Bedford Way
London WC1H 0AL
UK
e-mail: I.Schoon[at]ioe.ac.uk

Abstract

What are social competencies? How can they be measured? Do they remain stable over time? This report examines the difficulties encountered conceptualizing and measuring social competencies at different developmental stages and in changing social contexts. Existing measures and available data sources are reviewed and recommendations are made for future developments in data provision, data usage, and data access.

Keywords: social competence, social skills, social relationships and interaction

1. Measuring social competencies

Social competencies have been identified by the European Commission as one of the benchmark indicators of prosperity and well-being that must be targeted for improvement in Member States (EU 2005). Social competencies can be broadly defined as the capabilities that enable individuals "to live together in the world" (Arendt 1958), comprising aspects of interpersonal, intercultural, social, and civic competencies. Beyond such a broad definition, however, general social competencies are difficult to define because the skills and behaviors needed for living together in the world and for achieving social tasks and outcomes vary with age and with the demands of particular situations. The notion of social competence is of interest to social scientists across disciplines, since it relates to adaptive functioning in a variety of contexts and across the lifespan. Social competencies reflect adjustment within the family, school, work, in society at large, and to old age. Therefore, more context-specific definitions of the construct are required, in addition to a greater focus on particular facets of social competence, such as empathy, self control, trust, respect for other people, and civic engagement. In recent years, the study of social competencies has received increased attention from policy-makers and social scientists across disciplines, partly due to increased concerns about the lack or erosion of social competencies in modern society (see for example Putnam 2000).

1.1 Conceptual issues

A major concern for empirical research is that social competencies are generally not well defined or measured. Social competencies comprise interactions between individual characteristics, social demands, and situative characteristics. They have to be understood as relative, since very different kinds of social competencies are required and valued in different contexts

(Argyle et al. 1985). Behaviors that are functional in one context might be dysfunctional in another, implying that the assessment of social competencies involves culturally based value judgments. These values, however, are subject to change. For example, as a consequence of the massive economic transformations that have taken place there, new behaviors and qualities – such as assertiveness and autonomy – are now required in China to be successful, whereas characteristics that used to be beneficial for adjustment – such as obedience to authority – are now perceived as problematic (Chen and French 2008).

Social competencies are conceptualized differently across disciplines, and even within disciplines there is no consensus about their exact definition. Within psychology, for example, social competencies are defined variously as personality traits (Sarason 1981) that can manifest themselves in different capabilities such as empathy, tolerance, and conscientiousness; as the ability to cooperate; as a dynamic construct involving successful adjustment to and interaction in given social conditions (Argyle 1994; Tajfel 1981); as people's beliefs about their own efficacy (Bandura 1997), and as social (Gardner 1999) or even emotional intelligence (Goleman 1995). In a pedagogical context it refers to lifelong, intercultural, and social learning. In economics, social competencies are sometimes used to refer to "soft skills" comprising abilities such as flexibility, working in a team, and motivating colleagues and clients. Economic terms such as "social capital" are used in sociology and the social sciences in general to describe resources arising from social relationships (Putnam 2000; Halpern 2005). Given this variety of definitions it is necessary to establish a unifying working definition that acknowledges differences in focus, and which specifies particular domains of manifestation as well as specific components and skills. To avoid confusion researchers must be clear about their theoretical orientation and must identify the context and focus of their assessments.

1.2 Research questions

Development of competencies. Social competencies change over the life course and depend on the development of capabilities such as social awareness, social skills, and self-confidence. For example, young children learn to play games with others, such as peek-a-boo or let's-pretend games, but in the process also learn important forms of self-control, including patience, sharing, and temper management, as well as learning to empathize with others. Later on they have to develop more integrated forms of self-regulation, with an emphasis on "fitting in" and achievement, as well as increased coordination of social skills and understanding of social scripts as they unfold (Saarni 2000; Waters and Sroufe 1983). Certain behaviors may be appropriate at particular ages but not at others. We still know relatively little about the developmental antecedents, or about the outcomes of social competencies in areas such as health, well-being, socio-economic attainment, and social integration. Questions that need to be addressed include concerns with how social competencies are expressed at different periods during the life course, but also whether there are stages in life when it is too early to expect a sense of social responsibility or empathy. Are there particularly sensitive periods of heightened awareness? What is the potential for developing social competencies over the life course? To answer questions about the development and growth of social competencies, and to assess continuity and change in development over time, it is vital to be able to draw on longitudinal data that follows individuals from an early age onwards. Furthermore, there must be agreement on the key indicators of social competencies at different life stages based on a thorough theoretical understanding of human development in context.

Biological aspects. There may be links between social competencies and other enduring personality characteristics as well as genetic factors that shape social interactions. However, there is still little understanding of the association of social competencies and genetic factors or physiological measures of neural efficacy (Flashman et al. 1998; Grigorenko 2000; Bechara et al. 2000). Nor do we yet know whether there are some basic physical and psychological needs that have to be fulfilled before social competencies can be developed.

Social change. In recent years concerns have been raised about the erosion of social competencies as a consequence of socio-historical change and increasing globalization. Some have argued that there has been an increasing instrumentalization and individualization of social relationships (Putnam 2000), while others have emphasized the emergence of new values and lifestyles with greater tolerance for ethnic, cultural, and sexual diversity, more issue-oriented forms of participation, greater emphasis on self-expression, and a search for the meaning and purpose of life (Inglehart 1997). Until recently it has not been possible to analyze the linkages between macro-social change and individual level attitudes due to the lack of reliable time-series data measuring certain concepts repeatedly across many different societies, or large-scale longitudinal studies following the development of social competencies within individuals over time and across different birth cohorts. Today, however, a number of large-scale longitudinal studies following individual lives over time as well as international panel studies are accessible, such as the European Values Study and the World Values Survey (WVS), both of which have been used to test assumptions about changing social values and competencies (Arts and Halman 2004; Inglehart 1997).

Context dependency. Social competencies are essentially relational, describing how individuals behave within the context of interpersonal and group relationships. Characteristics of both the relationships in which individuals engage and their context offer opportunities to acquire and express social competencies. How are competencies influenced by interactions with family members, peers, at school or at work, or in one's neighborhood? What are the factors and processes that foster and promote social competencies? To answer these questions it is vital to assess information about contextual as well as individual characteristics. Questions about the transgenerational transmission of social competencies and values, a process not yet fully understood, require the assessment of social competencies across generations as well as a consideration of socialization practices and the availability of social support.

Another area of inquiry concerns general versus context-specific manifestations of social competence. To what extent can social competencies be generalized across groups and communities? How do opportunities, norms, and expectations for social connectedness and participation influence the development of social competencies over the life course? Key context-related indicators that must be considered include measures of social status (comprising socio-economic as well as family status, education, and income), gender, culture, and ethnicity, formal and informal settings, as well as age. Questions to be addressed by researchers include, for example, whether the gender or cultural differences that are often noted in the expression and/or manifestation of social competencies are a product of measurement, norms and socialization influences, or something else.

1.3 Measurement

There is no established consensus about how to measure social competence. The assessment of social competencies can comprise a variety of methods, ranging from self-ratings or self-reports of behavior, values, and motivations; direct behavioral observations (in natural situations or under experimental conditions); behavior rating scales (to be completed by parents, teacher, employer, subordinates, or self); the use of vignettes; interviewing; make-believe tasks and role-play; hypothetical scenarios; the interpretation of video clips; social network analysis and sociometric approaches; to computer simulations.

A widely used instrument to assess personality characteristics such as agreeableness, conscientiousness, or extraversion is the "Big Five" inventory and its abbreviated forms (Costa and McCrae 1992; Gosling et al. 2003; *McCrae and Costa 2004*). Other widely used self-reported measures are the Rosenberg Self-Esteem Scale (Rosenberg 1979), measures of self-efficacy (Bandura 1997; Schwarzer 1993) or locus of control (Rotter 1990), or the Interpersonal Reactivity Index (Davis 1983) that measures both cognitive and affective aspects of dispositional empathy. Useful scales for the assessment of social adjustment in children and adolescents are the social competence inventory (Rydell et al. 1997), the self-control rating scale (Kendall and Wilcox 1979), the child behavior checklist (Achenbach and Howell 1993), and the Strengths and Difficulties Questionnaire (SDQ), which contains subscales measuring peer problems and prosocial behavior (Goodman 2001). These questionnaires are by no means a complete list of available instruments. They are intended as examples of the many ways it is possible to conceptualize and operationalize social competencies. Generally it is best to select measures geared toward the context being addressed. There are also widely used single-item measures that are often included in large-scale surveys, which tap into conceptions of generalized trust (most people can be trusted), reciprocity, social networks and support, or social participation.

Concerns have been raised about the consistency and reliability of self-assessment as well as biases in reporting (Hagerty et al. 2007). Single-item measures, although attractive, are only suitable for the assessment of constructs that are simple and unambiguous. They are otherwise limited in several respects: they provide only one chance to capture a complex concept, they are likely to miss differences at the individual level, and they might be "contaminated" by the context in which they are collected. Psychometric scales comprising multiple items to measure a specific dimension – such as social intelligence, social responsibility, assertiveness, or empathy – are more reliable yet often take a longer time to complete and without abbreviation are not suitable for large-scale surveys. The same applies to attempts to measure social competencies on the basis of assessments in experimental settings, make-believe scenarios, or interpretations of video clips, which usually take more time to collect. A compromise might be to use or to develop brief multi-item scales for specific competencies. Another major concern is the lack of clarity or agreement on what indicators are relevant to establish construct validity. Definitions either focus on internal processes or external outcomes, although both aspects are important. Ideally the measurement of social competencies should involve different assessment modes – combining self-reports, rating scales completed by others, and observational data to obtain reliable and valid measures. Instead of direct assessments, multiple measures could be used as indicators of latent constructs, which would also facilitate comparative approaches of assessment and research.

2. Status quo: Databases and access

Free web-based access to national and international studies is available through a variety of social science data archives across Europe and the US. The UK based *Economic and Social Data Service (ESDS)* provides support for secondary use and facilitates access to an extensive range of key quantitative and qualitative economic and social data. The ESDS Qualidata archive provides access to qualitative data, such as the study "Inventing Adulthoods" that explores social relationships and interactions among young people living in the UK,[1] or the study, "Quality of Life in Older Age,"[2] providing information on social networks and support.

ESDS also assists users locating and acquiring international survey data,[3] as well as longitudinal data.[4] Data collections include, for example, the 1958 National Child Development Study (NCDS), the 1970 British Cohort Study (BCS70), the British Household Panel Survey (BHPS), the English Longitudinal Study of Ageing (ELSA), the Families and Children Study (FACS), the Longitudinal Study of Young People in England (LSYPE), and the Millennium Cohort Study (MCS). These studies contain a wide range of data on social competencies, comprising assessments in early childhood, adolescence, and adulthood. The MCS, for example, a study of over 18,000 children born between 2000-2002 includes measures of early social competence, using the Strength and Difficulties Questionnaire as well as a make-believe task (Sally-Anne task). NCDS and BCS70 contain measures of early behavioral adjustment, using the Rutter A Scale.[5] NCDS, a fifty-year-old study, contains measures of the NEO "Big Five" personality inventory. Most of the studies include assessments of social attitudes in adulthood, such as attitudes towards equality and fairness and information about social networks and civic activities – although mostly as single-item statements.

The *Council of European Social Science Data Archives (CESSDA)* is an umbrella organization for social science data archives across Europe. The CESSDA Portal[6] is a gateway to many kinds of research data and metadata, including, for example, international panel studies that have adopted a collaborative approach with other countries to provide comparative data. Studies accessible via this portal include the International Social Survey Programme (ISSP), the European Social Survey (ESS), the European Values Study, the World Values Surveys (WVS), and the International Social Justice Project (ISJP). All of these surveys contain items assessing generalized social trust

---

1 http://www.esds.ac.uk/findingData/snDescription.asp?sn=5777
2 http://www.esds.ac.uk/findingData/snDescription.asp?sn=5237
3 http://www.esds.ac.uk/international/
4 http://www.esds.ac.uk/longitudinal/
5 http://www.data-archive.ac.uk/doc/5805/mrdoc/ pdf/RutterBehaviourQuestions. pdf
6 http://damad.essex.ac.uk/portal/cessda.html

(using a question such as "most people can be trusted"), frequency of contact with friends and relatives, strengths of social networks, participation in social and civic activities, social attitudes, attitudes towards gender equality, and social justice.

The *Inter-University Consortium for Political and Social Research (ICPSR)*, based at the University of Michigan[7] is an organization of member institutions working together to acquire and preserve social science data, to provide open and equitable access to these data, and to promote effective data use. ICPSR is the world's largest archive of digital social science data. It provides, for example, access to the following longitudinal datasets that contain data on competencies, attitudes, values, and behaviors: the Panel Study of Income Dynamics (PSID), the National Longitudinal Survey of Youth 1979 and 1997 (NLSY79; NLSY97), data on the children of the National Longitudinal Survey of Youth (NLSYC), the National Longitudinal Study of Adolescent Health (Add Health), and Monitoring the Future. The NLSY studies, for example, contain information about self-esteem (Rosenberg scale), self-efficacy (Pearlin scale) of both mother and children, and information about behavior adjustment (Achenbach Youth Report), delinquency, social relationships, and social networks. The Child Development Supplement (CDS) of the PSID and the Add Health Study also contain information about self-esteem and self-efficacy as well as information on social support and social attitudes. The PSID CDS provides time-use diary data accounting for the social context of daily social activities. The Add Health Study contains information on dyadic relationships and social networks, enabling a close analysis of relationship symmetry, the strengths of friendship ties, and social integration.

3. Future developments

3.1 Data provision

Given the stock of available data resources and the multiple perspectives on how to operationalize social competences, future challenges for data provision include (a) the integration and consolidation of existing data resources and measures of social competencies, (b) the cataloging and documentation of topic-specific resources, (c) the promotion of data re-use, (d) the addition of data sources to the archives that have not yet been made available, and (e) efforts toward the harmonization of future data collection.

Integration and consolidation. So far, very few attempts have been made to take stock of and evaluate existing resources. Future efforts should attempt

---

7   http://www.icpsr.umich.edu/

to provide an overview of existing measures and approaches. Similarities and differences in approach, as well as unifying conceptual issues, must be identified to enable the development of integrative research.

Cataloging and documentation. Currently documentation exists for individual studies (most of which are multipurpose), yet topic-specific documentation of measures and methodologies across different studies is lacking. Combining topic-specific evidence from different studies, countries, populations, and age groups will facilitate comparative research and contribute to a more integrated conceptualization of research. In particular, information about types of assessment, age groups and populations under investigation, psychometric properties of assessment (i.e., reliability and validity), inter-linked context variables, relevant publications, and the strengths and weaknesses of the particular approach used, are needed.

Promotion of data re-use. To date, not all relevant studies have been made available for public access via data depositories. This includes large-scale multipurpose longitudinal data, as well as more focused specialized investigations. To gain a better understanding of the different approaches and contexts of assessment, it is necessary to overcome "proprietary" models of publicly funded social science research and shift toward a more open and collaborative paradigm in order to obtain as complete an overview as possible, drawing on existing evidence. Of course, studies should be vetted and evaluated for criteria of research excellence before they are added to the depositories.

Data harmonization. Future data collection should build on the existing evidence base and strive to promote coordinated collaborative efforts following best practices, ideally involving several countries to provide comparative data.

3.2 Data usage

Data usage in the future is likely to involve interdisciplinary teams and international research networks sharing and consolidating existing knowledge, working towards a coordinated, comparative approach, and preparing strategies for collecting new evidence. To facilitate such developments it is necessary to improve the infrastructure of international data provision – including data documentation across different studies and disciplines and possibly the creation of innovative examples that model how to use data from different studies.

3.3 Data access

Access to data should be expanded via remote access to sites and coordinated data archives. Consequently, resources must be invested in protecting the confidentiality of data, and consideration must be given to different levels of access depending on security clearance. Given the attractiveness of personal data for various interest groups and financial or market organizations, safeguarding the data while allowing access to bona fide users is a vital issue.

3.4 European and international challenges

A key issue in the collaborative use of data is the international comparability of data and the provision of internationally harmonized datasets. Such an endeavor has to build on collaborative agreements between contributors and joint research projects. Every effort should be made to preserve existing data and to enable its re-use, even with a different purpose or research question in mind. Language barriers have to be acknowledged and overcome, for example, through coordinated efforts in data collection and documentation. Another area of importance concerns culturally specific norms and resulting expectations about what constitutes social competencies. For such issues it is necessary to identify a common denominator or to develop culturally sensitive or culturally neutral measures.

Furthermore, existing data sources should be integrated, creating multipurpose studies. This might involve the linkage of panel and cohort studies to administrative data and expanding the scope of studies to assess predictors and outcomes of development across domains, such as education and health. Innovative tools for data collection and analysis have to be developed, making use of newly available technologies. For example, data collection can be conducted via mobile phone or the internet, even using advanced methods of assessment such as computer simulation or time-use diaries. Further consideration should be given to the development of new analytic approaches, enabling the analysis of mechanisms and processes across and within domains, contexts, cohorts, countries, and over time. Moving beyond population statistics, there is the potential to adopt new methodologies that enable the identification of patterns and a comparison of functioning both between and within subgroups of the population.

3.5 Recommendations

The measurement of social competencies involves the study of a complex phenomenon that occurs over time and in specific contexts. The following recommendations would advance our understanding and assessment of social competencies:

- Improved conceptual clarity and focus are needed to define what is being measured in the research. This should be achieved through efforts to develop an interdisciplinary, culturally sensitive, and relevant working definition of social competencies, integrating both general and specific components and skills.

- Appropriate methods are needed to map development over time and across domains and contexts. This implies the need for age-, domain-, and context-appropriate measures, enabling the assessment of growth and development over time. Methods should also be developed that are suitable for the examination of continuity and change in the acquisition and expression of competencies in different contexts.

- Since the effectiveness of social behavior can only be determined within the context of a particular social environment, it is necessary to include both individual and contextual characteristics in the assessment.

- The acquisition of social competencies is a developmental process, yet we have too little knowledge about how individuals learn and acquire social competencies in different contexts and settings, and how competencies develop and diversify over time. It is thus vitally important to increase the availability of longitudinal data, beginning at an early age to acquire information on different manifestations of competencies. Longitudinal data would also help clarify the factors and processes that facilitate the acquisition and expression of social competencies and promote adaptive interpersonal and personal environmental interactions at different life stages.

- There is a need for a better understanding of intergenerational transmission of social competencies as well as their biological foundations.

- To consolidate the research evidence, effort must be made to continuously update and advance the integration of existing data resources and to promote their re-use. Collaborative agreements to submit data to a publicly accessible data depository for the purpose of secondary analysis would pave the way for future shared research and training. Working toward the cataloging and topic-specific documentation of resources would provide the necessary infrastructure.

- To improve the possibility of collaborative and comparative research there should be integrated and harmonized approaches to data collection that draw on newly available technologies.
- Confidentiality of data has to be safeguarded, and specific modes of access to data depositories must be considered.

References:

Achenbach, Th.M. and Howell, C.T. (1993): Are American children's problems getting worse? Journal of the American Academy of Child and Adolescent Psychiatry 32 (6), 1145-1154.
Arendt, H. (1958): The Human Condition. Chicago.
Argyle, M. (1994): The psychology of interpersonal behaviour, 5th edition. London.
Argyle, M./Henderson, M. and Furnham, A. (1985): The rules of social relationships. British Journal of Social Psychology 24, 125-139.
Arts, W. and Halman, L. (Eds.) (2004): European values at the turn of the Millennium. Leiden.
Bandura, A. (1997): Self-efficacy: the exercise of control. New York.
Bar-On, R./Tranel, D./Denburg, N.L. and Bechara, A. (2003): Exploring the neurological substrate of emotional and social intelligence. Brain 126 (8), 1790-1800.
Bechara, A./Tranel, D. and Damasio, A.R. (2000): Poor judgement in spite of high intellect. In: Bar-On, R. and Parker, J.D.A. (Eds.): The handbook of emotional intelligence. San Francisco.
Chen, X. and French, D.C. (2008): Children's social competence in cultural context. Annual Review of Psychology 59, 591-616.
Costa, P.T. and McCrae, R.R. (1992): Revised NEO Personality Inventory (NEO-PI-R) and NEO Five-Factor Inventory (NEO-FFI) professional manual. Odessa.
Davis, M.H. (1983): Measuring individual differences in empathy: Evidence for a multidimensional approach. Journal of Personality and Social Psychology 44, 113-126.
EU (2005): Working together for growth and jobs: A new start for the Lisbon Strategy. European Commission, Communication 33. Brussels.
Flashman, L.A./Andreasen, N.C./Flaum, M. and Swayze, V.W. (1998): Intelligence and regional brain volumes in normal controls. Intelligence 25 (3), 149-160.
Gardner, H. (1999): Intelligence Reframed. Multiple intelligences for the 21st century. New York.
Goleman, D. (1995): Emotional intelligence. New York.
Grigorenko, E.L. (2000): Hertitablility and intelligence. In: Sternberg, R.J. (Ed.): Handbook of Intelligence. Cambridge.
Goodman, R. (2001): Psychometric properties of the strengths and difficulties questionnaire (SDQ). Journal of the American Academy of Child & Adolescent Psychiatry 40 (11), 1337-1345.
Gosling, S.D./Rentfrow, P.J. and Swann, W.B. Jr. (2003): A Very Brief Measure of the Big Five Personality Domains. Journal of Research in Personality 37 (6), 504-528.
Hagerty, M.R./Cummins, R.A./Ferriss, A.L./Michalos, K.L.A.C./Peterson, M. et al. (2007): Quality of life indices for national policy: Review and agenda for research. Social Indicators Research 55 (1), 1-96.
Halpern, D. (2005): Social Capital. Cambridge.
Inglehart, R. (1997): Modernization and postmodernization. Cultural, economic, and political change in 43 societies. Princeton.

Kendall, Ph.C. and Wilcox, L.E. (1979): Self-control in children: Development of a rating scale Journal of Consulting and Clinical Psychology 47 (6), 1020-1029.

Kihlstrom, J.F. and Cantor, N. (2000): Social intelligence. In: Sternberg, R.J. (Ed.): Handbook of intelligence. Cambridge.

McCrae, R.R. and Costa, P.T. *(2004): A contemplated revision of the NEO Five-Factor Inventory.* Personality and Individual Differences *36 (3), 587-596.*

Putnam, R.D. (2000): Bowling alone: the collapse and revival of American community. New York.

Rampus, K. (1947): Social Competence. Journal of Abnormal and Social Psychology 26, 681-687.

Rosenberg, M. (1979): Conceiving the self. New York.

Rotter, J.B. (1990): Internal versus external control reinforcement. American Psychologist 45 (4), 489-493.

Rydell, A.-M./Hagekull, B. and Bohlin, G. (1997): Measurement of two social competence aspects in childhood. Developmental Psychology 33 (5), 824-833.

Saarni, C. (2000): Emotional competence: A developmental perspective. In: Bar-On, R. and Parker, J.D.A. (Eds.): The handbook of emotional intelligence. San Francisco.

Sarason, B.R. (1981): The dimensions of social competence: Contributions from a variety of research areas. In: Wine, J.D. and Smye, M.D. (Eds.): Social competence. New York.

Sarason, B.R. (Ed.) (1981): The dimensions of social competence: Contributions from a variety of research areas. New York.

Schwarzer, R. (1993): Measurement of perceived self-efficacy: Psychometric scales for coss-cultural research. Berlin.

Tajfel, H. (1981): Human groups and social categories. Cambridge.

Walker, R.E. and Foley, J.M. (1973): Social intelligence: its history and measurement. Psychological Reports 33, 839-864.

Waters, E. and Sroufe, A.L. (1983): Social competence as a developmental construct. Developmental Review 3 (1), 79-97.

2.5 Subjective Indicators

Beatrice Rammstedt

Contact:

Beatrice Rammstedt
GESIS – Leibniz-Institut für Sozialwissenschaften
P.O. Box 12 21 55
68072 Mannheim
Germany
e-mail: beatrice.rammstedt[at]gesis.org

Abstract

Subjective indicators have been proven to possess predictive power for a large array of social and economic outcomes. However, most of these measures face serious psychometric shortcomings, namely that the items used are not psychometrically investigated. Furthermore, various different item phrasing and response formats are used in different surveys for the assessment of one and the same construct. The present paper makes several recommendations to improve the quality and thus also the acceptance and usage of subjective indicators. These include the development of more ultra-short but multi-item measures for subjective indicators. In addition, surveys should try to use the same form of measurement (i.e., the same item phrasings and the same response scales). In terms of psychometric properties, the report recommends that the reliability and validity of the indicators be investigated in as much depth as possible. In addition, suggestions are made regarding how best to investigate the respondent's judgmental process for the measurement of subjective indicators, which will allow researchers to obtain a clearer picture of how the item is understood by the respondent and the cues on which he bases his judgment.

Keywords: subjective indicators, reliability, validity, multi-item instruments, cognitive interviews

1. Introduction

Certainly it is possible to assess a person's state of health by investigating patient records, counting the number of sick days, or noting the amount of pharmaceuticals the person takes. However, these are only proxies for the actual state of health. What is more important is the perceived, that is, the subjective state of health. A person going to work even though he feels sick, who is not taking medication, and who does not visit a doctor will be much less productive than a person who perceives himself as healthy.

2. Definition: What are subjective indicators?

At first sight it might be assumed that the distinction between objective and subjective indicators is relatively unambiguous. Objective measurement is based on explicit criteria and is performed by external observers (e.g., Veenhofen 2007). Taking again the example of the individual's state of health, it can be assessed by objective indicators such as antigens in the blood or by the income level; it can be assessed by the annual pay check. However, such objective criteria may also be assessed by subjective measures, for instance, by use of self-ratings. Are such self-ratings (thus subjectively assessed measures of health or income) still objective or do they become subjective measures? Alternately, one could think of subjective criteria that is assessed by objective measures – such as individually perceived insecurity recorded by the installation of alarm systems or the training in self-defense. Would this be an objective or a subjective indicator? We thus need to differentiate between objective and subjective in both cases, the side of the criterion or substance that is being assessed as well as the assessment itself. Both can be either objective or subjective.

Subjective indicators are often defined as information that includes some kind of a subjective component, such as personal perception or a personal evaluation (e.g., Noll 2001). This definition focuses exclusively on the subjective measurement of any type of criterion. Following the above-described differentiation, this definition includes subjective measures of both objective and subjective criteria. In light of new thinking on this subject, however, this definition is far too broad because it includes any self-reported data and thus can in no way be differentiated by criterion. In the following report, subjective indicators are defined as subjective measures of a subjective criterion. Thus, a comparably strong definition is chosen, which, however, will make it possible to narrow the broad and often somewhat vague field of subjective indicators. Subjective indicators – in this sense – are defined as *subjective information about a subjective criterion*. Subjective indicators thus include constructs like satisfaction, worries, or trust.

3. The reason for assessing subjective indicators

Why do we assess subjective indicators at all, although we know that subjective measures like self-ratings have strong shortcomings since they are – as the label says – subjective. To answer this question we need to disentangle the subjective indicator once again in the subjective substance and its subjective measurement.

Why are researchers interested in subjective substances such as happiness, worries, or values? A common objection has it that such matters are unstable over time, that they are incomparable across cultures and even individuals, that they are unintelligible since they are implicit and therefore their "true score" can hardly be investigated (e.g., Veenhoven 2007). However, research findings have shown that these objections do not apply to *all* subjective criteria. There seem to be several subjective constructs, such as overall life satisfaction, of which individuals have a clear, stable, and comparable understanding. Therefore, even though the rating itself is subjective, the construct it is based on seems to be comparable across individuals. Furthermore, these subjective criteria often have a high impact on external and objective criteria, such as objective welfare or suicide rate. Thus, for the prediction of several important life or societal outcomes, the measurement of subjective substances is indispensible.

However, the question might also be raised, why are these subjective substances measured by self-reports rather than using more objective data, such as indicators for quality of life conditions, to estimate well-being? One reason is that it is often much more time-consuming to gather information on such objective measures than simply to ask the respondent about his or her well-being. The most important reason, however, is that such objective indices do not seem to be an appropriate proxy for the individually perceived criterion. The individual's "true score" in the subjective criterion is only partially based on objective measures, such as, for example, life circumstances. The other part of this "true score" is based on multiple aspects including the individual's fit within his or her environment and the capacity to cope with these life circumstances. This latter part, however, can hardly be assessed by objective proxies.

In sum, research has shown that subjective criteria are fruitful and valid predictors for an array of social and economic outcomes. These subjective criteria are best assessed by means of subjective measures and thus in the form of subjective indicators.

4. Typical subjective indicators in social and economic surveys

In social and economic surveys there are a number of subjective indicators which are assessed relatively regularly. Instead of providing a complete list, we will give a short overview of the most frequently assessed subjective indicators.

The most prominent criterion for a subjective indicator is *satisfaction* or *subjective well-being*. This can be either operationalized as satisfaction with life in general or as satisfaction with specific aspects of one's life, such as work, marriage, or living conditions. Satisfaction is regularly assessed in numerous studies, such as the German Socio-Economic Panel (SOEP, *Soziooekonomisches Panel*), the European Social Survey (ESS), the German Welfare Survey, the European Values Study, and the World Values Survey (WVS).

The counterpart to satisfaction is *worries*. Worries are often assessed in the field of job security or health. Thus, worries are usually assessed based on specific aspects of the respondent's life. Studies that regularly assess worries are again the SOEP and the German Welfare Study.

Another frequently measured complex of subjective indicators in social surveys are measures of *trust*, such as trust in government, in democracy, etc., or even general trust in other people. Various questions regarding trust have been asked in the German General Social Survey (ALLBUS, *Allgemeine Bevölkerungsumfrage der Sozialwissenschaften*), in the Eurobarometer, in the International Social Survey Programme (ISSP), and in the WVS.

5. The assessment of the most prominent subjective indicators

Usually satisfaction, worries, and trust are measured by single item indicators. Typical phrasings of these questions are given in table 1. Respondents are asked to rate their degree of satisfaction, worries, or trust as outlined in the given item formulation on a Likert-scale ranging from "not at all [satisfied, worried, trusting]" to "fully [satisfied, worried, trusting]."

Research, however, has shown that psychometric properties of multi-item scales, as used in psychology for example, are significantly higher than for single-item measures. In multi-item scales, item responses are aggregated to a sum or mean score of the underlying construct. In general, the broader the construct of interest is (e.g., general life satisfaction vs. satisfaction with income), the more multi-item scales should be used. Broader constructs cannot be validly assessed by only one indicator.

Surveys, however, face tight time constraints. Therefore, the number of items used for multi-item scales needs to be restricted. In recent years, efforts have been made to construct ultra-short measures for constructs like personality or values to obtain multiple-item measures that can be used under the tight time restrictions of surveys. This approach could also be very fruitful for subjective indicators. On the one hand it would be a way to reduce lengthy item batteries, on the other broad constructs could be assessed with greater validity.

6. How can subjective indicators be validated?

As mentioned above, subjective measures of subjective substances are hardly testable against their supposed "true scores." The ratings represent feelings, evaluations, or conditions within the respondent that can hardly be perceived from an outside observer. Thus, the respondent's "true score" remains a mystery.

There are, however, several means available to investigate the quality of a self-report and to gain insight into the process used in making the judgment. If the individual's response to a subjective indicator is reliable, respondents should answer the same question in the same way if asked again. To avoid memory effects when responding the second time, a substantial time interval should be established between the two administrations, since it can be assumed that a judgment about one's overall life satisfaction or job security is relatively stable over time, say across several weeks (given that no serious life event happens in that period of time). Therefore, one way of investigating the quality of a subjective indicator is to investigate its stability by administrating the same question to the same set of respondents twice. A measurement can be regarded as reliable if the retest stability, thus the correlation between the two administrations, is high.

Another way of investigating the reliability of a subjective indicator is to use multiple items for its assessment. Since all items are assumed to measure the same underlying construct, it can be assumed that all items are positively related to each other. The standardized intercorrelation among this set of items (Cronbach Alpha coefficient) could therefore be regarded as a measure of the measurement reliability.

Testing the validity of the measurement of a subjective indicator poses a larger challenge. Validity is usually investigated by comparing self-estimates to peer or expert ratings or by comparing it to an external (objective) criterion (e.g., self-rated health to results of bio-chemical tests or by the number of doctor's consultations). Such comparisons are difficult, if not impossible, if the substance rated is subjective and not objectively measurable and perceivable by others – as in the case of health, for example. The only way of shedding some light onto the validity of subjective indicators would be to investigate their construct validity. This could either be done – in the case of multi-item indicators – by a factor analytic approach to test, if all items assumed to measure one indicator from a common factor; or, in a multitrait-multimethod design, by testing several subjective indicators, for example, assessed by self-ratings and peer ratings.[1] Alternatively, this construct validation could be more theoretically driven by investigating

---

1   Peer ratings are also perceived as subjective indicators because they are a subjective judgment about a target person.

hypothesized external correlations. For example, it could be assumed that a person highly worried about his financial situation would be less likely to put high amounts of money in high-risk investments. This form of validation depends significantly on the creation of plausible hypotheses. To develop such hypotheses we first of all need to learn more about the respondent's process of understanding the question and – most importantly – about the respondent's process of developing the judgment that is then given as an answer to the item.

One way of investigating respondent judgmental processes that has been very prominent in recent studies is the qualitative approach of cognitive interviews. In these cognitive interviews, a small number of respondents (preferably rather heterogeneous with regard to their socio-demographic background) are asked to respond to the items in question. In doing so they are either invited to think aloud or to paraphrase specific terms or to explain why they chose a specific answer category. This approach can significantly increase our knowledge about the respondent's understanding, interpretation, and response to a subjective indicator item. This becomes even more valuable the less concrete an item is. Asking a respondent to think aloud while answering the item "Do you like to go to parties" – a typical extraversion item – would probably not give us as much insight into the respondents mind as letting him think aloud about whether he is satisfied with life in general. This latter investigation could help inform us about cues like health, partnership, children, a secure job, or the financial situation, that a person has used to perceive himself or herself as either satisfied or dissatisfied. These cues can then be used to develop hypotheses for assumable correlations. For example, if all respondents refer first to their health as a cue for their level of satisfaction, a significant positive relation between these two indicators can be assumed and tested in terms of validity. Health, however, will never be the only cue and cannot be regarded as a proxy for life satisfaction. Thus, a substantial but not maximal correlation can be anticipated.

Parallel to the development of cognitive interviews, an alternative quantitative approach to shedding light on the individual judgmental process has also been developed (Jasso 2006). In this factorial survey method, respondents are asked to rate the level of a specified outcome variable (e.g., well-being or healthiness) based on a given fictitious description of a person and its characteristics (age, gender, income, eating habits, housing, etc.). Respondents will be rating a large set of such fictitious descriptions, termed "vignettes." Based on these ratings, the implicitly used equations for assigning outcomes like well-being or healthiness can be retrieved using statistical techniques.

In sum, the quality of subjective indicators can be investigated by using methods such as test-retest reliability, Cronbach Alpha coefficients, construct validity in form of factorial structure or hypothesized correlations with external criteria and by use of cognitive interviews and vignette techniques.

7. Recommendations

Subjective indicators have been proven to possess predictive power for a large array of social and economic outcomes. For most of them, only single item measures are used. The phrasing of items and the response formats differ substantially across different surveys. The items used are in most cases not tested with regard to their psychometric properties. This, however, can be done with very simple means. We therefore recommend the following:

- Subjective indicators should become more widely accepted and investigated as they are proven to possess a substantial predictive power.

- More ultra-short scale measures should be developed and validated

- In order to reach more comparability across studies and thus more comparable results, and in order to profit most from validated measures, surveys should try to use the same form of measurement, (i.e., the same item phrasings and the same response scales).

- Even though the validation of subjective indicators cannot as easily be conducted as it is for objective ones, we strongly recommend that the reliability and validity of these indicators be investigated in as much depth as possible.

- Furthermore, we suggest investigating the respondent's judgmental process for subjective indicator measures by the use of cognitive interviews and/or by the vignette technique. This makes it possible to obtain a clearer picture of how the item is understood by the respondent and on which cues he bases his judgment.

- If results of cognitive interviews indicate that individuals strongly vary in their understanding of and in their way of responding to these single-item indicators, researchers should examine whether it would be more fruitful and thus more valid to use multiple indicators that could be, in turn, less abstract.

Table 1. Typical item phrasings for measures of satisfaction, worries, and trust.

General life satisfaction (WVS)	All things considered, how satisfied are you with your life as a whole these days? Using this card on which 1 means you are "completely dissatisfied" and 10 means you are "completely satisfied" where would you put your satisfaction with your life as a whole?
Domain specific satisfaction (GSOEP)	How satisfied are you today with the following areas of your life? How satisfied are you with... your health your sleep your job your housework your household income your schooling and professional education your place of dwelling your free time your family life the child care available?
Domain specific worries (GSOEP)	What is your attitude towards the following areas – are you concerned about them? General economic development Your own economic situation Your health Environmental protection Maintaining peace Global terrorism Crime in Germany Consequences of the expanding of the EU to the east Immigration to Germany Hostility towards foreigners or minorities in Germany *If you are employed:* Your job security?
Trust in others (WVS)	Generally speaking, would you say that most people can be trusted or that you need to be very careful in dealing with people? I'd like to ask you how much you trust people from various groups. Could you tell me for each whether you trust people from this group completely, somewhat, not very much or not at all? - your family - your neighbourhood

	- people you know personally - people you meet for the first time - people of another religion - people of another nationality
Trust in institutions (ALLBUS)	I am now going to read out a number of public institutions and organisations. Please tell me for each institution or organisation how much trust you place in it. Pleas use this scale. 1 means you have absolutely no trust at all 7 means you have a great deal of trust You can differentiate your answers using the numbers in between. What about the – Health service German constitutional court German Parliament Municipal administration Army Catholic church Protestant church Judicial system Television Newspapers Universities and other institutes of higher education German government Trade unions Police Job centres State pension system Employer associations?

References:

Jasso, G. (2006): Factorial survey methods for studying beliefs and judgments. Sociological Methods and Research 34, 334-423.

Noll, H.-H. (2001): Subjektive Indikatoren: Expertise für die Kommission zur Verbesserung der informationellen Infrastruktur zwischen Wissenschaft und Statistik. In: Kommission zur Verbesserung der informationellen Infrastruktur zwischen Wissenschaft und Statistik (KVI) (Ed.): Wege zu einer besseren informationellen Infrastruktur. Baden-Baden.

Veenhoven, R. (2007): Subjective measures of well-being. In: McGillivray, M. (Ed.): Human Well-Being – Concept and Measurement. Houndsmills.

3. EDUCATION AND RESEARCH

3.1 Education Across the Life Course

Hans-Peter Blossfeld

Contact:

Hans-Peter Blossfeld
University of Bamberg
Chair of Sociology I
Faculty of Social Sciences, Business Administration and Economics
PO Box 1549
Lichtenhaidestr. 11
96045 Bamberg
Germany
e-mail: Soziologie1[at]uni-bamberg.de

Abstract

There is enormous demand in Germany for high-quality longitudinal research on education. In particular, there is a clear need for both analytical and methodological progress in order to understand educational pathways through the life course and how they lead to different outcomes. This paper identifies the theoretical and methodological challenges of studying education across the life course and describes the structure of the National Educational Panel Study (NEPS) in Germany.

Keywords: competence development, educational decisions, formal, informal and nonformal educational environments, returns to education, educational trajectories, life-course research, longitudinal analysis, panel data

1. Research questions

Germany, like other modern industrialized societies, has evolved into a knowledge-based economy. More than in the past, today education is a lifelong process in which individuals continually learn in formal, non-formal, and informal environments. Individuals' educational careers and competencies and how they unfold over the life course in relation to family, educational institutions, workplaces, and private life are therefore a topic of considerable national interest. There are several social, economic and demographic changes that make education particularly important in modern societies. Some examples include:

- The dramatic decline in the number of unskilled jobs that has taken place over the course of technological change raises issues concerning the proportion of youth who leave the educational system with poor competencies and/or without a certificate. Questions thus arise, such as which factors influence educational participation and achievement in educational institutions? How are basic competencies related to school success, certificates, the transition into the labor market, and job careers?

- Technological change has also led to an increase in the number of service, professional, and engineering positions that require a range of social, communicational, and problem-solving skills. This upgrading of the job structure has enhanced the value of education, science competencies, and soft skills on the labor market and in society as a whole. Such changes inevitably affect the content and processes of learning in schools, vocational training systems, and universities, triggering questions such as what do students learn and which kinds of competencies do individuals need in a knowledge society? How can we engender motivation and interest in reading, mathematics, and science? How is the development of reading, mathematical, and science competencies affected over the life course by different learning environments such as school, work, home, and community? How can we quantify the economic and social benefits of these competencies?

- New information and media technologies continue to have a growing impact on our daily lives and work. They demand the ability to communicate and share information. This raises questions about how well the educational system provides the relevant training for ICT (Information and Communication Technologies) literacy, social competencies, and personal skills to meet these demands.

- Increasing worldwide competition and globalization are stepping up the pace of social and economic change, making it necessary for individuals to exhibit greater flexibility and adaptability both at their workplace and in society. The ability to learn new skills and to adapt has become an important requirement for securing jobs and being a successful citizen. Therefore, the question is, how does the initial full-time educational investment influence these learning skills and attitudes toward educational institutions, further education, and learning situations over the life course? How can we improve self-regulated learning so that individuals realize opportunities to take on challenging tasks, practice their learning, and develop a deep understanding of their subject matter?

- Germany is also undergoing considerable demographic changes: there is a decline in fertility, an aging population, an increasing diversity of ethnic background in the population, and a rising level of instability in family life. All these changes have direct consequences for individual educational processes (e.g., the impact of parental divorce on the educational careers of children and their competence development) and for educational institutions as a whole (e.g., when *Hauptschule* and *Realschule* are combined because of the declining number of students, or when older workers have to increase their participation in education during late adulthood). The capacity to follow individuals through the life course and to observe how educational experiences, competencies, and behavior are influenced by the formal, non-formal, or informal contexts in which they find themselves grants longitudinal studies a major role in understanding the role of education in modern society.

- Empirical studies such as PISA (Programme for International Student Assessment) demonstrate that the quality and quantity of schooling that individuals acquire still depend to a large extent on the advantages or disadvantages that parents confer throughout childhood, adolescence, and adulthood. However, most of these educational inequalities are only documented on the basis of cross-sectional data. The causal mechanisms that produce primary and secondary outcomes as well as the cumulative processes over the educational career are still subject to considerable controversy in the literature on educational inequality and can only be studied reasonably on the basis of longitudinal data. In particular, the complex and subtle role that schools, vocational training institutions, universities, and continuing education play in the maintenance of inequality and the allocation of persons to unequal positions in Germany across generations and within the life course is still not well understood.

2. Status quo: Databases and access

National and international school performance studies or student assessment studies such as TIMSS,[1] PISA, PIRLS,[2] or DESI[3] have developed competence tests in different domains (mainly in the domains of reading, math, and science literacy or in English as a second language). These studies provide information on the distribution of competencies within the Federal Republic of Germany in comparison with other countries as a function of school type attended, social background, and student gender. However, they are cross-sectional and therefore provide only a snapshot of different students at a particular point in their educational careers. Successive snapshots in a series of cross-sectional surveys highlight changes in the structure as a whole. Yet, they do not show the changing (and sometimes unchanging) experiences of individual students as their educational careers progress.

Several longitudinal studies have already been carried out in Germany that broaden the knowledge derived from these cross-sectional studies by providing more information about the causes of established competence development and educational decisions. The available longitudinal studies can be assigned to the following four areas: (1) childhood development, (2) transitions and competence developments in elementary and secondary school, (3) transitions from school to vocational training and university, and (4) life-course research with a strong emphasis on educational and employment careers and family-related processes:

---

1 Trends in International Mathematics and Science Study.
2 Progress in International Reading Literacy Study.
3 Assessment of Student Achievements in German and English as a Foreign Languag (DESI, *Deutsch-Englisch-Schülerleistungen-International*).

- The studies concerning childhood development are national (DJI[4] Children's Panel) or regional longitudinal studies (BiKS,[5] LOGIK[6]) on competence and personality development in children and on the transition from kindergarten to elementary school.
- The majority of longitudinal studies were carried out on educational development within schools. Among these regionally designed longitudinal studies, we can differentiate two types: The first concentrates on competence development within one level of education (SCHOLASTIK,[7] BeLesen,[8] and Hannoversche Grundschulstudie in elementary school; PALMA[9] in the lower secondary school), whereas the second type predominantly examines transitions between two stages of education (BiKS in Hesse and Bavaria, KESS[10] in Hamburg, Koala-S in Bavaria and Saxony). However, some studies have a strong focus on competence development as well as on transitions (ELEMENT[11] in Berlin, BIJU[12] in Mecklenburg-Western Pomerania, Saxony-Anhalt, North Rhine-Westphalia, and Berlin). Only two nationwide studies have a rudimentary longitudinal character: TIMSS 1995 and PISA 2003. TIMSS 1995 has tested students in the 7th grade (1994) and then again one year later (1995). PISA 2003 has been expanded by a second wave (PISA-I-plus). Ninth graders from the intermediate and academically oriented track were tested one year later in tenth grade in order to analyze how they had progressed in mathematics and sciences and what the determining factors were.

---

4   German Youth Institute (DJI, *Deutsches Jugendinstitut*).
5   Educational Processes, Competence Development, and Selection Decisions in Pre- and Primary School Age (BiKS, *Bildungsprozesse, Kompetenzentwicklungen und Selektionsentscheidungen im Vor- und Grundschulalter*).
6   German Longitudinal Study on the Genesis of Individual Competencies (LOGIK, *Longitudinalstudie zur Genese individueller Kompetenzen*).
7   Organized Learning Opportunities at School and the Socialization of Talents, Interests, and Competencies (SCHOLASTIK, *Schulorganisierte Lernangebote und die Sozialisation von Talenten, Interessen und Kompetenzen*).
8   Berlin Longitudinal Study on the Literary Development of Primary School Children (BeLesen, *Berliner Längsschnittstudie zur Lesekompetenzentwicklung von Grundschulkindern*).
9   Project on the Analysis of Performance Development in Mathematics (PALMA, *Projekt zur Analyse der Leistungsentwicklung in Mathematik*).
10 Competencies and Attitudes of School Students (KESS, *Kompetenzen und Einstellungen von Schülerinnen und Schülern*).
11 Study on Competencies in Reading and Mathematics (ELEMENT, *Erhebung zum Lese- und Mathematikverständnis*).
12 Learning Processes, Educational Careers, and Psychosocial Development in Adolescence and Young Adulthood (BIJU, *Bildungsverläufe und psychosoziale Entwicklung im Jugend- und jungen Erwachsenenalter*).

- For participation in the university and the labor market entries of academics, the Higher Education Information System (HIS, *Hochschul-Informations-System*) has conducted national longitudinal studies in which, however, no performance-based competence measurements were included. One of the HIS panels covers a cohort of secondary school graduates qualified for higher education, follows their transition into the university or vocational training programs and their subsequent educational career for a period of three and a half years after leaving school. The HIS survey of graduates concentrates on the transition from university to the labor market and into the professional career. The DJI Transition Panel, implemented by the German Youth Institute, focuses on the transition of "disadvantaged" students who have finished the lower school track, and follows their paths into the vocational training system and their entry into the labor market (no competence tests have been conducted). There is also the ULME[13] study in Hamburg that is testing competence development from entry until the end of a course of study at vocational schools, independent of whether the vocational school is full- or part-time.

- The following longitudinal studies differ from those previously summarized. Their focus is on a longer time span. The study of former students from academically oriented secondary schools (*Gymnasium*) follows student careers (beginning in the 10th grade) and examines college and professional education as well as gainful employment in North Rhine-Westphalia over a period of twenty-eight years. In addition, the GLHS (German Life History Study) collected data retrospectively from several birth cohorts on their previous educational and employment career as well as their family history in Germany. No competence tests were included in the GLHS. Since the beginning of the 1990s, individual biographies of East Germans have been surveyed in order to obtain detailed information on lives before, during, and after reunification. Finally, the German Socio-Economic Panel (SOEP, *Sozio-oekonomisches Panel*), a general public survey carried out every year in Germany since 1984, includes large samples of West and East Germans as well as various groups of immigrants. The SOEP combines retrospective data on the work and family-related event history with prospective panel data on, among others, job and income mobility, educational participation, family status, and life satisfaction in different domains.

---

13 Study on Achievement, Motivation, and Attitudes of Students at the Beginning of Vocational Education (ULME, *Untersuchungen der Leistungen, Motivation und Einstellungen zu Beginn der beruflichen Ausbildung*).

This short overview of available longitudinal studies conducted in Germany reveals that there is only one genuine nationwide panel study, the SOEP. However, this study includes no detailed data on changes in educational contexts and no information on the development of competencies. Based on the other longitudinal studies that do measure competencies, only limited conclusions can be drawn. This is because they either confine themselves to a certain region within Germany or concentrate primarily on one stage of education or a specific transition in the educational career. These studies make it impossible to understand how the competencies of individuals develop over the life course, how they interact with educational decisions at various critical transitions in their careers, and how competencies are influenced by the family and the arrangements of teaching and learning processes in kindergarten, school, professional education, and university. It is also unclear how competencies are related to the achievement of educational qualifications, and which competencies are responsible for labor market success and a successful private and social life.

Other European and North American countries have a longer tradition in conducting educational panel studies that include the assessment of competencies, skills, or intelligence components. Kristen et al. (2005) provide an extensive overview of studies conducted in Canada, France, the Netherlands, Sweden, the United Kingdom, and the United States. In these countries, different approaches have been chosen to obtain longitudinal information on education. These are mainly either long-running cohort studies that collect data on an individual's life over a long period or short-term studies on a specific stage of the educational career.

In the United Kingdom, large birth cohort studies have been carried out with educational topics. These studies started in 1958 with the National Child Development Study (NCDS), continuing with the British Cohort Study (BCS70) in 1970 and the Millennium Cohort Study (MCS) in 2000-2001. While in the 1958 NCDS, the distances between the panel points fluctuated between four and ten years, the Millennium Cohort Study intends to have a much smaller time span.

The Effective Provision of Pre-School Education (EPPE) project running from 1997 to 2003 is the first major study in the United Kingdom to focus specifically on the effectiveness of early childhood education (the EPPE 3-11 Project from the years 2003-2008 builds on the original EPPE study). The EPPE project is thus a large-scale longitudinal study of the progress and development of children in and from various types of preschool education (from ages three to eleven).

England and Wales used a research strategy to focus on a short relevant sequence of the educational career. The Youth Cohort Study (YCS) is a repeated short panel study providing insight into the transition from secondary school to further education and to the labor market. Another variant of a cohort study focusing on careers after completing compulsory education is the Canadian Youth in Transition Survey (YITS). This survey attempts to follow students over a longer period of time. The study started with two subsamples in 2000. The members of the first sample were 15 years old, those of the second aged from 18 to 20. For the younger cohorts, only competencies were tested within the framework of PISA 2000. A similar strategy has been implemented by the Swiss Transitions from Education to Employment longitudinal study (TREE), which also started in the year 2000 and measured competencies within the PISA framework only for this first year. Recently (in 2006), the Swiss Survey of Children and Youth COCON (competence and context), was also initiated. This study investigates the social conditions, life experiences, and psychosocial development of children and youth in the German- and French-speaking parts of Switzerland from a life-course perspective. The longitudinal part of this study follows up two cohorts: six-year-olds (middle childhood) and fifteen-year-olds (middle adolescence). In the United States, there have been a large number of different longitudinal education studies. Their main goal has been to analyze the educational, professional, and personal development at different points in the educational career and to identify the role played by personal, family, social, institutional, and cultural factors (NCES 2003). Most of these cohort studies have four or five observation points, and begin at Grade 10 or 12. These are high school studies focusing on the transition to postsecondary education and on labor market entries, including the National Longitudinal Study of the High School Class of 1972 (NLS-72), the National Education Longitudinal Study of 1988 (NELS-88), the Educational Longitudinal Study (ELS 2002), and High School and Beyond (HS&B). Some studies concentrate on students in tertiary education and their labor market entry, such as the Beginning Postsecondary Students Longitudinal Study (BPS), and Baccalaureate & Beyond (B&B). In recent years, as part of the Early Childhood Longitudinal Study (ECLS), two cohort studies have commenced that focus on development at early ages. One cohort starts with the newborn, the other with children attending kindergarten or preschool institutions. The situation for education data in the US can be described as an additive, repeated cohort sampling. This means that different cohorts are available for children and students at a specific stage in the educational career. The complete data pattern of these cohorts delivers sequences reaching from birth up to age thirty. However, there still remains a gap at the lower secondary level. Finally, there are international longitudinal studies on school-to-work transitions. Most of these longitudinal studies focus on educational biographies and transitions, some of them have conducted cross-sectional competence and/or skill measures (in different domains, mostly by including the youths tested in the PISA Studies), but only few have started to survey longitudinal competence developments.

This brief overview of different longitudinal studies using different longitudinal designs makes it clear that birth cohort studies take too much time to acquire a "complete" picture of the educational career. To study children's development and transitions until the end of the secondary school level would take nearly twenty years. Therefore, it is more efficient to concentrate on important sequences in the educational career. Samples must be drawn for every relevant sequence. Such a multicohort sequence design quickly provides the relevant information. In order to capture the influence of educational reforms and social change, new cohorts have to be sampled repeatedly. Such a strategy is comparable to the one followed by the US-National Center for Education Statistics.

In summary, there is enormous demand for high-quality longitudinal educational research in Germany. In particular, there is a clear need for both analytical and methodological progress in order to understand educational pathways through the life course and how they lead to different outcomes.

3. Future developments in Germany: The National Educational Panel Study

The National Educational Panel Study (NEPS), supported by funds from the Federal Ministry of Education and Research (BMBF, *Bundesministerium für Bildung und Forschung*), started in August 2008. The basic design and organization of the NEPS can be summarized as follows.

3.1 Theoretical framework of the NEPS

The key theoretical assumptions of the NEPS as an instrument for studying education over the life course can be best summarized in a diagram. Figure 1 shows that individuals' educational trajectories over the life course are the result of a dynamic system, creating a complex, time-related interdependence of educational decision making, educational processes within different learning environments, and competence development: (1a) Decisions (by parents, students, or teachers) determine whether and to what extent individuals participate in educationally relevant social and institutional contexts; (1b) participation in formal, non-formal, and informal learning environments, in turn, will influence further educational decision making; (2a) educational processes within learning environments are supposed to have an effect on competence development; (2b) competence development, in turn, will influence future opportunities to participate in social and institutional contexts; (3a) competence development will also affect the processes of educational decision making; and (3b) educational decisions will influence the future competence development over the life course. Focusing on these three key theoretical dimensions and their time-dependent interaction mechanisms, which generate change and development over the life course, establishes a foundation for powerful explanations and evidence-based research in the NEPS.

Figure 1: Dynamic Interdependence of Educational Decision Making, Participation in Learning Environments, and Competence Development Over the Life Course

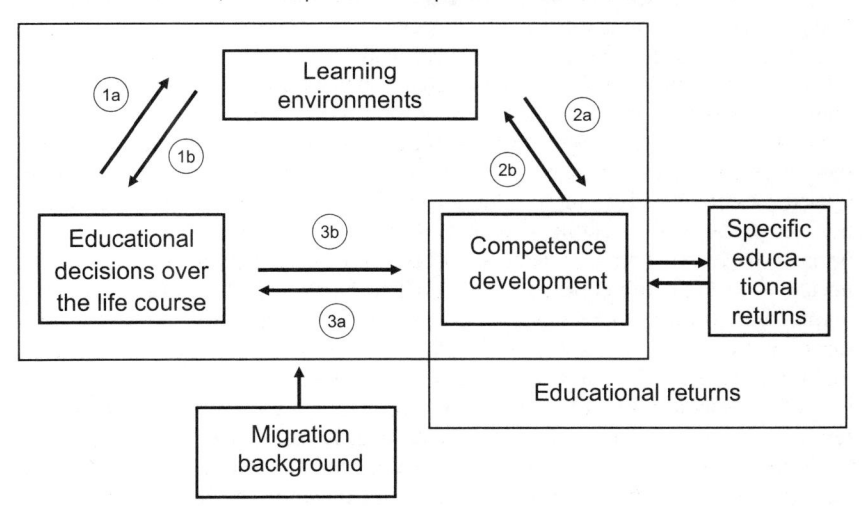

```
                        Learning
         (1a)         environments        (2a)
                (1b)                 (2b)

   Educational        (3b)       Competence        Specific
   decisions over  ─────────→    development       educa-
   the life course ←─────────                      tional
                       (3a)                        returns

                         ↑              Educational returns
                     Migration
                    background
```

It is well known from several recent studies that the educational outcomes of immigrants' children differ substantially from those of their peers from native families. These differences are likely to exist across the whole life course and are conditioned by several specific theoretical mechanisms. In addition to the three main theoretical dimensions, a fourth theoretical dimension of the NEPS is therefore concerned with the educational career of immigrants and their descendants. In order to account for ethnic inequalities, it is necessary to ask which specific resources and orientations on the level of the individual, the family, the learning environment, and the context (e.g., local community), as well as which institutional (e.g., regulation of transitions, availability of education in German as a second language), societal (e.g., acculturation orientations), and political conditions (e.g., regulations for residency status) impact systematically the success of immigrants and their descendants in the educational system and the labor market. The crucial theoretical and empirical task for the NEPS is therefore to identify the particular mechanisms affecting the competence development and the educational decision processes of immigrants.

Finally, there is a fifth significant theoretical dimension to the NEPS that concerns the issue of educational returns. Given that education unfolds over the life course and myriad interactions and relationships are involved, the measurement and modeling of these returns must concentrate on the changes of these outcomes over the life course and the complex dynamic interaction processes that take place when qualifications, competencies, and educational certificates at certain points in the life course are turned into future economic and noneconomic returns. Thus, at least three aspects are important for the returns of education over the life course: the first is that education is a lifelong and cumulative process, and that the educational events and experiences in earlier life stages have consequences for later educational processes and competencies. In other words, from a life-course perspective, later educational participation and competence development are themselves returns to earlier educational investments (see figure 1). Second, educational events, considered in causal process models as constituting the causes of economic and non-economic returns, are to a large extent shaped by these returns. Finally, the importance of the different non-economic and economic returns strongly varies over the life course, because they are often associated with certain development stages or are connected to specific life-course transitions. The NEPS will focus on three economic dimensions: (1) reconsidering the effects of education in classic estimates of monetary returns to years or level of education, job opportunities, and job mobility rates; (2) returns to educational reforms; and, most importantly, (3) returns to specific school institutions. Apart from the monetary economic returns and the returns in terms of later education, the NEPS will include additional nonmonetary returns to education in several areas. Nonmarket returns may come most notably in the form of (a) health, (b) family and fertility behavior, (c) reduced crime and deviance, (d) increasing political and social participation, and (e) subjective well-being.

These five theoretical dimensions are called "pillars," because they will help the consortium to integrate the multicohort sequence design of the NEPS in terms of content, theory, and method and provide a unified mold for the NEPS. In organizational terms, these five theoretical key perspectives are represented by five substantively focused expert groups. Since the NEPS is hosted at Bamberg University, the five pillars will be coordinated and integrated by experts from the Institute for Longitudinal Educational Research Bamberg (INBIL, *Institut für bildungswissenschaftliche Längsschnittforschung*). In addition, two expert groups will support the NEPS: an expert group that will take care of the most important methodological issues of the NEPS, such as sampling design, data cleaning, data archiving, data dissemination, as well as methodological analysis and training; and an expert group on technology-based assessment (TBA) that will support the NEPS with respect to issues involved in computer- and Internet-based assessments.

3.2 The multicohort sequence design of the NEPS

The aim of the NEPS is to provide fast and up-to-date information on educational processes in the various parts of the educational system. Thus, it cannot start with a single birth cohort and then follow it up for 20 years until some of the cohort members eventually leave university. Instead, the consortium has decided to start with several well-chosen cohorts at the same time and to follow these cohorts over longer time spans in their lives. The cohorts will be selected around crucial educational transitions in the German educational system. The multicohort sequence design of the NEPS is shown in figure 2. This design covers: (1) educational processes in kindergarten and the transition to elementary school, (2) educational processes in elementary school and the transition into the tracked secondary school system, (3) processes in the lower secondary school and the transition to upper secondary school, (4) processes of education in upper secondary school and the transition to university or vocational training, (5) educational processes at the university level and the transition of university graduates into the labor market, (6) vocational training and transitions into the labor market, and (7) processes of lifelong learning.

In other words, NEPS will start with five cohorts and follow them up over longer periods in the educational system (Figure 2). It is suggested that four of the five cohort studies begin in the fall of 2010 and then continue with annual observations (the vertical line in figure 2 marks the end of a first 5-year funding period). These five cohorts will be complemented by a panel survey of individuals aged 23 to 64 who have already left full-time education in order to collect data on adult education and lifelong learning. The Institute for Employment Research (IAB, *Institut für Arbeitsmarkt- Und Berufsforschung*) began this survey in 2007 (Figure 2) and it will be integrated into the NEPS in 2009. This multicohort sequence design repeats its structure after some time. However, the next new cohort will not start with kindergarten aged children but with newborn infants (at age six months, see figure 2), therefore allowing not only cohort comparisons but also the identification of age, period, and cohort effects – at least after some time.

In order to develop appropriate instruments for the different educational stages and transitions within the German educational system, the consortium will draw on seven expert groups. The idea behind this is that expert groups on each of the five pillars will cooperate closely with the expert groups responsible for the seven educational stages to develop the necessary questionnaires and competence tests for the NEPS. The representatives of these pillars will ensure that the unified research perspective represented by the five pillars is taken into account by all stage-specific research groups and that the measurement instruments are comparable across the various cohorts of the NEPS.

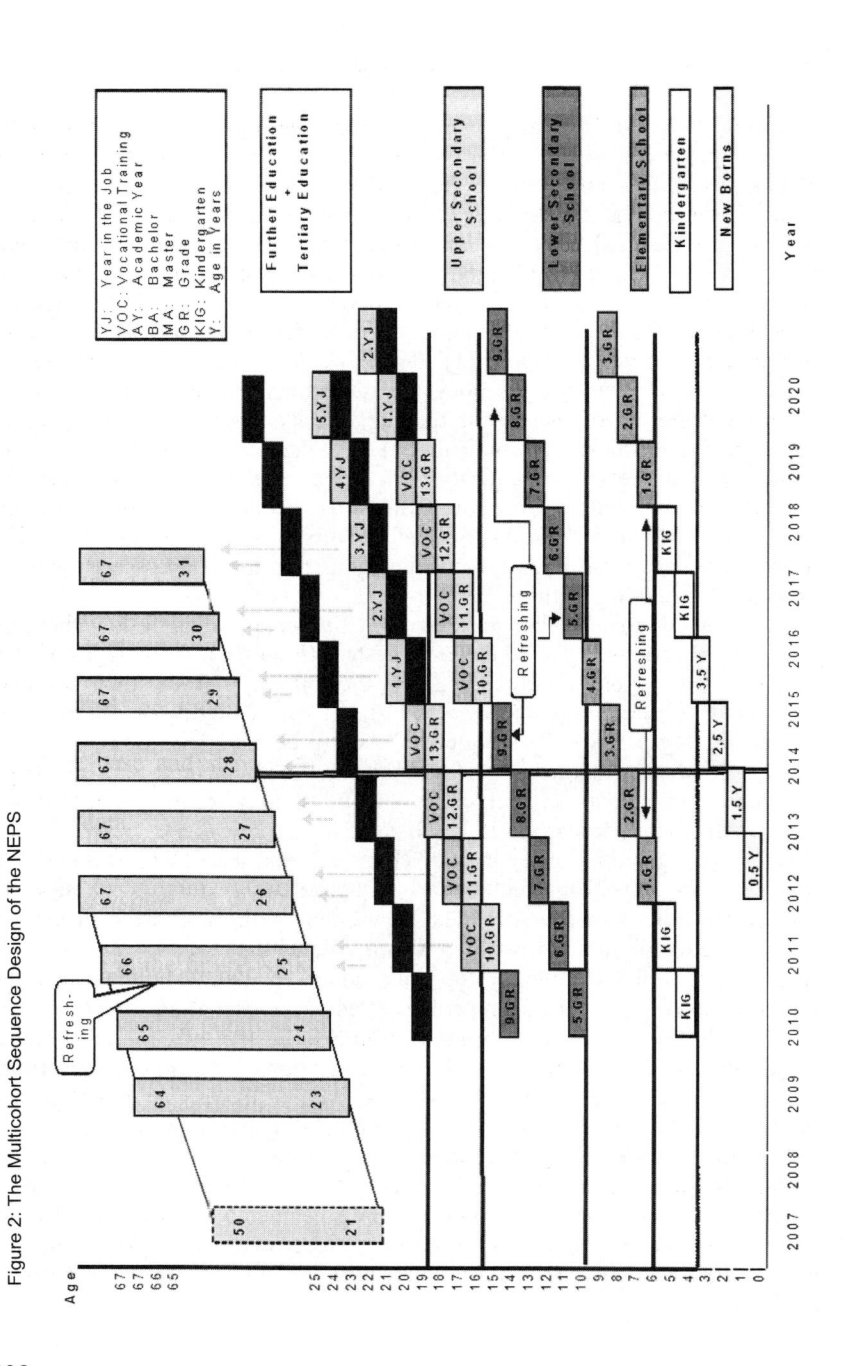

Figure 2: The Multicohort Sequence Design of the NEPS

4. Some concluding remarks

The center of the NEPS consortium is hosted at INBIL at Bamberg University. The role of the INBIL and the division of work between INBIL, the expert groups, and the survey institutes is described in detail in the research proposal (Blossfeld 2008): as a first step, the questionnaires and test instruments for the seven educational stages of the NEPS will be constructed in close collaboration between INBIL and the expert groups. Because the coordinators of the pillars are members of INBIL, it is guaranteed that the multicohort sequence studies will be integrated in terms of concepts, operationalizations, and measurements. After the measurement instruments have been constructed, INBIL will, in a second step, commission survey institutes to carry out the random sampling and the data collection. After data collection, the survey institutes will deliver the datasets to the data center of INBIL. INBIL will then perform data cleaning, validation, coding, scale construction, data weighting, imputation, anonymization, data preparation, data documentation, and so forth. After collection, cleaning, and archiving, the NEPS data will be disseminated to the scientific community as quickly as possible. For this purpose, the NEPS will produce a Scientific Use File and offer training courses on how to effectively exploit the potential of the NEPS for appropriate analyses of all forms.

In sum, the NEPS will establish an excellent scientific evidence base with which to address a broad range of both basic and applied questions in the field of education and to inform policymaking. In particular, the NEPS will provide representative data on the condition of all relevant parts of the educational system in Germany (system monitoring) and offer a better base of scientific evidence for educational reforms and political consultation (system improvement).

References:

Blossfeld, H.-P.(2008): Education as a lifelong process. A proposal for a National Educational Panel Study (NEPS) in Germany. Part A: Overview, Part B: Thoeries, Operationalizations and Piloting Strategies for the Proposed Measurement, and Part C: Appendices. Faculty of Social and Economic Sciences, Bamberg University.
Kristen, C./Römmer, A./Müller, W. and Kalter, F. (2005): Longitudinal Studies for Education Reports: European and North American Examples. Report commissioned by the Federal Ministry of Education and Research. Education Reform vol. 10. Berlin. [German version: Längsschnittstudien für die Bildungsberichterstattung – Beispiele aus Europa und Nordamerika. Gutachten im Auftrag des Bundesministeriums für Bildung und Forschung. Bundesministerium für Bildung und Forschung. Bildungsreform Band 10].

3.2 Preschool Education

C. Katharina Spieß

Contact:

C. Katharina Spieß
German Institute for Economic Research (DIW Berlin)
DIW Berlin
Mohrenstraße 58
10117 Berlin
Germany
e-mail: kspiess[at]diw.de

Abstract

Given the importance of the early stages in a child's life, and taking into account the various initiatives underway to improve preschool programs in Germany, it is remarkable only a few microdatasets cover the field of preschool education in Germany – and even fewer of these are nationally representative datasets. The majority of the existing data provide, at a minimum, basic information on attendance in preschool programs. In principle there are two main groups of data: data comprised of information collected by official statistics and survey data. However, hardly any data is collected that allow researchers to link preschool program information with child outcome data. There is an urgent need for better data on children from age zero to three, as well as for data on children from immigrant families. There is, in particular, a need for good panel data that would permit individual data to be matched with institutional information. Given recent developments in the German data infrastructure, the potential for preschool education research will certainly improve. Nevertheless, there are a number of significant gaps that need to be explicitly addressed. This contribution recommends several key improvements within the field, including better data on the quality of preschool programs, on family context, and on the cost of preschool education. Finally, the paper stresses the need for detailed intervention studies (on a representative, or generalizable level), which can help us to learn more about the most effective and efficient parameters of preschool programs.

Keywords: preschool education, day care, child outcomes

1. Research questions

Preschool education refers to education given children before the commencement of statutory education, often between the age of two and compulsory school age. The term "preschool education" generally refers to preschool programs in formal educational settings. The prevalent type of preschool programs in Germany are the "*Kindertageseinrichtungen*,"[1] the generic term that encompasses traditional *Kindergarten, Kinderkrippe,* and day care centers, which offer care to children ranging in age from birth to compulsory school age. A broader concept of preschool education might also include family day care (*Tagespflege*), or at least licensed family day care. This is a particularly relevant issue in Germany, where family day care is currently being considered as an alternative to traditional day care programs, at least for younger preschoolers.

---

1   In an even stricter definition the first tier of the German educational system, the so-called *Elementarbereich*, refers to the German *Kindergarten*, which starts at age three. However, a focus solely on the *Elementarbereich* seems too narrow for the analysis of preschool education in Germany today.

Preschool education is embedded in the broader field of early childhood education. This field of educational research views parents and families as integral parts of the early childhood education process, apart from formal educational settings. Thus, for this age group in particular, both the family as a context and the interaction between family and preschool education is of great importance.

Today more than ever, the importance of early childhood education is being recognized and investigated by a range of disciplines, including neuroscience, developmental psychology, educational research, educational economics, and sociology. In all these diverse strands of research there is broad agreement that these early years play a crucial role in the child's development, and are particularly important for his or her later performance.

Considering the importance of this early stage, a great deal of attention should be devoted to preschool programs, particularly if the broader goal is to improve the effectiveness and efficiency of the educational system as a whole. Preschool programs produce a wide range of positive effects. US studies have demonstrated that high-quality programs produce short-term gains in cognitive functioning and longer-term gains in school achievement, including special education placement, high school graduation, and college enrollment. Other positive impacts include better health as adults, reduced criminal activities, and an increase in lifetime earnings. High-quality preschool programs are particularly important for disadvantaged children.[2] Although most of these effects have been demonstrated in the context of model programs, high-quality preschool programs can be considered an effective tool to reduce the achievement gap between poor children and children from more affluent families. In a broader sense, high-quality preschool programs can contribute to increasing an economy's human capital.

Today more than ever before, preschool programs are attracting attention among the German public. Beginning with the "Schröder-government" and increasingly under the first "Merkel-government," initiatives have been launched to augment preschool education for children under the age of three. The Law for Expansion of Daycare (TAG, *Tagesbetreuungsausbaugesetz*) and the Law to Support Children (Kifög, *Kinderförderungsgesetz*) at the federal level represent major steps in this direction. These initiatives have been accompanied by various initiatives at the state and municipal level. The federal states and in particular the municipalities are the agencies actually responsible for the funding of preschool programs. Although these initiatives are motivated by more than just educational objectives,[3] they are critically important for the improvement of preschool education in Germany. The

---

2   For a summary of the results of the relevant US studies, see for instance Karoly et al. (2006).

3   Another important motivation behind these initiatives is the improvement of the reconciliation of work and family life in Germany.

federal government has set a target of providing preschool education or day care to 35 percent of children under the age of three by the year 2013. In addition to these efforts to increase the quantity of preschool in Germany, there are various initiatives to increase preschool quality. In providing these measures, the German government is trying to catch up with the preschool provision rates in other countries such as the Scandinavian countries, France, and Belgium. For instance, in Denmark almost 62 percent, in Norway 44 percent, and in Belgium 34 percent of all children under the age of three attend some kind of formal day care. In Germany the corresponding number was 9 percent (OECD 2006; 2007; UNICEF 2008). It is clear that countries like Sweden and Denmark, widely considered to be the childcare and preschool education leaders in Europe, offer their citizens universal–or nearly university – high-quality, publicly-funded childcare. However, there are other countries like Germany that have begun to promote increased preschool education attendance. The UK, for instance, has sought to learn from the Nordic childcare model by moving towards a model of universal childcare while focusing on an educational approach for early childhood services.

For older preschoolers (three years and over), the German discussion looks different. In Germany these children have the legal right to a place in a formal day care program, or *Kindertageseinrichtung*; however, at the federal level this legal right only covers four hours per day. The public debate here seems to favor an increase in the number of available slots covering more hours as well as the provision of a lunch. Again, this is an already established standard in some other European countries: in Sweden 63 percent, in Denmark 83 percent, and in France 45 percent of all children aged three to five are enrolled in full-time day care; in Germany the rate was only 29 percent (OECD 2006; 2007).

In terms of the educational aspects of preschool facilities, there is yet another issue that requires attention. Children from families occupying a better socio-economic position are particularly overrepresented in the German preschool system, especially up to age four. Empirical evidence suggests that this is different from other European countries, in particular from the Scandinavian countries (OECD 2006). After the age of four, almost all children in Germany attend preschool (87 percent of all 4–5 year-olds and 91 percent of all 5–6 year-olds).[4] Below the age of four, however, preschool attendance is higher amongst those children with a non-migration background compared to those with a migration background. Nonetheless, preschool attendance at later ages (4–5 and 5–6 year olds) does not differ anymore by migration background. This is significant as preschool education could be an efficient tool for integration.

---

4   See for instance, Konsortium Bildungsberichterstattung (2006: chapter C).

2. Status quo: Databases and access

There are only a few microdatasets covering the field of preschool education in Germany – even fewer of these are nationally representative datasets. The majority of these provide, at a minimum, information on attendance in preschool programs. There are two main groups of data: the first includes data collected by official statistics. The most important database of this type is the Children and Youth Services Statistics (KJH-Statistik, *Kinder- und Jugendhilfestatistik*) (see Schilling 2002; Kolvenbach and Taubmann 2006). Since 2006, KJH-Statistik has compiled information on the number of children attending a formal day care program and the number of children attending a publicly funded family day care facility (*Kindertagespflege*). They include information on the staff of these programs and facilities.[5] In addition, data on the age and gender of the children, the country of origin of the parents, the language spoken most at home, and information on special needs for support are also collected. The KJH-Statistik covers the number of hours in care as stipulated in the care contract[6] and the provision of school lunch. These data indicate the type of provider – whether a non-profit provider or for-profit provider. The information on staff details their gender and contracted working time. The information on age, qualifications, occupational status, and field of activity is collected for the majority of the staff members. All data are collected on a yearly basis.[7] Official reporting of these statistics differs by state and district. It is the task of the Office for Children and Youth Services Statistics (AKJ, *Arbeitsstelle Kinder- und Jugendhilfestatistik*) in Dortmund to analyze this data and to promote its use.[8] The microdata can be used via the Research Data Centers of the Statistical Offices of the German *Länder*. Other official statistics no longer cover preschool education: the German Microcensus stopped doing so in 2005. Thus, the Scientific Use Files from the Microcensus provide information on whether the children in the household attend some type of formal day care or preschool only until 2004.

The second set of data is survey data. This group covers the Children's Panel of the German Youth Institute (*DJI, Deutsches Jugendinstitut*).[9] This

---

5 Before 2006 these statistics included information on the number of places available in formal day care programs. This supply-side approach was changed to provide better information on actual attendance rates. For the relevant law, see the Act on the Further Development of Child and Youth Services (KICK, *Kinder- und Jugendhilfeentwicklungsgesetz*), which came into effect in October 2005 (Kolvenbah and Taubmann 2006). Information on family day care facilities was not collected before this date.
6 The daily care hours as contracted do not necessarily correspond to the actual amount of time in day care.
7 Before 2006, they were collected on a four-year basis only.
8 http://www.akjstat.uni-dortmund.de/
9 http://www.dji.de/kinderpanel. See also Alt (2005).

study was started in 2002 with two cohorts: one of children in their last year of preschool (age five), and one of children in second grade (age eight). In the first wave the sample size was over 2,000 children. Two more waves followed in 2004 and 2005. The DJI Children's Panel covers various topics in addition to information about the preschool education. These include whether a child attends a formal day care program, and information about the provider, actual daily care hours, costs, and the level of parental satisfaction with the preschool program. In addition, information on the child's health and personality is collected as well as data on the family and household. There is a special sample for the Turkish and Russian minorities. Given the panel character of the DJI Children's Panel, this dataset allows for longitudinal research, although the panel covers only three waves. In principle, the DJI study is open to the entire research community.

Another dataset covering preschool education is the German Socio-Economic Panel (SOEP, *Sozio-oekonomisches Panel*).[10] The SOEP is a representative longitudinal study of private households in Germany that has regularly surveyed the same private households, individuals, and families since 1984. Since this time, information on preschool education has also been collected, including data on preschool attendance and daily hours in preschool for all children in the household. Every four years, more information is collected on the type of provider, lunch provision, and parental fees. In 2003, the SOEP started collecting age-specific information as well. In the meantime, special survey instruments have been developed for children in their first year of life, for two- to three-year olds, and for children in their last year of preschool. For all these three age groups, the SOEP collects more detailed information on the child, including his or her preschool education and child outcomes (for more information, see Lohmann et al. 2008: chapters 3.1 and 8.1). Further age-specific survey instruments for children in school are planned up to age 16 or 17 (see Schupp et al. 2008). This is the age when the "children" are interviewed as regular SOEP respondents. Given the panel character of the SOEP, such data is especially useful for longitudinal research, in particular for the analysis of preschool effects. With the SOEP, the relationship between preschool education, family indicators, and child outcomes can be analyzed. The SOEP data are available to the entire research community.

Another group of surveys consists of those with a research focus other than preschool education. One example of this type is the German Health Interview and Examination Survey for Children and Adolescents (KIGGS. *Studie zur Gesundheit von Kindern und Jugendlichen in Deutschland*) by the Robert Koch Institute.[11] It was designed as a nation-wide health survey for the age group from 0 to 17 years. Between 2003 and 2006, around 18,000

---

10 http://www.diw.de/english/soep/26636.html. See also Wagner et al. (2007).
11 http://www.kiggs.de/. See also Kurth et al. (2008).

children were enrolled. The data obtained include a large number of objective and subjective health measures. The parents were asked if the child visits a childcare program and the age of entry. Here, preschool education is valued as one of numerous other environmental determinants of child health. These data thus are useful for the analysis of the relationship between preschool education and child health. There will be a Public Use File of the KIGGS data available starting in 2009.

Apart from these representative datasets with a panel character, there exist other cross-sectional or regionally limited datasets that include information on preschool education. Most of these represent regional cross-sections with a special focus on children. Such a cross-sectional study is the DJI Children's Panel,[12] which collects detailed information about preschool education. In the study, more than 8,000 parents of children up to the age of six were interviewed. An example of a regionally restricted panel study is the German Longitudinal Study on the Genesis of Individual Competencies (LOGIK, *Longitudinalstudie zur Genese individueller Kompetenzen*), started in 1984 with 200 nearly four-year-old children in the region of Munich (see Weinert and Schneider 1999). The study, which was designed to analyze the development of various competences of children, contains information on preschool education as an environmental determinant of child development. Another study by Tietze et al. (1998) in three German states was designed to study the effects of preschool program quality. The study started with children in preschool and followed them up to primary school. Given the focus of this study, it is one of the few that has collected detailed information on the structural and process quality of preschool education. All these very different datasets were produced by a particular research group or institution with a particular research interest. In general, they are not available to the broader research community. Nevertheless, they can serve as models for the development of an adequate preschool data infrastructure.

From a European and international perspective, it is important to note that other countries realized the importance of a solid data infrastructure for research on preschool education – and on early education in general – long before Germany did. The Anglo-American research community was among the first to take up this issue in depth.[13] Thus, such major household panel studies as the US Panel Study of Income Dynamics (PSID) with its Child Development Supplement (CDS)[14] and the National Longitudinal Surveys of Youth (NLSY)[15] have special child-related supplements or questions. A number of these include research questions related to preschool education

---

12 http://www.dji.de/cgi-bin/projekte/output.php?projekt=390. See also Bien et al. (2006).
13 For a brief summary of Anglo-American longitudinal studies covering the early years, see BMBF (2008: chapter 2).
14 http://psidonline.isr.umich.edu/CDS/
15 http://www.bls.gov/nls/

that collect information on household and family context in particular. Since they cover some measures on the cognitive and non-cognitive development of children, they allow longitudinal studies on the effect of preschool education. Apart from major household panel studies, the NICHD study,[16] which began in 1991, is an example of a study offering an extremely rich database for the analysis of preschool education. The Cost, Quality and Child Outcomes Study in Child Care Centers (e.g., Helburn et al. 1995) is one of the few examples that combine detailed information on the quality of preschool programs and detailed information on its costs. There are a few studies that focus on particular model preschool programs. They allow a very detailed analysis of their effects, benefits, and costs (e.g., Perry Preschool Project, Schweinhardt et al. 2005). Great Britain is another country that acted on the perceived need for a data infrastructure on early education many years ago, producing various cohort studies starting at birth like the British Cohort Study,[17] the Millennium Cohort Study,[18] and the Avon Longitudinal Study of Pregnancy and Childhood (ALSPAC).[19]

For comparable European and international research, it would be beneficial for comparable survey instruments to be used in the collection of data on preschool education and child outcomes. The European Statistics on Income and Living Conditions (EU-SILC) is designed to provide harmonized instruments to this end. The EU-SILC data cover some preschool information, such as the number of hours in preschool.

3. Future developments

Given the well-recognized importance of preschool education, it is surprising that there are so few initiatives that exist in this field of educational research so far. In response to the general lack of empirically based educational research, the Federal Ministry of Education and Research (BMBF, *Bundesministerium für Bildung und Forschung*) has launched various initiatives to stimulate empirical research on education in Germany over the last several years. One of the few initiatives to focus on preschool (and school) education, however, is the BiKS Project.[20] BiKS stands for educational processes, competence development, and selection decisions at preschool and primary school age. It is based at the University of Bamberg and began the first round of data collection in 2005. The BiKS studies are based on formal

---

16 http://secc.rti.org/
17 http://www.cls.ioe.ac.uk
18 http://www.millenniumcohort.org/
19 http://www.bristol.ac.uk/alspac
20 http://www.uni-bamberg.de/biks/

childcare programs and schools in Bavaria and Hesse. The longitudinal study "BiKS 3-8" involves the observation of approximately 600 children, beginning at age three and continuing up to the second grade of elementary school.[21] This project will help to answer questions about the effects of preschooling, taking various socio-demographic and socio-economic variables of family background into account. In addition, the project will be concerned with the quality of preschool education.

Another project that reflects the efforts of the federal government to stimulate empirical educational research is the German National Educational Panel Study or NEPS.[22] The panel started in 2009. First information for children aged four and older will be collected. It is planned to collect information for younger children later. The sample will be drawn from institutions such as preschool programs, day care centers and schools. Once these data have been collected, they will provide the basis for innovative research, particularly on the effects of preschool programs. The NEPS offers a highly promising infrastructure, with a research team that includes social scientists from different disciplines such as sociology, education, psychology, and economics.

4. Future developments: European and international challenges

A European target has been set by the Barcelona European Council to provide childcare services for 90 percent of children between three years of age and the mandatory school age by 2010, and for 33 percent of children under three years of age (European Council 2002). In light of this, and even more recent initiatives from May 2005 that consider the improvement of childcare an important tool for meeting this target, the near-complete lack of internationally comparable data on preschool education is a significant problem.[23] The only exception to this is the information in EU-SILC but, as indicated above, this contains little preschool information and does not include quality data or child outcome data in a strict sense, such as variables on skills or socio-emotional behavior, which is precisely the type of data needed to study educational effects of preschool programs from a European

---

21 The longitudinal BiKS 8-12 follows approx. 2,000 children from third grade through sixth grade.
22 http://www.uni-bamberg.de/neps
23 The expansion of early childcare and education is also a goal on a broader international level. One of UNESCO's medium-term objectives (2002–2007) is the expansion and improvement of comprehensive early childcare and education, especially for the most vulnerable and disadvantaged children (UNESCO 2003).

perspective. Apart from this, it is not clear what the different countries mean by the term "childcare" and thus whether this information can be used for research on preschool education.

In light of all these findings, it is clear that *there is need in most countries for a systematic procedure* to collect and provide consistent and comparable information on preschool education programs. Currently, the ministries responsible for young children use different indicators and diverse methods in collecting data on the preschool education of young children. Thus the definition of the population group considered to be in pre-primary education is often arbitrary. Moreover, program criteria are sometimes confusing. What is clear is that countries use different proxy measures to determine whether a program should be classified as educational or not. Variation in these proxy measures undermines comparability. Moreover, the weekly and annual durations of preschool education sessions are rarely taken into account. Thus it is obvious that the first future challenge to be faced is to provide comparable data on preschool education with respect to basic structural characteristics. Once these data exist, a further challenge will be to provide data on program quality, the costs and potential outcomes of preschool education programs in the European countries, or at an even broader level among the various OECD countries (on the need for comparable data, see OECD 2006, esp. chapter 8).

5. Conclusions and recommendations

Given the importance of improved preschool programs in Germany and taking into account the various initiatives underway on different levels, the following demands for a data infrastructure in this area can be summarized: (1) Current and detailed data on the development of preschool programs is needed (detailed with respect to age groups, hours of care provided, provider type, etc.). This is also needed to ensure that the current political initiatives are effective. This data should be available on a small regional level since there are great regional disparities that needed to be analyzed. (2) Data on attendance in these preschool programs are needed that cover the socio-demographic and socio-economic backgrounds of the children and their families. This will make it possible to address important questions such as whether disadvantaged children attend preschool. (3) Given the importance of preschool programs, data on the quality of these programs should be made available. These data should not focus on structural quality indicators alone (e.g., group size, child-staff ratios). As research has shown, other quality dimensions such as process quality (the interaction between child and teacher) are even more important for child development (see, for instance,

Roßbach 2005). (4) These data should ideally be linked to cost information. General information on the expenses of such programs is important, but not necessarily sufficient. What is ideally needed is data on the detailed costs of particular programs in relation to the level of educational quality. (5) Especially from a longitudinal point of view, it is important to have child outcome data[24] that can be linked to preschool information. This child outcome data should include cognitive measures as well as socio-emotional outcome measures. Only this linkage allows the effects of preschool programs to be analyzed in the short, medium, and long term. Given the fact that most of the empirical research on the effects of preschool programs has been conducted in Anglo-American settings, this type of analysis is widely missing in Germany, where the necessary microdata to support it is virtually non-existent. Up to now, there have only been few empirical studies on preschool effects in Germany, partly based on regionally restricted samples. Moreover, only a few of the existing studies were able to control for the quality of the preschool programs and even less for their costs (for a short summary of these studies based on representative microdata see Spieß 2008a).

Given the recent developments in German data infrastructure, the potential for preschool education research will certainly improve. Nevertheless, a number of gaps remain:

(1) First of all, groups of children under three or four years of age have not received adequate attention to date. This partly reflects the longstanding idea that preschool education begins with entrance to the traditional German *Kindergarten* at age three. Yet developmental psychologists and brain researchers have shown that education starts much earlier. Moreover, there is a new political commitment to increasing preschool attendance of children below the age of three. It is therefore recommended that the data infrastructure be improved particularly around this early stage of child development.[25]

(2) Given the importance of preschool for disadvantaged children – such as children from households with low socio-economic status – datasets covering this group should have an adequate sample size. An oversampling of this group in existing surveys might be one option; special surveys of these groups of children might be another. Nevertheless, future study designs should integrate the setup of a control group as well.

---

24 For a summary of relevant child outcome indicators with respect to various competencies in early childhood, see, for instance, BMBF (2008).

25 The SOEP data are almost the only publicly available dataset covering this early age. More data is also needed on family day care, which will probably play an increasingly important role in the future. Therefore, efforts to improve the data infrastructure for the younger age group should be linked with efforts to improve the data situation on family day care.

(3) Third, there are no representative data on the quality of preschool education programs if researchers do not want to rely solely on structural quality indicators (such as group size, staff-to-child ratio, or education of the staff). This is striking, considering that other quality dimensions, such as process quality, have been shown to be of much greater importance than structural indicators in explaining the variance in child outcomes. However, the lack of representative data on this aspect might be related to difficulties inherent in measuring process quality. There are a few instruments for quantifying process quality (for a summary, see Mc Cabe and Ackermann 2007), but they are costly and time intensive. Thus, on the one hand, greater effort should be put into the development of more efficient instruments for measuring process quality with respect to cost and time. On the other hand, more effort should be put into the application of existing instruments to a broader set of preschool programs.

(4) Fourth, given the significant impact of preschool quality on child development, measures of quality should be available in datasets that also include child outcome measures. Given the lack of efficient measures of process quality in the short-run, structural quality indicators can be used in a first stage. Official data such as the Children and Youth Services Statistic cover some indicators on the structural quality of preschool programs, while surveys such as the SOEP cover child outcome measures. At the moment, however, it is not possible to link this information. Therefore, serious investigation needs to be undertaken to determine how survey data can be linked with official data, and it is obvious that the preschool institution a child attends is the key indicator. The efforts of labor market researchers to link official data with survey data in their field of research might provide a useful model. Another option would be to enrich datasets like the SOEP with quality data on preschool by collecting additional quality data on preschool for the explicit purpose of linkage. This is possible once the respondent agrees to allow the institution that his or her child attends to be identified.[26] It is obvious that data security will play a major role in such an undertaking. But such efforts are of particular interest in the long run since they enable long-term analysis.

(5) Fifth, the crucial interaction between the family or home environment and preschool education can be analyzed using current and future data, but only to a very limited extent. This is particularly true with respect to the quality of these two educational settings, although it is known from international research that these quality aspects are of extraordinary

---

26 The SOEP has conducted a pretest asking respondents for information on the preschool or day care center that their child attends (see Schupp et al. 2008: 72).

importance. It is therefore recommended that greater effort be expended to provide data on the quality of the family/home environment[27] and the quality of preschool education simultaneously. Such data would be of particular interest for multilevel analysis.

(6) Apart from preschool quality and child outcome aspects, there is a dearth of information on the real costs of preschool programs. There are almost no options for combining detailed cost information with preschool quality and child outcome information. This is remarkable since pure information on cost is not very useful in itself for educational research, and the relationship between preschool quality and child outcomes and a given input (here, particular costs) is unknown. Better data on costs, preschool quality, and child outcomes are necessary for solid cost-benefits analyses of the German preschool system. A cost-benefit analysis based on such data would complete the set of first attempts for cost-benefit calculations in Germany (see Spieß 2008b).

(7) Nevertheless, it is clear that compiling nationally representative datasets that cover detailed cost information, quality information, and detailed information on various aspects of the cognitive and non-cognitive development of children is an extremely costly and time-consuming endeavor. To save resources, it might be possible to add the missing information to a preexisting dataset at a less detailed level. Alternately, one could focus on particular preschool programs or a particular group of children. In this case, we would recommend more intervention studies in the strict sense. These studies could have different foci, but should all aim at collecting more detailed information on preschool quality, child outcomes, and costs. They would also allow us to learn more about the effects of specific preschool programs with a special educational program.

(8) From an international, and in particular European perspective, there is a clear need for more, and more comparable data on preschool education in the various countries. As pointed out in section 4, the primary aim is to collect and provide more detailed information on preschool, with information on structural indicators. Such *datasets need to cover newborns to six-year-olds*, and include all forms of provision, regardless of administrative responsibility, funding source, or setting. What is needed is a collection of data over time. From a longer-term perspective, comparable data are needed, which offer more information on the quality, costs, and outcomes of such preschool education programs.

---

27 One example of a scale that could be used to measure the quality of a child's home environment, see the HOME scale as used in the NLSY (Bradely et al. 2001).

Apart from this, there is a special need for collecting and identifying preschool information for children from disadvantaged families.

(9) All these recommendations reveal obvious links to the current state of the data infrastructure in the field of families in general (see Huinink in this publication) and in the fields of abilities and competencies (see Stern, Trautwein and Schoon in this publication). Thus it might be of added value to develop the preschool data infrastructure in collaboration with the data infrastructure of the other fields mentioned. Although the foci might differ, the overlap between these various fields should be kept in mind and efforts should be made to foster exchange between the different interests, agencies, and organizations involved.

References:

Alt, C. (2005): Data, Design and Constructs – The First Wave of the Children's Panel. In: Klöckner, C. and Paetzel, U. (Eds.): Kindheitsforschung und kommunale Praxis. Praxisnahe Erkenntnisse aus der aktuellen Kindheitsforschung. Wiesbaden.
Bien, W./Rauschenbach, T. and Riedel, B. (Eds.) (2006): Wer betreut Deutschlands Kinder? Weinheim/Basel.
Bradley, R.H./Corwyn, R.F./McAdoo, H.P. and Coll, C.G. (2001): The Home Environments of Children in the United States Part I: Variations by Age, Ethnicity, and Poverty Status. Child Development 72, 1844-1867.
BMBF – Bundesministerium für Bildung und Forschung (Ed.) (2008): Kindliche Kompetenzen im Elementarbereich: Förderbarkeit, Bedeutung und Messung. Reihe Bildungsforschung des BMBF, Volume 24.
European Council (2002): Presidency conclusions, Barcelona European Council, 15-16 March 2002, available at: http://ue.eu.int/ueDocs/cms_Data/docs/pressData/en/ec/71025.pdf. [Last visited 02/03/2010].
Helburn, S. (1995): Cost, Quality, and Child Outcomes in Child Care Centers: Key Findings and Recommendations. Young Children 50, 40-44.
Roßbach, H.-G. (2005): Effekte qualitativ guter Betreuung, Bildung und Erziehung im frühen Kindesalter auf Kinder und ihre Familien. In: Sachverständigenkommission Zwölfter Kinder- und Jugendbericht (Ed.): Bildung, Betreuung und Erziehung von Kindern unter sechs Jahren. München.
Karoly, L.A./Kilburn, R.M. and Cannon, J.S. (2006): Early Childhood Interventions: Proven Results, Future Promise, RAND Cooperation. Santa Monica.
Kolvenbach, F.-J. and Taubmann, D. (2006): Neue Statistiken zur Kindertagesbetreuung. Wirtschaft und Statistik 2, 166-171.
Konsortium Bildungsberichterstattung (Ed.) (2006): Bildung in Deutschland. Gütersloh.
Kurth, B.-M. et al. (2008): The challenge of comprehensively mapping children's health in a nation-wide health survey: Design of the German KiGGS-Study. BMC Public Health 8, 196.
Lohmann, H./Spieß, C.K./Groh-Samberg, O. and Schupp, J. (2008): Analysepotenziale des Sozio-oekonomischen Panels (SOEP) für die empirische Bildungsforschung. SOEP Paper No. 110.
McCabe, L.A. and Ackerman, D.J. (2007): Child Care Center Quality: Measurement Issues and Links to Child Developmental Outcomes. DIW Data Documentation No. 25.
OECD (2006): Starting Strong II. Paris.
OECD (2007): Babies and Bosses. A Synthesis of Findings for OECD Countries. Paris.
Roßbach, H.-G. (2005): Effekte qualitativ guter Betreuung, Bildung und Erziehung im frühen Kindesalter auf Kinder und ihre Familien. In: Sachverständigenkommission Zwölfter Kinder- und Jugendbericht (Ed.): Bildung, Betreuung und Erziehung von Kindern unter sechs Jahren. Bd. 1. München.

Schilling, M. (2002): Die amtliche Kinder- und Jugendhilfestatistik. Dissertation am Fachbereich Erziehungswissenschaft und Soziologie der Universität Dortmund, November 2002.

Schupp, J./Spieß, C.K. and Wagner, G.G. (2008): Die verhaltenswissenschaftliche Weiterentwicklung des Erhebungsprogramms des SOEP. Vierteljahrshefte zur Wirtschaftsforschung 77, 63-76.

Schweinhart, L.J./Montie, J./Xiang, Z./Barnett, W.S./Belfield, C.R. and Nores, M. (2005): Lifetime Effects: The High/Scope Perry Preschool Study Through Age 40. Ypsilanti.

Spieß, C.K. (2008a): Early Childhood Education and Care in Germany: The Status Quo and Reform Proposals. Zeitschrift für Betriebswirtschaftslehre 67, 1-20.

Spieß, C.K. (2008b): Volkswirtschaftliche Bedeutung der Kinderbetreuung: Wie ist diese zu bewerten und was können wir dabei aus dem Ausland lernen? In: von der Leyen, U. (Ed.) (2008): Voneinander lernen – miteinander handeln: Aufgaben und Perspektiven der Europäischen Allianz für Familien. Berlin.

Tietze, W. (Ed.) (1998): Wie gut sind unsere Kindergärten? Eine Untersuchung zur pädagogischen Qualität in deutschen Kindergärten. Weinheim.

Wagner, G.G./Frick, J.R. and Schupp, J. (2007): The German Socio-Economic Panel Study (SOEP): Scope, Evolution and Enhancements. Schmollers Jahrbuch 127, 139-170.

Weinert, F.E. and Schneider, W. (Eds.) (1999): Individual development from 3 to 12: Findings from the Munich Longitudinal Study. New York.

UNESCO (2003): Medium-term strategy 2002-2007, available at: http://unesdoc.unesco.org/images/0012/001254/125434e.pdf. [Last visited 02/03/2010].

Unicef Innocenti Research Centre (UNICEF) (2008): The child care transition, Report Card 8. Florence.

3.3 Data in the Domain of Secondary School Education

Petra Stanat and Hans Döbert

Contact:

Petra Stanat
Humboldt-Universität zu Berlin
Institut zur Qualitätsentwicklung im Bildungswesen
Unter den Linden 6
10099 Berlin
Germany
e-mail: petra.stanat[at]iqb.hu-berlin.de

Abstract

Research on school education is exceptionally active at present. This heightened level of activity is partly due to the realization that, compared to other countries, Germany knows very little about its school system. Before the results from the first cycle of the Programme for International Student Assessment (PISA) were published at the end of 2001, for example, even the proportion of immigrant students attending German schools was largely unknown (Baumert et al. 2001). Although the situation has changed tremendously over the last 10 years, many questions remain open. One of the major research gaps pertains to how student competencies and other aspects of educational success develop over time and across different stages of the education system. Similarly, information on the factors that shape these developments is lacking. This is particularly the case for process factors within schools, classrooms, and families that affect student learning. Moreover, although considerable progress has been made in capturing cognitive competencies and skills, little is known about how they unfold over time. Also, the role that "soft-skills," such as social competencies, play as determinants and outcomes of educational processes remains largely unclear. To provide a basis for exploring these and other issues, it is necessary to make existing datasets available to researchers and to generate additional datasets with improved research designs and instrumentation.

1. Currently available datasets

Three types of datasets are currently available in the domain of school education in Germany: official and non-official school statistics (primarily the school statistics and the Microcensus), survey data (e.g., SOEP,[1] ALLBUS,[2] the HIS[3] survey of students eligible for university studies), and data from large-scale assessments of student performance (e.g., PISA, TIMSS,[4] PIRLS,[5] *Länder* assessments).[6] From the perspectives of educational monitoring and reporting, the usefulness of these datasets depends, among other things, on the extent to which they include information on (1) student educational participation (including the type of school attended within the

---

1 German Socio-Economic Panel (SOEP, *Sozio-oekonomisches Panel*).
2 German General Social Survey (ALLBUS, *Allgemeine Bevölkerungsumfrage*).
3 Higher Education Information System (HIS, *Hochschul-Informations-System*).
4 Trends in International Mathematics and Science Study.
5 Progress in International Reading Literacy Study.
6 Important additional data sources are research projects focusing on specific aspects of the school system, such as video studies on classroom instruction (e.g., Seidel et al. 2007), studies on transitions from elementary to secondary school (e.g., Ditton 2007), or studies on whole day schooling within the Study on the Development of Whole-day Schools (StEG, *Studie zur Entwicklung von Ganztagsschulen*) program (Holtappels et al. 2008). It is beyond the scope of this report, however, to cover these studies as well.

tracked system and grade retention), (2) learning outcomes in core domains, (3) family background, and (4) student development over time (preferably based on longitudinal data rather than on retrospective information). In terms of these features, each of the listed dataset has differential strengths and weaknesses.

- The main advantage of *school statistics* is that they are based on data collected for the entire school population. They include information on educational participation and grade retention. However, the data are cross-sectional and are provided at the aggregate level only. It is consequently neither possible to perform individual-level analyses nor longitudinal analyses based on school statistics. In terms of student background, the data include only rudimentary information, such as gender and nationality. Moreover, indicators of learning outcomes are not available. An attempt is currently being made to reform the data collection process for school statistics. This reform, which will be described in more detail below, would be in line with the approach taken in many other countries where school statistics are already based on individual-level data and include a student identification number.

- Although the *Microcensus* provides data on individuals within households, its usefulness for school-related analyses is also quite limited. In the past, the Microcensus asked respondents only whether or not household members attended a school and, if so, which grade they were in. Information on the type of school attended was not collected. This changed in the 2008 survey, which now includes questions on the types of school the household members visit. At the same time, however, questions on attendance of preschool institutions, such as kindergarten, have been eliminated from the survey. Moreover, although the Microcensus now collects more detailed information on family immigration background, some of the most important questions (e.g., country of birth) will only be asked every four years. Like school statistics, Microcensus data are cross-sectional and do not include any indicators of learning outcomes. Similar household surveys are also conducted in other countries, such as the Labour Force Survey (LFS) in the UK or the Swiss Labour Force Survey (SAKE, *Arbeitskräfteerhebung*).

- Among all the surveys carried out in Germany, the *Socio-Economic Panel (SOEP)* is the most frequently used dataset for individual-level analyses related to schooling. It provides information on school participation and on a large number of background factors over time. Since 2006, the SOEP has also collected data on various aspects of cognitive functioning (Wagner et al. 2007). Adolescents are tested with a measure of verbal, numerical, and figural intelligence, and adults complete short tests on processing speed and word fluency. This addition is useful for many analyses, yet its relevance for questions related to outcomes of schooling is limited. Although schools certainly affect students' intelligence development, their effects on such domain-general cognitive dispositions are considerably smaller than on subject-specific competencies, such as mathematics or foreign languages (Baumert et al. 2007). Again, similar longitudinal household surveys are carried out in other countries, such as the Longitudinal Household Study in the UK (UKLHS) or Labourmarket Monitoring (LAMO) in Austria.

- *Large-scale assessments of student performance* have gained in importance considerably over the past ten years. Due to factors such as a generally negative attitude towards testing that was shared by many members of relevant stakeholder groups in Germany, as well as the potential conflict associated with comparisons of student performance across the federal states, or *Länder*, Germany has, for a long time, refrained from measuring the output of schooling. In the aftermath of the first cycle of the OECD's Programme for International Student Assessment (PISA), whose results were published in 2001 (Baumert et al. 2001; OECD 2001), however, this changed dramatically. The disappointing results that PISA revealed for Germany has spurred a national paradigm shift, from an almost exclusive input-orientation in the school system to a considerably stronger focus on its output – a shift that many other countries, such as the Netherlands, Sweden, or the United States, have undertaken long ago. The Standing Conference of the Ministers of Education and Cultural Affairs of the *Länder* in the Federal Republic of Germany (KMK, *Kultusministerkonferenz*) decided to participate regularly in the international large-scale assessment studies PISA, TIMSS elementary school, and PIRLS. In addition, the KMK set up the Institute for Educational Progress (IQB, *Institut zur Qualitätsentwicklung im Bildungswesen*) whose task it is to coordinate the specification of national standards for learning outcomes in various school subjects and to develop test instruments that can be used to evaluate the extent to which the standards are met (Köller 2008). The IQB will administer these tests in representative samples in order to provide information on student performance levels in the 16 *Länder*.

In addition to these national activities, several of the German states have carried out their own assessment studies (e.g., LAU,[7] KESS,[8] MARKUS,[9]

---

7 Aspects of Learning Prerequisites and Learning Develompment (LAU, *Aspekte der Lernausgangslage und der Lernentwicklung*).
8 Competencies and Attributes of Students (KESS, *Kompetenzen und Einstellungen von Schülerinnen und Schülern*).
9 Rhineland-Palatinate Comprehensive Assessment in Mathematics: Competencies, Characteristics of Instruction, School Context (MARKUS, *Mathematik-Gesamterhebung Rheinland-Pfalz: Kompetenzen, Unterrichtsmerkmale, Schulkontext*).

ELEMENT,[10] QuaSUM[11]), and all of them are currently conducting "comparison tests" or *Vergleichsarbeiten* on a regular basis in selected grades (typically grades 3 and 8). The main purpose of the *Vergleichsarbeiten* is to provide schools, teachers, parents, and students with feedback on their relative learning results (Hosenfeld, 2008). Although the tests are developed centrally, they are administered and scored by the students' teachers, so the quality of the data is unclear. Moreover, whereas the international, national, and *Länder*-specific assessment studies typically measure a wide range of background variables, this type of information is either absent from or highly limited in the *Vergleichsarbeiten* datasets.

The international and national student assessment studies present an important data source for analyses on secondary schools. They provide highly reliable information on educational participation as well as learning outcomes. With the exception of a national extension to PISA 2003 (Prenzel et al. 2006) and the nationwide study on language competencies DESI[12] (Klieme et al. 2008), both of which included a longitudinal addition with two measurement points (PISA: from the end of grade 8 to the end of grade 9; DESI: from the beginning to the end of grade 9), the national assessments typically have cross-sectional designs. Longitudinal studies in selected regions of Germany include: BIJU[13] (grades 7–12 and transition to work), BiKS[14] (ages 3–8 and 8–12), DESI (beginning and end of grade 9), ELEMENT (grades 4–10), LAU[15]/ULME[16] (grades 5–13, vocational training), SCHOLASTIK[17] (grades 1-4), and TOSCA[18] (grade 10–vocational training or university).

---

10   Study on Competencies in Reading and Mathematics (ELEMENT, *Erhebung zum Lese- und Mathematikverständnis*).
11   Study on School Quality in Mathematics Instruction (QuaSUM, *Qualitätsuntersuchung an Schulen zum Unterricht in Mathematik*).
12   Assessment of Student Achievements in German and English as a Foreign Language (DESI, *Deutsch-Englisch-Schülerleistungen-International*).
13   Learning Processes, Educational Careers, and Psychosocial Development in Adolescence and Young Adulthood (BIJU, *Bildungsverläufe und psychosoziale Entwicklung im Jugend- und jungen Erwachsenenalter*).
14   Educational Processes, Competence Development, and Selection Decisions in Pre- and Primary School Age (BiKS, *Bildungsprozesse, Kompetenzentwicklungen und Selektionsentscheidungen im Vor- und Grundschulalter*).
15   Aspects of Learning Prerequisites and Learning Development (LAU, *Aspekte der Lernausgangslage und der Lernentwicklung*).
16   Study on Achievment, Motivation, and Attitudes of Students at the Beginning of Vocational Education (ULME, *Untersuchungen der Leistungen, Motivation und Einstellungen zu Beginn der beruflichen Ausbildung*).
17   Organized Learning Opportunities at School and the Socialization of Talents, Interests, and Competencies (SCHOLASTIK, *Schulorganisierte Lernangebote und die Sozialisation von Talenten, Interessen und Kompetenzen*).
18   Transformations of the Secondary School System and Academic Careers (TOSCA, *Transformation des Sekundarschulsystems und akademische Karrieren*).

In general, the types of datasets that are currently available in Germany typically also exist in other countries. Germany lags behind some international developments, yet the process of catching up with these developments is currently well under way.

2. New developments

2.1 Change of school statistics to individual-level data

In 2003, the KMK decided to change the school statistics to individual-level data and defined a core set of variables to be included in the dataset ("Kerndatensatz für schulstatistische Individualdaten der Länder"). The core dataset, which the individual *Länder* may extend as they see fit, encompasses the following variables:

- *Organizational characteristics of the school* (e.g., location, school type, legal status, number of delayed enrollments in first grade)
- *Individual background data of students* (e.g., sex, month and year of birth, nationality, year of immigration to Germany, language spoken in the family, country of birth, grade level, year of enrollment in first grade, school and grade attended the year before, type of grade repetition, focus of special support measures, attendance of all-day schooling programs and after-school care, place of residence)
- *Individual background data of school-leavers and graduates* (similar to data for students remaining in the school as listed above)
- *Individual background data of teachers and data on teacher fluctuation* (e.g., sex, month and year of birth, nationality, type of teacher training, teaching qualification by subjects, gross teaching load, type and hours of reduced or additional teaching load, number of lessons taught at the school, functions within the school's administration, beginning and end of employment at the school)
- *Data on classes/courses at the school*
- *Organizational data in terms of instructional units* (e.g., grade level, educational track, subject, lessons per week, course type)

The KMK had aimed to convert school statistics to individual-level data with the agreed-upon core set of variables by 2007. Since the process has not been finalized across the board, however, the time frame has been extended to 2008–2009. Some of the *Länder* already possess individual datasets with student identification numbers while others have not yet begun to change their statistics. Moreover, the *Länder* typically concentrate on public schools, and it is not clear whether the collection of individual school data will be extended to private schools in the future.

The conversion of school statistics to individual-level data is in line with international standards. Informal interviews with representatives from several Northern European countries (including Austria and Switzerland) in the technical group of the OECD's Educational Indicators Project indicate that individual-level data are the rule rather than the exception (Hetmeier and Leidel 2007). Among the eleven countries included in the interviews, five (Austria, Denmark, Israel, the Netherlands, Switzerland) collect individual-level data for students in elementary schools and all countries except Poland and Spain collect such data for students in secondary schools. Moreover, the datasets in these countries typically include identification numbers, making it possible to capture educational careers over time. Austria, the Netherlands, and – starting in 2011/2012 – Switzerland use the social security number for this purpose; Denmark, Finland, Norway, Poland, and Sweden use a general person registration number.

In Germany, the data protection commissioners of some *Länder* resist the introduction of pupil identification numbers as well as the establishment of a centralized national data pool. In an attempt to find a compromise solution for this issue, a hashcode is considered that would be derived from data that typically remains unchanged throughout a student's school career (e.g., date of birth, sex, name), thus making it possible to capture educational pathways longitudinally. However, it is highly uncertain whether such a solution will, in fact, be accepted and implemented by all *Länder*. It is also unclear whether individual-level data will be integrated into a national data pool and whether it will cover the entire school system, including private schools and vocational schools.

2.2 The National Educational Panel Study

Carried out by a consortium of researchers from various disciplines concerned with education, its outcomes and returns (education, psychology, sociology, and economics), the National Educational Panel Study (NEPS) promises to provide a dataset that meets the criteria outlined above (Blossfeld et al. 2008). It will include comprehensive information on the participants' educational careers, competencies as well as family background, and it will collect this information longitudinally. The panel is designed as a multi-cohort sequence study with eight stages that cover important transitions within the educational system. Secondary schooling will be analyzed in stage 3 (from elementary school to lower secondary school), in stage 4 (from lower secondary to upper secondary school), and in stage 5 (from lower secondary school to higher education, occupational training, or the labor market). The assessments will focus on five themes that are of particular relevance within research on education. These are (1) competence development across the lifespan, including German-language competencies and reading literacy, mathematical literacy, scientific literacy, foreign-language competencies, and social competencies; (2) educational processes in life course specific learning environments; (3) social inequality and educational decisions in the life course; (4) education acquisitions of immigrants and their descendants across the life span; and (5) education returns. The first assessments within the NEPS will start in 2009–2010 so that the results can be expected to become available in 2011–12.

The implementation of the NEPS is also in line with international developments. Several countries already have similar longitudinal studies in place, such as the 1970 Birth Cohort, the Millennium Cohort, and the Youth Cohort Studies in the UK; the National Longitudinal Survey of Children and Adolescents (NLSCY) in Canada; or the Survey of Children and Youth on "Competence and Context" (COCON) in Switzerland. However, the scope of these studies tends to be more limited than that of the German NEPS, both in terms of the age range included in the assessments and in terms of the covered research foci. A particularly innovative and challenging feature of the NEPS is that it aims at assessing central domain-specific competencies across the lifespan. In addition, while it would be possible to study educational careers based on adequate individual-level school statistics, NEPS will allow for more detailed and in-depth analyses of these careers within contexts. Thus, the NEPS is a highly ambitious program which goes beyond what is currently available internationally. If successful, the study will yield an important database for analyses of educational processes and outcomes.

3. Data access

Data from the Microcensus and such surveys as the SOEP or ALLBUS are typically available as Scientific Use Files. Within the limits of data protection regulations, researchers are free to use the data for scientific analyses. Similarly, the NEPS data will be made accessible to the scientific community as soon as the necessary data cleaning and scaling procedures have been completed. While the international dataset from such studies as TIMSS and PISA can be easily downloaded from the Internet, access to national data from assessments of student performance has traditionally been more restricted. The Federal Ministry of Education and Research (BMBF, *Bundesministerium für Bildung und Forschung*) is funding a Research Data Center at the IQB that is designed to make data from student assessment studies available to researchers and to provide training and support in using these data (IQB 2009). Researchers who want to work with a specific dataset have to submit a proposal, describing their research questions and the analyses they plan to carry out. Whether or not access is granted depends on the following criteria (IQB 2008):

(1) The data will be used for scientific purposes, not commercially.

(2) Individual data protection is secured.

(3) The planned analyses are in line with contractual agreements made with the owner of the data (such as the KMK). Comparisons between the German *Länder*, wich have not yet been conducted, need to be approved by the KMK.

(4) The planned analyses do not threaten theses (such as dissertations) or publications that are currently being written. The topics of these projects have to be specified at the time the researchers who have collected the data submit them to the Research Data Center. These topics are blocked for analyses with the respective dataset for at least nine months. This time lag may be extended to three years at the most.

(5) No additional issues are in conflict with the intended use of the data.

If these conditions are met, the Research Data Center at the IQB will provide the applicant with a Scientific Use File. Researchers who want to use sensitive data (e.g., the *Länder* codes) have to perform their analyses at the IQB or via remote computing.

Unlike the initial regulations of the Research Data Center at the IQB, which included an evaluation of proposals in terms of their theoretical and methodological soundness, the current procedure largely complies with the standards for Research Data Centers defined by the RatSWD. Nevertheless, a few open questions remain, such as who decides whether or not a proposal "threatens" theses or publications on the blocked topics and what kind of "additional issues" may be "in conflict with the intended use of the data." The transparency of the decision-making process should be increased by publishing a list of specified research questions that would be rejected on the grounds of the third or forth criteria. This would prevent researchers from investing time and effort on writing proposals that are bound to fail, and it would further increase the perceived fairness of the application process.

4. Current challenges and future development

Although the database for analyses on secondary schooling has improved considerably, a number of challenges remain. Most of these issues pose significant challenges not only in Germany but also at the international level, such as the problems associated with modeling input-process-output associations in education.

Variables in educational research can be categorized in terms of whether they pertain to the input, to the process, or to the output of education (Konsortium Bildungsberichterstattung, 2006). While more work is needed on the systematization and operationalization of variables in all three categories, the process dimension is the most challenging. From the perspectives of both educational research and educational reporting, it would be highly desirable to generate data and indicators that capture the process character of education. This pertains to characteristics of *interactions* in educational settings that are related to actual learning processes, such as approaches to structuring the teaching and learning process or the use of instruction time by teachers and learners, as well as to aspects directly relevant to the governance of educational *institutions,* such as the implementation of curricular requirements or measures of quality development and quality control. The central question is whether it is possible to develop indicators for basic dimensions of processes that can be measured across different educational institutions and across the sixteen *Länder* in reliable and valid ways. Since such measures are necessary to study the black box between the input and the output of education, it would certainly be worthwhile to invest into their development.

Within the output dimension, further work is needed on the assessment of so-called "soft skills," such as the various facets of social competence (e.g., the ability to communicate and cooperate with others). There is unanimous agreement that these skills present important determinants of learning processes as well as outcomes of schooling, and it has repeatedly been argued that they should be taken into account in educational monitoring. Thus far, however, no reliable and valid measure has been developed that could be included in such studies as PISA (Kanning 2003; Kunter and Stanat 2002). This is partly due to the fact that the appropriateness of social behavior is highly dependent on situational requirements; that is, a specific behavior may be quite competent in one situation yet largely counterproductive in another. Because it is typically not feasible to employ systematic observations in large-scale surveys or assessment studies, it would be necessary to develop more indirect measures. One promising approach might be to work with computerized scenarios that elicit student responses to simulations of various social situations. Yet, again, it would be a challenge to come up with scoring systems for the appropriateness of these reactions.

Even aspects of the output dimension for which well-established measures exist (e.g., reading, mathematics, and science), however, require further development for long-term longitudinal analyses. Most of the existing instruments were specifically designed for groups of students within a restricted age range, such as students in 9th grade or 15-year-olds. A major challenge the NEPS will have to tackle is to model these competencies and link the measures across the life span. If successful, however, the study will provide important insights into the ways in which competencies in the domains of language, mathematics, and science unfold and interrelate at different developmental stages.

The question of how to model change is a challenge for educational research that has only been partly resolved. It is relevant not only at the level of individual development, but also for the development of individual schools and school systems. In Germany, there is a dearth of research on the extent to which schools change over time and on factors determining this change (Klieme and Steiner 2008). This is mainly due to the lack of longitudinal data at the school-level. Although the comparative tests (*Vergleichsarbeiten*) discussed above could be used to perform such analyses, their results should be validated through studies employing more controlled data collection and scoring procedures. Several analyses of this type will be necessary to derive reliable estimates of changes occurring at the institutional level, the stability of these changes, and the effect sizes associated with potential determinants of developmental trajectories.

Even more complex is the attempt to capture and explain change at the level of school systems. The trend design of PISA aims at providing information on the extent to which school outcomes in the participating countries improve or do not improve over time, yet the interpretation of the findings has been controversial (Carstensen et al. 2008). This complexity is partly due to the changing focus of the PISA assessments, such that in each project cycle one of the three assessment domains (reading, mathematics, and science) is measured more comprehensively than the other, and to the multi-matrix design employed in the study. In PISA 2000 the focus was on reading, in PISA 2003 on mathematics, and in PISA 2006 on science. As a consequence, the overlap of items across the cycles has, so far, been limited. In addition, the composition of the test booklets varied in the different cycles, making it difficult to tease apart possible changes in item difficulty and changes in performance levels.

Still more complicated than estimating changes at the levels of schools and school systems is the attempt to explain the observed developments with multilevel analyses. Multilevel modeling presupposes that the variables included in the model are comparable across the units of analyses. This is particularly questionable for analyses of data from international assessment studies, as specific features of individual countries, such as approaches to ability grouping or types of curricula within the tracks, will almost inevitably be neglected (see Stanat and Lüdtke 2008 for a discussion of multilevel issues in international assessment studies). It is typically impossible to take such complex between-country differences into account in multilevel analyses. Therefore, quantitative multilevel analyses need to be complemented with qualitative data in order to generate more in-depth information on single cases (e.g., Döbert and Sroka 2004). One approach, for example, would be to submit countries deviating substantially from their predicted value in a multilevel analysis (Bowers and Drake 2005) to an intensive ideographical analyses. In addition to structural features of the school system, these analyses should take into account the country's historical complexity as well as cultural factors that are likely to affect teaching and learning processes (Stanat and Lüdtke 2007).

5. Recommendations

Based on the current situation outlined above, the following recommendations result:

School statistics

- School statistics should be changed to individual-level data in all *Länder*.
- To allow for longitudinal analyses of educational careers, school statistics should include a student identification code that remains the same across core educational stages. In the short run, the feasibility of different approaches to deriving such a code should be evaluated.
- Core characteristics, such as student socio-economic and immigrant backgrounds, should be represented by the same indicators in all *Länder*.
- More generally, the measures of core characteristics should be harmonized in the available statistical datasets (e.g., school statistics, youth welfare statistics, vocational training statistics).
- Data should also be collected for private schools.

Large-scale assessments (with *Länder* comparisons)

- Participation in international large-scale assessment studies, especially PIRLS, TIMSS, and PISA should be continued.

- In order to use the potential of these studies more fully, it should remain possible to add national options to the international designs.
- Assessments of competencies should be extended to the beginning of elementary school (including language skills) and to the transition into the labor market.
- In addition to the large-scale assessment studies, the German Time Use Study (*Zeitbudgetstudie*) and the Volunteer Survey (*Freiwilligensurvey*) should be continued as well. The Time Use Study is the only source of reliable data on the time people invest in education, and the Volunteer Survey allows for analyses of relationships between background factors and non-formal as well informal learning.
- Data from large-scale assessments and similar studies should be made available to the scientific community as soon as possible after they have been collected, cleaned, and scaled.
- The procedure of granting individual researchers access to data from large-scale assessments and similar studies should be completely transparent, including openness about the limitations of access in terms of the content of the proposed analyses. Such content-related limitations should be avoided.

Conceptual work and instrument development

- Theoretical models specifying the structure of competencies need to be refined as well as tested in various domains.
- In some domains, such as social or vocational competencies, the development of conceptual models is still in its very early stages and should be intensified.
- Substantive conceptual work is also needed with regard to the theoretical specification and empirical operationalization of process and context factors determining competence development and school success.
- Measures are needed that can be used to study competence development in longitudinal analyses over longer periods of time.
- Similarly, measures that are sufficiently sensitive to change are required in order to estimate the effects of interventions.
- Statistical methods need to be refined or developed for capturing change in data over time, not only at the individual level but also at the levels of schools and school systems.

- Technology-based assessment systems are needed to allow for the use of more complex and innovative test formats and, in the long run, to reduce the cost of testing.

References:

Baumert, J./Brunner, M./Lüdtke, O. and Trautwein, U. (2007): Was messen internationale Schulleistungsstudien? – Resultate kumulativer Wissenserwerbsprozesse. Eine Antwort auf Heiner Rindermann. Psychologische Rundschau 58, 118-129.

Baumert, J./Klieme, E./Neubrand, M./Prenzel, M./Schiefele, U./Schneider, W./Stanat, P./Tillmann, K.-J. and Weiß, M. (Eds.) (2001): PISA 2000. Basiskompetenzen von Schülerinnen und Schülern im internationalen Vergleich. Opladen.

Blossfeld, H.-P./Doll, J. and Schneider, T. (2008): Bildungsprozesse im Lebenslauf – Grundzüge der zukünftigen Bildungspanelstudie für die Bundesrepublik Deutschland. Recht der Jugend und des Bildungswesens 3, 321-328.

Bowers, J. and Drake, K.W. (2005): EDA for HLM: Visualization when probabilistic inference fails. Political Analysis 13 (4), 301-326.

Carstensen, C.H./Prenzel, M. and Baumert, J. (2008): Trendanalysen in PISA: Wie haben sich die Kompetenzen in Deutschland zwischen PISA 2000 und PISA 2006 entwickelt? In: Prenzel, M. and Baumert, J. (Eds.): Vertiefende Analysen zu PISA 2006. Zeitschrift für Erziehungs-wissenschaft: Sonderheft No. 10.

Ditton, H. (Ed.) (2007): Kompetenzaufbau und Laufbahnen im Schulsystem. Eine Längsschnittuntersuchung an Grundschulen. Münster.

Döbert, H. and Sroka, W. (Eds.) (2004): Features of successful school systems. A comparison of schooling in six countries. Münster.

Hetmeier, H. and Leidel, M. (2007): Internationale Praktiken in der Bildungsstatistik. Presentation at a workshop of the Standing Conference of the Ministers of Education and Cultural Affairs of the Länder in the Federal Republic of Germany. Berlin.

Holtappels, H.G./Klieme, E./Rauschenbach. T./Stecher, L. (Eds.) (2008): Ganztagsschule in Deutschland. Ergebnisse der Ausgangserhebung der "Studie zur Entwicklung von Ganztagsschulen" (StEG). Studien zur ganztägigen Bildung, Band 1. Weinheim.

Hosenfeld, I. (2008): Statewide monitoring and assurance of school quality: Principles of assessment and internet-based feedback of test results. In: Hartig, J./Klieme, E. and Leutner, D. (Eds): Assessment of competencies in educational contexts – State of the art and future prospects. Göttingen.

IQB (2008). Aufgaben und Verfahrensweise des Forschungsdatenzentrums (FDZ) retrieved on March 4, 2009 from http://www.iqb.hu-berlin.de/arbbereiche/ fdz/dateien/FDZ_VO.pdf. [Last visited: 02/12/2010].

IQB (2009): FDZ. Forschungsdatenzentrum am IQB (Research Data Center), retrieved on March 4, 2009 from http://www.iqb.hu-berlin.de/arbbereiche/fdz/ dateien/FDZ_VO.pdf. [Last visited: 02/12/2010].

Kanning, U.P. (2003): Diagnostik sozialer Kompetenzen. Kompendien Psychologische Diagnostik, Vol. 4. Göttingen.

Klieme, E./Helmke, A./Lehmann, R.H./Nold, G./Rolff, H.-G./Schröder, K./Thomé, G. and Willenberg, H. (Eds.) (2008): Unterricht und Kompetenzerwerb in Deutsch und Englisch. Weinheim.

Klieme, E. and Steinert, B. (2008): Schulentwicklung im Längsschnitt. Ein Forschungsprogramm und erste explorative Analysen. Zeitschrift für Erziehungswissenschaft, Sonderheft 10/2008, 221-238.

Köller, O. (2008): Bildungsstandards – Verfahren und Kriterien bei der Entwicklung von Messinstrumenten. Zeitschrift für Pädagogik 54, 163-173.

Konsortium Bildungsberichterstattung (2006): Zur langfristigen Sicherstellung der Datenbasis für die Bildungsberichterstattung. Deutsches Institut für Internationale Pädagogische Forschung (DIPF). Frankfurt am Main.

Konsortium Bildungsberichterstattung (2007): Das weiterentwickelte Indikatorenkonzept der Bildungsberichterstattung. Deutsches Institut für Internationale Pädagogische Forschung (DIPF). Frankfurt am Main.

Kunter, M. and Stanat, P. (2002): Soziale Kompetenz von Schülerinnen und Schülern: Die Rolle von Schulmerkmalen für die Vorhersage ausgewählter Aspekte. Zeitschrift für Erziehungswissenschaft 1, 49-71.

OECD (2001): Knowledge and skills for life. First results from PISA 2000. Paris.

Prenzel, M./Baumert, J./Blum, W./Lehmann, R./Leutner, D./Neubrand, M./Pekrun, R./Rost, J. and Schiefele, U. (Eds.) (2006): PISA 2003. Untersuchungen zur Kompetenzentwicklung im Verlauf eines Schuljahres. Münster.

Seidel, T./Prenzel, M./Rimmele, R./Herweg, C./Kobarg, M./Schwindt, K. and Dalehefte, I.M. (2007): Science teaching and learning in German physics classrooms – Findings from the IPN-Video Study. In: Prenzel, M. (Ed.): Studies on the educational quality of schools. The final report on the DFG Priority Programme. Münster.

Stanat, P. and Lüdtke, O. (2008): Multilevel issues in international large-scale assessment studies on student performance. In: van de Vijver, F.J.R./van Hemert, D.A. and Poortinga, Y.H. (Eds.): Individuals and cultures in multilevel analysis. Hillsdale.

Stanat, P. and Lüdtke, O. (2007): Internationale Schulleistungsvergleiche. In: Trommsdorff, G. and Kornadt, H.-J. (Eds.): Enzyklopädie der Psychologie: Kulturvergleichende Psychologie, Band 2: Kulturelle Determinanten des Erlebens und Verhaltens. Göttingen.

Wagner, G.G./Frick, J.R. and Schupp, J. (2007): The German Socio-Economic Panel Study (SOEP): Scope, evolution and enhancements. Schmollers Jahrbuch 127 (1), 139-170.

3.4 Knowing More about Vocational Training

Steffen Hillmert

Contact:

Steffen Hillmert
University of Tübingen
Department of Sociology
Wilhelmstr. 36
72076 Tübingen
Germany
e-mail: steffen.hillmert[at]uni-tuebingen.de

Abstract

Modern societies depend on the successful and comprehensive provision of skills. In younger cohorts, the majority of the population has received some form of vocational training, increasing the demand for timely information about the various forms of training and their relation to the broader societal context. Over recent decades, the patterns of participation in education and training have become more complex and heterogeneous, and extend further into the life course. In considering this development, this paper discusses the extent to which existing and projected data sources are suitable for investigating scientific and policy-related questions in this field. Among these questions are: what trends in vocational training can be identified over an individual's lifespan? What are the relative chances of receiving specific types of training? Who, in particular, is likely to receive the most attractive types? Are training measures effective? When reviewing currently available data, it becomes clear that progress has been made in the past few years. It is also obvious, however, that fundamental questions cannot presently be answered on the basis of the available large-scale data on vocational education and training. Some key recommendations are presented to remedy these gaps.

Keywords: vocational training, data, research infrastructure, overview, Germany

1. Analytical framework and research questions

Modern societies depend on the successful and comprehensive provision of skills. In younger cohorts, the majority of the population has received some form of vocational training, increasing the demand for timely information about the various forms of training and their relation to the broader societal context. This has raised questions like: what do participation rates in training currently look like? What are the relative chances of receiving specific types of training? Which groups are likely to receive the most attractive types? Are training measures effective?

Over recent decades, patterns of participation in education and training have become more complex and heterogeneous. Young people do not necessarily receive training from just one type of institution, but combine episodes of training in various ways (Hillmert and Jacob 2003). It therefore makes sense to speak of educational and training *careers*, which extend ever further into the life course. Today, many individuals participate in formal education for more than two decades. For research, this highlights the need for studying education and training from a dynamic, lifelong perspective based on empirically observed behavior, not administrative categories. Accordingly, the demand for detailed and reliable data is high, for such information provides a solid empirical foundation for future educational policies. While it is still important to know about aggregate numbers (such as training positions, participants, or applicants at a particular point in time), it is crucial to look at individual situations and the dynamic processes that take place within education and training. This means that it is essential to collect not only "snapshot" information about current activities in vocational training, but also information about connections with the individual's previous life history and subsequent career steps.

In Germany, recent and ongoing longitudinal studies (e.g., SOEP,[1] GLHS,[2] BIJU,[3] LAU,[4] ULME,[5] BIBB[6] Transition Study, DJI[7] Transition Panel) have compiled valuable data about educational careers – sometimes including measures of performance of competencies – and have thus enhanced our knowledge about likely causal relationships. Nevertheless, evidence-based policies continuously require differentiated, reliable, and up-to-date information. It is therefore necessary to improve the quality of process-produced data in line with new demands. Importantly, however, it is necessary to keep in mind that official statistics are constructed on a specific legal basis, so any recommendations for improvement have to take into consideration the details of these regulations. This may pose problems for the collection of comprehensive data on the training situation of the whole population, as this would require still more radical innovations in the information infrastructure such as the introduction of a population register. Even when ambitions are lower, there still exists an urgent need for improving the current data situation. Even a brief review reveals that very basic information about the situation of vocational training in Germany is not available. Measures to change this would often require no more resources yet still be of great value. In any case, research will continue to operate with a variety of different data sources, which should be coordinated as much as possible.

To overcome the aforementioned problems, a simplified framework should be used, containing basic requirements for the systematic collection of information on training. The initial focus of any approach proposing to assess the performance of the vocational education and training (VET) system should be to differentiate between its institutional characteristics; that is, em-

---

[1] German Socio-Economic Panel (SOEP, *Sozio-oekonomisches Panel*).
[2] German Life History Study.
[3] Learning Processes, Educational Careers, and Psychosocial Develpment in Adolescence and Young Adulthood (BIJU, *Bildungsprozesse, Kompetenzentwicklungen und Selektionsentscheidungen im Vor- und Grundschulalter*).
[4] Aspects of Learning Prerequisites and Learning Development (LAU, *Aspekte der Lernausgangslage und der Lernentwicklung*).
[5] Study on Achievement, Motivation, and Attitudes of Students at the Beginning of Vocational Education (ULME, *Untersuchungen der Leistungen, Motivation und Einstellung zu Beginn der beruflichen Ausbildung*).
[6] Federal Institute for Vocational Education and Training (BIBB, *Bundesinstitut für Berufsbildung*).
[7] German Youth Institute (DJI, *Deutsches Jugendinstitut*).

ploy an "institution-oriented differentiation" approach. Historically, vocational training statistics have been equated with information on apprenticeships, but today it seems useful to distinguish among three major areas of the VET system below the tertiary level (Baethge et al. 2003; Autorengruppe Bildungsberichterstattung 2008): the "dual system," i.e., apprenticeships organized as a combination of firm-based training and vocational schooling; (full-time) "school-based training"; and also a large "transition system" of measures including youth training schemes and basic forms of vocational training. Additionally, there exist special cases like training in the Civil Service.

A second issue to be considered when assessing the VET system is that one can differentiate among different analytical elements. These elements, also known as central "dependent variables" for empirical analyses, represent the basic building blocks of careers in education and training. They allow inferences to be made about mobility and developments in the training system. These elements relate to several different concerns, in particular, to

- access: the transitions to specific forms of vocational training and their determinants;
- outcomes: learning, competencies, and qualifications in vocational training; and
- impact: in the sense of transitions out of vocational training and their consequences, in particular labor market consequences.

Complementing the institution-oriented differentiation approach, and just as necessary, is an approach that considers non-institutional characteristics; that is, an "individual-level differentiation" approach. This approach allows researchers to compare the relative chances of particular groups in society to achieve particular educational outcomes and impacts. For empirical analyses, this approach would focus on the set of central "independent variables." These analytical dimensions are summarized in Table 1. While variables like age and gender are commonly used distinctions, differences in nationality and – even more important for meaningful analyses – migration background have only recently come into the focus of official statistics. Another important form of non-institutional differentiation is regional differentiation. Classifying various aggregate units may extend the database further towards a multilevel structure.

It is essential for the analysis of training careers to make use of longitudinal data. For research, *prospective* collection of information would be preferable, i.e., following the careers of individuals as they develop over time. However, such data designs have tended to be controversial with respect to data protection as they necessarily require matching information on individual cases across several waves of data collection. Hence, the second-best solution is collecting information on individual developments *retro-*

spectively, i.e., gathering time-referenced information about individuals' previous experiences and actions each time someone begins a (new) period of activities in VET.

This framework is rather simple and selective. When contrasted with the basic questions in the first paragraph, however, it does make clear that fundamental and highly relevant questions cannot presently be answered on the basis of the currently available large-scale data on VET. These questions have already yielded significant findings in small-scale studies and hence warrant further investigation. Among these questions are: how many people combine two or more episodes of VET? Do young people with and without a migration background have similar chances of access to training? How do people with a migration background perform within the system? Does training within the dual system and in full-time vocational schools lead to similar patterns of transitions to employment? Do training programs result in transitions to regular training and/or stable employment? What proportion of a cohort entering vocational training completes it successfully?

Table 1: Systematic information for a dynamic analysis of vocational training

Institution-oriented differentiation	Analytical elements in a life-course perspective	Individual-level and other non-institutional differentiation (examples)
- Dual system - School-based training - Transition system	- Access - Outcome/performance - Impact/consequences	- Individual history of education and training - Age - Gender - Migration background - Regional differentiation

2. Contrasting demands and available databases

This section discusses the extent to which existing and projected data sources can be used to investigate such questions. Compared to other industrialized countries, VET in Germany is formalized to a relatively high degree. Due to the differentiation and the complex institutional structure of the German education and training system, however, relevant information sources are very heterogeneous. Given this, any brief overview of relevant data and their characteristics – taking into account the basic distinctions between the three sectors of the VET system – is necessarily a selection (for a general overview on the information infrastructure in this area, see Weishaupt and Fickermann 2000; Baethge et al. 2003, 47-54; Bellmann 2005; Brosi 2005).

2.1 Data on vocational training within the Dual System

Historically, the data situation regarding apprenticeship training has been adequate. Given its dual nature, it is covered by various data sources. These include the School Statistics, which are collected by the *Länder*, and the Vocational Training Statistics of the responsible authorities, i.e., institutions such as the Chamber of Commerce, whose statistics are often referred to as *the* Vocational Training Statistics. Additionally, there are also statistics on the vocational training market that report the number of registered applicants and vacancies. These allow for calculations of supply and demand, at least in a simple form (BMBF 2007). Additional information about apprenticeships is provided by Employment Statistics and regular collections of firm-level data (IAB Establishment Panel).

The Vocational Training Act (BBiG, *Berufsbildungsgesetz*) is the central legal basis of the VET Statistics. As this is national law, it allows for standardized gathering of information. The Reform Act of 2007 has significantly improved the collection of mandatory data, in particular in terms of the shift from aggregate to individual-level reporting and the provision of more information on individual-level determinants of transition (Uhly 2006). Implementation of these changes is, however, still underway.

Despite some level of progress, there still exist considerable deficits for dynamic analyses: there is no linkage between years and no information on timing. In other words, there is information on transitions within a given year, but it represents a one-off snapshot. This means that there is insufficient information about the length of training careers, the structure of multiple training episodes, and in general on lifelong aspects. Since program termination rates are calculated on a yearly basis, it is not possible to distinguish between temporary and final dropout and hence to calculate cohort-specific rates of success within the apprenticeship system.

This situation could easily be remedied by the introduction of a personal ID number which would allow for connecting individual-specific data entries across different years. Currently, whilst information on previous education and training – including school-based training and qualification measures – is indeed collected (Statistisches Bundesamt 2007a), this information is restricted to type and level. Furthermore, the range of these statistics is limited. An implication of this is that matching person-specific data records across years (and institutions), which is the preferable solution for reconstructing training biographies, is not possible. As long as this cannot be done, it would be helpful to collect qualitative information on previous VET experience (most notably, occupation) and on the *timing* of previous experiences in training.

Another specific deficit with respect to currently available large-scale data on vocational education and training is the insufficient amount of information about possible migration backgrounds. This additionally required data needs to go beyond information about the individual's nationality. It would be helpful to coordinate the definitions of an extended set of collected variables with other central data sources in this area, such as the individual-level School Statistics, where information is made available about country of birth, parents' country of birth, and year of immigration, as well as language spoken at home. Including at least some proxy information on regional mobility among apprentices or previous performance in the form of grades may also be considered.

2.2 Data on full-time school-based training

The varying forms of full-time school-based training have become an increasingly important part of the VET system. They form a mixed category, but a major share consists of training in occupations outside the BBiG regulations. Whereas vocational schools are regulated by state law and covered by the School Statistics (Statistisches Bundesamt 2007b), data are collected by the *Länder* according to varying regulations and classifications. In many respects, the information collected and published has been limited and heterogeneous (Krüger 2005).

A fundamental systematic deficit of statistics that focus on secondary school students is that there is no information about applicants or the amount of space available in school programs. This means that – in contrast to apprenticeships – there is no information about relations of supply and demand in this sector of VET. Special problems are associated with data on school-based training in the healthcare sector. Data are incomplete (e.g., there is no reporting in the federal state of Hesse) and of varying quality. One of the reasons for this is that supervision lies with different authorities, some of them with no obligation to report.

A consequence of all this is that there is still no comprehensive account of the volume and the structure of school-based training in Germany. Given this heterogeneity and limitations, major improvements can be expected from the coordinated "core data" project on schools (KDS, *Kerndatensatz für schulstatistische Individualdaten der Länder gemäß dem Beschluss der Kultusministerkonferenz*) recently undertaken by the *Länder* – that is, as long as there is comprehensive coverage of all vocational schools in all federal states. Similar to the changes in the BBiG statistics, this undertaking would also mean a shift from aggregate reporting to the collection of individual-level information and an extension of collected variables. For this change to be of use for research on training careers, it is essential that individual records be able to be matched from one year to another. However, implementation of this measure has caused some controversy and has so far proceeded very differently in the various *Länder*.

2.3 Data on the "transition system" of training measures

The term "transition system" subsumes a variety of measures within the VET system, including both youth training schemes and forms of preparatory vocational training (including attainment of general school qualifications). It is a very heterogeneous category, but given its considerable size, it makes sense to include it in any regular assessment of the VET system. So far, it is not clear how permanent and successful the measures included in the transition system are as components of individual training careers. Empirical studies have hitherto relied on one-off samples or focused on special, temporary programs (Troltsch et al. 1999; Dietrich et al. 2002). For a specific sub-group of the training population, there is analytical potential in matching different sources of process-produced data on training and employment. Notably, this undertaking is an ongoing project, entitled "Integrated Employment Biographies," at the Institute for Employment Research (IAB, *Institut für Arbeitsmarkt- und Berufsforschung*).

Regular reporting about transition system measures is mainly based on the statistics of vocational schools and the statistics of measures financed by the Federal Employment Agency (BA, *Bundesagentur für Arbeit*). In terms of these reported figures, it is difficult to identify any overlap (Autorengruppe Bildungsberichterstattung 2008: 99). Clearly, there exists a need for better coordination between the two data sources. While there is some information available on transitions to employment after the end of particular measures ("integration into the labor market"), there is no comprehensive and permanent data source available that records intertemporal individual experiences within the transition system and links them to other forms of education and training.

The lack of transparency regarding empirical information about the transition system has further consequences. For example, as young people in these measures do not appear as applicants in other sectors, it is very difficult to assess the overall demand in the VET system. For this part of VET, it is especially important to know more about the incidence, duration, and success of training measures undertaken by individuals. To overcome the shortcoming that information across various years of data collection cannot be matched, information on previous experiences in the transition system needs to be collected when individuals enter training in either the dual system, school-based training or any another training measure. In order to relate this information to the relevant groupings of former participants in these training sectors, however, it would be most important to have information on the *timing* of these experiences. Again, it would also be essential to collect information on the individual migration background.

2.4 Additional data sources

Apart from data that have been designed primarily to inform about the VET system, there exist a number of other representative data sources that do not have such a specific focus, but nevertheless provide relevant information. The most prominent of these examples is the German Microcensus, which is a valuable source of information on the distribution of qualifications differentiated by individual characteristics. In contrast to many other data sources, recent releases of the Microcensus contain fairly comprehensive information about both nationality and migration background. Although conceptualized as a short-term panel, in principle the Microcensus is able to map educational transitions. Notably, there are a few direct indicators in the questionnaire that could be extended. For example, as of 2005, information on additional vocational degrees is available; however, this is restricted to graduates from higher education so it does not allow for the identification of multiple training episodes in secondary vocational training. In relation to additional data sources, such as the Microcensus, refining and harmonizing the definitions of specific variables may greatly enhance their compatibility and hence their value for empirical research on training issues. In general, conceptualizing and further developing these data sources should be done in close cooperation with potential users. One good way to accomplish this would be to conduct issue-specific expert workshops.

3. Questions of data access and use

Collecting adequate data is crucial, but for practical research, data availability and access are also key issues. In recent years, major progress has been made regarding the systematic and regular collection of individual-level data on the VET system. There is still a great need for well-regulated access to and systematic documentation of these data. However, up to this point it is not clear to what extent and in what form this information will be accessible to scientific researchers.

Other major advances can be expected from the recently established Research Data Center for vocational training data at the BIBB. Given that relevant data on the VET system are held by very different institutions, a common and regularly updated directory would be helpful for researchers.

Another concern regarding data access and use is the range of available databases beyond official statistics. While data access and support for established surveys like the SOEP are exemplary, many issue-specific datasets never become available or even known to potential users because the principal investigators are obliged by their funding contract to delete the data once the project is finished. In light of this, many researchers argue that it is crucial that the data collected for projects commissioned by public authorities be made available through the relevant data archive or Research Data Center.

4. Summary and recommendations

Contemporary, individualized knowledge-based societies require comprehensive, up-to-date, and dynamic data, that is, regularly collected data on individual histories of education and training rather than just aggregate snapshots. Taking this into consideration, the current data situation concerning the VET system can be summarized as follows:

Information about the dual system of apprenticeship training is fairly comprehensive, but the shift towards an individual-level statistical accounting system should be complemented by a systematic decision allowing for the study of longer sequences of training careers rather than single transitions. The simplest solution for this would be a permanent ID number.

In contrast to the data on the dual system, the data available on full-time vocational training is much more limited. This situation is unsatisfactory, not least in terms of the gender-specific participation in these institutions. It is also fairly heterogeneous due to the federalist structure of the German school system. Further efforts of coordination are necessary to build up a regular accounting system that allows dynamic analyses on an individual level. A further problem exists in that there is still no systematic reporting on transition system measures that may be related to transitions to regular forms of training.

In spite of the progress that has been made, a major deficit remains: all three main sectors of the VET system are covered by very different regulations and procedures for data collection. This means that transitions between these sectors can be analyzed only in a very selective and limited manner. Moreover, it is impossible to use process-produced data to study some very interesting research questions about the links between the VET system and other educational institutions as they are represented in patterns of educational careers. Nonetheless, it has been established in survey research that careers in education and training do transcend the borders of specific institutions and educational levels. Linking databases on different areas of education and training therefore remains a top future priority. Again, the introduction of a common ID number – in combination with a consistent concept of data protection and data availability – could help greatly in overcoming this deficit. Moreover, great care should be taken to harmonize the definitions and rules of data collection in the various sectors of the education and training system.

Considering the aforementioned shortcomings of currently available large-scale data on the VET system, there are major opportunities to improve the scope and the quality of regularly collected, process-based data. Nevertheless, despite the need for a shift towards more individualized data, large-scale surveys will continue to be indispensable and therefore still require adequate funding. Both aggregate and individualized data are necessary for studies of specific issues and causal relations. For rigorous empirical analyses of the VET system, a broader range of individual characteristics, including information about parents and families, are required. This is because educational careers are embedded in social relations, and the impact of families and life situations on educational decisions is strong. Moreover, it is necessary to include all three sectors, including the transition system, into systematic data collection, for example, in the multi-cohort National Educational Panel Study (NEPS), which is due to start in 2009/2010. Given its sample size and scope, as well as the comprehensiveness of its data, the NEPS can be expected to accomplish an unprecedented level of integration among analyses of various institutional stages of educational and training careers.

The expected trend towards international comparisons in all areas of education and training places extra pressure on the need for adequate data. These data requirements range from large-scale cross-sectional reporting and longitudinal studies to evaluation studies of specific institutions or measures. VET systems have become part of such endeavors at a relatively late stage, but large-scale assessments comparable to the Programme for International Student Assessment (PISA) (VET-LSA: Baethge et al. 2006; PIAAC, Programme for the International Assessment of Adult Competencies) have been announced. Coordination among various programs assessing both general education as well as vocational and academic training may provide new challenges. Cross-national research has shown that it is often more salient to compare whole systems of education and training than specific elements defined on the basis of nominal institutional classifications. To allow such a system evaluation, it is again important to link data from different parts of the education and training system and to harmonize the definitions used when collecting these data – on both the national and the international level.

References:

Autorengruppe Bildungsberichterstattung (2008): Bildung in Deutschland 2008. Ein indikatorengestützter Bericht mit einer Analyse zu Übergängen im Anschluss an den Sekundarbereich I. Bielefeld.
Baethge, M./Buss, K.-P. and Lanfer, C. (2003): Konzeptionelle Grundlagen für einen Nationalen Bildungsbericht: Berufliche Bildung und Weiterbildung / Lebenslanges Lernen. Bonn/Berlin.
Baethge, M./Buss, K.-P. and Lanfer, C. (Eds.) (2005): Expertisen zu den konzeptionellen Grundlagen für einen Nationalen Bildungsbericht. Bonn/Berlin.
Baethge, M./Achtenhagen, F./Arends, L./Babic, E./Baethge-Kinsky, V. and Weber, S. (2006): Berufsbildungs-PISA: Machbarkeitsstudie. Stuttgart.
Bellmann, L. (2005): Der Stand der Aus- und Weiterbildungsstatistik in Deutschland. In: Baethge, M./Buss, K.-P. and Lanfer, C. (Eds.): Expertisen zu den konzeptionellen Grundlagen für einen Nationalen Bildungsbericht. Bonn/Berlin.
Brosi, W. (2005): Anmerkungen zur Verfügbarkeit von Statistiken im Bereich der beruflichen Bildung als Basis für eine umfassende Bildungsberichterstattung. In: Baethge, M./Buss, K.-P. and Lanfer, C. (Eds.): Expertisen zu den konzeptionellen Grundlagen für einen Nationalen Bildungsbericht. Bonn/Berlin.
Bundesministerium für Bildung und Forschung (BMBF) (2007): Berufsbildungsbericht 2007. Berlin.
Dietrich, H./Behle, H./Böhm, R./Eigenhüller, L. and Rothe, Th. (2002): Design der IAB-Begleitforschung zum Jugendsofortprogramm im Kontext des IAB-Forschungsschwerpunkts School-to-Work-Transition. Nuremberg.
Hillmert, S. and Jacob, M. (2003): Bildungsprozesse zwischen Diskontinuität und Karriere: das Phänomen der Mehrfachausbildungen. Zeitschrift für Soziologie 32 (4), 325-345.
Krüger, H.(2005): Zur Datenlage vollzeitschulischer Berufsausbildung. In: Baethge, M./Buss, K.-P. and Lanfer, C. (Eds.): Expertisen zu den konzeptionellen Grundlagen für einen Nationalen Bildungsbericht. Bonn/Berlin.
Statistisches Bundesamt (2007a): Berufsbildungsstatistik – Begriffe und Erläuterungen. Wiesbaden.
Statistisches Bundesamt (2007b): Fachserie 11, Reihe 2: Bildung und Kultur – Berufliche Schulen. Wiesbaden.
Troltsch, K./Lásló, A./Bardeleben, R. von and Ulrich, J.G. (1999): Jugendliche ohne Berufsausbildung. Eine BiBB/EMNID-Untersuchung. Bonn.
Uhly, A. (2006): Weitreichende Verbesserungen der Berufsbildungsstatistik ab April 2007. In: Krekel, E.M./Uhly, A. and Ulrich, J.G. (Eds.): Forschung im Spannungsfeld konkurrierender Interessen. Die Ausbildungsstatistik und ihr Beitrag für Praxis, Politik und Wissenschaft. Bonn.
Weishaupt, H. and Fickermann, D. (2000): Informationelle Infrastruktur im Bereich Bildung und Kultur, Expertise für die Kommission zur Verbesserung der informationellen Infrastruktur zwischen Wissenschaft und Statistik. Erfurt.

3.5 Higher Education

Andrä Wolter

Contact:

Andrä Wolter
Dresden University of Technology
Faculty of Education
01062 Dresden
Germany
e-mail: andrae.wolter[at]tu-dresden.de

Abstract

During the last five years, higher education research in Germany seems to have taken a significant upturn. This is partly a side effect of the obvious boom overall in empirical research on education, and partly of the reform movement that has affected the German higher education system since the mid-1990s. The demand for data in the field of higher education will increase considerably in the future. The available data infrastructure for higher education research in Germany consists of two central and complementary sources: official statistics on higher education on the one hand and survey-based research on the other.

In principle, there are no serious obstacles to accessing the available data stock relevant to higher education. However, access to some of the most important surveys would be improved through the establishment of a Research Data Center at the Higher Education Information System (HIS, *Hochschul-Informations-System*). Furthermore, there are some significant shortcomings in the present data provision. New topics that place new demands on data provision must be integrated into official statistics and survey-based research alike (e.g., migration status, competencies, lifelong learning, quality of studies, institutional effects, international mobility, programs to promote younger scholars etc.). In particular there is a lack of panel designs. The recently established National Education Panel Study (NEPS) will eliminate some, but not all, of these deficiencies.

1. The development of higher education research in Germany: Old and new research questions

In Germany, as in other countries, higher education is faced with increasing pressure to justify its existence in terms of demand, outcomes, effectiveness, study success, and other issues that might be grouped collectively under the concept of accountability. Researchers and particularly politicians – at institutional, state, and national levels – are interested in information and data concerning the results and performance of higher education institutions, citing funding bottlenecks and growing competition for students, scholars, academic reputation, and resources. With the growing social and economic centrality of higher education, the academic and political interest in data on the development and functioning of its institutions is rapidly increasing.

Over the last five decades a wide range of academic and political issues in higher education have been the focus of empirical and non-empirical higher education research in Germany. Although higher education had already been the subject of various academic undertakings since the late 1950s, research on higher education in general remained on the periphery of social and educational research for a long period of time. As a result of the massive quantitative expansion of higher education over the past few decades, colleges and universities have become some of the most important institutions – sometimes regarded as the most important institution of professional education in modern, knowledge-based societies. In view of the overall trend toward upgrading the qualification structures of employment, higher education can be expected to become even more relevant as an institutional center of qualification. As a result, the academic and political interest in higher education can be expected also to increase considerably.

During the last five years, higher education research in Germany seems to have taken a significant upturn. This is partly a side effect of an obvious boom overall in empirical research on education, and partly a result of the reform movement that has affected the higher education system in Germany since the mid-1990s. As with empirical educational research in general, research on higher education seems to have profited from the new paradigm of evidence-based educational policy. One element of this is the establishment of continuous monitoring systems at different levels (international, national, state), including higher education, such as the German National Report on Education (*Nationaler Bildungsbericht*) (Avenarius et al. 2006; Klieme et al. 2008), which rapidly gave reinforcement to the need for an elaborated data infrastructure. The fact that the higher education system in Germany, as in other countries, is currently the subject of a lively public reform debate and faces several reform challenges (Wolter 2004; 2007a), has also stimulated the increasing interest in higher education research.

Higher education research covers a broad range of research questions and topics and it is difficult to reduce the diverse research activities that have been pursued in recent years to a selection of a few major themes. However, it may be possible to distinguish the following four main fields of research (Teichler 2002):[1]

- *Quantitative-structural changes in higher education.* This area of inquiry considers the development of the social demand for higher education, the consequences of the wholesale "massification" of the system, the particular institutions, the institutional structures of higher education and its changes (e.g., through diversification, profiling, or vertical and horizontal differentiation), the provision of studies, the interdependencies between the expansion, types of differentiation, etc.;

- *Transitions and processes of studies.* A significant amount of research has focused on topics dealing with the first transition point – the status passage between school and higher education, including issues such as access and admission, social inequality and opportunities to study, the social and economic conditions of studying, processes and success of

---

[1] Because research is the second pillar of higher education, another important field is represented by research on research or on science, the subject of another article in this volume by Stefan Hornbostel.

studying (including the drop-out phenomenon) and their determinants, teaching and learning, and student mobility. Also included under this heading are issues arising from a second transition point – from higher education to the labor market and employment, including early vocational careers, the match between higher education and employment, and similar questions;

- *Post-graduate training and academic staffing.* This field encompasses topics such as the different stages and paths to a professorship, the effectiveness and quality of doctoral programs, the main activities and time budget of the academic staff, faculty development, employment conditions, and the career perspectives, especially of young scholars, etc.;
- *Organization, management, and governance of higher education.* This field includes, at the systemic or institutional level, topics such as the external relationships between state and university, the internal organization of institutions, issues of efficiency, funding, professional institutional management, new concepts and procedures of steering and allocation, evaluation and quality assurance, etc.

The kinds of data required in these studies vary with the research questions and fields. Whereas the first three areas require primarily data at the national level, most research on steering and governance topics depends on the availability of data primarily at an institutional level. The following discussion focuses on available data stocks and new data requirements primarily at the national, rather than at the institutional level. For this reason, the new wave of ranking procedures with their enormous demand for differentiated data on the performances of individual institutions of higher education (Bayer 2004; Statistisches Bundesamt 2007) is not the subject of this report.

Sometimes it is difficult to differentiate strictly between old and new research questions. Old questions often remain relevant over time or become significant again in changing contexts. For example, the effect of the continuous expansion of participation in higher education on the changing relationships between higher qualifications, profession, and employment had already become a hotly debated issue in the early 1970s. But these issues have become relevant again with the new wave of expansion that has occurred since the 1990s. They will retain their relevance with the recent political consensus that higher education in Germany should aspire to a participation rate of 40 percent of the corresponding age group and a graduate rate of 35 percent (Wissenschaftsrat 2006) in order to keep pace with other highly developed countries. Therefore, issues such as the unemployment of graduates or whether there is an adequacy link between qualifications and employment have always been acute questions, even if now they are being analyzed in a methodologically more differentiated way and in the changed context of the rising knowledge-based society.

On the other hand, there are new questions and topics that have arisen in the context of these enormous changes to German higher education – which might even be called a fundamental transformation – during the last decade:

- *The impact of the Bologna Process.* During the last few years interest has grown considerably in the impact of the Bologna Process on studies and studying (Teichler 2008; ZSE 2008). At a structural level, changes in the relationships between different types of institutions (e.g., trends of convergence) and in the provision and organization of courses have been the focus of this interest. But the Bologna accords include more than new degrees and a consecutive structuring of studies. This notion indicates a radical change in educational culture that includes changes in teaching and learning styles. So, at an individual level, the motivation to study and the learning behavior of the students and their adaptation to the new configuration of studies is of great interest. This will result in an expanding demand for related data particularly from research on students.

    Since the Bologna Process has determined that employability – whatever this concept may mean (Schaeper and Wolter 2008) – is a primary objective of study, further research will also focus on transitions between higher education and work. Thus, there is (and will be) a demonstrable and increasing interest in graduate studies, manifest in cross-sectional or, more productive yet, as panel studies (HRK 2007). Furthermore, research will be concerned with the outcomes of studying, especially in terms of disciplinary competencies and broader, transdisciplinary "key competencies" (Schaeper 2005; Schaeper and Spangenberg 2007). Last but not least, the line differentiating initial and continuing studies has become blurred under the Bologna Process, which has strengthened the focus on lifelong learning as the primary mission of higher education. But the situation of continuing higher education is particularly problematic, with completely disparate and inadequate data provision (Wolter 2007b).

- *Internationalization of higher education.* The internationalization of higher education – due to globalization, Europeanization, or other processes (Teichler 2004) – has led to a growing need for internationally comparative data. Institutions of higher education today are often considered to be organizations acting on a global market with global competition. Research on higher education must take this international or even global character into account. During the last decade, this internationally comparative perspective has been reinforced for two major reasons. First, there is a political demand for comparative analyses that reveal the strengths and weaknesses of higher education systems and institutions, for information needed for the identification of concepts or models of institutional reform, and for establishing procedures of quality control. Second, the establishment of a "European Higher Education Area" in the course of the Bologna Process has reinforced the earlier interest in student and staff mobility. As a result, there is a growing need for valid international data on higher education, in particular on student mobility (Kelo et al. 2006).

- *Differentiation and governance of higher education.* The growing stratification of the German higher education system in the course of the Excellence Program and other mechanisms of differentiation is another area of growing interest. Although these institutions of "excellence" (in the three areas of graduate schools, clusters of excellence, and future development concepts) have been selected on the basis of a state-regulated nomination procedure rather than by a market-shaped process of competition (and thus is based on reputation and performance), in the long run the claim of excellence will require academic justification by measurable criteria. This will result in an increasing need for data pertaining to the achievements of higher education institutions, primarily in the areas of research, but probably also in teaching (Hornbostel 2008a; b). Research on the results and changes, generated by the progressive implementation of new governance and steering structures, will be another important future research area (Wolter 2007a). But both of these questions are still in their infancy, since the dynamic of these changes is at an early stage. Both require, as mentioned above, special data particularly at institutional rather than the national level.

2. The current state of data infrastructure and the challenges in higher education research

The available data infrastructure for higher education research in Germany consists of two main sources:

- official higher education statistics, which include information about students, personnel, and finance statistics; and
- data and results from survey-based research, in particular in the field of student and graduate research, which is conducted by research centers, such as the Higher Education System (HIS, *Hochschul-Informations-System*) GmbH Hannover, the International Center for Higher Education Research (INCHER) at the University of Kassel, the Research Group on Higher Education (*Arbeitsgruppe Hochschulforschung*) at the University of Konstanz, and other centers.

In principle, the availability of and access to public data and survey data is ensured. Yet, with the exception of official statistics, research institutes or centers are often faced with obstacles due to lack of personnel or technical capacity. From an international perspective, higher education research may be less developed in Germany than elsewhere relative to the size of its national higher education system. However, the main problem in German higher education research does not primarily consist of a lack of data but rather a lack of an extensive and methodologically sophisticated utilization of existing data stocks. Thus, access could be improved in a practical sense, rather than through legal changes.

As a result of the higher education statistics laws, official student statistics have been presented annually by statistical offices at the state or federal level since the early 1970s. These statistics provide a significant amount of data on the number of students (new entrants or all students), their distribution over institutions and subjects, some information on their composition (gender, nationality), their regional origin, types of study entitlement, and other variables. In contrast to official school statistics, the statistics on students in higher education have consisted of individual datasets since the 1970s, so it is not necessary to establish individual statistics in this field. The official student statistics allow for many very differentiated analyses, such as on the development of (realized) student demand, on regional student mobility, duration of studies, fluctuation between subjects, and other aspects. However, there are some important limits and deficits.

- First, it has not been possible to link organized school and higher education statistics individually. So, even if it were possible to calculate general transition quotas, the transitions from grammar school to university cannot be reconstructed as individual processes. The introduction of an overarching identity number in educational statistics would therefore be an important measure that would enable the analysis of processes and transitions. This step would nonetheless confront some serious problems with respect to data protection and public acceptance.

- Second, there are many important variables that are not part of the official statistics (e.g., social origin, migrant status of students apart from formal nationality, any subjective variables). The provision of these other types of data depends completely on survey research on students.

- Third, student statistics end with exmatriculation, so of course the further life course of graduates, in particular their professional or academic careers, is not part of the student (or other) statistics. Because of this, graduate survey studies are of great importance. Some data about the employment of graduates can be gained from the German Socio-Economic Panel (SOEP, *Sozio-oekonomisches Panel*) and the Microcensus, but these do not have the necessary depth of focus that could be obtained in graduate studies.

- Fourth, official statistics include only a very few variables (such as duration of studies) that can be used as indicators to assess the quality of studies. One of the most important gaps concerns the provision of valid and reliable data on students who drop out of programs. This is partly due to legal objections, and partly due to difficulties in the precise definition and measurement of the drop-out rate. Empirical information has primarily been generated so far by estimate models developed by HIS (Heublein et al. 2008). Currently, a joint project between the Federal Statistical Office and HIS is being carried out to deliver valid data on student drop-out.

- Fifth, official statistics do not include the universities of cooperative education (*Berufsakademien*) as a hybrid type of institution between tertiary and post-secondary education. *Berufsakademien* are not established in all German states, but where they do exist, they are often considered as the third pillar of the German higher education system, showing a high degree of curricular overlap with the universities of applied sciences, or *Fachhochschulen*.

Because of these deficits in official statistics, student survey research holds a key position in the data infrastructure of higher education research. In certain respects, official statistics on higher education and the survey-based research and data production can be seen as complementary parts of one system that shapes the research data infrastructure in the field of higher education. Survey projects can be conducted as single projects or as follow-up projects in order to build up time series. In Germany, several such follow-up studies with different target groups have been carried out since the late 1970s. They include school graduates with study entitlement, new entrants in higher education, students, and graduates.

HIS regularly undertakes various cross-sectional surveys among recent school graduates who have earned a particular study entitlement (who have an upper secondary school diploma, either the *Abitur* or *Fachhochschulreife*) and among new entrants in higher education. The focus of these studies is on the decision-making process surrounding whether to study, the choice of institution, subject of study, and the personal and social factors that determine these decisions (Heine et al. 2008a; b). The HIS survey of graduates has been partially continued as a panel during the first study sequence. On the basis of these surveys, it is possible to reconstruct the status passages between school and university as a time series for almost three decades. However, there are only a few longitudinal studies examining the complete transition process from school into higher education, starting from the upper stage of grammar school and ending at a later point in time during university study. Some of these panel studies show a very sophisticated methodological design, but are limited to a particular *Land*, such as the TOSCA study (e.g., Köller et al. 2004).

There are two larger projects worth mentioning which concern students (across all sequences of studying) that have generally been updated every three years. The social and economic situation of students and the conditions of studying have been examined in the Social Survey (*Sozialerhebung*), also carried out by HIS since 1982 (Isserstedt et al. 2007). As a part of what is called the social dimension of the Bologna Process, a European-wide study on the social and economic conditions of studying (called Eurostudent) has been established that is also coordinated by HIS (Eurostudent 2008). The study situation, study problems, and the individual orientations of students have also been investigated since the early 1980s by the survey of students conducted at the University of Konstanz (*Konstanzer Studierendensurvey*) (Multrus et al. 2008). Some additional differentiated special analyses on certain subjects (e.g., humanities or engineering) or certain groups of students (e.g., female) have been based on this survey. Most of this type of research on students has been conducted in the framework of cross-sectional surveys.

Study on graduate education is an exploding field of research. Most of these studies focus on a retrospective assessment of studies and their outcomes – the transition from university to employment, the occupational or academic career after the first degree, and other aspects of the further life course (e.g., mobility or participation in continuing education). Since the late 1980s, there have been two research contexts on a national and international level that have provided representative data for Germany. Beginning in 1989, HIS established a study of graduates not only as a longitudinal study but also as a time series. HIS surveys a large graduate sample representative for Germany every four years with up to three panel stages: during the first, fifth, and tenth year after graduation (Briedis 2007a; b; Kerst and Schramm 2008). Coordinated by the International Center for Higher Education Research at the University of Kassel (INCHER), two internationally comparative graduate surveys have also been undertaken – CHEERS[2] (Schomburg and Teichler 2006; Teichler 2007a) and REFLEX[3] – that also embrace a larger German graduate sample and place it in a European context for comparison.

Additionally, numerous studies have been carried out at local universities or faculty levels in recent years. Many institutions are interested in the success and careers of their graduates as an indicator of academic performance or quality of studies. In the meantime, studies of graduates have also been established in three German states (Bavaria, Rhineland-Palatinate, Saxony). Graduate studies are thus one of the main areas of growing

---

2   Careers after Higher Education – A European Research Study.
3   The Flexible Professional in the Knowledge Society.

research. Nevertheless, despite or even because of the proliferation of local and regional studies, graduate surveys at the national level will retain their relevance as a benchmark for these narrower studies.

All in all, the complementary relationship between official statistics on higher education and the diverse number of surveys undertaken in this field is not a bad basis for the data infrastructure of higher education research. Nevertheless, there are some essential deficits in research and data provision.

- First, there is a lack of longitudinal studies that follow a cohort of students from upper-level grammar school (or at least from their entry into higher education) through their studies until their transition to employment and the first phase of vocational activity (with the exception of the longitudinal study of Meulemann et al. (2001) based on a cohort of grammar school graduates). Most of the existing panel studies concentrate on only one transition point – either access to higher education or to employment. This deficit is another reason why the drop-out phenomenon has not been explained sufficiently.

- Second, despite the fact there are some student surveys exploring the situation and the difficulties of students during their studies, there is a lack of data concerning the interrelationship between institutional context and the processes and outcomes of learning in higher education institutions. The relationship between internal contextual and institutional conditions at different levels (classroom, program, faculty, the institution as a whole), personal attitudes and behaviors, and learning outcomes – as well as the influence of outside learning environments – is obviously an important research desiderata. Without data on these aspects, the actual impact of institutions on learning and its outcomes is not really that clear (Pascarella and Terenzini 2005). Of course, this is an area that is both theoretically and methodologically very ambitious in light of the multiple dependent, independent, and intervening causal variables. However, it is also a venture of central importance – not only academically but also politically. The manifest trend toward more differentiation in German higher education through profiling, ranking, and excellence inevitably provokes the question of the particular influence exerted by institutions and study programs on the learning outcomes and on the later employment situations and career courses of graduates from these institutions (Teichler 2007b).

- Third, there is a considerable deficit in research and knowledge about competence development in higher education. The subject of competencies in higher education research is still a relatively new field that has become increasingly important with the Bologna Process. First of all, it is necessary to distinguish between at least three different types of competencies: (1) subject- or discipline-specific competencies; (2) cross-curricular competencies (also called "key" or "generic" competencies that include social skills, and can normally not be acquired through learning processes independent of discipline-related learning, but which nonetheless need to be measured in their own way); and (3) competencies to act professionally in vocational demand situations. During the last ten years, there have been several attempts to measure student or graduate competencies in Germany, but these have mostly been only cross-sectional, primarily measuring for cross-curricular competencies and based largely on self-assessment or self-reporting measures (Schaeper 2005; Schaeper and Spangenberg 2007). Valid measurement procedures for competence development, based on competence tests, are very rare. In the field of discipline-related competencies, they do not even exist (apart from a very small number of pilot studies for selected subjects).

Attempts to develop and practice competence measurement procedures primarily have two main problems to confront: (1) the great diversity of discipline contexts in higher education, which is different than the school system with its core curriculum and a limited number of subjects; and (2) a completely different target group and institutional context, both of which make it more difficult to implement test-based procedures of competence measurement for students – and even more so for graduates – than is the case for pupils and classroom situations, including the acceptance of such procedures to graduates. However, there is no doubt about the relevance and necessity of the development and implementation of more elaborate procedures of competence measurement in higher education, in particular to address the question whether (or to what extent) institutions and programs actually impart the competencies they should and to what extent other formal or informal learning settings intervene in this process.

Some of these questions and issues are the subject of the recently established National Educational Panel Study (NEPS) (Blossfeld 2008; Blossfeld in this publication), which also includes a student cohort. The NEPS focuses on a number of aspects: first, on the development of competencies through higher education, mainly cross-curricular competencies; second, on the influence of institutional settings and contexts; and third, on the educational decisions and courses including the extent and conditions of success and drop-out. In the long term, the NEPS will provide empirical information and knowledge precisely in some of the deficit areas which have been specified before. However, the NEPS limits the measurement of subject-related competencies to two selected disciplines and concentrates primarily on cross-curricular competencies.

Gender problems and issues have been dealt with in many different forms in higher education research. Whereas the participation of women in higher education has continuously increased over the last decades and, in the meantime, has become higher than that of men at least at the university level, there are still large disparities in gender participation within specific subjects. Particularly the low degree of female participation in engineering and some of the sciences has caused concern and attracted special attention. The success rate of women is higher than that of men or, the other way round, the drop-out rate is lower. Since 2000, more females than males have graduated from universities every year, and since 2003, they have graduated in greater numbers from the higher education system in general (Klieme et al. 2008, 133, 302). It seems that the future of human capital, particularly of the highly qualified workforce, depends more and more on the supply of qualified women in the labor market. Based on these trends, some new questions arise with regard to the response of the employment system. For example, transitions of female graduates, their particular employment chances and conditions, career perspectives, and the compatibility of work and family will become or remain very important issues.

Migration has been a relatively marginal issue in German higher education research so far. First of all, it is necessary to distinguish between students with migration status and internationally mobile students who do not have residential status in Germany but stay here for the purpose of their studies. The official higher education statistics register migration only in a very narrow interpretation, based on nationality. According to this definition, approximately 3 percent of all students are migrants whereas the proportion of migrants in the population is about 9 percent (Avenarius et al. 2006, 140, 273). Based on a wider (but not exhaustive) definition of migration background, including educational residents (*Bildungsinländer*), students with double nationality, and naturalized students, the proportion of migrants in the student body comes to about 8 percent compared with a proportion of this group of about 19 percent in the population (Isserstedt et al. 2007, 435). Obviously, migration has been up to now only a peripheral topic in higher education research, resulting in a lack of data and empirical knowledge despite the fact that a higher rate of participation of migrants would be a new source of social demand.

Whereas research and data provision on students and studying is relatively well-established, the state of research and data in the field of academic recruitment and academic staff is not satisfactory in the same way. Even if the official personnel statistics can deliver a lot of quantitative and structural information, there have not been any regular parallel surveys up to now – either for young scholars or for the complete academic staff. Furthermore, the official statistics cannot deliver any reliable information about the volume, the paths, and the overall situation of the new academic generation. In this area a lack of quantitative information and some important research desiderata dominate (BMBF 2008; Burkhardt et al. 2008).

Because of the current generation, changes in academic staffing, and the high demand for scholars – not only from higher education institutions but also from the non-university research sector – the state of data provision in this area is absolutely unsatisfactory. However, some empirical, partly comparative studies have been carried out during the last years concerning the situation of young scholars and the paths of qualification and employment on the way to a professorship (Enders and Bornmann 2001; Enders and Mugabushaka 2005; Burkhart 2008; Kreckel 2008). These studies highlight the urgency of the problem. But neither the number of young scholars, currently employed at German universities as the coming generation of professors (*wissenschaftlicher Nachwuchs*), nor the number of PhD students, is precisely known. The same is true for the expanding group of postdocs.

Most quantitative information in this field is based on estimates, case studies or other limited projects. The success rate of PhD candidates is unknown as well. At best, the number, situation, and success of PhD candidates in graduate schools or with other institutions can be or has been examined, but this group represents only a small proportion. One reason for this insufficiency in data provision is the individual diversity and heterogeneity in the qualification routes, in particular to acquire a PhD degree, and in the employment conditions within and outside universities. Presently, some panel projects are being established or planned to collect more and better data on the number, routes, situation, problems, and success of this group, such as the PhD panel "ProFile" and the online panel "WinBus." Graduate panel studies with a sufficient sample volume could be another way to improve the state of information and knowledge in this area.

3. Conclusions and recommendations

The demand for data in the field of higher education will increase considerably in future. This growing need is due to the rising social and political importance of higher education in postmodern societies as well as to the implementation and extension of monitoring systems including higher education. In Germany, a complementary infrastructure of research data has been being developed since the 1970s, consisting of official higher education statistics and some survey-based regular data and information sources. In the future, the National Educational Panel Study (NEPS) will significantly extend the existing system of data provision. However, there are some obvious deficiencies in the present data infrastructure, and because of this the following measures should be taken.

- *Access to data stocks:* All in all, there are in principle no serious obstacles to access to the available data stock. This is true not only for official statistics but also for the survey-based data. But access could be improved from a practical point of view. Because HIS is the institution outside official statistics that provides the largest data stocks relevant to higher education research, a Research Data Center should be established at HIS.

- *Diversification of higher education:* In the area of official higher education, statistics on cooperative learning institutions (*Berufsakademien*) should be included in the student or personnel statistics (and also in surveys). This would take into account that fact that the structures of higher education in many countries have become blurred due to the hybrid status of some institutions – straddling post-secondary and tertiary education – and the increasing permeability between these institutions. Another important point concerns the revision of the list of disciplines in the higher education statistics, because the number and the degree of specialization within subjects have seen significant growth and provoked several serious problems of allocation.

- *Personal identity number:* The introduction of an identity number for all participants in educational programs would allow us not only to link future individual school statistics with the already given individual student statistics on pursuing transitions and additional routes of training and education, but also to improve processing data, particularly with respect to students who drop out and issues of national and international mobility. This will certainly be a delicate issue, but nevertheless is an important academic demand for the official statistics.

- *Continuation of survey-based time series:* A great deal of data and information in higher education depends on regular survey research. But this kind of survey research is based on applying for every individual project. The future availability of this data provision as the second pillar of the research data infrastructure depends completely on the continuation of these surveys. Therefore, the certainty of long-term planning is of almost constitutive importance for the data infrastructure in higher education research.

- *Indicators for quality of studies and studying:* Official statistics and survey-based research should collaborate to develop and implement a joint set of quality indicators to exploit the available data stock in a comprehensive way with regard to the increasing demand for quality assessment in higher education. Quality of studies or institutions will become one of the central issues in future higher education policy and research.

- *Longitudinal design and process data:* In student research, the most serious deficits are the lack of longer panel designs, of competence measurement, and of studies that can explore the interrelations between contextual and institutional features, personal characteristics, the processes of studying and learning, and the learning outcomes. The NEPS will probably improve the state of knowledge in this field considerably. But longitudinal research should be intensified in general, not only in the context of NEPS. Furthermore, there should be additional pilot projects to initiate and promote the development and testing of procedures for the discipline-related measurement of competencies. Initially these should focus only on a few selected subjects, primarily those not included in the NEPS.

- *Graduate and competence studies:* Graduate studies, especially panel studies, will become even more important at all levels – at the local, state, national, and international levels. At the national level, graduate studies are indispensable as a comparative point of reference. Particular attention should be drawn to the role of institutions and programs for the allocation of position and status in the employment system. Neither the match between qualifications and employment nor, in particular, the role of competencies acquired during studies in coping with later occupational requirements are very clear. It can be expected that the trend towards more horizontal and vertical differentiation between universities will also affect the importance of institutions for employment and the future career perspectives.

- *Academic careers and young scholars:* As a part of graduate studies research, attention to the situation and further development of PhD candidates should be intensified. The lack of reliable information on the employment conditions and career paths of the younger generation of scholars, even with regard to the number of young academics or PhD candidates or to their success rate, indicates one of the most alarming deficits in the data infrastructure of higher education research. Therefore, the improvement of data provision concerning the qualification routes to an academic career remains a matter of high priority.

To sum up, it seems possible to conclude that the current state of data provision in higher education research reflects (not completely, but in many aspects) the questions, issues, definitions, and methods that emerged during the 1970s and 1980s, to which the data infrastructure has only partially adapted up to now. Many new academic or political topics and demands on data provision have arisen since this time, including issues such as migration status, competencies, lifelong learning, quality of studies, differentiation, programs to promote younger scholars, international mobility, outcomes, employability etc. These have had to be integrated into existing data programs, a venture that obviously is still ongoing. In this respect, surveys have proven to be more flexible in many respects than the often quite inflexible procedures in official statistics.

References:

Avenarius, H./Baethge, M./Döbert, H./Hetmeier, H.-W./Klieme, E./Meister-Scheufelen, G./Rauschenbach, T. and Wolter, A. (2006): Bildung in Deutschland. Bielefeld.
Bayer, C.R. (2004): Hochschul-Ranking. Vorschlag eines ganzheitlichen Ranking-Verfahrens. Berlin.
Blossfeld, H.-P. (2008): Education as a Lifelong Process. A Proposal for a National Educational Panel Study (NEPS) in Germany. 3 parts. Bamberg (unpublished).
Bundesministerium für Bildung und Forschung (BMBF) (2008): Bundesbericht zur Förderung des wissenschaftlichen Nachwuchses. Bonn/Berlin.
Briedis, K. (2007a): Die HIS-Absolventenstudie. In: Hochschulrektorenkonferenz (Ed.): Potentiale von Absolventenstudien für die Hochschulentwicklung. Bonn. Beiträge zur Hochschulpolitik 4.
Briedis, K. (2007b): Übergänge und Erfahrungen nach dem Hochschulabschluss. Ergebnisse der HIS-Absolventenbefragung des Jahrgangs 2005. Hannover.
Burkhardt, A./König, K. and Krempkow, R. (2008): Dr. Unsichtbar im Visier. Erwartungen an die Forschung zum wissenschaftlichen Nachwuchs. Die Hochschule 17 (1), 74-90.
Burkhardt, A. (Ed.) (2008): Wagnis Wissenschaft. Akademische Karrierewege und das Fördersystem in Deutschland. Leipzig.
Enders, J. and Bornmann, L. (2001): Karriere mit Doktortitel? Ausbildung, Berufsverlauf und Berufserfolg von Promovierten. Frankfurt/M./New York.
Enders, J. and Mugabushaka, A.-M. (2005): Wissenschaft und Karriere. Erfahrungen und Werdegang ehemaliger Stipendiaten der DFG. Kassel.
Eurostudent, co-ordinated by the Higher Education Information System (HIS) (2008): Social and Economic Conditions of Student Life in Europe. Bielefeld.
Heine, C./Spangenberg, H. and Willich, J. (2008a): Studienberechtigte 2006 ein halbes Jahr nach Schulabschluss. Hannover.
Heine, C./Krawietz, M. and Sommer, D. (2008b): Studienanfänger im Wintersemester 2006/7. HIS-Projektbericht.
Heublein, U./Schmelzer, R. and Sommer, D. (2008): Die Entwicklung der Studienabbruchquote an den deutschen Hochschulen. HIS-Projektbericht.
Hornbostel, S. (2008a). Exzellenz und Differenzierung. In: Kehm, B. (Ed.): Hochschule im Wandel.
Hornbostel, S. (2008b): Evaluation der Exzellenzinitiative: Gibt es objektive Kriterien für Exzellenz? In: Bloch, R./Keller, A./Lottmann, A. and Würmann, C. (Eds.): Making Excellence. Bielefeld.
Hochschulrektorenkonferenz (HRK) (Ed.) (2007): Potentiale von Absolventenstudien für die Hochschulentwicklung. Bonn.
Isserstedt, W./Middendorff, E./Fabian, G. and Wolter, A. (2007): Die wirtschaftliche und soziale Lage der Studierenden in der Bundesrepublik Deutschland 2006. Bonn/Berlin.
Kelo, M./Teichler, U. and Wächter, B. (Eds.) (2006): Eurodata. Student Mobility in European Higher Education. Bonn.
Kerst, C. and Schramm, M. (2008): Der Absolventenjahrgang 2000/2001 fünf Jahre nach dem Hochschulabschluss. Hannover.

Klieme, E./Baethge, M./Döbert, H./Füssel, H.-P./Hetmeier, H.-W./Rauschenbach, T./Rockmann, U. and Wolter, A. (2008): Bildung in Deutschland. Bielefeld.

Köller, O./Watermann, R./Trautwein, U. and Lüdtke, O. (Eds.) (2004): Wege zur Hochschulreife in Baden-Württemberg. Opladen.

Kreckel, R. (Ed.) (2008): Zwischen Promotion und Professur. Leipzig.

Meulemann, H./Birkelbach, K. and Hellwig, O. (2001): Ankunft im Erwachsenenleben. Lebenserfolg und Erfolgsdeutung in einer Kohorte ehemaliger Gymnasiasten zwischen 16 und 43. Opladen.

Multrus, F./Bargel, T. and Ramm, M. (2008): Studiensituation und studentische Orientierungen. 10. Studierendensurvey an Universitäten und Fachhochschulen. Bonn/Berlin.

Pascarella, E.T. and Terenzini, P.T. (2005): How College Affects Students. San Francisco.

Schaeper, H. (2005): Hochschulbildung und Schlüsselkompetenzen – Der Beitrag der Hochschulforschung zur Evaluation der Qualifizierungsfunktionen und – leistungen von Hochschulen. In: Teichler, U. and Tippelt, R. (Eds.): Hochschullandschaft im Wandel. Zeitschrift für Pädagogik. 50. Beiheft. Weinheim/Basel.

Schaeper, H. and Spangenberg, H. (2007): Die Erfassung von Schlüsselkompetenzen in den HIS-Studienberechtigten- und Absolventenuntersuchungen. In: Jude, N./Hartig, J. and Klieme, E. (Eds.): Kompetenzerfassung in pädagogischen Handlungsfeldern. Bonn.

Schaeper, H. and Wolter, A. (2008): Hochschule und Arbeitsmarkt im Bologna-Prozess – Der Stellenwert von „Employability" und Schlüsselkompetenzen. Zeitschrift für Erziehungswissenschaft 11 (4), 607-625.

Schomburg, H. and Teichler, U. (2006): Higher Education and Graduate Employment in Europe. Dordrecht.

Statistisches Bundesamt (Ed.) (2007): Statistik und Wissenschaft. Amtliche Hochschulstatistik und Hochschulrankings. Wiesbaden.

Teichler, U. (2002): Hochschulbildung. In: Tippelt, R. (Ed.): Handbuch Bildungsforschung. Opladen.

Teichler, U. (2004): The changing debate on internationalisation of higher education. Higher Education 48, 5-26.

Teichler, U. (Ed.) (2007a): Careers of University Graduates. Dordrecht.

Teichler, U. (2007b): Studium und Berufschancen: Was macht den Unterschied aus? Beiträge zur Hochschulforschung 29 (4), 10-31.

Teichler, U. (2008): Der Jargon der Nützlichkeit. Zur Employability-Diskussion im Bologna-Prozess. Das Hochschulwesen. 56, 68-79.

Wissenschaftsrat (2006): Empfehlungen zum arbeitsmarkt- und demographiegerechten Ausbau des Hochschulsystems. Köln.

Wolter, A. (2004): From State Control to Competition. German Higher Education Transformed. The Canadian Journal of Higher Education XXXIV, 73-104.

Wolter, A. (2007a): From the Academic Republic to the Managerial University – The Implementation of New Governance Structures in German Higher Education. In: University of Tsukuba, Research Center for University Studies (Ed.): The 3rd International Workshop on Reforms of Higher Education in Six Countries/Regions – Commonalities and Differences. Tokyo.

Wolter, A. (2007b) Diversifizierung des Weiterbildungsmarktes und Nachfrage nach akademischer Weiterbildung in Deutschland. Österreichische Zeitschrift für Hochschulentwicklung 2 (1), 14-29.

Zeitschrift für Soziologie der Erziehung und Sozialisation (ZSE) (2008): Der Bologna-Prozess – Potenziale und Folgen für Hochschule und Studium. Vol. 28/No. 4. München.

3.6 Adult Education and Lifelong Learning

Corinna Kleinert and Britta Matthes

Contact:

Corinna Kleinert
Institute for Employment Research (IAB)
Regensburger Str. 104
90478 Nuremberg
Germany
e-mail: corinna.kleinert[at]iab.de

Abstract

Over the last years, political and scientific debates have stressed the growing importance of adult education. Currently important research questions call not only for data sources that collect detailed information on adult education with repeated measurements and in different cohorts, but they should also include data on other life spheres such as education and working histories, partnership and household information, as well as competence development.

In Germany, there are several large-scale datasets containing information on adult education. While general panel studies do not provide a systematic overview of educational activities of adults, studies focusing on adult education are either small-scale or cross-sectional and contain little contextual information. A study that covers information on all educational activities in the life course as well as repeated competence assessment is still missing.

In part, these deficits will be resolved by the large-scale longitudinal studies focused on adults and education that were either recently conducted or are currently being prepared. Thus, we do not call for new data sources on adult education. What is far more important in the next few years is analyzing the data of the new large-scale data sources thoroughly, but also developing new theoretical approaches to adult education.

Keywords: adult education, further education, lifelong learning, continuing training, life course, competencies, data access

1. The need for analyses in the area of adult education

Over the last few years, political as well as scientific debates have stressed the growing importance of adult education (Becker and Hecken 2005; European Commission 2000). The significance of this area is largely justified with reference to ongoing globalization, skill-biased technological change, and the development of the knowledge society – changes that have crucial effects on the working lives of the population in (post-)industrial countries. Education is no longer viewed as an asset achieved in youth that remains of constant value during an uninterrupted and stable employment career. Today and in the future, adults must learn continuously to keep up with the flexible requirements of the workplace and to be able to find employment in different and rapidly developing fields.

As a result, there is an urgent political need for knowledge about how to achieve the following goals: How can we enlarge the skill potential among those that have been largely underexploited up until now (e.g., the unemployed or marginally employed, low-skilled, or older workers)? Do these groups have the necessary prerequisites for continuous learning, particularly in terms of basic skills? How can we ensure that higher-skilled adults continue to learn after completing their initial education? How can they be enabled to flexibly adapt to the changing requirements and new technologies of working life, beyond their employers' immediate needs? How can lifelong learning be organized efficiently in society as a whole so that it reaches all groups of individuals – integrating all the different institutions and organizations involved in adult education? A great deal of empirical research is needed to answer these questions.

In contrast to this evident need, the first national report on education in Germany devoted only sixteen pages to adult education due to the "particularly difficult data situation of adult education" (Konsortium Bildungsberichterstattung 2006: 123). The report merely covered diverging participation rates of subgroups in different types of adult education in Germany, differentiated by educational background, age, gender, occupation, and position (Kuwan et al. 2006). Thus, we know that lifelong learning increases with growing education, occupation, and position, and declines with age (e.g., Pfeiffer and Pohlmeier 1998; Schömann and Becker 1995; Bellmann and Leber 2003; Schiener 2006). Furthermore, men participate more frequently in adult education than women, and natives more frequently than persons with a migration background (e.g., Pfeiffer and Pohlmeier 1998; Becker 2003). In comparison with other nations, we know that the participation rate in adult education in Germany is relatively low (OECD 2006). Finally, the costs of adult education in Germany are mainly borne by firms, the participants themselves, and the Federal Employment Agency (BA, *Bundesagentur für Arbeit*), but figures on financing vary according to different data sources (Beicht et al. 2005).

Apart from these facts, there are many research questions, particularly of a longitudinal nature, that have not yet been answered. This deficit becomes apparent for example when searching for results on *(cumulated) long-term returns of educational activities* in youth as well as in adult life. Since most of the existing data is only cross-sectional, this issue cannot be analyzed. The exceptions to this deficit are the training schemes financed by the BA. In various evaluation studies the success of these programs with regard to subsequent labor market integration is analyzed (e.g., Hujer et al. 2006; Schneider and Uhlendorff 2006). While the returns of (adult) education are mostly understood economically – for example by analyzing income, wages, labor market integration, mobility, or career development – a more pedagogically oriented approach would ask for *learning outcomes*. To answer this question, we need not only precise data on learning activities, but also on the development of individual competencies (for details see Trautwein and Schoon in this publication). Studies targeted at adult persons that combine both topics in a longitudinal design are currently underway (see section 4).

Learning activities are embedded in the adult life course. Up until now we have known little about these *framing mechanisms of adult education* and how they interact with participation, since research on educational pathways and how they are embedded in employment histories and other life domains is still at an early stage (Jacob 2004; Hillmert and Jacob 2004). The decision to participate in further education is connected to specific personal circumstances. Certain factors, such as unemployment, promote participation due to an expected increase in employment chances. Other circumstances may reduce participation due to the time restrictions they impose (e.g., childbearing) or because of the expectation that such education does not pay off anymore (e.g., in the case of older persons). To explore these research questions, rich data sources in a life course oriented framework are needed.

Another aspect of framing adult education within the life course is the *household,* since it determines the opportunities and restrictions surrounding participation in several respects: first, economic resources and their allocation among household members determine participation; second, the division of labor within households and partnerships has an impact on participation. Thus, the relative position of household members, their educational resources, and their time budgets decide about participation in adult education. These aspects are particularly important for assessing gender differences in lifelong learning. Another household characteristic that is primarily significant for self-learning processes is the learning environment at home. Finally, the household situation not only influences participation in adult education, but even more it affects the *decision-making processes that precede it.* In sociology particularly, there are highly-developed theories and many empirical results related to parental decisions about the educational choices of their children, but far less research is available concerning educational decisions made during adulthood.

Another important research question addresses further education in Germany among adults with a migration background. *Migrants and their descendants* are a group that, in part at least, is urgently in need of education during adulthood since their educational endowment is often inadequate and certificates acquired in their countries of origin are frequently not recognized in Germany.

Finally, many countries are struggling with an aging society; this is especially true in Germany (Fuchs and Dörfler 2005). Thus, it must be ensured that the older population will be equipped for participating in working life longer than it is today by providing access to continuing education. Yet, in contrast to these necessities, we find that older people participate less in continuing learning than younger ones (Kuwan et al. 2006). Thus, it is important that research can identify the *opportunities and barriers to continuing education in older age groups.* To do so, it is necessary to gain additional knowledge about the returns of educational activities later in life.

Taken together, these research questions call not only for data sources that collect detailed information on adult education with repeated measurements and in different cohorts, but they should also include data on other life spheres, such as education and working histories, partnership and household information, and competence development in different domains.

2. A complex field of research

The main challenge that faces data collection in the field of adult education is the complexity of the object of investigation. It is therefore fruitful to distinguish it analytically before describing the relevant data sources. For this purpose we classify adult education according to the form of learning, the learning location and context, and the purpose and contents of learning (Wohn 2007).

Generally, adult education can be defined as "the continuing or resumption of formal, non-formal, and/or informal learning with general or vocational content after completion of initial training" (Expertenkommission Finanzierung Lebenslangen Lernens 2002: 56). *Formal education* is institutionalized and leads to recognized certificates that strongly determine labor market chances in Germany. Therefore most existing data sources are limited to this type of education and the data situation here is well developed. A second – and in quantity and quality more important – type of adult education is *non-formal education,* which includes shorter institutionalized training courses that do not lead to certificates (or to certificates not fully recognized). This is the type of educational activity that is commonly understood when referring to "adult education." However, data on non-formal education is more difficult to collect: Participation differs individually and problems of recall and identification of these events are common. Even less is known about *intentional informal learning*, learning processes organized by the individuals themselves (e.g., by participating in conferences, reading textbooks, or learning a new computer program). This is particularly true regarding the decisions that lead to these learning processes or their (cumulative) returns. In this context, it is important to mention the limitations of standardized survey research. First, people have difficulty remembering such activities over a longer period of time. Thus, information on non-formal and informal learning can only be collected in a panel design or for a limited retrospective period. Furthermore, survey questionnaires cannot measure *unintentional informal learning* that takes place in the context of other activities – at least not directly. Still, we assume that this form of learning is very important, particularly when it takes place on the job. Many adults constantly obtain new skills, typically without being aware of it, simply by fulfilling their tasks and responding to the challenges of everyday working life or by performing voluntary activities. Thus, unintentional informal learning can be assessed only indirectly by measuring employment experience, activities and requirements on the job, and social engagement.

While most individuals participate in learning in earlier educational stages within the same predefined institutional contexts, learning processes of adults happen in a multitude of different *learning environments*. Firms are the major providers of adult education in Germany. Thus, certain kinds of information on participation in firm-based training and education cannot be accessed by individual and household surveys alone, but also by firm-level data (see Joachim Wagner in this publication). Other institutions are important providers of adult education as well. Second-chance programs *(Zweiter Bildungsweg)* allow people to complete upper-secondary qualifications and to proceed to tertiary education (evening schools, adult apprenticeships). Upgrade training for employed workers is offered by the Chamber of Industry and Commerce (IHK, *Industrie- und Handelskammer*) or by the Chamber of Crafts and Trades (HWK, *Handwerkskammer*) and allows for the acquisition of additional formal certificates in relatively short courses. A variety of shorter and longer training programs aiming mainly at reintegrating unemployed persons into the labor market are provided by the BA. Adult Learning Centers *(Volkshochschulen)* provide courses in many areas of self-development including languages, art and music, political developments, and information technology. Non-vocational adult education is also provided by a variety of voluntary and non-governmental organizations including religious groups. These courses often target specific sections of the population, such as women or migrants. This list of examples shows how difficult it is to gain a complete overview of the providers of adult education in Germany. This variety also limits the possible information on the institutional contexts of adult education in empirical data.

Finally, adult education covers many *fields*, ranging from basic cognitive competencies to vocational and non-cognitive skills. Adults do not only participate in further education with the objective of vocational training, but also for personal reasons. Researchers, however, are interested mainly in adult education relevant to working life, employability, active participation in society, or coping with everyday life. Whereas formal training undertaken for these purposes can theoretically be distinguished clearly from educational activities taken up for private reasons, such a distinction is not possible for non-formal education. Taking a foreign language course can, for example, be of central importance for the career advancement of one individual, whereas for another person it serves mainly private interests and has no effect on her or his further working life. This problem calls for relatively broad questioning strategies on the one hand, and for a detailed collection of the contents of further education on the other hand.

This brief overview already suggests that the data situation in the field of adult education may be both confusing and limited. In the next section, we describe and evaluate the most important data sources and their accessibility before presenting new developments in national and international data collection.

3. Status quo: Databases and access

In the following, we distinguish between the actors involved in adult education (providers, firms, or individuals) on the one hand, and cross-sectional and longitudinal data on the other hand. Our discussion of datasets is largely focused on German research and includes only selected examples of international and comparative studies.[1]

In Germany, a comprehensive *statistic* on adult education does not exist. Rather, different statistics are found that are only partly compatible (Weishaupt and Fickermann 2001), since they differ in definitions, variables, periods, etc. Official statistics, for instance, the Statistics of the General Education Schools (evening schools), the Statistics of Technical Schools, or the Statistics of Vocational Education provide information on the number of participants and their socio-demographic characteristics within the respective school types. In addition, the manifold providers of adult education produce statistics relating to their own programs (for example, the German Institute for Adult Education (DIE, *Deutsches Institut für Erwachsenenbildung*) generated the Statistics of the Adult Education Program).

More data sources are available for firms, the most important group of adult education providers. Regarding cross-sectional firm-level data, most important to mention are the IW Survey on in-firm further training conducted by the Institute of the German Economy (IW, *Institut der Deutschen Wirtschaft*) and the Continuing Vocational Training Survey (CVTS) con-

---

1 An overview on data sources concerning adult education in other countries is found in the article by Kristen and colleagues (Kristen et al. 2005). Additionally, Statistics Canada (http://www.statcan.gc.ca), the US National Center for Education Statistics (http://nces.ed.gov/), the Longitudinal Studies Centre (http://www.iser.essex.ac.uk/survey) and the Inter-University Consortium for Political and Social Research (http://www.icpsr.umich.edu/ICPSR/access/index.html) in the UK, and the Data Archiving and Networked Services in the Netherlands (http://www.dans.knaw.nl/en/) offer online information on studies referring to adult education. A web guide made available by the Mannheim Centre for European Social Research (MZES) supports searching for metadata of major European socio-economic surveys (http://www.mzes.uni-mannheim.de/projekte/mikrodaten/ drafts/index.html).

ducted by the Federal Institute for Vocational Education and Training (BIBB, *Bundesinstitut für Berufsbildung*). The IW Survey contains data on the provision of workers' educational activities initiated or financed by the firm (such as on-the-job training, reading literature, participation in internal or external seminars, informative meetings, or retraining) (Werner 2006). However, it is hard to gather information on the survey because there is no systematic overview and its data is not yet available. CVTS is a firm survey on the European level containing information on participation rates, hours, costs, and socio-demographic characteristics of the participants. The advantage of CVTS is its voluminous structural information on further education provided and financed by firms, but its value and comparative possibilities are limited, mainly by methodological problems, for example the change of research unit (firm vs. establishment), or the probable higher response rate of firms or establishments that do provide further education.

In contrast to these cross-sectional firm surveys, the IAB Establishment Panel is an annual panel survey of nearly 16,000 German establishments. One of main topics surveyed in this multi-issue study is further education, including information on evaluation of employee demands, provision of internal or external courses, on-the-job training, and participation in self-learning activities. Additionally, data on participant characteristics is available. Since the panel contains a wide range of firm characteristics, it also allows for an analysis of firm-based training in a longitudinal research design. The IAB Establishment Panel is available through the Research Data Center of the Federal Employment Agency at the Institute for Employment Research (IAB, *Institut für Arbeitsmarkt- und Berufsforschung* within the BA, *Bundesagentur für Arbeit*).

Regarding individual data, the most important data source in Germany has been the *Berichtssystem Weiterbildung* up until now, a national, repeated, cross-sectional survey dedicated specifically to further education (Kuwan et al. 2006). Its data – available for the years 1979 and 1988 to 2003 via the data archive at the Leibniz Institute for the Social Sciences (GESIS, Leibniz-Institut für Sozialwissenschaften) – mainly supports analyses of participation in adult learning. About 7,000 respondents have been asked every three years about their participation in a broad range of educational activities and their learning interests. Since 1994, non-formal education has been included, and questions about self-regulated learning have been asked since 2000, containing instruments to record learning environments, learning dispositions, and support by other persons. However, due to its cross-sectional structure, longitudinal analyses on educational careers are not possible.

Another large-scale dataset containing information on adult education activities of individuals is the German Microcensus, a one-percent sample of all German households conducted yearly by the Federal Statistical Office. Between 1970 and 1995, respondents were asked every two years about further education over the previous two years; since 1996 these questions have been surveyed on an annual basis. The advantage of the Microcensus is the obligation to participate as well as the high number of respondents, so that even results focusing on small subgroups are reliable. Unfortunately, in the Microcensus adult education is restricted to "training, further education and retraining" and there is no information on when exactly the relevant events took place. Furthermore, comparisons between different survey years are limited due to changing instruments and time references. Except for two four-year panel files (1996-1999, 2001-2004) covering 25 percent of the yearly sample, analyses are restricted to cross-sectional designs. The Microcensus data is available via the Research Data Center of the Federal Statistical Office, the Scientific Use Files via the German Microdata Lab at GESIS.

Finally, the *BIBB/IAB Surveys* are a series of large-scale, representative cross-sectional surveys of huge samples of the employed conducted in 1979, 1985/86, 1991/92, and 1998/99. Like all other previous waves, the most recent survey from 2006 *(BIBB-BAuA Survey)* will be available in 2009 via the data archive at GESIS. These surveys gathered rich representative information on qualification profiles and occupational developments, as well as the organizational, technological, and qualification frameworks at the workplace. They also contain limited retrospective data on former educational careers, in particular on initial training. The data on adult education is cross-sectional as well, but has the advantage of capturing formal, non-formal and informal training, as well as activities and requirements of the current job that can be used indirectly as proxies for informal learning activities.

In the field of cross-sectional individual survey data, the situation in Germany can be compared to many other Western countries. Regularly implemented surveys focused on adult education and available for scientific use can be found in the UK with the National Adult Learning Survey,[2] in Finland with the Adult Education Survey,[3] in Sweden's Staff Training Statistics,[4] or in the US Adult Education Survey.[5] In the future, national surveys in Europe – in Germany the Berichtssystem Weiterbildung – will be replaced by a common data source, the European Adult Education Survey (AES). AES was carried out for the first time in 2007 on a voluntary basis in over twenty European countries and provides information about adult participation in formal, non-formal, and informal training. The first round of obligatory data collection will be in 2011 (e.g., Gnahs et al. 2008; Rosenbladt

---

2 http://www.statistics gov.uk/StatBase/Source.asp?vlnk=1329&More=Y
3 www.stat.fi/meta/til/aku_en.html
4 http://www.scb.se/Pages/Product____9001.aspx
5 http://nces.ed.gov/nhes/

and Bilger 2008). The German AES data is available at the data archive at GESIS.

In the US, the long tradition of student assessment has also led to a comprehensive literacy assessment study focused on the adult population, the National Assessment of Adult Literacy (NAAL),[6] which was carried out in 1992 and 2003. This survey also set the groundwork for international studies on adult skills, learning, and competencies, including the International Adult Literacy Survey (IALS) from the mid 1990s with twenty-two participating countries, and the six-country Adult Literacy and Lifeskills Survey (ALL)[7] carried out in 2003. These studies combine questionnaire data on educational qualifications and different forms of learning with assessments of basic cognitive domains, such as reading literacy or numeracy. Germany participated in IALS, but not in ALL.

Longitudinal datasets on adult education from an individual perspective are available as well. Rich data on educational and employment careers can be found in the German Life History Study (GLHS) of the Max Planck Institute for Human Development, which collected retrospective data on educational, employment, and family histories of several birth cohorts (from the 1920s to 1971). A Scientific Use File is available via the data archive at GESIS or by contacting the Center for Research on Inequality and the Life Course (CIQLE) at Yale University. However, it is well known that the recall of continuing education, in particular of short or relatively minor courses, is restricted. Thus, the extent of non-formal educational activities is underestimated in this survey and probably systematically selective.

More respondents are interviewed in the German Socio-Economic Panel (SOEP, *Sozio-oekonomisches Panel*), a large general household panel survey that has been carried out every year since 1984. The data is made available to researchers by the Research Data Center of the SOEP. This survey focuses on economic issues and employment careers by combining retrospective information with panel data. Further education was the main topic in 1989, 1993, 2000, and 2004. These panel waves cover information on participation in adult education, the number of courses, their extent and duration, goals, providers, costs and financing, with additional questions on the general motivation to participate in adult education. However, the instruments were mainly focused on formal and non-formal training (Pischke 2001) and further education was not linked to the employment history or the employer (Kuckulenz 2007).

Another longitudinal dataset that can be used for analyzing a particular type of adult education – programs provided by the BA – is the Integrated Employment Biographies Sample (IEBS, *Stichprobe der Integrierten Erwerbsbiografien des IAB*). This process-produced dataset contains obser-

---

6   http://nces.ed.gov/naal/
7   http://nces.ed.gov/surveys/all/

vations on employment, unemployment benefits, job search, and participation in active labor market programs on a daily basis, combining records from four data sources: the IAB employment history, the IAB benefit recipient history, the participants-in-measures data, and data on job search originating from the applicant pool database. Thus, the IEBS enables detailed longitudinal analyses of the participation in measures of active labor market policy. This dataset is available through the Research Data Center of the Federal Employment Agency at the Institute for Employment Research (IAB, *Institut für Arbeitsmarkt- und Berufsforschung* within the BA, *Bundesagentur für Arbeit*).

In the field of longitudinal data on individuals, Anglo-American countries, having launched birth cohort panel studies focused on educational pathways already decades ago, play a leading role today. In the UK, these panels started with newborns (the National Child Development Study, or NCDS, with birth cohort 1958 and the British Cohort Study, or BCS, with cohort 1970[8]), while US studies began primarily with high school students (the National Longitudinal Study of the High School Class of 1972, or NLS-72; the High School and Beyond Longitudinal Study of 1980, or HS&B; and the National Education Longitudinal Study of 1988, or NELS:88[9]). Both approaches have certain disadvantages. The UK panel studies were followed up only in long intervals during adult life. The US surveys concentrate on transitions from training and higher education into employment and usually stop following up their respondents after their mid-twenties. Thus, these data sources are suitable only to a limited extent for analyzing questions about adult education.

To sum up, there are several large-scale datasets containing information on adult education in Germany. Since the publication of the initial expert report and recommendations on the improvement of the information infrastructure in 2001, the possibilities for data access have improved considerably. However, a representative longitudinal study with the main focus on educational issues, such as the birth cohort studies in Anglo-American countries, is still missing. Most large-scale panel studies in Germany still have a broader focus and thus do not provide a systematic overview of educational activities of adults in all panel waves. Studies focusing on adult education are either small-scale or cross-sectional and contain little context information. Moreover, most data sources do not cover all sources of educational activities, and thus do not provide a comprehensive view of educational histories over the life span. Finally, the field of adult education also includes the aspect of lifelong learning, at least from an educational science perspective. This view calls for instruments measuring competence attainment and development. A study that covers both – information on educa-

---

8   http://www.cls.ioe.ac.uk/
9   http://nces.ed.gov/surveys/

tional activities as well as the repeated assessment of competencies – is still lacking.

4. Future developments

These deficits will be partially resolved by large-scale surveys that have either been recently conducted or are currently being prepared: the IAB study Changing Conditions of Working and Learning (ALWA, *Arbeiten und Lernen im Wandel*), the adult stage of the National Educational Panel Study (NEPS), and the international survey PIAAC.

ALWA was designed to study relationships between formal education, basic cognitive skills, and the working life of adults from a longitudinal perspective (Kleinert et al. 2008). It focuses on recording detailed education and employment biographies of the respondents and on testing their literacy and numeracy skills. The design combines these two components in the form of computer-assisted telephone interviews and paper-and-pencil personal interviews. The target group of the survey is the German population, age 18 to 50. In the 2007-2008 survey, 10,000 persons, chosen on the basis of a random sample from the Resident Registration Offices, were questioned by telephone, and a subsample of 4,000 persons participated in the skills tests. In the CATI questionnaires, all formal educational activities over the whole life course were surveyed. Questions on non-formal education were integrated into the modules on employment, unemployment, and other events to ensure better recall. In addition, data on informal learning activities were collected for the last two years before the interview. Due to its complex structure, the dataset will not be made publicly available (via the Research Data Center of the BA at the IAB) until mid-2010.

From 2009 on, the ALWA participants will be followed up in the context of the adult stage of the National Educational Panel Study (NEPS), in a panel design with yearly intervals (for a description of the complete study, see Blossfeld in this publication). Additionally, the sample will be extended: the study will cover all adults (including migrants) of working age older than twenty-two years, regardless of employment status. In contrast to the ALWA study, the NEPS adult stage is more strongly focused on adult education and lifelong learning. Thus, it is planned to design, test, and implement more detailed instruments covering non-formal and informal learning activities for the retrospective period between panel waves, and to supplement them by indirect measures of informal learning such as job tasks and requirements, and volunteering. One of the main goals of NEPS is to make its data publicly available quickly after the data is gathered.

A second new development in the field of adult training was inspired by the realization that we need to know more about the providers of adult education in order to learn about training decisions and learning processes. Considering the multitude of actors in the field, this would be a difficult goal to achieve in the case of adult education in general; however, it is a more reasonable goal for firm-based training and education. One approach to this is combining individual and firm-level data, a method that is currently implemented in projects linking individual survey data and administrative data (for a detailed discussion, see Schnell in this publication). For instance, ALWA and NEPS will use record-linkage routines to enrich respondents' data on employment periods with establishment information from administrative data.

Another approach to data linkage was undertaken in the project 'Further Training as a Part of Lifelong Learning (WeLL). This project of RWI Essen, IAB, infas, and DIE aims at analyzing the joint training decisions of employers and their employees (Bender et al. 2008a; b). First, an employer survey was conducted in 2007, followed by a panel survey of employees in the respective firms. Both surveys focus on the collection of training information together with a variety of employee and employer background characteristics. Moreover, administrative longitudinal employee data can be linked with these data sources. In 2010, the project will provide its data via the Research Data Center of the BA at the IAB.

Finally, a large-scale international OECD survey on adult education is currently being prepared. The Programme for the International Assessment of Adult Competencies (PIAAC) will assess the level and distribution of adult skills by focusing on key cognitive and workplace skills across countries. PIAAC will also gather information on the antecedents and outcomes of skills, as well as on the use of information technology and literacy and numeracy practices in general. Its data will allow researchers to investigate links between key cognitive skills and a range of demographic variables, economic and other outcomes, as well as the use of skills in the workplace and other settings. The survey will be administered in 2011 and its results are scheduled to be released in early 2013.

5. Two final recommendations

The comparison between two important data sources on adult education in Germany results in astonishing disparities, even in terms of basic information. For example, according to the data of the Berichtssystem Weiterbildung IX, 41 percent of the adult population in Germany participated in further education in 2003, while the Microzensus reported only 13 percent

(Wohn 2007). The main reason for this significant discrepancy seems to be the highly different instruments of the two surveys. This problem arises not only around these particular studies. Most other surveys use specific, non-comparable instruments as well. Often, they are constructed ad hoc and not sufficiently tested. In part, this problem is simply a reflection of the complexity of adult education and its 'resistance' to standardized survey research. Thus, an important challenge to be met over the next few years is to develop standardized, valid, and reliable instruments representing the entire range of educational activities in adulthood, at least as far as they are undertaken intentionally and can be recalled. To a certain extent, these development tasks are central to the above mentioned new studies – above all to the National Educational Panel Study (NEPS). Moreover, the call for standardized instruments has also an international dimension. To date, the results of most German studies cannot be compared internationally, since instruments and item batteries differ considerably by country. This is not only a problem of poor international coordination, but also of different national meanings of adult education, educational cultures, and institutional conditions. Here, new international studies such as PIAAC could take a lead in helping to integrate instruments.

Since we are now (it is hoped) taking a step forward with tackling these problems by way of the new surveys mentioned above, we are not issuing a call for new data sources on adult education. What is far more important in the next years, in our view, is testing these new large-scale data sources, analyzing the data thoroughly, but also developing new theoretical approaches to adult education. It is from these areas that we will find the greatest challenges in the upcoming years. More researchers from diverse fields – including sociology, economics, psychology, and educational science – should work with innovative theoretical approaches and state-of-the-art empirical methods on the existing and new data to generate more knowledge about adult education and to explore its development and its relationship with structural changes in the labor market and the life course. This calls for a strong initiative in the training and promotion of young empirical researchers in these fields.

References:

Becker, R. (2003): Educational Expansion and Persistent Inequalities of Education: Utilizing Subjective Expected Utility Theory to Explain Increasing Participation Rates in Upper Secondary School in the Federal Republic of Germany. European Sociological Review 19 (1), 1-24.
Becker, R. and Hecken, A. (2005): Berufliche Weiterbildung – arbeitsmarktsoziologische Perspektiven und empirische Befunde. In: Abraham, M. and Hinz, Th. (Eds.): Arbeitsmarktsoziologie: Probleme, Theorien, empirische Befunde. Wiesbaden, 133-168.
Beicht, U./Berger, K. and Moraal, D. (2005): Aufwendungen für berufliche Weiterbildung in Deutschland. Sozialer Fortschritt 54 (10/11), 256-266.
Bellmann, L. and Leber, U. (2003): Betriebliche Weiterbildung. Denn wer da hat, dem wird gegeben. IAB-Materialien, 1/2003. Nürnberg.
Bender, S./Fertig, M./Görlitz, K./Huber, M./Hummelsheim, S./Knerr, P./Schmucker, A. and Schröder, H. (2008a): WeLL – Berufliche Weiterbildung als Bestandteil Lebenslangen Lernens. Projektbericht. FDZ Methodenreport, 5/2008. Nürnberg.
Bender, S./Fertig, M./Görlitz, K./Huber, M. and Schmucker, A. (2008b): WeLL – Unique Linked Employer-Employee Data on Further Training in Germany. Ruhr Economic Paper 67. Essen.
European Commission (2000): A Memorandum on Lifelong Learning. Brussels.
Expertenkommission Finanzierung Lebenslangen Lernens (2002): Auf dem Weg zur Finanzierung Lebenslangen Lernens. Zwischenbericht. Schriftenreihe der Expertenkommission Finanzierung Lebenslangen Lernens, Vol. 1. Bielefeld.
Fuchs, J. and Dörfler, K. (2005): Projektion des Erwerbspersonenpotenzials bis 2050: Annahmen und Datengrundlage. IAB Forschungsbericht, 25/2005. Nürnberg.
Gnahs, D./Kuwan, H. and Seidel, S. (2008): Weiterbildungsverhalten in Deutschland. Band 2. Berichtskonzepte auf dem Prüfstand. Bielefeld.
Hillmert, S. and Jacob, M. (2004): Multiple Episodes: Training Careers in a Learning Society. Universität Bamberg Globalife Working Paper 64. Bamberg.
Hujer, R./Thomsen, S.L. and Zeiss, Ch. (2006): The effects of vocational training programmes on the duration of unemployment in Eastern Germany. Allgemeines Statistisches Archiv 90, 299-321.
Jacob, M. (2004): Mehrfachausbildungen in Deutschland. Karriere, Collage, Kompensation? Wiesbaden.
Kleinert, C./Matthes, B. and Jacob, M. (2008): Die Befragung „Arbeiten und Lernen im Wandel". Theoretischer Hintergrund und Konzeption. IAB-Forschungsbericht, 5/2008. Nürnberg.
Konsortium Bildungsberichterstattung (Ed.) (2006): Bildung in Deutschland. Ein indikatorengestützter Bericht mit einer Analyse zu Bildung und Migration. Bielefeld.
Kristen, C./Römmer, A./Müller, W. and Kalter, F. (2005): Längsschnittstudien für die Bildungsberichterstattung – Beispiele aus Europa und Nordamerika. Berlin.
Kuckulenz, A. (2007): Studies on Continuing Vocational Training in Germany. Mannheim.

Kuwan, H./Bilger, F./Gnahs, D. and Seidel, S. (2006): Berichtssystem Weiterbildung IX: Integrierter Gesamtbericht zur Weiterbildungssituation in Deutschland. Berlin.

OECD (2006): Education at a Glance. Paris.

Pfeiffer, F. and Pohlmeier, W. (Eds.) (1998): Qualifikation, Weiterbildung und Arbeitsmarkterfolg. Baden-Baden.

Pischke, J.-St. (2001): Continuous Training in Germany. Journal of Population Economics 14 (3), 523-548.

Rosenbladt, B. v. and Bilger, F. (2008): Weiterbildungsverhalten in Deutschland. Band 1. Berichtssystem Weiterbildung und Adult Education Survey 2007. Bielefeld.

Schiener, J. (2006): Bildungserträge in der Erwerbsgesellschaft. Wiesbaden.

Schneider, H. and Uhlendorff, A. (2006): Die Wirkung der Hartz-Reform im Bereich der beruflichen Weiterbildung. Zeitschrift für Arbeitsmarktforschung 39 (3/4), 477-490.

Schömann, K. and Becker, R. (1995): Participation in Further Education over the Life Course. A Longitudinal Study of Three Birth Cohorts in the Federal Republic of Germany. European Sociological Review 11 (2), 187-208.

Weishaupt, H. and Fickermann, D. (2001): Informationelle Infrastruktur im Bereich Bildung und Kultur (Expertise für die Kommission zur Verbesserung der informationellen Infrastruktur zwischen Wissenschaft und Statistik. In: Kommission zur Verbesserung der informationellen Infrastruktur zwischen Wissenschaft und Statistik (KVI) (Ed.): Wege zu einer besseren informationellen Infrastruktur. Baden-Baden.

Werner, D. (2006): Trends und Kosten der betrieblichen Weiterbildung – Ergebnisse der IW-Weiterbildungserhebung 2005. IW-Trends – Vierteljahresschrift zur empirischen Wirtschaftsforschung 33 (1).

Wohn, K. (2007): Effizienz von Weiterbildungsmessung. RatSWD Working Paper No. 19.

3.7 Research, Science, Development

Stefan Hornbostel

Contact:

Stefan Hornbostel
Humboldt-Universität Berlin
Institut für Sozialwissenschaften
10099 Berlin

iFQ - Institut für Forschungsinformation und Qualitätssicherung
Godesberger Allee 90
53175 Bonn
Germany

e-mail: hornbostel[at]forschungsinfo.de

Abstract

As in other societal realms, in research, science, and development, governments have been increasingly placed under pressure to legitimize their actions. Accordingly, it is only natural that governments wish to base future activities on well informed and empirically grounded decisions. As a result, demand for performance measures, benchmarking, comparative analysis, and "foresight studies" has grown significantly. To meet this demand, rankings, ratings, and evaluations have been supposedly introduced to, on the one hand, produce transparency and, on the other hand, act as stimuli to improve performance. To date, however, central questions relating to the underlying methodologies and indicators used in evaluation measures have been left unanswered. These questions concern not only the availability and appropriateness of the data, indicator construction, and methodologies used, but also how to approach effects caused by disciplinary, sectoral, regional or national differences. Furthermore, questions regarding the intended and unintended effects of the evaluation instruments used have also been left unresolved. This article will describe and discuss these issues in greater detail. In Germany, infrastructural deficiencies, such as the fragmentation of research groups, have prevented open research questions from being addressed. Within this context, the two most important tasks identified are the development of a decentralized data collection system that would enable standard definitions, and the development of competitive research infrastructure.

Keywords: science indicators, R&D, research funding, governance

1. Research questions

On account of Germany's federal structure, its research and innovation landscape is both highly diversified and differentiated. Research is conducted in state and non-state institutions, institutes of higher education, non-university research institutions as well as in industry, which alone constitutes two-thirds of invested research funds.

On an international level, interest in assessments and comparative analyses of higher education and research systems has increased significantly since the 1970s. This growth in interest can be attributed to two closely-related factors. First, the development of a knowledge-based society whose interests are increasingly dependent on research and technology has inevitably contributed to the growing trend to evaluate higher education and research. Second, this development has been driven further by the fact that the quality of this research and technological progress in turn relies on the continual search for ideal conditions in which well-qualified junior scientists, innovation, and top-class research can be fostered. Additionally, in the name of legitimacy and planning, governments are progressively demanding more performance measures, international comparisons, and "foresight studies." In the course of the 1980s and 1990s, output-orientated research funding gradually increased and, in many European states, the competitive orientation of the academic system grew. Rankings, ratings, evaluations, and formula-based allocation schemes were deemed to provide the necessary transparency, problem diagnoses, and performance-raising stimuli.

Michelson (2006) describes the trend in research assessment in the US as follows:

"First, the standardization and harmonization of performance assessment methodologies has begun to spread across various federal R&D funding agencies. [...] Second, there has clearly been a turn toward employing quantitative methodologies as a major part of performance assessment initiatives. [...] Third, the growing use of quantitative bibliometric indicators is also being paired with a renewed focus on utilizing qualitative indicators in an effort to create more appropriate hybrid methodologies that can capture a wider range of variables related to a program's performance."

These three developments can also be observed in Europe.

When conducting analyses of the academic system, results can be systematically contrasted with relevant data or, for example, governance instruments, depending on the purpose. Assessment subjects can range from the academic performance of individuals, of organizations, of institutions (workgroups, institutes of higher education), or of branches of research (research fields, disciplines), through to national academic systems. Essentially, for such analyses, indicators and peer-review procedures are most often employed, as well as a combination of the two (this is known as an informed peer review). Because the use of data and assessment procedures in the academic world is as varied as the actors who conduct or commission them, only a few applications will be mentioned as examples. One such example is the German Council of Science and Humanities (WR, *Wissenschaftsrat*), which publishes nationwide research ratings for selected subjects. These ratings are based on series of output data about assessed research units, which are evaluated by peers according to a uniform scale and various criteria (WR 2008).

However, in contrast to the British Research Assessment Exercise, which utilizes a similar methodological structure, funds in Germany are not allocated according to ratings. Non-university research institutes, such as the Max Planck Society or Leibniz Association, conduct regular assessments of their member institutes and have their own departments for carrying out this task.[1] In such cases, typical indicators for measuring performance, which includes publications, third-party funding, patents, and services, are drawn upon and used to make decisions concerning the allocation of further funds to the establishments. Research funding bodies, such as the German Research

---

[1] Max Planck Society: http://www.mpg.de/ueberDieGesellschaft/profil/evaluation/index.html, Leibniz Assoziation: http://www.wgl.de/?nid=veva&nidap= &print=0.

Foundation (DFG, *Deutsche Forschungsgemeinschaft*), the Alexander von Humboldt-Foundation or the European Research Council, regularly evaluate the outcomes of their funding programs on a selective basis.

Additionally, such institutions have established monitoring systems, which regularly provide data concerning the performance of particular programs. The *Länder* and university faculties, for instance, make use of performance-based funding allocations to distribute part of their budget according to positive and negative performance indicators. Such systems are based exclusively on quantitative performance indicators relating to research, and in some cases teaching. Some federal states even have their own assessment centers, such as Lower Saxony's Scientific Commission (WKN, *Wissenschaftliche Kommission Niedersachsen*) or Baden-Württemberg's Evaluation Agency (EVALAG, *Evaluationsagentur*).[2] These assessment centers conduct regular or special-purpose assessments of academic establishments. Institutes of higher education also develop their own evaluation and reporting procedures to collect and disseminate information about performance in teaching and research. They link these assessments to target agreements, which are established by management and the corresponding faculties or institutes.

Until now in Germany, the use of performance indicators has not played a significant role in pay negotiations. But with the introduction of elements of performance-related pay, typical research indicators will play an increasingly important role in this area of individual agreements. In some disciplines already, but especially in the life sciences, the use of specific indicators is being used informally. Examples of this include the application of Journal Impact Factors for measuring publication activity or the Hirsch Index for quantifying individual research performance within the framework of employment and appointment negotiations (Jaeger 2006; Vahl 2008).

With the significant increase in quantitative indicators and the availability of complex indicators, expectations relating to data quality and knowledge of their governing factors have grown considerably, even among non-specialists. The error tolerance when small units are analyzed is drastically lower than when larger units are taken into account. This is also true of the use of indicators (which, it should be noted, are often not assessed) that are frequently used for a different purpose from that which was originally intended. The Journal Impact Factor, for example, was developed to characterize academic journals but is generally usually used to provide an indication of the quality of individual publications. It is difficult to assess the impact of bias effects, especially when small units are being compared, because there are very few foolproof error theories. Moreover, selected procedures and indicators cause learning effects among the concerned aca-

---

[2] Wissenschaftliche Kommission Niedersachsen: http://www.wk.niedersachsen.de, Evaluationsagentur Baden-Württemberg: http://www.evalag.de.

demics. Behavior, which is directly geared towards "indicator polishing," can, although not always, bring about unwanted effects (Moed et al. 2005).

1.1 Indicators

The call to develop appropriate indicators for measuring performance in research and development, as well as measures of potential indicators, was formulated within this context and still applies to this day. Central questions in this area are:

- What mechanisms can be used to measure academic performance? Apart from survey techniques (reputation surveys, Delphi surveys, etc.) and the analysis of funding data, bibliometric mechanisms have been developed as a method of measuring academic performance. Additionally, peer reviews of performance and, in particular, techniques used in patent data analysis have also become increasingly used.

- How can national, disciplinary, and sub-disciplinary specifics be taken into account when using publication and citation analyses as indicators? Publication and citation behavior, the intensity of third-party funding, or patenting strategies differ considerably according to discipline. A clear implication of this is that standardization mechanisms are needed for comparative analyses and descriptions. This point is also highlighted by the use of national languages in academic publications in the larger non-English speaking realm, as this equally makes comparison difficult. Publications in a national language necessarily reach a smaller audience and thus have fewer chances of being cited; a strong argument for developing appropriate indicators. Notably, although bibliometric mechanisms are mainly applied to the life and natural sciences, they are becoming increasingly used in the humanities and social sciences across Europe (Hornbostel 2008a). This trend allows for some degree of comparison, however, this single shared feature is relatively insignificant when compared to the remaining differences.

- How can research performance be assessed in the applied disciplines? Classic bibliometrics has a limited function in these areas and is often substituted by analyses of patenting activities. Here, too, exists a series of problems related to content and methodology. Questions that researchers (Butler 2006; Butler and Visser 2006) are currently working on within this field include: to what extent do the most-used triad patent data relate to the income from license agreements? What patenting strategies are used in which fields? How are patents related to the academic literature? To what extent do these indicators signal the existence of innovation processes?

- Can standard and internationally-applicable definitions of input, process, and output values be developed? Even within a national context, it is difficult to compare uniform compilations of input values (monetary values, personnel, etc.) due to the heterogeneity of research systems. This is undoubtedly also true of the international arena. In the 1970s, the OECD started standardizing the variables used for evaluating R&D. However, many problems remain unresolved – especially when institutions with different legal and organizational structures are compared.

- International cooperation has become a very important political issue over the course of the past 30 years. Indeed, foreign policy has expanded to include "academic foreign policy." In light of the growing trend towards specialization, the importance of international academic cooperation will most likely continue. The conditions for successful international cooperation, the consequences of such cooperation, and questions on the methodology of measuring the intensity and impact of international academic cooperation, are some of the chief current questions being posed by researchers and government alike. These questions are addressed mostly within the realm of the aforementioned indicators (co-authorship analyses, international patent announcements, citation networks, CV analyses, mobility analyses) (Schmoch et al. 2006).

- R&D expenditure is evaluated within the framework of official statistics and treated as far as possible according to international standards as specified by the OECD. In Germany, agreements have been met between the WR, the Federal Statistical Office, the Conference of the Ministers of Education and Cultural Affairs (KMK, *Kultusministerkonferenz*), and the Federal Ministry of Education and Research (BMBF, *Bundesministerium für Bildung und Forschung*) to compile data about academic staff (Hetmeier 1998). Questions regarding qualifications and subject expertise cannot, however, be answered with currently available data.

- Third-party funding is harder to assess. Competitive third-party funding that is granted after expert consultant approval is an important research indicator. This is because the approved funding is registered by the recipients and the pertinent funding bodies are also in receipt of the relevant data (Hornbostel 2001; Hornbostel and Heise 2006). After considerable teething problems, the situation concerning third-party funding has improved considerably. Nonetheless, it remains somewhat problematic, especially with regard to European funding (e.g., the Framework Programme). In particular, the blurred cut-off line between funds for basic research and those for development or contract research remains controversial. It is argued that the use of third-party funds can lead to considerable bias in disciplines or sub-disciplines that are often only in comparatively limited need for third-party funding. The interpretation of third-party funding indicators also creates problems because only the assessor's evaluation of *quality* is important during the approval process. The actual *quantity* of funds, which can amount to significant investments in a given project's research infrastructure, is often of comparably lesser importance.

- Data about junior scientists, especially the number of PhD candidates, are often used as research indicators. Doctoral candidates often find themselves on the border between teaching and research systems. The Bologna Process regards the doctorate as the third cycle within the academic training process. Unfortunately, apart from the number of completed doctorates, there exist very little data about the quality of academic training and the selection process. Equally, there is very little information available about the career paths of doctoral students. The increasingly used criteria of the number of doctoral students for allocating funds is, therefore, purely quantitative and does not take quality into account. This needs to be addressed urgently (Berghoff et al. 2006; Hornbostel 2008b).

- In the field of innovation research, the central question regarding performance measures revolves less around typical performance measures than it does around the identification of scientific "breakthroughs" and their possible application in products and services. Apart from the issue of how such "breakthroughs" can be recognized from an early stage, there is the related question of what conditions are needed to enable a rapid transfer of knowledge about essential research questions to other social sectors.

R&D data are not sufficient enough to address the aforementioned issues, especially as, for historical reasons, their compilation has very much been geared towards industry. Correspondingly, this makes it difficult to chronicle knowledge-based innovations in the service sector.

1.2 Effects analysis / governance

A second set of questions arises with respect to the topic of appropriate governance structures: which structures best generate conditions ideal for innovative and efficient research? Ideally, these conditions should enable a knowledge transfer between research and other social sectors, as well as establish linkages between economic growth and the breadth and type of R&D investment. However, the heterogeneity of research and funding systems only allows for analyses that provide limited information because of the lack of compatible data. This problem is exacerbated by several unresolved problems concerning indicators, especially in comparative analyses at an international level.

Over the past 15 years, the governance structures of the higher education system in Germany have changed dramatically. There has long been a shift in research funding due to an increase in third-party funding and simultaneous decrease in access to standard basic equipment. This trend has been augmented by the growing competition among institutes of higher education and within institutes themselves for basic equipment, which, increasingly, is allocated according to performance (Jansen 2007). At the same time, institutes of higher education have gradually gained more and more autonomy whilst having been compelled to develop stronger strategy and management skills. The driving forces behind these developments include the spawn of higher education representative bodies, internal organizations, and management structures, as well as pressure for the creation of a competitive profile in research and teaching. Other contributing factors include the distribution of expertise between the German Federal Government and the *Länder*, the "European research realm," and the general statutory framework. Additionally, in some cases even the statutory position of institutes of higher education themselves have contributed to the simultaneous growth in autonomy and management strategies.

In light of the aforementioned, information about academic performance has gained greater significance in numerous aspects – as comparative data for stakeholders, as an internal monitoring system, as an instrument of accountability for financiers, and as a component of governance systems (ESF 2008). This is true not only of institutes of higher education, but of all actors in the academic system. Until now, however, the necessary data have been compiled, if at all, *in situ* and according to contrasting standards. Similarly, performance indicators have also been defined in different ways. Technical systems have not been developed with interoperability in mind. This means that while data are often compiled several times, they do not necessarily exist in formats that easily enable their exchange.

1.3. Data compilation

At an early stage, the increased significance of R&D triggered attempts to compile data about input and output variables on a regular basis. The first international "Science and Engineering Indicators Report" was published in the US in 1973 by the National Science Board of the National Science Foundation. The OECD followed this up in the 1980s and has since regularly published the "OECD Science, Technology and Industry Scoreboard" and the "OECD Science, Technology and Industry Outlook" on an alternating basis. Each publication gives an overview of the trends in science, technology, and innovation policy, all of which are backed by data. Similarly, Eurostat has been compiling data since the beginning of the 1980s with its Science, Technology and Innovation in Europe series. In Germany, the "Report of the Federal Government on Research" (*Bundesbericht Forschung*) publishes information about R&D activity. Regular compilation of data also takes place within Germany at an institutional level or within the framework of research funding. One such example is given by the rankings created by the German Research Foundation (DFG, *Deutsche Forschungsgemeinschaft*) (National Science Board 2006a, 2006b; OECD 2008a, 2008b; BMBF 2008; Europäische Kommission 2008; Statistisches Bundesamt 2008; DFG 2006).

2. Status quo: Databases and access

Germany's "Report of the Federal Government on Research" records the growing demand for contemporary data about the development of investments in research. However, as yet, data about R&D investment tend to be published after considerable delay because data from the federal government, the states, and industry have to be combined. The data are not appropriate for an outcome-oriented analysis. This is due to the fact that, apart from the official data, although there is a wealth of data about rankings, ratings, and evaluations that are compiled more or less regularly, they are limited or not accessible and very different in terms of quality (Hornbostel 2007; 2006). In this regard, the WR is exemplary because it makes its ratings accessible in a format suitable for scientific use (WR 2008).

Publication and citation data are accessible thanks to two large commercial databases (Web of Science and Scopus) and an abundance of specialized subject databases. They do not, however, usually enable citation analysis. Recently, Google Scholar and researchable open access repositories have started providing publication and citation analyses. Many of these databases offer a series of bibliometric codes. But these impressive masses of data hide a series of problems. In Germany, for example, the few small database workgroups which have emerged are ill-equipped in terms of staff and, from a technical point of view, cannot afford to accumulate expertise over the long-term. In other European countries, however, over the past 20 years some extremely well-performing institutes have been established. These institutes, which have in-house databases and the capacity to develop specific indicators, empirically monitor the academic system and engage in infrequent bibliometric analyses. In light of this, the BMBF is promoting a consortium[3] of German establishments, which are intended to close the gap between German database workgroups and other European institutes by creating a "bibliometric expertise center."

Research about patent data can be conducted with the German Patent Information System[4] (DEPATIS, *Deutsches Patentinformationssystem*) of the German Patent and Trade Mark Office. The European Patent Office Worldwide Patent Statistic Database (also known as EPO PATSTAT[5]), however, on account of it having been specifically developed for use by governmental/intergovernmental organizations and academic institutions, is more appropriate. Distribution of this database is, however, restricted, and commercial use is not foreseen.

Substantial data compilation about academic performance and related staff and material inputs requires a combination of heterogeneous information from different sources. Sources of information include academics (self-input), institutes of higher education, third-party funding bodies, and bibliometric and patent databases, among others. A prime example of how output data is collected at institutes of higher education and combined with other data is given by the Norwegian research information system, entitled Frida.[6] Since 2004, Frida has been used as a quality-controlled author-based register of research publications and other types of research outputs. The catalyst for Frida's emergence was the new outcome-based financing system for Norwegian universities and colleges. Norwegian institutions must now document their actions in order to receive a full share of government funding. Frida is associated with the Norwegian Open Research Archives (NORA),[7] which were launched at the same time. The broader objective of these projects is to develop a central Open Archive Initiative harvesting service. It is intended that this service will be open to all Norwegian research institutions that have both online material in full text and metadata in harvestable format.

In contrast to Norway, Germany lacks such a coordinating body for collecting data. In Germany, not only are definitions of data very different, but technical systems have been developed on a decentralized basis and not generally geared towards an exchange of information. It would seem almost inevitable that chaos should ensue.

---

3   Consisting of the Institute for Research Information and Quality Assurance (iFQ, *Institut für Forschungsinformation und Qualitätssicherng*), the Fraunhofer Institute for Systems and Innovation Research (ISI, *Institut für System- und Innovationsforschung*), IWT University Bielefeld, and the Leibniz Institute for Information Infrastructure (FIZ Karlsruhe, *Leibniz-Institut für Informationsinfrastruktur*).
4   *www.depatisnet.de/*.
5   http://www.epo.org/patents/patent-information.html.
6   https://wo.uio.no/as/WebObjects/frida.woa/wo/0.0.27.2.
7   http://www.ub.uio.no/nora/noaister/search.html?siteLanguage=eng.

3. Conclusions and recommendations

Overall, data compilation about science and research in Europe is far from sophisticated and outcome-oriented. Further, it lacks in comparability, as data are by no means standardized, despite early attempts at standardization by the Frascati Manual (1963). In Germany, like in other European countries, interest in observing, analyzing and evaluating the academic system has increased substantially and this trend will presumably continue. The reasons lie less in an academic interest than in the consequences of higher education and research reforms, which have brought about some serious changes to governance mechanisms. Knowledge of both structures and of the effects of measures undertaken has a significant role to play across the board. Fast-growing competition worldwide, at an academic and technological level, especially from emerging nations, is also increasing the political pressure to act. The competition can already be perceived in the massive shifts in the worldwide distribution of publications, citations, and patents towards emerging countries.

Alongside qualitative analyses and peer review-based expert opinions, quantitative procedures in the compilation, analysis, and evaluation of research data are gaining in importance. There are several reasons for this, which range from an already perceptible overuse of peer reviews to the need for methodological, controlled comparisons and unanimous indicators. Another reason is that certain questions are deemed no longer answerable from the perspective of individual experts.

Overall, the status quo in Germany, in terms of the coordinated collection of data pertaining to the academic system, the training of experts for processing and evaluating this data, and the quality of the data itself, is deplorable. Data about certain important areas simply do not exist, the comparability of existing data is often limited, and in the field of bibliometric analyses Germany risks falling behind. The two most important tasks, therefore, consist, on the one hand, in developing a decentralized data collection system (CRIS, *Current Research Information System*)[8] that will enable standard definitions to be developed and for centrally-compiled data to be interoperable, as well as, on the other hand, developing a competitive research infrastructure.

---

[8] http://www.eurocris.org/.

References:

Berghoff, S./Federkeil, G./Giebisch, P./Hachmeister, C.-D./Hennings, M. and Müller-Böling, D. (2006): Das CHE Forschungsranking deutscher Universitäten 2006. Arbeitspapier 79. Gütersloh. http://www.che.de/downloads/CHE_Forschungs Ranking_2006.pdf. [Last visited: 02/26/2010].

Bundesministerium für Bildung und Forschung (BMBF) (2008): Bundesbericht Forschung und Innovation 2008. http://www.bmbf.de/pub/bufi_2008.pdf. [Last visited: 02/26/2010].

Butler, L. (2006): Research assessment: moving beyond journal outputs. http://www.sussex.ac.uk/Units/spru/events/ocs/viewpaper.php?id=96. [Last visited: 08/14/2009].

Butler, L. and Visser, M.S. (2006): Extending citation analysis to non-source items. Scientometrics 66 (2), 327-343.

Deutsche Forschungsgemeinschaft (DFG) (2006): Förder-Ranking 2006. Institutionen – Regionen – Netzwerke. DFG-Bewilligungen und weitere Basisdaten öffentlich geförderter Forschung. Weinheim.

Europäische Kommission – Eurostat (2008): Europa in Zahlen – Eurostat Jahrbuch 2008.

European Science Foundation (ESF) (2008): Window to Science. Information Systems of European Research Organizations. Report of the EUROHORCs – ESF Working Group on a Joint Research Information System. Strasbourg.

Hetmeier, H.-W. (1998): Methodik und Berechnung der Ausgaben und des Personals der Hochschulen für Forschung und Entwicklung ab dem Berichtsjahr 1995. Wirtschaft und Statistik 2/1998.

Hornbostel, S. (2001): Third Party Funding of German Universities. An Indicator of Research Activity? Scientometrics 50 (3), 523-537.

Hornbostel, S. (2006): Leistungsmessung in der Forschung. Von der Qualitätssicherung der Lehre zur Qualitätsentwicklung als Prinzip der Hochschulsteuerung. Beiträge zur Hochschulpolitik 1, 219-228.

Hornbostel, S. (2007): Theorie und Praxis von Hochschulrankings. In: Statistisches Bundesamt (Ed.): Statistik und Wissenschaft, Band 11. Amtliche Hochschulstatistik und Hochschulrankings, 6-13.

Hornbostel, S. (2008a): Gesucht: Aussagekräftige Indikatoren und belastbare Datenkollektionen. Desiderate geisteswissenschaftlicher Evaluierung in Deutschland. In: Lack, E. and Markschies, Ch. (Eds.): What the hell is quality? Frankfurt/New York.

Hornbostel, S. (2008b): Bologna und die Forschung. In: Rudinger, G./Krahn, B. and Rietz, Ch. (Eds.): Evaluation und Qualitätssicherung von Forschung und Lehre im Bologna-Prozess. Bonn.

Hornbostel, S. and Heise, S. (2006): Die Rolle von Drittmitteln in der Steuerung von Hochschulen. In: Berthold, Ch. (Ed.): Handbuch Wissenschaftsfinanzierung. Berlin.

Jaeger, M. (2006): Leistungsorientierte Budgetierung: Analyse der Umsetzung an ausgewählten Universitäten und Fakultäten/Fachbereichen. In: HIS (Ed.): Kurzinformation, A 1/2006.

Jansen, D. (Ed.) (2007): New Forms of Governance in Research Organizations – Disciplinary Approaches, Interfaces and Integration. Dordrecht.

Michelson, E.S. (2006): Approaches to research and development performance assessment in the United States: an analysis of recent evaluation trend. Science and Public Policy 33 (8), 546-560.

Moed, H.F./Glänzel, W. and Schmoch, U. (Eds.) (2005): Handbook of Quantitative Science and Technology Research. The Use of Publication and Patent Statistics in Studies of S&T Systems. Dordrecht.

National Science Board (2006a): Science and Engineering Indicators. Volume I, http://www.nsf.gov/statistics/seind06/pdf/volume1.pdf. [Last visited: 02/26/2010].

National Science Board (2006b): Science and Engineering Indicators. Volume II, http://www.nsf.gov/statistics/seind06/pdf/volume2.pdf. [Last visited: 02/26/2010].

Organisation for economic co-operation and development (OECD) (2008a): OECD Factbook 2008. Economic, Environmental and Social Statistics.

Organisation for economic co-operation and development (OECD) (2008b): OECD in Figures 2008.

Schmoch, U./Rammer, Ch. and Legler, H. (2006): National Systems of Innovation in Comparison. Dordrecht.

Statistisches Bundesamt (2008): Datenreport 2008. Wiesbaden. http://www.destatis. de/jetspeed/portal/cms/Sites/destatis/Internet/DE/Navigation/Publikationen/Quer schnittsveroeffentlichungen/Datenreport__downloads,templateId=renderPrint.ps ml__nnn=true. [Last visited: 02/26/2010].

Vahl, Ch.-F. (2008): Forschungsförderung durch leistungsorientierte Mittelvergabe (LOM): Argumente für eine medizinische Wissenschaftskultur jenseits der Impact-Punkte. Zeitschrift für Herz- Thorax- Gefäßchirurgie 22, 94-97.

Wissenschaftsrat (WR) (2008): Pilotstudie Forschungsrating. Empfehlungen und Dokumentation. Cologne.

4. Economy and Labor Markets

4.1 Data from the Federal Employment Agency

Stefan Bender and Joachim Möller

Contact:

Stefan Bender
Institute for Employment Research (IAB)
Regensburger Strasse 104
90478 Nuremberg
e-mail: stefan.bender[at]iab.de

Abstract

The supply of German microdata for labor market research has been rapidly growing in recent years. This paper reports on this development, focusing on three key aspects: the establishment of Research Data Centers, the creation of new anonymization techniques for establishment data and the spate of scientific analyses and evaluation studies of active labor market programs based on administrative data in the aftermath of labor market reforms, especially the new Social Code II. Substantial progress has been made in all these fields with respect to the availability of adequate data, for instance, through the combination of different datasets. However, there is still large room for improvements. For future development, we recommend to focus on three primary areas: (1) the influence of researchers on data production; (2) (internationally) combinable datasets, and (3) the establishment of an international infrastructure for data access.

Keywords: labor market, data access, administrative data, linked employer-employee data, Research Data Center, evaluation of labor market programs, Social Code II

1. Introduction

There are numerous reasons for collecting labor market data. One could stress the importance of having reliable data for research on changes in the wage and employment structure, or one could point to the fact that labor market policies require evaluation studies for selecting the most effective of efficient instruments. Since this is a report on data, and our aim is a description of the German information infrastructure and its development we do not intend to go into more details here. Instead, we will restrict ourselves to referring to the illuminating introduction in Dan Hamermesh's article, "Fun with Matched Firm-Employee Data: Progress and Road Maps." In this article, Hamermesh raises the question,

"What generates scientific progress (assuming that we can use the term science to talk about economics)? Does it matter whether causation runs from data to problems or from problems to data? I think it does" (2008: 664).

We agree with Hamermesh that without datasets like the Panel Study of Income Dynamics (PSID) in the US or the German Socio-Economic Panel (SOEP, *Sozio-oekonomisches Panel*) our knowledge about the intertemporal labor supply or the intergenerational transmission of inequality, for instance, would be very limited.[1] Without the availability of administrative data for the

---

[1] "In terms of issues of firm behavior in particular, I doubt that we would even have thought about the issues in the way we now do without the availability of this type of data. No doubt the opposite is also often true, but my purpose here is to talk about the former. To

evaluation of active labor market programs, we would know hardly anything about their effects. Kluve (2006), for example, reports that almost 80 percent of all microeconomic evaluation studies in Europe are based on administrative data. Without the relevant microdata on establishments, the work of, say, Dunne et al. (1989) or Davis and Haltiwanger (1992), would not have had the powerful influence that it has actually had.

Writing this motivational section during the first half of 2009, one cannot ignore the financial crises and its possible effects on the labor market. The World Recession triggered by the financial crisis hit economies surprisingly and had no predecessor in recent times. Moreover, it is an international phenomenon which requires a cross-border perspective. For such a situation the empirical basis is weak. Because of the lack of adequate data, deeper analyses are scarce and most researchers are more or less speechless when it comes to the concrete consequences of the crisis on firms' behavior and labor market outcomes.

Due to its rapid development in recent years, the German data infrastructure for the labor market has reached a satisfactory stage of completion. What we can learn from the current crisis, however, is that we need internationally comparable datasets at the micro-level and – more and more – a combination of these. These datasets should cover all important spheres of content, such as trade, foreign direct investments, offshoring, outsourcing, labor flows, earnings, strategic planning etc.

2. The situation before the 2001 KVI report[2]

Compared to the situation as it existed some years ago, access to confidential microdata – often critical for labor market research – has improved considerably. Prior to the 2001, the German Commission on Improving the Information Infrastructure between Science and Statistics, the creation of the FiDASt network "Firm-Level Data from Official Statistics" (*FirmenDaten aus der Amtlichen Statistik*), and the so-called *Schalterstelle* of the Institute for

---

paraphrase Matthew 5, 'Blessed are the data developers because they inspire the creation of knowledge.' Creating data is a very thankless task for which one gets very few points. Yet so many of our ideas are inspired by new data, and so much of research rests on innovations in questions and data collection that are barely, if at all, acknowledged by the more technical researchers" (Hamermesh 2008: 664).

[2] Our report will focus primarily on the current situation, developments since KVI in 2001, and the short-term developments needed in the Federal Employment Agency (BA, *Bundesagentur für Arbeit*) data and the Institute for Employment Research (IAB, *Institut für Arbeitsmarkt- und Berufsforschung*) data. The other report in this volume focusing on labor market data, by Hilmar Schneider, will elaborate on the situation outside the BA and IAB.

Employment Research (IAB, *Institut für Arbeitsmarkt- und Berufsforschung*) that provides remote data access, represented milestones in labor market data availability. The FiDASt project was based on the need for access to data from the various Statistical Offices of the German *Länder*. A network was created for analyzing firm-level data. In some cases, remote data access could be used, in others the researcher was given the status of an unpaid employee at the Statistical Office (see Wagner in this publication for more details).

At the time of the 2001 KVI report, the only available microdata for labor market researchers were the IAB Employment Sample and the German Microcensus. In their advisory report to the Commission, Falk and Steiner (2000) argued that additional micro datasets should be created for the scientific community including information on active labor market policies, the IAB linked employer-employee dataset, or aggregated information on establishments from employment statistics. Information on marginal employment and forms of work outside the standard working-hour arrangements, being typical in Germany (such as temporary employment, temporary contracts, and self-employment), should be improved and made available, too. The high demand for establishment and firm-level data should be taken into account. Since quantitative information on establishments and firms is hard to anonymize, effort has to be put into investigating how these data can be offered to researchers. Basic information on employment and income should be made available via the Internet for free (especially employment and unemployment rates by skill level and differentiated by age and sex). When compared to the data provision of the US Bureau of Labor Statistics, the information provided by the Federal Statistical Office and the Federal Employment Agency (BA, *Bundesagentur für Arbeit*) seemed inadequate and left much room for improvement.

3. Situation since the 2001 KVI report

3.1 The establishment of Research Data Centers and Data Service Centers in Germany

Following the suggestions of the 2001 KVI report, most of the important data producers in Germany – responsible for firm-level, organizational, and labor-market data as well as household income, poverty, and wealth data – have created Research Data Centers. Since 2000, one of the landmark developments in the improvement of the German data infrastructure was the establishment of four publicly funded Research Data Centers: the Research Data Center of the BA at the IAB, the Research Data Center of the German Pension Insurance (RV, *Deutsche Rentenversicherung*), and the Research Data Centers of both the Federal Statistical Office and the Statistical Offices of the

German *Länder*. Two Data Service Centers – the German Microdata Lab at the Center for Survey Research and Methodology (ZUMA, *Zentrum für Umfragen, Methoden und Analysen*) and the International Data Service Center at the Institute for the Study of Labor (IZA, *Forschungsinstitut zur Zukunft der Arbeit*) – were also established (see Bender et al. in this publication for more details).

The Research Data Center of the BA at the IAB was created in April 2004 and its micro datasets include the IAB Establishment Panel, the IAB Employment Sample (IABS), the BA Employment Panel (BAP), the Integrated Employment Biographies Sample (IEBS), the Establishment History Panel (BHP), the linked employer-employee dataset from the IAB (LIAB), the cross-sectional survey "Life Situation and Social Security 2005" (LSS 2005), and the first wave of the panel study "Labor Market and Social Security" (PASS, *Panel "Arbeitsmarkt und soziale Sicherung"*).[3]

3.2 New developments in anonymization techniques

In recent years, the public demand for microdata has increased dramatically. But statistical agencies face a dilemma. Although they might be willing to provide all the information required, it might not be possible to release these datasets for reasons of confidentiality. The natural desire to enable as much research as possible with collected data must take a back seat to the confidentiality that is guaranteed to the survey respondent. When confidentiality comes into play, potential respondents might be less willing to provide sensitive information, might intentionally provide wrong answers, or might even be unwilling to participate at all, with devastating consequences for the quality of the data collected (Lane 2005).

For this reason, there has been a variety of methods developed to provide as much information to the public as possible while satisfying the access restrictions needed to maintain the quality of the collected data (Willenborg and de Waal 2001; Abowd and Lane 2004). For German establishment datasets, a broad literature for anonymization approaches has developed, mostly based on perturbation techniques (e.g., Brand 2002; Gottschalk 2005; Rosemann 2006; Drechsler et al. 2008).

Official statistics in Germany, together with researchers using their data, carried out a research project on the "Factual Anonymization of Business Microdata," which was finished in summer 2005. For the project, a large amount and variety of perturbation approaches were tested. Moreover, test analyses with anonymized real data were undertaken and the results were

---

[3] Documentations in English can be found on the webpage for nearly all datasets. Descriptions are also published in the "Data Watch" section of *Schmollers Jahrbuch*.

compared with those obtained from analyses based on original data.[4] Several anonymized cross-sectional data were made available. They included data on cost structures in industry and in retail trade, as well as profit-tax data. Detailed descriptions of the Scientific Use Files can be found in Lenz et al. (2005), Vorgrimler et al. (2005), and Scheffler (2005). Recently, similar approaches have been used to anonymize business statistics. These include the German data of the Continuing Vocational Training Survey 1999 and the German Structure of Earnings Survey 2001.

The aim of the follow-up project "Business Statistical Panel Data and Factual Anonymization" (FAWE-Panel, *Wirtschaftsstatistische Paneldaten und faktische Anonymisierung*) was to improve researcher access to panel data from official statistical offices and the BA. In cooperation with different Research Data Centers and the Institute for Applied Economic Research (IAW, *Institut Arbeit und Wirtschaft*), the objective was:

- to expand the data supply for researchers by adding individual business statistical panels,
- to optimize the potential of business panel data for analysis, and
- to research the possibility of the factual anonymization of panel data in the field of economic statistics with the goal of ultimately making these available as Scientific Use Files.

Results from this project are published in a special volume of Advances in Statistical Analysis (Pohlmeier and Ronning 2008), and a special volume of Wirtschafts- und Sozialstatistisches Archiv (Bender et al. 2009).

While anonymization techniques have helped to make establishment and firm-level data more accessible, the degree of anonymization for some individual data has decreased over time. For example, panel anonymization was abandoned for the IAB Employment Sample.

3.3 A new and unexpected situation: The Social Code II[5]

With the deep changes to the German system of unemployment insurance and welfare benefits that took place through the labor market reforms in 2005 (Social Code II / SGB II), a new data infrastructure was implemented in Germany. These changes occurred in three main areas:

(1) Job search and participation in active labor market schemes
(2) Data stemming from the SGB II software, A2LL
(3) Data from 69 districts where local authorities (zkT, *zugelassene kommunale Träger*) are responsible for administering the unemployment assis-

---

4   For more information about this project see Lenz et al. (2006).
5   This section is taken from Koch et al. (2008). It is shortened and translated.

tance (ALG II, *Arbeitslosengeld II*). Data are available through the BA via the interchange program XSozial.

With the start of the SGB II, the BA expanded its IT administrative procedures. In July 2006, for example, the BA introduced an integrated program for occupational counseling and an employment service. The change in the procedures temporarily affected the quality of the data in the years 2006–2007.

Because the reform proceeded so rapidly, A2LL was very hastily implemented in 2004. As a result, a number of problems occurred. In addition to difficulties with the software, which made headlines in all the German newspapers, there was no interface between the data produced by A2LL and all the other datasets belonging to the BA and stored in the BA data warehouse. To integrate these data is time-consuming and costly. In 2005 and 2006, the A2LL data changed significantly due to the synchronization of individuals over time and due to the introduction of the concept of so-called "communities of need" (*Bedarfsgemeinschaften*) in the SGB II. This concept implies that individuals in disadvantaged households take responsibility for each other and, therefore, entails a different logic of representativeness of the data. Before SGB II, individuals were comprised in the data when they received unemployment insurance. Since SGB II, unemployed individuals living together with a partner whose earnings are above a certain level are no longer eligible for receiving unemployment benefits. The situation changed also for low income earners. Before SGB II, they were not eligible to receive additional money from unemployment insurance; after SGB II, this became possible.

The situation of the data from XSozial is rather complex. Because of the initial problems encountered by all participating institutions, there are no microdata available for the first few years. At the end of 2006, the BA began working to build up an adequate micro database. To date, this work is not finished and thus the data is not available for researchers. The main reasons for the delay are: missing data, the different time structure, and the different definitions and collection of variables in the different software systems. Because of the lack of information in the XSozial data, a harmonized dataset will end up with only a few basic variables.

At the IAB, SGB II data will be integrated into the Integrated Employment Biographies. At the moment, this is the dataset where employment information based on the social security system, receipt of benefits, participants in active labor market policy measures, and job seekers are integrated over time (since 1990) and harmonized.

Information on unemployment benefits between 2005 and the fall of 2007 can be distinguished between traditional unemployment benefits and the "new" Unemployment Benefit II (ALG II). Not integrated into XSozial are data from the 69 districts where local authorities are responsible for administering Unemployment Benefit II.

Everyone should be aware that – beginning in 2005 – Germany has some white regions on data maps where previously there had been information. There are no microdata covering the years 2005 and 2006 available for the 69 districts. This deficiency extended to statistics covering social benefits. As an unfortunate result there are no administrative microdata available covering one of the biggest changes to the labor market in German history (2004–2005).

The SGB II has introduced different possibilities for organizing social and unemployment assistance at the regional level – such as *Arbeitsgemeinschaften* (ARGE) – a joint organization between local authorities and the BA – or *Kreise mit geteilter Trägerschaft* where the different forms of assistance are separated. Due to these different organizational forms, non-compatibel software for job seekers and individuals in need under the SGB II has been used. Hence, the situation does not seem to be improving. Since 2006, nearly everyone has been using the same software (A2LL). All rescue efforts for gathering microdata for those white regions for 2005 have failed. XSozial data for 2005 will not be available if no techniques like imputation are used to replace missing data.

In addition to administrative data and "standard" surveys, two new survey tools can be used for analyzing the situation of households in need or individuals living in those households. The cross-sectional survey, "Life Situation and Social Security 2005" (LSS 2005) covers the period 2005–2006 and asked 20,832 recipients about unemployment benefits. It is a unique survey because it covers the time during which the Social Code II was first introduced. The panel study "Labor Market and Social Security" started its first wave in 2006–2007 and surveys the households of recipients receiving support from Unemployment Benefit II as well as low wage earners. The panel covers 12,794 households and 18,954 individuals. Both datasets are available for researchers via the Research Data Center of the BA at the IAB.

3.4 The new spirit: labor market research with administrative data

Until the late 1990s, the evaluation of active labor market policies was in a state of hibernation. Starting with the so-called Hartz Reforms at the end of 2002, the German Bundestag commissioned an evaluation of these reforms as a large research project (around 100 researchers in nearly twenty institutions with a budget of around 10.3 million Euros directed into different projects). These investigations into the evaluation of active labor-market policy were extensive, and point to a new quality in the discourse around policy and research in Germany. Based on empirical evidence, labor-market policy is now conceived as something like a "learning system." That is, new instruments are temporarily introduced and subsequently evaluated by researchers, which leads to im-

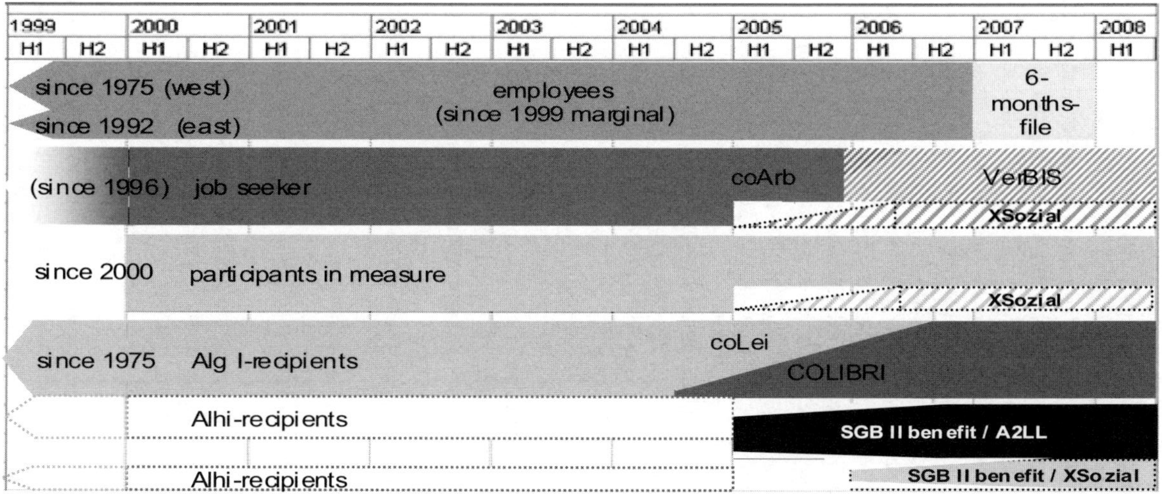

Figure 1: Short summary of the gaps in administrative data stemming from SGB II

proved instruments (if there is a need for improvements). In this framework, labor-market policy acts as a pioneer for other policy areas. This prescribes an important role for research (Social Code II and III) and to have a detailed, well-defined mandate. The evaluation of the so-called Hartz Reforms thus represents a significant and singular project that will influence future labor-market research in Germany and that exemplifies a new form of research-based policy advice (Heyer 2006).

Another milestone was the research network, "Flexibility of Heterogeneous Labor Markets" financed by the German Research Foundation (DFG, *Deutsche Forschungsgemeinschaft*). The network was established in 2004 with the objective of finding solutions to the permanent challenge of responding quickly and effectively to changes in the labor market. A central aim of the research program is thus to analyze rigidities that have developed historically in labor-market institutions and to investigate whether and to what extent deregulation is possible and/or necessary. The program has organized a research group to tackle the pertinent questions by actively drawing on data from the Research Data Center of the BA at the IAB as well as from other Research Data Centers. This research network and the Research Data Center of the BA at the IAB are also active in a more informal network and have jointly stimulated data production processes and higher data quality. The fruit of this work are several published articles in international journals.[6]

In addition to these networks, there are many researchers interested in labor market use of data from the Research Data Center (see Bender et al. in this publication for more details). As an illustration, in September 2008 there were already 341 publications drawing from data made available through the Research Data Center of the BA at the IAB. Twenty-seven of these were publications in SSCI journals and an additional forty-two appeared in peer-reviewed journals. Judging from this and the number of publications in process as indicated by an increasing number of discussion papers – Germany is no longer a wasteland for empirical labor-market research. To the contrary, a quantitative and a qualitative improvement is evident in papers presented at international conferences based on BA-IAB data, as well as those published in international, high-quality journals. There should and could be more done to improve research with German datasets, but it should be kept in mind that the starting point for significant change only dates to 2004, and that research with datasets is a slow process of diffusion. There must be some visible articles before other researchers begin working with the data.

---

6 See www.zew.de/dfgflex for further information.

4. What is missing?

In the wake of these developments over the past few years, some of the gaps mentioned by Falk and Steiner in 2000 have been closed while others have not. For example, the availability of establishment data, data for evaluating active labor-market policies, linked employer-employee data, and data for specific groups in the labor market are now available. But precise and comprehensive data for earnings and wages are still not available. Neither the employment statistics nor the German Microcensus have changed their concepts over the last few years, for example. An exception to this is the SOEP, which has raised the quality of its income and assets data (Anger et al. 2008).[7] Although some specific groups in the labor market, like the marginally employed, have been incorporated into the administrative microdata of the BA-IAB, there is still no information available for temporary employment, temporary contracts, or self-employment in Germany.[8]

Basic aggregated information for some labor market indicators (such as employment) is available via the Internet for free, but the information system in Germany still lags behind official statistics in other countries, such as the US Bureau of Labor Statistics. The information given by the Federal Statistical Office and the BA could be improved. Basic aggregated information such as wages or regional price indices are still missing.[9]

5. Outlook

Because researchers use administrative data more frequently, there is now a demand to change the production of administrative data to suit researcher needs in two respects: (a) to add additional variables like working hours, contract type, or anonymized case worker IDs to existing datasets; and (b) to provide more information about data-generating processes, because the quality of administrative data is an underdeveloped research field. Some planned changes in the development of variables are "automatically" benefitting researchers – like the addition of working hours or the inclusion of an internationally comparable occupation code in employment statistics (Stegmann 2009). However, the research community needs to exert constant pressure to make more relevant microdata from administrative processes available as well as to enhance data quality.

---

7   See the paper of Schneider in the same book for a deeper discussion of the topic.
8   The backbone of the administrative data in the BA / IAB will be changed in this direction (Stegmann 2009).
9   The RatSWD initiated expertises on regional price indices in 2008.

It is increasingly important to create reliable and precise microdata for topics of current relevance (e.g., innovation, globalization) and to ensure that it is available for research. For example, a "double" linked employer-employee dataset could be used for the project, "Further Training as a Part of Lifelong Learning," co-funded by the Leibniz Association. For the first time in Germany, data stemming from surveys and administrative data for both employer and employee groups are combined and available (Bender et al. 2008). Combining the available data (administrative data, survey data, commercial data, and Internet data) is extremely important. However, because we do not have comparable unique identifiers in German datasets, we need more research on record linkage techniques and also to engage in dialogue with representatives of data protection and with legislators (see the papers by Schnell and Metschke in this publication).

The projects Official Firm Data for Germany (AFiD, *Amtliche Firmendaten für Deutschland*) and Combined Firm Data for Germany (KombiFiD, *Kombinierte Firmendaten für Deutschland*) will extend the range of data in two directions: AFiD will integrate economic and environmental data from official statistics, and KombiFiD will link company data from official statistics, the Deutsche Bundesbank and the BA-IAB for the first time (Hethy and Spengler 2009). The project Biographical Data of Selected Social Insurance Agencies in Germany (BASiD, *Biografiedaten ausgewählter Sozialversicherungsträger in Deutschland*) will combine administrative data from the German Pension Insurance with IAB data. It will offer a Scientific Use File for researchers in Germany and abroad as well as on-site use. International datasets are needed because individuals are migrating and many firms no longer remain within national borders. Datasets should not have those restrictions either.[10]

It is becoming increasingly important to establish an international infrastructure for data access (including translation, harmonization, integrated metadata systems, integrated access, and remote access) and to coordinate the different developments taking place in different organizations and/or countries.

---

10 "However, an improved statistical infrastructure is needed not only on the national level. As the European research landscape evolves, it produces increased demands on the data infrastructure in order for the social sciences and economics to develop their full potential in the area of social comparisons as well. By actively participating in important developments at both the national and international levels, the RatSWD intends to work even more intensively in this important field in the future. It already provides a platform for a fundamental discussion and planning process that is almost one of a kind both in Europe and beyond. If international and interdisciplinary strategic planning is to be successful in fostering empirical research and improving the research infrastructure, however, greater involvement of the professional scientific organizations representing the social sciences and economics will be urgently needed. The RatSWD will endeavor to promote this involvement" (Solga and Wagner 2007: 4).

Through the activities of the German Data Forum (RatSWD) itself, German researchers and the Research Data Centers have started to present the German model of data access and data infrastructure to the international research community. The German experience of organizing access and building up an infrastructure could offer a blueprint for how an equivalent international system might be established. There is a need for both coordination and advocacy in this area to press for the activities necessary for its realization and to steer them in the right direction.

References:

Abowd, J.M. and Lane, J. (2004): New Approaches to Confidentiality Protection: Synthetic Data, Remote Access and Research Data Centers. Privacy in Statistical Databases. New York, 282-289.
Anger, S./Bowen, D.A./Engelmann, M./Frick, J.R./Goebel, J./Grabka, M.M./Groh-Samberg, O./Haas, H./Headey, B./Holst, E./Krause, P./Kroh, M./Kurka, C./Lohmann, H./Pischner, R./Rahmann, U./Schmitt, C./Schräpler, J.-P./Schupp, J./Sieber, I./Siedler, T./Spieß, C.K./Spieß, M./Tucci, I. and Wagner, G.G. (2008): 25 Wellen Sozio-oekonomisches Panel. Vierteljahrshefte zur Wirtschaftsforschung 77 (3), 9-14.
Bender, S./Rosemann, M./Zühlke, S./Zwick, M. (2008): Betriebs- und Unternehmensdaten im Längsschnitt – neue Datenangebote und ihre Forschungs-potenziale. Vorwort. Wirtschafts- und Sozialstatistisches Archiv. AStA 2, 189-191.
Bender, S./Fertig, M./Görlitz, K./Huber, M. and Schmucker, A. (2009): WeLL – unique linked employer-employee data on further training in Germany. Schmollers Jahrbuch. Zeitschrift für Wirtschafts- und Sozialwissenschaften 129, 637-643.
Brand, R. (2000): Anonymität von Betriebsdaten – Verfahren zur Erfassung und Maßnahmen zur Verringerung des Reidentifikationsrisikos. Beiträge zur Arbeitsmarkt- und Berufsforschung 237.
Brand, R. (2002): Masking through Noise Addition. Inference Control in Statistical Databases. Berlin/Heidelberg, 97-116.
Brand, R./Bender, S. and Kohaut, S. (1999): Possibilities for the creation of a scientific-use file for the IAB-Establishment-Panel. Statistical Data Confidentiality Proceedings of the Joint Eurostat/UN-ECE Work Session on Statistical Data Confidentiality Held in Thessaloniki in March 1999. Eurostat. Brüssel, 57-74.
Davis, S. and Haltiwanger, D. (1992): Gross Job Creation, Gross Job Destruction and Employment Reallocation. Quarterly Journal of Economics 107, 819-863.
Drechsler, J./Dundler, A./Bender, S./Rässler, S. and Zwick, T. (2008): A new approach for disclosure control in the IAB Establishment Panel – multiple imputation for a better data access. Advances in Statistical Analysis 92, 439-458.
Dunne, T./Roberts, M. and Samuelson, L. (1989): The Growth and Failure of U.S. Manufacturing Plants. Quarterly Journal of Economics 104, 671-698.
Falk, M. and Steiner, V. (2000): Informationsfeld Erwerbstätigkeit/Einkommen im KVI-Gutachten.
Gottschalk, S. (2005): Unternehmensdaten zwischen Datenschutz und Analysepotenzial. ZEW Wirtschaftsanalysen 76. Baden Baden.
Hamermesh, D.S. (2008): Fun with Matched Firm-Employee Data: Progress and Road Maps. Labour Economics 15 (4), 663-673.
Hethey, T. and Spengler, A. (2009): Matching process generated business data and survey data – the case of KombiFiD in Germany. FDZ Methodenreport 01/2009 (en).
Heyer, G. (2006): Zielsetzung und Struktur der "Hartz-Evaluation". Zeitschrift für ArbeitsmarktForschung 39 (3/4), 467-476.

Kluve, J. (2006) The Effectiveness of European Active Labor Market Policy. IZA Discussion Paper 2018.

Koch, S./Kupka, P. and Steinke, J. (2008): Aktivierung, Erwerbstätigkeit und Teilhabe – Die Wirkungen der Grundsicherung für Arbeitsuchende (Ergebnisse der Wirkungsforschung nach §55 SGB II von 2005 bis 2008).

Kommission zur Verbesserung der informationellen Infrastruktur zwischen Wissenschaft und Statistik (KVI) (Ed.) (2001): Wege zu einer besseren informationellen Infrastruktur. Baden-Baden.

Lane, J. (2005): Optimizing the Use of Microdata: An Overview of the Issues. Paper presented at the Joint Statistical Meetings. http://client.norc.org/jole/SOLEweb/ Accesstomicrodata%5B1%5D.pdf. [Last visited: 02/10/2010].

Lenz, R./Vorgrimler, D. and Rosemann, M. (2005): Ein Scientific-Use-File der Kostenstrukturerhebung im Verarbeitenden Gewerbe. Wirtschaft und Statistik 2, 91-96.

Lenz, R./Rosemann, M./Sturm, R. and Vorgrimmler, D. (2006): Anonymising Business Micro Data – Results of a German Project. Schmollers Jahrbuch 126 (4), 635-651.

Pohlmeier, W and Ronning, G. (2008): Microeconometrics and disclosure control. Advances in Statistical Analysis 92, 351-357.

Rosemann, M. (2006): Auswirkungen datenverändernder Anonymisierungsverfahren auf die Analyse von Mikrodaten.

Stegmann, M. (2009): Änderungen der Erfassung der Angaben über Bildung, Beruf und Beschäftigungsform im Meldeverfahren zur Sozialversicherung. Deutsche Rentenversicherung, 487-500.

Scheffler, M. (2005): Ein Scientific-Use-File der Einzelhandelsstatistik 1999. Wirtschaft und Statistik 3, 197-200.

Solga, H. and Wagner, G.G. (2007): A Modern Statistical Infrastructure for Excellent Research and Policy Advice – Report on the German Council for Social and Economic Data during its First Period in Office (2004 - 2006). RatSWD Working Paper No. 2.

Vorgrimler, D./Dittrich, S./Lenz, R. and Rosemann, M. (2005): Ein Scientific-Use-File der Umsatzsteuerstatistik 2000. Wirtschaft und Statistik 3, 197-200.

Willenborg, L. and de Waal, T. (2001): Elements of Statistical Disclosure Control. New York.

4.2 More and Better Data for Labor Market Research
Proposals for Efficient Access to the Currently Unused Potential of Official Statistical Data

Hilmar Schneider

Contact:

Hilmar Schneider
IZA – Institut zur Zukunft der Arbeit
Schaumburg-Lippe-Str. 7-9
53113 Bonn
Germany
e-mail: schneider[at]iza.org

1. Introduction

The economic assessment of issues related to the labor market requires a sound and comprehensive database. A key variable for understanding labor market processes is hourly wages. For example, hourly wages can explain whether people work or not, and if they work, how much they work. The related earnings are a major source of income and hence a key to explaining consumption. Hourly wages also explain why and how long people remain unemployed as well as how much they invest in human capital. On the employer's side, hourly wages explain the number of workers being hired or dismissed, the location of firms, and the optimal form of specialization. Last but not least, hourly wages have a crucial impact on income distribution. Given the importance of hourly wages, it appears more than surprising that official statistics provide little data support for this central part of the economy. With comparably little effort, significant improvements could be made to the utilization of existing data. However, it would require the support of the legislative. On the one hand, this affects the conception of official surveys, and on the other hand, it requires a legal basis for merging official microdata for scientific purposes.

The logic of the existing surveys is still rooted in an antiquated understanding of statistics that sees its objective in compiling aggregate figures with the aid of independent samples designed specifically for a particular purpose. Structurally related data like working hours and wages are collected by separate surveys. Hourly wages can therefore only be computed on an aggregate level. The analytical potential of such datasets will remain limited as long as it is impossible to create broad linkages with structural characteristics on the level of observation units.

If the samples were conceptualized to enable information on the firm level to be linked with information on the individual and household level, the analytical potential of the data would be significantly increased, while at the same time reducing the effort required for data collection. Indeed, it was for this reason that the 2001 KVI report called for legal regulations to provide a possibility for exact data linkage – without the express agreement of all respondents – for purely statistical purposes (see KVI 2001, recommendation 34).

Aggregated statistics are insufficient because they do not provide a basis for conclusive answers about the structural causes of differences or changes in aggregate indicators. In the scholarly literature, this phenomenon is known as an ecological fallacy (Robinson 1950). Typical questions of labor market research can only be answered based on microdata, in which micro-level heterogeneity in observation units – which, for labor market research, consist mainly of individuals, households, and firms – serves as the identifying moment. Here, two kinds of heterogeneity are relevant: heterogeneity between observation units on the micro-level (between variance) and heterogeneity over time (within variance). If the process under examination is a stationary one, and if characteristics with explanatory relevance are observable, it is sufficient to collect cross-sectional data; that is, to examine the heterogeneity between units of observation. Going beyond this to examine panel data is useful, first, when cohort effects are present, and second, when the observability of the characteristics with explanatory relevance is limited, which can essentially never be ruled out. With the aid of panel data, the potentially distorting effect of unobservable heterogeneity can be neutralized (see Baltagi 1995).

From this, it follows that there is a basic need to collect panel data on the micro-level. Numerous such data are already collected by statistical offices or originate from administrative processes. But there is still, to some extent, a lack of suitable means for researchers to access these data, and in some cases it would require that existing survey concepts be linked in a coherent manner.

The related request is not completely new. In an advisory report on employment and earnings for the 2001 KVI report, Falk and Steiner (2000) discussed the problems outlined above and formulated a series of recommendations to address them. The present chapter takes up these recommendations and assesses the hitherto achieved progress. Building on this, areas will be identified in which further action is needed. The focus here will be on the proposal for coordinated sampling procedures that would allow linkage of individual and firm-related data and can thus be seen as an extension of the recommendations by Falk and Steiner.

2. Prime example: Hourly wages

As already mentioned, hourly wages are the key driver for empirically based economic analyses of the labor market. This requires information about paid salaries as well as information about the related working time. However, in official statistics, information on these variables is not only collected in separate surveys, but also in an insufficient manner.

Respondents to the Microcensus, for example, are surveyed regarding hours worked, but not with respect to the wages earned. They are asked instead just to provide personal net income or household net income. Since these figures can also include unknown amounts of transfers and other forms of income, it is impossible to calculate hourly wages. Approximately one-sixth of all German households receive transfers, such as housing allowances and unemployment benefits (see Rudolph 2008). According to the Federal Statistical Office, almost one quarter of households receive child allowances or parental allowances. Additionally, the tax and transfer system provides very low wage earners with a major source of income compensation (BMAS 2008), meaning that the use of net income to approximate earned income will probably lead to completely erroneous conclusions.

Since 2003, the Income and Consumption Survey (EVS, *Einkommens- und Verbrauchsstichprobe*) has included survey questions not just on detailed income categories, but also on weekly working hours – albeit only the contractually stipulated working hours. Since overtime hours are also included in income earned, actual hourly wages are overestimated when dividing earned income by contractually stipulated working hours. Furthermore, the EVS is only conducted once every five years and is limited to specific household types (on this and other limitations, see Hauser 2010). In addition, the EVS is conducted on a voluntary participation basis, which can be accompanied by systematic selection bias, adversely affecting the representativeness of the survey further.

The Time Budget Survey carried out in 1991/92 and 2001/02 does not overcome the limitations mentioned above. Although the Time Budget Survey does contain a detailed record of time use over the course of the day, it is impossible to link this with earned income.

3. The recommendations of Falk and Steiner

Official statistical agencies possess a series of micro datasets that are relevant to labor market research. In this context, Falk and Steiner (2000) examine the following datasets:

(1) European Household Panel (EHP)
(2) Microcensus
(3) Income and Consumption Survey
(4) Time Budget Survey
(5) Salary and Wage Structure Survey
(6) Official Industry Statistics on Firms and Companies
(7) Social Security Statistics
(8) Cost Structure Survey

The report concludes with approximately 15 recommendations, eight of which are relevant to the datasets listed above. These recommendations are summarized in the following:

(1) Develop the Microcensus into a dataset relevant to labor market issues by including income characteristics.
(2) Develop the Income and Consumption Survey into an instrument for annual accounts and expand it to include data on working hours.

(3) Collect Microcensus data over the course of the year.
(4) Develop the Microcensus further as an access panel.
(5) Open up access to data for interested researchers.
(6) Provide individual-level microdata from official statistics in factually anonymized form.
(7) Provide firm- and company-level data from official statistics in simple anonymized form.
(8) Comparatively evaluate data access through computer centers and remote data processing facilities that are subject to federal data protection regulations in the framework of a pilot project.

The first two of these recommendations should be seen as crucial, and relate to the problem mentioned at the outset: that the existing microdata have been used relatively little in labor market research because central variables are not available. In the area of individual-level data, this is especially the case for hourly wages, and in the area of firm-level data, it is true for the decomposition of value added into its labor and capital components.

4. An assessment of progress achieved since 2000

To start with, on a positive note, the number of micro datasets of potential interest for labor market research has increased significantly with the establishment of the Research Data Centers of the Federal Statistical Office and the Statistical Offices of the German *Länder*. Nearly all of the data collected by official agencies are now available to interested researchers, either as Scientific Use Files (SUFs) or as onsite files. The demand to provide access to the data has thus been met to a large extent. But what still has not been adequately addressed, at least by official statistical agencies, is the need to provide controlled remote data processing – despite the emphasis on this point in the 2001 KVI report and the fact that this is an integral component of the newly founded Research Data Centers' work from the Commission's point of view (see KVI 2001, recommendation 29).

Along with Research Data Centers, two Data Service Centers have also been established on the KVI's recommendations. The task of these Data Service Centers is to provide special services to data users and data producers (see Schneider and Wolf 2008). The Data Service Center at GESIS (GMD, *German Microdata Lab* at GESIS, *Leibniz Institute for the Social Sciences*) has taken on the task of developing special aids in the documentation and use of official microdata. The International Data Service Center at the Institute for the Study of Labor (IZA, *Forschungsinstitut zur Zukunft der Arbeit*) aims to meet the needs of an international research community. The International Data Service Center provides, on the one hand, metadata on micro datasets relevant to the labor market, and on the other, assistance to foreign researchers in accessing German microdata. One of its outcomes has been the development of a tool for controlled remote data processing that goes by the name JoSuA (Job Submission Application) and can be used as a prototype for use in Research Data Centers. Up to now, however, it is used only by researchers from abroad who want to use SUFs from official statistics for projects conducted in cooperation with IZA. The researchers send their questions for analysis by JoSuA to the IDSC, where the actual data access occurs, after the International Data Service Center has checked the input for compliance with data protection regulations. Then, after the output is checked by the International Data Service Center for compliance with data protection regulations – and if permissible – the data are sent back to the researcher who made the request.

Although the number of micro datasets made available by statistical offices has increased substantially, quantity is not equivalent to quality. The value added of, for example, company data on continuing education collected in the framework of the European Continuing Vocational Training Survey (CVTS) remains very limited since this survey does not collect data on individual-specific characteristics, nor does it allow for linkage of existing individual datasets. Much the same is true of the statistics on students or marriages, to cite only two examples.

In regard to the two primary demands of Falk and Steiner, the progress achieved so far can be described as modest. With the new Microcensus Law of 2005, an opportunity to expand the survey to encompass measures of earned income has been lost for the foreseeable future. Nevertheless, the EVS has been surveying contractually stipulated weekly working hours since 2003. Before then, the survey was limited to surveying the categories of part-time and full-time employment as well as marginal employment. As mentioned above, the issue of the EVS's adequacy for computation of hourly wages has by no means been solved satisfactorily.

With the new version of the Microcensus Law, the call to conduct the Microcensus over the course of the year has been met. Previously, the Microcensus data always referred to the situation on a single reference date in April of the survey year, so the Microcensus was unable to reflect major seasonal fluctuations in employment behavior. Following extensive pilot surveys in the years 2003 and 2004, as of January 2005, the Microcensus is now conducted at monthly intervals. As a byproduct, the pilot surveys have provided labor market research with an interesting new micro database on the International Labour Organization (ILO) employment status.

The proposal to further develop the Microcensus as a so-called "access panel" has also been taken up by official statistical agencies. Since 2004, participants in the Microcensus have been asked for their agreement to participate on a voluntary basis in further official statistical surveys (see Körner et al. 2006). The advantages of this procedure consist of the possibility to draw random samples with great flexibility and the ability to achieve higher response rates than is possible with the usual sampling procedures. In addition, the adoption of this procedure has led to not having to collect the same already available data repeatedly. This could potentially overcome the limitations identified above in the separate surveying of related characteristics. In practice, however, the potential here has by no means yet been exhausted, since only a relatively small portion of the variables surveyed in the Microcensus are actually included in the corresponding master file. For example, among the variables on working hours, only normal weekly working hours are included in the master file. Linkage with the EVS, for instance, offers no new information for the generation of hourly wages.

The selection of potential survey participants based on the Microcensus is mainly utilized in sample selection for the European Statistics on Income and Living Conditions (EU-SILC). This panel survey, conducted for the first time in 2005, is the successor to the European Community Household Panel (ECHP), which was carried out until 2001. Unfortunately, this survey also passed up its chance to create a solid database on individual hourly wages. Although detailed information is collected on current working hours, in the area of income, only data on monthly net income is collected, without differentiation into income components. Differentiated income data is only collected retro-spectively for the previous year, but without corresponding data on working hours. Although it is conceivable to link current data on working hours with retrospectively collected earnings data at a later point in time, this is only useful for individuals with a continuous employment history. For those with career interruptions, or a change of their employer, retrospective annual income data do not match current working time data.

Even if little progress has been made so far in generating individual hourly wages based on official microdata, a development is currently underway that gives reason for hope. Here, efforts have been made to put the idea of merging microdata from various sources into practice as far as possible within the given legal constraints. This process has even succeeded in overcoming institutional boundaries, which should undoubtedly be counted as an accomplishment of the data infrastructure created so far. The effort that should be mentioned here above all is the project Combined Firm Data for Germany (KombiFiD, *Kombinierte Firmendaten für Deutschland*) (see also Möller and Bender 2010; Wagner 2010).[1] By linking firm-level data from the Federal Statistical Office, the Deutsche Bundesbank, and the Federal Employment Agency (BA, *Bundesagentur für Arbeit*), it aims at creating a combined database.

---

1   See also: http://www.kombifid.de.

There is unquestionably vast potential in the coordinated linkage of previously independent surveys for improving and enhancing official statistics. An important step in this direction can also be seen in the conception of the 2011 Census, which plans to link the available information on the individual or household level from diverse registers (see Statistische Ämter des Bundes und der Länder 2004; Heinzel 2006). The procedure developed for this purpose should provide a valuable impetus toward a reconceptualization of coordinated sampling procedures in official statistics.

5. Resulting or remaining needs for action

A comparison of the data requirements described above and the progress achieved so far results in four basic recommendations for action that can be summarized briefly as follows:

- Provide controlled remote data processing in the Research Data Centers of the Federal Statistical Office and the Statistical Offices of the German *Länder*.
- Expand the program of household statistical surveys to include questions on hourly wages.
- Legally regulate exact data linkage – without the express agreement of all respondents – for purely statistical purposes.
- Conduct coordinated statistical surveys to create possibilities for data linkage.

The call for controlled remote data processing needs no further explanation. A tension exists between the demand to expand the programs of household statistical surveys to include questions on hourly wages and the recommendations that follow here. If it were possible to link different data sources with each other, the demand to expand the program of questions in these surveys would be superfluous. This demand should therefore be seen as a second-best solution, for it would only solve a specific – although very fundamental – problem. Coordinating statistical surveys to facilitate data linkage, on the other hand, would not only overcome the lack of data on hourly wages but would also solve many other problems. Without a sound legal foundation, however, this is not to be expected.

As long as such a fundamental legal solution remains a distant prospect, there is no alternative to expanding the survey program of the Microcensus and the EVS. The next opportunity to do so will arise with the harmonization of national household statistics that is planned on the European level. The

Microcensus Law will remain in effect only up to the year 2012. One year later, the law governing the EVS will expire. It is probable that legislators will decide to pass a comprehensive law reconceptualizing statistics oriented toward European guidelines. Already in November 2007, a workshop took place in Mannheim organized by GESIS together with the German Data Forum (RatSWD), the goal of which was to foster dialog between scholars and official statistical agencies on the programs of household statistical surveys. The Federal Statistical Office is addressing this question within the framework of the project "Reforming Household Statistics". Beyond this, a steering committee was appointed by the federal and state governments to advise on how to proceed. In order for a coordinated concept to be introduced into the legislative procedure in a timely manner, it would have to be agreed upon by the end of 2010 at the latest. On a European level, these considerations have found expression in the planning for a new ECHP. A pilot study was already carried out in 2008.

The alternative of coordinated linkage of data sources, on the other hand, would allow the information basis to be expanded much more effectively. It would permit improvement in the quality of the data collected, on the one hand, and would reduce the effort required to collect the data, on the other. The possibilities for linking data also would not have to be limited to surveys by the statistical offices. One could conceive, for example, of linking Microcensus samples with administrative data from the BA. While the BA data lack information on working hours, the Microcensus lacks information on earnings. When each is taken on its own, the datasets offer a limited basis for drawing conclusions. But combining them would result in a powerful basis for analysis in which, for example, the Microcensus data would compensate for the lack of information on working hours in the BA data.

This kind of strategy also goes far beyond the recommendations of Falk and Steiner (2000). While their recommendation was limited to complementary collection of individual or household data by official statistical agencies, the project KombiFiD demonstrates the possibilities that result from the coordinated linkage of firm-level data with individual- or household-level data beyond institutional boundaries. With KombiFiD, the BA plans to contribute only aggregated individual data, such as number of employees, age structure of employees, etc. In principle, however, this opens up the possibility for the reverse perspective: that of linking individual data with firm-level data and thus expanding in the direction of a linked employer-employee dataset.

In this case, the coordinated linkage of data sources requires that the sample of households and firms be drawn in a coordinated manner. This may go in two directions, which are not equally useful. It would be possible, for instance, to generate the Microcensus sample no longer just as a population sample, but also as a sample containing all employed persons from a firm sample. The Microcensus sample, however, could not be drawn exclusively on this basis since otherwise, unemployed and non-employed persons would be excluded from the survey. It could therefore prove more sensible to take the reverse approach, using the employers of the Microcensus respondents as the basis for a firm sample.

Even if the perspective outlined here is of a more long-term nature, there is no reason to dismiss it as unrealistic. The reconceptualization of the 2011 Census as a register-based census has shown a promising way to overcome the basic obstacles. The priority should now be to exploit the potential of this path for research.

References:

Baltagi, B.H. (1995): Econometric Analysis of Panel Data. Chichester/New York/Brisbane/Toronto/Singapore.

Bender, S. and Möller, J. (2010): Data from the Federal Employment Agency. [In this publication].

Bundesministerium für Arbeit und Soziales (2008): Lebenslagen in Deutschland – Der 3. Armuts- und Reichtumsbericht der Bundesregierung. Bonn.

Falk, M. and Steiner, V. (2000): Expertise für die Kommission zur Verbesserung der informationellen Infrastruktur zwischen Wissenschaft und Statistik im Bereich Erwerbstätigkeit und Einkommen. Mannheim.

Hauser, R. (2010): Household income, poverty, and wealth. [In this publication].

Heinzel, A. (2006): Volkszählung 2001 – Deutschland bereitet sich auf den registergestützten Zensus vor. Berliner Statistik 7/ 2006, 321-328.

Körner, T./Nimmergut, A./Nökel, J. and Rohloff, S. (2006): Die Dauerstichprobe befragungsbereiter Haushalte. Wirtschaft und Statistik 5/2006, 451-467.

Kommission zur Verbesserung der informationellen Infrastruktur zwischen Wissenschaft und Statistik (KVI) (Ed.) (2001): Wege zu einer besseren informationellen Infrastruktur. Baden-Baden.

Robinson, W.S. (1950): Ecological Correlations and the Behavior of Individuals. American Sociological Review 15, 351-357.

Rudolph, H. (2008): Erwerbstätigkeit in Transferhaushalten – Arm trotz Arbeit. IAB Forum 2/2008, 34-39.

Schneider, H. and Wolf C. (2008): Die Datenservicezentren als Teil der informationellen Infrastruktur. In: Rolf, G./Zwick, M. and Wagner, G.G. (Eds): Fortschritte der informationellen Infrastruktur in Deutschland. Festschrift für Johann Hahlen zum 65. Geburtstag und Hans Jörg Krupp zum 75. Geburtstag. Baden-Baden.

Statistische Ämter des Bundes und der Länder (2004): Ergebnisse des Zensustests. Wirtschaft und Statistik 8/2004, 813-833.

Wagner, J. (2010): Firm-Level Data. [In this publication].

4.3 Interdisciplinary Longitudinal Surveys
Linking Individual Data to Organizational Data in Life-Course Analysis

Stefan Liebig

Contact:

Stefan Liebig
Bielefeld University
Faculty of Sociology
Postfach 10 01 31
33501 Bielefeld
Germany
e-mail: stefan.liebig[at] uni-bielefeld.de

Abstract

This paper starts with three fundamental insights from social science and economics: (1) that the conditions and consequences of individual behavior can only be studied empirically on the basis of longitudinal data, (2) that individual behavior is embedded in social contexts and social aggregates, and (3) that formal organizations – e.g., firms, schools, universities – are becomming more important for individual life courses. From this, it follows that social and economic research needs a data infrastructure which provides information on individuals over time and on the organizations those individuals are associated with. In the last nine years, there have been major efforts to provide scientific communities with linked individual-firm data in Germany. However, the available datasets comprise only limited information on individuals and organizations and provide no information on the household level. As the latter is becoming more important – e.g., in generating social inequalities – the existing data-stock should be complemented by longitudinal data linking individuals, their households, their firms, and other organizations they are members in. The recommendation is to enhance the German Socio-Economic Panel (SOEP, *Soziooekonomisches Panel*) with information from the firms the household members are presently employed in. Such a dataset can be useful for a wide range of social and economic research areas and would be unique on an international level.

Keywords: longitudinal data, surveys, linked employer-employee data, microdata, household data, life-course analysis, survey methodology

1. Research questions

One of the fundamental insights gained by the social and economic sciences is that empirically founded statements on the conditions and consequences of individual behavior or of social and economic change can only be formulated on the basis of longitudinal microdata. The observation of individuals, households, and other socio-economic units over long periods of time allows us to causally determine the reasons for social and economic stability and change. Moreover, socio-economic phenomena are particularly path-dependent. The opportunities and restrictions that individual or corporate actors face over their life courses – or more generally: over time – depend to a great extent on decisions and events earlier in time. The available individual and household-level datasets used in empirical social and economic research in Germany are capable of mirroring these path-dependencies.

But social and economic phenomena show another fundamental quality: they are embedded in social contexts and social aggregates (Granovetter 1985). Embeddedness means that actors are in most cases elements of a number of social aggregates. Their behavior is affected by these different memberships and the structures and processes that take place within these aggregates, whether households, social networks, schools, firms, associations, regional areas, or nations. Longitudinal microdata for assessing the effects of these different social contexts on individual decisions and behavior are available at the level of households, geographic units, or – within comparative research – at the national level. However, recent labor market and educational research shows that there is another type of social aggregate that is crucial for an individual's economic or social situation and his or her life chances: institutions and organizations like schools, universities, firms, or establishments (Baron and Bielby 1980; Coleman 1993; Hamermesh 2008; Heckman 2001).

For many years, organizations have played a subordinate role in German research on social stratification, the labor market, and the education system (Allmendinger and Hinz 2002). With regard to firms and establishments, this was justified with reference to the dominance of the tariff system and the longstanding practice of macro-level regulation. Today, there exist a range of empirical studies showing a general trend towards increasing heterogeneity on the organizational level in Germany and suggesting that labor market and educational institutions are developing more and more differentiated internal structures and processes. One consequence of this development has been that the distribution of goods, jobs, and life opportunities is determined increasingly by the "internal logic of organizations." Some of the main effects of this on individual career paths and employment histories can be seen at the establishment level and firm level (Bender et al. 2000; DiPrete et al 2001), on the level of wages (Kölling et al. 2005), in the duration of unemployment, and in qualification levels (Frederiksen et al. 2006), and even in the political attitudes of employees (Liebig and Krause 2007). Besides the classical variables such as number of employees (Heyman 2007), degree of unionization (Fitzenberger et al. 2007), and branch affiliation, a range of other important explanatory factors can be identified on the firm level and establishment level, such as a firm's age (Brixy et al. 2007), its socio-demographic structure (Krell and Sieben 2007), the magnitude of income disparities or mobility chances (Liebig and Krause 2007), and the particular form of work organization (Bellmann and Pahnke 2006).

The operative structures, processes, and strategies, as well as the business situations of employers are becoming increasingly important, and not only for employment revenues (Goedicke 2006; Lengfeld 2007). The variety of firm-specific operative time regimes, improvements in the compatibility between work and family, health promotion activities, and more flexible regulations governing working time and location (e.g., home workplaces) also affect an individual's social relations and his or her way of life in general (Düntgen and Diewald 2007).

As has already been outlined, organizations can control their members' access to jobs and goods. This is an assumption that takes on particular importance when analyzing durable structures of social inequality (Tilly 1998). The individual life course can also be understood as a sequence of different memberships in organizations (Figure 1). Individual life courses can thus be distinguished by the extent to which people succeed in joining organizations that offer better life chances. In this context, social stratification research tries to investigate whether this also results in path-dependencies, i.e., as people become members of advantageous or disadvantageous organizations, advantages and disadvantages are accumulated over the life course.

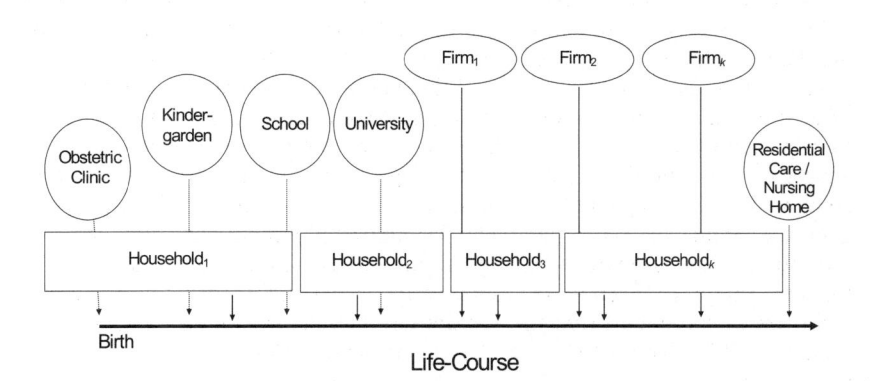

Figure 1: The individual life course and memberships in different types of organizations

2. Status quo

In order to empirically analyze the effects of the organizational level on individual career paths, the conditions and outcomes of employment, and different aspects of individual life courses, social and economic research requires adequate data linking personal and organizational information. Such matched organization-member datasets are available especially in the field of labor market research. These Linked Employer-Employee (LEE) datasets are characterized by a hierarchical multilevel structure, in which employees constitute the bottom level and the firms and/or enterprises constitute the upper level. The distinct feature of these LEE data is that they contain information about several – and in the optimal case, all – persons employed in a firm. In most cases, "process-produced" administrative data, on either the individual or the firm level, constitute the basis of analysis (Abowd and

Kramarz 1999). In contrast to other European and non-European countries, Germany recognized the potential of LEE data very late. This is why, in 2001, Martin Falk and Viktor Steiner concluded, in their advisory report to the 2001 KVI report: "The opportunities of matching firm and individual data were recognized much earlier in other countries. In certain areas, such as operative employment and income trends, German research is no longer competitive. In this domain, research is almost non-existent" (p. 8).

In the meantime, the data supply has been improved substantially, mainly because of the linked employer-employee dataset from the IAB (LIAB) (Alda et al. 2005) and the income and wage structure surveys conducted by the official statistical agencies (Stephan 2001), which are available in the Research Data Centers of the Federal Employment Agency at the Institute for Employment Research (IAB, *Institut für Arbeitsmarkt- und Berufsforschung* within the BA, *Bundesagentur für Arbeit*) and the Research Data Centers of the Federal Statistical Office and the Statistical Offices of the German *Länder*. Both data sources are "real" linked employer-employee datasets that offer information on all – or at least a sufficient number of – employees in each participating firm. Both datasets contain vast and diverse potential for analysis. The central difference is the degree of available firm information contained. The income and wage structure survey is a cross-sectional dataset; it only contains the basic parameters of the employment structure, sectoral affiliation, and degree of collective bargaining. Thus, it can be used primarily for the analysis of cross-sectional wage structures (especially after the inclusion of surveyed firms and sectors through changes in the legislation in January 2007). The LIAB, on the other hand, offers a broader base of information, ranging from detailed employment structures, the firm's economic situation, professional training programs, to labor time regulations, payment systems, and special measures to improve compatibility between work and family. Although this focus indeed requires further development – e.g., with regard to the existing mobility regimes or the firm culture, which is quite important to organizational research – on the operative side, the LIAB offers a potential for analysis that exceeds the classic labor economic or sociological questions, all the more so because it displays longitudinal processes on the firm level and on the individual level. This central advantage is diminished, however, by the restricted supply of information on the employee side. Here, the LIAB shares one of the main weaknesses of the income and wage structure survey.

Both available LEE datasets in Germany are characterized by restricted access to information on individuals and households. This applies to central features of current employment relationships (the LIAB does not identify, e.g., temporary employment or the supply of temporary workers), to information on the economic situation of an individual, and even more so to household data, the family situation, social origins, social preferences and personal characteristics, norm and value orientations, and political attitudes and membership in parties or other organizations. Since these topics are of central interest in empirical social and economic research, there is a strong need for a dataset that contains longitudinal information on the individual, household, and organizational level.

Against this background, an extension of the existing linked employer-employee data supply in Germany is desperately needed. This improvement needs to be promoted especially for the kind of information that goes beyond basic employment data. This can be achieved, for instance, by gathering information on family background, family and domestic situations, integration into social networks, as well as moral concepts and political attitudes. Improvements are also possible on the organizational side – the data catalog of the IAB Establishment Panel can, for instance, be expanded to include income and wage formation processes, elements of enterprise and firm culture, industrial relations, and the national or international competitive position of firms. Such a catalog of information can only be created on the basis of linked employer-employee surveys. In the present research, these kinds of data are produced using two different approaches:

2.1 Employer-first approach

In the first step of this approach, which has also been pursued by official statistics in the framework of the income and wage structure survey or the WeLL[1] project by IAB and RWI (Bender et al. 2008), suitable firms are selected. Individual information is collected from a sample of employees working in these firms (either all employees or a partial sample) (see the 2000 National Employer Survey, Capelli 2001). The advantage here is that the existing multilevel data structure prevailing in common LEE datasets is still existent. One problem, however, is that such samples quite rapidly go beyond realistic limits. This happens if the information on the employees is not supplied by the firm itself but gathered by employee surveys. The coordination and implementation of such employee surveys in more than 100 or 200 firms is hardly practicable in the framework of normal research projects – even when the surveys are conducted by survey institutes. Accordingly, a recent project in Germany utilizing this approach concentrated on a single-digit number of firms (Brose et al 2006).

---

1 Further Training as a Part of Lifelong Learning (*Berufliche Weiterbildung als Bestandteil Lebenslangen Lernens*).

2.2 Employee-first approach

In the second approach to generating matched datasets, not firms or organizations, but persons (employees), constitute the point of departure. The individual data, which are gathered through personal interviews, are later complemented by firm-level data. This again can be done in three different ways (a technique that is already being used in research projects) (see Kmec 2003):

(1) The information on the establishment or firm where the respondent of a population survey is employed are added using available commercial business datasets (in Germany: Creditreform or Hoppenstedt). Examples of this method are the New Worker Establishment Characteristics Database and the Decennial Employer-Employee Dataset. The problem of this approach is the limited scope of available firm information in the databases (e.g., number of employees, founding year, business volume). Although business databases can be used to assess an enterprise's liquidity or financial strength, they are less suitable for scientific questions.

(2) The second way is to complement the personal information with data from official statistics for the appropriate establishment or firm. In the framework of a study conducted by the Max Planck Institute for Human Development in Berlin, for instance, researchers asked the respondents for their social security numbers. Afterwards, the individual data were linked to the IAB Establishment Panel (Reimer and Kuenster 2004). If the employer was included in the IAB Establishment Panel, the firm information was added to the individual data record. Obviously the problem here is that the share of employees in a population survey who are covered at the same time by the IAB Establishment Panel is expectedly small. Another possibility lies in using the IAB Establishment History Panel (Dundler et al. 2006), but in this case, the available employer information is much more restricted than in the IAB Establishment Panel.

(3) Finally, one can use an individual or household survey to ask employees for the name and address of their employer, and can conduct a separate firm survey on the grounds of this information. The collected firm-level data can then be matched with the individual or household data. Examples of this approach are the Multi-City Study of Urban Inequality and most notably the National Organization Survey (NOS) from the years 1991 and 2002 (Kmec 2003). In the framework of the German General Social Survey (ALLBUS, *Allgemeine Bevölkerungsumfrage der Sozialwissenschaften*) of 1991 and 2002, all (1991) and, respectively, some (2002) of the currently employed were asked for the name and address of their workplace. Local business units in which people were gainfully

employed were the target units. On the basis of these entries, telephone interviews were conducted and postal questionnaires distributed. These data were matched to the individual data of the ALLBUS. The result is a linked employee-employer dataset (Kalleberg et al. 1996; Smith et al. 2004). In 1991, for a total of 51 percent of all cases (in 2002, 48 percent) the individual and firm-level data could successfully be matched. In contrast to the classical LEE data structure, this dataset does not possess a hierarchical structure. For one firm, the individual data are available for just one employee. Due to its cross-sectional character, this does not offer causal or longitudinal potentials for analysis. But through combined individual-firm surveys, it is possible to collect far more firm information than in a person-to-person interview, and the firm-level data, which are collected in combined surveys, are gathered independently from the interviewee's attitudes and perceptions (see Gupta et al. 2000).

In a current project underway at the University of Bielefeld, the design of the NOS study is being tested for its transferability to the German situation. For this purpose, all currently employed persons who are being surveyed in the ALLBUS 2008 (a nationwide reference survey) were asked for the name and addresses of their employers. Useful data is available for about 85 percent of those people who are employed in firms with more than six employees. On the basis of these data, a firm survey will be conducted in January 2009. The aim of this study is to assess the quality and methodological problems arising in connection to the generation of survey-based LEE datasets. Moreover, conclusions for future interview projects will be derived. As the willingness to participate in firm surveys has decreased constantly since the 1990s, another important task will be to find ways to maximize firm participation. A central problem of such a twofold survey-based approach is data protection. The respondents have to give permission for their firms to be contacted. Only then can individual and firm information be matched. A further problem is the re-identification of individuals and firms. However, the projects currently carried out by the official statistical agencies on the anonymization of firm and panel data already offer suitable tools that simplify data access – also for researchers.

3. Future developments

Empirical research shows that there is an increasing variety of organizing work at the firm level in Germany which affects labor market processes, social stratification, and other socio-economic phenomena (e.g., work-life balance). From this follows an increasing demand for socio-economic datasets that identify linkages between individuals and organizations. Especially in the field of educational research, the interest in particular educational institutions will increase in the near future (Klieme 2008). The efficiency and the evaluation of activities will be measured according to their impact on the student's performance and his/her educational achievements. However, if no further household information is available, the linkages between organizational and individual data are not sufficient – especially with regard to the educational system.

The linkages between different data sources (e.g., Bender et al. 2007) offer the chance to broaden the scope of survey-based organizational data and to match them with information from other data sources. This reduces interview costs and allows the researcher to conduct firm surveys that are more strongly focused on a specific topic. As socio-economic research has recognized the need for longitudinal data and the embeddedness of individual behavior, it seems to be more important than ever before to collect longitudinal information on the individual and the household level.

4. Recommendations

Against this background the following recommendations can be made:

(1) There is an increasing demand for linked data between individual, household, and organization information – especially with regard to the organization of the educational system and the workplace.

(2) As the available datasets only offer limited information, household and individual surveys should be matched based on adequate organizational data. This can be achieved by matching data from official statistics or from separate surveys.

(3) Linked individual/household and organizational datasets will be only feasible for socio-economic research if they contain longitudinal information.

(4) The best solution to achieve an adequate data structure is to enrich the SOEP with separate firm surveys (e.g., of nursery schools, schools, workplaces of other household members) at five-year intervals. Respondents to SOEP should be asked for the names and addresses of these organizations, and based on this information, organizational surveys should be conducted to achieve a three-level hierarchical and longitudinal dataset. In this way longitudinal information would be made available on the individual, the household, and the organizational level. Such a dataset would be internationally unique and would offer novel

potential for analysis in a variety of disciplines (education, sociology, economics, psychology).

References:

Abowd, J.M. and Kramarz, F. (1999): The analysis of labor markets using matched employer-employee data. In: Ashenfelter, O. and Card, D. (Eds.): Handbook of Labor Economics. Amsterdam.

Abowd, J.M./Haltiwanger, J. and Lane, J. (2004): Integrated Longitudinal Employer-Employee Data for the United States. American Economic Review, (94), 224-229.

Alda, H./Bender, S. and Gartner, H. (2005): The linked employer-employee dataset of the IAB (LIAB). IAB Discussion Paper 6/2005.

Allmendinger, J. and Hinz, Th. (2002): Perspektiven der Organisationssoziologie. In: Allmendinger, J. and Hinz, Th. (Eds.): Organisationssoziologie. Sonderheft der Kölner Zeitschrift für Soziologie und Sozialpsychologie 42/2002. Opladen.

Baron, J.N. and Bielby, W.T. (1980): Bringing the Firms Back, Stratification, Segmentation, and the Organization of Work. American Sociological Review, (45), 737-765.

Bellmann, L. and Pahnke, A. (2006): Auswirkungen organisatorischen Wandels auf die betriebliche Arbeitsnachfrage. Zeitschrift für ArbeitsmarktForschung, (39), 201-233.

Bender, S./Konietzka, D. and Sopp, P. (2000): Diskontinuität im Erwerbsverlauf und betrieblicher Kontext. Kölner Zeitschrift für Soziologie und Sozialpsychologie, (52), 475-499.

Bender, S./Wagner, J. and Zwick, M. (2007): Kombinierte Firmendaten für Deutschland. FDZ Methodenreport 5/2007. Nuremberg.

Bender, S./Fertig, M./Görlitz, K./Huber, M./Hummelsheim, S./Knerr, P./Schmucker, A. and Schröder, H. (2008): WeLL – Berufliche Weiterbildung als Bestandteil Lebenslangen Lernens. Projektbericht. FDZMethodenbericht 05/2008. Nuremberg.

Brixy, U./Kohaut, S. and Schnabel, C. (2007): Do Newly Founded Firms Pay Lower Wages? First Evidence from Germany. Small Business Economics, (29), 161-171.

Brose, H.G./Goedicke, A./Diewald, M. (2006): Beschäftigungsverhältnisse und sozialer Tausch. Wechselwirkungen zwischen Arbeitsangebot und Arbeitsnachfrage. Universität Duisburg-Essen/Universität Bielefeld. http://www.uni-due.de/beata/. [Last visited: 02/19/2010].

Capelli, P. (2001): The National Employer Survey: Employer Data on Employment Pratices. Industrial Relations, (40), 635-647.

Coleman, J.S. (1993): The Rational Reconstruction of Society. American Sociological Review, (58), 1-15.

Diewald, M./Brose, H.-G. and Goedicke, A. (2005): Flexicurity im Lebenslauf. Wechselwirkungen zwischen pluralen Lebensformen und betrieblichen Beschäftigungspolitiken. In: Kronauer, M. and Linne. G. (Eds.): Flexicurity. Die suche nach Sicherheit in der Flexibilität. Berlin.

DiPrete, Th.A./Goux, D./Maurin, E. and Tahlin, M. (2001): Institutional Determinants of Employment Chances: The Structure of Unemployment in France and Sweden. European Sociological Review, (17), 233-254.

Dundler, A./Stamm, M. and Adler, S. (2006): Das Betriebs-Historik-Panel. FDZDatenreport 3/2006.

Düntgen, A. and Diewald, M. (2007): Auswirkungen der Flexibilisierung von Beschäftigung auf eine erste Elternschaft. In: Szydlik, M. (Ed.): Flexibilisierung. Folgen für Arbeit und Familie Wiesbaden.

Falk, M. and Steiner, V. (2001): Expertise für die Kommission zur Verbesserung der informationellen Infrastruktur zwischen Wissenschaft und Statistik im Bereich Erwerbstätigkeit und Einkommen. In: Kommission zur Verbesserung der informationellen Infrastruktur zwischen Wissenschaft und Statistik (KVI) (Ed.): Wege zu einer besseren informationellen Infrastruktur. Baden-Baden.

Fitzenberger, B./Kohn, K. and Lembcke, A.C. (2007): Union Density, Collective Bargaining, and Individual Coverage: The Anatomy of Union Wage Effects. Mannheim.

Frederiksen, A./Ibsen, R./Rosholm, M. and Westergaard-Nielsen, N. (2006): Labor Market Signalling and Unemployment Duration: An Empirical Analysis Using Employer-Employee Data. IZA Discussion Paper No. 2132.

Goedicke, A. (2006): Organisationsmodelle in der Sozialstrukturanalyse: Der Einfluss von Betrieben auf Erwerbsverläufe. Berliner Journal für Soziologie, (16), 503-524.

Granovetter, M. (1985): Economic Action and Social Structure: The Problem of Embeddedness. American Journal of Sociology, (91), 481-510.

Gupta, N./Shaw, J.D. and Delery, J.E. (2000): Correlates of response outcomes among organizational key informants. Organizational Research Methods, (3), 323-347.

Hamermesh, D. (2008): Fun with matched firm-employee data: Progress and road maps. Labor Economics, (15), 663-673.

Heckman, J.J. (2001): Micro Data, heterogeneity, and the evaluation of public policy: Nobel lecture. Journal of Political Economy, (109), 673-748.

Heyman, F. (2007): Firm Size or Firm Age? The Effect on Wages Using Matched Employer-Employee Data. Labour, (21), 237-263.

Kalleberg, A.L./Knoke, D./Marsden, P.V. and Spaeth, J.L. (Eds.) (1996): Organizations in America. Thousand Oaks.

Klieme, E. (2008): Längsschnittuntersuchungen zur Schulentwicklung. Vortrag auf der 4. Konferenz für Sozial- und Wirtschaftsdaten. http://www.ratswd.de/kswd/download/4_KSWD_Klieme.pdf. [Last visited 09/20/2008].

Kmec, J.A. (2003): Collecting and Using Employer-Worker Matched Data. Sociological Focus, (36), 81-96.

Kölling, A./Schnabel, C. and Wagner, J. (2005): Establishment Age and Wages: Evidence from German Linked Employer-Employee Data. In: Bellmann, L./Hübler, O./Meyer, W. and Stephan, G. (Eds.): Institutionen, Löhne und Beschäftigung, Beiträge zur Arbeitsmarkt- und Berufsforschung Nr. 294. Nuremberg.

Krell, G. and Sieben, B. (2007): Diversity Management und Personalforschung. In: Krell, G./Riedmüller, B. and Sieben, B. (Eds.): Diversity Studies – Grundlagen und disziplinäre Ansätze. Frankfurt am Main.

Lengfeld, H. (2007): Organisierte Ungleichheit. Wie Organisationen Lebenschancen beeinflussen. Wiesbaden.

Liebig, S. and Krause, A. (2007): Arbeitsorganisationen als Kontexte der Einstellungsbildung. In: Hummell, H.J. (Ed.): Die Analyse von Gesellschaften, Organisationen und Individuen in ihrem Zusammenhang – Theoretische und methodische Herausforderungen. Tagungsberichte Band 13. Bonn.

Reimer, M. and Kuenster, R. (2004): Linking Job Episodes from Retrospective Surveys and Social Security Data: Specific Challenges, Feasibility and Quality of Outcome. Arbeitspapier Nr. 8 des Projekts Ausbildungs- und Berufsverläufe der Geburtskohorten 1964 und 1971 in Westdeutschland. Berlin.

Schnabel, C. (2006): Verbetrieblichung der Lohnfindung und der Festlegung von Arbeitsbedingungen. Arbeitspapier 118. Düsseldorf.

Smith, T.W./Kalleberg, A.L. and Marsden, P.V. (2004): National Organization Survey (NOS), 2002. Ann Arbor.

Tilly, Ch. (1998): Durable Inequality. Berkeley.

4.4 Organizational Data

Stefan Liebig

Contact:

Stefan Liebig
Bielefeld University
Faculty of Sociology
Postfach 10 01 31
33501 Bielefeld
Germany
e-mail: stefan.liebig[at] uni-bielefeld.de

Abstract

Organizational data describe central characteristics of organizations, their internal structures and processes as well as their behavior as corporate actors in different social and economic contexts. Firm and enterprise data are the most frequently used type of organizational data, but there is also a growing interest in data on schools, universities, and hospitals in the economic and social science research. In the last several years, there has been a substantial improvement in the accessibility and scientific usability of organizational data from official statistics. However, non-official organizational data produced within publicly funded research projects are practically impossible to obtain for secondary analyses. There is no documentation of the existing stock of non-official organizational data, and the methodological standards used for organizational research in Germany are low compared to the standards of international research. Against this background, it is recommended that efforts be focused on documenting and archiving the existing non-official organizational data for secondary analyses and on establishing higher methodological standards within this research field.

Keywords: firms, organizations, methods of organizational research, microdata, secondary analysis

1. Research questions

The most common form of organizational data used in economic and social research relates to firms as local production units, in which goods and services are produced, and to enterprises as the legal units of the private and public sector. The data describe central characteristics of these organizations, their internal structures and processes, as well as their behavior as corporate actors in different contexts. Besides these kinds of "classic" firm-level data, data referring to organizations within the educational system (nursery schools, schools, and universities) have recently also attracted attention in Germany (Klieme 2008). This interest has arisen in the context of an increasing awareness that the structures and processes existing on the school level – demographic composition of the school, quality of the cooperation among staff members – are important for individual educational success. Furthermore, an ongoing differentiation is being observed on the level of individual organizations within the German educational system, making it more important, for example, which university a person graduated from.

Each of the different disciplines focus on describing and explaining different structures and processes of organizations and their actions. The organizational research (business administration, sociology, psychology) is preoccupied with the structural characteristics of firms (degree of centralization, formalization, and standardization), the internal forms of organization of work, the design and practice of operational staff policy, the industrial relations or the reasons for growth and shrinking of firms. Moreover, organizational-level data offer the possibility to evaluate the effects of policy measures. In this case, the structural features of organizations and their behavior are the objects that are to be explained. The question here is how organizations react to changes in the legal, economic or social surroundings; in other words, which effects specific changes in the social, economic, and legal environment have on organizations. Vice versa, firm-level data can additionally be used for the explanation of other issues such as macro economic developments, job market dynamics, educational participation or the reproduction of social inequality. In this respect, external consequences of organizational behavior or their internal structures and their changes stand in the center of interest. In this context, organizations represent micro-level units that help to explain macro-level phenomena. Correspondingly, economic researchers have defined firm-level data thus far as microdata. Important questions are, for instance, the consequences of operative employment trends, apprenticeship and advanced training, productivity and investment in the different areas of interest to economic policy (see Wagner 2010). Topics of organization-centered education research are the relevant surroundings and arrangements of educational organizations, their composition with respect to their personnel (teachers) and clients (children, pupils, students), and the resulting effects on education performance, education participation, and social inequalities (see Klieme 2008; Garmoran et al. 2006; OECD 2005).

To answer these questions, information about organizations can be collected in two different ways: first, through primary data collection using reactive and non-reactive research methods. This can take the form of interviewing (reactive methods), in which information about the organization is gathered by persons inside or outside the organization using standardized (surveys) or non-standardized (case studies) questionnaires (Bryman 2000, Stablein 1999). In the framework of non-reactive methods, data on firm structures, processes, and behavior can be collected by making use of documents provided by the organization itself or archives in which data about organizations are stored. Second, organizational data can be collected by gathering information that accompany administrative processes. These "process-produced" administrative data arise either within organizations, e.g., in personnel administrations (see Brüderl et al. 1993), or outside organizations, e.g., in social security and tax administrations (see Wagner 2010). Currently, the most frequently used organizational data in Germany are survey data, qualitative case studies, and "process-produced" administrative data.

One of the major findings of organizational research is that organizations are not well coordinated units that follow strict and coherent bureaucratic principles (Hannan and Freeman 1977; Sørensen 2007). A number of organizational scholars hold the view that the complexity and diversity of organizations can solely be represented adequately on the basis of case studies with the aid of qualitative survey methods. As a result, the organizational research has given rise to a multitude of qualitative case studies. The use of qualitative methods and the concentration on case studies has long been a distinctive feature of the German organizational research by international comparison (see Grunow 1995). Case studies do in fact have an important heuristic function in the research process, yet they entail some major problems: due to the small number of cases, they cannot provide any generalized statements; inter-subjective validation of the findings is impossible; and they can have only limited significance for social and economic research, which is more oriented towards explaining and predicting phenomena (see Hauptmanns and Rogalski 1992). Accordingly, there is a need for quantitative firm-level data based on standardized survey methods that allow for utilization of econometric methods. At the same time, such datasets need to have a sufficiently large sample size: only on this basis can researchers conduct analyses on the level of economic sectors, sub-sectors, and regional units. Moreover, there is a need to adequately describe changes over time and to scrutinize causal explanatory models. Such questions can only be answered by analyzing longitudinal data. This is why panel data have taken a central role in organization-related social and economic research since the 1990s (Heckman 2001; Wagner 2008). Regarding the collection and provision of quantitative data on economic organizations in Germany, the situation since the 1980s has been as follows: most of the data outside official statistics were acquired by analyzing cross-sectional studies restricted to smaller, individual economic sectors, distinct types of enterprises, and single regions.[1] Only in the 1990s were a number of larger longitudinal firm-level datasets generated (e.g., the *NIFA-Panel),* which were then expanded to intersectoral and national scales (IAB Establishment Panel). Since that point, firm-level data from official statistics have been gradually made accessible to researchers (KVI 2001). However, only since 2001, with the creation of Research Data Centers, have these data found real applications in research. These conditions have not yet been achieved for data on organizations within the educational system (Stanat 2008).

Organizational data are only valuable for scientific purposes if data production is guided by methodological standards, and if the resulting fin-

---

[1] The only exceptions are the surveys within the framework of official statistics, the process-produced data of the Establishment History Panel (*Betriebs-Historik-Panel*) of the former Federal Employment Agency (*Bundesanstalt für Arbeit*), as well as a few individual studies, such as the IfO Business Survey.

dings can be reconstructed by other researchers and assessed on the basis of the data. The latter is only possible if data are made available in a broadly useable form. When it comes to methodological standards, most of the organizational research is concerned only with the quality of data analyses. But there is also the problem of data collection, which raises questions of survey methodology even in organizational research: the quality of data depends not only on the sample or the sampling procedures used, but also on the validity and reliability of the measures. In this respect one must ask: who in the organization provides the information on what basis? Does a question measure the same phenomenon in different sectors, sub-sectors, or firms?

The plea for making organizational data available is confronted by a fundamental problem of organizational research: with very little information, it is relatively easy to re-identify the firms and enterprises from which the data was collected (see Gottschalk 2002). Data collected on the basis of the compulsory duty-of-disclosure of official statistics, however, can only be made accessible if re-identification is impossible *(BStatG §16)*[2]. This does not apply to firm-level data, which are generated through voluntary participation. Nevertheless, anonymity is needed in order to convince firms to participate. The protection of participants' confidentiality prevents non-anonymous use of the data by a third party. However, in the last years, new methods and techniques have been developed that allow anonymization of firm-level data without diminishing its worth for scientific research (Drechsler et al 2007; Rosemann 2006; Wagner 2010).

2. Status quo

The organizational data used in social and economic research can be subdivided into three different groups: (1) data from commercial providers, (2) survey or "process-produced" administrative data from official statistics, and (3) data collected by research institutions or individual researchers.

(1) Currently, commercial firm-level data are available solely as enterprise data. The two most important databanks in Germany are the *Hoppenstedt-Firmendatenbank* and the *Creditreform-Firmenprofile*. Both contain a limited number of details (e.g., form of organization, sales figures, number of employees over the past years, contacts on top management level) about the enterprises as legal units. Therefore, they offer no information about the firms in terms of local units. Both suppliers exclude specific enterprise groups. *Creditreform*, for instance, rules out certain legal forms, *Hoppenstedt* excludes enterprises with an annual turnover below 1 million

---

[2] The citations to German legal sources have been left in German to guarantee accuracy.

euros or with less than 20 employees. The information is based on entries in commercial registries or on the suppliers' own research, in which case the entry is voluntary. An additional commercial dataset is *LexisNexis*, which collects information about enterprises thereby using different sources – *Hoppenstedt, Bundesanzeiger,* commercial registries, and press releases.

Besides the restricted information base for many scientific and applied questions, the problems of these data are that (1) data collection is not documented and not transparent, and (2) the enterprises listed do not necessarily constitute the respective universe. The access to data for researchers, however, is quite good, as the suppliers have specific and less expensive offers for scientific purposes. In addition, databanks are made available as a standard part of many universities' research resources. Moreover, there exists a range of other national, international, and comparative datasets on firm policies – also related to personnel policies – that are collected by private companies and consulting firms. They offer a broad range of information, but are in most of the cases not available for scientific use.

(2) Organizational data from official statistics are the firm and enterprise data collected by the Federal Statistical Office and the Statistical Offices of the German *Länder*, the Deutsche Bundesbank, and the Federal Employment Agency (BA, *Bundesagentur für Arbeit*). The data from the statistical offices are collected by legal order via surveys or are the result of administrative processes – e.g., reporting to the social security system or tax administration. The data are provided by the Research Data Centers of the Federal Statistical Office and the Statistical Offices of the German *Länder* via (1) Public Use Files with very restricted information, (2) Scientific Use Files, which are de facto anonymized,[3] (3) teleprocessing, and (4) on-site usage of the original data within the centers. The surveys are conducted separately for each economic sector, thereby producing different kinds of datasets that range from monthly figures and total surveys up to annual sample surveys (see: Brandt et al. 2007; Kaiser and Wagner 2008). Data on individual economic sectors (producing industry, trade, hotel industry, service sector) are accessible in the same way as other cross-sector surveys on wages and tax statistics.

Besides the data from the statistical offices, the BA offers two datasets: one of them is the Establishment Panel of the Institute for Employment Research (IAB, *Institut für Arbeitsmarkt- und Berufsforschung*), which is an annual, voluntary survey that offers information on 16,000 firms since the year 1993 (in East Germany: 1996). Of all the available official statistics, the IAB Establishment Panel offers the broadest scope of information. Quite recently, the Establishment History Panel has also been made available. As a "process-produced" administrative dataset, it aggregates information on

---

3 De facto anonymous data contain information that can only be traced back to the participant with time consuming and cost-intensive effort.

employees covered by the social security system in the period between 1975 and 2005 to the firm level, and creates a data stock with information on 1.5 to 2.5 million firms. Both datasets are accessible in the Research Data Center of the BA at the IAB for on-site use, and the Establishment Panel is also available via teleprocessing.

Due to the firms' legal duty of disclosure (which, however, does not apply to the IAB Establishment Panel), official organizational data are characterized by high participation rates – with even sensitive questions being answered thoroughly – and large sample sizes. This is why differentiated analyses are possible, even in small regional units. As most of the available microdata on establishment and firms are longitudinal panel data, it is possible to analyze processes of change and to test causal explanatory models (Brandt et al. 2007).

Data documentation and data access have been considerably improved in the last few years. In this context, the research project "De facto anonymization of business microdata" (Lenz et al. 2006) has played a decisive role here, by developing solutions to the anonymization problem. The follow-up project "business panel data and de facto anonymization" sets the ground for the expansion of available data (Scientific Use Files) through longitudinal panel data.

A central problem with organizational data from official statistics is that they only capture a small amount of information – mainly business and personnel statistics – which are useful only for specific fields of research in economics and the social sciences. Moreover, some of the surveys are restricted to single economic sectors. One possibility to resolve this problem is the inter-linkage of different datasets via the business register (which has been officially permitted since 2005). This is currently being investigated in the project Official Firm Data for Germany (*AFiD*, Konold 2007). The project Combined Firm Data for Germany (*KombiFiD,* Bender et al. 2007) even goes a step further by working on the linkage of data from the Federal Statistical Office, the Statistical Offices of the German *Länder*, and the Federal Employment Agency – which, however, is not yet legally permitted (see Wagner 2010). One central problem that has not yet been addressed by the ongoing projects is the quality of data collection (e.g., the problem of measurement error).

Data on organizations in the educational system – e.g., childcare facilities, schools, universities, as well as advanced training facilities – are collected by the Federal Statistical Office and the Statistical Offices of the German *Länder*, and are available on the micro-level at the respective Research Data Centers.

(3) Organizational data collected by research organizations or individual researchers generally have a smaller sample size. Since they are more strongly oriented towards substantive research questions, they contain more

information than the official data. In this regard, they offer a necessary extension of the official data sources, and they build the basis for organization-related research focusing more on the description and explanation of an organizational strategy, internal processes, industrial relations, etc. The relevant literature in this discipline shows that there exist a multitude of quantitative and qualitative (and in most cases cross-sectional) organizational studies, financed by public and private research organizations *(*e.g., DFG,[4] BMBF,[5] *VolkswagenStiftung, Hans-Böckler-Stiftung, Thyssen-Stiftung)*. However, in contrast to the official statistics, the existing data stock is not documented and the data are not available for secondary analyses.[6] Exemptions are only the data from Ifo Institute for Economic Research (Ifo Business Survey, Becker and Wohlrabe 2008), Centre for European Economic Research (ZEW, *Zentrum für Europäische Wirtschaftsforschung*) in Mannheim (datasets on innovation, business trends and the middle classes), the NIFA-Panel (Widmaier 2000), as well as the longitudinal firm-level data that have been collected since 2001 in the framework of *Sonderforschungsbereich 580* (SFB580-A2 manager survey and SFB580-B2 establishment panel, Krause and Martens 2008). Currently, only the NIFA-Panel is incorporated into the data catalog of the GESIS[7] Data Archive, Cologne. German firm and establishment data on working time and work-life balance are available as part of an international comparative survey conducted by the European Foundation for the Improvement of Living and Working Conditions (Eurofound). The data are archived and accessible at the Economic and Social Data Service (ESDS), UK.

One of the main reasons for the inadequate availability of organizational data for secondary analysis might be the problem of re-identification. This is especially true for qualitative organizational data. But it seems that researchers within the field of organizations have not yet noticed the progress regarding anonymization methods of firm-level data made by the abovementioned projects.[8]

Closely connected to restricted usage and lack of data documentation are central methodological deficits, which are visible in many research articles dealing with organizational data. First, in most of the cases publications relying on organizational data do not offer any methodological explanations regarding sample quality or data collection. In addition, the organizational data lack a well-documented, standard methodological set of measurement

---

4   German Research Foundation (*Deutsche Forschungsgemeinschaft*).
5   Federal Ministry for Education and Research (*Bundesministerium für Bildung und Forschung*).
6   According to the author's own research, even the funding institutions do not have detailed information about previously collected data and their availability.
7   Leibniz Institute for the Social Sciences (*Leibniz-Institut für Sozialwissenschaften*).
8   The qualitative interview data that were collected in Sonderforschungsbereich 580 are an exception.

instruments as it is common in survey research (see Statistisches Bundesamt 2004; Glöckner-Rist 2007). A strong need therefore exists to establish internationally comparable methodological standards and also for more research on organizational survey methodology, which concentrates on data collection methods, measurement errors, sampling, and unit- or item-non-response problems.

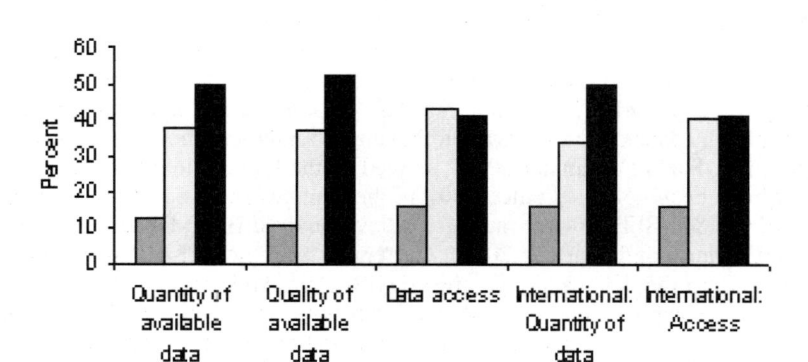

Figure 1: Results from an Expert Online Survey in Germany 2008.[9]

Notes: Relative Frequencies, Online Survey August/September 2008, N = 40.

The deficits in supply, methodological quality, and access – also in international comparison – have been articulated in an online survey among organizational researchers, which was conducted by the author and Alexia Meyermann in summer 2008. In this online survey, 50 percent of the participants assessed the data supply and the quality of content and methods as inadequate or insufficient. Forty percent criticized data access. A similar pattern can be found when looking at the numbers of participants who appraised the quantity of data and the access in international comparison. Overall, the researchers surveyed called for an improvement of the research situation. 74 percent of the researchers were prepared to make their data

---

9 The online survey was conducted by Stefan Liebig and Alexia Meyermann. A call for participation was sent via mailing lists to different sections of the German Sociological Association (Sociology of Work and Industrial Sociology, Economic Sociology), to the research group on empirical personnel and organizational research (*Arbeitskreis Empirische Personal- und Organisationsforschung*) and to the German Industrial Relations Association (GIRA) in August/September 2008. The survey homepage was visited by 121 people, of whom 40 completed the survey.

available for secondary analyses, but had not delivered them to a data archive so far due to the anonymization problem.

3. Future development

The future development of organizational research is characterized by an increasing demand for international comparative and longitudinal studies. This will be the only way to identify causal effects of the organizational level on macro-phenomena and vice versa. Especially under the conditions of an ongoing process of globalization, we will need this kind of data to study the relationship between macro-level economic processes and the behavior of organizations as corporate actors and their internal structures. Furthermore, European unification makes it necessary to broaden the narrow national perspective of organizational research. As the institutional conditions at the member state level are adjusted, we will need to investigate the accompanying restrictions and challenges for different organizations. For such international comparative and longitudinal organizational research, the implementation of methodological standards is necessary. At the same time, a broad base of information is decisive for the individual disciplines and for the evaluation of different policy measures. In the face of demographic changes and the debates on the work-life balance, not only personnel and business figures will be of interest but also the strategies and programs that are not covered by official statistics. Given the much higher obstacles to international comparative and standardized surveys, this will require the collection of non-official, comparative longitudinal organizational data. At the same time, the differentiation of the German educational system – which affects all levels – will increase the demand for a more detailed description of the internal structures and processes of nursery schools, schools, and universities (Klieme 2008).

All in all, the present progress in the field of official organizational data is positive. The improvements in data supply and data access are leading in the right direction. Further linkages among individual datasets and improved access – e.g., through remote access – have already been examined in different projects (see Wagner 2010). Furthermore, it will be essential not only to improve linkages within the official statistics, but to apply this same approach to the publicly and privately financed organizational surveys as well. While the official statistics offer exact longitudinal information on "hard" personnel and business figures, the advantage of non-official surveys can be seen in their thematic amplitude. Non-official organizational surveys can benefit from such linkages, since they do not bear the burden of data collection but can instead focus on specific research questions; initial efforts in this field are already underway (for more on this issue, see Reimer and Künster 2004).

However, the enhancement of the organizational data infrastructure in Germany will also lead to another, perhaps less obvious problem: for the production and use of organizational data, specific competencies are required that are only taught in academia to very low degree at present. Although organizational research also relies on the methods and techniques of general empirical social research, standardized organizational surveys pose specific challenges with regard to methodological issues. These include questions of how to draw the sample, develop the sampling instruments, and collect the data, and require knowledge of the respective statistical techniques. This implies that data producers should increasingly offer CAMPUS-Files for scientific education. Moreover, methodological training in organizational research should be professionalized and intensified.

4. Recommendations

Against this background, the following recommendations for improving the existing infrastructure of organizational data can be given:

(1) Documentation of existing non-official organizational data should be made easily accessible to interested researchers and enriched with detailed methodological information – at least including the publicly-funded data of the DFG, the BMBF, the Max Planck Society, and the Leibniz Association.

(2) Data producers from universities and publicly financed research institutes should be obliged to make the data they collect available for research. As with the social data on persons and households, these data should be centrally archived. This should be done not only for quantitative data but also for qualitative organizational data (e.g., it is currently done in Sonderforschungsbereich 580) as is the case within the Economic and Social Data Service (ESDS), UK.

(3) Research on organizational survey methods is urgently needed, as is enhanced academic training within the field of survey methods for organizational research.

(4) A network of projects should be established that deals with the implications of data protection laws, practical solutions to the linkage of official and non-official organizational data, and the promotion of analogous policy measures.

(5) The useable official statistics on organizational microdata should be enriched to include data on the educational system.

(6) In addition to existing Research Data Centers, a specific Data Service Center on firm and organizational data should be established. The task of such a center should not only be to document the existing data on organizations in Germany and archiving the data from non-official producers but also to offer expertise and service for researchers who are planning organizational studies and want to provide their data for secondary analyses. Such a center should work on developing solutions for the anonymization of quantitative and qualitative organizational survey data and boosting the establishment of and adherence to methodological standards in order to improve the quality of organizational data in Germany. Only by creating a center that is responsible for documenting, archiving, and providing a broad range of methodological services, can the gap be closed between German organizational research and the international standards and infrastructures that exist in other countries (e.g., the Data Archive in UK).

References:

Becker, S.O. and Wohlrabe, K. (2008): Micro data at the IfO Institute for economic research – The "IfO Business Survey" usage and access. Schmollers Jahrbuch 127, 307-319.
Bender, St./Fertig, M./Görlitz, K./Huber, M./Hummelsheim, St./Knerr, P./Schmucker, A. and Schröder, H. (2008): WeLL - Berufliche Weiterbildung als Bestandteil Lebenslangen Lernens: Projektbericht. FDZMethodenbericht 05/2008. Nuremberg.
Bender, St./Wagner, J. and Zwick, M. (2007): Kombinierte Firmendaten für Deutschland. FDZ Methodenreport 5/2007. Nuremberg.
Brandt, M./Oberschaltsiek, D. and Pohl, R. (2007): Neue Datenangebote in den Forschungsdatenzentren Betriebs- und Unternehmensdaten im Längsschnitt. FDZ-Arbeitspapier 23. Wiesbaden.
Brüderl, J./Preisendörfer, P. and Ziegler, R. (1993): Upward mobility in organizations. The effects of hierarchy and opportunity structure. European Sociological Review, (9), 173-188.
Bryman, A. (2000): Research Methods and Organization Studies. London.
Drechsler, J./Dundler, A./Bender, St./Rässler, S. and Zwick, Th. (2007): A New Approach for Disclosure Control in the IAB Establishment Panel. Multiple Imputation for a Better Data Access. IAB-DiscussionPaper 11/2007. Nuremberg.
Gamoran, A./Secada, W. and Marret, C. (2006): The Organizational Context of Teaching and Learning. In: Hallinan, M.T. (Ed.): Handbook of the Sociology of Education.
Glöckner-Rist, A. (Ed.) (2007): ZUMA-Informationssystem. Elektronisches Handbuch sozialwissenschaftlicher Erhebungsinstrumente. Version 11.00. Bonn.
Gottschalk, S. (2002): Anonymisierung von Unternehmensdaten: En Überblick und beispielhafte Darstellung anhand des Mannheimer Innovationspanels. ZEW Discussion Papers 02-23.
Grunow, D. (1995): Research Design in Organization Studies. Organization Science, (6), 93-103.
Hannan, M. T., and Freeman, J. (1977). The population ecology of organizations. American Journal of Sociology, (82), 929-964.
Hauptmanns, P. and Rogalski, W. (1992): Fallstudien in der Industriesoziologie – Zur Kritik der vorherrschenden Methode sozialwissenschaftlicher Technikforschung. In: Lehner, F. and Schmid, J. (Ed.): Technik – Arbeit – Betrieb – Gesellschaft. Neue Informationstechnologien und flexible Arbeitssysteme Bd. 1. Opladen.
Heckman, J.J. (2001): Micro Data, heterogeneity, and the evaluation of public policy: Nobel lecture. Journal of Political Economy, (109), 673-748.
http://www.ratswd.de/kswd/download/4_KSWD_Klieme.pdf. [Last visited 09/20/2008].
Kaiser, U. and Wagner, J. (2008): Neue Möglichkeiten zur Nutzung vertraulicher amtlicher Personen- und Firmendaten. Perspektiven der Wirtschaftspolitik 9, 329-349.
Klieme, E. (2008): Längsschnittuntersuchungen zur Schulentwicklung. Vortrag auf der 4. Konferenz für Sozial- und Wirtschaftsdaten.

Kommission zur Verbesserung der informationellen Infrastruktur zwischen Wissenschaft und Statistik (KVI) (Ed.) (2001): Wege zu einer besseren informationellen Infrastruktur. Baden-Baden.

Konold, M. (2007): New possibilities for economic research through integration of establishment-level panel data of German official statistics. Schmollers Jahrbuch 127, 321-334.

Konsortium Bildungsberichterstattung (2006): Zur langfristigen Sicherstellung der Datenbasis für die Bildungsberichterstattung. Frankfurt am Main.

Krause, I. and Martens, B. (2008): Wann lohnt sich die Akquisition nicht mehr? Antworten auf der Basis von Erfahrungen mit telefonischen Expertenbefragungen im Paneldesign. In: Martens, B. and Ritter, Th. (Ed.): Eliten am Telefon. Baden-Baden.

Lenz, R./Rosemann, M./Vorgrimler, D. and Sturm, R. (2006): Anonymising business micro data – results of a German project. Schmollers Jahrbuch 126, 635-651.

OECD (2005): Chapter 3: The relative impact of school climate, school policies and school resources on quality and equity. In: OECD (Ed.): School factors related to quality and equity. Results from PISA 2000.

Reimer, M. and Künster, R. (2004): Linking Job Episodes from Retrospective Surveys and Social Security Data: Specific Challenges, Feasibility and Quality of Outcome. Arbeitspapier Nr. 8 des Projekts Ausbildungs- und Berufsverläufe der Geburtskohorten 1964 und 1971 in Westdeutschland. Berlin.

Rosemann, M. (2006): Auswirkungen datenverändernder Anonymisierungsverfahren auf die Analyse von Mikrodaten. Tübingen.

Sørensen, J.B. (2007): Organizational diversity, labor markets, and wage inequality. American Behavioral Scientist, (50), 659-676.

Stablein, R. (1999): Data in Organization Studies. In: Clegg, St.R. and Hardy, C. (Ed.): Studying Organization. Theory & Method, 255-271.

Stanat, P. (2008): Daten der Bildungsforschung: Aktueller Stand und neue Entwicklungen. Vortrag auf der 4. Konferenz für Sozial- und Wirtschaftsdaten am 19. Juni in Wiesbaden.

Statistisches Bundesamt (2004): Demographische Standards. Wiesbaden.

Wagner, J. (2000): Firm Panel Data from German Official Statistics. Schmollers Jahrbuch 120, 143-150.

Wagner, J. (2008): Improvements and Future Challenges for the Research Infrastructure in the Field Firm Level Data. Working Paper Series in Economics No. 88. Universität Lüneburg.

Wagner, J. (2010): Firm Level Data. [In this publication].

Widmaier, U. (2000): Das NIFA-Panel und der deutsche Maschinen- und Anlagenbau. In: Widmaier, U. (Ed.): Der deutsche Maschinenbau in den neunziger Jahren. Kontinuität und Wandel einer Branche. Frankfurt am Main.

Zwick, M. (2007): CAMPUS Files. Free public use files for teaching purposes. Schmollers Jahrbuch 127, 655-668.

4.5 Firm-Level Data

Joachim Wagner

Contact:

Joachim Wagner
Leuphana University Lueneburg
Institute of Economics
PO Box 2440
21314 Lueneburg
Germany
email: wagner[at]leuphana.de

Abstract

This article discusses the use of enterprise- and establishment-level data from official statistics to document stylized facts, motivate assumptions used in formal theoretical models, test hypotheses derived from theoretical models, and evaluate policy measures. It shows how these data can be accessed by researchers in Germany today and reports on recent developments that will offer new and improved datasets that combine data collected in separate surveys and by different agencies. The paper makes three recommendations for future developments in this area: (1) change the law to make the combination of data collected by different producers easier, (2) combine firm-level data across national borders and make these data available for researchers, and (3) find ways to enable researchers in Germany to work with confidential firm-level data via remote access 24 hours a day and 365 days per year.

Keywords: firm-level data, Germany, FiDASt, KombiFiD, AFiD

1. What are firm-level data?

Firm-level data are data collected at, or related to local production units (establishments) or legal units (enterprises). The technical term used to describe this kind of data in official statistics is *wirtschaftsstatistische Einzeldaten*, or microdata for production units. This kind of data can either be collected in a survey (administered by a statistical office or by other institutions such as an opinion research institute or by a researcher at a university), or produced during a process that is related to administrative issues (for example, collection of taxes on sales or reporting to the social security system), resulting in what is named process-produced data.[1]

Usually, firm-level data are confidential – either by law (if they are collected in surveys from official statistics or are the outcome of administrative processes) or by an agreement between the (private, non-governmental) collector of the data and the firms that delivered the data. The reasons for confidentiality are manifold, including the fact that information delivered by firms that are required to report to surveys administered by official statistics has to be protected against competitors, and also that firms usually are only willing to respond to a survey voluntarily if they can be sure that any information considered to be "sensitive" will not be disseminated.

Confidentiality of firm-level data is a crucial issue for researchers who want to use microdata for production units in scientific studies. Although researchers are not at all interested in any of the establishments or enterprises

---

1   For a discussion of other organizational data (for example, data for organizations within the educational system) and publicly funded non-official organizational data collected by researchers, see the contribution by Stefan Liebig (2009).

per se, they need to access the data at the micro-level to perform their statistical analyses and econometric estimations and thereby to uncover patterns of firm behavior and test theoretical hypotheses. This paper discusses issues related to the use of confidential firm-level data by independent researchers (i.e., those who are not working for the data producers). It begins with a review of what firm-level data are good for (in section 2), who produces firm-level data in Germany, and how researchers can gain access to these data today (in section 3). In section 4, new and ongoing developments that are currently leading to new products are discussed – new types of firm-level data will considerably enhance the research potential available to researchers in the near future. Section 5 concludes with a wish list.

2. What are firm-level data good for?

Researchers use firm-level data in a wide range of areas in economics for four (not mutually exclusive) tasks, namely

- to document stylized facts that cannot be uncovered by looking at aggregate data for industries or regions,
- to motivate assumptions used in formal theoretical models,
- to test hypotheses derived from theoretical models, and
- to evaluate policy measures.

The following three examples from different areas of economics – firm demography, job creation and destruction, and international firm activities – illustrate the need for, and the research potential of, the use of firm-level data:

(1) Hopenhayn (1992) considers long run equilibrium in an industry with many price-taking firms producing a homogeneous good. Output is a function of inputs and a random variable that models a firm-specific productivity shock. These shocks are independent across firms and are the reason for the heterogeneity of firms. There are sunk costs to be paid upon entry and entrants do not know their specific shock in advance. Incumbents can choose between exiting or staying in the market. The model leads to three testable hypotheses, namely that firms that exit in year t were less productive at time t-1 than firms that continue to produce in t; that firms that enter in year t are less productive than incumbent firms in year t; and that surviving firms from an entry cohort were more productive than non-surviving firms from this cohort in the start year. Wagner (2007a) uses a panel dataset for all manufacturing plants from

Germany (1995-2002) to test these hypotheses econometrically, and finds that all three hypotheses are supported empirically.

(2) It is often argued that in Germany jobs are mostly created in small- and medium-sized firms, while large firms generally tend to destroy jobs. The *Mittelstand*, or middle class, is considered the engine of job creation. Using panel data for manufacturing firms, Wagner (2007b) demonstrates that this simple view is wrong. Growing and shrinking firms, entries and exits can all be found in substantial amounts in all size classes within each time period considered. Economic policy measures with a special focus on firms from different size classes, therefore, cannot be justified by pointing to an extraordinary large contribution of these firms to job creation.

(3) A large number of empirical studies for many countries (surveyed in Wagner 2007c) demonstrate that exporting firms are more productive than non-exporting firms of the same size from the same narrowly defined industry. This stylized fact motivated Melitz (2003) to set aside the standard assumption of homogeneous firms and to develop a model with heterogeneous firms where only the more productive firms in an industry export. This model has become the workhorse of a flourishing body of literature dealing with international firm activities. Using unique, recently released, and nationally representative high-quality longitudinal data at the plant level, Wagner (2007d) presents the first comprehensive evidence on the relationship between exports and productivity for Germany, a leading actor on the world market for manufactured goods. He documents that the positive productivity differential of exporters compared to non-exporters is statistically significant and substantial, even when observed firm characteristics and unobserved firm specific effects are controlled for.

All three examples demonstrate that using firm-level data is not only useful but indispensable for both sound empirical research (including the evaluation of policy measures and the derivation of policy recommendations) and crafting theoretical models that are relevant outside academic journals. In his Nobel lecture, James Heckman (2001, 674) named "the evidence on the pervasiveness of heterogeneity and diversity in economic life" the most important empirical discovery from econometric analyses using microdata. Everybody who ever worked with plant- or enterprise-level data will agree – there is no such thing as a representative firm, not even in 4-digit industries. We would not know this, and would be unable to base our theoretical models and the policy implications derived from these models on this knowledge if firm-level data was not accessible to researchers. Fortunately, such access is possible, as the next section discusses in greater detail.

3. Who produces firm-level data, and how can they be accessed by researchers today?

In Germany, the data for establishments and enterprises are collected or constructed by a number of institutions. The most important among them include:

- the Federal Statistical Office (Destatis, *Statistisches Bundesamt*) and the Statistical Offices of the German *Länder* (*Statistische Ämter der Länder*), which administer a large number of surveys as well as secondary statistics;

- the Federal Employment Agency (BA, *Bundesagentur für Arbeit*) and its research institute, the Institute for Employment Research (IAB, *Institut für Arbeitsmarkt- und Berufsforschung*), which uses information on employees covered by social security to construct establishment-level information on the number of employees and their average characteristics, as well as collects information on a wide range of issues for a panel of establishments in annual surveys for the IAB Establishment Panel;

- the Deutsche Bundesbank has a database with information from balance sheets and data on the foreign direct investments of German firms.

Furthermore, firm-level data are collected on a large scale by research institutes (including the Ifo Institute for Economic Research in Munich and the Center for European Economic Research in Mannheim) and by the KfW (*Kreditanstalt für Wiederaufbau*), a bank that is closely related to the German state.

It should be noted that some of these firm-level data include information on the employees working in firms, leading to what is named Linked Employer-Employee (LEE) data. LEE data for Germany are the salary and wage structure surveys (*Gehalts- und Lohnstrukturerhebungen*) from official statistics, and the LIAB, which combines information from the IAB Establishment Panel with employee information from social insurance records.

More information on the firm-level data for Germany, and references to papers describing their information content, are given in Kaiser and Wagner (2008).

In the past, some of the data producers provided access to confidential firm-level data for researchers on the basis of individual contracts and contacts. For example, various statistical offices of the *Länder* allowed researchers to work with firm-level data either via remote data access (i.e., by sending programs to the office, checking their output for violation of data protection rules, and then sending them to the researchers) or by giving them a special status as an unpaid employee, making it feasible for researchers to work with the microdata inside the office in strictly accordance with all relevant data protection rules. Projects that pursued this type of access formed the network FiDASt – an acronym for Firm-Level Data from Official Statistics (*FirmenDaten aus der Amtlichen Statistik*). Results from these projects are documented in various contributions to professional journals and in three workshop volumes (see Schasse and Wagner 1999; 2001; Pohl et al. 2003). Furthermore, the IAB offered researchers the option of using the data from the IAB Establishment Panel via remote data access and the so-called *Schalterstelle*, a contact person in charge of running the programs and checking the output afterwards (see Kölling 2000).

In recent years, following the suggestions of the German Commission on Improving the Information Infrastructure between Science and Statistics (KVI, *Kommission zur Verbesserung der informationellen Infrastruktur zwischen Wissenschaft und Statistik*), most of the important producers of firm-level data – including the Federal Statistical Office and the Statistical Offices of the German *Länder*, the IAB, and the Deutsche Bundesbank – established Research Data Centers that offer researchers convenient ways to work with confidential data via remote data access or by working in-house (see Zühlke et al. 2004; Kohlmann 2005; Lipponer 2003). Furthermore, Scientific Use Files (SUFs) were produced for several datasets that can be used by researchers on their own PCs in the office, as well as Public Use Files (PUFs), which can be used by anybody, including students during courses (see Zwick 2007). Other data producers (like the KfW) offer researchers the opportunity to use the confidential firm-level data in joint projects with employees of the producers, including access to the data while working in-house. A survey of who offers what to whom, and how, is given in Kaiser and Wagner (2008).

Most recently, further progress on the way to a less restrictive access to confidential data was made by locating a Research Data Center outside the data producing institution and inside the institution where the researchers are. The Statistical Office of Berlin and Brandenburg opened a Research Data Center in the building of the German Institute for Economic Research (DIW, *Deutsches Institut für Wirtschaftsforschung*), making the work with the microdata from German official statistics much more convenient for DIW researchers (and for researchers working in the universities nearby).

Compared to twenty, ten, or even five years ago, things have improved a great deal for researchers with regard to access to confidential microdata for establishments and enterprises. As the next section will demonstrate, there is more to come.

4. What will the near future bring? New products in the pipeline

Compared to firm-level data collected by research institutes, data from official surveys have several advantages: they often cover the whole population of targeted firms (not merely a small sample) and the firms are required to answer and answer correctly (there are no missing cases, no missing values, and – it is to be hoped – no wrong answers). Furthermore, the surveys are usually repeated periodically, and the data from various waves can be combined to build panel datasets. The extra costs associated with preparing data from official surveys for scientific research are not zero, but they are only a tiny fraction of what it would cost to collect data in a new survey. That said, there is one disadvantage of these data from official statistics. Usually, they cover only a small number of items, often fixed by law. This leads to severe limitations with regard to the potential use of these data for scientific analyses.

A promising way to increase the research potential of data from the surveys of official statistics would be to combine the information collected for a unit (enterprise or establishment) in different surveys. This is technically feasible if each unit has a unique identifier (a unit number) that is used in different surveys. Fortunately, this is the case with firms surveyed by the Federal Statistical Office and the Statistical Offices of the German *Länder*. Given that the law allows for matching data from various surveys administered by statistical offices, combined information from these surveys can be used in a single empirical investigation. The following example illustrates how such combinations can increase the research potential of firm-level data from official statistics.

Cost structure surveys collect information on, among other things, turnover and various categories of costs. From these data a rate of return can be computed to proxy the profit situation of the firm. How is this rate of return related to export activities of the firm? This question cannot be answered using these data alone, because no information on exports is collected in the cost structure surveys. Information on exports, however, is available in another survey – a report covering the activities of manufacturing firms, which does not, however, contain any information itself about the profit situation of the firm. Combining data from these two different surveys leads to a dataset that makes it possible to investigate the role of exports for profitability (see Fryges and Wagner 2008).

Matched data from surveys collected by the statistical offices have been used in a number of studies recently. The datasets for these studies have been tailor-made by the Research Data Centers to suit the purposes of each respective study. This is both expensive and time consuming. In the AFiD project (where AFiD is an acronym for *Amtliche Firmendaten für Deutschland*, or Official Firm-Level Data for Germany) several standardized datasets are prepared that are combinations of data from various surveys (for details see Malchin and Voshage 2009). These combined data are available to researchers via the Research Data Centers of the statistical offices.

Datasets from the AFiD project will offer a convenient way for researchers to investigate questions that could not be answered using data from only one survey. Furthermore, the content of datasets prepared in the AFiD project can be enhanced by adding information from other sources. On the one hand, it is both technically feasible and legal to add data collected in special purpose surveys that are administered by the statistical offices only once. A case in point is the survey on international outsourcing activities of firms recently performed by the German Federal Statistical Office (Statistisches Bundesamt 2008). The data from this survey have a limited amount of information, yet combined with all the other data for firms from the AFiD project, these data offer the opportunity for exciting empirical research on various topics related to the determinants and consequences of international outsourcing. Note that the extra costs of adding these data to the datasets already available are negligible. On the other hand, in accordance with the law, and given that it is technically feasible, data from publicly available sources can be matched with the AFiD data to further enhance the information content of these datasets. To give an example, information about patents granted to the firms can be added. Augmented datasets of this type – or what might be labeled AFiD*plus* data – will offer attractive opportunities for empirical investigations in innovative fields.

While combining information available for a single firm from various surveys done by official statistics (in addition to publicly available information from other sources) in the AFiD project is an attractive way to build new, rich datasets that are worth much more than the sum of their parts to a researcher, even more attractive datasets can be constructed when confidential firm-level microdata from the vaults of different data producers are matched on top of that. To give an example, information on the foreign direct investments of firms is not available from any survey done by the statistical offices, but rather from balance sheet data processed by the Deutsche Bundesbank. Combining AFiD data with the data for foreign direct investments leads to a dataset that makes it possible to investigate problems highly relevant for both scientific analysis and policy debates, including the consequences of foreign direct investments for jobs and wages in Germany.

Due to the sometimes tricky problems related to the definition of economic units, and the different identifiers used for firms by different data producers, this matching can be technically demanding. Furthermore, this is only legally allowed (in Germany in 2008) if each firm explicitly declares in a written statement which of the data it delivers to the different data producers can be used for the matching. This sets the benchmark fairly high for any project trying to observe this procedure. Recently, the German Federal Ministry of Education and Research (BMBF, *Bundesministerium für Bildung und Forschung*) funded the research project KombiFiD (an acronym for *Kombinierte Firmendaten für Deutschland*, or Combined Firm Data for Germany), a feasibility study in which a large number of firms are asked to agree to match their data and in which the technical problems of matching data across the boundaries of data producers are examined. The data from this feasibility study will be available at the Research Data Centers of the data producers involved in KombiFiD – hopefully beginning in the summer of 2009. More information and up-to-date news on the project can be found at the website: *www.kombifid.de*.

5. A "firm-panelholic's" wish-list

Even considering all the recent progress that has been made in the way that firm-level data are prepared and made available for the use of independent researchers, and even with all the datasets currently under construction in the projects described above, there are still several wishes left unfulfilled. If a good fairy granted me three wishes related to firm-level data, I would ask for:

(1) A change in German law allowing the matching of microdata for firms across the boundaries of data producers without requiring written consent from the firms. The reason for this wish is obvious from the discussion presented in section 4.

(2) Finding ways to combine firm panel data across national borders, and to give researchers access to these data (see the International Public Use Microdata Series Project[2] that collects census data for persons and households from all over the world for a role model dealing with individual level data). The main reason for this wish is the observation that we live in a time of increasing globalization. If the objects of our analysis – the firms – become more and more international, often controlling or being controlled by firms in other countries, the data we use should enable us to learn about the causes and consequences of their behavior by allowing access to micro-level data for all units connected to a firm, legally or otherwise, irrespective of the country these units are located in.

---

2   www.ipums.org/international.

(3) Finding ways to enable researchers in Germany to work with firm-level microdata via remote access, available 24 hours a day and 365 days per year, rather than requiring them to send programs to the Research Data Centers or to go there in person (see Hundepool and de Wolf (2005) for a description of a pilot project at Statistics Netherlands). The reason for this wish is obvious to any researcher familiar with the conventional ways of working with confidential firm-level data: while it is possible to work using the current means of access, and it is infinitely better to have this opportunity than not to have any opportunity at all – it remains a second-best solution. Time for research is the ultimate constraint faced by researchers and the means of access available today are extremely time consuming. (As an aside, I would like to add that the SUFs that can be used on the researchers' own PC are in my view no solution when it comes to firm-level data; see Wagner 2005.) While the space limitations for this report make it impossible to go into detail on this point, the example of Denmark (described in Kaiser and Wagner 2008) clearly demonstrates how such an "easy access" policy can be implemented. Based on an approved research proposal, researchers in Denmark can access the data on the mainframe computers in Statistics Denmark from their office PCs, with extremely high penalties for any misuse. Not that long ago, the Kingdom of Denmark began in what is today the northern part of Hamburg, some 40 kilometers north from my office at the Leuphana. Given the high price of beer in Denmark I am not sure that I would wish this still to be the case – yet when I look at the ease of access to all kinds of confidential microdata that my colleagues at Danish universities enjoy, I do feel some regret. So, at the end of the day, I do wish that we would start to learn from the Danish experience.

References:

Fryges, H. and Wagner, J. (2008): Exports and profitability – First evidence for German manufacturing firms. [Unpublished manuscript].

Heckman, J.J. (2001): Micro Data, heterogeneity, and the evaluation of public policy: Nobel lecture. Journal of Political Economy 109 (4), 673-748.

Hopenhayn, H. (1992): Entry, exit, and firm dynamics in long run equilibrium. Econometrica 60 (5), 1127-1150.

Hundepool, A. and de Wolf, P.-P. (2005): OnSite@Home: Remote Access at Statistics Netherlands. [Unpublished manuscript].

Kaiser, U. and Wagner, J. (2008): Neue Möglichkeiten zur Nutzung vertraulicher amtlicher Personen- und Firmendaten. Perspektiven der Wirtschaftspolitik 9 (3), 329-349.

Kölling, A. (2000): The IAB-Establishment Panel. Schmollers Jahrbuch 120 (2), 291-300.

Kohlmann, A. (2005): The Research Data Center of the Federal Employment Service in the Institute for Employment Research. Schmollers Jahrbuch 125 (3), 437-447.

Kommission zur Verbesserung der informationellen Infrastruktur zwischen Wissenschaft und Statistik (KVI) (Ed.) (2001): Wege zu einer besseren informationellen Infrastruktur. Baden-Baden.

Liebig, S. (2009): Organizational Data. RatSWD Working Paper No. 67.

Lipponer, A. (2003): Deutsche Bundesbank's FDI micro database. Schmollers Jahrbuch 123 (4), 593-600.

Malchin, A. and Voshage, R. (2009): Official Firm Data for Germany. Schmollers Jahrbuch 129 (3), 501-513.

Melitz, M.J. (2003): The impact of trade on intra-industry reallocations and aggregate industry productivity. Econometrica 71 (6), 1695-1725.

Pohl, R./Fischer, J./Rockmann, U. and Semlinger, K. (Eds.) (2003): Analysen zur regionalen Industrieentwicklung. Sonderauswertungen einzelbetrieblicher Daten der Amtlichen Statistik. Berlin.

Schasse, U. and Wagner, J. (Eds.) (1999): Entwicklung von Arbeitsplätzen, Exporten und Produktivität im interregionalen Vergleich – Empirische Untersuchungen mit Betriebspaneldaten. Hannover.

Schasse, U. and Wagner, J. (Eds.) (2001): Regionale Wirtschaftsanalysen mit Betriebspaneldaten – Ansätze und Ergebnisse. Hannover.

Statistisches Bundesamt (2008): Verlagerung wirtschaftlicher Aktivitäten. Erste Ergebnisse. Wiesbaden.

Wagner, J. (2005): Anonymized firm data under test: Evidence from a replication study. Jahrbücher für Nationalökonomie und Statistik 225 (5), 584-591.

Wagner, J. (2007a): Entry, exit and productivity. Empirical results for German manufacturing industries. University of Lüneburg Working Paper Series in Economics 44, March.

Wagner, J. (2007b): Jobmotor Mittelstand? Arbeitsplatzdynamik und Betriebsgröße in der westdeutschen Industrie. Vierteljahrshefte zur Wirtschaftsforschung 76 (3), 76-87.

Wagner, J. (2007c): Exports and productivity: A survey of the evidence from firm-level data. The World Economy 30 (1), 60-82.

Wagner, J. (2007d): Exports and productivity in Germany. Applied Economics Quarterly 53 (4), 353-373.

Zühlke, S./Zwick, M./Scharnhorst, S. and Wende, Th. (2004): The research data centers of the Federal Statistical Office and the statistical offices of the Länder. Schmollers Jahrbuch 124 (4), 567-578.

Zwick, M. (2007): CAMPUS files – Free public use files for teaching purposes. Schmollers Jahrbuch 127 (4), 655-668.

5. STATE, FAMILY, AND HEALTH

5.1 Public Finance

Thiess Büttner[*]

---

[*] The author is grateful to U. Rehfeld for helpful comments on an earlier draft. All errors remain the author's responsibility. The support of the German Data Forum (RatSWD) is gratefully acknowledged.

Contact:

Thiess Büttner
Ifo Institute for Economic Research
Poschingerstr. 5
81679 Munich
Germany
e-mail: buettner[at]ifo.de

Abstract

This paper briefly surveys the available data sources relevant to the empirical study of public finance in Germany and discusses future developments. It starts from the notion that public finance deals with decisions made by diverse agents, not only by different levels of government but also private households and firms. As a result empirical research requires different types of data. Budgetary statistics capture government decisions to some extent, although these statistics have shortcomings related to the quality of public service provisions and the revenue instruments. In order to study the decisions made by the other agents, individual-level data is also required. While there has been some recent progress in this direction, the combination of various datasets at the individual level is a key priority.

Keywords: empirical research, public finance, budgetary statistics, revenue statistics, micro-level data, taxpayer data

1. Research questions

Public finance is an area concerned with decisions made by collective agents and institutions with the impact of those decisions bearing on the economy and individual agents. This definition implies that, depending on the specific topic being researched, disparate types of data are used and may have to be combined.

Empirical research on public finance traditionally addresses the decision making of the public sector itself. This includes the substantial efforts that have been undertaken to monitor developments in the public sector in terms of the budget as well as with regard to service provision and inputs. In most countries the public sector shows a marked vertical and horizontal structure such that research addresses all levels of government including national and federal governments, state governments, and local governments, as well as separate bodies such as school districts and public enterprises.

With regard to policy areas, research on public finance tends to take a comprehensive view. In areas where policy implementation takes specific forms and includes private institutions, the research has developed into autonomous subfields. This includes areas such as Health and Education. While some research in these areas has close connections to public finance in the general sense, this paper will not discuss these specialized areas of empirical research infrastructure.

A significant part of empirical research in public finance focuses on the impact of instruments of public policy on the economy – including taxes and various types of government spending such as subsidies and transfers. A particular focus is on the impact of those instruments on individual agents, such as households and firms. This usually requires data about individual agents. At the same time, however, the study of long-term implications of policies requires not only cross-sectional, but also longitudinal data.

Due to its intrinsic complexity, research on taxation is often concerned with simulating rather than testing for tax effects. The corresponding simulation models need detailed information about the various components of the tax accounts and, hence, are ideally based on micro-level data for taxpayers.

Given the large share of resources expended by the public sector, empirical research is also concerned with the macroeconomic consequences of fiscal policies at an aggregate level such as the national, regional, or state levels. There is also empirical research that aims to provide a comprehensive picture of the economic consequences of government policies using general-equilibrium simulation models. These models require detailed information not only about the public sector but also about household and firm sectors and may also utilize input-output tables. Moreover, these models usually employ various parameters that originate in previous empirical research.

Empirical research on public finance, however, must not only concern itself with different types of agents, it also faces specific measurement problems with regard to government decisions and policies. Often, research is concerned with data on government spending or revenues. However, in many circumstances empirical research benefits from using more detailed information on specific government policies. This is particularly applicable in the context of taxation where the relevant policies are concerned with determining very specific parameters such as statutory tax rates, tax brackets, or tax incentives. Generally, a detailed knowledge of the law and its implementation is required. Measurement issues are also important with regard to the supply side of the public sector where the use of expenditure data is often not sufficient to capture government policies if the analysis is concerned with public service provision. As quantity and quality of public service provision are difficult to capture, research often must resort to using survey data where respondents assess the supply of public services.

2. Status quo: Databases and access

Given the various types of research questions, a useful way to structure a discussion of databases is to distinguish the agents whose decisions are under consideration as well as the type of policy under consideration such as taxes, public service provision, or social policies.

2.1 Data on governments

The basic data source for empirical research are the fiscal accounts that capture expenditures and revenues, as well as information on stocks such as government debt or assets. With regard to Germany, the Federal Statistical Office and the Statistical Offices of the German *Länder* offer a broad set of detailed data covering public spending, detailed by types of expenditure and categories of revenue. These statistics refer to the various fiscal tiers (federal, state, county, and municipality) and some important parafisci (para-fiscal organizations), such as social insurance. Quarterly data are provided about three months after the end of the respective quarter. Detailed data on government functions are based on the annual accounts available about two years after the respective year. Budget information is augmented by aggregate tax revenue statistics that report revenue pertaining to specific taxes. The standard set of statistics also includes information about the stocks of debt. The monitoring of government activities by the statistical offices further includes information about employment in the public sector. Finally, information about the annual accounts of state-owned enterprises is also available.

Data access is easy for federal- and state-level data as well as for the consolidated budget of the public sector: in all cases information is available on the website of the Federal Statistical Office. However, with regard to the state level, not all statistics are provided as part of the standard program. For instance, detailed data regarding both the type of expenditure and the function of government require separate requests. While a virtue of the German system of fiscal federalism is that the fiscal classification used for counties and municipalities is almost identical across the German states, or *Länder*, detailed data on government below the state level are only available for individual states subject to the approval of the Statistical Office in that respective state.[1]

Given the large share of public expenditure allocated to social welfare, several statistics of the statistical offices focus on specific programs, and the Federal Ministry of Labor and Social Affairs (BMAS, *Bundesministerium für Arbeit und Soziales*) provides even more comprehensive statistics (*Sozialbudget*).

Government statistical offices hold individual tax files for several major taxes that provide more detailed information and are made available for research as Scientific Use Files. Combination into panel data is possible if based on tax identifiers. However, with most other taxes the data are triennial starting with 1992 or 1995. Data access is restricted to the Research Data Centers at the national and state level and may be further restricted by remote processing of routines.

---

1   An exception is a study by Borck et al. (2007), which uses a comprehensive dataset for all German municipalities.

While the fiscal variables refer to the executive branch of the government, information about the legislature is also provided by the statistical offices. At the website *http://www.bundeswahlleiter.de*, detailed data on the results of federal, state, and local elections can be downloaded. Information about annual and medium-term budget planning is provided through the Federal Ministry of Finance (BMF, *Bundesministerium der Finanzen*) or through the Finance Ministries of the German *Länder* (*Finanzministerien der Länder*). Data on auditing is available for the federal and the state level only. Results from the auditing of lower-level governments are generally not available.

With regard to quantity and quality of public services provided by the various governments, the data supplied by the statistical offices are rather limited. Specific statistics exist for some functions of government. For instance, statistics on higher education provide data on enrollment at universities and the universities of applied sciences (*Fachhochschulen*) according to university and field of study and include additional information about the background of students. However student test scores as assembled in the OECD's PISA initiative are not provided at the state level in a way that allows meaningful cross-state comparisons. Since education is the key responsibility of the state governments in Germany, this restriction is a severe limitation for empirical research in Germany.

At the municipal level, the *Statistical Yearbook of German Communes* (edited by the German Association of Cities) provides some further information on the supply of government services, however, this data focuses on larger cities. Research that is concerned with the supply of public services at the local level might need to resort to survey data, where, however, the number of respondents is often small. An exception is the "Perspektive Deutschland" where waves four (2004/2005) and five (2005/2006) provide survey responses for several aspects of local living conditions including public services at county level. Data access is provided through the GESIS[2] Data Archive in Cologne.

2.2 Household data

An important part of empirical research in public finance is concerned with the impact of public policies on household decisions such as consumption, labor supply, or location. For this purpose, all sorts of household data are used such as the German Socio-Economic Panel (SOEP, *Sozio-oekonomisches Panel*), Mikrocensus, or the Income and Consumption Survey (EVS, *Einkommens- und Verbrauchsstichprobe*). The latter is particularly interes-

---

[2] Leibniz Institute for the Social Sciences (GESIS, *Leibniz-Institut für Sozialwissenschaften*).

ting as it offers some direct information about taxes paid whereas the SOEP employs imputed values (Becker et al. 2002).

Given the importance of the specific institutional details of the tax code, research often uses taxpayer panels (see below) even if these have limited information about household characteristics. This includes the *IAW-Einkommensteuerpanel* (Gottfried and Schellhorn 2001) that builds on individual tax information in the state of Baden-Wuerttemberg. More recently, the Federal Statistical Office has begun to provide an annual taxpayer panel, a project that makes taxpayer data available on an annual basis beginning in 2001 (see Kriete-Dodds and Vorgrimler 2007). While the taxpayer panel can only be used via controlled remote processing, the triennial micro-level income tax statistics is available as a Scientific Use File (FAST) in the Research Data Center of the Statistical Offices of the German *Länder*.

Another important area of research is concerned with the consequences of social policy on individual choice. However, the key issues in this context such as distribution or labor market participation suggest that the discussion of data availability and the conditions for empirical analysis are best addressed in the context of poverty (see Hauser, 2009) and labor market research (see Bender and Möller 2010; Schneider 2010).

2.3 Firm-level data

To study the impact of government policies on firm decisions, a large body of research utilizes firm-level data that capture investment, financial structure, and many other dimensions of firm decisions. However, financial statement data as provided by Hoppenstedt or Creditreform (DAFNE) usually report tax payments that capture not only the tax burden or tax incentives but also reflect firm performance and/or tax planning. The resulting problem of the endogeneity of tax variables has made it difficult to identify the role of the tax system for investment or the financial structure of firms. Rather than using tax payments, research might exploit differences between firms that lead to differences in taxation due to the specifics of the tax law, perhaps related to legal form or firm size.

Over the last decade, however, empirical research has been more successful in addressing these issues by employing data for multinational firms operating in different countries. The advantage here is that policies including tax policies show marked variation across countries that can be exploited for identification purposes. As a consequence, a great deal of research has been concerned with multinational data. Financial statement data for German and European multinationals or multinationals operating in Europe are provided by commercial providers such as Bureau von Dijk's Amadeus database. A unique data source for studying multinationals is the Bundesbank's MiDi database that currently provides annual firm-level panel data for the period 1996 to 2004. The collection of the data is prescribed by German law, which determines reporting mandates for international transactions (Lipponer 2006). A shortcoming of the MiDi dataset is that it provides limited information about the parent companies of domestic affiliates and German parents of foreign affiliates.

Alternatively, research in this area is concerned with data that exploits institutional variations across regions. In the context of company taxation, for instance, many studies exploit the local variation in the local business tax (*Gewerbesteuer*). Research opportunities are provided by the corporate balance sheet database (*Jahresabschlussdaten*) of the Deutsche Bundesbank (Stoess 2001), available within the bank's research center, by the IAB establishment panel (*IAB-Betriebspanel*), where Scientific Use Files are provided through the Research Data Center of the Federal Emloyment Agency at the Institute for Employment Research (IAB, *Institut für Arbeitsmarkt- und Berufsforschung* within the BA, *Bundesagentur für Arbeit*), and by the taxpayer data for the local business tax. The latter is a triennial micro-level dataset that currently provides information for 1998 and 2001. It can be accessed within the Research Data Centers of the Statistical Offices of the German *Länder*, though data access is further restricted by controlled remote processing.

Given the difficulties in identifying tax effects, research is also concerned with setting up simulation models. As with the analysis of household decisions, micro-level tax statistics are particularly helpful for this purpose. In addition to the local business tax, the triennial micro-level tax statistics for the corporation tax, and, with regard to the unincorporated firms, also the personal income tax statistic can be used – all of them are provided within the Research Data Center of the Statistical Offices.

2.4 Tax policy & institutional data

Typical of a large part of empirical research in public finance is a detailed characterization of institutions, including tax systems, social security systems, or specific laws that govern government policies. At the international level, however, there are some supra-national bodies such as the OECD and the European Commission that provide data on tax systems and institutional characteristics of countries such as the vertical structure of the public sector.

Generally speaking, data collection is easier for subnational entities. For instance, information about the tax burden associated with the local business tax (*Gewerbesteuer*) and the land tax (*Grundsteuer*) is provided by the statistical offices, at least at the level of counties.[3] However, the effective tax burden on land is not known due to the substantial discrepancy between market value of land and the assessed value. While land has been assessed for the estate and gift tax (*Erbschaftsteuer*) according to market prices since the mid-1990s, information about the assessment is not provided by the statistical offices.

3. Future developments

An important issue for the future development of research infrastructure is the combination of diverse data sources. This refers in particular to corporate and personal income taxation where taxpayer panel data so far have not been merged across different taxes. However, even at the level of the corporation, the tax burden consists of local business taxes as well as of corporate taxes. Moreover, a combination of taxpayer data with other firm-level data could yield substantially improved datasets where firm decisions as well as firm-specific conditions could be modeled much more precisely. The recent KombiFiD initiative of the Federal Statistical Office, the IAB, and the Deutsche Bundesbank, which aims at providing those combined datasets is to be greatly appreciated (see Bender et al. 2007). In particular, the combination with the Bundesbank MiDi data would vastly improve conditions for empirical research. Another promising data combination project is the Economics & Business Data Center (EBCD) initiative of Munich University in collaboration with the ifo Institute, which aims to combine ifo-firm survey data (Becker and Wohlrabe 2008) with commercial financial statement data including Amadeus and Hoppenstedt. An interesting aspect of this project is that it relies on randomized record linkage.

---

3   The common practice is to report weighted averages of municipal tax rates where the weights correspond to the municipal government's tax revenue. However, this practice is problematic. To see this, consider the weighted collection rate (*Hebesatz*) for a set of municipalities:

$$\frac{\sum_{i=1}^{N} h_i G_i}{\sum_{i}^{N} G_i}$$

where G_i is the revenue at a standardized collection rate (*Grundbetrag*). Since G_i is a declining function of the own collection rate and an increasing function of the tax rates of other municipalities, municipalities with high tax rates tend to receive a smaller weight. As a consequence, using the weighted average tends to yield biased results: tax increases are underestimated, tax decreases are overestimated.

A data combination that would help to address important issues pertaining to the tax system would be the combination of individual and firm-level taxpayer data. This would be an important step towards creating a reliable and comprehensive empirical basis for research on tax policy and reforms. The BMF has started an initiative in this direction. In this context, it should be noted that the growing complexity of tax issues has led other countries to set up micro-simulation models that are used for revenue estimation and also revenue forecasting purposes. However, currently no such attempts have materialized in Germany.

With regard to the analysis of the finances of subnational jurisdictions, the traditional financial accounting system is subject to change. As of 2009, North Rhine-Westphalia, the largest German state, introduced a new system of accounts, entitled "Neues Kommunales Finanzmanagement" (NKF), which replaced the current cash-based accounting. While this might systematically improve the information about controlled enterprises and liabilities, some new problems regarding assessment and valuation are coming up. Moreover, the data series will suffer from an important structural break.

As the current analysis of municipal finances has to resort to the last 1987 census, another important development for empirical research at the local level is the new census planned for 2011. While this update is important, it should be noted that current access to census data at the municipal level is difficult, since data access is restricted by the Statistical Offices of the *Länder*.

4. Future developments: European and international challenges

A large amount of research in public finance is concerned with the consequences of international economic and political integration for public policies. This includes cross-border flows not only of goods and services but also migration, factor movements, capital flows, and the emergence of multinational enterprises. Even if those cross-border issues are of particular importance in the European context, there is only very limited information available. Research so far has centered around specific datasets, many of which are subject to important qualifications. To merge those datasets with other more standard datasets of households and firms would substantially improve the conditions for empirical research using German data. Therefore, initiatives like KombiFiD are very welcome.

5. Conclusions and recommendations

Empirical research in public finance that aims at monitoring and assessing budgetary performance has access to a rich body of financial accounts that enables researchers to assess federal and state budgets. While the statistics for lower-level governments are available, data access is unduly restrictive. Since there is no justification to hold back financial data on these governments, the statistical offices should rethink their publication strategy.

With regard to statistics on major taxes, the Statistical Offices of the German *Länder* and the Federal Statistical Office have recently improved conditions for empirical research by providing micro-level taxpayer data. This is a major achievement. However, there are serious restrictions in data access and also the limited information about the background of tax payers in these statistics constitute a significant obstacle for the exploitation of this data.

Attempts to combine different data for research purposes are greatly appreciated. However, data combination should not be confined to providing firm-level data; it is also important to combine different taxpayer statistics in order to get a comprehensive and consistent data source for the empirical analysis of the tax system.

With regard to research on the supply side of public services, there is inadequate data availability. To some extent this reflects the fundamental problem of measuring public services – expenditure data offers only very limited information about the quantity and quality of public service provision. There has also been some progress made in specific areas of government policies such as social policy. However, in other areas, such as public education, the information about quality that is available in principle has not been made available for research.

References:

Becker, I./Frick, J./Grabka, M.M./Hauser, R./Krause, P. and Wagner, G.G. (2002): A Comparison of the Main Household Income Surveys for Germany: EVS and SOEP. In: Hauser, R. and Becker, I. (Eds.): Reporting on Income Distribution and Poverty. Perspectives from a German and European Point of View. Heidelberg.

Becker, S.O. and Wohlrabe, K. (2008): Micro Data at the Ifo Institute for Economic Research – The "Ifo Business Survey" Usage and Access. Schmollers Jahrbuch 128 (2), 307-319.

Bellmann, L. (2002): Das IAB-Betriebspanel: Konzeption und Anwendungsbereiche. Allgemeines statistisches Archiv 86 (2), 177-188.

Bender, S. and Möller, J. (2010): Data from the Federal Employment Agency. [In this publication].

Bender, S./Wagner, J. and Zwick, M. (2007): KombiFiD – Kombinierte Firmendaten für Deutschland. FDZ-Arbeitspapier Nr. 21.

Borck, R./Caliendo, M. and Steiner, V. (2007): Fiscal Competition and the Composition of Public Spending: Theory and Evidence. FinanzArchiv 63 (2), 264-277.

Gottfried, P. and Schellhorn, H. (2001): Das IAW-Einkommensteuerpanel und das Mikrosimulationsmodell SIMST. IAW-Diskussionspapier. Tübingen.

Hauser, R. (2009): Household Income, Poverty and Wealth. RatSWD Working Paper No. 53.

Kriete-Dodds, S. and Vorgrimler, D. (2007): Das Taxpayer-Panel der jährlichen Einkommensteuerstatistik. Wirtschaft und Statistik 2007 (1), 77-85.

Lipponer, A. (2006): Microdatabase direct investment – MiDi. A brief guide. Bundesbank Working Paper.

Schneider, H. (2010): More and Better Data for Labor Market Research. Proposals for Efficient Access to the Currently Unused Potential of Official Statistical Data. [In this publication].

Stoess, E. (2001): Deutsche Bundesbank's Corporate Balance Sheet Statistics And Areas of Application. Schmollers Jahrbuch 121 (1), 131-137.

5.2 Household Income, Poverty, and Wealth

*Richard Hauser**

---

* This advisory report reflects the state of affairs as at 2009.

Contact:

Richard Hauser
Goethe University
Department of Economics and Business Administration
POB 11 19 32
60054 Frankfurt am Main
Germany
e-mail: r.hauser[at]em.uni-frankfurt.de

Abstract

This paper concentrates on the official statistics on household income, poverty, and wealth. It characterizes the main research questions in this field, and presents an overview of the available statistics and Scientific Use Files produced by the four Research Data Centers in Germany: the Research Data Center of the Federal Statistical Office, the Research Data Center of the Statistical Offices of the German *Länder*, the Research Data Center of the Federal Employment Ageny at the Institute for Employment Research (IAB, *Institut für Arbeitsmarkt- und Berufsforschung* within the BA, *Bundesagentur für Arbeit*), and the Research Data Center of the German Pension Insurance (RV, *Deutsche Rentenversicherung*). We support the recommendations of a peer review group for the Federal Statistical Office based on the European Statistics Code of Practice, and suggest peer reviews for all data-producing bodies including ministries. We repeat a recommendation of a former commission to find ways of distributing Scientific Use Files to reliable foreign research institutes. Special recommendations refer to the improvement of survey methods and extended questionnaires of the Income and Consumption Survey (EVS, *Einkommens- und Verbrauchsstichprobe*) and the German contribution to the European Statistics on Income and Living Conditions (EU-SILC). We also recommend a harmonization of the administrative statistics on the various minimum benefit programs, and the development of a single Scientific Use File for all minimum benefit recipients.

Keywords: Research Data Center, Scientific Use Files, household income, wealth, minimum benefits, EVS, EU-SILC

1. Introduction

Individual and household well-being is strongly determined by income and wealth. The levels and distributions of these economic resources and their changes within a society over time are of utmost importance from a scientific and political point of view. A minimum amount of regular income is also a necessary although not always a sufficient condition for avoiding poverty. Strictly speaking, net equivalent income and net wealth are the main variables of interest here.[1] To calculate these variables, however, one needs information on all sources of income and all components of wealth, as well as on all personal taxes and social security contributions.[2]

---

1 Net equivalent income is a weighted per capita income derived from the net income of the individual's household. Net wealth is the difference between all of a household's assets and its debts.
2 The most important research questions and the current status of research can be gathered from Atkinson, A.B. and Bourguignon, F. (Eds.) (2000): Handbook of Income Distribution, vol 1. Amsterdam et al. The historical perspective on changes in the share of high incomes is presented in Atkinson, A.B. and Piketty, T. (Eds.) (2007): Top Incomes over the 20th

International comparisons of income and wealth distributions and of the size and composition of the population in poverty are in increasingly high demand both in the European Union[3] and worldwide.[4] These require comparable definitions of the variables measured in national surveys and administrative datasets.[5]

Income and wealth distributions are "anonymous" in the sense that the overall distributions do not change if individuals or households simply switch places in the distribution. When looking at the distributions of income and wealth from an individual point of view, however, one is also able to identify changes in the relative positions of concrete individuals in the income and wealth hierarchy. This is especially important for the analysis of changes in the composition of the poor population due to ascents out of and descents into income poverty.[6] If one extends the perspective from a short-run to a long-run view, it becomes possible to identify changes in individuals' economic resources over the entire life course. Part of an individual's life course may be as a member of a family, meaning that the life courses of other family members and their interrelationships are also of interest. Moreover, information about private transfers between households and intergenerational transfers of income and wealth (gifts, inheritances) is needed to gain a complete picture.

The first step of an analysis in the field of income, wealth, and income poverty is always to *describe* the present situation based on household income and wealth statistics. An even greater challenge, however, is to analyze the factors that have produced the existing distribution and that will cause

---

Century, A Contrast Between continental European and English-Speaking Countries, Oxford. An overview of wealth distributions is provided by Wolff, E.N. (Ed.) (2006): International Perspectives on Household Wealth, Cheltenham/UK and Northampton/MA, US. Problems of poverty are summarized in Huster, E.-U./Boeckh, J. and Mogge-Grotjahn, H. (Eds.) (2008): Handbuch Armut und Soziale Ausgrenzung. Wiesbaden; and in Jenkins, S.P. and Micklewright, J. (Eds.) (2007): Inequality and Poverty Re-examined. Oxford.

3   The EU has defined the so-called Laeken indicators which have to be calculated regularly by each member state to facilitate comparisons between its members.
4   Compare OECD (2008): Growing Unequal? Income Distribution and Poverty in OECD Countries, Paris.
5   See Expert Group on Household Income Statistics (The Canberra Group) (2001): Final Report and Recommendations, Ottawa. The Luxembourg Income Study (LIS) collects data on income and wealth for about thirty countries and takes great effort to make them comparable based on these recommendations.
6   A panel study on social assistance recipients gave rise to new insights. See Leisering, L. and Leibfried, S. (1999): Time and Poverty in Western Welfare States, United Germany in Perspective. Cambridge. Many studies on income mobility use data from the German Socio-Economic Panel (SOEP, *Sozio-oekonomisches Panel*), a social science based panel that is located at the German Institute of Economic Research (DIW Berlin, *Deutsches Institut für Wirtschaftsforschung*). Comparative studies of income mobility can be carried out based on the Comparative National Equivalent File (CNEF) that presently comprises the national panels of five countries (Germany, United Kingdom, Canada, Australia, The Netherlands). It is organized and distributed by Cornell University, Ithaca, NY, US.

changes in this distribution and in the relative positions of individuals in the income and wealth hierarchy, especially those in poverty. Our objective, therefore, is to find *explanations* and to make *predictions*. Although there is no comprehensive theory of the personal distribution of income and wealth, one can say that it results from an interaction among macroeconomic and demographic trends, institutional arrangements, and personal characteristics. Social and fiscal policy decisions that change the institutional arrangements work within this general setting. While information on macroeconomic and demographic developments, institutional arrangements, and policy decisions has to be obtained from other sources, information on relevant personal characteristics should be contained in the same data file with information on individual or household income. This is necessary in cross-sectional household surveys as well as in household panel surveys. While simulations of the first-round effects of social and fiscal policy changes usually neglect behavioral responses by assumption, the prediction of second- and third-round effects requires estimates of individual behavioral responses with respect to working time, consumption and savings, and changes in the portfolio structure of wealth holdings. Econometric estimates of these behavioral responses should therefore be based on variables contained in the same dataset as the income and wealth variables. Usually, however, one has to ignore the macro-level consequences of micro-level behavioral changes due to the lack of an integrated micro-macro model.

Given the current state of research, in the following we will examine the sources of official statistical data currently available for analyses of income, wealth, and poverty. On this basis, we will formulate recommendations for improving specific components of the information infrastructure in Germany. Cross-sectional and longitudinal household surveys conducted independently by social science research organizations will not be dealt with

2. An overview of public data sources and their availability for research on income, wealth, and poverty

Since 2001, when the German Commission on Improving the Information Infrastructure between Science and Statistics (KVI, *Kommission zur Verbesserung der informationellen Infrastruktur zwischen Wissenschaft und Statistik*) published its first set of recommendations, the German statistical infrastructure for empirical research in the economic and social sciences has improved dramatically.[7] For research on the distribution of income and

---

7 Towards an Improved Statistical Infrastructure – Summary Report of the Commission set up by the Federal Ministry of Education and Research to Improve the Statistical

wealth and of income poverty, the following Scientific Use Files are provided by public institutions through various Research Data Centers.[8,9]

2.1 Research Data Centers of the Federal Statistical Office and the Statistical Offices of the German Länder[10]

These Research Data Centers offer a range of Scientific Use Files and provide researchers in many fields diverse possibilities for working either on-site or via remote computing. In the following, only those files are listed that refer to income, wealth, and poverty.

(1) Microcensus (1973-2006)
(2) Income and Consumption Surveys (EVS, *Einkommens- und Verbrauchsstichprobe*) (1962/63, 1969, 1973, 1978, 1983, 1988, 1993, 1998, 2003)
(3) German contribution "Leben in Deutschland" to the European Statistics on Income and Living Conditions (EU-SILC) (2005), European Community Household Panel (ECHP) (1994, 1995, 1996)
(4) Income Tax Files (1992, 1995, 1998, 2001, 2004)
(5) Taxpayer Panel (2001, 2002, 2003, 2004)
(6) Inheritance Tax File (2002)
(7) Social Assistance Files (1998-2004)

Datasets (1), (2), and (3) are sample surveys, while (4), (5), (6), and (7) are samples of administrative datasets. All these datasets are relevant for analyses of income, wealth, and poverty, but we will only comment on the surveys. The relatively new tax files are very promising for distributional analyses.[11] Methodological research on problems in administrative datasets is still in progress.

Infrastructure in Cooperation with the Scientific Community and Official Statistics (KVI), reprinted in: Schmollers Jahrbuch 121 (3), 443-468.

8 Details of the four Research Data Centers are described in several articles in the volume Rolf, G./Zwick, M. and Wagner, G.G. (Eds.) (2008): Fortschritte der informationellen Infrastruktur in Deutschland. Festschrift für Johann Hahlen zum 65. Geburtstag und Hans-Jürgen Krupp zum 75. Geburtstag. Baden-Baden.

9 In addition to the distribution of Scientific Use Files, the Research Data Centers also provide workplaces for guest researchers on site and facilities for remote computing with all the surveys mentioned.

10 www.Forschungsdatenzentrum.de.

11 See Bach, St./Corneo, G. and Steiner, V. (2007): From Bottom to Top: The Entire Distribution of Market Income in Germany, 1991-2001. DIW Discussion Paper No. 683. And Bach, St./Corneo, G. and Steiner, V. (2008): Effective Taxation of Top Incomes in Germany, 1992-2002. DIW Discussion Paper No. 767.

2.2 Research Data Center of the Federal Employment Agency at the Institute for Employment Research *(IAB,* Institut für Arbeitsmarkt- und Berufsforschung *within the BA,* Bundesagentur für Arbeit*)*

(8) IAB Employment Sample (*IAB-Beschäftigtenstichprobe*) (1975-2004)
(9) Cross-Sectional Survey "Life Situation an Social Security" (LSS 2005, *Querschnittsbefragung Lebenssituation und Soziale Sicherung*)
(10) Panel Study "Labor Market and Social Security" (PASS, *Panel Arbeitsmarkt und soziale Sicherung*);
(11) BA-Employment Panel (BAP, *BA Beschäftigtenpanel*);
(12) Integrated Employment Biographies Sample (IEBS).

Dataset (8) is a valuable administrative dataset for research on the distribution of individual labor income, which can contribute to explaining the distribution of net equivalent income derived from household net income. These statistics only contain incomes of higher-earning employed individuals up to the ceiling on social security contributions. Dataset (9) is an individual survey that can be used for analyses of income distribution among households, but its comparability with other surveys is limited. Datasets (10) and (11) are based on surveys focusing on the long-term unemployed and thus can contribute to a partial explanation of net household income and of poverty, but only for this subgroup of the population. Dataset (12) is a sample from a longitudinal administrative data survey.

2.3 Research Data Center of the German Pension Insurance *(RV,* Deutsche Rentenversicherung*)*

(13) Cross-sectional files for the years 2003, 2004, 2005, and 2006 of the German Pension Insurance on pensions in payment (*Rentenbestand*), on new pensions awarded (*Rentenzugang*), on cessation of pension payment (*Rentenwegfall*), and on actively (currently) insured persons (only 2004 and 2005)
(14) Cross-section files on special topics and groups:

    a)   persons with reduction/loss of earnings capacity and their diagnosis (2003, 2004, 2005, 2006)
    b)   Scientific Use File with reduced information on pensions in payment, newly awarded pensions, cessation of pensions (1993-2005)
    c)   Scientific Use File on the qualifications of persons with newly awarded pensions (2003).

These various Scientific Use Files can only be used to describe the distribution of pensions by case and to explain their levels as determined by the pension formulae. Since individuals may receive more than one pension – from the German Pension Insurance as well as from other old age protection systems, these datasets are not sufficient to estimate the total pension income of elderly individuals. For this, one needs household surveys that record all types of old age income. Although there exist several very good household surveys on income of the elderly and even on pension entitlements accrued for persons over 40 (ASID, *Alterssicherung in Deutschland* 1986, 1995, 2003, and AVID, *Altersvorsorge in Deutschland* 1996, 2005), they are not available for independent scientific research but only for research commissioned by the Federal Ministry of Labor and Social Affairs (BMAS, *Bundesministerium für Arbeit und Soziales*).[12] This contradicts the recommendations of the 2001 KVI report that all surveys paid for by public money should be available to researchers.

3. Problems with the information infrastructure for research in income, wealth, and poverty provided by public bodies

3.1 Problems mentioned in a report by a European peer review group

The peer review initiated by Eurostat identified problems with the existing statistics of the German Statistical Offices and made recommendations for improvement.[13] This peer review, based on the *European Statistics Code of Practice*, dealt with how the German Statistical Offices produce their official statistics, internal organization, quality control, and the distribution of statistics to the public and the research community.[14] Some of the problems detected also apply to the quality of data distributed for scientific research.[15] The recommendations for improvement contained in the report implicitly

---

12 Results of AVID 2005 are published by: Frommert, D./Ohsmann, S. and Rehfeld, U.G. (2008): Altersvorsorge in Deutschland 2005 (AVID 2005) – Die neue Studie im Überblick. Deutsche Rentenversicherung 63 (1), 1-19. A critique of these results can be found in: Hauser, R. (2007): Altersarmut unterschätzt. Soziale Sicherheit, Zeitschrift für Arbeit und Soziales 56 (12), 416-419.
13 Peer review on the implementation of the European Statistics Code of Practice, Country visited: Germany, by Geert Bruinooge (statistics Netherlands, Daniel Defays (Eurostat), Paloma Seoane Spiegelberg (INE, Spain), March 10, 2008 (available at www.destatis.de).
14 The Research Data Centers of the Federal Statistical Office and of the Statistical Offices of the German *Länder* were accepted as "best practice."
15 See Peer review, section 7: principle 4 (quality commitment), principle 7 (sound methodology), principle 11 (relevance), principle 12 (accuracy and reliability), and principle 15 (accessibility and clarity).

indicate where the problems lie. The following are key elements of five of these recommendations:

- Depending on resources available and taking into account the cost-benefit ratio, an internal data quality network should be established to improve internal quality control and increase the transparency and comparability of statistics.
- Transparency in the methodologies and procedures used by the statistical offices should be improved through appropriate documentation measures.
- Customer satisfaction surveys should be conducted regularly.
- A concept should be developed for measuring errors and error sources from administrative sources.
- Quality reports should be systematically evaluated for information value and standardized.

We fully support these recommendations but will not consider them further in the final section of this contribution.

The peer review did not deal with some of the problems of the information infrastructure for empirical economic and social research on income, wealth, and poverty. Obviously, they were not within its focus.

3.2 Additional problems of the German information infrastructure with respect to scientific research on income, wealth, and poverty

Statistics that are relevant for research on problems of income, wealth, and poverty in Germany are produced by different public bodies: the German Statistical Offices, the German Federal Employment Agency, the Deutsche Bundesbank, the German Pension Insurance and other social security institutions, and some ministries. Either these statistics are collected in accordance with special statistics laws, or they are produced as part of an institution's general administrative activities, or they are based on surveys carried out by private market research companies and financed by public funds. Regular evaluation processes for these other data collection activities similar to the peer review based on the *European Statistics Code of Practice* for the Federal Statistical Office do not exist for all public bodies. This lack of systematic control casts doubts on the reliability of the various datasets.

Up to now, it has not been possible to draw a comprehensive picture of the distribution of income, wealth, and income poverty within the permanent population of Germany. The German Microcensus, which is compulsory and based on a random sample, covers in principle the entire resident population but does not contain sufficient information on income and wealth. It therefore only provides the basis for rough analyses of income and poverty.

The EVS contains detailed information on income, wealth, consumption, and savings, but does not cover some population groups, particularly households with very high incomes, persons living in institutions,[16] and the homeless. Additionally, persons with a migration background – especially if they immigrated recently – are grossly underrepresented. One reason for these gaps may be that the EVS is a voluntary survey based on a quota sample instead of a random selection of interviewees. It also uses German questionnaires sent by mail instead of multilingual questionnaires distributed by interviewers. These gaps cause biased results with respect to the distribution of income, wealth, and income poverty. Moreover, because the EVS is a quota sample, confidence intervals cannot be calculated. Although it is not possible to analyze annual income mobility using cross-sectional surveys carried out at five-year intervals, at least one can conduct pseudo-longitudinal analyses based on several of these surveys.[17]

The German contribution to the European Statistics on Income and Living Conditions (EU-SILC) also contains income sources and some indicators of the quality of life, but it neglects components of wealth, consumption, and savings. It is, therefore, only suitable for the analysis of income distributions and income poverty. Each year, one-fourth of the interviewees are selected at random. In its final stage, this survey will be a rotating panel with each interviewee participating for four consecutive years. This will make it possible to analyze annual income mobility and periods of income poverty lasting longer than one year. There are doubts, however, whether the basis for the random selection of interviewees – the so-called "access panel" – is itself a random representation of the resident population of Germany. Moreover, the German contribution to EU-SILC is a voluntary mail survey with questionnaires solely in German, meaning that various groups are underrepresented and that the results will be biased.[18,19]

The data sources are based on different income and wealth concepts: current quarterly household net and gross income, annual household gross

---

16 The concept of institutions is relatively broad. It includes, for example, hospitals, homes for the elderly, nursing homes and orphanages, homes for workers, barracks and prisons, homes for asylum-seekers, monasteries, and similar collective households.

17 See Hauser, R. and Stein, H. (2006): Inequality of the distribution of personal wealth in Germany 1973-98. In: Wolff, E.N. (Ed.) (2006): International Perspectives on Household Wealth, Cheltenham/Northampton, 195-224.

18 See Hauser, R. (2007): Problems of the German Contribution to EU-SILC – A research perspective, comparing EU-SILC, Micro census and SOEP. RatSWD Working Paper No. 20.

19 An extensive methodological discussion of the problems of EU-SILC in all Member States of the EU can be found in: European Commission (Ed.) (2007): Comparative EU statistics on Income and Living Conditions: Issues and Challenges, Proceedings of the EU-SILC conference (Helsinki, 6-8 November 2006), Methodological and working papers.

and net income from the previous year,[20] monthly gross income from earnings, different lists of components of household wealth, and so on. Although there may be good reasons for different definitions of the variable "income," it is difficult to combine information from different statistical sources. Moreover, the gross sums of the various kinds of income do not fully correspond with the same categories in the national accounts. For some income categories, these differences amount to more than 30 percent.[21] The differences are even greater with some wealth categories, especially with financial assets as compared to the sums published by the Deutsche Bundesbank. A second serious gap in the statistics on wealth is the neglect of the value of ownership rights in unincorporated businesses. Additionally, the value of consumer durables and cars, antiquities, jewelry, and the private ownership of precious metals is not recorded. The distribution of wealth of the resident population should include all assets, irrespective of whether estates and private businesses are located in Germany or abroad. The available household statistics, however, exclude assets located abroad that are not traded on the stock exchange. These various problems result in a considerable underestimation of inequality in the distributions of net equivalent income and net household wealth. To explain the distribution of net wealth, it would be extremely helpful to know the value of the inheritances and gifts inter vivo accrued up to the time of interview. Unfortunately, the Income and Consumption Surveys record this information only partially.

The IAB Employment Sample (IABS) contains administrative data on gross labor income of workers and employees, but only up to the limit for social security contributions. For those with higher incomes, the value contained is simply this income ceiling. It is therefore impossible to investigate the upper tail of the labor income distribution or to construct a complete distribution of income from labor.

Minimum benefit regulations, in principle, cover the entire population in the case of net household income below a certain threshold. More than ten percent of the resident population of Germany receives subsidies of various kinds, with standard minimum benefit coverage levels for the entire population. From a social policy point of view, it seems urgent to analyze this large segment of the population below or near the poverty line who have to rely on means-tested minimum benefits. There exist administrative statistics on recipients of minimum benefits under the Unemployment Assistance Law

---

20 This method is problematic because it only records previous income of persons who are still members of the household at the time of interview.
21 See Sachverständigenrat zur Begutachtung der gesamtwirtschaftlichen Entwicklung, Jahresgutachten 1998/99, Bundestagsdrucksache 14/73 table 57; and Hauser, R. and Becker, I. (2001): Einkommensverteilung im Querschnitt und im Zeitverlauf 1973-1998. Bonn. Table 4.1; and Westerheide, P./Ammermüller, A. and Weber, A. (2005): Die Entwicklung und Verteilung des Vermögens privater Haushalte unter besonderer Berücksichtigung des Produktivvermögens. Bonn. Table 9.

(*Arbeitslosengeld II* as defined in *Sozialgesetzbuch II*, second book of the German social code) and the Social Assistance Law (*Bedarfsorientierte Grundsicherung im Alter und Erwerbsminderung sowie Sozialhilfe* according to *Sozialgesetzbuch XII*). A unified Scientific Use File of minimum income recipients, however, is not available, although this would be of utmost interest for research.[22,23] Only a panel of a sample of the long-term unemployed will become available (PASS as mentioned above). Even the Scientific Use File of former social assistance recipients is no longer available because of changes enacted in 2003 and 2005 that altered the legal framework.

4. Recommendations

To remedy the problems described above, we offer several recommendations for improving the information infrastructure for research on income, wealth, and poverty in addition to the aforementioned recommendations of the Peer Review Group.

- To improve the possibility for in-depth research on recipients of minimum benefits, all statistics on minimum benefits should be harmonized and a single Scientific Use File should be created, similar to the former social assistance file.

- To improve the possibility for in-depth research on household wealth, missing elements of wealth, such as the value of ownership of unincorporated businesses and estates in foreign countries, should be included in the Income and Consumption Survey. It would also be very helpful if a question on the value of all inheritances ever received were included. Additionally, an accurate representation of the foreign population should be guaranteed so that special studies on foreigners living in Germany can be undertaken.

- To simplify work with Scientific Use Files, high-quality reports on all household statistics, including ex post checks based on the Microcensus

---

22 See Hauser, R. (2008): Mindestsicherungsleistungen in Deutschland – ein Plädoyer für eine harmonisierte Gesamtstatistik. In: Rolf, G./Zwick, M. and Wagner, G.G. (Eds.): Fortschritte der informationellen Infrastruktur in Deutschland. Festschrift für Johann Hahlen zum 65. Geburtstag und Hans Jürgen Krupp zum 75. Geburtstag. Baden-Baden, 359-368.
23 In 2008 the Statistical Offices published tables for the recipients of the various minimum benefits and for the recipients of other means-tested benefits. This publication underscores the necessity of harmonizing the concepts and making a Scientific Use File available for all the recipients of the various minimum benefits. See Statistische Ämter des Bundes und der Länder, Soziale Mindestsicherung, Wiesbaden 2008.

and various administrative statistics, should be made available to the scientific community. These reports should also show the differences between survey results and the national accounts and national balance sheets, and possible causes. Moreover, the reliability of the income data reported by the Microcensus should be evaluated.

- To improve the data available for research on income, wealth, and poverty, methods should be developed to combine household surveys with administrative statistics – especially tax statistics – while safeguarding this data for confidentiality. This could be done e.g., by statistical matching.

- To cover the entire resident population, new statistics on the homeless and persons in institutions should be developed, at least including standard demographic variables. Additionally, statistics should be collected on all the institutions in which individuals live.

- The German data from EU-SILC that are handed over to Eurostat should be made available to German researchers through the Research Data Centers. The anonymization undertaken by Eurostat should be considered sufficient for compliance with German data protection regulations since the entire dataset can be obtained for all countries in this form from Eurostat, but at a considerable cost.

- It should be checked whether methodological improvements to the German contribution to EU-SILC can be made. This is all the more important since it will become the main statistical source for the German Poverty and Wealth Reports and the National Action Plans for Social Inclusion. In the long run, this extremely important dataset should be improved by using truly random samples, five waves for each quarter of the rotating panel with the first wave only being used as a pretest, face-to-face interviews with multilingual questionnaires, guaranteeing sole responsibility of the German Federal Statistical Office, and outsourcing fieldwork to a private market research company with a well-trained and permanent staff of interviewers.

- The IAB Employment Sample (IABS) should be expanded to include more precise information on labor income above the limit for social security contributions. This could be done by extending the obligation of employers to report labor income of employees above this limit at least by income brackets.

- It should be guaranteed that the interviewees of all future household surveys financed by public money – especially the ASID (*Alterssicherung in Deutschland*) and AVID (*Altersvorsorge in Deutschland*) – give permission in advance to be included in Scientific Use Files derived from these surveys, in compliance with data protection laws. These datasets should either be made available for scientific research by transmitting them to the Central Archive in Cologne or by producing and distributing Scientific Use Files through one of the Research Data Centers.

- The problem that legal regulations forbid transmitting Scientific Use Files containing German data to reliable foreign institutions (e.g., universities) should be solved following the suggestions in the 2001 KVI report.[24]

- To improve the quality of statistics produced by public bodies outside the German Federal Statistical Office, a code similar to the *European Statistics Code of Practice* should be developed. Additionally, a regular review process for these other bodies should be introduced, especially for those statistics published by the German Federal Statistical Office but provided by other institutions.

---

[24] Kommission zur Verbesserung der informationellen Infrastruktur zwischen Wissenschaft und Statistik (KVI) (Eds.) (2001): Wege zu einer besseren informationellen Infrastruktur. Baden-Baden, 152-154.

5.3 Family Research

Johannes Huinink

Contact:

Johannes Huinink
University of Bremen
FB 08 / EMPAS
FVG-Mitte, Celsiusstrasse
28359 Bremen
Germany
e-mail: huinink[at]empas.uni-bremen.de

Abstract

Family research has become increasingly important in recent years, as reflected in the high public interest in family issues. A number of improvements have been made with regard to the provision of family related data in response to the 2001 KVI report. Family research has profited from these considerably. However, progress in data provision since the beginning of the 21st century has been limited, both in terms of the quality and quantity of data produced. In particular, there is still an urgent need for longitudinal data on social and family-related processes dealing with different levels and dimensions of family development. Data are needed not only to describe family change adequately but also to model the determinants and "outcomes" of couple and family dynamics or family relationships over time. What is needed most at present – aside from an improved family data reporting system provided by the official statistical agencies – are panel studies collecting longitudinal (socio-)structural and socio-psychological "on time" information on the dynamics of individuals' living arrangements over time.

Keywords: family research, longitudinal data, family dynamics

1. Introduction

Family research has gained considerable attention in recent years, and the need for more, and more precise, information on various aspects of family dynamics is urgent. This is reflected in the current high public interest in family issues of various kinds: not only family demography in the narrower sense (living arrangements, nuptiality and divorce, fertility) but also aspects of the internal dynamics of close relationships in unions and families (quality and benefits of intimate relationships, parenting, intergenerational relationships, effects of poverty, intra-family violence). These topics often lie on the borderline between social, economic, and psychological research.

Despite the high public interest, family research was not addressed in the first round of KVI advisory reports in 2001 explicitly. In KVI reloaded, aside from the reports on population (Kreyenfeld and Scholz) and intergenerational relationships (Nauck and Steinbach), only this report deals with family research. Family-related issues are still not well represented in a broad range of research fields.

In 2001 the KVI report made several recommendations of particular relevance for the field of family research. These include:

- conducting a census;
- providing long-term institutional support for the German Socio-Economic Panel (SOEP, *Sozio-oekonomisches Panel*);

- allocating more support for prospective and retrospective cohort studies to allow longitudinal analyses of individual development and life courses;
- continuing the German General Social Survey (ALLBUS, *Allgemeine Bevölkerungsumfrage der Sozialwissenschaften*) and the International Social Survey Programme (ISSP);
- improving access to aggregated as well as individual-level data, providing scientific use microdata files, and establishing Research Data Centers; and
- creating opportunities to link data from different data sources.

In nearly all of these areas, improvements made since 2001 have benefited family research considerably. Particular progress has been achieved in access to large datasets (Microcensus) of the official statistical agencies, allowing more valid and detailed description and analysis of changing demographic family structures over time. A census has not materialized up to now, but is in the planning phase. The body of family related panel data allowing longitudinal studies is growing. Family issues have also been addressed in more detail in recent ALLBUS, ISSP, and European Social Survey (ESS) surveys. However, in terms of sample sizes and content, progress since the beginning of the 21st century has been limited. It will be argued below that the longitudinal data needed to study social and family-related processes on different levels of family development is still not adequate. The newly launched Panel Analysis of Intimate Relationships and Family Dynamics (pairfam) is one step in overcoming this lack of data in Germany.

2. Research in family science

2.1 Main research fields

Family research is multidisciplinary by definition, spanning the disciplines of demography, psychology, sociology, economics, anthropology, education, political science, and law. In the following, the main research fields will be addressed systematically from an analytical point of view (Huinink 2008).

Family and social structure (the macro perspective): This research field deals with demographic and socio-structural changes in family and living arrangements as well as their structural and institutional embeddedness in our functionally differentiated society. Subfields of research are:

- demography of the family and family types;
- social structure and social inequality of families;
- family as a social institution in welfare states; and

- family and subsystems of the society: demands and achievements of the family related to other subsystems of society.

Family as a social group (the meso perspective): This field of research looks at the dynamics of social relationships in private households and families of different kinds and during different phases of family development. Subfields of research are:

- social interaction in couples and families;
- household production and organization of everyday life in couples and families;
- socialization, parenting, and parental transmission; and
- intergenerational relationships.

Family development over the life course (the micro perspective): This research field addresses the behavior of individual actors and their motivational structure connected with family development as an interdependent part of the individual life course. Subfields of research are:

- mating, establishing partnerships, family formation and extension;
- stability and disintegration of couple and family relationships; and
- family life and its effects on other domains of the individual life course.

2.2 Development in theory and methodological challenges

Investigations in these fields of family research are connected to different theoretical approaches, each requiring different data for empirical investigation and different methods of data analysis. Even a brief overview of the theoretical developments and methodological challenges accompanying them, as well as a review of progress in methods of data analysis, very clearly shows what kind of data are needed to make further progress in family research. Theoretically and methodologically, family research in the social sciences has made considerable progress by overcoming cross-sectional concepts and implementing longitudinal approaches of theoretical and empirical analysis. Family research has profited from new strategies of data collection, especially panel and retrospective survey designs (Mayer 2000; Seltzer et al. 2005). Refined methods of panel and event history analysis allow consideration of different levels of analysis and different dimensions of the life course in the study of couple and family dynamics (Blossfeld and Rohwer 2002 Wu 2004; Singer and Willett 2003, Halaby 2004).

There already exists a broad *theoretical framework* for family research that is still being expanded. The main theoretical paradigm follows a multi-level life-course approach of individual welfare production over time. The rationale for welfare production can be based on different versions of a theory of individual action over the life course. It makes assumptions about the interdependency among individual action, its contextual conditions on different levels of social processes, and the various closely interrelated dimensions of the individual life course – of which family life is one (Feldhaus and Huinink 2008).

On the macro level, research focuses on social change in the family's structural and institutional context in society. Cohort analysis makes it possible to distinguish period, age, and cohort effects. Research on the meso level addresses the impact of the medium-range social context, the local infrastructure (e.g., child care systems), social networks, working conditions, neighborhoods, etc. On the micro-level of family units and couples, family research examines dynamics of interpersonal relationships of different kinds over time. Here, individual family-related behavior is examined in context, since it is embedded in diverse strata of constantly changing situational conditions.

These fields of family research require specific kinds of data and methodologies. Particularly, family research faces the following *methodological challenges*:

Third variable phenomenon: The question of spurious correlation is particularly critical in longitudinal research, especially in self-referential or path-dependent processes like the life course of individuals. One theoretical approach in family research addressing this phenomenon is Hakim's preference theory. It assumes that much of the relationship between family activities and work in later life is preconditioned by early adopted attitudes (Hakim 2000).

Selection and adaptation: Processes of selection and adaptation over the life course have to be considered (Lesthaeghe 2002). Intentions, values, aspirations, and frames of action (socio-psychological indicators), shape individual behavior (selection). At the same time new biographical statuses and life course decisions affect individuals' values, attitudes, and aspirations (adaptation). Also individuals' social networks are formed by processes of selection and adaptation.

Substitution and complementarity: The life course is a multidimensional process, but little is known about relations of substitution and support between different dimensions of welfare production in different life domains such as family and work.

Anticipation: Social actors learn from the past and are restricted in their degrees of freedom for action by past decisions and past behavior. Knowing this, they anticipate future consequences as well as expected changes in the conditions of their action. Future life-course transitions or the "shadow of the future" therefore take on increasing importance in decisions on current behavior (Nauck 2001).

Couple perspective: Individual-level family research in sociology is still strongly focused on individual actors and often fails to integrate the perspectives of partners and family members (Lyons and Sayer 2005).

Cultural comparison: A great deal of international diversity in family dynamics is due to cultural differences, which are often rooted in processes that took place centuries ago. An example demonstrating the impact of cultural differences that were emerging only decades ago are the different patterns of family development and parental living arrangements in East and West Germany. Up to now, the crucial cultural parameters have not been clearly identified empirically even though we know that socio-structural differences between the populations of the "two Germanys" do not fully explain the divergent behavioral patterns.

Still, there are blind spots in our understanding of the complex individual decision making processes that take place over the life course. In particular, we observe an evident lack of interdisciplinary theory integrating demographic, economic, sociological, and psychological approaches, and a lack of adequate longitudinal data for empirical analysis.

3. Status quo: Databases and access

Although considerable improvements have been made in data provision – with respect to the requirements mentioned above – there are still severe deficits to be noted.

Following the recommendations of the 2001 KVI report, great progress has been made in structural macro and microdata for the demographic analysis of family dynamics. This is thanks to improvements in access to data from official statistical agencies, and in the provision of family-related data from social surveys in the national and international context. However, most of the data available are cross-sectional data enriched by retrospective information. Non-structural information (socio-psychological indicators) is usually only available from cross-sectional surveys or panel studies with long gaps between the few panel waves, while longitudinal data of this type is still lacking.

3.1 Official statistics

Data from official statistical agencies is useful primarily for descriptive purposes, for example, in reporting changes in family structure. But increasingly official statistical data are also used to model and investigate family dynamics analytically, thanks primarily to improved access to the Microcensus data.

Statistics on marriage, divorce, and fertility are available but can only be used for descriptive purposes. Up to the year 2007, parity-specific birth statistics cannot be calculated on the basis of data from vital statistics, and the proportion of childless men or women in a particular cohort cannot be estimated accurately.

Major progress has been made in regard to the use of Microcensus data in family research, especially in family demography. Not only are the Microcensus data being used to an increasing degree for descriptive purposes, they are also used more and more in highly differentiated and sophisticated statistical models of family formation and development (e.g., Duschek and Wirth 2005; Kreyenfeld 2001; Kreyenfeld and Geißler 2006; Lengerer and Klein 2007; Lengerer et al. 2007; Wirth 2007; see also the report on demography in this publication).

Up to now, however, users have to struggle with a number of shortcomings. One widely discussed shortcoming is that the Microcensus only considers children of respondents who live in the same household. And surprisingly, questions on day care provisions were not covered in the last Microcensus Act of 2005.

Another problem with using Microcensus panel data is that respondents who change their place of residence drop out of the sample. This means that the panel subsample becomes more and more selective because mobile respondents are underrepresented. If migration behavior is correlated with a dependent variable of interest, biased results can be expected. Nonetheless, it has been investigated whether Microcensus panel data can be used for longitudinal analyses. Kreyenfeld et al. (2007) show that selectivity does not seem to be problematic in case of studying family formation.

Some other surveys by the Federal Statistical Office that are useful for family research should be mentioned. The second time use survey provided considerable information for research on household production in families and households. The Sample Survey of Income and Expenditure (EVS, *Einkommens- und Verbrauchsstichprobe*) can be used to study the economic situation of families and households. The social assistance statistics (*Sozialhilfestatistik*) and youth welfare statistics (*Statistik der Jugendhilfe*, various micro datasets on institutions providing services for children and adolescents) are relevant for family research and are available for several years. These opportunities are not yet being utilized extensively in family research.

3.2 Survey data

Longitudinal data for family research are currently available from large-scale studies like the SOEP (Wagner et al. 2007), the German Life History Study (GLHS) (Mayer 2000), the Family Survey of the German Youth Institute (DJI, *Deutsches Jugendinstitut*) (Bien and Marbach 2003), and the Cologne study of upper-level secondary students (*Gymnasiastenstudie*) (Meulemann 1995). The part of the SOEP relevant for family issues has been extended considerably over the years. A questionnaire dealing with newborn and very young children (aged two to three and four to six) and the subsample of adolescents (aged 16-17) provide important data in this context.

The SOEP, the Family Survey, the GLHS, and the Cologne *Gymnasiastenstudie* have brought about a considerable shift in the longitudinal analysis of family dynamics. The SOEP and the GLHS focus on socio-structural as well as demographic data and socio-economic issues. However, they do not allow the study of the interrelatedness between psychological and social dynamics and processes of decision-making about family or intimate relationships.

Studies on fertility and family dynamics that go beyond this "structural bias" are primarily cross-sectional surveys such as the Family and Fertility Surveys (FFS) conducted in the early 1990s and used to this day in international comparative studies. The same is true of the ALLBUS, the European Social Survey (ESS), and the German Family Survey. The latter includes a three-wave panel as a subsample but with a lag of six years between the waves. The Generations and Gender Survey (GGS) conducted under the auspices of the United Nations Economic Commission for Europe (UNECE) (Vikat et al. 2007) will also provide panel data. The time interval between the waves is also quite large here (three years). The German partner in this program is the Federal Institute for Population Research (BiB, *Bundesinstitut für Bevölkerungsforschung*). The first wave of the German GGS was conducted in 2005; in 2006 a migration sample was added (Ruckdeschel et al 2007; Ette et al. 2007); and data collection for a second wave of the German sample started in 2008.

The DJI is running several surveys that are relevant for family research. Among the most important are the Youth Surveys addressing the living conditions and social and political orientations of adolescents and young adults (started in 1992; cross-sectional representative surveys of young people in Germany aged 16 to 29 or 12 to 29), and the Children's Panel, a longitudinal study started in 2001 that provides data on children's living situations and the impact of living conditions on children's individual development.

Socio-psychological determinants of couple and family behavior are being studied more and more in prospective surveys. Yet family behavior is still not being studied extensively in regard to social embeddedness (social networks, kinship networks) or from the perspective of "linked lives" (Elder 1994). Very few studies so far have attempted to use multi-actor designs to obtain original data on attributes of several related persons. An important exception in Germany is the SOEP, which makes it possible to combine information on the different members of a household.

Longitudinal data on living arrangements of the elderly are provided by the Survey of Health, Ageing and Retirement in Europe (SHARE) (Börsch-Supan et al. 2003). Two waves with respondents aged 50 and higher have been collected so far; the third is on the way. Also, the first and the second versions of the German Ageing Survey (DEAS, *Alterssurvey*) should be mentioned, which have contributed substantially to knowledge on this aspect of family life. But these studies have not been designed as panel studies and are limited to analyzing the dynamics of elderly people's family lives (Kohli and Szydlick 2000; Tesch-Römer et al. 2006).

To summarize: nearly all fields of family research are making use of information provided by large-scale datasets, and the research infrastructure has improved considerably. However, the richness of the data is often still quite limited due to the theoretical and methodological challenges referred to above.

3.3 International perspectives

An adequate overview of the international situation is impossible to provide in the limited space of this report. Some of the aforementioned German surveys have international counterparts (like the SOEP) or are part of international programs. This is true, for example, of the GGS, the ESS, and the SHARE project.

One international prospective longitudinal study that focuses on family issues and meets the conditions listed above is the Netherlands Kinship Panel Study. It is conducted by the Netherlands Interdisciplinary Demographic Institute in cooperation with several Dutch universities (NKPS; Dijkstra et al. 2004). The research questions focus on issues of intergenerational relationships and solidarity in kinship systems. Two waves of extensive face-to-face interviews have been conducted so far (Wave 1 in 2002-2004, Wave 2 in 2006-2007).

In Britain, important longitudinal data sources (besides the BHPS[1]) are provided by the National Child Development Study and the 1970 British Cohort Study, followed by the National Child Development Study and Millennium Cohort Study. These studies are run by the Centre for Longitudinal Studies UK. The Millennium Cohort Study (MCS) is the UK's latest longitudinal birth cohort study and follows the lives of a sample of babies

---

1 British Household Panel Study.

born 2000 to 2002. The studies collect information on education and employment, family and parenting, physical and mental health, and social attitudes of large numbers of respondents of selected birth cohorts (Ferri et al. 2003; Dex and Joshi 2005).

4. Future developments: Data provision and data access

4.1 Requirements in regard to data

Although considerable theoretical and methodological progress has been made, some aspects of family research seem to have reached an impasse that crucially needs to be overcome. This is primarily a problem of data, not of theory. Data are needed not only to adequately describe family changes but also to measure the structural and especially socio-psychological determinants and "outcomes" of couples' and family dynamics and family relationships over time – both retrospectively and prospectively. The resulting data requirements are obvious:

(1) Data on all levels of analysis are needed. Macro-level data mainly provide information about demographic trends in changing living arrangements, family developments, and social structure. However, these data are also indispensable to multilevel analyses of family processes. We need information about societal conditions of family life (macro-economic, political, and cultural conditions). On the meso-level, what is needed most is information on the regional circumstances (opportunities and restrictions) of parenting, family life, and intergenerational support (support systems and institutions for various needs of couples and families at all stages of their development, labor market conditions, information about company support to families, programs providing childcare for working parents, etc.) as well as data dealing with the social context, kinship structure, and social networks. On the individual level, data are needed to model individual decision processes over time. Moreover, it will be increasingly important to be able to combine data from different sources and different levels of analysis.

(2) Not only do we need (socio-)structural information (demographic variables; the indicators of "standard demography" as provided by the ALLBUS) on the macro- and micro-levels, but also data on cultural factors impacting family development. Measurement of these factors must be improved by developing instruments to study national or regional cultural patterns in ideas about family or religiosity. The attitudes and socio-psychological dispositions of individual actors will have to be considered in order to model multilevel decision processes

over time, to test bridge hypotheses, and to include the developmental dimension.

(3) Panel data are needed to test multilevel, dynamic theories of couples' and family development. Cross-sectional data only serve descriptive purposes and help to obtain correct correlations. Data from retrospective surveys are not sufficient, because they can only provide structural information ("life histories") of sufficient validity. At least panel data are needed providing information on life events and socio-psychological dispositions over time. Here, it may even be necessary to implement event-based sampling strategies. Only prospective methods of data collection deliver valid information on social-psychological indicators.

(4) Because we are dealing with intimate social relationship decisions, individuals (partners, parents and children, grandparents and parents, siblings, etc.) have a strong impact on each other's behavior. Therefore, a multi-actor design is often necessary. In particular, it is virtually impossible to obtain valid proxy information on socio-psychological attributes (such as attitudes) of another person, whether the person reporting is a friend, member of the social network, partner, or parent of the individual being reported on.

To summarize, we need longitudinal, "on time" data from all levels of analysis. At the micro-level, we need more socio-psychological information and multi-actor designs, and high-quality data enabling a differentiated description of family dynamics and changing living arrangements in Germany.

4.2 Official statistics

Many improvements have been made in data from official statistical sources to implement a descriptive reporting system in the field of family research (see the report by Kreyenfeld and Scholz). The quality of the vital statistics of the Federal Republic of Germany on family issues has improved since 2008: they now provide the opportunity to study fertility in line with international standards. The same is true of the Microcensus: at least now, female respondents are asked about their total number of children. This is a very small improvement, however.

Here, more effort should go into using other micro datasets that are relevant for family research, such as the *Statistik der Jugendhilfe* and the like.

4.3 Surveys

The empirical basis for descriptive analyses and analytical models in different fields of family research has to be strengthened. Surveys like the Family Survey of the German Youth Institute should therefore be continued: they serve both purposes, as past experiences show. Furthermore, they are essential to a reporting system on family issues, which cannot be created solely using data from official statistical sources (Engstler and Menning 2003).

The other longitudinal research and survey programs mentioned above also have to be continued. A major contribution has been made by the newly launched pairfam with a yearly data collection schedule. Members of three age cohorts (15-17, 25-27, and 35-37 years old in the first wave) will be followed up over subsequent years. The study will provide longitudinal data on the basis of a multi-actor design. Additionally, the partners, parents, and children of the anchor persons will be interviewed. The questionnaires include detailed structural and non-structural information. Particular emphasis is placed on psychological and sociological instruments to obtain prospective information on determinants of establishing intimate relationships and their stability over time; the timing and spacing of fertility; intergenerational relationships and parenting; and social networks. It is important to continue this panel on a long-term basis.

Internationally, the Netherlands Kinship Panel Study will be continued. Also a third wave of the GGS is planned in different European countries.

5. Conclusions and recommendations

First of all, there is good reason to demand more attention to the various issues of family research from the German Data Forum (RatSWD) in its efforts to improve the data infrastructure for the social sciences. This need should not be addressed strictly from a demographic perspective – as important as this perspective is. Major aims of such an effort should include:

(1) Continuing initiatives to improve the family reporting system of the official statistical agencies, allowing for refined description and analysis of family structure and changing living arrangements in Germany. It should be consistent with respective reporting systems in other European countries. The probability of success would increase if scholars from different disciplines of family science in Germany undertook a coordinated initiative, potentially under the auspices of the German Data Forum (RatSWD).

(2) Providing opportunities to combine data from different sources, allowing the use of more refined models of multilevel analysis in family research. One possibility would be to combine individual-level information of different origins (register data of different kinds) with data on the local family-related infrastructure (day care provision) and data on workplace benefits supporting family needs (working hours policies).

(3) Continuing and optimizing prospective longitudinal studies collecting structural and socio-psychological information on the dynamics of individuals' living arrangements over time. Because of the special importance of longitudinal research for social research in general, major German panel studies such as pairfam should be integrated into a panel infrastructure covering different fields of social research. Family research would benefit from this considerably.

(4) Developing new instruments and methods of data collection going beyond the strict panel design with equidistant waves and testing methods of event-based sampling (see the report by Riediger).

(5) Improving the conditions for comparative longitudinal research by pursuing closer international cooperation.

References:

Bien, W. and Marbach, J.H. (Eds.) (2003): Partnerschaft und Familiengründung – Ergebnisse der dritten Welle des Familien-Survey. Opladen.
Blossfeld, H.-P. and Rohwer, G. (2002): Techniques of event history modeling. New approaches to causal analysis. Second Edition. Hillsdale (NJ),
Börsch-Supan, A./Jürges, H. and Lipps, O. (2003): SHARE - Measuring the aging process in Europe. ZUMA Nachrichten 53, 96-113.
Dex, S. and Joshi, H. (Eds.) (2005): Children of the 21st century: From birth to nine months. Bristol.
Dijkstra, P.A. et al. (2004): Codebook of the Netherlands Kinship Panel Study, a multi-actor, multi-method panel study on solidarity in family relationships. The Hague.
Duschek, K.-J. and Wirth, H. (2005): Kinderlosigkeit von Frauen im Spiegel des Mikrozensus. Eine Kohortenanalyse der Mikrozensen 1987 bis 2003. Wirtschaft und Statistik 8/2005, 800-820.
Elder, G.H. Jr. (1994): Time, Human Agency, and Social Change: Perspectives on the Life Course. Social Psychology Quarterly 57, 4-15.
Engstler, H. and Menning, S. (2003): Die Familie im Spiegel der amtlichen Statistik. Berlin.
Ette, A./Hullen, G./Leven, I. and Ruckdeschel, K. (2007): Generations and Gender Survey. Dokumentation der Befragung von türkischen Migranten in Deutschland. Materialien zur Bevölkerungswissenschaft, Heft 121b. Wiesbaden.
Feldhaus, M. and Huinink, J. (2008): Family Research from the Life Course Perspective. International Sociology. [Forthcoming].
Ferri, E./Bynner, J. and Wadsworth, M. (Eds.) (2003): Changing Britain, Changing Lives: Three generations at the turn of the century. London.
Hakim, C. (2000): Work-Lifestyle Choices in the 21ist Century: Preference Theory. Oxford.
Halaby, Ch. (2004): Panel Models in Sociological Research. Annual Review of Sociology 30, 507-544.
Huinink, J. (2008): Gegenstand der Familiensoziologie. In: Schneider, N.F. (Ed.): Lehrbuch Moderne Familiensoziologie. Opladen.
Kohli, M. and Szydlik, M. (Eds.) (2000): Generationen in Familie und Gesellschaft, Opladen.
Kreyenfeld, M. (2001): Employment and Fertility – East Germany in the 1990s Rostock. [Unpublished dissertation].
Kreyenfeld, M. and Geisler, E. (2006): Müttererwerbstätigkeit in Ost- und Westdeutschland. Zeitschrift für Familienforschung 18, 333-360.
Kreyenfeld, M./Zühlke, S. and Konold, M (2007): Ökonomische Basis der Familiengründung – Analysen mit den Daten des Mikrozensus-Panels. Presentation on the 5. Nutzerkonferenz „Forschungen mit dem Mikrozensus: Analysen zur Sozialstruktur und Arbeitsmarkt", 15-16 November 2007, Mannheim.
Lengerer, A./Janßen, A. and Bohr, J. (2007): Familiensoziologische Analysepotenziale des Mikrozensus. Zeitschrift für Familienforschung 19, 186-209.

Lengerer, A. and Klein, Th. (2007): Der langfristige Wandel partnerschaftlicher Lebensformen im Spiegel des Mikrozensus. Wirtschaft und Statistik 4, 433-447.

Lesthaeghe, R. (Ed.) (2002): Meaning and Choice: Value Orientation and Life Course Decisions. NIDI/CBGS Publication. The Hague/Brussels.

Lyons, K.S. and Sayer, A.G. (2005): Longitudinal Dyad Models in Family Research. Journal of Marriage and Family 67, 1048-1060.

Mayer, K.U. (2000): Promises fulfilled? A review of 20 years of life course research. Archives européennes de sociologie 41, 259-282.

Meulemann, H. (1995): Die Geschichte einer Jugend. Lebenserfolg und Erfolgsdeutung ehemaliger Gymnasiasten zwischen dem 15. und 30. Lebensjahr. Opladen.

Nauck, B. (2001): Der Wert von Kindern für ihre Eltern. „Value of Children" als spezielle Handlungstheorie des generativen Verhaltens und von Generationenbeziehungen im interkulturellen Vergleich. Kölner Zeitschrift für Soziologie und Sozialpsychologie 53, 407-435.

Ruckdeschel, K./Ette, A./Hullen, G. and Leven, I. (2007): Generations and Gender Survey. Dokumentation der ersten Welle der Hauptbefragung in Deutschland. Materialien zur Bevölkerungswissenschaft, Heft 121a. Wiesbaden.

Seltzer, J.A. et al. (2005): Explaining Family Change and Variation: Challenges for Family Demographers. Journal of Marriage and Family 67, 908-925.

Singer, J.B. and Willett, J.B. (2003): Applied Longitudinal Data Analysis. Oxford.

Tesch-Römer, C./Engstler, H. and Wurm, S. (Eds.) (2006): Altwerden in Deutschland – Sozialer Wandel und individuelle Entwicklung in der zweiten Lebenshälfte. Wiesbaden.

Vikat, A. et al. (2007): Generations and Gender Survey (GGS) Towards a Better Understanding of Relationships and Processes in the Life Course. Demographic Research, 17, pp. 389-440

Wagner, G.G./Frick, J.R. and Schupp, J. (2007): The German Socio-Economic Panel Study (SOEP) – Scope, Evolution and Enhancements. Schmollers Jahrbuch 127 (1), 139-169.

Wirth, H. (2007): Kinderlosigkeit im Paarkontext von hochqualifizierten Frauen und Männern – Eine Folge von Bildungshomogamie? In: Konietzka, D. and Kreyenfeld. M. (Eds.): Ein Leben ohne Kinder? Kinderlosigkeit in Deutschland. Wiesbaden.

Wu, L.L. (2004): Event History Models for Life Course Analysis. In: Mortimer, J.T. and Shanahan, M.J. (Eds.): Handbook of the Life Course. New York.

5.4 Intergenerational Relationships

Bernhard Nauck and Anja Steinbach

Contact:

Bernhard Nauck
Anja Steinbach
Chemnitz University of Technology
Department of Sociology
Thueringer Weg 9
09107 Chemnitz
Germany
e-mail: bernhard.nauck[at]phil.tu-chemnitz.de
          anja.steinbach[at]phil.tu-chemnitz.de

Abstract

Intergenerational relationships within family and kinship structures have become a salient issue in scientific research. The major reasons for this are the intense demographic changes that occurred throughout the twentieth century, such as an increased life expectancy in combination with decreased fertility, and the implications of this for the major institutions of the social welfare state. This has resulted in several larger studies that can serve as the basis for an analysis of the situation as it impacts older people, including the German Socio-Economic Panel (SOEP, *Sozio-oekonomisches Panel*), the Generations and Gender Survey (GGS), the Family Survey, the German Ageing Survey (DEAS, *Deutscher Alterssurvey*), the Survey on Health, Ageing and Retirement in Europe (SHARE), and the Panel Analysis of Intimate Relationships and Family Dynamics (pairfam). However, an overarching theoretical and research perspective on intergenerational relationships from their creation (fertility) through parenting to the longest lasting relationships between adults of different generations is still lacking. In order to overcome this deficiency, this paper recommends that future data structures obtain information on intergenerational relationships through data that is obtained (1) simultaneously and is theoretically complete, (2) in a lifespan perspective, (3) from a panel design and (4) a multi-actor design. Studies should (5) account for cultural variability of intergenerational relationships and (6) for institutional settings in cross-national comparisons.

Keywords: intergenerational relationships, intergenerational solidarity, life course, demographic change, ageing, panel studies

1. Introduction

Intergenerational relationships within the family and kinship structures have become a salient issue in public discourse as well as in scientific research. The major reasons for this are the intense demographic changes that occurred throughout the twentieth century, such as an increased life expectancy in combination with decreased fertility and their implications for the major institutions of the social welfare state. Since the end of the 1990s in the social sciences, this has resulted in the planning and realization of several larger studies on the situation of older people in Germany and Europe, including their relationships to family members. It has also resulted in the implementation of instruments measuring parent-child-relationships in already existing or newly initiated longitudinal surveys. Due to the urgent political issues surrounding these questions, initial research on intergenerational relationships in families in the context of demographic changes has focused on relationships between *aged* parents and their *adult* children, focusing generally on the question of family-based care and intergenerational solidarity in later stages of life. Accordingly, data collection has concentrated on relationships between children and their (very) old parents. The research domain has therefore been located at the intersection of family research and research on aging. Labeled *research on intergenerational relationships*, it is at present clearly distinguished from *research on parent-child relationships* as a classical research domain of parenting within developmental psychology and socialization research. *An overarching theoretical and research perspective on intergenerational relationships from their creation (fertility) through parenting to the longest lasting relationships between adults of different generations is still lacking.*

2. Theoretical developments and research questions

2.1 Theoretical developments

Most literature on intergenerational relationships starts with a reflection on the family-in-crisis hypothesis. To test this hypothesis, but also to give a descriptive picture, various aspects of these relations are considered. The most important contributions to this framework include the theory of intergenerational solidarity (Bengtson and Roberts 1991; Bengtson 2001) and work on ambivalence (Lüscher and Pillemer 1998; Pillemer and Lüscher 2004). These contributions to the discourse consider many different aspects of contact and supportive behavior within the family and between generations. Based heavily on social exchange theory, intergenerational relationships are understood as any form of exchange between generations. Six exchange dimensions are distinguished, namely structural, associative, affective, consensual, normative, and functional solidarity.

The *structural dimension* refers to the opportunity structure that determines the specific ways that family interactions are realized. Typical measurements are geographical distance and residential proximity, but availability of kin, parents, children, and siblings, as well as their age, sex, marital status, health status, and working arrangements are also seen as important factors in structural solidarity. The *associative dimension* refers to the amount and kind of intergenerational contact, either face-to-face or by phone, e-mail, or other means. Therefore, frequency and intensity of contact can be distinguished. The *affective dimension* comprises emotional closeness as well as conflict as measures of the quality of the relationship between children and their parents. The *consensual dimension* measures the degree of agreement in values and beliefs – whatever the specific content of these convictions may be. The *normative dimension* refers to the extent of commitment to filial and parental obligations by the respective members of intergenerational relationships. The *functional dimension* measures all kinds of financial, instrumental, and emotional support that are exchanged between parents and children.

However, the various types of interaction between generations are not always positive. Intergenerational relations can – and typically do – comprise both positive and negative components, and thus are to some extent *ambivalent*. This is due to the social character of intergenerational relationships, which is in most cases unavoidable and inescapable, rather "diffuse" in their exchange, and thus "packaged." It is an open debate whether ambivalence should be measured directly, for example by asking about the amount of simultaneously positive and negative (i.e., ambivalent) emotions or whether conclusions about ambivalence should be arrived at indirectly, from the extent of simultaneous emotional closeness and conflict between generations.

For a long time, theoretical discussions around intergenerational relationships were (and to some extent still are) limited to the question of whether these named dimensions are adequate (Szydlik 2000) or complete (Bengtson et al. 2002; Lüscher and Pillemer 1998). More recent discussions have become increasingly critical and point out the theoretical deficits of the well-established paradigms (Dallinger 2002; Hammarström 2005; Katz et al. 2005; Grünendahl and Martin 2005). However, serious attempts to provide theoretical explanations for the emergence of and changes within and between the respective dimensions of intergenerational relationships are still very rare (Merz et al. 2007; Steinbach and Kopp 2008a). In summary, one may state that apart from the heuristic model of Szydlik (2000), which includes the associative, affective, and functional dimensions and relates them to opportunity, need, family, and cultural-contextual structures, there is no elaborated theory of intergenerational relationships.

2.2 Research questions

Empirically, several different analytical strategies can be distinguished with regard to the respective aspects of intergenerational relationships (Steinbach and Kopp 2008a).

2.2.1 Intergenerational solidarity

Within this research domain, a first group of studies focuses on the internal structure of the dimensions of intergenerational solidarity (Atkinson et al. 1986; Roberts and Bengtson 1990; Rossi and Rossi 1990). A second group of studies tries to combine these different dimensions of intergenerational relations, aiming at the construction of family typologies (Bengtson 2001; Giarrusso et al. 2004; 2005; Katz et al. 2005; Van Gaalen and Dykstra 2006;

Silverstein et al. 1994; Steinbach 2008). A third group of studies deals with the different perspectives that parents and children have on their respective relationships. This research has resulted in the so-called "intergenerational stake hypotheses" (Bengtson and Kuypers 1971), and has recently initiated several subsequent replications (Aquilino 1999; Giarrusso et al. 1995; Trommsdorff and Schwarz 2007). The fourth and largest group of studies can be characterized by varied attempts to identify independent socio-structural, intrafamilial, or intergenerational factors that determine intergenerational relationships. Determinants of the degree of emotional closeness, the frequency of contact, and the level of exchange are of particular interest (Attias-Donfut 2000; Hank 2007; Kaufman and Uhlenberg 1998; Klaus 2009; Kohli et al. 2005; Lawton et al. 1994; Parrott and Bengtson 1999; Roberts and Bengtson 1990; Rossi and Rossi 1990; Spitze and Logan 1991; Steinbach and Kopp 2008b; Szydlik 1995; 2000). But also, for example, conflict (Szydlik 2008), ambivalence (Pillemer and Suitor 2002), and inheritance (Kohli 2004; Lauterbach and Lüscher 1996; Nauck 2009b; Szydlik 1999; 2004; Szydlik and Schupp 2004) are important empirical research subjects. The results of all these studies stand in sharp contrast to the popular perception of weakening ties between generations in "postmodern" families. Instead, intergenerational relationships have become – despite changing demographic structures – increasingly important for family members and are obviously one of the major mechanisms of social integration in functionally differentiated societies.

2.2.2 Gender

One structural variable that has played an important role over the years and thus will be given particular attention at this point is that of gender. Empirical results show consistently that the respective combination of gender across generations structures the relationship considerably; that is, there is a rank order in the closeness of the relationship from mother-daughter to mother-son, father-daughter and father-son relationship (Kaufman and Uhlenberg 1998; Nauck 2009a; Rossi 1993; Szydlik 1995). Women – especially from the older generation – function as "kinkeeper" (Atkinson et al. 1986; Rossi and Rossi 1990), maintaining the relationships and providing support. Moreover, women are prone to find themselves in a "sandwich" situation, with simultaneous care activities for both the older and the younger generation within the family. However, this phenomenon becomes rarer with increasingly healthy aging and extended age differences between generations (Kohli and Künemund 2005a; Künemund 2006).

2.2.3 Life course

In recent years, research on intergenerational relationships has also adopted a life-course perspective. Although cross-sectional data are predominantly used, the interesting research question has become whether early life stages have an important impact on the intergenerational relationships in later life. From this perspective, one topic of investigation has been the degree to which parents' early transfers to their young adult children affect the children's propensity in middle age to provide social support to their aging parents (Silverstein et al. 2002) and how life-course transitions experienced by each generation affect the quality of relationships between adult children and their parents (Kaufman and Uhlenberg 1998). In particular, the separation and divorce of parents as a potential obstacle in later life intergenerational relationships has become an important research question (Aquilino 2005; Kalmijn 2008; Lin 2008). Likewise, the relationship between attachment patterns in early childhood and the exchange of support in later life stages has arisen as a significant theme in the research (Cicirelli 1993; Merz et al. 2008; Schwarz and Trommsdorff 2005).

2.2.4 Cross-national comparisons

The establishment of cross-national and cross-cultural comparative datasets has made it possible to investigate intergenerational relationships in a comparative perspective. Such research programs, predominantly based on cross-sectional data, exist especially for East Asian societies (Hermalin 2002), for Europe (Albertini et al. 2007; Brandt and Szydlik 2008; Haberkern and Szydlik 2008; Hank 2007; Katz et al. 2005), and to some extent for comparisons across continents (Nauck 2009a; 2009b; Nauck and Suckow 2006; Nauck and Yi 2007; Trommsdorff and Nauck 2005). The predominant focus in cross-national research is the interrelationship between the social-political regimes on the one hand and the structure of intergenerational exchange relationships on the other, for example, whether social-political measures and incentives may deteriorate intergenerational support and solidarity (crowding out) or whether they enable and enhance them (crowding in) (Künemund 2008). Empirical research provides some evidence that economic transfer and care provisions by the welfare state do not edge out intergenerational support – both seem to complement each other (Armi et al. 2008; Attias-Donfut 2000; Brandt and Szydlik 2008; Künemund and Vogel 2006). Moreover, empirical evidence has suggested that social-political regimes and individual involvement in intergenerational support interact strongly (Haberkern and Szydlik 2008).

2.2.5 Social and demographic change

Major demographic trends in the twentieth century had a strong impact on the analysis of intergenerational relationships. One emerging research domain is the analysis of intergenerational relationships beyond the parent-child dyad, namely grandparent-grandchildren relationships (Hank and Buber 2009; Harper 2005; Hoff 2007; King and Elder 1995; 1997; Mueller and Elder 2003). Increased life expectancy in welfare societies has not only resulted in the prolonged common lifetime of parents and children, but also in the increased existence of families with three and even four generations (Hoff 2006; Lauterbach 1995; Lauterbach and Klein 2004). This phenomenon, together with the decline of horizontal kinship relationships because of reduced fertility, was coined as the "beanpole family" (Bengtson et al. 1990) and described as a multi-local extended family structure (Bertram 2003; Lauterbach 2004). This development has stimulated questions about the extent to which relationships between generations are interwoven (Friedman et al. 2008) and the extent to which grandparent-grandchildren relationships are comparable to parent-child relationships (Hoff 2007).

Another major demographic trend is the increased number of immigrants and their aging patterns (Dietzel-Papakyriakou 1993; Nauck 2007). Empirical research has been dedicated to the question of whether intergenerational relationships differ between migrant and native families, between immigrant families of different origin and within different receiving contexts, and how these relationships are maintained across national borders (Attias-Donfut and Wolff 2008; Baykara-Krumme 2008a; 2008b; Komter and Schans 2008; Nauck 2001; Nauck and Kohlmann 1998).

3. Status quo: Databases and access

Meanwhile, several datasets exist that can be used for the analysis of intergenerational relationships. In Germany, these include on the one hand the large-scale datasets like the SOEP, the GGS, and the Family Survey, which encompass large age brackets. On the other hand, datasets from aging research are also available, such as the study Old Age and Autonomy: The Role of Service Systems and Intergenerational Solidarity (OASIS), DEAS or SHARE, which mostly concentrate on the population from age forty onwards. Additionally, the dataset of pairfam will be available soon, which will provide data on the intergenerational relationships of younger respondents (aged between fifteen and fifty) with their respective parents. GGS, OASIS, and SHARE are cross-national comparative research programs that allow for analyzing the German situation in an international perspective.

Other important international studies of intergenerational relations without German samples are the Netherlands Kinship Panel Study (NKPS) (Dykstra 1999; Dykstra et al. 2006) and two studies from the United States: the Longitudinal Study of Generations (LSOG) (Mangen et al. 1988; Giarrusso and Zucker 2004), and the American National Survey of Families and Households (NSFH) (Sweet and Bumpass 2002). A systematic comparison of the existing datasets on an international level is provided in the appendix. The following brief description concentrates on German datasets and those with German participation.

German Socio-Economic Panel. The SOEP of the German Institute for Economic Research (DIW Berlin, *Deutsches Institut für Wirtschaftsforschung*) has collected detailed annual data to measure the stability and change of living conditions in Germany since 1984 (Frick 2007). Since the early 1990s, it has extended its scope to include some instruments on intergenerational relationships, such as residential distance and emotional closeness to biological parents and to the closest living son or daughter (if the respondent has more than one) (1991, 1996, 2001, 2006). Since 1984, the amount of financial transfers between generations is also captured (exception: 1992 and 1994), including intergenerational donations, inheritance, and bequest.

Generations and Gender Survey. The GGS is the German version of an international research program in sixteen countries. It is merged into the "Generations and Gender Program" (GGP) of the United Nations Economic Commission of Europe (UNECE) (Ruckdeschel et al., 2006). The first two waves were completed in 2005 and 2008. The GGS contains questions regarding residential distance, frequency of contact and emotional closeness to parents and children, filial obligations, and daytime care of grandchildren. Financial, instrumental, and emotional support is captured with a network generator, within which family members can be named.

Family Survey. The Family Survey of the German Youth Institute (DJI, *Deutsches Jugendinstitut*) (Bien and Marbach 2008) includes a three-wave panel as a subsample but with a lag of six years between the waves (1988, 1994, 2000). Emotional closeness and exchange of financial support is captured with a network generator, within which family and kinship members can be named. For all named individuals, information on relationship quality, residential distance, and frequency of contact are available.

Old Age and Autonomy: The Role of Service Systems and Intergenerational Family Solidarity. OASIS is conducted in five countries, including Germany (Tesch-Römer et al. 2000; Lowenstein and Ogg 2003). Data collection took place in 2000 in urban regions only. The disproportionate stratified sample starts at twenty-five years old and over-represents individuals older than seventy-five. Intergenerational relationships are measured based on the dimensions residential distance, frequency of contact (to parents and all children), emotional closeness, conflict and ambivalence, consensus (degree of similarity on opinions and values between parents and focus child) and the agreement on filial obligations. Mutual support is captured by data on financial, emotional, and instrumental help within the last twelve months. Moreover, grandparent-grandchildren relationships are covered with regard to residential distance, frequency of contact, and support.

German Ageing Survey. The DEAS of the German Center of Gerontology is a study of the living situation of people aged forty and older in Germany. Three waves were completed in 1996, 2002, and 2008 (Kohli and Künemund 2005b; Tesch-Römer et al. 2002; 2006). For all children and for individuals with whom the respondent predominantly grew up, and for up to eight additional network members, the following dimensions of intergenerational relations are captured: residential distance, frequency of contact, and emotional closeness. Exchange of support is part of a network generator, within which up to five persons may be named with whom the respondent exchanges financial, instrumental, and emotional support. Daytime care of grandchildren is also captured, as well as inheritance and bequest.

Survey of Health, Ageing and Retirement in Europe. SHARE is an international longitudinal research program and comprises fifteen countries in Europe (Bösch-Supan and Jürges 2005; Bösch-Supan et al. 2005) with three panel waves in 2004-2005, 2006-2007, and 2008-2009. The first wave captured target persons of fifty years and older and their household partners. Intergenerational relationships are covered by the dimensions residential distance, frequency of contact, and emotional closeness to parents and all children living outside the respondent's household. Received help was captured by questions surveying sources of material and financial transfer within the last twelve months and whether caring, if necessary, was received. Up to three individuals can be named. Daytime care of grandchildren is also captured.

Panel Analysis of Intimate Relationships and Family Dynamics. pairfam is a comprehensive research program about partnership and family development in Germany (Huinink and Feldhaus 2008). It is based on a cohort design, comprising three cohorts of 15 to 17, 25 to 27, and 35 to 37 years-old target persons respectively in combination with a multi-actor design, including the respective partner, both parents, and children of eight years and older. Data collection of the first wave takes place in 2008-2009, with thirteen further waves currently planned. In the first wave, short versions of instruments on intergenerational relationships are applied (residential distance, frequency of contact, and emotional closeness). From the second wave onwards, comprehensive instruments on residential distance, frequency of contact, emotional closeness, conflict, ambivalence, and agreement to filial obligations, as well as material, financial, instrumental, and emotional transfers will be used, targeting the relationship to both biological parents and, if relevant, stepparents. The multi-actor design implies that from the second wave onwards, (step)parents will provide information about their perspective on the intergenerational relationship towards the target person and his or her respective partner, and that the partner will provide information on his or her relationship to the parents-in-law.

Although surveys that include topics around intergenerational relationships have grown considerably during the last decade, there are still obvious data deficits – especially in Germany:

- As the data on intergenerational relationships are in most cases limited to the measurement of selective dimensions of intergenerational solidarity, their internal structure and mutual influences can not be tested.
- Most studies originate in the field of social gerontology with a focus on the elderly, their family support, and its relation to institutional caretaking.
- Most studies are highly selective in the choice of the studied intergenerational relationships, such that only the relationship to the emotionally and geographically closest child or parent is surveyed, resulting in a positive bias in the scientific description of intergenerational relationships.

For a better understanding of intergenerational relationships in present society, a life-course perspective that covers the development of intergenerational relationships across the entire lifespan and under varying family settings, including non-biological forms of parent-child relations, is needed. Only then can valid measurements of intergenerational solidarity, conflict, and separation in their various dimensions be obtained and thus also allow researchers to make informed estimates about the future potential and development of intergenerational solidarity and social integration.

4. Future developments and recommendations

The diagnosis of these deficits allows us to suggest some recommendations for creating the data structures necessary for future research.

- Data on intergenerational relationships should be *obtained simultaneously and should be theoretically complete*. That is, all dimensions of the well-established model of intergenerational solidarity and its extensions into conflict have to be measured. Only this will allow for the investigation of the interrelationship between the various dimensions of intergenerational relations – an issue of significant scientific and practical interest.

- Data on intergenerational relationships should be targeted to a *lifespan perspective*. Intergenerational solidarity in later life stages depends on intergenerational experiences in formative life stages, trajectories, and alternate options and obligations during the previous life course, and is therefore path dependent. The interdependence of generations during the entire lifespan is one of the most important desiderata in this research domain.

- The study of intergenerational relationships needs *panel designs*. Only panel designs allow for the analysis of the creation and the development of intergenerational relationships in specific stages of the life course. They should be complemented by retrospective information on critical life events and related to intergenerational relationships in the past biography of the respondents and his or her family members.

- Methodological research is urgently needed with regard to the *measurement intervals* for intergenerational relationships. Since previous research has concentrated on the most stable and most harmonious relationships in later life, this research provides no knowledge base for an adequate measurement of instable, disruptive, or conflictual parent-child relationships.

- The study of intergenerational relationships should include a *multi-actor design* in order to include the perceptions, evaluations, needs, and resources on both sides of an intergenerational relationship, which is, by nature, asymmetrical and thus prone to differences between members. Moreover, each individual operates and can be statistically modeled within the context of other's actions. Comprehensive analyses of multilevel panel data on intergenerational relationships will be a major research agenda in this realm.

- The study of intergenerational relationships should account for *cultural variability and diversification*. The increasing number of individuals with a migration background is resulting in an increased variability of values related to filial and parental obligations, of arrangements in intergenerational support, and of wealth flows between generations. Thus, specific measurements should be included not only to accommodate migrant and minority situations, but also a range of cross-culturally informed adaptations, which still have to be developed and tested.

- The emergence of multi-local and multi-generational family structures demands special provisions in the collection of data, and, in most cases, a *multi-method-design*. As the study of intergenerational relationships cannot be based on a standard representative survey design, where all respondents are accessed with the same data collection method, it will be necessary to use a combination of various obtainable methods, such as mail survey, computer-assisted telephone interview (CATI), computer-assisted personal interview (CAPI), computer-assisted self interview (CASI), paper and pencil interview (PAPI), or computer-assisted web interview (CAWI). However, no systematic results are available yet to allow for estimation of the respective advantages and disadvantages of each method within this specific research field.

- For a full understanding of the interplay between institutional settings in the respective social context and the specific structure of intergenerational relationships, *cross-national and cross-cultural comparisons* are needed. To achieve this goal, concepts and measurements have to be standardized and tested for linguistic and functional equivalence. These efforts require a specific infrastructure and extended time for development, both of which are typically disregarded in the funding of comparative research programs. Effective international collaboration needs an additional infrastructure from which standardization and equivalence testing can be coordinated.

The study of intergenerational relationships is an emerging and expanding research domain in the social sciences. It is situated at the intersection of a micro-social level of interactionist family sociology, the meso-level of network analysis and human ecology, and the macro-level of societal integration and social inequality. Its constantly developing nature requires one to adopt a lifespan perspective, which both asks for and permits interdisciplinary cooperation, including a large array of disciplines including developmental psychology, social gerontology, demography, economy, and sociology.

Appendix: Overview of surveys which include measures of intergenerational relationships

Study	Full Name	Institution	Data Collection	Unit of Observation
SOEP	German Socio-Economic Panel Study	German Institute for Economic Research, Berlin	Since 1984 IGR: 91, 96, 01, 06	Households (n=10,000) Individuals (n=20,000)
Family Survey	German Family Survey	German Youth Institute, Munich	1988/1990 1994 2000	Individuals (n=10,000)
GGS	Generations and Gender Survey	Federal Institute for Population Research, Wiesbaden	2005 2008 (2011)	Individuals (n=10,000)
OASIS	Old Age and Autonomy: The Role of Service Systems and Intergenerational Family Solidarity	The German Centre of Gerontology, Berlin	2000	Individuals (n=1,300)
DEAS	German Ageing Survey	The German Centre of Gerontology, Berlin	1996 2002 2008	Individuals (n=5,000)
SHARE	Survey of Health, Aging and Retirement in Europe	Mannheim Research Institute for the Economics of Aging, Mannheim	2004/5 2006/7 2008/9	Individuals (n=3,000) Partner
pairfam	Panel Analysis of Intimate Relationships and Family Dynamics	Universities of Bremen, Chemnitz, Mannheim, Munich	2008/9 + 13 waves	Individuals (n=12,000) Partner, Children, Parents

Universe	Countries	Migrant Sample	Dimensions of Intergene-rational Relations
18+ Panel	DE	684 Foreigners (1994+)	Distance, Contact, Emotional Closeness, Transfer
18-55 Mixed Design	DE		Distance, Contact, Emotional Closeness, Satisfaction, Transfer
18-79 Mixed Design	DE (AU, BE, BG, CZ, EE, FR, GE, HU, IT, JP, LT, NL, NO, RO, RU)	4,000 Turks (in 2006)	Distance, Contact, Satisfaction, Filial Obligations, Transfer
25+ Cross-sectional	DE (IL, NO, ES, UK)		Distance, Contact, Emotional Closeness, Consensus, Filial Obligations, Transfer
40+ Mixed Design	DE	586 Foreigners (in 2002, 2008)	Distance, Contact, Emotional Closeness, Transfer
50+ Panel	DE (AT, BE, DK, FR, GR, IT, ES, CH, NL/CZ, IE, PL/SI)		Distance, Contact, Emotional Closeness, Transfer
15/25/35 Panel	DE	300 Turks (in 2008)	Distance, Contact, Emotional Closeness, Conflict, Filial Obligations, Transfer

Study	Full Name	Institution	Data Collection	Unit of Observation
NKPS	Netherlands Kinship Panel Study	Netherlands Interdisciplinary Demographic Institute, The Hague; NL	2002/4 2006/7	Individuals (n=10,000) Partner, Children, Parents, Siblings
LSOG	Longitudinal Study of Generations	University of Southern California, Los Angeles, USA	1971, 1985, 1988, 1991, 1994, 1997	Families (n=300) Members of four Generations (in 2000)
NSFH	American National Survey of Families and Households	Center for Demography, University of Wisconsin, USA	1987/8, 1992/4; 2001/2	Individuals (n=13,000) Partner, Children

Universe	Countries	Migrant Sample	Dimensions of Intergenerational Relations
18-79 Panel	NL	1,400 Migrants (in 2002, 2006)	Distance, Contact, Relationship Quality, Conflict, Filial Obligations, Transfer
18+ Panel	US		Distance, Contact, Emotional Closeness, Conflict, Consensus, Filial Obligations, Transfer
18+ Panel	US	Oversample of Blacks/Puerto Ricans/Mexicans	Distance, Contact, Relationship Quality, Transfer

References:

Albertini, M./Kohli, M. and Vogel, C. (2007): Intergenerational transfers of time and money in European families: common patterns – different regimes? Journal of European Social Policy 17 (4), 319-334.

Aquilino, W.S. (1999): Two Views on One Relationship: Comparing Parents' and Young Adults Children's Reports of the Quality of Intergenerational Relations. Journal of Marriage and the Family 61, 858-870.

Aquilino, W.S. (2005): Impact of Family Structure on Parental Attitudes toward the Economic Support of Adult Children Over the Transition to Adulthood. Journal of Family Issues 26 (2), 143-167.

Armi, F./Guilley, E. and Lalive D'Epinay, Ch.J. (2008): The Interface between Formal and Informal Support in Advanced Old Age: A Ten-Year Study. International Journal of Aging and Later Life 3 (1), 5-19.

Atkinson, M.P./Kivett, V.R. and Campbell, R.T. (1986): Intergenerational Solidarity: An Examination of a Theoretical Model. Journal of Gerontology 41 (3), 408-416.

Attias-Donfut, C. (2000): Familialer Austausch und soziale Sicherung. In: Kohli, M. and Szydlik, M. (Eds.): Generationen in Familie und Gesellschaft. Opladen.

Attias-Donfut, C. and Wolff, F.-Ch. (2008): Patterns of Intergenerational Transfers Among Immigrants in France: Comparative Perspective. In: Saraceno, Ch. (Ed.): Families, Aging and Social Policy. Intergenerational Solidarity in European Welfare States. Cheltenham/Northampton.

Baykara-Krumme, H. (2008a): Migrant Families in Germany: Intergenerational Solidarity in Later Life. Berlin.

Baykara-Krumme, H. (2008b): Reliable Bonds? A Comparative Perspective of Intergenerational Support Patterns Among Migrant Families in Germany. In: Saraceno, Ch. (Ed.): Families, Aging and Social Policy. Intergenerational Solidarity in European Welfare States. Cheltenham/Northampton.

Bengtson, V.L. (2001): Beyond the Nuclear Family: The Increasing Importance of Multigenerational Bonds. Journal of Marriage and the Family 63 (1), 1-16.

Bengtson, V.L. and Kuypers, J.A. (1971): Generational Difference and Developmental Stake. Aging and Human Development 2 (4), 249-260.

Bengtson, V.L. and Roberts, R.E.L. (1991): Intergenerational Solidarity in Aging Families: An Example of Formal Theory Construction. Journal of Marriage and the Family 53 (4), 856-870.

Bengtson, V.L./Rosenthal, C. and Burton, L. (1990): Families and Aging: Diversity and Heterogeneity. In: Binstock, R.H. and George, L.K. (Eds.): Handbook of Aging and the Social Sciences. 3rd edition. San Diego.

Bengtson, V.L./Giarrusso, R./Mabry, J.B. and Silverstein, M. (2002): Solidarity, Conflict, and Ambivalence: Complementary or Competing Perspectives on Intergenerational Relationships? Journal of Marriage and the Family 64 (3), 568-576.

Bertram, H. (2003): Die multilokale Mehrgenerationenfamilie. Von der neolokalen Gattenfamilie zur multilokalen Mehrgenerationenfamilie. In: Feldhaus, M./ Logemann, N. and Schlegel, M. (Eds.): Blickrichtung Familie – Vielfalt eines Forschungsgegenstandes. Würzburg.

Bien, W. and Marbach, J.H. (Eds.) (2008): Familiale Beziehungen, Familienalltag und soziale Netzwerke. Ergebnisse der drei Wellen des Familiensurvey. Wiesbaden.

Bösch-Supan, A. and Jürges, H. (Eds.) (2005): The Survey of Health, Aging and Retirement in Europe (SHARE). Methodology. Mannheim.

Bösch-Supan, A./Brugiavini, A./Jürges, H./Mackenbach, J./Siegrist, J. and Weber, G. (Eds.) (2005): Health, Aging and Retirement in Europe. First Results from the Survey of Health, Aging and Retirement in Europe (SHARE). Mannheim.

Brandt, M. and Szydlik, M. (2008): Soziale Dienste und Hilfe zwischen Generationen in Europa. Zeitschrift für Soziologie 37 (4), 301-320.

Cicirelli, V.G. (1993): Attachment and Obligation as Daughters' Motives for Caregiving Behavior and Subsequent Effect on Subjective Burden. Psychology and Aging 8 (2), 144-155.

Dallinger, U. (2002): Das ‚Problem der Generationen': Theorieentwicklung zu intergenerationellen Beziehungen. In: Dallinger, U. and Schroeter, K.R. (Eds.): Theoretische Beiträge zur Alternssoziologie. Opladen.

Dietzel-Papakyriakou, M. (1993): Altern in der Migration. Die Arbeitsmigranten vor dem Dilemma: zurückkehren oder bleiben? Stuttgart.

Dykstra, P.A. (1999): Netherlands Kinship Panel Study. A Multi-Actor, Multi-Method Panel Survey on Solidarity in Family Relationships. The Hague.

Dykstra, P.A./Kalmijn, M./Knijn, T.C.M./Komter, A.E./Liefbroer, A.C. and Mulder, C.H. (Eds.) (2006): Family Solidarity in the Netherlands. Amsterdam.

Ette, A./Hullen G./Leven, I. and Ruckdeschel, K. (2007): Generations and Gender Survey. Dokumentation der Befragung von türkischen Migranten in Deutschland. Materialien zur Bevölkerungswissenschaft, Heft 121b.

Frick, J.R. (2006): A General Introduction to the German Socio-Economic Panel Study (SOEP). http://www.diw.de/documents/dokumentenarchiv/17/43529/soep overview.pdf. [Last visited 01/18/2010].

Friedman, D./Hechter, M. and Kreager, D. (2008): A Theory of the Value of Grandchildren. Rationality and Society 20 (1), 31-63.

Giarrusso, R. and Zucker, D. (2004): The USC Longitudinal Study of Generations. Time-1 Thru Time-7 Codebook. Ann Arbor.

Giarrusso, R./Stallings, M. and Bengtson, V.L. (1995): The "Intergenerational Stake" Hypothesis Revisited: Parent-Child Differences in Perception of Relationships 20 Years Later. In: Bengtson, V.L./Schaie, K.W. and Burton, L.M. (Eds.): Adult Intergenerational Relations. Effects of Societal Change. New York.

Giarrusso, R./Feng, D. and Bengtson, V.L. (2004): The Intergenerational-Stake Phenomenon Over 20 Years. Annual Review of Gerontology and Geriatrics 24, 55-76.

Giarrusso, R./Silverstein, M./Gans, D. and Bengtson, V.L. (2005): Aging Parents and Adult Children: New Perspectives on Intergenerational Relationships. In: Johnson, M.L./Bengtson, V.L./Coleman, P.G./Kirkwood, Th.B.L. (Eds.): Cambridge Handbook of Age and Aging. London.

Grünendahl, M. and Martin, M. (2005): Intergenerative Solidarität und praktische Implikationen. In: Otto, U. and Bauer, P. (Eds.): Mit Netzwerken professionell zusammenarbeiten. Band 1: Soziale Netzwerke in Lebenslauf- und Lebenslagenperspektiven. Tübingen.

Haberkern, K. and Szydlik, M. (2008): Pflege der Eltern – Ein europäischer Vergleich. Kölner Zeitschrift für Soziologie und Sozialpsychologie 60 (1), 78-101.

Hank, K. (2007): Proximity and Contacts Between Older Parents and Their Children: A European Comparison. Journal of Marriage and the Family 69 (1), 157-173.

Hank, K. and Buber, I. (2009): Grandparents Caring for Their Grandchildren. Findings From the 2004 Survey of Health, Aging, and Retirement in Europe. Journal of Family Issues Vol. 30 (1), 53-73.

Hammarström, G. (2005): The Construct of Intergenerational Solidarity in a Lineage Perspective: A Discussion on Underlying Theoretical Assumptions. Journal of Aging Studies 19, 33-51.

Harper, S. (2005): Grandparenthood. In: Johnson, M.L. (Ed.): The Cambridge Handbook of Age and Aging. London.

Hermalin, A. (2002): The Well-Being of the Elderly in Asia. A Four-Country Comparative Study. Ann Arbor.

Hoff, A. (2006): Intergenerationale Familienbeziehungen im Wandel. In: Tesch-Römer, C./Engstler, H. and Wurm, S. (Eds.): Altwerden in Deutschland. Sozialer Wandel und individuelle Entwicklung in der zweiten Lebenshälfte. Wiesbaden.

Hoff, A. (2007): Patterns of Intergenerational Support in Grandparent-Grandchild and Parent-Child Relationships in Germany. Aging and Society 27 (5), 643-665.

Huinink, J. and Feldhaus, M. (2008): Beziehungs- und Familienentwicklung – eine konzeptionelle Einführung in ein Forschungsprogramm. In: Feldhaus, M. and Huinink, J. (Eds.): Neuere Entwicklungen in der Beziehungs- und Familienforschung. Vorstudien zum Beziehungs- und Familienentwicklungs-panel (PAIRFAM). Würzburg.

Kalmijn, M. (2008): The Effects of Seperation and Divorce on Parent-Child Relationships in Ten European Countries. In: Saraceno, Ch. (Ed.): Families, Aging and Social Policy. Intergenerational Solidarity in European Welfare States. Cheltenham/Northampton.

Katz, R./Lowenstein, A./Phillips, J. and Daatland, S.O. (2005): Theorizing Intergenerational Family Relations. Solidarity, Conflict, and Ambivalence in Cross-National Contexts. In: Bengtson, V.L./Acock, A.C./Allen, K.R./Dilworth-Anderson, P. and Klein, D.M. (Eds.): Sourcebook of Family Theory and Research. Thousand Oaks.

Kaufman, G. and Uhlenberg, P. (1998): Effects of Life Course Transitions on the Quality of Relationships Between Adult Children and Their Parents. Journal of Marriage and the Family 60, 924-938.

King, V. and Elder, G.H. (1995): American Children View Their Grandparents: Linked Lives Across Three Rural Generations. Journal of Marriage and the Family 57 (1), 165 – 178.

King, V. and Elder, G.H. (1997): The Legacy of Grandparenting: Childhood Experiences with Grandparents and Current Involvement with Grandchildren. Journal of Marriage and the Family 59 (4), 848-859.

Klaus, D. (2009): Why Do Adult Children Support Their Parents? Journal of Comparative Family Studies 40 (2), 227-241.

Kohli, M. (2004): Intergenerational Transfers and Inheritance: A Comparative View. In: Silverstein, M. and Schaie, K.W. (Eds.): Intergenerational Relations Across Time and Place. Annual Review of Gerontology and Geriatrics 24. New York.

Kohli, M. and Künemund, H. (2005a): The Midlife Generation in the Family: Patterns of Exchange and Support. In: Willis, S.L. and Martin, M. (Eds.): Middle Adulthood: A Lifespan Perspective. Thousand Oaks/London/New Delhi.

Kohli, M. and Künemund, H. (Eds.) (2005b): Die zweite Lebenshälfte. Gesellschaftliche Lage und Partizipation im Spiegel des Alters-Survey. 2nd edition. Wiesbaden.

Kohli, M./Künemund, H. and Lüdicke, J. (2005): Family Structure, Proximity and Contact. In: Bösch-Supan, A./Brugiavini, A./Jürges, H./Mackenbach, J./Siegrist, J. and Weber, G. (Eds.): Health, Aging and Retirement in Europe. First Results from the Survey of Health, Aging and Retirement in Europe (SHARE). Mannheim.

Komter, A. and Schans, D. (2008): Reciprocity Revisited: Give and Take in Dutch and Immigrant Families. Journal of Comparative Family Studies 39 (2), 279-298.

Künemund, H. (2006): Changing Welfare States and the „Sandwich Generation". Increasing Burden for the Next Generation? International Journal of Aging and Later Life 1 (2), 11-29.

Künemund, H. (2008): Intergenerational Relations Within the Family and the State. In: Saraceno, Ch. (Ed.): Families, Aging and Social Policy. Intergenerational Solidarity in European Welfare States. Cheltenham/Northampton.

Künemund, H. and Vogel, C. (2006): Öffentliche und private Transfers und Unterstützungsleistungen im Alter − „crowding out" oder „crowding in"? Zeitschrift für Familienforschung 18 (3), 269-289.

Lauterbach, W. (1995): Die gemeinsame Lebenszeit von Familiengenerationen. Zeitschrift für Soziologie 24 (1), 22-41.

Lauterbach, W. (2004): Die multilokale Mehrgenerationenfamilie. Zum Wandel der Familienstruktur in der zweiten Lebenshälfte. Würzburg.

Lauterbach, W. and Klein, Th. (2004): The change of generational relations based on demographic developments: The case of Germany. Journal of Comparative Family Studies 35 (4), 651-663.

Lauterbach, W. and Lüscher, K. (1996): Erben und die Verbundenheit der Lebensverläufe von Familienmitgliedern. Kölner Zeitschrift für Soziologie und Sozialpsychologie 48 (1), 66-95.

Lawton, L./Silverstein, M. and Bengtson, V.L. (1994): Affection, Social Contact and Geographic Distance between Adult Children and Their Parents. Journal of Marriage and the Family 56 (1), 57-68.

Lin, I-F. (2008): Consequences of Parental Divorce for Adult Children`s Support of Their Frail Parents. Journal of Marriage and the Family 70 (1), 113-128.

Lowenstein, A. and Ogg, J. (2003): OASIS − Old Age and Autonomy: The Role of Service Systems and Intergenerational Family Solidarity. Final Report. Haifa.

Lüscher, K. and Pillemer, K. (1998): Intergenerational Ambivalence: A New Approach to the Study of Parent-Child Relations in Later Life. Journal of Marriage and the Family 60 (2), 413-425.

Mangen, D.J./Bengtson, V.L. and Landry, P.H. (Eds.) (1988): The Measurement of Intergenerational Relations. Newbury Park/Beverly Hills/London/New Delhi.

Merz, E.-M./Schuengel, C. and Schulze, H.-J. (2007): Intergenerational Solidarity: An Attachment Perspective. Journal of Aging Studies 21, 175-186.

Merz, E.-M./Schuengel, C. and Schulze, H.-J. (2008): Inter-generational Relationships at Different Ages: An Attachment Perspective. Aging and Society 28, 717-736.

Mueller, M.M. and Elder, G.H. (2003): Family Contingencies Across the Generations: Grandparent-Grandchild Relationships in Holistic Perspective. Journal of Marriage and Family 65 (2), 404-417.

Nauck, B. (2001): Social Capital, Intergenerational Transmission and Intercultural Contact in Immigrant Families. Journal of Comparative Family Studies 32, 465-488.

Nauck, B. (2007): Immigrant Families in Germany. Family change between situational adaptation, acculturation, segregation and remigration. Zeitschrift für Familienforschung 19 (1), 34-54.

Nauck, B. (2009a): Patterns of Exchange in Kinship Systems in Germany, Russia, and the People's Republic of China. Journal of Comparative Family Studies 40 (2), 255-278.

Nauck, B. (2009b): Intergenerational Relationships and Female Inheritance Expectations. Comparative Results from Seven Societies in Asia and Europe. Asian Journal of Social Psychology (12).

Nauck, B. and Kohlmann, A. (1998): Verwandtschaft als soziales Kapital – Netzwerkbeziehungen in türkischen Migrantenfamilien. In: Wagner, M. and Schütze, Y. (Eds.): Verwandtschaft. Sozialwissenschaftliche Beiträge zu einem vernachlässigten Thema. Stuttgart.

Nauck, B. and Suckow, J. (2006): Intergenerational Relationships in Cross-Cultural Comparison: How Social Networks Frame Intergenerational Relations Between Mothers and Grandmothers in Japan, Korea, China, Indonesia, Israel, Germany, and Turkey. Journal of Family Issues 27 (8), 1159-1185.

Nauck, B. and Yi, Ch.-Ch. (Eds.) (2007): Intergenerational Relationships in Cross-Cultural Perspective: Fertility, Interaction and Support. Special Issue of Current Sociology 55.

Parrott, T.M. and Bengtson, V.L. (1999): The Effects of Earlier Intergenerational Affection, Normative Expectations, and Family Conflict on Contemporary Exchange of Help and Support. Research on Aging 21 (1), 73-105.

Pillemer, K. and Lüscher, K. (Eds.) (2004): Intergenerational Ambivalences. New Perspectives on Parent-Child Relations in Later Life. Oxford.

Pillemer, K. and Suitor, J.J. (2002): Explaining Mothers' Ambivalence Toward Their Adult Children. Journal of Marriage and the Family 64 (3), 602-613.

Roberts, R.E.L. and Bengtson, V.L. (1990): Is Intergenerational Solidarity a Unidimensional Construct? A Second Test of a Formal Model. Journal of Gerontology 45 (1), 12-20.

Rossi, A.S. (1993): Intergenerational Relations: Gender, Norms, and Behavior. In: Bengtson, V.L. and Achenbaum, W.A. (Eds.): The Changing Contract Across Generations. New York.

Rossi, A.S. and Rossi, P.H. (1990): Of Human Bounding. Parent-Child Relations Across the Life Course. New York.

Ruckdeschel, K./Ette, A./Hullen G. and Leven, I. (2006): Generations and Gender Survey. Dokumentation der ersten Welle der Hauptbefragung in Deutschland. Materialien zur Bevölkerungswissenschaft, Heft 121a.

Schwarz, B. and Trommsdorff, G. (2005): The Relation Between Attachment and Intergenerational Support. European Journal of Aging 2 (3), 192-199.
Silverstein, M./Lawton, L. and Bengtson, V.L. (1994): Types of Relations Between Parents and Adult Children. In: Bengtson, V.L. and Harootyan, R.A. (Eds.): Intergenerational Linkages. Hidden Connections in American Society. New York.
Silverstein, M./Conroy, St.J./Wang, H./Giarrusso, R. and Bengtson, V.L. (2002): Reciprocity in Parent-Child Relations Over the Adult Life Course. Journal of Gerontology: Social Sciences: 57B, 3-11.
Spitze, G. and Logan, J.R. (1991): Sibling Structure and Intergenerational Relations. Journal of Marriage and the Family 53, 871-884.
Steinbach, A. (2008): Intergenerational Solidarity and Ambivalence: Types of Relationships in German Families. Journal of Comparative Family Studies 39 (1), 115-127.
Steinbach, A. and Kopp, J. (2008a): Intergenerationale Beziehungen. Theoretische Diskussionen, empirische Befunde und offene Fragen. In: Feldhaus, M. and Huinink, J. (Eds.): Neuere Entwicklungen in der Beziehungs- und Familienforschung. Vorstudien zum Beziehungs- und Familienentwicklungspanel (PAIRFAM). Würzburg.
Steinbach, A. and Kopp, J. (2008b): "When will I see you again?" Intergenerational Contacts in Germany. In: Saraceno, Ch. (Ed.): Families, Aging and Social Policy. Intergenerational Solidarity in European Welfare States. Cheltenham/ Northampton.
Sweet, J.A. and Bumpass, L.L. (2002): The National Survey of Families and Households – Waves 1, 2, and 3: Data Description and Documentation. Center for Demography and Ecology, University of Wisconsin-Madison. http://www.ssc.wisc.edu/nsfh/home.htm. [Last visited 01/18/2010].
Szydlik, M. (1995): Die Enge der Beziehung zwischen erwachsenen Kindern und ihren Eltern – und umgekehrt. Zeitschrift für Soziologie 24 (2), 75-94.
Szydlik, M. (1999): Erben in der Bundesrepublik Deutschland. Zum Verhältnis von familialer Solidarität und sozialer Ungleichheit. Kölner Zeitschrift für Soziologie und Sozialpsychologie 51 (1), 80-104.
Szydlik, M. (2000): Lebenslange Solidarität? Generationenbeziehungen zwischen erwachsenen Kindern und Eltern. Opladen.
Szydlik, M. (2004): Inheritance and Inequality: Theoretical Reasoning and Empirical Evidence. European Sociological Review 20 (1), 31-45.
Szydlik, M. (2008): Intergenerational Solidarity and Conflict. Journal of Comparative Family Studies 34 (1), 97-114.
Szydlik, M. and Schupp, J. (2004): Wer erbt mehr? Erbschaften, Sozialstruktur und Alterssicherung. Kölner Zeitschrift für Soziologie und Sozialpsychologie 56 (4), 609-629.
Tesch-Römer, C./Engstler, H. and Wurm, S. (Eds.) (2006): Altwerden in Deutschland. Sozialer Wandel und individuelle Entwicklung in der zweiten Lebenshälfte. Wiesbaden.
Tesch-Römer, C./Kondratowitz, H.-J. von/Motel-Klingebiel, A. and Spangler, D. (2000): OASIS – Old Age and Autonomy: The Role of Service Systems and

Intergenerational Family Solidarity. Erhebungsdesign und Instrumente des deutschen Surveys. Berlin.

Tesch-Römer, C./Wurm, S./Hoff, A. and Engstler, H. (2002): Die zweite Welle des Alterssurveys. Erhebungsdesign und Instrumente. DZA Diskussionspapiere, Nr. 35.

Trommsdorff, G. and Nauck, B. (Eds.) (2005): The Value of Children in Cross-cultural Perspective. Lengerich.

Trommsdorff, G. and Schwarz, B. (2007): The „Intergenerational Stake Hypothesis" in Indonesia and Germany: Adult Daughters' and their Mothers' Perception of their Relationship. Current Sociology 55, 599-620.

Van Gaalen, R.I. and Dykstra, P.A. (2006): Solidarity and Conflict Between Adult Children and Parents: A Latent Class Analysis. Journal of Marriage and the Family 68 (4), 947-960.

5.5 Administrative Data from Germany's Statutory Health Insurance Providers for Social, Economic, and Medical Research

Günther Heller

Contact:

Günther Heller
Research Institute of the Local Healthcare Funds (WIdO)
Rosenthaler Straße 31
10178 Berlin
Germany
e-mail: guenther.heller[at]wido.bv.aok.de

Abstract

This article gives a short description of the administrative data sources used by Germany's statutory health insurance providers. These data sources are of potential interest for social, economic, and medical research. We first briefly outline the legal regulations applying to these sources, the structure and contents of the most relevant databases, as well as current and future access to these data sources in the context of legal and data privacy protection issues. We then discuss issues of data validity and completeness of different data sources in relation to a recent example of health care research using administrative data. In conclusion, we discuss the potential and limitations of research using administrative medical data from Germany's statutory health insurance providers.

Keywords: administrative data, claims data, health service research

1. Introduction

Recent years have seen growing importance of administrative medical data for scientific purposes. Clinical research, health service research, and the health care economy all increasingly demand medical data not only from surveys and clinical trials, but also data on entire populations. This demand stems from a need to analyze and evaluate medical innovation and developments more broadly based upon real-life settings. In light of this, it is only fitting to address the topic of administrative medical data in terms of its structure, availability, and usefulness.

To avoid confusion about the term "administrative medical data," the following short description is given: the term refers to data that has been established for administrative purposes in the field of health care provision. In most cases, administrative medical data has been collected for the reimbursement of health care providers (e.g., doctors, nurses, or hospitals), for usage in official statistics, and other administrative purposes. Thus, in the context of scientific research, administrative medical data are secondary data. Other frequently used or similar terms are "administrative data," "claims data," or "reimbursement data." Administrative medical data may be contrasted with data from medical surveys, medical trials, or data derived directly from medical records.

There are numerous examples of administrative medical data from the international field. Some well-known examples are the Hospital Episodes

Statistics (HES) from Great Britain,[1] the Veterans Affairs data collections, or the Medicare databases from the US.[2]

In this advisory report, the focus will be on the administrative medical data of statutory health insurance providers in Germany. The structure and availability of these data depend on which part of the health care sectors they pertain to. An example from the field of health service research will be provided and future developments will be discussed.

2. Administrative medical data of German statutory health insurances

For 125 years, medical care in Germany has been financed through the health insurance system. Currently, approximately 86 percent of the population is insured under the statutory health insurance system (GKV, *Gesetzliche Krankenversicherung*), while the remaining 14 percent is insured by private health insurance (PKV, *Private Krankenversicherung*) (Jacobs et al. 2006). Health insurance is largely governed by the Code of Social Law V (SGB V), however several smaller parts are covered by the Code of Social Law IX (Rehabilitation) (SGB IX) and XI (Nursing) (SGB XI). The collection of routine medical data, as well as its transfer to statutory health insurance providers,[3] is also regulated by these Codes.

The provision of health care in Germany is divided into different sectors, each of which is regulated individually. For the sectors listed in table 1, health care providers are obliged to provide individual-specific medical data when submitting an invoice for reimbursement from the statutory health insurance. It is, however, unclear whether all statutory health insurance providers have established databases that allow these data from different health sectors to be linked at an (anonymous) individualized level. Table 1 provides an overview of the different laws pertaining to different health care sectors according to SGB V, as well as examples of the most important medical data required to be transferred to statutory health insurance providers. Additionally, a list of the currently available anonymous individualized-level databases within the Research Institute of the Local Healthcare Funds (WIdO, *Wissenschaftliches Institut der AOK*) is provided. The WIdO is responsible for the databases for German regional healthcare funds (AOK, *Allgemeine Ortskrankenkasse*). Currently, approximately 24 million people

---

1   http://www.hesonline.nhs.uk/Ease/servlet/ContentServer?siteID=1937&categoryID=537, cited on 09/27/2008.
2   An overview of "coded data from administrative sources" in the US is provided by Iezzoni (2003).
3   Or maybe different insurance providers when referring to SGB IX and XI.

are insured by the AOK, making it – compared with other health insurance providers – the largest database of this kind in Germany.

Table 1: Health Care Provision according to Code of Social Law V (SGB V) in different medical sectors and the data transfer to statutory health insurance providers in Germany

	Medical Sector	Main Medical Contents (Examples)	WIdO Database since (2)
SGB V § 295	Ambulatory care	Diagnosis, type of medical care provided	2004
SGB V § 295	Incapable of work	Diagnosis, time being incapable of working	2006
SGB V § 300	Pharmaceutical prescription	type of pharmaceutical product, price, quantity of prescribed pharmaceutical	1998
SGB V § 301	Hospital care	Admitted hospital, diagnoses, operations, procedures, length of stay	1998
SGB V § 302	Prescription of remedies and medical aids (1)	Diagnosis, type, and quantity of medical care provided, price	2004
SGB XI § 93 – 98	Nursing Care	Diagnoses, type of care	-
SGB IX	Rehabilitation	Admitted hospital, diagnoses, operations, procedures, length of stay	2004

(1) e.g., massages, ergo therapy, physical therapy, prosthesis, etc.
(2) case specific, able to be linked on a anonymous individual level

In general, the described administrative medical data contain the following information, which are usually stored in Structured Query Language (SQL) databases:

- personal identifier
- date(s) of medical care provision (episode)
- type of disease (e.g., International Statistical Classification of Diseases and Related Health Problems, also known as ICD)
- type of treatment (e.g., procedural classification)
- invoice
- other information

These data may be linked to additional administrative data related to the insured individual. Therefore, information about, for example, the individual's place of residence, status of insurance, or end of insurance may be used for further scientific purposes.

In light of this, information collected from medical sectors and during an individual's contact with the medical system has potential to be used for individual longitudinal analyses. This would be of great interest for research purposes.

2.1 Accessibility of data

It may be seen as a serious drawback that the data described is currently only available to health insurance providers and to researchers performing research in cooperation with these health insurance providers (AOK-Bundesverband et al. 2007; Bramesfeld et al. 2007; Geyer 2008; Grobe et al. 2008; Heller et al. 2004; Heller 2006; Heller 2007; Heller et al. 2007; Ihle et al. 2005; Müller and Braun 2006; Schubert et al. 2007; Swart and Heller 2007; Swart and Ihle 2005). This limited data access is a direct result of the protection of the private data of insured individuals and the involved institutions, such as hospitals. However, there are currently at least two regulations which have the potential to make these data available to the scientific community in the future; namely, § 303 SGB V Data Transparency and § 137 SGB V Quality of Medical Care.

According to § 303 SGB V Data Transparency, administrative medical data from all health insurance providers is to be pooled in a data trust center. These data should be made available to health insurers, health authorities, and several other defined user groups, such as, for example, independent scientific organizations. However, the level of aggregation at which the data can be made available is not fixed. Thus, data may be distributed on an individual level, or on an aggregated level. However, it remains unclear how expensive it would be to use these data for external research. How the data are to be compiled and distributed, and at which expense they are to be provided, are issues still being debated.

In the latest health care reform of March 2007, § 137 SGB V Quality of Medical Care was renewed. According to this reform, a quality agency shall be assigned to develop and provide "inter-sectoral" comprehensive quality assurance. The agency that is to be developed for this purpose has additionally been granted permission to use administrative medical data. Consequently, for future considerations relating to administrative medical data, it may be of interest to direct attention towards this agency. Which institution will assume the role of this quality agency is, however, still unclear, as the pan-European tendering process for this agency is still in progress.

2.2 Aspects of data quality

For numerous research-related enquiries, one central question relating to administrative medical data is whether the required information is present in the data. Interesting information might or might not be sufficiently present. For example, the social status of an individual or issues pertaining to an individual's quality of life often play an important role in a person's health, however, administrative medical data often do not include such information.

Currently, for example, there is much debate as to whether administrative medical data provides sufficient information to perform risk-adjusted analyses when comparing hospital performance measurements, such as, for example, 30-day survival rates after diagnosis of acute myocardial infarction. While the effectiveness of risk-adjusted analyses using administrative medical data has been questioned for some time, recent research from Great Britain and the US reveals similar performance of administrative medical data compared to clinical data or clinical register data when predicting survival after admission to hospital due to tracer-diagnoses or procedures (Aylin et al. 2007; Pine et al. 2007). It should, however, be noted that good prediction is only a poor indicator for good risk adjustment (Heller and Schnell 2007).

Another important issue related to administrative medical data is data validity. It should be noted that while administrative medical data is secondary data, how valid the data is depends on the primary purpose for which the data was collected. For example, reimbursement data from the hospital sector is usually checked by health insurance providers in terms of the accuracy of invoices. This is done using plausibility checks (internal validity). In addition, health insurance providers also conduct audits comparing the transferred administrative medical data with clinical data from medical records (external validity). When scrutinizing reimbursement data, several data elements are typically considered unimportant. Items such as time of coded procedures or admission diagnoses are, for example, neither checked nor corrected. Nevertheless, such information may be of great importance from various analytical perspectives. Thus, when performing medical administrative data analyses for various purposes, one should take note of the data available as well as its validity.

To my knowledge, there have hitherto been no studies from any German health care sector examining the validity of administrative medical data from a medical or scientific perspective. Before using any administrative medical data for such purposes, first undertaking an external study would seem appropriate. Generally, it is reasonable to assume that the validity of administrative medical data increases with time as administrative procedures regarding data transfer become more established. In light of this, administrative medical data from hospital care or pharmaceutical prescriptions – in both of which areas data transfer practices were established in 1998 – are usually considered valid and reliable. Data transfers from the ambulatory sector, on the other hand, were not established until 2004 and have thus been called into question (Gerste and Gutschmidt 2006; Giersiepen et al. 2007; Trautner et al. 2005).

An interesting matter connected to data validity is whether information that may be of potential interest to researchers is linked to reimbursement. For example, the type and amount of prescribed pharmaceuticals is directly linked to reimbursement, which is thoroughly examined by insurers and thus deemed to be of a high level of validity. Documentation of primary and secondary diagnoses in the hospital sector, which are used to verify data validity, has dramatically increased since the implementation of Diagnosis Related Group (DRG) hospital reimbursement schemes. Diagnoses from the ambulatory sector, on the other hand, are not directly related to reimbursement, not scrutinized by insurers, and have accordingly been shown to be invalid in many cases (Gerste and Gutschmidt 2006; Giersiepen et al. 2007; Trautner et al. 2005). However, in light of the recent "morbidity-orientated risk-structure compensation" (*Morbititäts-Orientierter-Risikostrukturausgleich*), this may change considerably in the near future.

In addition to the validity of the data, one must also take the completeness of the data into consideration. Administrative medical data is typically considered to be complete when all relevant cases are present in the data. Administrative medical data need to be comprehensive, as these data are utilized by several different health care sector bodies for various purposes, such as, for example, the DRG-based statistics on hospital diagnoses compiled by the Federal Statistical Office (Spindler 2008). Another example is the use of administrative medical data by the Federal Office for Quality Assurance (BQS, *Institut für Quatlität und Patientensicherheit*) to create quality benchmarks (Veith et al. 2008).

Several years ago, a working group entitled the Working Group for Secondary Data Analysis (AGENS, *Arbeitsgruppe Erhebung und Nutzung von Sekundärdaten*) was created to assess the contents and possible uses of administrative medical data. In addition to AGENS, a handbook was also created to provide a detailed overview of administrative medical data in Germany (Swart and Ihle 2005). A more compact, updated version of this handbook is currently available (Swart and Heller 2007). In addition to this handbook, the same authors have developed a set of guidelines addressing "Good Practice for Secondary Data Analysis" (Swart et al. 2005). Since these guidelines were formulated, they have been adopted by several scientific societies as well as funding agencies.[4]

---

[4] http://www.gesundheitsforschung-bmbf.de/_media/GPS.pdf, cited 02/10/2008.

3. A health service research example using administrative medical data

As mentioned, administrative medical data can be used for various research purposes. One such example is the "volume outcome relationship" of very low birth weight infants (VLBWs). In Germany, the issue of whether a minimum level of provision be introduced for hospitals treating VLBW infants has been addressed by a Federal Joint Committee (Gemeinsamer Bundesausschuss). Before the decision of the Federal Joint Committee was reached, it commissioned the Institute for Quality and Efficiency in Health Care (IQWiG, *Institut für Qualität und Wirschaftlichkeit im Gesundheitswesen*) to evaluate whether a "volume outcome relationship" for this patient group exists. In its final report, the IQWiG used analyses by Heller (2007), based upon administrative Hospital claims data (IQWiG 2008). These analyses have since been extended to include spatial simulation analyses for different "minimum provider volumes." The analyses conducted by Heller first measured distances from patients' residences to hospitals providing care. Second, a simulation was conducted measuring the extent to which these distances changed after "minimum provider volumes" were introduced. Additionally, the changes in survival rates after introducing various levels of "minimum provider volumes" were estimated (Heller 2009). These and several other similar analyses are currently being used by the Federal Joint Committee.

4. Discussion and conclusion

- Three points on administrative medical data in Germany are to be noted:
- administrative medical data provide detailed information about medical care provision for large samples or even entire populations;
- these data provide information about existing diseases, medical therapy, and health outcomes; and
- researchers with clinical economic and social research interests have shown particular interest in performing individual longitudinal analyses using individual identifiers.

With this article, I aimed to give the reader a brief description of the most important administrative medical databases in Germany, and to address issues like data validity, completeness, and accessibility of administrative medical data. Additionally, to illustrate the importance of administrative medical data, I provided an up-to-date example of its use in health service research on very low birth weight infants.

One point which should be kept in mind, however, is that health and illness also exists outside the official medical system within the lay system (Borgetto and Trojan 2007). The onset of a disease might occur long before a doctor is contacted or self-administered treatments are undertaken (such as using readily available over-the-counter drugs, which have been known to cure numerous diseases without the patient ever coming into contact with the official medical system). Incidence or prevalence studies may be difficult to justify under this restriction.

From this perspective, the administrative medical data of statutory health insurance providers tell only part of the story. Thus, depending on the research question, it is in most cases desirable to complement administrative medical data with other data sources.

References:

AOK-Bundesverband, Forschungs- und Entwicklungsinstitut für das Sozial- und Gesundheitswesen in Sachsen Anhalt (FEISA), HELIOS Kliniken, Wissenschaftliches Institut der AOK (WIdO), Editor. Qualitätssicherung der stationären Versorgung mit Routinedaten (QSR).

Aylin, P./Bottle, A. and Majeed, A. (2007): Use of administrative data or clinical databases as predictors of risk of death in hospital: comparison of models. BMJ 334 (7602), 1044.

Borgetto, B./Trojan, A. (2007): Versorgungsforschung und Laiensystem. In: Janßen, C./Borgetto, B. and Heller, G. (Eds.): Medizinsoziologische Versorgungsforschung. Theoretische Ansätze, Methoden, Instrumente und empirische Befunde. Weinheim.

Bramesfeld, A./Grobe, T. and Schwartz, F.W. (2007): Who is treated, and how, for depression? An analysis of statutory health insurance data in Germany. Soc Psychiatry Psychiatr Epidemiol 42 (9), 740-746.

Gerste, B. and Gutschmidt, S. (2006): Datenqualität von Diagnosen aus dem ambulanten Bereich. Gesundheits- und Sozialpolitik 2006, (3-4), 29-43.

Geyer, S. (2008): Social inequalities in the incidence and case fatality of cancers of the lung, the stomach, the bowels, and the breast. Cancer Causes Control 19 (9), 965-974.

Giersiepen, K./Pohlabeln, H./Egidi, G. and Pigeot, I. (2007): Die ICD-Kodierqualität für Diagnosen in der ambulanten Versorgung. Bundesgesundheitsblatt – Gesundheitsforschung – Gesundheitsschutz 8, 1028-1038.

Grobe, T.G./Gerhardus, A./A'Walelu, O./Meisinger, C. and Krauth, C. (2008): [Hospitalisations for acute myocardial infarction – comparing data from three different sources]. Gesundheitswesen 70 (8-9), e37-46.

Heller, G./Swart, E. and Mansky, T. (2004): Qualitätsanalysen mit Routinedaten. Ansatz und erste Analysen aus dem Gemeinschaftsprojekt "Qualitätssicherung mit Routinedaten" (QSR). In: Klauber, J./Robra, B.P. and Schellschmdit, H. (Eds.): Krankenhaus-Report 2003. Stuttgart/New York.

Heller, G. (2006): Sind risikoadjustierte Analysen mit administrativen Routinedaten möglich? In: Hey, M. and Maschewski-Schneider, U. (Eds.): Kursbuch Versorgungsforschung. Berlin.

Heller, G./Günster, C./Misselwitz, B./Feller, A. and Schmidt, S. (2007): Jährliche Fallzahl pro Klinik und Überlebensrate sehr untergewichtiger Frühgeborener (VLBW) in Deutschland. Eine bundesweite Analyse mit Routinedaten. Z Geburtshilfe Neonatol 211 (3), 123-131.

Heller, G. and Schnell, R. (2007): Hospital Mortality Risk Adjustment Using Claims Data. JAMA 297 (18), 1983.

Heller, G. (2009): Auswirkungen der Einführung von Mindestmengen in der Behandlung von sehr untergewichtigen Früh- und Neugeborenen (VLBWs). Eine Simulation mit Echtdaten. In: Klauber, J./Robra, B. and Schellschmdit, H. (Eds.): Krankenhaus-Report 2008. Stuttgart.

Ihle, P./Köster, I./Herholz, H./Rambow-Bertram, P./Schardt, T. and Schubert, I. (2005): [Sample survey of persons insured in statutory health insurance institutions in Hessen – concept and realisation of person-related data base]. Gesundheitswesen 67 (8-9), 638-645.

Iezzoni, L.I. (2003): Coded data from administrative soruces. In: Iezzoni, L.I. (Ed.): Risk adjustment for measuring health care outcomes. 3rd ed. Chicago.

IQWiG (2008): http://www.iqwig.de/index.681.html.

Jacobs, K./Klauber, J. and Leinert, J. (2006): Fairer Wettbewerb oder Risikoselektion. Analysen zur gesetzlichen und privaten Krankenversicherung. Bonn.

Müller, R. and Braun, B. (Eds.): Vom Quer zum Längsschnitt. Möglichkeiten der Analysen mit GKV-Daten. St. Augustin.

Pine, M./Jordan, H.S./Elixhauser, A./Fry, D.E./Hoaglin, D.C./Jones, B. et al. (2007): Enhancement of Claims Data to Improve Risk Adjustment of Hospital Mortality. JAMA 297 (1), 71-76.

Schubert, I./Kupper-Nybelen, J./Ihle, P. and Krappweis, J. (2007): [Utilization patterns of dementia patients in the light of statutory health insurance data]. Z Arztl Fortbild Qualitatssich 101 (1), 7-13.

Spindler, J. (2008): Fallpauschalenbezogene Krankenhausstatistik: Diagnosen und Prozeduren der Patienten auf Basis der Daten nach § 21 Krankenhausentgeltgesetz. In: Klauber, J./Robra, B. and Schellschmidt, H. (Eds.): Krankenhaus-Report 2007. Stuttgart.

Swart, E. and Heller, G. (2007): Nutzung und Bedeutung von (GKV-)Routinedaten für die Versorgungsforschung. In: Janßen, C./Borgetto, B. and Heller, G. (Eds.): Medizinsoziologische Versorgungsforschung. Theoretische Ansätze, Methoden, Instrumente und empirische Befunde. Weinheim.

Swart, E. and Ihle, P. (Eds.): Routinedaten im Gesundheitswesen. Handbuch Sekundärdatenanalyse: Grundlagen, Methoden und Perspektiven. Bern.

Swart, E./Ihle, P./Geyer, S./Grobe, T. and Hofmann, W. (2005): GPS – Gute Praxis Sekundärdatenanalyse. Arbeitsgruppe Erhebung und Nutzung von Sekundärdaten (AGENS) der Deutschen Gesellschaft für Sozialmedizin und Prävention (DGSMP) [GPS – good practice secondary data analysis. Working Group for the Survey and Utilization of Secondary Data (AGENS) of the German Society for Social Medicine and Prevention (DGSMP)]. Gesundheitswesen 67 (6), 416-421.

Trautner, C./Dong, Y./Ryll, A. and Stillfried, D.G. (2005): Verlässlichkeit von Diagnosen niedergelassener Ärzte in Niedersachsen. Gesundheits- und Sozialpolitik (1-2), 36-42.

Veith, C./Bauer, J./Döbler, K./Eckert, O./Fischer, B. and Woldenga, C. (2008): Qualität sichtbar machen. BQS-Qualitätsreport 2007. Düsseldorf.

5.6 Provision for Old Age: National and International Survey Data to Support Research and Policy on Aging

Hendrik Jürges

Contact:

Hendrik Jürges
Mannheim Research Institute for the Economics of Aging
University of Mannheim
L13, 17
68131 Mannheim
Germany
e-mail: juerges[at]mea.uni-mannheim.de

Abstract

This report reviews recent trends in the collection of multidisciplinary and longitudinal data in the area of aging research, both in Germany and internationally. It also discusses important developments such as linkage with administrative records, the inclusion of health measurements and biomarkers, and the inclusion of populations in institutions, particularly nursing homes.

1. Research questions

Population aging is one of the megatrends of the twenty-first century. In almost all countries of the developed world, mortality rates are falling, birth rates are below replacement rate, and work rates are falling. World wide, the number of people aged 60 and over is expected to triple until 2050. The aging of the population will shape the world to come and its political agenda. The main policy issues that arise with an aging population concern providing income and health security during old age at affordable budgets. To cope with these particular challenges of rapid population aging, it is important to improve the current scientific understanding of complex linkages between economic, health, and social factors that determine the quality of life in the older population. These interactions primarily take place at the individual level, they are dynamic – aging is a process, not a state – and are related to a country's welfare regime.

To improve our understanding of population aging and its policy implications, researchers need multidisciplinary and longitudinal data. Over the past decade, the international research community has responded to this need by starting to create a worldwide microdata infrastructure that helps researchers to better understand the individual and population aging processes. The aim of this special report is to document the contents and degrees of access to existing national and international datasets containing household- and individual-level information on the economic well-being and health of older populations. In this context, the international perspective is of great importance. Internationally comparative data is necessary in order to exploit the rich variety in policies, institutions, and other factors across different countries. The impact of public policy can be much better understood if one can observe one policy in relation to other policies. Many of the policies that might be considered as solutions to address future public policy challenges resulting from an aging population have already been implemented in some form in some country. For instance, comparisons of different pension systems and their impact on old age poverty rates, savings decisions of the working population, or the role of the family and intergenerational relations, can inform policy-makers about the likely consequences of pension reform.

In addition to briefly describing the contents of and access to existing survey datasets, the present report also discusses future developments and further needs in the area of aging research. Three important areas in which such developments are likely and needed are (1) linkage with administrative records, (2) the inclusion of (more) health measurements and biomarkers, and (3) the inclusion of populations in institutions, particularly nursing homes.

2. Status quo: Databases and access

This section briefly describes a selection of important national and international databases for multidisciplinary research on aging. Summary information and details on data access are given in tabular form in the appendix. Only databases that fulfill several criteria are listed. First, they must of course include – although not exclusively – coverage of the older population (defined as individuals aged 50 and older). Second, they must be based on non-administrative *research-driven* surveys. Third, they must be multidisciplinary; that is, they must include data with some detail from at least two of the following fields: medicine, economics, sociology, and psychology. Fourth, they must have a longitudinal design, because many events associated with aging are dynamic or longitudinal in nature. Obviously, these four criteria together seem to be fairly restrictive. For instance, they exclude the European Community Household Panel (ECHP), many of the health interview surveys carried out on national levels, and also the current European Health Interview Survey (EHIS).

2.1 National data sources for Germany

German Socio-Economic Panel (SOEP, Sozio-oekonomisches Panel*):* arguably, the most important data source of longitudinal microdata is the SOEP, which has collected detailed annual data mainly on housing, employment, and income since 1984. One advantage of the SOEP is the large sample size. The sample currently includes about 22,000 respondents of which some 10,500 are aged 50 and above. Another advantage is the length of the panel. The SOEP now spans 25 years of annual data on the lives of a substantial number of respondents, following individuals from middle age into old age. The usefulness of the SOEP for certain aspects of aging research, however, has been limited by two facts: first, until recently, it contained little health-related information. For instance, self-rated general health has been included only in 1992, and information on respondents' smoking behavior, height, and weight has been only available since the late 1990s. However, a more systematic approach to the measurement of health has been taken since 2002, when SOEP included a version of the SF-12 health questionnaire. A more recent development has been the inclusion of physical measures or biomarkers, such as handgrip strength (in 2006). Second, although some broad information on savings and household assets is available annually, the quantitative composition of household assets was covered only in 1998, 2002, and 2007, making it difficult to track in detail changes in the asset portfolios or in the amount of wealth.

The German Ageing Survey (DEAS, Deutscher Alterssurvey*):* DEAS is a cross-sectional and longitudinal survey of individuals aged 40 and over. The main topics it covers address circumstances and attitudes in later life, particularly related to housing, employment and retirement, volunteering, family, leisure activities, and social participation. Data collection started in 1996 and is repeated every six years. In the first two waves, samples included about 5000 respondents. One advantage of the DEAS is that it collects highly detailed information from the respondents, particularly around psychological variables, whereas panel mortality due to the large gap between waves clearly is a disadvantage. Only 32 percent of the original sample members in 1996 could be reinterviewed in 2002. Also, data on the oldest-old (85+) are only available for reinterviewed panel data members, since the baseline sample in 1996 was restricted to individuals up to age 85.

Sparen und Altersvorsorge in Deutschland (SAVE): SAVE is the most elaborate survey on savings behavior in Germany. It contains detailed factual information on the current financial situation of households (including asset components), savings behavior, psychological determinants of saving, and health. SAVE was started in 2001 and data for several waves are now available. One drawback of the data for longitudinal analyses is the somewhat complex mixture of different samples that comprise it, which limits the exploitable longitudinal dimension.

2.2 International data sources

The *Cross-National Equivalent File (CNEF)* is an *ex post* harmonized dataset containing annual panel data from the US Panel Study of Income Dynamics (PSID), the German Socio-Economic Panel (SOEP), the British Household Panel Study (BHPS), the Household Income and Labour Dynamics in Australia (HILDA), and the Canadian Survey of Labour and Income Dynamics (SLID). Future releases of the CNEF will include data from the Swiss Household Panel (SHP). Even for researchers planning research on only one of the contributing countries, CNEF offers the distinct advantage of providing a set of generated and fully imputed variables (in particular income components and equivalence weights) that are not directly available with the original surveys. These generated variables can be merged with the original survey data (and are part of the data distribution, e.g., of the SOEP). While being an excellent data source for comparative analyses of retirement and income security in old age, comparability issues have somewhat limited the use of the data for other fields such as health (the 2006 CNEF release added a set of variables that measure health behaviors and health outcomes). One disadvantage of CNEF as a multinational dataset is that the data cannot be accessed jointly and access is not harmonized across surveys.

The *Survey of Health, Ageing and Retirement in Europe (SHARE)* is a multidisciplinary and cross-national panel database of microdata on health, socio-economic status, and social and family networks of individuals aged 50 or over. Individual interviews (overall N=33,000, about 3,000 respondents in Germany) are conducted with primary respondents and cohabitating partners. Fifteen European countries including Israel have so far contributed data to the first and/or second waves of SHARE conducted in 2004 and 2006 respectively. The survey's third wave of data collection will collect retrospective life histories in sixteen countries in 2008-09. SHARE is partly harmonized ex ante with the US Health and Retirement Study (HRS) and the English Longitudinal Study on Ageing (ELSA) (see below). Data collected include health self-reports, some biomarkers, psychological variables, economic variables (current work activity, sources, and composition of wealth and current income), and social support variables (e.g., assistance and transfers within, volunteer activities). One noteworthy feature of the international SHARE database is the inclusion of anchoring vignettes for internationally comparative studies on a wide range of subjective survey data, such as health self-reports, life satisfaction, job satisfaction, satisfaction with health care, or political efficacy. Future waves of SHARE will include the collection of biomarkers and linkage with administrative records.

The *Generations and Gender Survey (GGS)* is a cross-national, multidisciplinary study of the dynamics of family relationships, covering non-institutionalized individuals aged 18-79. The main topics of the survey are related to the respondents' current and past family situation and family-related events, such as partnership formation, childbearing, and leaving the parental home. The GGS is designed as a panel survey with at least three waves at an interval of three years. GGS wave 1 data are currently available for Bulgaria, France, Georgia, Germany, Hungary, and Russia.

The *English Longitudinal Study of Ageing (ELSA)* is an interdisciplinary biannual panel survey on health, economic position, and quality of life of older adults in England. ELSA covers the range of topics needed to study the economic, social, psychological, and health elements of individual and societal ageing. The initial ELSA sample (N=12,000), interviewed in 2002, was drawn from respondents (aged 50+) to the Health Survey for England (HSE), contributing baseline data on respondents' health (details of morbidity, lifestyle, diets, and blood samples). Covered topics are similar to SHARE: health and disability; cognitive functioning; income and wealth; employment and retirement and post-retirement activities; social networks, support, and participation. Biomarkers (blood pressure, blood samples, including genetic information, measured height and weight, lung function, grip strength, balance) are collected every four years during a separate visit by trained nurses. A life history interview has been conducted between regular waves in 2007.

The *Italian Survey on Household Income and Wealth (SHIW)* is unusual in the sense that it is conducted by a government agency (the Italian central bank – Banca D'Italia), has a strong research component, and grants free public online data access. All documentation is available in English. SHIW was started in the 1960s collecting data on income and savings. The survey has developed into a general household survey which includes detailed information on employment, wealth, financial decision making, and financial behavior.

The *Irish LongituDinal Study on Ageing (TILDA)* will interview a sample of some 10,000 individuals aged 55 and older living in the Republic of Ireland and collect detailed data on social networks and support, economic circumstances and health, including biomarkers. Three main waves of data collection are planned in 2008, 2013, and 2018, with annual telephone follow-ups and smaller-scale add-on studies. TILDA is specifically designed to deliver data comparable to the US HRS and ELSA. Data access is not yet possible but planned to be free to scientific users.

The *US Health and Retirement Study (HRS)* is the role model of many aging surveys currently conducted throughout the world, in part due to its scientific productivity. Since 1992, the HRS has generated more than 500 papers in peer-reviewed journals. Today, some 60 papers using HRS data appear in a refereed journal every year. The HRS is a biannual panel survey of Americans aged 50 and over, started in 1992. The current sample consists of about 22,000 respondents, providing detailed information on their physical and mental health, insurance coverage, financial status, family support systems, labor market status, and retirement planning. In addition to standard HRS questions, HRS has recently introduced an "enhanced" interview, collecting physical performance measures (grip strength, puff test, timed walk, balance), anthropometry (height, weight, waist), blood pressure, dried blood spots (HBA_{1c}, cholesterol, high-density lipoprotein, C-reactive protein), even salivary DNA (for extraction and storage only).

The *Mexican Health and Aging Study (MHAS)* is a panel study of respondents aged 50 and over in Mexico. At baseline (in 2001), about 15,000 individuals have been interviewed, providing information on health (self-reports and biomarkers), financial and time transfers between generations, sources, amounts of income, types and value of assets, and housing. The survey design closely follows HRS. MHAS provides comparable data. Respondents were reinterviewed once in 2003. New interviews are planned with MHAS wave 1 & 2 survivors and a representative sample of cohorts born 1951-1959.

The *Korean Longitudinal Study of Ageing (KLoSA)* is a biannual panel survey of approximately 10,000 South Korean residents (excluding Jeju Island) aged 45 or older, started in 2006. The 2006 main survey includes only respondents living in private households. Collected data include employment status, income, asset, family relations, health, and subjective judgment. KloSA was designed to allow comparative studies with HRS, ELSA, or SHARE.

Based on the SHARE baseline questionnaire, the first wave of data collection for the *Japanese Study on Aging and Retirement (JSTAR)* took place in the first half of 2007. Interviews have been conducted with some 4,300 individuals from five municipalities (Takikawa, Sendai, Adachi, Kanazawa, and Shirakawa). A second wave of data collection (extending the sample to include a sixth municipality) is currently being prepared and will begin in January 2009. Although JSTAR features many design elements of SHARE and HRS, there are also a few major differences. First, the sample was drawn in only five municipalities. One of the reasons for this design is that administrative health records are stored at the municipality level. Data linkage between these records and the survey data is planned. Second, the initial sample is restricted to individuals aged 50-75. Third, JSTAR interviews only one respondent per household. However, some limited information on cohabitating spouses or partners is gathered during the interview.

Aging studies for China, India, Thailand: Planning for initial waves of panel surveys comparable to HRS and SHARE is underway in further Asian countries. These are the Chinese Aging and Retirement Longitudinal Study of Aging (CHARLS), the Health and Retirement Study for Thailand (HART), and the Longitudinal Survey of Aging in India (LASI).

3. Recommendations for future research

This section describes selected future needs in the area of empirical research on aging. The selection reflects ongoing innovative efforts in connection with some of the surveys described in the previous section (e.g., biomarkers), but also identifies issues that have hitherto received little attention, such as the systematic inclusion of individuals living in institutions (i.e., nursing homes).

3.1 Data linkage

Survey data, as described above, cover a wide range of topics. Information provided by respondents, however, is often incomplete and inaccurate. In contrast, administrative data are (ideally) complete and accurate but contain only very limited information, typically only information that is immediately related to the purpose of the data producer. The advantages of both types of data can be combined by linking administrative records to survey data. Benefits of linkage include (1) validation of respondents' self-reports, in particular if these reports are potentially subject to recall bias; (2) improved measurement of explanatory and dependent variables, reducing bias and increasing precision of model estimates; (3) reduction of respondent burden. For instance, aging surveys can benefit from adding social security records to explain retirement behavior or measurement of economic resources during retirement. Doctors' or health insurance records can be used to improve the measurement of health.

Researchers trying to link administrative data with survey data face several challenges. First, they need to get a unique ID from the respondent (e.g., social security number), which is needed to actually link the data. Asking for this ID (in some countries together with a written consent to link data) can have adverse effects on response or retention rates. Second, the availability of data that could be matched to general population surveys may be limited or require a great deal of cooperation from many agencies (such as getting medical records for German residents from public or private health insurers). Third, due to privacy legislation, data dissemination rules are often not able to conform to the standards set by the survey data to which the administrative data are linked. Restricted access to linked data will make cross-national analyses using linked data a very difficult enterprise. Here, new cross-national solutions of data access that fulfill all legal confidentiality requirements are needed.

3.2 Biomarkers

One important recent development in social survey research is the integration of biomarkers. Biomarkers are often associated with genetic information such as DNA samples. The purpose of genetic research in social sciences is not to find *the* gene for some socially relevant trait. Rather, the collaboration of geneticists with social scientists is fruitful because social scientists are experts in measuring social phenomena that may or may not be associated with genes. The two important contributions of social scientists to genetic research are, first, to help to establish the importance of non-genetic factors or interactions of genes and environment, and second, their familiarity with using large scale social, nationally representative samples to help verify associations found in small-scale medical studies.

The vast majority of biomarkers currently collected and analyzed are non-genetic: anthropometric measurements (height, weight, waist circumference, lung capacity, grip strength, balance), and blood and saliva samples. The scientific value of collecting such biomarkers in large surveys is promising: first, biomarkers improve the measurement of health. Self-reports of health are subject to considerable under-, over-, or misreporting, depending on the circumstances and dimensions at hand. Objective information can be used to validate respondents' reports and to study the amount and determinants of under-, over-, or misreporting in population surveys. However, self-reports of health have their own distinct scientific value. Thus, biomarkers should be seen as complementary measurements rather than substitutes. Second, biomarkers allow studying physiological pathways in the complex relationship between social status and health, providing information on important links that can be used to identify causal relationships. Third, biomarkers provide direct information on pre-disease pathways, in particular by measuring physiological processes that are below the individual's threshold of perception. Combined with longitudinal data on individuals, this information helps to identify the role of the environment in turning health risks into manifest diseases.

Several constraints have been identified for the collection of biomarkers in social surveys. First, collecting biomarkers increases the cost and complexity of data collection. Additional costs, like those associated with visits by trained nurses (practiced by ELSA, for example), may seem prohibitive. Recent developments in minimally invasive methods which allow collection by trained survey interviewers have led to considerable cost decreases. For instance, it is now possible to measure HbA1c (as a measure for diabetes), cholesterol (to measure risk of cardiovascular disease) or C-reactive protein (to measure risk of cardiovascular disease and chronic stress) in dried blood spots. Thus, the most important risk factors for chronic disease and work disability in early old age can be measured through the collection of a few drops of blood taken from the finger tips. Together with measuring blood pressure and tobacco consumption, these data allow forecasting for the incidence of cardiovascular disease 10 years hence. Thanks to advances in technology, the costs of collecting blood and analyzing the samples in laboratories are now down to a few Euro per respondent.

Still, while the research potential of collected biomarkers is large, the training of lay interviewers and the logistics of storing and sending specimens should not be underestimated. Second, collecting biomarkers increases respondent burden and may affect the willingness of survey participants to cooperate in future waves. Third, biomarkers are potentially sensitive information and raise a lot of ethical issues surrounding confidentiality, storage, and respondent information. Survey researchers planning to include biomarkers in their data collection efforts need to be aware of these constraints.

3.3 Coverage of nursing home residents

In the US, some 15 percent of individuals aged 85 or older live in nursing homes. Thirty percent of all individuals die in nursing homes. However, the social and health determinants of nursing home admissions and the living conditions and quality of life of nursing home residents is greatly under-researched. The main problem faced by survey researchers probably is that in many countries, including Germany, no sample frames exist that include reliable information on nursing home residents (or other institutionalized populations). The typical approach taken so far is to draw a baseline sample from the non-institutionalized population and to follow respondents who move into nursing homes between waves. In principle, this approach should lead to samples of nursing home residents of reasonable size if panel surveys mature. In practice, however, there is substantial under-coverage due to the problems involved with tracking respondents, gaining access, and also due to a lack of respondents' ability to answer (and an increased need for proxy respondents). The oldest-old are the fastest growing segment of the population, and dementia – already a leading cause of nursing home admissions – is likely to be an increasing concern among the oldest-old. Despite the challenges of collecting data on them, neglecting a significant proportion of the older population in social surveys is hard to justify. Recent experience, for example from the Danish Longitudinal Centenarian Study, shows that many concerns voiced about conducting interviews in nursing homes (e.g., unethical, too costly) are unfounded. The primary impediment in most countries is the lack of a suitable sample frame such as a nationwide person register.

4. Conclusions

The collection of multidisciplinary, longitudinal data on aging is one of today's most active and innovative fields in survey data collection. This report has documented the host of data available to researchers from various disciplines working in the field of individual and population aging. We can observe several exciting developments. First, researchers across different countries (including emerging economies) are trying to collect data that are comparable internationally. Comparability is sought mainly with US surveys, because the US not only plays a leading role in survey methodology, but also because it is an important reference country, due to its size and due to the particularities of its welfare state. Second, data access for secondary analysis has become easy and quick, thanks to developments in information technology. With few exceptions, data are released after some cleaning often less than one year after they were collected. For many surveys, released data are downloadable from websites literally within minutes. Thus, the concepts of primary and secondary analysis become meaningless. Rather, it makes more sense to speak of overlapping groups of data producers and data users. Third, researchers are currently trying hard to bridge boundaries between disciplines, especially between social sciences and medicine. Some biomarkers are already routinely included in a number of ongoing surveys, and the scope of measures that can be collected during normal face-to-face interviews is increasing due to technical progress.

5. Appendix: Summary information on current aging surveys

Survey	Country	Age range	Sample size*	Survey Years
SOEP	Germany	17+	22,000	1985-2007
DEAS	Germany	40-85	6,000	1996, 2002, 2008
SAVE	Germany	18+	3,000	2001-2007
CNEF	USA, Germany, UK, Australia, Switzerland, Canada	17+	181,000	1980-2007
SHARE	Denmark, Sweden, Austria, France, Germany, Switzerland, Belgium, Netherlands, Spain, Italy, Greece, Poland, Czechia, Israel, Ireland	50+	35,000	2004-2008 (biannual)
GGS	Bulgaria, France, Georgia, Germany, Hungary, Russia	18-79	60,000	2005, 2008
ELSA	England	50+	12,000	2002-2008 (biannual)
SHIW	Italy	18+	20,000	1977-2006
TILDA	Ireland	55+	10,000	2008
HRS	USA	50+	22,000	1992-2008 (biannual)
MHAS	Mexico	50+	15,000	2001, 2003
KLoSA	Korea	45+	10,000	2006, 2008
JSTAR	Japan	50-75	4,300	2007, 2009

Access

SOEP data are available for all academic users from DIW upon signature of a user contract.
Access to the first two waves of DEAS data is provided via the central archive for social science data (ZA) at the University of Cologne (Study Numbers. 3264, 4304), access class C: data access is granted to academic users upon approval of the primary researchers.
SAVE data are available through the central archive for social science data (ZA) in Cologne (Study-Numbers: 4051, 4436, 4437, 4521, 4740), access class C: data access is granted to academic users upon approval of the primary researchers.
The PSID-CNEF file is public use and can be simply downloaded from the CNEF website. Access to BHPS-CNEF, SOEP-CNEF, or HILDA-CNEF requires approval by the BHPS, SOEP, and HILDA primary researchers, respectively. SLID data (a non-research driven survey conducted by Statistics Canada) can only be accessed via remote computing.
SHARE data are available online to academic users via the SHARE website (upon signature of a data confidentiality statement) or through the central archive for social science data (Zentralarchiv) in Cologne (Study-Number: 4560), access class C: data access is granted to academic users upon approval of the primary researchers.
Data access is granted only after a research proposal submitted to the data administrators has received a positive review "for relevance to research". Who the reviewers are and what critera for relevance they use is as yet unclear.
Online access to Scientific Use Files for waves 0 (i.e. HSE data) through 3 (i.e. the 2006 data collection) is available via the UK Economic and Social Data Service (Study-Number 5050).
Microdata are freely available from the Banca D'Italia website.
Data are not yet available.
Original HRS data are available to researchers after a simple online registration process.
Additionally, a user friendly combined and harmonized HRS file is made available by RAND.
Data collected so far are freely available from the MHAS website after a simple registration process.
The 2006 data and English documentation are freely available from the KLoSA website after a simple registration process.
Public release of wave 1 data planned for 2009.

* Note: Sample sizes may vary from year to year.

5.7 Income Provisions and Retirement in Old Age

Tatjana Mika, Uwe Rehfeld and Michael Stegmann

Contact:

Tatjana Mika
Federal German Pension Fund
Deutsche Rentenversicherung Bund
Research Data Center of the German Pension Insurance
Ruhrstraße 2
10709 Berlin
Germany
e-mail: tatjana.mika[at]drv-bund.de
          uwe.rehfeld[at]drv-bund.de
          michael.stegmann[at]drv-bund.de

Abstract

Research on the income situation of current and future retirees often requires record-based data. Because records include accurate information on the life course, they can also, when linked to survey data, make interviews shorter and less demanding for the interviewed persons. Process-produced data from the German Pension Insurance are already available for research topics in this area. The data include details about employment histories and other life-course events insofar as they are considered in the calculation of pensions. Nevertheless, additional sources are needed if research projects are to address the income situation in more detail, in particular the question of poverty or affluence in old age. The pension reforms of the past decade have strengthened the importance of the second and third pillar, thereby increasing the importance of occupational pensions and private savings for future old age income. There are already some detailed and inclusive data for research on old age income and retirement that have been collected for government reports, but not all this data is available for scientific research yet. Furthermore, the exchange of data between social security and/or tax institutions should be combined more often with the collection of statistical data in order to improve the possibility of record-to-record linkage.

Keywords: retirement, old age provisions, public pension fund, process-produced data, data linkage

1. Research questions

A principal theme in current research on old age provision is that of income after retirement for current and future retirees. For an analysis of the current retired generation comprehensive data on all income sources are needed. For in-depth research on the reasons for specific income situations among retired persons, the data should include life-course information on employment and income over the life cycle until retirement. Process-produced data from the German Pension Insurance are especially useful for these research topics because the public pension scheme is the most inclusive old age provision and it also contributes the largest share of income received in old age. These data include details about employment history and other life-course events insofar as they are considered for the calculation of pensions. The life-course information collected is very broad because of the far-reaching evaluation of social situations and activities dictated by past and current pension law. Nevertheless, additional sources are needed if research projects are to address the income situation in more detail, in particular if they are to answer questions about poverty or affluence during old age. Occupational pensions and private savings are important additional components in old age provisions. The pension reforms of the past decade have strengthened the importance of the second and third pillars of occupational and private pensions, thereby increasing their importance for future old age income. The generally lower income of women in the older population, especially in West Germany, also requires information on household income in order to assess the real economic situation.

The central focus of social research is the age of retirement, which is largely determined by social security law. The pension law determines overall retirement behavior among those who are socially insured. Process-produced data are the best choice for this kind of research question, including information on legal background that is unknown even to the pensioners themselves. However, process-produced data do not include subjective information on the motives behind early retirement. The data are not accurate for persons who retired earlier from lifetime civil service employment or from being self-employed, but who only received their public pension later. As a result, pension insurance data alone lead to an overestimation of retirement age.

To assess future old age income requires a different approach and more adequate data. To begin with, the forecast of future income requires a thorough collection of all information about old age provisions undertaken up to the date of retirement; including acquired social security rights, private insurance, and other savings and occupational pensions. These data then form the basis for estimates of future old age income.

2. Databases and data access

2.1 Databases for current old age income

Data on the income situation of the current aged population are available in many surveys like the German Socio-Economic Panel (SOEP, *Sozio-oekonomisches Panel*), the Microcensus, and the EVS (*Einkommens- und Verbrauchsstichprobe*). The varying income structure of retired people nevertheless requires a special survey design. Difficulties may arise because persons over a certain age are often difficult to interview and can be hard to reach if they live in an institution and no longer in a private household. Process-produced data are therefore helpful to estimate the number of elder people who are not or no longer available for surveys. They also offer information about the legal conditions of a granted pension.

2.1.1 Pension Records (RTBN, *Rentenbestand*) and Completed Insured Life Courses (VVL, *Vollendete Versichertenleben*) samples

The sample of the pension records includes all pensions paid from the German Pension Insurance at the last day of each year. These data are a useful basis for the validation of other sources on the retired segment of the population. Participation in the public pension insurance scheme is mandatory for all persons in Germany employed in the private or public sector. Additionally, contributions are paid out of unemployment insurance in the case of the unemployed, out of health insurance in the event of long-term illness, and from the state for people in military or civilian national service. The majority of the population thus comes into contact with the pension insurance system at some point or another in life, and the pension insurance system has data on about 90 percent of the entire population. The statutory old age and disability pension – due to its income replacement tasks and broad social basis – provides the main income source after retirement. Survivor pensions are the main source of income for widowed women.

The special survey, Completed Insured Life Courses, (VVL 2004) is a useful source for empirical analysis about retirement age and income in relation to the life course. A 20 percent sample of newly granted pensions in a particular year is the basis for this longitudinal data. The calculation of the pension is one important source of information, in combination with the longitudinal dimension of information about the past – from age fourteen until retirement. The sampling of data from one year of newly granted pensions enables researchers to compare different life courses, ending in the social status of becoming a pensioner in the same year in East and West Germany and abroad. At the time of retirement, the pension fund has gathered all information on a life course as far as the activities, contributions, and legal entitlements are relevant to the pension benefit. The moment of retirement is the point where people hand over all necessary proofs to the pension insurance office in order to receive a pension on the basis of all the relevant facts. From the statistical point of view, it is therefore the point in time at which information about the life course is most accurate. The sample drawn from all newly granted pensions is so large that all social strata and many different types of life courses are represented in sufficiently large numbers to enable empirical research on many different questions. Only old age and disability pensions are selected for this sample, excluding survivors pensions.

For the dataset "Completed Insured Life Courses," all pension funds send the information on the completed biography – from secondary school to the moment of retirement – to the Research Data Center of the German Pension Insurance (RV, *Deutsche Rentenversicherung*) (Stegmann 2007). The Scientific Use File for social research combines the longitudinal life-course information with the result of the pension calculation as a cross-sectional part of the dataset. The cross-sectional part includes additional demographic information. This means that demographic variables mirror the social situation at retirement. However, in some cases, the socio-demographic position might have changed over the lifetime, for example, if immigrants with foreign nationality are naturalized at retirement or if marital status changes over the lifetime. The longitudinal information is presented on a monthly basis. For each month the data shows whether the person was gainfully employed or was in another social position such as unemployment, care-giving, or sickness. Childcare is assumed to be the main occupation if the birth of a child is registered and no gainful employment has taken place afterwards.[1] Employment has priority status in the data and all other social situations are second in rank. A lack of information means that a person is in none of these social status situations at this time in Germany. Such a gap in information can stand for self-employment without social insurance obligation, unemployment without being entitled to benefits from the Federal Employment Agency, or working abroad. However, in most female biographies a gap in information stands for a period of housekeeping.[2] The main drawback of these data is the lack of information on other sources of income before and after retirement.

The data are accessible at the Research Data Center of the German Pension Insurance. A smaller sample is drawn for the Scientific Use File, which can be ordered for use in research institutions. Larger samples up to full samples in the case of data on recorded pensions can be use on-site at the Research Data Center.

2.1.2 Survey on Old-age Pension Schemes in Germany (ASID)

It is the aim of the research project called Old-age Pension Schemes in Germany (ASID, *Alterssicherung in Deutschland*) to provide up-to-date and representative data organized according to various socio-demographic groups that describes the income situation of the older population in West and East Germany. The first survey was realized in 1986, the last and current study was carried out in 2007. The law requires that the ASID survey be conducted once every legislative period because it is the basis for an official government report on the income of the older population (*Alterssicherungsbericht*). The study has so far been carried out six times. The population studied

---

[1] The birth of a child is registered in the pension record of one of the parents. In most cases this is the mother, because there is an income cap that hinders higher earners from profiting from the child benefit. The child benefit in the German Pension Insurance credits one point for children born before 1992 and 3 points for children born after 1992.

[2] This fact can be proven with the data from the AVID (*Altersvorsorge in Deutschland*) 1996 project, where process-produced data were combined with survey data.

includes all those older than fifty-five, including those living in residential homes.

The centerpiece of the survey is the collection of data on over twenty-five types of income. In the case of couples the data include the income of both spouses and in the case of widows income is disaggregated into self-acquired and derived benefits. Like all old age pension provision systems, the ASID collects information on income from various sources, but also includes income from private sources like private insurance. Thus, the ASID shows not only the level of overall gross and net income but also allows for varied analyses of income patterns. This is supplemented by information about the course of working life and the current life situation. In the case of couples, relevant data is acquired for both spouses, in case of widows the late husband is also taken into consideration. The gross incomes are finally converted into net incomes by way of an income tax and social insurance contribution model.

For the ASID, a representative sample is taken for this particular purpose from the local registers, where all people living in Germany must register. This is the best and most expensive method of sampling survey data. It can only be used if there is a public interest in the conducted survey. Irrespective of marital status, both men and single (i.e., widowed, divorced, and unmarried) women were chosen at random as target persons. The data of married women were collected together with the data gained from their spouses. The survey thus includes married couples and single persons. The data of the ASID 1992, 1995, and 1999 can be ordered via the GESIS Data Archive for the Social Sciences (*Datenarchiv für Sozialwissenschaften* des *Leibniz-Instituts für Sozialwissenschaften*) in Cologne using the keyword "Alterssicherung in Deutschland." For later surveys, the data have not been published and a date of publication has not yet been announced.

2.2 Old age provisions of future pensioners

The estimation of future old age income on the basis of current acquired pension rights and savings is a particularly daunting task. It requires the assessment of contributions to public, occupational, and private schemes up to the present and the prospect of future old age income streaming from these sources.

2.2.1 Sample of the insured population pension fund records

The sample of all actively insured persons in a specific year, called the insurance account sample (VSKT, *Versichertenkontenstichprobe*), is the best source for acquired rights in the public pension scheme. The longitudinal information is presented in the same format as in the "Completed Insured Life Course" data, but the former sample includes 500,000 people from the insured population aged seventeen to sixty-seven. Insured persons with non-German citizenship are over-sampled because they have a high percentage of incomplete records due to migration. In this case, transnational mobility severely limits the collection of complete life-course information.

The social situations of persons sampled are recoded from the original mainframe data into similar social situations consistent with the "Completed Insured Life Courses" survey described above. Future old age income is estimated in the data on the basis of contributions paid up to the time of sampling. The estimated pension included in the data is calculated as if the insured person retired with a disability pension for health reasons at the date of sampling. All information used for the calculation of a pension from the public pension scheme is also included in this estimate. This includes raising children, periods of education and training, as well as phases of unemployment and care-giving. The sample size and accurate information on employment and socially insured gainful employment make the VSKT attractive for social research, but the lack of information on other sources of income and the household income are a drawback for research on future old age income. A selectivity problem arises insofar as people who were employed as lifetime civil servants after less than five years of socially insured employment are not registered. Self-employed professionals have, on the other hand, a very incomplete socially insured life course, but are often covered by other compulsory old age provision schemes. The selectivity problem could only be undone if all compulsory old age provision schemes would send their data to a common statistical collection point. For occupational pension schemes data are still lacking, but the Federal Statistical Office is conducting a feasibility study about the future collection of data on this retirement income source.

2.2.2 Combination process generated with survey data from Retirement Pension Provision Schemes in Germany

The last decades have shown a diversification in and growing heterogeneity of (empirical) life courses in Germany as well as in many other welfare states. Facing this evolution, the German Pension Insurance and the Federal Ministry for Labor and Social Affairs (BMAS, *Bundesministerium für Arbeit und Soziales*) commissioned an elaborate study on future old age incomes with a strong biographical focus called the Retirement Pension Provision Schemes in Germany (AVID, *Altersvorsorge in Deutschland*).

The target persons of the first AVID Study (AVID 1996) stem from a representative random sample drawn from the panel of samples of statutory pension insurance accounts. A tailor-made projection of the data guarantees that the outcome of analyses of those contributors to the statutory pension scheme aged forty to sixty and their spouses will have a representative character. The projection method chosen makes both single person and spouse-related evaluation possible. The universe of analysis of the AVID 2005 was extended to include the entire population of Germany born between 1942 and 1961 (and their spouses), irrespective of any entitlements to pensions from the German Pension Insurance. As a result of this decision, the representative sample had to be derived from a different source and was in this instance taken from an access panel. The record to survey data match of the first wave had the advantage that the quality of the pension insurance data was the same as for the "Sample of the Insured Population Records." The price for this was that the data were representative only for the population who had a pension insurance account on the date of sampling. The second survey to record paths ensured representativeness for the whole population, but created a more troublesome process in the collection of process-produced data afterwards (Frommert and Heien 2006; Bieber and Stegmann 2002).

The objective of this project is to identify the type and amount of entitlements to old age income for individuals and married couples, that is, for pension-insured persons between forty and under sixty years of age (age groups born between 1936 and 1955, Germans living in Germany and – irrespective of nationality and age – their spouses). Thus, in AVID 1996 for the first time entitlements to payments from the statutory pension insurance for those between forty and under sixty years of age among married couples are shown, the accumulation of entitlements within the statutory pension insurance are covered (including entitlements arising from other standard and supplementary pension systems), previously unavailable information in terms of gaps in the insurance biographies of the statutory pension insurance is gathered, and extrapolation data are supplied for the analysis of future developments. Moreover, various data concerning life and working biographies are supplied that are not included in the individual pension accounts.

The AVID studies are characterized by an innovative mix of methods and data sources. They are composed of several steps, each of these and their combination as a whole are rather unique in the context of old age security research.

The survey comprises all the important schemes for retirement in Germany. Apart from the German Pension Insurance, the most significant system, this includes private and public supplementary systems, the civil servants' pension scheme, farmers' old age pensions, and schemes for independent professions. Private provisions such as life insurance and private pension insurance, ownership of property, as well as maintenance payments made by children and partners are also taken into account.

After the deduction of income tax and statutory contributions for health and old age insurance, the net old age income shown is the sum of benefits due to personal entitlements arising from the pension schemes described above, including private provisions such as life insurance and private pension insurance, survivor income, or other benefits, if any, arising from such schemes. Other sources of income such as earned income or transfer payments (i.e., housing subsidies, welfare benefits, and other forms of unearned income) are not taken into account. In the second step, the individual pension insurance accounts of the AVID respondents are clarified by the (federal or regional) institutions that manage the accounts; the entire process takes about eighteen months. These two datasets are then matched with the respondents' consent and checked extensively for consistency, resulting in a highly valid and reliable dataset on (past) life courses and pension provisions. The design of the survey also allows for the identification of married couples so that at least some measure of household context can be included in the analyses. In the third step, the individual (work) biographies are projected to the age of 65 – at the time of the surveys the legal retirement age in Germany – using a specially developed micro simulation model. Biographical events like unemployment and long-term illness are taken into account as well as individual decisions to interrupt or end employment for purposes such as housekeeping, raising children, or looking after relatives in need of care. The projection is based on a projection corridor using individual data on the years 1992 to 1996 for the AVID 1996; the projection corridor for the new study is correspondingly longer (1992 to 2002). The simulation model does not take into account socio-demographic processes, so marital status represents the status of the survey year and any mortality is excluded.

The findings are based on the projected old age income that is calculated in the final step: the gross old age income at the age of sixty-five is calculated on the basis of individual biographies, taking all the relevant pension schemes – the statutory pension insurance, the civil servants' pension scheme, the farmers' old age pension scheme, special schemes for the liberal professions, the public and private supplementary systems and private provisions for old age (life insurance, private pension insurance) – into account. Finally, the net incomes are generated by taking into account current income tax regulations and a specially designed social insurance contribution model.

The results of the AVID Studies are published as reports and charts. The data have not been published for the scientific community. However, due to its combination of process-produced data from the records of the federal pension insurance and survey data, the AVID sets an example for future data based on survey-record linkage.

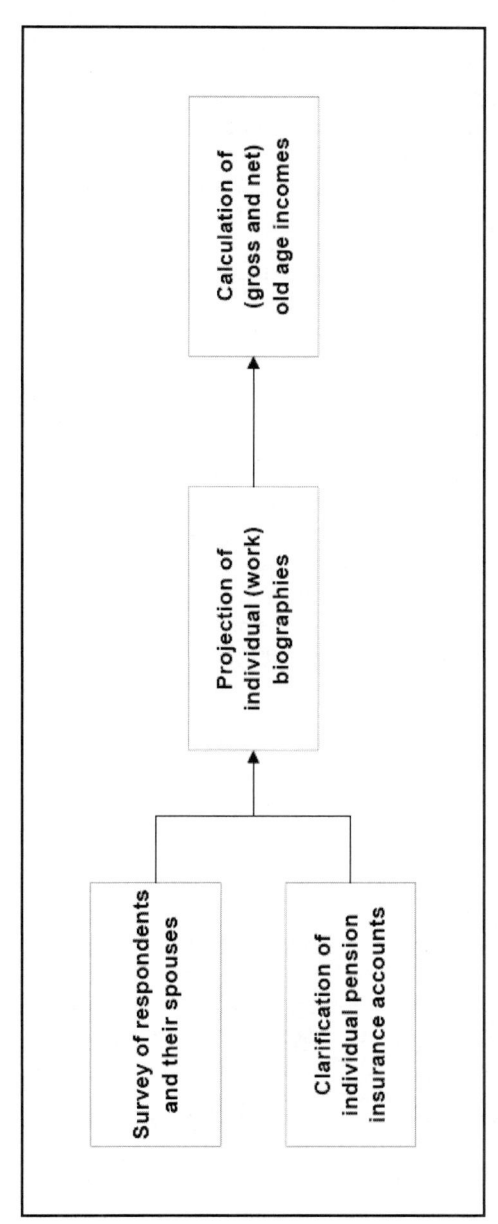

Data sources of the AVID:

```
┌─────────────────────────────────────────────────────────┐
│                                                         │
│   ┌──────────────────┐                                  │
│   │ Survey of        │                                  │
│   │ respondents      │──┐                               │
│   │ and their spouses│  │   ┌──────────────┐   ┌──────────────┐
│   │                  │  │   │ Projection of│   │ Calculation of│
│   │                  │  ├──▶│ individual   │──▶│ (gross and net)│
│   ┌──────────────────┐  │   │ (work)       │   │ old age incomes│
│   │ Clarification of │  │   │ biographies  │   │               │
│   │ individual       │──┘   └──────────────┘   └──────────────┘
│   │ pension          │                                  │
│   │ insurance accounts│                                 │
│   └──────────────────┘                                  │
└─────────────────────────────────────────────────────────┘
```

Source: Dina Frommert und Thorsten Heien (2006)

3. Future developments

3.1 Record-to-record linkage

Record-to-record linkage would improve data where other social security or tax institutions gather information unknown to the pension fund. In the case of the Federal Employment Agency, there are relevant data on training and other benefits from unemployment insurance. In the case of public health insurance, such data would include information about prescriptions and health treatments.

Record-to-record linkage is not an easy task for the Research Data Center of the German Pension Insurance (RV, *Deutsche Rentenversicherung*), because the social security number is not known for persons included in the data gathered for statistical purposes which is the case, for example, for the 500,000 persons included in the insurance account sample (VSKT). The public pension fund itself is a federation of several regional and two federal insurance programs that keep the records on the persons insured by them. For statistical purposes all pension insurers send data to the central statistical collecting point, not including the social security number. The Research Data Center is therefore unable to re-identify the persons included in the data provided for scientific research. Record-to-record linkage must therefore be supported from all pension insurers by sending the data including the social security number for a particular research project and a particular year and data source. These projects must therefore be presented to the self-governing boards. Strict data privacy rules also apply because the Research Data Center is not allowed to have the social security number in its reach. A regular procedure is not yet in place for record-to record-linkage, but if convincing new results from research projects using improved data were presented, a recurrent regular procedure could become possible. The next step in record-to-record linkage would be matching data that have other identifiers other than social security numbers. These could be tax data or data from the old age provision schemes.

3.2 Matching process-generated data with survey data

The linkage of pension insurance records with survey data would improve the life-course information for many surveys, which suffer from recollection errors by interviewed persons or left censoring. Research on retirement or disability would, on the other hand, gain from subjective information gathered via the survey. Self-assessed health and retirement planning would give crucial insights about early retirement, a research topic of the utmost importance. Objective indicators of health status could also be included (biomarkers). However, for survey-to-record linkage re-identification is likewise not an easy task. The self-governing boards of the pension insurances have to give their consent to the project, because the cooperation of all pension insurances is here again essential. The survey must include the informed consent of the interviewed person, who must also provide his or her social security number. The collected number must then be searched for in the central register of all socially insured persons. The next step is the collection of the data from pension insurance records.

4. Future developments: European and international challenges

The German Pension Insurance exchanges data with most public pension funds worldwide because social security treaties require that migrants should not be discriminated against and should have an easy one-step procedure to apply for their pension in just one country. The most important partners in data exchange are the Member States of the European Union, who act under the common framework of the same regulations. The exchanged information is only minimally included in the statistics. A common effort to gather more information on transnational working biographies would be a step toward improving the data.

A common international pool of data on public or publicly supported old age provisions would promote comparative research. This would require improved multilingual metadata and very accurate documentation, because the differences between national security systems could easily lead to misconceptions.

5. Conclusions and recommendations

Research on the income situation of current and future retirees often requires record-based data. Because of their accuracy in providing life-course data they also can, if they are linked to survey data, make interviews shorter and less demanding for the interviewed persons. However, the projects leading to this improved data are time-consuming, because privacy laws demand extensive data protection requirements. Furthermore, social security laws require that the collected data are for research projects on social security related topics like health status and early retirement. Record-to-record linkage does not require informed consent to protect privacy, but extensive technical provisions separate the data from the identifier at an early stage. Both methods of matching greatly improve data quality at a reasonable price, but require an established infrastructure that is able to handle the procedures required by privacy laws and regulations.

References:

Bieber, U. and Klebula, D. (2001): Kräftiger Aufholprozess: ASID 1999. Bundesarbeitsblatt 9/2001.
Bieber, U. and Stegmann, M. (2002): Sozialer Ausgleich in der gesetzlichen Rentenversicherung. Empirische Ergebnisse auf Basis der Untersuchung AVID 1996. Deutsche Rentenversicherung 11/2002.
Federal Ministry of Labor and Social Affairs (2001): Old Age Pension Systems in Germany 1999. Summary of results.
Federal Republic of Germany (2005): National Strategy Report on Old-Age Pension Provision 2005 (NSR 2005).
Frommert, D. and Heien, Th. (2006): Retirement Pension Provision Schemes in Germany 1996 and 2005. Schmollers Jahrbuch 126 (2), 329-336.
Kortmann, K. and Schatz, Ch. (1999): Altersvorsorge in Deutschland 1996 – (AVID'96). Zusammenfassung wichtiger Ergebnisse der Untersuchung „Strukturen und Trends der Altersvorsorge von 40- bis 60-jährigen Rentenversicherten und ihrer Ehepartner". DRV 10-11/1999, 573-597.
Roth, M./Stegmann, M. and Bieber, U. (2002): Die Aktualisierung der Studie Altersvorsorge in Deutschland – Inhaltliche und methodische Neuerungen der AVID 2002. DRV 11/2002, 612-641.
Stegmann, M. (2007): Biografiedaten der Rentenversicherung und die Aufbereitung der Sondererhebung „Vollendete Versichertenleben 2004" als Scientific Use File. DRV-Schriften Band 55/2006, 82-95.
TNS Infratest Sozialforschung (2005): Alterssicherung in Deutschland 2003 (ASID '03) – Zusammenfassung wichtiger Untersuchungsergebnisse, Forschungsbericht Bd. 346/Z des Bundesministeriums für Arbeit und Soziales. Berlin.
TNS Infratest Sozialforschung (2007): Altersvorsorge in Deutschland (AVID) 2005: Alterseinkommen und Biografie. Forschungsprojekt im Auftrag der Deutschen Rentenversicherung Bund und des Bundesministeriums für Arbeit und Soziales. Berlin.
Verband Deutscher Rentenversicherungsträger (VDR) (2000): Special Survey „Old Age Pension Provision in Germany (AVID'96)" Old Age Provision of Statutory Pension Insurance Contributors – Birth Years 1936 to 1955. Übersetzung des Projektdesigns. VDR. Frankfurt/M.

6. Political and Cultural Participation and the Role of the Media

6.1 Political Participation – National Election Study

Rüdiger Schmitt-Beck

Contact:

Rüdiger Schmitt-Beck
University of Mannheim
Chair of Political Science I (Political Sociology)
68131 Mannheim
Germany
e-mail: schmitt-beck[at]uni-mannheim.de

Abstract

This advisory report gives an overview of recent developments in political participation and electoral research, and discusses the current state of affairs with regard to data provision and access. It concludes with several recommendations: (a) to retain a small number of key political variables in the future German General Social Survey (ALLBUS, *Allgemeine Bevölkerungsumfrage der Sozialwissenschaften*) and the German Socio-Economic Panel (SOEP, *Sozio-oekonomisches Panel*) questionnaires to create substantial amounts of synergy at little marginal cost; (b) to establish a National Election Study in Germany by providing the current German Longitudinal Election Study (GLES) project[1] with a constant logistic and methodological support infrastructure through the Leibniz Institute for the Social Sciences (GESIS, *Leibniz-Institut für Sozialwissenschaften*). It is recommended that in the long run a regular follow-up study to this project be provided with stable public funding and a firm institutional embedding, preferably by including it in the remit of GESIS; (c) to align the data services of statistical offices more closely to the data requirements of participation and electoral research; (d) to establish a formal obligation for public agencies to submit survey data collected under their auspices in due time to the public domain for purposes of secondary analysis.

Keywords: political participation, political behavior, elections, electoral behavior, voting

1. Introduction

The notion of political participation, in the sense of voluntary activities undertaken by free and equal citizens to influence the course of government, is at the heart of the idea of representative democracy (Dahl 1972). To be sure, in liberal democracies no one is obliged to take part in politics. But if large majorities of the citizenry abstained from any political involvement, there could simply be no democratic politics. Hence, a substantial amount of political activity on the citizens' part is essential for the functioning of democracy. Therefore, describing and explaining how people participate in politics is a vitally important task for political scientists. Consequently, patterns and dimensions of political participation, which encompass a whole range of activities, from contacting local officials to engaging in acts of political violence, have been scrutinized extensively since the 1960s (van Deth 2003). Among the many avenues by which people can make their needs and interests count in political decision-making, casting votes at general elections has always been the most important one. To the present day, it is by

---

1 The GLES is funded by the German Research Foundation (DFG, Deutsche Forschungsgemeinschaft) to study the 2009, 2013, and 2017 national elections.

far the most widely used and most egalitarian form of political action. Moreover, it stands out as the one form of political participation that, by its very nature, is inextricably tied to the core principle of representative democracy. It decides who is granted access to public office and thus to the levers of power. It is a sharp weapon in the hands of citizens that enables them to hold officials accountable to the will of the people. It seems just, then, that electoral behavior is one of the most intensely explored political phenomena. Most of this research has concentrated on explaining citizens' vote choices, while studies about turnout and its preconditions are less numerous (Falter and Schoen 2005; Lewis-Beck et al. 2008).

Seven years after the 2001 KVI report, the present advisory report will attempt to take stock of the current state of data provision and access with regard to the various aspects of political participation and, in particular, electoral behavior in Germany. It first gives an overview of recent theoretical and methodological developments within the field of participation research, especially electoral research, that appear particularly important from the perspective of data provision and access. It will then discuss the current state of affairs with regard to these two foci in Germany, including developments that have taken place since the 2001 KVI report. The chapter concludes with a brief summary of recommendations, directed at either policy-makers or scientific infrastructure organizations.

2. Recent developments in participation and electoral research

Since Milbrath's (1966) seminal study on political participation in the United States in the 1960s, participation studies have flourished, and quickly developed into a respected subfield of political research. In the 1970s, the first large-scale internationally comparative projects were undertaken, and comparative survey research has, to the present day, remained the hallmark of this strand of studies. Between them, these studies have greatly enhanced our understanding of political participation – the incidence of its various forms, its dimensionality, and its backgrounds, i.e., the factors that facilitate or impede citizens' active involvement in politics (van Deth 2003; Kaase 2007). Since the 1990s, the field of participation studies has expanded and become part of a broader paradigm of research into modern democratic citizenship. This recent conception conceives political participation as one of but a whole range of facets of citizens' orientations towards their political system, including social participation (such as associational membership and activity; see the chapter on civil society by Alscher and Priller in this publication), socio-political norms and values (such as civic obligations, tolerance, norms of reciprocity, or inclusion/exclusion); and support for democracy and its institutions (Pattie et al. 2004; van Deth et al. 2007).

The special field of electoral research has also substantially expanded its scope in several ways. Traditionally, it has been guided by a small set of related questions: who votes, and for what reasons? Which candidates and/or parties are chosen, and, again, for what reasons? Typically, these questions were focused at particular national elections. Representative surveys of voters (often cross-sections, sometimes short-term panels) were the method of choice to answer these questions. In recent projects, this rather narrow frame of surveying and collecting data has given way to a broader perspective that seeks to understand elections as part of broader processes of political representation. This includes manifold and dynamic interactions between citizens and office-holders, as well as candidates for electoral office, with political parties and the mass media functioning as mediating agencies. The broadening focus of electoral research has also been accompanied by a pronounced interest in the dynamics of the communicative processes taking place between citizens on the one hand, and parties and their candidates on the other. An implication of this is that study designs have moved from a cross-sectional to a longitudinal approach (Romer et al. 2006). Further, this shift in electoral research has forced researchers to go far beyond mere voter surveys in data collection. Consequently, researchers have also added candidate surveys, party campaign studies, media content analyses, and contextual data. Moreover, electoral studies are even coming to see inter-election periods as similarly important for election outcomes (Güllner et al. 2005). This development has heightened the increasing data requirements of studies not only during the few weeks of the "hot" campaigns immediately preceding elections, but also at more or less close intervals during entire electoral cycles. As voters' political behavior tends to become more and more individualized and volatile, it seems clear that ideal designs to study contemporary elections need to include specific components for capturing short-term campaign dynamics immediately preceding elections, on the one hand, and for tracking the long-term changes that take place over whole electoral cycles, on the other.

Closely connected to this is a recent tendency of electoral studies to become less sociological and more political. Traditionally, election studies tended to see individual voters and their attributes as the sole key to understanding the outcomes of elections – as if these were occurring in a political vacuum. Recent studies, in contrast, try to explore how elections can be better understood by taking into account the institutional and situational political contexts within which they take place. These typically include the behavior of parties, candidates, the media, and other actors. Naturally, such a perspective would require attention to be directed beyond individual elections by comparing various elections in both cross-national and longitudinal perspectives. Hence, elections themselves become units of observation in complex longitudinal and multilevel research designs (Franklin and Wlezien 2002; Thomassen 2005). Obviously, such studies are far more demanding than traditional ones in terms of data requirements.

Although older than participation studies, electoral studies lag behind this field with regard to internationally comparative projects – for obvious reasons. National elections are in many respects idiosyncratic affairs (beginning with their dates), and studying them in an internationally comparative perspective poses serious challenges in terms of study designs and instrumentation. Recent years have seen the development of measures which may be used to successfully deal with these problems. One is the Comparative Study of Electoral Systems (CSES), a collaborative program of research among election study teams from several countries around the world, including Germany. These study teams include a common module of survey questions in their own post-election studies which are further enriched with system-specific macro variables to allow for multilevel analyses and the study of interactions between system characteristics and individual behavior at elections (Klingemann 2009).[2] Another is the European Voter Project (Thomassen 2005), which, jointly with the GESIS Data Archive, successfully undertook the formidable task of harmonizing data from national election studies from six countries over more than four decades (Mochmann et al. 1998). It has additionally started a successor project, entitled COST Action "The True European Voter."[3]

Of particular relevance for this advisory report is yet another recent trend: a palpable strengthening of interest within the political science community to move beyond single election projects and engage in creating permanent, integrated data infrastructures for electoral research. More and more countries are institutionalizing National Election Studies as part of their social science data infrastructure. In Germany, a concerted attempt to establish such a study started in 2007, which is described in more detail below. Teams of French and Austrian political scientists are also engaged in similar activities in their respective countries. It also deserves mention that a multinational team has been awarded funding under the EU's Seventh Framework Programme to carry out a pilot study for the creation of an extensive European data infrastructure for research into citizenship, political participation, and electoral democracy at the level of the EU.[4] Moving beyond an exclusive emphasis on surveying voters, this project impressively illustrates the trend towards broadening the scope of election studies towards dynamic studies of political representation. Importantly, such data infrastructures are not intended to serve exclusively the data requirements of

---

2   http://www.umich.edu/~cses/
3   http://true-european-voter.eu/
4   http://www.piredeu.eu/

scientists specializing in electoral research, but also to address – by appropriate means of data dissemination – the information needs of the general public. This includes political actors ranging from MPs, government agencies, parties, and organized interests to journalists and members of civil society.

3. Data provision and access

The 2001 KVI report did not include a special section on political participation, but it did contain an excellent, highly detailed stock-taking of provision and access to data on elections and political parties (Niedermayer 2001). With regard to elections, this report evaluated the availability of data for purposes of scientific research on the whole quite positively, although it also emphasized – to adopt Lipset and Rokkan's (1967, p. 50) famous phrase – a "few but significant exceptions" to this. One of the most significant gaps mentioned concerned the general dearth of data concerning elections at the local level. This bleak state of affairs has remained virtually unchanged. In stark contrast to European, national, and *Länder* elections, local elections have remained a "blind spot" and are therefore still extremely difficult to analyze.

Official electoral data are reliable and can therefore be used as benchmarks for data collected by means of sample surveys. Importantly, some research problems can only be addressed using this kind of data. These research problems typically include analyses aimed at understanding how political behavior is embedded in broader socio-spatial contexts, which requires advanced methods of multilevel analysis. While provision of data from official electoral statistics is generally satisfactory, from the perspective of electoral research, revisions of current practices seem desirable with regard to a number of details. One concerns the residual category of "other" parties. As a matter of information efficiency, it seems appropriate to use such condensed categories in official publications, but the results of these parties should, as a rule, always be reported separately in computerized data collections. In an age of ongoing party system fragmentation, from the perspective of electoral research, it is desirable to obtain easier access not only to data pertaining to the larger established parties, but also to marginal parties. These comparatively smaller parties are an important, albeit neglected, research object in their own right. They are of importance as, while they can only be appropriately studied using official electoral records, no one can tell whether or not they are indeed bound to remain marginal in the future.

Moreover, it would be desirable if election results at all levels of the political system were, as a rule, added to all regionalized data files provided by statistical offices. An even better alternative would be to set up a comprehensive database at the community (and city district) level, containing results of elections at all levels of the political system. A final desideratum concerns the data gained through the Representative Election Statistics program. Research possibilities could be substantially improved if these data would be made public not only at the level of the states, but also at the level of electoral districts. Participation studies, in their turn, could profit from access to process-produced data, such as data on extremist organizations collected by the State Offices for the Protection of the Constitution (*Landesämter für Verfassungsschutz*). Police records of demonstrations and estimated head counts of their participants could also greatly benefit participation studies. In the United States, such data have been successfully used to analyze the selection bias of mass media with regard to coverage of such protest events (McCarthy et al. 1996).

Survey data of high potential value for research into political attitudes and participatory orientations are constantly collected under the auspices of public agencies, such as the Press and Information Office of the Federal Government, and the public broadcasters ARD and ZDF. At present, only a small portion of these data are routinely submitted to the GESIS Data Archive. This seems hard to justify for data whose collection has been financed by public funds. Indeed, publicly funded projects can be seen as public property, which naturally the public has a right to access. In this regard, the German Freedom of Information Act (FOIA) clearly lacks bite. Under the US FOIA, data collected by public agencies are required to be made accessible to the public after three years at the latest. For three decades now, the Politbarometer surveys, as well as election studies conducted by the Forschungsgruppe Wahlen e.V. under the auspices of the ZDF, have been passed to GESIS. Cumulated over this long period of time, these data are a treasure trove for longitudinal political research, without which many important academic projects of electoral and participation research never would have seen the light of day. Starting with the data collected in 2008, the monthly Deutschland-Trend survey series conducted by Infratest dimap for the ARD is also made accessible through the GESIS Data Archive – a highly welcomed recent development. It would be desirable if this policy would also extend to other data collected under the auspices of the public broadcasters, in particular the exit polls conducted at elections, as already emphasized by Niedermayer (2001: 38). Moreover, in view of the increased interest in the role of media and communications for citizens' participation in politics, it would be highly desirable if the data collected by programs such as the ARD/ZDF's Mass Communication and Online Studies would be routinely submitted to the public domain (on media data see also the advisory report by Meulemann and Hagenah in this publication).

Concerning the access of the scientific community to political surveys conducted by private survey institutes either for clients from the private sector or for their own purposes, one can only appeal for an increased readiness to submit these data to the GESIS Data Archive on the part of these institutes *and* their clients (who typically own the data). In this respect, at least one quite large recent project deserves highlighting: a public/private partnership between a group of academic researchers and the FORSA institute. Although it only partly improved data access for the scientific community at large, it provided a creative and original analysis of the dynamics of the 2002 parliamentary election by utilizing a very unusual and innovative database (Güllner et al. 2005). Private survey institutes also have been collecting data on media usage for decades. These data are of high interest for participation researchers, but so far the scientific community has only been granted limited access to these data (see the advisory report by Meulemann and Hagenah in this publication).

Turning to science-based programs of data collection, of the various ongoing replicative survey programs, two are of particular interest to researchers studying political participation and electoral behavior in Germany; namely, the German General Social Survey (ALLBUS, *Allgemeine Bevölkerungsumfrage der Sozialwissenschaften*) and the German Socio-Economic Panel (SOEP, *Sozio-oekonomisches Panel*). The ALLBUS is an indispensable resource for the long-term observation of trends in political participation and related topics. Fortunately, from its beginning, it has always carried political variables, and every ten years it has adopted political participation values and attitudes as core themes. It is strictly recommended to carry on with this rotating system in the future. For participation researchers in particular, it is considered vitally important to receive updates of key measures of political participation and related concepts at regular intervals (as well as data pertaining to new participatory phenomena). In doing so, the ALLBUS key working principle of combining replicative components with new, pre-tested instruments to catch up with recent societal developments seems highly appropriate.

In addition to the cyclical inclusion of political topics at a broader scale, each ALLBUS has always carried a small set of political indicators. However, the partial lack of long-term continuity with regard to these is disadvantageous. In the past, ALLBUS surveys included a number of important instruments, but several of them disappeared from time to time, either temporarily or permanently. Thinking about the future, in all upcoming waves of the ALLBUS, permanent inclusion of a small set of standard instruments would be extremely valuable for research into political participation and electoral behavior. Here, a commitment on the part of the ALLBUS program to include them permanently as part of the essentials of the questionnaire would be welcome. These instruments should include:

- voting intentions and recall of vote decisions to record turnout and party vote at previous elections. These should pertain to national parliamentary elections. Additionally the recall question should ideally relate to the previous state and European elections;
- party identification (existence, strength, and party);
- party membership;
- left-right self-placement;
- interest in politics; and
- satisfaction with democracy.

It would be highly recommendable to include this same set of variables also into the standard SOEP questionnaire. This excellent database has so far not found many users among political scientists due to its glaring lack of political measures. Traditionally, the SOEP has carried only the standard indicator of party identification. It would therefore be highly welcome if the SOEP adopted at least the same small set of political standard instruments as essentials for its future surveys. For three reasons this would – at little cost – greatly enhance the utility of this impressive database: the uniqueness of the SOEP's panel design would open up unprecedented opportunities for analyzing change and stability of political orientations; the fact that it does not sample individuals, but households, would allow for analyses of the interdependence of individual orientations (Zuckerman et al. 2007); and, last but by no means least, its core content of socio-economic variables could be related to basic political attitudes (and their change).

While these steps towards increasing the value of the ALLBUS and SOEP programs would be highly desirable in view of the criterion of greatly enhanced synergy at little marginal cost, they could by no means replace a genuinely institutionalized program of research into citizens' political orientations. Although on the whole rather sanguine about the state of data provision and access for electoral and other political research in Germany, the 2001 KVI report emphasized a glaring gap in the otherwise very well developed German social science research infrastructure; namely, the lack of an institutionalized German National Election Study (GNES) that at each election reliably produces high-quality data as a public good (KVI 2001: 66; Niedermayer 2001: 33; Kaase and Klingemann 1994: 351-356; Kaase 2000: 32-34; Schmitt 2000; Gabriel and Keil 2005: 635-636). A significant step towards remedying this disadvantageous state of affairs has been made very recently. Starting with the 2009 Federal Election, a major research project, entitled the German Longitudinal Election Study (GLES), is funded by the German Research Foundation (DFG, *Deutsche Forschungsgemeinschaft*). The goal of this project is to cover the next three Federal Elections (Rattinger et al. 2008). The GLES is exceptional in that it is a continuous program of empirical social research that meets the highest methodological standards, rests on a solid organizational base and transparent governance structure, enjoys the security of long-term funding, and is accountable. Furthermore, the GLES is open to the entire scientific community of academic empirical social researchers both with regard to the input side (i.e., with regard to developing the study design, questionnaires, etc.), and the output side (i.e., with regard to data availability and distribution). In light of this, it does not seem farfetched to claim that the GLES displays all the trademarks of the best election studies worldwide. In bearing with the previously described general trends, the GLES encompasses not only voter surveys, but also other components such as a candidate survey, interviews with party officials, and media content analyses. In this way, the GLES is in a unique position to place voting behavior in the broader context of the parties' campaign communications and the mass media's political coverage. Moreover, the GLES includes several longitudinal components (both repeated cross-sections and panels) that are to capture both the short-term dynamics taking place during election campaigns, and the long-term dynamics over entire electoral cycles. The study will also routinely include the CSES question modules (see above).

Overall, the GLES constitutes an important element of an emerging international infrastructure of high-quality data production and dissemination related to vitally important questions of the empirical foundations of democracy. It is conducted in close cooperation with the German Society for Electoral Studies[5] and GESIS. The former serves as an organizational network for linking the study to the scientific community, while the latter provides the study at all stages with logistic and methodological support, from developing research instruments to distributing the data via a web-based system. However, while being conducted according to the principles characteristic of high-quality National Election Studies worldwide, the GLES is still deficient with regard in one important respect – it will create unprecedented data infrastructure for the next three German national elections, but not beyond these. It would therefore be ideal if, in the long run, the study would be continued under the auspices of GESIS. In this respect, the GESIS could follow the model of the ALLBUS, which years ago mutated from a DFG project into an indispensable part of Germany's social science data infrastructure (within the remit of GESIS).

---

5 http://www.dgfw.eu

4. Recommendations

- The ALLBUS is a replicative survey program of immense value to political research. For political scientists, it is essential that the ALLBUS carries on with its tried and tested rotating system of integrating broad political topics at regular intervals in the future. Moreover, it is strongly recommended that both the ALLBUS and the SOEP tag a small number of key political variables (listed above) as constant elements in their future question programs, ideally to be included in each wave. For the scientific organizations responsible for these two research programs, "value-adding" the ALLBUS and the SOEP in such a way would open the possibility of creating substantial amounts of synergy at little marginal cost.

- Responding to a grave deficit diagnosed by the 2001 KVI report, a determined collective attempt was recently initiated to close a glaring gap in the otherwise very well-developed German infrastructure of high-quality programs of replicative social science data collection. The ultimate goal of the effort leading to the German Longitudinal Election Study (GLES), which is at present funded by the DFG, is the institutionalization of a German National Election Study (GNES). In the long run, following the model of well-established continuous research programs, such as the ALLBUS and the SOEP (which are mostly designed to cater to the data requirements of sociologists and economists), this study should be granted permanent funding and become institutionally integrated into the overarching infrastructure of the social sciences. Permanently establishing this study beyond the present DFG project, which covers the three German Federal Elections 2009, 2013, and 2017, would create an ideal supplement to the existing programs of replicative surveys in Germany. It also would generate unprecedented synergies with these pre-existing surveys. It is therefore to be recommended to policy-makers and research administrators to follow the model of other countries by providing the GNES with a stable financial basis of reliable public funding and an institutional embedding beyond the present GLES project. Ideally, this would occur by including it into the remit of GESIS.

- Concerning electoral data provided by the statistical offices, several improvements to data services are to be recommended. These include, for example, better provision of data on local elections, ideally as part of a comprehensive database at community (and city district) level. These data should contain results of elections at all levels of the political system. Further recommendations include detailed provision of electoral data on marginal parties in computerized form, the addition of electoral data to regionalized data files, and publication of data from the Representative Election Statistics at the level of electoral districts. In addition, it is recommended to grant greater access to process-produced data pertaining to acts of collective (unconventional) participation.

- It is to be recommended that policy-makers establish a formal obligation for public agencies, including public broadcasters, to submit survey data collected under their auspices in due time to the public domain for purposes of secondary analysis. For this purpose, GESIS appears appropriate for archiving and disseminating such data. In particular, data of immediate relevance to participation, electoral, and political communication research is of importance.

References:

Dahl, R. (1972): Polyarchy. Participation and Opposition. New Haven.
Falter, J.W. and Schoen, H. (Eds.) (2005): Handbuch Wahlforschung. Wiesbaden.
Franklin, M. and Wlezien, Ch. (2002): Reinventing Election Studies. In: Franklin, M. and Wlezien, Ch. (Eds.): The Future of Election Studies. Amsterdam.
Gabriel, O.W. and Keil, S. (2005): Empirische Wahlforschung in Deutschland: Kritik und Entwicklungsperspektiven. In: Falter, J.W. and Schoen, H. (Eds.): Handbuch Wahlforschung. Wiesbaden.
Güllner, M./Dülmer, H./Klein, M./Ohr, D./Quandt, M./Rosar, U. and Klingemann, H.-D. (2005): Die Bundestagswahl 2002. Eine Untersuchung im Zeichen hoher politischer Dynamik. Wiesbaden.
Kaase, M. (2000): Entwicklung und Stand der Empirischen Wahlforschung in Deutschland. In: Klein, M./Jagodzinski, W./Mochmann, E. and Ohr, D. (Eds.): 50 Jahre Empirische Wahlforschung in Deutschland. Wiesbaden.
Kaase, M. (2007): Perspectives on Political Participation. In: Dalton, R.J. and Klingemann, H.-D. (Eds.): The Oxford Handbook of Political Behavior. Oxford.
Kaase, M. and Klingemann, H.-D. (1994): Electoral research in the Federal Republic of Germany. In: Thomassen, J. (Ed.): The Intellectual History of Election Studies, European Journal of Political Research 25 (3) (special issue), 343-366.
Klingemann, Hans-Dieter (Ed.) (2009): The Comparative Study of Electoral Systems. Oxford.
Kommission zur Verbesserung der informationellen Infrastruktur zwischen Wissenschaft und Statistik (KVI) (Ed.) (2001): Wege zu einer besseren informationellen Infrastruktur. Baden-Baden.
Lewis-Beck, M.S./Jacoby, W.G./Norpoth, H. and Weisberg, H.F. (2008): The American Voter Revisited. Ann Arbor.
Lipset, S.M. and Rokkan, S. (1967): Cleavage Structures, Party Systems, and Voter Alignments. An Introduction. In: Lipset, S.M. and Rokkan, S.(Eds.): Party Systems and Voter Alignments. New York.
McCarthy, J.D./McPhail, C. and Smith, J. (1996): Images of Protest: Dimensions of Selection Bias in Media Coverage of Washington Demonstrations, 1982 and 1991. American Political Science Review 61, 478-499.
Milbrath, L.W. (1966): Political Participation. Chicago.
Meulemann and Hagenah (2010): Mass Media Research. [In this publication].
Mochmann, E./Oedegaard, I.C. and Mauer, R. (1998): Inventory of National Election Studies in Europe 1945-1995. Bergisch Gladbach.
Niedermayer, O. (2001): Wahlen und Parteien. Expertise für die KVI. In: Kommission zur Verbesserung der informationellen Infrastruktur zwischen Wissenschaft und Statistik (KVI) (Ed.): Wege zu einer besseren informationellen Infrastruktur. Baden-Baden.
Pattie, Ch./Seyd, P. and Whiteley, P. (2004): Citizenship in Britain: Values, Participation and Democracy. Cambridge.
Rattinger, H./Roßteutscher, S./Schmitt-Beck, R. and Weßels, B. (2008): The Dynamics of Voting: A Long-term Study of Change and Stability in the German Electoral Process, Application to the Deutsche Forschungsgemeinschaft for long-term funding. Bamberg/Frankfurt/Mannheim/Berlin.

Romer, D./Kenski, K./Winneg, K./Adasiewicz, C. and Jamieson, K.H. (2006): Capturing Campaign Dynamics 2000 & 2004. The National Annenberg Election Survey, Philadelphia.

Schmitt, H. (2000): Die Deutsche Nationale Wahlstudie – eher kollektive Aufgabe als aktuelle Realität. In: Klein, M./Jagodzinski, W./Mochmann, E. and Ohr, D. (Eds.): 50 Jahre Empirische Wahlforschung in Deutschland. Wiesbaden.

Schmitt-Beck, R./Weick, S. and Christoph, B. (2006): Shaky attachments: Individual-level stability and change of partisanship among West German voters. European Journal of Political Research 45, 581-608.

Thomassen, J. (Ed.) (1994): The Intellectual History of Election Studies. European Journal of Political Research 25 (3) (special issue).

Thomassen, J. (Ed.) (2005): The European Voter. A Comparative Study of Modern Democracies. Oxford.

Van Deth, J.W. (2003): Vergleichende politische Partizipationsforschung. In: Berg-Schlosser, D. and Müller-Rommel, F. (Eds.): Vergleichende Politikwissenschaft. Opladen.

Van Deth, J.W./José Ramón Montero and Westholm, A. (Eds.) (2007): Citizenship and Involvement in European Democracies: A Comparative Analysis. London/New York.

Zuckerman, A.S./Dasovic, J. and Fitzgerald, J. (2007): Partisan Families: The Social Logic of Bounded Partisanship in Germany and Britain. Cambridge.

6.2 Civil Society

Mareike Alscher and Eckhard Priller

Contact:

Mareike Alscher
Eckhard Priller
Wissenschaftszentrum Berlin für Sozialforschung
Reichpietschufer 50, 10785 Berlin
e-mail: alscher[at]wzb.eu
priller[at]wzb.eu

Abstract

Despite the obvious existence of civil society organizations (CSOs) and forms of civic engagement, the data available for this sector remain inadequate. This advisory report provides a comprehensive view of the current data situation, reveals existing gaps, and offers suggestions on how these gaps might be closed.

The empirical material currently provided by existing data sources – the Federal Statistical Office, statistics from the CSOs themselves, as well as special data and surveys – only register this area separately and to a limited extent, and even then not in a consistent manner. With respect to both CSOs and forms of individual engagement, the data situation is inadequate. Questions pertaining to whether CSOs will remain oriented toward civil society within a context of increased economic pressure cannot be answered. Similarly, it is nearly impossible to analyze whether civic engagement stands at odds to the increased tendency towards monetarization.

Since civil society will undoubtedly continue to gain in political and social importance, the long-term task will be to set up a meaningful and a predominantly self-contained system of data collection and provision. This goal can be reached by using the existing surveys and databases described in this paper.

Keywords: civil society; civil society organizations; civic engagement; Volunteers Survey; Johns Hopkins Comparative Nonprofit Sector Project; Handbook on Nonprofit Institutions in the System of National Accounts

1. Introduction

The term "civil society" attracts a range of paraphrases and definitions. One of the most common definitions is action-oriented and focuses on four distinct attributes (Kocka 2003; Gosewinkel et al. 2004: 11). These attributes include (1) qualities of self-organization and independence; (2) an emphasis on actions taken in the public domain nurturing exchange, discourse, and understanding but also conflict; (3) the acknowledgement that conflicts and protests are included in this concept of civil society but they are associated with peaceful, non-violent, and non-military actions; and (4) a course of action that considers the common good above and beyond individual, specific, and particular interests.

This advisory report conceives of civil society in accordance with the logic of this field. As such, civil society can be perceived especially as characterized by (a) the self-organization of citizens and (b) their voluntary engagement in a number of organizational forms, such as clubs, associations, initiatives, or foundations. These organizations are generally regarded as the institutional core or infrastructure of civil society and are often collectively referred to as the "third" or "non-profit" sector as a way of separating them from state and market sectors (Anheier et al. 2000). Civil society organizations (CSOs) thus constitute that area of society located between the boundaries of market, state, and family, and are characterized by their formal structures, organizational independence from state control, autonomous administration, non-profit approach, and voluntary engagement. Engagement in civil society organizations includes both unpaid voluntary work in traditional membership-based organizations and nonprofit-oriented activities in unconventional forms of organizations.

CSOs can be found in a variety of areas and perform diverse roles. Whether in recreational or cultural spheres, as part of social service facilities, or as other types of local, professional, and political advocacy groups (e.g., clubs, associations, foundations, not-for-profit Public Limited Companies, cooperatives, etc.), they have collectively become an essential part of society's workings.

As contemporary forms of civic self-organization and self-responsibility, CSOs possess considerable abilities in terms of the concentration, expression, and representation of interests. They are assigned responsibility for implementing important tasks, in promoting the development of democracy, providing welfare state services, as well as integrating citizens into coherent collectivities and thereby ensuring social cohesion.

A number of factors have led to the increased importance of this sector of society in recent years. On the one hand, citizens have become increasingly conscious of their own skills. On the other hand, social change has led to changes in social roles and functions, resulting in an increasingly stark division of tasks between state, market, and civil society. The growing significance of CSOs has manifested itself through increases in the number of CSOs, in the number of people working in them, and in the services they offer. At the same time, the number of voluntary workers also continues to grow.

Despite the obvious existence of CSOs and forms of civic engagement, the data available for this sector remains inadequate. Due to the relatively late development of the study of CSOs as an independent scientific discipline, the empirical information available on this constantly evolving sector is incomplete. Even official statistics and other data-providing information systems mark this area separately to a limited extent, and even then not in a consistent manner. For instance, CSOs and their services are often subsumed within the categories of state and economy, with data gathered from disparate surveys seldom taking their autonomous forms of organization into account.

CSOs tend to highlight the fact that they break down the classic dichotomy of state and citizen, replacing it instead with the three social spheres of state, market, and civil society. In the past, however, the autonomy of this sector did not prevent the use of CSOs for political ends in order to carry out those inconvenient tasks for which no one was – or considered themselves to be – responsible. With this in mind, some social actors view CSOs as simply a form of cheap "repair service," a way of balancing out the social deficits caused by the failure of the market, state, or family sectors.

Generally speaking, the growing demand for data on civil society can be explained by the increasingly autonomous significance of civil society in economic, social, and cultural life. Yet the current data situation is extremely complicated, not least because civil society has its own particular logic of action, and possesses unique functions and organizational structures, all of which have until now received only a modicum of direct attention and consideration. Data is lacking on the size of this sector, the extent of the services it offers, and its degree of socio-political integration. Current yet differentiated information is needed in order to more accurately define the significance of civil society, its development, and its contribution to providing solutions for current and future social challenges.

This expert report provides a comprehensive view of the current data situation, reveals existing gaps, and offers suggestions on how these gaps might be closed. Whereas in Germany relatively little data on civil society is available, other countries, such as the US, Australia, Italy, Belgium, and even Hungary, have progressed much further with regard to data collection and the long-term observation of civil society. Corresponding data is already an important component of these countries' official statistics.

2. The current data situation in the civil society sector

Empirical research on civil society can be divided into investigations aimed at three distinct levels. At the macro-level, CSOs are collectively analyzed as a field or sector. At the meso-level, research focuses on the CSOs, their specific tasks, and the way they function. Finally, at the micro-level, public activity in and for these organizations is investigated, with the key concerns in this context being membership, volunteering and donation behavior.

A considerable step toward improving the relatively awkward data situation was made with the Johns Hopkins Comparative Nonprofit Sector Project,[1] a large-scale, internationally comparative project with a scope spanning more than thirty countries. Under the coordination of the Johns Hopkins University Institute for Policy Studies (Baltimore, US), this project provided the results of data collected in Germany for the 1990 and 1995 reporting periods. The project was launched in 1990, and encompassed a

---

[1] The project included formally structured, state-independent, and non-profit-oriented organizations. These organizations were also administered autonomously, funded to a certain extent by voluntary contributions, and could not in any sense be called an "administrative union" (Anheier et al. 1997: 15).

group of seven industrialized and five developing countries. In the meantime, the number of countries taking part has increased significantly. During the second phase (1995–1999), countries in North and South America, as well as both Western and Eastern Europe were heavily represented. Existing gaps in Africa and Asia have also been closed in more recent years thanks to the provision of additional country reports. Germany has been involved in the project from its inception.

The project collects quantitative data at national level on the structural dimensions of the non-profit sector, and investigates qualitatively how the sector is embedded within national structures. During the second phase, the German component of the project was located at the Social Science Research Center Berlin (WZB, *Wissenschaftszentrum Berlin für Sozialforschung*) and the Westphalia Wilhelm University of Münster's Institute for Political Science.

It was agreed that during the course of this international comparative project, empirical data on the CSOs would be collected according to the following targeted items:

- Number of CSOs
- Number of staff, based on number of hours worked (paid and voluntary staff)
- Financial volume
- Proportion of different funding sources within financial volume
- Expenditures
- Fields of activity
- Services provided

The well-established International Classification of Nonprofit Organizations (ICNPO) also formed part of the uniform research design. The nonprofit sector was then divided according to activity into twelve distinct fields, thereby allowing for an investigation into the internal structure of the sector. The ICNPO lists the following fields:

- Culture and recreation
- Education and research
- Philanthropic intermediaries and voluntarism promotion
- Health
- International
- Social services
- Business and professional associations, unions
- Environment
- Religion
- Development and housing
- Not elsewhere classified

The Johns Hopkins Project also developed a corresponding methodology, thereby establishing the essential groundwork for long-term observation. In collaboration with the Johns Hopkins University Center for Civil Society Studies, the United Nations Statistics Division produced the *Handbook on Nonprofit Institutions in the System of National Accounts*. This publication offers recommendations and guidelines for setting up national information systems. A host of countries (including Belgium, Italy, and France, among other European countries) have already adopted this approach. In Germany, however, no comparable administrative decisions and effective measures have been taken. Nevertheless, the implementation of this methodology is conceivable and could indeed be achieved on account of the close cooperation between the research community, the Federal Statistical Office, and CSOs.

In order to establish long-term and sustained observation of German civil society, data from official statistics as well as additional data stocks from CSOs, federal ministries, and other institutions and associations – including the research community – must be integrated. Despite endeavours to secure the continuous generation of reliable data on the social impact and performance of civil society in Germany, up to this point only partial and very basic data have been made available. Yet it would be possible to draw from sources ranging from official statistics, information from the CSOs, and, above all, data from scientific surveys. It is thus critical that the current data situation be fundamentally reshaped and improved; this must be set as a goal for the future. Greater coordination will be required in order to organize the amalgamation of the various data stocks. Moreover, scientific research, especially with regard to CSOs, must be undertaken. The current situation for the individual fields is as follows:

2.1 The Federal Statistical Office

The Federal Statistical Office provides diverse statistics, although they do not fully conform to the methodology laid out in the *Handbook on Nonprofit Institutions in the System of National Accounts*. The information gathered from this source during the investigation referred to the number of CSOs, the number of staff, the CSO's financial volume, as well as the services offered, results, and capacities. These data do not, however, offer a full picture of the CSOs. Some of the surveys used to collect data are based on the 2003 German Classification of Economic Activities (WZ03) and use business entity classifications that are not consistent with the typical fields of activity and business entity classifications developed by the Johns Hopkins Project. Thus, the significance of these data is, generally speaking, limited. The following summarizes the individual data and data sources pertaining to CSOs within official statistics:

a) *Economic accounts*
   - Data on gross value added and staff
b) *Business register*
   - Data on turnover, number, and staff
c) *Income tax statistics*
   - Data on financial volume (income) acquired through donations from private households
d) *Corporation tax statistics*
   - Data on finance volume (income acquired through donations and the expenditure of donations; profit and loss information)
e) *Survey on private schools (no current data available – last surveyed in 1995)*
   - Data on the number, income, and expenditure of private schools
f) *University statistics (manual allocation of type of business entity necessary)*
   - Data on the number of universities, their staff, expenditure, income, and services provided
g) *Research statistics of non-university research institutions*
   - Data on the number of institutions, their staff, expenditure, and income
h) *Child and youth services statistics*
   - Data on the number of institutions, results, and income
i) *Health service statistics*
   - Data on the number of institutions, their staff, services provided, and capacities
j) *Continuous household budget surveys*
   - Data on financial volume (obtained through information on income, donations, and membership fees)
k) *Income and consumer sample*
   - Data on financial volume (obtained through information on income, donations, and membership fees)
l) *Time use survey (no current data available – last collected in 2002)*
   - Data on the engagement/volume of voluntary work

2.2 Statistics from Civil Society Organizations (CSOs)

Data received from umbrella organizations represent another important source of information for statistical analyses. However, the material provided from these sources is marked by certain gaps and irregularities. These gaps are caused by a number of factors. On the one hand, transparency is not particularly well developed in civil society organizations; the corresponding tax legislation means that only limited support is received from the state. On the other hand, the member organizations of these umbrella organizations – or even their regional branches at the level of the *Länder* – are themselves autonomous and independent legal entities and thus not obliged to provide data. Finally, incapability and noncompliance inevitably lead to gaps and loss of information.

At this point, it is useful to observe that when one considers the combined statistics available from all of the non-statutory welfare services in Germany (i.e., the voluntary welfare organizations of *Caritas, Diakonie,* the *German Red Cross, Paritätische*, and the *Central Welfare Office of Jews in Germany)*, the combined statistical data in all the museums in Germany, and the database of the Association of German Foundations (*Bundesverband Deutscher Stiftungen*), it is very clear that CSOs could play a much larger role as potential suppliers of data in the future. The information gathered whilst conducting surveys such as the European Social Survey (ESS), which is a representative social survey that was first established in 2002/03 at the suggestion of the European Science Foundation (ESF), refers to the number of CSOs, the services offered and capacities, as well as the number of staff. The varying forms of data on CSOs in Germany are:

a) *Overall statistics of the non-statutory welfare service sector*
   - Data on the number of institutions, staff, and their capacities
b) *Overall statistical data for museums in Germany*
   - Data on the number of institutions, services provided, and number of staff
c) *Association of German Foundations database*
   - Data on the number of foundations, their assets, and outputs

3.3 Special data and surveys focusing on a micro-level

a) The Volunteers Survey

The German Volunteers Survey consists of a representative data collection in which around 15,000 German citizens over the age of 14 are queried about their level of civic engagement. To date, the survey has been carried out twice – in 1999 and 2004 respectively. The next survey is planned for 2009.

The survey's data – which have been scientifically verified – provides a number of opportunities for carrying out extensive analysis on the orientation, extent, and potential of civic engagement in Germany. At the same time, the survey provides information on the willingness of individuals to participate in civic activities (see Gensicke et al. 2006). Furthermore, the German Volunteers Survey offers insight into the motives behind civic engagement and the social structure of volunteerism. The differentiated data were collected according to socio-structural criteria.

b) The German Socio-Economic Panel (SOEP, *Sozio-oekonomisches Panel*)

By focusing on "social participation and time use," the SOEP represents another crucial source of data in the combined statistical measurement of the level of engagement in civil society. Data from this source focuses on the types of engagement associated with certain forms of CSOs. At the same time, activities that fall within the purview of informal personal and community networks are also taken into account. Although the data gathered are not differentiated by specific fields of engagement, it is well-suited to the illustration of general trends and developments over time, and can also be used to implement time series analyses and analyses on socio-structural factors.

c) The IAB Establishment Panel

Data from the IAB Establishment Panel is primarily evaluated at the Institute for Employment Research (IAB, *Institut für Arbeitsmarkt- und Berufsforschung*). The survey gathers data from organizations that have at least one staff member subject to social insurance contributions. Therefore, the sample only contains those CSOs with paid staff. The survey thus provides information relating to staff and the CSOs. However, because it concentrates on economically active establishments, the broader spectrum of CSOs remains poorly represented.

d) European Social Survey (ESS)

As previously mentioned, the ESS is a representative social survey that was established at the suggestion of the European Science Foundation (ESF) and carried out for the first time in 2002/2003. In the first round, twenty-two countries participated (Austria, Belgium, the Czech Republic, Denmark, Finland, France, Germany, Great Britain, Greece, Hungary, Ireland, Israel, Italy, Luxemburg, the Netherlands, Norway, Poland, Portugal, Slovenia, Spain, Sweden, and Switzerland). With the exception of Switzerland and the Czech Republic, data on the level of engagement in civil society was provided for the remaining twenty countries. The long-term goal of the ESS is to investigate the interaction among political and economic institutions in transition, as well as the attitudes, convictions, and behavioral patterns of each country's population. The first round of the ESS focused on the themes, "Citizenship, Involvement, Democracy." The 2002/2003 survey used a four-step approach to gathering data on civic engagement, including: (1) being a member of a CSO, (2) working for a CSO, (3) donation behavior, and (4) civic engagement within a CSO.

3. Gaps, progress, developments, and tendencies of the current data situation

This portrayal of the current data situation makes it abundantly clear that a comprehensive and developed information system on civil society simply does not exist at this point. While individual engagement can be analyzed through different scientific surveys, other areas show distinct deficits. Data gaps exist particularly where it concerns CSOs and their concrete fields of activity. To date, the current picture – including over 600,000 associations, more than 14,000 foundations, around 8,000 registered cooperatives, and numerous other organizations – is more than a little hazy. Information on newly established or disbanded CSOs can, as a rule, only be found by searching through special registers existing for different forms of organizations. One particularly significant gap is the absence of broader scientific surveys that cover all of the different organizational forms of CSOs; other countries (e.g., Austria) have already embraced this approach in recent years and integrated such broad scientific surveys on CSOs as part of their federal statistics. These extensive surveys offer insight into the dynamic changes in the orientation and activities of different CSOs. In light of the increasing economic pressure on organizations, which tend to react to such strain by improving their management techniques or by tapping into additional financial resources (e.g., donations), the importance of extensive surveys offering insight into the inter-temporal changes of CSOs has grown. This increased financial strain simultaneously raises the question of whether CSOs intend to remain oriented toward civil society. A change in orientation could lead CSOs to regard the engagement of the population in civil society as less important. Economic factors can therefore lead to the neglect of civic engagement and volunteerism on the part of the CSOs.

Moreover, irrespective of all that might be done at the organizational level (of CSOs), many questions that concern the civic engagement sector at the individual level remain unanswered: either no data are available or existing data cannot come up with adequate answers. As a consequence, it is almost impossible to analyze whether civic engagement stands at odds with an increased tendency towards monetarization. This would seem to confirm theories which declare an increased tendency towards the dissolution of boundaries between paid and unpaid work vis-à-vis gainful activity. Research is also needed to ascertain whether value change is taking place within the context of civic engagement and whether forms of a stronger, non-organized engagement, one which requires no concrete membership, are becoming increasingly prevalent.

Alongside these obviously significant gaps in the data, however, some developments and tendencies can be detected that point to improved data collection and analysis.

a) Civil Society Data Collection Project

Due to the grossly inadequate data situation that exists with regard to civil society, several foundations have decided to sponsor a new intervention. The aim of this project, which will run until 2010, is to establish a reporting system based predominantly on the Federal Statistical Office's data stocks. The reports will focus on providing an economic balance sheet and social service profile for CSOs. The project is located at the *Stifterverband Wissenschaftsstatistik GmbH*, the research and development branch of the Donors' Association for Promotion of Science and the Humanities in Germany (*Stifterverband für die Deutsche Wissenschaft*), and will provide basic data for further investigations. Based on the concepts and methods of the Johns Hopkins Comparative Nonprofit Sector Project, with existing international standards that have developed in the meantime, the midterm goal of the project is to establish a national accounting satellite system.

b) Report on Donation Behavior

So far there have been a number of investigations that deal with donation behavior. Among these we find the "Donations Survey" (*Spendenmonitor*) by EMNID and the "Gfk Charity*Scope" survey of the GfK Group, an international market research company.

Amidst calls for greater transparency in the donation sector and increasing competition among non-profit organizations, plans are underway to publish a national report on donation behavior. The Social Science Research Center Berlin (WZB, *Wissenschaftszentrum Berlin für Sozialforschung*) has developed the report methodology which contains, among others, information on donation volume, donors, purposes, and motives. The project is to be conducted by the German Central Institute for Social Issues (DZI, *Deutsches Zentralinstitut für soziale Fragen*).

4. Future requirements and perspectives for civil society data

Civil society will undoubtedly continue to gain in political and social importance as we move into the future. It is therefore highly likely that the demand for data and analyses will also increase. The long-term task, as it has been in many other areas of society, will be to set up a meaningful and predominantly self-contained data collection and provision system. This goal can be reached by using the existing surveys and databases that have been described in this paper. Along with more substantial and better methods of coordination, the criteria and categories for civil society must be integrated into other data collection activities. Considerable progress could be made by ensuring that the type of business entity represented by CSOs, or their nonprofit orientation, is considered as a specific criterion throughout. Subsequent analyses could also be strengthened by integrating questions about civic engagement into other specific large-scale surveys (e.g., the annual Microcensus). Experience in Austria has shown that using this approach significantly improves the availability and quality of data.

More effort must be directed toward carrying out larger surveys on CSOs. The impact of research in this field and the evaluation of particular structures and practices will have increasing significance.

References:

Anheier, H.K./Priller, E. and Zimmer, A. (2000): Die zivilgesellschaftliche Dimension des Dritten Sektors. In: Klingemann, H.-D. and Neidhardt, F. (Eds.): Zur Zukunft der Demokratie. Herausforderungen im Zeitalter der Globalisierung. WZB-Jahrbuch 2000.

Anheier, H.K./Priller, E./Seibel, W. and Zimmer, A. (Eds.) (1997): Der Dritte Sektor in Deutschland. Organisationen zwischen Staat und Markt im gesellschaftlichen Wandel. Berlin.

Gensicke, Th./Picot, S. and Geiss, S. (2006): Freiwilliges Engagement in Deutschland 1999 - 2004. Wiesbaden.

Gosewinkel, D./Rucht, D./van den Daele, W. and Kocka, J. (2004): Einleitung: Zivilgesellschaft – national und transnational. In: Gosewinkel, D./Rucht, D./van den Daele, W. and Kocka, J. (Eds.): Zivilgesellschaft – national und transnational. WZB-Jahrbuch 2003.

Kocka, J. (2003): Zivilgesellschaft in historischer Perspektive. In: Forschungsjournal Neue Soziale Bewegungen 16 (2), 29-37.

van Deth, J.W. /Montero, J.R. and Westholm, A. (Eds.) (2007): Citizenship and Involvement in European Democracies. A comparative analysis. London and New York.

6.3 Culture

Jörg Rössel and Gunnar Otte

Contact:

Jörg Rössel
Gunnar Otte
Universität Zürich
Soziologisches Institut
Andreasstrasse 15
8050 Zürich
Switzerland
e-mail: roessel[at]soziologie.uzh.ch
        otte[at]soziologie.uzh.ch

Abstract

The term "culture" is notorious for its multitude of meanings. This advisory report strictly focuses on culture in terms of the arts. We adopt a sociological as well as an economic perspective. Research questions are subdivided into three spheres: artistic production and its organization; the distribution and valuation of culture; and the consumption and reception of culture. The data requirements and the availability of adequate data vary substantively, depending on artistic branches (music, performing arts, etc.) and specific research questions. In order to make the empirical investigation of culture a flourishing field, we recommend the following improvements in data infrastructure: first, comprehensive surveys of artists on the one hand, and cultural consumption on the other, should be carried out with the support of public funding; second, a national cultural statistic should be established, illuminating the size, impact, and evolution of the cultural sector in comparative perspective; third, the public availability of organization-level data as well as communal surveys on cultural production and consumption issues should be improved; fourth, the transparency of existing data sources and their accessibility should be improved by archiving them centrally, e.g., at the GESIS[1] Data Archive.

Keywords: culture, arts, artists, production, distribution, consumption, reception, cultural sector, cultural industries

1. Definition of culture

The term "culture" is notorious for a multitude of definitions. In our advisory report we strictly focus on culture in terms of the arts. Issues that are sometimes included under the superordinate concept of culture, like religion, ideologies, values, norms, and patterns of everyday life, are not considered in this paper. Including these topics would necessarily lead to a superficial treatment of each because of the numerous and heterogeneous data sources in these areas. However, even the concept of "arts" itself must be differentiated. Generally speaking, the arts include objects and services of primarily aesthetic expression. These are, first, differentiated according to the implied aesthetic criteria. In public as well as scientific discourse, high culture, popular culture, folk culture, and youth culture are typically distinguished even if these terms are difficult to mark off in their boundaries (Gans 1974; Schulze 1992; Hügel 2003). While folk, popular, and youth culture are often normatively devalued, all of these aesthetic forms have to be included in empirical research from a value-free scientific point of view. This is because conceptions of beauty are socially constructed and historically variable.

---

[1] Leibniz Institute for the Social Sciences (*Leibniz-Institut für Sozialwissenschaften*).

Secondly, the arts have to be differentiated into core branches like music, performing arts, literature, visual arts, and film. Since these areas exhibit varying forms of social organization (Deutscher Bundestag 2007, chap. 3), most research questions have to be applied separately to these fields. These internal differentiations of the arts lead to a multiplication of the data sources required for empirical research.

2. Theoretical developments and research questions

In the last major German publication of the sociology of the arts, Gerhards (1997: 7) concluded that this field is not at all established in German sociology. The situation has remained nearly unchanged. German sociology has not participated in the international boom of the sociology of the arts and culture.[2] Most sociologists in the field prefer qualitative methods – if they do empirical research at all. To be sure, qualitative research and case studies are important complements of the standardized data that we focus on here. We do not further discuss this strand of research because it almost always involves primary data collection. Due to this basic research orientation and because of other reasons to be described in section 3, adequate data enabling scholars to tackle central research questions are scarce.

Contemporary sociology of the arts and culture is not about the interpretation of artistic content. Although this orientation can still be found in the literature, the main focus is – in accordance with Max Weber – on the description, understanding, and explanation of social action related to goods and services of primarily aesthetic expression. Research questions are usually subdivided into three different spheres of action: first, artistic production and its organization; second, the distribution and valuation of culture; and third, the consumption and reception of culture (Becker 1982; Blau 1988; Gerhards 1997; Schneider 1993; Zolberg 1990). Apart from sociology, the field of cultural economics has developed recently. Therefore, we include research questions and data requirements of economists of the arts and culture in our report (Blaug 2001; Caves 2000; Frey 2000; Ginsburgh and Throsby 2006; Throsby 1994).[3]

---

2   In the most important journal of empirical research in the arts (Poetics), we find only one article from Germany and one from Austria in the issues from 2003 to 2007. In comparison, economists from Germany and Austria have published nine articles in the major journal in the field of cultural economics (Journal of Cultural Economics).
3   Although being very important for the explanation of phenomena related to the arts and culture, we do not discuss psychological research because it is mainly based on experimental data.

2.1 Artists and production of culture

The sociology and economics of artistic production deal with four broad research questions. They are, first, concerned with the socialization, recruitment, and training of artists, as well as the social inequalities connected with artistic career paths that vary in terms of social class background, general and artistic education, gender, ethnicity, earnings, and social security (Menger 1999; Caves 2000, chap. 4; Janssen 2001; Haak 2008). Second, inter- and intra-individual variations in living and working conditions are supposed to have an impact on artistic output, creativity, and aesthetic development. Both questions necessitate longitudinal data that link artists' labor market positions and integration in artistic networks with their aesthetic expression and that track stability and change over their life courses (Thurn 1983; Simonton 1997; Bourdieu 1999). Third, scholars are interested in the institutional organization of artistic production, its conditions, and consequences. They try to explain why organizational forms of artistic production vary enormously between cultural branches and between countries. They also try to assess the impact of these variations on artistic outcomes: bureaucratic organization vs. short-term projects, public vs. private funding, types of contracts between artists and support personnel, organizational structures dealing with market uncertainty (Peterson 1976; Caves 2000; Dowd 2004; Deutscher Bundestag 2007, chap. 3; Gebesmair 2008, chap. 4). Finally, the production of culture may be considered from a macro perspective. The importance of culture for the economy has become an important issue for research and official statistics as several German states and cities have published reports on the cultural sector (*Kulturwirtschaftsberichte*). Currently, a lively political debate centers on the establishment of a unified statistic of the cultural sector in Germany and Europe (Statistisches Bundesamt 2004; Deutscher Bundestag 2007, chap. 5; Eurostat 2007, part II).

2.2 Distribution and valuation of culture

Producing a good or providing a service does not make it art. The status of art is based on the authentication of a good or service as art by accepted authorities like critics, curators, gallery owners, and ministries of culture. Therefore, the development of aesthetic criteria to evaluate art and the canonization of artists and art forms is a central research area (Bevers 2005; Baumann 2007). However, cultural authorities do not only consecrate goods or services as art; they recommend and interpret art works for the lay public and are thereby actively engaged in the creation of markets for art and in price formation on these markets (Shrum 1997; Caves 2000, chap. 12; Beckert and Rössel 2004; King 2007). Social scientists depend on data about cultural authorities and critical evaluations, which are essential for artists' reputations, as well as on market data, like prices for art works and box office results, which reflect their commercial successes.

Other actors and organizations, like gallery owners, museums, concert halls, and radio stations, are decisive for the supply and distribution of cultural goods and services. They perform gate keeping functions in artistic fields, create artistic repertoires, and thereby advance or hamper artistic careers (Greenfeld 1988; Mark 1998; Giuffre 1999). Again, we find a vast array of different organizational forms in the distribution and valuation of culture. Explaining why certain forms emerge and which consequences they imply are central topics for both sociology and economics (Frey 2000; Kirchberg 2005). Data on cost and finance structures of institutions are of further importance from an economic perspective, as they enable researchers to evaluate the efficiency of the provision of culture, e.g., theatres in the profit- vs. non-profit sector.

2.3 Consumption and reception of culture

Questions of the consumption and reception of culture have generated the bulk of empirical studies in sociology. A lot of research has been devoted to inequalities of social class, gender, ethnicity, age, and generation in cultural consumption, especially with regard to the use of publicly funded cultural institutions (Dollase et al. 1986; Klein 1990; Rössel et al. 2005; Kirchberg 2005; Bourdieu et al. 2006). However, much of this research is of a rather descriptive kind and the data usually collected do not allow scholars to test rival hypotheses and reveal explanatory mechanisms. For example, there is a long-standing and still open debate about whether the well-known educational effects on high-culture consumption are based on information-processing or status-seeking mechanisms (Ganzeboom 1982; Otte 2008). In order to fill these research gaps, scholars are dependent on adequate survey data containing theoretically derived indicators. In particular, longitudinal individual-level data are of prime importance for the analysis of the biographical formation of aesthetic preferences (Hartmann 1999; Katz-Gerro et al. 2007). In this respect, findings in the sociology of culture are of a more general interest, as the origin of preferences constitutes a central question in the behavioral sciences. Closely related is research on the symbolic boundaries people draw in order to express their likes and dislikes for different aesthetic forms and genres (Lamont and Molnár 2002). A major international debate circles around the thesis of so-called "omnivorous" tastes. This implies a reorganization of traditional taste hierarchies: the educated classes in Western societies are said to have stopped using high culture as the main aesthetic format of distinction vis-à-vis the lower classes, and instead to have broadened their taste repertoire with popular genres and to display wide-ranging competences as new status-markers (Peterson 2005). High-quality time series data are needed to study such preference and consumption patterns over time, comparative data are required to find out about international variation.

3. Databases and access

In comparison with other research areas, the data infrastructure in the field of culture is not well-institutionalized. In academia, there has been no establishment of a research program based on comprehensive, recurrent nation-wide surveys on cultural production and consumption, let alone panel studies. In official statistics, the cultural domain falls under the sovereignty of the federal states and communes. A standardized, unified cultural statistic on the national level is nonexistent. In this regard, the conclusion of the 2001 KVI report still holds: reporting on cultural issues is rather unsystematic (Weishaupt and Fickermann 2001: 50).

This does not mean that there is a scarcity of data on culture. Rather, as has been noted by the KVI report (2001: 16) for other fields, the current situation resembles a fragmented mosaic of various data lacking comparability, being frequently intransparent or inaccessible, and thus inhibiting cumulative research efforts. We will shed light on this situation according to the three main spheres of research that we distinguished in the last section. We consider both aggregate- and individual-level data from various sources.[4] Although we wish to emphasize the much greater analytic potential of individual-level data for most research questions, aggregate-level data are valuable especially for some applied and policy-relevant questions.

3.1 Artists and production of culture

Artists' socialization processes and careers are of interest from a double perspective: the formation of aesthetic expression over the life course and social as well as material inequality within the cultural field. Both questions can be addressed most systematically by using surveys tracking artists' retrospective careers and using a research design like the German Life-History Study (Mayer 2008). Assessing individual artists' development of aesthetic expression and productivity can be further improved by linking respondent data to documentary sources on art works for a subset of cases. While, to our

---

4 Aggregate data are data that have been aggregated from smaller units of analysis and cannot be easily disaggregated again. Individual-level data, in our case, refer to both persons and organizations.

knowledge, such datasets are nonexistent, the situation is somewhat better for questions of inequality. In order to study patterns of intergenerational social mobility and reproduction among artists, cumulative ALLBUS- and SOEP-data may, in principal, be used (Jonsson et al. 2007). However, the number of respondents is very small; artistic branches cannot be differentiated. The German Microcensus has the great advantage of large numbers, but lacks sufficient biographical information. Still, it has been used to investigate the effects of socio-demographic variables on artists' employment relationships and earnings (Haak 2008).

In this context, limitations become apparent regarding data from official statistics of artists' earnings and material living conditions.[5] The main data sources are the German Microcensus, the Employment Sample of the Institute for Employment Research (IAB, *Institut für Arbeitsmarkt- und Berufsforschung*), the statistics of the German Artists' Social Insurance Company (KSK, *Künstlersozialkasse*) and sales tax statistics (*Umsatzsteuerstatistik*). They differ substantially in their coverage of the artist population. The Microcensus, for example, counts everyone who works at least one hour per week in his or her main occupation as employed – and thus includes individuals regarded as not employed by the IAB's Employment Sample. The latter considers employees who are subject to social insurance contributions, work at least 15 hours per week, and earn at least € 400 per month. Because it does not cover, among others, the self-employed, it may be combined with KSK statistics, a social insurance institution open (on a voluntary basis) for self-employed artists earning at least € 3,900 annual artistic income. The sales tax figures include businesses with more than € 17,500 annual turnover and thus exclude self-employed "starving" artists. The databases also differ in their classifications of cultural occupations: the Microcensus defines occupational affiliation according to respondents' self-assessments, the Employment Sample according to employers' reports, and the sales tax statistics according to tax inspectors' assignments. The Employment Sample and sales tax statistics can be broken down to low occupational levels, but they do not contain enough individual-level information to model explanatory variables in statistical analyses. The Microcensus as a household survey may be preferable in this respect, but it does not offer a fine grouping of occupations. None of these data sources properly comes to grips with multiple job holdings and the mixture of dependent and self-employment typical for the artist population (Haak 2008).

---

5   Haak (2008, chap. 3) gives a detailed discussion of the problems the Microcensus and the IAB's Employment Sample have. Apart from problems due to the incomplete coverage of the artist population and the aggregation of occupational subcategories, inconsistencies of educational variables, censored income variables, the lacking differentiation of income sources, and multiple job holdings are considered problematic.

Because of these coverage, classification, and measurement problems, estimates of the number of artists, their education, and earnings differ depending on the data used (Haak 2008, chap. 4; Deutscher Bundestag 2007: 289ff).[6] Against this background, an explicitly designed survey on the living conditions of artists would be highly desirable. More than thirty years after the pioneering work of Fohrbeck and Wiesand – "Autoren-" and "Künstler-report" (1972; 1975) – primary data still need to be collected on a large representative sample of artists and other persons close to the creative core of the cultural sector.[7] Nevertheless, official statistics will be important for continuous social reporting and construction of time series. Therefore, an integration and standardization of current statistics is needed.

A similar conclusion holds for the effects of the cultural sector on the economy, usually measured in turnover and employment figures. Problems of definition, classification, and comparability, pervade the currently popular *Kulturwirtschaftsberichte* (Weckerle et al. 2003; Statistisches Bundesamt 2004; Deutscher Bundestag 2007, chap. 5). The relevant target population extends far beyond those occupations that would count as "cultural" according to our definition. Usually, all self-employed and dependently employed people in the production and distribution of goods and services in the visual and performing arts, publishing, press, radio, television, music, film, architecture and design, cultural education, and maintenance of cultural heritage, are subsumed under the label "cultural industries." This already broad category is sometimes expanded to include those in the advertisement, software, and games industries, and correspondingly entitled "creative industries."[8] There is disagreement, however, on the following (Deutscher Bundestag 2007: 340ff): is cultural employment in the public sector to be counted among the cultural industries? Are non-profit, voluntary, and lay cultural

---

6   The boundary problem of who is an artist is difficult to solve because the arts are not as professionalized as other occupations (Karttunen 1998). A minimum proportion of income earned or of hours worked can serve as criteria. In addition, the subjective self-categorization as an artist, educational credentials, and institutional affiliations, have some plausibility. Notably, artistic status is professionally or publicly ascribed and undergoes historical change. Current examples of boundary cases – sometimes legal cases about inclusion in the KSK – comprise assistant directors, disc-jockeys, web designers, and curators. A classic, prevailing controversy is related to the boundary between arts and crafts (Becker 1982: chap. 9).

7   In connection with an inquiry into "Culture in Germany" (Kultur in Deutschland), a large-scale online and mail survey addressing self-employed artists was launched by a culturally committed consultant, Christian Scheibler. In various aspects, e.g., sampling procedure and questionnaire construction, it did not follow standards of scientific research (Kressin 2008). This example highlights the urgency of a methodologically sound "status-of-the-artist" survey in Germany. Otherwise, we see the danger that the artist population, known to be particularly hesitant to provide personal information, may lose trust in future survey efforts.

8   Söndermann (2005) combines data from the Microcensus, Employment Sample, and sales tax statistics, to make estimates of employment in the cultural industries, differentiated by branches, employment status, regional distribution, and development from 1999 to 2004.

activities to be included (e.g., choirs, music clubs, theatre groups) – and how can they be reliably captured? Are both a narrow and a broad definition necessary, and if so, which cultural branches belong to the core of the cultural sector? Are whole branches to be incorporated or just the creative parts of them (e.g., writers, but not printers)? A consensus on these questions is needed to guarantee the comparability of future reports on cultural industries in different countries, federal states, and cities.

The Federal Statistical Office (Statistisches Bundesamt 1994; 2004) has suggested a conception for a nationally unified culture statistic and illustrated the potential of standardized indicators in a recent publication (Statistische Ämter des Bundes und der Länder 2008).[9] Cultural statistics have also been presented at the European level (Eurostat 2007). They are based, among others, on the EU Labour Force Survey, Structural Business Statistics Survey, EU Household Budget Survey, Harmonized European Time Use Study, and the Eurobarometer, but provide a rather incomplete and tentative picture. From a scientific point of view, cultural statistics and reports on the economy of culture encompass important macro indicators, allowing researchers to make spatial-temporal comparisons and to identify broad trends. The more aggregated the data are, however, the less potential they have for revealing social processes at the micro-level within the cultural sector.

3.2 Distribution and valuation of culture

Research on the distribution and valuation of culture requires organizational and archival data. In order to learn more about the types of cultural products and services which are distributed, longitudinal data on artistic repertoires of institutions and companies are needed, e.g., repertoires of theatres and orchestras, inventories and exhibitions of museums, circulation and sales figures of books and records. In the case of public sector institutions, especially theatres, operas and orchestras, such information is accessible via archival documentation of single institutions and increasingly via internet websites. This information can then be used to generate datasets (Mark 1998; Gerhards 2008). The situation becomes worse, however, the smaller the organizations are (e.g., free theatres) and the more profit-oriented they are (e.g., musicals, record companies).

For such purposes, publications of professional associations are important sources. These include, for example, the Institute for Museum Research

---

9   For the Federal Statistical Office's enquiry into "Culture in Germany" (Statistisches Bundesamt 2004: 208-311), it produced an advisory report, which contains an extensive account of the official data sources currently available for the creation of a federal culture statistic.

(*Institut für Museumsforschung*), the German Theatre and Orchestra Association (*Deutscher Bühnenverein*), the German Publishers and Booksellers Association (*Börsenverein des Deutschen Buchhandels*), the Confederation of the Film Industry (*Spitzenorganisation der Filmwirtschaft*), the Association of the German Music Industry (*Bundesverband Musikindustrie*), the German Confederation of Socio-cultural Centers (*Bundesvereinigung soziokultureller Zentren*), and the German Choral Association (*Deutscher Chorverband*). Data reported in the annual reports of such institutions are based on (a) routine surveys of samples of cultural institutions or of their member organizations, (b) questionnaires on special topics, and (c) sales tax statistics. Official statistics often rely on these figures in their yearbooks. Additionally, collecting societies, such as GEMA, GVL, and VG Wort,[10] hold data on musical and literary publications.

A central shortcoming of these data sources is that they are subject to high aggregation levels and information scarcity. Reports usually aggregate figures of single organizations on turnover, ticket prices and sales, utilized seat capacity, persons employed, and other indicators, without differentiating sufficiently between organizational forms and sizes. For scientific purposes, disaggregated organizational-level data are most desirable because they allow researchers to classify organizations according to the question at hand. Also, information about concrete repertoires is frequently missing. If concrete products are mentioned, they are often confined to successes, e.g., the top 50 movies of the year. However, similar annual "flop" lists (in combination with production costs) would be of equal importance because they constitute negative cases for comparative analyses.

For economic analyses, more data on organizational cost and finance structures are of high importance. Most detailed information can be found in the theater statistics of the German Theatre and Orchestra Association (Deutscher Bühnenverein 2008a; 2008b). Down to the organizational level, it provides data on repertoire, performances, seat capacity, visitors, personnel, revenue, and cost structures, as well as prices. This detailed data provision could serve as a model for the museum statistic (Institut für Museumsforschung 2007). A further improvement would be electronic access to these organizational-level data because, otherwise, data preparation for statistical analyses is very cumbersome.

A second problem has to do with organizational coverage, sampling, and response bias. The coverage of cultural institutions and organizations is often

---

10 GEMA (Gesellschaft für musikalische Aufführungs- und mechanische Vervielfältigungsrechte) is a non-profit organization representing the copyrights composers, lyricists, and music publishers, GVL (Gesellschaft zur Verwertung von Leistungsschutzrechten) is an association representing the copyright interests of performing artists and record manufacturers, and VG Wort (Verwertungsgesellschaft Wort) is a copyright association of authors and publishers.

intransparent or – as in the case of the theater statistic – biased towards large, professional, publicly funded or member organizations. Precise methodological information on the target population of organizations, sampling issues, and the data collection methods of participating organizations are necessary to assess the quality and information content of the data.[11] A potential problem of unclear incidence might result from organizational interests of professional associations and their influence on questionnaire content, question design, organizational population covered, and statistical reporting. The availability of data from professional associations varies between cultural branches. There is, for example, relatively rich information for theatres, museums, the phonographic and film industries, some information for publishing, and poor information for socio-culture and the primary market for visual arts (Statistisches Bundesamt 2004: 312-423).

Data on valuation processes in the arts are most useful when collected through content analyses of documentary sources. These include reviews in journals, newspapers, and art history books, as well as coverage and accounts of artistic products in school books (Bevers 2005). Scientific access to these sources exists via the German National Library (*Deutsche Nationalbibliothek*), other libraries, and archives of journals and newspapers. It seems important to broaden the coverage of libraries and archives to smaller art periodicals.

3.3 Consumption and reception of culture

As mentioned above, most empirical studies in the sociology of culture focus on consumption and reception issues and utilize survey data. Modules on culture in our sense appear in various surveys and are largely accessible via the GESIS Data Archive. These typically include general social surveys like the Welfare Survey (*Wohlfahrtssurvey*) 1993 and the German General Social Survey (ALLBUS, *Allgemeine Bevölkerungsumfrage*) 1998, youth surveys like the Shell-Jugendstudie, comparative surveys like the Eurobarometer 67.1/2007, studies on media consumption like "Massenkommunikation I-VI," and surveys on reading conducted by the Stiftung Lesen in 1992, 2000, and 2008 (not available at the GESIS Data Archive). These studies usually ask respondents about the frequency of consumption of a set of artistic goods and services. However, they do not go into details of the specific contents being consumed and the ways they are consumed, while these studies sometimes

---

11 The advisory report of the Federal Statistical Office (Statistisches Bundesamt 2004: 312-423) describes non-official data sources extensively. Among the statistics of professional associations, the museum statistic is also exemplary in its methodological documentation and its efforts to achieve a high response rate. Taking into account that methods of annual visitor counts vary enormously between museums – from cash registers to pure estimates – however, reliability problems even in quite simple indicators become apparent.

employ multidimensional categories like "theatres and concerts" and they contain little information on the biographical formation of consumption and reception practices and their embeddedness within social networks. Thus, currently available data are not suitable to test rival hypotheses about the origin and development of aesthetic preferences. Nor are they sufficient to reconstruct modes of cultural education or the ways symbolic boundaries are drawn. It is therefore clear that academic research in Germany has hitherto not developed a comprehensive, recurrent survey on the cultural consumption and reception of the general population.[12]

The survey that comes closest to an institutionalized reporting on cultural tastes and activities of the population is the "Kulturbarometer." This survey has been conducted eight times since 1991 by the Centre for Cultural Research (ZfKf, *Zentrum für Kulturforschung*), Bonn – the same institute that was responsible for the "Künstlerreport." Although the published results of these surveys are sometimes accompanied by extensive and informative tables, the data are currently not accessible for secondary analyses. Because the ZfKf is built on project-specific funding, continuous cultural reporting is currently not ensured.[13]

Since the 1990s, survey research on local-level cultural participation has flourished in cities and municipalities. These data are usually compiled by local statistics agencies or, sometimes, by academic or commercial research institutes on behalf of local authorities. The existing data infrastructure is very intransparent because these research activities are scattered all over the country, results are not made accessible to the wider public, and data are not centrally archived. There are efforts by the Union of German Municipal Staticians (VDSt, *Verband Deutscher Städtestatistiker*) to coordinate and standardize surveys in order to achieve better comparability of local results via programs such as KOSIS ("Kommunales Statistisches Infrastruktursystem") and UrbanAudit. Recommendations for questionnaire construction have also been made (Deutscher Städtetag 1994). Notably, a database for research reports and questionnaires of communal surveys ("komm.DEMOS") is located at the German Institute of Urban Affairs (Difu, *Deutsches Institut für Urbanistik*), Berlin (Bretschneider and Schumacher 1996). This database

---

12 The situation is, as far as we know, not much better in other countries. In the US, the replicative survey SPPA ("Survey on the public participation in the Arts") was conducted in 1982, 1992, and 2002 enabling scholars to make temporal comparisons (DiMaggio/Mukhtar 2004). However, it was an add-on to other surveys and impaired by methodological problems (Peterson 2005). Quite extensive surveys on culture are carried out in the Netherlands, but we do not know about recurrent social reporting on this topic.

13 As a response to our request for opening its databases for scientific secondary analyses, the director of the ZfKf, Andreas Johannes Wiesand, signaled a general willingness to make primarily older data available to the GESIS Data Archive. However, some of them – e.g., data of the "Künstlerreport" – frequently do not exist in electronically readable form. Resources are needed to convert them.

currently comprises about 2,000 standardized study descriptions, 400 of which are culture-related. It is accessible free of charge primarily to communes having provided financial contributions ("Zuwenderstädte"), but not for the scientific community. Komm.DEMOS, however, does not archive the survey data itself, nor does any other central archive for communal surveys exist.[14] We expect communal survey data to vary in quality, depending on issues of survey administration and methodological rigor. Individual-level data of well-organized surveys are of great scientific value as they are more context-sensitive than nationwide surveys. They entail information on a broad range of the locally available cultural infrastructure, enabling researchers to map the participation of different population groups in a local social space of various scenes (Otte 2004, chap. 11).

Related to these communal citizens' surveys are audience and visitor surveys borne by cultural institutions like museums and theatres. Here we expect even greater variation in data quality. A careful methodological assessment should be made before using data for secondary analyses. This survey approach is insightful because the composition of the audiences consuming concrete aesthetic products and services can be studied on the basis of actual (not reported) behavior. Such data enrich aggregate visitor statistics that are reported by cultural institutions and professional associations. Informative spatial-temporal comparisons are enabled by combining various audience samples (Dollase et al. 1986; Klein 1990; Rössel et al. 2005). Unfortunately, documentation of such studies is even scarcer and access to datasets more problematic.

Finally, we would like to mention three more sources of individual-level survey data which could be usefully employed for scientific analyses. First, official statistics, such as the Sample Survey of Income and Expenditure (EVS, *Einkommens- und Verbrauchsstichprobe*), the Household Budget Survey (LWR, *Laufende Wirtschaftsrechnungen*), and the Time Use Survey of the Federal Statistical Office, do not sufficiently differentiate cultural consumption activities and expenditures internally. Instead, they tend to merge "culture" and "leisure" categories. These categorizations could be improved. Second, the media research departments of the public radio stations, ARD and ZDF, carry out nation-wide studies (e.g., "ARD/ZDF-Onlinestudie," "ARD-E-Musik-Studie," surveys employing the "MedienNutzerTypologie") and even more studies confined to single transmission areas on various

---

14 Susanne Plagemann, responsible for documentation issues at the Difu, gave us rich information about komm.DEMOS. It is accessible on a "fee for service" basis via the IRB Stuttgart (www.irb.fraunhofer.de/datenbanken.jsp). The study descriptions contain information on the primary researcher who might be asked for the release of survey data for secondary analyses. Where ever local statistical agencies collected the data, chances are great that the data are still existent. Only in exceptional cases were they given to the GESIS Data Archive. Rudolf Schulmeyer, chairman of the VDSt, promised to put our request about the trans-communal data infrastructure on the agenda of the next executive board meeting.

aspects of media consumption and musical preferences. Only a few of these data have been made accessible for scientific secondary analyses. In particular, the older data could be placed at the GESIS Data Archive's disposal, like those of the Leser- and Media-Analyse recently have been (Hagenah et al. 2006).[15] Third, cultural preferences and activities are frequently part of market research surveys. Some have been given to the GESIS Data Archive, such as, "Outfit 1-4" or "Typologie der Wünsche," but many more could be made available.

4. Recommendations

Taking into account the research needs in the sociology and economics of culture, the status quo of data infrastructure, and current debates in official statistics and cultural policy, we conclude with the following recommendations:

(1) A double-task of prime importance that has to be accomplished by scholars in academia is the theory-driven development of two comprehensive, large-scale "baseline" surveys. The first one has to follow the "social-status-of-artist" and "Künstlerreport" tradition, but should also contain detailed life-course information enabling analyses of artists' careers. The second one has to be a representative population survey on cultural consumption and reception comprising current preferences and behavior. Additionally, retrospective biographical and social network information should be included. These surveys call for public funding (e.g., by the DFG). They can serve as baselines for the construction of more elaborate panel studies on culture, as well as replications in an international or European comparative context.

(2) We support the inquiry into "Culture in Germany" (*Kultur in Deutschland*) in its recommendation of the construction of a nationally unified and standardized cultural statistic, mainly based on aggregate data, borne by the Federal Statistical Office and compatible with efforts at the EU level. It should allow researchers to distinguish at least between the core of the cultural sector and a wider notion of the cultural industries (KEA European Affairs et al. 2006), between the public, private, and nonprofit sectors, and different cultural branches. For adequate scientific research, differentiated data on low aggregation levels are needed.

---

15 We contacted Dr. Ekkehardt Oehmichen, director of media research at the Hessischer Rundfunk, who promised to address this topic at the next meeting of ARD media researchers.

(3) Organizational-level data, especially those collected for the theater and museum statistics, should be made available in a computer-readable format in order to facilitate statistical analyses.

(4) The large pool of communal citizen surveys on cultural topics and of organization-based audience surveys should be documented and made accessible in a central archive. Three options seem to be practicable. First, the German Institute of Urban Affairs' (Difu, *Deutsches Institut für Urbanistik*) database "komm.DEMOS" should be financially supported in order to enable scientific access free of charge. We recommend this step even if the database is not expanded to cover survey datasets. Further funding would enable archival storage and administration of such data at the Difu. Second, the GESIS Data Archive for the Social Sciences, with its approved data infrastructure, could be an alternative archival location. Third, a Research Data Center for data of communal statistical agencies could be established at the Federal Statistical Office. In all cases alike, studies should be carefully selected and documented according to scientific requirements of data quality.

(5) Access to data on culture collected by statutory bodies (media research of public radio stations), by the Centre for Cultural Research (*Zentrum für Kulturforschung*) (e.g., "Kulturbarometer," "Künstlerreport"), and by market research institutes, should be improved. These data are promising for building up time-series and analyzing trends in cultural preferences and behavior. The GESIS infrastructure would be suited best as an archive for these data. Conversion of data from the 1970s into electronically readable files would also be worthwhile funding if data quality is satisfying and studies are important for historical-comparative work.

Neither in Germany nor abroad is the field of culture well-institutionalized in its current research infrastructure. The field is of growing importance, though, not only in the social and economic sciences, but also in society and the economy in general. Improving data access and supporting large-scale surveys would assist scholars in Germany greatly in their effort to reach a leading international research position in this thriving field.

References:

Baumann, Sh. (2007): Hollywood Highbrow. From Entertainment to Art. Princeton.
Becker, H.S. (1982): Art Worlds. Berkeley.
Beckert, J. and Rössel, J. (2004): Kunst und Preise. Reputation als Mechanismus der Reduktion von Ungewissheit auf dem Kunstmarkt. Kölner Zeitschrift für Soziologie und Sozialpsychologie 56, 32-50.
Bevers, T. (2005): Cultural Education and the Canon. A Comparative Analysis of the Content of Secondary School Exams for Music and Art in England, France, Germany and the Netherlands, 1990-2004. Poetics 33, 388-416.
Blau, J.R. (1988): Study of the Arts: A Reappraisal. Annual Review of Sociology 14, 269-292.
Blaug, M. (2001): Where are we now on Cultural Economics? Journal of Economic Surveys 15, 123-143.
Bourdieu, P. (1999): Die Regeln der Kunst. Genese und Struktur des literarischen Feldes. Frankfurt a.M.
Bourdieu, P. and Darbel, A. with assistance of Schnapper, D. (2006): Die Liebe zur Kunst. Europäische Kunstmuseen und ihre Besucher. Konstanz.
Bretschneider, M. with assistance of Schumacher, J. (1996): DEMOS – Eine Datenbank zum Nachweis kommunaler Umfragen auf dem Weg zum Analyseinstrument. ZA-Information 38, 59-75.
Caves, R.E. (2000): Creative Industries. Contracts between Art and Commerce. Cambridge.
Deutscher Bühnenverein (2008a): Theaterstatistik 2006/2007. Deutschland. Österreich. Schweiz. Köln: Deutscher Bühnenverein, Bundesverband der Theater und Orchester.
Deutscher Bühnenverein (2008b): Wer spielte was? Werkstatistik 2006/2007. Deutschland. Österreich. Schweiz. Bensheim.
Deutscher Bundestag (2007): Schlussbericht der Enquete-Kommission „Kultur in Deutschland". Berlin: Deutscher Bundestag, Drucksache 16/7000.
Deutscher Städtetag (1994): Methodik von Befragungen im Kulturbereich. Eine Arbeitshilfe zur Planung, Durchführung, Auswertung und Präsentation von Besucherbefragungen in Museen und Theatern sowie von Befragungen über Kultur in allgemeinen Umfragen / Bürgerbefragungen. Köln: Reihe H-DST-Beiträge zur Statistik und Stadtforschung, Heft 40.
DiMaggio, P. and Mukhtar, T. (2004): Arts Participation as Cultural Capital in the United States, 1982-2002: Signs of Decline? Poetics 32, 169-194.
Dollase, R./Rüsenberg, M. and Stollenwerk, H.J. (1986): Demoskopie im Konzertsaal. Mainz.
Dowd, T. (2004): Concentration and Diversity Revisited. Production Logics and the U. S. Mainstream Recording Market, 1940-1990. Social Forces 82, 1411-1455.
Eurostat (2007): Cultural Statistics. Luxembourg.
Fohrbeck, K. and Wiesand, A.J. (1972): Der Autorenreport. Reinbek.
Fohrbeck, K. and Wiesand, A.J. (1975): Der Künstler-Report. Musikschaffende, Darsteller/Realisatoren, Bildende Künstler/Designer. Munich.
Frey, B.S. (2000): Arts and Economics: Analysis and Cultural Policy. Berlin.

Gans, H.J. (1974): Popular Culture and High Culture. An Analysis and Evaluation of Taste. New York.
Ganzeboom, H.B.G. (1982): Explaining Differential Participation in High-Cultural Activities. A Confrontation of Information-Processing and Status-Seeking Theories. In: Raub, W. (Ed.): Theoretical Models and Empirical Analyses. Contributions to the Explanation of Individual Actions and Collective Phenomena. Utrecht.
Gebesmair, A. (2008): Die Fabrikation globaler Vielfalt. Struktur und Logik der transnationalen Popmusikindustrie. Bielefeld.
Gerhards, J. (1997): Soziologie der Kunst: Einführende Bemerkungen. In: Gerhards, J. (Ed.): Soziologie der Kunst. Produzenten, Vermittler, Rezipienten. Opladen.
Gerhards, J. (2008): Die kulturell dominierende Klasse in Europa. Eine vergleichende Analyse der 27 Mitgliedsländer der Europäischen Union im Anschluss an die Theorie von Pierre Bourdieu. Kölner Zeitschrift für Soziologie und Sozialpsychologie 60, 723-747.
Ginsburgh, V.A. and Throsby, D. (Eds.) (2006): Handbook of the Economics of Art and Culture. North-Holland.
Giuffre, K. (1999): Sandpiles of Opportunity. Success in the Art World. Social Forces 77, 815-832.
Greenfeld, L. (1988): Professional Ideologies and Patterns of „Gatekeeping". Evaluation and Judgement in Two Art Worlds. Social Forces 66, 903-925.
Haak, C. (2008): Wirtschaftliche und soziale Risiken auf den Arbeitsmärkten von Künstlern. Wiesbaden.
Hagenah, J./Meulemann, H. and Akinci, H. (2006): German Media-Analyse (MA). A Large-Scale Commercial Data Source Available for Secondary Analyses on Media Use and Social Change. Schmollers Jahrbuch 126, 129-137.
Hartmann, P.H. (1999): Lebensstilforschung. Darstellung, Kritik und Weiterentwicklung. Opladen.
Hügel, H.-O. (Ed.) (2003): Handbuch Populäre Kultur. Begriffe, Theorien und Diskussionen. Stuttgart/Weimar.
Institut für Museumsforschung (2007): Statistische Gesamterhebung an den Museen der Bundesrepublik Deutschland für das Jahr 2006. Berlin: Staatliche Museen zu Berlin – Preußischer Kulturbesitz, Institut für Museumsforschung.
Janssen, S. (2001): The Empirical Study of Careers in the Literature and the Arts. In: Schram, D. and Steen, G. (Eds.): The Psychology and Sociology of Literature. Amsterdam.
Jonsson, J.O./Grusky, D.B./Di Carlo, M./Pollak, R. and Brinton, M.C. (2007): Micro-Class Mobility. Social Reproduction in Four Countries. Mannheim: MZES Working Paper No. 100.
Karttunen, S. (1998): How to Identify Artists? Defining the Population for "Status-of-the-Artist" Studies. Poetics 26, 1-19.
Katz-Gerro, T./Raz, Sh. and Yaish, M. (2007): Class, Status, and Intergenerational Transmission of Musical Tastes in Israel. Poetics 35, 152-167.
KEA European Affairs, Turku School of Economics and MKW Wirtschaftsforschung (2006): The Economy of Culture in Europe. Study prepared for the European Commission, Directorate-General for Education and Culture. Brussels.
King, T. (2007): Does Film Criticism Affect Box Office Earnings? Journal of Cultural Economics 31, 171-186.

Kirchberg, V. (2005): Gesellschaftliche Funktionen von Museen. Makro-, meso- und mikrosoziologische Perspektiven. Wiesbaden.

Klein, H.J. (1990): Der gläserne Besucher. Publikumsstrukturen einer Museumslandschaft. Berlin.

Kommission zur Verbesserung der informationellen Infrastruktur zwischen Wissenschaft und Statistik (KVI) (Ed.) (2001): Wege zu einer besseren informationellen Infrastruktur. Baden-Baden.

Kressin, J. (2008): Zwischen Autonomie und Abhängigkeit. Empirische Analysen zur Marktsituation selbständiger Künstler in Deutschland. Leipzig: Universität Leipzig, Institut für Kulturwissenschaften (Magisterarbeit).

Lamont, M. and Molnár, V. (2002): The Study of Boundaries in the Social Sciences. Annual Review of Sociology 28, 167-195.

Mayer, K.U. (2008): Retrospective Longitudinal Research: The German Life History Study. In: Menard, S. (Ed): Handbook of Longitudinal Research: Design, Measurement, and Analysis. Burlington.

Mark, D. (1998): Wem gehört der Konzertsaal? Das Wiener Orchesterrepertoire im internationalen Vergleich. Wien/Mülheim.

Menger, P.-M. (1999): Artistic Labor Markets and Careers. Annual Review of Sociology 25, 541-574.

Otte, G. (2004): Sozialstrukturanalysen mit Lebensstilen. Eine Studie zur theoretischen und methodischen Neuorientierung der Lebensstilforschung. Wiesbaden.

Otte, G. (2008): Lebensstil und Musikgeschmack. In: Gensch, G./Stöckler, E.M. and Tschmuck, P. (Ed.): Musikrezeption, Musikdistribution und Musikproduktion. Der Wandel des Wertschöpfungsnetzwerks in der Musikindustrie. Wiesbaden.

Peterson, R.A. (Ed.) (1976): The Production of Culture. Beverly Hills.

Peterson, R.A. (2005): Problems of Comparative Research. The Example of Omnivorousness. Poetics 33, 257-282.

Rössel, J./Hackenbroch, R. and Göllnitz, A. (2005): Soziale Differenzierung und Strukturwandel des Hochkulturpublikums. In: Institut für Kulturpolitik der Kulturpolitischen Gesellschaft (Ed.) (2005): Jahrbuch für Kulturpolitik 2005. Essen.

Schneider, M.A. (1993): Culture and Enchantment. Chicago.

Schulze, G. (1992): Die Erlebnisgesellschaft. Kultursoziologie der Gegenwart. Frankfurt.

Shrum, W.M. (1997): Fringe and Fortune. The Role of Critics in High and Popular Art. Princeton.

Simonton, D.K. (1997): Creative Productivity: A Predictive and Explanatory Model of Career Trajectories and Landmarks. Psychological Review 104, 66-89.

Söndermann, M. (2005): Beschäftigung im Kultursektor in Deutschland 2003/2004. Ergebnisse der Kulturstatistik. In: Institut für Kulturpolitik der Kulturpolitischen Gesellschaft (Ed.) (2005): Jahrbuch für Kulturpolitik 2005. Essen.

Statistische Ämter des Bundes und der Länder (Eds.) (2008): Kulturstatistiken. Kulturindikatoren auf einen Blick. Ein Ländervergleich. Wiesbaden: Hessisches Statistisches Landesamt.

Statistisches Bundesamt (Ed.) (1994): Im Blickpunkt: Kultur in Deutschland. Zahlen und Fakten. Stuttgart.

Statistisches Bundesamt (2004): Methodenkritische Analyse von Basisstatistiken zum Kulturbereich und Fragen zu einem Anforderungsprofil an eine bundeseinheitliche Kulturstatistik für die Bundesrepublik Deutschland. Gutachten für die Enquete-Kommission „Kultur in Deutschland" des Deutschen Bundestages. Langfassung. Wiesbaden.

Throsby, D. (1994): The Production and Consumption of the Arts: A View of Cultural Economics. Journal of Economic Literature 32, 1-29.

Thurn, H.P. (1983): Die Sozialität der Solitären. Gruppen und Netzwerke in der Bildenden Kunst. In: Neidhardt, F. (Ed.): Gruppensoziologie. Perspektiven und Materialien. Opladen.

Weckerle, Ch./Söndermann, M. and Hochschule für Gestaltung und Kunst Zürich (2003): Das Umsatz- und Beschäftigungspotential des kulturellen Sektors. Erster Kulturwirtschaftsbericht Schweiz. Zurich.

Weishaupt, H. and Fickermann, D. (2001): Informelle Infrastruktur im Bereich Bildung und Kultur. Expertise für die Kommission zur Verbesserung der informationellen Infrastruktur zwischen Wissenschaft und Statistik. CD-Rom Attachment in: Kommission zur Verbesserung der informationellen Infrastruktur zwischen Wissenschaft und Statistik (KVI) (Ed.) (2001): Wege zu einer besseren informationellen Infrastruktur. Baden-Baden.

Zolberg, V. (1990): Constructing a Sociology of the Arts. Cambridge.

6.4 Mass Media Research

Heiner Meulemann and Jörg Hagenah

Contact:

Heiner Meulemann
Jörg Hagenah
Forschungsinstitut für Soziologie
Universität zu Köln
Greinstraße 2
50939 Cologne
Germany
e-mail: meulemann[at]wiso.uni-koeln.de
hagenah[at]wiso-uni-koeln.de

Abstract

Mass media are defined as media that have their own, self-defined program and solicit their own audience. Accordingly, mass media research deals with the production of programs and the consumption of programming by an audience. This report discusses the justification for both perspectives on the topic, introduces the relevant data sources, and makes recommendations for the research infrastructure. In terms of media production, the discussion recommends the establishment of a central media content archive where content analytic time series of public agencies as well as the work of individual researchers can be collected. Furthermore, the development of a unified system of content analysis and the promotion of cross-national comparisons are recommended. In terms of media consumption, the provision of privately funded data to the scientific community, the promotion of cross-national comparisons, and the linkage of programs and audience data are recommended.

Keywords: mass media, data archive, content analysis, survey research

1. Introduction

Media can be defined as a set of technologies designed to store and distribute meaning. Among media in general, *mass* media can be singled out by both the types of meaning it produces and by the audience receiving these messages. In terms of meaning, mass media content is produced by specialized agencies according to a predetermined schedule of "(daily) actuality" within a particular national or linguistic community (Reitze and Ridder 2006). Mass media have a program: they pre-package content and distribute it according to a thematic structure and a time schedule – they are media for masses of meanings. Regarding the audience, the use of mass media is delineated by the technical requirements and possibilities of mass media themselves, together with the given language, so that in principle they are available for each member of a nation or language community, rather than for socially circumscribed groups only – they are media for masses of people.

Mass media, therefore, can be distinguished from individual media, such as the book, the letter, the telephone, and the internet. The meanings of individual media are produced by persons individually; they are derived by individuals according to personal needs and have a small, socially restricted audience, such as friends, the family, and professional or intellectual peers, audiences that often can be named, for example, the "intellectuals" or the "*Bildungsbürgertum.*" Mass media are anchored in a national society; individual media are anchored in – as internet jargon has it – "communities" that rest on personal, although not face-to-face, relationships.

As mass media address nations, their development is one strand in the modernization of nations (Hallin and Mancini 2004: 261). Up to now, modern societies have only had three forms of mass media: (daily) newspapers (including periodicals), dating back to the seventeenth century; radio, originating in the 1920s; and television, taking the lead after the 1950s. These three will be dealt with in the following expert report. The internet, however, will not be dealt with, since it is an individual rather than a mass medium. It is a technical platform, which is primarily used for personal communication and for personal services, but which can also be used in order to distribute the three above-named mass media (Meulemann 2009). Therefore, it has been identified as a "converged medium" (PriceWaterhouse-Coopers 2007: 53).

If mass media have a program and solicit their own audience, mass media research comprises both a communicator-oriented perspective on the production of programs and a recipient-oriented perspective on consumption by audiences. In the following, we describe the research topics of both perspectives in section 2, their data sources in section 3, and give recommendations for the research infrastructure of both in section 4. For the sake of simplicity, we speak of media only although we refer to mass media throughout.

2. Research topics and research questions

2.1 Production of programs

The appropriate method to analyze the production of media programming is content analysis. Its topics can be broadly grouped, as one view from media studies journals explains (Bonfadelli 2002: 33), into two classes: *analyses of information structure* and *analyses of social problem areas*. The former purport to examine whether the media fulfill their social function as a "fourth public authority" and satisfy the information needs of the audience. The latter intends to examine whether the media discriminate against social groups or represent them adequately.

Analyses of information structure

The core questions treated in this research area concern whether and how the introduction of the dual broadcasting system in the middle of the 1980s has marginalized public stations or assimilated them into new private ones. The *marginalization hypothesis* contends that public stations have lost audience share to private stations from the lower social strata (Krüger 1992). As a result of this loss, public broadcasting might suffer from a legitimacy crisis concerning their "public mandate of a basic provision" (Bomas 2005) or their "cultural mandate" (Rossen-Stadtfeld 2005) as well as their mandatory dues system (Kleinsteuber et al. 1991). The *convergence hypothesis* contends that the public stations tend to neglect their "public mandate" in devoting an ever larger part of their program to mass-entertainment (Brosius and Zubayr 1996, 186), and that private stations have improved their informational broadcasting in order to catch up in this area to the public stations (Saxer 1980; Schatz et al. 1989).

Numerous content analyses, mostly concerned with television and seldom with radio (Marchal 2004: 704ff), have examined these two hypotheses (Maier 2002: 83; Brosius and Zubayr 1996). However, the results have remained contradictory. On the one hand, Krüger (Krüger and Zapf-Schramm 2008; Krüger 2005b; Krüger 1992; 2001; Krüger and Zapf-Schramm 2002) has compared genres, broadcasts, and contents of public and private stations annually since 1985 and regularly detected differences between both groups of channels on all three levels (Weiß 2007; Trebbe 2004; Trebbe and Weiß 1994: 175; Meier 2003). On the other hand, assimilative tendencies between public and private stations in the program structure (Faul 1988; 1989; Schatz et al. 1989; Donsbach and Dupré 1995; Hallermann et al. 1998; Sutor 1999; Rossmann et al. 2003), in the presentation of newscasts (Kaase 1989; Pfetsch 1991; Greger 1998; Goertz 1996), and in sports reporting (Scholz 1993) have also been shown to exist.

Apart from this core question, content analyses about daily newspapers have only been used in a few stand-alone studies (Meier 2002: 192; Maurer and Reinemann 2006: 83). These studies are hardly comparable, because they refer to different titles and use different content analytical categories. However, a few tendencies relating to the content areas of politics, economics, and sports can be summarized. Thus, in all newspapers examined – with the exception of the tabloid "Bild" (Schulz 1970) – politics and economics have dominated since the 1950s, and sports have captured a considerable portion of the news content in each newspaper (Held and Simeon 1994; Hüther et al. 1973; Schulz 1970; Schwantag 1974; Hagemann 1958).

Analyses of social problem areas

The question posed in this category of research concerns whether social groups are adequately reflected in media content. In the simplest case, this has been done by comparing the shares of groups represented in the media with their share in the population (Bonfadelli 2002, 33ff), particularly the share of foreigners (Bonfadelli 2007; Bonfadelli and Moser 2007; Ruhrmann 2002), of poor and old people (Burgert and Koch 2008; Davis and Kubey 1982; Bosch 1988), and of men and women (Gnändiger 2007; Petersen 2006;

Hesse 2001; Jud-Krepper 1997; Fröhlich and Holtz-Bacha 1995; Werner and Rindsdorf 1998; Weiderer 1992; Schmerl 1985; Ulze 1977; Küchenhoff 1975) have been compared.

More complex studies of media representation examine specific social problems. Thus, the presentation of crime and violence has been investigated with respect to their possibly detrimental effects on social integration (Kunczik 2008; Petzold 2008; Gerbner et al. 1979; 1980; Stein-Hilbers 1977; Groebel and Gleich 1993). In a similar vein, reports on racism (Handel 1998; Ruhrmann and Kollmer 1987), on conflicts and wars (Fröhlich et al. 2007; Kolmer 2004; Hallin 1997; Olien et al. 1989), on drug abuse (Fleming et al. 2004; Rose 1995), and on pornography (Scheufele 2005; Brosius and Rössler 1999; Amann and Wipplinger 1997) have been subjected to content analysis.

2.2 Media consumption

In order to investigate the media audience within a particular country, nationally representative population samples have to be surveyed. This results in a *micro perspective* which examines persons which use and do not use mass media and why (Lindner-Braun 2007; Meyen 2004; Schweiger 2007). If replicated, they also provide information relevant to a *macro perspective* on media systems and their development.

Micro perspective

As research on media consumption is initially driven by the needs of advertising research (*Werbeträgerforschung*), it begins with (1) the *socio-demography* of media use that allows producers to find their audiences and to calculate their advertising price. This very purpose, moreover, requires frequent replications of the surveys with the same question wording. The socio-demographic variables thus surveyed encompass the basic opportunities and restrictions of media use, such as the resources of education, occupation, and income and the obligations associated with being employed and having a family. Thus, the relative impact of these factors on media use can be studied. However, advertising research has already gone well beyond that in collecting information on (2) *time budgets* of work, leisure, and media use, so that media use can be related to its most important resource – leisure time. Thus, it is possible to examine how all these resources determine media use; moreover, this impact can be followed up over time.

Nevertheless, media use – like all forms of consumption – depends not only on resources but on (3) *preferences* as well. These determine how time is allocated to work or leisure, to indoor or outdoor leisure activities, and to competing media sources. But preferences for information or entertainment or for political and fictional contents in the media, for active or passive leisure pastimes in general, or for leisure or work are never investigated in advertising research and only rarely in academic research.

Finally, media use depends on (4) *attachments* to and (5) *images* of specific media. Questions such as how much one would miss a specific medium, or how trustworthy a specific medium is assessed to be, have been repeatedly asked in both advertising and academic research (Reitze and Ridder 2006: 26-32, 80-95).

Macro perspective

Taken as a whole, replicated surveys delineate changes in media use and in the underlying social structure. There are two ways to examine the relation between these two levels of change. First, once social structural developments have been controlled for, the (1) *total and net change of media use* can be compared. For example, Fürtjes (2008) examined whether the changing composition of a German soccer fan magazine between 1954 and 2005 reflected concurrent changes among the media or in the social structure, and demonstrated that only the latter was responsible for changes in the readership. The phenotypic change disappeared once changes in population composition had been controlled for; there were no genuine media developments in this domain beyond social structural changes. Moreover, changes in media use can be at least partly (2) *explained by cohort succession*. Thus, the cohort that first experienced television might become "the television cohort" and stick more than other cohorts to television viewing during their lifetimes – which was indeed examined and did not turn out to be true (Peiser 1996). Similarly, the cohorts that first experienced private television might stick more than others to private programs – which indeed did turn out to be true, but which only partly explained the audience movements from public to private broadcasters (Meulemann et al. 2009).

In addition, since Germany, like all other European countries, switched during the 80s from a monopoly of public broadcasting to a dual broadcasting system, (3) the *effects of organizational change on media use* can be examined within the total audience as well as specific segments.

Finally, as advertising research often contains information on the use of a whole range of media used by a person, changes in the (4) *media repertory* as well as in the encompassing *consumer repertory* can be assessed. Is the increasing number of television broadcasters and the decreasing number of newspapers reflected in corresponding changes in personal repertories? Similar questions can be treated on the aggregate level: which media gain at the cost of which others? Which media compete within a specific market of, say, periodicals, which substitute for each other?

If content analyses and population surveys are combined, the perspective can be broadened from communication to social research in general – as illustrated in the case of two topics: leisure and politics. In studying leisure, the combination of media content analyses and time budget surveys of media use allows for a more convincing investigation into why people prefer the media to other leisure pastimes, and in particular why the preference for the media, as measured by their share of leisure time, has increased in Germany after the introduction of the dual system, although the supply for other leisure time activities, such as theaters and museums, clubs and associations, has risen simultaneously as well (Gilles et. al. 2008). As for politics, the combination of media content analyses with surveys on the perception of politics and politicians and on voting decision allows for an investigation of media effects on the political process (Petersen and Jandura 2006; Semetko 2009). The "political communication" (Schulz 2003) between citizens, media and politicians could be followed up, not only on the aggregate level, but also on the individual level.

3. Sources for media research

3.1 Production of programs

Archiving institutions

In principle, all mass media can be archived continuously so that they can be content analyzed even decades after they have been issued or broadcasted. In practical terms, however, print and electronic media are accessed in different ways.

In the case of *print media*, supra-regional and above all also regional daily papers are archived in municipal libraries or city archives that want to keep track of their own history. Beyond this, a copy of each paper must be held by the German National Library (*Deutsche Bibliothek*) in Frankfurt. For some newspapers, even digital versions are provided by the internet software of the commercial info service LexisNexis.[1]

As for *electronic media*, broadcasting contents are less systematically archived and therefore less easily accessible. The public stations archive their program galleys in the German Broadcasting Archive (*Deutsches Rundfunkarchiv*) in Frankfurt and their self-produced broadcasts in archives of the ARD and ZDF stations. In analyzing these archives two content analytic strategies have been followed. Either current programs are video- or DVD-

---

[1] www.lexisnexis.de

taped or the program structure published in program magazines is analyzed (Merten 1996: 156). The first strategy permits broad investigations of current programs, but allows no longitudinal designs. The second strategy permits longitudinal analyses, yet has some shortcomings, since published programs are changed in the short run to give space to unforeseen events and do not allow deeper analyses with fine-tuned categories.

Using these archives, time series which refer to the program structure of television and radio in general and to news broadcasts of the television specifically have been constructed.

Time series: The program structure of television and radio in general

With regard to the structure of television programs, national[2] time series are regularly constructed by four research groups. (1) the Institute for Empirical Media Research (IFEM, *Institut für empirische Medienforschung*) has been tracking the genre profiles of public stations *ARD* and *ZDF* and private stations *RTL, SAT.1* and *Prosieben* since 1985 annually on the basis of four broadcasting weeks (Krüger 2005a: 302; Krüger and Zapf-Schramm 2008). These analyses aim at examining whether there is a convergence of public and private programming or not. (2) GöfaK Media Research (*GöfaK Medienforschung*) analyzes most of television programs since 1998 on behalf of the Association of State Media Authorities for Broadcasting in Germany (ALM, *Arbeitsgemeinschaft der Landesmedienanstalten*). One broadcasting week of the public stations *ARD* and *ZDF* and of the private stations *RTL, RTL II, Vox, Sat.1, Prosieben* and *kabel 1* are videotaped each spring and each autumn (Weiß 2007; Trebbe 2004; Weiß and Trebbe 2000; Weiß 1999). These analyses aim at giving private stations some feedback about their success within the dual broadcasting system. (3) The most elaborate analysis is commissioned by the Consortium for TV Research (AGF, *Arbeitsgemeinschaft Fernsehforschung*). Since 1963, the telemetric data – at that time still only of *ARD* and *ZDF* – have been linked with program data such that social profiles of the program use can be established. Since 1985, these measurements, which as of today cost 17 million Euros per year, are performed by the Society for Consumer Research (GfK, *Gesellschaft für Konsumforschung*); Hagenah and Meulemann 2007: 157f). The data are collected to calculate advertisement prices in specific program areas. (4) Using a different source, namely the television listings magazine *Hörzu* from 1980 to 1993, Merten (1994; 1996), commissioned by the German Association of Private Broadcasters and Telemedia (VPRT, *Verband Privater Rundfunk und Telemedien*), analyzed the content of eighteen public and

---

2 Furthermore, there are stand-alone studies of regional television programs, e.g., in Thüringen 1999, 2002 and 2006 (tlm.de 2000; Moses and Heyen 2003; Giewald and Heyen 2007).

private television stations. The analyses aimed at showing that private full programs[3] provided information in a manner comparable to the public stations.

As for the structure of *radio* programs, time series that compare several *Länder*[4] are regularly constructed by three research groups. (1) The yearbooks of the *ARD* report the percentages of word and music broadcasts from all *ARD* stations since 1969 (Gleich 1995: 555). Using this source, each of the *ARD* stations has analyzed the content of its programming extensively; unfortunately, they have changed their analytical categories between time points. (2) Wichert (2008; 1997) has examined the content profiles of private radio programs in comparison with public programming in Berlin-Brandenburg for the State Media Authority of Berlin-Brandenburg (*Landesmedienanstalt Berlin-Brandenburg*) since 1994. (3) Heyen (2001) has examined the program structure of *Antenne Thüringen*, *Landeswelle Thüringen*, *Jump*, and *MDR 1 Radio Thüringen* on behalf the State Media Authority of Thuringia (*Landesmedienanstalt Thüringen*) since 1996.

Time series: News broadcasts of television

As for the structure of the *news broadcast,* time series have been constructed by four research groups. (1) The *InfoMonitor* of the IFEM institute has examined all the main newscasts of *ARD, ZDF, RTL,* and *Sat.1* according to the structure of their topics on behalf of these public stations since 2005 (Krüger 2008; 2005b). (2) Maier, Ruhrmann and Klietsch (2006) have analyzed the topic structure for the main newscasts of *ARD, ZDF, RTL, RTL II, ProSieben, Vox,* and *kabel 1* on behalf of the State Media Authority of North Rhine-Westphalia (*Landesmedienanstalt Nordrhein-Westfalen*) at five time points between 1992 and 2004. (3) The Institute for Media Research (IMGÖ, *Institut für Medienforschung*) examines the regional news reporting in the *Länder* of former West Germany broadcasted by *RTL* and *Sat.1* on behalf of the ALM annually since 2005 (Volpers et al. 2008).

(4) The private institute *Media Tenor* has constructed the most encompassing content analyses since 1993. It has no commissioning agency, but sells its analyses to enterprises who are interested in gaining knowledge about their representation in the media. It scans approx. 700 media every day worldwide – among them the most important German television and radio

---

3   Full programms offer a programm-mix, they are not only specialised in themes like music, entertainment, news or sports.
4   There are also stand-alone studies of regional radio broadcasting programs that have been commissioned by the media authority of the *Länder* (*Landesmedienanstalten)*, for example in Schleswig-Holstein (Hasebrink 2006), Niedersachsen (Volpers 2009), Mecklenburg-Vorpommern (Rager et al 2005), Nordrhein-Westfalen (Volpers and Schnier 1996), Hessen (Brosius and Weiler 2003), Rheinland Pfalz (Rager and Siebers 2006), Saarland (Bauer 2003), Baden-Württemberg (Schönbach et al. 1993), and Bayern (Stuiber 1990).

stations, all supra-regional, and the most important regional newspapers, the news magazines, and the most important news sites and news blogs available on the Internet (mediatenor.de 2009).

3.2 Audience media consumption

Surveys commissioned by broadcasting agencies

Three large-scale sources provide answers to the questions about audience described in section 2.2. (1) Every half decade from 1964 to 2005 the *ARD-Werbung Sales & Services* has commissioned the Long-Term Study on Mass Communication (*Langzeitstudie Massenkommunikation*), which surveys the use of the daily media (newspapers, radio, and television) and the internet, the time budgets of media use, audience attachment, and the image of the media (Reitze and Ridder 2006). This source contains answers to nearly all the questions relevant to a micro perspective. In terms of macro perspective, its datasets cumulatively describe the often dramatic changes in media use (Schweiger 2007: 42-48), such that it can be explained by cohort succession (Peiser 1996; Engel and Best 2001; Reitze and Ridder 2006: 134-165).

(2) Since 1954 the Consortium of Media Analyses (AG-MA, *Arbeitsgemeinschaft Media-Analyse*) has commissioned the Reader Analysis (LA, *Leser-Analyse*), which since 1972 has been called the Media Analysis (MA, *Media-Analyse*). They survey the use of many print media titles and electronic media stations minutely through a series of question modules in order to establish the "advertising currency" of each. Since 1987, they have also administered a time budget question module (Hagenah and Meulemann 2009a; b). In order to do this for specific titles, samples have to be very large (more than 60,000). To detect general developments in media use, however, titles and programs have to be regrouped into genres. For example, periodicals have to be grouped into title categories such as politics, sports, etc.; and radio programs must be grouped into tune in and go along programs (*Einschalt- und Begleitprogramme*), predominantly devoted to information or to entertainment. The Center for Teaching and Research in Media Science (*Medienwissenschaftliches Lehr- und Forschungszentrum*) has accomplished this sometimes extensive work, together with the technical preparation of the datasets. In addition, it has constructed time series of the use of all types of media and of social structures from the MA datasets, which are available on their website.[5] Thus, the LA and MA present many options to researchers for describing changes in media use in the context of changing social structure from a macro perspective. Since quite a few of the MA even contain a

---

5   http://www.mlfz.uni-koeln.de/index.php?id=106.

question on party preference, they also can also be used for political analyses.

(3) The MA discontinued its survey of the use of specific television stations in 1997 and only continues to report the total television time. Since then, only telemetric information is available for specific stations. Telemetric research started in Germany already in 1963, commissioned by the public stations. At present, the AGF has commissioned the Society for Consumer Research (AGF/GfK, *Gesellschaft für Konsumforschung*) to measure for every second of television use by each member of a panel of households telemetrically in order that results are ready the day after broadcasting (Lindner-Braun 2007: 127-139). These data – as well as their predecessors – are not available to the public. However, on request the AGF delivers the reaches and the market participation of several age brackets of each broadcasting for each station immediately in the following week.

Apart from these studies of media use in general, there are three further kinds of studies partly or completely commissioned by broadcasting agencies that either put media use in the broader perspective of consumption and survey the total population (4-6) or that put media use in the deeper perspective of the evaluation of programs and survey restricted populations, either regionally (7) or according to age (8).

(4) The Consumer and Media Use Analysis (VUMA, *Verbrauchs- und Medienanalyse*)[6] research media use in the context of general consumer behavior in order to detect complementarities and substitutions within each and between both. The samples are nationally representative and somewhat smaller than those of the MA (about 24,000). VUMA started in 1995 and has been replicated annually since 2000. The same aim is served by (5) the Allensbach Market and Advertising Media Analysis (AWA, *Allensbacher Markt- und Werbeträger Analyse*)[7] and by (6) the survey, Typology of Needs (TDW, *Typologie der Wünsche*)[8]. AWA started in 1959 and has been replicated annually with samples of about 20,000. TDW started in 1974 and has been replicated annually since 1986 with samples of about 20,000.

(7) For quite a few of the German *Länder*, *state specific MA studies* on the use of radio and television have been administered. They have their own names, such as the Bavarian Broadcasting Analysis (*Funkanalyse Bayern*)[9] that started in 1989 and is replicated annually and comprises samples of about 23,000 for radio use and a further 16,000 for television use. These studies have two primary goals. First, they provide data on small and local stations. Second, and more interesting for academic purposes, they survey the

---

6   www.vuma.de.
7   www.aw-online.de.
8   www.tdw.com.
9   www.funkanalyse.tns-infratest.com.

evaluation of specific programs. Depending on the specific *Land*, some of these surveys are replicated annually, others less often.

(8) As the MA only surveys a population older than fourteen years old, the KIM und JIM surveys, commissioned by the Research Consortium on Media Pedagogy (*Medienpädogischer Forschungsverbund Südwest*)[10] specifically analyze media use by youth between the ages of six and thirteen, and between twelve and nineteen respectively. KIM started in 1999 and JIM in 1998; both are replicated annually and have sample sizes of about 1,200. In addition, for each child KIM surveys the legal parent or guardian (*Erziehungsberechtigte*) so that pairs of respondents can be analyzed. The topics of the KIM and JIM surveys include media use, leisure interests, sources of information, and – something unique for media studies – also television *preferences*. KIM additionally surveys media use in the context of the family.

The results from most of the above-mentioned studies are published in the monthly journal edited by *ARD-Werbung Sales & Services*, called *Media-Perspektiven*, which is considered even by the academic world to be one of "the three leading periodicals in communications science" (Hanitzsch and Altmeppen 2007). Thus, *Media-Perspektiven* continuously reports on the most recent trends in the use of periodicals (Vogel 2006), radio (Klingler and Müller 2008), and television (Zubayr and Gerhard 2008). Additionally, results are compiled in a yearly brochure, *Media-Perspektiven-Basisdaten*, the content of which can be found on the *Media Perspektiven* website, where this brochure can also be ordered.[11]

Surveys commissioned by the Federal Statistical Office and Academic Associations

Four sources respond to the questions discussed in section 2.2. All of them are multi-purpose surveys in the sense that they allow researchers to investigate attitudinal and behavioral correlates of media use. The first two allow for comparisons between European countries. (1) The 1999 Eurobarometer (EB), a survey commissioned by the EU every year, solicited information on media use from the then fifteen Member States. As these surveys also obtained information on environmental behavior and social capital (Schulz 2003; Wilke and Breßler 2005), the impact of media use on these domains could also be assessed. We strongly recommend to replicate the 1999 EB in future years. (2) The European Social Survey (ESS), which is financed by the European Science Foundation together with national funding agencies within individual European countries, has been administered since 2002 every second year in about twenty-five countries of East and West

---

10 www.mpfs.de.
11 http://www.media-perspektiven.de/3921.html.

Europe. Its core module, that is, the questions to be replicated in each wave, surveys the frequency of newspaper, radio, television, and Internet use for general and political purposes as well as voting behavior and some political, social, and religious attitudes. Thus, the ESS provides an opportunity to compare changes in media use in a macro perspective between European countries. More importantly, it allows researchers to asses the attitudinal and behavioral correlates of media use in the domains of politics, civil society, and religion.

Furthermore, two German sources provide time series on media use and attitudes to the media. (3) The General German Social Survey (ALLBUS, *Allgemeine Bevölkerungsumfrage der Sozialwissenschaften*) surveyed the use of and interest in many media in 1998 (Weiß 2001) and 2004. Furthermore, it surveyed trust in media in 1984, 1994, 2000, and 2002 (Schweiger 2007, 259). (4) The Time Budget Study of the Federal Statistical Office, administered in 1991 and 2001, describes the development of media use in the context of how leisure time has developed (Ehling 2004; Jäckel and Wollscheid 2004).

Both of these types of resources are underexploited today. However, it is generally the case that surveys commissioned by broadcasting agencies seem to contain a greater potential for analyzing media change, while the surveys commissioned by the Federal Statistical Office and academic associations provide more opportunities for examining attitudinal and behavioral correlates of media use.

4. Recommendations for the research infrastructure

4.1 Production of programs

(1) *The establishment of a central media content archive.* In this archive, the contents of all media should be stored in digital form so that primary computer-aided content analyses (Maurer and Reinemann 2003, 62f) become feasible and available for secondary analyses. The following substantive orientations are proposed for this archive:

- It should archive current productions, but simultaneously should also gather all materials already available in private or semi-private archives.
- It should be more concerned with electronic media than with print media, given the current status of media content archiving.
- It should archive video-type broadcasts as well as content analytic datasets constructed for their analysis – that is, code plans, results of

coder reliability tests with different category systems, and other materials required for replications and longitudinal analyses.
- It should instigate a call for content analytical longitudinal research projects, specifically in social problem areas where stand-alone studies up to now have prevailed. Moreover, it should support such projects while they are under way.

Formally, the archive should consist of at least two permanent positions devoted to data service funded by scientific agencies. It should rest on the open source principle, but it could – after it has been successfully established – require a fee for its services. Since up to now there have only been a few regional archives, such as the data archive of the Institute of Journalism (*Institut für Publizistik*) at the University of Mainz, these may form the core of the planned central archive.

In brief, to catch up with what has been accomplished in survey research since the 1950s, this report proposes the creation of a central infrastructure for content analyses – similar to the Leibniz Institute for the Social Sciences (GESIS, *Leibniz-Institut für Sozialwissenschaften*) but to serve the needs of survey research.

(2) *Archiving content analytic time series of public agencies.* One of the tasks of the state media authorities for broadcasting in Germany (*Landesmedienanstalten*) and often also one of the voluntary endeavors of public broadcasting stations is to establish longitudinal data. They should be asked to extend their current research programs and to hand this over to archive the following data:

- The biennial longitudinal content analyses of the radio program structure of the private radio stations financed by the media authorities for broadcasting of some of the German *Länder*. In the future, moreover, this research should be expanded to all the *Länder* and to public radio stations as well. Possibly, the ARD could take over part of the financing.
- Thus far, the structure and quality of print media content have not been systematically evaluated. For this purpose, a research department should be established at the central institute.

(3) *Archiving content analyses of individual researchers.* In contrast to public agencies, individual researchers are interested in specific theoretical questions rather than in long-term descriptions. Consequently, the content analyses of their stand-alone projects use different category systems. Nevertheless, these analyses should be gathered and prepared for secondary analyses in the archive as well. These systems are useful in the construction of more integrated and enduring category systems in future research.

(4) *Developing a unified content analytical category system.* The German professional associations in the social and communication sciences should advocate the development of a system that contains the most general categories for the measurement of the program structure and quality in all media that establishes guidelines for more specific research projects. The research funding agencies should support this endeavor.

(5) *Furthering cross-national comparisons.* The national professional societies in Europe should prepare a common core of content analytical categories. The European Science Foundation and individual national science funding agencies could finance pilot content analyses with the same category system in all European countries.

4.2 Media consumption

(1) *Providing privately funded data for the scientific community.* The German professional societies of the social and communication sciences should secure access to important surveys funded by media stations for scientific use. In particular, these are:

- *AGF/GfK data.* As competing stations may understandably have some provisos against a premature release, a waiting period of some years should be contracted. Furthermore, as the AGF/GfK data are much richer and much more complicated than the MA data, a research project devoted to their transformation into meaningful indicators and, ultimately, time series that continue the ones constructed from the MA is recommended.
- *the latest two editions of the Long-Term Study on Mass Communication (Langzeitstudie Massenkommunikation), 2000 and 2005.*
- *Consumer studies, regional studies, and studies of specific audiences*, as mentioned in section 3.2.

(2) *Enhancing the analytical potential of privately funded data.* Understandably, privately funded media surveys have been rarely concerned with more general social and political attitudes – the occasional questioning of party preferences in the MA being one of the rare exceptions. Yet, adding such questions can strongly enhance the public visibility of these studies and their funding agencies, once analyses are publicized. Therefore, the national professional associations should urge funders to include at least three more very brief, and therefore inexpensive, general questions that have been widely used in academic research: on party preference, church attendance, and union membership. If private funders cannot be motivated by appealing to their self-interest in terms of public

attention to future results, some financing through national academic funding agencies should be considered as well.

(3) *Data linkage of programs and audience data.* Although the MA data, for example, contain exact information about the time someone uses a specific medium, content analysis and survey data are rarely linked, and programs and audiences are rarely analyzed simultaneously. Therefore, research projects that link content analyses and survey analyses should be supported.

(4) *Feasibility project on comparisons of national data between countries.* Since there are consortia similar to the AG-MA in other countries that commission market research on the "advertising currency" and the quota of stations and broadcasting, a feasibility project that explores the possibility of comparisons should be launched. As national broadcasting stations will increasingly cooperate, their genuine commercial interests should be appealed to in order to support such an endeavor.

(5) *Promoting cross-national comparisons.* Cross-national comparisons are rare in media research (Kleinsteuber 2002: 56). Moreover, the cross-national comparison of media uses and media effects is on the bottom rather than on the top of the agenda of the German media research community (Wilke 2002: 18-31). There are two reasons for this

- on the macro-level there is a lack of systematic research of media systems backed by quantitative indicators (Hallin and Mancini 2004). A European media indicator databank that collects indicators from the various sources mentioned (e.g., Thomaß 2007) would stimulate comparative research.
- on the micro-level there is a lack of knowledge within the research community about existing cross-nationally comparative datasets (Livingstone 2003, Hanitzsch and Altmeppen 2007).

Therefore, the EU should be asked to replicate the 1999 EB on media use. Moreover, cross-national research using the above mentioned EB and ESS data should be encouraged.

References:

Amann, G. and Wipplinger, R. (1997): Sexueller Missbrauch in den Medien. In: Amann, G. and Wipplinger, R. (Eds.): Sexueller Missbrauch. Überblick zu Forschung, Beratung und Therapie. Ein Handbuch. Tübingen.
Bauer, G. (Ed.) (2003): Programm-Profil-Analyse saarländischer Hörfunkprogramme 2003. Schriftenreihe der LMS Landesmedienanstalt Saarland, Band 10. Studie erstellt durch die Arbeitseinheit Medien- und Organisationspsychologie des Saarlandes. Projektleitung: Frank Schwab, Dagmar Unz.
Bomas, W. (2005): Der duale Rundfunk. Sein Bedeutung für die Entwicklung des Rundfunkmarktes. Köln.
Bonfadelli, H. (2002): Medieninhaltsforschung. Konstanz.
Bonfadelli, H. (2007): Die Darstellung ethnischer Minderheiten in den Massenmedien. In: Bonfadelli, H. and Moser, H. (Eds.): Medien und Migration. Wiesbaden.
Bonfadelli, H. and Moser, H. (Eds.) (2007): Medien und Migration. Wiesbaden.
Bosch, E.M. (1988): Exkurs: Alter in der fiktiven Fernsehrealität – Eine Analyse der Konstruktion von Altersdarstellungen und ihrer Rezeption durch ältere Menschen. In: Eckhardt, J. and Horn, I. (Eds.): Ältere Menschen und Medien. Eine Studie der ARD/ZDF-Medienkommission. Frankfurt/M.
Brosius, H.-B. and Rössler, P. (1999): Die soziale Realität in einfacher Pornographie und Softsex-Filmen. Ein Beitrag zur Pornographie-Diskussion. In: Rundfunk und Fernsehen 47 (1), 25-42.
Brosius, H.-B. and Weiler, S. (2003): Programmanalyse nichtkommerzieller Lokalradios in Hessen. Eine Inhaltsanalyse im Auftrag der Hessischen Landesanstalt für privaten Rundfunk (LPR Hessen), München 2000, Schriftenreihe der LPR Hessen, Bd. 10.
Brosius, H.-B. and Zubayr, C. (1996): Vielfalt im deutschen Fernsehprogramm. Eine empirische Anwendung eines Qualitätsmaßstabs. Rundfunk und Fernsehen 44 (2), 185 -214.
Burgert, C. and Koch, T.K. (2008): Die Entdeckung der Neuen Alten? Best-Ager in der Werbung. In: Holtz-Bacha, C. (Ed.): Stereotype? Frauen und Männer in der Werbung. Wiesbaden.
Davis, R. and Kubey, R. (1982): Growing Old on Television. In: Pearl, D./Bouthilet, L. and Lazar, J. (Eds.): Television and Behavior. Ten Years of Scientific Progress and Implications for the Eighties. Rockville.
Donsbach, W. and Dupré, D. (1995): Mehr Vielfalt oder „more of the same" durch mehr Kanäle? In: Mitchell, J. and Blumler, J.G. (Eds.): Fernsehen und Zuschauerinteressen. Baden-Baden.
Ehling, M. (2004): Zeitbudgeterhebungen 1991/92 und 2001/2002 – Kontinuität und Wandel. In: Statistisches Bundesamt (Ed.): Alltag in Deutschland. Analysen zur Zeitverwendung. Wiesbaden.
Engel, B. and Best, S. (2001): Mediennutzung und Medienbewertung im Kohortenvergleich. Media Perspektiven 11/2001, 554-563.
Faul, E. (1988): Die Fernsehprogramme im dualen Rundfunksystem. Wissenschaftliche Begleitkommission zum Versuch mit Breitbandkabel in der Region Ludwigshafen/Vorderpfalz. 10. Band. Berlin.

Faul, E. (1989): Die Fernsehprogramme im dualen Rundfunksystem. Rundfunk und Fernsehen 37 (1), 25-46.

Fleming, K./Thorson, E. and Aitkin, C.L. (2004): Alcohol Advertsing Exposure and Perceptions: Links with Alcohol Expectancies and Intentions to Drink or Drinking in Underaged Youth and Young Adults. Journal of Health Communication 9 (1), 3-30.

Fröhlich, R. and Holtz-Bacha, C. (1995): Frauen und Medien. Eine Synopse der deutschen Forschung. Opladen.

Fröhlich, R./Scherer, H and Scheufele, B. (2007): Kriegsberichterstattung in deutschen Qualitätszeitungen. Publizistik 52 (1), 11-32.

Fürtjes, O. (2008): Die Entproletarisierung des Fußballpublikums im Kontext des gesellschaftlichen Wandels. Eine empirische Längsschnittanalyse zur Ursächlichkeit der schichtungshierarchischen Veränderung des Fußballpublikums, exemplifiziert an der Leserschaft des Kicker-Sportmagazins von 1954 bis 2005. Köln.

Gerbner, G./Gross, L./Signorelli, N and Morgan, M. (1980): The „mainstreaming" in America: Violence Profile No. 11. Journal of Communication 30 (3), 10-29.

Gerbner, G./Gross, L./Signorielli, N./Morgan, M. and Jackson-Beeck, M. (1979): The demonstration of Power: Violence Profile N. 10. Journal of Communication 29 (3), 177-196.

Giewald, O. and Heyen, A. (2007): Lokales Fernsehen in Thüringen 2002. http://www.tlm.de. [Last visited 11/11/2008].

Gilles, D./Hagenah. J. and Meulemann, H. (2008): Freizeit zunehmend durch Fernsehen bestimmt. Freizeit und Fernsehnutzung in Deutschland 1987-2005. Informationsdienst Soziale Indikatoren 40, 11-14.

Gleich, U. (1995): Hörfunkforschung in der Bundesrepublik. Media Perspektiven 11, 554-564.

Gnändinger, C. (2007): Politikerinnen in deutschen Printmedien. Vorurteile und Klischees in der Berichterstattung. Saarbrücken.

Goertz, L. (1996): Zwischen Nachrichtenverkündung und Infotainment. In: Hömberg, W. and Pürer, H. (Eds.): Medien-Transformation. Konstanz.

Greger, V. (1998): Privatisierung politischer Berichterstattung im Fernsehen? In: Imhof, K. and Schulz, P. (Eds.): Die Veröffentlichung des Privaten – Die Privatisierung des Öffentlichen. Opladen.

Groebel, J. and Gleich, U. (1993): Gewaltprofil des deutschen Fernsehprogramms. Schriftenreihe Medienforschung der Landesanstalt für Rundfunk Nordrhein-Westfalen; Band 6. Opladen.

Hafez, K. (Ed.) (2002): Die Zukunft der internationalen Kommunikationswissenschaft in Deutschland. Hamburg.

Hagemann, W. (1958): Der Wochenrhythmus der westdeutschen Tagespresse. Publizistik 3, 259-271.

Hagenah, J. and Meulemann, H. (2009a): The Analytical Potentials of Survey Trend Data from Market Research. The Case of German Media Analysis Data. To appear. In: Baur, N. (Ed.): Historische Sozialwissenschaft, Sonderheft.

Hagenah, J. and Meulemann, H. (2009b): Alte und neue Medien: Medientrends und sozialer Wandel. In: Hagenah, J. and Meulemann, H. (Eds.): Alte und neue Medien – Zum Wandel der Medienpublika in Deutschland seit den 1950er Jahren. Münster.

Hallermann, K./Hufnagel, A./Schatz, K. and Schatz, R. (1998): Grundversorgung: Pflichten und Rechte. Eine Langzeit-Inhaltsanalyse zum Informationsangebot von ARD und ZDF. Bonn.

Hallin, D.C. (1997): The Media and war. In: Corner, J./Schlesinger, P. and Silverstone, R. (Eds.): International Media Research. A Critical Survey. London/New York.

Hallin, D.C. and Mancini, P. (2004): Comparing Media Systems. Three Models of Media and Politics. Cambridge.

Handel, U. (1998): Tatort Hannover. Ausländer und Deutsche in der Kriminalitätsberichterstattung im Vergleich. In: Quandt, S. and Gast, W. (Eds.): Deutschland im Dialog der Kulturen: Medien, Images, Verständigung. Konstanz.

Hanitzsch, T. and Altmeppen, K.-D. (2007): Über das Vergleichen: Komparative Forschung in den deutschen kommunikationswissenschaftlichen Fachzeitschriften. Medien & Kommunikationswissenschaft 55 (2), 185-203.

Hasebrink, U. (2006): Hörfunklandschaft in Schleswig-Holstein. Bestandsaufnahme 20 Jahre nach Einführung der dualen Rundfunkordnung. Kiel.

Held, B. and Simeon, Th. (1994): Die zweite Stunde Null. Berliner Tageszeitungen nach der Wende (1989-1994). Marktstrukturen, Verlagsstrategien, publizistische Leistungen. Berlin.

Hesse, M. (2001): Wer macht die Nachrichten. Über die öffentliche Sichtbarkeit von Männern und Frauen in den Medien 2000. Forschungsbericht Nr. 105. Bonn.

Heyen, A. (2001): Programmstrukturen und Informationsangebote im Radio. Ergebnisse und Erfahrungen aus sechs Jahren Programmforschung der TLM. In: Rössler, P./Vowe, G. and Henle, V. (Eds.): Das Geräusch der Provinz – Radio in der Region. München.

Hüther, J./Scholand, H. and Schwarte, N. (1973): Inhalt und Struktur regionaler Großzeitungen. Düsseldorf.

Jäckel, M. and Wollscheid, S. (2004): Mediennutzung im Tagesverlauf: Ausweitung des Angebots und Strukturen der Zeitverwendung. In: Statistisches Bundesamt (Ed.): Alltag in Deutschland. Analysen zur Zeitverwendung. Wiesbaden.

Jud-Krepper, H. (1997): Das Mädchen- und Jungenbild im Fernsehen und seine sozialisierende Wirkung. In: Erlinger, H.-D. (Ed.): Neue Medien, Edutainment, Medienkompetenz. Deutschunterricht im Wandel. München.

Kaase, M. (1989): Fernsehen, gesellschaftlicher Wandel und politischer Prozeß. Kölner Zeitschrift für Soziologie und Sozialpsychologie, Sonderheft 30, 97-117.

Kleinsteuber, H.J. (2002): Mediensysteme im internationalen Vergleich: Ein Überblick. In: Hafez, K. (Ed.): Die Zukunft der internationalen Kommunikationswissenschaft in Deutschland. Hamburg.

Kleinsteuber, H.J. and Wiesner, V. (1992): Szenario des Niedergangs. Die Entwicklung des öffentlichen Rundfunks in Australien und Kanada als Modell für Europa? Medium 22 (1), 57-60.

Kleinsteuber, H.J./Wiesner, V. and Wilke, P. (1991): Public Broadcasting im internationalen Vergleich. Analyse des gegenwärtigen Stands und Szenarien einer zukünftigen Entwicklung. Rundfunk und Fernsehen 29 (1), 33-54.

Klingler, W and Müller, D.K. (2008): Radio II: Stabile Nutzungsmuster auch bei erweiterter Grundgesamtheit. Radionutzung erstmals inklusive EU-Ausländer und Kinder ab zehn Jahren. Media Perspektiven 10/2008, 502-515.

Kolmer, C. (2004): Krieg im Fernsehen 2001-2003. Eine Inhaltsanalyse der deutschen, englischen, südafrikanischen und US-Fernsehnachrichten. In: Zeitschrift für Kommunikationsökologie 6 (1), 37-43.
Krüger, U.M. (1992): Programmprofile im dualen Fernsehsystem 1985-1990. Baden-Baden.
Krüger, U.M. (2001): Programmprofile im dualen Fernsehsystem 1991-2000. Baden-Baden.
Krüger, U.M. (2005a): Themenprofile deutscher Fernsehnachrichten. In: Media Perspektiven 7/2005, 302-320.
Krüger, U.M. (2005b): Sparten, Sendungsformen und Inhalte im deutschen Fernsehangebot. Media Perspektiven 5/2005, 190-205.
Krüger, U.M. (2008): InfoMonitor 2007: Unterschiedliche Nachrichtenkonzepte bei ARD, ZDF, RTL und Sat.1. Media Perspektiven 2/2008, 58-83.
Krüger, U.M. and Zapf-Schramm, T. (2002): Öffentlich-rechtliches und privates Fernsehen: Typische Unterschiede bleiben bestehen. Media Perspektiven 4/2002, 178-190.
Krüger, U.M. and Zapf-Schramm, T. (2008): Sparten, Sendungsformen und Inhalte im deutschen Fernsehangebot 2007. Programmanalyse von ARD/Das Erste, ZDF, RTL, SAT.1 und ProSieben. Media Perspektiven 4/2008, 166-189.
Küchenhoff, E. (1975): Die Darstellung der Frau und die Behandlung von Frauenfragen im Fernsehen: eine empirische Untersuchung. Stuttgart et al.
Kunczik, M. (2008): Medien und Gewalt: Der aktuelle Forschungsstand. In: Dittler, U. and Hoyer, M. (Eds.): Aufwachsen in virtuellen Medienwelten: Chancen und Gefahren digitaler Medien aus medienpsychologischer und medienpädagogischer Perspektive. München.
Lindner-Braun, C. (2007): Mediennutzung. Methodologische, methodische und theoretische Grundlagen. Berlin.
Livingstone, S. (2003): On the challenges of Cross-national Comparative Media Research. European Journal of Communication 18 (4), 477-500.
Maier, M. (2002): Zur Konvergenz des Fernsehens in Deutschland. Ergebnisse qualitativer und repräsentativer Zuschauerbefragungen. Konstanz.
Maier, M./Ruhrmann, G. and Klietsch, K. (2006): Der Wert von Nachrichten im deutschen Fernsehen. Ergebnisse einer Inhaltsanalyse 1992-2004. Düsseldorf. http://www.lfm-nrw.de. [Last visited 01/18/2009]
Marchal, P. (2004): Kultur und Programmgeschichte des öffentlich-rechtlichen Hörfunks in der Bundesrepublik Deutschland. Band II: Von den 60er Jahren bis zur Gegenwart. München.
Maurer, M. and Reinemann, C. (2003): Schröder gegen Stoiber – Nutzung, Wahrnehmung und Wirkung der TV-Duelle. Wiesbaden.
Maurer, M. and Reinemann, C. (2006): Medieninhalte. Eine Einführung. Wiesbaden.
mediatenor.de (2009): Media Tenor – Medien-Monitoring & Medieninhaltsanalyse. http://www.mediatenor.de. [Last visited 01/18/2009].
Meier, H.E. (2003): Beyond Convergence. European Journal of Communication 18 (3), 337-365.
Meier, K. (2002): Ressort, Sparte, Team. Wahrnehmungsstrukturen und Redaktionsorganisation im Zeitungsjournalismus. Konstanz.
Merten, K. (1994): Konvergenz der deutschen Fernsehprogramme. Eine Langzeituntersuchung 1980-1993. Münster.

Merten, K. (1996): Konvergenz der Fernsehprogramme im dualen Rundfunk. In: Hömberg, W. and Pürer, H. (Eds.): Medien-Transformation. Konstanz.

Meulemann, H. (2009): Verdrängt das Internet die Massenmedien? Medienpräferenzen und die Individualisierung der Mediennutzung. Schriftenreihe des Instituts für Rundfunkökonomie an der Universität zu Köln.

Meulemann, H./Hagenah. J. and Gilles, D. (2009): Neue Angebote und alte Gewohnheiten. Wie und warum das deutsche Publikum zwischen 1987 und 1996 vom öffentlich-rechtlichen auf das private Fernsehen gewechselt hat. Publizistik 54 (2), 240-264.

Meyen, M. (2004): Mediennutzung. 2nd edition. Konstanz.

Moses, K. and Heyen, A. (2003): Lokales Fernsehen in Thüringen 2002. http://www.tlm.de. [Last visited 12/12/2008].

Olien, C./Tichenor, Ph. and Donohue, G. (1989): Media Coverage and Social Movements. In: Salmon, C. (Ed.): Information Campaigns. Balacing Social Values and Social Change. Newbury Park/London/New Delhi.

Peiser, W. (1996): Die Fernsehgeneration. Eine empirische Untersuchung ihrer Mediennutzung und Medienbewertung. Opladen.

Petersen, J. (2006): Männlichkeit. Eine Inhaltsanalyse ihrer Darstellung in Männer- und Frauenzeitschriften in Deutschland. Berlin.

Petersen, T. and Jandura, O. (2006): Testing visual signals in representative surveys in combination with media content analyses of the 2002 German Federal election campaign. International Journal of Public Opinion Research 19 (1), 89-96.

Petzold, T. (2008): Gewalt in internationalen Fernsehnachrichten: Eine komparative Darstellung medialer Gewaltpräsentation in Deutschland, Großbritannien und Russland. Wiesbaden.

Pfetsch, B. (1991): Die Fernsehformate von Politik im Dualen Rundfunksystem. In: Gellner, W. (Ed.): An der Schwelle zu einer neuen deutschen Rundfunkordnung. Berlin.

PriceWaterhouseCoopers (2007): Report for BBC Trust Unit. BBC On-Demand Proposals – Assessment of BBC Managements's "New Media" Assumptions and Assertions. http://www.bbc.co.uk/bbctrust/assets/files/pdf/review_report_research/pvt_iplayer/bbctrust_pwcreport_pva_annexe.pdf. [Last visited 12/12/2008].

Rager, G. and Siebers, T. (2006): Inhaltsanalyse des Senders RPR 1. Ludwigshafen. [Unpublished research report].

Rager, G./Siebers, T. and Hassemer, G. (2005): Hörfunk 2005 in Mecklenburg-Vorpommern. Programmanalyse, Strukturen und Potenziale. Schwerin.

Reitze, H. and Ridder, C.-M. (2006): Massenkommunikation VII – eine Langzeitstudie zur Mediennutzung und Medienbewertung 1964-2005. Baden-Baden.

Rose, C. (1995): Die Drogenberichterstattung der deutschen überregionalen Tagespresse. Ergebnisse einer Inhaltsanalyse von FAZ, FR, taz und Welt. Sucht 41 (1), 34-42.

Rossen-Stadtfeld. H. (2005): Funktions und Bedeutung des öffentlich-rechtlichen Kulturauftrags im dualen Rundfunksystem. Köln.

Rossmann, C./Brandl, A. and Brosius, H.-B. (2003): Der Vielfalt eine zweite Chance? Publizistik 48 (4); 427-454.

Ruhrmann, G. (2002): Wie regionale Tageszeitungen über Migranten berichten. Das Beispiel Thüringen. In: Meier-Braun, K.-H. and Kilgus, M.A. (Eds.): Integration durch Politik und Medien? Baden-Baden.

Ruhrmann, G. and Kollmer, J. (1987): Ausländerberichterstattung in der Kommune. Inhaltsanalyse Bielefelder Tageszeitungen unter besonderer Berücksichtigung ausländerfeindlicher Alltagstheorien. Opladen.

Saxer, U. (1980): Führt ein Mehrangebot an Programmen zu selektivem Rezipientenverhalten? Media Perspektiven 6/1980, 395-406.

Schatz, H./Immer, N. and Marcinowski, F. (1989): Der Vielfalt eine Chance? Empirische Befunde zu einem zentralen Argument für die Dualisierung des Rundfunks in der Bundesrepublik Deutschland. Rundfunk und Fernsehen 37 (1), 5-24.

Scheufele, B. (2005): Sexueller Missbrauch – Mediendarstellungen und Medienwirkung. Wiesbaden.

Schmerl, C. (Ed.) (1985): In die Presse geraten: Darstellung von Frauen in der Presse und Frauenarbeit in den Medien. Köln.

Scholz, R. (1993): Konvergenz im TV-Sport. Eine komparative Studie des „Dualen Fernsehsystem". Berlin.

Schönbach, K./Feierabend, S. and Möhring, W. (1993): Lokale Hörfunksender in Baden-Württemberg. Eine Inhaltsanalyse ihrer Berichterstattung, LFK-Schriftenreihe Dialog, Bd. 7. Stuttgart.

Schulz, W. (1970): Der Inhalt der Zeitungen. Eine Inhaltsanalyse der Tagespresse in der Bundesrepublik Deutschland (1967) mit Quellentexten früher Inhaltsanalysen Amerika, Frankreich und Deutschland. Düsseldorf.

Schulz, W. (2003): Mediennutzung und Umweltbewusstsein: Dependenz- und Priming-Effekte. Publizistik 48 (4), 387-483.

Schulz, W. (2003): Politische Kommunikation. In: Bentele, G./Brosius, H.B. and Jarren, O. (Eds.): Öffentliche Kommunikation. Wiesbaden.

Schwantag, K. (1974): Die betriebliche Anpassung lokaler und regionaler Abonnementszeitungen an die durch intra- und intermediären Wettbewerb der Massenkommunikationsmittel ausgelösten Veränderungen der Leserbedürfnisse. In: Presse- und Informationsamt der Bundesregierung (Ed.): Kommunikationspolitische und kommunikationswissenschaftliche Forschungsprojekte der Bundesregierung (1971-1974). Bonn.

Schweiger, W. (2007): Theorien der Mediennutzung. Eine Einführung. Wiesbaden.

Semetko, H.A. (2009): Election campaigns, partisan balance, and the news media. In: Norris, P. (Ed.): The Roles of the News Media: Watch-dogs, Agenda-setter and Gate-Keepers. Washington.

Stein-Hilbers, M. (1977): Kriminalität im Fernsehen. Eine inhaltsanalytische Untersuchung. Kriminalität und ihre Verwalter, Bd. 6. Stuttgart.

Stuiber, H.-W. (1990): Landesweiter Hörfunk in Bayern – Programm, Publikumswünsche und Bewertungen: Inhaltsanalyse, Image- und Akzeptanzstudie zu den Hörfunkprogrammen Antenne Bayern, Bayern 1 und Bayern 3. München.

Sutor, S. (1999): Programmbeobachtung der BLM. In: Jarren, O. (Ed.): Rundfunk in öffentlich-rechtlicher Trägerschaft. Modell für modernes Rundfunkmanagement / BLM Symposium Medienrecht 1999. München.

Thomaß, B. (Ed.) (2007): Mediensysteme im internationalen Vergleich. Konstanz.

tlm.de (2000): Lokales Fernsehen in Thüringen 1999. http://www.tlm.de. [Last visited 12/23/2008].

Trebbe, J. (2004): Fernsehen in Deutschland 2003-2004. Programmstrukturen, Programminhalte, Programmentwicklungen. Berlin.
Trebbe, J. and Weiß, H.-J. (1994): Öffentliche Streifragen in privaten Fernsehprogrammen. Opladen.
Ulze, H. (1977): Frauenzeitschrift und Frauenrolle: eine aussagenanalytische Untersuchung der Frauenzeitschriften Brigitte, Freundin, Für Sie und Petra. Berlin.
Vogel, A. (2006): Stagnation auf hohem Niveau. Media Perspektiven 7/2006, 380-398.
Volpers, H. (2009): Hörfunklandschaft Niedersachsen 2009. Projektbeginn: Januar 2009, Auftraggeber: Niedersächsische Landesmedienanstalt (NLM). http://www.alm.de. [Last visited 02/09/2009].
Volpers, H. and Schnier, D. (1996): Das WDR-Hörfunkprogramm Eins Live. Ergebnisse einer empirischen Programmanalyse. Media Perspektiven 5/1996, 249-258.
Volpers, H./Salwiczek, C. and Schier, D. (2008): Die Regionalfenster von RTL und Sat.1 im Jahr 2006. Ergebnisse einer kontinuierlichen Programmanalyse. ALM Programmbericht 2007.
Weiderer, M. (1992): Das Frauen und Männerbild im deutschen Fernsehen. Eine inhaltsanalytische Untersuchung der Programme von ARD, ZDF und RTL plus. Regensburg.
Weiß, H.-J. (1999): Programmalltag in Deutschland. In: Arbeitsgemeinschaft der Landesmedienanstalten in Deutschland (Ed.): Programmbericht zur Lage und Entwicklung des Fernsehens in Deutschland 1998/99. Berlin.
Weiß, H.-J. (2007): Private Fernsehvollprogramme 1998-2007. Eine 10-Jahres-Bilanz der kontinuierlichen Fernsehprogrammforschung der Landesmedienanstalten. In: ALM Programmbericht 2007.
Weiß, H.-J. and Trebbe, J. (2000): Fernsehen in Deutschland 1998-1999. Programmstrukturen – Programminhalte – Programmentwicklungen. Schriftenreihe der Landesmedienanstalten, Bd. 18.
Weiß, R. (2001): Der praktische Sinn des Mediengebrauchs im Alltag. In: Maier-Rabler, U. and Latzer, M. (Eds.): Kommunikationskulturen zwischen Kontinuität und Wandel. Konstanz.
Werner, P. and Rinsdorf, L. (1998): Ausgeblendet? Frauenbild und Frauenthemen im nordrhein-westfälischen Lokalfunk. Opladen.
Wichert, L. (1997): Radioprofile in Berlin-Brandenburg 1996. Zehn privaten und ein öffentlich-rechtliches Programm im Vergleich. Schriftenreihe der mabb, Band 6.
Wichert, L. (2008): Radioprofile in Brandenburg. Fünf Lokalprogramme im Vergleich 2007. Schriftenreihe der mabb, Band 23.
Wilke, J. (2002): Internationale Kommunikationsforschung. Entwicklungen, Forschungsfelder, Perspektiven. In: Hafez, K. (Ed.): Die Zukunft der internationalen Kommunikationswissenschaft in Deutschland. Hamburg.
Wilke, J. and Breßler, E. (2005): Europa auf dem Weg in die Informationsgesellschaft? Eine Auswertung von Eurobarometer-Daten. In: Rössler, P. and Krotz, F. (Eds.): Mythen der Mediengesellschaft – The Media Society and its Myths. Konstanz.
Zubayr, C. and Gerhard, H. (2008): Tendenzen im Zuschauerverhalten, Fernsehgewohnheiten im Jahr 2007. Media Perspektiven 3/2008, 106-119.

6.5 Judicature

Wolfgang Heinz

Contact:

Wolfgang Heinz
University of Constance
Faculty of Law
Universitätsstraße 10 · Box D 119
78457 Konstanz
Germany
e-mail: wolfgang.heinz[at]uni-konstanz.de

Abstract

The German crime statistics system should provide an adequate database for addressing questions about the level, structure, and variation of crime rates; prosecution and sanctioning by the authorities; the level and types of criminal sanctions imposed; and the enforcement of sanctions and reconviction rates. In these areas, the German criminal statistics system suffers many deficiencies. It is therefore necessary to improve the existing statistics by carrying out periodic crime and victimization surveys, surveys of suspects in the preliminary stages of public prosecution, and by compiling statistics on the enforcement of criminal offenses and reconviction rates.

But comprehensively optimizing the criminal statistics system would require a statistical database that contains all the data from police crime statistics and all judicial decisions relevant for criminological research, and then linking these data with pseudonymized individual data. This statistical database would solve the problems of the existing German crime statistics and would offer a basis for new, regularly compiled federal statistics, in particular on the execution of sentences and recidivism, as well as for caseflow statistics and cohort studies.

Keywords: caseflow statistics, cohort studies, conviction statistics, crime, sanctions, criminal, police crime statistics, prison statistics, probation service statistics, recidivism, reconviction statistic, statistics of criminal courts, statistics of the public prosecution offices, victimization survey

1. The existing criminal statistics system

The criminal statistics system in Germany consists of statistics that cover the areas of the police, public prosecutors, criminal courts, probation services, and prisons. The data is collected at the state level, where it is checked for plausibility and published in the statistics of the *Länder*. The Federal Criminal Police Office (BKA, *Bundeskriminalamt*) and the Federal Statistical Office summarize the aggregate data from the *Länder* statistics (see figure 1).

The statistics compiled by the public prosecution offices and criminal courts are procedure statistics (the statistical units are procedures), while the other statistics mentioned in figure 1 – Police Crime Statistics, Conviction Statistics, Probations Service Statistics, Prison Statistics – are personal statistics (the statistical units are individuals). In the personal statistics, the statistical units always designate the sex of the individual as well as their age

Figure 1: Overview of the crime and criminal justice statistics in the Federal Republic of Germany

Stage of Procedure (statistical unit)	Data collection (statistics published at the federal level)
Preliminary proceedings	
Police Investigation (Criminal suspicion: case, criminal suspect, victim)	**Police Crime Statistics (*Polizeiliche Kriminalstatistik*)** (Federal Criminal Police Office) (since 1953)
Public prosecutor's decision on the result of the investigation (Cases dealt with by the public prosecution office. Statistical unit is procedure; since 1998 the statistics also contain information on individuals)	**Statistics of the public prosecution offices (StAStat, *Staatsanwaltschaftsstatistik*)** (Federal Statistical Office) (since 1981)
Main proceedings	
Proceedings of the criminal courts (Criminal prosecutions processed by the courts. Statistical unit is procedure; since 1989 the statistics inform also on persons)	**Statistics of criminal courts (*Justizgeschäftsstatistik in Strafsachen*)** (Federal Statistical Office) (since 1959)
Decisions of the criminal courts (sentencing, conviction, based on persons)	**Conviction Statistics (*Strafverfolgungsstatistik*)** (Federal Statistical Office) (since 1950)
Conviction / prison	
Suspension of sentence for parole (Placed under the supervision of a full-time probation officer) (Waiver/revocation of parole is based on the subject)	**Probation Service Statistics (*Bewährungshilfestatistik*)** (Federal Statistical Office) (since 1963)
Execution of a prison sentence (Number and type of prisons, actual population, capacity, demographic characteristics of the prisoners)	**Prison Statistics (*Strafvollzugsstatistik*)** (Federal Statistical Office) (since 1961)

(in age groups[1]). These statistics also contain the citizenship of the person, which in the Police Crime Statistics (PCS, *Polizeiliche Kriminalstatistik*) is determined by using a comprehensive citizenship key (*Staatsangehörigkeitsschlüssel*) covering all nationalities. Currently, only the citizenship of the main guest worker countries is accounted for in the criminal justice statistics (this will be changed in 2009; see section 3.2.2 below). For the particularities of the statistical units and statistical variables, refer to the overview in the First Periodical Security Report (Federal Ministry of the Interior and Ministry of Justice 2001b: 15; see also Heinz 2003; 2008).

2. Research questions

The central issues that should be answered by the criminal statistics system are questions about the level, structure, and variation of crime rates; prosecution and sanctioning by the authorities; the level and types of criminal sanctions imposed; and the enforcement of sanctions and reconviction rates.

3. Status quo of the crime and criminal justice statistics: databases and access

3.1 Information deficits in the existing criminal statistics system

When measured against the aforementioned research questions, the existing criminal statistics system in Germany has many shortcomings, despite the fact that it has been progressively expanded to include new statistics in various sectors (see figure 1) and additional or more differentiated statistical variables. Yet even with these improvements, the following fundamental problems have not been overcome:

- The existing criminal statistics system is limited to officially reported crime.

---

[1] In the Police Crime Statistics (PCS), children are assigned to the following age groups: under 6, 6–8, 8–10, 10–12, and 12–14. For persons above the age of criminal responsibility, the PCS, the Conviction Statistics, and the Probation Service Statistics contain the following age groups: youth (in the PCS and in the Probation Service Statistics 14–16, 16–18), adolescents (18–21), young adults (in the PCS 21–23, 23–25), 25–30, 30–40, 40–50, 50–60, 60 and older (in the Conviction Statistics 60–70, 70 and older). In the Prison Statistics the age groups are even more highly differentiated in some areas.

- The current crime and criminal justice statistics are not coordinated either in content or methodology. Statistical units and variables are only partially compatible. The statistics are compiled according to different measurement and processing standards; an input-output analysis of the system is therefore not possible. Additional data collection beyond the stipulated statistical variables is a rare exception. The lack of compatibility is not just a problem between the PCS and the criminal justice statistics, but also among the different sets of criminal justice system statistics.

- The process of prosecution and sanctioning cannot be examined for specific offense groups. To do so one would need to be able to link data collected at the individual level to different sets of statistics (caseflow statistics), which is currently impossible. This in turn would require the transmission and storage of pseudonymized individual data.

- Data collection is carried out by authorities of the *Länder*. Checking the validity of the data in terms of both content and adherence to formal requirements is only possible at the state level; at the federal level it is only possible to conduct plausibility and consistency tests.

- Until very recently, Criminal Police Offices and Statistical Offices of the *Länder* did not provide federal statistical authorities (BKA, Federal Statistical Office) with any individual statistical data (microdata) (see section 3.2 below for recent changes).

- Regional criminal justice statistics are partially incomplete. In some cases they are not reported at all. For example, conviction statistics were not compiled in Saxony-Anhalt until 2007; probation service statistics are not being compiled in three out of five of the new *Länder*; and statistics on persons committed by a criminal court to a psychiatric hospital or institution for drug rehabilitation are not being compiled in four out of five of the new *Länder*. In other cases, compilation of the statistics has been suspended (e.g., the probation service statistics in Hamburg since 1997 and in Schleswig-Holstein between 2002 and 2006). This is due to the fact that there is no federal law that compels the *Länder* to collect the data for criminal justice statistics.

- The PCS cover only a portion of the actual registered crime rates; road traffic crime rates, for example, are left out. Due to a lack of adequately differentiated statistical variables in the criminal justice statistics, the statistics do not accurately reflect the decisions of the public prosecutors or the criminal convictions or executions of sanctions.

- Given the statistical units and variables as well as the measurement and processing standards currently available, the existing criminal statistics provide a very inadequate basis for fundamental scientific research. This is due in part to the fact that the crime and criminal justice statistics are collected and processed according to regulations stipulated by federal and state government committees in which there is no one representing the research community.

- Scientific research is most productive when it has access to individual data records rather than aggregate data for statistical purposes. At present, only the individual data records of some of the criminal justice statistics are available from Research Data Centers of the Federal Statistical Office and the Statistical Offices of the German *Länder*. The individual data records of the PCS are not available through the Research Data Centers.

The 2001 KVI report already listed several of these deficits and emphasized the need for improvement by collecting caseflow statistics and additional information. These improved statistics would better meet the research demand for high-quality data linked to individual data records at the state level and the need for statistics on the enforcement of criminal sanctions such as fines or educative and disciplinary measures under juvenile law (see Albrecht 2001: 66f).

3.2 Changes in databases and data access since the 2001 KVI report

3.2.1 Extension of the criminal statistical systems on unreported crimes, on fear of crime and on the subjective recognition of crime rates and crime control

In its First Periodical Report on Crime and Crime Control, the German Federal Government stated that continually updated research in the area of unreported crime is "a necessary instrument for measuring developments in crime for those types of offense where this is appropriate" (Federal Ministry of the Interior and Federal Ministry of Justice 2001b: 600). In early 2002, a working group (AG BUKS) was set up by the Ministry of the Interior and the Ministry of Justice with the task of creating a concept for a periodical crime survey in order to gain insight into the extent of victimization, the scale of reporting behavior and experiences of crime victims when reporting to the police, and public attitudes on various aspects of crime and the fear of crime. The final report of this working group was submitted to the commissioning ministries in September 2002 (Heinz 2002). The recommendations have not yet been implemented, mainly due to the costs involved.

3.2.2 Changes in databases and data access in the field of crime and criminal justice statistics

3.2.2.1 Databases

Police Crime Statistics (PCS). In 1997/98 the police internally developed a plan to install "PCS-new" as a component of a comprehensive executive information system, which was abandoned in 2002 due to serious difficulties in implementation. From this date on, the further development of PCS-new has been carried out solely in the framework of the police information system INPOL (*Informationssystem der Polizei*) analysis. At the end of 2004, the "old" database of the PCS was integrated to the new Oracle database of the INPOL systems. PCS-new will be introduced in a two-stage procedure. Basically, inputting of the individual data records to the current PCS and conversion from a four-digit to a six-digit criminal offense code will take place in the first stage. The second stage will include expanding the PCS system to incorporate additional catalogs that allow more differentiated collection of individual variables.

Since 1 January 2007, the BKA has been collecting pseudonymized individual data records. Since not all of the *Länder* were in a position to provide this data at the outset, a transitional period was established. During this period, individual data records were provided to the BKA along with the aggregated tables. It was planned that by 2008, the delivery of individual data records would be carried out nationwide, at which point aggregated delivery would be discontinued. Ideally, the BKA should currently be in a position to compile statistics for each of the *Länder* as well as for the federal government on the basis of these individual data records.

The pseudonymized individual data records allow personal data to be collated in order to determine the "real" number of suspects at the federal level. Furthermore, by providing access to the individual data records, the BKA makes it possible for the first time to link the variables collected and to use different methods of statistical analysis.

The previous four-digit criminal offense code will be converted to a six-digit code. This will lay the foundation for a far more complete and differentiated record of criminal offenses than under previous standards. It will increase the currently 421 code numbers to approximately 1,500 code numbers.

Statistics of the public prosecutors offices and criminal courts. Since the reporting year 2004, the Federal Statistical Office provides (anonymized) individual data from the *Länder* to the public prosecutors offices and criminal courts for use in their statistics. This enables the Federal Statistical Office to flexibly analyze data available beyond the regularly published statistics on public prosecutors and criminal courts whenever a need arises.

Since 2004, criminal proceedings initiated by public prosecutors have been categorized following a subject matter catalog of the penal provisions violated, in which there are currently 30 categories. Detailed information is published on only six of these categories.

Conviction Statistics, Prison Statistics, Probation Service Statistics. For 2007, the specific offense codes used in each set of criminal justice statistics were replaced by a uniform recommended code system for all personal statistics. This will enable better comparison of the results of the three statistics in regard to convictions for felonies. This will constitute a major advance in the field of personal criminal justice statistics.

From 2009 on, the conviction and prison statistics were to have removed the previous restriction on data collection concerning citizenship, which had been differentiated only according to either German or non-German citizenship as well as citizenship of a few important guest worker groups. In the future, citizenship of convicted criminals or prisoners and detainees will be contained with the complete area and citizenship code in the official population statistics. In contrast, probation service statistics will continue to differentiate only between Germans and non-Germans.

Conviction Statistics. Since 2007, conviction statistics have been compiled in Saxony-Anhalt, making it possible to now publish statistics covering all of Germany. From the reporting year 2009 forward, the levels of criminal sanctions currently recorded in fixed categories will be recorded in a non-categorized manner.

3.2.2.2 Data access by data users

Since 1997, the annual report of the PCS has also been published on the Internet; the annual tables and time series dating back to 1987 can be downloaded as PDF files;[2] interested users can also receive this data as an Excel file. Up to the end of the 1990s, the Federal Statistical Office published the technical series *Strafrechtspflegestatistiken* exclusively in printed format, and for a few years in both printed and electronic form. Since 2004, only the electronic version has been provided[3] (Excel or PDF). Time series on convicted criminal offenders as well as convicted Germans and foreigners are also available for downloading.

Since autumn 2005, microdata from the Conviction Statistics (StVerfStat), Prison Statistics (StVollzStat), and since summer 2008 also from the Probation Service Statistics (BewHiStat) on the reporting years since 1995 have been made available for scientific analysis through the Research Data Centers of the Federal Statistical Office and the Statistical Offices of the

---

2   http://www.bka.de/, click on Reports and Statistics, Crime Statistics.
3   https://www-ec.destatis.de

German *Länder*.[4] At present the data in the judicial statistics are solely available through controlled remote data processing.[5] In addition, what is known as a "Public Use File" is being prepared for the Conviction Statistics.

The annual reports of the PCS contain not only data in tables, but also detailed explanatory reports, time series, graphic visualizations, and interpretations.

On the other hand, the Federal Statistical Office limits itself primarily to the publication of the criminal justice statistics in tabular form, which are supplemented by several datasets with time series. There are, however, noteworthy exceptions to this publication system. In 1999, the results of the various criminal justice statistics were summarized by the Federal Statistical Office in the publication *Justice as Reflected in the Criminal Justice Statistics*. The brochure *Justice at A Glance*,[6] published in 2008, included data provided by the statistical offices as well as results of scientific research.

For the first time in 2001 and again in 2006, the federal government sought to present a comprehensive picture of the crime situation in Germany in its two *Periodical Reports on Crime and Crime Control in Germany* (Federal Ministry of the Interior and Federal Ministry of Justice 2001; 2006). The aim was

"to put together the most comprehensive picture possible of the crime situation in Germany. For the first time in a report, it will draw together findings taken from the existing pool of official data [...]. At the same time, the report will provide a useful reference on the results of scientific research into the incidence and causes of crime" (Federal Ministry of the Interior and Federal Ministry of Justice 2001a: 3).

Through the inclusion of data from other data sources and the results of scientific research (e.g., victim surveys), the two reports provided a synopsis of the state of knowledge in the field of crime and internal security.

---

4   http://www.forschungsdatenzentrum.de/en/
5   On remote data processing, or "remote execution," see http://www.forschungsdatenzentrum.de/en/datenzugang.asp
6   http://www.destatis.de/jetspeed/portal/cms/Sites/destatis/Internet/DE/Content/Publikationen/Broschueren/JustizBlick,property=file.pdf

4. Optimizing the existing criminal statistics systems: Recommendations of the German Data Forum (RatSWD) working group

4.1 Tasks of the working group

On the 27 October 2006, the German Data Forum (RatSWD) hosted the workshop "Data Problems in the Crime and Criminal Justice Statistics" in Berlin. Participants at this workshop adopted a memorandum in which the RatSWD was asked to assemble a working group tasked to create "proposals for a comprehensive optimization of the existing criminal statistics systems."[7] In response to the memorandum, the RatSWD assembled a working group of elevn members. The task of the working group was to deliver proposals for the "optimization of the existing criminal statistics systems" within a year. The constitutive meeting of the group took place in Berlin in July 2007.

With regard to the aforementioned deficits listed in the 2001 KVI report and additional information gaps (see 3.1 above) that the working group had noted as deficiencies, proposals were made to redress these deficiencies in the short, medium, and long term. These recommendations were delivered to the German Data Forum (RatSWD) in September 2008 and were published in 2009 (RatSWD 2009).

4.2 Recommendations of the working group

4.2.1 Short- and medium-term recommendations

In the view of the working group, deficiencies in the existing criminal statistics system can only be resolved effectively if the official data on crime, convictions, and prisoners are linked together in a single statistical database. Overhauling the criminal statistics system therefore means, first and foremost, creating such a database. This, however, will presumably only be accomplished in the long term. The working group therefore outlined a number of measures that could be implemented in the transition period, enabling short- and medium-term improvements of the data situation in the field of crime and crime control. These improvements serve the purpose of rectifying acute problems and are also – at least partly – necessary intermediate steps for the establishment of a statistical database. The recommendations differentiate between short- and medium-term measures that would expand and improve the existing criminal statistics system, and long-term measures that would fundamentally overhaul the system:

---

7 http://www.ratswd.de/download/veranstaltungen/Memorandum_KriminalWS.pdf

(1) Measures to improve the existing components of the criminal statistics system:

- Expanding the crime and criminal justice statistics system to include periodic crime and victimization surveys.
- Creating a new statistic on suspects facing preliminary proceedings by public prosecutors based on data from the Central Public Prosecutors Procedural Register (ZStV, *Zentrales Staatsanwaltschaftliches Verfahrensregister*).
- Creating a periodic reconviction statistic based on register data, which could enhance the ongoing research on criminal recidivism.
- Expanding the Prison Statistics, which are currently collected on a single fixed date each year, to include entry and release statistics.

(2) Measures to fundamentally overhaul the system:

- Ensuring that personal data for the Criminal Justice Statistics is collected and compiled nationwide.
- Providing pseudonymized individual-level data records from the Criminal Justice Statistics that have been checked for plausibility to the Federal Statistical Office.
- Improving the compatibility among the Criminal Justice Statistics at the individual level as well as with the PCS.
- Supplementing the criminal offense code with criminological-criminalistic characteristics including a severity index.
- Providing greater flexibility in data collection and data preparation by supplementing the original dataset with additional information on specific regions and/or time frames. These data may be collected by the authorities of the *Länder* or by a research network of statistical authorities and scientific researchers. The additional data can help answer existing questions or act as a trial run for future changes to the original dataset.
- Expanding the data available from the Research Data Centers of the Federal Statistical Office and the Statistical Offices of the German *Länder* for use in all individual-level statistics on crime and criminal justice.
- Publishing time series in digital spreadsheet form allowing for subsequent processing.
- Periodical publishing of Reports on Crime and Crime Control.

Carrying out at least some of these recommendations will require the passage of a federal law on individual-level statistics on criminal justice. This is the only way that will ensure that data collection and preparation is completed nationwide, that the budget is maintained, and that the pseudonymized individual-level data records of the statistics for criminal justice are delivered successfully to the Federal Statistical Office.

The Criminal Justice Statistics on legal proceedings (compiled by the public prosecutors and criminal courts) should remain unchanged. Their goals are predominantly administrative in nature, for example, to calculate the manpower needed in the judicial system.

4.2.2 Long-term recommendations

Admittedly, the fundamental problems of the existing criminal statistics system will not be resolved through these short- and medium-term improvements to the data situation. The working group suggests replacing the previous system with a statistical database containing all judicial decisions of relevance to criminological research, linked with pseudonymized individual data. The problems with the current crime statistics system can be solved through this conversion. It also offers a foundation for new federal statistics collected on a regular basis, particularly regarding the preliminary proceedings of public prosecutors, remand custody, execution of sentences, and recidivism. The working group is aware, however, that this proposed system conversion will require significant organizational and technical advances. For this reason, the database presumably cannot be created until the longer term.

In an optimized criminal statistics system, the police data should also be integrated into the new database. However, due to the organizational separation of the PCS and the Criminal Justice Statistics, it is likely that this integration will not be possible in the near future. A more efficient comparison of police and court data can be achieved by harmonizing the criminal offense data collection and measurement standards.

In the opinion of the working group, the judiciary does not need to carry out any additional data collection for the criminological-statistical database system. Instead, data that have been collected for other purposes and are therefore generally available electronically should be made accessible for statistical analysis. To this end, the working group proposes that not only should the Justice Administration report to the Central Public Prosecutors Procedural Register and the Federal Central Register, but also that extensive parallel data be provided to the official statistical agencies as has been put into practice already in several *Länder*.

The working group believes that to comprehensively optimize the current criminal statistics system in Germany, the following requirements have to be met in order to enable the required system conversion:

- The existence of possibilities for identification or linkage that enable personal classification through a pseudonymized encryption process.
- Pseudonymization of the individual data records, plausibility check at *Länder* level, and provision of pseudonymized individual data to the federal level.
- Storage of the pseudonymized individual data records in a protected database at the federal level and personal linkage of the data.
- Independence of the data processing sites.

The implementation of these basic requirements calls for the establishment of a federal law:

- governing the delivery, processing, linkage, and storage of pseudonymized individual-level criminal justice data in a database,
- governing the regular compilation of the (improved) criminal justice statistics based on this dataset,
- regulating the scientific access to the individual data and the integration of the data into the institutional framework through further development of the database.

5. European and international developments

5.1 *European developments*

5.1.1 *European Sourcebook of Crime and Criminal Justice Statistics*

In 1993, the Council of Europe charged a group of specialists with the preparation of a feasibility study concerning the collection of crime and criminal justice data for Europe.[8] The first study, which was limited to ten countries, was met with a positive response. In 1995, the expert group was therefore expanded; the first publication of the European Sourcebook of Crime and Criminal Justice Statistics in 1999 contained information from 36 European countries, covering the period 1990 to 1996.[9] The second edition was sponsored by the governments of Switzerland, Great Britain, and the Netherlands and published at the end of 2003.[10] It contained data from 40 European countries between 1995 and 2000. The third issue, which appeared in 2006, covers the period between 2000 and 2003 with data from 37

---

8 http://www.europeansourcebook.org/
9 http://www.europeansourcebook.org/sourcebook_start.htm
10 http://www.europeansourcebook.org/esb2_Full.pdf

countries.[11] The publication of the fourth edition has been announced for 2009 and will cover the time period 2004 till 2007.

5.1.2 The Hague Programme 2004 and its implementation

Hague Programme 2004 and EU Action Plan 2006–2010, "Developing a Comprehensive and Coherent EU Strategy to Measure Crime and Criminal Justice."

The establishment of a comprehensive European crime statistics system has been recommended repeatedly. The most significant effort in this direction was the Hague Programme,[12] accepted by the European Council in 2004. The Council welcomed

> "the initiative of the Commission to establish European instruments for collecting, analyzing and comparing information on crime and victimization and their respective trends in Member States, using national statistics and other sources of information as agreed indicators."[13]

The communication from the commission "Developing a Comprehensive and Coherent EU Strategy to Measure Crime and Criminal Justice: An EU Action Plan 2006–2010,"[14] maintains that "one of the main deficiencies in the area of Justice, Freedom and Security is still the lack of reliable and comparable statistical information."[15] The goal is to assemble "statistical information on crime (including victimization) and criminal justice at European Union level,"[16] which should enable the comparison between Member States and their regions. For this purpose, the "available national data will be collected and quality-assessed to form the first Community statistics on crime and criminal justice"[17] in the short term, and in the medium term the attempt will be made to collect data "in a harmonized manner."[18] The Commission proposed to establish an expert group representing data users and a second working group should be formed to represent data producers.

---

11 http://www.europeansourcebook.org/esb3_Full.pdf
12 Programme for the strengthening of Freedom, Security and Justice in the European Union (http://ec.europa.eu/justice_home/doc_centre/doc/hague_. programme_en.pdf).
13 Hague Programme (note 12): 25.
14 http://eur-lex.europa.eu/LexUriServ/LexUriServ.do?uri=COM:2006:0437:FIN:EN:PDF
15 EU Action Plan 2006-2010 (note 14): 3.
16 EU Action Plan 2006-2010 (note 14): 2.
17 EU Action Plan 2006-2010 (note 14): 3.
18 EU Action Plan 2006-2010 (note 14): 4.

Actions for the implementation of the Hague Programme and the EU Action Plan 2006–2010

Expert group of the Directorate-General for Justice, Freedom and Security within the EU Commission (DG JLS): pursuant to the EU Action Plan 2006–2010, the DG JLS set up a group of experts on the policy needs for data on crime and criminal justice (PNDCCJ).[19] Among other things, this group had the task of creating an indicator list on the comparison of criminal statistics in Europe and of developing the content requirements for a Europe-wide population survey on crime rates and safety concerns. The expert group identified human trafficking and money laundering as issues on which urgent comparative data should be gathered across Europe.[20]

Working group on Statistics on Crime and Criminal Justice: also in 2006, the Directors of Social Statistics of the National Statistics Departments in Europe (DSS) created a representative working group for data producers "Statistics on Crime and Criminal Justice."[21] It was tasked with the responsibilities laid out in the Hague Programme 2004 of supporting in data collection, analysis, and comparison in the field of crime and criminal justice in the Member States, and ensuring that the EU Action Plan is implemented effectively by working closely with other supranational organizations that are already active in the field of crime and judicature, for example the European Sourcebook Group,[22] the United Nations Office on Drugs and Crime (UNODC),[23] and the United Nations Economic Commission for Europe (UNECE).[24] Additionally, the working group will pass their work and results onto the statistical systems of the Member States. Moreover they will be required to appoint specific task forces[25] and to cooperate closely with the expert group of the Directorate-General for Justice, Freedom and Security within the EU Commission (DG JLS) (see above).

Statistics in focus: Crime and Criminal Justice: it was proposed in the Hague Programme that Eurostat should use European instruments for the collection, analysis, and comparison of information on crime and victimization and also draw on the developments of the individual Member

---

19 Commission Decision of 7 August 2006 setting up a group of experts on the policy needs for data on crime and criminal justice, Official Journal L 234, 29/08/2006 P. 0029 – 0032. http://eur-lex.europa.eu/LexUriServ/LexUriServ.do?uri=OJ:L:2006:234:0029:01:EN:HTML
20 http://www.crime-prevention-intl.org/filebin/Generating%20Links%20for%20Website/Other%20ICPC%20Events/Rencontre%20des%20Observatoires%20de%20Paris/Liens/Olivier.Bardin.Paris.ENG.pdf
21 http://eur-lex.europa.eu/LexUriServ/LexUriServ.do?uri=OJ:L:2006:234:0029:01:EN:HTML: 2
22 http://www.europeansourcebook.org/
23 http://www.unodc.org/unodc/en/about-unodc/index.html
24 http://www.unece.org/Welcome.html
25 Currently two task forces exist on "victimization" and "crime data availability."

States. Additionally, they were to use national statistics and other information sources as agreed indicators. In 2007, the first copy of Statistics in Focus: Crime and Criminal Justice[26] was published; in the meantime the first updated version has been released.[27]

The publication contains the most important results of the Member States' "Crime Data Request" led by Eurostat. While the publication only identifies trends, absolute numbers are available on the Eurostat website.[28]

Europe-wide Population Survey on Crime Rates and Safety: in the implementation of the EU Hague Programme and the EU Action Plan 2006–2010, Eurostat plans to conduct a European victimization survey in 2010/2011 on victimization and general safety issues. In preparation, a survey of previous victim surveys conducted in Europe was created. On this basis – and using the manual on victim interviews developed by the UN – a questionnaire were developed and tested.

The European Institute for Crime Prevention and Control affiliated with the United Nations (HEUNI)[29] was commissioned to conceptualize the design and the questionnaire material (Heiskanen and Viuhko 2007; Thomas 2007). The individual methods of such a population survey should be tested using different surveying methods in the individual Member States. Germany wants to participate in the pilot survey; therefore the Federal Statistical Office, four of the Statistical Offices of the German *Länder,* and the BKA collectively developed an operating concept that they submitted to Eurostat.

5.2 International developments

International Crime Victimization Survey (ICVS) and International Self-Report Delinquency Study: the major advantage of crime surveys is that they have a standardized inventory and are independent of national crime definitions, convictions, and registration practices. They are therefore suitable for country comparisons.

In the 1980s the International Crime Survey (ICS) was established, which has been known as the ICVS since its renaming in 1996. The survey has been repeated using the same instruments and most of the same methods[30] four times since 1989 – that year also with German participation.[31]

---

26 http://epp.eurostat.ec.europa.eu/cache/ITY_OFFPUB/KS-SF-07-015/EN/KS-SF-07-015-EN.PDF
27 http://epp.eurostat.ec.europa.eu/cache/ITY_OFFPUB/KS-SF-08-019/EN/KS-SF-08-019-EN.PDF
28 http://epp.eurostat.ec.europa.eu/portal/page?_pageid=1996,45323734&_dad=portal&_schema=PORTAL&screen=welcomeref&open=/&product=EU_MASTER_crime&depth=2
29 http://www.heuni.fi/index.htm
30 http://rechten.uvt.nl/icvs/

Germany participated again in the fifth survey that was carried out in 2004/05 (Van Dijk et al. 2008). The sixth survey is planned for 2009.

An "International Self-Report Delinquency Study" took place in 1982 (Junger-Tas et al. 1994). The second International Self-Report Delinquency Study occurred with German participation.[32]

Comparative international crime and criminal justice statistics: The International Criminal Police Organization (ICPO, *Interpol*)[33] gathers data from the police crime statistics of their Member States and then summarizes these data at regular intervals. These reports were previously available upon request and for a few years they were even universally accessible on the Internet. However, for the past few years, they have only been available for (internal) official use. In 2006, the 75th General Assembly passed a resolution[34] that brought an end to the International Criminal Police Statistics.[35]

United Nations Survey on Crime Trends and the Operations of Criminal Justice Systems (World Crime Survey): following international trends, the United Nations compiles data on international crime developments as well as sentencing and conviction by law enforcement agencies.[36] The United Nations Survey on Crime Trends and the Operations of Criminal Justice Systems (World Crime Survey) has been executed in eleven phases since 1970. The accuracy and reliability of this survey is naturally dependent on how accurately the comprehensive questionnaire is filled out.[37]

---

31 At the first ICVS in 1989, 14 countries including Germany participated. The following surveys took place in 1992 with the participation of 33 countries, and in 1996 and 2000, 48 countries participated. Germany did not participate in these latter two surveys. Germany only took part again in the fifth survey of 2004/2005.
32 http://www2.jura.uni-hamburg.de/instkrim/kriminologie/Projekte/ISRD2/ISRD2.html. The final report has been announced for the summer of 2008.
33 http://www.interpol.int/
34 Resolution No AG-2006-RES-19.
35 http://www.interpol.int/public/ICPO/GeneralAssembly/AGN75/resolutions/AGN 75RES19.asp
36 http://www.unodc.org/unodc/en/data-and-analysis/United-Nations-Surveys-on-Crime-Trends-and-the-Operations-of-Criminal-Justice-Systems.html
37 For the comparison of data quality and individual internationally comparative analyses, see the second Periodical Report on Crime and Crime Control (Federal Ministry of the Interior and Federal Ministry of Justice 2006: 39ff.).

References:

Albrecht, H.-J. (2001): Informationsfeld "Rechtspflege/Gerichtsbarkeit/innere/äußere Sicherheit". In: Kommission zur Verbesserung der informationellen Infrastruktur zwischen Wissenschaft und Statistik (KVI) (Ed.): Wege zu einer besseren informationellen Infrastruktur. Baden-Baden.

Federal Ministry of the Interior and Federal Ministry of Justice (Ed.) (2001a): First Periodical Report on Crime and Crime Control. Abridged Version. Berlin. http://www.uni-konstanz.de/rtf/ki/Download_Abridged_Version.pdf. [Last visited: 02/19/2010].

Federal Ministry of the Interior and Federal Ministry of Justice (Ed.) (2001b): First Periodical Report on Crime and Crime Control. Berlin.

Federal Ministry of the Interior and Federal Ministry of Justice (Ed.) (2006a): Zweiter Periodischer Sicherheitsbericht. Berlin. http://www.uni-konstanz.de/rtf/ki/links.htm#PSB2. [Last visited: 02/19/2010].

Federal Ministry of the Interior and Federal Ministry of Justice (Ed.) (2006b): Second Periodical Report on Crime and Crime Control in Germany. Abridged Version. Berlin.

Heinz, W. (2002): Final Report by the Working Group of the Ministry of the Interior and the Ministry of Justice on the Regular Execution of Victim Surveys. [Unpublished paper].

Heinz, W. (2003): Soziale und kulturelle Grundlagen der Kriminologie – Der Beitrag der Kriminalstatistik. In: Dittmann, V. and Jehle, J.-M. (Eds.): Kriminologie zwischen Grundlagenwissenschaft und Praxis. Mönchengladbach.

Heinz, W. (2008): Kriminalstatistik – quo vadis? In: Festschrift für K. Tiedemann. Cologne.

Heiskanen M. and Viuhko, M. (2007): European Victimization Survey. In: Aromaa, K. and Heiskanen, M. (Eds.): Victimization Surveys in Comparative Perspective. Papers from the Stockholm Criminology Symposium. http://www.heuni.fi/uploads/ojyw1estdwh5b.pdf. [Last visited: 02/19/2010].

Junger-Tas, J./Terlouw, G.-J. and Klein, M.W. (Eds.) (1994): Delinquent behavior among young people in the western world: first results of the international self-report delinquency study. Amsterdam.

Kommission zur Verbesserung der informationellen Infrastruktur zwischen Wissenschaft und Statistik (KVI) (Ed.) (2001): Wege zu einer besseren informationellen Infrastruktur. Baden-Baden.

Rat für Sozial- und Wirtschaftsdaten (RatSWD) (Ed.) (2009): Optimierung des bestehenden kriminalstatistischen Systems in Deutschland. Baden-Baden.

Thomas, G. (2007): Development of a EU Victimization Module. In: Aromaa, K. and Heiskanen, M. (Eds.): Victimization Surveys in Comparative Perspective. Papers from the Stockholm Criminology Symposium. http://www.heuni.fi/uploads/ojyw1estdwh5b.pdf. [Last visited: 02/19/2010].

Van Dijk, J.J.M./van Kesteren, J.N. and Smit, P. (2008): Criminal Victimization in International Perspective. Code findings from the 2004-2005 ICVS and EU ICS. The Hague. http://rechten.uvt.nl/icvs/pdffiles/ICVS2004_05.pdf. [Last visited: 02/19/2010].

6.6 Environment

Cornelia Ohl and Bernd Hansjürgens

Contact:

Cornelia Ohl
Bernd Hansjürgens
Helmholtz Centre for Environmental Research – UFZ
Department of Economics
Permoserstraße 15
04301 Leipzig
Germany
e-mail: cornelia.ohl[at]ufz.de
        cornelia.ohl[at]uba.de
        bernd.hansjuergens[at]ufz.de

Abstract

Many environmental problems are large in scale, both geographically and temporally. A natural implication of this is that numerous environmental events and consequences often tend to coincide with one another, therefore making inferences about causal relationships between humans and nature is difficult at best ("transparency challenge"). Consequently, we see a need for innovative analytical methods and modeling approaches to supplement the traditional monitoring-based approach to environmental policy. These methods and modeling approaches should make it possible to capture different degrees of uncertainty, which are generally beyond the scope of the control variables used in traditional monitoring activities. Moreover, due to the difficulty associated with distinguishing the boundaries between natural and social systems, the monitoring approaches should be based on the collection and connection of data from different fields. For this, comparable and often very large datasets are needed, ("availability challenge" and "compatibility challenge"). Even if these obstacles are overcome, data processing will remain a very complex and time-consuming task. It is therefore crucial that the data infrastructure is user-friendly. We see an advantage here in using the Geographical Information Systems (GIS) technology as well as a nested structure for data provision. This structure should aid the upwards and downwards scaling of information as well as facilitate access to data by the relevant parties – polluters, victims, and regulators ("connectivity challenge").

Keywords: coincidence of causes and impacts, transparency, availability, compatibility, connectivity, GIS technology, nested structure for data provision

1. Research questions

At present, various data sources indicate that human interferences in nature have reached unprecedented levels (Vitousek et al. 1997; Nelson et al. 2006). Disturbances in ecological systems have increased in magnitude, and impact not only ecosystems, but also human wellbeing (IPCC 2007; MEA 2005). Unsurprisingly, this has led to increased questioning of contemporary management strategies. In order to effectively monitor human impact on his surroundings, new monitoring approaches and strategies are required. Ideally, these strategies should better capture the interplay between humans and nature in terms of the associated varying degrees of uncertainty and unpredictability involved.

The fact that many environmental problems today are large in scale both geographically and temporally poses several problems for the design of data provision. Specifically, these problems pertain to the collection, processing, and accessibility of information. Reasons for this are: (1) the fact that a majority of environmental problems are long-term in nature, which frequently makes it impossible to distinguish between overlapping causes and impacts. (2) Furthermore, many environmental problems are characterized by "true uncertainty." This means that neither the expected damages and costs nor the probability of their occurrence are adequately understood. In turn, (3) this makes it difficult to monitor policy interventions due to changes in relevant state variables and (4) undermines the evaluation of policy success or failure. Hence, any monitoring activity aiming to capture changes in complex environmental phenomena is doomed to fail. Thus, the critical questions to answer are: how does one monitor changes in complex environmental phenomena characterized by human interference and human-nature feedbacks? How does one measure the success of policy interventions given that environmental problems are large-scale and long-term?

To answer these questions, we see a need for innovative analytical methods and modeling approaches that supplement the traditional monitoring-based approach. Traditional monitoring is based on indicator-orientated environmental assessments of typically a single (often well-known) source or pollutant that causes specific ecosystem disturbances. Analytical methods and modeling approaches are required in order to better understand correlations between multiple interferences in natural and societal systems as well as the interplay of different sources and pollutants. We call this the "transparency challenge." It is the challenge of separating multiple interferences at different levels of interplay (e.g., the level of drivers and responses). As a prerequisite for defining policy responses aimed at halting undesired environmental changes, these innovative methods and approaches require descriptive informational inputs about the natural system being assessed. This includes information not only about internal pressures affecting the state of the ecosystem, but also about external pressures, such as the effects of various sectors of the economy, local planning bodies, etc. We label this the "availability challenge." It is the challenge of delivering sufficient information about different facets of a problem to researchers, policy-makers, and the public. Here, problems may arise if data are non-existent or not accessible. In this regard, it is important to note that environmental problems are of a particular nature; they are characterized by problems of fit, interplay, and scale (Young 2002). The notion of fit refers to the natural and socio-economic boundaries of an environmental problem. While natural boundaries are determined by the "natural properties" of an ecosystem, for example, the boundaries of a river basin, the socio-economic boundaries are mainly administrative ones, for example, national, regional, or local governmental units. From the perspective of providing adequate data, this leads to a misfit such that the environmental problem under concern cannot be adequately captured in a quantitative dimension. We call this the "compatibility challenge." It is the challenge of avoiding a mismatch of available datasets. Problems of interplay refer to the fact that many environmental problems are cross-cutting by nature. This requires that data from several policy fields be combined. Making proposals for alternative land use, for instance, requires information on agriculture, urbanization, the water sector, and other environmental media. In most cases, existing databases have not been developed for cross-cutting research questions like this, so major changes with respect to data processing have to be undertaken. Finally, problems of scale refer to the need to scale data up and down. Many environmental data are gathered on a scale different from that where policy recommendations are developed. This leads us to formulate a fourth challenge, the "connectivity challenge." This is the challenge of combining the available datasets in such a way that information is accessible from different perspectives (e.g., from the victim's,' policy-maker's,' and pollutant's points of view). These challenges require new and innovative methods of data management.

2. Status quo: Databases and access

In recent years, considerable progress has been achieved in the provision of both natural and social science data on environmental issues. Today, it is undisputed that social and behavioral science data are complementary and supplement natural science data. At an international level, four major data approaches can be identified (Ohl et al. 2009):

(1) *The media approach:* focused on environmental components, such as air, land, water, and the human-made environment;

(2) *The stress-response approach:* focused on human impacts on the environment and subsequent transformation ("responses") of environmental systems;

(3) *The resource accounting approach:* focused on the natural resources flow beginning at extraction, then following different resource uses throughout the lifetime of a product, and ending at the final return of the resources (e.g., as emissions, wastewater) into the environment;

(4) *The ecological approach:* based on models, monitoring techniques, and ecological indices. This approach draws on the notion of pressures, states, and responses (PSR) with regard to data organization, but applies these concepts only to ecological zones within a country. For example, the Geographical Information Systems (GIS) use the ecological approach.

Additionally, different combinations of these approaches are used on all scales of environmental statistics (local, regional, national) (Ohl et al. 2009):

- FDES: a Framework for the Development of Environmental Statistics, developed by the United Nations Statistical Office;
- PSR: Pressure-State-Response framework, developed by the Organization for Economic Co-operation and Development (OECD);
- DSR: Driving forces-State-Response framework, developed by the Commission of Sustainable Development;
- DPSIR: Driving forces-Pressure-State-Impact-Response framework, used by the European Environment Agency (EEA) and the Statistical Office of the European Communities (Eurostat).

The use of these approaches and frameworks has led to extensive data on all kinds of environmental issues. These occurred not only in Europe, but all over the world. To some extent, these approaches complement each other, as each emphasizes different aspects of an environmental issue. The differences in viewpoint, however, are sometimes confusing. For example, the collection of data on drivers and pressures in abstract of one another is only used in the DPSIR framework. The other frameworks do not differentiate between them.

Despite this disparity among approaches, the overall experience in collecting and reporting environmental data has led to the development of several useful environmental indicators since the 1970s. These indicators allow reporting on, for example, environmental conditions, environmental performance, and progress towards sustainable development. These indicators are judged as powerful cost-effective tools for tracking environmental progress, providing policy feedback, and measuring environmental performance (OECD 2003). Their development has catalyzed fruitful cooperation among a great number of countries and international organizations, for example, between the OECD and the United Nations Statistics Division (UNSD), the UN Commission for Sustainable Development (UNCSD), the United Nations Environment Programme (UNEP), the Commission of the European Communities, Eurostat, and the European Environment Agency (EEA).

In addition, considerable progress has been made regarding the development of a System of Integrated Environmental Economic Accounting (SEEA). This has occurred at both the UN level and at respective national levels, for example, in the German Environmental Accounting Framework (UGR, *Umweltökonomische Gesamtrechnung*). The UGR was developed in the 1990s and delivers the most comprehensive framework for capturing the relationships between environment and economy today. Both approaches, the SEEA and the UGR, are characterized by an integrative perspective that makes use of common concepts, definitions, and classifications in order to allow for the direct observation of links between economic and environmental development. Importantly, these approaches serve as a basis for providing indicator-based information to policy-makers and the public. Moreover, the integrated accounting approaches allow for drawing conclusions about the macroeconomic costs of policy measures by modeling sector-specific economic and environmental behavior under certain policy constraints. These approaches are currently being evaluated and revised by the UN Committee of Experts on Environmental Economic Accounting and Statistics (UNCEEA), with the aim of developing an international statistical standard.

Against this background, deficits in data provision are hardly found on the macroeconomic level. What is missing is the provision of adequate datasets on the microeconomic level. If made available, these micro-level datasets could be linked with already readily available macro-level data to enhance our understanding of the vulnerability of individuals and social groups subject to environmental change on the level of small scale regional units.

3. Future developments

3.1 Data provision

In addition to the information provided by statistical institutions and other organizations, there are several other networks responsible for data provision. One of these is, for example, the Global Earth Observation System of Systems (GEOSS), which, within the next decade, is expected to provide a further large amount of new datasets. These include several products such as maps on river systems, infrastructure, land cover, and land use, all of which are expected to be available for common use. To interpret and use these products for society's benefit, the earth observation data need to be linked to social science information on human related drivers and consequences of change. Currently, there are two problems associated with data provision in GEOSS. First, socio-economic data providing this kind of information is very often on administrative scales that differ from natural scales, creating a problem of fit (see above). Second, socio-economic data and indicators are rarely delivered and visualized in maps. Nonetheless, it should still be noted that some progress has been made in the technical support of this kind of data provision, especially since GIS[1] technology has improved the effectiveness and analytic power of traditional mapping.

---

1 GIS application tools support users in analyzing spatial information (i.e., data that refers to or is linked to a specific location), in editing data, and in visualising the results of operation

Today, in several fields of application, GIS not only provides maps on socio-economic developments in space and time, but also supports analyses of social science data for decision-making. For marketing purposes, for instance, demographic information is used to determine how many individuals with a certain socio-economic classification (e.g., age, sex, or income) live in a given spatial area. Another prime example is the CompStat approach used in New York City, which uses GIS for crime mapping and analysis (e.g., crime forecasting and geographic profiling) to formulate strategies, target resources, and evaluate crime reduction programs. Data held by GIS may also be used as a spatial decision-support system. In the US, time-specific population data, which deliver insight into humans' daily routines, are used to track and model patterns of commuter behavior. Projecting these data forwards into the future is helpful in assisting the local planning bodies in analyzing and testing different types of policy decisions.

In the field of the environment, the most prominent example is the use of GIS to understand the impacts of global climate change. So far, however, the focus has mainly been on combining various maps and satellite information sources to simulate interactions of complex natural system phenomena (e.g., the impacts of climate change on coastal areas, including flooding due to sea-level rise and storm erosion). According to these data, the exposure of individuals, societal groups, or regions to climate change risks and impacts can be visualized. A future challenge will be including anthropogenic factors in order to better understand the capacity of the entities considered to cope with climate change impacts. Relevant questions in this regard are: which individuals or social groups are affected by global climate change? What is their regional distribution (e.g., within the boundaries of an urban agglomeration)? What are the housing conditions? Are individuals able to protect their homes against flooding or to cope with flooding events? Is it possible to combine global climate change data with data on social segregation? Can changes in lifestyle or socio-economic adaptation measures be captured? The final goal of adding these data to the existing global climate change data is to get a deeper understanding of the vulnerability of individuals, social groups, societies, and regional units. This includes data on both the exposure of "elements at risks" as well as coping capacities.

Further questions arise with respect to the measurement of the success of policy responses: how should a new type of regulation consider variables on the state of the natural and social system? Who will be affected by current and future regulations and how? Answering these questions should deliver the blueprint for building modern data provision infrastructure. And, of course, this infrastructure will have to be updated whenever a new policy problem materializes. Here, the challenge is that for the observation of newly

---

in maps. GIS can, for example, be used for urban planning, resource management, and environmental impact assessment.

emerging environmental problems, the existing infrastructure needs to be flexible enough to adapt to and be merged with newly emerging demands for data provision. A second important challenge is to identify overlaps of natural and social systems, especially with regard to the social entities affected. This concern is related to the problem of interplay (see above) as well as correlations between the new and past chain of causes and impacts.

3.2 Data usage

The most important deficit in the field of data usage is the improper provision of information for the implementation of policy responses. The provision of data does not sufficiently take into account the needs of data users. This primarily holds for trans-boundary and global environmental phenomena (Neßhöver et al. 2007: 120), but also at the regional and local level. To overcome this shortcoming, the design of monitoring activities needs to stringently take policy considerations and users' needs into account. Questions concerning design need to be asked in a targeted manner: which information is required for which purpose, at which point in time, and by which user (e.g., at which governmental level)? Very often, data collection, processing, and publication are driven by the providers, the "supply side." It will be, however, crucial to strengthen the interests of users in the process of collecting and processing data and thereby strengthen the "demand side."

The environmental data available is often insufficient not only for policy evaluation, but also for public communication purposes. One important goal of the collection and distribution of environmental data is to inform the general public. In order to achieve this goal, information has to be prepared in a way that stakeholders who are not experts in a particular environmental field are able to understand and interpret the data.

However, public participation and the involvement of user groups can even go a step further. To foster public involvement in policymaking as well as to promote the goals of nongovernmental organizations, grassroots groups, and community-based organizations, data infrastructure should broaden its view to public participation. In this regard Public Participation GIS (PPGIS, Sieber 2006) can be used as a supportive tool. Ghose (2001) reports a case study where residents of an inner city neighborhood became active participants in building a community information system. The participants learned to access public information and create and analyze new databases derived from their own surveys. In this manner, participants became engaged in city management and the formation of public policy. Use of PPGIS is motivated by the expectation that access to information is the key to more effective government and community empowerment. As a top-down approach, PPGIS could also be used to analyze the spatial differences in access to environmental services (e.g., with reference to the social and economic background of relevant actors) and thus support making adjustments and improvements in environmental management.

3.3 Data access

The vast amount of data provided by institutions and organizations is easily accessible via the Internet. However, datasets are often dispersed and disconnected and thus inconvenient for users to handle. In cases where datasets are centrally archived, for example, on the homepages of the United Nations Framework Convention on Climate Change (UNFCCC) or the Convention on Biological Diversity (CBD), the sheer amount of information available often exceeds the time constraints of the users seeking it.[2] The speed of progress in computer technology and widespread Internet access, together with the complexity of the problems under consideration – especially if they are global in scope – are some of the reasons why desired information is not always easily accessible. This holds true not only for third-party users in the general public, but also for individuals responsible for the provision and analysis of the datasets. Hence, it is unsurprising that the relevant data suffer from time lags in provision and do not qualify as up to date.

Thus, although data provision has considerably improved in recent years due to technological progress in the information sector, the main factor hampering information processing is human: too much complex information for a normal human being to process, and time constraints create bottlenecks. To deploy and process more of the information provided by administrative sources, it is thus necessary to assist the users with improved search functions and an infrastructure that allows for individual ways of data connection. One promising route to follow in this regard is again the development of a GIS based system of data storage and processing.

To fully utilize the societal benefits of environmental data, it is crucial to share the data across national and international administrative boundaries. In this regard, the GEOSS data-sharing principles could work as a model for future developments in national and international data-sharing. In recognition of relevant international instruments and national policies and legislation, GEOSS will support the full and open exchange of data, metadata, and products, not only within the GEOSS community, but also beyond. For research and education, all shared data, metadata, and products will be provided free of charge or at no more than the cost of production. For other users, these

---

[2] One example is reporting by CBD signatories on measures undertaken and their effectiveness in accordance with article 26 of the Convention. So far there are 191 CBD parties, of which 143 have delivered the third national report (NR3); see http://www.cbd.int/reports/ (accessed Novemsber 30, 2008). Going through all these reports to find country-specific information on a particular measure is an extremely time-consuming task.

data will be provided at minimum cost. Use of the data or products need not necessarily imply agreement with or endorsement of the purpose behind the gathering of the data, which will be made available with minimum time delay.

At the local and individual level, the security of environmental data may remain a problem for the social sciences. While data collection on a very small scale is usually not a problem in the natural sciences, the collection of such data in the socio-economic fields can become a problem if individuals, households, or companies can be identified due to the small number of units in the sample. Here, the legal protection of the private sphere of individuals, households, and companies may lead to conflicts with research interests.

4. Future developments: European and international challenges

Despite important progress in the field of international environmental statistics, differences among countries remain. In order to make progress in providing environmental data tailored towards policy needs, we must establish closer links between the data gathered on natural systems and the data on social systems at different scales. In this respect, linking national accounts with international datasets seems to be most important. A nested structure of data provision that provides the datasets from various points of view seems appropriate. These include:

- Polluters: focusing on, e.g., consumption behavior and production processes.

- Victims: focusing on, e.g., the consumption of harmful goods, or vulnerability of specific sectors in the economy due to climate change.

- Regulators: focusing on an inventory of policies affecting, e.g., environmental pollution behavior and reducing social vulnerabilities.

Coordinated data management by national and supra-national bodies should center on *environmentally relevant core activities*. Determination of these core activities requires an approach that includes the interests of (national) users. Such an approach would facilitate agreement on the objectives of data gathering and sharing as a prerequisite for developing a common data infrastructure. Guiding questions in this regard are:

- What are the most important environmental problems that need to be solved on a supranational level (climate change, biodiversity loss, water scarcity, deposition of nuclear waste, etc.)?
- Which state variables describe the problem under consideration (e.g., emission levels, damage costs, stock of resources)?
- What are the key variables that require monitoring and policy control (e.g., sectors, inputs, outputs)?
- What are the most important channels for transferring impacts from one administrative unit (governance level) to another (e.g., import and export of goods, unidirectional or reciprocal externalities, etc.)?
- Within which time horizon do the problems need to be solved and should a policy phase-out take place (considering delays as well as persistence and irreversibility of causes and impacts)?
- Which policy measures already affect or are expected to affect the problem under consideration?

With regard to the organizational infrastructure, an improved systematic horizontal and vertical integration of datasets from different types of administrative, research, and business units is urgently needed. The key aim of horizontal integration is to develop standards for the integration of important private (business) and project-related research data in official accounts at all administrative levels. The key aim of vertical integration is to derive national accounts data from datasets collected on the lower (sub-national) administrative units and vice versa. This requires developing ways of combining electronic surveys with new sampling techniques and/or algorithms that are capable of exploiting data at different levels of generalization. This in turn involves cross-linking statistical data, including its combination with text- and image-based information available from different sources. For this purpose, it will be crucial to develop a sophisticated infrastructure for data storage and provision (e.g., development of statistical and machine learning algorithms that have the capacity to cope with massive amounts of data, development of methodologies and semantics for statistics, integrated with metadata construction and retrieval systems to handle statistical requests and improve the access to datasets). Only the future will show whether the improvements needed here will be made.

References:

Global Earth Observation System of Systems (GEOSS): 10-Year Implementation Plan (As adopted 16 February 2005), accessed http://www.earthobservations.org/documents/10-Year%20Implementation%20Plan.pdf [last visited: 02/17/2010]; see also http://www.earthobservations.org/ [last visited: 02/17/2010].

Ghose, R. (2001): Use of Information Technology for Community Empowerment: Transforming Geographic Information Systems into Community Information Systems. Transactions in GIS 5 (2), 141-163.

Intergovernmental Panel on Climate Change (IPCC) (2007): Climate Change 2007 – Synthesis Report. IPCC Fourth Assessment Report. Cambridge: http://www.ipcc.ch/pdf/assessment-report/ar4/syr/ar4_syr.pdf. [Last visited: 02/17/2010].

Millennium Ecosystem Assessment (MEA) (2005): Ecosystems and human well-being. Washington.

Nelson, G.C./Bennett, E./Berhe, A.A./Cassman, K./DeFries, R./Dietz, T./Dobermann, A./Dobson, A./Janetos, A./Levy, A./Marco, D./Nakicenovic, N./O'Neill, B./Norgaard, R./Petschel-Held, G./Ojima, D./Pingali, P./Watson, R. and Zurek, M. (2006): Anthropogenic Drivers of Ecosystem Change: An Overview. Ecology and Society 11 (2), 29. http://www.ecologyandsociety.org/vol11/iss2/art29/. [Last visited: 02/17/2010].

Neßhöver, C./Berghöfer, A. and Beck, S. (2007): Weltranglisten als Beratungsinstrumente der Umweltpolitik – Eine Einschätzung des Environmental Performance Index. Marburg.

OECD (2003): OECD Environmental Indicators: Development, Measurement and Use. Paris. http://unpan1.un.org/intradoc/groups/public/documents/apcity/unpan015281.pdf. [Last visited: 02/14/2010].

Ohl, C./Bezák, P./Palarie, T.A./Gelan, A. and Krauze, K. (2009): DAPSET – Concept for Characterising Socio-Economic Drivers of and Pressures on Biodiversity. UFZ-Discussion Paper 2/2009.

Sieber, R. (2006): Public Participation and Geographic Information Systems: A Literature Review and Framework. Annals of the American Association of Geographers 96 (3), 491-507.

Vitousek, P.M./Mooney, H.A./Lubchenco, J. and Melillo, J.M. (1997): Human Domination of Earth's Ecosystems. Science 277 [25 July 1997], 494-499.

Young, O. (2002): The Institutional Dimension of Environmental Change. Fit, Interplay, and Scale. Cambridge.

Terminology

English Name[1]	Original German Name
Research Data Center of the Federal Statistical Office	Forschungsdatenzentrum des Statistischen Bundesamtes
Research Data Center of the Statistical Offices of the German *Länder*	Forschungsdatenzentrum der Statistischen Landesämter
Research Data Center of the Federal Employment Agency (BA) at the Institute for Employment Research (IAB)	Forschungsdatenzentrum der Bundesagentur für Arbeit (BA) im Institut für Arbeitsmarkt- und Berufsforschung (IAB)
Research Data Center of the German Pension Insurance (RV)	Forschungsdatenzentrum der Rentenversicherung (RV)
Research Data Center of the Federal Institute for Vocational Education and Training (BIBB)	Forschungsdatenzentrum im Bundesinstitut für Berufsbildung (BIBB)
Research Data Center at the Institute for Educational Progress (IQB)	Forschungsdatenzentrum am Institut zur Qualitätsentwicklung im Bildungswesen (IQB)
Research Data Center of the German Socio-Economic Panel (SOEP)	Forschungsdatenzentrum des Sozio-oekonomischen Panels (SOEP)
Research Data Center ALLBUS at the Leibniz Institute for the Social Sciences (GESIS)	Forschungsdatenzentrum ALLBUS bei GESIS
Research Data Center "International Survey Programs" at the Leibniz Institute for the Social Sciences (GESIS)	Forschungsdatenzentrum "Internationale Umfrageprogramme" bei GESIS
Research Data Center "Voting Behavior database" at the Leibniz Institute for the Social Sciences (GESIS)	Forschungsdatenzentrum "Daten der Wahlforschung" bei GESIS
Research Data Center of the Survey of Health, Ageing and Retirement in Europe (SHARE)	Forschungsdatenzentrum des Survey of Health, Ageing and Retirement in Europe (SHARE)
Research Data Center of the German Ageing Survey (DEAS)	Forschungsdatenzentrum Deutscher Alterssurvey (DEAS)
German Microdata Lab (GML) Service Center for Microdata at the Leibniz Institute for the Social Sciences (GESIS)	German Microdata Lab (GML) Servicezentrum für Mikrodaten des Leibnitz-Instituts für Sozialwissenschaften (GESIS) / MISSY
International Data Service Center at the Institute for the Study of Labor (IZA)	Internationales Datenservicezentrum des Forschungsinstituts zur Zukunft der Arbeit (IZA)

---

[1] For the purpose of standardization, the German names of the Research Data Centers have been translated into English using the American spelling.

Frequently used Abbreviations:

A

AES	(European) Adult Education Survey – *Berichtssystem Weiterbildung*
AFiD	Official Firm Data for Germany – *Amtliche Firmendaten für Deutschland*
ALL	Adult Literacy and Lifeskills Survey
ALLBUS	German General Social Survey – *Allgemeine Bevölkerungsumfrage der Sozialwissenschaften*
ASID	Old-age Pension Schemes in Germany – *Alterssicherung in Deutschland*
AVID	Retirement Pension Provision Schemes in Germany – *Altersvorsorge in Deutschland*

B

BA	Federal Employment Agency – *Bundesagentur für Arbeit*
BAMF	Federal Office for Migration and Refugees – *Bundesamt für Migration und Flüchtlinge*
BAP	Employment Panel of the BA – *BA-Beschäftigtenpanel*
BBR	The Federal Office for Building and Regional Planning – *Bundesamt für Bauwesen und Raumordnung*
BCS	British Cohort Study
BHP	Establishment History Panel – *Betriebs-Historik-Panel*
BHPS	British Household Panel Study
BiB	Federal Institute for Population Research – *Bundesinstitut für Bevölkerungsforschung*
BIBB	Federal Institute for Vocational Education and Training – *Bundesinstitut für Berufsbildung*
BIJU	Learning Processes, Educational Careers, and Psychosocial Development in Adolescence and Young Adulthood – *Bildungsverläufe und psychosoziale Entwicklung im Jugend- und jungen Erwachsenenalter*
BiKS	Educational Processes, Competence Development, and Selection Decisions in Pre- and Primary School Age – *Bildungsprozesse, Kompetenzentwicklungen und Selektionsentscheidungen im Vor- und Grundschulalter*

	BMBF	Federal Ministry of Education and Research – *Bundesministerium für Bildung und Forschung*
	BStatG	Law on Statistics for Federal Purposes – *Gesetz über die Statistik für Bundeszwecke (Bundesstatistikgesetz)*

C

CAPI	computer-assisted personal interview
CASI	computer-assisted self interview
CATI	computer-assisted telephone interview
CESSDA	Council of European Social Science Data Archives
CNEF	Cross-National Equivalent File
CSES	Comparative Study of Electoral Systems

D

DDI	Data Documentation Initiative
DEAS	German Ageing Survey – *Deutscher Alterssurvey*
DESI	Assessment of Student Achievements in German and English as a Foreign Language – *Deutsch-Englisch-Schülerleistungen-International*
DFG	German Research Foundation – *Deutsche Forschungsgemeinschaft*
DGS	German Sociological Association – *Deutsche Gesellschaft für Soziologie*
DJI	German Youth Institute – *Deutsches Jugendinstitut*

E

ECHP	European Community Household Panel – *Europäisches Haushaltspanel*
ELSA	English Longitudinal Study of Ageing
ESAC	European Statistical Advisory Committee
ESDS	Economic and Social Data Service
ESFRI	European Strategy Forum on Research Infrastructures
ESOMAR	European Society for Opinion and Marketing Research
ESRC	Economic and Social Research Council
ESS	European Social Survey
EU-LFS	European Labour Force Survey
EU-SILC	European Statistics on Income and Living Conditions
Eurostat	Statistical Office of the European Union

	EVS	Income and Consumption Survey* – *Einkommens- und Verbrauchsstichprobe*

F

	FiDASt	Firm-Level Data from Official Statistics* – FirmenDaten aus der Amtlichen Statistik

G

	GEOSS	Global Earth Observation System of Systems
	GESIS	Leibniz Institute for the Social Sciences – *Leibniz-Institut für Sozialwissenschaften*
	GfK	Society for Consumer Research – *Gesellschaft für Konsumforschung*
	GGS	Generations and Gender Survey
	GIS	Geographical Information System
	GLES	German Longitudinal Election Study
	GLHS	German Life History Study – *Deutsche Lebensverlaufsstudie*
	GNES	German National Election Study

H

	HILDA	Household, Income and Labour Dynamics in Australia
	HIS	Higher Education Information System – *Hochschul-Informations-System*
	HRS	Health and Retirement Study

I

	IAB	Institute for Employment Research – *Institut für Arbeitsmarkt- und Berufsforschung*
	IAB-PASS	IAB panel study "Labor Market and Social Security" – *Panel "Arbeitsmarkt und soziale Sicherung" des IAB*
	IABS	IAB Employment Sample – *IAB-Beschäftigtenstichprobe*
	IALS	International Adult Literary Survey
	ICPSR	Inter-University Consortium for Political and Social Science Research
	ICT	Information and Communication Technology

---

* Inofficial translation.

IDF	International Data Forum	
IEBS	Integrated Employment Biographies Sample – *Stichprobe der Integrierten Erwerbsbiografien des IAB*	
Ifo	Ifo Institute for Economic Research – *ifo Institut für Wirtschaftsforschung*	
ILO	International Labour Organization – *Internationale Arbeitsorganisation*	
IQB	Institute for Educational Progress – *Institut zur Qualitätsentwicklung im Bildungswesen*	
ISI	International Statistical Institute	
ISR	(Michigan) Institute for Social Research	
ISSP	International Social Survey Programme	
IZ	Specialized Information for the Social Sciences – *Fachinformation für die Sozialwissenschaften*	
IZA	Institute for the Study of Labor – *Forschungsinstitut zur Zukunft der Arbeit*	

K

KombiFiD	Combined Firm Data for Germany – *Kombinierte Firmendaten für Deutschland*
KVI	German Commission on Improving the Information Infrastructure between Science and Statistics – *Kommission zur Verbesserung der informationellen Infrastruktur zwischen Wissenschaft und Statistik*

L

LAU	Aspects of Learning Prerequisites and Learning Development[*] – *Aspekte der Lernausgangslage und der Lernentwicklung*
LEE data	Linked Employer-Employee data – *kombinierte Arbeitgeber-Arbeitnehmer Daten*
LIAB	Linked Employer-Employee Data from the IAB – *Linked-Employer-Employee Daten des IAB*
LIS	Luxemburg Income Study
LOGIK	German Longitudinal Study on the Genesis of Individual Competencies – *Longitudinalstudie zur Genese individueller Kompetenzen*

---

[*] Inofficial translation.

	LSS 2005	Cross-sectional survey "Life Situation and Social Security 2005" – *Querschnittsbefragung „Lebenssituation und Soziale Sicherung 2005"*

M

	MCS	Millenium Cohort Study

N

	NCDS	National Child Development Study
	NEPS	National Educational Panel Study
	NLSY	National Longitudinal Survey of Youth
	NORC	National Opinion Research Center
	NSF	National Science Foundation
	NUTS	Nomenclature Of Territorial Units For Statistics / Nomenclature des unites territoriales statistiques – *Systematik der Gebietseinheiten für die Statistik*

O

	OECD	Organisation for Economic Co-operation and Development – *Organisation für wirtschaftliche Zusammenarbeit und Entwicklung*
	OECD/ SOPEMI	Continuous Reporting System on Migration / Système d'observation permanente des migrations

P

	pairfam	Panel Analysis of Intimate Relationships and Family Dynamics – *Beziehungs- und Familienentwicklungspanel*
	PIAAC	Programme for the International Assessment of Adult Competencies
	PIRLS	Progress in International Reading Literacy Study – *Internationale Grundschul-Lese Untersuchung (IGLU)*
	PISA	Programme for International Student Assessment – *Programm zur internationalen Schülerbewertung*
	PSID	Panel Study of Income Dynamics
	PUF	Public Use File

R

RatSWD	German Data Forum (formerly named as German Council for Social and Economic Data) – *Rat für Sozial- und Wirtschaftsdaten*
RV	German Pension Insurance – *Deutsche Rentenversicherung*
RWI	Rhine-Westphalian Institute for Economic Research* – *Rheinisch-Westfälisches Institut für Wirtschaftsforschung*

S

SHARE	Survey of Health, Ageing and Retirement in Europe
SLID	Survey of Labour and Income Dynamics
SOEP	German Socio-Economic Panel – *Sozio-oekonomisches Panel*
SUF	Scientific Use File

T

TIMSS	Trends in International Mathematics and Science Study

U

UKHLS	UK Household Longitudinal Study
ULME	Study on Achievement, Motivation, and Attitudes of Students at the Beginning of Vocational Education* – *Untersuchungen der Leistungen, Motivation und Einstellungen zu Beginn der beruflichen Ausbildung*
UNECE	United Nations Economic Commission for Europe

V

VET	Vocational Education and Training
VET-LSA	Large-Scale Assessment of Vocational Education and Training
VSKT	Insurance account sample – *Versichertenkontenstichprobe*
VVL	Completed Insured Life Courses – *Vollendete Versichertenleben*

---

* Inofficial translation.

W

WGL Gottfried Wilhelm Leibniz Scientific Community – *Leibniz Gemeinschaft*

WR German Council of Science and Humanities – *Wissenschaftsrat*

Z

ZUMA Centre for Survey Research and Methodology – *Zentrum für Umfragen, Methoden und Analysen*

Unsere Fachzeitschriften auf www.budrich-journals.de

- **Einzelbeiträge im Download (Micropayment)**

- **Kombi-Abos für AbonnentInnen**

- **IP- und Domain-Zugänge (Mehrplatzlizenzen)**

- **Großer *open access*-Bereich**

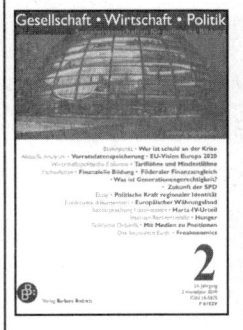

Wir haben unsere Fachzeitschriften für Sie online gestellt. Als AbonnentIn z.B. mit Kombi-Abo bekommen Sie weiterhin Ihr Heft wie gewohnt bequem nach Hause geliefert und Sie haben Zugriff auf das gesamte online-Archiv.

Zu günstigen Preisen. Fragen Sie uns!

**Verlag Barbara Budrich •
Barbara Budrich Publishers**
Stauffenbergstr. 7. D-51379 Leverkusen Opladen
Tel +49 (0)2171.344.594 • Fax +49 (0)2171.344.693 •
info@budrich-verlag.de

www.budrich-verlag.de • www.budrich-journals.de

Geisteswissenschaften & Beruf

Budrich UniPress

HEIKE SOLGA • DENIS HUSCHKA • PATRICIA EILSBERGER • GERT G. WAGNER (HRSG.)

Findigkeit in unsicheren Zeiten

Ergebnisse des Expertisenwettbewerbs „Arts and Figures – GeisteswissenschaftlerInnen im Beruf", Band I
2008. 205 S. eBook im open access und Printing on Demand. Dieses Buch können Sie als pdf-Datei kostenlos von unserer Internetseite herunterladen oder als gedrucktes Buch gegen Rechnung bestellen.
Kart. 39,90 € (D), 41,10 € (A), 56,90 SFr
ISBN 978-3-940755-12-4

HEIKE SOLGA • DENIS HUSCHKA • PATRICIA EILSBERGER • GERT G. WAGNER (HRSG.)

GeisteswissenschaftlerInnen: Kompetent, kreativ, motiviert – und doch chancenlos?

Ergebnisse des Expertisenwettbewerbs „Arts and Figures – GeisteswissenschaftlerInnen im Beruf", Band II. 2008. 144 S.
eBook im open access und Printing on Demand.
Kt. 39,90 € (D), 41,10 € (A), 56,90 SFr
ISBN 978-3-940755-13-1

Bestellen Sie jetzt:
Budrich UniPress Ltd. Stauffenbergstr. 7. D-51379 Leverkusen-Opladen.
ph +49.2171.344.694. fx +49.2171.344.693. buch@budrich-unipress.de

www.budrich-unipress.de